St. Charles College

August 5, 1949

Eugene J. Smith
151 E. Wooster St.
Bowling Green, Ohio

*The Story of*

# CIVILIZATION

## MAN'S OWN SHOW

# The Story of

# CIVILIZATION

## MAN'S OWN SHOW

*by*

GEORGE A. DORSEY, Ph.D., LL.D.

AUTHOR OF

"WHY WE BEHAVE LIKE HUMAN BEINGS"

HALCYON HOUSE

*New York*

PRINTED IN THE UNITED STATES OF AMERICA
BY THE CORNWALL PRESS, INC., CORNWALL, N. Y.

TO

My Wife Sue

# CONTENTS

vii

*PART TWO*

## OUR CULTURAL INHERITANCE; OR, HOW WE CAME BY OUR CIVILIZATION

# CONTENTS

## PART THREE

## WHAT SHALL WE DO TO BE SAVED?

# CONTENTS

# PREFACE

It is next to impossible, I suppose, for anyone to see his belongings or himself without some prejudice; nor, presumably, can any human being write about human beings or civilization quite free from personal bias. Yet that is what I have attempted to do in this volume: discuss human beings and civilization as objectively as though I were neither human nor civilized, but nevertheless had retained my human right to be curious about everything, my acquired interest in anything or anybody, and my constitutional privilege to speak my mind about anything I am taxed to support. On the other hand, I have not tried to prove something or improve anybody; exploit somebody or expound anything; point a moral or point with pride; sound a warning or forecast the future.

Man has done the few simple things he has to do (or die) in so many different ways, and has thought up so many ways to beat death, that the anthropologist has been swamped in the attempt to find out and describe the vagaries of human culture. He could not see Man for the men, women, and children; he could not see Civilization for the manners and customs; he could not see Life for the skulls and souls.

Man had to take to culture or perish: no man-made additions to man's natural endowment, no human race. Culture was a biologic necessity. As culture helped man to supply his physiologic needs, it had survival value in the struggle for existence—and still has. As culture was man's answer to the will-to-live, civilization is his answer to the will-to-power, to live more, bigger, faster, longer, for ever: insurance for life and immortal glory in death; to live like a magician, like a king, like a demon, like a god.

More questions are asked today about more things than our ancestors had names for, and about thousands of things they took for granted because named or unheard of, or because grandfather had divined or grandmother dreamed the answer. This revolt against ancient beliefs and vested ignorance has produced a new world—

as our forefathers' revolt led to a new nation. Truth evolves, as surely as do species, nations, or means of transportation. Is this a better nation than the one Washington led a revolt against? That is not the question. *The new truth is here;* does it yield more light than the old? That is the question. It seems to.

It was something of a shock for a good hundred-per-cent American to discover how well people who never heard of American or European civilization could get along, and how well they got along thousands of years before America was "discovered" or Europe "civilized." They had even risen to superb heights of human achievement, had made great discoveries, conquests, and voyages; had domesticated useful animals and plants; practised medicine and surgery; built great cities, fine roads, gardens, playgrounds, and temples; had worked out adequate systems of agriculture, government, education, ethics, art, and religion; and a better calendar than the one we borrowed and hang on to just because we are used to it.

Biology is so modern it has not yet discovered what life is; but it has thrown light on what living beings are, and how they live, and what they must do to keep alive, and what goes on after death in a body that is no longer being but has been. Biology helps us understand human beings, and gives us light on why man—and man alone—developed the manners and customs, cultures and civilizations, the anthropologist discovers and digs up.

We look to psychology for light, for the laws which govern the bents human appetites and desires take, and the ways we learn to fit into the fabric of civilization woven in answer to nature's demands and in response to the demands we have laid upon ourselves in our attempt to outstrip nature, pull ourselves up by our bootstraps, and without food or mate, bone or flesh, live among the stars like a perpetual-motion machine, like an ion, a moonbeam, a sigh, a longing, a ghost.

And so, as an anthropologist, with the aid of biology and psychology, I look at Civilization: the stereotyped patterns which we were taught to fit into and live with, and which vary from place to place and age to age—faster these days than we can keep up with.

Prejudiced—yes; not in favour of my belongings or myself, but against having to put up with more stupidity and incompetence, hypocrisy and sham, selfishness and greed, and plain or fancy living, than is compatible with the fact that we are well along in the twentieth century A.D. and can read and write.

To the following scientists who have given me of their time and learning, I here offer my grateful thanks: Dr. W. I. Thomas, who read the entire manuscript; Professor W. K. Gregory of Columbia University, who read Chapter I; Edward Sapir, Professor of Anthropology and Linguistics, Yale University, who read Chapter II; Professor A. L. Kroeber of the University of California, who read Chapter IV; Professor Robert H. Lowie of the University of California, who read Chapter V; Professor George Grant MacCurdy of Yale University, Director of the American School of Prehistoric Research in Europe, who read Chapter VI; Dr. James Harvey Robinson, who read Chapter X; and Dr. Herbert Grove Dorsey, Physicist and Research Engineer, United States Coast and Geodetic Survey, who read Chapter XII.

GEORGE A. DORSEY.

*New York City*
*Spring, 1931.*

# ACKNOWLEDGEMENT

Following is a list of the authors whose works principally have been consulted and referred to in the preparation of this book:

Barton, G. A.
Bewer, Julius A.
Bingham, Harold C.
Boas, Franz
Bölsche, W.
Breasted, James Henry
Bridgman, P. W.
Briffault, Robert
Burkitt, F. C.
Carpenter, E.
de Laguna, G. A.
Eddington, A. S.
Einstein, A.
Ellis, Havelock
Frazer, J. G.
Haddon, A. C.
Haggard, H. W.
Haldane, J. B. S.
Hall, H. R.
Harrison, J. E.
Hobson, J. A.
Jeans, Sir James
Keith, Sir Arthur
Köhler, W.
Kroeber, A. L.

Laufer, B.
Lowie, Robert H.
MacCurdy, G. Grant
Malinowski, Bronislaw
Millikan, R. A.
Ogden, C. K.
Pearson, Karl
Reinach, S.
Robertson, J. M.
Robinson, James Harvey
Rohde, E.
Russell, Bertrand
Sapir, E.
Shotwell, James T.
Singer, Charles
Smith, G. Elliot
Smith, W. Robertson
Thomas, W. I.
Thorndike, Lynn
Watson, John B.
Whitehead, A. N.
Wilson, E. B.
Woolley, C. Leonard
Yerkes, Robert M.
Zuckerman, S.

# PART ONE

## AS IT WAS IN THE BEGINNING

### OR

## MAN'S NATURAL ENDOWMENT

*The Biological Foundations of Human Society; the Psychological Processes of Becoming Cultured; and the First Great Steps in Becoming Civilized.*

CHAPTER ONE

*The Significance of Being Born Human*

1. "We Have Developed a Great Civilization." 2. We Are Domesticated Animals. 3. Fossils, Dead and Living. 4. Man Is a Rational Animal; Easily Excited. 5. The Upright Gait Freed the Larynx. 6. Our Contemporary Ancestors. 7. The Banyan Tree of Culture.

I

W*E HAVE developed a great civilization,* said the radio tonight. I pricked up my ears, hoping I might hear who "we" are, how civilization is "developed," what makes it "great," and possibly what constitutes "civilization"; for to the answering of such questions I have devoted most of my life. But it was not that kind of speech; it was the voice of the propagandist—from Washington, pleading for the enforcement of the Eighteenth Amendment. I listened just long enough to learn that there are twenty (or is it twenty-five?) million automobiles on our roads—each a "potential engine of death."

From the radio I turned to the evening paper, and learned that these potential engines are actually lethal to the extent of about thirty thousand human lives a year—the number "steadily mounting." The same paper described an arsenal found by chance in the apartment of a gunman: a gallon of tear-gas, eight bombs, two dozen hand-grenades, eight pieces of steel armour, twenty-two "fountain-pen" pistols, four rifle-"silencers," two machine guns, etc.

Fountain-pen pistols, machine guns, tear gas, *silencers!* Ours; we have developed them. In that private arsenal the armour only is ancient. To the other strictly modern improvements add automobiles, radio, television, movies that talk, airplanes that fly: evidence, surely, of a great civilization. And *we* have developed it! Yet, lying on the radio cabinet is my friend Lowie's book, *Are We Civilized?*

*Are* we? And if *we* are not, who *is* civilized? But Lowie is not

3

all shooting at civilization, weighing it and finding it wanting. Not one credits *us* with having "developed" it; nor do any two agree on who "we" are or what civilization is. Light on these and similar problems can only come, it seems to me, from a knowledge of *how* we became civilized. This book attempts to answer that question.

The African Bushman is not civilized in the sense that we are, but he is human; he can do that which no infrahuman animal can do. Call it culture, or even *Kultur*, if you please; and if you insist that he is not so cultured as, or is less civilized than, the Dry propagandist speaker tonight, even Lowie would not quarrel with you.

"Culture" the Bushman certainly has, though possibly not so much as he had before modern civilization entered "primitive" or "savage" Africa. Presumably we have more civilization than he has and are more civilized; yet conceivably he is as good a man as we are, and possibly his ancestors were earlier civilized than ours and contributed more to the beginnings of civilization.

We were not always civilized. Were we savages? The Bushman is no savage—though he probably would behave like one if you tried to steal his wife or child. We never were "savages" as that term is generally misunderstood. Our ancestors were natural, children of nature; they began without culture. With the first cultural traits they ceased to be mere animals and began to be human.

A digging-stick is a cultural trait just as a radio set is. Not long ago there was no radio; once upon a time there was no digging-stick. The waves which make radio possible, and the sticks our forbears turned into digging-tools, are far older than human beings.

Roughly, but not inaccurately, we may say that civilization (or "culture") is man's unnatural way of living naturally. Birds build nests and beavers dams because they are built that way. Building nests comes "naturally" to birds; dams, to beavers. There are bird nests and beaver dams because there are birds and beavers. Man became civilized because he is that kind of animal; it is his nature. Civilization had *survival* value in man's early struggle for existence. If man had not become civilized, there would be no human beings.

We are prone these days to think of "struggle for existence" in terms of wars between classes or nations. That is not the struggle I am referring to, but rather the struggle *man*—not class or nation

—made to live his life out and leave offspring to carry on the race. "Struggle" is used figuratively, but behind the figure are great facts; and greatest of all is the fact that man alone of all animals is self-domesticated and thereby unique. Civilization itself is unique.

Ours today is a civilization of a kind. We have not developed it. We have changed it, modified it; especially, we have added to it. In the sense that this century, like all preceding centuries, is unique, ours is a unique civilization. The Empire State Building is unique, but its uniqueness extends only to certain features. The idea of such a building is fairly modern; the idea of *a* building is fairly ancient. In other words, much of our civilization—more than we realize at first thought—is part of our social heritage; every trait and every element in it had a beginning, and the beginnings of every human cultural trait are to be sought in human nature. If civilization, as I have said, is unique, it must be because man himself is unique. In that uniqueness we may expect to find the beginnings or germs, not only of our own but of all civilizations, and of all the cultural traits which collectively make up what is called civilization.

Part I of this volume, then, is an attempt to understand human nature—both for its own sake and for the understanding it alone can give us of the historic development of the civilization we use— or abuse—in our business of life.

## II

In becoming human man learned to walk on his own self-made crutches. By the time he had developed enough artificial limbs to survive the struggle for existence, he had become fully domesticated. He runs wild now and then, but no feral tribe of humans has ever been discovered.

"Crutches" represent a uniquely new phenomenon in the world. In the entire animal kingdom there is nothing comparable to man-made props. Nests of birds, lairs of mammals, and various contrivances of the insect world, are the nearest approaches to human culture. But nests and lairs are primarily nurseries—abandoned when the young can travel on their own or fend for themselves.

The prevailing rule in animal evolution was specialization of a part or trait: tusks or daggers from teeth; digging-tools from snouts; armour-plate from skin; paddles from feet; horns or antlers from hair; stilts from legs; etc. To these endless special adaptations we must add such general life-savers as fleetness of foot, sheer brute strength, sharpness of vision, acuteness of smell or hearing, fecundity, etc. Mammals alone tried out, and succeeded in becoming adapted to, every clime, every zone, every milieu.

Man also goes everywhere, lives wherever there is food; but in a peculiar sense he carried his board and bed with him—in his head. Any human being can. That is the significance of being born human. It is not that the human youngster has a superior body, but rather that he can learn to carry so much in his head, so to speak, that he need carry little on his back or in his hands. He can supply his natural deficiencies.

Man's answer to change in environment is change in habits, not change in physical structure. That enables him to enjoy a kind of freedom denied all other animals. He defies his environment, as it were; changes it to suit his fancy. In this sense man has profited enormously from his self-imposed domestication. His life is not only freer, but his freedom gives him an incomparably richer life than is possible to any other animal.

Culture freed man from the natural struggle for existence; it thereby stabilized his physical structure. Why, then, so many kinds and colours of men? No satisfactory solution has yet been given, nor is it worth our time to discuss them. We may look at a fact or two.

Animals in a state of nature vary—in certain features or traits as much as thirty per cent. Given a pair of parents with an excess variation of some physical feature—pigmentation, kinky hair, "Mongolian" eye-fold, etc.—inbreeding among their offspring would tend to emphasize and fix such a trait. The Eskimo, for example, shows a few strongly emphasized physical features, due presumably to centuries of inbreeding. Such a social condition must have prevailed for thousands of years in the human race.

While the influence of such factors as climate, food, etc., are not at all well understood as yet, man, as Wissler says, bears in his own person what he has imposed on his dogs and pigs. We might conceivably breed human beings, but. . . . BUT, who is going to take care of such a stock-farm and what is he going to aim at—more brains? The human pelvis has already decreed that the human brain must be reasonable in size or mother and infant perish. What would man do with more brains, anyhow, seeing that he has not yet made the most of what he has?

No, *natural* selection seems to help us little in trying to account for the diversity of physical types we find on earth today. We are forced back, as was Darwin, upon sexual selection. But even if we grant the validity of that hypothesis, we need not assume that there was universal selection toward any one particular type. The grounds for selection were not necessarily what *we* call physical beauty. As a Potawatomi chief said, some foolish young men fall for beauty, but they are few, and soon learn to take *good* wives, without minding their charms.

Corpulence and beauty are synonymous terms throughout black Africa. "Getting ready for the wedding" means getting the girl fat—so monstrously beautiful she can't get up without help. A fat woman, says the Kafir, can weather famine better than a lean one. No hour-glass figures for Africa; nor are such figures found in the ancient deposits around the Mediterranean. Fat figures do abound, from Crete to Egypt, from Dalmatia to Spain.

Beauty, after all, we are agreed, is only skin deep. The fattest bride in Equatorial Africa is a human being, and hence as unique as the slimmest beauty in our underwear advertisements. Our uniqueness is more than skin deep.

In one important respect we are not unique at all. Vital processes are fundamentally the same in man as in beaver and bird—yes, and in the fly that just buzzed by and in the amœba which infests the mouth of man and monkey and gives one in every five of us pyorrhœa.

Animals *live* by procuring, eating, and digesting food; excreting waste; and by growing and reproducing their kind. *How* they perform these vital processes depends on their endowment of mechanisms, organs, etc., for maintaining life. And these fundamental mechanisms became stabilized early, for, as Cannon says, the dynamics of digestion, circulation, respiration, and of the endocrine and neuro-muscular systems, are essentially the same from fish to man and show little evidence of progressive evolution. We can claim no halo for merely being alive.

Man's glory is in his capacity for discovering and inventing new mechanisms for securing the means of life to supplement those nature gave him. Therein lies his uniqueness—his urge to do new things; to discover new ways is his ruling passion.

The equipment we are born with is unique only in quantity, not in quality or kind. Bone for bone, muscle for muscle, nerve for nerve, eyes to see, ears to hear, nose to smell, tongue to feel and taste, fingers to monkey with, the chimpanzee is about as good a man as we are; in some respects the gorilla is a better man than either of us. Why, then, has no ape become human?

One did. It took a million years to do it; and because bones are naturally hard and resistant and under certain conditions easily fossilize, the steps or structural changes an ape took to become human enough to begin civilization are now pretty well known— so well, in fact, that we could wish we knew man's future as well as we know his past. History will not help us predict that future; it can give us grounds for understanding the present and suggestions for preparing the stage for tomorrow's play; but just what kind of play man will enact tomorrow we cannot know, for, as a Chinese sage remarked, man is a "bundle of possibilities."

### III

The first step in becoming human was taken when the ancestors of the Primates became arboreal. That one line of Primates became tailless is significant; but taillessness is only a concomitant of even more significant changes of millions of years ago. Just where or when that step was taken is not yet known, but probably will be some day. No fossil apes have yet been found in the New World; many have been found in the Old World. Man and civilization began in the Eastern Hemisphere.

The next step involved an outlook on life. The ape took to an upright gait. That meant compensating changes in all bones, muscles, every organ in the body.

Why any apes at all today? Why did certain land mammals, such as whales and seals, take to the sea? others, like bats, to the air? Why are some bats hairless, some clothed in fine fur? Why do our finger tips have thirty times as many touch-spots as our upper arm? Why do our nerves carry impulses five times faster than a frog's? No one knows; but such facts are known, and even much of the *hows* of heredity. The evolution of man is a long story in which geographical distribution and climatic changes play important rôles. Certain apes persisted: it is a fact of heredity that the parent stalk often persists long after daughter species appear. The line which became human presumably had to change or become extinct.

In fact, there are not only extinct species of monkeys and apes, but also extinct "races," so-called, of man. *Dryopithecus,* for example, was an *anthropoid* or manlike ape—more *man*like than any living ape. Its remains have been found in Miocene deposits in France; it became extinct in the Pliocene Period. Even more *man*like (especially in teeth and chin) is the fossil *Australopithecus,* found in 1924 in Bechuanaland, South Africa. It is assigned to the Pliocene Period, and is especially interesting in view of Darwin's idea that Africa may have cradled the human race.

The fossil bones found in Java in 1891 by Dubois were properly dubbed *Pithecanthropus erectus.* It was not a man, it was not an ape; it was an upright ape-man. No better "missing link" has ever been or is likely to be found. With *Pithecanthropus erectus* of a million years ago, we can say that one ape at least was looking in our direction. It is a *link* that up to a few years ago was missing.

Did he leave any children? Are we his heirs? The answer still awaits pick and shovel. Dozens of fossil links binding man to a geologic past are known, and new ones keep turning up—in Europe, Asia, Africa. An enormously important link from China has only recently been described by Davidson Black. His *Sinanthropus* had more brains than *Pithecanthropus*; less than the so-called Neanderthal man. Its age is put at between a half and one million years. It also is a link that was missing—as perfect as though made to order. It fits into the hypothesis of man's origin as neatly as the new planet, Pluto, fits into the hypothesis of celestial order.

It is not known just when or where man left off being an ape, or what natural or cultural trait, if any, marks the transition from ape to *Pithecanthropus,* from *Pithecanthropus* to *Homo Sinanthropus,* from *Homo Sinanthropus* to *Homo Neanderthalensis,* or from *Neanderthalensis* to *sapiens.*

To reconstruct the story of man's transition from an animal, we have at least six fossil "missing links" and thousands of rude artifacts. Are the fossils *human?* Some undoubtedly, some probably, some possibly. And the artifacts? Again, some undoubtedly, some possibly. Why the doubt? Because it is not yet known just how far an ape can go in aping a human being and still remain an ape. Hence the importance of studies now being made in ape behaviour. I do not wish to overrate that importance—nor, in fact, do I see how I can.

Apes are *living* fossils, as it were, of human forbears. They are *almost* human; the nearest approach, presumably, we shall ever get to infrahuman cultural beginnings. They are not ideal sub-humans; they have evolved a long way in this direction and that from the original ape branch of our family tree. But they are the best witnesses we have. Insect behaviour is enormously varied and astoundingly complex—even modifiable to a degree; but to my way of thinking a fair knowledge of Mr. and Mrs. Congo will let us farther into the Adam and Eve that are in us—yes, and into such behaviour as marriage, homosexuality, nose-rings, tantrums, and Einsteins—than encyclopædias of ant behaviour or X-ray motion pictures of anthills. In short, we are willy-nilly forced to ask our ape cousins where grandfather got it.

Ape studies have really only just begun. The results are astounding and illuminating, but there is much that is not yet known; we do not yet know all the light that can come out of Darkest Africa. We do not know all the outer limits to a chimpanzee's capacity to learn; we know very little about that "hypersensitive introvert," the gorilla, but suspect that much of his hypersensitiveness may have been forced on him by whites armed with rifles and by natives who dearly love human and almost-human flesh. He seems to be more savage than he used to be. In captivity he dies of *ennui*.

With our heads full of primitive and Biblical ideas about man's genesis, it was all too easy to discover an impassable gulf between humans and apes; but when apes are viewed honestly and impartially by anatomists and by our Köhlers, Yerkes, and Binghams, the gulf becomes passable and we discover that humans do a great deal of monkeying, and the apes are so childish as to seem almost human. Prone as we are to exaggerate every practice or profession which removes us from our "inferiors," we do not easily see how far we fall from our vaunted superiorities. But that we colloquially turn apes and monkeys into nouns, verbs, and even adjectives, to

characterize certain norms of human behaviour, is a naïve confession of factual kinship with these almost-humans. In very fact
we may say that in sensory equipment and emotional endowment
there is no essential difference between ape and human.

Apes can make ("invent") tools, but only in simple or primitive
forms. Lacking all the verbalized, socially valuable stimuli which
spur us on, they soon tire in any pursuit unless driven by such
primitive emotions as hunger (food or sex), jealousy, etc. Such
"learning" as they acquire (even the act of copulation, for example)
seems to begin in kindergarten play and to come more or less by
accident. Their curiosity is almost insatiable and leads to what appears to be wanton destructiveness; out of such destructiveness man's
early inventiveness may have sprung. They are fond of display, of
a kind we call exhibitionism as well as personal adornment or ornamentation—a forerunner of athletics and the root of clothing. They
are as afraid of the unknown or the *super*natural as we are, and
hence have the psychological foundation of a religious attitude.

In other words, the very foundations, not only of our so-called
material, but of our social, æsthetic and spiritual culture as well,
are older than man; they are rooted in ape nature. No emotion,
no emotional attitude, known to civilized man, is without its beginning in ape behaviour. We may not always correctly interpret their
behaviour, but among themselves there is, as Köhler puts it, "sure
and mutual comprehension." He believes the chimpanzee's emotional register even greater than that of the average human being
today; its exhibitions of pain, pleasure, playfulness, pleading, desire,
rage, terror, despair, grief, jealousy, satisfy the most exacting demands for realism.

So social are chimpanzees that one in solitary confinement is not
a real chimpanzee at all. With them, as with us, an "outsider" is a
*foreigner* and treated with suspicion. They throw stones at newcomers. The social group is made up of those "used to each other."
A single cry of anger is enough for "a wave of fury to go through
the troop; from all sides they hurry to the joint attack. In the sudden transfer of the cry of fury to all the animals, whereby they
seem to incite one another to ever more violent raving, there is
demoniac strength, coming, surely, from the very roots of their
organism."

Apes seem to love to do things for the sheer love of it: to fish for ants in cracks in the wall with wet straws, to dip bread in the water-bucket and let it drip into their outstretched lip, to climb up on boxes, to climb to the top of poles before the poles fall over, to splice short bamboo rods into a rod long enough to draw in bananas. In short, they love to "fool around"—and that is all the more reason why we should not ape them.

When Köhler handed a small mirror to an ape, it did just what a New Guinea native did when I handed him one. Children of nature—curious, quaint, lovable, excitable, ingenious, emotional. Boundless youthful curiosity, tireless energy, endless playfulness, are part of our ape inheritance.

We marvel at the infinite wisdom of our Darwins and our Einsteins resuming nature in a phrase or the universe in a mathematical formula, but when they tire of the pursuit of knowledge they do just what their nature bids them do—turn to the bosom of their family, or go fishing, for their deepest joys and satisfactions. Human nature is founded on visceral needs working through glandular secretions; but older than physiological laboratories or knowledge of glands of internal secretion is that now nearly extinct little band of apes, keen for action, full of feeling. With them and their forbears nature became almost human.

Why, then, we ask again, if apes are almost human, can't they learn to behave like human beings; why, if they can construct and invent, have they not laid such cultural foundations of civilization as are represented by the so-called palæolithic implements of the Chellean period of half a million years ago? Well, why did it take a half-million years for the Old to become the New Stone Age? That second question is not easily answered. The answer to the first is: not enough brains. A tablespoonful more, conceivably, would have enabled them to turn the trick. Man has no new kind of brain cells, no new brain cell connections—simply larger association areas in his cerebrum; more brains.

Neanderthal man of more than a quarter-million years ago not only had enough brains to be human, but, despite his beetling brows, was a man in the very image of God. With Cro-Magnon man of thirty thousand years ago, we come to a human form divine that to the Greeks would have seemed Jovian. Possibly earth never held more shapely human forms; certainly none with larger brains.

Cro-Magnon is not only man but *Homo sapiens.* He was tall, had a broad face, long head, a big and shapely skull. He was a wonderful artist; his mural decorations are our earliest known masterpieces. For his time he was as *sapiens* as we are, and possibly as "civilized" as were the Australian blacks a hundred years ago. Where that "race" began, where it left off, where it came from or where it went, is not yet known. In fact, we have much to learn yet of the laws of human heredity.

Nor is it yet known where, when, or how certain groups or families of human beings became taller or shorter, more or less pigmented, longer- or shorter-headed, bigger- or smaller-brained, thicker- or thinner-lipped, longer- or flatter-nosed, more or less hairy, than certain other or all other groups. Such physical types did develop; they can be seen on Main Street in almost any city in the world.

Pigmentation is a biological factor, a heritable trait; modifiable, of course, but how long it takes or what factors are involved is not yet known. It is believed that Negroid peoples abounded in Europe about thirty thousand years ago; it is known that whites today will spend months on the sand to acquire a dark-brown skin.

Physical traits (pigmentation, stature, head form, shape of eyes, nose, etc.) are one thing; they belong to our natural inheritance and are governed by their own laws, as yet not at all well known. Behaviour, action (how one makes love, blows one's nose, or eats snails), is not only a horse of another colour, but a different horse. We may like a Hittite nose, or see beauty only in a snub. The fate of empire has hung on such preferences and prejudices. But a preference is a preference, prejudices are prejudices—part of our training. They are not innate characters; they are cultural acquisitions.

Cro-Magnon was not only as good a man as Gunga Din, but had a better brain than Kipling. "Better?" Well, bigger. Why, then, don't we know his fate? Possibly because he became too spiritual or intellectual to breed. In a way a brain is like a motor-car—it may be used to go somewhere, or it may be used just for a ride.

What we do with our brain depends, roughly, less on its size than on the knocks we get on the head and the kicks on the shin.

For at least a quarter of a million years, children born of human parents have inherited human-sized brains. "Civilization" is not dependent on brain size, but on the way brains are used; and no one has yet *proved* that, provided an individual has as large a brain as an African Pygmy, the use made of brains is in any way innately connected with mere brain size—or with any other anatomical trait. A black skin, biologically useful under a tropical sun, is a social handicap on the sidewalks of New York.

*Pithecanthropus* of a million years ago was an upright creature. His brain was not large enough to be quite human, much too large for a mere ape. What he did with it we do not know. We do know that it enlarged his possible range of behaviour; made him more adaptable, more plastic, and therefore removed him farther from a vegetative existence. He had more brain for the binocular, stereoscopic eyes to see with; more brain for the hearing ear to understand with; more brain for more perfect control over all motor mechanism. In short, greater freedom from purely visceral demands because better control over striped, to satisfy the demands of unstriped, muscles. Complicated actions became possible to satisfy the simplest needs. He had travelled far; not far enough to build a cathedral to pray in, but far enough to get ready to-begin-to-commence to think about such things.

### IV

The upright gait freed the hands; an expanding brain made speech possible and dexterity profitable.

What is a brain? A trite answer is that it is the most complex structure in the known universe; and that is some excuse for the prevailing ignorance about it. That a human brain is a more wonderful structure than an elephant's trunk is merely a human way of viewing nature. That its chief function in textbooks on psychology is to provide an excuse for pictures in otherwise dry and monotonous texts, is Lashley's point of view.

Well, the pictures are often excellent, and the brain is no longer a refrigerator for an overheated heart—as Aristotle thought it was; nor is it merely a model of a central to an automatic telephone system whereby messages from sense organs can be executed by muscle organs. Whatever it is, large animals as a rule have a larger brain than smaller animals. But, with insignificant exceptions, no animal has a brain relatively so large as man's, nor has any animal but an ape a brain of the same architecture.

While man shares this relatively large-sized brain with his simian cousins, his brain on the average is two and one-half times as large as that of the largest ape. A sixty-pound human dwarf may have a larger brain than a 600-pound gorilla. But, as Huxley said of a famous Palæolithic skull, it might have belonged to a philosopher or held the brain of a thoughtless savage.

That brings us back to man as a "bundle of possibilities." The size of the brain is roughly—and roughly only—a measure of the size of the "bundle." The outstanding difference between man and ape is speech, language. Now, man can suffer enormous brain injury and still live, but even a slight injury to the brain can upset his speech. Yet one may still speak intelligibly, and show otherwise orderly behaviour, despite great lesions in the brain.

In short, there is as yet no theory which reconciles the problems of human and infrahuman behaviour with the known facts of brain anatomy or neural physiology—even though, as Lashley says, no fact in the field of neurophysiology is more firmly established than the functional differentiation of the various parts of the cerebral cortex. Hence no neurologist can predict human behaviour or define its normal organization in terms of neurons, nerves, or brains.

Can nothing more be said? Much. Man is not a cabbage; he is an animal. And of all that distinguishes animal- from plant-behaviour and is summed up in such words as plasticity, teachability, adaptability, irritability, excitability, man has more than any other animal. Plants can be trained, but only within set limits soon reached. As we ascend the tree of animal life, the limit of educability keeps ever widening. The most highly trained horse, seal, or elephant is a poor show compared with even a poorly trained chimpanzee.

Plasticity, adaptability, power to organize forces to meet change in environment, power to reorganize forces when the existing organization is upset, as by brain lesion—all such biologically useful equipment reaches a height in monkeys and apes not found elsewhere on this earth. And man has more of it than any monkey or ape. His larger brain, his larger area of cortex, is the necessary organ for making possible the realization of his human opportunities. But man could not have put his expanding brain to human purposes had not his hands been set free by his upright gait; nor could an upright gait have made hands *human* without a brain big enough to organize handiwork for human needs.

While the most striking differences between any human being and any ape or monkey are the upright gait and a relatively big head, no feature in all animal creation is more striking than the "adolescent drag," as Todd calls it, of human beings. A rat reaches skeletal maturity in two months and a dog in two years, but an ape requires seven and a human being twenty-three years.

Prenatal ape life is, roughly, 220 days; human, 280 days. The human infant's head is so large as to seem out of all proportion to its body. That big head means big brain. *Life* itself does not hang on cerebrum; *learning* does. The human infant's huge brain gives it enormous capacity to learn.

Human nature, then, is more than an upright gait or a big brain—vastly more. And any attempt to explain man or to understand civilization which leaves prolonged infancy and childhood out of the count is doomed to failure. A colt is a horse in four years, and at no time much trouble to its mother and less to its father. But, I repeat, an ape requires seven years to mature. Prolonged infancy began with Primates. It is as truly a distinguishing feature of apes and man as any physical trait.

There is nothing simple about human behaviour or brains, but human behaviour can be observed. It has been observed, and a large amount of factual material has been gathered—also from observation of apes and other animals. And I know no simpler way of emphasizing the difference between a lion, an elephant, a chimpanzee, and a Congo Pygmy, than by comparing the amounts of their natural curiosity about their respective worlds and the way they spend their spare time. The elephant's trunk is good; the hand is a really handy tool. But the little Pygmy can talk it over far into the night and so lay the foundation of what is often called reflection, intelligence, "consciousness"—all of which require, not brains, but a *talking* brain.

It has been suggested that the brain may be a wen or a non-

malignant hereditary tumor; or a superfluity, as Ritter says, like the hump on a camel's back or the querl in a pig's tail. It may be. But if man is a rational animal (and I believe he often is) and if there is such a thing as intellect (and I believe there are often signs of it) the human brain is the responsible party. Man's ability to gather, collect, select, stop fooling around with things and choose those he wishes to work with, is the mark of intellect, the sign of reason, the evidence of will. We enjoy "free" will if and when we are free to choose.

In other words, as Ritter also points out, it is not enough to call man "nothing but" an animal. No other animal talks. That uniqueness is dependent on his uniquely large cerebral cortex.

But while man is a rational animal, he is easily excited. By nature. In fact, all protoplasm—the stuff oak trees, catfish, and Nordics are made of—is naturally excitable. The foundation of the facts that I am writing these words and that you believe in freewill, was built into the first molecule of protoplasm called to life by the sun hundreds of millions of years ago. Excitable, irritable, dynamic protoplasm—especially in such highly organized beings as monkeys, apes, and humans.

Rage and fear are manifestations of excitability. Rage blinds us to reason, makes us throw caution to the winds, provokes us to thoughts or deeds of murder, makes madmen of us. Rage is an emotion. As is fear—which moves us to pause, lie, run, hide, play 'possum, or fall in a faint. Strong fear led our brutish ancestors to defecate—a purely physiological reflex and biologically useful in lightening the load in flight.

Squeamish souls with a high-strung olfactory sense discovered in the London Underground "tubes" during German air raids how easily the bejewelled and embroidered mantle of civilization slipped off in the crush of panic-stricken mobs scuttling downstairs for their lives. Both rage and fear make for indigestion and inhumanity, and dethrone intelligence.

It has always been so; it was so when we were Cave-men and when we were just plain monkeys. Rage and fear are biologically useful emotions, ancient and honourable institutions in the evolutionary history of higher mammals. Without such devices it is

difficult to see how man could have evolved. They have played important rôles in the drama of civilization and appear on every page of human history.

The far-reaching changes which take place within our body when we are moved by rage or fear are so well known since Cannon's physiological classic that I need go no further, except to add that this body of ours not only *changes* under rage and fear, but also in pain and hunger. *Bodily Changes in Pain, Hunger, Fear and Rage* is the expressive title of Cannon's volume.

That pain and hunger *move* us must be obvious; it is not so evident that rage and fear follow close after in their biologic usefulness. While all of us presumably have been driven out of our course, or out of our "minds," by intense pain, gnawing hunger, abject fear, and towering rage, only recently have we been able to understand just how these bodily states can be, and frequently are, so devastating. They *change* us: we are not ourselves; we become irrational, driven by pain to commit suicide, by hunger to steal, by fear to die of fright, by rage to murder our dearest friend.

Families, tribes, nations, get that way. *Why* this war, that migration, this religious frenzy, that inhuman butchery? The obvious reasons are generally mere rationalizations hardly scratching the surface; the real reasons are rooted in our animal nature. I find no evidence that that nature has greatly changed since the wind blew through our cradle in the tree-tops. Our structure has changed somewhat; our viewpoint, enormously.

It does seem, however, that blind, brutal behaviour which once had biologic usefulness in man's struggle for existence among the wild beasts of the forest, should by now have become obsolete. The good things in human lives have been won by the use of brains and not by blind, unreasoning brute strength. So far have brains triumphed in man's conquest over nature that he can now use his brain to march on to even greater conquests—fear of death and hatred of his fellow-men.

### V

In turning from the horizontal to the upright gait something else happened, something that added enormously to the importance of a larger brain; a talking brain is worthless without a talk-

ing mechanism. That erect gait not only freed the hands; it freed the larynx for speech.

There are many things—physical, chemical, emotional, etc.—that render us speechless or upset our speech, but the outstanding fact of human nature is that we are born speechless, though not voiceless. And the outstanding fact of civilization is its foundation in organized articulate speech.

It is speech which makes possible the social systems, or patterns, into which we fit ourselves and through which we relate ourselves to our social and physical world. These systems, or patterns, are unique. That uniqueness did not spring full-grown, like Athene from the head of Jove or Adam from the breath of Yahweh, but grew slowly and from small seeds. One of the "seeds" of that uniqueness had its soil in the first pair of vocal cords on earth. In the primeval swamps a small voice was worth more than a test tube or a pair of binoculars. If the bullfrog had not found his mate there would have been no amphibia, no land vertebrates. Not only the voice-producing but the sound-receiving mechanism began with the earliest tetrapods—as all four-footed vertebrates are called. Nor is it at all inappropriate that the Frogs' Chorus of Aristophanes should be heard in the Bowl of a great seat of learning.

Man can talk because he can control his talking mechanism; that control is learned and is dependent on a brain cortex capable of assuming certain functions and the striped muscles necessary in the production of speech. Thinking is just as mysterious as playing the piano—no more, no less. Civilization could get along without pianos; it began with thought, and fails when it thinks to no purpose: *no brains*. No key unlocks so many puzzling problems of human behaviour as does the one fact that man is a talking animal.

Our upright gait does not free us from, but is responsible for, our proneness to hernia, falling of the womb, varicose veins, and the many disabilities which bedevil our throat. We have not yet stopped paying the price for turning vertical; nor, presumably, for a million years will our body forget that it was quadruped before it was biped, reptile before it was mammal, amphibian before it was reptile, and fish before it was amphibian. Just what it was before it was fish is not yet known, but it is known that at one stage our fœtal neck is more fishy than human and that by the time it becomes human it has a thyroid gland with a fish ancestry.

The thyroid is an energy regulator. When it is upset, we are upset. Hair requires energy to "bristle," to keep it oiled and growing. When our prenatal life was extended from 220 to 280 days— as it was while we were becoming human—a train of consequences was to ensue. Aboard that train were factors which make for civilization. Longer fœtal growth made bigger heads possible. But the human infant cannot hold up its head; it needs parental care. That in itself was a problem our ancestors had to solve; it was solved *culturally*, not biologically. Prolonged prenatal life also cut down our allowance of hair—another problem for our early ancestors, and solved culturally.

Now, without hair, the thyroid need direct no energy to the upkeep of a hairy coat; more energy was available for discovering a fur coat. Cold is cold to such a warm, even-temperatured creature as man; much cold is pain, too much is death. To keep the internal fires burning meant more food, much more in winter than in summer. Hunting food prolonged growth, retarded sex maturity, and thereby added another to the ever-growing load of problems our early ancestors had to solve, because back in Tertiary times certain apes had begun to specialize in no one direction, with the result that one of their descendants some millions of years later could specialize in civilization, which requires wits.

Monkeys have more wits than lemurs, apes than monkeys, man than apes. When the infant's skull bones ankylose, thereby permitting no further growth of brain, the result is an idiot—even though the ankylosis may be caused by a brain which for any reason prematurely stops growing. "At his wits' end"; an imbecile.

## VI

While human history, civilization, is the answer to human nature, it seems worth pointing out here that in addition to the facts usually set forth in histories and in works on civilization, three categories of evidence are available for the better understanding of the problems of civilization.

First is the evidence afforded by studying the behaviour of the animals most closely related to us by all known blood tests, immunization, etc., by anatomical structure, and by physiological functionings—the four anthropoids. They are so like us, and in so many ways, that we infer we can learn of man from them. We already have had them on the witness stand.

Second is the evidence found in caves, rock shelters, graves, etc., left by man himself ages ago. That evidence is not all in yet, for there are thousands of unexplored sites where the workings of early man's hand and brain may be brought to light.

Third is the evidence afforded us by observing the behaviour of our "contemporary ancestors," as Thomas calls them; natives, aborigines, primitives, savages, they are also sometimes called. It seems worth while to be clear about these peoples at the start.

These primitive folk, roughly speaking, comprised the peoples of the earth beyond the ken of the Mediterranean world, where our particular form of civilization got its early slants and tints, and were brought within range of European eyes through such voyages of discovery as those of Marco Polo, da Gama, Diaz, Columbus, Magellan, Cook, etc. They are—or were—the natives of the Americas, Australasia, and the South Sea Islands, the "jungle" folk of South Asia, and the tribal folk north of China and Mongolia.

All these folk, together with Africans south of the Sahara, are . . . what? Well, many of them have become as extinct as the mastodon. While being exterminated they fought for their homes as well as they knew how, naturally; and finding bow and arrow a poor answer to powder and shot, in sheer desperation took to ways well known to their white exterminators and called "savage."

Illiterate—yes. Most of them when discovered were without letters—as were all peoples a few thousand years ago and all North Europeans two thousand years ago; not only illiterate, but to the Græco-Roman world savages. Those savages finally learned to read and write, and some of them conquered America and became our revered ancestors. But the aborigines of Mexico and Central America were not illiterate, nor were they primitive. The real *savages* in Mexico and Central America were the murderous Conquistadores, one of whom did not hesitate to consign to the flames hundreds of native books because they set forth a religion so like Christianity they thought it must have been inspired by the devil himself!

Nor were the natives of Australia or the South Sea Islanders, etc., savages. True, Captain Cook was killed by Hawaiians, and many a white man found his way to native stomachs; but everywhere the white explorers found, not savages, but childish, simple folk, ready to lend a hand or a ham; it was the *second* exploring party that found "savages." We speak of those early travels as voyages of exploration, as though they had been financed by a Carnegie Institution to explore some unknown land or investigate some particular problem. They were nothing of the kind; the explorers were out for what they could get: a new route to some point, or a new source of supply for something—principally gold or human slaves. Excepting Cook, who had a true scientific spirit, they were mostly sublimated pirates and buccaneers. They had no more compunction about cheating the natives than had our own Plymouth Rocks.

The Veddahs of Ceylon, the hill tribes of Central India, the Semang and Sakkai of the Malay Peninsula, the Pygmies of Central Africa and the Philippine Islands, the Bushmen and Hottentots of South Africa, and the aborigines of Australia and Tasmania, lived simply and in conformity with their physical and cultural environment. They were on the fringe of more civilized peoples; they lived down by the gasworks beyond the railroad yard, as it were. It had been home before gas and railroad moved in. They were pioneers.

If we can explain why life in a hilltop village within sight of Rome, or in a village at the foot of a castle-fortress in Sicily, goes on today as it did one, two, or three thousand years ago, we will know why the Veddahs, for example, use a bow and arrow instead of a sawed-off shotgun, or why the Australians prefer grubs to caviare, or why Boer children use diamonds for marbles.

Do we speak of the washwoman down by the gas-house as primitive? She may be an excellent mother, a clever laundress, a skilful seamstress. She may be even a marvellous lace-maker. Her home may be scantily furnished, her wardrobe as bare as her cupboard. Her only decoration may be a violet in her hair; her jewels her children, whom she loves with a passion only exceeded by that which goes into slaving for them or would go into fighting for them when endangered. Primitive? Jungle folk, the same way.

Reading, writing, and arithmetic are marvellous cultural achievements, and among people who read, write, and figure they are valuable tools for being sociable and for finding one's place in society. But they are tools—and, among unlettered folk in illiterate lands, valueless. So recently have our priests and rulers *allowed* us to learn to read, that in our pride we can't help feeling sorry for poor illiterates. We wonder how they can get along at all; and are often astounded to learn how well they do get along, and how rich their lives are, in so many different ways.

## VII

We think of the human race as a family tree—with ourselves, of course, at the top. It is a tree, but not a redwood; it is a banyan tree.

A big banyan tree is a small forest, often covering a half-dozen acres. It grows this way. Seed; parent stem; branches shooting almost straight out. From the branches hair-like processes grow downward till they touch the ground; then they root. The processes grow bigger and stronger, like the parent stem. And so the tree spreads on and on, wherever a tiny process can get a roothold and become a trunk. All one tree: one in many, many in one. One banyan conceivably could cover the earth if all conditions were favorable. Man did. White man does.

Civilization spread that way, but we can no more distinguish its parent stem now than we could the banyan's. There was a parent stem, and that stem was human nature. When it got firmly on its feet and could walk like a man, it was ready to branch out; and when it learned to build a boat, it took to water and finally covered the earth. Same stuff as the original stem, but as shoots (families) settled down, some here, some there, some way way off, to take root and draw their nourishment from the soil and not from the stem they left behind, they encountered varying conditions: rocky soils, sandy plains, mountains, rich river valleys, etc. And when man finally reached Tasmania, he was in a sense out of luck: he got there too soon. Being first on the spot gave him no title the next man respected, for *he* was civilized and armed to the teeth.

Is it plain? Well, it will be after a while. As a Tlingit clam-digger says to the fast-retreating clam, we must not go too fast or we will hit our mother-in-law in the face!

No human family left the parent stem without enough culture to live by, to take root and get enough from soil or sea to grow on and raise up seed. In passing, say, from one island to another, they did not have to take a clam-digger with them: all they needed was an appetite and a clam-digging idea. This earth was not peopled by idiots or by solitary males, as we sometimes seem to think, but by families, human families—pa, ma, and the baby.

Primitives, we may call them. Some were more primitive than others: they had no time for frills, no chance to get ahead; they had to keep their noses to the grindstone. Most of us could live beautiful lives if we had three cars, sixteen servants, a yacht, a house on the Avenue, one at Palm Beach, and one at Cannes. We could even afford to be noble and unselfish; possibly a philanthropist, a founder, a benefactor! No such high living for our contemporary ancestors. Their minds are on their work.

As we look at ape families and primitive society, we are struck by their need for getting along as a family, as a society. Really human virtues have family and social value. These simple families must live, breed, and rear their young to adult life, or they become extinct.

They cannot eat when they are in pain or too tired or too frightened or angry; or, if they do, they cannot digest their food. Care cannot kill a cat, but worry shortens ape and human life, banishes food and sex hungers, and steals sleep. Whatever makes for peace and tranquillity in such families has survival value. Without peace they cannot function, cannot survive the keen, ceaseless struggle for a livelihood, cannot find proper mates, enough food and shelter, and protection and food for the children.

The unfaithful wife, the lawless brother, the immoral or incestuous father, the indecent, thieving, deceitful child, etc., are lawbreakers; such ways are unethical. Even among the Trobrianders, the female who is always pestering the males, seeking and demanding attention, favors, applause, is regarded as immodest, a shameless hussy.

There must be norms of social behaviour if one is to live in a society which functions through its conditioned, acquired appetites and likes and dislikes, and not through its innate reflexes. To be liked, one must learn likable, socially approved ways. The chief difference between gorilla, Bushman and Doughboy ethics is that gorilla and Bushman have a code and live up to it; the Doughboy has several, including one for Saturday night and one for Sunday.

Primitive morals are especially shocking to those accustomed to tyrannical, male-made, bisexual codes founded on neither rhyme nor reason and biologically silly, psychologically crazy, and socially worse than Masai morals.

Without going further, we seem justified in asserting that everywhere early human society was based on families founded on true marriage. Sexual disabilities or degradations were rare or unknown. Families functioned through strict codes whereby descent, inheritance, habitation, etc., were orderly and ethically systematized. Parents coöperated in rearing, sheltering, protecting and instructing their young. Children obeyed, honoured, and respected their parents. Boys and girls were formally instructed in the technique of such arts, handicrafts, etc., as were in regular use. Through broad extensions of kinship terms into complex systems, families were socially and emotionally knit into one large clan or brotherhood. Strangers were hospitably received, prisoners of war were adopted. Government was democratic, leadership being given to elders of prestige.

This is not whitewash for the "noble" savage; it is an honest and reasonable inference from what is known of apes and primitive peoples. Here and there we encounter forms of ethics which seem horrible; and those are the ones we hear about oftenest and loudest—they make a "good story." But when such horrors—cannibalism, killing off the hopelessly infirm or aged, female infanticide, etc.—are investigated, they are found to be norms of behaviour fitting in with the social and economic background.

We say we have one standard of conduct—and drop it overboard when we go to war or to Paris. The primitive has two standards: one within the tribe; one for the enemy. Law is neither a force nor a code of morals; it is simply custom, sublimated public opinion. Custom is king. Infraction of any custom which habitually provokes punishment is illegal—a "violation" of the law.

Without such social conditionings there can be no peace within the gates. Peace makes for solidarity, for strength, for the common weal; it does *not* make for kings, pontiffs, Crœsuses, nor encourage selfish ambition to gratify personal vanity by hogging power or wealth. That memorable epoch was to come later; it was to yield impressive results, but its cost in human woe did not contribute to human weal. Nor did any civilization so founded endure.

Vanity, yes; ambition, yes; personal gratification, yes; even selfishness plays its useful rôle among primitives, in any society. But when vanity, ambition, personal gratification, selfishness, pass the legitimate requirements of the tribe or nation, or are satisfied at the expense of the tribe or nation, or are pursued as mere means to vanity, power for power's sake, or wealth for wealth's sake, they inevitably become socially destructive engines.

Being born human, then, is not a figure of speech, for the family complex is a biologic factor of great import. It is unique for human beings; unique in that it places man's fate in his own hands rather than in the workings of nature. Evolutionary change is irreversible change. Man transcends that law of evolution through his brain, the organ of his plasticity. He needs no specific instincts, for life itself is an instinctive force; nor does he need to ape anyone, for he can learn better ways. He thereby learns from experience, and thus gains insight, foresight, ever wider vision.

Note again, please, that in all nature there is nothing like man's prolonged immaturity—in bone, muscle, brain; and that only in the anthropoids is there anything approaching this uniqueness of human nature. With that immaturity goes plasticity, unique plasticity. This uniqueness came slowly, painfully, haltingly, and began in the uniqueness of higher animals over lower, of lower animals over plants, and of plants over less highly organized, more simple structures. Man's real and distinguishing uniqueness goes back to Tertiary times, to the early mammals.

Mammals only have plastic brains. With mammals brain cortex becomes the distinguishing feature: bigger brains, specialization of certain parts. Tree life made for agility, and was followed by higher brain for the seeing eye and understanding ear. Then the upright gait, setting the hands free. And at last man, *Homo sapiens*, not a freak of nature, nor yet a special creation, but the perfection of hundreds of millions of years of animal effort toward greater freedom from physical environment.

The real significance of being born human, then, lies, not in the upright gait, for that is older than man, but in a big brain. Without that brain no infant could learn to behave like a human being; nor would its curiosity lead to discovery or invention; nor could it learn the meaning of the sounds its ear hears, or realize the significance of human speech, or reflect about feelings, things, and actions. "Dumb as an animal," without a brain big enough to learn to talk.

We have travelled so far from the dumb brutes that the voice "on the air" seems a miracle; and so the "mike" would seem to our grandfathers. The wisest man on earth could not have predicted the radio on the day our Unknown Soldier was born; nor can any marvel of our civilization be understood except as viewed against the background of its history and the nature of man who developed it. For the real beginnings of civilization we must go to the beginnings of speech.

# CHAPTER TWO

## In the Beginning Was the Word

1. No Articulate Speech, No Civilization. 2. The Rôle of Language among Infrahumans. 3. The Evolution of Articulate Speech. 4. The Mechanism of Speech. 5. Language as a Mode of Action. 6. The Technique of Belief. 7. Languages and Linguistic Change. 8. The Rôle of Language in Social Organization. 9. Sacred and Profane Scriptures.

I

*IN THE beginning was the Word . . . and the Word was God . . . and the Word was made flesh, and dwelt among us.*

But the first voice that cried out on this earth was that of an amphibian, and the "wilderness" was a frog-pond. It wasn't a very good voice, it wasn't a nightingale's voice; but it was a call to nature, the first vocal music on earth—and it got results. Words can do no more. As the infant in its second year learns that things have names and so makes the most important discovery of its life, so man himself made that discovery and thereby began civilization.

What a story between that first mate-call and the love lyrics now nightly put on the air! Millions of years behind that story, geologic ages of changing structure—and to what purpose? That with words man might woo woman, with words be wedded to her, and with words teach their offspring the ways of human folk? Was that the purpose of evolution from amphibia to man?

The *purpose* of evolution is as yet beyond man's ken. But looking at that story as it is revealed in the book of the earth and in the structure and behaviour of living animals, we seem justified in saying that, beginning with amphibia, first of land vertebrates, and ending with man, highest of land vertebrates, we can discover an increasing amount of socialization. This socialization among Primates is based on the facts of their sex life and the use made of the voice.

28

At any rate, it may be asserted that man is primarily a social animal, and that speech is his most socializing instrument. We may go further and state that man began when articulate speech began, and that the odyssey of his achievements and wanderings is inconceivable without words.

All this seems obvious. It is obvious that speech, or language, is a tool, an instrument, an invention, a man-made device. It is not so obvious that of all man-made devices it is the most important, the most human, the most humanizing, and incomparably the most socializing. Nor is it so obvious that social processes are primarily intercommunication processes; nor that the "real world" we live in is largely a word-world, that there are as many "worlds" as there are languages, and that every social reality is essentially dependent on the particular language habits of the society; nor that human experiences—through eyes, ears, etc.—are mostly interpreted against linguistic predispositions.

In short, it is not obvious that the world every human being has to face is a named world, and that behind some names there may be nothing more substantial than a bad verbal habit passed on from some ancient inspired lunatic who today would be adjudged insane and treated accordingly.

Free speech is a fine ideal, but ears trained to "see" through words is a sounder ideal. Our civilization, as we shall see, wabbles because there are too many hollow, unsocial, word-made ideas in its foundation, too many false words in its vocabulary. The tribute this nation alone pays to the voices of the dead is incalculable.

Yes, the word made man possible, language made civilization possible; and our present task is to see as far as possible into words as words, and language as language. Without such insight civilization is a mystery. And if there could be no civilization without articulate speech, we must look first at infrahuman activities for the beginnings of human speech. There, and there only, shall we discover the biologic nature of language, for human articulate language began with the tone language of animals. Even the mechanism amphibia employed to voice their mate-hunger is fundamentally the same mechanism humans use to voice their hungers, real or imagined.

II

*Moved* by emotion; to cry out, to voice a hunger: *tone language*.

Most of us are more or less familiar with the voices of animals—cats, dogs, horses, pigs, cattle, etc.—under emotional excitation; and while we can often distinguish the "meaning" of these voices—as in fear, rage, hunger, pleasure, satisfaction, pain, etc.—we cannot be certain in every case, we can only infer. What matters, however, is not whether *we* understand these cries, but . . . do the animals themselves?

Judging by their behaviour, they do. The voice excites the interest of other animals of the same kind, and they respond "appropriately." Hence we may say that the function of the animal voice is to arouse interest and bring about or prevent a change in behaviour. It is both a form of social control and a means of social organization. The animal voice is primarily a proclamation—"danger," "food," etc.—but only for a general situation. The human voice is more specific; it says "snake," "fried chicken," etc. But not at first. The child's world is emotional rather than objective: nice, horrible, nasty, strange, satisfactory, unsatisfactory. It is years before it learns to distinguish between the noise a thing or person makes and the thing or person that makes the noise. Its early "names" are not names for its mother, but cries for help, for food, for relief from distressing or unsatisfactory situations.

Craig's studies on pigeons, as analysed by de Laguna, are illuminating. They show such varied and important specific uses of song as personal control—male over mate; suggestion—nest-call coo and challenge coo; stimulation—with reference to sex, inhibition, adultery, nesting sites, etc.; coördination in space—leading male and female to use same nest; coördination in time—leading male and female to synchronize brood activities; proclamation—of sex, identity, rights.

What an astounding repertoire of pigeon voiced-behaviour! Birds are not simple. A society as flexible as theirs requires a varied voice control; they have a language that meets their requirements. It is a *tone* language—as far from articulate language as bird society is from human society.

As against the range of bird tone language, note the range of

emotional cries employed by those highest of all animals but man—
the monkeys and apes. And what are their screams, whines, wheed-
lings, coaxings, and cooings, but voiced forms of efforts to control
their social environment—tools, as it were, with which to bend an
outside environment to an inside need; a special kind of bodily
behaviour in one individual as an instrument for exciting a change
of behaviour in another individual; a bit of verbalized behaviour in
one to induce a change of behaviour in another.

Apes have no words, no articulate speech or language; simply
social tools for social purposes. Every ape has a kit of such tools
and knows how to use them. Such tools bring results from the
mother-ape. Ever hear an ape scream? Blood-curdling! It gets results from every ape within hearing. Ape ears, like ours, soon
become attuned to the significance of these emotional cries.

In short, apes have a language of a kind; when they have something "to say," they do their best to say it, not only by the use of
appropriate cries from an extraordinarily large repertoire, but also
by grimaces, gestures, grins, by hopping up and down, banging
a cup on a table, rattling a chain, pounding a box with fists. They
have a strikingly human-like talking mechanism. Anatomically
speaking, apes *can* talk; factually, they never do, nor even try. No
ape has been known to *talk* more than a normal half-year-old baby.

What touches a bird off in song, or an ape to scream? What
excites us to talk, to think, to sing? A stimulus, within or without.
"Within," hunger for food or mate, a mature egg in the oviduct, an
overladen milk gland, etc.—physiological stimuli; and they are as
numerous as life is complex, and end only in death. To be "adjusted" is to be all set for readjustment. "Without," of course,
means that particular and restricted part of the cosmic universe
accessible to the animal's senses.

But with words man has built additions to the sensible cosmic
universe—heavens, hells, and purgatories—and peopled them with
gods and goddesses, devils and imps and ghosts, and supplied
angelic messengers or go-betweens. These word-annexes to our sensible cosmic universe, with their word-inhabitants, rouse us to action
no less than the sensible world under our feet and before our eyes.
Nay, more, this word-world can regulate our hopes and fears and
even mould our entire life.

Note that bird song, animal cry, and human speech are specific forms or modes of behaviour and perform similar functions; but, while the animal cry occurs as a mere element of a larger response, human speech is an independent form of behaviour. For example, a girl can say "No!" while nodding her head and pursing her lips; inwardly she may be cursing a corn or thinking about the dress she will wear.

Speech, as a tool to provoke speech in others or call out a reciprocal response, is better than any tool possessed by animals lower than man; without speech, no animal could have become a human being. That is why speech evolved. It could not have evolved if the ape's voice had not had latent possibilities beyond those needed to act like an ape; just as culture, tools and weapons, industries and arts, could not have developed had not our ape ancestor been handier with his hands than he had to be to live like an ape. The adult ape, as we shall see, seems to lose his youthful interest in life: folds his hands, so to speak, and sits . . . but does *not* think, because he has no words to think with. That does not mean that he has no "feelings." It does mean that the ape never developed human speech.

III

Somehow, somewhere, sometime, cries good enough for ape society developed into human voices crying in the wilderness: just when, where, or how is idle speculation. Into that "development" went larger brains and better organization of facial muscles, making possible better facial and vocal control. The ape's face is expressive; it falls short of the human face in expressiveness. The progressive changes in the muscles of an ape's face in becoming human required a million or more years to effect, and would require a volume to describe in detail.

What I learned forty years ago about the evolution of human speech was the best guess the Whitneys of that day could make without leaving their chairs or looking out of the window. True, those guesses made no reference to Genesis ii or the Tower of Babel; but they were armchair guesses, hypotheses which could stand the test of no known or ascertainable facts such as any hypothesis must stand before it can enter into the kingdom of science.

Paget has recently propounded a hypothesis of the evolution of human speech which seems plausible and worth looking at. It rests on the idea that most languages are based on whispered or subvocal speech, and that *phonation* is only an auxiliary device by which certain important qualities are added to whispered speech, which thereby becomes more audible and produces a more emotional and artistic appeal.

I have, let us say, no words by which I can get what I want from my fellow-men. I do have a body, arms, legs, fingers, etc., over which I have fair control; also lips which I can purse, eyes I can roll, a head I can nod or "point" with; and a voice I can coo, grunt, or scream with. A clever mime gets along with less. I can make gestures; I am a fairly good pantomime artist.

Now I am hungry, let us say, and must go hunting for food. I want you to go with me. I grunt. You hear, and, having two ears, can detect direction; you look up. I go through the motions of sprinkling salt on a bird's tail or catching a bear by the tail. You understand, for you have done these things yourself. You are favourably inclined, and nod; or perhaps you go through the same pantomime, grunt as though you had eaten a bird or a bear-steak, possibly rub your stomach in anticipation. Then you get up, and off we go without another "word." No more "conversation" needed for the moment.

We need follow this hunt no farther. Have you not said to someone or thought to yourself, after seeing some silent picture without titles, "That's the best movie I ever saw"? Why the best? It was so good you needed no titles; it "acted" itself and you understood every *word* of it.

Watch an old Kiowa tell an old Cheyenne about his trip to Washington: why he went, what luck he had (he hadn't had any —Indians never do when they go to see the Big White Father), what he ate, what it cost, and so on. And he never says a word; in fact, he knows neither Cheyenne nor English, nor does the Cheyenne know Kiowa or English. He tells his long story in the famous sign-language of the Indians of the Great Plains, the *lingua franca* of the West of buffalo days. That Plains sign-language is a special language evolved, presumably, since the horse made the physical environment of the Plains a new problem of great practical importance, just as the automobile has transformed the country and ushered in new problems—of morals, manners, laws, language, etc. But note that while speech has a biological basis different from that of gesture, our deaf-mute language is a kind of phonetic writing and not at all comparable to the Plains sign-language.

In using the sign-language to communicate his story, the Kiowa was doing just what you and I were doing before we went bear-hunting—talking by gestures, pantomime. But that is only a small part of the story.

When the hero in the movie is riding like mad to save the beautiful but dumb Cinderella from going off with the villain, we help him ride, our arms tingle, our knees press the horse's sides, we use the spurs, and we muffle a whoop when he gets there just in the nick of time to foil the villain. But human nature at its very lowest animal level may best be seen at a million-dollar prize fight. Seven men got so wrought up listening in to one fight over the radio that they died of exhaustion! Or watch a small boy with his first copy-book. What is he writing with? Mind, body, and soul. His feet are wrapped around the chair, his mouth twists like a gyroscope, every muscle in his body is taut, and he actually *sweats*.

Even as a Kiowa would sweat trying to tell his story to his Cheyenne friend if there were no Great Plains gesture *language*.

Gestures can be wonderfully expressive signs, and one soon learns to "read" them. But, though I follow Charlie Chaplin easily, when I face a Balinese dancer pantomiming the loves of Arjuna, I am lost—in admiration of her grace and chagrin that I don't know more about Arjuna. She excites me; I want to follow the story she is portraying; I strain to catch the significance of every movement of her lithe body, her supple arms and hands.

To *strain* is to become more excitable: more nervous energy available. Perhaps Lamarck was not so foolish as instructors in zoology think. Conceivably, straining to make a sign like "Come on, you; let's go after birds," put a strain on tongue and lips, and on muscles which control movements of tongue and lips; conceivably, better controlled speech mechanism arose in, or as response to, the straining of that mechanism to carry more load.

That theory will not work? Well, Darwin liked it. It will not endow a blacksmith's son with huge fist and brawny arm; nor did anyone say it would. Conceivably, Lamarck's hypothesis has merit. Darwin, I repeat, thought well of it, and was not at all dogmatic about his own hypothesis of natural selection.

The next step follows naturally. As I "point" with my hands or head, I point with my tongue. Tongue, lips, and jaws come to understudy hand and body gestures. But none of these gesture-words will carry around a corner or pierce a wall on a dark night; besides, with my hands full of firewood and your eyes glued to a snake, we are both *hors de combat* in the game of conversation.

Conversation requires speaker and listener; I cannot "speak," for my wood; you cannot "listen" for your snake. That fact alone puts an enormous strain, or added stimulus, on my getting more work out of that part or segment of my body which I do not require for carrying wood, seeing snake, skinning a bear, painting a bear, or for holding, hanging, or turning my head—namely, my mouth, tongue, lips, epiglottis and glottis: my voice mechanism, my throat segment. Impelled to certain action to bring about a certain reaction in a fellow-creature, and with most of my body mechanisms already engaged, I fall back on the only mechanism available, my sounding box, my voice mechanism.

Having trained my tongue to gesture *up* or *down*, and my lips to "say" *over yonder* or *off in that direction* (as I have repeatedly seen Navajos do), I begin to use them more and more instead of hands or legs. Note, too, that the waving of my arm or stretching out of my leg burns up some calories—not many, of course, but more than a wagging tongue will consume in an hour's conversation. If talking took us to the filling station as often as walking, most of us would have to talk less and walk more.

But suppose I grunt or sing while I am pantomimically asking you to go "bearing" or "birding," as I might to sharpen your attention. That brings about an important result: *a modification of the laryngeal sound*. I hear it; you hear it. Suppose I repeat that trick that night in the dark. I hear it; you hear it: you and I have taken our first step in learning a new language. That modified grunt need not be called a *word* yet: it is a symbol, a sign, a certain special sound I can make which you can hear and *understand*. Is that *symbol* a "part of speech," a word, or possibly a sentence? We shall look into that later.

The gamut of these voiced mouth-gestures is soon run; mere lateral movements of lips, tongue, and jaw can alter the quality of the voice very little. Thus, they would necessarily be limited to up-and-down or to-and-fro movements: two-dimensional movements. And that helps to account for the fact that in all languages the same word is often forced to bear several meanings. The gestures of articulation in speech are limited in number; the hand can gesture in three dimensions.

We need not push this gesture hypothesis further. It works. It is at least as old as Socrates. In Plato's *Cratylus* he asks: If we had no voice or tongue and wished to make things clear to one another, should we not try, as dumb people do, to make signs with our hands and head and person generally?

Wallace pointed out many cases in English of words produced by appropriate gestures of our speech mechanism, bringing "sense and sound into union." Try it *up* and *down* on your own jaw; or note the gestural significance in consonants—the *continuous* motion in *fly, run, swim, move*; the abrupt endings to motions with stopped consonants, as in *stop, leap, pat, stab, kick,* etc.

What "catches" our ear as we listen to speech—the sounds themselves, or the evidence the sounds afford as to the gestures of the speech mechanism? The latter, presumably, as otherwise it would be hard to understand the ease with which the deaf learn speech (lip-reading) by mere sight, and limited at that to the movements of the lips alone.

Well, if this pantomimic hypothesis be sound, it must apply to all languages—and does. But that does not signify that a Chinaman will halt when I say *stop*. Our voice gesture *stop* might also and easily be stip, stap, stup, etc. Alternative sounds for the same gesture may be produced, using more or less rigor, or by slight changes in the position of the mouth. Our own, and presumably every speech, has and has had its *homophones*: words with several distinct or even opposite meanings. Hence the more than a thousand vocabularies on earth today. As Sapir says, we can hardly expect to reduce the present babel to its pristine unity—for there never was unity.

To sum up Paget's hypothesis: Man *naturally* tends to express his ideas in pantomime, his tongue "understudying" his hands. Hence it follows that in forming spoken words the tongue tends to keep in gestural relation to the ideas that are to be expressed. If this principle underlies all philologic changes, it confers immortality upon all good pantomimic words.

IV

We pretend to know how thunder and lightning ("God Almighty's artillery") are produced, but we do not know how the voice of man is framed—"that poor little noise we make every time we speak," said Sir William Temple some four centuries ago. We shall have many occasions to contrast what was known 400 years ago with what we "pretend" to know today; but, curiously enough, our scientific laboratories can turn out a machine that produces real thunder and lightning, whereas their efforts to make a machine that will really talk are as yet only moderately successful. The noise we make every time we speak may be poor and little, but there is nothing simple about our speech mechanism; in fact, it is so complex that it is not yet all understood; otherwise we should have a more perfect speech-producing machine than Sir Richard Paget's clay model. I said *pro*duce, not *re*produce.

It must be obvious from what has been said that human speech is unique, not so much as vocal music, but in such control over a musical instrument that it can be made to speak as well as to sing, to produce words, thousands of words, as well as vocal music of widely varying emotional intensities. It is the control—*vocal* control—which is unique; a control which only human beings can learn because of their unique capacity to learn. But first let us look at the marvellous "sound" mechanism, or organ of speech, with which we are born and which we learn to control for such varied human ends.

Our speech-and-song-producing mechanism is a wind instrument. Our lungs correspond to a pair of adjustable bellows which deliver air through our trachea, or windpipe, which in turn ends in our larynx, or Adam's apple. In passing up toward our mouth, the air passes through a pair of "vocal cords" in our larynx. These cords, genetically the primary opening or air valve of the vertebrate larynx, resemble the lips of our mouth, but are only half as large, and can by muscle control be "tuned" up or down or thrown out of action. As Paget puts it, these cords amount to a vibrating reed; their vibration produces the "poor little noise."

Just above the cords is our epiglottis, which, with the soft palate in the roof of our mouth, forms a resonating cavity. The size and shape of this cavity are regulated by the tongue and lips. Thus, the cavity can be subdivided, closed off from the nose, etc.

Human speech (says Paget) is really two separate acts: producing the sound, or phonation; and modifying it into words, or articulation.

*Phonation,* the tone language of the emotions which corresponds with the natural cries of animals, is due to the reed-like action of the vocal cords, and is used to express such emotional states as fear, anger, pleasure, affection, or the like. *Articulation,* due to the various movements of the jaw, lips, tongue, and other movable portions of the vocal cavity, is the language of the mind. This language may be produced as whispered (or breathed) speech, when the vocal cords are held apart, so as not to vibrate as the air passes between them, or as "voiced" speech when the vocal cords are pressed together so as to vibrate (like the lips of a cornet-player) as the air from the lungs is forced between them on its way to the mobile cavities where "articulation" is produced.

Acoustics, or the business of hearing, was an obscure point until cleared up by the great Helmholtz, who in the middle of the last century formulated the principles of Resonance. Later, Graham Bell showed that most of our English vowel sounds are due to at least two resonances set up in different parts of our vocal cavity or resonator.

Air, being elastic, acts like a spring in a cavity. When disturbed it begins to surge in and out of the resonator, producing "sound" waves. The size of the resonator and of the opening through which the air surges, governs the rate of surging, or number of pulses per second. Thus, a large cavity produces slow pulses (sound as a low note); a large opening, permitting the air to surge in and out quickly, gives rise to a high note, because the larger the cavity, the longer time needed for the pressure to pile up, and pile out. Further, any change of shape (by obstruction, etc.) of vocal cavities changes the stream of pulsating air passing through; and that, in turn, disturbs the air in every accessible part of the vocal cavity.

As a result of these physical phenomena, a complex compound sound-wave comes out of the speaker's mouth. One of the first tasks we had to learn as little children was what these sound-waves meant: in short, what mother was saying; for these sound-waves are the words of human speech.

Most words consist of vowels and consonants. Vowel sounds result from tongue and lips so posed as to form two or three connected cavities, which thereby produce corresponding numbers of resonant notes. Vowels are produced by *postures*; most consonants, by *gestures* of tongue, lips, etc. Thus, open your mouth quickly; that "p" that came out is a consonant. Now say "k." How did you do it? And all so easy! Some day the radio will fling a deaf-mute's "speech" to Penguin Island: the mute will simply operate the keyboard of a machine that will make any speech one can think up if one knows the necessary words and can spell them phonetically.

Could a deaf-mute learn to use a mechanical phonetic speaker? When Laura Bridgman "talked" in her sleep, she spoke the only "language" she knew, the gesture-language of deaf-mutes. Helen Keller is a different case; she had a wonderful teacher. I still recall, after nearly forty years, guiding her hand over the body of a mummified dog I had dug up in Peru. She recognized it almost instantly, her face lit up, and in a mechanical voice that I shall never forget she uttered the one word, *dog*. Both Miss Keller and Miss Bridgman talked as children; their misfortune was not congenital, but befell them at the age of two. Presumably, congenital deaf-mutes cannot learn "speech" as that term is generally understood, nor learn to speak phonetically through a mechanical talking robot.

Just here it is worth noting that when some Graham Bell or Thomas Edison patents a real talking machine and puts it on the market as a commercial product, he will go down in history as *the* inventor; Paget's preliminary laboratory model will have been forgotten—like the experiments of Wheatstone, Kratzenstein, and de Kempelin of 150 years ago. De Kempelin's "speaker" could be made to produce sentences in French, though it spoke its native German tongue better.

Fleas and lice may still be "born" from the dust of Babylon, as the natives say they are; inventions such as the telegraph, telephone, radio, steam engine, etc., are not born of single brains or individual men, but are rooted in the soil of human nature and nurtured by human society. They begin as tiny germs, and usually require long incubation.

V

Just so human speech was born, for its germ, in all literalness, goes back to that old frog-pond. There, I repeat, the first voice was lifted up. Our ears may find no music in a frog's voice, but every human voice owes its vocal cords to amphibia. That primeval vocal music was a sex call, evolved to meet a need only the voice could supply in a swamp; it had survival value.

It is a far cry from that first croak to the song of the lark or the impassioned plea of a pulpit orator; but no farther than from amphibia to man, or from the lowly, insecure life of a frog in a swamp to the rather more secure life of a man in a cave or in a modern city.

Just what life in a cave and in a modern city means we shall endeavor to ascertain later; but as one of our chief concerns is to discover the "meaning" of man himself, we may pause here long enough to make certain that we are on the right track. I am far from certain that I know what the right track is, but I am equally far from doubt that failure to recognize the biologic significance of speech is fatal to a scientific understanding of human society or modern civilization.

Take John's famous lines again: "In the beginning was the Word . . ." It is no exaggeration to say that millions of words have been spoken and written about and around these lines or equally hollow phrases. William James spoke of the metaphysical theologians who shuffle and match pedantic dictionary adjectives; Ogden, of the ablest logicians who evolve fantastic systems by the aid of verbal technique. Every known form of social injustice or sex inequality has been backed by quotations from some Holy Writ.

Aristotle's catchwords have ruled human thought for over 2,000 years—and still furnish enough food for thought for those who find thinking more profitable than observing. The Classics still "train" minds, as candles "save" souls. Not one single step in advance did modern civilization take until it had cast off the chains of some ancient system of words. Even philosophy, as a discipline of ancient lineage, at last tends to evaporate before the modern scientific attitude which demands that language be understood if knowledge or the meaning of symbols is to be understood. To transform grammatical forms and linguistic processes into metaphysical entities and then talk about them as though they were primary symbols of fundamental human needs or wants, may be an intellectual pastime; it cannot be a useful pursuit for modern society.

Of all this, more anon; much more. But when we come to look at human history, we want to be able to look at it with a modern, critical eye, which means without blinders or rose-coloured glasses. No historical or human-behaviour problem can be understood without understanding language mechanisms in general and our own language habits in particular.

Up to the beginnings of the modern scientific point of view, no system of words that left out of account some anthropomorphic magician-creator was thought adequate to describe nature; and how many today can think of human evolution without dragging in such Aristotelian phrases as mind, intellect, consciousness, mental faculties, intellectual traits, etc.? What are our Animal Mind and Ape Consciousness but relics of Middle Age Scholastic verbiage?— long-winded arguments about hypothetical entities that are as useless in anthropology as are gods and demons in astronomy. There may be gods and demons, but they are not scientific concepts and are not useful in describing celestial phenomena. So, also, there may be souls, minds, faculties, etc., but such entities cannot be observed, and such concepts are not needed to describe human behaviour or to understand human beings. I know no better way of bringing this point into relief than by sketching briefly the processes of learning to talk, think, etc.

Here is an ape, let us say. I brought him up, fed him, cared for him. He knows me, and under certain internal drives exhibits certain forms of behaviour toward me. What does he think of me? Nothing. Or, to speak loosely, he "thinks" of me in terms of hugs, mouth-waterings, grins, silly little squeals and coos of delight, heightened excitement, etc.; in terms of words, speech, thoughts, just *nil*. And without speech or thoughts, the ape can have no mind or consciousness.

If I have anything the ape has not, it is language; if I can do anything the ape cannot, it is think it over with myself and then say it. Or put it this way: Speaking is a mode of action. The bodily segment involved in speaking is the throat—the speech-mechanism. Ape and I both have such a mechanism, just as we both have arms and hands; but, through cerebral control, I can get more action, a wider range of action, out of my speech-mechanism or organ of speech than the ape can. Why? Because the human speech organ is a *better* organ for articulate speech than the ape's; it has a more flexible musculature and is dominated by a larger or more flexible nervous organization. The ape is more immediately under the influence of his emotional drives; through words I may postpone for months or years my response to an intolerable situation, or, having consigned the "intolerable situation" to the lowest pit in hell, I may "grin and bear it"—or write a book.

I no more need a "mind" than I do a "faculty" to put these words down on paper. What I need to "put it down on paper" is, briefly, a certain type of manual organization; and I had to learn that. To "say" it, I have to have a certain kind of verbal organization; and I had to learn that.

The ape is curious, energetic, persevering; he experiments, experiences, learns. He becomes clever, learns lots of tricks. He has habits of response: bodily, or manual; visceral, or emotional; and both become well organized. But of verbalized (voice, speech) behaviour he has at twenty years practically no more than he had at twenty days: enough for being an ape. Our speech, as de Laguna says, applies to a world of things and qualities, acts and relations; this world, in distinctiveness and in interconnections, does not exist for dogs or apes, but only for human beings.

One word more to emphasize and clarify how human beings organize their verbalized behaviour. If I say, "I play golf," you understand me, and realize that I had to learn it and could learn it only by getting out on the field and whacking the ball with a club—by effort, experience, trial and error. My *manual* organization includes golf.

If I say, "I hate golf; the sight of a ball makes me sick!" you may smile indulgently, but you know there *are* people like that, "squeamish." About most things, however, I am not squeamish at all; almost nothing makes me sick; not moth balls nor tumble-bug balls—only golf balls. My *visceral* organization includes a certain particular reaction at the sight of golf balls.

You hear a lecture on golf and say: "Grand! Such a well-trained mind! Such a clear thinker! What an intellect!" But neither "intellect" nor "mind" is needed to talk well or clearly or intelligibly about golf, or about anything. One does need words, and practice in stringing them along so that they sound plausible, reasonable, "worth-while." In short, to evoke your "Grand!" on the golf course, one must play a good game of golf; on a lecture platform one must, and easily can, "play" a good game with words.

In learning to play golf we call upon muscles already fit for many forms of bodily or manual behaviour; by trying these muscles we learn comparatively new ways of action in response to new stimuli. It was hard work at first, and may be yet; our visceral organization may be so poor that we are unfit for *any* competitive or public sport. But if we are good, golf is easy, a joy; no sweat, no bad words. A habit. That means millions of muscle engines exploding at the right time, in the right amounts, and being kept supplied with enough "gas"; sensory and motor nerves functioning to a T. That is *kinæsthetic* organization, or motor-feel sense.

How does one learn to *talk* golf? By the same road the human infant travelled to learn "Dada" 100,000 years ago. The human infant can cry, make noises; it can hear these cries, noises. It fumbles and explores with that "original endowment" of voice mechanism and stumbles upon a phonetic combination that gets results—a smile, a gumdrop; it heard the sound that proved a winner, and makes it again. We are imitators, but the people we imitate are ourselves. Learning is a process of climbing up the ladder we build as we learn.

The child learns to attach vocal significance to an object. It does not thereby "name" the object; it has merely learned a new kind of response to the object. Its learning (both verbal and manual) is part of the family game. Parents help, applauding successes, frowning on failures. By and by the child learns that there is a specific response (word) to be learned for each object. That in itself becomes a new game, and the child is as delighted in trying out its powers as is the lamb gambolling on the green or the ape monkeying with an alarm clock.

And all the while, in these trial-error experiments with voice, not only is the child taking on or organizing speech (verbalized) behaviour as such; it is organizing the behaviour or learning the control of muscles of lips, tongue, larynx, etc., into definite and useful modes of response. Speaking involves neuro-muscular activity. Just as our kinæsthetic organization (of muscles and tendons of back and legs, and balancing organ in middle ear) tells us when we have made a false step, so that same body-feel or kinesthetic sense in the throat-mouth segment tells us when a word has been fumbled.

The child soon becomes a fluent talker. Then come the "Shut-ups!" It keeps right on talking—to itself. It becomes proficient in that form of verbalized behaviour, and is now a thinker. Talking is *explicit*, overt verbalization; thinking, *implicit*—and so easy that we think the grandest thoughts, or commit the foulest murders even though our lily-white hands could not harm a kitten.

We are born into a world of language and things; we have to learn to use them. There is a *technique* of language—as there is of ice-skates or chopsticks. Mastery of the technique means more power; more work from the mechanism involved, less sweat in working it.

Language can work wonders on land and sea—through rousing enemies and mobs of men to action. Language is the mightiest of all instruments in its power to play upon human nature, to provoke men to climb to the stars or slink to obscurity. Words can kill as well as cure. Yet how little time we give to the perfection of this most potent of all tools and the one we use most. Besides, it is far easier to hurl an epithet than a brick at our enemy.

Hurl an epithet. That is an old habit in human history. It wasn't only bombs that were hurled across the lines in the World War. Presumably, verbal bombs have been plentiful in every war since war became an institution for making peace.

We learn more than mere *words* and how to use them; we learn their *weights*, kicks, explosive powers. Probably none of us realizes the potency of a string of words to affect us: some little, some greatly, some like poisoned arrows. Think of the fate of the poor wretches upon whom the Church had pronounced sentence of excommunication! Sentence of death today were more bearable.

If some extraordinarily delicate instrument were attached to us, capable of registering our slightest reaction in respiration, heart-beat, resistance to a string galvanometer, etc., it would be found that few words would weigh the same to any two of us. Many experiments have been made to test these reactions. One such is before me, and not the least interesting part of the result is the discrepancy between what the mechanical Sherlock Holmes recorded and what the subjects themselves reported. I ask you, for example, what is your reaction to the word *moron*; you reply, "Little, if any." The instrument might show a violent reaction. You might resent my using that word as possibly being personal.

The ten most heavily loaded words, as shown by mechanically recorded reaction time, were: "name", naked body, kiss, husband-wife, intercourse, self-abuse, Jesus Christ, the dean's office, prostitute, disappointment in love. But the *last* ten words of a long list were: immoral, mother, frigid-impotent, ambitious, hot-headed, father, undersized, childish, stupid, lonely.

Of the first ten words, no less than seven have a sexual significance; yet to two of these words—intercourse and disappointment in love—the students *claimed* practical immunity. That is, they lied; for the mechanical detective showed that the words *moved* them. Still more significant is the fact that among the least heavily loaded words occur "mother" and "father." That also is against the rules.

When the entire list of words is arranged according to the load the students *said* they carried, we have: "name", Jesus Christ, kiss, mother, father, lover, ambitious, success, kicked out, self-abuse. Which means that we can lie one way and emote another way at the same time. We can say—as did Rip Van Winkle after each drink, "We won't count it this time"; it is counted just the same somewhere inside us, and thereby becomes part of us. Lip-service, it is often called. It can also be done with hands; as when we make the sign of the cross with a hand that has just thrown a brick. The amount of lip-service at large in our civilization is staggering, and possibly an insupportable burden.

Later, we shall look into some of the beliefs that have enormously influenced the growth and direction of civilization. Critically examined, many of them, as we shall see, are childish; others, stupid; while still others have proved almost insuperable barriers against the formation of new and more socially serviceable creeds. But to say that a belief (for example, that the earth is flat or that woman was created from a rib) is childish, is one thing; it is quite another thing to understand the technique of believing or the mechanism involved in coming to or arriving at a belief.

If I say, for example, that Frank Smith believes in ghosts and is afraid of a Holy Ghost, I have stated a fact, not as to ghosts, but as to his belief. But if I say, let us see if we can find out why Smith, in other respects a hard-headed man, should be so gullible and credulous in this one respect; or, if we go farther back in time and try to find out why *any* human being ever began to believe in ghosts and to behave as though he had seen some, we leave history and turn to human nature to help solve our problem. That is what we are doing here. We are not now concerned with beliefs in a flat earth or in ghosts, or in any particular belief, but in the behind-the-curtain part of our make-up where beliefs are born.

Knowing the genesis of beliefs in general, we can the more easily understand how even today certain primitive, ancient, childish beliefs not only persist, like our coccygeal bones, but, not content to blush unseen like our atavistic tails, grow strong enough to "wag the dog."

Do dogs believe; do apes have beliefs? The answer, of course, is no. Beliefs, judgments, opinions, etc., as we commonly use these terms, are as far beyond the reach of dogs and apes as is human verbalized behaviour (speech, language, thought). But as dogs can lead a dog's life and apes an ape's life without word or speech, so they can react to dog- or ape-universe without beliefs or opinions.

Before we have beliefs we have thoughts: we weigh evidence; balance the pros and cons; come to a decision, have a belief. No belief, presumably, springs up full-grown in any one individual; it has its very humble and often unrecognizable beginnings, as does every tool, any invention. Conversation is the great garden for growing beliefs. They pop up like weeds, jostling, crowding one another, fighting for a place in the sun. Those that get to the top, to be carried off and pressed to the bosom or dried and shown to friends, are not necessarily the sanest, wisest, or most useful. What carries most of us away is not so much the belief as the tone or the appearance of the man who voices it. We can almost as easily accept the beliefs of our enemies as love them.

Conversation in ancient days probably passed through two stages or phases: first, a long pow-wow to settle the big features of a situation—a hunting expedition or defence preparations for an impending attack, leading to some general agreement as to the main facts of the situation; then some more conversation in which plans or a plan of action were determined. But I suspect that then, as now, the *chairman*—Dominant Male, Big Chief, Largest Stockholder, Best Mind—told them where to stop but not why: and that was the real "topic" of the conversation.

As de Laguna says, language can become so autonomous as to transcend and defy all known laws of nature and go on its own for hours. Conceivably, a roomful of talking machines, their keyboards operated by boys shooting phonetics at them with peashooters, could "converse" with as much rhyme or reason in solving the problems of human society as half the gabble that passes today for "conversation."

But as language was the greatest social builder of all human inventions, for it is a tool easily acquired and easily carried, so conversation is the great instrument for bringing about social solidarity. Greetings are exchanged; deeds and events, real or imagined, are recounted; and so forth. It is a major human activity, and for many their sole sport, source of greatest satisfaction, their Field of the Cloth of Gold. What was once useful and necessary in making preparation for primary human action has come to be the "medium for reliving the past, enjoying imaginary worlds of delights, deeds and triumphs unattainable in primary life."

And how is thinking or believing related to conversation? Two are company; three are a crowd. *Alone* one can think things out for oneself. After all, "we" are society, and three are pa, ma, and the baby; but we act, live, behave, think, believe, not as society nor as pa, ma, and the baby, but as pa, ma, *or* the baby—as individuals.

"Society" is a word, a concept, an idea; it existed before it was named, conceptualized or abstracted, before groups of individuals of varying size were resumed or summarized for purposes of convenience under the word "society."

Great thoughts! Great thinkers! Too often nothing more substantial, more useful, more wearable or livable, proceeds from these Best Minds and Intellectual Giants, than a lot of words any child could easily find in a dictionary. We once had to think (make a word-plan of action) how and where we could get our next meal; and having thought that out (reached a conclusion as to how we could get it and where) we had to go "there" and get it. And that was a marvellously useful tool for getting meals. Now we do not have to do any thinking; the radio tells us what to do, be, wear, eat, and believe. All we have to do is believe and buy it. One of the first things we learn is to believe what we are told; and one of the hardest things to learn is to outgrow our early beliefs.

I need a new dictionary; but will it tell me how to be honest, faithful, beautiful, good, or give me more freedom, more energy, or enlighten me as to the least common denominator in a good meal, a good hug, a good baby, and a good God? It will define these words—in terms of other words. It is, as Ogden says, "a list of substitute symbols": if you do not know what that word means, substitute this or that word. It "serves to mark the overlaps between references of symbols"; it does not define their fields.

When to Polonius' "What do you read, my lord?" Hamlet replied, "Words, words, words," I infer he was reading philosophy, theology, or the dictionary.

Our own English language is strewn with barbaric relics and needless complications, irregularities and ambiguities; and it should be spelled as it is spoken, without dictionary, with phonetics. Our alphabet is an antique hand-me-down, as modern as an ox-cart. It has twenty-six letters, but as a matter of fact we require, and actually use, about forty sounds to speak our "minds." The way a word is spelled in the dictionary gives us only a clue, often misleading, as to how to pronounce it to put it into circulation; for speaking purposes we require a *pronouncing* dictionary.

We have, and can have, only vague notions of Greek and Latin phonetics—or of any dead language. They left no pronouncing dictionaries; we have to infer. A modern Neapolitan or Roman probably could not understand enough of *De Senectute* as spoken by Cicero, to discover whether he was talking about hay fever or a trip to Sicily; and Demosthenes' *De Corona* might be a description of *Cuba Libre*, for all a modern Greek could make of it.

VII

Language is primarily a tool for social purposes, and is as truly a cultural product as a prayer-meeting or a wedding ring. Not every society—or culture—has a prayer-meeting or a wedding ring, but every society has a language: human society and human culture are dependent on language. If children are the cement of society, language is the "real world" in which society functions and into which babies are born.

In other words, every human being is born not only into a big world of objects and a little world of social activity, but also into an English- or German- or Chinese-speaking world. And every human being must learn the language of that world, not only that he may communicate with its people, but that he may know just what the "real world" is that is to be his home for the few decades nature allots human life. What we individuals see, hear, feel, taste, touch, desire to possess or fear to think, or what we experience, is largely predetermined for us by the language habits of our social environment.

In sober truth, it is far easier to say that we are at the mercy of our language habits than to realize the significance of that fact; just as it is easier for us to realize that many of our language habits are primitive and inhuman, than to overhaul our primitive institutions, laws, and practices, which, however reasonable once, are now known to be dangerous to civilization and destructive of human health and happiness.

Our concern here, however, is to realize that language is a unique product of human culture, the supreme tool for social intercourse, for reproducing and sharing experience, for getting and giving information, for expressing and communicating emotions, and for so labelling or symbolizing the nominal, phenomenal, and epiphenomenal world that it can be manipulated in thought, without turning a hand or lifting a foot. We cannot stop here to inquire into the distinction between these or between the subjective and objective worlds; but we do insist that the difference between the world Mussolini, let us say, lives in, and the world we live in, is not merely in the label attached but in the world itself: they are different and distinct worlds. As Sapir says, there are as many distinct "worlds" as there are different societies, and each has its own language.

The Lapps, for example, are said to have twenty-four words for ice, forty-one for snow in different forms, eleven for cold, and twenty-six for freezing, thawing, etc.; also words for all the species of reindeer. Just what does "cattle" mean in English—livestock of all kinds, or merely the species *Bovidæ*? There is no confusion in the words bull, cow, ox, steer, calf, heifer, etc. Yet these sex and age distinctions, which for us have practical use, are without value to a Masai cattle-owner. His world is different from ours, as is also the Lapp's; even as ours is different from that of our forefathers.

Man can talk, but not until he has acquired his language. There is an organic basis for language, but its environment is superorganic, cultural. Hence cultural change makes for linguistic change. As culture in general has evolved without benefit of clergy, rhyme, or reason, and as there are many cultures, so languages have evolved and are as numerous as cultures. Nor has any language yet passed its primary, rudimentary stage as an instrument for symbolizing human thought.

The Bible uses 7,200 words; Milton, 17,000; Shakespeare, 24,000; a good dictionary, 100,000. My medical dictionary has 76,000 words; my chemical dictionary, about 30,000; and both must be revised every few years, so rapidly does the world of medical and chemical science change and grow. Probably two or three thousand words sufficed to symbolize primitive man's activities in play, war, ritual, and art, as well as in food and shelter.

When primary symbols were supplanted by secondary or referential symbols is quite unknown. But this is known. When Babel was built man had already built Babels and Pyramids, and with words had named the world he knew through his eyes and that other world that came to him in his dreams: shadows and night-mares that arose in response to his need to calm his fears and fertilize his fields and keep things going on forever in the "same old way."

All humanity talks through the same kind of vocal cords and gets its hot air from the same kind of bellows. To speak of a *parent* language of human speech is to talk nonsense—as it is to speak of Adam and Eve, or of any one pair, as the parents of the human race. Yet St. Basil in the fifth century was accused of being an "atheist" because he held that babies had to *learn* to talk. It took away another instinct and seemed impious—as though God had forgotten to endow us with one of our most necessary gifts! Then there was King James of Scotland, who decided to decide not only whether infants had to learn to talk, but what the original tongue was. He turned two "bairns" over to a dumb woman to be brought up on an island; and sure enough, at the right age they could speak! In what tongue? The "original": Hebrew. And "guid" at that! Thousands have burned at the stake for doubting such fairy stories.

No one language is older than another; all go back to unknown and unsung beginnings. Nor can we say of any known language that it is more primitive or more rudimentary than, for example, English or Chinese. Every known language bears the marks of great antiquity.

We no longer, therefore, seriously hope or attempt to arrange languages in their order of development or to grade them in an evolutionary series—as "races" are sometimes arranged. Analysis of the language of any backward people—the Arunta of Central Australia, for example—would reveal an astounding and bewildering complexity.

Even the scheme in vogue a few years ago, of classifying languages according to one or another formal process, is being discarded. True, some languages do consistently follow a definite grammatical process which seems to be typical of a group of otherwise unrelated languages. But, like "races," they overlap. The scheme is found to be purely arbitrary—as are most schemes for classifying human beings or human achievements. As it keeps popping up, however, we may look at it—if only to get it out of our systems.

In the so-called *Isolating* type of language, words are fixtures—

entities, as it were; they are not modifiable grammatically. Chinese is the prize-winner in this class. Chinese grammar is taken care of when the words are arranged in ways that may be dark to us but which are quite clear when one understands Chinese. Thus, to use Sapir's example, the four words "Woo pu pa ta" mean "I do not fear him"; but, shuffled up as "Ta pu pa woo," they mean "He does not fear me." In other words, grammar (subject, predicate, object) is a matter of arrangement; just as 1234 is quite different from 4321 or 3412.

In the *Agglutinative* type of language, words are not entities, like colored beads on a string; they are agglutinous, like the carbon chains in a molecule of fat. Turkish is the stock example. Thus, "Dzan u gonul-den unan-a gel-ir-ler" means "Heart and soul-from belief-to coming-ings"—or, "They were converted to the true faith with heart and soul."

With the *Inflective* type, we find ourselves more at home. We used to know something about Greek and Latin inflections—so much, in fact, that we knew little Latin or Greek. If no sample rises to the surface easily, say "I see the men" as *video homines.* It seems like an old friend, a "good" language, *civilized,* Classical.

*Polysynthetic* used to be said to characterize the morphology of the American-Indian languages; but not only do they vary enormously, some are Inflective, others Agglutinative.

When the classification scheme was *au courant* it was the fashion to grade them, Latin at the top, Chinese at the bottom. But . . . English was once Inflective, is becoming Isolating; so we now say, put Chinese at the top as a type—but find extenuating circumstances for putting English in a class by itself.

But, as Kroeber points out, if mere wealth of grammatical apparatus be made the criterion, Latin stands higher than French and Anglo-Saxon higher than English; and if lack of declensions be a virtue, Chinese stands higher than English by about ten per cent. Sapir, if pressed to name the language logically of "most perfect linguistic form," would nominate Chinese: a "language that, with the simplest possible means at its disposal, can express the most mechanical or philosophical ideas with absolute lack of ambiguity and with admirable conciseness and directness."

But Chinese is so sing-songy! So it is. It is a musical language.

Why not? Musical accent can be as effective as phonetic characteristics, and is, not only in degrees varying from a musical scale of
two up to one of seven in Chinese dialects, but also in many other
Asiatic, African, and even a few American-Indian languages.
Musical accent was employed by the Homeric Greeks, and is today
by the Lithuanians. Possibly our school began as a singing-school.
My father sang his geography lessons.

Lord Raglan has an idea which may illuminate this subject.
His idea is that "hilltop" peoples (as Italians in Europe and Lotuka
in the Sudan) *shout* their language; and that "plains" peoples
(Germans, Dinkas of the Sudan) do not. Basque and Japanese
(hilltop peoples) are "shouting" languages; Chinese is not. From
which he infers that to such factors as "degeneracy" and "foreign
influence" which produce linguistic change, physical environment
should be added. Maybe.

One thing is certain: we never transcend our physical environment. It may not mould us; it weighs on us—fifteen pounds to the
square inch at sea-level. Remove that pressure: we do not go up
like a balloon; we die like a candle in a vacuum. It is also certain
that, despite divergences, all languages agree fundamentally in
structure and means of expression; and that the categories in all
languages are largely childish and primitive, irrational and unsys-
tematic. Even poets, painters, and priests, however high their
spiritual heads, never quite succeed in their efforts to transcend the
struggle for existence nature imposes on men. They may develop
their own linguistic rituals, but their mother-tongue must reflect
a practical attitude toward a practical world.

"Mother-tongue" is spoken of as a linguistic *stock* or *family*.
Thus, English is a dialect of the far-flung Indo-European or Aryan
stock, which includes all the early languages or dialects of Europe,
Persian or Iranic, Armenian, and several modern Sanscrit-derived
languages of India. Homeric and modern Greek would have to be
classed as distinct dialects, as would English and German, the
various Slavic languages, and the Latin-derived languages—Spanish,
French, Portugese, Italian, and Rumanian. There are two other
stocks in Europe: Ural-Altaic (Finnish, Magyar or Hungarian, and
Turkish); and Basque, of the northern and southern slopes of the
Pyrenees.

The number of linguistic families on earth today has never been accurately determined; but about ninety per cent of all the people on earth can be put in eight great families: Indo-European, Ural-Altaic, Semitic, Sinitic, Dravidian, Japanese, Malayo-Polynesian, and Bantu. Of these families, the Semitic is of the greatest historic interest. Babylonians, Assyrians, Phœnicians, Carthaginians and Hebrews were all great Semitic-tongue nations; and since the rise of Mohammedanism, Arabic, chief living Semitic tongue, has supplanted Hamitic, the tongue of ancient Egypt, as the great language of Africa north of the equator.

It need hardly be said that there is no innate connexion between language and physiognomy or physical features, or between language and culture. It is therefore as nonsensical to speak of a "Semitic" or an "Aryan" race as of a Catholic physique or a brunette linguistic type. While the laws of physical heredity are not yet at all well understood, it is known that they are different from those which govern the diffusion of culture traits—of which some spread rapidly, others slowly or not at all. The diffusion of language is something different again. Words may be borrowed more easily than sounds or phonetics, and grammar rarely passes beyond its own home except when carried by those who speak it as their mother-tongue.

As blood circulated millions of years before Harvey discovered the fact, so grammar is older than the grammarians; and languages change despite the authorities. "I ain't" and "he don't" will be good grammar when enough good people habitually use these expressions. The King's English is not what it used to be. But the mere fact that there is no rational basis for any given linguistic or cultural usage is no reason for stigmatizing it. There is as much sense in a patent-leather shoe as in the word "thou"; no more reason for discarding one than the other. The plain fact is that man is an enormously complex and generally highly irrational creature, not easily grasped by the hand or encompassed by words.

VIII

Families of two, of ten thousand; social and religious organizations; fraternities, sororities; age and military societies; states,

United States. Is there strength in union, or is man just a natural-born "joiner"?

Human societies; social *instinct!* Recall the many uses the turtle-dove has for its voice. But here is another dove, fundamentally different from the one that used its voice for so many social purposes. It is a "dumbbell" of a dove; it does not know how to coo. When it hears another dove singing, it looks bored. Is it an idiot? Not at all. It was born in a dovecote, but was brought up by the jays. It never learned how to "talk" like a dove. In other words, even a dove has to learn to behave like a dove. It learns that in dove society. Brought up with blue jays, it does its anatomical best to talk blue jay.

Social organization in all higher animal society is voiced organization. Animals with voices hear other voices, and also their own. Some of the best "music in our ears" is the music of our own voice. Nor can we understand the beginnings of social organization without some notion of the process whereby our whole body easily and naturally becomes a receiving instrument, as it were, for voices and sound-waves in general.

To illustrate. I sit down before the radio, and, closing my eyes, slowly move the dial across the plate. I keep picking up sounds: voices, male and female, singing, speaking, declaiming, selling, "blah"-ing; music, vocal, instrumental; and so on. Within an hour I have been *moved*, emotionally aroused, in many ways: moved to a smile, to a frown, to laughter, and to anger.

We are harps, of thousands of strings, and the whole buzzing world plays on us. Most of the buzzes fall on deaf ears, set no string vibrating in us; some of them plunge us into grief, some move us to laughter, some to anger. Our "strings" are extraordinarily sensitive; they become insensitive to certain voices and ideas, sensitive to others.

I said moved, emotionally aroused, and spoke of tears, smiles, laughter, etc. We know what we cry with, smile with, laugh with. We can feel the tear trickle down our face, hear ourselves sob. There is no mystery about all this; it is sensible behaviour, sensed in ourselves and when exhibited by our fellow-creatures. And it is all highly verbalized; we have names for tears, sobs, frowns, winks, blinks, scowls, smiles, pouts, laughter, grins, blushes, etc.

The *feel* behind the emotion that moves us to tears, etc., is deep within us, in the very bowels of our nature; we have no words to describe our visceral heavings while our harp-strings are being played upon. When we can describe the second-by-second behaviour of our thirty-foot-long alimentary canal, with its countless muscle engines and secreting glands, and of our almost as complicated urino-genital system, as well and as vividly as we now describe our manual behaviour, we shall have progressed in understanding ourselves and human society. Our autonomic nervous system is of very humble parentage, but without it there would be no higher life for us, nor idea to be voiced. If, as Mark Twain said, ours is an inherent right to say one thing and do another, that right would disappear if we had no autonomic nervous system.

Over a clump of trees in an open country flew a flock of possibly two thousand birds. Close together they circled, spiralled, and looped the loop, chittering all the while. Marvellous manœuvring. And then, so suddenly that it was startling, there wasn't a bird in sight! We gasped, strained our eyes, and there they were in the trees, out of sight but not quite out of hearing. No army could manœuvre like that—so surely, swiftly, up and down, round and round, long spirals, short spirals, and, in the twinkling of an eye, quite disappear.

That was in Kenya Colony, East Africa. I do not know what the birds were. But I think I know what vocal cords are, and how sensitive ear-drums are. My guess is that had our ancestors been deaf, we should be dumb. The human voice is the tie that binds human society. Will the society please come to order!

My next guess is that the first cry for order came from the lips of Madame President. Why not? She was the First Lady of the Land, the cornerstone of the family, fount of wisdom, source of love, and natural-born school-teacher. She had more at stake, more varied interests, jumped oftener, and was more on the jump. When the mere male had satisfied his two primal wants, his day's work was done; but *woman's work is never done!*

IX

If language be the tie that binds human society, *written* language is the bridge between the present and the past and hangs the future on the present. In the beginning was the Word, but when it was written down—or up—it acquired posthumous value. And the very fact that we of the twentieth century still pay homage to certain writings of an ancient and primitive world, is evidence of the value man attaches to this, possibly the most far-reaching and influential invention ever made.

In our enthusiasm for this important tool for making progress, let us not fail to realize its potential evil in civilization. Like every other man-made tool, it can be used to good purpose or turned into a weapon to serve selfish or class interests. Almost all progress in the knowledge which underlies modern civilization, and which uniquely distinguishes it from all past civilizations, was made after it was discovered that the mere fact that it had been written was no proof that it was true. Not without reason has some tough-minded man from time to time risen up and said in effect: Let's burn the books; let us shake off the authoritative voice of the dead past and do some investigating of our own!

History, as we usually use that term, begins with *recorded* events; but the great events which made civilization possible had nearly all happened before man discovered that he could make his mark. With that discovery recorded history begins, and human culture passes into what we usually call civilization. In the history of the civilization which became part of our cultural heritage, the invention of writing must certainly be rated as the most decisive single step.

Of that heritage we shall have much to say, but it seems well to point out here the far-reaching influence of the fact that our fore-fathers landed on American soil with at least one book in their hands. That book was their sanction for living, the dominating influence in their lives.

The written is something more than a new kind of language; much more. Through the written word one can go anywhere, be anybody, do anything—if the writer has been anywhere, been anybody, done anything. It affords an extension, as it were, of our senses and activities; spreads us around the earth, so to speak, and often at one sitting. With television perfected. . . . But think what the camera has already done to short-cut experience! and what else is civilization but an aggregate of tools, mechanisms and devices to save time, save energy, save labor, in order that life may be lived on a higher, richer, and more secure level? Writing is such a tool.

Make his mark. When our Indian chiefs signed the scraps of paper (usually called treaties and supposed to be perpetual) that our government offered them as the price of moving on to some Bad Land, they made their mark: the picture of their totem or crest. Every system of writing, presumably, began with pictures of things or symbols of ideas. The prehistoric pictures on the walls of caves, on cliffs, and on boulders, were symbols, signs, marks. Picture-writing is the oldest written language, and in many cultures never passed beyond that stage.

Pictures, of course, can be sculptured as well as drawn. The Eskimo carves his pictures rather than draws them—as Cave-man often did. But graphic is older and far more common than plastic picture-writing.

One of the earliest known symbols is a dotted circle—presumably a sun symbol. It is found in French caves, in Egyptian hieroglyphs, and in the prehistoric dolmens of Europe. The circle without the dot passed into ancient alphabets and is still found in ours.

Early Babylonian boundary stones bore signs of the heavenly bodies or star deities: sun, moon, stars, scorpion, goat, etc. Our almanac astronomical signs are merely these pictorial symbols. Our "digits" (*digitus*) I, II, III, IV, V, are survivals of primitive pictured fingers of the hand held up in counting. Our Arabic 1, 2, 3, 4, 5, etc., are of no known phonetic value. And our silent movies are but a revised and improved form of picture-writing.

We can "read" the silent movies because they employ a symbolic language with which we are familiar. A shrug of the shoulders, a handshake, a kiss, a hat tipped, etc., are all so many symbols which, like shorthand signs, dots, dashes, flag signals, crosses, crescents, eagles, swastikas, etc., in certain places or under certain conditions stand for or represent facts or ideas and function as tools. Of such symbols are the languages of arithmetic, music, weights and measures, shorthand, Morse code, etc.

While the picture or *icon* stage of writing was reached early and widely, but few people passed to the next or *rebus* stage: ideographic or hieroglyphic writing. Only where the need for a mechanism to convey the spoken word instead of an idea became a compelling stimulus was that important and difficult stage reached.

In rebus or ideogram writing, qualities, attributes, and similar ideas are expressed by a glyph of the significant part of the picture or by combinations of such parts. Thus, a conventionalized glyph of a hand signifies power; of a leg, movement; of an eye, seeing; of an arched sky with a star, night. Our Plains Indians used such ideograph writing; as did the Chinese, the early Egyptians, Sumerians, Hittites, Minoans, and Mexicans. The Mayas of Yucatan, in fact, passed this stage and were on the road to phonetic writing; symbols had begun to represent sounds.

The Chinese written language is still based on ancient, clumsy ideographs. It is neither pure pictograph (ideograph) nor alphabetic (phonetic), and hence is specially interesting because it represents phonetic writing in a state of arrested development. Its ideographic basis consists of some 600 fundamental characters and more than 200 classifiers or radicals, which are also ideograms, and all of which are highly conventionalized pictures. The Japanese borrowed this language, but to write it invented forty-seven purely phonetic characters to express grammatical elements, proper names, etc. Less than half that number of phonetic sounds would have sufficed.

The third stage, most difficult and important of all, involved substituting a character representing a certain sound or phonetic value for the ideogram; that is, a *sound* picture for a *thing* or *idea* picture. Thus, the eye picture of our rebus signifying *seeing*, now signifies the sound of the word eye—"i." It has lost its primary or pictographic significance (eye) and its secondary or ideographic significance (seeing) and has become a sound picture—the vowel "i."

Thus, the first four letters of the Hebrew alphabet are highly conventionalized pictures of an ox, a house, a camel, and a door—*aleph, beth, gimel, daleth*; or, in their Greek form—*alpha, beta, gamma, delta*. But a few thousand years had to pass before the large number of highly conventionalized phonetic symbols were used as syllables in other words and finally reduced to the few fundamental sounds required to produce, by proper combination, any word in the spoken language.

The compelling stimulus behind every written language was the felt need for accuracy, precision, speed. Under such a drive alphabets grew up; evolved slowly, painfully, and often without rhyme or reason. That our own is far from perfect as a *phonetic* alphabet may be inferred from the fact that the one word "scissors" can be spelled in eighty-two million different ways. Why don't we reform our alpha beta, or at least adopt phonetic spelling? Or, if we wish to preserve it in its pristine purity, why don't we return to the original pictures, to rebus writing? Because charades are a good game for children, but not good enough for business purposes or scientific accuracy.

Hieratic writing is good enough for priests, for *hier* means "sacred"; but people, as in democracy, need demotic writing, for *demos* means "people." That epitomizes the history of our alphabet.

Egypt by 4777 B.C. had a fully developed system of picture-writing, called by Herodotus *hieroglyphikos* because the writings which were translated for him were "sacred." These pictures—about six hundred in number—had phonetic value, like syllables. But Egypt had also evolved a demotic language of twenty-four signs, each representing a letter: an alphabet. This demotic language was virtually a shorthand for the more picturesque hieroglyphic language, and was used in legal and business documents and in civil and domestic letters. But as there was nothing *holy* or even "refined" about it, Egypt clung to her old sacred bull, cat, and crocodile syllabary.

Not later than 1600 B.C. nor earlier than 2000 B.C. the Phœnicians, driven by the need for a written language fit to trade in, took over twenty-two Egyptian alphabetic signs, arranged them in a fixed order, and gave each letter a name: *aleph* (ox), *beth* (house), etc. That alphabet was the father of all alphabets.

Taken over by the Arameans, together with a curious Phœnician script, it gradually replaced the cuneiform (wedge-shape) writing in western Asia, and later became the alphabet of Persia, etc. In short, all Asiatic alphabets, Mongol and Manchu, Indian, Arab, Nestorian, Hebrew, and Sanscrit, are derived from the Aramean, which in turn was derived from the Phœnician.

In the mouths of the children of the Greek traders, the aleph beth of the Phœnicians became alpha beta: our *alphabet*.

With the borrowed and transformed Egyptian alphabet went Egyptian paper (*papyros*), pen and ink—thereby driving out the wedge form of writing on soft clay tablets. The Aramean tongue in Palestine replaced the Hebrew and became the language of Jesus and contemporary Jews.

Papyrus paper was a marvellous invention; it marked enormous progress over stone and clay tablets and made literature possible. India developed a palm-leaf-fibre writing material, but Mesopotamia turned to leather. Leather at Pergamum underwent a new process of tanning and became the *pergamena charta* or parchment of Europe. As it could be easily cleaned or scraped, old parchment writings became the palimpsests (*palin*, again; *psao*, scrape) of mediæval scribes; and what they wrote over what they often failed to wash completely off is far less precious today than the pagan writings they held so lightly. It is a bit ironical, as Shotwell says, that the books of devotion used in the Church which denounced pagan vanity, should have preserved for modern times the very texts they denounced.

As a medium for handing the good word on to posterity, papyrus was only a medium-good paper, but it was better than our fragile stuff of today. "We are writing, not upon sand, but upon dust heaps."

Papyrus, in use at the papal court up to the eleventh century, began to be replaced by rag paper, but not until the fourteenth century was this in general circulation in Europe—twelve centuries after it had been invented in China. When the Crusaders were fighting Saladin for the Holy Sepulchre, China was printing a commentary on her Classics in 180 magnificent volumes. And she was printing playing-cards and paper money with movable type five centuries before Gutenberg "invented" the printing-press. What China knew, the Moslem world learned—and Europe borrowed.

The Holy Writ our ancestors brought over here to begin its deadening sway over human lives in a new world gets its name from the town Biblos, whence Europe used to import its papyrus paper. We also speak of that Bible as a "tome" because a length of *charta* (or papyrus) when cut off was *tomus*, or as a "volume" because the Latins called a wound-up papyrus roll *volumen*. And when we call the Bible a "library," as it really is, it is because *liber* also means *volumen*, and was originally applied to the bark of a tree used to write on. And, finally, our "book" is Anglo-Saxon *boc*, a variant of the old Latin root word for beech tree; Anglo-Saxon runes were written on beechen boards. The Romans displayed notices on oak boards in the Forum; board, *tabula,* our word "tablet." Our "pen" is *penna,* feather; and our "style" is the *stylus* or pointed bodkin anciently used for writing on wax tablets.

That the real foundation of a real university is a well-chosen library of books is less true today than it was in Carlyle's time. A dictionary is "interesting," as the Swede said, "but the chapters are too short." At best, it is a necessary evil. If we must see through others' eyes, hear with others' ears, and get all our thrills second hand, we must keep going to the dictionary. But after all, the words in our dictionary employ only twenty-six letters; we have a quarter of a million nerve fibres in our eyes. Can the dictionary, with its puny twenty-six characters, see as far or as deeply into life as we can with our eyes? If I want more sense I do not go to the dictionary; I must use my senses more. The man with the least common sense of any man I have known was a bookworm.

Written language is a marvellous vehicle for getting about and for finding out what has been found out. But a library of books is not civilization, nor is a big library necessarily a more healthy sign of civilization than a big lot of automobiles or radio sets; nor is it a better educator of youth than a live teacher. And when Bertrand Russell turns up his nose at female school-teachers, who "irretrievably" ruin children, we may meet him with a line of a nineteenth-century physician: "If the early part of education, which concerns us most, had been designed for fathers, the Author of Nature would doubtless have furnished them with milk for the nourishment of their children."

No, language alone cannot build civilization nor domesticate wild animals. The milk of human-kindness can. To stress the important fact that man's innate equipment includes the capacity to learn articulate speech, to stress language as a primary factor in making human behaviour the complex, baffling thing it is, is to put stress where the facts warrant. The word *was* in the beginning; one word led to another; and it was not long before there was a vocabulary and set rules for saying the words and set habits for responding to words. But long before a word was said, there were infants crying for food, for protection, for attention.

In the beginning were hunger for food and mate and varied ways of finding means to satisfy these natural drives. In the beginning was love. And whereas the Romans thought it wise to keep reminding themselves that they were human and must die, we may keep reminding ourselves that we were once monkeys, and that while every mammal has a voice-box, monkeys have enough hearing mechanisms to initiate and control speech, and a third frontal convolution which is supposed to be a talking brain. Why they do not talk is, as Cannon says, a riddle.

Why we talk so much to such little purpose is also a riddle. It must be because it is so easy. Is man to talk himself to death or become the slave of the printed word, or is the printed word to prove that earth is not his home and that he can defy all earthly virtues in the hope of a reward hereafter? Believing that man is a rational animal, my guess is that he will learn to take the printed word for what it is worth and for no more.

# CHAPTER THREE

## *In the Beginning Was Love*

1. The Rôle of the Family. 2. Apes Are the Real Primitives. 3. The Mechanism and Significance of Perennial Desire. 4. Family Life on "Monkey Hill." 5. Courtship Under the Trees. 6. The Genesis of Family Love. 7. Aberrant Sexual Behaviour. 8. The Totemic Family. 9. The Rôle of the Incest Taboo. 10 The Function of the Marriage Ceremony. 11. The Story of the "Stork." 12. The Family Becomes Society. 13. "The Home Is on the Rocks!"

I

NEITHER speech nor family ushered in civilization, but both preceded it; both were essential to the humanizing of the simple-minded, chattering, primitive man of Eolithic times. Indeed, without family life and without true speech or language, the transition from *natural* to *cultural* behaviour is inconceivable; and while vocal cords are as old as amphibia, bisexual reproduction is almost as old as life itself. True, man makes a cult of virginity, but parthenogenetic reproduction in higher animals (including the *Hominidæ*) is as fabulous as the creation of man from clay; both fables may be admired as literature, or, depicted in stone or on canvas, as works of art. Virgin mothers and magicians are man-made, and will be looked at in due time; our concern now is with the makings of the human family.

That family life is based on bisexual reproduction must be so obvious as to need no argument, and I offer none. But what is a "family," and why are there old maids and old bachelors, and even professional celibates of both sexes, and why are there homosexuals? Is Lesbos merely an island, was Sappho merely a poet, Narcissus a fable, Sade a French count, and Masoch an Austrian writer? Or did Sappho make a cult of tribadism in Lesbos? Does Narcissus symbolize hopeless self-love? Are sadism and masochism supernormal passions—one finding outlet only in the infliction of

64

pain, the other in submission to pain, serving as escape from normal sexual relationships and masking ascetic impulses, and both socially aberrant and biologically useless forms of sex behaviour?

More specifically, is the human family a cultural product or is it grounded in nature; and if the latter, what is its biologic rôle? The answer to that question should give us a background against which we may view the family as it is today, and an opportunity to weigh its enemies in the scales of social usefulness, biologic utility, and physiologic well-being.

In these days especially, with marriage as an institution called a failure and derided as obsolete, and free love proposed as a panacea for social ills, we need a sound hypothesis of family life.

That our civilization is chaotic and society shot through and through with insane demands and idiotic notions, there is no doubt. Possibly marriage *has* failed as an institution; but that promiscuous sex-relationships (sometimes called "individuality") are not a panacea for anything except licentiousness and would destroy human society, I am in no doubt.

In no other respect, it seems to me, have we reached such a pinnacle of fatuity as in proclaiming the sacredness of individuality. No individual is sacred. Individuality, in almost every species of higher vertebrates, is biologic suicide. Perfect individuality in human society is perfect monstrosity. Man is a *social* animal—by nature, by endowment, by training; sociability is his nature by every known law of biology; the extent of his sociability is the measure of his humanness. And of all man's human qualities, the most distinctively human and socially valuable is, not individuality, but individual responsibility.

Strip man of his responsibility to the society which bore him, nurtured him, and makes his life possible, and you have, not a human being, nor even a good-natured brute: you have an anarchist, a monstrosity. Every virtue of proved worth in every human society has been a variant of that responsibility.

What are discipline, tolerance, decency, sportsmanship, perseverance, frankness, reasonableness, and honesty, but expressions of individual responsibility—the mantle of charity, of sociability, of sweet reasonableness, which raises man above and distinguishes him from all brute creation? Some humans may be in rags and some may drag the royal mantle in the mire; and there are also those inhuman monstrosities who would usurp the purple and proclaim themselves divinely favoured, uniquely blessed. While such behaviour fills pages of history, it never had value in promoting human society or in furthering humane causes and endeavours.

Throughout history the family has played the rôle of fundamental civilizing element, and it is not without significance that no tribe of human beings has ever been discovered that does not recognize the principle of family life and honour the institution of marriage.

Children are the cement of society; and since man began to talk, marriage has been the catalyzing force binding male and female molecules into the protoplasmic units of which society consists. Marriage—by capture, purchase, or decree, and whether monogamous, polyandrous, or polygamous—is marriage; and may or may not be founded on love. Man by nature is a marrying animal and all marriages presuppose an urge called love—desire to possess a mate.

What, then, is the nature of love? What are the biologic beginnings of the oldest, noblest, and most civilizing of all human institutions?

Where shall we go for our answer? To the "primitive" tribes, such as the Veddahs of Ceylon, the Tierra del Fuegians, the Australian aborigines, the Shoshoneans of Nevada, or the Pygmies of Africa? They are illiterate; they have only the simplest, most "primitive" culture. But their culture is as old as ours; their history is as deeply rooted. They have the same biologic equipment we have, and hence the "psychological equivalents," as Lowie calls them, of every cultural phenomenon known to modern civilization. A study of their culture is useful in many ways and often most illuminating, but is not to be stretched out of all semblance of reality.

Biologic equipment is one thing; historic development, or how that equipment has been invested, is quite another thing. Hence we are no more justified in inferring that a certain Australian marriage system, for example, represents a stage all mankind passed through, than we are in assuming that subincision of the male generative organ was once a universal initiatory rite. As practised by the Australians, system and rite are complex and specialized, even "advanced," if you please; they are no more necessarily "primitive" than Ford's first model or Al Smith's brown derby.

In other words, just as we cannot recover "original" speech by studying primitive languages, so we can learn nothing certain of *original* family life by studying primitive family systems or marriage customs. We are forced to turn to the "living fossils," our Primate relatives. They really are primitive. Among them we shall find the germs of every form of sex behaviour known to humans. But, be it noted, while speech—or symbols or insignia of language—holds complex human societies together, it is sex behaviour that underwrites human society.

II

Having no words, apes have no thoughts, mind, consciousness, or conscience—though they can be made cowards. Having no ideas, they can have no ideals. Having no slogans, they make no progress. Without souls, they care nothing for immortality. And having become sexually mature and sexually adjusted, they become less excitable, more irritable; less curious, more stolid; less playful, more indolent; as though, having perfected their food and sex reflexes, there was nothing more to learn in life. Almost human.

The ape, we may remind ourselves, is biologically almost human. It can invent tools of a simple kind, and can learn to use rather complicated tools. It can be sexually aroused any day in the year. Excepting possibly masochism, it can learn any kind of sexual perversion known to man, and can contract every known form of venereal disease.

The ape can become a prostitute; the female will "sell" her favours for food, protection, defence. It can be a strict monogamist, prefers monogamy; it insists upon fidelity in the wife. It can be promiscuous in its sexual gratifications, and is, in youth and until it forms a permanent association. It can rear its young without the aid of the male. It shows sex "love": mates, for each other; mothers, for offspring. It is, in captivity at least, an exhibitionist, shameless, frankly indecent and obscene. It has keen vision and nimble fingers. Its see- and feel-senses are extraordinarily acute; it has as many senses, and possibly as much sense, as we have. It is vastly more playful than a kitten, and sexual interest begins early, in play. It has no idea of incest—that is exclusively human, though the practice is not. It can hug, spit, and be taught to brush its teeth, eat with a knife and fork, jump when spoken to, say grace, kneel down as if in prayer, and kiss the Bible. But it cannot pass the word along.

Ape behaviour in a zoo is zoo-ape behaviour: unnatural, artificial. But aren't *we* in a zoo, and isn't *our* behaviour unnatural and artificial? That is what civilization does to us; and we are so well adapted to it we could not go back if we wanted to. As an ape in captivity soon learns to depend on its new and artificial environment, so we learn to depend on an environment as artificial and unnatural as a city slum. For gaining insight into our prehuman or natural behaviour, these infrahuman apes are priceless.

### III

Primates reveal a unique kind of social life. Its chief feature is enduring associations of the two sexes. Why this seemingly insatiable sex life in apes and man? *Because Primates differ from all other mammals.* Man is largely what he is because sociability had selective value in his ancestors; behind "sociability" is an almost perennial fount of love—a sex attractiveness which suffers few interruptions.

In its ultimate analysis, every animal reaction is a response to some physical or chemical (physiological) stimulus. The noticeably large difference in sexual activity between mammals and higher Primates is primarily physiologic; it is in the blood. This difference is well summarized by S. Zuckerman.

Cows, horses, pigs, and mammals generally confine their sex activities to certain definite seasons of the year—as every farmer used to know before he bought his milk and ham at a chain store and Fordson antiquated his horses. Out of "season," or during the anœstrous (no-egg) period, they are quite asexual; they show no sexual or reproductive behaviour of any kind. (The dog is seemingly an exception—perhaps that is why he is called a "dog"; the bitch is not that kind of dog.) Primates, on the other hand, especially apes and man, have no clearly recognized anœstrous period. Unlike lower mammals, even the few species of monkeys known to reproduce seasonally show no quiescent period in their reproductive organs.

This difference in sex activity is far-reaching. During the anœstrous period the lion, for example, lives a solitary life; seals and buffaloes separate into male and female herds. In fact, in most species of mammals the sexes separate during their asexual periods. Mammalian anœstrous associations are generally offensive packs or defensive herds. For most mammals, it is as though there were no such thing as sex most of the year, and they behave accordingly. With the approach of the mating season they change anatomically and physiologically—a kind of metamorphosis. Some even experience a change of voice. Changes in olfactory sense and in gland odors are common.

Among these *seasonal* mammals there is family life, but not of the Primate kind. There are no true monogamous marriages. The males mate till they are exhausted; the females during, and only during, "heat" or œstrus. Pregnant females neither mate nor are they stimuli to males. The bull moose, said to be monogamous, is known to change his wife once a week; the fact that he does not keep a harem is no proof of monogamy.

These specific forms of mammalian sex behaviour are regulated by *changes in sex apparatus*, especially in the female. She mates only when she is physiologically prepared to begin gestation. At that time she is in heat (*œstrus*); an egg (*ovum*) is ready for fertilization. Most larger mammals are monœstrous: only one ovum available during the mating season.

Period to period (ovum to ovum) constitutes a regular recurrent cycle—the œstrus. Sexual activity or impulse is dependent on a specific hormone (exciter) found in the fluid of the ripening egg-producing follicle. This hormone (*œstrin*) excites change in behaviour, in outward visible activities and in the reproductive organs themselves. In short, only when the mammalian female is in heat will she submit to or seek a mate, and only at that time does she look or smell like a mate to the male.

After "successful" mating, the female's sex behaviour enters a new phase, the luteal, due, presumably, to a hormone secreted by the *corpus luteum* which develops in or on the follicle which has just produced a matured, and now fertilized, ovum. This hormone drives her, prepares her for maternity, physically and otherwise. During this luteal phase she ceases to exist as a sexual stimulant for the male. Not until the follicular phase of her œstrous cycle comes round again will she excite interest in the male of the species.

Primates have a twenty-eight day menstrual cycle with a follicular and luteal phase, ovulation occurring about midway between. But—and this is an important point—œstrin activity continues through the monthly period or menstrual cycle. True, certain anatomical variations and obvious sex behaviour during the cycle, in certain species of monkeys, suggest that the female is more sexually excitable at certain times and more of an excitation or stimulus to the male; but in man and higher apes there is no obvious change that can be ascribed to œstrin variation. Their sexual activity is not dependent on the moon, like the tides, nor on a waning and waxing supply of a certain drug secreted by the ovary. It is as though, in our ascent from monkeys, we had transcended the need of being periodically spurred on to seek a mate. If, then, sexual activity looms large today, and has so loomed throughout human history, there is a reason, a natural reason.

The "flesh" and the devil may be synonymous terms, but the flesh is older than Adam and will not wash out, whatever name we give it. Carnal it is, also sensual and animal. But to call sexual activity sin, immoral, loathsome, Satanic, is not wisdom; as well rail at the sun, author of life itself on this earth. The sun's work is not to be judged by the ethics of a Mosaic cosmogony. The Romans knew better; they enshrined and endowed with its own deity every phase of reproduction: menstruation, pregnancy, birth, even the sex act itself. To them Love was a goddess; the phases of reproduction, divine.

Apes explore, embrace, mate; the female then temporarily loses her charm, the male his desire. But sex is not all of the higher life; other requirements must be met. Time out for food, for relaxation, for sleep. Fatigue susceptibility is a big factor in active, high-strung lives; muscle engine cells must have new supplies of sugar, brain cells must be recharged with bioelectricity.

Meantime the mating, let us say, has been "successful." Apes know nothing of that yet; there is no change in their behaviour, no provision for what the stork may bring. Apes are not birds; they have no nest-building reflexes. They just go on living day by

day; sufficient unto the day is the evil thereof. We are more prov-
ident because we are so taught. Our nesting activities are *culturally*
conditioned; we are no more natural home-builders than apes. In
fact, hundreds of centuries passed before man had built himself
a house as snug as a wasp's nest or as big as a Rhodesian anthill.
That meant that he had learnt better control over autonomic nervous system: visceral wants had to bide their time while cultural
demands were being satisfied. But visceral wants cannot be kept
sublimated or starved with impunity; they are too deeply rooted
in our nature.

## IV

Deeply rooted; we often speak of it as "mother" nature. Can we
learn anything of that nature from a baboon? Much; but not so
much as from the still higher Primates. Nor, may I suggest, may
we learn much from any Primate except as we realize that man
is a Primate, and that to be a Primate is to be genetically, anatomically, biologically, physiologically, and psychologically, uniquely
distinguished above all other living creatures on earth.

Baboons are notoriously cross; they have what we may call a
*mean* disposition. And while they represent a divergent line of
Primate evolution, they may be looked at with profit for such light
as they may shed on potential human nature. At any rate, they have
a code of morals of their own, and a certain kind of social organization. Their mean disposition seems to grow naturally from that
organization.

Jealousy, for example, is one of the meanest, most devastating
and abnormal of all human emotions. Endless murders have been
committed in jealous rage: rage at some one who has stolen, or
threatened to steal, a loved *possession*. Is jealousy purely human,
cultural—a deficiency in the capacity to love, a sign of weakness, a
guilty fear; or does it have a biologic history? And is murder from
jealousy a "natural" reaction?

Such questions are pertinent; they bear upon the problems of
civilization.

We do not know how anthropoid sex behaviour would answer
such questions, because of our lack of complete knowledge of their
family life. Anthropoid colonies, for various reasons, cannot easily

be made available. Their sex behaviour or family life is known only
from the few samples that can be kept in captivity. London and
Munich have large baboon colonies which are allowed to live in
large enclosures and as close to nature as possible. The London
colony, Monkey Hill, has been carefully studied and sheds extraordinarily interesting light on certain infrahuman practices—so much
that the Hill might, not without propriety, be called the "Sacred
Mount."

These baboon colonies consist of harems: "dominant" males,
wives, children; and "bachelors"—males that cannot get wives because they lack dominance. The bachelors live more or less by themselves, fighting and scrapping over trifles, "flea"-ing each other, and
engaging in unnatural practices. But note that the heads of families
mind their own business and pay no attention to the bachelors—
unless, indeed, one of them approaches a spot regarded as private.
The tyranny goes even further: when a dominant male starts
toward a spot occupied by a bachelor, the latter promptly moves.

Any unseemly move of a bachelor toward any lady of the harem
promptly leads to a fight, and frequently to the bachelor's death.
The moral seems to be that virility once had survival value. Bachelors are biologically useless and should be killed; humans used to
alter them and use them as domestics in the harem or sopranos in
the choir. But note, also, that fighting the bachelors is based on true
jealousy: *fear* of losing a possession, not fear of losing the love of a
wife. A jealous human being lacks self-confidence.

But if a sexually immature baboon approaches a harem he is
tolerated by the overlord, even if he engages one of the wives in
the sex act. He is condoned, as if to say, "Only a child." The child
may even be allowed to join the harem—to be thrown out violently
later on. The limit of baboon altruism is soon reached.

A newcomer is sometimes added to the Monkey Hill colony.
He is likely to be killed, sometimes is. If allowed to live, he is
"shown his place"; and if food is scarce, he is allowed to die of
starvation.

Because of this dominance of the "married" males, ape associations are "closed societies." The dominant males are not only
sexually dominant, they are dominant in all things. They dominate
their wives—terribly, we should say. Wherever he goes, she goes;

she rarely makes the first move. But when she is sexually disinclined or disabled, she may sit three yards off. When she wants her own way and cannot get it otherwise, she tempts him—and Adam generally falls. She also uses her sex appeal to divert her lord's wrath. No female in the colony has been known to commit adultery —and the colony has been carefully watched. That may prove uxorial fidelity; it may prove nothing more than male dominance. It does prove *permanent sexual association* in Hamadryas baboons. Such associations are inherent in human culture.

While human society is rooted in infrahuman social life or "organization," the unit of ape society is a variable, even as it is with man. Of some seventy-five (out of a total of 450) species of monkeys I have met in the forests of the New and Old Worlds, I have seen bands ranging from a dozen to a few hundreds. Only once have I met a solitary monkey, and that was the anthropoid gibbon. Its mate was probably near-by.

Colonies, hordes, bands, gangs: but what is the *unit* of monkey society? It varies. One harem may be a "society"; or several harems may live as a horde society. I saw one in Kenya that must have numbered between three and four hundred. Or, two or more harems may temporarily unite—perhaps driven by food supply, enemies, forest fires, floods, etc. Such temporary unions may conceivably become permanent.

In the Monkey Hill colony, eight of the thirty-nine adult males possessed the only nine females—which suggests monogamy; but, says Zuckerman, in the Munich colony, of twenty-five pairs of adults and a hundred children, five males owned all the females, the Brigham Young of the lot resting content with seven. Possibly, capacity to satisfy is as important a trait in male dominance as in cigarettes.

Each male wants and secures as many wives as possible. He is "faithful" to them only if he can add no more. The family is polygynous, the number of wives depending on the supply, and especially on the dominance of the males. Conceivably, if no dominant males turn up in any given colony, monogamy rules.

Are orangs exclusive, leading solitary lives? Did segregation of the sexes begin with them? Are they pure monogamists? Or do they favour plurality of wives and lead a humdrum, solitary kind of existence in the bosom of their harem? They have been accused of all these practices. We do not know their social organization. We do know that the skin of the male orang shows signs of the prize-ring. What was the prize? *Cherchez la femme;* wanted to enlarge his harem, presumably. If he keeps his harem in the background, as the gorilla seems to do, it may be set down to fine fatherly protection or mere masculine jealousy. Even a Moslem does not wear his wives on his sleeve.

Males of all Primates are larger than the females, though there is no uniformity. Thus, there is little difference in chimpanzees and gibbons; more in orangs; much more in gorillas and baboons. Does this account for the known prevalence of polygyny among baboons and gorillas, and the reported existence of monogamy among gibbons and chimpanzees? Possibly. In which case those favouring monogamy should take steps to reduce the discrepancy in size between men and women. In fact, such steps have been taken; girls are growing up as big as men. If now the men can be restrained a little bit more, the disparity in size will disappear; there will be no more weak sisters, and monogamy will reign supreme—unless men allow the pendulum to swing too far, inaugurating afresh Tibet's polyandrous scheme.

Monkey Hill children fare badly; the Hill, big as it is, is not big enough. Altruism has little chance to expand. The baboon mother faithfully nurses her baby and rarely lets it out of her reach until it can run on its own; but she will not share her food with it and the father pays almost no attention to it. From six months on, if it survives, it must fend for itself: if a male, among the bachelors; if a female, in a harem, for females are promptly annexed by some dominant male even before sexually mature. With one exception only, no mother has been seen to pay any motherly attention to any baby but her own. At large, in their native habitats, the amount of "motherly" love would, of course, generally suffice; the youngster would learn to take care of itself—would have to learn or die in the struggle for existence.

It is all right to say that we have become chicken-hearted, that our pampering of weaklings makes for a weak-kneed civilization; but it is even more right to say that just on that very account have we become civilized. Altruism of a kind came to have selective

value in Oligocene times, and from that day to this it has done more
to get us where we are than any selfish anarchistic scheme of civilization yet propounded.

I say it has; I should not like to have to prove it. But facts are
facts. One big fact is that we have travelled far beyond harem-
horde baboon society, but that society gave us *permanent* sexual
association—the beginnings of man and wife, the foundation of the
family, the cornerstone on which our civilization has been built.
Those who would usher in promiscuity in sexual relations forget
that fact, and think, not in terms of infrahumans, but of infra-
primates: cats and dogs.

"*Cornerstone* . . . and no father?" Well, he did have the domi-
nant-male rôle in the monkey play we have been looking at. In that
rôle he was thoroughly sensual and thoroughly selfish—far, far
removed from father in human society; and as for "chivalry" . . .
he had less of it than a bantam cock; in fact, hardly more of it
than the Knights of Old who locked their wives in chastity belts
and rode off on love hunts—again to kiss and ride away. And what
else did those belts mean but baboon-like jealousy of possession—
property rights? The Gallas of Africa invented an even more fiendish "belt": infibulation, a frightfully painful operation.

Then, too, a baboon is only a baboon, a mean brute in a Primate
colony where might makes right. The almost-human apes tell a
better story. With them, courtship precedes mating, and right makes
might. Sex becomes love.

### V

Human sex life, family life, *unnatural* life, is what it is because
man is born curious for curiosity's sake. That trait we inherited
from our ape ancestors. Highly excitable, high-strung, nervous, on
the jump, eternally fooling around, monkeying with everything:
these terms are as applicable to apes as to humans, and are especially applicable to chimpanzees and gibbons; gorillas and orangs
are more stolid. Fumbling about, trying things out, learning by
trial and error, discovering relationships, using objects as implements, manipulating mechanisms—often with great patience and
long attention: this fits a healthy child as snugly as it describes a
chimpanzee.

Try, and try again. If hungry for food, try anything within reach. How does it feel to the tongue; how does it strike the taste-buds; how easily does it slip down; how does it rest on the stomach? If all right and no ill effects, eat more of it when hungry. Hunger is a drive—and a grand sauce.

There is another hunger—for a mate. But young apes and children know nothing of mates. They are driven just the same; superabundant energy is crying out to be spent.

Tumescence (blood-engorged genitalia, involving delicate tactile nerves) appears early in apes and children. Meanwhile play has begun. Among apes it soon becomes, or develops into, sex play, and so continues for years before real adjustment takes place. Bingham, in fact, thinks that among chimpanzees the fundamental features of copulatory adjustment develop years before they are reproductively mature. He speaks of their pre-maturity sex play as the most surprising he has ever seen: "remarkable coöperation between the pair," astounding "functional adequacy," "never expected to see such pre-adolescent behaviour," and was "surprised at the front-to-front position," the first ventroventral position in apes ever recorded.

Bingham thus summarizes this amazingly human-like courtship behaviour: unorganized movement contact; clinging, nuzzling, sucking; genital contact; embracing, cuddling, exploring; erection; attack—flight, retreat, evasion; playful aggression; tantrums; manipulation—ornamentation, coquetry; all leading, in the course of years, to sex adjustments. Add words—sighed, spoken, sung or written, and nothing more than a rite or ceremony is needed to bring this picture down to date.

Chimpanzees apparently mate only after courtship and when there is mutual consent; rape seems to be a purely human phenomenon. And, with Bingham's findings, we cannot wonder at the amount and precocity of sex play that naturally goes on among children from four to ten years of age. "Naturally." Factually, such play is generally rudely interrupted, and the children, especially girls, are made to feel that they are branded, if not damned, for life. But not everywhere. There are still large populations where such natural preliminary and investigatory play goes on without parental hindrance, and some with a frankly naïve indulgence amounting to encouragement.

In fact, society is so organized among certain South Sea Islanders that sex play has its own place in the general scheme of routine life. While children of tender age must shift for themselves in the preliminaries of love-making, and adolescents must build their own love-nests, for their more enduring liaisons youths and adolescent girls require some special institution, definitely established, physically comfortable, and socially acceptable. Such an institution, as Malinowski shows us, the Trobriand Islanders provide—"limited bachelors' houses," of which he found fifteen in one village.

But is this not the "group marriage" of the old speculative philosophy—the primitive "promiscuity stage" hypothecated for the whole human race? "Nothing of the kind," says Malinowski. We are dealing with a limited, socially designated number of couples who sleep in a common house. "Limited," also, in the sense that the house is not *furnished* as a home. Each couple is in an exclusive liaison; there is no promiscuity, no exchange of partners, no poaching or complaisance. "Poaching is bad, like adultery with a friend's wife," say the natives.

Malinowski throws a curiously interesting sidelight on "morality." Whereas a Trobriand unmarried girl may share a man's bed, she may never allow him to take her out to dinner. To share his meal would bring the same disgrace on her that sharing his bed would with us.

These liaisons may or may not lead to marriage. They are *not* "trial marriages" as we use that term. Marriage with these islanders is an institution—ordered "as simply and sensibly as if they were modern European agnostics, without fuss or ceremony, or waste of time and substance." Once the knot is tied it is tied for good, "firm and exclusive," in the light of tribal law, morality, and custom. The liaisons are liaisons and nothing more—exclusive, decorous, proper; "decent," we should say if we approved of them. And the decline in the number of bachelors' houses, due to decreasing population, missionary influence, etc., has not "enhanced true sex morality."

Those children have progressed beyond Bingham's apes; they have institutionalized a *natural* mode of behaviour—codified it, as it were, given it a definite set of rules. Formalized, it becomes part of their *life*; and because they have a name for it, it becomes more or less permanent, passed on by the children themselves from one generation to the next. Even games which make for bodily contacts among the children are traditional and socially heritable, as "post office" used to be with us. And such songs as they do sing with their games, "Fire," "Parrot," "Bananas"!

## VI

Venus is no "seasonal" goddess among humans; she is a hardy perennial. Her cycle runs from puberty at fourteen or thereabouts, to menopause at forty-five or fifty. She always "looks good" to the normal male of the species. But why so much perfume?—for scent is no clue to loveliness; our nose does not lead to Venusburg. What does?

We still perspire, and urea is an odor of a sort; but ages ago we definitely and forever parted company with odoriferous glands, and with them most of our capacity to smell. In fact, noses such as ours are fairly modern, largely ornamental, and easily damaged; evolved, possibly, in very cold climates to warm the air on its way to the lungs. As a smell organ, it is fitter for food purposes than for sex-hunger. The human nose is as asexual as that of the proboscis monkey of Borneo.

As our sense of smell slipped away, our vision sharpened. Life in the trees did that for us: seeing was believing, and much more important than smelling. I can smell Limburger for only a minute or two; I can see it for hours. How long does it take the average visitor to "see" the Victory of Samothrace in the Louvre, and how long the Venus of Melos? The Victory is taken on the run; they stop at Venus and crowd up close to the rail. Why rail? Against vandals—but mostly against finger-marks; human beings are prone to handle things. This proneness to manipulate objects, to be handy with our hands, is an honest trait; we came by it also in the trees while our vision was becoming stereoscopic binocular.

Ever watch monkeys "flea" each other? Wrong again. A flea has no chance with a monkey: eyes too keen, fingers too clever. That finger-cleverness goes with vision-keenness and makes for very delicate eye-hand coördination, so extraordinarily developed in Primates as to amount to a new sense. Primates' sensori-motor apparatus is vastly superior to that of all other mammals; and our young Beethovens should thank their ape ancestors for this apparatus and not use it to thumb their noses at their poor relations.

No, monkeys do not "flea" each other; they pick each other, looking for dandruff or bits of dried skin secretion. Seemingly they like to pick: the activity in itself is satisfying to nerves of fingers; and they like to be picked: skin sense nerve-endings are thereby gently stimulated. Do we not scratch and like to be scratched? "Scratch my back and I'll scratch yours" even "subs" for rolling each other's logs. There is not only the "skin you love to touch" but the skin that loves to be touched.

What do two-year-olds do when brought together for the first time? Touch each other—with fingers, and with lips and tongue. But not for long. They are soon told, "Touch not, taste not, handle not." They get no sense because they cannot use their senses.

Ape "picking" leads naturally to discoveries and not infrequently to sexual activity; it is one way of making love. It often leads to patting, petting, cuddling, kissing, embracing—boxing even; all in the way of experimentation, as it were. We cannot say they want to know; we can say they do explore, and develop certain patterns of exploration. Sexual activity, for example. The first thing Schultz's chimpanzee does when handed a dressed doll is to make a definite kind of exploration; it lifts the dress, to discover, as it were, the doll's sex.

Apes and man have keen eyes, but the beginnings of love are felt rather than seen. Bodily contact: tactile nerve-endings; fingers; erogenous zones. No instinct of love, no instinct of motherhood or of fatherhood; capacity to learn to love. It is on record that a mother monkey carried her dead infant in her arms till it rotted and fell away. Instinct of motherhood? Well, if it is, it is a poor instinct. She did not know her child was dead. She was conditioned to carrying it; "fond" of having it in her arms; "loved" it, if you please.

Original mother-love begins with milk-laden mammary glands crying out for relief—pain, a stimulus for action; and an empty stomach growling for food—stimulus for action, squirms. By the good old process of trial and error the fumbling, experimenting mother finally solves two pressing problems. As a result, the infant is fed, she is relieved, and both are adjusted. In being relieved the mother is sexually stimulated; nipples are more than mere pipes or ducts, they are *special* tissue, abundantly innervated. In a word, they are "erectile" tissue, subject to tumescence, detumescence; they are part of her erogenous (love-making) mechanism, and a highly sensitized part. Result: the child becomes a new kind of stimulus, pleasurable, a sexual excitant. She has begun to *love* her child.

And while that love is the finest thing in the world, it may take such selfish turns that the child can be tied to her for life. But note, please, that whether mother-love takes its natural altruistic bent or develops into an artificial egoistic orgy, love as a fundamentally important emotion in apes and man is not a word but a force, a moving force. The mechanism behind that force is specialized tissue; its specialty is love-making.

Paternal love is a different story. There are fathers and fathers. In our society, until lately, he was still the same old dominant male we saw on Monkey Hill. He quarrelled with his wife, bullied her, brutalized her, tyrannized over her; he allowed her neither rights, prerogatives, nor personal property. But he claimed his "rights" of cohabitation; and as for permanent sexual association with his mate, he resorted to the practices of the baboon, without the baboon's honesty or frankness. He even wrote books about his wife's "inferior" brain, and tested her "intelligence."

That male baboon kept a harem, which meant plenty of children about. He tolerated them—to keep peace in the family, for the mothers naturally became strongly attached to their offspring. Under changing conditions—and conditions have changed enormously during the last million years—harems again and again were forced to unite.

These larger associations put new values on brains, gave a new meaning to self-control, and elevated the doctrine of live-and-let-live to the rank of a prime virtue. In short, the evolution of the loving father is bound up with the evolution of monogamic marriage. Let us see.

Growth in monkey and man means learning, conditioning, habituating. Sex play, satisfactory and pleasurable in itself, leads to sexual activity, even more satisfactory and pleasurable; the pair thereby become "attached," are in love. Each is a fairly vital stimulus to the other. They become conditioned to each other in hundreds of ways, in all of which all their senses and millions of nerve cells are involved. Thus their "living together" is facilitated; it becomes a "natural" condition, a habit. Being physiologically perennially sexed, enduring monogamous relations are as psychologically natural as polygamous. Whatever made for monogamy made for fatherhood; and the same psychological process also makes a wife *his* wife, her offspring *his* children.

Wife and children are stimuli calling forth responses: wife, of a certain kind; children, of a certain kind. The ape overlord of a harem evolved into the husband of one woman and the guardian, protector, playmate, of her children. Does he know they are *his* children? No more than the Trobriand Islander does. In fact, the Islander does not even know that nature created sexual pleasure as a bonus for the perpetuation of the species.

We may feel sorry for the abysmal ignorance of this poor South Sea heathen who thinks of life in terms of magic, and of sex in terms of pleasure. Yet on this vital matter he could shake hands with Aristotle and join in thanks to God that they were not, like the Chosen People of Israel, born miserable sinners. The Islander, in fact, is generous enough to think the pleasure a boon granted by his wife and great enough to repay him for services rendered, among which is helping her to care for her children. In *caring* for them he learns to love them.

Where do children come from, then? They have their own brand of "stork" story—not to fool their children, but because they themselves are ignorant of the fact that the male plays a physiological rôle in procreation. The husband does not even call himself *father*. He is merely the husband of the mother of certain children. They belong to her, but he loves them as though they were of his flesh and blood, because he has learned to love them by playing with them.

Blood should be thicker than water—though not much thicker than salt water. Children love papa when papa is lovable. Conditioned reflexes do it. Recall Pavlov's salivary-gland trick. For salivary, substitute any gland, including sexual; for hand, substitute anything the eye can see, ear hear, nose smell, or fingers feel—not forgetting that our entire skin is "feeler."

This hypothesis of the genesis of family ties is founded in sound psychology: good for apes, good for a pair of congenital mutes cast away on a desert island. Without language, no mother could tell her daughter what to do for the pain of swollen breasts, or how to still her hungry child; she would have to learn. But if the daughter were not blind, she could see what other mothers do with their babies, and that would be of service to her.

The amount of time, worry, vexation, and fumbling that can be saved by a few words from a mother or nurse is to be reckoned, we may remind ourselves, as among the countless drops which make up the sea of advantage that is man's because he can communicate experience through speech.

The psychologic beginnings, then, of love as the chief factor in the founding of the human family, lie in the fact that the mother becomes organized to care for the child. As Watson says, she reacts to "its cries, its comings and goings, its contacts. It becomes something to play with. It brings in the element of companionship. As it gets older, it learns to fetch and carry and help out in the business of securing food and preparing it. The economics of child labor becomes a definite factor. The father learns to accept the child at first as a part of the mother. Interference with the child means a lack of mutual sex coöperation on the part of the mother. Collateral conditioning comes in for the father also, just as it does for the mother. The family unit is thus completed by the joint acceptance of the child."

The Trobriand family is no less a unit because the father knows no more of the physiology of reproduction than an ape. It is a unit because he accepts responsibility for his wife's children. He learned to love his wife; he learns to love her children. All of which makes for family ties—a family.

## VII

There are no statistics on civilization; there are on insanity. One-tenth of us now living in the United States are in asylums, or will be before we die; and ten per cent of us over forty-five are neither fathers, mothers, nor married. Is there possibly some connection between the two facts? There is certainly some connection between them and the important fact that in the lower levels of humanity practically every adult is married and "bachelors" are as rare as lunatics.

Possibly all bachelors are lunatics. Certainly love is at the foundation of the noblest edifices reared by man, with word, in stone, or in bronze. Yet how infinitely man can debase sex, descending to the love level of a male frog mounted like a maniac on a piece of wood! A mating frog without a mate does act like a maniac. Even cutting off its head does not cause it to relax its embrace of the senseless object held by its "claspers." Which means that the mating frog is not *driven* to find a mate, but something to embrace. Having found "something," it can't let go till the drive is spent.

Homosexuality; bestiality, corpses, sadism, manikins, mechanical devices, grotesque contortions; jaded appetites lashed by whips, humiliations, pains, drugs: these and countless other aberrant sex practices make up, as Bölsche says, a serio-comic chamber of horrors into which a healthy man or woman gazes as into the torments of Dante's Inferno. And except for the philosophizing, the frog did it all first!

Such abnormal behaviour only occurs in higher animals when normal mating is thwarted; it is aberrant, unnatural, monstrous behaviour. Yet half the slogans man has fought for have been put forward by men who were sexually abnormal. Possibly there is some connection between that and the fact that man has been asked to put love of truth above love of discovering new truths.

Any unnatural sex practices among such "primitive savages" as the South Sea Islanders? They have names for practically all the sex aberrations known to psychoanalytic literature; from which we infer that they know the practices themselves. But they abhor them. To them, autoeroticism, homosexuality, bestiality, exhibitionism, and other perversions are *perversions*—improper, inadequate, contemptible substitutes. By invective and comic anecdote they brand sex aberrations as ridiculous and improper. In short, their mental attitude is much like ours, only their success in making such practices undesirable is greater than ours because social tradition weighs more heavily on them and natural outlets for the sexual impulse are within reach.

Where such natural outlets are not within reach—on training-ships, in girls' boarding-schools, boys' academies, and among apes, monkeys, horses, and dogs in captivity—unnatural practices may be expected. Girls in boarding-schools, boys in academies, and sailors on long cruises do not, however, always or inevitably develop homosexual tendencies or resort to aberrant forms of sexual gratification; nor do adults who for one reason or another eschew marriage and are otherwise normal, inevitably resort to one or other of the possible ways of cheating the normal sex-impulse outlet. But there is more cheating than is generally supposed. Dr. Katherine Davis' findings, in her study of autoerotic practices among college women, must have surprised the women themselves. Incidentally, these results helped to make plain that the more human nature changes the more it remains the same, and that Mother Nature had sense enough to make the weaker sex the stronger in the more important business of sex.

Monkeys and apes readily take to unnatural "vices." Bingham's chimpanzees, even though the sexes were not separated, showed manifestations of what we may call a willingness-to-try-anything-once. Under the drive of innate curiosity they discovered, among countless other things, their sexual organs. They manipulated them; the male with hand, foot; the female with hand—and a mango. Such manipulatory tendencies appeared early and seemed to be provoked or intensified when enraged or when scratching or pulling their hair in a tantrum. One young ape's unexpected masturbatory behaviour seemed to have been associated with his heightened irritability while cutting his second molars. Often when performing experiments, such as piling boxes, the young males were observed to make sexual movements toward a box. The female not only "tried out" a mango, but "varied its position as though to improve her technique"—bring about more friction. She kept at it for ten minutes, then tried her finger, then the stem of a leaf, and finally a pebble.

Depraved behaviour? No; surplus energy; experimental, exploratory, investigatory behaviour. Without such experimentation, exploration, and investigation there can be no learned behaviour. Primates are not innately nice, only innately curious. But note, please, that as a result of such curiosity, these young apes discovered not only themselves but each other; and long before they were sexually mature they had learned bisexual behaviour. Their early autoerotic and homosexual practices never became bad habits because the sexes were not segregated.

Appropriate bisexual behaviour is learned, acquired, conditioned behaviour; learned easily when the learning conditions are favourable, and easily learned so well that it becomes a habit, "second" nature. What we too often forget is that it is just as easy to acquire the habit of indifference to any particular stimulus as a positive-attitude habit. That this must be so the history of the human family offers abundant proof. In fact, civilization could not progress without this capacity of human beings to learn restraint.

So important is this principle of acquired indifference that we may well look into it; we shall thereby better understand that humanizing of the love impulse which helped to make human families possible and human culture easy. The principle is often called inhibition, or negative response. And so strong are our inhibitions against plain language in sexual activities that I shall use "food" as a symbol for *sex*.

"That is my dish," I say, but only after trying it out. I taste it, swallow it, digest it; then, having added these individual experiences together and found them satisfactory, I am satisfied. I have fully "experienced" it, and as a result of that crowning experience I proclaim *that* to be my dish.

An untried, untasted, unexperienced dish can whet my appetite if it looks, smells, feels, or sounds like a dish I have already learned to like—one toward which I am already positively conditioned and one which I have found by experience to be satisfactory. To that new and as yet unexperienced dish I also respond positively. It is a *collateral* conditioned reflex.

Now, I see in a cookshop window a certain dish which *excites* me; it "looks good," and, if I am hungry, makes my mouth water. I want it. But for any one of dozens of possible reasons I cannot have it. Yet I must pass that shop daily for months. How long is that dish going to continue to excite me? That depends, also, on many circumstances; but it is not going to excite me for the rest of my life. Being human, I can learn, and sooner or later do learn to pass it by without a drop of mouth-water or a sigh of regret. Without such power of inhibition we could not even go to sleep.

Sister, or home-town girl, comes at last to be inhibited. She can be seen, and may excite to play, but as an exciter to sexual activity she ceases at last to be a possible "*my* girl." And with girl as with puddings, the proof is in the eating.

This power of inhibition, or capacity to accept some things as mere scenery, has biologic usefulness.

You have a dog, let us say, which jumps up every time you enter, wags its tail, and gives silly, coaxing little barks. "Nice doggy," you say, patting it on the head and scratching its back—possibly even kissing it. "Nice doggy. Go lie down now." It obeys.

Now for the experiment.

You enter. The same nice doggy jumps up, wig-wags tail, barks, and with trusting eyes looks into yours—to meet a stony stare. Dog looks fussed, is fussed, quite upset in fact.

Second day. You enter, and meet the same nice doggy—just a trifle less certain—with the same stony stare.

Third day. Fourth . . . twentieth. Look at the dog now. When you enter it does not move an inch—just rolls one eye round to see that it is the same old you and goes back to sleep.

In the higher animal world it is biologically useful to investigate *moving* objects; to animals in society it is useful to investigate social customs and to respond in social ways to biologically useful stimuli. In the case of the dog, you became such a stimulus and your soothing voice and hand were biologically useful. You had come to be a stimulus calling out certain dog behaviour meritorious in dog-man society. Responding to your entrance in a certain way "bought" the dog something, got certain results which a dog could use in its business of living like a civilized dog. But getting up, wagging tail, barking, are energy-consuming processes—biologically useless and socially stupid if they bring home no bacon. And the dog finally "realizes" that it can get more out of scratching fleas than it can out of jumping up and doing its stuff every time you enter the room.

In short, the dog no longer responds to your entrance because for its dog's purposes you have ceased to exist; it has inhibited you. Just as Johnny learns to inhibit his father's eternal barking. Just as Christianity finally stopped jumping every time somebody yelled "Hell-fire!" It is useful to read civilization's story in terms of what made it bark and wag its tail; it is also worth knowing why it so often reverted to flea-scratching.

It is a long road man has travelled in becoming civilized, but it is still dark under the tree of knowledge. However freely we may want to love, what embraces us, as Bölsche says, is "the claws of fear, anxiety, shame, prudishness, moral scruples, a million forms of inhibitions and doubts—stuck fast in sweat and torments, no longer a tree or a mussel, but not yet a man of knowledge."

Malinowski expresses it even better: With us soon comes the world of lawful, normal, nice things, and the world of shamefaced desires, clandestine interests, subterranean impulses. Two categories of things, decent-indecent, pure-impure, crystallize; in some, the indecent become suppressed and right values of decency become hypertrophied into virulent Puritan virtue or the hypocrisy of the conventionally moral; or the decent is smothered through pornographic satisfaction.

If we only knew just what the *right* values of decency are! We do know that we are not born with any sense of decency, or we could never have become as decent as we are, nor could our acquired decency fall from us as it often does in certain forms of insanity. Indecency, in the form of orgiastic rites rationalized to relieve physiologic tensions, has been institutionalized again and again by different peoples at different times in the course of history, and generally under the guise of religion.

Does it not become increasingly plain that between us and the ape world we left behind is a vast gulf filled with cultural traditions and materials, possible because man's is a world of human voices? Deprived of this symbolic world, we soon become animals searching for food and mates or fleeing from our enemies. So completely have our simple wants been buried under verbal meanings that millions of human beings wait resignedly for the "next" world to enjoy themselves. We have so conditioned our lives by our civilization that we forget it was made by illiterates and could be remade by a first-class engineer.

VIII

Just what is a family? One thing is certain: the term itself is obfuscated by terminology. "My family" means one thing in this country; any one of several things in India; still quite a different thing in Central Australia; in China it might cover ten thousand individuals.

Which means that our few and simple relationship terms, as we use them, do not at all necessarily fit family life or social organization in other parts of the world. We may not know who sired us, but *father* to us means male parent and no one else. So with the other relationship terms in common use: mother, brother, sister; grand- and great-grandparents; paternal and maternal uncles and aunts; first and second cousins. Blood relationship, or consanguinity, is the tie that binds us—though not necessarily into a happy family.

Genetics is one of the newest sciences and "blood" relationship is still a figure of speech. Families were organized long before man attributed babies to sexual intercourse. Millions of people are still ignorant of the facts of biologic fatherhood. They know much of bird, snake, and turtle eggs; nothing at all of mammalian ova. Ignorance of these biologic facts and failure to infer that babies and sexual intercourse are necessarily connected, have led man's fancy all the way from the stars to the underworld to account for life. He has invented menageries of "storks"—from grubs to crocodiles, pee-wees to eagles, snakes to moonbeams. These "ancestors" are not superstitions; they are *totems*, and spring from the kind of ignorance that has led man into many wild beliefs, inhuman performances, ridiculous taboos—and muddied the pages of religion.

Family organizations based on ignorance of the physiology of reproduction are technically called "classification systems of relationships." Some of these systems are enormously complex—in fact, painfully so. Let us look at a "very simple system," as Mrs. Seligman calls it.

The mother-child relationship seems a sensible and reasonable idea, but there are many civilized societies which abhor sense and reason. The child not only calls his *mother* "mother," but also all her sisters and *all* the women she *calls* sisters; to all these women, the child is *their* child. If this system embraces the Mormon idea also, as it sometimes does, *all* the wives of the father are "mothers" also of all the children. That is not all. If all real or make-believe mothers' sisters are mothers, then *their* children are sisters or brothers. And so on. That is one of the simplest systems.

Systems of what? Family? Not at all. Systems of classificatory terminology: puzzles which drive students of primitive sociology to tear their hair, and fill endless pages with discordant and controversial theorizing. Into that esoteric mass of kinship algebra and geometry, as Malinowski calls it, we need wade not another inch; for, though in the simplest system of classificatory relationships a man may seem to have a thousand-eyed mother, man himself knows better. As the Nigerian puts it, one can always get a second wife, but not a second mother.

These systems are purely cultural, highly complex, highly specialized; and they vary enormously. They can no more be reduced to law than fashions in head-dress. At most, they are symbols for social relations—such relations as underlie *clan* and *social* organization, and not family relations. In other words, society, or clan, is not a domestic institution; the family *is* such an institution, and the only one yet devised by man which performs the necessary primary functions of procreation, rearing children, and furnishing outlets for emotional attitudes which alone make continuity of cultural heritage possible.

Society or the clan, on the other hand, is a non-reproductive, asexual, non-parental organization. Its functions are primarily legal, and often ceremonial and economic. Clan organizations among illiterate folk today are as a rule based on common totems and myths of unilateral descent from a (totemic) ancestor or ancestress, and perform certain appropriate religious or magical rites and duties.

In other words, the human family is organic; clan organizations are superorganic. And all arguments as to "original" promiscuity, communism, matriarchy, patriarchy, etc., based on existing conditions, "survivals," are idle speculations.

### IX

In such a "simple" family system as the one just looked at, does a man ever take his mother to mate, or his sister; a woman, her father or brother? No; that would violate the incest taboo—or, as we say, would be illegal.

Incest was, and is, outlawed the whole world around. But the custom of brother-sister marriage prevailed at certain times and in

certain places; among the royal families of Egypt, Peru, and Poly-
nesia, for example. These exceptions, however, merely prove the
rule; and besides, they are far from primitive.

Incestuous marriage is universally tabooed; of all sexual relationships it alone is uniquely tabooed. Even among the Australian Bushmen. A boy, for example, of the *Emu* clan may not marry an Emu
girl, even if she came from Brooklyn. Blood counts, but so do names
and ideas; and if he married a Brooklyn Emu, dire events would
follow the breaking of a high-tension taboo. To commit incest in
Borneo is to cause the very earth to quake, the volcanoes to erupt;
in Mindanao, to cause floods; nearly everywhere, to bring disease—
to the guilty, their offspring, relatives, the whole tribe even. Upset
of big ideas causes big commotions.

Many theories have been proposed empirically to justify the out-
lawing of incest, such as danger from inbreeding, economic burden
of intermarriage, "familiarity breeds contempt," etc. They will not
work; they are too easy. Nor does an anti-incest *instinct* theory
help: the universal taboo is too often violated!

Enter Freud with his cyclopean family: brothers ate their fathers
in order to marry their mothers and sisters—but were so ashamed
of themselves that they outlawed incest forever! Uncle Remus could
do better; and in fewer than the 144 pages Freud requires in his
recent attempt to dissect *Civilization and Its Discontents*. Freud's
error, it seems to me, is in his assumption that because *our* world
is neurotic it was always neurotic: hence his postulate of the
primal neurosis. But to picture, as he does, a monstrous and unnatural family situation—sons torn between love for and fear and
hate of their father—as the setting for a universal remorse- or
guilt-complex, is pseudo-science and an unwarranted rationalization.
If Freud's claim is founded in fact, if such "discontents" are inherent
in human nature, this world is indeed a mad-house and only neu-
rotics are normal.

An Englishman may now marry his deceased wife's sister; since
1907 such marriages have not been incestuous. But marriage with
his deceased brother's widow is still illegal—incestuous. The law
started when younger, unmarried sisters generally lived with older,
married sisters. The idea was good: there must be peace in the
family. The law was bad: it added to whatever stimulus the younger

sister may have had, thereby provoking "incestuous" relations but not violation of the law.

Did that old law grow from a tap root of human social behaviour? Apes have no horror of incest, and violations of the taboo against parent-child, brother-sister relationships are notoriously frequent, especially in our crowded city tenements. But human is not ape society, nor is a cave a tenement. Society must have peace, or there is anarchy. Peace-in-the-family, and more especially peace-in-the-tribe, had survival value ten thousand years ago, and have today.

Man succeeded where other Primates failed, not because he is a social animal, but because he had brains enough to learn that being sociable paid. He learned it by experience, not through remorse. There were no rules, no codes, no textbooks of sociology, to tell him how to behave; there was continuity of life. Families died or were wiped out; other families carried on; society never died out. I can conceive of an ape-family experience yielding results in moulding succeeding generations. Multiply that ape-family by ten and endow that ape-society with speech, and it will not be long before there is a common social heritage. We are apes with human conventions. Long before we experience sex we experience sex attitudes. These collateral conditioned reflexes play important rôles in our experiencing sex. These attitudes spring from the collective wisdom and folly which form part of our social heritage.

While we were once apes and are animals, the fact is that we are human. Human social heritage is ape social heritage plus all that has been learned and said about that heritage. Results that papa-ape can get only by armwork, papa-man can get by a "Don't!" By ethics. But when to the incest taboo he added, "The devil will get you if you do," he had substituted a theological for an ethical reason; and thereby started the categorical-religious-imperative snowball rolling. And it is still rolling, but melting.

When an ape mates he has already played with sex for years and has experienced some of its "deepest facts," as Havelock Ellis calls them. Mating is the deepest fact of all sex experience, and if both are perfectly happy they just naturally experience it again and again. The stage is now set for a happy home. If, some months later, the male finds his mate preoccupied, he seeks another. Every ape, in short, has the makings of a Solomon in him. But it took man thousands of years to become unsocial enough to collect wives as fighters collect medals or as Magyar peasant wives collect feather pillows. Before he could become Solomon, he had to add sensual, lustful ideas to his sex-hunger nature.

Our ancestral fathers probably had harems, but of modest proportions; and everybody was satisfied. They loved their wives; and were beloved. The harems were necessarily restricted in size. Man has his physiological limits; nor were there yet animal husbandry or agriculture.

A happy family; but if, and only if, they kept the peace. That meant: no overt and explicit parent-child sexual behaviour. The parent-child is the oldest of all incest taboos—enforced at first by physical or manual means, later by verbal taboo, which had all the force behind it that the law against incest has today.

How the brother-sister marriage taboo started is not so clear: possibly through extension of the parent-child incest idea. To fathers, daughters are *hors concours* as wives; but daughters are females— potential wives if the taboo *must* be broken. Sons, to mothers, stand in the same light. Hence, conceivably, parental restrictions, frowns, slaps, and repression of sex play between brothers and sisters. They do not mate because desire was "nipped in the bud" before it ripened into overt sexual behaviour.

Marriage outside the family unites two families. The bond may be strong, it may be weak; it is a *bond*. As the number of families thus united in marriage increased, their strength increased; social organization was on its way. Plausibly, the brother-sister taboo carried within itself the germ of another socially useful tool. Denied by the incest taboo opportunity to indulge in sex play, their natural energies sought other outlets; they thereby developed a kind of solidarity and a degree of comradeship useful to them and serviceable to society in general.

This hypothesis possibly gives us a clue as to why certain early experiments ·at being human—Neanderthal, for example—failed. Their families were not well enough founded to survive: too much internal dissension, too little solidarity, not enough "all for one, each for all."

The early family may have been polygamous or monogamous;

it certainly was farther from "general promiscuity" than is ours. But if polygynous, the harem was necessarily restricted to a biologically satisfactory size. It could not have been polyandrous—even though such systems are found in Tibet and among the Todas of South India. As Mrs. Seligman points out, and as common sense indicates, a family of one woman and seven men cannot satisfy anybody. In Tibet, only the agricultural portion of the population is polyandrous; the Todas kill off the "surplus" girl babies. The idea makes for biological suicide, social impotence. The biggest mark the Todas have left in history is Rivers' 700-page account of their queer practices.

Man can be queer. He talks today about abolishing the very thing that made it possible for him to be human. We can no more abolish the human family than we can abolish childhood. I can bring about endless reforms and build finer republics than Plato's —if you will let me make people over to my order, as a tailor makes shirts to fit my proportions. But you will not turn your child over to me—and quite properly; nor can I by any stretch of imagination change human nature. We do not cry, "Scrap the stomach," just because we have too much stomach-ache—though we do hear more complaints about poor stomachs than about poor food-habits or the colossal ignorance as to why stomachs get upset.

If the home is diseased—and too many are—it is not the fault of the idea. It is the fault of a society which pretends that it can progress by going backward; that the way to sanity is through the perpetuation of social conditions which breed discontent and insanity.

The home—the place where father, mother, and the children lived in peace, whether in a cave or over a cowshed—was the cradle of human culture. Human culture increased in length, breadth, and height when the family in that home united with other families in other homes to build simple cultural traits into great cultural complexes. The history of civilization shows ever larger social units. A society is just as stable as its family units are biologically sound; no society can be sane or sound if the families are at war one with another. This and that are said to be "divinely appointed." If we of this earth have an institution that is divinely appointed, it is the family home. But asking God to bless it does not fill it with peace, happiness, or bliss.

Safe, sane, sound homes are founded on love—the love that naturally accompanies the complete and perfect sexual adjustment of two human beings of opposite sex. And is it or is it not significant that the darkest of all ages in human history was the age when the fear of hell-fire was thrown into what should be and naturally is the finest, deepest, and most soul-satisfying experience in human lives? The phantasmagoria of assorted lunacies and idiocies spewed out in those centuries is beyond belief.

We speak of the burden this generation bears, and must hand on in part to future generations, because of the World War. Well, it is a burden, and a heavy one; but it is light compared with the burden imposed upon our section of the human race by the thunderings from pulpits that this world is full of sin and sorrow and vampires and devils—and all because of that one phase of our nature which more than any other made a man out of a monkey by forcing him into a home where he could become a family man. We could become civilized because we did become human.

x

What the dominant male of an ape harem does with brute strength, human beings do with a marriage ceremony—inform the world at large that the party of the second part is definitely and permanently satisfied and may be crossed off the list of possible sex stimuli. Marriage had social survival value, just as the home with its incest taboo had family survival value. The taboo made for peace in the family; the ceremony, for peace in society. Hence, everywhere, marriage ceremonies. No tribe so low as to be without it; few societies so sophisticated as to think they could get along without it.

It was a grand idea and a most useful device; but some of man's best laid schemes, as Burns reminds us, "gang aft agley": how far "agley" is only too evident by looking around us, or into Westermarck's *History of Human Marriage*—which is not history, yet something more, something less, than the history of marriage.

Crawley's *Mystic Rose* is different; parts of it are almost pornographic. That fact alone made it worth reprinting, and the fact that it is still cited in sociological literature as science—thereby colouring the views of students of sociology—makes it worth noticing.

*The Mystic Rose* claims to be a "study of primitive marriage and of primitive thought in its bearing on marriage." It does abound in strange and fantastic beliefs, rites, and ceremonies; but that any study, however exhaustive, of all that can be gathered from existing customs or customs recorded within historic times, helps us to read primitive thoughts, I do not believe. We can know almost nothing about primitive thought because early man had almost no thoughts. All "primitive" living tribes are sophisticated; they have rationalized themselves out of really primitive ways of life almost as far as we have. Their world is as complete and perfect and self-evident to them as ours is to us.

To say, as Crawley does, that human nature remains "fundamentally primitive," is to say less than that Fundamentalists remain children, though dressed up in the antiquated clothes of Middle Age bigotry. "Primitive thinking does not distinguish between the natural and the supernatural." How much of ours does? And that we can squeeze enough juice out of fifty or five hundred assorted marriage ceremonies, or out of an equal number of assorted sex taboos and puberty rites, to predict the asininity or the alkalinity of future ceremonies, taboos, rites, etc., I do not believe. Viewed objectively and from an easy-chair, certain ceremonies, taboos, etc., in Crawley's hands become as funny as Freudian dreams.

Horror at the possibility of incestuous marriage made man fear matrimony itself! Here is Crawley's argument. All human beings— so primitive man "thinks"—are potentially dangerous; do not touch them or you may "catch" something. That belief makes for universal human "egoistic sensibility," intensified when any new act is about to be performed. Sex itself carries an especially heavy current of potential death and destruction. Hence the paralyzing fear in contemplating the nuptial bed. Something must be done to allay that fear, *hence the marriage ceremony*. That ceremony prevents either of the contracting parties from catching anything dangerous from the other. And that is the idea behind all moral and social ideas—in short, the cornerstone of human society!

Well, if true, it is a serious indictment of the human race. But just as Burke was right in saying that you cannot indict a nation, so I think the human race cannot be held guilty of that particular form of insanity. That a portion of the human race has been guilty of such fantastic beliefs, and has done its best to live up—or down —to them, is a fact, and significant of the stranglehold a belief, howsoever absurd, can get. And that again merely proves that man by nature is credulous and can easily be led to trade his birthright for a Woolworth Building or a corner lot in the sweet by and by —and on the instalment plan.

Sex as a broad and intricate complex means more to woman than to man. It must. Woman is the logical and inevitable centre around which the whole sexual complex revolves and from which the family evolves. That fact is so striking that no man, however credulous or childish, could fail to be moved by it. Woman is the deadlier of the two contracting parties.

Woman's potentiality for weal or for woe may be small; her potentiality for *something* is greater. She arouses more emotion; she is the greater emotional stimulus. In countless ways man has gone crazy about her; but he never went more crazy about anything than when he made her responsible for Original Sin.

See how theology handles this delicate situation—all because *she* is Original Sin. Continence is advised because "taught by the counsel of the Blessed Son of God and confirmed by the example of Tobias." Tobias survived the first night with Sarah by being good. He left Sarah alone. Sarah's preceding seven husbands had dropped dead! Sarah had a mean lover, Asmodeus, who, although he loved in vain, was so jealous that he slew anybody who approached Sarah's bed.

Tobias had a friend, the angel Raphael, whose *medicine* was more powerful than Asmodeus'; he told Tobias how to make it. So Tobias put the heart and liver of a fish into a smouldering incense-burner. That stank Asmodeus out, and he fled to Egypt. And Tobias, having a clear field, took Sarah by the hand and led her to the bed, where they both knelt down in prayer and prayed all night. They kept that up three nights more, and lived happily ever after!

Asmodeus is *taint*—the taint of Original Sin. It can be cured: by being driven out, even to Egypt—as though poor old Egypt had not had enough troubles of her own. This form of magic, as we shall see, is far-reaching and widespread. It takes a thousand forms and pursues a thousand ways. Basically, it is always the same game: by making the right kind of "medicine" you can cure any kind of disease.

Original Sin was the original disease. Its cures have filled apothecary shops with everything under the sun. Then came a Master Mind with something better than a cure, a really bright idea. And the Church sold dispensations for ten francs apiece. A dispensation on the mantel would drive "Asmodeus" out as efficiently as fish-liver in an incense-burner, and the uxorious flesh, as Langdon-Davies puts it, could forthwith safely wed the misogynist spirit.

While many Catholics (Langdon-Davies says) still cling to the Tobias and Sarah pattern, the Anglican Church has recently substituted that of Abraham and Sarah as its warrant for preaching first-night continence. In Brittany, continence was obligatory for three nights: the first night belonged to the Good God, the second to St. Joseph, the third to the husband's patron saint; the fourth was the husband's. But all this is mere detail. The larger point is the widespread belief that the bride is dangerous and that something must be done about it before she is safe for the nuptial couch. What to do? The answers (cures) are many and interesting.

Surround the bride and groom with so many bridesmaids and groomsmen that *taint* (evil spirits, imps of Satan) could not tell which was which. Or cover the bride with a veil; the taint cannot see through the veil and will fly away. In New Guinea they carry the bride home nicely camouflaged in mats and palm-leaf fans. Or fool the evil spirit by substituting a mock bride at the ceremony. The Bretons used to rig up a little girl, or the mother, or an old grandmother, as the bride, to mislead the hovering taint-imp. Or, marry the girl to a tree—in the belief that evil will take out its spite on the tree. Objects other than trees have been used in various quarters.

Another widespread and efficacious trick was to get some one else to break the ice, so to speak—catch the taint first. Hence the widespread custom, in places elevated into the *jus primæ noctis*, of inaugurating the bride into wedded life by a priest or the god's delegate, acting for the god. It looks as though the now privileged kiss of the best man were a relic of what was once a purely self-sacrificing act of purification, of immunizing her from taint.

These charms vary because simple-minded humanity has never agreed on just what it is that must be charmed away. If the devil had only shown himself in the very beginning and in his own true colours, or if Original Sin had not been discovered so many times and in so many guises, there would not be so many kinds of simple-minded Simple Simons, or so many simple-minded ways of beating the devil around the stump. To look further into these folk-ways, or at more guises of sin, is to take us into the very core of religion and too far from *The Mystic Rose*.

Our ring, rice, old shoes, veils, kissing the bride, etc., says Crawley, are not mere survivals of primitive customs and beliefs, but are *natural* to man; they spring "from functional causes constant in the human organism." Well, if we throw rice, not as an antique way of saying "Multiply and be fruitful," nor as a pure though mild form of hedonism, but because some form of childish action and moron belief is a "functional" *constant* in our mating behaviour —why, I am for more and bigger world wars and free sex for all! Possibly we are all stark mad; but I cannot see the idea that man is inherently and forever crazy, nor do I believe our earth is merely a reserve for lunatics at large. Better be an electron and lead a really fast life!

Once upon a time, says Crawley, there was no marriage ceremony, but "the ideas of such were latent in the actual union of man and woman." *Latent?* That word acts like one of Mr. Freud's trained animals: it will do anything you want it to do; and incidentally it explains everything you have made it do. It is like Morgan's "Emergent Evolution." Such concepts cover so much they cover nothing; they say so much they say nothing. Even if we are now "emerging" lunatics, criminals, and parasites faster than ever before in human history, that does not prove that we are latent lunatics, criminals, or parasites!

Superstition clutched man's throat early in his human career, and gradually strangled the life out of certain functions which, let alone or given a chance, would have pursued the even tenor of their way. Marriage was such a function. We fight today to scrape these barnacles from our lives. But if Crawley's implications are correct, we might as well go to La Mancha and fight windmills.

Advance cannot be made as long as human desires are thought of as unnatural or supernatural, sacred or profane, devilish or divine. Human relations, family, religion, government, are human and of the earth earthy. What we call morality, chastity, virtue, sin, etc., are human, habits of behaviour; but they are no more sacrosanct than mice or mouse-traps, and the sole test of their validity is no more, no less, than that for mouse-traps: are they good, will they work, are they worth the price we pay, are we getting the results out of them we think we are? There is no more reason why any particular form of marriage, morality, religion, or government should be withdrawn from scientific observation, than that certain strata of the earth's crust or certain fossilized human bones should be fenced off from human eyes.

In the race to become human the ape that won paid more attention to his duties than to his rights. There were then no supermen, nor superboobs: just enough flesh, bone, and good red blood to make man. To endow man with the idea that sexual contacts are inherently dangerous is to make lead pencils latent in cedar trees and graphite. Then to take that idea as proved and formulate a hypothesis which will explain all the known superstitions about primitive and modern marriage, is to take a mean advantage of the Rose.

And so we turn from *The Mystic Rose* to the fact that sex play is the ape and primitive way of learning about sex. But with man, everywhere, there comes a time when play ends and work begins. The fact is announced to the neighbours in such a way that they can see and hear it, and by the same old ceremony and ritual *their* ancestors used. Thereafter they are man and wife—with all the exceptions, reservations, conventions, separations, divorces, widow immolations, etc., yet devised by human ingenuity.

In most of the infraliterate world, sex is almost as free as cocoanuts up to the time of the marriage ceremony—but with all the restrictions of certain specific taboos as to who's who and what's what and when's when that make up the mores of each particular culture. But that sex, as sex, is dangerous, or that girls, as girls,

are she-devils to be handled with gloves, or that chastity is a virtue
—of all this, not a trace.

As a result, sex repression, in the many manifestations which
drive us insane, is practically unknown in primitive society. All
the slimy phenomena the Freudians discover in our world and hang
on human nature are diseases of our times and our society. Most
of the mental disorders, diseased personalities, etc., that bedevil
us are the result of conflicting social heritages, growths from a
soil reeking with the débris of early Oriental superstition and mysticism, and fertilized by Middle Age Scholasticism.

Yet, as Dr. Cabot says, we go right on speaking contemptuously
of "mere lust," "merely physical," etc., as though these terms were
scientific descriptions, whereas they are but attempts to push a
living act out among the dead. "When an act needs improvement,
we damn it with a phrase." Love is an *elemental* force, a groping
force, and "should be helped to find its goal and not be branded
as an outcast."

And this is no plea for a "return" to promiscuity, or divorce for
the asking, or free and unrestricted prostitution. Nothing of the
sort. Anyone who reads such a plea into it has learned about love
from a book.

Human beings, we may remind ourselves, are not dogs, even
though some yelp like curs and in rage show their canines. Sex
in dogs is blind, seeks its own selfish ends, is without conscience
or discretion, and is heedless of weal or woe; it is seasonal, and
nature cares for her own. In human beings it begins in play and
ends in love: love so strong that when two souls have but a single
thought and two hearts beat as one, nothing can separate them.
If a Twentieth Amendment tomorrow dissolved every marriage
vow in America, thousands no doubt would avail themselves of
the opportunity for freedom; and that, plus the number already
divorced, would show how far, and why, the American family
has failed to function. No law is needed to hold a happy family
together.

When a man is found with manners and morals fitter for a
kennel than for a home, we may lay it to his masters and his early
associates and not to human nature. It is human nature to mate
and common sense to inform the world when he has mated.

Nothing is wrong with marriage, nor with the family, nor with society, nor with human nature, nor with civilization. The "wrong" lies in the fact that our pace-makers have become megalomaniacs, and we poor mortals, in our fear of being left behind, have no time to marry, or if we do, to accept full responsibility for parenthood and citizenship. All of which makes for chaos in society, anarchy in government.

Healthy society begins with healthy families; it ends with diseased marriages. Some human relationships cannot be tampered with recklessly, and when man gets bigger than his innate nature allows, he bursts like an over-inflated frog. Nothing is so valuable as human values—values which proved their worth during the long years man was struggling up and out of and away from brute creation. When man ceases to be born of woman—and not before— he can disregard the obvious biologic facts of his bisexual world, the psychological consequences of loveless marriages, and the sociological consequences of warring homes.

This is not a dictum, but a conviction founded on what seems to me to be scientific evidence; inference that may be drawn, not from academic discussions of marriage or lists of social taboos, but from common sense and such light as is shed by recent studies of the sexual behaviour of our closest infrahuman relations, the almost-human apes.

## XI

Peace in the family: tribe, clan, state, league, nation. Loyalty, solidarity, conformity. These were desirable qualities in becoming human and in building civilization. But there is another side to the story. Even today few "inferiority complexes" are so compelling as to make the admission of ignorance easy. As a result, man has found himself again and again stranded by a high tide or holding an empty sack.

Man's desire for Reality leads him to speculate; speculations easily become traditions which soon fossilize, thereby becoming the tribal Bible or Law and Order, whereby sin is cast out and purity and peace maintained.

How does the family, tribe, or nation justify its conduct? How do beliefs which to us seem unreasonable, unjustifiable, illogical, get their start, soon becoming self-evident, fundamental truths, infallible guides to action and rules of conduct, warrants for cruelty, murder, torture, slavery and war? Religion, obviously, is the best field for a study of the growth and consequences of the errors of ignorant speculation or primitive philosophizing; but Malinowski's researches among the illiterate South Sea Islanders afford unparalleled materials for seeing into the working of a universally employed psychological principle of enormous portent in all human society. Incidentally, we shall see how primitive beliefs about such natural facts as reproduction become sanctions for endless cultural acts.

Primitive man knows nothing of the physiological facts of conception. He does know babies, and he invariably has a theory of their origin. Those theories vary endlessly, hence the endless variety of customary religious, magical, or legal practices, rites, and taboos associated with puberty, menstruation, pregnancy, and birth—in short, with all the striking phenomena of life and death. Even simple biological kinship facts become extraordinarily complex cultural facts. It is these "cultural" facts which make up our cultural world and prescribe the pattern of our behaviour, no less nor more than that of primitive man.

Children ask questions; parents will try to answer them. Where *do* babies come from? There are probably mothers today who give their children toy trains, but make the old stork story carry its burden of tiny human freight.

Parthenogenetic birth makes a nice story and even made the Parthenon, but Athene the Virgin had no children. Our Virgin, as I read my Bible, was *visited* by the Holy Ghost. But belief in magic is far older than knowledge of human ovum, and of how, and how only, that ovum may be fertilized. The male element can, however, find its way to an ovum if left on the doorstep, as it were; in other words, coitus is not an absolute *sine qua non* in fertilizing a human ovum. Nor was the true nature of the male discharge at all understood until within modern times. Which means that false ideas easily arose, and persist, as to the physiological function of sexual intercourse. So primitive man accepted the act for what it seemed to be, and what he found it to be by personal experience, and invented various stork stories to satisfy his own and his children's curiosity.

Babies begin as spirits, says the Trobriand variant; they are brought by a "spirit-carrier" and laid upon the woman's head. This *causes* the blood to rush up to her head to meet the fœtal spirit, pick it up, and carry it down to the womb.

Note the logic. Knowing nothing of procreation, much of the endless stream of life from infancy to death, they infer that life is immortal and is reborn as a spirit. It *must* come somehow: it is *brought*—by a spirit-carrier. How do they know the blood "rushes up" to meet the fœtal spirit? Because the woman's menses stop, and stop "because" the blood has gone to her head! She does not resume her periods "because" her normal menstrual blood is required to nourish the spirit. When the fœtal spirit has matured, it just naturally appears—is born. All this is so self-evident to the Trobriander that he *knows* it.

Tell him there is no spirit for the spirit-carrier to bring, that coitus is the *cause* of pregnancy: he will laugh at you and pity your ignorance. Unmarried girls, he will tell you in refutation of your claim, have more sexual intercourse than married women, but they have no children! Then there is So-and-so, married these many years, who has had frequent intercourse but has never had a child. Then So-and-so left his wife for two years; no sexual relations at all; yet on his return she presented him with a new baby. Then there is that repulsive albino; she has two children; she never had a lover. Babies are brought! Coitus has nothing to do with procreation.

For every argument Malinowski had, they had a better one. His facts were not their facts. To his "What are testes?" they reply, "Ornaments!" Great physicians of the Middle Ages made mistakes as great.

What started this primitive thinker on the wrong track? The same fact that led so many other "savages" into fanciful beliefs, or rather the same complex of facts. First, the sex act itself: what is it; why? "Pleasure! Why do I eat? I like it." Note that while fertilization *may* follow coitus by hours or days, nobody is aware of the fact; neither mother nor gynæcologist can be *certain* of pregnancy till months after fertilization: the mother, by quickening; the doctor, by fœtal heart-beat. It is only natural that the native sees no necessary connection between an oft-repeated act of purely sensual pleasure and the quickening of pregnancy four and one-half months later. The woman notices that her menses have ceased, but sees no reason why she should associate that fact with one she cannot sense for months later—because, as Ashley-Montagu points out, she may have had intercourse that very day, or not for several weeks. In other words, her lunar cycle is a *period* cycle, but in regard to follicular ovarian change and not to a variable number of sexual acts.

If we who count ourselves wise do not reason out the connection between what we ate last Saturday night and how we feel this Monday morning, how can we expect a South Sea Islander or our ancestors to exhibit much common sense? In terms of logic, we get a cold the same way a South Sea mother gets a baby.

Where *do* babies come from? Some are brought by spirit-bearers. Some are carried in the foam of the sea; take care while bathing! Some are generated from saliva or from a drop of blood. Some are caused by eating a certain kind of egg or some particular animal or vegetable food; some from the glance of a god; or from swallowing a jewel; or from eating a hermit's heart, the ashes of a human skull, or a bit of the placenta, or the sex organs themselves.

Everything, anything, causes pregnancy somewhere. Hence the endless, "Don't do so-and-so, or . . ." Or more often, for babies are generally regarded as gifts of the gods, "Do this or that, eat this or that, and . . ." World of fanciful beliefs without end! Hence, too, the amazing number of love philtres. There are probably six in the nearest drug store: "medicines" to compel love, increase powers, etc., *ad nauseam*. Add credulity, also ignorance. The more superman we try to be, the more superboob we become.

By such reasoning cultural complexes are built, and collectively become both citadel and encircling wall. Into these man is born; into these he learns to fit—easily, because he is trimmed to fit the garment.

In other words, to the Trobriander, with his fundamental truths to protect him from every evil eye, I need not come with my physiological facts about procreation or contraceptives; to him they are all superstitions, absurdities, magic contrivances. He can *prove* his case; he *knows*; and a camel could not get its nose under his fundamentalist tent. Whether I am laughed at for my "absurd" arguments, or hanged because I am absurd, is determined by time, place, and power.

The South Sea Islander's reasoning seems primitive, we say, and certain religious and social practices growing out of this reasoning seem absurd. So they do; but think of the reasoning behind the note accompanying a monk's Christmas present of honeycake, mead, and capon, to his sister:

The mead is the blood of Christ, the honeycake and the capon are His body, which for our salvation was baked and pierced at the Cross. The Holy Ghost baked the cake in the Virgin's womb, in which the sugar of His divinity amalgamated with the dough of our humanity. In the Virgin's womb the Holy Ghost also spiced the mead and prepared it from wine; the spice is divine virtue, the wine is human blood. In addition He caused the holy capon to issue from the egg; the yolk of the egg is the deity, the white is humanity, the shell is the womb of the Virgin Mary. . . .

Even Plato held that the womb is an animal which demands food to become fecund; if allowed to go hungry, it wanders around, tormenting the body and causing *hysteria*—Greek for uterus. If Plato's reasoning was more logical than the South Sea Islander's, his facts were just as childish and uncritical. The great fact is that most facts must be dug out with the hands; they cannot be reasoned out. Yet there are those who maintain that the illiterate "savage" remains primitive because he has a constitutionally primitive mind, and that only whites can reason!

## XII

Families grow larger, unite, grow into societies. Society for its governance splits up again into smaller organizations for the carrying on of certain functions: to regulate descent, maintain order, keep off evil spirits, insure abundance—in families, fields, herds, etc. The emphasis is now here, now there. Woman—a goddess, empress, slave, prostitute, chattel, thing. Man—a god, king, tyrant, despot, slave, eunuch. Leaders and led; priests, prophets, shamans, soothsayers, witch-doctors, medicine-men; aristocracy, commoners; Brahmans, pariahs; public assemblies and secret societies. For everything we have, they had something just as good; it served their purpose.

Organizations, societies, fraternities, sororities, age societies, guilds, professions, heads, chiefs, executives, come into existence to supply human needs when society grows unwieldy, impracticable, unmanageable.

Disease began, as for most people today it ends, as something supernatural. And man explored the supernatural world for ease for diseased minds. Taking advantage of his greater freedom from family cares, he "improved" his freedom by finding unnatural uses for his wife whereby he could realize his own ease; he used his fellow-men also, even his children. There is nothing this man-afraid-of-himself has not used, nothing he has not prostituted to his own selfish and greedy ends—even his wife, his daughter. Prostitution began as an idea, a physical cure for a real or imagined condition.

Early ignorance of the facts of procreation was only natural, but man's equally fanciful interpretations of fertilization processes in herds and crops were astounding—and incidentally led to some of the foulest and unholiest deeds of history, as well as some of the finest and loveliest pages of literature.

We may stop to look at but one example. Some 5,500 years ago Gudea, a Lagash king in Babylonia, rebuilt his temple, and into the holy of holies led his wife. There she found a couch and the god's agent, to whom she gave herself, with the result that: "The holy bowl of the terrace of the great dwelling was submerged, the great watercourses that were low became like water that bowls will not hold; it stood on their plantations; from the Tigris and Euphrates it joyfully overflowed; whatever was needful for the city and temple it caused to grow satisfactorily."

With man creating gods in his own lusts and out of ignorance of the natural processes of fertilization, it was a foregone conclusion that temple prostitution should become a regular practice. But to reach such heights of socially destructive behaviour, man had to become highly civilized. The Prophets in Israel finally turned from such fraudulent and unholy god-of-fertility marriages to means more socially sane but quite as inefficient.

It may be that prostitution and seduction can disappear only with pre-marital sex freedom. That freedom, for a while at least, probably would be followed by licence; but, what is important, it *might* lead to more lasting marriages, sounder and saner homes, and a healthier society. But it has a long, hard road before it. Our ideas about marriage and sexual life in general are not South Sea Islander; but large and firmly entrenched portions of our society revolve in a fundamental-truth vacuum-tube as hard to penetrate as the Trobriander's island home, fortified by its own pragmatic, self-evident Facts.

The body is older than the heart; society, in higher apes, is older than the individual. The strength of every society depends primarily on peace, health, well-being, in the home; and is as strong as its weakest family. This or that individual can go far, or high, or low, but society pays his passage and has a right to ask what he is doing up or down there and whether his solo flight is of any possible earthly use to society.

Looking at history, one sees men breaking away from time to time, penetrating hitherto unexplored worlds, and returning laden with rare and usable goods. Not all those men were burned at the stake; many of them even got a respectful hearing for their pains. Many of them today adorn public squares and occupy niches in halls of fame, but did they leaven any dough, is society as stale and sour as ever?

### XIII

Marriage has *failed*; what shall we do to be saved? One silly proposal follows another. What are the facts?

Delayed marriages founded on intelligence and endowed with wealth may, and often do, endure; but their permanence is precarious, and they are generally sterile in children and in social, serviceable, humanly sensible goods. Marriages founded on sex love are biologically sound and psychologically sane. When they are not permanent, and often they are not, the reason must be sought in social environment and not in human nature.

The most significant fact, as I see it, is the slow but sure decline of our inherited Middle Age belief that sexual desire is man's most devilish enemy; its fulfilment, an act of degradation. As a result, the facts and problems of our bisexual world can not be recognized and dealt with honestly, critically, scientifically, and without squeamishness, prudery, or shame. The hypocrisy behind the Christian male's demand for sexual "purity" is no longer necessary.

But our newly won freedom from the dead hand of an irrational past will avail little unless the two sexes clearly recognize that their sex problems can be solved satisfactorily only if they are understood to be *bisexual* problems; there must be mutual understanding, sympathy, and coöperation. There should be no "woman" problem, no "child" problem, but rather problems of the home, of society, of the common weal.

There are forces at work today which tend to disrupt the home, to imperil marriage, and to swell the flood of the socially irresponsible, biologically useless, and psychologically neurotic. How these forces got started, and whether they are waxing or waning, are real problems that can be profitably investigated. But, as Sapir points out, a sociology which treats of family morals in terms of sex desire, mating, economic security, or care of children, and avoids the word *love* as though it were a sentimental bugaboo, is not a realistic but a stupid sociology.

As monks once thumbed the pages of St. Augustine's *City of God* for their philosophy of life, while pondering wistfully on the sin they had fled the world to escape, so there are those today who thumb the pages of our sociologies in search of a philosophy of life. There can be no *science* of society that knows nothing of love.

That our Machine Age, in altering the relation of the family to property and in liberating work and love from parental "wisdom" and authority, has, as Floyd Dell maintains, made real courtship and true love-marriage possible, seems likely. But whether the credit be given to the Machine Age or not, the fact remains that love today has a chance it has been denied since the Christian mystic and unnatural "pure" and "impure" concepts made emotional happiness next to impossible between man and wife.

It is significant that the century which produced Rousseau's *Nouvelle Héloïse*, the first story of sentimental love, made a hero of Casanova, chief libertine of an age of unparalleled sensuality. Sexual relations, long stigmatized by the Church as evil, had become obscene. Love degenerated into lust; its gratification the chief form of amusement.

That form of degeneracy is no less socially dangerous than other forms, and today we face that danger. The legitimate demand that sex be returned to its proper place has been made a smoke screen to hide the forcing of it into improper places. Freud, primitive art, naturalism, individualism, are only a few of the modern justifications for sex licence. To use "love" as justification for lust is to tear it from its biologic and psychologic settings.

Sex, as we have seen, becomes love among the higher Primates, and is altruistic. Sex "freedom" has been made a symbol for egoism in sex satisfaction. Egoistic sex, as Sapir says, is narcistic; and applied narcissism is promiscuity, enemy of social sanity and destroyer of every sound sentiment of love. Every divorce presumes an unhappy marriage; and the unhappy marriages that never seek dissolution are known to be numerous. All unhappy marriages are potential nurseries of social misfits and criminals. Unhappy marriages are loveless marriages, sexual incompatibility. What are the divorce court records of "cruelty," "incompatibility of temper," "adultery," etc., but euphemisms for homosexuality, parental fixations, infantilisms, sadism, masochism, and other unnatural sex habits which make bisexual love difficult or impossible?

These evils spring, not primarily from the family, but from society itself, from our civilization. The ancient and honourable institution of the family is not to be made the scapegoat for our cultural institution, backed as it is by Roman and Germanic law and custom and Christian asceticism.

Woman is no longer a necessary evil or slave to an overlord, but we still make marriage a contract till death, and legally dissoluble only by gross physical misbehaviour; and we rail at the number of women who live useless lives, vainly seeking outlets for their lost domestic responsibilities. "Useless" is a sinister word, but I wonder how many men of our day are leading *useful* lives, accepting their share of domestic responsibility?

Which—the old "holy" family, or the much older "erotic" family? Of this we may be certain: the erotic family is founded in sound psychology; and that is the only hearth where children may learn to know and appreciate altruistic love—greatest of all boons known to mankind.

Chastity is a virtue only when some authority calls the lack of it a vice. Man had travelled far and grown grey before he became so virtuous. Love was once free to choose, as it was meant to be, and when two choosers had really become lovers they were so attached to each other through the countless fibres of their being that they founded a *home*. Homes otherwise founded are always and eternally shaky and easily bowled over. In other words, primitive man was a clean-minded animal. He knew sex perversion, but only as rare and silly foolishness. Knowing that there were two sexes, he wisely did not bother his head about which was the inferior. And he learned that the old grey mare was the better horse.

The home on the rocks? I venture to say that nowhere else on earth, nor at any previous period since our own civilization began, have marriages founded on nothing but mutual love and understanding been so prevalent as in America today. With so many marriages founded on the rock of love, the home cannot go on the rocks.

Hands off the home!—especially the dead hands of superstition and ignorance, and more especially the hand of the Church! No home can be brave that is moved by fear. What needs to be saved is lives, not souls.

# CHAPTER FOUR

## In the Beginning Were Joy and Art for Life's Sake

1. Playing the Game; or the Rôle of Customs and Manners. 2. The Æsthetic Sense; or "Damn it, I like to be liked." 3. The Skin that Loves to be Tattooed. 4. The Virtue of a Perfect Charm. 5. Ethics— for Men Only. 6. Genuine Old Masters. 7. Listen, my Children, and You Shall Hear. 8. The Fundamentals of Song, Music, and Dance. 9. The Divine Drama. 10. Madame Grundy Speaking. 11. The True, the Good, the Beautiful, and the Bunk.

I

LIFE among human beings is a game which must be played according to the rules. Without rules there can be no joy in life, and without joy there can be neither art nor opportunity to develop æsthetic sense. This seems obvious; it is not so obvious that joy has biologic value, that the artistic is a human quality, that man has an innate æsthetic sense and is by nature an artist. Were it not so, man could not have become cultured, could not have built a great civilization.

If we of today are not enjoying life or making life an art, there must be a reason—which will be discovered in our cultural heritage and not in our natural inheritance. My aim in this chapter is to examine these fundamental qualities of human nature in so far as they bear on the joys of life and give us, as part of our birthright, a love of art and the impulse to express ourselves artistically.

"According to the rules." In a society so complex and fluid as is ours today, one would be bold indeed to say just what the rules are which govern our game of life. I need not stress this point here; I only mention it to emphasize the necessity of turning to a civilization less advanced, a society less confused and complex than our own, to get at the beginning of that side of human nature which makes joyous living profitable and artistic expression the finest of all fine arts. We shall see this side of human nature at work in our historic examination of the facts behind our civilization; those facts make an interesting story in themselves, but we want here to get closer to the nature of the animal responsible for them.

What I have called "rules" are often spoken of in anthropologic literature as Customs and Manners. But on our first view of a new and strange people, are we not likely to concur in the opinion of the investigator whose "Customs, beastly; manners, none" covered all there was to be said about the people he was supposed to investigate?

It must be obvious that behind every set of customs and manners is a tribe, society, or group of human beings who have learned to live according to their lights, the lights they learned to see by. I have seen four kinds of light in my life—tallow candle, kerosene, gas, electricity. But this century is unique.

It must also be obvious that without customs and manners man could not have become civilized. In fact, common usage with us restricts civilization to those whose customs and manners are in general agreement with ours. It is always the outer world that is savage or barbaric or uncivilized, we and our kind who are cultured and civilized. There is nothing new in this usage, nor was the Kaiser the first to restrict *Kultur* to the Fatherland. The Egyptians, Babylonians, Semites, Greeks, Romans, all viewed outsiders as "outlanders." We meet the same difficulty in talking about religion. It is always *our* religion that is True and Authorized; all others are pagan, or damned with faint praise. Orthodoxy is always *my* doxy.

Here, then, we have the fundamental psychology of customs and manners: they are *good* because they are ours, just as what I do with my right hand is *right*; and if my right hand is big enough, that makes *might*. Hence might is right. We are always right; or if we individually are wrong, society is right—and generally has the might to enforce its opinion. So in the religious field. We do not question our sins; we accept them as facts and lay the burden on bad luck, or on our stupidity, or on fate. We do not question the wisdom of God in making sin inviting and often inevitable.

To lie, steal, murder, or rape was unnatural, abnormal, insane behaviour in all primitive societies. Their crimes seem cruel to us because ours is a different code. Primitive and modern societies have codes of conduct; fundamentally the codes are the same and are founded on biologically useful principles, namely, respect for the liberty, life, health, and personal belongings of fellow-men, and avoidance of conduct harmful to society at large. With them as with us, breach of that code was punished. But the life, health, liberty, well-being, and property that are to be respected may mean one thing in one society, quite a different thing in another. Even among us these words mean different things in different ranks of society. "Respect" may mean almost anything; often Yes for public exhibition, No for private practice.

In other words, there is no reason for customs or manners outside society. Society itself is the stimulus evoking steadfastness in morals, efficiency in the routine business of life, and interest in life itself. But we assume that law can replace society; and turn its enforcement over to the police. The result is that we have as many grades or prices of justice as we have grades of social wealth. That result is inevitable, and judging by present tendencies it must become even more destructive.

In former times I could look about to see what my neighbours were doing as my guide to righteousness and proper moral conduct, and if there were no neighbours near-by I could turn to my Bible. We have lost both guides. Many of us do not know a single person in our block, and communities grow like weeds and as aimlessly. We are here today and who knows where we'll be next week? The press is no longer an authority on customs or manners, and blind submission to the Church, except in a limited respect on the part of a large but limited number, has become as out-of-date as the old-fashioned family. Custom has given way to individual whim, fancy, greed, lust for power; manners, to "What will pay most?" or, "What can I get away with?" or, "How far can I pursue my individual career before somebody decides something must be done about it or me?" That does not make for righteousness or propriety. Civilization was not founded on such codes, nor can a nation live on them.

It is human nature to want to excite admiration in the family or community; otherwise no one will be proud of us, nor will posterity point to us with pride. Pride is rooted in ape behaviour; it has biologic value.

There must be discipline, of course; anarchy is as suicidal to apes as to humans. The youngster who displeases the dominant male or the nursing mother gets a slap for its pains; it thereby becomes expert at avoiding slaps, and so becomes the one the fond mother can point to with pride. If the youngster gets nearly killed for some particularly flagrant breach of ape-family morals or manners, or for venturing too far from the beaten path, that breach or venture drops out of the youngster's repertoire then and there. It has no confidence in that particular field of endeavor—in fact, it has ceased to be a "field"; the youngster turns "naturally" to other fields. And by manhood can find in the words Freedom and Liberty all the freedom his liberty allows him.

The "customs" may be bad, the "manners" next to none; rules there must be if the stage for life's game is not to become a prison for the criminal insane.

## II

Natural activities are naturally enjoyable. Joy has biologic value. The lamb gambolling on the green is innate nature expressing itself. Man is primarily a social animal. Certain activities are naturally enjoyable, and as he can only function as a member of society he naturally desires recognition, approval. When Charles Lamb said, *Damn it, I like to be liked*, he spoke for humanity. Man *naturally* likes to be liked. He can make himself more likable by discovering new things or ways socially valuable. To make discoveries he must manipulate, examine, observe, try, experiment; and to gain recognition he must exhibit his achievements, talk about them, pass them on, participate in the activities of the crowd. That, please note, is man's innate equipment as a social animal: the will or desire; the mechanism or "constitution" to make the will effective, to carry out the desire.

And so we may say that while any human activity can assume more than one form, certain forms have *æsthetic* value: they give joy to the doer, pleasure to the beholder. Our ear is so attuned that harsh noises seem *harsh* because our ears were not evolved in a boiler factory, or beside a rivetting machine, or over a street-car track. Human eyes were evolved primarily to pick up and follow movement. Certain classes of stimuli are more fatiguing to the eye than others, just as harsh and clanging noises more easily disturb our ears.

And so, as we might expect, we find Primitives everywhere dancing rhythmically, singing in sequence of tones, and making things which "feel good" to nerve-endings in hand and fingers and "look good" to human eyes. Such activities give pleasure to those who see, hear, and handle, and also to the dancer, singer, or maker himself. We are not natural-born contortionists; our motor mechanism learns to function along lines useful to us in life's routine. To the healthy body natural movement is a natural performance, an enjoyable activity. In rhythmical movements in dancing there are both the personal joyous feeling in kinæsthetic sense—muscles, tendons, joints, etc.—and the added stimulus which comes from being in contact with and in sight and hearing of one's fellow-men.

Thus we find, everywhere, dances, songs, stories, carvings, paintings, sculptures—activities which please one or more of the senses. The natives *enjoy* these for the same reason we enjoy the song of birds and shadows dancing on the water. In that sense, beauty is beauty the world over. Anything which pleases the senses is beautiful, everywhere. Beauty is perfection. A perfectly beautiful thing is a thing which both pleases and satisfies the senses. The mere fact of the universality of a sense of beauty is evidence of an innate craving to make or do things which satisfy, and an innate capacity to sense beauty in them—to enjoy them.

While growing up we learn to attach relative values to things which please or displease our senses. We become emotionally slanted toward the objective world. The odor of cheese moves us one way; of a rose, another. The taste of a pie "like mother used to make," the sight of a glen like the one we learned to love in, the song of birds like the kind we used to hear when the world was fresh and young: these and all such are not only sensed—smelled, tasted, seen, or heard; they are *felt*, they arouse us emotionally, they move us with a thrill, a sigh, a longing, a yearning, or even poignant grief or a mad passion to live our lives over again.

The things we feel most deeply are the feelings we cannot put into words. Man named all the stars before he named all his feelings.

These emotional slants, these family conditionings, become more or less systematized, organized into social, tribal, national attitudes. We have, for example, a certain type of woman we call beautiful. "She," we say, "is my type," or "my style." But if we were trying to sell a magazine by its cover to a Hottentot, we should hurry to inform him that there were other types inside. Beauty is beauty the world around, but the Hottentot likes them fat, so fat they seem repulsive to us. He can see no beauty in the American girl. To him a girl is not a picture to be looked at—on magazine cover or in bathing-suit; but a potential wife who must live in the desert and may have to live for weeks off the stored-up fat of her posterior. "Beauty? Why, she's a scarecrow!" His young, buxom, steatopygous wife is not only useful and beautiful, she has æsthetic value in his eyes. She is so artistic she appeals to him; she is one of the loveliest works of God.

Which is, of course, but another way of saying that the Primitive cannot afford to indulge his eye or ear at the expense of tangible, livable values; he does not go in for beauty contests; he goes in for beautiful wives. The *perfectly* beautiful wife is the one who satisfies all his senses. So, everywhere, we find styles or types of beauty, fixed forms, standards by which perfection is measured.

The foundations of æsthetic enjoyment, then, are to be sought not in books, but in our eyes, ears, nose, nerve-endings in skin, muscles, and tendons—in our sense organs; in stimuli which please. Art uses materials of the material world, but the drive in art comes from pleasure-giving stimuli. And there we see the reason for the distinction we make at times between art and æsthetics.

A lamb gambolling on the green may be good dramatics; it may be æsthetic; it is not art. What counts in the distinction is the actor— who is doing the gambolling? We do not speak of a lamb's dramatic antics as a production; but when Pavlova danced, we spoke of it as an æsthetic production or dramatic art. Likewise we speak of sculpture, music, painting, etc., as arts, as æsthetic productions.

We find artistic effects either in form alone or in ideas which we are wont to associate with form. Herein we have the reason for our failure to find Hindu sculpture artistic. We concede its marvellously perfect technique, but it is not easy for us to discover art in a six-armed god dancing in a circle of flame. We admit the supreme skill shown in producing that dancer; it is wonderful, and the flaming circle is most beautifully done. But a six-handed man! And what funny things he has in his hands! No art in that! But when we get far enough away from our conviction that no god should have more arms than we have, and allow Siva the Creator and Destroyer as many arms as we sometimes wish we had, and realize that those "funny" things are sacred symbols and no funnier than those we endow our Apostles with; when, in short, we can forget our *ideas* of a two-armed God in some well-known, conventionalized attitude, and look at that Siva as it is, we must admit that it is Art, and one of the most artistic creations in the world. Yet people go to Madras to see Annie Besant, and fail to see those dancing bronze Sivas!

Even the elephant-headed Ganesh seems not without artistic merit after one has been in India for a few months. Much "art" was called into being by purely emotional impulses and for religious purposes. We look upon certain religious paintings and sculptures through the smoked glasses of our infantile fears and awes. If we were to remind ourselves that these horrors are not designed to please, but to teach, we should stop calling them great art. Some of them are not art by any reasonable canon. They have no more and no less æsthetic value than the implements of torture of an Inquisition court. Looking upon tears and agony no more drives tears and pain away from human lives than looking at a bowl of soup satisfies hunger.

Why the craze for antiques? Vanity, the joy that comes from mere possession, for one thing. With a good set of antiques I am armed; I can hold my own among the antique-crazed crowd. And as that crowd has money, and as money has social value, I thereby become more valuable in my own eyes and am at least on a par with the crowd.

But let us look at some real antiques: a grandfather clock, a Haida masque, a Maori war club, a Pomo basket, a Hopi pot, a Papuan drum—at all the things one finds in a good ethnologic museum. What have they in common? Why house them at all? Because, whether or not they conform to our ideas of art, they so excel in sheer technical excellence that they compel our admiration.

When we recall that those stone axes, fish spears, tobacco pipes, food bowls, drums, canoes, masks, house-posts, and the thousand

and one other things, were practically all made with stone, shell, or bone tools—tools so primitive we could not catch a fish or fell a tree with them—our admiration mounts so high that we must concede them to be works of Art.

Robinson Crusoe without materials salvaged from his ship would have been a sorry mess indeed. But his man Friday could build a boat that would take him and his family round the world—and did. More than that, he decorated every inch of it above the water line. Marvellous carving—and with a stone ax! And by carving I mean *carving*. Cellini himself never did *finer* work with his sharp knives and engraving tools than thousands of Primitives have done with the rudest, simplest tools, and with no greater hope of reward than a smile of approval from their fellows.

Art is expression. The oldest artifact known is a chipped flint tool. In the chipping of flint early man found outlet for his deepest æsthetic joy. The tool meant a way, a means of life. He saw the tool as life-giving. To the making of the tool he gave the best he had. As the tool expressed something vital, he put vitality into it, expressed himself in it.

Where was the added stimulus to put his whole soul into canoe, food bowl, or house-post? *Skill*: no dumbbell, loafer, or lounge lizard could do that! He'd show them! Mere skill, technical skill, itself became stimulus for more skill. That is why the capitalist who has made a hundred million dollars breaks his neck to make another hundred million. The native puts skill into making a more beautiful canoe, the capitalist into making "another." One is Fine Art; the other is High Finance. One creates something; the other creates nothing. One is a manufacturer, makes his canoe with his hands; the other is a juggler.

These "antiques" are so well made they are artistic. How did they start? In play, manipulating materials at hand. We have got our feet so far from the earth that we have forgotten how to play or what play is. Nothing counts any more but the score. Our "play" costs, so Chase estimates, over twenty billion dollars a year—including, among other items, two billion dollars for candy, gum, and pop. Thirty million people "listening in" to sounds issuing from a small box; a million rural matrons listening in on the party line as their major indoor sport. Our second-hand play is so thin we have to salt it with bets. We gamble as a revolt against boredom.

In making a better canoe our Primitive finds expression for his varying emotions—none socially destructive—and for his thinking apparatus and manual skill. When he has put "all he has," as we say, of these three behaviour elements into his canoe, he has put *himself* into it. It satisfies; he has pleasure from its beautiful form, joy because his masterly technique has triumphed over technical difficulties. It is a work of art—a thing of beauty, a joy for ever. And after he has christened it with the well-tested rite of his fore-fathers—"I shall fly, I shall become like smoke, I shall become invincible, I shall become as a world eddy"—that canoe is a *speed* boat; and its maker knows why England calls her flagship the *Invincible*, and why Britannia rules the waves.

Before we abandon the canoe let us note two points bearing on art and life. A canoe is a tool—an easy way of walking on the water; it is also a surface. That surface easily becomes stimulus for other activities. We do not carve canoes, we paint them; nor do we decorate their prows with sea-shells or carved figures, or with anything at all. Native canoes are not everywhere decorated, of course. A dugout good enough to cross a creek may not be deemed good enough to cross a creek full of crocodiles; that makes it another kind of creek entirely. Better do something to propitiate the crocodiles. So they carved the prows in the form of crocodiles.

Here is the other point. I am, let us say, the maker of that canoe. My canoe is *me*, as are my house, my garden, my dances, my pleasures, my games, my manners, my customs, my religion, my philosophy; all belong to me and mine. We made them; they represent us. In making them we found our joy, through them we are rooted in the past, by means of them we live and have our being. Then you come along with your steel knives, calico dresses, motor-boats, tin pans, canned food and canned music, and say, "Don't do this," and, "You can't do that. If you do this I'll put you in jail; and you've got to pay your head tax or I'll make your son work it out on the government farm." Just what have you done? Cut all the joy of living out of my life, torn me loose from the soil. Yet we wonder why natives do not love missionaries, give up making beautiful things, and die from sheer ennui!

Beauty is as beauty does, and there is nothing beautiful in life without love, dignity, exultation, joy, health, virility.

The traditional ways of work and play hold these Primitives together as in a silken net. Cut that net and they fall apart, to become the loafers, dreamers, vagabonds, renegades, and prostitutes that hang around the fringe of the white settlements. Their life is finished; they have nothing more to do; they are waiting to die. Such social excrescences are no more *natural* to primitive society than they are to ours. Wherever found, there is a reason.

Our Primitive, in other words, does not work to earn a living; he lives to gratify his needs, satisfy his impulses, find expression for his fancies and his talent. When he met a tough knot he had time to tackle it; the tougher the knot, the more he felt impelled to master it. The time he spent in finding suitable, workable materials for his tools, utensils, weapons, etc., was possibly as great as the time he spent in getting results once he had selected his material. So, we should say, he often went too far; he put more time and zeal and patience into getting a good food bowl than the bowl was worth after it was finished. But that is not his way of looking at it. He did produce many economic monsters, but he did not so regard them; in his eyes they were his most valued worldly possessions. He rated values not in terms of rarity, but of perfect skill, fine material, and inexhaustible zeal and patience. Everything he used had meaning for him; it affected him emotionally. The more he had put himself into it, the more it meant to him.

"But he had no originality!" Well, if he did not, there is no such thing on earth in art or in anything called into being by man the creator. Go to a New Guinea village and collect a thousand gourds such as the native keeps his male organ in. Every gourd is decorated; no two are alike. Go to a Hopi village and collect a thousand earthenware bowls. Every bowl is decorated; no two are alike.

Tribal styles, regional styles, national styles, yes; and generally easily distinguishable. I do not believe you can bring me a decorated garment, an ornamented earthenware vessel, or a carved bowl, spoon, mask, or idol, from any region in the world, which I cannot assign to its proper place in a museum. Form alone is generally distinctive enough to settle its origin. Forms and decorations are standardized, but infinite variation is found within the limits of the standard.

How styles change, new standards replacing the old, is a psychological problem in itself and will be attended to in due time. But we may notice that great changes in Art may and do come about through changes which affect tribal or national outlook.

Thus, as Boas points out, Primitives feel the need of beautifying their lives more than we do. Our desire for beauty has been overlaid by a desire for comfort. Utility first—and if that will not sell, paint it another color, put it in a new frame, or give it a new name.

To our remote ancestors, the Beautiful was what was good; Goodness, what was beautiful. But within the horizon of their activities, their eye for æsthetic appreciation was at least as keen as ours. As our horizon is wider, our society more complex, our interests more varied, we can see beauties as yet undisclosed to their senses. Not that we put more meaning into life, but that life demands more from us; we are subject to a wider range of stimuli, from which we must choose those which mean most and those which mean least in our lives. Their lives were probably lived on a more exalted plane than ours; we are more restrained by convention. What we call "abandon" among Primitives is merely a form of exaltation which, formalized, finds expression in song, dance, ceremony—art in all its forms. Our art differs from theirs primarily because our experiences are not theirs—and so our appreciation, tastes, are different.

### III

If our snap judgment says, "Manners, none," what should we say of the morals of a country where high-born ladies went about naked? Pepys testifies that this was not unknown on the streets of London; it was the custom in parts of Ireland in the seventeenth century. Eccentricity? Shocking? Immoral? Why, they weren't even tattooed!

Some years ago I was set down on a beach in Bougainville, the largest and then unexplored Solomon Island. I encountered some hundreds of stark-naked natives at work and at play, moving in and out of their huts; all ages and sizes and both sexes. Was I shocked? For a fleeting moment only. Going from India to Java, past New Guinea, and so finally to the Solomons, one passes gradually from clothed to naked people: scantier and scantier, fewer and fewer garments, and finally complete and perfect nudity. It is the sudden, the unexpected, that shocks.

No clothes at all, not enough to wad a gun, as we used to say. Young and old, both sexes. "Indecent, immodest! Have they no sense of shame at all?" you say. And quite properly. We learned to *wear* clothes, our naked body learned the *feel* of clothes, and our larynx learned what to say when shocked—as, for example, by a naked body. But *you* do not see these Islanders, you simply read about them. Shocked, just the same. It *is* shocking, and they must be shameless, indecent people! So they must—to comply with our verbal reaction to verbally undressed savages. But if I add that that was twenty years ago and their immodesty is now decently clothed in our cast-off garments carried down there by the missionaries, you would probably feel that this world *is* more decent than it used to be and that there is still hope of civilizing the shameless savage.

"Manners" are but ways of getting along socially, routine ways if they are conventionalized and we have learned to respect the conventions—that is, to be nice, refined, ladylike, modest, loyal, respectful. Then, too, they serve as time-savers, conveniences in understanding one another, ways of showing our hand to strangers. I go to Africa and a man spits toward me. Is he insulting me or welcoming me to his city—sending part of himself out to meet me, as it were? I give a dinner to an Afghan chief and he ends the meal with a resounding belch: is he unspeakably rude or merely expressing his enormous pleasure at my hospitality? Two men call on me at my home; one removes his hat, the other his shoes. Which one thereby "dishonours" me?

We find Parisian open-faced public conveniences "shockingly" disgraceful. A South Sicilian town, such as Vittoria or Sciacca, is "unspeakably" filthy. Perhaps that is why we always speak of it. Our manners vary individually because we acquire them early and as individuals, not as a class or in a Sunday school. There are, of course, big differences in the run of manners between Flatbush and Hell's Kitchen; between upper and lower Fifth Avenue; between U. S. A. and U. S. S. R.; between England and Peru. The manners we like best and approve of most are our own. And that is natural, too, for they are acquired psychologically and are generally socially useful—though they may be, and often are, socially absurd, economically monstrous, and biologically destructive.

But, you say, Here is modesty: see how coy she is. Here is chastity: pure as the driven snow. Here is elegance: look at those jewels. Here is decency: bustles, corsets, hoop skirts. Here is breeding: what a perfect gentleman, and such refinement! Here are Master Minds: look at their masters. Here is . . . Rubbish? No, not rubbish; samples of manners, with most of which we are all, no doubt, on speaking terms.

Samples. Note, please, that my manners may be bad, but they are mine, come by honestly and as we come by anything—I learned them. I reveal them in dozens of ways—in personal habits, in verbal habits. My manners may be sufficiently like yours to be merely criticized as "mannerisms." The manners that offend us most are generally those which are most different from our own accustomed and habitual ways of satisfying our primary wants and needs.

Let us return to the Solomons for further light. After a few minutes' brisk trading with the natives, a girl of about fourteen came out of a hut and at once caught my eye; she alone of the crowd was not naked. Around her waist was a tiny cord, from which hung a big red leaf.

That leaf was an ethnological specimen and I wanted it. I went through the motions of offering her a stick of "trade" tobacco for it. She hung back "coyly" and was promptly reproved by the old women; a stick of tobacco was a worth-while article! I offered two sticks. She came up, removed the leaf, and the trade was made. She then walked over to a tree of the *ficus* genus, plucked another red leaf, and tied it to her waist string.

That coyness was a feminine trait; its exhibition had nothing to do with modesty or immodesty, or with leaf or nudity. She hung back and made a coy gesture because she had been spoken to by a strange male. It was a natural gesture, a feminine gesture—as though to say, "Come and catch me."

Those Islanders were then cannibals and fairly untouched by white influence. The leaf was obviously an ornament—decoration, perhaps it should be called. It certainly was not a dress, nor even a garment. Presumably it was a "custom," signalizing the onset of adolescence. There may have been nothing more behind it than the natural impulse which led our black boys, when ashore, to crown themselves with a wreath of scarlet hibiscus.

Girl's leaf and boy's crown were ornamental, decorative. They added a distinctive feature to a body otherwise undistinguished except for the usual tribal tattoo marks.

Tie a cord around a young ape's waist and hand it a bright red leaf: it is not inconceivable that it would try to attach the leaf to the cord. Why to the cord? Because it has nothing else to attach the leaf to. The big red leaf will stimulate the ape to some kind of action. The fondness of apes for placing ribbons or garlands around their necks or over their shoulders has been noted repeatedly; they have also been observed to smear their faces and bodies with powdered paint. Those apish performances were accompanied by signs of pleasure. Infrahuman Primates habitually clothed manifest what we might call a preference for being clothed. The satisfaction they get from ornamenting or decorating themselves is obvious and beyond question. Having learned to wear clothes, they feel "natural" when clothed; without, unnatural.

Were I to return to Bougainville today, I suppose I should find that the natives had been taught "modesty" by the missionaries and are now as fully clothed as the natives of the other Solomons. The women probably wear Mother Hubbards; the men, short calico skirts. And probably no amount of tobacco would induce man or woman to trade skirt or Mother Hubbard—if they had to undress in public. Pruriency is founded, not on the naked body, but on the unclothing of the body.

Barton in his *The Half-Way Sun* says that when the headhunting Filipino lads were rounded up for educational purposes and forced into shirt and trousers, they insisted on retaining their tiny loin-cloth. Trousers are trousers; but, to their way of thinking, a loin-cloth, even though only a half-inch wide, is the only "natural and proper" garment for certain parts of the human body. With trousers they are covered, but without the g-string they feel "exposed"—immodest and indecent. Up to the beginning of this century it was not only indecent but almost a crime to name any part of the human body within a radius of twenty inches from its centre.

Before we clothe the body—with modesty or ornament or comfort—let us remind ourselves again that we are all born naked and unashamed, without customs, manners, or morals; that by the time we are six we are clothed in breeches or panties and are shocked at nakedness; and that by the time we are ready to leave the home nest we have been painted, tattooed, scarified, or circumcised; had our ear, nose, or lip bored; had one or more teeth filed to a point or knocked out; and our head so permanently waved that forever after it will bear only a general resemblance to a normal head and will have more museum value than an ordinary skull.

Some of these mutilations must hurt, but the physical pain is soon over; without them, the social pain would endure for life. We cry "Ouch!" when a pin pricks us: suppose every inch of our body were pin-pricked? Or suppose, instead of having our ear lobe pierced, we had the rim of our ear pierced in a dozen places, or the lobe so distended that we could use it as a bracelet; or our upper lip pierced and then stretched so far that we could put our foot through it. We have all enjoyed the dentist's drill and take pride in our front teeth. How would we like to have all our front teeth filed to a point with a sandstone file, or have them knocked out?

Scarifications (slits in the skin, and earth and ashes rubbed in to delay healing, thereby raising great welts); tattooings; hole-plugged ears, nose, and lips; heads deformed by steady pressure while the bones are soft and modifiable; ribs bent out of shape by corsets; muscles of calves and arms atrophied from being wrapped in copper wire during childhood; feet deformed out of all semblance of and value as a human foot; external genitals slit wide open and looking like nothing human: just what are these man-made mutilations?

Style or fashion; customs or manners? All, and more. These terms really lead us nowhere. What is fashionable is style; what is customary is manners. What a diamond dog-collar does for a Manhattan dame, a Haida hag achieves with a big ivory lip-plug. The frat pin which marks the freshman's initiation into he-manhood is for the Australian lad a penis slit wide open.

Tribal customs. In most tribes the sexes are differently branded; in some, only one sex is branded. Except in the case of foot or skull deformation, which must be begun in infancy, and lip, ear, or nose piercing, which begins early and the holes gradually extended, mutilations or branding usually form part of more or less elaborate initiation ceremonies which signify love's coming of age. They are puberty ceremonies, marking the turning of a crisis in sexual life.

Roughly speaking, these mutilations are clothes that will not come off. They have nothing to do with modesty as we use the term; they have much to do with custom. They are tribal customs. They brand the tribe, as it were, with a brand that will not wear off. A much-travelled Uganda Negro could, I suppose, distinguish twenty or thirty strangers, not by their physiognomy, but by their tribal scarifications.

Tattooing and scarifications are always in patterns, often elaborate and even beautiful patterns. No particular part of the body seems to have been favored over any other part, though the face has certainly not been neglected. No stocking ever worn by man or woman comes within miles of being so elaborate or decorative as the stocking the Caroline Islanders tattoo on their legs. It is like beautiful lace. An incised and tattooed Maori chief's face is one of the wonders of the world. His entire body is also tattooed, from eyelids to genitalia. He is less a walking picture-gallery than a sailor, but more a work of art.

Why not? Man likes pretty things; he has a talent for decorating, a sense of the æsthetic. His body is a surface: decorate it. He does—or rather he did, and in countless ways. Paints and pigments which easily wash off were generally reserved for special occasions—initiation rites, magical practices, ceremonial performances. Thus, one wears "the paint of the god," thereby becoming endowed with his magic power, or proof against evil power, etc.

The first fig-leaf garment was probably more ornamental than useful. In fact, the idea of ornament is probably older than the idea of clothing. Aurignacian caves furnish evidence that both the dead and the living were painted. Necklaces and waistbands of perforated shells and teeth have been found, chiefly on the skeletons of males. That was forty thousand years ago. Within twenty thousand years shells and teeth were imitated in ivory.

But long before Magdalenian man made imitation teeth and shell girdles and necklaces, he had taken to clothes—possibly even to fitted or made-to-order clothes. At any rate, with Solutrean times, some twenty-five thousand years ago, bone needles begin to be found in the cave refuse. Man had already learned to make and use bone awls, but *needles*, as Kroeber says, imply thread and sewing.

What earliest man wore we of course do not know. Probably dressed skins; skin scrapers of worked flint probably go back a hundred thousand years. But why did man wear skins at all, what was the matter with his own skin? It is thick and tough, and can resist great cold when habituated to cold.

A white trapper in our far north, shivering though heavily clad, petulantly remarked to his practically naked Indian guide that he didn't know why he didn't freeze to death. "No freeze!" said the Indian, pointing to the white man's face. "No; my face is used to it." "Indian all face," was the Indian's come-back. And it was a good reply.

That Indian and his tribe are exceptions—at least in the northern hemisphere. Eskimos and northern Asiatics are carefully protected against cold, in snugly fitting fur garments. The Tierra del Fuegians were notoriously scantily clad.

Our original fur coat was hair. Just when did we lose it, and why? Many theories have been proposed, but no one theory is generally accepted. If the sun played lady's maid to help undress man, why not the other Primates also? Monkeys and apes retain their hairy coats, and where food is to be found the year around can withstand great cold.

Man can feel a gentle breeze on the hairs of his head, but hair itself is not sensitive; he "feels" it only as the motion is transmitted to skin nerve-endings at the base of the hair. To say that shedding our hairy coat made us more sensitive is, to my way of thinking, to say nothing that gets us into a fur coat. What we can say to the point is that at the seventh month of our prenatal life we have a coat of down, *lanugo*, which is absorbed before birth and replaced by the kind of hair we wear during life.

The hairy coat we are born with varies enormously among groups of men, and among individuals. A really hairy man is, I believe, never found among heavily pigmented or dark-skinned peoples. Very hairy individuals are often found in light-skinned peoples. The light-skinned aborigines of northern Japan are the hairiest people on earth, and are often spoken of as the Hairy Ainu.

We cannot prove anything from these Hairy Ainu; they too are all dressed up. But here is a curious thing. All those beautifully dressed Hyperboreans are keen on ornament. They *decorate* their clothes. Did they invent clothes for æsthetic rather than for calorific purposes? It seems certain that they did not invent clothes to "cover their nakedness." The first thing an Eskimo does when he enters his snow house is to strip. He is then ready for work, play, or company.

Wearing-apparel may be roughly divided into two great categories: the tailored, the draped. The Near East went in for draped garments; the Far East, for tailored. The Peruvians used both, of both cotton and wool, and as Montell says in his *Dress and Ornaments in Ancient Peru*, their draped garments especially, in fineness and variety of weave, in artistic and technical skill, and in marvellously beautiful colours, have never been surpassed and approximated only in southern India. They were also masters of the technique of cloth-printing and of tie- and other forms of resistance-dyeing, including batik. In fact, it is possible that the batik process is older in Peru than in the Gobi Desert, its oldest known home in the Old World.

Some day we shall realize the greatness of the indigenous civilizations of the two Americas, which have been swept out as ruthlessly as a housewife sweeps out dust—to make room, in the field of textiles, as Crawford says, for bad colours and insipid or bizarre patterns, "fabrics without interest or charm."

IV

Grant, as we well may, that clothing was biologically useful in man's evolution in lands with severely cold winters, we must infer that personal adornment, body decoration in general, had social value, charming power. The psychology of clothing and body decoration is plain and simple; man just naturally likes distinction. A red fig-leaf, a garland of scarlet hibiscus, is an easy and cheap decoration. Everywhere, and for at least a hundred thousand years, man has been pinning decorations on himself.

Failure to win a medal or to be decorated caused more grief in the World War than failure to win a battle. Military officers especially, accustomed as they are to gold lace and other distinguishing devices, often develop a mania for decorations, and whenever occasion offers strut around in them, proud as peacocks—and refer to their wives as the Vain Sex.

Innate desire to be conspicuous, to look well in the eyes of society, is reinforced by the attention one gets when conspicuous; one not only looks well but feels well. At this point another element comes in. You and I grow up together, and I think I am as good as you; but in some contest—over a maid, let us say—you wear some gewgaw on your arm—and win. But I am as good a man as you are. Why did I lose? It must have been the gewgaw. Possibly maids like gewgaws; I will try one. If you wore a dog's tooth on your arm, I will try a shark's tooth; and if I win with my shark's tooth, I have started something. Or, if I cannot be an Eagle, I will be an Elk.

Some particular gewgaw wins; and possibly for thousands of years thereafter is *the* "medicine" for a certain kind of contest. It becomes the emblem, badge, banner, of a warrior society, an age society, a dynasty, a religion. When Constantine in 312 fought Maxentius just outside Rome, his banner bore the words *Hoc signo vinces,* instead of *Sol invictis,* emblem of Mithra, his previous and favorite religion. He won. As he had witnessed the atmospheric phenomenon of a solar cross some time before the battle, he interpreted the cross as the sign of victory: it was an *omen.* A Cross was better war-medicine than Sol. He thereafter "permitted," and a dozen years later "embraced," Christianity.

By such hairs hang heavy destinies. A Christian sees "destiny" in Constantine's victory; Constantine saw destiny in the cross. Science sees destiny as "x"—an unknown, something to be investigated. History and psychology help to solve such problems.

Human nature demands distinction, but the form the distinction takes is a cultural trait. The traits are not to be thought of as psychological exhibits, but as historically derived products, human creations, superorganic. They are, therefore, variables. Man *must* satisfy his innate hungers, and as his innate equipment did not suffice, he discovered cultural ways. One thing leads to another; culture piles up, becomes specialized, complex. But culture is always historic, not biologic or psychologic.

Man is a domesticated animal, but his behaviour is always conditioned by historic, cultural, factors. These factors make him what he is. Taboos, restraints and sanctions become specific—for time and place, age, sex, class, rank, etc. Every problem, then, of human personality or tribal culture, is primarily a historic problem, and every specific cultural trait has its history. That history may be ten thousand years old; it may be but a day.

On the banner carried into Mexico by the mounted soldiers of Cortez was a double-headed eagle. The Indians liked its decorative character and adopted it as a symbol in their textiles and embroideries. That double-headed eagle is older than Emperor Charles V of Spain and Austria; its history goes back to ancient Egypt, to the great god Sun, which furnished the central disc, and to the divine hawk and vulture, which supplied the two outstretched wings. That common Egyptian device was carried to the Assyrians about 4,000 years ago. They, or the Hittites, for symmetry's sake added a second head, and carved it on monuments on a cliff, where it was seen and so admired by a Turkish prince in 1300 that he used it as a symbol on his coins. Crusaders carried that coin to Europe, where, Kroeber says, it proved a welcome addition to the lions and unicorns. Austria-Hungary and Russia adopted it as their national emblem. The Russians probably thought it ancient Russian; the Huichols of Mexico thought it ancient Indian.

Why should the lion and the unicorn fight for the crown, and why should the lion beat the unicorn all round the town? Or, more specifically, does that jingle refer to the heraldic supporters of the royal shield of Great Britain? Possibly; but the fact is, as pointed out by Cyril Bunt, that mediæval Europe used the unicorn (gazelle) as a symbol of Christ and as an emblem of purity. It is also a fact that one of the squares of a gaming-board—possibly chess—of prehistoric Ur, figures a lion and unicorn in shell inlaid with lapis-lazuli.

Why lion and unicorn? Because when that chessboard was made the solstitial signs were not Cancer and Capricorn as in classical times, but Leo and Aquarius. And when the summer solstice was in Leo (the lion) the spring equinox was in Taurus (the bull—or unicorn). Summer conquers spring; the lion beats the unicorn. The cross beat the sun. We put the eagle on one side of our coins and trust in God on the other. But 5,000 years before America,

Russia, Austria, and Prussia had put their trust in eagles, the city state of Lagash had used as its coat of arms a lion-headed eagle clutching the backs of two lions. Man could not have found so many symbols had he not found so many pictures in the sky and read so much fate in the stars. Decorations are good; charms are better.

For any one of a dozen possible psychological reasons, some form of body mutilation, body adornment, or body covering, or banner, emblem, symbol, or motto, becomes the custom: the habit for a tribe, for a class, for a sex, for an age, for an event, for a special purpose. It becomes established, and thereafter functions automatically. With us, deviation from the expected, the habitual, makes one merely ridiculous or objectionable; in societies more bound by tradition, it may entail serious consequences.

Thus, without a ten-inch skewer through my nose I may not be a he-man; without my teeth filed I may not be anything the tribe recognizes. A visitor from Mars, unacquainted with our brand of civilization, might infer that we dress our corpses for burial so that they may be easily recognized in the hereafter.

In a thousand ways and in as many respects, man has insured his bet on himself by looking for, and finding, magic power ("virtue") in plants and animals, and then adding that power to his own. With but few exceptions, all "medicines" in the world are magic, based on man's inability to distinguish likeness from sameness. *Similia similibus curantur.* And so, to his honest desire to *look* well he adds an attempt to look better than nature allows him: he "dresses up."

Necklaces, armbands, aprons of sharks' teeth, dogs' teeth, boars' tusks, eagles' talons, bears' claws; lions', tigers', leopards' skins; tigers' and leopards' bristles; birds' feathers; coral, crystal, agate, moonstone: nothing has been overlooked, no stone left unturned in the endless search for things which will adorn, fortify, add virtue. The *perfect* charm is the one which both catches the eye and "knocks it out," be it eye of friend or foe.

Possibly the psychology behind the "evil eye" idea is responsible for the almost universal prevalence of some form of covering for the genitalia of both sexes: the power of the human eye to look "daggers," to give "withering" glances, to cast "spells." The eye is a powerful weapon, and wins many battles in love and war. The prevalence of genitalia coverings in peoples otherwise practically nude has been attributed to the alleged fact that "what the eye does not see the heart does not covet." That explanation seems too simple.

In fact, man is so complex that most simple explanations are too simple. Man has two hands; their business is to handle anything which attracts his eye. The natural, the usual, the habitual, ceases to charm. Probably the least sexually stimulating sight is the unarmed, unaffected, unclothed body. The completely or partially clothed body whets the imagination, artificially stimulates the appetite. Briffault says that Flaubert nearly fainted the first time he saw a woman's breasts uncovered. The sex taboo itself provokes lubricity.

Look at the eye again, its potency to kill or cure. The man or woman who has not been stared out of countenance is a man or woman who has not yet met his or her match as a starer. Many a time when among primitive people I have observed some child shielded from my admiring eyes by brother, sister, or parent. They did not know my eyes were admiring—they might have been evil!

Remember, too, that the primitive man's world is thickly populated with spirits, ghosts, disembodied souls—though never quite so crowded with evil spirits as was our Christian world a few centuries ago. Evil spirits are worse than evil eyes, for they can enter holes no eye can see into. And they are always up to some mischief, seeking a place to enter.

Protection against their entrance must be added to the reasons for covering so much of our nakedness as seems particularly liable to be injured by magic. Between the Moslem woman, so completely protected that not a hair of head or eyebrow is visible, and the woman of some Brazilian tribes who "protects" her vulva by an inch-wide ribbon and is otherwise quite nude, there is every gradation—from the hoop skirts of our grandmothers to the one-piece bathing-suits of our granddaughters.

Taking the primitive world as a whole, the male seems to think he requires more "protection" than his better half. And the vanity he puts into decorating his protection is only exceeded by his ingenuity in devising bizarre protectors. Throughout India one sees swarms of little tots quite naked but for their little silver sex amulets. These amulets, generally shaped like a fig leaf, are in no sense of the word coverings; they are charms pure and simple, and to be without one would be "extremely unlucky." In South Europe mothers usually hurry to cover their breasts while nursing their children if they are looked at—not from modesty, but from a possible evil eye.

Modesty, then, began as habituation to ornament, which passed into protection from magic—an evil eye, a dirty look, an evil spirit. The form the protection takes becomes the custom, the right thing, good manners, "becoming modesty." It was because the external genitalia were susceptible to magic and were themselves a source of magic, that they received so much attention. Otherwise there is no more logic in covering them than in covering the ears or the feet. In fact, the supreme height of immodesty in a Chinese woman is to undress her feet; and in a test recently made in a Chinese boys' school, the foot rated first as a secondary sexual stimulus. The Chinese woman of "perfect" form has a perfectly straight front and monstrously small feet. A common prayer with Central African maids is that their breasts may fly away.

The sentiment of modesty, then, primarily refers to the sexual organs; with us it generally relates to sex morality. Neither is anywhere conceived in reason nor founded in sound biology. Clothing began as adornment, soon became magic, and has been crazy as a loon ever since.

Immodest ideas are not, strictly speaking, confined to public behaviour. It is not modest to eat with one's wife in Brazil, or with one's inamorata in New Guinea. And in South Africa it is most immodest to bow to a chief; one bows from a chief. Privacy is not necessary for modest sexual intercourse in Australia and in some parts of Africa; nor is the open-air defloration of maidens demanded by tribal custom deemed immodest in several parts of the world. Why deflower the girls, and in public? Why do we baptize girls, and in public? Same reason: it makes them pure and everyone should know it. Yet we speak of privacy!

The perfectly virtuous person is the one with the perfect charm. Or, *Honi soit qui mal y pense!*

## V

Ethics is the art of living like a scholar and a gentleman. Our scholars and gentlemen are assumed to be Christians. It is also assumed that they derive their ethics from their religion. Hence, it is inferred, ethics is Christianity, and without Christianity there can be no ethical life.

It may be asserted here and now that no ethical principle can be found in the Old or New Testament which cannot be matched by one just as sane and sound from Egypt or Assyria, Greece or Rome, India or China—or from a Red Indian. "We dry him if he is wet," said an Onondago chief to Morgan; "we warm him if he is cold, and give him meat and drink that he may allay his hunger and thirst, and we spread soft furs for him to rest and sleep on. We demand nothing in return. But if I go into a white man's house . . . 'Where is your money? . . . Get out, you Indian dog!' "

Primitive man lived ethically—because he had to or go down; but with the new physical environment which agriculture brought into certain regions, the old decalogues of ethical living became mottoes for business purposes only. From that time on, civilization was a dog-fight; ethics, a dream to come true in heaven.

The big winner in the dog-fight was the male. Henceforth, with but few exceptions, woman was the under dog and could choose only between becoming cow or courtesan. In Athens, the courtesan played the higher and more profitable rôle.

"Where thou art the bull, I am the cow" (*"Ubi tu gaius ego gaia"*) was the old Roman formula spoken by the bride at her marriage ceremony. Gaia was the earth goddess, symbolized as the cow—to be fertilized by the heavenly male power. But that ceremony was not a sacrament; it simply signalized a civil contract—as did marriage ceremonies in the early Christian days. Not till 1735, with the Hardwick Act, did marriages in England have to be legalized by a religious ceremony.

We have made some advance toward freeing human relationships from the clutches of religion, but we are still dominated by the absurd mediæval idea that "purity" is sexual morality, and that it is the woman who must be pure. In other words, she was damned if she did and damned if she didn't. We have been reaping the harvest. The idea came late in our civilization, but it dug in deeply. The reign of the double standard is dying, but it dies hard, for it has much "spiritual" life in it yet.

By "double standard" I mean, of course, the popular notion that the bride must be a virgin; as to the groom's purity, *caveat emptor*; it is nobody's business but his own. That idea is not new in civilization, nor uniquely Christian. It is held by certain tribes of East and West Africa and of northern Asia. Those tribes buy their wives as they do their cattle. They demand purity, and chastity in unmarried girls is safeguarded.

A chaste or virgin bride, on the contrary, is widely looked upon as an unknown quantity. To contract marriage with such a girl is like buying a pig in a poke. She may be sterile! Sterility, almost universally, is ground for divorce; if gifts have been made they are returned, or another woman is supplied by the bride's parents. In one Central African tribe, pregnancy makes a spouse valuable, and she is paid for accordingly. A virgin is worth a goat in Nigeria; the mother of a child, a horse. The disparity in value between virginity and proved fertility in Congoland is much greater. Similar ideas are found in some of our Indian tribes and in northeastern Asia. According to Marco Polo, the Tibetan girl who carried the most lovers' tokens around her neck got married soonest and had the most virtue in the eyes of her husband.

Even more significant is the very widespread idea of the necessity for prenuptial intercourse. Many reasons for this are found. Most of them spring from false inferences about fertility—in nature in general, in game and domestic animals, in fields, etc. We find ritual defloration by prince or priest, hierodulic, mechanical; presumably every conceivable idea, some time, some place, has been utilized to prevent the possibility of a virgin bride. The most widespread of these ideas was based on the belief that up until actual marriage sexual relations were and should be free, restricted only by specific incest taboos. That idea prevailed till recently among the peasantry of most of Europe, especially in Holland, Norway, Bavaria, Austria, Hungary, and Switzerland. There was little, if any, retrospective jealousy.

Among peoples where prenuptial chastity was demanded, defloration was the ruling practice. "Holy" matrimony with the deity's representative secured the fertility of woman, crops, and cattle, and protected the husband from the perils of defloration.

This "medicine" operation to remove the magic power or "take the curse off" the woman was early and thoroughly performed in India, China, and the Far East generally—by nurses in China, by mothers elsewhere; with shark's tooth, flint knife, stone phallus, razor. It was a regular practice in Egypt and among the Arabs, and was performed by Hagar on Sarah.

China, by most accounts, ranks highest in her standard of female virtue. The early Jesuit missionaries thought Chinese modesty unparalleled in all the world. Hundreds of girls cast themselves into a well in Hangchow rather than fall into the hands of the Taiping rebels. Hundreds of memorial arches in China commemorate such acts of virtue.

The practice of infant betrothals, accompanied by religious rites and exchange of gifts, presumably started the idea of value in virginity. In high society of mediæval Europe this became a common practice and "proofs" of virginity were demanded—and looked for by the mothers, who examined the nuptial couch. Thus, the assembled grandees solemnly inspected the "proofs" of Braganza Isabel's virginity on her marriage to Emperor Charles V.

What we call virtue and purity had no merit in Greek eyes. Plato and the Cynics preached what the Spartans and Epicureans practised—sex communism; they saw no merit in chastity. Roman opinion put sex virtue on the plane of civic secular duty—an ideal for both sexes. But neither in the Greek nor Roman world, nor in savagery, do we find the concepts of sin and impurity; or sex, the mystical and paramount factor in morality.

It was the Church which made that synthesis. Our concepts of morality as pertaining to the realm of sex alone, of sex activity as inherently "beastly," of continence having magic power, of the virtue of chastity as ritual purity, are hangovers from those dark days when St. Gall found a deacon bathing, shaving, cutting his hair, etc., quite the reverse of ritual purity. Purity to Eastern ascetics meant magical purity for magical purposes. Incontinence among Jewish priests made them so impure they dared not handle the pure ritual vessels. The "cleanliness" that was next to Godliness had nothing to do with taking a bath or washing the hands: it meant scrupulous respect for the taboos—the *don'ts*! Some people still think a dirty pew sprinkled with holy water cleaner than one washed with soap and water; to *wash* is to be unclean, to play into Satan's hands.

That life has become a business instead of a pleasure is possibly because love has been taken from human arms and turned over to Morality—in the name of the Law or the Church. Morality never cured cholera or tuberculosis; it cannot cure venereal disease or any of the ailments which bedevil Venus. For thousands of years man has maintained that woman was easily corrupted; what he refused to see was that it was he who had corrupted her. His ethics was *his* ethics.

VI

Art was born of magic, it has been said; it would be equally to the point to say that magic was born of art; even more to the point to say that art and magic were born of man—and at times behaved like naughty children and cost him more than he could afford. But in impoverishing himself to gratify them, he probably said to himself: "It's all right; I prefer the Higher Life."

Art, in other words, ran a course somewhat comparable to speech. Just as certain words, formulas, and rites came to have emotional value because they were the sounds or spoken representatives of certain symbols, so certain forms—in graphic, plastic, art of any kind—just because they are stereotyped or standardized, become effective emotional stimuli. The *forms* (in dance, decoration, music, literature, carving, painting, etc.) mean something; they stand for or are symbols of an idea complex.

Hence my reference to art and magic as naughty children. Having created them, man is not allowed to neglect them. They become embedded in his ways of living. They move him; he moves through them, and gets results. Man, ancient or modern, easily becomes a confirmed pragmatist: hence the amazing amount of superstition among athletes, prize-fighters, gamblers, and farmers. Their charms work because they have worked, because they have always worked. And if they don't? Well, it was not the charm's fault. "Lady Luck wasn't good to me *today*." We can hardly expect Cave-man to be a harder-boiled reasoner than a 'varsity quarterback.

The Eskimos are very clever artists and artisans, especially in carving stone and ivory. Boas gave one pencil and paper and asked him to draw a walrus hunt. He tried, and tried again; and finally gave up and *carved* the scene on a piece of ivory! A capital illustration of man's inability to move out of his art forms into a new field.

Art presupposes surplus energy, leisure, and opportunity. Not much art can be expected of a people who have to spend all their time hunting food and water. With no more worldly belongings than would fill a flapper's vanity case, the Bushman of the Kalahari Desert had to limit his artistic yearnings and output. But when he found a cave and had plenty of game, he could and did become wonderfully clever at drawing pictures on the walls. He was a first-class graphic artist. Some of his paintings are worth going halfway round the world to see. They are Old Masters, indeed!

Here is a curious thing: In European caves, especially those on both sides of the Pyrenees, wall paintings very like those of North, Central, and South Africa have been found; also figurines of humans not unlike the Bushman. More: skulls of a Negroid type have been found in some of these caves. From which inferences have been drawn. In fact, L'Abbé Breuil only recently bade us "be prepared to admit a real relationship between the paintings of eastern Spain and those of South Africa."

Some of those ancient French and Spanish masters are only twenty thousand years old; some over fifty thousand years. What did those artists paint? Scenery, still life, portraits of leading citizens or famous women, allegories—Fall of Man, Temptation, Flood, Hell Fire? Why should they? Such ideas roused no creative spark in them. They painted *food*, food on the hoof; especially the animals that tasted best, could be got most easily, and were most needed to replenish their larder.

Our Cave-man ancestors of fifty millenniums ago went in for good red horse meat and red deer. Did they paint them because they were fond of them? They did. They were fonder of horse and deer meat than of lion and hyena, so fond that they seemed to have an idea that by painting them on the walls of their caves they could prevent them from becoming extinct. And they painted more females than males. Their knowledge of procreation may have been two miles below the Trobriander level, but they could see that for breeding purposes one stag was as good as a dozen, but one hind was worth only one hind.

The picture of a hind was the symbol of fecundity. And what is that picture—magic, superstition, religion, art? It is man trying, through such materials as he knows, to force nature to feed him. That picture is a prayer for more deer.

"Cushy," or white-collar, jobs require little food; hunting wild horses afoot, dodging wild beasts, and keeping warm at the foot of a glacier require great amounts of food. And what meat-eaters they were, especially horse meat. Apparently horse meat is the oldest dish in France—and just as good as cow if one thinks so.

Our Cave-man ancestors painted big-game animals primarily; they were big-game hunters. As MacCurdy says, the number of animals represented by bones in refuse heaps, and by paintings on cave walls, is directly proportionate. On the Spanish side of the mountains they preferred red deer meat; hence more red deer than horse bones and pictures.

Other animals depicted were bison, wild goat, cattle, reindeer, deer, mammoth, wild ass, chamois, elk, wolf, lion, fox, hare, hyena, musk ox, otter, rhinoceros, antelope, seal, wild sheep, cave bear. Not all these necessarily represent food or "game" animals; many were enemies pure and simple. Birds and fish were rarely painted or sculptured—though fish vertebræ were used for necklaces. The invertebrate kingdom did not appeal to man in those days—no need to express himself by depicting bugs; only five in all have been found, one, a ladybug, carved in ivory.

Human are much rarer than animal forms in earliest known art creations. Female forms predominate, especially of the Bushman physical type—pendent breasts, hypertrophied buttocks.

The famous "Venus of Willendorf" may be an object of the cult of fertility, as has been urged, but I agree with Luquet that such obese figures sprang from pure joyous art—the "wish-fulfilment dream" of a voluptuous artist who resented skinny women.

Human forms, as a rule, were more summarily treated than animal: small and sketchy, generally of the entire figure. Small sculptured figures, or painted arms, legs, and emblems of both male and female sexual organs, have been found; but they are rare as compared with the number of times the human hand appears, and always represented in a technique of its own.

One way was to place the hand, with outstretched fingers, flat on the cave wall and make a "negative" of it by sprinkling dry powdered paint around it; or the hand, covered with paint, was applied to the wall, leaving a "positive" imprint. A negative hand imprint in a French cave near Gargas, MacCurdy thinks is the oldest example of mural art in the world. Possibly the hands depicted, showing the loss of one or more joints from one or more fingers, record man's earliest human sacrifice.

What an emblem of our becoming civilized that ancient, painted, mutilated red hand is! A blood-red hand: art, religion; the handiwork of man!

Make no mistake, those Pyrenean and Bushman mural paintings or petroglyphs are art, and most realistic art; and those artists show an astonishing sense of perspective in both rest and motion. Note, also, that even then there were styles: the paintings in Altamira Cave represent one school; those in Gourdan, another. But behind both, and behind all those early French and Spanish schools and the Bushman of Rhodesia, is a Hunter of Big Game.

Many of the game are depicted wounded and bleeding from arrows; some of the animals sculptured in high relief on the floors of caves are literally riddled with punctures, as if from arrows. To these add Frobenius' account of the doings of a Central African Pygmy who had just killed an antelope with his arrow. He drew a picture of the antelope on the ground; then shot his arrow into the neck of his image; took blood and hair from the dead antelope; pulled out the arrow, and into the hole poured the blood and stopped it up with the hair.

And what are those extraordinary sand paintings or dry mosaics of our Hopi and Navaho of Arizona and the wild tribes of Australia? Dozens of volumes have been written describing the ceremonies based upon and surrounding those very artistic productions. Even I have tried my hand at it. What are they? We call them this and we call them that, but is it not becoming plain that separately and collectively they are nothing more than 'man trying to get such control over the general situation that he would be at peace with himself and his fellow-men?

Nothing less than peace satisfies human nature—food, mate, children, shelter, hearth, friends. For a hundred thousand years man has been fighting to make the world safe—for Democracy? For himself and his loved ones. "Women and children first" were the first words man spoke when he faced his first panic.

Women and children are biologically more important than men. Man's first prayer was for peace. That mutilated human hand is the emblem of that prayer. It is not art, it is not prayer, it is not religion: it is man ready to give his right hand for his loved ones. It is human nature at its highest. It can never get higher, but it can and will improve the tools it must work with to fulfil its potential destiny.

Possibly we are as close to that fulfilment as we shall ever be; possibly the whole human family has become so enamoured of its artificial props and has leaned so long on them that reason and common sense have become permanently out of the question. And possibly man can never face the fact that he does not know why he is here and never will know; but possibly he will accept life as he now accepts the briny deep and the starry vault overhead, as a fact which can yield great pleasure and happiness. Man is by nature an optimist; my share of it still holds out.

One phase of Cave Art already hinted at needs further attention because of the light it throws on many problems involved in our becoming civilized. Female figures, as we have seen, predominate. Many of the human figurines are of the pregnant woman. In one cave painting (Trois-Frères) a male reindeer pursues the female; in another cave (Tuc d'Audoubert) the artist has modelled on the floor a realistic bison cow awaiting the bull—a masterpiece of plastic art. And behind all this . . . shall we call it art? They are clever, well done, artistic; but had you called them art to the artist's face, he would have given you a blank stare. Those figurines, wall paintings, plastic representations, were to him, roughly, what the medical and agricultural sciences are to us today—"medicine" to make the necessaries of life plentiful. More, it was his cry for peace—life everlasting for his race, an unfailing supply of human food.

When Cave-man left his retreats in the deep rock caverns and took to a vegetable diet in the fertile river valleys, he soon became a good farmer, but not for ten thousand years did empirical farming become science and big business. He was as intent as ever on handing on his own seed, and kept up, even improved, his technique for insuring that very thing—by handing his wife over to the god. But how about the fields; how insure their fertility?

In short, the world the farmer faced was a new world again. He had to find new tricks—new arts, new magic, new gods; agricultural arts, agricultural magic, agricultural gods.

In changing from nomad hunter to dirt farmer, we do not say that man passed to a *higher* plane or that all hunters became farmers. There is a vast difference between organic evolution and cultural development. Some American Indians, for example, were skilful agriculturalists and had domesticated many valuable plants, but of animals, except the dog, they had domesticated not one. Why not? Roughly, for the same reason the Greeks did not sacrifice hippopotami and crocodiles to their gods.

As there are no evolutionary levels of culture, so there are no distinct levels of art or religion, or of magic, or of any cultural phase. That excuses us from trying to decide whether the art of agricultural Egypt was "higher," "finer," or "poorer" than that of the big-game hunters of Aurignacian Europe. But Egypt does best illustrate certain rules of art. In Egypt more than in any other country culture developed almost continuously under the same psychological and social conditions; yet nothing got steadily better. After the great initial flowering, many phases of culture seem to move backward. We stand amazed at King Tut's jewelry, but much of it is mere mud-pie art compared with First Dynasty work. It is, however, "pure" Egyptian; there is no mistaking any cultural artifact in five thousand years of Egypt.

Those early types became so definitely established that all later art seems to have been cast in the same iron mould; they got a stranglehold on every form of life. Ikhnaton had the cards stacked against him; to overthrow one cat-god was to overthrow all Egypt. And Egypt did not propose to be overthrown—not by any one man, however clearly he saw the sun. Early Egyptians made Egyptian culture; and it was extraordinarily sublime in many respects. Old Egyptian culture made young Egyptians old before they were born. All they had to do was to find a suitable spot for a tomb and engage a decorator for its interior. Their greatest book was the Book of the Dead.

And so from one art we pass to another, the Literary.

## VII

If my standing in the moron class depended upon my ability to define Literature, I should be at the foot. But I think I know how what we call Literature and the literary arts got started; and why, for example, I might return a book you handed me as Pure Literature with the comment, "Impure rot!" and we should both be right!

As grammar is merely how the king or the Oxford dons talk, so literature is merely what the "upper class" reads; that is why their talk is always good grammar, and why their reading is always good literature. Hence the Bible translated from Latin into English became the Vulgate—something vulgar the common people could read. A prose translation of Homer ceases to be literature and hardly remains a classic; it is just a story, a curious mingling of historical fact, traditional lore, and mythology.

Father tells the children about the fish that got away; that is a story, and it may be a historic fact, but was more likely a *big* fish. The "fish" rarely grows smaller; no point in telling a little fish story. It gets bigger and bigger. By the time the children grow to be fathers, that fish has grown several feet; by the time it gets its final growth, it is a miracle-performing whale, a sea serpent, a leviathan, a behemoth. The original story has now become a myth.

Put that myth into an inspired book and it becomes a fact, part of Revealed Religion; put it in Homer and it becomes Literature (in metrical form, Poetry) and a Classic; put it in the *Ramayana* and it becomes silly superstition; put it on the stage and it becomes drama; put a moral in it and it becomes church literature; dress it up a bit and it will be fit for a fable or a child's book; whittled down a bit, it becomes natural history (old histories are full of such gurglings); reduce it to an incident and it may be built into an odyssey.

Put it this way. This earth, home of man, is a most extraordinary world. It is easy to be born into it, but not easy to learn how to take it. Man, the speaking animal, has spent much time on that problem; in fact, he solved vast numbers of problems by just plain or fancy lying about them. But these fish stories served their purpose in a way, and in another way served it only too well. Almost everything having been decided, in words, man had to learn and accept the decisions passed on to him.

The genesis of literature, then, in over-simplified form, is a wise and loving father and an ignorant but curious child. The father has to answer the child's questions—and of course his own, should he retain enough curiosity to ask any.

This or that band of Primitives may do little of this, have little of that, and care for the other not at all, but the band has its literature, its Bible from Genesis to Revelation, and its history, poetry, song, drama, comedy, tragedy.

In short, we need not invoke any "faculty" for literature any more than we do for marriage, religion, art, magic, or speech. We need invoke only human nature in a male and in a female, on the kind of unknown earth this planet used to be. Children will come, will ask questions. Parents are ignorant and "just naturally" hate to confess it. And the whole family is easily moved by fear to wonder. From that biological and psychological background literature was created. There is so much of it because there are so many of us and it is more easily stored than corn or silver, more easily carried about than a dictionary; it is the perfect *vade mecum*. And if we run short, we still have the makings in our head. Shakespeare needed only 24,000 words for all the literature he created. Our beauty contests need only a tenth of that number.

We must invoke one thing more before we go ahead with nearly all early and most late literature—man's love of drawing analogies and his almost fatal tendency to draw them painlessly. Abigail's husband's name suggested *folly*. "Nabal is his name, and folly is with him."

A child stumbles on a stone, turns around and kicks it, and adds insult, "Naughty stone!" Man is more careful whom he insults. The biggest and roughest ocean is called the Pacific; the most inhospitable sea, the Euxine, "Hospitable." But we brand our "undesirable" immigrants with a dozen undesirable epithets, and invoke eugenics to prove that they should be kept out.

Wherefore do the wicked live, grow old, and wax mighty in

power? asks Job. Plutus, the god of wealth, is blind! Jacob wrestles with God: the mere "fact" changes him; he must have a change of name; they call him *Israel*. Abram, father of *many* nations, becomes Abraham. Simon "believes," and is changed into Rock, Peter. Romulus, mythical founder of Rome, goes to heaven and is called Quirinus—like the hill on which the Quirinal, or royal palace, stands. Helen, sister of Castor and Pollux, becomes St. Helena, patroness of August 18th in the Roman calendar; and in corrupted form, St. Elmo's fire.

Twins on earth. There must be twins in the sky. Castor and Pollux. But why twins at all? According as that question was answered in literature and life, we have Yama and Yami; Romulus (Romus) and Remus; Huppin and Nuppin; and Shakespeare's cobbler-martyrs, Crispin and Crispianus. When a pair of twins was engendered by a demon, the mother was hanged, beheaded, and drowned, and the child pronounced "bad" by lot, strangled; or the "odd" one might be considered specially "good," thereby raising respect for the mother and creating veneration for the child.

The really old literature has of course passed away, but we can make a pretty good guess at what it was from what has come down and from what can be learned from the literature of the Primitives. The myth seems to form the background of all literature and to contain within it the germs of future epic, romance and drama, especially tragedy. The great myth, of course, is always genesis, the myth of creation. Our own Genesis will be looked at later. Let us take two forms of the same myth.

What is the most striking feature of northern skies in winter— when a pastoral people has time to observe the heavens? The constellation Orion, I think we should agree. What is Orion? To the Israelites, Kesil the Fool. He was a mighty hunter, but in his vanity he tried to scale Heaven to dethrone Yahweh; so Yahweh took him between thumb and finger and bound him, to teach him submission. "Canst thou bind the sweet influences of the Pleiades, or *loose the bands* of Kesil?" Part of the year we cannot see him because Yahweh sent him to Sheol to learn more wisdom.

And what a lovely story the Greeks made of this victim of Apollo's strategy, all because his sister Artemis fell in love with him! Odysseus, you will recall, saw him in Hades. That is what

Orion was. And we still speak of his belt and sword and are entranced by the loveliest constellation in the sky.

Why did Frazer call his gigantic collection of myths *The Golden Bough*? Because it is typical of a category of great myths. In a certain tree near Lake Nemo in Italy lived Nemorensis, the Tree King. On that tree hung a golden bough. To any man who could pluck it would be granted immortality; it would carry him to Hades and back, that bourne whence no traveller has yet returned. The bough is the sun.

A great myth must be a good story; it must have human interest. Greek myths appeal to us because the Greeks personify nature; they read themselves into sun, moon, stars, and natural phenomena, and make human stories out of them. As magic and religion are closely associated with human passions, so the great and widespread myths deal with love, death, genesis, loss of immortality, the Golden Age, the Fall of Man, the banishment from paradise, incest. They are dramatic stories and recount happenings of great import in human lives. Hence the important function of myths in tribal life, second only to tribal legends.

Tribal myths, I repeat, form the tribal Bible. They state what happened and what is, and thereby, as Malinowski says, supply a retrospective pattern of moral values, sociological order, and magical beliefs. That is, myths are not mere narrative, science, art, history, or explanation. They strengthen tradition and endow it with special value and prestige because they give it a background of supernatural reality.

The fact that the myth is supernatural is all the more reason why it is true. The mythical past is quite as much alive and true to the Trobriander as it is to the believer in Genesis: If man could recover the power he once had in supernatural times, he could again fly, defy the devil, and be immortal. Myths do not narrate events that happen, but events that happened. The earth as it is here and now is proof that they happened!

Most human are the so-called Culture Hero myths, anthropomorphic beings who set the pace, established things as they are. Man is powerful, but the Culture Hero was more powerful. A rain-doctor can make rain—and it falls on the just and the unjust;

the Culture Rain-maker could make just enough rain to water his own garden; other gardens could look out for themselves!

The literature of our North American Indians is full of Culture Hero tales. Each tribe has its own type of hero, who remains true to character in the entire cycle. In one cycle his predominant trait may be superhuman strength; in another, voracity; in another, sensuality. In Alaska, the voracious raven; among the Great Plains tribes, the sensual coyote; among the Algonquin, the rabbit and turtle—as in Uncle Remus. The fox is the Culture Hero in South Africa.

Culture Hero deeds strung on a string result in an odyssey. Boas has pointed out the general but striking resemblance between the Greek and Eskimo odysseys. Both really amount to tales of travel and adventure, with lots of "fish stories" for seasoning. The Eskimo hero escapes a storm which had been created by magic; then encounters many sea dangers, which are described in detail; reaches a cannibal coast, encounters other dangers; triumphs over all and reaches home at last.

The buffalo naturally abounds in the tales of our Plains Indians, which are still told around the hearth though the buffaloes have all gone to the Happy Hunting-ground. These tales were created when there were buffaloes and a Happy Hunting-ground future. They agree with existence as it used to be, and picture cultural conditions as they were a century or more ago. Thus, in literature as in art, the determining factors are the existing cultural states.

The fairy tales we tell our children are comparable to the Indian culture tales. They reflect, as do Indian tales, customs and culture existing when these tales took formal shape; through them we can picture rural life in semi-feudal times.

Tales may and will be borrowed when they seem useful or can be fitted into tribal conditions. But sometimes they undergo curious transformation. Thus, Dr. Benedict found that in the Pueblo Indian variant of the story of the Nativity, Jesus is a baby girl, daughter of the sun; all the domestic animals lick the newborn infant, except the mule; for its disobedience it is punished with sterility, while the other animals are rewarded with increased fertility. A combination of natural history and moral teaching well known to Middle Age schoolboys.

In all Primitive literature, we may expect to find its character and type of narration in agreement with the cultural background. As mode or manner of living determines motives for action, we may expect to find their chief interests pictured in their plots. In short, the yarns they spin are yarns about the things, actions, and beings which most excite them. Hence the great differences between Homeric Greek literature and that of the Ionian Greeks a few centuries later, or between Greek and Semitic literature, or between either and Eskimo literature. These differences are often more apparent than real—the story has changed with change of narrator; but such as they are, they are based on different cultural outlooks. Hence the same story may come to have as many faces as it has cultural settings and cultural motivations. One culture plays up one element or idea in the story; another makes another element its key. Hence the 360 varieties of Cinderella, and the even larger number of genesis myths.

As any stick will serve to beat a dog, so any tale can be made to point any moral desired or prove any point in question.

Literature somehow seems to carry a heavier load than art. Words may be lighter than feathers, but they can brand like hot iron or crush the very life out of a people. This fact should not be lost sight of in considering the rôle of literature in human lives. For every graven image man has bowed down to, he has worshipped a thousand verbal images; for every fact man has sensed, there are thousands he has thought of; for every problem man has solved with his hands, there are thousands he has solved with his imagination. Were this not so, we should not be so glib with our tongues, and we should have less literature and more art.

Mark Twain said he liked a thin book because it would steady a table; a leather-covered book because it would strop a razor; and a heavy book—to throw at a cat. But we may remind ourselves that Homer, the blind, itinerant minstrel, did more to nationalize the Greeks than all their statesmen. The *Iliad* and the *Odyssey* were authority for their past, sanction for their beliefs, and pattern for their politics and language.

In literature, as in other forms of human expression, it is the same old story. A start from scratch: some travel far, some stay at home; some go in for this, some for that. West Africa went in for proverbs and has as many pithy ones as Europe. *If your stomach is weak, don't eat cockroaches.* The Old World in general went in for riddles and moralizing fables, and man the world over used animal fables to explain natural phenomena. Europe and Central Asia went in for epic poetry. Some day we may have an epic which will sing our historic deeds.

Had our European forefathers not brought with them to this continent romance, epic poetry, and proverbs, it is not at all certain that such literary arts ever would have appeared in America. And they brought something else till then foreign to this side of the world, and of no solid worth or with any valid excuse among civilized people: belief in the evil eye and in obsessions; and formalized justice based on oath or ordeal. America for thousands of years had got along without these monstrosities; and could today.

### VIII

We stamp our feet and clap our hands to synchronize with the accent of the song. It seems so natural that we assume it is universal, but many Primitives employ a different synchronization. Song accents and patterns of rhythmic body movement are far from homologous in Negro and Northwest Coast Indian music; in some examples they even seem independent of one another.

Rhythm is kinæsthetic or body-movement sense and has emotional quality; hence it enters into any activity related to our emotional life. Religious songs, for example, are likely to be accompanied by one kind of dance; war songs, by another; melodies, by another. In other words, rhythm is not born of religion or of any special form of social activity; it is born, rather, of the emotional states which go with religious or social activity. Emotional states produce rhythm; rhythm arouses emotion.

Dancing and other forms of regularly repeated body movement intensify the feeling for rhythm; hence Wundt inferred that ceremonial song rhythms are derived from dance-movements, working songs from work-movements. But this is a purely technical explanation of the origin of rhythm and is inadequate. Bücher (*Arbeit und Rhythmus*) gets nearer the truth when he derives songs from work. The regular and repeated movements in stringing beads, in embroidery, painting, etc., are pleasurable, not because the technique determines the movements, but because any regularly repeated movement, in work or in play, individually or collectively, intensifies the feeling for rhythm.

Our earliest musicians were singers. The song is older than the poem. We still dance to music, but when poetry was freed from song, music was freed from speech, and finally started a career of its own.

Our ancient narrator was more or less of an actor and probably excelled in pantomime; he knew how to use his face, roll his eyes, wave his arms. Then, too, if we may infer from what we hear when watching men work in any part of the world outside of our civilization, early man in taking *his* "exercises" sang or chanted. Every form of violent body movement seems to have a particular grunt of its own. Again, strong emotions find expression, unless thoroughly controlled, in bodily movements and voiced sounds. We also have our way of emotional speaking.

Hence the natural and almost universal association of song with dance, song with games, and gestures with spirited speech. We still dance to music, as I have said, but our music generally comes from a box; and some of our poets trust more to hair than to music to put their messages across. It is a mistake; music hath much more power to soothe the savage breast than hair. If it were not so, most of the love lyrics that now compete with static for our attention would seem worse than the static if merely recited. Poetry without music is modern sophistication.

Melody began at home, and begins early. Early, because the child utters a sound and hears it at the same time, and makes no distinction between uttering and hearing. A musical prodigy—like Handel or a thrush—need not speak to produce melody. As an Indian said to Frances Densmore, "There are no words in that song; it's just *singing*."

Whether music, as music, had artistic meaning to the ancients we cannot know, but throughout the primitive world songs with fixed rhythms may be found; also songs "carried along on a meaningless burden," as Boas puts it. They either do not know the words or use meaningless vocables of syllables.

Gradually, songs carried by the burden alone passed into songs containing meaningful words. A verse may contain a single word only, but "as we use the apostrophe for syllables not ordinarily slurred, expand a long vowel over several tones, or utilize archaic pronunciation for meter's sake or when wrong accents are intro-'duced," so do primitive people. For example, here is Boas' example of an Indian song: "I saw-haw the gre-heat sp'rit tra'ling 'bout, ham, ham."

Primitives also are likely to find value in borrowed songs—not in the words of the song, but in the emotions aroused by the song itself. As these emotions are fundamental and universal, we all have in us the makings of a poet. Lyrical at that. Only sophistication puts into poetry elements based on sensible ideas. Our earliest cry is emotional; it neither informs nor predicts. When poetry or religion becomes informative, it cuts off its nourishment; when it predicts, it cuts off its head.

Those unfamiliar with the literature of our Indians, or of any primitive literature, would be amazed at its richness, variety, and depth. The songs sung, for example, by the Navaho in their great ceremonies reveal a poetic appreciation of natural phenomena as fine as may be found in any literature. Such appreciation varies from culture to culture, and in form and depth. The world around, we find poetic feelings on planes quite creditable to the human race.

I sit down before the radio to have my ears tickled; more especially, to be stirred to my deepest nature. And when I hear tears, laughs, and thrills made to fit the public taste as a suit of clothes might be made for Uncle Sam, I am not thrilled, nor do I laugh or shed a tear; they move me like a Santa Claus parade on Fifth Avenue. But when I hear half a dozen Negroes singing spirituals, I stop. They move me because they themselves are moved; the tears in their voices are human tears, not drops of glycerine or paraffin. I can no more keep myself calm inside while they sing than I can during a storm at sea. When we become so intellectual that we cannot find a thrill, it is time to get out the embalming fluid. Intellectual music always looks better than it sounds.

The key to music must be sought in song; song alone in the realm of music is universal. All song has two common elements —rhythm, fixed intervals. Rhythm is so universally employed in primitive art and music that it may be said to have natural æsthetic value. As rhythm in primitive art runs to complexity, so it does also in their music. Their measures, says Boas, are not so rigidly confined to two-, three-, or four-part time; five- and seven-part tend to predominate: five in North America, seven in South Asia. They also employ to us unfamiliar alternations of rhythm, and complex sequences which cannot be reduced to measures.

Musical interval is comparable to melody of language, which, as we have seen, may have great significance in articulation. We pitch our voices higher, lower, etc., under emotional stress, but these pitches are not formalized elements of our language as they are in some. So, in singing, intonation is an emotional dependent; hence the fixed intervals in singing are rarely quite accurate.

Boas thinks it conceivable that early speech used fixed intervals and musical phrasing of vowels and voiced consonants, as well as different timbre of vowels, to express ideas. Presumably musical tone, in such languages as employ it, is secondary and due to the disappearance of formative elements. In the so-called drum languages—in Africa, Malaysia, Melanesia, etc.—the fixed interval is as keenly felt as in a Morse code.

Transposability of fixed intervals is a fundamental factor of all music. All intervals are subdivisions of an octave—though the subdivisions are not always founded on harmonic principles as with us, but by equidistant tones. Our scale is really a compromise; we divide the octave into twelve equal parts—good enough for all but highly trained ears.

The Javanese, with their great orchestras of bronze drums and gongs, divide the octave into seven equidistant steps; the Siamese, into five.

To drums, gongs, and rattles of every conceivable form and material, add still other noise-making devices, and you have a worldwide collection of the one universal type of musical instrument whereby man the singer can beat rhythm to carry his song. Callwhistles are almost as widely distributed, wind instruments much less. Both flute and pipe were well known and widely distributed in both Americas; but stringed instruments, ranging from the rude musical bow of Africa to the various complicated instruments of Asia, are common to the Old World. Recent excavations made by Woolley in Ur of the Chaldees brought to light a marvellous harp of eleven strings, of exquisite workmanship and at least 5,000 years old. It was found in the arms of a girl musician in the outer chamber of the queen's tomb. It is the oldest harp in existence.

One of the curiosities of distribution is that of the so-called pipes of Pan—Solomon Islands and South America. They have been found in the ancient graves of Peru, and may still be heard in the high Andes.

The Greek lyre, together with the Greek system of musical notation, probably came from Babylonia. The lyre of eight strings was a modified harp of Ur. Their chorus of boys and girls was the beginning of orchestral and choral music in Europe. Poets (Pindar of Thebes was the greatest) wrote verses to be sung with the lyre; hence *lyrics*.

Part-singing seems to have been unknown to primitive music. African music is famous for its solo singing and responsive chorus; it also has true part-singing.

Music, like other cultural traits, goes in areas, and each is recognizable by its common fundamental traits: the kind of accompaniment of song; use of purely instrumental music; narrow compass of tunes; varying systems of tonality; antiphony—as among our Negro songs; etc.

Music as we know it today is of comparatively recent origin. Up to the eighteenth century it was largely personal, or an accompaniment to the other arts, "embroidering the ritual of the church, setting the figures and movements of the dance, lightening the labors of sailors," etc. Our symphony orchestras came in with the factory age.

IX

Every form of art must have some *formal* element. Mere work, however complicated, does not yield artistic joy; it must have form. An idea. Play, as play, is not art; it may become art. Random or violent jumping about is not necessarily dancing; formalized, its movements controlled, it becomes dancing, an art—in Pavlova, divine art.

Bodily movements release voiced sounds. Rhythmic bodily movements release rhythmic voiced sounds—song. Song is an emotional release, which in turn releases bodily movements fitting to the rhythm of the song—dance. The song conditions the dance.

Most primitive dances, strictly speaking, are beyond the range of art. Their value is not based on æsthetic enjoyment; they are symbolic accompaniments of ceremonial rites or religious (magic) performances; or, more commonly, a form of exhibitionism or show-off behaviour for frankly erotic purposes—girls are supposed to lose their hearts. Our dancing has been shorn of symbolism and has become purely formal. It depends for its æsthetic effect almost entirely on the joy of bodily movement plus the emotional excitement released by the movement.

Symbolic movements presumably are older than the purely formal dance. Even today the formal dance is practically unknown in Asia; symbolic dances form characteristic features of the Buddhist and Hindu worlds. They are entirely pantomimic in character, forerunners of the drama. The drama began in gestures culturally patterned, body movements accompanying the song.

Our theatrical performances have travelled far from the drama of ancient days. In fact, many of our activities have been "big-business-ized" out of recognition, quite divorced from the human nature which called them into being. Oberammergau's divine play takes us back toward the birth of drama, back to the time when man thought he could bring to pass that which once had happened by mimicking it, rehearsing it, re-acting it.

The psychology behind ancient drama was the psychology behind magic in general, behind mimicry, behind the mime, behind pantomime. That psychology is based on man's proneness to fail to distinguish between the shadow and the substance, between the image and the reality. He readily jumps to the conclusion that things that look alike must be the same. We shall see the same principle in early medicine: *similia similibus curantur*—like cures like.

Passion plays, all dramas, presuppose a certain amount of leisure and fixed family abodes. Wandering hunting tribes have neither time nor social background for the production of drama; they resort to "one-act" sketches, easily put on wherever they happen to be. Magic for this, magic for that, but no real dramatization of world creation. In fact, they needed no such re-creation of the world; all they needed was an unending supply of certain animals—and we have seen their magical workings to insure their fertility. We spoke of those workings as magic, as art, as religion; but the god the Cave-man was working for was his stomach. His impulse was gastronomic rather than spiritual. As Luquet says, he was an artist before he was a magician. The man always antedates the medicine-man. His "medicine" was his own, popular, democratic. Millenniums were to pass before his medicine was to become a great ceremony backed by the Vested Interests of religion and staged by its College of Priests. If Cave-man's magic was religion, it was most parochial.

From that magic rite to insure animal food let us in one long jump turn to the great dramas of antiquity. In that jump man passed from the forest to the farm—and sank so deep in the slime of superstition that his superiors still speak of him as a hayseed.

What Cave-man failed to observe about his supply of red meat the farmer was forced to observe about his supply of corn—it was seasonal. With the general world-shaking changes which agriculture brought about we are not at present concerned; they were world-shaking, momentous; they changed man himself as he had not been changed since he acquired language. But by the time man had become a farmer he had also become a devout believer in anything the priests told him. The priests had plenty of time to think up new things to tell, because agriculture made a new kind of leisure possible, a new kind of power profitable—power over men's actions and beliefs.

The thing that counted most was, of course, to keep the seasons rolling along. What is a season? A god. Why do seasons change? Because the god changes. But suppose he should forget to change? Remind him, by mimicking him, by changing like a god. Then and there the divine drama was born. Oberammergau repeats it every tenth year, because its townspeople vowed they would eternally repeat it every tenth year if the Lord would rid them of the plague then scourging Europe.

And who is the Lord? A name found hundreds of times in the Bible for Yahweh, whose real name was Tammuz—still the name of the month of June in the Jewish calendar.

Tammuz, the Saviour, the Divine Son, is one of the oldest elements in Babylonian religion. In Sumerian cities of 5000 B.C. he was the great Culture Hero, creator of the vegetable world. He was the lover of Ishtar, the great goddess of nature. Once each year he dies, goes below; Ishtar goes to fetch him. Meanwhile nothing can grow. So a messenger is sent to Hades' queen to beg permission for Ishtar's return. Permission is granted. Ishtar, sprinkled with the water of immortality, returns to earth, bringing Tammuz with her. The seasons roll on again as before.

So much for the Word. Now for the divine drama. With autumn, Tammuz' "death" is mourned with a funeral dirge. A rough log effigy is set up, washed or "anointed" with water, and dressed up in a blood-red robe; women weep and sing mourning songs over the image of the dead god. The log (the dead Tammuz) is then cast into the water—sacrificed by drowning.

By the Babylonians, Tammuz was also called the Anointed; by the Hebrews, the Messiah; by the Greeks, the Christos.

Remember Ezekiel's vision, when the Spirit lifted him up by the hair of his head so that he could see over into the temple of Jerusalem? "Behold, there sat women weeping for Tammuz." But there were "greater abominations . . . five and twenty men . . . and they worshipped the sun toward the East." My Bible dictionary defines Tammuz as a "Syrian idol corresponding to the Greek Adonis," lover of Venus.

Of the many Babylonian trinities, the "son" is always a saviour, Tammuz, Ninib, Abu, Nergal; Melkarth at Tyre; Gilgamesh was a saviour god; Bel-Marduk, Lord of Lamentations, was a divine son; Yahweh began as Tammuz. All waxing-waning gods were divine sons, saviours. Throughout Mesopotamia and Syria the cult of Tammuz prevailed under one name or another. There was even an Adonis shrine at Bethlehem in the shade of a grove specially dedicated to him. "The very grotto," says St. Jerome, "where the infant Christ uttered his first cries, resounded formerly with the lamentations over the lover of Aphrodite."

And what were the great Greek tragedies but divine dramas? But far older than Æschylus or Sophocles were the orgiastic rites connected with the worship of Dionysus and the rites of the Eleusinian mysteries. Both verged on true drama. There were a stage, light, darkness, singing, dancing, voices, entrances, exits. The rites were "seasonal," held only at times appropriate to the worship of the god. In a sense they were amateur performances: local talent, localized by the god's shrine. Oberammergau is not the Holy Land, scene of the Passion; they only *play* the Passion. Such mystery plays were common during the Middle Ages. It was out of such Oriental and Greek Passions that tragedy was born.

The same devolutionary process can be traced in China. Orgiastic rites, with ecstatic dances, dialogue between spirits and priestesses, are known accompaniments of the worship of earth deities and the powers of fertility in early Chau Dynasty times. From such purely ceremonial divine comedies Chinese drama derived, just as the Grecian did. And in China, as in Greece, the drama developed in its own peculiar way. What was a purely magical performance for the initiates or believers became a secular performance for the masses. But China more than Greece, or more than any other country, has had an unbroken cultural history for thousands of years. Hence it is still possible—or was recently—to see in China many archaic forms of dramatic art. Shadow-plays are indigenous to China —and, with Laufer as our guide, well worth looking at for the light they throw on many phases of cultural development.

To Wu-ti, a Han (c. 200 B.C.-200 A.D.) emperor, disconsolate over the loss of his favourite wife, came a magician who threw her shadow on a transparent screen. It was a good trick and a good idea, and the idea grew. It is just as easy to throw a shadow on a screen as it is to raise a shadow at a spiritualistic *séance*.

Those early "shadows" were true shadows cast on a screen by placing a lighted candle behind thin rawhide silhouettes; the spectator sat in front on the other side of the screen. Thus, the magician threw up or projected the shadows as souls of the departed, "summoned back" by his magical powers.

Within a thousand years this purely spiritualistic or religious performance had become the people's drama. Romantic elements from China's age of chivalry gradually replaced the earlier ghostly elements; scenarios from the literary drama of the now legitimate stage were adopted. With the Mongols in Peking, and the influx of foreigners from the entire Eastern world, shadow-plays became not only popular but widespread. By the fifteenth century they formed a favourite pastime at Sultan Saladin's court in Egypt. Selim carried it to Constantinople, and it reached France in 1767—to be carried to London in 1776 as *Ombres Chinoises*. What was once a purely religious performance now had no function other than entertainment.

Shadow-plays reached Java by the eleventh century, and there they still preserve traces of their religious origin. Their scenarios are founded chiefly on the great Indian epics of *Mahabharata* and *Ramayana*—superhuman heroes and deities. Hence, before each performance, food is offered to the spirits and incense burned.

Puppet plays, or marionettes, were not invented by Tony Sarg, but presumably started in Greece. At any rate, marionettes identical in idea with those used in China are found in Greece, Italy, and Egypt. Their original function was possibly pure entertainment. By 630 they had reached China; and as women were barred from the public theatre in China, they soon became popular entertainment for the women and children in the courtyards of private houses. But by the time of the Sung Dynasty they had taken on a religious significance, being performed after funerals in honour of the dead.

Plots for Chinese dramas, whether performed by living actors, marionettes, or puppets, are drawn from Buddhistic or Taoist lore, from historic tradition, and from Confucian ethics—filial piety, devotion of servant to master, loyalty of friend to friend, the worth of learning. Hence one need not be surprised to see a servant offer his son to the jaws of death to save the life of the crown prince; or a soldier cutting off his arm and feigning surrender to a barbarian king that he may the better serve his own king. Hence, too, the swarms of Buddhist nuns and lazy, licentious monks, and the hordes of Taoist demi-gods, fairies and fabulous animals. The result is a curious and purely Chinese blending of religion, superstition, and ethics.

Shadow and marionette plays especially excel in comedy and satire. Human frailty, official corruption, and social and political evils are shot at with keen arrows. In short, they are, as we should say, moral and instructive as well as entertaining. That is, they are *fit* for women and children.

A familiar group in Chinese dramatic art is a pair of dancing lions or strolling mimes. They came from India and are Buddhist in origin. The lion is Buddha's emblem or "vehicle." Great stone lions in front of Chinese Buddhist temples "protect" his religion; dancing lions dispel or expel demons.

Hence lions in Trafalgar Square and on the steps of our Public Library; and the lionizing of matinée idols; and the thousands of lion crests, brands, emblems, on fakes masquerading in the clothes of a big cat.

While the idea of lions as "protectors" entered China late in the Tang Dynasty, the dog-temple idea is much older. Erh Lang, prince of the wonder-working Tao, is the patron saint of dogs. He owned a "medicine" dog, which he carried in the sleeve of his coat; it could devour any enemy it was set on. In a Tao temple in Peking, many clay dogs may be found at the foot of the altar. To cure a sick dog, one goes to this temple, takes some ashes (*medicine*) from the censer, and administers according to instructions. If the dog gets well, one is supposed to add another clay dog to the collection.

Before we leave China, let us look at a sign on a house door-post. It says: *Mr. Kiang is here.* Of course there is no "Mr. Kiang" there; but he is a dramatic figure in China's literature: his spirit goes marching on, and his name is as good as a horseshoe or a saint's relic for frightening off evil spirits. Mr. Kiang is powerful "medicine," a sort of Chinese St. Francis. At the age of eighty, it seems, he gave up his post as chief counsellor of a Chau Emperor and took to fishing . . . but without hook or bait. So attracted were the fish by his virtue that they allowed themselves to be caught on a straight iron rod. Against the virtue of such a name no evil spirit can hope to prevail.

All the world's a stage, but the play became serious when man went in for divine drama. It took the joy out of life. It bade man to a feast, but, like the Feast of Hussein, son of Ali and Fatima, it was but to rehearse a massacre at Kerbala. Ali himself was cruelly murdered—as was Jesus, as was Tammuz, as was Osiris, as was the sun, as was the moon. The moon influences tides; it has influenced human beings even more profoundly, flooding them with false and misleading hopes, causing their lives to ebb away in vain lamentations.

Art—in any and all forms—has no quarrel with the joys of life, nor with a scientific attitude toward life. The play is the thing; but may we not also ask, *At whose request do these men play?*

The divine drama has become secularized; the human drama is becoming more humanized.

### X

Any innate sexual differences in æsthetic sense, artistic faculty, or creative ability? We may rule "faculty" out at once. It is simply another name for another unknown variable, often called instinct: faculty sounds more intellectual. Æsthetic sense we may also rule out. Woman has all the senses man has; and though she may at times seem to have less sense, that is only man's seeming, and he is generally biassed in his opinion. Woman has all the senses and all the emotional endowment man has. She shares human nature equally with her bearded spouse. If she has not created *this*, she has created *that*. *Creation is her business.*

The reason why woman has not turned her hand to many phases of the arts is not to be found in her nature but in her preoccupations. Her hands are fuller of the things that count most in human lives. Wherever we find society so organized that industries requiring high mechanical skill and permitting artistic productivity are allotted to women, the output in skill and artistry measures up to any male standard. Virtuosity goes hand in hand with artistic productivity.

Of the two greatest factors in civilization—agriculture and language—woman contributed at least fifty per cent of one and probably ninety-five per cent of the other. She is rarely now harnessed to the plough beside a cow, as she was until recently in eastern Europe, and she is still allowed her share of speech—although most pulpits are still closed to her. Didn't she bring wisdom into the world? And at what a price! It took the supreme genius of a Persian to contend that not God but the devil created woman; but it was the infamous bigotry of the early Christians that hunted out the eleven books of the world's greatest poetess and burned them in the public square.

It is not known that Sappho leaped to her death from the Leucadian rock, as Ovid claimed in his *Heroides*. That is probably a fable, as is her reputed unrequited love for Phaon—and a vicious fable at that, invented by the Attic Greek comic poets, who knew women only as property or as playthings. Sappho was an Æolian

Greek, and as such could enjoy life and liberty, and find room in society, literature, or philosophy to express herself. But whether "violet-crowned, pure, sweetly smiling" Sappho, as Alcaeus called her, was a native of Mytilene or Lesbos, is not known.

Among the Æolian Greeks there were social clubs or literary societies of women whose business it was to foster the religion of the gods and train youth in the ways of virtue and to the service of the muses. They also acted as a chorus to sing songs of praise at fashionable weddings, for which they were liberally paid. Sappho headed such a club. She wrote the songs herself. They were highly original in airs and words. Her lyrics, sung with simplicity, directness, warmth, and high fervor, were in praise of the gods of love, Eros and Hymen. They reveal her passionate love for her maiden pupils, and her sorrow as they passed from the service of Apollo to the cares of family life. They were the favourite songs of a thousand years—to be burned by the priests of Christianity, who misunderstood them even more than had her calumniators of Athens. Neither could understand sentimental love, nor qualify for the Order of the Garter.

There is no proof, nor any evidence at all, that Sappho was a Lesbian. The fragments of her poems which escaped the hands of the Christian destroyer are evidence of the enormous loss the world of literature sustained when the work of the greatest poetess of antiquity, if not of all time, was nearly expunged from the record.

Our art today is enormously complex, extremely subtle—even as are our lives. Our latest art is the movietone news; but news is much older—far older than the oldest newspaper. And the first broadcaster, we may suspect, was a weazened old widow, Dame Grundy. She doted on scandal and loved to hear her own voice; was no good on the farm and a nuisance in the kitchen. But she had to express herself. Her footprints are still visible at the edge of the cave where she put herself on the air in a high-pitched voice full of static. Poor old soul, there was nowhere else she could expend her pent-up energy with such great results and with so little effort, no other way to get so much out of life while putting so little into it. She was a Patron, if not the Founder, of the Literary—oldest of all arts.

XI

Of all modern social parasites claiming respectability, the æsthete is perhaps the most light-headed and empty-handed. He toils not nor spins, nor breeds. He is as anæmic as a jellyfish, as little rooted in the social fabric of life as an assembler in a Ford plant. He is æsthetic, and his name is Art. His motto is "Art for Art's sake." Yet society cherishes him—for Art's sake. We must look him over.

*How, why,* did our hard-headed, horny-handed ancestors fall for the buncombe behind the True, the Beautiful, the Good? They did, though not so hard as we do. Man had to become very sophisticated before he could kiss a toe to save his soul and pay a king's ransom for an oil-painting. Gullible, trusting man; easily fooled by such laryngeal grunts as *Precious, Priceless*—sometimes called universals.

It was William of Occam who held that "the *universal* is merely a concept for many singulars and has no reality beyond that of the mental act which produced it and of the singulars of which it is predicated."

Art, Beauty, Truth, Virtue, Freedom, Liberty, Nobility, Patriotism, are sample universals; and may we note here that of all the tyrants the world has known, no one has ever wielded such tyranny as names can wield.

Low down in the scale of civilization man found certain simple, harmless adjectives—fine, good, bad, true, etc.—useful for expressing his attitudes toward the weather, his ax, his child, his food, etc. But when from the things and persons that satisfied or dissatisfied him he sublimated such universals as Beauty, Goodness, Evil, Truth, etc., he then and there created a superhuman world which still bedevils our systems of thought and religion. These universals—in Law, Politics, Government, Business, Commerce, Religion, Society, Family—become systematized. They change, of course, but not necessarily to meet the demands of living human beings for more air and sounder food, or for a better chance to live and learn and more opportunity to love.

The Middle Ages went crazy trying to find the *essences* of words and the *Realities* in Plato's dead world of Ideas. We can lighten our burden, it seems to me, by dumping overboard a lot of the verbiage foisted on us by those who live by selling it. We submit to countless restrictions because everything is restricted but the cease-less flow of high-pressure Slogans, Watchwords, Mottoes, Platforms, Labels, Banners, Emblems.

"They sold me the box but they didn't the sox," Frank Daniels used to sing; "and I'll never go there any more." But we do; and if it was an *art* store, we treasure the box as a venerable relic or priceless work of art. Socks? Oh, we can get along without socks. Art's the thing.

It is the *word* that is handed on from adult to adult, shaman to shaman, priest to priest, body-snatcher to body-snatcher, cradle-robber to cradle-robber, Good to Good, True to True. . . . And to sanctify the relics, to make the "medicine" more magical, the Good more refined, the True more desirable, the Beautiful more divine, Art more "arty"—ever new and cleverer ways.

While the High Priests of Art, Religion, Fashion, and of the True, the Beautiful, and the Good, continue to improve their selling tech-nique by making their wares more precious (more expensive), they must solve the vitally important problem of maintaining a steady supply of "patrons." Catch them young. Get a stranglehold on the mothers!

What is the inevitable result of "selling" Art, Literature, Truth, Goodness, Beauty, to the masses, or of storing it in books or museums, or of building it in tombs, temples, churches, and palaces?

Let us look at human nature again. I am, say, a healthy boy of six, and you are Santa Claus. Of all the conceivable things you can bring, which do I choose; what do I want in my stocking? Do you let *me* choose? Do you weigh my choice by your judgment? Or do you go to a shop and buy me a mechanical toy such as you think *you* would like if you were a child? Santa Claus dumps tons of such toys into children's laps these days—and then spends half an hour enjoying himself, showing them how to wind them, what to do with them, what not to do with them, etc.

What experience can I, a boy of six, get from that toy; what can I learn from it? It excites me, I am curious about it; but after a few hours I grow indifferent, lose my curiosity, and by the end of the week the toy is added to the scrap heap.

But suppose you give me a few simple tools, some nails and soft pine, and opportunity? I smash my thumb, quite likely; lose a finger, possibly. What of it? I am learning, and by the only way possible, to train my hands and eyes; acquiring valuable kinæsthetic sense. I may never become a master carpenter; I may never build a museum piece. But the home Abraham Lincoln was born in needed but four tools and no great architect or master builder; Darwin's entire scientific equipment cost less than the mechanical toys you gave your child last year.

What of it?

The higher the cathedral spires towered toward the heavens, the flatter the homes in which human lives were lived. The faster Art, Truth, Beauty, and Goodness went into dead parchment, dead marble, dead formulas, the faster they disappeared from human lives.

Man eternally builds monuments to Honour, Virtue, Nobility, Character, Patriotism; and behind each monument is a Vested Interest, a High Priest, a Superman. "The poor we have with us always. Nature must take its course!" But we may remind ourselves that when the powers of peace are usurped by the powers of war, there can be no peace; and when the powers of Salvation, Art, Truth, Beauty, are monopolized by their High Priests, we lose sight of the fact that human lives are to be saved, that art is merely a way of life to be enjoyed in living and doing, and that there is no Good or True outside man's capacity to do good and be true to his fellowmen.

It was a great game, but while king, priest, or Midas was growing omnipotent, thousands were losing their potency; and the game ended in a smash. It always does when civilization becomes lopsided through building to any one Great Idea—or any dozen small ideas that choke the life out of human beings.

What has become of the great military civilizations, the great theocratic civilizations, the great artistic civilizations? Disappeared under the dust of their own earthquakes or smashed to pieces by the raw-beef-eating savages from the hills. They fell because they fostered everything but the opportunity for their peoples to live sound, sane, healthy, happy, virile human lives.

Top-heavy, lop-sided. Those Military machines, those Fine arts, those Gargantuan festivals, those huge hives of monks and nuns, those Scholastic halls, those quests for truth for Truth's sake, were biologic parasites—lice, fleas, leeches, book-worms, tape-worms; and most of them, in the long run, as useful as the itch.

But they made contributions to knowledge? Yes; but *whose* knowledge? And what in the name of heaven is knowledge good for, anyway, if somehow, somewhere, it cannot be built into a social fabric and made available for human beings—as something to nourish, protect, and prolong human lives? Call this "materialism" if you please, but note that you have not thereby added one jot to the inescapable fact that we are material and live in a material world; that the thinner the air, the faster we must breathe; and that spiritual food may be good enough for a ghost, but it has never been known to prolong a human life or keep a body alive. The marvel is that any Pure Soul should ever eat steak, fish, or string-bean. If they object to the idea of materialism, why make a material gesture—with larynx or hand—toward it?

What if the physicist *has* pushed matter out of the universe? He can still hear the rustle of a banknote and feel the chill of winter; he shaves with a razor and toasts his toes by the fire. Man has developed some extraordinarily keen extensions to his sense organs; but for all eternity, so far as I can see, he will be feeling his way about this world with his fingers—and always in quest of something to satisfy his animal nature. Ours are not the first scientists to wonder whether life is but an empty dream or to decide that things are not what they seem. Like the Pure Souls, however, they keep on making laryngeal noises, eating three meals a day, and (some of them) propagating their kind in the same good old way.

It was natural that our forefathers should have paid more respect to men of words than to men of brawn and action. A rain-maker calls down rain and saves the tribe from famine—by merely lifting up his voice. Mere brawn can perform no miracle like that.

Look at a modern miracle-maker. A *famous* doctor charges, and gets, ten thousand dollars from a millionaire for a "cure." Is the millionaire *cured*? He is. Being a *practical* "business man," he knows what a dollar will buy and that ten thousand is a lot of money. When he spends ten thousand he *always* gets his money's worth! Had the doctor given him not one single bread pill, he would have been *cured*; the fee alone had therapeutic value! And his respect for that doctor is enormous. Because the doctor cured him or because he took ten thousand dollars from him?

It is not that we are born so dumb that hurts; it is that we are so easily fooled by the shadow-world of words. Does this shadow-world rule us, or do we control it and thereby find it an invaluable instrument for controlling the world we were born in and must live and die in?

Plato's immortal *Republic* is as full of noble sentiments as a modern sermon or a President's speech, abounds with fine maxims, has all our own unctuous moralities. Freedom rings out, Liberty wins, Democracy is triumphant. Let us remember it when we think of that mighty creative spirit of the Greeks which produced art, poetry, music, eloquence; the Parthenon, the Acropolis, the groves of the Academy; Phidias, Praxiteles.

"Marvellous," *classical*. So they are, and we shall look more closely at them later. But the republic the author of the *Republic* lived in was an oligarchy; his "freedom" took slavery for granted—and slaves as two-footed beasts of burden, as we did a few years ago. Apart from public buildings, stately Athens was a jumble of huts and hovels amid dunghills, facing alleys and lanes full of dust, dirt, rubbish, filth, mud-holes. There human beings lived, amid squalor, "riff-raff, terrors, brutalities, pleasure boys, phallic worship, and imperial orgies."

Euripides lived like a troglodyte in his cave at Salamis, but was better housed than most Athenians. Existence then was as uncertain as it is in Chicago today. The city was in a perpetual reign of terror; war was always at the gates. Athenians warred on their neighbours without scruple, killing the men and selling their wives and children into slavery—even to the brothels of the Levant.

All that we call Art and the higher life in general, came into being in answer to the call in human nature to win the applause and approval of our fellow-men; it had social value—it always will have. But when it becomes an end in itself and lives for itself, it becomes parasitic, biologically useless, socially destructive—in short, it gets into the realm of psychopathology and functions best in an asylum or a cathedral, or on a battlefield.

As Ogden truly says, psychologically all æsthetes are non-starters. Certain it is that "arty" people find what they set out to find.

Ruskin, Tolstoy, Bosanquet, Santayana, Croce, are all equally enthusiastic, equally dogmatic in their conclusions—and all differ from one another and from all who have gone before. Which recalls Hume's comment called forth by the wranglers over Beauty:

*Disputes are multiplied, as if everything was uncertain, and these disputes are managed with the greatest warmth, as if everything was .certain. Amidst all this bustle 'tis not reason which gains the prize, but eloquence . . . The victory is not gained by the men-at-arms, who manage the pike and sword; but by the trumpeters,. drummers, and musicians of the army.*

Any discussion of Art, or of the Beautiful, the Good, and the True, as objective entities, in terms of intrinsic qualities of artistry, beauty, goodness or truth, is twaddle—sometimes called Intellectual Conversation.

When Richard Wagner spoke of art as a confession of impotence, and said that art begins where life leaves off and if we had life we should not need art, he may have been speaking for himself, or for Greenwich Village, or for the Quartier Latin; he was not speaking for mankind. Nor is it true to say, as he did, that art lies to hide truth's ugliness. Nor is it true, as some one has said, that poetry, drama, music, etc., are spiritual soothing-syrups, balms, fairy tales, make-believes for stern realities. Nor does art, as some one else has said, stand as a symbol for escape from the world of actuality. Nor is art, as Professor More seems to think, merely a means of communication.

Art is not so simple, for it is human life at its supremest moment of elation, at its acme of perfection. Man can live that kind of life because, I repeat, it is in his nature; he brought the æsthetic germ up with him in his ascent from apes.

Hands, fingers: *touch*—extraordinarily clever tactile sense; stereoscopic binocular *vision*, and close examination possible because of hands. Primates, especially man, can get kinds and degrees of information denied all other creatures. Information through eyes, added to that from handling, made for a degree of appreciation of form and texture, of estimating weights, distances, and proportions, entirely beyond the infraprimate world. Then came that supremely valuable and uniquely human advantage of labelling the information acquired by this æsthetic sense—and Art was in the offing.

Æsthetics, says my dictionary, is the science of the beautiful. And what, pray, is an anæsthetic? Well, chloroform is an anæsthetic. Under its influence I cannot *feel*; I have lost my sense, have no sensibility. In anæsthesia, I may be a sensation, but I have no sensation; I am no longer *æsthetic* and can no longer weigh the æsthetic qualities of my fellow men.

What else but this æsthetic sense was behind Darwin's theory of *sexual* selection? At any rate, I agree with Elliot Smith that the appeal of physical beauty—the æsthetic sense—must have helped to transmute the uncouth ape into the graceful human figure. That the general form of the body has been profoundly altered, the features enormously refined, there is no doubt. Not all these changes can be easily ascribed to natural selection; sexual selection is a tenable hypothesis.

During that transmutation, work had to be done; activities had to be undertaken for purely material purposes, to keep the wolf from the door. But, I repeat, Primates do not like work; they do not take kindly to pure labor; they prefer to play.

Play is pleasurable; it is its own reward. But it gets no chores done, no trees felled, no fires kindled, brings home no "bacon." It was man's business to discover a way of turning work into play. Art was the answer. Art is a means and an end. In art, work is the means; play, enjoyment, the end. To *work* for a living is to take the joy out of life.

To draw the further inferences these fundamental biologic considerations warrant would take us too far out of our way. But one fact does stand out, and it bears on our own social and economic problems.

Life as drudgery is for man not natural; nor is that society organically sound which makes art a plaything or a means for the rich to exaggerate their self-importance; nor is the alumnus who would turn college games into gladiatorial shows to enhance his own and his college's prestige any more civilized than the patriarch of old who would prostitute his wife and daughter to fertilize a field. If society must seek vicarious enjoyment as a reward for unsatisfactory labors, let it turn to professional entertainers. If

youth can find no joy in play, it is not likely to discover the way
to make living a joy. The finest of all arts is the art of living.
When that art is lost, all that makes for humanity is lost.

Our purely conventional categories—art, literature, poetry, music,
dancing, etc.—are useful symbols for handling certain forms of
human activity; but we have paid dearly for formalizing these
natural ways of human æsthetic expression and appreciation. We
have lifted them out of the range of normal human activities, the
inevitable result being that we have "artists," "art buyers" and
"dealers," and "just people." Nor does taking a "course" in an art
*subject* have more value in making for artistic living than taking
a course in politics makes for good government. But as we have
given up most of the sympathetic-magic procedure in sexual activities, we shall probably abandon that procedure as a means of making life enjoyable—as it must be if it is to be sane and healthy.
Beauty is as beauty does. To say, as does Ducasse in his recent *Philosophy of Art*, that art and beauty are "essentially distinct," is to
anæsthetize life for dissection purposes only.

We need hardly remind ourselves that Primitives knew nothing
of "Art" or "the Arts" or "Æsthetics"; they did make things, skilfully, cleverly, artistically, æsthetically. That made living a joy and
life an art.

And then somebody who had failed in life began to throw the
fear of God around. The æsthetic in man gave way to the ascetic.
There was no more joy on earth.

In the battle of Megiddo, fought 608 B.C., King Josiah was killed.
Twenty years of anarchy followed; Jerusalem was taken three times
and destroyed. It was a terrible trial for the Jews. How *could* God
allow it! In Revelation, the battle that will end the world is
Armageddon; the war that ended the lives of thirteen million
young men was Armageddon.

# CHAPTER FIVE

## Primus in Orbe Deos Fecit Timor

1. The Religious "Instinct." 2. The Biologic Value of Beliefs. 3. The Stuff Souls Are Made of. 4. The Nature of Religion. 5. The Nature of God. 6. The Mystery of Magic. 7. Sex as Divine Mystery. 8. The Blood Sacrifice Complex. 9. Totem, Taboo: Categorical Imperatives. 10. The Divine Afflatus. 11. The Word of God.

I

*NO OTHER book has ever been associated in the same way with the joys and sorrows of human life, with births, marriages and deaths; and no other would we care to have read over the casket of our beloved dead.*

These closing words of the Reverend P. Marion Simms's *Bible from the Beginning* seem a fitting introduction to a discussion, not of Christianity nor of the Christian religion, but of religion in general, of the biologic roots of all religions.

Whether ours is or is not a "Christian" civilization, our society is saturated with beliefs and practices which antedate Christianity and have the sanction of divine law. We shall look at that religion later, but, isolated from human nature and from its cultural beginnings, it cannot be at all understood. If, as I believe, the Dead Hand of the past still clutches our throats, sanctifies tradition, and authorizes existing beliefs, practices and social injustices, we shall want to know where the Hand came from, how it came to be, and what is behind its claim to authority.

Beyond that, we must know the mainspring of the religious attitude if we are at all to understand human history; for the rôle that attitude has played, the rôle religion has played, in all civilizations, can hardly be overestimated. Let us be certain of this at the outset. So important has been the rôle of religion that we are constantly being warned that its destruction would inevitably involve the destruction of civilization itself. I do not say that these warnings are not founded in reason; we do want to know if the "reasons" are well founded, or if they are as unreasonable as most of the rationalizations man uses to cloak his ignorance and justify his faith.

The facts which supply the knowledge necessary for reasonably sound judgments on religion, as on language, marriage, or any cultural phenomenon, can be found only in history as it mirrors the workings of human nature.

Religion is a phase of culture. It has had a function in human society, has played a rôle in civilization, and today has a powerful hold on the beliefs which sanction the actions of hundreds of millions of human beings.

Think of the cultural accompaniments to Tutankhamon's mummy: almost all the arts—architecture, sculpture, music, dancing; almost all the crafts; and technical and engineering skill of an order hardly yet excelled. And was there really a causal connexion between disturbing that tomb a few years ago and the death of several of the excavators? Thousands of people so believe. Which means that the body of a lad dead some thirty-one hundred years still influences men's activities, if not their destinies.

What is a mummy—religion? But let us come closer to home—and look at a circular recently mailed, presumably, to all the names on a certain "sucker" list. First, let us ask, what is the sensible way of getting rid of a corpse—for a corpse must be got rid of, because, while little is known of death, much is known of the ways of corpses. They do something; they change. These changes are potent stimuli to induce action in the living. What is the simplest, easiest, sanest, and safest method of disposing of a dead body: cremate it, feed it to the fishes, or to the fields as fertilizer, turn it over to a medical school to advance knowledge, or send it to a mausoleum? And if to a mausoleum, should a mortician or a clergyman "officiate"? (And what, by the way, should we do for a mausoleum had not the wife of King Mausolus of Caria built for him twenty-three hundred years ago the most magnificent tomb of the ancient world?)

*Los muertos mandan,* said Ibañez of his Spain. But who of us, or what nation, is free from the commands of the dead?

With the circular comes a post-card. If I mail it, so I am informed. I shall receive architect's plans. For a home for crippled children? No; for a beautiful mausoleum, "right in my own home town"—which happens to be one of the most crowded and deadly on earth. It is "sponsored by leading business men and approved by leading ministers." But I had "better hurry, for much space is already gone"—to leading families. And I can get it on the instalment plan, "terms arranged."

I buy a mausoleum, let us say, at a cost of $50,000, on the instalment plan—and spend the rest of my life trying to pay for it. Then a panic wipes me out and I die of heart failure. But my widow cannot live in our mausoleum, or even use it as a summer garden, as Mr. and Mrs. Shah Jehan used their world-renowned Taj Mahal.

No, she can't do that; but Society—leading business men and ministers—will expect her to *bury* me in the style to which I *was* accustomed. For $25,000 she can get a "noble" casket; and for disposing of my "remains" (worth just ninety-eight cents for their sugar, sulphur, lime, and other chemicals) in that beautiful "Home of the Departed," she will get a bill for only $3,217.54.

Why so expensive? Well, a "noble" casket is a *noble* jewel-box. And there are incidentals, all necessary for a noble funeral in a big city: face veil, slumber robe, floral door-pieces, palm decoration; special car for flowers, "evergreen" lining for the grave; special device for lowering a dollar's worth of raw chemicals into a grave. As Blanshard says, my widow could ship me to effete Europe and get rid of me cheaper than that. Switzerland would bury me free of charge. In Germany she could count her money, if any, and choose between a Class A or a Class B funeral. And if she went to Munich and spent more than $176.83 to put me away, she would be arrested for speeding.

That New York funeral, by the way, was without "benefit" of clergy, which would cost more. *Whose* benefit?

Think again of the time, pains, effort, skill, technique, and craftsmanship that went into the mummification of that boy king's body. Try to think of Egypt without a "mummy" idea, and what becomes of those mighty pyramids, those gorgeous mastaba tombs, and those enormous temples? When I think of China I think of temples and interminable burying-grounds.

Think of the ways man has devised to dispose of the remains:

in urns, boxes, coffins, caskets, or in canoes, or under houses, or in trees, or under thousands of tons of rock or earth. And why unflesh the bones, or carve the skull and keep it in the house? Why eat the body, or the ashes of the cremated? Why kill the wife, children, slaves, horses, and bury them with the master? Why bury with the dead, food, clothing, toys, trappings, tools, weapons, jewels and ornaments? Why bury a smallpox victim one way, an executed murderer another, a suicide another, and an infant still another? Why do we speak of the dead as the "departed," or as having "passed away"? In short, why such a cultus of the dead that a hundred volumes would not describe its beliefs, rites, rituals, practices, and implications?

Are we far from religion? Well, we have looked at some hard, cold, very expensive facts. That cultus of the dead is a fact of a large order, and it began not as ancestor-worship but as fear of souls. The souls of the dead must be treated with respect or they will haunt us!

Let us now look at another very significant fact—nor ever lose sight of it in trying to understand human culture.

The fact of birth. No infant, ape or human, is born in a vacuum, but into a particular family, at a particular time and in a particular place, a *made* world, a going concern in every sense of the word. And plenty of time is allowed to learn its ways before one is expected to become a member in full standing.

The infant needs no instincts to learn the world's ways: it must have appropriate reflexes for all vital activities and the capacity to learn its social or cultural ways; and it must have teachers.

There is no religious instinct. There are human beings, and within each a trinity of heart, lungs, and brain, which functions best during crises. Religion supplies one answer to a crisis; it is a purely cultural answer, hence uniquely human, even as is articulate speech. Science supplies another answer.

Science and religion—in attitudes, methods, practices, and results —are irreconcilable; they can no more meet than Euclidean parallel lines. Science does not know what life is; it knows much of the behaviour of a corpse—and asks, What is a sensible way of dealing with corpses? Religion knows what life is, and just what should be done to and with corpses. Neither proceeds on instinctive or innate lines; both proceed along historic lines. As infancy precedes man-hood, immaturity maturity, and ignorance knowledge, so it was as inevitable that religion should precede science as that magic should precede electric power.

Ours is a word-world; and for all of us the real world is the world we believe in. Names are but signs, the symbols of a reality they can never replace. Thoughts are true only to the extent that they are honest signs of sensible things in the world of reality. *Religious* thought can never be true thought, for it thinks of a supersensible, metaphysical world beyond reach of fingers and eyes. Religious thought is religion, and has no existence outside language.

Religion, then, is belief in insensible, insensate, invisible powers; action whereby such powers are appeased or controlled. And every religious belief in . . . began with a fear of . . . With the fear of death began the belief in souls.

## II

Reality for man, let me say again, is the world of his ideas, the world he believes in. But antiquity or universality is no proof of a belief's usefulness today. It may be the rankest kind of rationaliza-tion, thereby evidencing the fact that rationalization is easy and good reasons may be poor excuses, or at best palliatives for ignorance. In short, religion is not insanity, but it is born of the stuff which makes for insanity.

We speak of the "sting" of death; but it is we, mourners of a beloved one, who are *stung*. We get rid of the sting by robbing the grave of its victory. The problem our ancestors faced was not what is *death* or *why* did she die, but a prolonged emotional crisis. That crisis had to be resolved before they were fit for food or mates. Their visceral tensions had to be relieved before they could resume normal activities.

A splendid mausoleum and a noble casket are one way of re-lieving grief; a confident belief in reunion "over there" is another. Widows rarely die of grief, though they may lose many kilos be-fore their appetite is restored. They sometimes suffer delusion, their confidence or "reason" being thereby restored.

Delusions, like fever, are nature's remedies for alleviating the toxins of disease. Grief is a disease, as are anxiety, apprehension, worry—any unresolved emotional crisis arising from anger, pain, hunger, or thirst.

Now, an intolerable situation is not easy to live with, nor can it be lived with in comfort, tranquillity, and serenity until it is resolved. To our steadily rising tide of thwarted, prostrated, hypersensitive, bereaved, unloved, and childless, delusions come naturally and spontaneously—to compensate, reconcile, cure. Life thereby becomes tolerable again. Confidence is restored. Confidence in all higher animals is ease; lack of it, disease.

Comforting beliefs have biologic value. Yes; but where is the value in spending the night under the bed on hands and knees, under the delusion that one is a cat watching for mice? That thirteenth-century nobleman suffered from melancholia—why, Bartholomew does not tell us. Being a *cat* was his way of being *something*; it was a good delusion; it may have saved his life. At any rate, if one believes oneself a cat, one must behave like a cat.

That nobleman was disordered, diseased; his delusion that he was a cat put him at ease. Possibly many of our beliefs, attitudes, values, standards, habits, are of the stuff "mental" disorders are made of. It is certain that a large body of the beliefs of orthodox religion are of the stuff dreams and delusions are made of.

Every religion is, of course, *orthodox;* and all religions perform the function of delusion. Their business is to make life tolerable. Too often they devote their energies to making life intolerable for unbelievers.

Birth, marriage, death—crises. There are also unexpected crises of life, upsets which must be righted, insults avenged, hungers satisfied; crises without end—individual, family, tribal, national. The World War was a colossal crisis, not only for millions of homes but for all humanity; nor will any one now living see the end of it. Every war is a crisis, and too easily turns men into unspeakably murderous, butchering, burning, mutilating, ravaging, looting savages—like the very imps with which man fills his hells.

Anger, rage; blind, unreasoning, murderous passion. Jealousy which leads to murder. Hunger, for food or mate, which can drive to theft, murder, cannibalism, rape. Pain so agonizing that every muscle in the body is put in action. Fear—chattering teeth, knocking knees, skin cold and clammy and of the pallor of death; cowering, frightful, ghastly, sordid fears.

Fear of dying, of poverty, of disgrace; fear of hunger, disease, pain. Dread has driven man to fashion the sword which hangs over his head like an avenging Fate, like a curse. How escape the curse, how avoid the avenger?

Savings-banks, storehouses, hospitals, anæsthetics, and insurance provide escape from many of our fears. Savings in turn support almshouses, asylums, and prisons for those sunk in or beyond reach of fear. Religion supplies the escape for the most dreaded of all fears—death. But all that can be symbolized as Salvation can be laid at the door of our deepest nature, our viscera; they made man so afraid of failure that he lost interest in life itself and took refuge in the delusion that life here and now is a snare and a delusion. Faith in his belief that life is a snare discounted failure in life and calmed his fears.

Faith does for man what he cannot or will not do for himself. But his burden of wrongs, poverty, and defeats had to accumulate mightily before he felt that only bliss in a Golden City could square the account.

We are fearful of losing our powers, our virility, our manhood, our life—and other abstractions shed as normally as milk-teeth. No one has personal knowledge of dying. We do not know that dying is horrible or terrible, nor even that it is painful. But we have reservoirs of emotionally loaded ideas about death, which drive us to fear it, to fight to stave it off, to grieve and mourn the loss of friends, relatives, loved ones. We even release much energy in self-pity because we too must grow old and die.

To transform that emotionally overwhelming foreboding, with its lurking, ruthless fatality, the optimist has one way, the pessimist another, the spiritualist another; and primitive man had still another. Then there are Hindu, Moslem, Shinto, Buddhist, and hundreds of Christian ways, from the sleek bishop's to the gaunt ascetic's.

It was a long, hard job to lay the foundations of civilization; it required enormous energy. No animal naturally transforms energy more easily than man, but man could not build anything on a sick stomach; he had to have peace in the home, and enough serenity at all times to get from hands and brain what was required to provide for the home and make provision for the future. He had to be at peace with himself and in love with life to get enough work out of himself and enough joy out of his work to become the master builder of the earth. Before he could enjoy health and multiply in prosperity he had to get the habit of enjoying life. Health and joy then came naturally.

"The world is at an end for me," said Queen Victoria, broken-hearted over the death of her mate. Well, what does she do with her ended world—accept its end as a fact and prepare her own shroud? Not at all. She plays make-believe that it is not ended, that Albert has not "passed away," that he still lives and will return in an hour or so. And so for forty years she kept his room ever ready, had his evening clothes and fresh linen laid out every day. She kept the world from ending by pretending that Albert was not dead.

Not all mankind can play valet to an irreversible phenomenon, but it generally finds ways of reconciling itself to catastrophic losses, cataclysmic changes, and such emotional crises as upset routine habitual activities.

Emotional crises not only change routine habitual behaviour, they release floods of surplus energy; heightened activity becomes possible. Nerves tingle like power wires surcharged with bioelectric current. Result, figuratively speaking: the experience, whatever it was that provoked the crisis, is burned into the fibre of our body— "seared in our brain," as we sometimes say; something to be talked about for days or years or generations.

The ape is never quite free; it has its enemies, must be alert; but man, with his unique capacity to name his forest and endow natural forces with verbal symbols of voiced human qualities, desires, hungers, yearnings, and passions, soon becomes so enmeshed in his verbal or supernatural world that he cannot get out. Many of us, like the Indians in old Veddic hymns, waste our days on earth waiting for Varuna's heaven, "where loves and longings are fulfilled and all desire is satisfied."

Religion is made, not born; it is the creation of a disease meant to restore ease. It symbolizes human distress, and by hocus-pocus cures the symbols. That restores confidence and puts man at ease.

Hence the prayers, incantations, and rites which collectively represent man's religious response to his huge assortment of verbal and visceral, dreamed or imagined, ills, and his voiced and unvoiced, explicit and implicit yearnings and aspirations. Not knowing how to "cure" them by the sweat of his brow, or by staying in bed, or by frankly realizing his limited powers, he calls on Powers. The flesh is made whole by the spirit; the sensible is satisfied by the senseless; the sensual is spiritualized by denying its existence.

And the process whereby all this magic comes to pass has a thousand names—among which Christian Science rises first to mind. It may be Christian—Christians say it is not; in procedure and results it certainly is as far from science as is the African rain-doctor's "rain," or the Crow medicine-man's "cure" when his magic removes a quartz pebble from a sick child's stomach.

I can remove the snake from your boot with my hand—but only if you have faith in my hand. As the pen is mightier than the sword and the Voice mightiest of all, I can get your confidence in my voice more easily than in my hand. Faith cures are therapeutically useful and psychologically sound devices for curing snakes. But most of our "snakes" are misbeliefs, false inferences, illusions, unfulfilled wishes, visceral tensions, unsatisfied yearnings, etc. Failure, in short, to accept failure, and inability to get relief from our own powers, are the motors which drive us to Higher Powers.

Fear does not generate religion, but timidity drives man to whistle to keep up his courage lest fear paralyze his legs. Fear is disease. Beliefs which stifle fear and restore confidence are biologically useful, though not necessarily valuable to human society or to any one who is not a coward or a sinner.

III

This is a world of rain, snow, earthquake, volcano, storm, thunder and lightning, flower and fruit, grass and forest, cat and crocodile, snake and tiger, summer and winter, waxing and waning moon, sunlight and shade, day and night, babbling brook, sighing pine and rustling leaf. The world makes men shiver and sweat; it blisters their skin, freezes their fingers. It also sways and rocks under their feet, belches forth fire which runs down mountainsides like rivers; it washes away houses and crops, drowns their cattle. It snows them under, freezes them in, or crashes down upon them like an avalanche. It gives; it also takes away. Then there are gnats, flies, mosquitoes, fleas, lice. "The worm ate half the crop and the hippopotami ate the other half," the steward of an estate wrote his master thirty-three centuries ago. "The fields were full of rats, a swarm of locusts settled down and fed, the sheep also ate and the birds stole."

The world also speaks, in sighs, murmurs, moans, whispers, in lightning flash and thunderburst, in voice of storm and crashing trees, in thousand-ton boulders ripping, tearing down the mountainside. The moon plays hide and seek, and ever waxes and wanes; the sun has its own carryings-on; and there are eclipses. It is a living world.

It is an animate world that responds to every touch. Throw your voice at the wall, the wall throws it back; your face at the pool, the pool throws it back; your fist against the rock, the rock smashes your fist; thumb your nose at the lightning, it strikes you dead; defy the storm, it blows you flat. A very living world. Cross it, and it double-crosses you.

For ages this world talked to the animals, and they responded with heavier coats of fur, armour-plate, speedier limbs, etc.; also with sweat and shiver, seeking shade from blistering sun, shelter from blinding sleet and icy wind. But man, the talking, high-strung, highly sensitive animal, came, and began to talk back. And he used the only words he could find. With no trouble at all he could find a replica in nature and a symbol for every family virtue and vice.

Is Nature alive? He would have smiled at such a question. Any fool could see it was; one only had to stop, look, listen.

Even for us the brooks have not stopped babbling, the winds sighing, the waters laughing, or the sunbeams dancing. It is a changing world and physicists may say what they please about these changes, it is still a withholding or a bounteous world, or an avenging, cruel world. It smiles, beckons, frowns, blesses, and impoverishes, gives and takes away. In very truth are we of the earth earthy. And considering his first-grade teachers, it is no wonder that early man read himself into its every nook and cranny, its every sigh and groan—in short, that he endowed the world with human qualities and then created a god in his own image as the easiest and simplest way to account for everything. What science does with its formulas, laws, hypotheses—as far from complete yet as is the earth itself—religion does with the Word.

In its infancy religion was not religion at all; primitive man did not have enough voiced yearnings, his fears were too vague, his struggle for existence too precarious. He had to become a man of culture before he could add such a cultural luxury as religion to his overhead. He had to accept the world as he found it. It worked; he was content. Only later did he think it all out and devise rites, magic, "medicine," and incantations to keep it rolling along. Nature had her tricks; he had his. There were many powers; but, thanks to culture heroes, beneficent animals, etc., he also had powers. Jonathan Edwards' Heaven, Hell, Father, Son, and Holy Ghost were as far from early man's beliefs as Karnak, Vestal Virgins, and the Spanish Inquisition were beyond his practices.

Just what the earliest religious or magic practices were we do not know, but practices which can best be interpreted as magic appeared very early in human history. We cannot reconstruct the history of religion, for the same reason that we cannot reconstruct the history of language. The actual first steps left no footprints, or have been buried under the accumulated debris of the ages.

Certain phenomena, for obvious reasons, made a big appeal to early man's emotional nature. He was impelled to investigate them —as is the scientist today. He made certain preliminary guesses, drew certain inferences which seemed justifiable and inevitable— and then set his hand to such work as seemed appropriate. Not always did his guess or inference provoke his hands to action. The stars, for example, might stimulate him to invent a story; it did not necessarily follow that the "story" would impel him to "do something about it." Eclipse of sun or moon was another story; in many parts of the world "something" just had to be done. Even today we refuse to let an eclipse alone, although we no longer try to prevent or hurry it, or to assist sun or moon to escape the eclipsing monster.

Even in the infancy of the human race one group of phenomena put a great burden on the imagination and taxed man's ingenuity in thinking out "what should be done about it"—that group which today comprises the biologic sciences and which forms the background of medical schools and agricultural colleges. But whereas we emphasize the *bios* (life), the ancients were more excited about the *psyche* (soul), or, in Latin, *anima.*

We in our ignorance probably make too sharp a distinction between animate and inanimate nature; our ancestors made no distinction at all; in fact, they so animated all nature that primitive religion has been called *Animism.* In Tylor's epoch-making (and too oft forgotten) *Primitive Culture,* Animism plays the leading rôle; and of all the articles in the 10,000 pages of my twelve-volume *Encyclopedia of Religion,* few indeed are free from the direct or implied taint of Animism. And of the twelve volumes of Frazer's monumental *Golden Bough,* how many pages would remain if man in his divine ignorance had not postulated a soul and then felt that he just must do something about his own, or become one with the Creator of immortal souls? No other doctrine ever devised has had such far-flung consequences as the doctrine of souls.

*Los muertos mandan.* They do; their souls go marching on. Did Hamlet believe in ghosts? His creator certainly did; and clearly distinguished "honest" (by "St. Patrick") from "familiar" ghosts or devils. It even seems probable that Shakespeare had read Lavater's *Ghostes and Spirites Walking by Nyght.* No ghost, no Hamlet. Early man was no artist, poet, sculptor, mortician, magician, or priest, but when he invented ghosts ghostly things were in the offing; spirits generated spiritual values; and souls soon animated the universe from highest heaven to deepest underground.

And so a corpse became a job for the grave-digger, sculptor, painter, poet, metallurgist, carpenter, mason, stonecutter, musician, realtor; especially for the mourners, and for the medicine-man, shaman, diviner, divine, experts in souls. They put their *soul* into their work; the *spirit* deeply moved them. And if the soul is in danger of annihilation or lasting torment, there is still more work to be done, more jobs.

Well, what is a soul? I do not know. Shall we consult a wild woman of Borneo, a dictionary of folklore, Plato, or the Bible? But if we ask, what is a sneeze, we need go no farther than our family physician for light.

When mother sneezes, do you get her a pinch of soda or in a solemn voice say, "God bless you"? A Borneo mother does neither;

she knows neither soda nor God. But she knows souls and how they get away; so, when her baby sneezes, she cries out, "Soul, come back!" And the soul comes, and the baby lives! A Hindu carefully sneezes in the direction he wants to go; he would not dare walk away from his soul.

There are languages in which one's name is equivalent to one's soul. If such a tongue be mine, I shall be wary of trusting my name to possibly hostile hands. Some years ago the King of Dahomey would not sign his name to his letter to the French Republic lest President Carnot use it to bewitch him.

As the dead do not breathe, the soul must be breath, air, wind, life. How did life start? Some supernatural force or being *breathed* the breath of life into a clay body—so say half the known creation myths; the body thereby became a *living* soul or thing of wind. *Pneuma* in Greek and *spiritus* in Latin mean wind, soul. "Thou takest away their (beasts' and birds') breath, they gasp, and *return* to their dust." (The italics are mine, not the Psalmist's.)

A "little bird" tells; so Ecclesiasticus warns us not to curse the king or the rich in our bedchamber, "for a bird of the air shall carry . . . and tell the matter." Re-read the story of Abigail and David for a paraphrase of the idea behind "He's got all your souls in his box," said when an Eskimo group was photographed. The idea in Ezekiel that souls could be caught in handkerchiefs is put to practical use by Samoan sorcerers, who set snares around houses in order to catch the souls of the inmates.

Even if childish, uncritical man had nothing more substantial than dreams, he still could be easily convinced of the dual nature of living creation: that there are souls and bodies, and that souls can and do "live" apart from or independently of the body. But dreams have played such an important rôle in human history that we may well look at the outer and inner workings of the dreamer —at the physiology and psychology of dreams.

It is not yet safe to be dogmatic, but it seems probable that all dreams spring from unresolved emotional or visceral tensions. Not all dreams are "nightmares," nor should we expect them to be, for emotional stress and sleep are incompatible. The business of emotion is to prepare the body for *action*, not to relax it for *sleep*. But we rarely go to bed without some unresolved emotional problem—

from childhood's scary days, or from last week or today, or of a week or a month hence. We may even carry to bed such a weighty problem as the fate of our soul after death. We cannot, of course, solve that problem, because we cannot know the future, but it can plague us, torment us, haunt us, even put us in a cold sweat or keep us on the anxious seat.

Is the dreamer sleeping peacefully, like a child? Hardly. His muscles twitch, his fists are doubled up, he snarls, shows his teeth, mutters imprecations, cries out warningly, screams with fright; in short, he is almost pure animal. His cortex (organ of learned behaviour) has gone out of action—otherwise he could not sleep; he is solving some cultural emotional problem in the old animal way.

This means enormous activity in the subcortical nervous system. And so it is only natural that such a life-or-death struggle should wake the dreamer—to find himself bathed in the cold, clammy sweat of fear, or weak with the exhaustion that follows a fight-to-the-death struggle. Is it any wonder that such dreamers evoke terror in bedfellows? They do act as if they were "possessed"!

Do we remember such dreams? Do we ever forget them! But what do we do about them—consult a dream-book? Some do. Dream-books could be had in Rome, Athens, and by the waters of Babylon and the Nile; and they can be had today in almost any bookshop. Dreams keep cropping up throughout recorded history as signals for action, even for war. Dreams *meant* something! They do indeed; but, like the stars and many other natural and "psychic" phenomena, they have passed from the realm of the mysterious, occult, spiritual, supernatural, into the realm of things to be investigated without emotion, prejudice, or bias, but with brains, sense, and honesty.

The stock use made of dreams by students of primitive cultures was the "evidence" they gave uncritical man of souls, of immortality. But dreams themselves are uncritical—uncortical, if I may so say. Our criteria, or critical attitudes, are cortical, for the cortex is our organ of discrimination, deliberation. Dreams are careless, lawless, spontaneously uncritical.

And so it is that in our dreams we travel long distances, perform physically impossible feats, talk to friends long dead, and so on.

"Strange!" They are all that, let us admit. And how few of us like strange things or care to examine them closely or calmly. Primitive, fearful man probably would have been willing to let dreams alone, but dreams would not let him alone; they kept coming back. Whatever they were, whatever was to be made of them, they could only reinforce a conviction forced upon him by his infantile interpretation of certain other phenomena: that the body has a *soul*, a something which comes and goes in ways all its own, and which persists after the body has been fuel for fire or food for worms.

A full description of what that thing of uncritical thinking, asleep or awake, can do, of what it has done, of the rites and tribute that have been paid to it, would fill a thousand volumes and take us round the world and into every house and through every graveyard —and back to the time when man discovered that it was easier to speculate in words than to investigate with hands. Metaphysics began then and is far from dead yet, though its fruits have fertilized fewer fields than the dead. We may people our world with spurious entities and even work for them, but no soul has yet turned a wheel for man or lightened a human burden.

And note that neither as tribe nor nation, family nor individual, do we put away childish things as easily as Saul of Tarsus claimed he did. If we could, we should not so easily behave like gullible children. Suppose Saul really had put away his childish credulity: there would have been no St. Paul and Christianity might have been a saner and wiser force in the world. Paul was steeped in the debased Greek mysticism.

Souls are not so popular as they used to be, and ghosts are rarely seen; but countless candles are burning on the altars, and presumably will long after we are dead and gone. I think the weirdest sight I ever saw was a Chinese cemetery on All Souls' night. Myriads of lights flickered over the hillside like fireflies, as the ancestor-worshippers moved hither and yon searching for their particular family shrine, to burn incense, "stage" money, and sundry other worldly valuables.

This recurrent desire for immortality becomes the dominant passion of nations, especially in the East. Their whole span of life is regulated by this one idea. As Laufer says, the Chinese live merely to be buried, spending fortunes on their coffins and funerals, beggaring the living to enrich the dead. We no longer kill our wives, children, slaves, cattle, dogs, cats, and canaries that their souls may accompany ours to the spirit world, but the spirit world collects its tribute just the same.

IV

"Fifty million Frenchmen *can't* be wrong!" There *must* be "something" behind the spiritual world or so many hundreds of millions of human beings would not have been *moved* by it. There must be a Creator or there could be no creation! And that, for many even today, closes the argument. The religious is a Closed mind, hence the incredible number of religions. As Robinson says, from the endless disputes as to just what religion is there issues one agreement only: *Yours* is false! Paul knew that Peter was wrong; Luther denounced Erasmus; Calvin executed Servetus. There are eleven different Bibles, all canonical.

Words fail to describe us, but they suffice to build heavens and to devise innumerable ways of getting there without walking a foot or sweating a drop; and those who have no yearning for heaven, yet seek escape from reality, readily find it by creating an Eden or writing philosophy.

Even a superficial glance at the religious world shows certain general and practically universal beliefs: supernatural beings—fairies, gnomes, djinns, hobgoblins, gods, tree-spirits, etc.—who never were human beings but act superhumanly; a soul in every living organism—which may or may not be released or freed at death; superhumans—angels, saints, the Greek lesser gods, etc.; and the original creative Powers or fundamental sources of energy.

Certain religions (Christian, Mohammedan, Mormon, for example) stress the "fact" that they are *revealed*. So Mormons, Moslems, and Christians believe. They are so strong in that belief that they *know*. How do they know? The *Book* says so. But the Sioux is just as strong in his belief in a divine authority. He *knows*. How? A sacred buffalo told him. Tell him that buffaloes do not talk, and he replies, "Well, one did." Others got their "medicine" from an eagle, the sun, morning star, etc. They *know*. Theirs is a *revealed* religion, and their traditional beliefs are to them as truly the Word of God as are the Holy Writs of literate religions. Beliefs do not have to be set down on paper or engraved on stone to become the Word.

Nor is the distinction between animism and theism at all sharp or significant; nor even that so often made between monotheism and polytheism. Certainly Ikhnaton's hymn to the sun reveals a monotheism as pure as was the Jews' Yahweh, and far less anthropomorphic. Mohammedanism is theoretically monotheism, but Islam's world is crowded with saints, djinns, and peri. As Swanton points out, many American tribes—Iroquois, Ojibwa, Pawnee, for example—show strong monotheistic tendencies in their worship of the sun or sky. "Supreme" deities are also fairly common in Africa, and even among Siberian Primitives; nor is the idea unknown to the natives of Australia. We cannot say that Christianity is *pure* monotheism—or, judging by its works and dissensions, pure anything. Half the Christian churches of the world exhibit monotheism as a form of idolatry, Mariolatry often playing the leading rôle.

Nor does a map showing the distribution of the adherents of the great religions—Protestant, Catholic, Mohammedan, Hindu, Buddhist, etc.—tell us anything about the nature of religion. We are no more born Catholic or Hindu than we are born Elk, Mason, or Rotarian. We conform because conformity pays in social values. Conformity becomes orthodox, Right, Best, True; a habit, automatic. To me, a Conformist, you are a nonconformist in so far as "true" religion is concerned; and if my religion is soulful, you are a lost soul. It is the essence of religion that there can be only one "true" way—though bewildered Chinamen have been known to embrace several. Even a Chinese agnostic demands a Buddhist, as the Western atheist expects a Christian, burial.

Every religion says: There is a *way*—but you must *believe*. Some Christian sects add baptism. But baptism alone is not enough; there must be a credo. Nothing is more important. Even a Congo witch-doctor would not minister to an unbeliever. For believing in and "loving" God, the Christian Fundamentalist expects God to play wet-nurse to him for the rest of his days and give him a place in a heaven built on the plan of his desires. It is a marvellous system and easy to sell to trusting humanity. No wonder millions accept it and live lives that even from a gnat's point of view must seem dull and empty. Little wonder that we must go to graves to find out how people lived, what they were, what they ate, what life meant to them.

Religion can be anything because man can believe in anything that makes his wish come true—even though he has to work like a slave all his life for a reward "hereafter." In every religion is something of what Sapir calls man's never-ceasing attempt to discover a road to spiritual serenity across the perplexities and dangers of daily life. "Where the need for such serenity is passionately felt," he says, "we have *religious* yearning; where it is absent, religious behaviour is no more than a socially sanctioned form or an æsthetic blend of belief and gesture. . . . Religious sentiment is typically unconscious, intense, and bound up with a compulsive sense of values."

Attempt, spiritual serenity, dangers of daily life—what does that mean but an easy way to beat the game? Life—yours, mine, everybody's—is beset with perplexities and dangers, trials and tribulations. There are injustices, unrequited loves, empty stomachs, heart-burnings, growing and labour pains, accidents, earthquakes, thieves, vandals, wolves, scorpions, disease, and death. And the greatest of these is death.

How can *all* wrongs be righted, all insults avenged, death itself evaded, and immortal bliss attained? Only a perfect religion could furnish such a perfect prepaid perpetual insurance policy. Such have been written ever since man learned to write.

Primitive man could not write such a policy. He did not lean so heavily "on the Lord"; he resolved most of his problems with his own hands. He had to; there were no established church, great social injustice, or caste stratifications. His religion was primitive, but it was far less savage than the one Luther protested or Jonathan Edwards preached. No Primitive could consign his enemies or his infants to hell fire for eternity. Scalp them, yes, and burn them at the stake, or roast them for "long pig" and eat them; but to sink them forever in boiling oil and molten brimstone takes a monster with a mind so closed to the joys and delights this world affords, and to the realities of health and happiness, that it must be diseased and debased.

If primitive religion does not reach to the sky, at least it does not

stoop to hell. Only "higher" religions have hells. Let us look at one
—possibly the *original* and certainly as ingenious as any yet devised.
To look into this hell will also help us to see into the growth of
insane, monstrous ideas. In this respect the growth of Buddhism is
analogous to that of Christianity. It is "followers" who *found* religions; they "put their shoulder" to the wheel to help the good
cause—thereby helping to keep their own shoulders from the wheel.

This is a terrible world, said Buddha: sickness and sin, crime
and poverty, injustice, toil, trouble—everywhere; I'm sick and tired
of it. A king's son who had never done a day's work in his life!
Psychopathic, of course. A hundred thousand years of rebirth before he could become *purified*. Suicide would only prolong the
agony. How to beat the horrible game!

Legend says he sat with his head in his hands and turned the
problem over for *seven* years—contemplating his navel all the while.
Finally. . . . Eureka! He had it—a way to stop this foolishness of
being handed down as a worm or a man from one generation to
another for a hundred millenniums.

What was the *way*? Well, for one thing, it is now a topic of
Intellectual conversation in Los Angeles. But, curiously enough,
Buddha's way has no real hell, nothing suggesting everlasting torment—merely a final funeral pyre for purification purposes only, to
remove the last speck of dust from the soul's wings.

Some hundreds of years later that idea got to China. The Chinese
are clever; they know human nature, what the masses want. They
turned Buddha's final funeral pyre into hell. And a Tang artist,
says Laufer, painted it so hot that its sight made beholders sweat
and their hair stand on end, and butchers and fishmongers so
anathema they had to abandon their trades. That Hollywoodized
hell was really eight hells so subdivided that there were 128 separate
and individual hells, each a gem of fertile imagination. Sinners
spent only 500 years in each hell—but there were 84,000 of them!

What that Tang painter could accomplish with paint, a Christian
divine could do with words.

Hell ideas are easy to build up, hard to tear down. "Well, if there
isn't one, there ought to be." We proceed to invent one; and it is
no work at all to fill it. Hells are still being painted, with words
and in oils, all round the world—and, curiously, seem to follow a

more uniform pattern than do the heavens and paradises. Which means, I infer, that man finds it easier to agree on a plan of damnation than on one of salvation.

Religion, of course, is no more responsible for heavens and hells than Art is. Man is the responsible party—wonderful, wondering, fearful, hopeful man: the Don Quixote, the St. Francis, that are in us all, and also the Dominant Male who knows how to scare women and children out of their senses with Jacks-in-the-box.

Time and again a Voice has risen above the buzz of the masses to proclaim itself Son or Prophet of Infinite Power or Wisdom, spokesman of the Voice of the Universe, Creator of heaven and hell. And if it speaks with authority, it can generally make itself heard. As children we heard and learned to obey that kind of voice. If gorillas were to be miraculously endowed with speech and some particularly dominant male proclaimed himself Author of the Universe, he would be mobbed. But if he knew how to play on the hopes and fears of his congregation and proclaimed himself spokesman for that Author, he would get an audience; and by and by some believers.

We assume that we regulate our actions by our beliefs, and in a sense we do, but in a stricter sense our actions regulate our beliefs. We carry from childhood to manhood certain fairly settled ways of responding to our innate needs and acquired wants. Among these "ways" are our beliefs.

What is spoken of as an emotional or unscientific attitude is really a set of conditioned manual, verbal, and visceral responses to a set of emotionally conditioned stimuli, which in turn are a *credo*. In short, we believe with our whole "body and soul." Such beliefs are hard to shake or change because they involve emotional habits—feelings, strong feeling. Hence, as we shall see, centuries had to pass before man felt he dared take his beliefs in hand and examine them critically.

A few years ago I sat through a revivalist meeting down South. "All up for Jesus," shouted the Big Voice. I got up—as we do between halves of a game, even though we prefer to sit.

An important psychological principle which has played a big rôle in human affairs is involved here; mob psychology, it is often called. "No congressman can possibly be as big a fool as Congress," nor does a man easily become as savagely murderous as a lynching party or as cowardly as a panic-stricken crowd. It is the "last straw breaking the camel's back" principle; intensification or stepping up of stimulus, the *summation* of stimuli. A screaming child can excite us, but a screaming mob can send us crazy. Trained as we are to accept the verdict of society and to conform to its code of behaviour, we easily let go or revert to more unlearned forms when society—as mob, crowd, panic, lynching-party—lapses, "loses its head." Brain work, or higher cerebration, rarely issues from a mob. It does not need a brain; its behaviour is primarily emotional— easily moved, easily intensified, easily brainless. A mob, as mob, does not *create* panics of fear, murderous lynchers, or religious frenzies; it does intensify the primary kill-or-cure passions once they are let loose. A mob sweeps me off my feet, beyond limits I consider prudent; I thereby become an additional charge to blow you off your feet.

A group of mourners, for example, is a real group; the mingling of their grief draws them closer together, thereby affording better compensation for the loss of one of their members. Under heightened group stimulus, mourners often pass from tears to more violent forms of grief, wailing, tearing their hair, lacerating their flesh. At certain times and in certain places, veritable orgies of self-inflicted tortures became the customary norms of mourning.

A big church can make a big noise, a big emotional appeal; and every child joins. It is in a way the old story of mass production—which can so reduce the cost of salvation that, as Haldane says, a death-bed administration of Extreme Unction costs less than one of oxygen.

The principle of mob psychology, I think, helps to account for the savage excesses state religions often exhibit. If it is good psychology to excommunicate an unbeliever, it is better psychology to torture him and burn him at the stake. As worship of the emperor was once Rome's religion, it seemed only fitting that burning Christians should be a light to point the way to reason for those who withheld their adoration. By the same token the Afghan king, Habidullah Khan, two years ago decreed that anyone mentioning the name of his rival claimant to the throne should be nailed to a wall by the ears, and after all had seen him, blown from a gun.

Only state religions or states at war can be as inhuman as fiendish mobs. Religion and war are cousins under the skin, and though one may provoke great art and the other great discoveries, they function best when fear and hatred are released from honest, critical restraint.

A state, in short, can be as monstrous as an individual, and tends to be when it makes slogans or creeds objects of worship rather than social justice. When a man murders a pregnant woman and cuts out the fœtus and eats the throbbing heart, he is both insane and dangerous—and was of course hanged, in Bayreuth, about two hundred years ago. His *intent* was laudable, and if he had waited for two centuries he might have become an airman; his idea was wrong, because based on the belief that a diet of throbbing hearts makes one invisible, which in turn enables one to fly.

Monster? Yes; but no mystery about it. He took current beliefs—in souls, angels, throbbing hearts, etc.—and, adding them up, had a brainstorm which he believed would gratify his ambition. And he had the courage, if you please, to try out his scheme.

Europe and parts of the United States are still saturated with beliefs founded on false inferences, unsatisfied yearnings, unadjusted tensions, illusions, hallucinations, and spiritual cravings which do not stand the test of reason. We do not have to go to Australia to study totemism, to Africa for fetishism, to China for ancestor-worship, or to ancient Greece for a cult of souls. We can find them all in our own home town.

It is of the nature of religion to fall back on tradition; it is the business of education to train youth to understand tradition, so that the useful may be preserved and the destructive transferred from general circulation to special museums and libraries. Our educators are not minding their business. In spite of our Constitution and the plain intent of the founders of the Republic, ours is a religious state.

But it is equally true that no past age has seen so many children carry into manhood so few infantile longings, so much youthful fire. That is the spirit that is revolutionizing the world, that particularly makes this age worthy of its hire. Things undreamed of before are accomplished now because energy is spent on attainable things.

Indeed, we might say that the less man thinks of God the more

Godlike he becomes. When longing for Paradise is turned into working for Paradise the foundations will have been laid, and by the time our children's children are grown up it might easily have become the finest thing on this earth. And when better foundations are laid, it is common sense that will do the work. Man has already paid too much for inspirations, bowed down too long before voices from the grave, fed too many fakirs from the desert.

v

> The little wheel runs by faith,
> And the big wheel runs by the grace of God

runs the spiritual. To all God's "chillun," nothing runs by itself. What runs things? Science has one answer, religion another.

Science and religion started on equal terms, but religion soon got so far ahead that it almost cut the very earth from under science's feet. Science, having no place to go, nothing to investigate, nobody to talk to, and with no taste for theology or demonology, was forced to make a metaphysical world where nothing grew but words. But it could not live long or happily on words, and finally went to work for a living.

Our "Christian" world owes much to the fact that its real founder was steeped in Greek metaphysics, mysticism, and spiritualism. That unseen world of the spirit got more attention than the world of physical reality and human values. It was that word-world which for a thousand years men got excited about, took seriously, grovelled before, sweated for, venerated, worshipped, and died for in poverty, squalor, and disease. But it was the Spiritual, the Higher, Life.

Such behaviour was not inherent in Christianity alone; it inheres in every system which denies social values and ignores the plain evidence of the senses. Buddhism ran the same course; and there are today, sealed up in stone huts on the "Roof of the World," men who have been there for forty years. In all that time they have seen no human face, heard no human voice, felt the touch of no human hand. Once every fortnight food is placed within reach of what was once a human hand. There, amid inconceivable squalour and filth, these Tibetan hermits live the Higher Life. One was recently dragged out into the sunlight after sixty-nine years in a cave; he was bleached white as a corpse, even his eyes were colourless, and of course blind; his body had shrivelled to child's size. He died at once. He had escaped reality! So he had; but it was real food that had kept his little flame alive and a real hand that had brought the food to him.

It is not the original cost of the ideas of the Spiritual Life, but their upkeep. Somebody must gather the faggots to keep the Vestal Virgin's fire burning.

We live in a world which moves, creaks, groans, sobs, sighs, rumbles; has moods, is sad and gay; has emotions, passions, frightful outbursts of anger; is vengeful, resentful; gives and takes away, rewards and punishes, coaxes and cajoles. We call that world "nature"; and not infrequently personify it as Mother Nature.

What is nature—Mother, Father, or God? Or entelechy, Purposive Striving, Holism, or Creative or Emergent Evolution? Or is it Wakanda or Mana? Personally, I do not believe that we shall ever know what nature is, nor do I know of any reason why we should; but it is certain that more is known about many things today than ever before. This is so because the nature of many things has been investigated. No one knows what thunder is, or lightning, but General Electric knows enough to be able to roar like thunder and flash like lightning. In fact, it knows so much about electricity that it can generate it, control it, make it perform incredible labors. In short, General Electric knows enough about electricity to put it to work for human ends.

The *nature* of electricity is what man knows about electricity. To gain that knowledge—which is power—man had to stop wondering why it thunders and lightens, and begin to ask, what *is* thunder, what *is* lightning? And to make advance in answering these questions he had to be honest and impartial, keep cool, and use his brain. This did not mean that he never got excited about his problems; it did mean that he put his emotionally produced energy at the service of his investigating, rather than into his kill-or-flee, mechanism.

As one cannot kill thunder or easily escape lightning, any emotional attitude they might arouse, unless expended upon observation and experimentation, could only result in childish speculations, coloured by emotional slants, dreads, and fears, longings and yearnings. Thus, it would be easy to anthropomorphize: that is, interpret natural phenomena in terms of human feelings—wants, aspirations.

Where science admits ignorance or says, let us investigate, where it knows enough to do this or that, predict thus and so, is ready to revise the old in the light of the new, and to seek new ways of grasping realities, new ways of getting closer to the truth, religion must discover Cause, Finality, Truth, Purpose, God. It asks why, and so cannot discover how or what, but can and does discover gods, Powers, anthropomorphic beings, spirits, essences, souls. In other words, religion stops where science begins, and in finding God finds what science can never hope to find. Science aims at more truths, closer approximations; religion begins with the Truth.

Whether we look at Christianity or Judaism, Shintoism or Animism, we find anthropomorphism—power or powers which can be pleased or displeased, angered or placated; which reward or punish, give or take away. The religious spirit is the childish spirit; no Father, no religion—whether "Father" means God, as to the Christian; the sun, as to the Ojibwa; Wakanda, as to the Sioux; or Mana, as to the Polynesians. The fasting Indian on a lonely hill as surely hears his god's voice as ever did Mohammed or Moses, prophet or saint; and further, his religion is as "true," as inspired, as revealed and as authentic as was Paul's or Mohammed's. And if Paul's God is not an anthropomorphic being, the whole structure of angels, saints, and prophets is founded on less reality than dreams are made of. The voice of God is the voice of human hopes and fears. God's "inscrutable" ways are expressions of man's ignorance of nature's ways, or rationalizations of social injustice.

We cannot, or at any rate we certainly do not, know the truth about anything; nor can we know about things except as they are observed or "sensed," from their behaviour. What do they do? How do they behave? We know the nature of nature in so far as we know the nature of the things, beings, forces, energies, of nature.

Science asks: Is it necessarily so? Are these phenomena related in causal sequence? Are they genetically related? Is there a factual basis for this or that inference?

Religion says: I want, *ergo* I will have it; I believe, *ergo* it is; it ought to be, *ergo* it will be; it was said, *ergo* it must be so. Of such stuff is the religious spirit born, creator of gods to serve human desires. The nature of God is the nature of man. But the gods man relies on measure the limit of his reliance on himself. In other words, man may be known by the gods he keeps; civilization, by the gods it worships.

## VI

Last week I prayed for rain, a boy baby, and the death of my worst enemy; on Monday, the stork brought a boy, it rained all day, and my enemy was killed by lightning. That was a "good" prayer. Good for what? Make wishes come true. Do my prayers always come true? Then it was my fault. I lacked faith, didn't believe in prayer whole-heartedly enough, wasn't sincere, didn't have God on my side, didn't use the proper words; or it wasn't to my best interests to have the prayer answered, for God in his "infinite wisdom" always knows "best."

But if you "believe" in prayer, and pray for rain and it rains, how can I *prove* that the rain was not an answer to your prayer? I cannot. No one can prove that prayers are not answered. No one can prove that Joshua, by commanding the sun to stand still, did not save enough daylight to win his battle; nor can anyone prove that wars cannot be won today with God's help, or that rain does not fall in answer to prayer or by some other trick of magic.

And so it is that prayers are prayed, magic formulas or rituals are recited, magic rites are performed, somewhere on earth every second of the year, in the belief or hope that something will happen *because* of the prayers, rites, etc. *Post hoc, ergo propter hoc.*

As a matter of fact, most prayers are answered; and would have been "answered" without prayer, ritual, or candle. Man rarely calls on his god for more than he thinks the god will grant. Even a hungry, penniless Christian doesn't pray for a banquet here and now.

If I pray for rain and it doesn't rain, there is nothing more I can do about it except offer up more prayers; no frenzy of mine will *force* the rain. But my frenzy will heighten my capacity for thanksgiving when at last the rain does fall. I have seen Indians break out in copious tears of joy when their rain-making magic "made" the rain fall. If, on the other hand, I have prayed for strength in a certain undertaking where success depends on strength, my prayer will have energy-yielding power—if I am a *true* believer. As belief in success has biologic value, so prayer to the believer has therapeutic value. Failure in itself is hard enough to bear, but to have our faith in our god shaken is real calamity. And so we may break our record in some critical endeavour when we have called supernatural powers to our aid.

If I depend on magic for success, I must see to it that it is good, authentic, "true" magic, and then get behind it with might and main and *prove* that it is good.

We are warned to be careful of our childhood wishes lest they come true to plague us in our old age.

Given a world of unseen, unknown powers—and such was the world of early man—what was the best way to cope with, defy, outwit, those powers? That was man's problem then, and is now. We of today are only fairly successful. Certain diseases still baffle medical science; certain "powers" of the air still make air transportation hazardous. Ships, trains, and automobiles are still subject to wreck. We do our best, as we say, and strive eternally by experiment, by try and try again, to lessen the hazards of living. We solve air, sea, and land transportation problems by appealing to science; we put our trust in the findings of certain sciences, and build our craft accordingly.

Primitive man built his craft with craftsmanship and called on magic to see that it was good. Look, for example, at a South Sea Islander building a canoe. He must put a lot into it; it will mean much in his life. It must be fast, steady, strong, beautiful, for, as Malinowski says, it is more than a canoe: it is a means (and vital) to an end (life itself). He does not trust Lady Luck to get him home through angry seas; he builds a seaworthy boat, and thinks nothing of a thousand-mile sail.

Our Islander hunts the forest over and chooses his tree; cuts a little hole in it, then feeds the tree-sprite some food: "Come down, O wood-sprites, dwellers in branches, come down, come down; eat; then move to some other tree and be at ease."

How do they *know* there are tree-sprites? They have *seen* them! Some trees are full of them. They are brown-skinned, long-haired, and have long beards. They often come at night and scare people. They can be heard wailing through the branches. They even come to houses and steal food.

*I give. Be not angry; go elsewhere and be happy.* An ancient formula for little imps; it takes the curse out of the tree.

After the tree is felled, more rites follow—to make the log lighter, swifter: "I lash you, O tree. The tree flies; the tree becomes like a breath of wind, like a butterfly, like a cottonseed fluff." That is a *ritual*, a trick; a piece of property also that may be transmitted, traded, sold. It is a secret, handed down from tribal lore—"whence these songs and traditions." Another rite causes the canoe to "make up its mind to go fast"; and there are other rites for carving, sail-making, etc.

This is not hocus-pocus. It is sacred, holy, supernatural, magic—magic power. It puts magic power into that canoe, so that it will ride out the storms, go like the wind. We still "christen" battle-ships—with "pop."

Magic makes the canoe go faster, but the real magic was human nature playing that it could defy the storm, beat the gale at its own game. Work? Of course not. The sheer play of competitive sport for its own sake.

Mightiest magic-maker, wonder-worker, and thimble-rigger is the Word. Had I dared whisper "Holy Ghost" when a child, I should not have been surprised to be struck dead. I was afraid of it; it was *wrong* to utter it.

What is right? Anything I do with my right hand. My right hand becomes so habituated to manipulating certain things that I handle them through sheer "second" nature. That makes the things I handle "right." We are a "righteous" people, as Ingalls points out, because our ancestors were *right*-handed. We can solve some problems with both hands, but most of our problems require close observation, and one, the right, hand came to be used more than the other. Why is not known. Our ancestors put more meaning into the superiority of the right-handed way of doing things than we do. For most things they used the right, for certain things the left hand exclusively.

"For he hath done marvellous things: his right hand hath gotten him the victory." Rarely do we ask what is in the left hand, for, being human as we are, we do not always let the right hand know what mischief the left hand is up to. The right "wing" is generally in power; the left is generally Red. But do not offer your left hand to your Moslem friend!

Rivers, investigating a South Sea tribe, learned the words for "dead," "living"—*mate, toa.* One day, while orderly preparations were going on for a burial, he noticed one old woman behaving in an unusually lively manner: she was the "corpse"! As she was valueless to the community, she ought to be dead; for all practical purposes she was *mate,* so they buried her. "Death" means whatever is customarily meant at a particular time and place. The old lady was "dead"; quite *right* to bury her. In parts of Scotland, to spin with an unburied corpse in town would be *sinister* (left-handed), not *right.*

Not only was I not to utter "Holy Ghost"; I was not to take the Lord's name in vain, even in thought. There was magic in that name; it must be used for magical purposes only. "He" would be personally offended—as we all are when our name is desecrated, bandied about lightly. A boy was burned to death under Henry VIII because he had written down some names he had heard used in connection with the sacrament.

Even hard-headed Herodotus did not dare mention the name of Osiris—often mentioned in the pyramid texts as *The Word.* Orthodox Jews do not call Yahweh by name. And the "Lord" said unto Moses, thou hast found grace in my sight and I know thee by name. Revelation speaks of "names of men seven thousand" as having been killed in an earthquake.

What's in a name? A soul, something mysterious, supernatural power. To have men's names is to have power over their souls. And there are mothers on earth today who would almost as soon trust their child itself to a stranger as its name—or its finger nail, or a lock of its hair, or its photograph.

Every language, as we saw, has its grammar; but *our* categories of things and their attributes, persons and their actions, functions, relations, substances, causes and effects, are *ours.* These twentieth-century categories no more coincide with the categories of former times than are our chemical "elements" the elements the ancients knew. But the pin a bare foot picks up in the dark can be damned today as easily as ever. Our tendency to "curse" things is the work of the same old human nature which could find evil in anything or anybody that scared it.

We may say in general that one or other of the following four principles is behind all superstitions and magical practices:

*Contagious* or sympathetic magic: Love me, love my dog; what hurts my dog hurts me; to take my name in vain disgraces me; to injure my food, nail parings, hair clippings, or my shadow, etc., injures me.

*Homœopathic:* Like cures like, also kills; "kill" an enemy by killing his picture or wax image; make rain by sprinkling water, sunshine by kindling a fire; fertilize field, cattle, or woman by exposing naked women to men.

*Telepathic:* No knots in the house of an expectant mother, lest the unborn child get entangled in the umbilical cord; wives whose husbands are at war or on a hunt must not oil their hair, lest their husbands slip; Moses sets up pole and brazen serpent, to cure the fiery serpents of lust.

*Doctrine of Signatures:* The Essence, Soul, Spirit or "Reality" of things can be extracted by means of charms, incantations, hocus-pocus, and then transformed or wielded for purposes of curing or cursing.

Behind the magic—rite or ritual—is a belief. Use lots of words to express the belief, and you have a myth. The myth then becomes commentary, warrant, charter, guide to behaviour—a Bible. It supplies motives for ritual and moral actions, and also rules for the game. A precedent stated or formalized in myth and rite constitutes an ideal.

Magic revealed in myth, rite, or ritual is infinitely varied. We may expect to find it accompanying any form of behaviour in which pure "chance" or accident is likely to play a *big* rôle, thereby keeping us hanging between hope and fear. Hence the ready sale of "rabbits' feet" to athletes and gamblers. What is a rabbit's foot, horse shoe, rosary, cross, relic, amulet, lucky piece, or hair from the dog that bit you? Magic, pseudo-science; and still employed in war, love, disease, wind, and weather. It makes for confidence, bodily poise, and mental integrity, and is a magic cure with real therapeutic value in despair, worry, anxiety, fear, enmity, impotent rage, and unrequited love.

But at what a price!

As old human emotional nature makes all religions possible, so religion can call out man's finest handicraft, as well as its humanest thoughts and foulest deeds.

Astrology, necromancy, palm-reading, crystal-gazing, fortune-telling with cards, dice, tea leaves, etc. Our bookstores carry all the latest methods of reading fate. Charlatans readily find soft spots in human credulity and know what to say and do. "Dope" sheets on Wall Street or the races are bad enough, but "dope" on the outcome of a future event which depends on a million unpredictable variables is more than gullibility: it is plain Simple Simon ignorance.

Yet for thousands of years man has been consulting everything from stars to entrails for omens, seeking signs, looking for portents, and importuning oracles from Apollo to the latest, fattest "medium."

An African witch-doctor will sit down before an outspread leopard skin, sing to the spirits, sound his musical bow, and jerk an indefinite number of small seeds from a gourd. Now the fun begins. He counts out the seeds in tens. If they come out even tens, he puts them back in the gourd and throws again; again counts, and if there is one left over, that is *bad*; two, doubtful; three, good; four, good for a woman, bad for a man—if he is sick he will die; five, good; etc.

Sounds a little like Fan-tan, as played in Macao.

Watch a Chinaman get the "dope" on the races. He goes into the joss-house and up to the table in front of the God of Luck. There he drops a coin in the box, lights a joss stick, and prays. Then from a bamboo holder he picks a random number of long flat bamboo splints, which he drops on end on the table. He is drawing lots. Each splint is two-faced, and from the lie of the splints he finds the right horse.

Suppose the "right" horse drops dead?

Generally we blame it on ourselves. The "medicine" was all right, but we did not take enough of it, or too much, or our spirit was bad, or our faith too little. But when an African witch-doctor's rain-maker idol fails him, he kicks it and burns it up. He cannot afford to appear to be the inefficient party.

Culin, in his *Korean Games*, held that all modern card games went back ultimately to Chinese dominoes, which in turn were once bamboo slips, derived from the markings on feathered cere-monial arrows used in divination. It is certain that devices such as dice, knuckle-bones, etc., for divining, were invented early. Dice from a Second Dynasty tomb, in size, shape, and markings, would still shoot craps or show the will of Fate.

What stupendous energy man has put into guessing the will of the gods he called into existence to mask his ignorance and make life safe and easy!

VII

As sex, after food and life itself, is man's chief concern, it was impossible, as Leuba points out, for it to keep clear of religion or free from magical practices; and as magic and religion are the ways of ignorance to maintain and enhance life, we may expect a literature of supernatural even more imposing than that of natural sex activities. In fact, this literature is so enormous and reveals such varied and close connexions between sex and religion, that some have maintained that religion is rooted in sex. And so it is, to the extent—and to the extent only—that sex is a fundamental need of man. But man has other needs no less fundamental, though none which can be so aborted, debased, depraved, or can so easily de-throne reason and common sense. The mere fact that reproduction is bisexual, however wild its interpretation, must have been a powerful incentive to speculative manipulation, which in turn led to magical practices.

The complete secularization of sex is for us still in the distant future, for mysticism is mysticism and the autoerotic easily turns mystic and becomes fit for a "pure" life only. All of which pro-longs the superstition that sex is mysterious and prevents our sens-ing the incongruity of worshipping a God of Love while sanctifying the perfection of chastity and continence.

It is such addled thinking that justifies the brute in a father who kills his daughter to save her "honour," or forces an unmarried woman to proclaim herself the spouse of a spiritual lover, or the wife of a priest, or both Virgin Mary and God.

As Elijah mocked the prophets of Baal, saying, "Cry aloud, for he is a god: either he is musing, or he is gone aside, or he is on a journey," peradventure our God of Love sleepeth and should be awakened. At any rate, he is a non-functioning deity these days, and cannot reign again until the God of War is dethroned.

Despite the fact that we are today closely knit by a common language and through newspapers, magazines, movies, and radio, we each live in a different world. But what a gulf between our worlds and those of St. Paul, Homer, Sargon, Adam and Eve!

A prostitute, for example, to us is one kind of animal; to the ancient world, quite another kind—in fact, she was not a bawdy woman at all. She was an instrument of magic—and sacred. Let us see.

Our Sioux Indians used to "marry" a woman to a bull buffalo—ceremonially, of course. Such "marriage" was once a fairly widespread practice. In Tudor England, a sleek white bull that had never been yoked was led by singing monks in a procession, through shouting crowds and accompanied by women stroking its sides, to the monastery gates. The bull was then dismissed, and the women entered the church and paid their vows at the altar of St. Edmund, kissing the stone and with tears entreating the magic power for fertility.

There we have one of the earliest forms and most widespread connexions of sex with religion—the worship of the Procreation Power in whatever animal or god embodied it.

Our Old Testament repeatedly witnesses the fact that prostitution was pleasing to Yahweh. Profane prostitution in Europe probably sprang from organized sacred prostitution; brothels are still spoken of as "abbeys" in some parts of Europe. Queen Joanna of Naples founded such a house in Avignon; it was regulated like a religious house, closed on Good Friday and Easter, and admitted only Christians. Julius II, by papal bull, instituted a similar brothel in Rome. The inmates of Japanese *yoshiwaras* are in a sense *sacred* prostitutes.

Those sacred marriages of women to gods, those holy prostitutes, and the sexual orgies that characterized the worship of Ishtar, Venus, and Aphrodite, were not marriages or prostitutions or "orgies": they were fertility rites—more children, more crops, more cattle, more buffaloes; and for Japanese and European peasant girls, a dowry, so that they could marry and have children.

What do we men do when the stork hovers nigh? Beat a drum, and join the other members of the Superior Sex at the village club-house, where we rinse our mouths with ginger beer and perform other antics to fumigate ourselves against the dreadful infection the newborn has brought to town? Well, if we did, we should be less foolish than fathers who follow the *couvade* system.

Under that widespread system, the wife labors and then goes about her business—which, for a few weeks, is to wait on her husband while *he* recovers from the pangs, discomforts, and im-purities attendant on childbirth. That is male dominance carried to a logical conclusion.

How the early Church Fathers hated women! "Sack of dung"; "temple above, sewer below": these were common characteriza-tions. To Tertullian, woman was more than "impure"; she was the "gate of hell." Clement of Alexandria thought every woman ought to be filled with shame at the very thought of being a woman. Some of them are—and are often sent to the asylum. But where could those Fathers be sent if hell were abolished?

One world-religion, as Bölsche says, relegates the love of the senses to hell and sends the naked body after it; another world-religion elevates the emblem of sensual life to an object of venera-tion and worships it accordingly. Only state or world religions can achieve zeniths and nadirs of fatuity.

Phallic worship is rarely found among Primitives, only among the "higher" civilizations—Egypt, Greece, Rome, India, Japan, and Christian Europe. Primitive man seems to have used his powers wisely and well; he had no need to resort to magic. Children came, anyway, and on their own, as it were. Besides, the act of inter-course itself brings perfect adjustment: physiological relaxation, in-difference. Hence the almost universal belief that it is weakening, and the endless taboos against the act for warriors, etc.

Phallic worship, or Priapism (Priapus, son of Dionysus and Aphrodite), does not imply sexual licence or prove depravity or degeneracy. It is, rather, a sign meaning "Children wanted." When a Japanese prostitute deposits a paper prayer with a small coin in the god's gift-box, she is not praying for carnal pleasure but for customers. She needs money—for a sacred cause. The ancient Egyp-tian or modern Italian woman is not praying for pleasure but for children. Children she must have. The husband's rôle is merely that of accessory, a vehicle for the divine or magic power.

Hamilton, in his *Worship of St. Cosmo and Damiano*, describes a festival (1780) of these two saints in Isernia, attended by a large number of women. Wax phallic emblems were hawked about in baskets. Each woman bought one, and offered it, with prayer, money, and thanks, to a canon of the church seated at a table. She was not worshipping Priapus; she was worshipping the powers that send children.

If the charms worked and prayers were answered, why can't wax phalli still be bought in Isernia? For the same reason that mixed bathing and phallic emblems are hard to find in Japan today. Public opinion; in both cases from the outside world; shame. But women still kiss St. Cosmo's big toe in Naples, and his renown for curing sterility may outlast his statue or his bones in the reliquary. Plenty of "emblems" can be found in any big museum: in the British Museum, for example, the actual prayers offered at Isernia; and in the Women-and-Children-Forbidden hall of the Naples Museum, Priapus himself in bronze.

The worship of Priapic saints survived in France into the sixteenth century, Sts. Pothinus, Guerlichon, Gilles, Réné and Regnauds being the best known. The wooden phallic images used in the rites were anointed with wine, which, when scraped off, was used as a fertility decoction.

In other words, phallic worship runs true to form: to fulfil a want or cure a "disease," one makes a symbol of the want or disease and then does something to or with the symbol.

If a fertility rite can increase a crop of children or of corn, why shouldn't the mere presence of a sterile woman sterilize a cornfield? It does. In Uganda a sterile wife is not allowed to enter one; she would cast a "spell" over it.

Just what a baby is no one knows. But every infant is a new and positive stimulus; something must be done about *it*, and with the baby. Then there is the "after-birth," which often causes more trouble than the baby itself. What is a placenta? A "cake," as the Greeks said; the container of the double of our immortal soul, an "egg" laid by the moon which hatches into a baby; or just a bit

of magic, some mysterious thing? It has been called almost everything under the sun, and has raised almost as much fanciful speculation as Old Sol himself.

Think of the appallingly long and varied list of idiotic beliefs
and crazy practices because of the simple fact that woman has her
periods, the moon hers, and that both form cycles of twenty-eight
days. Hence the euphemism, woman's lunar cycle.

These crazy notions die hard. Isn't it almost incredible that there
was a serious correspondence in the *British Medical Journal* not
very long ago, as to whether *a menstruating woman could cure
bacon*? The doctors agreed that the belief that she could not was
universal in England, but disagreed as to the *facts*. Some said she
could, but one, a Fellow of the Royal College of Physicians, was
certain she could not, cure bacon. "None but an Australian black
would deny it!"

In all outdoors Pliny could find almost nothing so "monstrous"
as a menstruating woman: her look would kill bees in their hives,
rust iron and steel—even brass, and make dogs mad!

Even expectant motherhood, somehow, somewhere, gets into
every magic picture. Pregnancy, of course, is just as natural a phenomenon in human lives as death itself; yet man has buried the
expectant mother under a load of fictions, taboos, rites, and lunacies, which, heaped up, would rival the Himalayas in height, fright,
and inaccessibility.

Samples of the power of the gravid uterus to addle the brains of
men may easily be found in our own Book of Books. To the writer
of the sacred book of Zoroaster, a menstruating or child-bearing
woman is a "fiend"—worse than devils, for she can smite with a
look. *Ergo*, she must not look on fire or on water—that would be
pollution of two *sacred* things; nor may she talk with a man. No
fire is to be kindled in the house; all firewood must be removed
and the floor sprinkled with dust (in the name of "purity," of
course). Her food must be cooked separately; any worn clothes
must be destroyed. And the poor woman herself must be "purified"
by being washed with bull urine.

Into the further vagaries of human sexual activities when withdrawn from natural and social control by the hand of superstition,

we cannot go here. Possibly we have already gone so far as to obscure the main issue, which is this:

Sex inevitably forced itself on "thinking" man. Man in the infancy of the race was a child in thought, and jumped at conclusions. Knowing nothing of the endless and infinitely complex processes whereby life in plant- and animal-world reproduces itself, it was inevitable that man should make a mystery of what is really a complex of mysteries, the solution of which is yet far from perfect. And to make a mystery of any process, thing, matter, or power is to withdraw it from critical observation, for it is the essence of mystery to mystify.

The mysteries of birth and death, of winter and summer, are enormously mysterious. To ascribe such mysteries to magic or supernatural power is to turn them loose for emotional, uncritical, biassed manipulation, which easily and rapidly transcends all bounds of reason and becomes an uncontrollable perpetual motion machine, as it were. It runs wild; it becomes abhorrent, unnatural, debased. Hence the, to us, idiotic "marriages" of women to incredibly ridiculous objects and beings; hence the unlovely sacrifice of virginity on every conceivable altar and to innumerable gods—generally understudied by a priest in full flesh; hence the monstrous idea that virginity or celibacy is pleasing to the gods and sexual activity the root of all evil. Not all religions went so far. In fact, no religion could reach that height of absurdity until it had developed a taste for inspiration and was ready to support a class of inspired prophets —super- or hypo-sexed mystics.

Thousands of superstitions, magic rites, religious practices and entire mythologies are explicable only as we realize that there is no force of nature that cannot be made mysterious, no mystery that cannot be solved in terms of mystery. As a Pawnee said to a missionary, "The corn is the same to us as Jesus Christ is to you." And if Eros is a god, there must be ways of securing erotic magic. Our drug stores sell it; there are abundant references to it in Vergil, Ovid, and Horace. In fact, the "secret" is known to all mankind. But nowhere is it to be had for nothing. Altruism, the quality that once had so much power to work wonders, ceases to be a virtue when religion makes a mystery of life and love.

## VIII

"Out, damned spot!" Just a little blood. But, as Mephistopheles said to Faust, blood is *ein ganz besondrer Saft. Saft*: that is the kind of *juice* blood is—mysterious. It was not the blood that provoked Lady Macbeth's cry of horror, it was the mystery of it; it might *curse* her. For blood is life, as we learn in Deuteronomy. We may eat the flesh; we are warned not to eat the life with the flesh. But a Roman woman suffering from epilepsy might, on the dying gladiator's cry, *Ave! Cæsar, morituri te salutant,* rush up and drink of the life-giving blood gushing from his wounds. To rejuvenate himself Louis XI is said to have drunk the fresh blood of children.

Gods in man's image are accredited with superhuman powers, but they have very human tastes, ambitions, passions, and frailties— and so can be fooled as easily as man can be foolish. Hence man often treated his god like a child and took away his candy; and as man himself is easily pacified, he found pacifiers for his gods.

Bloodthirsty man makes bloodthirsty gods, and, conversely, downtrodden worms in human guise demand immortality, omnipotence, omniscience—behind pearly gates in a city of pure gold.

How does one do business with superhuman beings or supernatural powers? One pays. Even electrical power is not to be had for nothing. Every good god or evil power is a symbol of something that can give or withhold, bless or curse, and must be treated accordingly. Wars especially make bloodthirsty demands, and are always made in some sacred *name*—God, Patriotism, Honour, even Peace! We find bloodthirsty gods by the hundreds.

Human beings and human blood have been sacrificed to promote crops, success in war, love, and business, to make strong the foundations of temples, palaces, houses, lodges, and ideas. Any idea will do; almost every idea has served. The victims vary from enemies to friends, hags to virgins, children to the king himself. By roasting, boiling, impaling, flaying. Blood flows through human history like a crimson river.

The food quest, however, is far older than any idea of sacrifice; human flesh always was, and always will be, a possible answer to a gnawing stomach. Human beings were sacrificed to human, before they were sacrificed to spiritual, stomachs. But once the idea of sacrificing human beings to spirits, gods, God, or to Magical or Spiritual Powers, got started, it easily grew into a vast cultural blood-sacrifice complex.

Man takes as readily to "long" as to "short" pig, if his taste runs in that direction. And it can. For 30,000 years not a century has been free from cannibalism. Hunger has always been the best sauce; dire hunger, rather than a finicky stomach, has driven men literally to try anything. If it tastes good, if it satisfies, a new taste has come into existence, a new dish upon the market. Roughly speaking, that principle is behind every menu, every altar, every work of art, and every form of sexual gratification.

Look at that crowd of dusky natives dancing and crowding around a human torso roasting on the grill. Human sacrifice, magic power, superstition? Not necessarily; they may be dancing for sheer joy, working up an appetite for a gorge.

Central Africa until recently reeked with the blood of humans, sacrificed, we should say, to a "depraved" taste. They liked it. Wild game abounded, but human game was easier to catch. The Australians also sacrificed human beings for their stomach's sake, and with no other idea. But most South Sea Islanders combined business with pleasure, so to speak. A Fiji chief would eat his wife if she displeased him, and his enemy for whatever virtue there might be in him.

Animals, under stress of hunger or strong emotion, will eat their young. But man alone has found *taste*, backed by crooked thinking, excuse enough to make cannibalism a practice and human sacrifice pleasing in the sight of God.

We drop a thin dime in the offering box. If ours is a bloodthirsty god we shed a drop of blood: hence blood-letting in general, by flint knife or finger nail. But if our god demands flesh and blood, it need not be a pound; an ounce will serve. Hence the widespread rite of circumcision, by which a few drops of blood and a little bit of unnecessary foreskin are sacrificed.

While circumcision is a form of *human* sacrifice, it may well also be, as Lehner argues, a symbolic sacrifice to the generative powers. At any rate, the bloodthirsty god is "satisfied," the victim is soon as good as new, and fertility reigns. Female circumcision (a cut along the clitoris) Loeb thinks is probably a late form of blood sacrifice and limited to parts of Africa.

Male circumcision in one form or another was an almost worldwide custom; it is today the recognized practice throughout the Mohammedan world, and is the "tribal badge" of the Jews. While the rite today is a *relic* of an ancient sacrificial rite, various reasons have been proposed to account for it—hygiene, for example. Mosaic law does talk much of purification and cleanliness. But animals in nature are naturally clean, and if not clean they are pure. Man started the cleanliness idea and Leviticus is mostly ways to keep clean—but it is all *ritual* cleanliness. As Loeb points out, it is as far from *hygiene* as a rusty knife is from a surgeon's scalpel.

Still more fantastic is the idea that circumcision arose from man's desire to prepare youth for sexual life, correcting a mistake of nature, as it were. If nature made one-tenth the mistakes about the business of sex that man does, we might all become St. Basils. Nature needs less correction and more observation.

In Central America the blood of the circumcised victim was spread on the idol's mouth; in Fiji, the foreskins were placed on graves or in the temples. Mexicans and Peruvians got immunity for all within by rubbing human blood on their door-posts—as we may infer from Exodus xii, 22, the Hebrews once did. But Yahweh finally forbade the use of human blood; lambs' blood became just as efficacious.

The Old Testament abounds in explicit directions for various bloody rites of sacrifice or expiation—to avert death, defeat, plague, etc. The Abraham-Isaac incident illustrates the Hebrew obsession that they ought to sacrifice their first-born to their jealous God. The Gezerites regularly sacrificed their first-born—as witness the many tiny skeletons crushed into jars and found buried under the shadow of sacred stones. The Canaanites burned "even their daughters" to their gods. Moab's king, facing the defeat of his army, gave his son for a "burnt offering on the wall." The Carthaginians, to propitiate Baal and save their city, sacrificed two hundred children of good families. Achilles sacrificed twelve noble Trojan youths to appease the soul of his dead friend.

Our Aryan ancestors were cannibals and freely fed the flesh and blood of human beings to the bloodthirsty maws of their deities.

Human sacrifice existed in Sweden up to 1350. Not till 97 B.C. did the Romans abandon the practice of sacrificing human beings when distress threatened the state. Augustus is said to have had three hundred noble Persians immolated on the altar of Cæsar, his great-uncle.

Blood taboos are thicker than flies across the pages of history. Blood *is* mysterious. Cain kills Abel—and Abel's blood's voice cries to Yahweh from the ground; the blood sinks into the earth, but the earth does not like it and so informs Yahweh. Blood must not be drunk because it is still living—like a soul; or it is drunk and one thereby gets whatever of virtue there was in it while it was the flesh.

One of man's earliest recorded ideas is that of the imprint of a human hand in red on the wall of a French cave. One finger has lost a joint. Just what particular idea cut off that joint, and what spirit appreciated the imprint of that red hand, we do not know. We do know that carved human bones have been found in ancient graves in almost every part of the world. Magic, spirit control of one sort or another, or just trophies? Trophies hang on the walls of huts, houses, castles, palaces, even on altars and walls of churches. And what cathedral in Europe is without its reliquary?

Why collect skulls? Power; the kind that knowledge is supposed to be and the kind that makes for magic. I may think myself powerful, but with your skull in my house I have additional power—especially if you were powerful. In other words, a skull is one thing to an anatomist, another thing to a head-hunter, and a drinking-cup to a Tibetan monk.

Head-hunting is still an outdoor sport in the Balkans, and was once common in Great Britain; traces of it persisted until recently. The Fitzgeralds collected the heads of the slain on a Leinster battlefield, and the Moss troopers of the Scottish marshes decorated their castle walls with the enemy heads they brought home on their saddlebows.

Murderers in Prussia and South Italy have been known to eat part of their victims to conciliate their ghosts. And it was not so long ago that a Scottish fisherman would think twice before he tried to save a drowning man or hook a corpse from the water; the "Poseidon" of the North might resent losing a sacrifice and demand a new victim! Which means that one does not "drown," but that a water-god has claimed a sacrifice. Recall Mark Twain's Missourians feeding the Father of Waters a loaf of bread loaded with mercury, to tempt him to disgorge a human corpse.

Possibly the future will find our World War, with its millions of victims, the most iniquitous and futile blood sacrifice exhibition in all human history.

## IX

Categorical imperatives begin with primitive taboos. When a fast-thinking medicine-man learns the trick, he soon has a complete armoury for compelling obedience. He is on the road which ended with an Emperor-Pope.

What happens when I break a taboo? It all depends. If I am a Zoroastrian, I commit a horrible crime and am properly and publicly flogged. The Jews do not deny themselves pork because they do not like it or because it might injure their health, but because it injures a particular food taboo—pork is "unclean." One can't keep clean by eating unclean food; one can become godly by eating the Eucharist. The Egyptians ate the wafer after it had been consecrated to the sacrament of the resurrection of Osiris. The Grand Lama of Tibet celebrates the sacrament with wine and bread.

As primitive man in many parts of the world looked upon some animal as his ancestor or source of power, he naturally regarded himself as being of the same flesh as that animal or totem. The totemic animal was rarely used as food, but the ceremonial eating of the totem became an essential practice in totemic societies. The Jesuit missionaries in Canada were struck by the fact that the Indians never ate without making a sacrifice to their totemic ancestor.

We may call these practices what we will: they played the important rôle of tying the clans into an emotional unit.

Taste and disgust are the two factors behind every food taboo. What disgusts is not violation of a taboo, but seeing some one eat, or being caught by some one eating, something *prohibited* by custom. Tastes become so individualized that untried foods, to adults, are generally "disgusting." Both tastes and disgusts are acquired: hence national dishes. Frogs' legs are disgusting to many—and the people who eat them are "Frogs."

As a matter of fact, a young ape, or an infant son of a Catullus, will try anything once, and if it does not bite will try it again—and by and by will have a taste for it. Bourke's *Scatalogic Rites of All Nations* spreads an extraordinarily disgusting table, before which only the most hardened stomach could keep quiet.

We *rest* on Sunday. Do we need rest, are we worn out, will that particular day off help us to grow healthy, wealthy, and wise? Perhaps I sprained my ankle on Monday and have been laid off all week. Sunday comes; I am quite fit now; my life work calls and I obey. That would be rational, reasonable, sensible. But no, I must *not* work on Sunday; it is a Day of Rest. Why? Because, said Plato, "the gods, in pity for the toils which our race is born to undergo, have appointed holy festivals, by which men alternate rest and labour." And that, as Webster says in his *Rest Days,* indicates "rationalization."

"And God . . . rested on the seventh day from all his work which he had made. And God blessed the seventh day, and sanctified it," is the Hebrew rationalization of the fact that the seventh is a holy day. Another rationalization sanctifies the seventh day as a memorial for the Chosen People's escape from Egypt. Anyway, the seventh day is *holy*, and Deuteronomy tells us what not to do on that day. But if I had taken my grandmother to task for slaving the whole Sunday through to feed her own big family and from ten to twenty guests from the near-by meeting-house, she too would have rationalized: "Well, *somebody* must feed them!" They were certainly fed, and she surely slaved.

Before going further we need some facts. Hawaiians call our Sunday *la tabu*—a word found in varying forms throughout the Polynesian world, with always the same meaning: Taboo, don't. Thus, to put a taboo on real or personal property meant, Keep off, or, Don't touch! Recall the stones Laban heaped up as a witness between himself and Jacob. Those stones were taboo, dangerous to anyone who moved them, as were the boundary stones set up in Babylon. The power to curse was in the stones themselves. Later, the power to curse anyone disturbing the boundary stones was assumed by Yahweh himself.

Taboo, then, is an appellative meaning dynamite. Is dynamite dangerous? Not if let alone; but, handled roughly, without gloves, it may send one almost to hell. The same with taboo—something dangerous, forbidden, prohibited, unlucky. Some taboos are more heavily loaded than others: Forbidden Fruit, Holy Ghost, Incest— and not so long ago, going to the movies on Sunday. Things *taboo* are the collective "don'ts" of the dominant male or medicine-man, or shaman, as he is called by Arctic peoples.

Thus, Christian missionaries to the Eskimos were *shamans*; their "don'ts" were new taboos. And they thought the Christians clever to taboo an entire day (Sunday)!

The Babylonians also had a taboo day, Shabattu. It was a day of abstinence and propitiation: Don't eat broiled flesh or oven-baked bread, nor change your clothes, nor offer sacrifice; the king must not ride in his chariot or deliver judgment; nor may the priest give oracles in secret; nor physicians lay hands on the sick. Just one "don't" after another.

And what was this *taboo, don't,* day—*Shabattu?* The seventh! Seven is my lucky number. If Cain be avenged seven times, surely Lamech seventy and seven. Pythagoras, level-headed, wise man in many respects, went quite mad over seven. He found seven sages, seven wonders of the world, seven gates to Thebes, seven heroes against Thebes, seven sleepers of Ephesus, seven dwarfs beyond the seven mountains—and so on, up to seventy times seven.

Look at the moon, that "golden hand on the dark dial of heaven"; then look at a Babylonian tablet in the British Museum with a calendar on it. Every month is divided into four weeks of seven days. Every seventh day is Sabbath, *taboo*. Why? Four times seven equals twenty-eight. Who first thought that out we shall look into later. It was thought out.

Now, those seventh days—seventh, fourteenth, twenty-first, twenty-eighth—on that Babylonian tablet are taboo days, as we have seen. Why taboo? They were Ishtar's *unlucky* days. Who was Ishtar? The Moon Goddess. Greece and Rome had Moon God-desses. All the peoples of old had them. Even the Jews—for they sojourned also in Babylonia. But they finally made Yahweh's their taboo day: our Day of Rest.

Moslems and modern Jews begin their "day" at sunset because

their ancestors reckoned time by the moon. The first crescent moon in the western sky is new moon; that begins the first day of the new month (moon). "He appointed the moon for seasons," says Psalms CIV, 19. In I Samuel xx David says to Jonathan: "Behold, tomorrow is the new moon, and I should not fail to sit with the king at meat." The new moon, thinks Webster, was a general rest day until possibly after the Exile.

A fortnight ago; a sennight hence.

Leda bore Apollo of the golden sword on the seventh of the month; that is why it is holy, says Hesiod. In the Babylonian Flood myth, rain falls for six days, ceases on the seventh; seven days must elapse before Noah can turn the animals loose and abandon ship. The Babylonians "kept" their Sabbath holy—by doing nothing that would arouse their gods' anger.

Poor old Friday the thirteenth; or any Friday but Good. The good and bad in Fridays arose chiefly from Middle Age theologic vapourings. Adam sinned on a Friday, as did Cain in killing Abel; Friday also saw John the Baptist beheaded, the innocents slain by Herod, the first day of the Deluge, the confusion of tongues on Babel, and the plagues in Egypt. The combined result was to give dog Friday a very bad name. The Passion made one Friday Good. But I do not yet know whether next Easter will come in March or April.

Taboo days, holy days. If not *too* holy, holidays, market days, fairs. The Romans called their taboo days *feriati*. There were sixty-one such public *feriæ*, each sacred to a god of the state religion. The ancient Greeks did better, in fact as well as the Ashanti of West Africa; they had about a hundred and fifty days of rest.

Who sets holy days? Holy men, of course. Who profits by them? Does any priest lose any weight or prestige on any holy day? Who started the calendar? The priest. People consulted him as to the best time to plant their corn, etc. The priests studied the stars, especially the changing moon. How many days in the week; how many planets? Hence *Sun*day, *Moon*day, and a day for Mars, Mercury, Jupiter, Venus and Saturn.

Jupiter and Venus play the leading rôles in star myths, and were probably the first planets named: Jupiter (Jove), because of his brilliant light; Venus, because she looks different preceding rising and following setting sun.

Just why the thirteenth was given the double cross I do not recall. It was; and in many hotels we easily perform the miracle of passing from the twelfth to the fourteenth floor in one jump—a harmless superstition if not taken too seriously. But do not forget that the Spartan army never got to Marathon because they would not begin a march before full moon. Some of man's most egregious failures may be charged to the same account.

Equally true is it that there could be no human civilization without taboos. Without "don'ts" there could be no peace in the family, no order in any human society. Taboos, as Havelock Ellis says, are an absolutely indestructible element of social life. They cannot be flouted with impunity. Nor, on the other hand, should they be regarded as sacred or immune.

Every taboo began with a reason—often most unreasonable. It makes for enlightenment that we look at our taboos with open eyes—and look at them twice before we discard them, three times before we decide to enforce them by law or replace them by new laws. It is well that all our "don'ts" lose all their religious sanction, but it is even better that they should have the sanction of reason and common sens^ and that they should make for tolerance and social order.

x

*It is so inspiring!*

All religion, art, literature, higher animal activity, in a sense are inspired; much of them is called inspirational. Clear thinking here will help us to understand civilization.

When I breathe in, I *inspire*; when I breathe out, I *expire*. Inspired air has more oxygen, less carbon dioxide, than expired air. We cannot live without oxygen or with excess carbon dioxide. For life is a flame; breathing fans life's flame. That flame expires with our last inspiration. Inspired air makes for vitality, is power.

From this bit of physiology, let us jump back to prescientific days. "Air" is a spirit, a soul, a psyche, something mysterious, something supernatural.

To revive the flickering flame of life today, science administers oxygen; to help the "spirit" on its way, religion administers Extreme Unction. Unction costs less than oxygen, but is it more inspiring? More divinely inspired, yes.

To be divinely inspired is to be one or in union with, or possessed by, whatever it is that is divine. And that, as Leuba points out, throws no light on the nature of inspiration; for *divine* merely signifies whatever the one "possessed" has experienced, "gets whatever significance it may possess from the experiences to which it is applied."

In other words, the dictionary helps us not at all to understand divine possession or inspiration; psychology does—and, viewed historically, inspiration falls largely into the field of psychology. But as I have insisted before, from the lunatic's point of view lunacy is normal behaviour. If I am possessed and you are not, I obviously have something you lack; and because of my possession it is not to be wondered at that I can see farther than you can, that I have insight which is better than your eyesight, that my intuition will enable me to discover more than you can learn with your learning tools!

I spoke of inspiration and psychology. Let us dig still deeper and speak of physiology and pure inspiration—of the anxiety neurosis behind all inspired fanaticism.

Anxiety, worry, is born of fear—forebodings; fear of the consequences of a past event or of future failure. Even mild worry or anxiety slows down normal healthful activity in the colon and in all organs innervated by the sacral division of the autonomic nervous system. That is the kind of animal man is. If he had no physical body or physical function, he need not eat, excrete, or reproduce; he could be *pure* spirit, *pure* inspiration.

But man must perform these "lowly" activities, and perform them well, or he is low in more ways than one. And when he is low he easily turns to delusions, hallucinations, daydreams, haunting dreams. The exalted, eccentric ascetic, emancipated or virtuous, is as likely to be diseased as his extreme opposite. All fanatics, religious or otherwise, are deranged, diseased. They cannot use their brains for solving their family, social, and economic problems, because their visceral or emotional tensions drive them to resort to elemental activities below or outside known and approved forms of behaviour which make for peace on earth and good will to men.

The difference between a man in an insane asylum whining like a monkey for a peanut while proclaiming himself God, and a Mohammed who proclaims himself the inspired prophet of God, psychologically speaking is not great; historically, it may be the difference between a paranoiac with specific delusions of grandeur and the founder of an inspired world religion. Conceivably, in other times, under other circumstances, the man of our illustration might also have had believers who would follow him and in *their* fits of inspiration evolve the mad dances of the Dervishes, the mystical doctrines of the Sufis, or the orgiastic rites of the Holy Rollers.

Back to normalcy, if we go back far enough, is back to lunacy; and, unfortunately, all too easy these days. A doctrine may be impressive; it may also be misleading and quite inapplicable to individual cases. Abnormality is such a doctrine; it implies a distinction between normal and abnormal which has no factual basis. Nor do many other categorical terms in common use help us to understand either religious or secular behaviour. Divine is such a term; also, inspiration, insanity, sin, guilt, inferiority, mind, faculty, soul, heredity, instinct. These terms are impressive, the ideas behind them may be excellent; the queston is, are they factually founded?

"Factually founded:" there's the rub, and we shall look into it later; but it is a historic fact, confirmed in our own experience, that in passing from childhood to maturity man passes from more or less make-believe to more or less disillusion. The result is dualism, the ages-old conflict between idealism and realism.

There are endless ways of resolving this conflict, but, roughly speaking, only two great categories of ways: use brains to acquire better knowledge or more understanding; use existing fear-rituals which serve as shock-absorbers for the reality of disharmony, imperfection, evil, and make it easy to create a world of harmony, perfection, good.

Behind these fear-rituals are such concepts or ideas as magic, magic power, divinity, God, evil, sin, death, immortal souls, etc. Life is not *lived*, but spent in perfecting the technique of fighting evil, wooing good. For such human existence the knowledge that comes from use of brains is a real hindrance. For such humans ignorance is bliss, and truth, as illusion, an object of worship; as disillusion, an object of mistrust or downright hatred.

Now, as religion is rooted in death, in the fear its mystery evokes, the unendurable thought of individual annihilation or extinction, its main function is to preserve life. It performs that function, not by handing on the germplasm, but by *saving* "souls." Human society, on the other hand, is rooted in peace and love in the family: the family being a biologic necessity because of prolonged childhood, and peace and love being psychological necessities for mating, procreation, and the rearing of children. What is religion's answer to that?

"Think not that I am come to send peace on earth: *I came not to send peace, but a sword* . . . to set a man at variance against his father, and the daughter against her mother. . . ."

That, in essence, is the message of every reformer known to history. Is it any wonder that this is a topsy-turvy world, or that there is no peace among nations, and none, too often, in the home? Impotence preaches continence to cover its defect; joins a purity league and slanders women; becomes a vice crusader to protect itself from its fear of women; or becomes a sex pervert to avoid loss of freedom, or a religious fanatic to cloak its lack of social standing. Bunyan's conscience was a disease. Pascal thought his mother's kiss a crime. Augustine, Assisi, and Loyola became saints— after they had spent their youth in riotous living.

Behind every fanatic, ascetic, prophet, saint, miraclemonger, revivalist, reformer, founder, or iconoclast is a man or woman with a collection of manias or phobias. Not being able to fit into the world as it is, they needs must create a world of their own. They are proof against society, against its religion; they fear the crowd, they hate the world. The monastery, the cloister, afford them asylum, or they preach a crusade.

The paranoiac thinks he is persecuted because he is great. The fate of the megalomaniac may hang in the balance for centuries. Rarely can he convert more than a handful of his contemporaries and become a local hero; more often he is regarded as a harmless, even though radical, dreamer. Today we think of Pythagoras as a philosopher or even as a mathematician; to the centuries following him, he was saint, prophet, founder of a fanatically religious society.

In other words, Pythagoras was inspired. No one can be truly inspired who is not a fanatic. Fanaticism is divine inspiration, and is what it is, and was what it was in Christianity, because of what it was in ancient Greece. In Rohde's account of the orgiastic rites of Dionysiac worship we meet many old friends, and much that helps us to understand a Hopi snake-dance, an Arapaho sun-dance, a Billy Sunday revival, and Christian beliefs and practices, prophets, and preachers.

Hashish, even synthetic gin, makes for exaltation, intoxication, hallucination, visions, possessions; but true religious madness— *ekstasis*, as the Greeks called it—comes only when the god enters into men and liberates the soul from its cramped prison.

Midnight on the mountain top; flickering torches; deep-toned flutes, clashing bronze cymbals, thunderous roar of kettledrums; frantic, whirling, headlong eddies, mostly women; long, flowing garments floating in the wind; snakes in their hands and daggers with points concealed in ivy leaves. They dance till they are in a sacred frenzy, then fall upon their beast victim and tear it limb from limb, devouring it raw. They have burst the physical barriers of their soul. A magic power has taken hold of them. They share in the life of the god himself; the superhuman and infrahuman are mingled in the dancer's person. A religious drama, visionary exaltation, a divine orgy. Such, in brief, was the ceremony around the oracle of Dionysus under the charge of his *prophetai*; but I doubt if it was a better show than a Hopi snake-dance.

"I adjure you by Jesus Christ that thou come out of her. And he came out that same hour." Remember the woman Paul met in Philippi? He was driving a snake out of her. Now, the woman herself thought she was possessed, as did Paul; but her "possession" was the spirit of Python, sacred serpent of Apollo, God of Wisdom, and that filled her with wisdom beyond ordinary mortals. But Paul thought Apollo a devil, and that he himself, filled as he was with a good spirit, could exorcise evil spirits.

Only last week I heard a preacher cry out over the radio: As sure as our Lord cast out *devils*, so we must drive *sin* out of our lives. He evidently thought sin a possession. John Wesley said that if you did not believe in sin, you must cease to believe in the Bible.

That same radio preacher declared that we must all be prepared to make sacrifices in a good cause. Well, we "sacrifice" a dollar in a "good" cause; Abraham would have sacrificed his son in a good cause; the Aztecs sacrificed scores of people in a good cause. The Egyptians, in dog-days, sacrificed people on bonfires and scattered their ashes in a good cause. And why do we electrocute criminals if not in a good cause?

We beat a bush and a bird flies out; a carpet, dust; man, evil. Fathers used to beat their children to drive the devil out of them; and still beat them, presumably in a "good" cause, if not to drive the mischief out of them.

In the days of Pericles, Lysias speaks of the "sacrifice" (execution, as we should say) of a criminal in these words: "We must needs hold that in avenging ourselves and ridding ourselves of Andokides we purify the city and perform apotropaic (purifying) ceremonies, and solemnly expel a *pharmakos* and rid ourselves of a criminal: for of this sort the fellow is."

How modern that sounds! *Pharmakon* is Greek for anything that heals, dyes, poisons, or cures. Such stuffs in large varieties can be got at the corner drug store. *Pharmakos* is Greek for any human being so infected that he is a walking pollution; in short, he is a holy horror and should be killed for the good of the community, as we kill a criminal. He is a criminal. That seems to make drugs and criminals related. Some mystery here.

Medical science began when diseases were haled before the court of common sense; when they were looked at as ailing human beings and not thought of as sinful or polluted souls. We have travelled far, but not far enough to make it incredible that a woman should spend her life in an insane asylum washing her hands to cleanse herself of guilt and purify her soul; nor so far as to have given up the superstition that sacrificing a human being on what today I heard called the "hot seat," will rid us of social or moral iniquity. To continue such practices is to remain in Old Testament times, when the goat bore all our "iniquities into a land not inhabited."

Let us now look at a special form of lunacy of ancient origin and not known today, for the light it throws on man's infinite capacity to make long flights when he travels solely on his imagination.

What is the sun—Apollo, God, just what? Whatever it is believed to be, the sun is almost always less mysterious than the moon. Are you just a little bit luny, or have you any moles?—"moon-calves," as Pliny called them, and found only on those immaculately conceived, if one may speak of fertilization by the moon as "immaculate." At any rate, to credulous man the moon giveth, the moon taketh away. It took away a wart for me once!

We call the moon *she* because our early Anglo-Saxon ancestors, in their scramble to become "civilized," pilfered right and left from the classical world, and replaced their he-moon with a new kind of lunacy.

We know the answer to lunacy and a moon(luna)-struck maid, and the Bible relates how Jesus cured lunatics and epileptics. Eugende, a Christian saint, even cured a girl of "lunatic fits" by tying this incantation around her neck: "In the name of the Father, the Son, and the Holy Ghost, I adjure thee, thou spirit of gourmandise, anger, and fornication, thou lunatic spirit, leave this woman!"

In most parts of the world "lunacy" is *divine* madness, "possession." Hecate is the shining example. Most of the saints in Egypt are lunatics (moonstruck); they go about naked, are often highly venerated by the women, and commit excesses with impunity—on the excuse that their *sanctity* takes their "minds" off worldly things! It is a good reason but a poor excuse.

Most lunar divinities are trinities. Some icons depict God with three heads and three faces—like the Hindu Brahma. The human trinity idea came easily to childish fancy. Commonest is the idea of a white or old woman and her two sons, waxing and waning. The Babylonians had three moon-gods, sickle, crown, and kidney representing the three phases. The Greek prophetesses, sibyls, were lunar. Artemis, *the* Moon Goddess, was chief sibyl. Vergil speaks of a prophesying sibyl in referring to the will of Phœbus.

In fact, it is astounding how much of man's activity seems to be lunacy writ large; but behind customs, rites, and practices which to us seem abhorrent, idiotic, or savage, will be found beliefs which justify if they do not explain all, or rationalizations which serve the same purpose. It was inevitable that man, having once "discovered" that he could control the unseen powers of nature, should easily learn how to play upon the spiritual powers of his fellow-men. Why throw the fear of God into man unless he can be induced to submit to an operation to have that fear removed? Some one had to bear the burden of sin, and ignorance makes a good goat to bear it away.

The net result of all these divinely inspired paranoiacs was that gullible man found himself between Scylla, or the devil, and Charybdis, or the deep sea. And down below him was the realm of Pluton, with Churlish Charm, the ferryman, holding out his hand for the coin that was buried between the teeth of the dead. Some Minoan genius first thought out that brilliant idea—still turned to good account today, though we put the coin in the Holy Man's hand and not in the dead man's mouth. That keeps it in "circulation."

Ideas are born, some of them from brains addled by the sort of shrieks that curdle blood and scare the very life out of us; hence the birth (no *Primitive* could have conceived it) of the big idea that if life itself is so perilous, birth must be the one grand mistake of life. That was inspiration! And what was the answer—contraceptives, universal suicide? Nothing of the sort. Systems of philosophy, one of which is still peddled about by Yogis; another was practised in Greece and was known as the Orphic life. The Orphics were "pure" and addressed each other as we say "Brother" and "Sister" to our fellow-communicants. It did not mean that they were *pure*, however; only that they were purified.

Man invented thousands of one-hundred-per-cent purification ways before he thought of soap and water; and the best we claim for our soap still falls short of the standard we set for a pure American.

To the Greeks of one period there were only two kinds of people—the pure and the uninitiated. Watch out for the initiates in history. Initiation always does something, even to a freshman; it makes him a Greek. But initiation into the Eleusinian Society made him pure; communion with its *mystery* saved him.

In union there is strength; in communion there is salvation; and both are ancient institutions. One is psychologically founded; the other is, psychologically speaking, therapeutic—good "medicine."

And along comes old Diogenes with a lantern in his hand and a sneer on his face: Pataikon, the thief, will have a better fate after death because he had been initiated at Eleusis, than Epaminondas, the saviour of Orchomenos.

To understand the infancy of Christianity one has only to study the "dark ages" of Greek religion, with its unattached, wandering prophets, exorcists, and ascetics: medicine-men all, and all called by "grace." They too, as we have seen, had their communion— bread and wine sacraments.

Pisa's leaning tower, where Galileo started modern science, over-looks the Campo Santo—holy, sanctified earth brought in sailing-ships from the Holy Land. Burial in that sacred soil *sanctifies* the corpse, *purifies* the soul.

Fear drove man to talk about death, and hope led him to believe in life everlasting; but it is hatred that drives man out of all reason. Misogynists hate all women, and find refuge in clubs where they may give expression to their philosophies. Ascetics hate everybody and everything. The compulsion neurosis to which their obsessive thinking drives them is a disease which for short may be called bio-geo-phobia. The only cure for that disease is solitary confine-ment, or flight to a cell, a cave, a monastery, to drown themselves in their own brain-brewed world of fancy. Some of them do a bit of fancy-work now and then; and some of it is so fancied that it brings fancy prices as an *objet d'art* or a church relic. Some of them became so holy, because of their self-immolation or their fancy-work, that their very bones have become holy and are to be found in reliquaries, at the base of Buddhist dagobas, in Moslem shrines, in Christian churches.

The Church still canonizes its wonder-working possessed. Society only a century ago ceased to look upon its lunatics as possessed: hence to be "cured" only by flogging, beating, pricking, torment-ing, half-drowning, or even hanging. We may yet see the day when criminals also will be recognized for what they are, and not treated as scapegoats to bear our sins away.

We solve too many modern problems against the background of a divine afflatus, stale, unsocial, and inhuman. There was little enough excuse for the vagaries of a religious *enthusiasmos* which could treat souls; there is no excuse for our enthusiasm in curing diseased human beings by judicial murder.

## XI

Down through the ages man is for ever burying the dead and caring for the living. Life itself, as symbol, is no stimulus for action; birth and death are—as are recurring seasons, phases of the moon, eclipses, and all striking, exciting, terrifying phenomena of nature. Death becomes an obsession, and with high death rates man must give much thought to the matter. *Death* may mean next to nothing to him; the *dead* do arouse him to action. Something must be done.

The corpse must be disposed of, for one thing; but that does not dispose of the formidable, haunting idea that death is terribly real, terribly earnest, and an ever-impending threat. That horrible thought, added to grief over the loss of a beloved one, is the real stimulus to further action: an emotional stimulus that will not rest till a satisfactory answer is found.

How can death be explained away, made unreal, the grave robbed of its victory, the loss of the beloved compensated? Everywhere the answer is the same: Deny death. Every "Bible" does it; every "Bible" is a testament, an explicit act of faith born of emotional reaction—that death is not what it seems.

Don't try to explain away death to me, Achilles said to Odysseus; for, "Who knows whether Life be not Death, and what we here call Death be called Life there below?"

Ask primitive man why, for example, he performs a certain rite, and he tells you the story as it was done in the beginning. The story is the guide to action—warrant, charter, commentary, all in one; is, in short, the reason why—in morals, manners, customs.

Why does he believe in immortality, eternal youth, immortal souls? Well, that's how it is in the tale. The story says that is the way it happened, this is *why* it happened. As Malinowski says, it is to him what Genesis, Fall, and Redemption are to the Christian. It is not an intellectual explanation, nor artistic imagery; it is a "pragmatic charter of faith and moral wisdom"—an explicit act of faith. The stories may be *myths* to us; they are the Word of God to the believer.

What is Homer—history, fiction, literature, poetry, mythology,

fairy tale, folklore, sacred book, religion? Homer himself probably would not have understood such a question any more than
would the authors of the Bible. What the Bible is, Homer once
was—a story of how things happened "once upon a time." "As
it was in the beginning" is primitive man's reason for the way it is
now, and the foundation for his prediction that it evermore shall be.

Until recently, "in the beginning" was not so very long ago.
Time-sense came to man slowly, as does space-sense.

Primitive man's "in the beginnings" are myths, but they are
*true*; they record supernatural happenings, but they happened.
Beginnings are always supernatural; that is why man's powers are
so limited—he has lost his pristine power. And there is always a
reason why, there is always a "goat"; Eve in the Garden is the one
we know best.

But, you say, that is an *inspired* story. So it is. In the same sense
the Wichita Indian genesis story is inspired—and in my opinion
a more interesting and credible story than the one Israel borrowed
from Babylon. Behind every "true" inspiration is a simple-minded
man; the simpler, the truer the inspiration.

Let us see how man fell from his former state of immortality
into sinful, mortal, human ways, in a South Sea Island myth recorded by Malinowski; it shows some real observation and fair
biological reasoning.

In the beginning, people lived under the earth. There were
villages, clans, districts, distinctions in rank, rights and privileges,
property, etc.—just as now. Thus endowed, people emerged, bringing their culture, manners and customs with them. When they
grew old they sloughed off their dead skin and became rejuvenated
—like a crab, like a snake. (And note, in passing, that rejuvenating
medicines and eternal-life elixirs are not born in senile brains, but
spring from the hope that doddering, decaying senility will never
overtake *us*.)

Well, there was a village, and in it lived a woman, her daughter,
and the grandmother. One day the girl and her grandmother went
to bathe in a tidal creek. The grandmother decided to become
young again, and so, unknown to the girl, she sloughed off her old
skin, which was carried up the creek by the tide. When the girl
saw her rejuvenated grandmother, she thought it was a strange

flapper and naturally tried to drive her away. That so enraged the rejuvenated grandmother that she decided then and there to put an end to rejuvenescence: she would die, as would the girl also after she had grown old and ugly.

South Sea Islanders die because a silly girl chased a maiden. We die because a silly girl was not chaste!

And the Islander's landscape, no less than our Holy Land, is pockmarked with crosses to prove that it all was so: special holy spots, grottoes, clumps of trees, coral outcrops, and springs. These spots are sanctions for certain social, industrial, totemic, and magical practices. Thus, a certain spot or spring may not look holy, but the "it is said" distinguishes it as the spot where something happened "in the beginning"; it is thereby no longer merely a spot or a spring, it is a marked spot, a peculiar spring, *sacred*. Put off thy shoes from off thy feet, for the place whereon thou standest is holy ground. Holy Land—the Land of the Book; as the Islander's is the Land of the Word.

Moral? Some day we may get up enough courage to take our antiques at their face value. Worm holes are worm holes. If grandfather was a kindly, decent old boy, and if his clock keeps good time, is easily kept in repair, and is not too hard to look at or too big to fit into the hall, keep it and cherish it for what it is—a good timepiece, a stimulus which causes you to behave kindly and decently. If the answer to all these "ifs" is *No*, donate it to the local museum, scrap it, or sell it to Mr. Ford.

Vandal? Well, if the Vandals had not sacked Rome, the Christians would have had more to sack. As it was, they had to work long and hard to turn the pagan idols into lime. Most of these idols were easy on the eye, much easier than those which have replaced them.

The more complete a religion, the holier its Book, the more devastating its power to close human eyes to the known joys of life and to paralyze human feet from walking in that direction. That is to say, some religions seem so biologically harmful that one wonders how they are perpetuated; their adherents, it seems, should all have died out long ago. Not the least amazing thing about man is that he can and does live despite his best efforts to slow life down and crush it out of his life. Had we not had a long line of agile ancestors, we could not be so clever at juggling heavens and hells.

Ever-living, ever-dying. Shelley called his lament for Keats *Adonais*—the ever-living, ever-dying god.

The living are warm. Dead, the body grows cold; the spark of life has gone out, like a flame. Recall Macbeth's "Out, out, brief candle"; Othello's "Put out the light, and then put out *the* light"; and the souls that mount up to God like thin flames.

More frequently, the souls return to the cavern they came from, there to dwell as they did before coming out on this stage.

Hence the big part cremation has played in human funeral rites. Fire releases the soul and purifies it. Thus, the Greeks needed no embalmers or morticians, nor do the Hindus; fire hastens the return of dust to dust, speeds the immortal soul on its way.

The "below" was not hell, but Hades, Erebus; below, where the shades, psyches, dwell as images. Thus, Odysseus saw the "images of those that have toiled," like smoke, on the edge of Hades. He also recognized his mother and his companions in the Trojan War.

Dead Patroklos prays to Achilles for immediate burial, that his *psyche* may at once pass through the door and not wander restlessly about the house of Ais (Hades).

Why those great burial mounds of Greek heroes on the plains of Troy if the dead are cremated and the souls gone to rest? Homer tells us: that their fame may remain imperishable among men; that future generations may not be ignorant of their history; that their glorious names may live on.

Human nature does not change; human culture does—human values and methods of attaining them.

Mohammed put a hell in his Bible; he also painted a heaven of known human delights. For the faithful, to die on the field of battle was no death: it was immediate translation to a land of sweet meadows, babbling brooks, peaceful shade, lovely houris— a sensual heaven it has been sneeringly called. It almost conquered the world. It did save Greek science, kept its spirit alive, kindled it anew, and handed it back to Europe a living flame.

And so we may say that, while God in the beginning made fear and fear was not long in finding God, man at last found courage to take God in his hands and examine him with open eyes—to discover that God is nature, infinitely complex and infinitely mysterious. But as to *why* there is a nature . . . I doubt if we will ever get beyond: *It is God's will.* I certainly know no better reason for human existence or wiser use for human hands and brains than Walter Savage Landor put in these words:

We are on earth to learn what can be learnt upon earth, and not to speculate on what can never be. . . . Let men learn what benefits men; above all things to contract their wishes, to calm their passions, and, more especially, to dispel their fears. Now these are to be dispelled, not by collecting clouds, but by piercing and scattering them. . . . Much of what we call sublime is only the residue of infancy, and the worst of it.

# CHAPTER SIX

## *The First Million Years; Or, The Foundations of Civilization*

1. The Dynamics of Cultural Change. 2. Patent No. 1,787,423; or the Mechanism of Discovery and Invention. 3. The Prehistoric Time-table. 4. Cave-Man, the Real Culture Hero. 5. Cro-Magnon and End of the Old Stone Age. 6. The New Stone Age. 7. The Domestication of Plants and Animals. 8. The Dawn of the Age of Metals. 9. Counting the Days and Numbering the Years. 10. Just How Painful Was Man's Ascent?

I

CIVILIZATION, human culture, is an extra-natural, superorganic, artificial burden man had to assume in order to survive the struggle for existence. Natural man was no match for natural environment; without having improved his natural equipment he could not have overrun the earth. He did improve that innate equipment; one improvement led to another. He probably overran the earth and reached security as a species in shorter time than any other species of animal. Today the world is at his feet as it never has been to any other species of animal. That position has been won by the use of artificial, man-made tools.

That man's position is not higher, more secure, more satisfactory, more enjoyable, is due to man himself. There has been scarcely one single labor-saving invention in all history that has not been wrecked on sight, and the inventor himself reviled, mobbed, or nearly killed. We of today do less wrecking, reviling, and mobbing because we know that an invention is not necessarily a devilish contraption and contrary to the will of God, but may be useful and possibly ornamental.

Civilization for intellectual purposes may be broken up into parts or complexes, and these in turn into elements or traits. Such analyses are necessarily superficial, for by the time we have analyzed civilization it is a museum of relics and a library of books. Just

229

what civilization is we shall never know; we can learn something about it by using our senses.

The most valuable of all senses in understanding civilization is the historic sense. For this reason. The strength and weakness of human nature are to be discovered in human deeds; human history is the final answer to human nature; and the earth's most gorgeous pageant is the birth and growth of civilization. But before we take our seats to become spectators at what is really our own show, we must consider certain general problems, especially those of the discovery or invention of cultural traits and their dissemination: in short, the dynamics of civilization.

These problems are sometimes spoken of as "academic": which means, as I understand that term, that they may be discussed only in halls of learning, by the learned, and not in the market place by mere hucksters. Well, by now we should have some idea of the nature of the man who retires behind an academic gown. Stripped of their trappings, priests and professors are found to be human. That they too often withdraw from, or "wash their hands" of, current problems of human interest, many of them now realize. More especially they begin to realize that Plato's Republic, for example, or Hammurabi's Code, or the Hebrew Decalogue, or even the Glory that was Greece and the Grandeur that was Rome, are not the answer to our civilization. Even Spengler speaks of civilization as though he were a pathologist at an autopsy and civilization itself a morgue of exhibits on marble slabs.

Invention, discovery, and the spread of cultural complexes are not academic problems; they are living problems, more vitally important today than ever before. And if knowledge is a valid tool for the understanding of any problem, knowledge of the nature of invention and of the dynamics of civilization's growth is the sharpest tool for an understanding of our own civilization.

Every civilization, all cultures, may for convenience be broken up into categories of activities. We have been dealing with certain activities, especially those which spring from the deepest wells of human nature. We have seen how certain biologic needs came in the course of time to be answered in certain ways, and how some of those ways actually distorted certain fundamental needs out of all semblance of human requirements. The original idea may have been sound; carried through to what seemed a logical conclusion, it made not for humanity but for inhumanity—anarchy, disease, insanity, disorganization. In other words, the answer to a crisis or an emotional need may become a decisive factor in provoking other crises, for which there is no sane, sound, humane solution. Wars, famines, plagues, revolutions, anarchy, become "logical" solutions—like avenging gods in armoured tanks ploughing through kindergartens.

An armoured tank is a cultural trait; a G.H.Q. is a cultural complex. We may even characterize a culture or civilization by its dominant complex, if it has one. It is evident that the dominant complex of Mississippi, for example, differs from that of Connecticut. Assyria was once dominated by the military-complex; Egypt, by the Osiris-complex; Greece, by the "Glory"; Rome, by the "Grandeur"; and so on.

While a cultural trait in a way is older than the complex or whole of traits, it must be obvious that man has always been at the mercy of complexes. Thus, before he had flint tools, he had a food-complex; and there was a family-complex long before there were wedding bells.

In every culture or culture-complex there are always certain known, certain unknown, factors—physical, biological, psychological. Knowledge of two of these is rarely enough to solve the unknown third.

The older anthropologists—Tylor, Spencer, McLellan, Morgan, Frazer, Balfour, Westermarck, Crawley—saw culture in terms of evolution; in fact, they make up the Evolutional or Unilineal school of culture historians. They say in effect: Give a people stone, copper, tin, zinc, gold, silver, iron, and enough time, and they will give you a stone, bronze, copper, iron, and steel age.

The second "school"—led today by Elliot Smith and including Perry, Rivers, Laufer, Schmidt, and Gräbner—finds only diffusion at work; they are the Diffusionists. There have not been volcanoes, but one volcano, erupting culture. From that one centre, culture has flowed like lava round the world. Their business is to show how contact, infiltration, and transmission have influenced culture.

Anthropologists who see culture in terms of sand dunes and swamps, valleys and mountains, forests and plains, are practically non-existent. It is only those who get their geography first-hand, and their anthropology second-hand and take of it only as much as they need to bolster up their theory, who constitute the Environmental or Geographical Determinant school, of which Buckle was, and Huntington is, the chief protagonist. Ratzel was one of the first to study human culture and race in terms of environmental influence, but he never allowed his studies to lead him to absurd conclusions.

"Don't talk to me about environmental determinants," said Hegel; "where the Greeks once lived the Turks live now." Geographical distribution may be interesting from a geographical, but it is not necessarily so from a cultural, point of view—except, as Boas says, "in so far as geographical contiguity may indicate trends of cultural dissemination."

Even the concept of Cultural Centres or areas is at best valuable only as a device for classifying cultures. First used by Klemm in 1840, in his *History of Human Culture*, and by Waitz a generation later—also by Ratzel, and by most museums as a basis for their exhibits—it can serve no purpose beyond that of mere device in classification. It solves no real problem in culture.

How about environment? At a superficial glance, environment does seem to explain many cultures, many cultural complexes. It has, in fact, been made to "explain" China, Babylon, Egypt, Greece, Great Britain, Japan, etc. Does our civilization reflect our American environment? Or, to put it another way, how far is civilization moulded by environment? To both questions the answer is, very little.

Man makes civilization and in so doing chooses his environment, then moulds it to his heart's desire. If he cannot do that, he migrates. Every animal does the same: adaptation, emigration, or death. Man, because of his extraordinary sensitivity to physical and social environment, and his capacity to acquire control over his motor mechanism, can manipulate his environment as no other animal can; he is the most adaptable of all animals. He can adapt himself to his environment, can force his environment to adopt him. Environment neither creates nor explains culture; it does set limits: a glacier is a glacier and a desert is a desert. But when man drains the glacier onto the desert, the desert soon becomes an orange grove.

In other words, the old limiting factor of environment tends to give way before civilization. A seemingly impossible environment may prove to be the necessary stimulus for man to find ways of turning it into real estate. In fact, it has taken man some 50,000 years to discover how good he is, how clever he can be. Nine-tenths of the time man has been on earth he has bowed down to something or somebody to save him; he now begins to realize that he can save himself, and with his own wonder-working hands.

The peculiarly and highly individualized culture of our South West Pueblo Indians has been explained by environment; but how about the fundamentally different cultures of their close neighbours, the Navaho and Apache? Our Plains Indians' culture was largely a buffalo culture, yet they never domesticated the buffalo. The Zulus have domestic cattle, but use them only for milk; the Masai keep cattle primarily to enhance their social value, using them only for their milk and blood. The Chinese had sheep and goats, but dressed in cotton and silk. They never used woollen clothing, and they learned to make felt and weave carpets from Mongol nomads. Mongols and Turks rely largely on dairy products, yet China with the same resources never took a fancy to milk. For their koumiss the Kirgis use horse's milk. To ancient India, Babylonia, Egypt, and China, the horse was a draught animal. To Cave-man and poor Frenchman, the horse is horse flesh. To Central Asiatics, the horse was something to ride; they invented the saddle. Kafir corn is eaten in Africa; fed to livestock in America.

Environment furnishes the bricks and mortar, as Lowie says, but no plan. Man combines the materials primarily to suit his tastes rather than his requirements. He also chooses, of the many materials available, those which he fancies. In short, man can never transcend his environment beyond his biologic requirements, but, being a creature of whims and strong likes and antipathies, he manipulates his environment and from it chooses what he likes or what law and custom allow him.

Civilization is unique; every culture is unique; it can only be explained in terms of its creators. Its creators can only be explained in terms of animal wants set to words and music and directed by the big chief. Time is a big factor in the stage settings; chance and accident are important factors. The biggest factor of all, possibly, is the big chief, the leader. Now and then a leader arises who seems to transcend all previous records. He not only blazes forth with startling brilliancy, but seems to set his people on fire and they transcend themselves—for a while, and are then snuffed out. Like a meteor, like a star, like a comet. Why?

We have already looked into the sources of inspiration. How explain such a career as that of Genghis Khan, a mere medicine-man of the primitive Mongols? He pops up out of nothing, as it were, and soon dominates all Asia and menaces Europe. More than that, the Mongols themselves become civilized overnight almost— embrace Buddhism and the Higher Life generally. Then there was the meteoric rise of the Arabs from crude nomads to a world power and for centuries the most cultured people on earth.

How explain these flashes of brilliancy in cultural achievement? Well, the Mongol flash is, roughly, comparable to Japan's modern career. Neither, of course, started with nothing. As Japan found China, so the Mongols found Asia unprepared for a certain kind of military enthusiasm and arms; one armoured carload of our best bootleg bandits could conceivably have whipped the entire Continental Army or have beaten Napoleon's time in conquering Europe. The Mongols created almost nothing. They got their Buddhism from India, their alphabet from Syria, their writing from Tibet, and the art of printing and many characters from China.

The rise of the Arabs is another story, and certainly one of the most extraordinary in all history. I spoke of them as crude, but so were our Embattled Farmers, so was Lincoln. The Arabs were crude, but they were sound physically, and having once started, found inspiration in every triumph to make the next one bigger and better. Their triumphs were real. They did not win against bow-and-arrow Indians, as did our American forefathers, but against their equals in arms. They did create a distinctive culture of their own. They made possible the reawakening of Europe. We shall see them again in these pages.

And let us not overlook the fact that the Arabs proved quite as original as ourselves, or as the Japanese. In other words, civilization cannot be explained in terms of race or physical type. The conquering Mongols and Manchus are blood kin to the still primitive Siberian tribes. The Mayas of Yucatan and the Incas of Peru were kin to peoples who never rose above the average American level— a level which compares favourably with that of northern and central Europe of 1 A.D. Arabian civilization was far higher than European of the Middle Ages. For hundreds of years China was the most civilized country in the world. After reading Marco Polo, turn to the magnificent era of the Grand Moguls of India. From every point of view, Akbar's fifty years' reign must be rated among the most glorious in all history; and Akbar himself was a descendant of the Mongol Tamerlane, one of the world's most brilliant and enlightened rulers.

Luck. The fates do seem to conspire now and then to raise men, tribes, and nations aloft; but history abounds also with the falls of men, tribes, and nations that depended on their luck to keep them aloft. Mount Everest is the highest peak in the world today, but it is being worn down by wind and ice. Will it be the highest peak a million years hence? There were hundreds of high peaks in the Alleghenies hundreds of millions of years before the Himalayas were born. What of it? Nothing; certainly nothing that we can do anything about. We can, however, get a better understanding of civilization if we stop assuming that our mind is better than was our Cave ancestors', or that theirs was better than their cousins' who stayed behind in Asia or wandered off to Tasmania or Manhattan Island.

The common assumption that primitive cultures are set in cast-iron moulds is not justified. Their simplicity only seems so to our ignorance. They are in truth enormously complex, and, psychologically speaking, as rich, full, and complete as ours. There is something doing all the time. These cultures inevitably change.

I spoke of "levels" and of "higher" civilization, and of the "fates"; I spoke figuratively, of course. I get no sadistic delight by feeling that just because I can read and write and wear clothes and sit in an easy-chair and toast my toes, I am morally superior to or more civilized than a naked cannibal of the Solomon Islands. I have grave doubts if I get more out of life than he does, or if my life is more "worth while." I do have two advantages over him: I can enjoy taking off my clothes; I can see more of the world's sights.

It must have taken his people hundreds of years to get to the Solomons; I can get there in a few days.

I keep this digression in the first person because I realize that many Americans look upon our civilization as something created by their own lily-white hands and therefore incomparably higher than any other. And by "higher" they mean nobler, purer, more genteel, more refined—in short, *higher*! Illusion is so deeply embedded in man's melodramatic nature that I cannot expect them to give up the thrill they get from feeling so morally superior.

As Boas convincingly demonstrated years ago, and as all anthropologists now agree, there is no innate connection between race, culture, and language. The more individual cultures are studied in terms of historical contacts and accidental discoveries, the less important, relatively, appears the factor of innate ability. Any attempt to correlate race with culture is precarious, to say the least; and so far no attempt has been convincing.

The complexity of historical events [says Boas] is such that the cultural life of any people and of any tribe can be understood only as an outgrowth of those unique conditions under which it has lived. An attempt to explain the details of the behaviour of a people on purely psychological grounds can never give an adequate understanding of the cultural life as it exists today, no matter how intimately we may be acquainted with the reactions of the individual to his social environment.

Culture is human history writ large; it is an historical science. Psychology supplies the reasons for individual cultural behaviour, but it can never replace the necessity of looking at cultural phenomena from a historical point of view.

These psychological "reasons," may we remind ourselves again, are legion. Roughly, they are our emotional slants, passions, appetites, tastes, prejudices, aspirations, wants, dislikes, fears; our manual habits and our kinæsthetic organization; our verbalized habits, implicit and explicit, thinking and speaking; and the infinite permutations of all these factors. When from the permutations certain unique individuals arise and the historic factors conspire to set the stage aright, we have such revolutionary leaders as Alexander, Mohammed, Luther, Columbus, Copernicus, Newton, Watt, Darwin —men whose lives have really changed human history. But the really world-shaking revolutions were brought about before the dawn of recorded history, and for them we are presumably indebted to Man and not to individual men.

Nietzsche's idea of a ruling class making progress over the backs of slaves is on a par with Plato's Republic and the rabid modern Eugenics programme; but his idea of characterizing cultures by their dominant traits is not without merit, though the extension of the idea in Spengler's hands gets us no closer to reality. Dr. Benedict has shown how Nietzsche's idea is useful, for example, in emphasizing the cultural differences between our South West Pueblo Indians and their neighbours the Pimas. Pueblo culture is dominantly "Apollonian." "They have a religion of fertility without orgy, high development of the dance without using it to arrive at abnormal psychic experience either individually or as a group, an order of priests who attain their dignity through status relationships and the knowledge of ritual." In other words, they are sane; they practise what the Greeks would call the "mean"—normal psychic experience, formal living.

The Pimas' dominant trait is "Dionysian": "The universal acquisition of power through a stress experience pushed to psychopathic extremes, the peyote and datura cults which attain similar ends, the frenzy of mourning ceremonies and the institutionalized uncleanness of menstruating women, the conventionalization of religion under the figure of intoxication."

In other words, to the historic factors in culture and the psychological factors in behaviour there must be added the nature of the culture itself; it is a *dynamic* force.

Our civilization is dominated by big business in charge of supersalesmen. This does not mean that that necessarily will be the dominant tone fifty or even ten years hence, nor even that the tone is necessarily discordant to human ears. It does mean that while it endures it acts. We have to reckon with it. It does something to us.

What brings about change in dominant cultural tones—the class in power? History teaches no such lesson. It is the business of the ruling class, whether religious, political, social, economic, racial, or intellectual, as Briffault says, to falsify and oppress rational thought, fetter the growth of social organisms, and sterilize the development of the class its object is to promote. In other words, the influence of the class in power is a *limiting* influence. Apply this principle to our control over the Philippines, or Haiti, or Cuba; or Britain's over India; or Holland's over the East Indies. Apply it to any page of human history since history began to be committed to writing.

Suppose the state is a theocracy or a military despotism, their virtues, spirit, and discipline are necessarily far removed from humanitarian ends or rational society. Supernaturalism and superhumanism are equally incompatible with sane, sound, enduring cultures. Making war and making myths are self-fertilizing pursuits, ends in themselves. The trappings of one and the phantasmagoria of the other are arts—appealing to the æsthetic sense, hence all the more dangerous. They easily absorb interest, stop the play —remove large fields of activity from too many hands, and thereby restrict socially important pursuits in which every normal person naturally likes to compete and in which approbation and prestige yield their choicest rewards.

Ethical ideals are always higher among the ruled than in the ruling class. Their feet are on the earth; they are closer to their fellow-men; they have more to gain, less to lose. The ruling classes love power as a kitten loves cream. Expect no social innovations or common-weal ideas from them—or much else than a nasty look or cries of "traitor," "treason," "iconoclast," "blasphemer," when reform is suggested. They have their own scale, their own touchstone, to weigh and test new ideas, proposals, suggestions. If the new looks like cream for the classes, it is "good," "valuable," "patriotic," in keeping with "manifest destiny"; but even milk for the masses is false, bad, "disruptive of society," "anarchy."

Our forefathers, after centuries of plodding effort, fashioned tools and weapons to fit the human hand and serve human society. These were great inventions, useful for hewing out the cornerstones on which all civilization has been built.

Among our forefathers also was a principle that effort should be rewarded; the most useful man won the acclaim of his fellowmen. It was right, proper, and natural that cunning, valour, wisdom, bravery, ingenuity, should be rewarded. But when some "city slicker" conceived the idea that that reward should be transmitted to his children and their assigns for ever, he conceived the most diabolical idea that ever entered the head of man. And when mankind accepted the principle of heredity in titles, emoluments, and property, it accepted a yoke centuries will not remove.

Most of mankind has broken from the fetters of the hereditary vice-regents of God, but hundreds of millions are yet without voice in their government; and still other hundreds of millions are without voice in the disposal of their country's natural resources, for they have been withdrawn from the public domain and are held as heritable private property.

What a puny, insignificant thing was that first stone ax compared with a tool which commands the labour of hundreds of thousands of human hands! Surely ancient society suffered from no disease comparable to this, so destructive of humanitarian ends, so incompatible with sane society.

II

In his *Inventions and Patents*, Wright speaks of a clerk resigning from the Patent Office years ago because there would soon be no more inventions to patent. That would close the Office, and he wanted to play safe, to desert the ship before it began to sink.

Our Patent Office was opened in 1836. Within fifty years it had granted 500,000 patents; the next eighteen years, another half-million; the next thirteen years, still another half-million; and on December 30, 1930, patent No. 1,787,423 was issued.

Many of these nearly two million patents are called *basic*; some fundamental principle is said to be involved—milking cows or rolling cigarettes by machinery, for example. It seems very wonderful. But suppose we had to catch the cow, find the tobacco, domesticate them, and invent paper, first; would these be grounds for basic patents? We keep extending the profitably cultivable area of wheat, making more grains grow on one stalk, and milling the wheat finer, faster, and whiter. Again, very wonderful. But suppose we had to discover a wild grass fit to tame and capable of becoming wheat; what kind of basic patent could we get on that? Just how *basic* are our patents?

If man's two eyes and two hands and the necessary neural structure to make marvellous eye-hand coördination possible, represent his highest natural endowment—and I think they do; and if continued activity in pleasurable and socially useful pursuits represents man's highest achievement—and I think it does; then in my opinion the compound achromatic microscope represents the most valuable single tool ever invented by man to help him on his way.

For over a century now, new and basic facts have steadily flowed from the physical and chemical laboratories and have been put to use in this age of power from coal and water. These utilities have revolutionized transportation and communication, have turned night into day; they have revolutionized the art of war and have been enlisted in the arts of peace.

This modern extension of capacity for physical power and increased control over the chemical elements is, without doubt, the greatest step man ever took in his march toward omnipotence. But aside from this momentous leap, the great steps, the basic discoveries, which removed man from the level of nomadic bands existing precariously to prosperous nations and powerful city states, were made from five to fifty millenniums ago.

Our civilization did not begin with the founding of Harvard College or with the discovery of the West Indies by Columbus; it began with the very beginnings of civilization. Our concern now is with those beginnings: the foundations of our material culture, the bases of our economic life—yes, and of our aims in life.

Basic patents, yes. How about basic *aims*? What are we aiming at today? What *can* we aim at? What is there to aim at? Merely to ask these questions is to take us back to the beginnings and into the heart of civilization.

In the beginning man's aims sprang from his need for food, the necessity to move about to secure food, and his desire for warmth and shelter. He found the means of satisfying these aims in his environment. And note here that while the story of man's discovery of the means to satisfy the aims that sprang from his fundamental needs and desires is wonderful, there would have been no story to tell had not Nature herself been a generous mother. She it was, rather than man's foresight, that made it easy for man to earn a living.

Man is wonderful; nature is wonderfully generous. We are the "heritors of the ages," but our real inheritance is an earthly home that was prepared for man and higher animals only after many hundreds of millions of years. I am not suggesting that we give thanks or anything of that sort; merely that we should be rather less vainglorious than we usually are and give the earth a little credit for the fact that we are here and have done so well.

Now, the *means* by which Cave- or city-man achieves his primary ends make up "material" culture; they are the *materials* of civilization—including, of course, methods, tools, implements, machines, etc. Our secondary or less material aims, arising from our æsthetic sense, love of adornment, desire for comfort and fear of annihilation, also find satisfaction only through materials. Hence the necessity for man to manipulate the materials of the objective world even for his spiritual existence. The Vice-Regent of the Supreme Spirit does not live in a vacuum, but in a very grand palace made of materials fashioned by horny human hands. With him, as with us all in this highly developed civilization, the means of life have become the aim of living; and, as Harrison says, the aims have become aspirations and ambitions.

To Cave- and city-man it is the environment which suggests the means of life—and most of the aims. It is still an open question whether in giving man enough brains to think up new luxuries, nature did not overshoot the mark. I cannot decide that question, but we may look at it again when we have become better acquainted with the means man has discovered for living a life of luxury and ease.

Under normal conditions I can sweat enough to keep cool enough to keep alive on a day too hot to live with if I could not sweat. With an electric fan, a hot day is something else again. The fan is an invention. Apes—and bees—make discoveries; man alone can invent. There could be no real inventions without articulate speech, nor cultural continuity, nor growth of civilization. Only as precept and practice were passed on was it possible to turn discoveries into inventions.

Discovery does not mean finding, but *finding out*. But man has never transcended his experience and his knowledge, nor presumably ever will; nor has he ever preconceived his means and his aspirations.

Man did not need metals until he had discovered them; nor would he have discovered their uses if he had not already become a tool-user. He was a tool-user before he was a tool-maker. Copper at first was not copper, but a peculiar kind of stone—malleable. By using stones and discovering that broken stones were better for certain purposes than natural forms, he began to break stones. Some stones do not break easily, but chip readily. Flint was man's earliest and best friend. Flint and obsidian behaved so unexpectedly under certain treatment that they stimulated him to more discoveries. One thing generally leads to another; the unexpected always leads to something.

Take that youngster again, man or ape: always tasting things—sometimes with fatal results; martyrs to humanity if the fatalities were duly recorded and passed on as valuable discoveries. Only by trying, monkeying with things—but not aping—can the unpredictable or unpredicated be discovered; only by manipulation are properties discovered, yielding experience which can be put to use or result in adoption. By such simple and perfectly natural processes or steps were flint, bronze, copper, pottery, fire-making tools, agriculture, and domestic animals discovered and put into circulation.

Thus, any great cultural complex, such as stone-working, pottery, bronze-casting, basketry, corn, wheat, milk, artificial fire, tobacco, is not to be thought of as an invention, but as an evolution involving a series, often a long series, of discoveries. The evolution, or history, of man's early arts and crafts came about through substituting one material for another, or through the transfer of method or idea from one substance to another. Melted beeswax or fat, when cooled, takes a form, as in a mould; that suggests moulds for anything that can be melted—copper, for example.

To discover flint is one thing; to discover what flint does under certain circumstances is another thing; to discover what can be done with flint—in hammering, stabbing, cutting, perforating, scraping, sawing, etc.—is still another thing. It is applied discovery: finding out the use and using, and then making. With applied discoveries material progress began; material objects and phenomena began to be moulded, manufactured, shaped into means for satisfying human aims.

Edison can put no more brains into his inventions than Cro-Magnon could put in his. Neither is an originator. The most that either can do is to adapt and combine the known to produce the new; they are wise only to what is known. Having discovered something, they are reassured by success, and promptly forget the fumbling that preceded success. Even a designer—of gowns or radio sets—does not design something new outright; he selects from the variants which result from trying the old in different lights.

Invention follows, not precedes, discovery; and the discovery is often accidental. Any stick is good to beat a dog or a carpet; but a short stick with a heavy end is a good war club, a longer one sharpened at one end is good for digging, and a still longer stick with a hard, sharp point makes a good spear. Throw that spear with a "throwing-stick," and you use a machine; you have used an important physical principle and you are an engineer. A stone in a sling, or an arrow in a bow, is an invention; both are machines; both use the well-known mechanical principle of "distortion of an elastic system"; the user is a mechanical engineer. There were bridge-builders when man threw a log across a stream; naval architects, when man made a dugout canoe.

Engineer-inventors preceded the Pyramids by thousands of years. Metallurgists and metallurgical engineers began with the bronze-workers in prehistory days.

A pick is a pick, but with a broad end and mounted it becomes an adze or a hoe; pull the hoe through the earth, and it is a plough —ox, horse, Fordson. Necessity may be the mother of invention, but, as Harrison says, prosperity is its fairy godmother. The first "fire-drill" was probably a drill for boring holes. Change of method of use, change of function. Substitute materials. Turn the knowledge of a way of attaching *a* to *b* to produce *c,* to a way of combining two other parts to produce another whole.

Is man far-seeing? Look at Edison's first lamp, the first "horse-less buggy," Langley's airplane; or at any of the first models in any museum of science and industry.

Why the endless patents these days? Canalized opportunism. What else were automobile and airplane? With the advent of rapid transportation on land and sea, possible because of the steam-engine, speed—faster, faster—became an *aim* in life; in a life so high-geared as ours, a huge aim. Schools had been turning out mechanics, engineers. Intelligence recognized the opportunity, and training and ingenuity began to design to meet it.

The prime difference today which makes for rapid advance in invention is the perfected technique of *designing* inventions and then testing the designs or models: experiment. Tens of thousands are behind the would-be inventors seeking discovery—fumbling, trying, looking. One Armageddon produced a war chariot; another, a tank. What the next one will produce the Lord only knows: certainly no General Staff does.

From this hurried sketch of the general procedure in discovery and invention, let us turn to the story itself, reconstructed from such remains as the first discoverers, inventors, mechanics, and engineers left behind. Ours is an industrial age, a mechanical era, but industry began with man; the first bow and arrow was a machine. Man is that kind of animal. The Machine Age has only begun to come into its own.

### III

The preface to the Holy Bible before me says that it is the "oldest record in the world which lays any claim to being a trustworthy history. It traces that history back to its very beginnings." Those "beginnings," as worked out after years of study by Bishop Lightfoot, Hebrew scholar and Vice-Chancellor of Cambridge University, were found to be 4004 B.C.; and that is the date at the top of the first page of my Bible. Sir J. G. Wilkinson, a distinguished Egyptologist, discovered a date on an Egyptian monument which *antedated* 4004 B.C.; and being a good Christian, he falsified the date!

The story of the discovery of prehistoric human relics, first in France, then in other parts of Europe, Asia, and Africa, the piling up of the evidence, and the complete demonstration of their great antiquity to the satisfaction of all people above the intelligence of a moron, is one of the most fascinating chapters in the history of civilization. The foundation of that chapter was largely due to the indefatigable zeal and scientific honesty of a Frenchman, Boucher de Perthes. Galileo was forced to recant; de Perthes was permitted to live in peace. And a hundred years after man's great antiquity has been proved by direct sensible evidence, Bibles are still being printed with 4004 B.C. as the beginning, not only of man, but of the earth, sun, moon, and stars.

That prehistoric chapter is so long and so wide it makes a big book in itself—in fact two volumes, as beautifully told by Mac-Curdy in his *Human Origins*; but the important, significant facts of the story can be set forth in a table which resumes, as it were, the first million years of civilization. This table—a composite based primarily on MacCurdy—is not, I need hardly add, to be considered perfect or final.

To the making of such tables many hands must contribute: prehistoric archæologists, palæontologists, anatomists, geologists, glaciologists, etc. Glaciologists especially, for the beginnings of our civilization are read between those recurring and retreating ice sheets which once covered so much of Europe: the Alpine glaciers being the surviving relics of the last great glaciers which covered the northern half of Old and New World northern hemispheres.

The table is really a compromise between observed facts and reasonable deductions. The *facts* are fossils—remains of men and animals, both living and extinct; artifacts—objects of stone, bone, clay, etc., indisputably worked or fashioned by human hands; and glacial markings, alluvial or flood deposits and drifts. From such facts the story of early man is deduced.

In a certain cave, for example, fossilized skeletal remains of men and certain artifacts are found above the fossils of certain extinct species of mammals. The presumption is that man lived in that cave at a time at least as long ago as that now extinct mammal. The next question is, when did that mammal become extinct, and how old are these indisputably human remains and artifacts? Geologist, palæontologist and glaciologist are appealed to for the answer.

Again, in a certain cave or on a certain "site" is found a slab of fossil ivory on which is etched a faithful picture of the noblest mammal that ever lived, the hairy mammoth. The artist did not dream or imagine that colossus; he must have seen it alive, on the hoof. That picture antedates the death of the last hairy mammoth. When did it become extinct? Man is older than that. Some deductions are so conclusive that they are accepted by all prehistorians. The matters still most in dispute are the fossil skeletal remains: do they represent *Homo sapiens* or just what kind of *Homo*, where did he come from, and what became of him?

One more point. The table is for Europe alone, especially France. Somebody has said that man is an adaptation to the Ice Age. Possibly; but Europe alone, especially France, has been thoroughly explored. There man can be definitely traced to a greater antiquity than elsewhere. That does not mean that man, or civilization, began in Europe; in fact, the presumption is against it.

Each year sees an extension of knowledge of prehistoric man across Asia down into Africa, and the returns are far from all in from these two vast land masses. Only recently, worked flints of very great antiquity have been found in Kenya and elsewhere in Africa. So-called *palæoliths* have been found in India, China, and elsewhere in Asia. They are of the same type as the artifacts of the Old Stone Age of Europe. Are they as old, do they go back to the same great antiquity, or are they older? These and similar problems are now under investigation. Their solution is difficult because geologists have not yet everywhere correlated their geological horizons with those of Europe.

The table, then, simply epitomizes the prehistoric civilization of the best-known region. It seems rather probable that man and culture passed into Europe from Egypt or from Mesopotamia. Certainly the first great beginnings of advanced civilization were borrowed by or were brought into Europe from the Near East.

"Historic" age or culture means recorded, written. As we saw, writing was a comparatively late, and by no means universal, achievement. Most of our American Indian culture was, in that sense, prehistoric. Long before writing had been invented in the Near East, man had overrun the habitable globe. But man certainly appeared in America later than in the Old World; he was an immigrant in pre- as in historic times. Prehistoric, therefore, is simply a convenient term; it is not a date—as, for example, 4004 B.C., 1492, or 1776.

Palæolithic (Old-stone) likewise carries no birth-death dates. Among the earliest stone tools were roughly flaked flints, of which the hand-pick (French *coup de poing*) is the most typical form; it is often called a palæolith. Such roughly flaked flints abound in America, but they are not called palæoliths—for they are rejects or unfinished spear or arrow points, and are not necessarily even pre-Columbian. In a stout hand this *coup de poing* could be a formidable weapon or a handy tool. It played a far more important rôle in human history than can ever be played by automobile or airplane.

Palæoliths were certainly made by man; they are unquestionably artifacts. They armed man with a weapon he could drop. Until this time, animals had to grow their arms, weapons, tools, and carry them about. The ape could use a stone or a stick, but that old palæolith was a *fashioned* stone, a formidable extension of fist, fingers, finger nails. It could cleave a skull. The flakes that came off in the process of chipping could cut skin, could cut like a razor. In fact, many tribes till recently used flint flakes as razors.

The Neolithic (New-stone) Age, again, is only an approximate time measure. It is even doubtful if it marks a real advance in utility. A good chipped tool or weapon requires great dexterity, fine skill; only an expert could chip out a fine flint knife or ax. Many of the "new" stone tools were ground smooth. That required great patience. A fool could grind a good stone ax.

Then there are the disputed *eoliths* or "dawn stones" from the Eolithic or Dawn Stone Age. These flints were not certainly fashioned; they do seem to have been used. They are tools in the sense that a stick is a tool. They were used as tools. They were cutting-tools a million years older than the cutting-tool I use to sharpen my pencil; Osborn thinks they are *six* million years older.

## IV

The Dawn Stone Age is reckoned roughly from 1,300,000 to 500,000 B.C.; but if to or from that estimate you add or trim off one or two hundred thousand years, no one can prove that you have falsified the dates—and Osborn will think you have greatly underestimated them. The only monument Piltdown man of the Eolithic Age left was his broken skull—beneath many feet of glacial-drift gravel.

That glacial drift marks the first of the four epochs of what is known as the Ice Age, which lasted from the end of Pliocene times of the Tertiary Period through Pleistocene times of the Quaternary Period: roughly, from 1,000,000 years ago down to 25,000 years ago.

Between these epochs the climate at times was as warm as, or warmer than, it is today in Europe.

The first Interglacial epoch found Europe as far south as Hamburg, Berlin, and London, covered with ice, and the Alpine snow line 1,200 feet lower than now. It left drift deposits of sand and gravel 100 feet thick. Eolithic "tools" have been found in these gravels. Dawn man's companions were the gigantic hippopotamus, sabre-toothed tiger, Etruscan rhinoceros, and southern mammoth.

The second Interglacial epoch was a long warm period. Among the many mammals which then entered Europe from the east or south were the broad-nosed rhinoceros, African lion and hyena, straight-tusked elephant, bison, and wild cattle. Man was still in the making, but, judging from the Heidelberg jaw, presumably of this epoch, more human than ever before.

With the retreat of the third ice sheet begins the third Interglacial Period, from 100,000 to 50,000 years ago. The climate was semitropical; the fauna, of the big game variety—elephant, Merk's rhinoceros, hippopotamus, giant deer, sabre-toothed tiger, wolf, hyena, bison, wild ox, etc. Man was a nomad hunter, and existence must have been precarious. Near Chelles on the Marne one of his camps has been found, one of the earliest known human habitations. His only known tool or weapon was a rough hand-ax. Artifacts older than this period are sometimes called pre-Chellean.

*Chellean* culture is characterized by a very rough type of chipped flint ax or pick from four to six inches long, and equally effective as knife, saw, ax, pick, or scraper. With this, man was armed as no man was ever armed before, and his advance in culture begins to speed up accordingly. Just how he looked is unknown. He must have been far from handsome, but in brain size and upright gait had travelled far from the ape he had left behind. He was definitely human; he had come finally to put his trust in the things he could make with his hands and use in his hands.

The second cultural period of prehistory, the *Acheulian*, takes its name from St.-Acheul, near Amiens, France. It was characterized by a specialization of flint tools—knives, scrapers, borers, etc. Man had become a better craftsman, had enlarged his tool-chest. The old *coup de poing* was flatter, neater, more a work of art.

Competition was beginning to tell; tools must be *good*, not just good enough. No fossil skeletal remains are associated with this culture.

With the fourth and last Glacial Period the climate becomes colder and damper. There is snow, deep and heavy, and swollen rivers. The hippopotamus, elephant, and other tropical animals have been replaced by reindeer, the woolly rhinoceros, and the hairy mammoth. Horse, bison, and wild ox abound. Man can no longer live in the open river valleys under skins or boughs. Exit Alluvial or River Drift man—or Diluvial, as he was called when science had to square itself with Noah's Deluge. Enter Cave-man.

Neanderthal man was the first cave-dweller—a child of the ice. He had a good big brain, but was still redolent of his ape ancestry. His culture, *Mousterian,* is named from the rock shelter near Le Moustier, in Dordogne, southern France, which now became the capital of the prehistoric world. Man was no beauty yet, but his cave was castle, home, nursery, workshop, tomb. He used finer tools than ever before, and discovered a new process—a basic patent! He fashioned the flakes into tools instead of the cores. He learned to strike off tiny flakes by pressure. And he learned to do better than Prometheus: he did not have to go to the gods to steal fire; he could now make it himself.

And may we note in passing that man everywhere has looked upon fire as a gift of the gods—or at least as divine magic. To record the *Myths of the Origin of Fire* has been the latest task of that prodigious worker, Sir J. G. Frazer, in a volume of 240 pages. I have so far resisted the temptation to grow enthusiastic over man's ancient conquest of fire: the rôle it has played in taming and civilizing man must be obvious; it can hardly be overestimated.

What a victory that was, my countrymen! One million years' ceaseless fighting against the most powerful mammals this earth has ever seen—lions, sabre-toothed tigers, rhinoceros with three-feet-long horns, huge elephants, still huger mammoths, wild horses, wild cattle, alligators basking in the sun on every sand-bar, hippopotamuses bobbing up and down in every river. Warm, enervating climate; icy cold climate. No friend, every beast his foe; even friend dog still a snarling jackal or fiercer wolf. No domestic animal at all, nor friendly plant. Nothing in his hand but a flint pick with which to fight the world.

Mousterian man was no child of paradise, was born with no silver spoon in his mouth; and he went in for red meat. One cave in Sicily yielded the bones of 2,000 hippopotamuses; a cave in France, a six-foot-thick layer of wild-horse bones big enough to cover four city blocks.

No, we have no reason to be ashamed of that ape-man that became a human being in a million years. It is a more edifying epic than that which began at 4004 B.C.—or at 1492 A.D. It is man's one really great epic. Earth has never witnessed another such astounding evolution.

With the close of Mousterian culture the lower stage of Old Stone culture closes, to pass some ten or fifteen thousand years later into the Upper Palæolithic Period. The climate changes again, from heavy rains and snows to intense dry cold. Forests become rare and scrubby. The mammoth and the woolly rhinoceros roam over wide, open, grassy spaces. Man has driven the cave-bear and cave-lion from their lairs. The caves and rock shelters are his alone now. A new stage in human civilization has been reached; a handsome man has appeared upon the earth. And we call him Wise, *sapiens,* because we are supposed to favour him.

What became of Mousterian man (*Homo Neanderthalensis*) is a mystery. Did he win the million years' war only to lose it? Did he lose his fight with nature? Or was he driven out by a better man? It is not yet known. It *is* known that this man who spread culture throughout Europe during the early part of the last Glacial Period disappeared as completely as though he and his family had been translated to another sphere. Why not? He was a true Culture Hero if ever there was one. He was a mighty hunter; he had tamed fire, man's most invaluable ally; had laid the foundation stones of industry; and could talk enough to be religious-minded. Why shouldn't he have been translated? Why shouldn't we canonize him?

With Neanderthal man the ape disappeared for ever from the human body. That body, now endowed with great brain power, was to begin a new series of conquests, which could have supported the human race in peace and tranquillity had not the arts of peace been prostituted to the arts of war and religion. In the mighty empires that were to come man was to become the most terrible monster the earth had yet produced. Kings, emperors, magicians, priests, popes, were to begin to drill men to obey and bow their heads. The human race, as such, was to disappear—to be replaced, not by humanity, but by Ruler and ruled, Freeman and slave, Brahman and pariah, Rich and poor, High and low, Civilized and uncivilized.

## V

True man (*Homo sapiens*) appeared in Europe some 25,000 years ago as Cro-Magnon man. His skeletal remains were found first in a rock shelter at Les Eyzies, Dordogne, in 1868; later, in many other caves. But whether the so-called Cro-Magnon "race" came from Africa or from Asia, or evolved from Neanderthal man, is not yet known. He was tall, with a well-developed chin and forehead and a brain large enough for an Einstein; and, like Mousterian man, was a victim of pyorrhœa.

The culture of this period is known as *Aurignacian* (from Aurignac in the province of Haute-Garonne), first of the three stages which make up the Upper Palæolithic Period. This culture girdled the Mediterranean and extended to the Baltic Sea on the north. It was characterized by a better equipped tool-chest—including new types of flint scrapers, borers and drills, as well as bone, ivory, and horn javelin points, knives, awls, needles, fishhooks, arrow-straighteners, and graving tools; and by real works of art and the symbols of religion. In fact, it is not too much to say that the fine arts and certain elements of religion were definitely born in the Dordogne caves of the Aurignacian stage of civilization.

That art has been considered elsewhere, but we may note here that it was real art, not yet surpassed in line, relief, or colour. The colours were ground on stone palettes and kept in bone tubes. The human forms were all portrayed nude, but decorated with necklaces and bracelets. From the presence of black manganese and red, orange and yellow ochre in the caves, it is inferred that they decorated their bodies. The skeletons generally show traces of red paint.

The second, and brief, stage of Upper Palæolithic culture is *Solutrean*, named after a station at Solutré, near Lyons, where 35,000 worked flints and the remains of 100,000 horses were found.

Man again was a craftsman rather than an artist. He made beautiful flint tools, needles with eyes for sewing, and engraved rather than painted his few wall pictures.

Central Europe meanwhile had grown steadily colder; lichen and moss, food for reindeer, had replaced prairie grass. Chamois and mountain-goats were forced down to the plains for food. The mammoth and woolly rhinoceros became almost extinct and horses comparatively rare.

With *Magdalenian* (from La Madeleine, a monastery ruin in Dordogne), the third and last stage of Upper Palæolithic culture came to a close about 20,000 years ago, and in a fog. This culture, extending from Europe far into Asia, saw ancient civilization's art reach its grandest heights in the marvellous polychrome master-pieces of the Altamira Cave in Spain and the extraordinarily fine bison modelled in clay in the Cavern of Tuc d'Audoubert in France. Art was in full stride; religion, superstition, taboo, and magic were all going concerns.

Nor were the material sides of culture less prominent. Exquisitely fashioned, excellently made tools of flint, bone, ivory, and horn abound. Daggers, harpoons, javelins, spear-throwers, graving tools, lances; tools with which to make tools and weapons; saws, drills, borers, scrapers of many varieties; needles, awls, fishhooks, pol-ishers; paint-tubes, whistles, decorated ceremonial batons of rein-deer horn; and ivory buttons, pendants, amulets. A regular museum of antiquities, a long catalogue of assorted gadgets to make life more secure, more human. Heat and lights, clothing, fine arts, re-ligion, everything a Cave-man required for hunting and fishing, and to be an artist, an artisan, and a god-fearing man.

As the Magdalenian ice retreated the reindeer retreated also, and this "Reindeer period" ends. Cold rains now add their floods to rivers already swollen by melting glaciers, and this fertile and magnificent culture of art and industry vanishes. What happened? Had man overreached himself, or had he settled down in sheer stagnation to slumber on till roused again by newcomers from the east or south? It is not yet known.

Looking back over these first hundred millenniums, certain things stand out in bold relief. An apelike man had become as human as we are. He had virtues and morals, manners and customs, art and industry. Neanderthal man buried his dead, and with the bodies placed food and their belongings. This means funeral practices, and presumably ritual and beliefs. We infer that he believed in spirits and immortality. He knew fire at least from Mousterian times, possibly a half-million years earlier.

Pre-Cave-man, we must remember, lived in the open; we know his culture only through such imperishable artifacts as flint tools: hence any possible advance he might have made in carving or fashioning wood to his will has been lost forever. That Mousterian man mounted flint arrow and spear points in wooden shafts seems probable. Magdalenian man is known to have had a short detachable harpoon shaft, hurled with terrific force from a spear-thrower. This artificially lengthened the human arm enormously. Our Eskimos still use spear-throwers, as did the ancient Mexicans.

There is no evidence that Palæolithic man made pottery, invented the bow, or domesticated any animal or plant, but on the whole he saw straight and used his hands to supply the tools and weapons necessary to lead a fairly secure and serene life. Had he thought as straight, he might have paid less attention to fertility cults and funeral rites and domesticated the horse. But we can excuse him for his ruthlessness and his superstitions; we exterminated the buffalo and preserve our Cave-man funeral rites. And we can gaze in wonderment at his outstanding achievement in the realm of æsthetics. In learning the control of fire, to cook food, clothe and decorate his body, live in his own house, and be a member of a social organization with law, order, justice, and religion, with graphic and plastic arts, songs, rituals, and legends, he laid the ground plan of a civilization on which man has been building ever since.

It was at the close of this Pleistocene Period that there was a gradual sinking of northern Europe. The British Isles were cut off from the continent. Cave-man and his art disappeared; there was a gradual transition from the Palæolithic to the Mesolithic period, and then to the Neolithic.

VI

Just what happened at the close of the Palæolithic period, or what closed it, is an unsolved mystery. Art, the reindeer, mammoth, and woolly rhinoceros disappeared. Then, some 22,000 years ago,

came a cultural period known as the Mesolithic (Middle-stone) or
*Azilian*, from Mas d'Azil in the Pyrenees, where curious painted
pebbles of unknown significance have been found. There is reason
for believing that during the next ten thousand years man was
beginning to dabble in clay, and play with certain animals (especially the dog) and plants; but not until the next cultural stage
are pottery and domesticated plants and animals known.

The Neolithic (New-stone) Age, or Prehistoric Period, as Daw-
kins calls it (12,000-3000 B.C.), all things considered, is the most
astounding period in human history. It was not that the new stone
tool became a polished stone ax so good that a modern Danish
woodsman could cut the timber and build a house in eighty-one
days with one, but that man suddenly decided that the old ground
plan of civilization was not big enough for the life of a gentleman
farmer, however suitable it might be for a nomad hunter. It was
this Neolithic culture that spread over the entire world.

The capital of Neolithic culture, in Europe at least, was the Swiss
Lakes. And what a life it was! Village life; villages on piles in
the lakes. Fifty thousand piles discovered at Wangen alone; also
one hundred bushels of grain, buried for thousands of years in the
mud. And that is not all. From these Swiss Lake villages have
been recovered barley, millet, pease, lentils, beans and apples; also
bones of dogs, cows, pigs, sheep and goats; and ploughs. The man
with the hoe had become the ox with the plough. Nomad hunters
and village fishermen had become farmers with domesticated plants
and animals, living in fixed houses, in permanent villages, with an
abundant food-supply at their beck and call, and flax for their linen
fishing-nets. And east of the Danube, far into Asia, man became a
pastoral nomad, following his herds as they moved from one pasture to another.

Meanwhile pottery had been fully developed. That meant porridge, soup, and stews—with rabbits and game birds, for the bow
had also been invented, and with it man could now stretch out
his hand, as it were, and gather in any small animal in sight. It
was a new deal in life. Civilization had taken a long stride forward
in assuring man a full belly during the long winter months, thereby
releasing energy to be spent in making mythology and otherwise
cultivating his spiritual nature.

With the full tide of Neolithic culture real houses begin to appear, partially excavated in the earth and roofed over with timbers covered with sod—not unlike the Pawnee earth-lodge or the houses of the Amur peoples. There also date from this period—though some belong to the Bronze Age—those remarkable megalithic tombs or dolmens (table-stones), menhirs (stones on end), and "alinements" of Brittany, and the great megalithic circles of Avebury and Stonehenge in England. A new kind of town life had come to all Western Europe. There were chariot races, athletic games. Where did the chariots come from? Did Europe ever invent anything so astounding as a wheel—or a draught horse? But let us go on a bit.

Neolithic Man was a great weaver of linen and wool (silk and hemp were to come later). His flax breaker and comb are well known to us, as are the plans of his house, his kitchen with hearth and hand-mill, his living-room with fireplace, loom, beds; and his dugout canoes. He was a fair surgeon, successfully trepanning the skull to relieve depressed fragments of bone, and without doubt knew more about medicine in general than a modern Healer.

Call it 3000 B.C., and Europe is still in the Stone Age—no metal, no writing, no sailing-ships.

Suddenly and without warning, metal begins to appear in Europe; the New Stone Age had passed imperceptibly into a Bronze Age culture. The Homeric Greeks had known iron for hundreds of years, but the *Iliad* mentions iron 23, bronze 270, times. Bronze was the weapon of nobility, and was used for vessels of state.

The first of the two Iron Age epochs in Europe is known as the Hallstatt, after an important site in Austria. Before it closed, (500 B.C.) pocket knives with bone handles and articulating iron blades had been invented; but not until the second epoch (La Tène) were shears invented, or iron locks and keys. Painted pottery and glass vases appear for the first time in northern Europe. But Europe north of the Balkans and the Alps was still barbaric, without cities, stone architecture, bridges, paved roads, writing, coins, millstones, wheels, or metal ploughshares—and so it remained until 200 A.D., when in its savage zeal for the blessings of civilization it began to penetrate the Roman Empire.

In other words, Europe, having weathered the Lower Palæolithic Age with the aid of fire and flint, and the Upper Palæolithic Age

with flint, bone, and art, began to invent pots and bows and polished stone tools in the Neolithic period. Possibly she did not
*invent* her pots and bows, for they were certainly known to the
East before they appear in Europe. It is certain that for her domestic plants and animals, for her Bronze and Iron Ages, and for her
metallurgy, masonry, alphabet, glassware, etc., Europe had to rely
on Asia and Africa—as she did later for her religion. Europe north
of the Alps, even well on into the Christian Era, was little, if any,
more advanced in civilization than were our Iroquois Indians, and
was far behind the Incas of Peru and the Mayas of Yucatan.

Or, to be personal, Babylon and Assyria had disappeared, Egypt
had become senile and Troy forgotten, a thousand years before we
Nordics had learned the first of the three R's.

I spoke of bronze, iron, wheat, cattle, pigs, etc., appearing suddenly in Europe. Where from? Who made these world-shaking
discoveries and inventions? Europe had large, long-horned cattle, the Urus; but the bones of the domestic cattle found in the
Swiss and Italian Lakes are of the short-horned variety. Pile-dwell-
ing pigs are small and long-legged, not at all like the native wild
boars. As a matter of fact, Europe had representatives of most of
the animals that suddenly appear as domesticated, but the work of
domestication was done in the East. Those other basic patents—
wheeled vehicles, horses, domesticated grains, etc.—were also taken
out in the Near or Far East.

The Near East gave the Far East metals, glass, wheat, cattle,
horses, cotton, architecture, religion, and writing; and in return got
silk, porcelain, gunpowder, movable type, and paper. The Nordic
world rode from savagery to civilization on borrowed horses, in borrowed clothes, with borrowed ideas.

Why did our Indians never pass from an age of stone, copper, and
bronze to an age of iron? Why did Scandinavia leave her copper
deposits untouched for fifteen hundred years after she had learned
to make marvellous bronze weapons and implements, and even
continue to import the tin she required for her bronze?

The history of most of these great and fundamental prehistoric
culture complexes is not, nor can be, well known; but it has been
worked out well enough to enable us to trace most of them back
to their beginnings. To those beginnings we now turn—not pri-

marily as problems in history, but as solutions prehistoric man reached in his effort to insure peace and plenty, and power in general over his physical environment.

VII

Domesticated animals are tamed animals. They are not born tame; they are tamed by kindness, by associating with and being fed and petted by kind people. Any animal caught young can be tamed; not all equally easily, of course, but they can be tamed. Snakes, lizards, birds, armadillos, skunks, seals, deer, camels, elephants, the *Felidæ* from cats to lions, the *Canidæ* from foxes to wolves, have all been petted by man. And note that, whereas man began to domesticate animals a few thousand years ago, ants began it millions of years ago. Just what lesson, if any, may be drawn from that fact I am not certain.

One rides over a hill into an African game reserve to find oneself suddenly in the midst of an astounding variety of game. Do they run? Not unless a horn is honked, or a gun fired, or they are chased. They are tame, but they can be frightened. Catch one young, feed it, never scare it, and it will follow you like a dog.

It is the business of every animal to know its "natural" enemies; of every flesh-eating animal, to know its meat. Nature takes care of that. Lions, tigers, etc., kill for food or for protection. Short-sighted rhinoceroses, buffaloes, elephants, etc., kill strangers on suspicion for purposes of defence. An African buffalo or a Philippine carabao that would charge you or me on sight (chiefly *scent*) will permit a naked tot to lead it by the nose or beat it with a club; it knows the tot, it takes no chance with strangers.

Man tames the animal by kindness, by feeding and protecting; especially by accustoming the animal to human society. Animals are astoundingly adept in acquiring a sense of security in man's presence. The terror-stricken face of a friendly human being is enough to let loose a shriek of terror in a pet ape. A horse will stand at ease at a cross-road and see its first train go thundering by, if some man in whom it has confidence stands at its head; confronted by a shrieking engine alone, it would break into a panic and run for its life. A great psychological factor is involved.

Certain animals are especially useful to man. They have been tamed, domesticated; turned back to nature, they become wild in a generation. I spent two weeks on a tiny island off the coast of Ecuador. It supported a small herd of cattle, loosed there many years ago from a wrecked ship. So wild were they I never even caught sight of one.

Behind animal domestication, then, are biology and psychology: animal needs; animal likes and dislikes. The dog presumably was man's first animal friend, and certainly followed him around the world; but whether the first "dog" was a coyote, fox, jackal, or wolf is not known, nor is it known just when or where such a canine was tamed. Allen believes the ancestor of domestic dogs to have been a wolf—possibly a small and now extinct species, possibly a hybrid. Like our own, the dog's ancestral tree is somewhat tangled.

Given a permanent settlement and a refuse heap of scraps, if you catch the young of the prowlers, wolves or foxes, tame them, and keep on taming their young: they are domesticated. It is a simple process and holds good for all animals that have been domesticated. Which means that the idea, as well as the achievement, of domestication might have arisen independently in different parts of the world.

Man has domesticated many animals quite out of nature. The llama, for example, one of the four small camel-like animals of the Andes, was quite weaned from nature long before the "discovery" of America. The Incas used it for its flesh and as a pack animal; it is *the* pack animal of the high Andes today. Of its long wool they wove clothing and made ropes, slings, etc. They made effigies of llamas in stone, copper, silver, and gold, and gave young llamas human burial. A volume could be written on the llama-complex.

Both species of Asiatic camels were early domesticated, and one, the dromedary, or one-humped, was at the dawn of history unknown in a wild state. The Bactrian, or two-humped, camel has almost ceased to exist wild. Without its camel-complexes, Asiatic culture would be a very different story. The camel, it seems likely, was domesticated earlier than the horse.

The Arab Midianite raiders whom Gideon defeated were mounted on camels. Camel transport made the Persian Empire possible, and carried Alexander to India and to Egypt. Under the Ptolemies, the camel spread across northern Africa. With the Nile alone as highway, Egypt could become great, but without the camel the empires to the east could not have become so great. It was the light cavalry that made Assyria's great conquests possible. With camel and horse transport available, new and subsidiary problems arose—roads, maps. Knowledge along many lines now had new value.

The dog was man's first and universal friend, but the horse was by far his most valued friend. Toy horses from a Kish palace go back five thousand years, but the horse probably was domesticated on the great plains east of the Caspian Sea a thousand years earlier. From that region hordes of nomad invaders repeatedly descended upon the Near East, the last horde being the Huns. These invaders were horsemen, hence the ease of their conquests. Pushing on to the Far East, they provoked the Chinese into building the Great Wall. They also repeatedly made trouble for the agricultural peoples of Chaldea and Babylon.

Armed and mounted Kassites overran Babylon about 2000 B.C., introducing the horse culture. By 1750 B.C. the horse was in use by the Babylonians. From Egypt, where the horse had been introduced by the Hyksos, it passed to Greece, and finally to Europe in general.

It was the horse-drawn chariot that helped to enrich the Amarna Age. Horses were still sacred in David's time. But while to Egypt the horse was simply part of the military machine or war-complex, it was a large part of the Asiatic nomad's life. He rode not only to war but to all his activities; everybody rode. His life centred about the horse. Only in the days of chivalry was there a widespread horse culture in Europe, and that was largely a special class culture.

The nomads of the steppes rode horseback; the Babylonians, Egyptians, and Romans used chariots. The oldest known wheel is from Ur; the Babylonians used ox-carts. When they got the horse, they put him to the cart.

The horse probably originated on this continent, but had become extinct in geologic times. To the Aztecs the horse-mounted Spaniards were two-headed monsters; yet within a century the horse had spread over most of the Americas and in parts had completely changed the culture of the aborigines. By 1669 wild horses were so numerous in Virginia as to be a pest. The horse culture was perfectly at home on the Plains before 1650, and the first white man on the Saskatchewan, in 1754, found all the Indians on horses.

Our Indians not only took over the horse, but the entire horse-complex, from the Spaniards—saddle, stirrup, crupper, quirt, and lariat. When the Easterner moved onto the Plains he took the same complex over from the Indians, and from the Mexicans sombrero, heavy spurs, and chaps. Which means that when the English Colonial became a cowboy he abandoned his English horse culture with its small saddle and small spurs, and took over a horse culture introduced by the Arabs into Spain and by the Spanish into Mexico.

Our Indians had used dogs to drag their V-shaped dog-travois for transporting their belongings. They promptly made horse-travois, and having become dependent upon buffalo meat for their food, became in a sense nomads instead of settled agriculturalists. That, in turn, necessitated easily portable houses; the *tipi* was the answer.

The horse made the Plains Indians, but while there was no Indian element in the horse culture except the Indian himself, the horse made a new kind of culture possible for the Indian—the buffalo culture. We stopped that culture dead in 1876—by finishing the slaughter of the buffalo. The noble red man had to make peace with the paleface.

It has been argued that man's first culture-complex was a horse hunt, and that while the men hunted in packs the women hunted berries and roots. That is too simple. We might as well say that man is a natural big-game hunter; woman, a natural truck farmer. Man is naturally born good for nothing but to monkey around and taste anything he can get his hands on. He is naturally a family man, but nothing more may be predicated of him. Even Biblical prophecies were written after the event, and at that are not always reliable. The "primal horde" of Atkinson and Freud is fiction and Trotter's "herd" is speculation; neither is factually founded.

The primitive family ate anything they could find that was good to eat. The horse-flesh trait was a special development in a special region, under special circumstances. Palæolithic man also ate the flesh of bears, elephants, and rhinoceroses, and we have already seen the piles of hippopotamus bones from the gargantuan feasts. Does this mean that man had to become "adapted" to a meat diet?

Man's alimentary canal does show a slightly closer analogy to carnivorous than to herbivorous animals, but his dentition belongs to neither. Man and other Primates alone among mammals have an *omnivorous* set of teeth, not specialized for any particular diet, good for any food that tastes good and satisfies.

The great civilizations of both New and Old Worlds were founded upon agriculture. Cereals are as easily domesticated as animals. Some cereals, like some animals, have been completely domesticated out of their natural state; some varieties bear no more resemblance to the original than a poodle-dog does to whatever it was that man made his dogs from.

Once the technique of crops was discovered in the Nile Valley, for example, Egyptian life began to blossom like a garden. Not that every "blossom" was beneficial to mankind; but life, freed of the haunting fear of want, began to blossom out in new fields of endeavour. Life was so rich and so easy that they could afford to spend an enormous amount of time on trying to make life eternal. Comparable phenomena took place in other agricultural cultures—Mesopotamia, India, China, Peru, Mexico. We have already seen how life in Europe seemed to leap forth when agricultural-complexes were adopted.

In other words, a new and valuable food-complex becomes stimulus to provoke the invention of other collateral or subsidiary complexes. Think of the science, art, industry, commerce and trade that have gone into the can of pork and beans on our pantry shelves. It is hardly too much to say that half of civilization, since beans and pigs were tamed, has conspired to produce a can of pork and beans: something an army can travel on, something a nation can live on.

Not only did agriculture and husbandry make great empires possible; they also changed the map of nature for man. He was stimulated to re-read that map. Hence the rise of great fertility cults, new gods and goddesses, new rites, new prayers, new incantations, new superstitions.

Certain regions are especially favoured for agriculture, others for grazing. Both types of life give man great freedom; but agriculture, with its fixed abodes, gave an additional freedom—freedom to build, to collect, to hoard, to amass wealth, to speculate about nature, about the stars, to found schools, maintain priests, astrologers, diviners, etc. Then fine clothes, endowed temples, rich trappings of state and church, gold and jewels, become so much tempting bait for the man on the horse. The cowpuncher sacking the town is a very old story.

Agricultural life is inherently peaceful. Peace is its life blood; it waxes fat and grows rich with peace. Thus Egypt, Sumeria, Babylonia, India, China, cultivated the arts of peace and grew rich— only to be despoiled by Assyrians, Arabs, Persians, Mongols. The year-by-year, century-by-century history of the cradles of great civilizations is comprehensible in the light of such facts as these. But the "cowpuncher" usually succumbs sooner or later to the refinements of the city—sometimes only after he has sacked and burned it, sometimes by taking charge of it and sacking a few old idols and ideas. He may even think up some new ones. Thus are cultures and peoples always being mixed; fertilization and cross-fertilization.

Trait-complexes spring up out of brains fertilized, as it were, by domestication-complexes; new deals in human relations are possible. Hyksos kings introduce horse-drawn chariots into Egypt. Within a few centuries Pharaoh's chariot-drawn archers have carved out the first world-empire. Egypt entered international politics thirty-three centuries before we did.

But there is no inherent reason why pastoral peoples should become bandits. When Abraham of Ur of the Chaldees wandered with his flocks into Canaan, he sought a parasitic life among the Canaanite farmers. Hebrew history enters a new phase—or rather begins.

The consequence of domesticating a wild plant or tree is not fundamentally different from domesticating a wild animal. The plant, tree, or animal is thereby largely freed from the natural struggle for existence. As human culture protects human beings from the rigours of adverse environment, so plant- or animal-complex frees the plant or animal from the strain of strife. Competition for a place in the sun among plants, for pasture or prey among animals, is a real struggle, a veritable fight for life. Hence energies that in a state of nature must go into certain biological traits—cellulose in plants, bone in animals—may go into sugars and fats. Increase in sugars and fats makes plants and animals just so much more valuable as food-supplies.

The process of domestication is, of course, different: there can be no such intimate bond between man and the vegetal world; but as I have said, the consequences of domestication are analogous. The plant is tended, protected, and defended from its enemies, lifted out of competition with similar organisms which might in a free and open fight win out because of their sturdier vegetal skeleton.

The Wisconsin Ojibwas had no rice gardens, but they had property rights in patches of wild rice, and they sowed rice in swamps where none had grown before, thus artificially increasing its area. They collected rice, hulled, winnowed, stored, and ate it; they had a well-developed wild-rice-complex. It requires only a struggle among humans for more rice, or in the rice swamps for more water or more favourable conditions to grow at all, to set human machinery in motion to solve the problem.

That problem has repeatedly come up in human history. Threatened, the wild plant-child of nature suddenly acquires new value, a heavier load of stimulus. Because of this stimulus the "child" is adopted into the human family, tended, protected, defended, cultivated—in a word, domesticated—and becomes the favourite child of the family. True cultivation implies tillage of the soil and an artificial interference with the soil to promote growth.

Who started agriculture? Merely to ask that question is to prompt another: Did "civilization" begin in Egypt or in Mesopotamia? Agriculture probably began in one or the other, possibly in both, presumably in Egypt. Quite possibly the date-palm was cultivated before any cereal; it has been an invaluable friend to man in the Near East. To pass down the Nile Valley in autumn, when the date-palms are loaded with enormous clusters of golden-brown dates, is a revelation.

It is, says Breasted, a "finally established fact that civilization first arose in Egypt." And when Breasted says it is a fact, we may begin at that point and go confidently forward to examine some other facts which bear on our problem. The first is Egypt's physiographic uniqueness. Egypt is the Nile—nothing more. But what a river, what fertilizing floods, what verdure when the floods subside, and what a desert frame for that verdant valley! If nature anywhere in the world pointed the way to agriculture, forced its possibilities on man, and encouraged him on to success, it was in that same Nile Valley.

Nowhere else on earth does stark death meet such lush life face to face and for so many hundreds of miles as in Egypt. That flooded Nile is most opportune; it comes at the end of summer when the soil most needs moisture. With coming cool weather there is little evaporation and the soil retains the moisture. But it does not get so cold during the winter months that grains, flax, etc., stop growing. Therein does nature conspire. Seasonal cycle of flood and cool weather is made to order for a good crop of millet and barley. Before the flood has completely subsided the green stalks appear; they ripen before the heat of summer burns the earth to brick, but not the seeds to death—they are ready to sprout with the August-September floods.

Those floods, a billion cubic yards a day, are as steadily recurrent as the tides, and if Uganda scants the White Nile's waters, Abyssinia can be counted on to flood the Blue Nile. White and Blue, of course, are figures of speech—like the "Blue" Danube. In flood, they are liquid mud, nature's own fertilizer, fresh from the tropics. It doesn't rain in Egypt. That again is a blessing for the farmer; he not only can count on his water, he is freed from mildew and the usual weevil pests which plague the rain farmer. And he could store his grain safely. Clay for granaries was under his feet; the sun would bake his bricks.

We examine the contents of the oldest known human stomach for our next fact. The last meal eaten by Egyptians 6,000 years ago, as discovered by Elliot Smith, was barley and millet and root-tubers of the nut-rush. These foods came from Egypt itself, or were imported; there is no evidence that they were imported or used elsewhere at that time for food, and it seems fairly certain that they were home-grown. Those oldest-known stomachs are pre-Dynastic. In a First Dynasty tomb (3400 B.C.) an ear of bearded grain carved on ivory was found; it may have been barley, but presumably was wheat—though possibly wheat was first cultivated by the Babylonians. A few centuries later, unmistakable references to both wheat and barley (and brewed beer) begin to abound, centuries before Biblical references to the "corn" of Abraham and Isaac.

Once the Egyptians had mastered the main principles of taming cereals, the next stage—controlling the water supply by means of dams and irrigating canals—would easily follow. The two oldest known agricultural cultures were Egypt and Sumer; both developed irrigation. Their neighbours—Assyria, Persia, Phœnicia, Syria, and later the Kassites, Mitanni and Hittites—all became skilful irrigation agriculturalists.

Barley and wheat, then, presumably began to be cultivated in Egypt, or somewhere in the Fertile Crescent, at least seven and possibly ten thousand years ago. Romaine salad, domesticated from a wild state, and many other garden vegetables, were known to Egyptians of the Pyramid Age; also marvellously fine linens and tapestry. Indo-China originated the rice-complex; also leaks, onions, pulses, hemp, and oats. China seems to have originated the soya bean, peach, and apricot. It is certain that Egypt had domesticated the wild ass, bred cattle, practised irrigation farming, was using metals, had invented writing, and had developed government on a big scale, before Europe had seen the last of the Ice Age.

This "emergence" Breasted calls the "most important event in the universe." I can think of three I should rate higher: the blow that freed this earth from the sun; the evolution of protoplasm from a few common elements; and the passing of a gibbering ape into a speaking man. But that our own civilization was cradled outside of Europe there is no doubt; nor, presumably, is there any doubt that its rebirth into something finer, simpler, more rational, more humane, will take place outside of Europe.

With agriculture the economic basis of life, great culture-complexes begin to spring up like mushrooms. Domesticated animals that had been used exclusively for food and hides begin to be used for transportation or draught purposes. Also for milk, cheese, and butter. Saddles, chariots, carts, wagons, ploughs. All well known in Asia from one to three thousand years before they passed into Europe.

Just why a particular people domesticated a particular plant or animal at a given time can be understood only as certain historic and environmental facts are known. One such fact is, of course, that before any animal or plant could be tamed, it must be found wild. On this score aboriginal America stands very high. She tamed the best beast of burden she had and made astoundingly good use of her vegetal resources. She was even on the way, as we have seen, to taming the wild rice of the Great Lakes. In artificial irrigation and in the construction of terraces, she stands high among the earth's best; in fact, the miles of artificially irrigated terraces of dressed stone reaching altitudes of 14,000 feet near Cuzco, Peru, are unsurpassed elsewhere on earth, in ancient or modern times, not even by the rice-growing peoples of the Far East.

Those marvellous Peruvian terraces could not have been built had not full granaries ensured full stomachs, thereby giving man time to plan new improvements. Therein lies the significance of agriculture in human history.

While native American civilization in general influenced ours only indirectly, we may stop here to pay our respects to the astounding contribution to the world's larder made by the American Indian—all aboriginal food-complexes, each with its own distinct history. That contribution, as Laufer says, is the most extensive, recent, prominent, universal, and momentous in the world's history; it has been felt everywhere, "has changed the surface of the earth."

Take tobacco; or perhaps we should take corn first, for corn was king on this continent thousands of years before the Pilgrims ate their first dish of succotash or smoked their first pipe of tobacco.

Wild wheat still grows on Mount Hermon, and the wild prototypes of all other cereals are known—all but corn. That is one reason, argues Collins, that corn may be the oldest domesticated cereal, with a continuous history behind it on American soil of 10,000 years. His other reasons are that corn is the only cereal completely dependent upon man for existence; that it is the only cereal known in a fossilized existence; and that no other cereal compares with it in diversity of forms. It probably arose in Mexico as "a hybrid between a *teosinte* and an unknown plant with edible seeds."

*Teosinte* is the *teocentli* of the Aztecs, the "grass of the gods," the only known plant that will hybridize with corn, and found only in the highlands of central Mexico, where corn presumably was domesticated—probably by the Mayas, the Egyptians of the New

World. But, as Morley points out, it was in the highlands of Peru that corn reached its greatest number and variety of types. Peruvian civilization is old, but its chronology cannot be read. That of the Mayas can—definitely, back to 400 B.C.; and it was then an old civilization with a highly developed and intricate calendar system and an absolutely unique chronology. Civilization in the New World was as surely founded on corn as it was on wheat in the Old World. "Higher" civilizations are indissolubly linked with agriculture.

Our ancestors, says Wissler, not only took over the Indian corn-complex bodily, but in the form which survives to this day—even to the number of grains planted in a hill, the interval between the hills, the beans and squash among the corn, the testing of the seed in warm water, the use of fish (one to a hill) as fertilizer, the husking-pin, and the idea and architecture of the corn crib. Even the methods of cooking, the roasting ears, the mush stirred by wooden ladles, lye hominy, the name *hominy* itself, corn and beans or succotash, corn-husk mats: all are Indian in origin. And our old-fashioned husking-bees strongly suggest the religious ceremonies the Indians used to perform because of the divine honours they bestowed upon this gift of the gods.

Of this purely American complex only the plant itself went to Europe, and thence spread all over Africa and Asia, where its culture took two different forms. Maize as a food plant in Africa, for example, ran a course of its own. It had to compete with other food-complexes, fit into established cultural traits.

America gave the world another equally democratic plant—the potato. First domesticated in Peru and Chile, possibly 2,000 years ago, it reached the New England colonists, says Laufer, from England *via* Bermuda. But it did not really dig in in England till the eighteenth century. It never became a favourite in the Far East—as did the American sweet potato, or *batata*, which was received with ecstasy in China, Luchu, and Japan, and under the Spaniards spread over the Philippine Islands.

The sweet potato's career in the Far East, says Laufer, is sheer romance. In 1593 the Chinese province of Fukien was famine-stricken. The governor sent a commission to Luzon, then thickly settled with Fukienians, to search for food plants. But the Spaniards had prohibited all export; so the Chinese wrapped the plants in cordage to look like ship cables, and thus they reached Fukien. In a short time, agricultural treatises and poems in honour of the *batata* had spread like prairie fire. From Fukien it was transplanted to Formosa and to the little Luchu kingdom as early as 1605, where it was found by a visiting Japanese farmer and carried back to Satsuma Province for cultivation. From this point it was disseminated all over Japan. The tomb of its discoverer, Riuemon, was known as the Temple of the Sweet Potato, and offerings were made to him every spring and autumn. The earliest Japanese treatise on agriculture (1695) gives a full account of its cultivation. During the famine years of 1832, 1844, 1872, and again in 1896, the *batata* was to be their sole means of subsistence.

The pineapple, queen of fruits, was a thoroughly domesticated plant in pre-Columbian Brazil, Guiana, and Colombia—cultivated practically out of its seeds and propagated only by crowns, slips, or suckers. According to Laufer, the pineapple is first mentioned in English literature in 1568, when Evelyn "first saw the famous queen-pine brought from the Barbadoes and presented to H. M. Charles II." Before the seventeenth century it had reached the East Indies, and shortly afterwards China, where it is cultivated in enormous quantities. Fibre from its leaf is the staple dress-goods of the Philippine Islands.

Another American food-complex that spread with amazing rapidity was the *manioc*. Tapioca originated with the Indians north of the Amazon. Its preparation from the root of the *manioc* requires special apparatus and the riddance of poisonous alkali. Call it the manioc-complex. One hundred years after its introduction into Africa it had overspread that vast continent—and without one line of advertising or one word of propaganda. It supplied a "long-felt want" and spread like wildfire.

Then there is tobacco, so purely American that only its scientific name owes anything to the Old World—and that to Jean Nicot, who presented Queen Catherine de' Medici with ground dried tobacco to be used as snuff to cure her headache. She was the first European woman known to use tobacco. The earliest mention of the use of snuff is by a friar who accompanied Columbus on his second voyage. Long used as a medicine, snuff became a luxury early in the seventeenth century. The snuff-box used by Newton at Cambridge has never been allowed to run dry. The first snuff factory started in this country still grinds out its quota of the annual output of 41,000,000 pounds.

Laufer, after long investigation, found only one tribe in the world that does not use tobacco in some form, and all adopted since 1492. It is the most universally consumed of all narcotics, profoundly influencing national economics and social customs. As the pipe of peace was the Indian emblem of friendship, so the Chinese and Japanese call tobacco the "herb of amiability, on account of the affectionate feelings entertained by all classes of mankind since its use has become general": the world's greatest maker of peace, tranquillity, comfort, and happiness.

That tobacco originated on this and on no other continent, botanists are now agreed. Even the name tobacco, Indian for cigar, was borrowed. It was not long before all Europe was smoking the weed. In an incredibly short time the tobacco-complex found its way across Africa, Asia, the East Indies—and even into the far interior of New Guinea long before a white man ever saw New Guinea. In one sense, no lovelier works of art have ever been made by man than some of the tobacco pipes of the Ohio Mounds, nor finer idea developed than the Indian Pipe of Peace.

Americans were also cultivating before 1492 cotton, coca, cacao, sunflower, the "Jerusalem" artichoke, the wild grape, wild plum, and the wild cherry. Peanuts were probably more widely cultivated before than after Columbus. Maple sugar was also purely American; its whole complex was taken over bodily by the English Colonists.

With America's corn, peanuts, potato, sweet potato, and tobacco, this earth is richer than it used to be. Potato and sweet potato especially have been invaluable famine crops in Ireland and in Central and South East Asia. For thousands of miles up and down and across Africa, one is rarely out of sight of a patch of corn (mealies), potatoes, sweet potatoes, peanuts, casava, or tobacco, all domesticated by the American Indians.

While alcoholic drinks were made in many parts of prehistoric America, our word alcohol comes from the Arabic chemists, and our word "booze," thinks Laufer, is possibly the old Persian-Arabic word *boza* or *buza* applied to an alcoholic drink made from millet, barley, or rice, and widely distributed across Asia, Europe, and northern Africa.

There are no less than two hundred passages referring to wine, strong drink, or other alcoholic beverage in the Old Testament. Wine or beer was the great stimulant of the East before the days of tea and coffee, and each country had its own alcohol-complex. The Jews used wine both as a food and as a heart stimulant; and the Bible reveals an extraordinarily sound and up-to-date account of the various physiological, pharmacological, and toxicological properties of ethyl alcohol. Among the earliest pictured scenes that have come down to us from antiquity are "wet parties" having a good time watching a ballet with orchestral accompaniment, while being attended by slaves. The Norse mead-hall probably goes back to Palæolithic times. With but very few exceptions, no tribe has been discovered without some form of alcoholic or narcotic complex.

For thousands of years agriculture remained just about where the ancient farmers left it: same old ox-drawn plough with wooden share, same old sowing by hand and same old hand-sickle, same old treading out of grain by cattle's hoofs, same old winnowing fans, same old hand or wind or water mills. For thousands of years these old complexes persisted without change, handed on from one generation to another. Buckwheat was cut with a hand-sickle and threshed with a hand-flail in Licking County, Ohio, last year. A poor man's crop, a small patch of ground: no need for modern machinery; the old way was good enough. A wheat-field of sub-continental proportions is different. But no McCormicks or Deerings could have inaugurated a new agriculture had there not been a new industry of cheap iron and steel.

VIII

The Near East planted the first garden and built the first forge; the two cradled civilization. That civilization was Oriental; it was as much an organic unity, and for as long a time, as European civilization.

Emphasis on our own Industrial Age tends to obscure the great fact that man is naturally industrious and had become a manufacturer before he had become quite human. Neanderthal Man's "palæolith" was a manufactured product; the Industrial Age was already well on its way into the first of the two great epochs of industry. The basis of that industry was stone; it was the Stone Age of industrial history. It was followed by the Metal Age—the age we are in now, the beginnings of which follow neither rhyme nor reason, because just as there are stones and stones, so there are metals and metals and each has its own peculiar behaviour. Some of these ways are so peculiar that they remained profound secrets until quite recent times. Our Industrial Age is backed by an enormous amount of high-geared scientific study, long and costly experimentation requiring a synthesis of the knowledge of a dozen or more special sciences.

There was no sharp break between Stone and Metal Age. Opportunities for lucky chance discoveries are not equally distributed over the earth. There was a most excellent reason, for example, why ancient Peru had begun to use bronze, and why our Mound Builders knew nothing of bronze but employed much copper and iron. Yet the use of iron as the great industrial metal was long delayed in the Old World. Egypt, in a sense, had gone into a decline before she began to produce iron. The Great Pyramids had become hoary with age before the mud of the Nile was stirred with iron hoes. Only with Ramses II, 1,600 years after Cheops, did Egypt's Iron Age begin. Western Europe knew no "cast" iron before the fifteenth century. China had cast-iron cookstoves, and in fact was master of the art of casting iron, as early as the Han Dynasty; yet their wrought-iron swords and knives are inferior to those of Central Africa or of the head-hunters of Borneo.

Most of those metalliferous puzzles disappear when viewed against the background of a few hard facts—such as, that there is meteoric iron and that there are iron ores. Meteoric iron is easily discovered if it is discoverable. Meteoric dust presumably, like rain, falls upon the just and the unjust, but meteoric iron falls according to no known law. There is nothing at all easy about iron ore. Even at a temperature of 900° C. it is only a pasty mass or "bloom," which only by hammering is "wrought" into anything fit for use; only in a furnace heat of 1535° C. does it fuse or "melt." That discovery came late in human history. To bury Tutankhamen in concentric coffins of pure gold was cheap and easy compared with a cast- or even wrought-iron burial.

In the eyes of our Mound Builders iron was "precious" enough to cause them to go to the trouble of iron-plating gold and silver ornaments. But it was meteoric iron; "black iron of heaven from the sky," the Hittites called it; "marvel from heaven," a Sixth Dynasty Pyramid text calls it. And what were the "swords from heaven" of Attila and Timor but meteoric iron, or the magic sword Hephæstus, "whose breath was fire," gave Pelias?

Meteoric iron is not iron of the earth, it is iron from heaven; and practically all meteoric iron is malleable; it makes wonderful swords, magic swords. A 100-pound meteorite that fell near Cordova, Spain, in the twelfth century, was promptly beaten into swords. Zimmer cites more than forty instances of the use of meteoric iron for knives, weapons, etc., by primitive tribes. But no amount of hammering of meteoric iron or realization of its excellence for industrial purposes could suggest the wealth locked up in hematite or magnetite, or any of the iron ores. Some discoveries are hard, some easy.

An easy and early discovery was gold. It too has a behaviour of its own. It exists in a pure or "free" state and is widely distributed; is comparatively insoluble, does not tarnish or oxidize—hence is relatively imperishable and remains bright and shiny; is one of the heaviest metals—hence concentrates easily; is comparatively soft, and so is easily hammered; melts easily—hence is easily moulded. These are among the reasons why gold was probably the first metal man discovered: not as gold or as metal, but as a peculiar kind of stone—"yellow stones." One, found in Ballarat, Australia, weighed 190 pounds. And a native Australian would gladly have traded it for an empty beer-bottle: with its glass he could chip knives, razors, arrow-heads—things he could use; that big nugget to him was a yellow stone and nothing more. He knew nothing about the glamour of gold; or that it is the symbol of immortality and untarnishable incorruptibility; or that it is the seed of Agni, source of life and light, fire and fertility.

To the Pyramid Age gold was the Sun God Re, who begat the kings in whose veins coursed "the liquid of Re, the gold of the gods and goddesses, the luminous fluid of the sun, source of all life, strength, and persistence."

To primitive man almost everywhere gold was good for nothing but personal ornament or god-metal, to hang around his neck or from his ears, or to make images. No wonder it became precious and glamorous, and even today makes honest thinking about values almost impossible. But the really precious metal of antiquity was the "red stone"—native copper.

In an abandoned trench in Minnesota a six-ton mass of copper was found which had been raised five feet by the Indians. In the vicinity were ten wagon-loads of stone hammers. Aboriginal America had its Copper Age as surely as did the prehistoric Old World. But it was a hammered copper culture—even as it was in Chaldea 6,500 years ago, and possibly even earlier in Egypt. The smith preceded the metallurgist.

It was copper as a stone that could be beaten into any desired shape and hardened perceptibly during the process—if not excessively hammered—that marked the transition in industry from stone to metal. But the true Age of Metals did not begin until man had discovered the basic fact of metallurgy—that metal could be melted out of rock. This discovery was presumably purely accidental and may have been made more than once. Rickard thinks a camp fire the most likely first metallurgic hearth. Given a hot fire enclosed by a ring of stones containing an oxide or carbonate of copper, beads of copper would result.

In the history of material culture was there ever a more momentous discovery? Real tools, at last; and the use of other metals. But it is a metallurgist's story. Let Rickard speak through the smoke of that lonely camp fire in the remote past, of the vision that rises

. . . of achievements unbelievable, of devices to assist human muscle, of bridges thrown over gulfs of space, of steel roads that thunder with the traffic of continents, of whispering wires that flash the news of the day round the earth, of other metallic threads that bring the energy of the mountain torrent into the innermost chamber, of many-storied towers that top the tallest trees; of boats that mock the vagrant wind and dive beneath the restless wave, of machines that fly above the mountain crests and thread the clouds of heaven, of all that brought man from the darkness of the jungle into the glory of the sunlight, from savagery into civilization.

Breasted locates this happy accident in the Sinai Peninsula about six thousand years ago. But globules of copper at first led to nothing more than beads for necklaces for the women. Later, copper was cast into blades, replacing ancient flint knives.

Although copper was discovered a thousand years before Egypt's era of great masonry, it was not until the pyramid-tomb idea was well started that copper tools developed rapidly: six-feet-long rip-saws to cut the limestone blocks for the Pyramids; 1,300-feet-long copper pipe to drain the Pyramid Temple.

There is no tin in the Sinai Peninsula, nor is it known where or when bronze was invented. It was probably discovered by accident. Egyptian copper contains arsenic; German, nickel; Hungarian, antimony; Indian, zinc; Saxony, tin. Copper alloyed with zinc makes brass; with tin, bronze. Generally speaking, tin is usually associated with copper in northern Europe and in Asia. No bronze period in North America because its tin ores are not associated with copper ores: no chance to discover that some copper ores are harder than others. Bronze was produced and its underlying idea of a metallurgic flux discovered long before tin was discovered.

With the addition of two-per-cent tin, copper hardens perceptibly; with five-per-cent it makes efficient weapons and tools. Bronze was known in the Near East by 4000 B.C.; in Spain and Italy by 2000 B.C.; in Egypt by 1580 B.C. Ægean civilization is Bronze Age civilization.

Bronze stimulated enormously the arts of war. The sword became the badge of rank; sword-making, an important industry. A flint dagger in Egypt, then cast in copper, then in bronze, the sword, according to Kroeber, took two lines of development. The one-edged cutting or hewing sabre developed in Asia Minor and was the ancestor of the Saracen and Italian scimitar and the Samurai sword of Japan. The two-edged sword with sharp point was the one favoured by Europe. In northern Europe, after the Iron Age began, it reached a greater length than the Greek and Roman swords. The Teuton two-handed hacking sword was very effective —if the victim could be detained long enough to be hacked.

Iron is known to have been used by 1400 B.C. in India, where it was called "dark-blue bronze." Phillips argues that India was its original home. Rickard thinks the art of iron-making originated in the mountainous country between the Caspian and Black Seas. The first real developers of iron were probably the Hittites; they are known to have used iron by 1350 B.C. According to Breasted, an iron sword was sent to an Egyptian king as a gift in the thirteenth century, and a Hittite king was ordered to send to Ramses II a shipment of "pure iron." The first large army known to have been equipped with iron weapons was the Assyrian. They obtained their knowledge of iron from the Hittites. Sargon's arsenal contained 200 tons of iron weapons and siege implements.

In the eighth century B.C. iron was so abundant in China that it was taxed, but it did not replace bronze for weapons till 500 B.C. A century later it had crossed over to Japan.

The Iron Age of Europe began in the Ægean Islands. Iron reached Greece by 1300 B.C. and was used by the Greeks in the Trojan War. Greek civilization may be said to have begun with the Iron Age, 1000 B.C., but to Æschylus 500 years later, iron is still the "Chalybean stranger."

The famous prehistoric cemetery of Hallstatt in the Austrian Tyrol yielded an astonishing number and variety of iron objects—proof of a great industry: long and short swords, daggers, scabbards, bracelets, etc. La Tène on Lake Neuchâtel, Switzerland, has yielded iron swords, sickles, rings, bars, brooches, spear-heads, etc. The Hallstatt "period" is reckoned from 1000-500 B.C.; La Tène, from 500-50 B.C. But Hallstatt's seemingly high civilization was based on its work in iron alone; in the other arts of civilization it was behind from one to two thousand years.

Egypt of the Pyramid Age (3000-2500 B.C.) was using closed furnaces to protect the firing of pottery from the wind. The principle of glass was soon discovered—accidentally, of course. At first it was used for glazing only; later, for bottles. Glass as art and industry was taken up and highly developed by the Phœnicians.

Glazed pottery, so far as can be ascertained, was invented independently in the Old and New Worlds. But the pottery idea is very widespread. Given the right kind of clay and enough heat, the surface of the vessel will vitrify—glaze. The discovery of that fact had no far-reaching consequences in America; it had in China. Our chinaware is proof enough.

And speaking of China reminds me of the bow and arrow—not

a Chinese invention but a Chinese specialty; it was the chief weapon in their military-complex and could not compete on equal terms with European bullets driven by gunpowder. The Chinese invented gunpowder. Out of that culture trait they built up a fireworks- and firecracker-complex, and did it so well that Western civilization finally took that over also; and now China is forced to take over the Western military-complex.

Bows and arrows are enormously useful go-getters for food and are found practically everywhere. But a good bow must be long and of good wood. Its length is against it as a military weapon either on horseback or in chariot. The Tartars invented a special type of compound bow. Its chief distinction was its sinew back; thus it could remain short and still be powerful. It spread across North Asia to the Ural Mountains on the west and to Siberia on the east. From Siberia it spread to Alaska, eastward among the Eskimos, and southward to California and northern Mexico; also, from China to India. It was known to Egypt of the Sixteenth Dynasty and to the Homeric Greeks. The Scythians used it against the Persians. Arabian horsemen carried the same Tartar bow across northern Africa and into Spain. It hung on in Italy until it was replaced by a steel bow of the same pattern. With gunpowder, the steel bow was as out-of-date as the man who hid behind steel armor and called himself a knight.

## IX

*Even* numbers are "soluble"—therefore ephemeral, feminine, earthly; *odd* numbers are "indissoluble"—hence masculine, celestial. But *one* is not odd, because it is the source of all numbers! "Superstition erected into a system," Dantzig calls it; but I infer that he thinks the idea good, for he says "only through number and form can man grasp the nature of the universe." My guess is that man's best graspers are his hands, and that the universe whose nature he grasps with mathematics is one that can be put in a pill-box or reduced to chalk marks. But of that, more later. What interests us now is why man began to count and how he came by numbers, that marvellously useful tool for the acquisition of knowledge. That quest takes us back to the beginnings again, to a great fact: that without signs, symbols, and words for things, qualities, relationships and natural phenomena in general, man's world could hardly have progressed far beyond the ape's world.

The ape, as we have seen, can discriminate, can do what Dantzig describes as recognizing "that something has changed in a small collection when, without his direct knowledge, an object has been removed from or added to the collection."

But we need not call that capacity to discriminate a "faculty" or a "number sense," as Dantzig does, for that, it seems to me, obscures an enormously important point, which is that man, through words, can refine his sensory discriminations—even to counting them. Counting involves or implies arbitrary, but fixed, words or symbols. Man alone of the animal world can count; that is, as Dantzig says, an exclusively human attribute. But no "intricate mental process" is involved; rather, brains and a human-speech mechanism.

Nor is "number the language of science," though man is the measure of all things and arithmetic has proved extraordinarily useful for prying into things that needed measuring—so useful that progress in the knowledge of many categories of phenomena would have been next to impossible without arithmetic, the foundation of mathematics. But numbers are older than arithmetic. In fact, arithmetic is a modern art; numbers, or *arithmos* as the Greeks called it, an ancient art. Pythagoras and other Greeks contributed greatly to the evolution of number concepts; but Pythagoras was a numerologist rather than a mathematician; to put it bluntly, he was "crazy" about numbers, as the Chaldeans were about the stars. But the difference between anthropomorphizing stars and numbers is all in favour of the stars.

Four is a *perfect* number; there are four sides to a square, four virtues, four seasons, four elements, four evangelists. There are four letters in God's (Latin) name—*D e u s*; and four in *A d a m*. "A" stands for *anatole*, Greek for east; "d" for *dysis*, west; "a" for *arktos*, north; and "m" for *membrion*, south; and these are the four quarters of the world. Four is a very wonderful number.

Forty days and forty nights' rain to make a Deluge; forty days and forty nights for Moses' visit to Yahweh on Sinai; forty years' wandering in the wilderness; and forty stripes, kine, cubits, baths, shekels, camels, and sockets of silver.

*Three* carries a mixed burden. There are three principal sins, three ways to satisfy sin, three persons offended by sin, three degrees of penitence, three furies, three virtues, three enemies of the soul, three principal things in Paradise, and three things especially displeasing to God.

Four is a good number, but *six* is better—in fact, it is the perfect number, not because God created all things in six days, but that all things were created in six days *because* six is perfect. So perfect, thought one early Master Mind, that it would still be perfect had there been neither God nor creation!

But in some games *seven* is even more perfect. It wins, on the first pass. By faith, says Paul, the walls of Jericho fell down, but more potent than faith in their fall, I suspect, was the magic number *seven*: seven priests blasting on seven trumpets for seven days and encompassing the city seven times. Then there were the seven deadly sins, virtues, spirits of God, joys of the Virgin, and seven devils cast out of Mary Magdalene.

Come seven! (One of the early uses for lead, by the way, was to load dice!) But the point is that every number up to sixty, some time, somewhere, has been more than a mere number; it has been a *loaded* number—a portent, a sign. We speak of cardinal and ordinal numbers, but to modern numerologists, Mediæval Schoolmen, and superstitious men everywhere, numbers are dynamic—some more dynamic than others. It was Pythagoras who made a religion out of numbers; his followers were so afraid of them that they endowed every number up to sixty with divine power or magic significance.

A moron can be a numerologist or even a Christian Scientist, but astrology is heavy thinking.

Astrology and numerology ran somewhat parallel courses, but what the Chaldean read into his stars was a milder form of lunacy than what the Pythagorean philosophers read into numbers. Nor would star- or number-worshippers be worth our attention were they not with us today—though often so disguised as to seem plausible, so plausible as to pass for scientists.

When Poincaré said that religious values vary with longitude and latitude, he merely said that mysticism, occultism, or religion varies with the world of words and numbers, stocks and stones, stars and seasons, man happens to find himself in, and to which he turns for "readings" of his fate or for the signs, symptoms, or agents of his destiny.

The sun was one thing to an Eskimo, quite another thing to a Chaldean. The Eskimo had more use for lamps than for astrology, for light than for arithmetic; little need for many numerals. He did have use for such concepts as one, two, etc., but he especially needed such words as *twins, team, couple, pair, brace*: with them he could not only say *two*, but convey additional and more concrete information. With such words as pack, flock, herd, lot, bunch, heap, mob, crowd, gang, etc., he could express more than "many."

Note that when we wish to express a *collection, congregation*, or an *aggregation,* we have to go to Latin for our words. Note also that the short, simple words above cited, while expressing *two*, are not really abstract, but concrete. We do not speak of a *brace* of deuces or *twin* treys. But *thrice* will serve for three times or repeatedly, even as does the Latin *ter*.

But for concreteness so extreme as to appear to us absurd, we look to the Tsimshians of the North West Coast. They have numerals—in fact, seven sets of number words: one for flat objects and animals; one for round objects and time; one for counting men; one for long objects and trees; one for canoes; one for measures; and one which is no longer a genuine antique, but which is a true homogeneous abstract number concept—that is, one that can be used for counting things regardless of their heterogeneity. Only when numbers were freed from all connection with concrete notions did "pure" mathematics become possible.

The freeing of numbers from all concrete implications was a slow process and did not proceed everywhere at the same rate. It would be advantageous for a Manhattan Island Solomon to be able to enumerate his wives, keep tally on his children, and calculate his income, but such arithmetic would have no great value for a Solomon Islander Solomon. The "learning" he would need would include the names of his wives and a collective name for plenty of cocoanuts.

In other words, man did not begin to count things till he had learned to name them; nor did he require a numerical system until he had freed objects of their individuality. Counting votes is important, but before election day the precinct captain sees his men not as 1, 2, and 3, but as Tom, Dick, and Harry; and the fact that the captain cannot count above six is no sign that his party cannot count on the 606 voters in his precinct.

Now for the next important step: finding means or methods of keeping track of the count. We "keep tally," as we say, and we "calculate"; *talea* is Latin for counting, and *calculus* is a stone— in the bladder or on the beach. But older, presumably, than keeping count by cutting notches in sticks or transferring pebbles, is counting by fingers. In many languages *five* means hand; *ten*, two hands or man. Our *decimal* system is a ten-finger system. Even our *eleven* and *twelve* were once *elf* (*ein lif*) and *zwölf* (*zwo lif*). *Lif* is old German for ten.

The Greek *pompazein* (to count by fives) and the Roman numerals point to a one-hand count or quinary system. Our "score," "two-score," "threescore," and the French *vingt* (twenty) and *quatre-vingts* (eighty) are hands-and-feet systems, or vigesimal.

Tally-sticks of ancient vintage were used for British Exchequer accounts up to 1826. Small notches represented pounds sterling, larger notches ten pounds, still larger ones one hundred, etc. Such records were purely *cardinal* in principle, each numeral up to nine being a collection of strokes, as it is in the most ancient known systems of written numerals. Units such as tens, hundreds, etc., were represented by special symbols: in Roman, for example, X stood for ten, C for hundred, M for thousand. The Greeks employed the *ordinal* system, the letters of the alphabet representing numbers. This was the system used by the Phœnicians and Hebrews. Roman numerals, though not so clumsy as the Greek, were so clumsy that Mediæval arithmetic was busy finding devices for using them. Any man who could do sums fit for our second-grade children was a specialist in mathematics.

Among the many devices for manipulating numbers were the tally-sticks already mentioned, the abacus, and counting-boards. But how represent the fact, for example, that the second, or "ten," square of the board had nothing in it? Just what does "III  II" mean—32, 302, 320, 3002, 3020, 300020, or what? What was needed, as Dantzig says, was a *symbol for an empty column*, for an empty class, for the fact of *nothing*.

The answer seems to us so simple that we wonder it could have been a problem. But let numbers become as loaded as they were to the ancients, and how is one to invent or discover a symbol for nothing? They did not make that momentous discovery.

The Hindu term for zero was *sunya*, but it meant *empty* or *blank*. The tenth-century Arabs adopted Indian numeration and translated *sunya* into *sifr—empty*. Arab numeration passed into Italy, and *sifr* was Latinized to *zephirum*. In passing from Italy to Germany *zephirum* became *cifra*; to England, *cipher*. In Italy it became *zero*.

*Cipher* today in English means something that one *deciphers*, any Arabic numeral, or nought, zero. Into the story of the introduction of Arabic numerals into Europe and the centuries-long struggle between the *Abacists*, fighting for the old Roman system, and the *Algorists*, advocating reform, I cannot go further—except to say that the Arabic numerals might have lost out had they not been prohibited. They were bootlegged in by merchants, who used them as a secret code! But when in the seventeenth century they had finally crowded out the Roman system, the Germans did not call them Arabic, but *Deutsche*, numerals.

Four centuries ago the masses of Europe were counting on their fingers, and the professional calculators were using counting-boards or notched sticks and the Roman numerals. The Indian *sunya* was the turning-point in the history of modern science and industry. That zero raised arithmetic to a place among the greatest of all human inventions; yet, as Laplace said, zero escaped the genius of Archimedes and Apollonius, two of the greatest men of antiquity. But note two things: that invention (o) which made higher mathematics possible, resulted from blind fumbling, a chance discovery; it was put into circulation only after a 400 years' fight against prejudice, bigotry, and obscurantism.

And my first sheepskin in this age of science and higher mathematics is in Latin and dated in Roman numerals—MDCCCLXXXVIII: thirteen letters to express a date in a patched-up calendar system older than Rome or Greece, inferior to a system discovered and in use on this continent before the beginning of the Christian Era and employing a zero symbol, invented at least six centuries before the Hindu *sunya*.

That Maya-Aztec calendar has functioned for two thousand years without losing a single day. Judging by the time required for Christian Europe to adopt Arabic notation, we may in another century have a calendar fitted to the needs of our civilization, founded on modern science and not on Chaldean astrology. But before we look at calendars, let us note that with the ten Arabic counting symbols and the metric system of weights with the unit of one gram—one twenty-eighth of an ounce—it is possible to match the weight of one electron against the weight of the universe, by such simple devices as $10^{-28}$ and $10^{57}$ x 2—more than man could count in a hundred million years. In short, as a phonetic alphabet suffices for recording the names of all things, Arabic numerals suffice for recording the measure of all things. Both devices are at the service of all men, everywhere.

Strictly speaking, time is a cultural concept, and every culture has its own "clock"; all, like all religions, orthodox. Even in our age there are those who object to daylight-saving shifts because they interfere with "God's own time"; but "God's time," again like religion, varies with latitude and longitude, with cultural needs, and with advance in scientific procedure.

As counting began with concrete terms for special cultural needs, so time reckoning began with concrete natural phenomena which forced themselves upon man's routine life or excited his curiosity. An eclipse of sun or moon is a thought-provoking phenomenon, but as man cannot see in the dark or pick berries in winter, darkness and winter had to be answered; he might wonder what he could do about eclipses, but he *had* to do something about darkness and winter. Presumably, concrete word symbols for day and night or darkness and light, for dawn and sunset, for blossoming and bird-nesting time, for dying vegetation and winter-time, and for similar diurnal, lunar, seasonal, and annual phenomena, antedate chronologies.

Why bother with years when there are days and nights and seasons to be wrestled with? As a matter of fact, primitive folk are notoriously short on annals, but strong on such time measures as bear directly on their material welfare and security.

To us on the farm it was more important to know the seasons than the years. Dawn and dusk regulated our days; the position of the sun and hunger pangs made a clock good enough to eat by. We had as much use for a chronometer as we had for a silk hat. As we enjoyed the blessings of civilization, we had almanacs to tell us the passing months and years, but the years that we *talked* about were the Year-of-the-Tornado, the Year-Uncle-John-Died, the Year-We-Painted-the-House, the Year-of-the-Centennial, etc., rather than 1876, 1886, or 1896. The "year-counts" our Indians used to paint on buffalo robes were not 1820 or 1830, for example, but the Year of the Shooting Stars, the Year of the Smallpox Epidemic. The Eighteenth Amendment does not date from 1914 or even from the year we entered the war, but "pre-war" dates certain goods, just as the "World-War" marks an era, epoch, age, a period or phase, as the case may be, in passing time. "Before-the-war" a few years ago meant pre-Spanish-War; a few years earlier, pre-Civil-War. *Ante bellum* days are still a distinct cultural period in Dixieland, a concrete period which needs no calendar or refined chronology to set it off.

So, too, what mattered in ancient days was not what year it was After the Flood, but what year it was of So-and-so's reign. Early chronologies were on the order of, "And all the days of Noah were nine hundred and fifty years, and he died." It was not one year after another, but one generation or one king after another. The Year-Arthur-Cumnock's-Team-Beat-Yale is more vivid to me than the year 1890 A.D. What American can look upon 1776 as "just another year" in the history of the universe!

It is the *loaded* years, seasons, days, that get attention—and not as years, seasons, or days, but as critical, epochal years, seasons and days.

Numbers—3, 4, 6, 7, etc.—as we saw, become loaded. *Seven* carries an extra heavy load in lands which depend on Babylonian superstitions for their weekday count. Every seventh day was dynamic, dangerous, taboo; on such days certain things *should* be done, certain other things simply *must not* be done. Being Christian farmers, we were under that Seventh Day spell. It mattered little whether we ploughed on the first or the second day of the week, but it mattered enormously that we did not plough on the *seventh*; there was the haunting fear that we might be struck dead!

And so it was of no great consequence whether we knew the first from the second day, or the fourth from the fifth; what mattered was that we should know the sixth day and get no hay down that we could not get in that night, for we simply dared not touch it on the Holy Day. In other words, we had to know the taboo days, even if we had to support a priest to keep count for us.

There were enough Jewish converts to Christianity to force the Church to recognize Saturday as holy. Constantine's Edict of 321 is the earliest known Sunday law, but it was not based on existing Christian practices. During the next three centuries Sunday labor was more and more restricted by imperial decrees.

It was during the Middle Ages that Friday became loaded with the superstitions we have already seen. And not only every Friday, but many other days of the year became loaded with bad luck during that period: *dies Ægyptiaci* they were called, with true Christian charity. They were *Don't* days. "Don't," or *nefasti*, days had grown so numerous in Rome in Cicero's time that the rich could evade justice, criminals escape punishment. We think of holidays as escape days, but with 175 days set aside as holy in honor of saints, and fifty-two more reserved for the Lord, the year was so used up that it was good for nothing but the Mediæval Greek Church.

This brings us to Christmas Day in the year 1. Suppose our Holy Land had been Australia, would we celebrate December 25th as Christ's birthday, or January 6th as *the* Epiphany of Epiphanies—miracle of water-wine, baptism with dove, star of the Magi, and even the Nativity itself? Or would the marriage at Cana have been celebrated on the 6th of January? Would Christ have made his appearance in the temple in his twelfth year? Would the twelve days between Christmas and Epiphany have been loaded with superstitious practices, such as sprinkling holy water on houses, making crosses on doors, burning candles, lighting bonfires, making new fires on hearths—all because werewolves roam abroad, witches and demons swarm about, and the dead revisit the living?

One miracle begets another. One of the miracles of nature in the northern hemisphere is the winter solstice; another, the vernal equinox. To match these "natural" miracles, man in his divine ignorance spun verbal miracles and invented chronologies, or time-tables, and with time opened accounts or calendars.

The calendar before me has 365 days, divided into twelve months, and weeks of seven days. "Thirty days hath September," but whether March hath thirty or thirty-one I still have to recite the old jingle to find out.

Why this nonsense? Because man tried to regulate his moon-clock by the sun. Result: our calendar system—as old-fashioned as an ox-team, as clumsy as a water-clock.

Yet we hang on to such fossils as though they were saints' bones we dare not drop into the ash-can lest they explode and blow us to bits. Reform in our calendar would take less time and be more profitable than the attempt to reform morals by law. Weights, measures and numbers are tools—devices for supplementing and correcting our inferior time, weight, and measure sense. We can improve them by laying down the law to them—which is more than we can do to human character. But as long as mothers bring up children on prayer-books founded on a divine chronology with appropriate festivals for such cosmic processional phenomena as solstices, equinoxes, phases of the moon, and movements of planets, we shall have a child's-play calendar.

"Child's-play" is hardly the word. No child could have worked out our calendar, or our almanacs; nor any farmer or astronomer on Manhattan Island. To study the stars one must be able to see them night after night and year after year, and keep track of what is seen—stars moving across the heavens in stately procession, planets zigzagging among the stars. To make anything of all this requires not only enormous and long-sustained patience, but an amount of mathematics that baffles any but the professional star-gazers—paid servants of the state.

We have such state servants because our government has intri-cate problems of navigation to solve—to name but one of many state problems requiring the most refined methods of astronomy and the highest mathematical skill. The ancients needed expert star-gazers because their days and seasons became loaded with magic, with mysterious or divine power. Holy days, holy weeks, even holy years. Lucky times, unlucky times. Evil days, evil times. Days, weeks, months, times, became consecrated to this or that god.

Reaping-time "belongs" to the god of the harvest. Calendars, like theologies, were born of fear of failure, fear of the unknown or the uncanny. The same sort of vague fear that clutches human throats today and prevents the fearsome from being grasped boldly with hands and viewed with enlightened eyes.

If time is God's, why shouldn't we rebel at setting our clocks back an hour? If our days are "appointed," why shouldn't we object to any revision of the calendar which might cause us to *lose* one or more days out of life?

What is a day? What is God's time? Is there a *natural* day of twelve hours, an hour of sixty minutes, a minute of sixty seconds? Is there a *natural* month, or a *natural* year? In short, is there a heavenly or an earthly "clock" which beats annual time? There are three; and that is one of the baffling things which take chronology out of the kindergarten.

There is a *natural* month—the lunar cycle of twenty-eight days; and a lunar year. There is also a *natural sidereal*, an *anomalistic*, and a *tropical* year—all different. Confusing, isn't it? That is only part of it. Even the length of days varies naturally, but the *mean* solar day in sidereal time is not twenty-four hours long, but 24 hours, 3 minutes, and 56.5 seconds. Our "civil" day begins at midnight—for obvious reasons; the "astronomical" day begins at midday—for obvious reasons. But there are twenty-four hours in the astronomical day; two sets of twelve hours in the civil day.

Then think of going to bed Sunday night, January 1st, and waking up next morning to find that it is Sunday or Tuesday according to whether one has crossed the 180th meridian from east to west or from west to east. Admiral Byrd's voice came up from New Zealand in less time than is needed to blink an eye—but there was a day's difference in the time just the same.

Calendars are not child's-play, but think of the time and patience required to work out a *saros*, the interval of time (6,585 days, 8 hours) between eclipses! Easy enough now, for with telegraph we can "see" eclipses visible only on the other side of the globe. Not so easy for the Chaldeans; it meant accurate and recorded observations over long periods of time. They recorded the present that they might calculate the future, not as chronology in the abstract, but as God's time for God-given purposes; for the *signs*

set in the heavens for the ordering of human lives. Signs of the
zodiac, for example, or the belt of the twelve animals—constellations—within eight degrees of the ecliptic, beginning with the Ram
and ending with the Fish. Each animal is a "sign"—but of what,
depends upon religion rather than upon astronomy. Even as
religion the signs have varied as they slowly moved from Babylon
to the city of Los Angeles.

Look into the Temple of Denderah and you will find the sky
with the zodiac, the Virgo as a woman, and Isis near by with the
infant Horus in her arms: there, presumably, was the germ of the
worship of the Virgin and the infant Saviour. Into the parallelism
between the sequence of Christian festivals and ancient Oriental
divine chronologies we need not go; it is enough to point out
that the great divine mysteries—including the "Labours" of Hercules, the Virgin birth in cave or stable on December 25th, Candle-
mas, Lent, death of Lamb-God on Good Friday, Easter, the Crucifixion, empty grave, Resurrection, Twelve disciples, betrayal by one
of the Twelve and on the day of the winter solstice, when doubt
of the rebirth of the sun seems justifiable—all become intelligible
only as reflecting man's attempt to read the heavens, not as natural
phenomena, but as Heavenly Hosts. The Divine Drama is the
cosmic drama of the sun moving through certain constellations,
"signs" or "houses," and changing from equinox to equinox.

Our calendar reflects that drama; it is a historic creation, a
cultural product, and there is no reason to expect it to be more
scientifically accurate or more fitted to the needs of modern civilization than any other discovery made in Babylon and patched up
from time to time to prevent Christmas from falling on Easter.
In other words, not a single phase of our calendar—either units
of time or names for units—is an invention of, or has resulted from,
astronomic science.

A Babylon calendar of 700 B.C. shows a week of seven days, each
devoted to one of the "divine" planets, which in their reckoning included sun and moon, Marduk (Jupiter), Ishtar (Venus), Ninib
(Saturn), Nabu (Mercury) and Nergal (Mars). As the Babylon
week was borrowed their god names were translated into local god
names, but in passing to Egypt and Europe the order was changed.
Our Sunday is of course the old sun- as Monday is the old moon-

day; Tuesday is German, *Tiu* (Mars); Wednesday, *Woden* (Mercury); Thursday, *Thor* (Jupiter); Friday, *Frija* (Venus). As the Germans had no good god for Saturday they used *Saturnus* in corrupted form; but the French *Mercredi, Jeudi,* and *Vendredi* are survivors of Mercury, Jupiter, and Venus.

Early Christian Europe followed the Jewish week and fought shy of the pagan god-names. The first five days were numbered—a usage still retained in Portugal.

Some 5,000 years ago the Babylonians were using a year of twelve lunar months or 354 days, adding an extra month now and then to bring religion and business into closer harmony. The Egyptians divided their year into twelve months of thirty days each, and added five days—won at play by the god Thor from the moon-goddess—to the end of the year. By an edict of 238 B.C. the leap-year device of 366 days was inaugurated—and promptly forgotten.

In 46 B.C. Julius Cæsar decided it was time to make their old moon-clock strike sun-time; their old lunar year was three months out with solar time. Why celebrate a harvest festival in the spring-time? The "Julian" calendar was the answer—every fourth year a leap year. That was good enough for the Eastern Church down to September 30th last year, when it dropped thirteen days as "lost" out of its life to bring it even with the Julian calendar as revised in 1582 by Pope Gregory XIII by dropping ten days from that year and three leap years out of every succeeding four centuries.

As the revised Gregorian calendar was *Catholic*, England, being Protestant, hung on to the Julian calendar up to bed-time September 2nd, 1752—to wake up New Style (N. S.) September 14th. But one section of the Christian world (Ruthene Uniat) still so hates the Greek and Roman Catholic Churches that it refuses to celebrate the divine mysteries with them and clings to the O. S. pagan calendar of Julius Cæsar.

"Thirty days hath . . ." Cæsar's months, except February, were to have alternate lengths; odd months thirty-one days; even, thirty. But the eighth month (fifth in the old year) was named after Augustus and given an extra day to make it as long as Cæsar's month. That brought three thirty-one-day months together—July, August, September. So September and November were reduced to thirty and October and December raised to thirty-one. And our "hath" still pays for that august vanity.

A calendar is one thing, chronology another. Historic chronicles began as rude annals, lists of the chief doings of the chiefs from year to year, the year being named 1 or 21 Sargon as the case might be. In Sparta the years bore the names of the ephors; in Athens, of the first archons; in Rome, of the consuls; and in Egypt and Babylon, of the kings. But a "year" in Babylon was not necessarily a year in Egypt. Intricate problems of chronology were involved. How astronomers worked that out is outside our province; but as we are about to become "historically-minded," a few facts will be of interest as well as pertinent.

Egypt numbered the passing years as events, campaigns, etc.; the Babylonians and Assyrians named their years rather than numbered them. It was Alexandrian mathematicians who laid the foundations for a sound chronology and in the canon of Ptolemy handed down accurate dates of Assyrian kings from 747 B.C.

About 530 A.D. a Scythian monk, abbot, and astronomer of Rome was commissioned to fix the day and year of Christ's birth. To him we owe our Christian Era—although 1 A.D. should be either 3, 4, or 5 B.C. His fixing December 25th for the Birth was of course pure fiction, although founded on ancient usage in celebrating cosmic phenomena.

Presumably the Babylonians also invented the clepsydra, or water-clock—in principle not unlike our sand "hour-glass" for three-minute eggs. Water escaped through a small outlet into a second vessel and was then weighed: equal weights of water, equal intervals of time. The Greeks used such "clocks." When Demosthenes was interrupted while making a political speech against time, he did not cry, "Time out," but "Stop the water!"

And now a minute for the sixty seconds. Sixty was a magic number in the number cult of Babylonia and Persia; possibly a combination of the ten-finger or decimal system and a magic six. But our 360 degrees, our 60 minutes, and our 60 seconds, come straight down from the Land of the Two Rivers, where priests spun myths, custom established taboos, and poets perpetuated both; where, also, priests worked out the fundamentals of writing and mathematics. Myth and epic have had to give way before science and art; calendars and chronology have brought history within the realm of science. And of all the knowledge science discovers and accumulates, none is more useful than that discovered by the historian. The real pity is that it is still regarded as literature and not as something to be applied to the art of living.

## X

A million years' climb up to the higher levels of economic security—and generally spoken of as "painful". I think that figure of speech is worth a glance. We call it painful because we read our own painful experiences in learning our early lessons in human behaviour in terms of a million years of drudgery doing chores and lessons. We speak of Early Man, but early man, after all, was just one man after another, each (barring accidents) living out a normal span of life. Life as dog-fight or foot-race came late in human culture.

For thousands of years life must have been lived much as it was lived two centuries ago by the natives of Australia. No one to crack the whip or call the faithful to prayer five times a day; no fierce competition; no school at all; no higher education for women; no mad scramble for power, for wealth, for fame, for the spotlight; no sackcloth and ashes in the name of Sanctity; no forced marches and sudden death in the name of Patriotism; no clocks or calendars; no birthdays or holy days.

No, it was not a painful climb. It was, on the whole, I suspect, a fairly even, uneventful existence, and lived day by day as life only can be lived before it must become adjusted to a supernatural world of hidden meanings and metaphysical values attainable only in a supersensible word-world.

It is not easy for us to live in imagination an Alluvial or a Cave life without suffering twinges and pangs and pains. I can twinge now when I think of getting out of a warm bed before dawn in winter, landing on an ice-cold floor, breaking the ice in the bucket, etc. Ugh! Seems terrible! But it did not seem terrible then. That was *life*. So it was on the morning of, say, December 31st 499,999 B.C. The bed one got out of may have been boughs on a floor of sand, the roof above a smelly hide. But it was Home, Sweet Home, just the same.

We don't miss the water till the well runs dry; we don't miss what we've never had or heard of. Man becomes accustomed to his surroundings. He is not born on a bed of boughs or in a manger, alone. He is not expected to hunt his first meal. He is born into a family, among friends. They have survived, they have had enough, they like life. The youngster will learn that life and like it; and, grown to manhood, will find his greatest joy in teaching his youngster how to shoot.

There is nothing fanciful about this picture; it has a biologic foundation; it is based on sound psychological principles. No ethnologist, I feel certain, who has really caught the spirit of any so-called primitive people, has failed to note the joy they get out of their feasts, let us say. That joy is not primarily in the mere eating of food: it is in the preparation of the food, the commingling of souls, the rubbing of elbows, at the feast. In short, doing things socially.

We like our ways of life because they are *our* ways. Our bodies feel peaceful, tuneful, when they are doing the habitual things. We try new things before we become set in our habits; after that, we like to keep on in the old habits. We can get so set that a new thought is too painful to contemplate. Why should we contemplate it, we say to ourselves; we have contemplated enough for all practical purposes.

Time's clock ticks on, the seasons roll along: "If winter comes, can spring be far behind?" Enough culture to live by is handed on from one generation to another, practically without change. The tangible results of change in culture from December 31st, 499,999 B.C. to December 31st, 99,999 B.C. could be put in a vest pocket.

No progress at all, you say. But where is your Progress bound for? What is its destination? What is even the next station on its line? Take life itself as a criterion. Can it be asserted of any one living human being today, of the age of ten or twenty, that his or her health or happiness twenty years hence is more certain than was that of any boy or girl of the same age five, three, or one hundred thousand years ago, or fifty, twenty, or five thousand years ago, or even five, three, or one century ago? But, you say, the existence of the human race is more assured today than it ever was before. Is it? And if so, by what count, by whose assurance?

Is it because of Progress or of sound human nature? Remove from this earth every living human being save one youth and one maid. Allow them a normal span of life and an average old-time family, and their descendants two hundred years hence could match the earth's present population. Nature seems to have assured the existence of the human race ages ago.

Well, what did happen, then, during those hundreds of thousands of years? Nothing of any particular consequence apart from becoming really human. Language signalized that momentous event. And then civilization suddenly dawned upon man—in Egypt and the Near East. In an incredibly short time man passed from poverty to affluence. But he was not necessarily happier, healthier, or wiser, though some of the population were immeasurably wealthier than before and began to live lavishly and luxuriously; like kings and gods, claiming omnipotence and omniscience.

The great Oriental civilization rested on five pillars—domesticated animals, agriculture, metals, writing, and arithmetic. Great weights were moved, great buildings erected, and great commerce was developed to distribute surplus metals, textiles, glass, and paper. Roads and bridges were built; the seas were sailed freely and far.

With this civilized Orient, Stone Age Europe traded, or "looked to the Nile," as Breasted says, "as American Indians must have looked to the first Europeans." By 3000 B.C. Europe was getting her first taste of metals *via* the Ægean Islands and Greece. At about the same time she began to get cattle and domestic plants *via* Sicily. But by 2000 B.C. the best Europe could show was Stonehenge and the dolmens. While she plodded along, content with a culture not one whit better than, and in many respects far inferior to, that of the Maoris of New Zealand or the Zulus of South Africa, the Near East had, as summarized by Breasted, invented, discovered, or developed stone masonry, colonnade, arch, tower, or spire; refined sculpture from wonderful portraits and colossal statues to exquisite seals; writing, earliest alphabet; earliest known tales in prose, poems, history, social discussions, drama; the calendar we use; began mathematics, astronomy, and medicine; administered machinery of government; paid officials to collect taxes and disburse payments; government on a big scale—both of single great nations and of empires of groups of nations; and a fatherly god of questionable ethics.

What Breasted does not mention explicitly is that the East had discovered a lot of things that are not so, developed a large number of ideas that are eternally socially destructive, and in general had withdrawn so much of life and the world in which life lives from human vision that Europe was to flounder about in darkness for a thousand years before it dared begin to ask the reasons why or inquire into the cause of things.

What is generally called inertia in human beings is merely force of habit. Europe inherited some bad habits from the Near East, and our American ancestors brought most of them over here. Some of them are still venerated as priceless heirlooms, as holy and untouchable as was ever bone of Buddha or Christian saint, or hair of Prophet's beard.

Heritors of all the ages we say we are, and properly. So far our curiosity about this cultural heritage has been chiefly concerned with its genetics—its biologic evolutionary basis, its psychologic meanings. We shall now look at it as a historic fact. How did it develop among the peoples whose heritors we are?

# PART TWO

## OUR CULTURAL INHERITANCE
### OR
## HOW WE CAME BY OUR CIVILIZATION

*The Story of the Growth of Empires; of Religion;
and of Science*

# CHAPTER SEVEN

## The Great Civilizations of the Near East

1. Predynastic Egypt and the Pyramid Age. 2. Egypt's Feudal and Golden Ages. 3. The Death Pits of Ur in the Land of Shinar. 4. The Babylon of Hammurabi. 5. The Original Flood Myth. 6. The Rise and Fall of Assyria. 7. "God's Victorious Armies." 8. The Persian Empire and the Behistun Tablet. 9. Thus Spake Zarathustra. 10. The Land of the Book and Its Chosen People.

I

WHEN the curtain goes up on the Nile Valley at the dawn of history, an astounding scene is disclosed and one as far from primitive as the Café de la Paix. In fact, many of the baubles which tempt tourists from Rue de Rivoli shop-windows are imitations of Egyptian charms older than Chapter I of our old Universal History. The solid foundations of civilization had been laid; civilization was full-blown, as it were, and in full working order. Yet what mighty structures were to be erected on those foundations as the next three millenniums were ticked off on time's clock! And to be read in sequence and in detail as nowhere else on earth. Fifty-three centuries of unbroken history!

Opportunity and desire met in the Nile Valley. Conditions for rapid advance were also favourable in the Land of Shinar, but Sumer and Akkad seem to trail a little behind Egypt. Their story in a way is as remarkable and possibly older, but the cradle of *our* civilization was rocked by Egypt rather than by Babylonia. So we excavate Egypt first. But we must dig fast and read as we run, for Egypt's story is long in years, rich in colour, and splendid in achievement. It is worth looking at, both for its own sake and for the light it sheds on our own civilization.

Let us note here and now that history is chiefly a record of successes and failures to live splendidly and rule majestically. But human nature being what it is, the record is punctuated by raucous cries from the man in the street: All is vanity; or, Take your foot off my neck! That makes the record interesting for us. If we cannot play the leading rôle, we can get a thrill from reading ourselves into a minor rôle in the mob scenes.

Up to the time Alexander relieved the Egyptians of the trouble of ruling themselves, Egypt had had just thirty dynasties. Before dynasties were kings—of Upper and Lower Egypt, and of unknown names.

These Predynastic kingdoms were really tribes with tribal totems or ancestral gods. One in Lower Egypt, according to Weigall, had had some sixty kings before the union. Its totem was the Hornet; its head-dress, or "crown," a curious low red cap with a high peak at the back. Its cobra ornament seems to have been derived from a conquered neighbouring tribe. Farther south was the "Reed" kingdom; its head-dress was a tall white crown. Still further south were two "Hawk" kingdoms. By a historic process not unlike that in fifteenth-century Spain, these kingdoms were gradually united through marriage or by conquest. It was Menes' father who as ruler of the united kingdoms of the Hawks and Reeds of Upper Egypt, conquered the Hornets of Lower Egypt. It was Menes who combined the white and red crowns into the well-known double crown of United Egypt.

Most of the confusion in Egyptian religion grows out of the difficulty of reconciling such totemic gods as Hawk, Cobra, Vulture, Reed, Hornet, and Sun—to mention only the most important—and arranging them into a working pantheon. The ancestral gods of the Hawk kingdoms were Osiris and Horus; of the Cobra-Vulture kingdom, Isis. Horus became the son of Osiris and Isis, and the three were worshipped as a family. Set, once a brother of Osiris, became the evil demon who had murdered Osiris. But in all this, as in legendary Greece, it is rarely possible to distinguish—nor have I tried—pure culture-heroes from totemic gods or semi-historic personages. These early First Dynastic days were the times of religion in the making and of myths in the process of crystallization.

Menes, long thought to be a mythical figure, is now known to have been a historic personage, founder of the First Dynasty of the Ancient Empire (3407-2270 B.C.). Memphis, his capital, a thousand years later was to become the greatest and most renowned city in the world.

What had the Egyptians been doing before Menes? Roughly speaking, just what we are doing now—working out their salvation. They did not invent as rapidly as we do, but theirs were *basic* inventions. With twenty-six letters at my disposal I could invent a hundred new words in a night, but would they be of any value to anybody? They would to me—if I could exchange them for merit or money. The alphabet was a basic invention.

Agriculture was also a basic invention; a written language was another. Then there were looms, weaving, linen, chronology, calendar, sea-going ships, chairs, beds, cushions, jewellery, jewel cases, lamps, musical instruments, games, razors, combs, spoons, wigs, hats, kilts, sandals, face paints; ornaments of great variety; dozens of kinds of earthenware vessels; and vessels and vases of hard stone of such marvellously perfect technique and masterful patience that they have never been surpassed—except, possibly, by Chinese jades.

Egypt's Predynastic imports are suggestive of what went on in those prehistoric times: gold, silver, iron, copper, tin, lead, hematite, galena, emery, obsidian, turquois, lapis-lazuli, serpentine, tortoise shell, coral. What a list! And these materials were worked into fine useful and useless arts, with such skill and cunning as might provoke Renaissance admiration or modern bewilderment. What could not skill and patience do with such raw materials!

That Predynastic culture was not thrown up in a day or a year. It did speed up, as the Great Pyramids were to climb up, once the two fundamental requirements for advance had been met: vast reservoirs of human energy available because agriculture had insured full granaries; engineers to direct the flow of that energy into supplying the accessories of art and religion demanded by society and the church, and the trappings of power demanded by kings and court—though it is only fair to say that at the very height of Egypt's magnificence her kings depended on their own almost naked majesty and not on vainglorious gewgaws. Her kings were kings, not clothes-horses.

The culture of that Predynastic period has been called Amratian. Before that (5000 B.C.) was the Badarian culture. Who the Badarians were is unknown; they are now being rather intensively investigated. What's in a name, anyhow? Men, tribes, kingdoms, come and go; human culture flowers, now here, now there, but never dies —nor will, as long as there is a pair of human beings to inherit it and remould it to their hearts' desire.

The Badarians, according to Brunton, kept oxen, sheep, and goats, hunted birds, caught fish with hook, line, and sinker and with nets. They grew emmer wheat and cooked their porridge and stew in earthen pots; used ivory dippers and ostrich-egg cups; wore woven kilts; and blew their noses on handkerchiefs. They also used dressed antelope skin for clothing, combed their hair with ivory combs, and bound it with fillets of Red Sea shells. They wore tiny stone studs in their nose and ears, necklaces with ibex-headed or hippopotamus amulets, and massive bracelets of ivory. The men wore belts with thousands of blue glazed steatite beads. Men and women rouged their cheeks and painted circles round their eyes with malachite paste.

They had beds and pillows. They wove mats and baskets, made rope, carved ivory, and decorated their pottery. They were a peace-loving people: plenty of aged skeletons without sign of injury, and no weapons of war in the graves. They believed in a life after death, and so prepared their bodies that they would wake up from sleep in a life everlasting, in the west. Gazelles and oxen were sometimes given ceremonial burial.

Call that Badarian culture "primitive"; it was Predynastic, prehistoric—8,000 years ago. Before that was the Tasian culture, still more primitive. Before that was the New Stone culture. And lower still, thirty feet deep in Nile delta soil, are accumulations which go back 18,000 years. Even Palæolithic and Eolithic implements have been found in the river terraces and plateaus—wrought perhaps several hundred thousand years B.C. In fact, a succession of cultures comparable to the Chellean, Acheulian, and Mousterian types of ancient Europe, are now being laid bare in or near the Nile delta.

Were these earliest Egyptians kin of Europe's early Stone Age man? Did they reach Africa *via* the then land bridge across Sicily? More likely the reverse was true, but no one knows. Borings in Lower Egypt at ninety feet have shown traces of pottery of an estimated age of 18,000 B.C.—ten thousand years before pottery reached the Baltic Nordics. Old Egypt is old.

Menes was king of several millions of subjects. There were taxes, governors, law courts, high society, great gods, royal palaces, stately temples, beer, hogs, ass transport; sun-dried brick; wattle cities. The king was so holy he must not be called by name but by that of his palace, hence *Pharaoh*, "Great-house."

Egypt had been merely playing at being civilized. Within four hundred years she decides to "show the world." She does. And ever since, the world visits Egypt to look at the world's most impressive monument, the royal tomb of Khufu—or Cheops, as the Greeks called him—second king of the Fourth Dynasty.

Rome's Colosseum is 600 feet long, and hollow; the Great Pyramid is 755 feet square, solid, and 481 feet high: thirteen acres of rock, its stones averaging two and a half tons in weight, and by Petrie's calculation there are 2,300,000 of them. Herodotus says that 100,000 men worked on it for twenty years. Their onion, radish, and garlic bill alone amounts to nearly two million dollars in our money. What must their beer bill have been!

It was a great tomb; it set a mark in tombs that has never been surpassed, in sheer size at least, or in perfect workmanship—it fits like a watch. It was greater than the idea which prompted it—though there was nothing puny in the idea of being buried in the heart of a vast emblem of the sun-god Re. The tomb, of course, was rifled and the royal mummies carried off. But the idea goes marching on. The idea was old; we saw its workings in Badarian cemeteries.

Zoser of the Third Dynasty began the pyramid tomb with the so-called "Step" Pyramid, each step smaller than the one beneath. A portrait statue of this king has only recently been found. The next king, Seneferu (Snofru), founder of the Fourth Dynasty, built the first true pyramid, with straight sides. He was the first really great Pharaoh. He built ships 170 feet long; sent a fleet of forty ships to Lebanon for cedar logs; worked the copper mines of Sinai; and returned from an expedition into the Sudan with 7,000 prisoners and 200,000 head of cattle.

Egypt now was the best organized, the most cultured, and the most enlightened country in the world. And Cheops' Great Pyramid was still in the stone quarry. But magnificent fluted (Doric) columns were already in existence—twenty-five centuries before the

Greeks were to use them in their temples at Olympia and on the Acropolis. Nor is there anything known about sculpture today that was not known to the Pyramid Age.

Within ten years from Cheops' death, Khafre (Chephren of the Greeks) had begun his great pyramid tomb on the same stupendous scale. But that was not enough glory. He built a massive granite temple for it, lighted by small oblique openings or roof windows —an architectural feature which was to become incorporated 3,500 years later in the naves of Christian basilicas. Its great halls, with their huge monolithic pillars and pavements of alabaster, alone would make Egypt famous. But this temple idea was to be carried far beyond the pattern set by Khafre; in fact, he himself cast a shadow of the coming event by carving a mass of near-by rock into an enormous recumbent lion with a king's head crowned with royal head-dress and cobra diadem. (With a cobra on my head, you are not likely to tweak my nose.)

That king's head is a portrait of Khafre himself; that human-headed lion is the original Sphinx—the most astounding statue ever carved from living rock.

Pyramid Age art—and architecture and civilization—reached its apogee in the Fifth Dynasty, and every succeeding period in Egyptian art that was not shamelessly decadent was a Renaissance. Even the foundations of the "wisdom of the Egyptians," in which Moses was said to be learned by the writer of the Acts, were laid during this dynasty.

In one of the oldest manuscripts in existence, a thousand years before a possible Moses, Ptah-hotep, the king's prime minister, admonishes his reader: "Let thy countenance shine joyfully as long as thou livest: did a man ever leave the coffin after having once entered it?" "Terrify not men, or God will terrify thee." "Be not puffed up because of the knowledge that thou hast acquired, and hold converse with the unlettered man as with the learned, for there is no obstacle to knowledge, and no handicraftsman hath attained to the limit of the knowledge of his art."

But the best part of Ptah-hotep's book of maxims is his introduction, where he explains why he wants to resign his office:

O King, my lord, grey hairs have come upon me: old age is advancing, and the years of my decline have arrived. Decrepitude has taken the place of freshness, and some new defect descends upon me every day. My eyesight is failing, my ears are deaf, my vigour is diminished, my brain is dull, my mouth is dumb and speaks not, my mind forgets, and cannot even recall the events of yesterday. Every bone in my body aches, pleasure is turned to discomfort, and the flavour of everything is vanished.

Ptah-hotep's king was himself a scholar and an antiquarian, and was the first to style himself Si-Re, or Son of the Sun, a title thereafter employed by every Pharaoh of Egypt. But in the Twelfth Dynasty, Amon had become identified with Re, and in the New Empire became the national god as Amen-Re.

3407 B.C. First Dynasty begins.

2420 B.C. Fifth Dynasty ends.

Between these dates Egypt's civilization reached its zenith. What characterizes it, what are its outstanding marks—art unparalleled in its perfection, Great Pyramid, unique Sphinx, matchless mastaba tombs, Khafre's splendid valley temple? These are the tangible, visible marks—and certainly worth going round the world to see; but the workings of a Great Idea are the characteristic feature of this zenith: the idea that if you did certain things to a dead body it would come to again and live a life of infinite joy for ever in the Isles of the Blest, in the west.

What confusion there would be in cemeteries, tombs, temples, churches, and cathedrals, and in all rebirth and rejuvenation rites, if the sun were to rise in the north and set in the south for just one day! That ancient superstition is still strong enough to make a Mott Street Chinaman save up enough money to defray the cost of transporting his mortal remains back to China, to come to life again amid familiar scenes and faces.

Blot out all that Egypt did to make effective its belief in an immortal body, and what is left in the Nile Valley for you to gaze upon in open-mouthed wonder? No, Egypt's real gifts to civilization, with a few notable exceptions, antedate its first Pharaoh—and he was long assumed to be mythical.

Between Menes and Onnos, last king of the Fifth Dynasty, the cult of the dead had made great strides. Mummification of the corpse had become a fine art and a regular practice. Belief in the immortality of the physical body as well as of the soul stimulated both art and science. The ages-old practice of burying the dead in simple brick-walled pits had developed into the mastaba tombs of the aristocrats of the Ancient Empire. By the Fifth Dynasty, these "Everlasting Abodes" had become veritable mortuary palaces: suites of rooms for the master, another suite for the harem, another for the son; and storerooms. In all the world there is nothing quite like these mastaba tombs. Long inscriptions, or realistic scenes in coloured relief of the deceased's usual activities, cover the walls and ceilings, the idea being that life as it is will continue in the life to come. Where undisturbed by vandals, these scenes picture ancient life as faithfully as, and more fully than, our life is portrayed by our Sunday rotogravure sections. Nothing is omitted. It may all be seen today, and in many mastabas as vividly as the day after they were sealed.

To describe the scenes on the walls of one tomb would require a volume. Even then words would fail to convey their wondrous brilliancy, their ineffable charm. Not only was daily life—hunting, fishing, playing drafts, playing the harp, Pan pipe and lute, dancing, children at various sports, ball games, dolls, jumping-jacks, tame birds, and monkeys, etc.—portrayed, but in the statues of the deceased and his family we can see how the people themselves looked in life. These are the earliest known human portraits; for life-likeness they have never been surpassed, and in my opinion never will be.

Into a later tomb of cliff-chambers the eighteen-year-old Pharaoh, Tutankhamon, was carried in state amid the clash of sistra and the laments of the multitude, 3,281 years ago—a tomb that was to be partly rifled at once, and then to rest undisturbed till opened by Howard Carter in 1922, to astound a callous world with the magnificence of a boy king till then unheard of by the world at large.

Those mastaba tombs, Everlasting Abodes, were not only decorated or embellished, they were furnished with everything used during this life and which would be needed in the life hereafter. Whatever was too large to be accommodated in the tomb chambers was duplicated in small models—of which hundreds of thousands have been "rescued" to fill museums everywhere and to adorn whatnots in Keokuk, Iowa.

By the time of the Twelfth Dynasty these models had grown prodigiously in number, especially models of *Ushebiu*, or "Answer-ers," miniature replicas of servants whose business it was to answer when the master required work to be done in the underworld: "Here am I, whensoever thou callest me." It seems like a silly idea, but it was an improvement on the idea of killing slaves and servants that they might wait upon their masters in the hereafter.

There was nothing silly in the idea, of course, if one expected a bodily resurrection in another world—which the Egyptians certainly did. And their beliefs and practices, especially their worship of Osiris, god of resurrection, certainly enormously influenced the Greek mysteries of Eleusis and Orpheus, at which we shall look later. The crux of Egyptian belief was that every soul would have to stand trial before the judgment-seat of Osiris. The key to their religious practices was preparation to pass that test, and performances of the Passion play. In that play as seen by Herodotus, the resurrection of Osiris was the chief theme; but by the time the Osiris mystery reached Rome, Isis, bringing the dead god back to life, was the central figure. Before Rome became Christian she had to make a choice, as we shall see, between the cult of Isis, of Mithra, and of Christ. Fundamentally, there was no choice. Even the hope of a joyous life after death that finally crept into Greek religion was born in and borrowed from Egypt.

Among the unforgettable scenes depicted on the walls of the Egyptian tombs is one of the jackal-headed Anubis weighing hearts in the balance before the judgment-seat of Osiris. Others are texts from the Book of the Dead—or rather Books, for there were many, and only "canonized" last century by pioneer Egyptologists.

The function of the Book of the Dead is that of any Holy Writ or Quiz book. Such functions are also performed by priests, confessor, or tutor. Thus, the 125th chapter enumerates the sins that displease the gods, and supplies the proper formulas for repudiating sin. So it is in all religions: one doesn't have to live a blameless life if one knows how to appear blameless at the last judgment.

Thus, on entering the Hall of Maati where Osiris sits in judgment, it is right and proper to say these words:

Homage to thee, O Great God, Lord of Maati, I have come to thee, O my Lord, that I may behold thy beneficence. I know thee, and I know thy name. . . . I have brought truth, integrity, to thee. I have destroyed sin for thee. I have not sinned against men. I have not oppressed (my) kinsfolk. I have done no wrong in the place of truth. I have not known worthless folk. I have not wrought evil. I have not defrauded the oppressed one of his goods. . . . I have not vilified a servant to his master. . . . I have not let any man hunger. I have made no one to weep. I have not committed murder. . . . I have inflicted pain on no man. . . . I have not diminished from the bushel. . . . I have not added to the weights of the scales. . . . I have not taken milk from the mouths of children. . . . I am pure. I am pure. I am pure. I am pure. . . .

All Books of the Dead begin with a hymn to Re, who, as we have seen, was king of kings and of gods in Egypt. This hymn, supposed to be sung by the deceased, dates from the Fifth Dynasty:

Homage to thee, O Re, at thy beauteous rising. Thou risest, thou risest; thou shinest, thou shinest at the dawn. Thou art King of the Gods, and the Maati goddesses embrace thee. The Company of the Gods praise thee at sunrise and at sunset. Thou sailest over the heights of heaven and thy heart is glad. Thy Morning Boat meeteth thy Evening Boat with fair winds. Thy father is the Sky-god and thy mother is the Sky-goddess, and thou art Horus of the Eastern and Western skies. . . . O thou Only One, O thou Perfect One, O thou who art eternal, who art never weak, whom no mighty one can abase; none hath dominion over the things which appertain to thee. . . . When thou risest men and women live. Thou renewest thy youth, and dost set thyself in the place where thou wast yesterday. O Divine Youth, who art self-created, I cannot comprehend thee. Thou art the lord of heaven and earth, and didst create beings celestial and beings terrestrial. Thou art the God One, who camest into being in the beginning of time. . . . O thou Divine Youth, thou heir of everlastingness, self-begotten and self-born, One, Might, of myriad forms and aspects. . . . Lord of Eternity, Everlasting Ruler, the Company of the Gods rejoice in thee. . . . Thou art unknowable . . . thou existest alone. Millions of years have passed over the world, I cannot tell the number of those through which thou hast passed. . . .

"Enough is as good as a feast," said a Fourth Dynasty philosopher. But long before the sun reached Copernicus it had shrivelled to a mere toy a Joshua could order about; and the earth itself had become a sad mistake less than 6,000 years old.

Not that all religion in Egypt was above that of an African cannibal king. Certain Fifth Dynasty spells form striking contrasts to both earlier and later splendid hymns to the sun; and some from the pyramid of Onnos are sheer diabolical black magic. "The heavens open and the stars tremble when this Onnos cometh forth as a god." Why shouldn't they? Onnos had a magic which would enable him, when dead, to kill the gods for food: "The old gods shall be thy food in the evening; the young gods shall be thy food in the morning"; and we have, as Hall says, the weird picture of the dead king boiling the bones of the gods in a cauldron to make his bread. But nowhere in Egyptian religion do we find portrayed any such bloodthirsty, revengeful god as the Yahweh of the Hebrews.

That the scarab, or "tumble-dung," should have been regarded in ancient Egypt, as it is in modern Africa, as a self-producing creature and so fit emblem of immortality and resurrection, is not to be wondered at. Some of Aristotle's natural history was on no higher plane; nor were many of the mediæval spontaneous generation arguments so plausibly founded.

On the whole, however, the religion, art, and civilization in general of the Pyramid Age were on a high plane, in many respects much higher than during the Cathedral Age of Europe.

## II

With the end of the Tenth Dynasty (2100 B.C.) the Ancient Empire gave way to the Middle Empire or Feudal Age, which lasted four centuries and reached its climax during the Twelfth Dynasty (2000-1790 B.C.), Egypt's most prosperous period and an era of great building.

But there was more to this Feudal Age than prosperity and huge public works; there was progress in rational thought, if not in humane conduct. We begin to hear more about moral values. The literature speaks of the faults of human society, the sufferings of the poor and humble, the wickedness of man, and the hopelessness of the future. Do justice; comfort the mourner; oppress not the widow; expel no man from the possessions of his father.

The prophecy in this age of a coming saviour who would bring coolness to the fevered, was a curious anticipation of the Hebrew Messiah by two thousand years. "He shall be the shepherd of his people, and in him there shall be no sin. When his flocks are scattered, he shall spend the day in gathering them together."

There was progress also in industry and science. For thousands of years Egypt had been building huge dikes and storage basins for

Nile flood-water, but irrigation was now undertaken on a really big scale. Even the Suez Canal idea was anticipated; fleets were sent to the Red Sea by canal from a branch of the Nile. Government was better administered; census lists for taxation purposes still survive. There were great advances in astronomy and geography, in arithmetic and algebra, and the beginnings of geometry and a decimal system.

Perhaps the greatest advance of all was in medicine and surgery. Even an Ancient Empire king had a court physician. Later, there were eye and stomach specialists, and a successful operation for an abscessed tooth. There were treatises on surgery and medicine, and the earliest known observations on the brain—the word "brain" occurring for the first time. Dissection was practised. Surgical stitching and adhesive tape were used. Dislocated and fractured bones were scientifically set. But creditable as were these ancient advances in the healing art, medical practice itself proceeded on the false hypothesis—not yet entirely eradicated—that disease is an entity, due to evil spirits.

Then followed a period of decline. Egypt was invaded by a wandering Semitic-speaking people called the Hyksos—the "Shepherd Kings" of the Fifteenth and Sixteenth Dynasties (1675-1600 B.C.). They brought horses and chariots into Egypt, and the idea of the war-horse. They were driven out by Amasis of the Seventeenth Dynasty, their exit possibly forming the background of the Biblical Exodus story. Egypt was once more united and about to become great and do things again.

With the Eighteenth Dynasty (the "Golden Age" of Egypt) begins the New Empire (1555-712 B.C.); and in Thutmose III (1501-1448 B.C.) Egypt was to have one of her most notable kings, her mightiest warrior, and the world its first Napoleon and one of the greatest builders of all time. We hear more about Ramses II—he was the world's first great advertiser—but Thutmose III was the greater man.

Thutmose's conquering arm covered Syria and reached far over into western Asia. The result was plenty of easy money for Egypt. Most of it went into Thebes, which had been made the capital after the expulsion of the Hyksos kings; it was now to become the world's first monumental city—which, in my opinion, it remains today. The temple of Karnak alone, to use Breasted's words, is a historic volume in stone, telling the story of the New Empire. And what a story! What a temple! What a city! Even Homer had heard of it; and of it Nahum the Prophet said: "Nubia and Ethiopia were her strength, and it was infinite; Phut and Lubim were her helpers." But the "strength" of Thebes was more than Nubia and Ethiopia; it was the civilized and barbaric world pouring booty and tribute into Thebes—most of it for the local deity, Amon, till then unknown in the next county. The Greeks called Thebes *Diospolis*, "City of God." Amon had become the national god: Amen-Re, the great sun-god. His "vehicle" was a ram.

Karnak is primarily Amon's temple. It has been built, rebuilt, plundered, and shaken by earthquake, time and again; but there it stands today, the world's greatest ruin, its hall the greatest ever built. The capitals of the twelve columns along its central aisle could accommodate a hundred men each, and each column is as thick as Trajan's column in Rome or the bronze column in the Place Vendôme in Paris. The roof was supported by 134 columns, and in the space thus roofed over you could drop Notre Dame de Paris in its entirety. And if to this huge hall the space within the walls of Karnak were added, you could drop still other great cathedrals, to wit: St. Peter's, Milan, Seville, Florence, St. Paul's, Cologne, York, Amiens, and Antwerp—the nine largest in the world. The Tower of Babel was no toy complex of religious building, but it was a mud pie compared with Karnak. Amon's temple alone of Karnak has an area equal to that of St. Peter's, Milan, and Notre Dame combined.

Yes, Thebes must have been an imperial city indeed at the height of its splendour. Thutmose III started it on the road to glory. Ashurbanipal (Sardanapalus), the Assyrian, did his best to wreck it; but it still stands—Karnak, the wonder of the world. Of the great obelisks Thutmose III built all over Egypt, not one stands where he left it; vandals saw to that. The most interesting of his obelisks stands today in the old Hippodrome of Constantinople; the finest one is in Rome; one is in London on the banks of the Thames, its twin in Central Park, New York.

Less than forty years after Thutmose III came another master builder, Amenhotep III, the world's first Louis XIV; the so-called

Memnon of the Greeks; he whom Baikie called "the great Jove, who assumes the God, affects to nod, and seems to shake the spheres."

Egypt's Pharaoh was now easily the world's First Man. Tribute poured into Thebes in floods. The temples blazed with jewels and gold behind huge bronze doors. The whole civilized world—Babylon, Assyria, Mitanni—courted the smile of Amenhotep III the Magnificent. Their correspondence, as well as that of the vassal states of Syria and Phœnicia, can still be read on the celebrated cuneiform tablets found at Tel-el-Amarna and now mostly in the British Museum. His warships policed the Mediterranean, his trading-ships went everywhere to gather *objets d'art* for Theban palaces and temples—damascened bronzes from Knossos, wonderful figurines, and other products of Minoan art.

In 1375 B.C. this super-Solomon, mightiest ruler of the ancient world, was succeeded by his son, Amenhotep IV—a strong man and fearless, says Breasted. Maybe; but he was not strong enough and he was too fearless for his generation. He was the world's first known monotheist, and he proceeded forthwith to throw a monkey wrench into the state religion. He did his best to destroy the old gods: closed their temples, drove out the priests, and effaced the names of the old gods from the temple walls—especially the name Amon. But as his own name was Amenhotep ("Amon is satisfied"), he dispensed with that too, and changed it to Ikhnaton ("profitable to Aton, the sun-god"). To get away from the shrines of the old gods he even built himself a new capital—Amarna; and there he carved on stone his hymns of praise to the sun—Aton, Creator of the World, King of Kings. Of the hymns themselves I may quote a few lines only, from Breasted's translation:

Thy dawning is beautiful in the horizon of the sky,
O living Aton, beginning of life!
When thou risest in the eastern horizon,
Thou fillest every land with thy beauty.
Thou art beautiful, great, glittering, high above every land,
Thy rays, they encompass the lands, even all that thou hast made,
Thou art Re, and thou carriest them all away captive;
Thou bindest them by thy love.
Though thou art far away, thy rays are upon earth;
Though thou art on high, thy footprints are the day. . . .

The trees and the plants flourish,
The birds flutter in their marshes,
Their wings uplifted in adoration to thee.
All the sheep dance upon their feet,
All winged things fly, . . .
Thy rays are in the midst of the great green sea.

Creator of the germ in woman,
Maker of seed in man,
Giving life to the son in the body of his mother,
Soothing him that he may not weep,
Nurse even in the womb,
Giver of breath to animate every one that he maketh! . . .

When the fledgling in the egg chirps in the shell,
Thou givest him breath therein to preserve him alive. . . .

How manifold are thy works!
They are hidden from before us,
O sole God, whose powers no other possesseth. . . .

All the distant countries,
Thou makest also their life. . . .
How excellent are thy designs, O lord of eternity!
There is a Nile in the sky for the strangers,
And for the cattle of every country that go upon their feet.

Thy rays nourish every garden;
When thou risest they live,
They grow by thee. . . .

Thou art in my heart,
There is no other that knoweth thee
Save thy son Ikhnaton.
Thou hast made him wise
In thy designs and thy might.
The world is in thy hand,
Even as thou hast made them.
When thou risest they live,
When thou settest they die. . . .

Nobility, spirituality, catholicity. The Hebrew psalms—still a
thousand years in the future—seem, as Baikie said, only an echo of
Ikhnaton's song of praise. No one, says Breasted, ever before caught

such a vision of the great father; or with such simplicity, honesty, frankness, and sincerity, preached the doctrine of peace. And when he died, there "died with him such a spirit as the world had never seen before—a brave soul, undauntedly facing the momentum of immemorial tradition, and thereby stepping out from the long line of conventional and colourless Pharaohs, that he might disseminate ideas far beyond and above the capacity of his age to understand . . . became the world's first idealist and the world's first individual."

Ikhnaton was a visionary, an idealist; he tried to rule his conduct by his creed—"Living in Truth"; "the most remarkable genius of the Oriental world before the Hebrews," says Breasted. "*Before* the Hebrews?*" Where in the whole Hebrew Bible is there a suspicion of the simple but inescapable fact that the sun is Creator, Generator, Author, Maker, of this earth and all that lives thereon?

Ikhnaton's idea of sweeping out the cat and dog gods and replacing them with a monotheistic god was a good idea, especially as his "true" god was the sun; but it did not spark. The zoo gods were too heavily entrenched. Cats and crocodiles, jackals and hawks, are more wonderful to morons than sun or any other "true" god. His was indeed a voice crying in the wilderness.

But there is a limit to every towering genius; he left no son to carry on his revolutionary reform—else Egypt might be our Holy Land today. He married his eldest daughter to a young noble, who died while co-regent. His second daughter died. His third daughter was married to the boy Tutankhaton ("Living-image of Aton"), who became co-regent. Amon's priests, however, came out of hiding and bestirred themselves; they forced the boy king back to Thebes and changed his name to Tutankhamon. He lived, a mere puppet of the priests—to die at the age of eighteen. Ikhnaton's idea of a true monotheistic god was promptly buried in the sands of the desert, to be hauled out by a Hebrew eight centuries later; Ikhnaton himself became known as the "criminal of Akhetaton."

With troubles at home and abroad, this amazing Eighteenth Dynasty went out in darkness.

In peace or war, Egypt was always doing something "for the first time in human history." One Pharaoh, dying full of years and "rich in possessions, like a flood, and like a sea, splendid in glory," has the names of his four favourite dogs ("Gazelle," "Greyhound," "Blackie," and "Hotpot") carved on his tombstone. Not far from Tutankhamon's tomb is that of Thutmose III's general who captured Joppa *à la* Ali Baba and his forty thieves—by sneaking in his soldiers in panniers on the backs of donkeys. At any rate, there is the general's tomb; Joppa was taken; and that is how he took it, according to the story. In other words, Egypt seems to have been the source of inspiration, not only for much sacred, but for much profane literature, including Sindbad the Sailor, Cinderella, Machandel, the disguised prince, the foredoomed prince, the faithful wife, the unfaithful wife, the hidden heart, the sad marriage between a vestal and a god, and wise men who wander beyond the Red Sea and perform magic—as did Moses at Pharaoh's court.

During the Nineteenth Dynasty (1350-1200 B.C.), under Seti I and Ramses II, Egypt again became a world power. In some respects Ramses II was Egypt's most remarkable king. He reigned sixty-seven years; waged long wars with the Hittites; built half the temples now extant in Egypt; and carved his name on all the others. Some of his portrait statues of monolithic granite weigh a thousand tons and would tax a modern freight engine to haul. His queen, Nefritiri, was made the presiding divinity of one of his temples—and, judging from her portrait statues, fully deserved the honour.

With Ramses III, the priests of Amon at Thebes began to become the great feudal power in the state, the king having presented them with 113,433 slaves in thirty years. The Twentieth Dynasty ended with a high priest on the Pharaoh's seat. With the Twenty-first Dynasty (1090-945 B.C.) the empire fell to pieces. Royal princes were content to be priests of Amon. But Sheshonk (the Shishak of the Bible) of the Twenty-second Dynasty captured Jerusalem in the fifth year of Rehoboam and robbed the Temple of Solomon of its treasure, including his golden shields—in conquests many of which may be read today on the wall of a pylon in Karnak. To be seen there also is Amon with a rope in his hand, binding the Jewish prisoners, and Sheshonk clubbing a group of cowering Asiatics whom he holds by the hair.

Egyptian history thereafter is not entirely without interest, but for us it is practically without importance. She remained wealthy

and refined, but after the Assyrian conquest in the seventh, and
the Persian in the sixth, century B.C., she ceased to be creative; in
fact, since her kings had become priests, in the eleventh century
B.C., she had ceased to be the world's chief creator and exporter of
civilization. The balance of cultural trade was against her—and has
been ever since. Only in medicine did she continue to hold her
supreme position. Homer rated Egyptian physicians above all others
in skill; Cyrus depended upon them; and Darius believed in them,
notwithstanding the high reputation of Greek medicine.

The scene of paramount interest had moved to the Tigris and
Euphrates valleys—the Land of the Two Rivers. There the torch of
civilization had long been blazing. Great ideas had already been
born; more were in process of incubation. The time was coming
when western Asia was to have its revenge on poor old Egypt. Let
us go to Ur of the Chaldees and again be with the winners. We
shall be among Semitic-speaking peoples. The Egyptians were a
Hamitic-speaking people, as are their cousins today, from Somali-
land to Morocco.

## III

Having decided that civilization began in Egypt, and having
sketched its growth from prehistoric times through its zenith to its
bankruptcy, we are now to see that civilization possibly began in
Mesopotamia or even farther east. Certain it is that in the silt of
great rivers ancient man found the spur he seemed to need to pass
from his long hand-to-mouth struggle to affluence and wealth.
Which river first spurred him to take this step is not yet certainly
known—presumably the Nile; it may have been the Euphrates, or
the Indus, or the Ganges, or even possibly the Yangtze. The Nile
has been most deeply prodded for its secrets and has yielded most.
What is under the accumulated silt of rivers farther east is yet
unknown.

It is known that men lived in the Syrian Desert, and on toward
the east in Mongolia and the Ordos region of China, in prehistoric
times; and that they used flint implements of the Mousterian type,
and presumably as ancient as the corresponding Palæolithic Age in
Europe. Why not? It is also known that when the curtain went up
—or when the archæologist's spade went down—on Ur, Kish, and

Eridu, an amazing culture was revealed, as beautiful to our eyes as it was ghastly.

That culture is not Egyptian; it is of the soil itself, Asiatic, Sumerian, Akkadian. But let us first emphasize the complexity of the problems involved, their similarity to and difference from those of Egypt. The Nile Valley is unique. But the Tigris and Euphrates are not unlike the Nile. They flow from the same mountains, and for much of their course are parallel. With the melting snows in spring they begin their annual inundations, bringing down silt and setting an agricultural stage not unlike that in the Nile Valley.

The entire lower region of the two rivers has natural boundaries, though not so sharp as those of the Nile. There are mountains to the east, a desert to the west. The upper and more elevated part of the country between the rivers is the Land of the Two Rivers—*Mesopotamia*. In that region Assyria rose to empire. The lower part, from modern Bagdad to the Persian Gulf, is a rich alluvial plain about 30,000 miles square. This was the scene of the great Chaldean-Babylonian empires.

That plain was called Sumer and Akkad by its earliest kings. Akkad ("the mountains") was the more northerly region, and the site of such cities as Akkad, Sippar, Kish, Opis, Cutha, and Babylon. In Sumer ("the river valley"), around the head of the Gulf and extending from Babylon to Kaldu (Chaldea), were the cities of Erech, Ur, Larsa, Lagash, Umma, Isin, and Eridu. This was the Land of Shinar—stretching east for some thirty to fifty miles to the mountains of Elam, and ending in the desert some twenty-five miles to the west. The problems already uncovered by excavations in and below these ancient cities have become numerous and conflicting, but there is no disputing the evidence itself. The big questions—who, when, and how related—can only be answered after further investigation.

Who these Sumerians and Akkadians were we do not know. The Akkadians possibly came from the desert to the west; the Sumerians, from the Elamite hills to the east. If they lived today, we should probably call them Arabs; but if they lived in Afghanistan, we should call them Afghans. Perhaps they were prehistoric Mongols.

"And it came to pass, as they journeyed from the east, that they found a plain in the land of Shinar, and they dwelt there." The plain is lower Mesopotamia; "they" were the Sumerians. That statement in Genesis presumably is based on an old Sumerian legend of their migration from the Elamite hills.

"Mankind," says a Sumerian hymn, "when created, did not know of bread for eating or garments for wearing; they ate herbs with their mouths like sheep, and drank ditch water." That hymn presumably refers to the people the Sumerians found dwelling in the river marshes. Recent excavations show that they lived in wattle huts of reed covered with pitch or mud plaster and protected by wooden doors. They had cows, sheep, goats, and pigs; grew barley; ate porridge, but lived chiefly on fish. They used more stone than copper tools; their sickles were baked clay set with flint teeth. They used earthenware vessels, some painted. They wore sheepskin and homespun cloth; seem to have tattooed their bodies; wore stone bead necklaces and ear ornaments. They buried their dead, and with them food, tools, ornaments, etc. They had a rude picture writing, which finally became a system of 350 signs representing syllables or words. They developed the cuneiform type of writing.

The age of these pre-Sumerians is, of course, unknown; but it is not likely that the swamps of this region would have permitted of occupation earlier than 6000 B.C. The earliest settlements were probably on islands formed by the recession of the Persian Gulf. Ur was probably on such an island.

The Sumerians came. Their deepest tombs are thirty feet below the level of the time of Sargon, 2750 B.C. Sumer early became a land of small city states ruled by chief priests, the gods' personal representatives on earth. Their favourite outdoor sport was civil war. Their chief contributions to our civilization were the wheeled cart and chariot; towers—leading to the Tower of Babel and all church steeples; a numerical unit of sixty for astronomical purposes—still used to divide our circle into 360 degrees, our hour into sixty minutes, our minute into sixty seconds; and a seven-day week with a taboo, or Sabbath, day. Also the original or oldest known Flood myth.

They really believed in their Flood. Who in the Mississippi Valley does not believe in a flood? There probably was a rare and extraordinarily high flood at some time in the Euphrates Valley.

At any rate, the Sumerians *claimed* to have had ten Antediluvian kings, with a combined reign of 456,000 years.

One of these "kings" was our old friend Osiris, Tammuz, Adonis, under the name Dumuzi—god of vegetation, who died every winter and came to life every spring. He reigned a modest 36,000 years. Of Gilgamesh, hero of the Flood epic, we shall see more later. These Antediluvian king lists vary: each Sumerian city state had its own list; they all agree there was a Flood. Let us look at one of these city states—at Ur, the most famous because of the extraordinarily interesting discoveries recently made among its ruins.

The dates of Ur's First Dynasty (3100-2930 B.C.) are possibly as well fixed as those of the First Dynasty in Egypt. But, as in Egypt, civilization is already in full bloom and, again as in Egypt, is known from the contents of graves—"death-pits," as they may appropriately be called. Some Predynastic Ur graves possibly date from 4000-3500 B.C.—contemporary with, or possibly older than, Menes.

On the brick floor of a twenty-five-feet-square death-pit, Woolley made an "astonishingly rich" haul: the remains of no fewer than seventy-four bodies, carefully arranged in overlapping rows. Sixty-eight bodies were of women; the other six, of men servants armed with daggers, used presumably to slay the women before the thirty-feet-deep tomb was sealed. The contents of that pit may be seen in the British Museum, including the restored head of one of the lady victims.

Besides astounding and costly personal adornments of gold ribbons, wreaths of gold leaves, inlaid beads, hair combs, and necklaces of gold and lapis-lazuli beads worn by the victims, four extraordinarily beautiful eleven-stringed harps of wood overlaid with silver or gold, and with a bull's head mascot, were found. Also wooden statues covered with gold, lapis-lazuli, and shell, of rams rampant. In design and execution all these things are little short of marvellous.

To these add the contents of royal tombs of about the same age—especially the "standards" and plaques of wood covered with significant scenes on mosaics of lapis, pink stone, and shell. One standard shows war scenes in marvellous detail. Chariots drawn by four asses, each chariot carrying a driver and an armed warrior. A phalanx of infantry wearing copper helmets and leather kilts and armed with short spears; other warriors, armed with ax and scimitar or with short spear and dagger. Another scene portrays the king with his officers and servants, the victors with arms, cloaks, and helmets, and their tattered and tattooed enemies. In another scene the king sits at a banquet; his sons or officials drink from wonderful goblets, while female singers and harpists entertain them; a queue of servants bring food and the spoils of war; teams of asses and pack-carriers bring supplies and more spoils. Also gold helmets; dice and gaming-boards with their sets of "men"; a king's ring, a queen's garter; fluted gold tumblers and chalices. Unparalleled works of art.

What does all this signify?

For one thing, a far richer and older treasure than that from the famed Minoan palace in Crete, or the equally famed treasure of Agamemnon of Mycenæ; and nearly two thousand years before the boy king Tutankhamon was born. There is also evidence of writing as advanced as that of Egypt; a lapidary art in hard stone never surpassed and still influencing our own decorative art; and a general technique in arts and crafts as fine as Egypt ever produced. In the beaten-gold head of a bull from one of the harps, the art of the goldsmith reached a height possibly never before or since surpassed.

Herodotus speaks of "all the Babylonians" having seals, but the seals they had are as the seals sold by the corner bookshop compared with the cylinder seals of Ur. What scenes those gem-cutters engraved on those little stone cylinders: farming and agriculture in all its phases, animals in the field, orchards, hunting scenes, court etiquette, temple worship, ritual scenes, scenes from myths—in short, the entire pageant of an ancient civilization, from daily life to the mythologic age. Infinite patience, marvellous technique, incomparable lapidary art. Nearly six thousand years ago.

But there is also all too unmistakable evidence of a highly developed war machine; and of a highly developed cult of the dead, including human and animal sacrifice. In short, we have at Ur and neighbouring cities the very foundations of civilization: absolutism on the part of king over the bodies of his subjects; of priest over their souls. Combine these powers in one divinely appointed ruler and we have the makings of a Babylon.

Ur was a city state, a little kingdom of Sumer; and there were other city states. There were no natural frontiers, nor was there enduring peace among the petty kingdoms; now this, now that one, was supreme. But to the northern or Akkad end of Sumer there came new blood, a Semitic-speaking people from the Arabian Desert. One of them, a chief who had become cup-bearer to the king of Kish, rebelled, and at Agade proclaimed himself king of Sumer and Akkad. That was Sargon I, who "knew not his father," hence probably was the son of a temple prostitute, and who founded a Semitic dynasty. He was the first to rule the whole of Akkad and Sumer. He pushed his conquest to Elam on the east and to the Mediterranean on the west—and was the first great conquering king known to history. The Akkadian masters of Sumer took over its civilization: war-complex, business methods, calendar, numerals, measures, weights, wigs, razors, dress, and helmets of leather and copper.

And we may emphasize here that Semitic-speaking people did not begin civilization; they took it over from the Sumerians. Who the Sumerians were, I repeat, is not known. It is known that they were neither Semite nor Aryan; nor, we may note in passing, were the Hittites, Trojans, Cretans, Lydians, Etruscans or Iberians, Aryan; not for nearly two thousand years yet do we even hear of Aryan-speaking people. To call the Sumerians Elamites is as yet to call them nothing, for nothing is known of the Elamites, except that at Susa in Elam huge mounds at a depth of a hundred feet show adobe brick, painted pottery, and copper.

The dynasty founded by Sargon of Agade ended about 2470 B.C. Meanwhile the Semites had gained control over all Shinar. But about two hundred years later Ur came to the front again with Ur-Nammu, founder of the Third Dynasty of Ur (2278-2170 B.C.). Again a non-Semite was king of Sumer and Akkad. By the twelfth year of his reign his son Dungi was accepted as a god by all Sumer and Akkad.

Ur-Nammu seems to have been "the merciful Lord who brought prosperity to Ur," as he titles himself on a stele set up in his capital. This stele shows the king in an attitude of worship, with an angel flying down to him from heaven, pouring the water of fertility upon the earth. Another scene is of cattle, and men milking cows. He built great irrigation canals, one connecting Ur with the Gulf.

His greatest building operations, however, were temples—a work carried on by his son, who succeeded him after eighteen years, and who reigned fifty-eight years.

The Ziggurrat, or staged tower of Ur, was the greatest of many religious buildings. As it still stands, a colossal ruin, while Babylon's Ziggurrat (Babel) has vanished, we may look at it. It is of solid brick, rectangular in shape, 250 by 150 feet, and was originally seventy feet high. Big; but a mere anthill beside Cheops' tomb. The Ziggurrat was not a tomb; it was an artificial mountain, the base of a shrine, the Hill of Heaven, the Mountain of God. Its stages, thinks Woolley, symbolized cosmic divisions: Underworld, Earth, and Heaven or House of God.

Within the vast double wall enclosing the tower, its Great Gate adorned with silver and gold, were quarters for the priest and for the temple officials and the cabinet: Ministers of the Harem, War, Agriculture, Transport, and Finance, and their secretaries and accountants. For the temple was a Vested Interest and heavily endowed. To its great storehouse the farmers brought their cattle, sheep, and goats, their cheese and barley, pots of clarified butter, and bales of wool—and got a receipt on a clay tablet looking like a dog biscuit.

Another temple, protected by a maze, housed the moon-god's harem, of which the head woman was the god's real wife. The concubines might bear children, but their fathers would remain unknown. They owned property and could carry on business in their own name; they might even be of royal rank; they were rich and honoured, high above the common temple prostitutes.

In the house of the keeper of the temple archives, thousands of clay tablets were found, showing profit-and-loss book-keeping, amazingly business-like. And in a room in the courtyard was a furnace for melting the temple's metal income into ingots for storage. Just like a mediæval monastery.

Even the houses of Ur's Third Dynasty well-to-do can be pictured. They were two stories high and had from twelve to fourteen rooms, kitchen with brick fireplace, lavatory with drains, servants' rooms, private chapel, etc. And tables and bedsteads; utensils of clay, copper, and stone; rugs and carpets; wall relief amulets; and, last but not least, a family burial vault of brick, under the chapel—

or, if no chapel, under any room. Sometimes they walled up the front door and turned the house into a mausoleum. The graves of thirty infants were found under one chapel.

Then came the Amorites and the Elamites; and a little later Ur and other Sumerian cities were plundered and burned—to lie forgotten for four thousand years, till yesterday's shovel lifted them into the light again.

Forgotten, yes; but Sumer's laws became Babylon's code. Her gods, too, lived on under their new Semitic names; even her literature, first to flourish in Asia, lived on in Semitic translation. In fact, Sumerian civilization came to new life in Babylon, and the traditions of her art were to influence eighth-century Assyrian sculpture. The true arch, the dome, and the vault can be traced from 3500 B.C. Sumer, straight through to Europe.

As Kroeber says, Indian architecture is not Indian; nor is Gothic connected with the Goths. Nor did the Arabs invent the dome. The Etruscans were using the true arch and vault by 700 B.C. The Greeks took over the Egyptian columns, but the Romans took over the rows of arches for their façades—arches which had been used in Sumer two thousand years before Romulus and Remus were suckled by a wolf. The Arabs twisted the columns and bent the arch into a horseshoe. The Gothic cathedrals, aiming at height, developed vertical lines at the expense of horizontal; but the fundamental engineering problems had all long been solved. Egypt was building with stone, and Nippur with true brick, 5,000 years ago. The main features of private houses and the architectural problems of arch, dome, and vault were thus solved in Egypt and Sumer over five thousand years ago.

Finally, from the Sumerians, says Woolley, "the Hebrews derived the ideals of social life and justice which informed all their history and have by Christian races been regarded in theory if not in practice as criteria for their own customs and enactments."

Just how Sumerian civilization would strike an unbiassed observer I cannot know, for there are no unbiassed observers. To an Apache Indian, I suspect, her ethics would have seemed savage and her "death-pits" incredible—though an Aztec would have understood them. Certain it is that her religion was based on childish superstitions, not one whit more refined, more sensible, or more

intellectual, than those of a South Sea Islander. Her religious practices—temple prostitution, wholesale human sacrifice—may be part
and parcel of early high civilization, but they are a disgrace to the
human race just the same and would have made Neanderthal man
blush for them.

To the credit of the Sumerians, their supernatural world had
neither heaven nor hell. They did recognize a land from which
there was no return. The way to get there was to be "decently"
buried—with plenty of food and enough of the goods of this life
to carry on there. If a master, "goods" included servants. We have
seen what it meant for a royal personage. The carrying off of their
conquered enemies' gods and the destruction of their temples were
logical processes—and were faithfully carried out by those who
followed, even by the Christians when they got hold of Rome,
and by Christian missionaries when they get hold of savages.

"Logical:" their gods were human passions writ large, in more
potent anthropomorphic form. When they destroyed an enemy,
they naturally destroyed, or adopted, that enemy's gods; it is only
human nature that every great god should be a jealous god. The
same sadistic spirit, plausibly rationalized, prompted us to compel
our Indians to stop the sun-dance.

Sumer's gods had, of course, different functions: of waters, of
wisdom, of rain and wind, of vegetation, plague, justice, love,
childbirth; but the local god of the city state naturally became the
High God. When Babylon became the capital of the Empire, her
god Marduk became Creator of the World.

It is worth noting that Ur was the centre of moon-god worship.
There was a great temple to Nannar and his consort Ningal. Even
up to the sixth century B.C. the eldest daughter of the king of
Babylon became high priestess of the moon-god Nannar—as did
Sargon's daughter more than two thousand years earlier. Haran to
the north, possibly settled about 2000 B.C. by Chaldeans from Ur,
was also a moon-god worshipping centre. What of it? Wasn't Abraham born in Ur? Didn't he tarry a while in Haran before he went
to Canaan? The Bible says so; and his family record is incomprehensible without a moon-worshipping-complex in the background.

It is not that the idea behind most Oriental religion was childish,
but that the idea put into practice—in the hands of greedy human

beings—became monstrous. It bled the people white. If "the earth is the Lord's," the Lord is the landlord. Ground rent is the logical step. But to whom must it be paid? To the Lord's agent, of course—his steward, the priest.

It is recorded on a baked clay tablet that for reading a burial service a priest received 7 urns of wine, 420 loaves of bread, 120 measures of corn, a garment, a kid, a bed, and a stool. It is to the priest's interest that the farmers depend on his magic mummeries for their corn, calves, and children, rather than on their own labours and intelligence. It is to the priest's interest that ignorance prevail, that no human being build a house, turn a sod, name a baby, eat a meal, take a breath or sneeze, without his advice or sanction.

Sumerian civilization made some progress in Babylonia, but in which direction it is not always easy to determine.

Let us go to Babylon.

### IV

The early history of Babylonia is the archæology of Sumer and Akkad. We saw how the desert Arabs (Bedouins) filtered into Sumer and became engulfed in its civilization; and how Sargon I of Agade was the first Semite to rule the whole of Akkad and Sumer, the first to conquer and plunder, if not to rule, nearly all western Asia. That Sargon became the semi-mythical hero of the Babylonians—their Menes, Charlemagne, Alfred the Great. They studied his successes and tried to follow in his footsteps, omen for omen.

As power waned in Sumer and Akkad because of civil wars, other Semitic-speaking people entered the Euphrates Valley, especially more Amorites from Syria. Till now, Babylon had been an obscure town in Akkad. The Amorites seized it (about 2225 B.C.) and founded the First Dynasty of Babylon, with Sumu-Abu as its first king.

The sixth and ablest king of that line was Hammurabi—possibly the "Amraphel king of Shinar" with whom the Hebrews' legendary hero, Abraham, came into warlike contact. Hammurabi (2123-2080 B.C.) was the real founder of Babylonia, and Babylon, his capital, thereafter was the capital of Mesopotamia throughout ancient history. But South Sumer, the "Kingdom of the Sea Land," lived on three centuries longer and then utterly disappeared, leaving its dead language, the "Latin" of Mesopotamia, to the scribes and priests.

In the reign of the eleventh and last king of the First Dynasty Babylon was stormed and sacked by a king whose name is not even known, and Kassite horse-breeders founded a dynasty which lasted six hundred years. Who the Kassites were, how they looked, or what language they spoke, is unknown. Not for a thousand years was Babylonian civilization to be revived by the Chaldeans.

The Sumerian foundations of that civilization we have seen. We have now to see how it was moulded and became fixed, crystallized, even codified, as few civilizations have ever been. On all this rests the genius of Hammurabi. He was the first and one of the greatest organizers in all history. Great in war, he was greater in peace. He was a great king and is one of the best known of the ancient world.

It is one of the ironies of fate that Hammurabi's claim to fame rests largely upon the fact that nearly 1,500 years after his death Ashurbanipal (Sardanapalus), last great Assyrian king and one of history's most bloodthirsty butchers, was a bibliophile. The "books" he prized most were antiques—the Classics, Babylonian clay tablets. He literally filled rooms of his palace and the royal library at Nineveh with them—to be found by Layard between 1848 and 1876, and to become, with the great hauls a few years later, the greatest archæological treasure of the British Museum. These now number 30,000, and, with the 20,000 from Nippur in Philadelphia, give us an unparalleled insight into the mind of an ancient people.

That "mind," as revealed in clay-tablet "books," included medical texts, language text-books, grammars, commentaries on texts, school editions of their "classics," hymns, sacred and penitential prayers, rituals, magic and incantations, dream and omen books, prescriptions for driving out demons, witches, and sorcerers, divination handbooks, myths of Creation, of the Flood, etc.

To this amazing literature must be added the famous Code of Hammurabi, to be read in Paris, inscribed on a magnificent diorite stele, found by French explorers at Susa. Drawn up about 1900 B.C., it is the oldest surviving law code and the farthest-reaching in its influence in all history. It was a reduction and codification of old local codes and customs brought up to date—and, says Woolley, was based primarily on a code of Dungi, a Third Dynasty king of Ur. Its great merit lay in its nationalization of local law.

Women, as in ancient Egypt, suffered few discriminations; they went unveiled, held high positions, did business on their own account, were professional scribes, could form partnerships with men, owned dowries and could transmit them to their children, etc. Marriage was legally protected. In fact, women enjoyed more freedom and independence of their husbands than they did in Great Britain till the Married Women's Property Act of 1870. Justice was to be done widows, orphans, and the poor; and the relations of borrower and lender were so carefully attended to as to show skill in banking business. Shylocks were watched—and in the interest of the needy borrower. The jerry-builder was provided for: if the house he built collapsed and killed the owner, "that builder shall be put to death." If a freeman's slave died because of an operation for a severe wound, the surgeon "shall restore a slave of equal value."

Babylonian saloon-keepers four thousand years ago were women: "If a wine-seller do not receive grain as the price of drink, but if she receive money, or if she make the measure for drink smaller than the measure for corn, they shall call that wine-seller to account, and they shall throw her into the water. . . . If outlaws collect in the house of a wine-seller, and she do not arrest these outlaws and bring them to the palace, that wine-seller shall be put to death." The trade was legal, but evidently in no high repute. Specific laws aimed at checking the greedy from exploiting the vice and weakness of their fellow-citizens.

As contrasted with older Sumerian codes, Hammurabi's marks an advance in severity against family tie offenses. Whereas adultery formerly did not even necessarily mean divorce, it now meant death for both guilty parties. To harbour a runaway slave formerly was atoned by restitution or fine; it now became a capital offence. Formerly, a quarrelsome slave was sold; now he paid the penalty of having his right ear cut off.

Every temple was a justice court; every priest could pronounce judgment. There were also, however, courts with judges appointed by the king. An eye for an eye, a tooth for a tooth, was the rule. The death penalty for serious offences was not rare, and mutilations were inflicted for certain others. Slaves could own property, give evidence, engage in business in their own names, borrow money, buy their freedom. They might be flogged and branded, but there is no evidence that they were ever regarded, as they were in our South, as outside the pale of humanity. Parents might sell their children into slavery; husbands, in payment of debts, could sell their wives to their creditors for three years. A free woman could marry a slave without disgrace, and their children were free.

By the fifth century B.C., according to Herodotus, every woman in Babylonia had to offer herself to a stranger in the temple before she was eligible for marriage. This custom was unknown in Hammurabi's time, though the temples maintained many prostitutes under the cloak of religious respectability.

All in all, it was a good code. It aimed at justice; it frowned on injustice. *Noblesse oblige* was its motto. It imposed heavier punishments on the rich than on the poor. How many modern codes come up to its high standard? How near do we come to it in actual practice? That code became the basis of the Mosaic code. Its influence has been inestimable. It began in a prehistoric age— as did most of the really important things of civilization.

"He who shall excel in tablet writing shall shine like the sun," is the motto on a clay tablet. Temples were the centres of education. The number of illiterates in Babylonia four thousand years ago was probably not greater than in some provinces of Spain today. With the finger of the law in every pie, and every transaction necessarily recorded, excellence in "tablet writing" must have been at a high premium, the number of professional scribes great.

From surviving tablets it is easy to reconstruct practically the whole course of study. The teacher would write the copy on one side of the unbaked tablet; the pupil, after studying it, would reproduce it on the other side. First, they had to learn the signs with phonetic value—the "alphabet"; next, the ideograms or signs for words or ideas of generic value. Then came short sentences, etc., on up to paradigms of verbs and declensions of nouns. Then came mathematics: tables of multiplication and division, for the extraction of square and cube roots; exercises in geometry; lists of weights and measures; etc.

A clay tablet bill of lading is extant, of a temple ship which returned (2080 B.C.) with a cargo of gold, copper ore, ivory, precious woods, and fine stone for statues and vases.

Life in Babylon, as revealed by the tablets, was in many respects essentially modern—certainly more modern in spirit than during the life of Charlemagne; and their ethical standards were at least as high as the Hebrews'. The family rather than the individual was the ethical unit. The individual, in respect to adultery, bearing false witness, theft, and murder, was held to strict account.

But life then was not all beer and skittles: "His ass I am; I am harnessed to a mule; a wagon I draw; to seek reeds and fodder I go forth." Nor was it always evident that goodness was its own reward: "He is altogether good, but he is clothed with darkness." Nor was it always plain sailing: "My knees go, my feet are unwearied; but a fool has cut into my course."

In short, in the realm of human affairs, as in the physical world, it was not impossible for Babylonians to take a scientific point of view. The foundations of a scientific attitude were laid in Babylonia. Even their Flood myth is their own answer to certain physical phenomena.

v

While Babylonian history in its Sumerian beginnings is not unlike that of Egypt, the Babylonians were more curious about the origins of things and paid more attention to their ancient literature, which, of course, was made up of pseudo-science—the myths they spun in answer to their curiosity. Those myths interest us, for, preserved and transformed by the Jews, we have inherited them in the Book of Genesis.

Their Creation myth, found a few years ago on seven tablets, is long, involved, and repetitious; in Genesis it is reduced to a few paragraphs. They also had a myth of Adapa, or Adamu, who broke the wings of the South Wind; he is the first man, like our Adam, but unlike our Adam, a true hero. He was warned by his father, Ea, Water God of Eridu, Sumer's traditionally oldest city, not to eat of the food the gods will offer him. He obeys his father's warning, and thereby misses eternal life. This and other myths, including that of the Flood, are part of Babylon's great epic of Gilgamesh, found on twelve closely written tablets in Ashurbanipal's royal library.

Gilgamesh, according to the legendary king lists, was fifth king of the First Dynasty of Erech, and ruled 126 years. It was on his wanderings in a mysterious far western country that from Noah's own lips he learned the story of the Flood, Babylon's most beautiful and impressive poem.

The angry gods decide to drown the human race. But Ea, the Water God, goes to the hut of a good man in a village on the Euphrates and betrays the secret in this whispered cryptic message:

> Reed-hut, reed-hut, wall, O wall,
> O reed-hut, hear, O wall, understand.

"Noah" understands, and builds an "ark."

What I had, I loaded thereon, the whole harvest of life
I caused to embark within the vessel; all my family and relations,
The beasts of the field, the cattle of the field, the craftsmen, I made
    them all embark.
I entered the vessel and closed the door. . . .

I sent forth a dove, I released it;
It went, the dove, it came back,
As there was no place, it came back. . . .

I sent forth a crow, I released it;
It went, the crow, and beheld the subsidence of the waters;
It eats, it splashes about, it caws, it comes not back.

So "Noah" leaves his ship and sacrifices on a mountain top. The gods, hungry because the flood had also drowned their food in the temples, "scented the sweet savour, and like flies gathered above the sacrifice"—and decide there will be no more floods. And "Noah" is told to be "fruitful and multiply, and replenish the earth."

The Babylonian "Noah," Woolley thinks, may have been a Sumerian settler among the Akkadians; the "wickedness" may merely reflect the racial animosity between the Sumerians and the Semite Akkadians. Having drowned out the Akkadians, the Sumerians by multiplying could replenish the now empty land. Kish and Erech are the first post-diluvial dynasties of Sumer.

At any rate, like all primitive Creation myths, these Babylonian myths point no moral, nor were they supposed to exert a moral influence. Only after the myths became transformed by successive editions in Jewish literature did they begin to be pointed with moral teachings. In Babylon's Creation myth, Marduk with magic spells creates the firmament out of the body of a slain monster and makes man out of mud and dragon's blood—merely that the gods may be fed. Babylonian gods, in short, are all-powerful, capricious, and unmoral. Mere virtue will not keep their favour; sacrifices of beer, wine, bread and milk, dates and flesh, will. "The lamb is the substitute for humanity; he hath given up a lamb for his life, he hath given up a lamb's head for the man's head," said their litany: relic of the human sacrifice we saw in Ur's prehistoric graves. Gilgamesh was a sort of Herakles: Hall thinks possibly the original of the Biblical Nimrod.

One of the finest bits of Babylonian poetry tells of Erech's dire straits after a three years' siege:

> Men cry aloud like beasts,
> And maidens mourn like doves;
> The gods of strong-walled Erech
> Are changed to flies, and buzz about the streets;
> The spirits of strong-walled Erech
> Are changed to mice, and glide into holes.
> For three years the enemy besieged Erech,
> And the doors were barred and the bolts were shot,
> And Ishtar did not raise her head against the foe.

Farther into this curious and interesting maze of Babylonian mythology we cannot go. We may not forget, however, that Syria and Palestine were culturally very dependent on Babylonia, especially in important matters of literature and religion. That dependence began with Sargon of Agade and lasted until the fall of Persia. But our Biblical temptation of Eve and the destruction of the Tower of Babel are of Jewish origin—or, at any rate, are unknown in Babylonian literature.

"For the king of Babylon," says Ezekiel (xxi, 21), "stood at the parting of the way . . . to use divination . . . he looked in the liver." The key to that liver may be found in the British Museum: a sheep's liver modelled in clay in Babylon over 4,000 years ago.

It is divided into fifty squares, and in each square is written the omen for that particular spot. What is ominous? Every accident, everything unusual, everything with a chance element in it. Ominous of what? Kill a sheep, examine its liver, and read the answer in the clay-model "dream-book." It was the business of the priests to keep track of omens and portents, to be expert in reading signs, to compile books of good omens. Within a block of where I sit I can buy a *Babylon Book of Omens* for half a dollar.

Last week a trained nurse caring for a paralytic aunt of mine entered a closet in the early morning and found an electric light burning. No one would admit having turned it on. "It's a portent!" she muttered; and no 2100 B.C. Babylonian was ever more serious about a portent than this trained nurse of 1930 A.D. And if my aunt had died that night or the next day, the light would have been more than a portent: nobody on earth could have convinced her that light and death were not related.

The Babylonians studied the stars as they studied livers, and for the same reason—for portents. Astrology, or astrophie, was an important branch of the magic art. Stars are beings, gods, demons; they change—frown, smile, are propitious, unpropitious; they *cause* events on earth. To know star change is to forecast the future, to hold fate in learned hands. They studied the stars—and really learned much of their movements. But in their intent they were no more moved by a scientific spirit than I would be if I were to "look up your record" with the hope that I might thereby gain power over you. The real religion of Babylonia was in its rites and liturgies; these sources of magic power were in the hands of priests whose main business was to bleed the people white in the guise of protecting them from the fearsome gods and demons.

And so we may say that while the gift of grain was of inestimable benefit to mankind, the gift of the gods of the Nile and Euphrates was almost fatal. Agriculture freed man from the endless drudgery of hunting the food his animal nature demanded, and released energy for the finer things his human nature craved. But the gods enslaved him to a false and vicious idea, forced him to trust the supernatural rather than cultivate his own innate powers, and withdrew nature so far from his vision that (with the exception of the brief emancipation under Ikhnaton) nearly four thousand years had to elapse before man dared call his soul his own or look at nature with his own eyes. There was an intellectual awakening, as we shall see, in Greece, which was to be buried in metaphysics. But throughout the East the critical thought of the Chaldean, Magian, or Brahmanical cults promptly soured into another form of magic and superstition.

Even in China we see the same process. Lao-tse speculates profoundly on secular affairs: these speculations turn into a gross religion called Taoism—ghastly hells and grinning demons in charge of unspeakably filthy and ignorant priests. Kong-fu-tse discusses family and state morals wisely, soundly, and practically: his teachings become another great cult with endowed' temples and fat priests—Confucianism.

Obsessions can ruin empires as well as individuals. The great obsession of Egypt and of Babylon, and of the entire East—Sumerian, Semite, Iranian, Indian—was a fixed belief in the intellectual supremacy of the priest. He represented God; he must know. There could be no questioning his decisions. He was a Magian, a mystic wonder-working magician, and held a tighter rein on men's thoughts than secular kings on their actions. Ikhnaton, the only king who dared ignore the teachings of the priests, was destroyed by them.

From the silt of the Nile, the Euphrates, and the Indus, civilizations sprang up like weeds, bearing lovely flowers of promise and hope—to bloom thereafter only in temples and palaces as sacred possessions of the priests, who in their god's name cast a palsied spell over them. And they lived on century after century, millennium after millennium, fixed, charmed, bewitched, entranced, unchanged, unchanging, cursed.

Yet to those Egyptian, Sumerian, and Babylonian priests our civilization is profoundly indebted. They laid its foundations. Our mechanics and engineers are their cultural descendants, even as are our astronomers and mathematicians, our architects, our builders of stone and makers of brick. They founded a hundred industries and crafts, taught us how to hammer and inlay metals, glaze pottery and tile, blow glass, weave and dye rich fabrics. They invented writing and recorded their knowledge on stone, clay, and papyrus, and they started the bent of our laws, warfare, and religion.

The embodiment of all this is the Chaldean star-gazer, the priestly caste of Babylon. He has, if I may figuratively individualize him, more profoundly influenced the thoughts of more people for a longer time than any other one man in all human history. He is the embodiment of the Rise of Civilization and the Fall of Man.

Just the same, I should like to have seen Babylon's vast temple of Marduk—enormous complex of priestly palaces, guarded treasuries, maze-enmeshed harems, huge towers, lofty white walls, great bronze doors encrusted with gold—the very essence of human presumption, as the Jews thought. I should like to have walked down Procession Street, flanked by glittering palaces, high ramparts, magnificent bronze gates, Ishtar Gate. "Is not this Great Babylon, that I have built for the house of the kingdom, by the might of my power, and for the honour of my majesty?" That Babylonian king was almost as modest as the Kaiser; but he had indeed built a house.

We may not agree with their idea of civilization, but they were very human and we owe much to them. They were not very critical, but they were curious, and we can· understand them. Some 1,800 years after Hammurabi had lifted Babylon high above the ancient world of Sumer and Akkad, Nabonidus, Babylon's last king, ran true to form: he was a great builder and an enthusiastic archæologist rather than a warrior. Cyrus the Persian was getting ready to strike, and was soon to enter the gates of Babylon at the head of his conquering army. But Nabonidus, absorbed in architecture and archæology, went on digging down through the debris of his city for the foundations of his new temple, leaving the direction of the empire to his son, Belshazzar—called "king" by the Hebrews—he who saw the "handwriting on the wall." And Nabonidus enthusiastically records how he dug up a foundation stone "which no king before me had seen for 3,200 years."

## VI

If we handle Assyria without gloves, no true Assyrian could object. Her contributions to civilization can be told in few lines; her contributions to the story of man's inhumanity to man would require pages.

For sheer downright ruthless brutality, the Assyrians outsavaged the entire savage world. We might omit Assyria from our record but for the fact that her idea of world power and her war machine for putting that idea into effect were to reach their culmination in the Roman Empire, and that her prowess in international affairs and in arms was to inspire the Hebrews to revise their conception of their God as they matched him against Assyria's God of War. We may remind ourselves that our own civilization is not entirely unacquainted with ruthless warfare and inhuman persecution in the name of God.

"Their booty and possessions, cattle, sheep, I carried away; many captives I burned with fire. I reared a column of the living and a column of heads. I hung up on high their heads on trees in the vicinity of their city. Their boys and girls I burned up in the flame. I devastated the city, dug it up, in fire burned it; I annihilated it."

So boasts the first Tamerlane in history—Ashurnatsirpal III (884-860 B.C.), and records it on a monument with all the pride of a proud king in glory or of a pope exulting in God's name in his triumphs over the infidels. As Hall says, he crushed his tortured, defeated enemies as though they were ants. He would capture a city, burn it, and then "mutilate all the grown men prisoners by cutting off their hands and ears and putting out their eyes; after which they were piled in a great heap to perish in torture from sun and flies, and from their wounds and suffocation. Children, boys and girls, were burnt alive at the stake; and the chief was carried off to Assyria to be flayed alive for the king's delectation." "I have not left a tree on which a bird could perch." On a black stone obelisk can be read the record of his son's twenty-two campaigns in thirty-five years. It was to that son, Shalmaneser III, that Jehu paid tribute in 842 B.C.

Who were these inhuman monsters who for nearly three hundred years inflicted incredible physical sufferings on the then civilized world? Just ordinary human beings, as all upstarts are before they arrive; a mixed population of northern mountaineers and Semitic Bedouins from that old breeding-ground of Arabia, who moved up into the upper reaches of Mesopotamia and settled at Asshur on the Tigris, about two hundred miles north of Babylon.

There, about 3000 B.C., they founded a tiny city kingdom. Hammurabi, about 2125 B.C., in pushing his conquests north of Akkad, reached Asshur and made its king pay tribute to Babylon.

Asshur is Assyria's earliest known sanctuary. About 1900 B.C. its chief calls himself "King of the Universe." But a thousand years had yet to pass before an Assyrian king could act as though he owned the universe and could torture its people with impunity. That was our friend Ashurnatsirpal III. Meanwhile the Assyrians had moved on to the west, by 1300 B.C. had swept the Hittites from the Euphrates, and turning south, had captured Babylon, which they thereafter looked upon as their mother-country—as, indeed, it was culturally.

Tiglath-Pileser I, about 1100 B.C., set a high mark for future Assyrians. Within five years he had subdued forty-two lands, "made them one tong." He was also a mighty hunter before the Lord, a real Nimrod; of wild bulls he had slain scores, also ten bull elephants, 120 lions afoot and 800 from his chariot. He forced Babylon to loose her hold on her western possessions, even looted Babylon twice, and called himself king of Sumer and Akkad. He marched across Syria and Palestine like a lord, took a deep-sea trip, and added a dolphin to his big-game bag. He looked so much like a stormcloud to the now priest-ridden Pharaohs that they sent him a peace-offering of a crocodile and a hippopotamus—which were duly carried off as curiosities to Nineveh, the Assyrian capital. That peace gift was characteristic of the end of the Egyptian Empire, and utterly unlike the end of the Assyrian Empire, which was now well started on its road to glory and ruin.

The Assyrians travelled in chariots drawn by fiery horses, and used iron weapons borrowed from their enemies. We have already peeped into Assyrian Sargon's well-stocked arsenal; but we may note here that Assyria's war machine was Assyria herself, the most terrible the world had yet seen. A big well-trained army, armed with iron weapons, riding to war in chariots, using battering-rams and siege machinery, and employing a well-developed postal system with royal messengers, was new in the world—and it was invincible. But . . . He who liveth by the sword shall perish by the sword.

Assyria was irresistible, and under Shalmaneser III again pushed on to the west, subdued Syria, demolished Damascus, and overran

Palestine. Assyria was an empire. Then came trouble, and in 745 B.C. a usurper who significantly took the name of Tiglath-Pileser IV, after Assyria's first redoubtable king. He added new lustre to the name and in a reign of eighteen years conquered Armenia, Syria, Phœnicia, Judah and Israel. He carried off the tribes of Reuben and Gad into captivity and annexed Philistia and all of Palestine and Syria, except Phœnicia and Trans-Jordan Galilee. He was the first king to systematize enslavement of his conquered captives. About his last act was to "take the hand of Bel" and by the priests of Baal be confirmed king of Sumer and Akkad.

Shalmaneser V followed. Hosea of Israel neglected to send in his yearly tribute, and after two years all Samaria was laid waste; Hosea was blinded, and his land and people annexed to Syria. Shalmaneser was murdered, and again the throne fell into the hands of a usurper who, two thousand years after Sargon of Agade had become Sargon I of Akkad and Sumer, took the name Sargon II (722-705 B.C.). His descendants were the great emperors of Assyria.

After defeating the Egyptians, Sargon took up Shalmaneser's unfinished business in Palestine. Of the flower of Israel 27,290 were carried into captivity and—according to the chronicler of II Kings—settled in Assyrian territory. Their places were filled by a mixed horde of Syrian and Babylonian prisoners. These, admixed with the remnant of Israel, were to become the Samaritans. Israel was now a province of Assyria.

Nineveh was yet to become great, but Sargon II seems to have been the first ruler to anticipate the idea which two thousand years later prompted an Indian emperor to build an entirely new capital for himself. Not content with Kalah's old royal palace or Nineveh's temples, he built the great royal city of Dur-Sharrukin (Sargonsburgh), now known as Khorsabad, excavated by the French to the enrichment of the Louvre, and finally by the Americans. Khorsabad was Sargon's great monument.

To Sargon's son Sennacherib (705-681 B.C.) fell the honour of crucifying three thousand of Babylon's leading citizens, razing walls, palaces, and temples to the ground, and turning the waters of the canal over them. He returned in triumph with Babylon's god Marduk in his pocket, as it were, and proceeded to rebuild

Nineveh, now his mighty capital, so that it would eclipse Babylon. Great double walls—"the wall whose splendour overthrows the enemy" and "the wall that terrifies the foe"—pierced by fifteen gates, were carried around the city. No other city had ever climbed so fast or so high—or was so soon to fall so hard. "An exceeding great city of three days' journey," was Jonah's impression of it. And today, only Babylon and Rome vie with its power to thrill men's imaginations.

Sennacherib was more than mere destroyer of a splendid rival city or builder of a splendid city; he was an empire-builder and bestrode the world like a colossal superdemon. How he appeared in his own eyes we may learn from Isaiah: "By the strength of my hand I have done it, and by my wisdom, for I am prudent; and I have removed the bounds of the people, and have robbed their treasuries, and I have put down the inhabitants like a valiant man: and my hand hath found as a nest, the riches of the people; and as one gathereth eggs that are forsaken, have I gathered all the earth; and there was none that moved the wing, or opened the mouth, or chirped."

He shut Hezekiah up in Jerusalem "like a caged bird," as he himself tells us. He ravaged all Judea, regarding its "200,150 people" as spoil. Hezekiah's attempts to negotiate with Assyrian officers, their insulting reply, the prayer of the Jews that the Assyrians would talk Aramaic and not "the Jews' language in the ears of the people that are on the wall"—all may be read in II Kings, xviii. Also the Assyrian king's reply:

What confidence is this wherein thou trustest?

Thou sayest (but they are but vain words), I have counsel and strength for the war. Now on whom dost thou trust, that thou rebellest against me?

Now, behold, thou trustest upon the staff of this bruised reed, even upon Egypt, on which if a man lean it will go into his hand, and pierce it: so is Pharaoh king of Egypt unto all that trust on him. . . .

Hath any of the gods of the nations delivered at all his land out of the hand of the king of Assyria?

Where are the gods of Hamath, and of Arpad? where are the gods of Sepharvaim, Hena, and Ivah? have they delivered Samaria out of mine hand?

Who are they among all the gods of the countries, that have delivered their country out of mine hand, that Yahweh should deliver Jerusalem out of mine hand?

Who, indeed? And the people held their peace and answered him not a word.

Then Hezekiah prayed:

Lord, bow down thine ear, and hear; open, Lord, thine eyes, and see; and hear the words of Sennacherib, which hath sent him to reproach the living God.

Of a truth, Lord, the kings of Assyria have destroyed the nations and their lands,

And have cast their gods into the fire; for they were no gods, but the work of men's hands, wood and stone; therefore they have destroyed them.

Now therefore, O Lord our God, I beseech thee, save thou us out of his hand, that all the kingdoms of the earth may know that thou art the Lord God, even thou only.

The Assyrians, weary of the siege, accepted a modified surrender and tribute, which they carried back home. Hezekiah turned mono-theistic—Yahweh had delivered him; Nahustan, the brazen serpent Moses had set up in the wilderness, and possibly originally brought from Egypt, was broken to pieces.

After rebuilding Nineveh on a more magnificent scale, Sen-nacherib was murdered by his two elder sons. A third succeeded him, Esarhaddon (681-668 B.C.). He kept up the pace; restored Babylon; reconquered Syria, Phœnicia, Cyprus, and part of Arabia; invaded Egypt, stormed Memphis and put it to the sword, con-quered Lower Egypt, and styled himself "King of Kings of Egypt." And eight centuries earlier, an Assyrian king had begged Amen-hotep III for twenty talents to help build his palace! Assyria was a world power now, her empire the widest the world had yet seen.

Ashurbanipal (668-626 B.C.) captured and sacked Thebes, invaded the old kingdom of Elam and captured and destroyed Susa, its cap-ital; built more royal palaces, made Nineveh still more a right royal city; built that royal library the spoils of which we saw in London; brought Assyrian art to its most superb height. He destroyed Thebes, stripped its temples of their valuables, and for its inhabi-tants whom he carried off as slaves to Assyria he sent Elamites. Susa he also utterly destroyed—to become centuries later the splendid capital of a great empire; Elam, the kingdom, passed from the stage of history for ever. Yet Elam may have been the scene of the world's first "civilization."

Ashurbanipal was the culmination of a long line of war lords, the embodiment of the God of War, the logical product of the military machine. What he could not carry off he sank without a trace.

We now come to one of those awful climaxes in human history which prove fact stranger than fiction—the closing scene of the third act of life's melodrama, when the villain of the play gets his just deserts. The villain was Assyria, upon whom at the height of her pride Isaiah had pronounced judgment in these memorable words: "Woe to thee that spoilest, and thou wast not spoiled; and dealest treacherously, and they dealt not treacherously with thee! when thou shalt cease to spoil, thou shalt be spoiled; and when thou shalt make an end to deal treacherously, they shall deal treacherously with thee!"

Inhuman brutality, senseless cruelty, and incredible mercilessness could not go on for ever, even though art flourished in the capital, and kings rode to chase and to war and patronized archæology. As a matter of fact, the Assyrian kings had ceased to hunt lions on foot or ride to war in chariots. Sennacherib was the first Sargonid to stay at home and take the credit of his generals' victories. Esarhaddon, in rehabilitating Babylon, had become smitten with its hoary superstitions. Why develop muscle if one's gods will do the hard work?

This was quite a new note in Assyria's war cry. Once it was, "We can't lose"; it had now become, "The gods will give us victory." Increasing dependence upon superstition seems inherent in every line of the war lords. It reached its logical conclusion in Ashurbanipal. Before a campaign was ventured, he must consult the oracle of Ishtar, the "Prostitute Compassionate." Early Sargonid kings had been mighty men, manly men, brave before lions, intrepid before foes; the peasants were manly, sturdy farmers. With such material incomparable armies were possible; armed with superior weapons, they became invincible.

That was not all. Victories brought home much gold and many idols—but no "bacon." As in France in Napoleon's time, all industries died but war and splendour. There was no one to till the fields

but slaves. All commerce had passed into the hands of alien Arameans of Syria. The rank and file of the armies also had to be
filled with foreigners. Even Sennacherib had to fill the gaps in
his army with alien subjects.

What a fall from former greatness, when the historian of Sennacherib's army could say of an Elamite army: like a "great swarm
of locusts which spreads itself over the land, so marched they in
warlike array against me. The dust of their feet rose before me like a
heavy stormcloud, which coloured the copper-coloured face of the
wide heavens. . . . But I prayed to Ashur, Sin, Shamash, Bel, Nebo,
Nergal, Ishtar of Nineveh and Ishtar of Arbela, the gods in whom
I trusted, for the defeat of the mighty foe." The historian says the
gods helped the king; but history says the king retreated to Assyria, leaving the Elamites in possession of the field.

Assyria was first of all a war machine; it rode over all, above
everything. There was no chance for the development of civil government or home rule in the provinces. Below the emperor were
governors-general. Civil administration, such as held Egypt and
even Babylonia together, no matter who ruled, could not thrive in
Assyria. Society itself had dissolved. There were still the linguistic
differences as of old, but the chief difference now was not between
free citizens of this and that country, but between citizen and slave
of an Oriental despot.

That was enough; but it was not all, not nearly all. An empire
may be a tottering degenerate and still live on indefinitely—if no
one takes the trouble to give it a push. There were plenty ready to
push Assyria and regard it as a favour—poor old Babylon, for
example.

However, there is no factual basis for the Greek legend of the
tragic end of "Sardanapalus." Ashurbanipal seems to have died (626
B.C.), says Hall, of old age and in bed, like Louis XIV, amid destruction but not in ruin. It also seems that before his death the
terrible Scythians had crossed the upper Euphrates gorges, overrun
Syria, and ravaged western Assyria. Those Scythians seem to have
caught the spirit of the old Assyrians. They inspired terror even in
Judah: "They lay hold on bow and arrow," said Jeremiah; "they
are cruel and have no mercy; their voice roareth like the sea, and
they ride upon horses." In Assyria's loss of her western possessions

Judah saw her chance, and under Josiah established an independent kingdom.

Babylon was next. Shortly after Ashurbanipal's death, a Chaldean native of Babylon proclaimed himself king of Babylon under the name Nabopolassar. The two puppet successors to the throne of Assyria could not dislodge him. There was nothing left of Assyria now but the homeland and a small portion of Babylonia. This remnant of an empire was the heritage of Sinsharishkun, last of Assyrian kings.

When it appeared that Assyria was impotent to stop an Egyptian king marching to the Euphrates, the Medes (of "unchanging laws" fame) thought it a sign that the times were ripe for a change. Nabopolassar also saw that sign. He joined the king of the Medes, and in 612 B.C. they laid siege to Nineveh's mighty walls. The Assyrian king died game. He heaped his palace treasures in a huge 400-feet-high funeral pyre, set it on fire, and threw his wives and himself into the flames. And the Assyrian Empire, excommunicated by the world, went down to Sheol amid the curses of the nations.

The nations rubbed their eyes—it was too good to be true—and burst into shouts of joy. Immortal among those shouts is the Prophet Nahum's grim poem on the news that Judah's and Yahweh's archenemy is no more:

Behold upon the mountains the feet of him that bringeth good tidings, that publisheth peace! O Judah, keep thy solemn feasts, perform thy vows, for the wicked shall no more pass through thee; he is utterly cut off. . . . The Lord is good; a stronghold in the day of trouble; and he knoweth them that trust in him. . . . Woe to the bloody city. . . . Behold, I am against thee, saith the Lord of Hosts, and I will discover thy skirts upon thy face, and I will shew the nations thy nakedness and the kingdoms thy shame. And I will cast abominable filth upon thee, and make thee vile, and set thee as a gazing-stock. And it shall come to pass, that all they that look upon thee shall flee from thee, and say, Nineveh is laid waste; who will bemoan her? . . .

Behold, thy people in the midst of thee are women, the gates of thy land shall be set wide open unto thine enemies: the fire shall devour thy walls. . . .

Thy shepherds slumber, O King of Assyria; thy nobles shall dwell in the dust; thy people is scattered upon the mountains, and no man gathereth them. There is no healing of thy hurt; thy wound is grievous;

all that bear the bruit of thee shall clap their hands over thee; for upon whom hath not thy wickedness passed continually?

Xenophon, like the rest of the world, had heard of mighty Nineveh; yet two hundred years after its destruction his guides could not even tell him which Mesopotamian mound was its ruin. As Layard put it, up to 1842 one could put the remains, not only of Nineveh, but of Babylon, in a Saratoga trunk. Great halls in London and Paris museums are now needed for the priceless treasures rescued from those vast shapeless mounds.

In one respect the sculptures of Ashurbanipal's palace reached a height never before, and rarely since, equalled in all the world. The Assyrians not only hunted lions, they knew how to depict lion hunts on stone—and with a keenness of eye, a love of truth, and a skilful hand, that put their sculptures among the immortal masterpieces of all ages.

Early Greek sculpture is crude, Egyptian and Minoan highly conventionalized; they could not catch the spirit of the wounded lion dragging its hindquarters, paralyzed by an arrow through the spinal column, or of the fiery heads of wild horses. Life, wonderfully sensed, masterfully portrayed; worth the trip to the British Museum to see. The masterful Nisaean steeds from Media, according to Hall, were carved by an unknown sculptor from Nineveh, and are not surpassed by the horses of the frieze of the Parthenon. In Assyria's art contact with Greek Ionia, the Ionian was the borrower, not the Assyrian. The genius of the Assyrian sculptures of Ashurbanipal was Assyrian—not Greek, Phœnician, or Syrian. Give the devil his due!

VII

The editor of my Bible says that the Book of Nahum was written in 713 B.C., and to Chapter II gives this headline: "The victorious armies of God against Nineveh." It is time that date was revised and that we saw what became of "God's victorious armies" which laid Assyria in the dust. We take Babylon first.

I spoke of Nabopolassar as a native of Babylon and as a Chaldean, but just who this rejuvenator of Babylon was, or for that matter who the Chaldeans were, no one knows. They seem to have been Semitic-speaking tribes of the southern shore of the Persian

Gulf. Just when they first entered Babylonia is not known. It is known that Shalmaneser II drove them out of Babylon in 851 b.c. A century later they had again crept around the Persian Gulf and conquered Babylon. In 731 b.c. Tiglath-Pileser III drove their chief back to the Gulf, and shortly after the Chaldeans ("of the Sea-Lands") submitted to the Assyrian yoke. Three years after that, Tiglath-Pileser "took the hand of Bel." Nabopolassar founded a Chaldean dynasty and Babylon's new empire blazed up like an oil-well afire—and was nearly as short-lived.

Assyria's downfall not only let loose much pent-up feeling, it also loosed some dogs of war—Necho, Pharaoh of Egypt, for example. On the plains where the great Thutmose III had fought the first battle of Megiddo in 1478 b.c., Necho fought the second, destroying Josiah and his army. He then made himself master of all Palestine and Syria. But that was bringing Egypt too close if Babylon were to be a true successor to Assyria; so the issue was decided (605 b.c.) at Carchemish on the Euphrates—Carchemish, which had been captured by Sargon of Assyria in 717 b.c.; Carchemish, which, more than a thousand years before that, had been the capital of a great Hittite empire.

Necho's army fled toward Egypt before the pursuing Babylonian army, whose leader stopped only when news came that Nabopolassar was dead. He returned to Babylon to assume the throne of his father as Nebuchadrezzar (604-561 b.c.).

Syria to the Egyptian frontier was now part of this new Babylonian Empire. Judah, under King Jehoiakim, paid tribute for several years, but, inspired by Josiah's fanaticism, revolted. Nebuchadrezzar captured Jerusalem (596 b.c.); also the Phœnician cities of Tyre and Sidon.

Meanwhile Judah's king, Zedekiah, despite Jeremiah's gloomy prophecies, again refused to pay tribute to Babylon; whereupon Jerusalem was besieged, captured, destroyed, and its temple burnt (586 b.c.). Zedekiah saw his sons slain, and was then himself blinded. The majority of the Jews left alive were carried to Babylon. It was during this captivity that they adopted the Garden of Eden myth and the Deluge tradition; also, presumably, the belief in immortality. The wretched remnant of Jews, led by Johanan and the Prophet Jeremiah, emigrated to Egypt.

Thus ended the kingdom of Judah at the hands of Babylon 154 years after Sargon II the Assyrian had captured Samaria and destroyed the kingdom of Israel.

Nabopolassar was a great builder, but his son Nebuchadrezzar was the builder of the new Babylon. He rebuilt the temples and palaces, and around the entire city a huge wall. He bridged the Euphrates and built the famous "hanging gardens" of the traditional palace of Semiramis. Babylon was now easily the greatest city in the world. But so engrossed was the pious Nabonidus in his architectural plans and his archæological explorations that he turned most of the civil and military affairs over to his son Belshazzar.

After a two years' siege, Babylon was captured (538 B.C.) by a Persian army led by Cyrus in person; he incorporated it into the Persian Empire he himself had founded in 550 B.C., when he deposed the last king of the Medes. Thus, sixty years after its fall, the Assyrian Empire had become part of a great Persian Empire stretching from the Hellespont to India and China. That Empire, the first great political fact of post-Assyrian times, after a world rule of 220 years, was to go down to defeat at the battle of the Granicus (334 B.C.) before the new world-conqueror, Alexander the Great.

Cyrus then was the successor to the empire Hammurabi had established and Nebuchadrezzar had restored. Babylon, queen of the Land of the Two Rivers, rejuvenated during the New Empire, seems the real Eternal City beside upstart Nineveh, its rival for a fleeting moment but whose very site was promptly forgotten. To that Babylon returned the great Alexander after he had conquered the world, to bury his favorite Hephaestion with magnificent obsequies. And there, in Babylon, the great conqueror died; in the city he had destined to be the capital of his new empire. With Alexander's last breath the light goes out in Babylon. A few centuries later it is deserted, in ruins; but its name and its site are imperishable.

And I saw a woman sit upon a scarlet-coloured beast, full of names of blasphemy, having seven heads and ten horns. And the woman was arrayed in purple and scarlet colour, and decked with gold, and precious stones, and pearls, having a golden cup in her hand full of abominations and filthiness of her fornication: And upon her forehead was a name written, MYSTERY, BABYLON THE GREAT, THE MOTHER OF HARLOTS AND ABOMINATIONS OF THE EARTH.

The author of the Apocalypse certainly shed no tears over the fall of what had come to be regarded as the quintessence of human depravity.

## VIII

Before we look at the Persian Empire, checked at Thermopylæ, humbled at Salamis and Platæa, and ended at Granicus, let us note just what the rise of that empire meant to the Near Eastern world. To certain empires and kingdoms—Babylonia (including Assyria, Elam, Israel, and Judah), Syria, Media, Phœnicia, Lydia and Egypt—it meant *finis*.

What were these empires and kingdoms—nations, specific peoples, specified territories, certain social organizations? Not at all. They were an indefinite and indeterminate number of human beings held together for the time being by a sovereign. The sovereign was the king or the emperor. When a king of Egypt added an Assyrian king's daughter to his harem and the favour was reciprocated, Egypt and Assyria became friends, allies; that made their subjects friends, allies. It was a royal game; the stakes were royalty. The people went with the crown; they had no more say in the matter than you and I have in the tariff on sugar. It is only within the memory of men now living that that game really went out of vogue as the prevailing fashion in European politics. The idea that a nation or a people has an inherent right to a voice in its affairs is modern and not yet universal.

That empire built to end empires is often spoken of as Medo-Persian; the Medes began the good work and spoke a dialect of a great linguistic stock—as did also the Persians. We look at that stock, not because it makes any difference what particular language anybody spoke twenty-five hundred or twenty-five thousand years ago, but because that language is a cousin of our own. So, of course, is a chimpanzee's, but more distant.

Some call it Aryan, some Indo-European; "Indo" because Aryan-speaking people are supposed to have entered India about 1800 B.C., where they met Dravidian-speaking peoples. Where the Dravidians originally came from—or anybody, for that matter—no one yet

knows. Possibly they were part of the folk that started a great civil-
ization on the Indus which, as I have said, may have been a parent,
or a child, of the civilization which has recently been dug up at
Ur and which we recently looked over and saw that it was good.
Apart from Dravidian tongues and Urdu—a bastardized Semitic
(Arab) tongue—Aryan is the language of India today, Hindustani,
Bengali, Gujerati, for example, being modern dialects. Sanscrit is
the earliest known Aryan tongue. Its literature is the *Vedas*. The
Scythians and Parthians also were Aryan; as were, and are, the
Armenians.

About the time one Aryan group was supposed to be moving
into India, another group entered Asia Minor, especially the Iran
plateau between the Indus and the Two Rivers. Their language was
Iranian, the tongue of the Bactrians, Medes and Persians, the tongue
of modern Persia—Aryan, Indo-European.

Breasted sees ancient history largely as the struggle between a
southern Semitic line which came from the southern grasslands,
and a northern Aryan line from the northern grasslands. Persia's
victory over Babylonia broke the right wing; Rome's victory over
Carthage broke the left wing. But both Semite and Aryan fought
over a civilization not of their own making.

Thus, Asia Minor at the beginning of history was occupied by
non-Aryan-speaking people; at present it is occupied by Turkish-
speaking people. Turkish civilization is really Persian; Persian is
really Babylonian; and Babylonian is really Sumerian.

The kingdom of the Medes got under way early in the sixth
century B.C. Its capital was Ecbatana. It paid tribute to Assyria—
which meant that it could live. By 650 B.C. the Persians, under the
Achæmenian Dynasty, were strong enough to trouble the Medes.
After Cyaxares, the Mede, with Nabopolassar had destroyed Assyria, the Median Empire included the country to the north and
east of the Tigris and was the most powerful in Asia; which meant
next to nothing, for the Medes were to have just one more king.
It was Persia's turn. Cyrus of the tribe of Achæmenes deposed that
last king, and in thirty years (558-528 B.C.) had founded the Persian
Empire.

Included in that founding was a successful war against the little
kingdom of Lydia—remnant of the ancient Hittite Empire—which

under the famous Crœsus had reached its highest prosperity. Crœsus was captured at Sardis: his cavalry would not face Cyrus' camels. Tradition says that Crœsus, to appease his gods' anger toward himself and his country, threw himself into the fire, but that the gods refused the sacrifice and put out the fire with rain. Herodotus says the idea of that fairy-tale was Cyrus'. But Cyrus was no Semite; to the Persians fire was sacred and not to be contaminated. Crœsus probably died of old age at the court of Cyrus, having been treated as a friend and adviser.

It would be more interesting if Crœsus had left us his opinion of the value of oracles. When he heard that the Median king had been deposed he thought he saw a ripe plum, but before moving to pick it he consulted the Oracle at Delphi in Greece. A tortoise and a lamb were duly boiled in a brazen kettle, and the omens said that if he crossed the Halys he would destroy a great kingdom. What the Oracle did not tell him was that it was his own kingdom he was to destroy.

Cyrus completed his work in the west by conquering the Greek cities of Ionia. We have already seen him add Babylonia to his empire, but we have not seen him send the Jews home to Palestine. That was in 538 B.C. He did not send them—he allowed them; only a small proportion went, as we shall see later.

Cyrus was truly the Great; but not, as Breasted says, the first great conqueror of "Indo-European blood." There is no more Indo-European blood than there is Portuguese blood. Blood is biology. Language is history. Biology and history will mix, but they are not inherently related.

Part of Cyrus' programme was the annexation of Egypt. His son, Cambyses, who had been governor of Babylonia, succeeded to the throne in 528 B.C., and within three years had carried out the programme.

Egypt at that time was helpless, or fascinated rather, like a bird before a serpent. Egypt's king had to rely on mercenaries from Ionian Greece. One of them had deserted to the Persian side, leaving his children behind. Herodotus tells how the remaining mercenaries, to "hearten" themselves, slew the children over a brazen bowl, then added wine and water to their blood and drank it—

a sacrifice of enemy's blood not unlike that of the Greeks before Salamis.

Egypt was defeated at Pelusium. Memphis was taken shortly after, and the Egyptian king was deposed and sent to Asia. Cambyses took his seat on the throne of "Horus of the Living" as Pharaoh of Egypt. But on learning that an army corps he had sent to Upper Egypt had been lost in the desert, he ran amuck in his rage and slaughtered the sacred bull, Apis, and violated the royal mummy of Amasis, who had been presumptuous enough to capture Cyprus a few years before.

Cambyses was followed by Darius, also the Great (521-485 B.C.). Persia was now really a vast empire stretching from the Nile to the Ganges. This empire Darius organized as no empire had ever been organized before. With the old Assyrian military organization as model, he divided his empire into twenty-one satrapies, the satraps, or civil governors, being independent in internal affairs. To simplify the collection of the fixed quota of tribute from each satrapy, coined money of fixed standards was used—first by the Lydians and Greeks. The "daric" of Darius was one of the purest gold coins ever struck. Where possible, native rulers were appointed satraps. It was a bilingual empire, as the officials adopted Aramaic.

Darius was a great king, a great ruler, the first in history to organize subject peoples. His organization brought peace and prosperity to the empire—five hundred years before *Pax Romana* was to attempt the same thing, and fail in the end. But Rome fell into the hands of barbarian savages and fanatical mystics; Persia fell into the hands of Alexander. How that came to pass is Greek. Before we discuss Persia, let us see how the great Darius wrote his name on high—and left us one of the wonders of the world and one of the world's most precious historic records.

First, let us see just what he had done in his thirty-six years' reign, just what his claims to greatness were. To start with, he had to *win* his throne; he did not inherit it. Cambyses, before setting out for Egypt, had privately murdered his brother Smerdis. When news of the defeat of Cambyses' army in Upper Egypt reached Persia, the Prime Minister (a Mede of its priestly tribe, the Magi— like the Levites of Israel) thought he saw a fine opportunity to do something for his family. He produced his own brother and declared him to be the true son of Cambyses. The lie "multiplied in the land." The impostor was proclaimed king.

When Cambyses heard the news he started home with Darius, son of an Achæmenian prince and a devout Zoroastrian. Cambyses died on the way. We do not know how. Darius and the army pushed on. The Magian upstart fled to a royal castle in old Media, where Darius and six other nobles found and murdered him. Darius was now, and properly, made king; but he had to prove himself king, for the provinces had revolted.

Babylon, among the revolters, was captured only after a siege of twenty months. Revolts in Elam, Armenia, and Media were put down. Then Persia itself revolted under another pseudo-Smerdis. Babylon revolted again, and was now destroyed. Finally, Darius was forced to lead a land force of 700,000 men against the Scythians.

We now come to the point. Returning home, he decided to commemorate his victories, and in the best regal tradition. On an overhanging and almost inaccessible Gibraltar-like cliff three hundred feet above the highway between Mesopotamia and Persia, he caused to be chiselled a great tablet picturing him with his conquered rebels—the "*Behistun* tablet." To the scene he added a long inscription setting forth his glorious deeds: "I am Darius, the great King, the King of Kings, the King of Persia, the King of the Provinces, the son of Hystaspes"; to which he added a curse upon vandals, ending with: "But if thou seest this inscription beside these sculptures and destroyest them not, but guardest them as thou livest," you would win Aramazda's friendship, long life, and blood perpetuation.

It was not the curse that kept vandals from battering the royal pictures or prevented the priceless records from being carted off to Rome, Paris, or London; it was sheer inaccessibility. Herodotus saw, and marvelled. For two thousand years men gazed upon this unique monument. Grotefend, a German scholar, saw it in 1821, and suspected its true nature. And finally a young English officer of the Indian army, Henry Rawlinson, saw it in 1837, at the risk of his life copied the texts, and after fourteen years of rare scholarship translated them—one of the most brilliant feats of scholarship ever accomplished.

"Texts?" There were three: Persian, Susian, and Babylonian—all in cuneiform characters. This Behistun tablet was a "Rosetta" stone —the first key to unlock, not only the mysteries of Darius' early campaigns, but, what was far more important, of cuneiform writings. Without that key there would be no unlocking of Hammurabi's Code or of the original Flood myth, nor knowledge of the history of Mesopotamia outside the records of Herodotus and Xenophon.

About a century after Alexander the Great destroyed the Persian Empire, a new empire arose, in practically the same vast territory as the Persia of Darius. This was the Parthian. Its last king, in 226 A.D., was slain by a Persian, who refounded the Persian Empire, which under the Sassanian Dynasty lasted until 641 A.D., when it became part of the Moslem world under the rule of the Caliphs.

IX

The Persians, said Herodotus, taught their sons three things: to ride a horse, use a bow, and tell the truth. The greatest disgrace, next to sin, was debt—"for a man who is in debt must of necessity tell lies."

Darius was a devout Zoroastrian; the usurper he replaced was a Magian. A magus is a wise man who knows everything, even the will of the gods—a medicine-man, a shaman, a priest; a Brahman in India; a flamen in Rome. The Magi began as the high priests of the prehistoric Iranians; they told the ignorant what to pray for and when to sacrifice to the gods. They became a caste, the highest caste, as also in Aryan India. Their chief deities were Indra and Varuna, Agni and Soma—as they were of the early Aryans in India.

Some time between the tenth and sixth centuries B.C. Zoroaster (Zarathustra), a Magian priest, turned prophet and founded a religion, Zoroastrianism. Breasted speaks of him as the "first great founder of a religious faith"; Jackson, as "the clarion voice of reform six centuries before Christ"—a high standard of morality, a noble code of ethics. It was a monotheistic religion—an imageless worship of one God supreme above all others.

The Zoroastrian doctrine, hymns, etc., were brought together in twenty-one books of two million verses, written on twelve hundred cowhides. Little except one book, the nineteenth, survives; this is the Avesta, the Bible of the Persians.

Zoroastrianism is really a religious philosophy of dualism, two primeval principles—good and evil, light and darkness. One could take one's choice, but choose one must. Evil was not to be propitiated, but resisted, fought to the death. All good was personified in the great god Ormazd—the Aramazda of Darius' inscription, the "Mazda" of the electric age. One of Mazda's helpers was Mithra, an old Iranian sun god; one of his angels was recorder of good and bad deeds. The Persian Bible also alludes to records being kept in the "account book," and to deeds being "weighed in the balance," and contains the earliest known recorded belief in an inescapable Last Judgment for all mankind—in contrast with the earlier Egyptian judgment of each individual separately immediately after his death.

Zoroaster's special mission, for which he thought himself divinely sent, was to guide men to choose good rather than evil. Chief of the evil spirits, opposed to Mazda, was Ahriman, inherited by Jews and Christians as Satan. As there is no evidence that the Jews believed in immortality before the Captivity, it is possible that they also borrowed the idea from Zoroaster. Even at the time of Christ the Sadducees regarded such a belief as foreign to Jewish doctrine: "Woe unto you, wicked people, who maintain that the dead will rise."

Ahriman, by his evil eye, created 99,999 diseases in the form of evil spirits or demons. Mazda thereupon appealed to the god of heavenly light, who destroyed diseases by reciting the Holy Word. He also took the ten thousand healing herbs which grew around the Tree of Life and gave them to Thrita, an old sage, upon whom the god of metals had bestowed a gold-mounted knife. Thrita was thus a forerunner of Æsculapius, healing god of the Greeks. Even Dante's vision of hell was forestalled by a Persian saint who pictured the sins, vices, and faults of the then prevailing society.

Curiously enough, the Avesta favoured incestuous marriages—parent-child, brother-sister—to preserve family unity and perpetuate the bonds of religion in the community of the Faithful.

Centuries later, Mithraism, an outgrowth of Zoroaster's teaching, was to compete with Christianity in Rome for the imperial throne; but in its own land the religion of Zoroaster, the reformer, was to become debased in the hands of the Magi into a thing of taboo and magic and the worship of the four elements as fetishes.

True Zoroastrians were not fire-worshippers, as is commonly supposed. Fire was simply one of the pure elements; like water and earth, it must not be defiled. There were special rules for preserving that purity—one result of which may be seen today in the Towers of Silence of the Persian Parsees of Bombay. As a corpse defiled fire, earth, and water, its disposition became a serious problem. In Bombay it is laid on gratings over charcoal, within open-topped, gas-tank shaped towers; and that accounts for the vultures which make the only sound heard around those gruesome Towers of Silence.

Thus spake Zarathustra.

x

Ancient Babylonia, 3500-2100 B.C.; the Assyrian Empire, 750-612 B.C.; the New Babylonian or Chaldean Empire, 612-539 B.C.: three great, triumphant periods in civilization's career in the Land of the Two Rivers. All Semitic; and Semitic Islam's triumph after the death of Mohammed yet far off. Alexander stopped the East's march upon the West; Islam was stopped at Tours in France and at the walls of Vienna. But from Palestine, football of thousands of years of struggle, was to come the Semites' greatest triumph— though without the intervention of Aryan-speaking peoples it seems likely that "God's victorious armies" would have fought Nineveh in vain. Semitic leadership gave way to Aryan Persians; Aryan Romans were to adopt Semitic religion and pass it on to Aryan Europe, which in turn was to carry it around the world. That religion we shall look at in due time. We now look at the people whose Bible we worship.

That Bible—our Bible—was once the name of a Phœnician city, Byblos. It came about this way. We speak of the porcelain dishes on our table as chinaware, or simply as china, although they may have been made in East Liverpool, Ohio. "Chinaware" started in China; anything that looks like it is *china*. Byblos, in the days when "books" were rolls, was a great exporting centre for papyrus paper; hence rolls were *byblia*.

Palestine, home of the Hebrews, is without impropriety called the Land of the Book. It really is not much longer than an old roll-Bible unrolled—about the size of Vermont, and about as rough. The comparison stops there. Vermont is between next to nothing, whereas the Land of the Book is between the desert and the deep sea—and that was a large factor in Palestine's history. To pass from the fertile Nile Valley to the fertile Land of the Two Rivers, it was necessary to traverse Palestine. Its maritime plain was the highway of all the ancients fighting for the crown. Pharaoh's armies had to cross Palestine's front yard to get into Syria. The Hyksos had already passed that way to get into Egypt, followed later by the fiercer Assyrians. For centuries Palestine was the cockpit of the East, as Baikie said, as the Low Countries were of Europe. From 1479 B.C., when Thutmose III scattered the army of the Syrian League at Megiddo, till 1918 A.D., when Allenby routed the Turks on the same field, the tide of war has surged up and down Palestine.

Just north of Palestine and without any intervening natural boundary is Syria. Syria is linked to Palestine by other ties. She entered history first; let us get rid of her first.

The narrow coast land of Syria, from the third millennium B.C., was occupied by small city states collectively known as Phœnicia, whose first powerful city was Byblos, mentioned in Egyptian texts well back toward 3000 B.C. The Phœnician cities were the middlemen between Egypt and Babylon. Byblos was perhaps the world's first sea power; it was followed by Sidon, likewise perhaps first to found colonies: on the islands of the Ægean, in Sicily, in southern Spain, and in the *Fortunate Isles*—probably Madeira and the Canaries. It possibly even traded with the "Islands of Tin" (Great Britain), and with the Baltic coast for amber. For five hundred years the Phœnicians were the hucksters of civilization. Their sea travels and exploits inspired many Greek myths.

Tyre, twenty miles away, took the lead from Sidon, and under Hiram (1001-967 B.C.), David's contemporary and Solomon's friend, reached great prosperity. Hiram's workmen built most of

Solomon's Temple—"for thou knowest that there is not among us any that can skill to hew timber like unto the Sidonians." When Tyre fell upon evil days following the murder of Hiram's last descendant by a high priest of Astarte, many families emigrated to the African coast, and, near the present city of Tunis, founded Carthage. The Carthaginians for three hundred years were the merchants of the 3,000-miles-long Mediterranean world.

The Phœnicians were great traders and had great industries, especially in metal-work; but they did not invent the glass, porcelain, linens and dyes, or the hammered, engraved, and cast metal-work they hawked about the Mediterranean. They were not inventors, they were borrowers; wonderful artificers, and, primarily, traders. They did play a most creditable part in spreading the alphabet we use today. To the Phœnicians the Greeks especially were indebted for styles in art and dress and for the technique of craftsmanship. Homer mentions their tunics and chains of worked gold; Ezekiel, their carved ivories; and Chronicles, their skill in gold, silver, brass, iron, stone, and timber, their fine linens of purple, blue, and crimson, and their cunning in graving. Their religion has been characterized as consecrated licentiousness and sanctified cruelty. Children were burnt alive to Baal or Moloch; and when Carthage was besieged in 307 B.C. they burned two hundred boys of the best familes to Saturn.

The Phœnicians were a Semitic-speaking people; as were also the Arameans who also had trekked into Syria from the Middle Euphrates, where they had been Bedouin nomads, and by the time of Thutmose III had made Damascus an important settlement. Possibly Abraham's family was of Aramean stock. Assyria, as we have seen, was tinged with Aramaic influence; perhaps half its people talked Aramaic. Aramaic writing, a cursive script drawn from the same source as the Phœnician, supplanted cuneiform in all western Asia; it was one of the official scripts of Persia in the fourth century B.C., and its alphabet is at the bottom of all Asiatic alphabets. Aramaic was the commerce language of Palestine, and became the language of Jesus.

In crossing from Syria back into Palestine we cross no visible barrier, meet no really new peoples. In the early days we are now considering, there was as yet nothing that could be called a nation or a kingdom of Israel; the Semitic nomads were organized on tribal lines, much as were our Plains Indians two hundred years ago. They had flocks of sheep and goats; and hereditary chiefs. Their family organization was what is known as patriarchal. The immortal tales of the patriarchs Abraham, Isaac, Jacob, and Joseph, as related in Genesis, are tinged with mythology, but they are also in part factually founded; their authors are among the earliest known historians. Beyond these tales, neither Hebrews nor Arameans have any authentic history antedating the twelfth century B.C.

Hebrews and Arameans were practically the same people in origin and early culture—and blood and culture kin to the Phœnicians. In moving into the hill country just back of the coast and behind the Lebanon range, they separated, the Arameans settling in the north, the Hebrews in the south. According to tradition, they left the desert about the same time and more or less in alliance; but when is not known. It is known that from about 1400 to 1350 B.C. the old midland cockpit where Egypt, Babylon, Hittite, Khatti, and Assyria had met and fought for dominion, enjoyed a period of respite from invasions of the great powers. The empires of Egypt and Babylon were for the time being degraded, as Hall says; the kingdoms of Khatti and Assyria were paralyzed.

The Hebrews found Palestine occupied by Canaanites, living in walled towns and as luxuriously as Egyptians or Babylonians. They were "civilized"; but, as Baikie said, Palestine never was cursed with originality. Hebrews and Canaanites were neither builders nor artists. The best the Canaanites did was a feeble imitation of the handicrafts of better men. Little of material civilization has come from Palestine because little was produced there. The alphabet was the achievement of the Phœnicians and Arameans or their predecessors.

The booty Thutmose III captured in 1479 B.C. at the battle of Megiddo throws interesting light on Canaanite wealth: 924 chariots (some of gold), 200 suits of armour, and large flocks and herds.

Among the Ikhnaton correspondence found at Tel-el-Amarna is a passport, probably issued by Babylon's king: "To the Kings of Canaan, vassals of my brother, the Great King [Ikhnaton]. Verily, my messenger have I sent to the King of Egypt in order to condole

with him. Let none detain him. In safety to Egypt bring him. . . .
And let no violence be done him." How modern this incident of
thirty-three centuries ago seems!—one king sending condolences
to another on the death of his father, and by a messenger carrying
a passport. One wonders if it had to be visaed.

Not long after that the Canaanites, "vassals of the Great King,"
had no great king to call on for aid. The Hebrews saw their opportunity; but they could capture only the weaker of the Canaanite
towns—to be captured, in turn, by Canaanite civilization.

Hence the long bitter feeling between the Hebrews of the north
and of the south—Israel and Judah. The southerners remained nomads for centuries; the kingdom of Judah was always poor, and,
with the exception of Jerusalem, had no real cities. The northern-
ers, who had adopted and were changed by Canaanite civilization,
were city folk; the kingdom of Israel was prosperous, rich. In time,
Israelites and Canaanites became indistinguishable.

The enemy the Hebrews dreaded was not Amorite, Canaanite,
Phœnician or Aramean, but the Philistines: Greeks, "remnant of
the dying glories of the vanished empire of the sea-kings of
Knossos"—Cretans, in short. "Caphtor" of the Book of Amos, Biblical origin of the Philistines, is *Keftiu* of the Egyptians—Crete.

Those Cretans, or Philistines, were fighting-men. Against their
thick corselets, bronze bucklers, great broadswords, and huge spears
of iron, the Israelites could offer little resistance. They were a formidable "oppressor" indeed, as we may read in the Book of Judges
—that is, "Leaders." The legend of Goliath in Samuel even more
vividly testifies to the impression this new oppressor left on the
Israelites.

"Canaan" was Yahweh's land; the Israelites were Yahweh's
people. But Palestine originally was the land of the Philistines—
*Pelishtim*, the coast. Only later did the Egyptians and Greeks apply
the term Pelishtim to what we now call Palestine and what the
Hebrews called the Promised Land: the land Yahweh promised to
the children of Israel.

Accepting the story in Exodus as history—which it probably is
not and is certainly mostly legend—it is certain that only a portion,
if any, of the Hebrews ever migrated into Egypt. If they did, it
was the tribe of Joseph, and about 1460 B.C. And if they were led

out, it was by Moses, if such a person ever lived, and that was about 1230 B.C.—or hundreds of years before the "Books of Moses" were compiled, edited and reëdited, from ancient legends.

With about 1220 B.C. we begin to get on firmer ground. An inscription of the Pharaoh Menephthes (1225-1215 B.C.) says: "Isirail is desolated, his seed is not." That seems to imply that the Israelites were then a settled nation in Palestine—probably in Mount Ephraim —and powerful enough to be mentioned by name by an Egyptian king.

With little time for the Israelites to recover from their desolation, the curtain goes up again, and the scene is "in Taanach by the waters of Megiddo," "where the kings came and fought, then fought the kings of Canaan." But let us hear the song itself, Deborah's magnificent song in Judges:

> Awake, awake, Deborah;
> Awake, awake; utter a song;
> Arise, Barak, and lead thy captivity captive,
> Thou son of Abinoam. . . .

> They fought from heaven;
> The stars in their courses
> Fought against Sisera.

> The river of Kishon swept them away,
> That ancient river, the river Kishon.
> O my soul,
> Thou hast trodden down strength.

> Then were the horse-hoofs broken
> By the means of the prancings,
> The prancings of their mighty ones. . . .

> He asked water, and she gave him milk;
> She brought forth butter in a lordly dish.

> She put her hand to the nail,
> And her right hand to the workman's hammer;
> And with the hammer she smote Sisera,
> She smote off his head,
> When she had pierced and stricken through his temples.

At her feet he bowed, he fell, he lay down:
At her feet he bowed, he fell:
Where he bowed, there he fell down dead.

The mother of Sisera looked out at a window,
And cried through the lattice,
Why is his chariot so long in coming?
Why tarry the wheels of his chariots?

Her wise ladies answered her,
Yea, she returned answer to herself,

Have they not sped?
Have they not divided the prey;
To every man a damsel or two;
To Sisera a prey of divers colours,
A prey of divers colours of needlework,
Of divers colours of needlework on both sides,
Meet for the necks of them that take the spoil?

So let all thine enemies perish, O Lord:
But let them that love him be as the sun
When he goeth forth in his might.

And the land had rest forty years.

And the land had rest forty years. What a commentary on human history! Forty years' rest. We are not old as a nation, but we have yet to see a forty-year period of rest in American history.

In the fourth chapter of Judges we learn that Sisera, leader of the Canaanites, "lighted down from his chariot and fled away on his feet"—like the Negro recruit who preferred infantry to cavalry because when the bugle blew the retreat he "didn't want to be bothered with no horse!" This is the first known time that the Israelites fought the Canaanite chariotry to a standstill.

It may be pointed out in this connection that the horse not only changed the art of war but made a deep and lasting impress on thought. Even in the Wisdom literature of the fourth century we find that bold, blaspheming freethinker Job apostrophizing the horse in one of the finest poems in the Bible; and in his "He saith among the trumpets, Ha, ha! and he smelleth the battle afar off, the thunder of the captains, and the shouting," we have two immortal lines. Even as late as Revelation, as Thorndike reminds us, it is the four horses of the Apocalypse which are to bring death and destruction.

With the issue of mastery between Israelite and Canaanite decided, the Israelites could mix with and absorb Canaanites and Amorites. They were kin in their Semitic tongue and in their Semitic practice of circumcision.

What, or who, broke that forty years' rest is not known, but it is known that about 1100 B.C. the Philistines appeared and were soon established in Gath, Ashdod, Gaza, Ashkelon, and Ekron. In Judges and Samuel we read of their temples and palaces, and of their theatres crowded with nobles and their retinues. The theatre at Gaza, for example, "was full of men and women; and all the lords of the Philistines were there; and there were upon the roof about 3,000 men and women, that beheld while Samson made sport"—just as was the custom in the palaces of Knossos in Crete a thousand years earlier, and as, presumably, other Israelite captives would continue to do until the Philistines finally succumbed to Israelite prowess. Within a hundred years they had become Semitized; but there could be no confraternity between them, for the Philistines were uncircumcised.

Samson, with his final victory in death, is the Semite Culture Hero, a sun god, kin to Babylon's Gilgamesh. Sports such as Samson's are seen in II Samuel, where Abner said to Joab, "Let the young men now arise, and play before me." Twelve of Benjamin's side arose, and twelve of the servants of David. "And they caught away one his fellow by the head, and thrust his sword in his fellow's side; so they fell down together." That was sport in the good old days.

Next, "Israel was brought very low because of the Midian"; so low that they fled to the caves in the hills. Midianites, Moabites, and Amorites, jealous because their cousins the Israelites beat them into Canaan, seem ever to have been hovering about on the edge of the desert, like vultures, only awaiting signs of distress to fall upon the Chosen People.

Presumably the Midianites could not have driven the Israelites to the caves had not the latter been overwhelmed by the Philistines and driven from the plains to the hills. This invasion seems to have been about 1080 B.C.—at the end of Eli's high-priesthood and just before the birth of his grandson, Ichabod. At the battle of Ebenezer, as told in I Samuel, the Israelite army was annihilated; the Ark of the Covenant, produced to scare the Philistines, was captured; and the national sanctuary at Shiloh was destroyed. Yahweh had delivered His people into the hands of the Philistines: and "so the Philistines held rule over Israel."

To make that rule secure, the Israelites were not only disarmed, but "there was no smith found throughout the land"—"lest the Hebrews make them swords or spears." Fifty years later, the Israelites revolted. That revolt resulted in Samuel (last "Judge in Israel") anointing Saul "King of the Hebrews" (1025 B.C.). Not that he wanted a real king, but a leader who would drive out the Philistines and then become his puppet. Saul was the leader he wanted, but not the kind of king he wanted. After initial victories over the Moabites he turned unexpectedly on the Philistines and smote them "from Michmash to Ajalon." Then he smote the Amalekites, whose captured king, Agag, was brought before Samuel —to be hewed in pieces before Yahweh in Gilgal.

During these successful smitings "David behaved himself more wisely than all the servants of Saul." But Saul became so jealous of his son-in-law's victories and his intrigues with Samuel that David had to flee for his life and take refuge among the Philistines, becoming a vassal of the king of Gath. A few years later Saul, worsted by the Philistines (1000 B.C.) "leaned upon his spear," the first recorded instance of a king committing hara-kiri.

With the murder of Saul's son Ishbosheth (Ishbaal) and Abner his general, the field was clear for David's *coup de main*, by which he got hold of Jerusalem and made it his residence and the abode of the Ark of the Covenant, Israel's palladium, the most potent "medicine bundle" of the Hebrews. The entry of the Ark into Jerusalem was a sign that Israel at last was free from its hated oppressor.

David's kingdom was primarily military; the organization of the army, a rude and puny imitation of Egypt's and Babylon's, was the state's chief concern. There was next to no learning and David's chief scribe was a Babylonian, but whether Aramaic or Phœnician script was used is unknown. David did rule a Hebrew kingdom, and at its highest power. He conquered the Arameans and annexed Damascus; he made an alliance with Hiram of Tyre; he did not conquer Philistia. He begat sons. One, from the loins of Bathsheba, he appointed his successor.

This son, Solomon (960-933 B.C.), had become one of the East's biggest business men; he was also a horse-trader and joint owner with Hiram of a trading fleet. He was rich enough to marry a Pharaoh's daughter, and with Phœnician help to build a "gorgeous temple of bad architecture and worse taste." Born to the purple, he was no warrior like Saul or bandit like David, but, as Hall says, "a typical Oriental sultan, magnificent (so far as his means would allow), wise (in the belief of the vulgar), and without doubt tyrannical."

"Wisdom" was his keynote; amassing a fortune, his passion. His Phœnician sailors perhaps reached India, or got their apes, ivory, and peacocks from Arab traders. The visit of the Queen of Sheba is pure legend. Heavy taxes led to discontent; "adversaries were raised up" against him. His business dealings with Hiram were astute rather than wise. At his death the Hebrew kingdom of David had shrunk to Saul's size. David, Solomon, and Rehoboam, says Hall, correspond to Henri IV, Louis XIV, and Louis XV.

And so, before the kingdom of the Hebrews was a century old, it had split on a rock. The south had never forgiven the north for its prosperity. Rehoboam, son of Solomon, ruled a kingdom of Judah from Jerusalem. Israelites under Jeroboam, having revolted, started the kingdom of Israel, with their capital first at Sichem, later at Samaria. We have already seen how Sheshonk (about 930 B.C.) invaded Judah and sacked Jerusalem; and how Sargon II, the Assyrian, captured Samaria and destroyed the kingdom of Israel. Sheshonk carried off Solomon's golden shields and the service vessels used in Yahweh worship, to enrich Amon's temple in Thebes. Sargon carried off part of the population itself. But *the* Captivity was in Assyria under Nebuchadrezzar.

After Cyrus the Persian had allowed the Hebrews to return to Palestine, the rebuilding of the temple was begun, but was not finished till the time of Darius (515 B.C.). When Alexander succeeded to the Persian Empire, Palestine began its existence under its sixth alien ruler. The Ptolemies of Egypt made the seventh, and the Seleucid king of Syria the eighth. And then came the emancipation by the Maccabees between 167 and 130 B.C. In other words, so far as participation in the making of civilization is concerned, we might omit Syria and Palestine.

Archæological research carries us back to Palæolithic remains in Palestine, but the archæologist has found next to nothing of originality or imagination in the material foundations of its civilization. He has found massive stone walls (in Jericho, now being excavated, 20 feet thick), fortified high places, brothels, and in pots beneath houses the skeletal remains of children, perhaps sacrificed.

But the Jews gave us the Old Testament, and whatever we think of its religion, we may agree with Hall that in dowering · the world with a poesy, a music and frenzy of words, the poets and prophets of Israel gave our civilization one of its greatest possessions —if one likes that kind of poetry, that kind of frenzy of words. Certain it is that some of it, isolated and brought together in a brochure with reasonably complete explanatory notes, would break up the Sunday schools and violate the law against obscenity. As a source book for students of anthropology, sociology, and psychology, it is priceless and too much neglected.

Jewish history, from the death of Solomon to the canonization of the Old Testament, is religious rather than political: one superstition fighting another for the crown, Baal against Yahweh, Yahweh against the field. We shall later review that struggle, and the ultimate triumph of Yahweh, Jehovah, God.

While the Hebrew kings were the Lord's Anointed, they never assumed godship, as did the kings of Egypt and Babylon, and later the emperors of Rome, but they did hope to have a king who would be the son of God. We may also note here that the Egyptian, Babylonian, and Assyrian tendency of religion to call a priestly ruling caste into existence and to foster a society founded primarily on the one relation of lord and servant, is much less evident among the Hebrews—presumably because Hebrew priests and prophets never commanded vast wealth; they remained closer to the people because they lacked the wherewithal to climb above them. But they were none the less essential to the man in the street or field for interpreting signs and omens and the will of heaven. They were reverent, and some of them fine men with lofty ideas of moral duty. Fundamentally, however, their superstitiousness was colossal and infinitely self-centred. It led to mild forms of insanity. All wars must be inhuman; religious wars must be insanely inhuman.

Our business now is to transfer civilization from the Orient to the Occident—an event which occurred long before the Bible passed from Palestine to Rome, leaving the Jews to follow later.

## CHAPTER EIGHT

### *The Glory that Was Greece and the Grandeur that Was Rome*

1. The Land of the Classics, and Minoan Civilization. 2. The Homeric Age and the Olympiads. 3. The Persian Wars and the Age of Pericles. 4. The Ionian Greeks and the Birth of Science and History. 5. Alexander Hellenizes the World for Cæsar. 6. Rome's "Manifest Destiny." 7. The Golden Age of Augustus. 8. Rome's Grandeur and Intellectual Achievements. 9. The Greek Snake Dance; and Orpheus the Good Shepherd. 10. The Religion Christianity Supplanted.

### I

PALESTINE is the Land of the Book, but Greece is the Land of the Classics. Even the Romans sat at the feet of their Greek masters; their classics are all rooted in Greek. Only today I read of discoveries on Italian soil of Greek artifacts that throw new light on ancient problems which form part of our Greek inheritance, problems which still confront us. For weal or woe, the Greek hand touched every phase of this civilization of ours that was born in the Near East—and, touching, left a mark. Our Lincoln bade us nobly resolve; Pericles of Athens bade his countrymen nobly resolve. We honour the Unknown Soldier; in the funeral processions Athens held to honour her war dead, there was an empty coffin to represent those who were missing.

Who were those Athenians? What is our legacy from Greece? What happened to civilization when it landed in Greece and was taken up by Rome? And how did civilization reach Europe? We shall have to hurry; we can only look at the high spots, the significant things.

Before Athens, there were Greeks; before Greeks, there were Ægeans. The oldest known Ægean civilization has, to the world's astonishment, been uncovered in the Isle of Crete in this generation. Civilization, as we are here using that term, passed from the

Orient to the Occident *via* Crete. In Crete it was modified, but not beyond recognition. The great kings of Egypt and Babylon would have thought Knossos a good show—not so great as those which had been staged on the Nile and the Euphrates, but worthy of its masters, and especially of Egypt, the master.

We have already met the Cretans. We saw the trouble they gave the people of the Land of the Book, and how, unwittingly, they gave that Land their name. The Philistines originally were Cretans. We now meet the real Cretans.

Need I say again that we do not know where the Cretans, or the Greeks, or any ancient people, came from? We know peoples only when somebody discovers them and learns their names or gives them a name. We have no idea what the Cretans called themselves; nor in Homer's time was there even a collective name for the Greeks. Homer knows only Achæans, Argives, Danaans, etc. To Hesiod, the Greeks were the *Hellenes*; and thereafter all non-Hellenes were *barbaroi*, the "bar-bar"-ians—or, as we might call a people whose tongue we did not understand, the *Blah-blahians*. So far as is known, the Romans were the first to use the term *Græci*.

Early wandering tribes had names for their enemies—presumably uncomplimentary; and for themselves—presumably complimentary, such as, *We, THE People*. If they left writings and we can read what they wrote, we often get much information about them —not always true, of course. The Cretans left much writing. As early as 2000 b.c. they had ground picture-signs down to sound-signs; that is, they had phonetic writing. Of clay tablet writings they left literally thousands; but the writings might as well be bird-tracks, for no one can read them. No key, no Rosetta or Moabite Stone, nor Behistun tablet, has yet been found to unlock their literature. The Cretans are known by their works, uncovered by pick and shovel, and read by the light of the known. They traded with Egypt. If Egypt were not well known, Crete would be even less known than it is.

When the Egyptians were building pyramids, the Cretans were using bronze vessels, baking their bread in closed ovens, turning out earthenware vessels on potter's wheels, and imitating Egypt's beautiful stone vessels. They were "civilized." Their kings lived in palaces built in the Egyptian style. With Sixth Dynasty Egypt, Crete was undoubtedly on familiar terms—creditor terms.

Crete's earliest civilization was contemporary with the earliest Egyptian dynasties—Early Minoan, 3000-2200 B.C. Before that was a Cretan Neolithic Age, which goes back to the tenth millennium B.C.

The Second Minoan period (2200-1600 B.C.), contemporaneous with Egypt's Golden Age (the Middle Kingdom), was marked by the beginnings of beautiful polychrome pottery; it reached unparalleled heights in the Third or Late Minoan period (1600-1400 B.C.).

This was Crete's Grand Age. She produced the most beautiful decorative art the world had yet seen or was again to see for a thousand years; also masterpieces in gold and bronze and sculptured ivory. Her civilization was far and away ahead of any other on the Mediterranean. Egypt was her inspiration.

So "staggeringly modern" was this Late Minoan civilization, says Evans, that it would pass for Mid-Victorian. Decorated palace walls reveal wasp-waisted Minoan dandies—an ideal, by the way, of male physical fitness alluded to by Aristophanes a thousand years later. Ladies wear elaborate dresses that might have come from a Paris *couturière* of our grandmother's day: *decolleté* evening gowns, puffed sleeves, skirts flounced from hem to waist, hair frizzed and curled.

The king's palace at Knossos must have been as great a revelation to the peoples of Greece and Italy as were the palaces of the Cæsars to the savage Teuton invaders fifteen hundred years later. Not only were there court ladies and dandies, feathered page-boys, marvellous wall decorations and ceiling frescoes, gorgeous furniture, monumental throne-rooms, splendid staircases, gold and bronze arms and utensils; there were *miles* of water-pipes, for baths, latrines, etc. The commoners' houses show comfort, high standards of living; even labourers' houses had from six to eight rooms. Illiteracy was less prevalent than it is among modern Greek peasants. There is no sign of the classic Greek's disdain for women. The Minoan king was surrounded by men and women who enjoyed beauty and the good things of life with him. His court, says Hall, "must have resembled the joyous surroundings of a European prince of the thirteenth and fourteenth centuries, with a touch of the Tuileries of the Second Empire."

Why "Minoan"? Recall your Greek mythology: the story of Perseus and the Minotaur. Crete was the traditional home of many Greek heroes. Zeus himself was born there. Also his son Minos; Europa was his mother. Minos was the Culture Hero of Crete.

The legends which cluster around Minos suggest certain Biblical characters. As Abraham is the "friend of Yahweh," so Minos is the "gossip" of Zeus. Like Moses, he received a code of laws on a mountain top, from the hand of Zeus. Every ninth year he went up to the Dictæan cave to talk with Zeus. He finally died, went to the underworld, and judges the dead in Hades.

According to Thucydides, Minos was also the great king who was first on earth to build a navy. The Cretans certainly were the earliest naval power in that part of the Mediterranean and the first sailor nation in history. Possibly they were the first to sail to Britain and the Baltic.

The wife of Minos, legend says, because of an unholy and unnatural passion, gave birth to a human-headed bull-calf, the Minotaur. Minos kept this monster in a labyrinthian palace. Athens, defeated in war, was compelled to pay tribute to the Minotaur—seven youths and seven maidens each year. Enter Perseus. Exit Minotaur. Enter Sir Arthur Evans. He found an opening to an artificial cave which possibly was a lair for lions; also extraordinary wall paintings of bull-fights: boys and girls leaping over bulls at the peril of their lives. They lived, says Hall, cruelly perhaps, and possibly, according to our ideas, wickedly, but they certainly lived beautifully—as æsthetes, unrestrained by all known conventions.

Who burned the palace of Knossos is unknown—or when, or why. Possibly its fate was that of Sodom and Gomorrah! Its light ceased to shine about 1200 B.C.—to blaze up a century later on the Greek mainland. Sea power had passed to the Greeks.

II

Greek history as I studied it began 776 B.C., the date of the First Olympiad. That seems pretty modern now. To 1930 add 776; to 2706 add 1535 more years, and we have travelled back to the day Egypt discovered there were 365 days in the year. Seven centuries before the Greeks took to jumping high hurdles, the Cretans were jumping wild bulls.

Greece passed—as did much of Europe—from Neolithic to Bronze Age; it was one single continuous transition, without new blood. But in passing from Bronze to Iron Age, Greece was invaded by Aryan-speaking people from the north. Bronze Age Greeks came from northern Africa; they were Mediterraneans, as were the Egyptians and Semites.

Cyprus—the Copper island—seems to have been the original home of the workers in copper. But whereas in Egypt bronze did not supplant copper till about 1700 B.C., the Ægeans had made bronze their chief metal a thousand years earlier. It seems likely that the Ægeans got their art of alloying copper with tin (or antimony) from the same source as the Babylonians—from the region beyond Akkad and Sumer. Babylonian seals of 2650 B.C. have been found in Cyprus; and when Sargon of Akkad and Sumer "crossed the Sea of the West," he probably landed in Cyprus. Possibly Egypt got her knowledge of bronze from Crete, foremost of Ægean Isles to climb up out of the Stone Age into civilization. That Greece got her Bronze Age from Crete is practically certain.

In fact, not before Late Minoan culture traits begin to appear in Mycenæ and Tiryns are there any signs of civilization in Greece. We may call this culture Mycenæan and set its age at 1500-1200 B.C.; but it is Greek neither in origin nor in inspiration. It is Ægean—as is that of Troy. Its makers were non-Aryan-speaking peoples, kin to the Philistines. There were no Greeks yet. Many Mycenæan artifacts are imports from Crete or other Ægean Isles. Greek mythology is full of legends crediting the foundations of their civilization to "Bringers from across the sea." Those bringers were Ægeans. Not for a thousand years yet were the Hellenes to make that civilization their own and transform it into what we know as Greek civilization—un-Egyptian, un-Asiatic. But games, sports, art, politics, city life in general, flourished on Greek soil centuries before they were to be lifted to the immortal heights of the "Glory that was Greece."

Before we trace that uplift, let us glance at the fortress-like palaces of Tiryns, with their fifty-seven-feet-thick cyclopean stone walls; at the fortress of Agamemnon of Mycenæ with its fifty-six-feet-thick walls; at his tomb with its stupendous eighteen-feet-high doorway, the lintel of which was thirty feet long and weighed 113 tons. It was in that tomb that the so-called Treasury of Atreus, of gold weapons and ornaments, was found.

Mycenæ and Tiryns are merely the most striking examples of this Ægean culture transplanted to Greek soil to flourish behind the massive walls of nests of robber barons on hilltops dominating the plains. There were other settlements well on into Greece above the Isthmus of Corinth. Even the Acropolis at Athens has recently yielded Ægean art of the Mycenæan Age. The artifacts from these sites show that while art of the Mycenæan Age was Ægean, it was becoming something else; it had begun to go on its own, as it were. The famous Golden Goblets, with pictures of tame cattle grazing in the field and of a wild-bull hunt, show a keenness of eye rarely surpassed anywhere. In the dagger blades with scenes pictured in inlaid gold and silver, from the royal tombs of Mycenæ, technical skill and artistry are marvellously mated.

Mycenæ—"rich in gold"—was the home of Agamemnon, leader of the Greek princes who warred on Troy to recover his brother Menelaus' wife, Helen, abducted by Paris, son of Ilium's king, Priam the Trojan.

At any rate, that is how the blind poet Homer sang it; and it was about the same time that David, the Hebrew poet, was singing his immortal song. Both songs were to inspire men down through the ages. But I know no case of happier inspiration than that of the American-born German lad, Heinrich Schliemann, at the age of seven, when he was living with his parents in Germany. It is an old story now, but will bear repeating.

On a Christmas Day young Schliemann and a girl playmate were turning the pages of a History of the World. They came upon a picture, pure fiction, of course, of Æneas, with his father Anchises on his back, fleeing burning Troy. The two youngsters then and there decided they would marry and together discover Troy. Fate decided otherwise, but human nature is human nature, and when it gets set—in a Schliemann, a Darwin, a Faraday—it will not be denied.

After being shipwrecked on the Holland coast, Schliemann at the age of fourteen was apprenticed to a grocer and transferred to Amsterdam. While dispensing smoked herring and similar delicacies, he learned English and French, and taught himself Greek and began to read Homer. And kept on saving money. Then he learned Spanish, Italian, and Portuguese. He became a rich grocer, and richer from Russian oil; and at forty-one retired with a fortune—as many men do, but without a hobby that can yield huge joy to its rider and knowledge to mankind.

Schliemann began his life work at Troy in 1870. Within four years he had uncovered parts of nine cities. We cannot say that he made history; we can say that he was one of the great modern uncoverers of thousands of years of making of history. A vandal in a sense, but the vandals of old were robbers searching for gold to be spent in riotous living; the Schliemanns, Layards, Rawlinsons, Nevilles, Petries, Breasteds, Carters, Reisners, de Sarsacs, Garstangs, de Morgans, Winklers, Burkhardts, Winckelmanns, Evanses, Meyers, and Woolleys search for facts, and, guarding the artifacts they discover as a mother guards a fragile baby, lay facts and artifacts before the reading and seeing world. Before these modern archæologists our knowledge of ancient history was not only scanty, vague, much of it legend and some pure fiction, but it was tinged and biassed by the viewpoints of the comparatively late Greek historians and the Hebrew writers of the Bible.

And what of Troy, and of Paris and Helen? First, note that the story of Paris and Helen survived Troy by nearly three thousand years. Words can be more immortal than monumental bronze.

Troy in 1500 B.C. was a splendid city, as civilized as its rival Knossos of Crete; about 3000 B.C. it was just a shabby little Stone Age village. In fifteen hundred years Troy had become Big Business; the city was prosperous, its kings were rich. Their palace is the earliest known fortress in the Ægean world. Its civilization was Ægean—brother under and on the skin to Knossos, to Mycenæ and Tiryns: in short, Minoan.

How about Homer? The *Odyssey* is gorgeous adventure, and Odysseus' twenty years on the way home to Ithaca from Troy is typical of countless odysseys, characteristic of man's wanderings from nowhere to where-he-is. It is also characteristic that the divine Autolycus, grandfather of Odysseus, was by grace of Hermes renowned among men for his cunning in thieving and for his false oaths. But it was all according to the rules of the game. It is also characteristic of the *Odyssey*, though not of later Greek society, that women directed the councils and protected the men; they ruled—alone, or with a mere man as consort.

The *Iliad*, written (perhaps generations) before the *Odyssey* and not before 800 B.C., is surcharged with the fire of the brave deeds of mortal men and the exploits of the Immortals among mortals. As a source book for light on obscure prehistoric beliefs it is priceless; it throws the spotlight on the doings of souls and illumines the Land of the Shades. As history . . . Well, Homer was the Bible of the Homeric Greeks, and was accepted as such by the early Christian fathers. But whether Peisistratus in the sixth century B.C., as is claimed, got specialists together to edit an orthodox text of Homer, as did Nehemiah for certain books of the Old Testament, is not at all certain. Shotwell thinks the Alexandrian Greeks responsible for the text of Homer as we now have it. Homer was not a historian; he was a poet, a romancer, an artist, a genius, greatest of all ancient bards. There were Troys before Troy, but no pre-Homeric Homer has yet been found.

There was a Troy. There was a city on the plains of Hissarlik overlooking and commanding the Hellespont, the Dardanelles, the seaway to the Black Sea. That made it a menace to anybody travelling that way, but whether Hissarlik was Troy or a fortified camp of the Greeks is still in dispute. If we could only read more Hittite or *any* Minoan clay tablets! We do not even know who the Hittites were.

It is known that the Hittites distributed iron to the ancient world and that some extraordinary upsets followed, one of which we have already seen down in Egypt. It is known that they learned cuneiform writing from the Babylonians, possibly before 2000 B.C. Although they were the neighbours of the Phœnicians on the north, they did not use a phonetic but a syllabic alphabet of some 160 signs, of which only about forty cannot be identified; but no Hittite inscription has yet been satisfactorily translated. Possibly the Hittites taught their writing to the Ægean world. Peake and Fleure date the emergence of the Hittite Empire—and the true Bronze Age— at about 1900 B.C. It is known that the Hittites were the ruling power in Asia Minor, a broken country as big as Texas, from before 1400 to 1200 B.C.; and that at that time they used horses and horse-drawn chariots, presumably their own invention.

It is also known that the discoverer rarely gets the most out of his discovery and that the inventor is often slain with his own weapon. We have seen what an Assyrian army of iron-armed fighters on horse-drawn chariots could do. We know that shortly after 1200 B.C. the Assyrian army began to squeeze the Hittites, drive them back toward the west. Did that put the Hittites between the two jaws of a nutcracker, and were the expanding Greeks the other jaw? Was the Greeks' assault on Troy but an episode, as Breasted thinks, in a Greek invasion of the Western Hittite frontier? It may well be. At any rate, after the twelfth century the Hittites fade from the picture.

In fact, about that time there seems to have been a general fading from the picture all along the line. History was being made, but not recorded; the makers were too busy fighting, and the faders had nothing worth while to record. Man sings his own pæan of victory, not the other fellow's. The Homeric songs were but old tradition handed on, modified, glorified, redacted—as were those of the Hebrew patriarchs.

By about 1400 B.C. Knossos had gone up in smoke, and by 1200 B.C. had changed hands; by about 1200 B.C. Troy had shared the same fate; by 1100 B.C. Mycenæ had given up; and by about 1000 B.C. all the Isles of the Ægean Sea had changed hands. The Greeks, in short, had come into what they were to make their own. They had been making history, but four centuries had to elapse before they began to write it; five centuries, before Greek became a "classic."

The Greeks of the Classic Age, in blood, language, and culture, were a mixture. Their blood was Alpine mixed with Mediterranean; their language was Indo-European, overlaying an as yet unknown tongue; their culture began as Ægean, Minoan: some of it they jettisoned, most of it they made Greek.

The migrations of these prehistoric Greeks southward into Greece and the Ægean world are still in the realm of speculation. The Greeks themselves called the "aborigines" Pelasgians. By 2000 B.C. the immigrants had settled all over Greece: their descendants, mixed presumably with Ægeans, may be the historic Arcadians and

Ionians. The ancestors of the historic Achæans—"the fair-haired sons of Achaia"—may have entered Greece by 1800 B.C. The last wave of immigrants seems to have been the Dorians; that wave may have started by 1500 B.C., ending at 1100 B.C. It is plausible that these Achæans were responsible for the upset in Crete which loosed the Philistines upon the Hebrew world. It is even more likely that the Dorian wave was armed with iron which had been learned in the Danube. That was when Greek met Greek. The ironclad Dorians won. The Dark Ages of Greece are the centuries when iron was hacking down Ægean civilization that a new civilization might have room to grow up.

Homer's pictures are primarily of an Ægean civilization between the twelfth and tenth centuries B.C. Iron is known, but bronze is the weapon of war and of the gods. By the time of the *Odyssey* there were Dorians in Crete. By the ninth century B.C. Dorian emigrants had founded a new Doris in Asia Minor. A hundred years later began another wave of Greeks—Ionians—to the west of Asia Minor. These Ionian Greeks, on the Asia Minor coast and adjacent islands, were the real school-teachers of Greece; they taught her letters, poetry, art, and gave her coined money. While Greece was still in darkness, a great light had been kindled in Ionia. There, across the Ægean Sea on the coast of Asia, Greek civilization was born anew, and from there it was carried to the remote ends of the known world.

Before Persia had drawn Greece into a life-and-death struggle on behalf of these Asiatic Greeks, Greece in a sense had done nothing. There was no Greece. There were Greeks—held together by no king or priest, but only by common tradition, language, manners, and customs. They were all Hellenes; Hellen was the mythical common ancestor of all "true" Greeks. They had no *national* tradition, but they had Homer, and in his songs their common cultural traditions, their national heroes. Homeric tradition, Homeric heroes, were a high mark to aim at, a noble goal of endeavour.

True, the Homeric gods cheat one another; commit adultery, fornication, and seduction; do deeds of violence; are whimsical and often vindictive; they even persecute mortals from sheer envy. But what ancient gods didn't? Life in Homer, as Shorey points out, was held in as high esteem as it is today in Chicago or New York—

and was safer from sheer accident. Homer's characters are certainly more worthy of respect and sympathy than are those of many modern novels. They are not criminals, they rarely lie or steal; there are no unnatural vices, drunkenness, or gluttony. And with all their frailties, the gods are guardians of the moral law.

There are no kings in Homer; *basileus* means prince. There were kings just across the water and in Crete. Greece's ancient kings are chiefs, with dwindling powers. The office became elective—*archon*; for life at first, then for ten years, then for a year.

The Greeks began with tribal democracy; they never got far beyond it. The spirit which leads to kings reigning by divine right found little nourishment on Greek soil. Even when little Attica made her imperial gesture, we find four slaves for every free citizen; but we find no slave revolts. There is nothing to show that the lot of the slaves was as bad as is the average miner's today in West Virginia. Grecian struggles are not between master and slave, but between city and city, faction and faction, citizen and citizen. The Pyramid architects commanded the services of tens of thousands of slaves; the Acropolis was built by free craftsmen.

With Greece, we have parted company, not with superstition— for there was plenty of it—but with organized superstition making for power and privilege, endowing kings with divinity, priests with omniscience. For the first time in from five to ten millenniums an essentially human society replaced theocracy, with the result that the energy the Jews spent in theology the Greeks spent in philosophy (which began as science) or in art (which demanded science). Therein lay the supremacy of Hellenic achievement as an enduring factor in the advance of civilization.

Quite likely, part of the credit for Hellenic uniqueness in sceptical criticism should go to stony soil as much as to the Greeks themselves. It is significant, as Briffault points out, that Thessaly, mother of witches, and Bœotia, home of oracles, were lands of rich soil tilled by backward farmers far from the centres of culture. Greece was always a poor country.

Five hundred years before the Persians burned Athens and destroyed the temples on the Acropolis, that hill was occupied, presumably, by what we may call the Castle. Vacated at the king's death and allowed to fall into ruin, it became a shrine, and then a temple; Athens had become a little city state. There must have been a score or more in Greece by the ninth century B.C. But that is still the prehistoric age. The first date we can tie to is 776 B.C., the First Olympiad.

The name of the winner of the Olympian games that year was Korœbus, the earliest known name of a winner; hence "Olympiad," hence *First* Olympiad.

Just when those games were inaugurated, or by whom, is unknown. The Greeks, of course, ascribed their origin to the gods—to the god Herakles (Latin, Hercules), to be more specific. But not the Herakles of popular mythology; rather the Idæan Herakles, from Crete, older than Zeus and present at his birth. The other and later Herakles, the most popular Culture Hero of the Græco-Roman world, took part in the games after he had cleaned out the Augean stables and slain King Augeas. Legend also tells of a king of the district who forced all suitors for the hand of his daughter to compete with him in a chariot race; the king always won, of course, and slew the loser. Then Pelops came along, beat the king, married his beautiful daughter, and restored the games in unparalleled splendour.

It seems certain that the games are very old, that Olympia was the site of an ancient shrine, and that Lycurgus, the Spartan lawgiver, in the ninth century B.C. reorganized the games. That, tradition says, was in obedience to the oracle of Apollo at Delphi, and with the object of staying the hand of the turbulent Greek city states. The "Peace of God" was to reign over Greece during the games. Hence the dignity which soon shone around them like a halo. They became veritable national festivals, and exerted enormous influence in unifying Greek sentiment.

As the sacred month of the first full moon after the summer solstice approached, heralds set out to proclaim peace throughout the Grecian world. From Ionia, from far off Sicily and Italy of *Magna Græcia*, contestants and spectators began to head for Olympia. After fitting sacrifices to Zeus and the lesser gods, the games were on.

The original contest was a footrace in the *stadion*. With the Eighteenth Olympiad in 708 B.C. (they were held every fourth year) the *Pentathlon* (fivefold) was introduced. The events—jumping, discus-throwing, running, wrestling, and boxing—were elimination contests, so arranged that the final issue lay between the two best boxers. In 648 B.C. four-horse chariot races were introduced.

No one with a blemish on his character could compete. Ten months' training was required—the last month in Olympia. Near an image of Zeus (He-of-the-Oath) all the athletes, with their fathers, brothers, and trainers, swore on a piece cut from a boar to be guilty of no foul play. The oath was in the nature of a *devotion*. As the boar or victim had been cut to pieces—destroyed, sacrificed, devoted—so they swore they would be "devoted" to Zeus if they committed perjury.

The prizes were simply branches from a wild olive tree said to have been planted by Zeus himself. The prize was not worth a penny, but it made the winner the greatest man in Greece. Pindar oded him, Myron sculptured him. It also distinguished him for life and brought honour to his family, his home, and his town. On returning he was met by a triumphal procession and given a public banquet—and sometimes exempted from taxes.

Besides athletic, Olympia was sometimes open to intellectual, contests. Thus, Herodotus is said to have read there portions of his immortal history; hearing it, Thucydides was inspired to become a historian. Celebrated orators, such as Gorgias and Lysias, went on the Olympian air. Painters exhibited their works. Themistocles, hero of Salamis, was applauded there, as was Plato. Greece died; the Games lived on.

Under the Roman emperors, Olympia every fourth year became the Mecca of the empire. Two emperors—Tiberius and Nero—even won prizes. But one of the first things Emperor Theodosius did after embracing Christianity was to stop all this "foolishness." That was 394 A.D. Such was "progress" from 776 B.C. to 394 A.D. Oh well, the Games should have been suppressed: they had become professional; a beautiful cult had become Big Business; "spotless character" had given way to prize-ring ethics; the olive branch had been replaced by cash prizes.

It was the archon Solon, of Constitution and Law fame, who told the world that "money makes the man." He was a great statesman. His Constitution, among other things, provided for a popular assembly (*ecclesia*) of all citizens over twenty years of age. It did not free the slaves; it did give all free men equal rights before the law. This was 594 B.C., thirty years after Draco's Law—"written with blood," because of its heavy hand on the poor. The modern world could trade some Dracos for a few Solons.

About the time of the First Olympiad, the Greeks began to expand toward the west. They pushed the Phœnicians to the far end of Sicily and founded such famous colonies as Syracuse (735 B.C.), Girgenti, Catania, Taormina, and Selinunte. They swarmed all around the Italian mainland, as far north as Naples (*Neapolis*, New city) on the west, to Bari on the east. Marseilles (*Masselia*) was a flourishing Greek city twenty-five hundred years ago and commercially of great importance, controlling as it did the overland route to the British Isles and the Baltic lands. The Riviera was studded with Greek cities. There were Greek colonists also in Spain and on the African coast. Naucratis in the Nile delta was a Greek city by 650 B.C. In short, the Greeks carried building and the fine arts, writing and literature, to the barbarians.

They had become a great sea power. They had given up their ponderous fifty-oar galleys and adopted swifter sailing-ships such as the Egyptians had owned a thousand years before. By 500 B.C. they had fleets of men-of-war and merchantmen.

Greek artists began to be artists! By 700 B.C. they thought enough of their work to sign it. With another century their work was good enough for export; they could surpass their Eastern teachers. Individual fame spread to far off lands. The name of a Greek vase painter may be found on vessels in the Nile Valley, in Etruscan tombs of Italy, and in the heart of Asia Minor. All over Grecian lands superb temples sprang up, many in white marble.

Greece, I repeat, has no history. It was never an empire, a kingdom, a nation, or even a union of states. A great patriot, statesman, warrior, appears in this place or that; something happens; it looks promising: the promise is never fulfilled. A brilliant light blazes up, now here, now there; it seems as though it might light up the world: then darkness reigns again. A clarion voice rings out, loud, strong, pure; but it is not heard five miles away and is promptly forgotten. A superlative democracy arises: it was founded on slavery. Rational thought is born again and again: to be thrown away with the bath water, or drugged with hemlock.

The very cradle of Greek civilization was Ionia in Asia; its largest temple was built in Sicily. *Magna Græcia* (Great Greece) was Sicily and southern Italy. Its master minds were Asiatic and Egyptian Greeks. Its great world-empire builder came from the barbaric north. And then, nearly strangled to death by Persia and delivered to Rome, Greece rose up and almost conquered the world.

Not with arms; with intellect. Therein lies the immortality of the Immortal Greeks. That is why the fifth century B.C. is closer to us of today than is the fifth, tenth, or fifteenth century A.D. Their language may be "Greek" to us, but we can understand their thoughts. All that has made our civilization unique had its beginnings twenty-five hundred years ago. The Greeks did not "save" Europe, as has often been said. There was less in Europe at that time more worth saving than the Norse Vikings found in America in the tenth century. The Greeks made Europe worth saving. They planted the germ of secular thought, of thought freed from priestly obsessions. In short, they did for men's minds what Lincoln did for certain men's bodies—turned them loose.

### III

The significant side of Greek history is not What's What and How, but Who's Who and Why. Our concern, then, is primarily with brains and ideas; with bone and muscle, only incidentally. But first let us build enough of a skeleton to accommodate a brain. Ideas no more spring from nothing than do violets or skunk cabbage; there must be seeds, soil, and seasons; a conspiracy, if you please; but nature can no more conspire in a vacuum than brains can.

Let us start with a defeat and a victory. It is also a convenient date in Grecian history. No better than other dates, nor a decisive date—simply a good date and easy to remember, like 1873 for Chicago. By 480 B.C. Athens was big enough to incite the Persians to burn it; the Greeks were strong enough to defeat the Persian fleet. And it was a brilliant victory, for the Greeks lost forty ships to the Persians' two hundred. That was the famous Battle of Salamis, September, 480 B.C. Xerxes, the Persian king, leaving his army of a quarter of a million men in Thessaly, retreated to Asia.

Themistocles was the *Strategus* of that victory and the leading statesman of Athens, having "potsherded" Aristides, his chief rival, to ten years' exile. We should call it banishment or exile; the Greeks called it *ostrakosmos*.

An *ostrakon* was a potsherd, a "scrap of paper," something that could be written on. A reformer named Cleisthenes invented the idea. Think of it: a secret ballot nearly twenty-five hundred years ago. A Greek invention. That is the kind of people the Greeks were. They had a flair for politics, a passion for democracy, but not enough machinery to build a lasting democracy. By means of Cleisthenes' law of *Ostrakon* a secret vote could be taken on anyone who endangered the public safety.

Three years before Salamis the Athenians decided that Athens, with Persia knocking at the door, was not big enough to hold two great statesmen who disagreed on everything. Instead of hanging one of them or suggesting that they fight a duel, they put the matter to a vote. Themistocles won by six thousand potsherds. It worked out all right too, for he was a Big Navy man. He began adding twenty triremes a year to Athens' fleet. Salamis proved he was right.

One month before Salamis, the Spartan, Leonidas, had won undying fame and put the Warm Gates of a mountain pass forever on the map. But the story of the battle of Thermopylæ is best told in the words on the monument the Greeks erected over the remains of their heroes: "Stranger, tell the Spartans that we are lying here in obedience to their commands." The command was, Hold that pass! But Leonidas had not the slightest chance of holding it; his forces were hundreds to the Persians' thousands, and he knew it. Their one idea was to sell themselves as dearly as possible, and they died to the last man. But not in vain. The Greeks never forgot their heroic patriotism, nor the Persians their valour.

Ten years before Thermopylæ the Greeks, led by Miltiades, had defeated the Persians at the battle of Marathon—not an endurance contest for the delectation of morons, but a contest between professional bowmen and a tiny citizen army armed with spears.

Two years before Marathon, the Persians had suffered their first defeat on European soil, and in 499 B.C. the whole trouble had begun. The Ionian Greeks, who had made extraordinary advance in rational thought and in science, had revolted against the civilized but despotic Persians. They had been aided in their revolt by the Greeks of Greece, especially by twenty ships from Athens. That fact had taken the Persians far from home, had led Darius from Asia to Europe in a struggle that was to wreck Persia and make immortal names in Greece.

After Salamis the Persians tried, for the fourth time, to crush Greece. In the battles of Platæa and Mycale (479 B.C.) the Greeks won great booty and thereafter took the offensive. In the naval battle of Salamis, off Cyprus, they won another brilliant victory. That ended the war; the Persians had had enough. Since their first invasion (499 B.C.) till their fleet went to the bottom off Cyprus (449 B.C.) they had met nothing but humiliation and defeat. They had wasted two million men and untold wealth; but they had given the Greeks something to be proud of. And now see Athens rise from her ashes and the Golden Age of Pericles break out in dazzling brilliancy.

Having learned how to fight and having driven the Persians from the land and waters of Europe, why didn't the Greeks go on and really conquer somebody? Were they too proud to fight? No; but they would rather talk than fight. Another thing: they could never get together; they were suspicious of one another, even unusually jealous. The city states fought one another after the fashion of our city gangs. They fought before the Persian threat and after Persia had ceased to threaten; there were fraternal wars between east and west, north and south; between Athens and the Dorian confederacy of Peloponnesus; between Greece and *Magna Græcia*; between Spartans and Persians; between Thebes and Sparta.

Presumably they would be fighting yet had not Alexander knocked their heads together and fought his war to end wars. Suppose he had lived twenty years longer, or had left a son who had learned the game from the Great Master? We should still have the Age of Pericles to marvel at, and possibly more of it. Alexander might have hastened civilization in Europe by two thousand years. As it was, Athens never recovered her prestige or again became the centre of learning after the migration of her scholars to Alexandria. Nor, indeed, did Greece herself ever recover from the wastage of her resources in her wars against *Magna Græcia*; nor did Athens ever recover her supremacy after her suicidal war against Sparta.

In fact, that fratricidal Peloponnesian War marks the beginning of the end of Greece as a political power in the world.

The entire population of the Athens Persian torches set aflame, sending its inhabitants flying to the coast where the Greek navy was soon to take revenge, could have been housed in two New York skyscrapers. Apart from its temples, there was nothing splendid about Athens. Its houses were of sun-dried brick, without conveniences or chimneys. The streets were narrow and crooked, and muddy or dusty, without pavements or sidewalks, and foul with rubbish and garbage. People lived out-of-doors, without pretence. Girls' schools were unknown. Boys were guarded on their way to school by old slaves (*pedagogue*, "leader of a child"). The "Lyceum" at one side of the city was then merely an athletic ground; only later was it used as a place for lectures. The Academy, a tract of ground on the north side of the town, dedicated to Athene, was at first merely a gymnasium; only later was it laid out with walks, trees, and fountains, its olive groves to be haunted by teachers such as Plato, for example.

The total income of the Athenian state, says Breasted, could hardly have been more than $750,000. Greek soldiers would furnish their own arms and fight for anybody for five dollars a month. An architect got about twenty-five cents a day. The luxury of Minoan city life was quite unknown. Athens never was famous for her riches or splendour. Her patriotism was inspired by the heroic valour of her supermen; that was her national religion. Her public buildings were temples in their honour.

One of the results of the Greek victory over the Persians was to make Athens rather than Sparta the head of all war activities, and that precipitated a contest for the control of political power in Athens. Into the resulting charges and counter-charges of treason, the ostracisms and banishments, we cannot go. It was an era of particularly "dirty" politics. The issue was finally narrowed down to Cimon, the aristocrat, and Pericles, the democrat. The democrat won; the aristocrat was potsherded from Athens. Thereupon Athenian democracy began to decline and the Golden Age of Pericles dawned.

As Pericles triumphed in 461 B.C. and died 429 B.C., we have thirty-two years for the most brilliant epoch in the history of

Athens. Philosophers: Socrates, Zeno, Anaxagoras, Protagoras. Historians: Herodotus, Thucydides. Tragic dramatists: Æschylus, Sophocles, Euripides. Comic dramatist: Aristophanes. Architects: Ictinus, Callicrates. Painter: Polygnotus. Sculptor: Phidias. And, last but not least, Aspasia, who possibly wrote the wonderful speeches of Pericles recorded by Thucydides. All from a state with a population no larger than that of Delaware in 1910, and from a city of less than 30,000 citizens. Nor did that Golden Age turn to brass at once. Greece went right on turning out master minds for centuries. Plato's "Academy" continued for a thousand years. The epoch following Pericles was possibly even greater.

"How did it happen? What happened?" The Persian wars woke Greece up, stirred the bones of the dead, let loose a torrent of emotional energy seeking outlets in thoughts and things finer, deeper, greater, nobler, truer, more profound, more beautiful, than before. In short, Greece was inspired. And the prosperity which came in as the Persians went out made for business; Greece was now commercially supreme in the Orient. They had begun as landlubbers, they had become sea-rovers—intelligent pirates; they were now the common carriers of the vast and rich Mediterranean maritime world.

To that world and its hinterland the Greeks exported their new goods and ideas: utensils, furniture, interior decorations, drama, theatres to stage it in, arms and weapons, military tactics; noble ideals, sane, sound ideas. Greece had the world at her feet; not in abject awe, as before a divinity, nor in slavish fear, as before a fiend, but in open-eyed youthful astonishment that man himself was the measure of all things, that man himself could discover virtue, truth, beauty, and honesty without the need of a mumbo-jumbo priest as interpreter, that the world was an oyster to be opened by the hand of man.

What the Greeks themselves discovered was astonishing, but somebody had to break through the wall of tradition. That wall had become so sanctified that men were afraid to think of questioning it, much less to break through it. Because of the sequence of events, and because of the lay of the land, it was possible for the Greeks. They did break through—not all of them, but enough to set a mark so high that not all of the civilized world of today has yet reached it.

Athens herself could and did rise to dazzling heights, but let us not forget that Athenian society was not founded on sound principles. It was a slave society; it was also a society which forced woman to the status of slavery. Her position, socially and culturally, was not one whit better than it was among the Turks of the last generation. She was essentially a purdah woman. Only the Aspasias, the *hetairai*, could flirt with a Socrates, sit at the feet of a Plato, or perhaps write the speeches of a Pericles. A society so founded was easy prey for organized mysticism; superstition was inevitable and became rampant.

Nor did Greek pupils always measure up to their masters. Socrates propounded ideas that had value in a world of living human beings. Plato, his pupil, after travelling in Egypt, set up his famous school in the Academy, and handed on those teachings in the famous *Dialogues*. But he had grown old; his *Republic* was as practicable as the electric engine I might design. As Rohde says, he discarded without regret all that Greek culture—in politics, society, custom, and art—stood for, and demanded instead an aristocracy beyond the possible reach of any human society, even that of Athens herself, saturated as she was with aristocratic ideas.

Plato was a philosopher. His teachings were as far from reality as was a ceremonial Japanese tea in the days of the Shogunate; but they made a tremendous splash in the sea of thought and nearly wrecked the craft of human lives. In seeming to confirm man's hope of, and strengthen his belief in, immortality, he has wielded incalculable power.

Socrates alone had the courage of his convictions. He did not pretend to know everything, not even whether life or death were better: that, he said after he had drunk the hemlock, "is known only to the gods." His gods were very human. They must exist— "how otherwise could you serve them?" Holiness to him was an *art*: during life one must do business with the gods; if one does one's part, the gods will do theirs. But sin, atonement, sacrifice, purification, fear of judgment, beatific yearning, were not the problems of religion to Socrates; for him it was enough that man mind his business of living. That was a new idea in the world of

Athens, though not in the world of the Ionian Greeks. The Athenian world was not ready for it. His execution was worthy of a Papal Inquisition—and had there been one at the time Plato would have been its Torquemada.

When a deformed ram's head with a single median horn was brought to Pericles he called in a soothsayer, who promptly began to draw omens. That was answer enough for a great statesman. But a scientist was present—Anaxagoras; he wanted to know why that ram had only one horn. He split the skull and showed that the single horn was due to maldevelopment of the cranial bones.

It was Athens' proud boast that "not only in politics are we open-minded: without a scrap of jealousy we tolerate peculiarities of all sorts in each other's daily lives; we have no objection to our neighbour following the bent of his humour; nor do we put on black looks, innocuous maybe, but annoying."

But Athens was not ready to tolerate rational thought. It was not safe to question or discredit the national gods or to expose the follies of the time; to do so was to imperil one's life. They had no trouble trumping up excuses; their hypocrisy in that regard was as shameless as it ever was in Rome or Christendom. Socrates "corrupted the minds of the youth," and had to drink poison. Anaxagoras, for presuming to question the gods, was tried and persecuted; as were also Æschylus, Phidias, Euripides, Aristotle, Alcibiades, Diogenes, Damon, Protagoras, Aristarchus, Theophrastus, Theodoris, Phormius, even Pericles himself and Aspasia. What talent, an all-star cast of genius! After 415, all impiety was punished. Diagoras was charged with having made firewood of an image of Herakles—telling him to cook turnips and thereby perform his thirteenth "labour"; a silver talent was offered for him dead, two for his capture alive.

## IV

Athens was not the first, nor certainly the last, state to handle rational thought as though it were a dangerous disease, or to treat critics as though they were dangerous animals. Nor was Athens herself the birthplace of the honest, critical questioner. For that we have to cross the Ægean Sea to semi-Asiatic Ionian Greece, home of the great Anaxagoras, who brought some science to Athens and taught Euripides atheism. Ionia alone in all the world of the sixth century B.C. could inspire a man to proclaim: "Of uncertainty and mystery there is, by Zeus, enough in this strange, rich life, and to spare. But how shall the myths and mummeries of a barbarian priest help it, or make it less or otherwise? What can be known we shall seek to know with all the might of the honest means of knowledge whereof we dispose; and what we cannot know we shall face fearlessly with no less honest ignorance."

Greatest of all Ionians was Thales of Miletus. He visited the Nile land, sought wisdom wherever he could find it. He obtained lists of observations on the heavens and from them calculated eclipses—for example, the total eclipse of the sun on May 28, 585 B.C., which interrupted the famous battle in which the Medes and the Babylonians destroyed Assyria. From calculating eclipses, Thales advanced to the next and possibly the longest and most important step ever taken by a human being. He took the stars from the hands of the gods and declared that they moved according to fixed laws. One of his pupils made a map of the world. The gulf between a Thales and a sixth-century B.C. Egyptian or Chaldean star-gazer was so wide it was not crossed again for more than fifteen centuries. In fact, the mental discipline which Thales set in motion, and which alone can save humanity, is far beyond the reach of many of our academies today.

From Samos of Ionia came that curious mixture of science and crank, Pythagoras. He too visited Egypt; and settled in Italy. He was a natural scientist, a mathematician. He proved by the use of fossils that the sea had once covered the land. But his greatest discovery was that the earth was a sphere and had a movement of its own. And then the earth was put back into the Bible again, only to emerge centuries later.

From Abdera in Thrace, founded by Ionians, came the great thinker Protagoras; and Democritus, one of the most original thinkers of all antiquity, with his hands full of atoms, more than two thousand years before atoms became entities—if they are. It was Protagoras who read a treatise at the house of the freethinker Euripides, declaring that life was too short to think about the gods. The story was "Butler"-ized and Protagoras had to flee for his life. His book was publicly burnt, and press censorship had begun.

It was Democritus that Plato said he would like to burn—only there were too many copies!

From Ephesus came the "Ionian Nietzsche," Heraclitus, denouncing the "vulgar instincts of the herd, who, like asses, prefer chaff to gold." In an absolute sense, said Heraclitus, there is no such thing as death; it only marks a point, the point where one condition gives way to another, where something becomes something else. He also had strangely modern ideas about the never-resting force and activity of becoming without beginning or end. Philosophic speculation, if you please, but ask a modern physiologist what death is, or a modern physicist what life or an atom is; they do not sneer at this old Ionian. Even his *psyche* as "fire" is quite as tangible as the psyche of some psychologies.

The amazing thing is that despite their tendency to speculate in abysmal waters and empyrean skies, so many of them kept so sober so much of the time. Empedocles, for example, claimed he was once a boy, also a girl, a bush, a bird, and a voiceless fish in the salty flood—sheer transmigration nonsense, of course; but when he claimed that attraction and repulsion, love and hate, are the four roots of things, he said something.

Also from Miletus came the "Ionian Darwin," Anaximander, proclaiming that men and higher animals were descended from fishes. And from Colophon came the Ionian, Xenophanes, who railed at Homer's immortal gods—"created in man's image"—and taught Parmenides, who in turn taught Plato, who in turn taught Aristotle, who tutored Alexander the Great, who founded Alexandria, which founded a school of science, which inspired Bagdad and Cordova and finally was reborn in Europe.

Before we part with these Ionian forerunners of science, let us make certain that we understand their weakness as well as their strength. They *loved knowledge*, hence the name *philosophia*; that is why they are called "philosophers." And they liked to speculate about what they knew; but too often their speculations took them into a shadow-land of words. They did not go out into the world enough; they got their feet too far from the ground; they did not go into workshops and laboratories and match things against words. No scientist gets far without speculation or without a love of knowledge, but he advances only as he keeps a critical eye on his knowledge, a tight rein on his speculation. When sheer love of knowledge gave way to a keen hunt for facts, and when speculation was not allowed to get beyond the control of facts, modern science began to grow into a forest. The significant thing is not that such men as Socrates, Anaxagoras, Phidias, Euripides, Aristotle, and Theophrastus were persecuted, but that there were such men on earth. Only a Christian Inquisition could torture and burn such men at the stake.

That old Ionian love of knowledge for its own sake began a new page in human history. They were not seeking power, salvation, dominion, or wealth; they were preserving their youth in the only way they knew how and as well as their times permitted: they kept on being curious about things. They put the will-to-know above the will-to-possess; they would live richly rather than be rich. Some of them, as we have seen, did travel—with their eyes open—and saw sun, moon, stars and earth almost as we see them, and not as gods, not as demons, not as the paraphernalia with which some mighty magician performed tricks to bewilder and edify puny earthly talking animals.

And that, I repeat, was a mighty step, one never taken before. They left no empire, no lists of kings or pontiffs; they had no career. But our indebtedness to them is no less great than it is to Old Egypt, Old Babylon, and Old Sumer.

Facts must precede speculation. Let us look at the first man in history who loved to seek facts even though it took him all over creation. I have mentioned Herodotus before, but he is worth more than honourable mention: he is worthy of the highest honours. He was the world's first great historian; he set a pace for historians of all time.

Homer made no pretence of writing history. He was a bard, a poet, an epic poet. He dealt with men, mortal combats, life and death, heroic deeds, dire tragedy, the restless activity of the heroic age. For him, for every epic poet, the story was *the* thing.

Hesiod was neither poet nor historian; he was a moralist. His *Theogony* is a cosmogony, the Greek Genesis—a straight-out account of the mythic basis of the beginning of Greek society. His *Works and Days* was first to propound the scheme of Gold, Silver, Bronze and Iron Ages "which has beguiled the fancy of so many a dreamer in later centuries—in that long 'Age of Iron' in which all dreamers live."

A *histor* to the Greeks was an arbitrator, one so versed in the manners and customs of the tribe that he could settle disputes, determine which disputant was right judged by tribal customs. Thus in the *Iliad*, during a dispute at law some one shouts out, "Let's make Agamemnon our *histor*!"—as though to say, He'll know what's what.

When Cambyses, the Persian, captured Memphis in 525 B.C., Egypt was thrown open to the inquisitive world. It became a great university for the Europeans and Asiatics of the entire Mediterranean world. There, later, went that very inquisitive Greek, Herodotus, whose life began in the year of Salamis (480 B.C.) and ended the year following the death of Pericles. His life, therefore, coincides with the years of Athenian supremacy. Neither he nor Pericles could have dreamed that they just barely escaped seeing that supremacy destroyed forever.

Herodotus went to Egypt armed with vivid curiosity, an insatiable desire to acquire knowledge, and a resolve to acquire it. Had he possessed the normal superstitious reverence of the non-Grecian world, he could not have acquired that encyclopædic wealth of information which made his history what Shotwell calls the "first single masterpiece in the history of history."

He went to Thebes and talked with the priests; to Phœnicia and talked with the priests; met Babylonian caravans in Lydian bazaars. He went to Babylon and talked with the priests. He talked with everybody worth talking to, saw everything worth seeing. And remember that at that time Babylon was to Greece what Peking was to eighteenth-century Europe. He was no snapshooting tourist. He was an explorer, an investigator, a searcher, a discoverer. And the things and peoples he discovered were put on the map, so to speak. Darius and Xerxes are immortal chiefly because this Ionian Greek talked about them and thereby immortalized them. Till the modern archæologist began, less than a hundred years ago, ancient history was not buried in the earth; it lived on in the immortal pages of the first Universal History, a monumental epos in the history of civilization.

Some of those pages, read within Olympia's sacred precincts, inspired a young Athenian aristocrat; that young man became the worthy successor of a worthy teacher. I do not mean to imply that Thucydides "went to school to" or "sat under" Herodotus. I speak of Herodotus teaching the young nobleman in the sense of a match that can touch off a keg of·gunpowder. An hour's contact with a human dynamo can charge a young man with more inspiration than four years' contact with two dozen spent dry batteries.

In Thucydides Shotwell finds great independence of thought and a unique detachment of mind; "Descartes was much less free from metaphysical preoccupation," and beside him "Socrates appears superstitious." Robertson thinks Thucydides not only the greatest of the old historians, but the greatest of all time; that he treated human affairs so rationalistically he might be called an atheist. His was the first History of Our Own Times—the Peloponnesian War; severe, impartial, proud, isolated, self-contained. His work became what he designed it to be, "an eternal possession"; the *ne plus ultra*, Macaulay called it, of human art.

Could more be said of any genius—the *ne plus ultra* of human *art*? Model he has been to historians ever since; and of how many of those who consciously strove to attain his heights, the *despair!* How many historians have seen what Thucydides saw so clearly, that wars cost Greece her very soul? Athens had loved liberty, had reverenced law, had been moderate in her treatment of enemies, had been a leader in art, science, and literature, had been really democratic; the long Peloponnesian War changed all that and she became the most aggressively intolerant and tradition-mongering city of Hellas—"crowning herself with crime," as Robertson says.

What Thucydides was to Herodotus, Tacitus was to Livy in Rome nine centuries later. If those four meant no more to us in college days than hurdles on the road to sheepskins, it was not their fault. They did their work well; their achievements are the common possession of the entire world of culture.

Xenophon, thinks Shotwell, would make a fortune today as a war correspondent, or win fame as a journalist and pamphleteer. His *Anabasis* is a memoir of the retreat (400 B.C.) of the 10,000 Greek mercenaries who took part in the fratricidal battle of Cunaxa, when young Cyrus attacked the Persian king, Artaxerxes II, near Babylon.

When Xenophon returned to Athens, his old master, Socrates, was dead. He proceeded to write his recollections. The *Memorabilia* is one of the earliest and most priceless of all "human documents." Its style became the pattern in Greece and was adopted by Cicero, who passed it on to mould countless pages of modern prose.

The rise of the scientific method was more significant than that of the Roman Empire; and I agree with Shotwell in finding Polybius, last great Greek historian, an exalted example and a noble exponent of that method. "As a living creature is rendered useless if deprived of its eyes, so if you take truth from History, what is left but an idle, unprofitable tale?" Truth—even if one must sometimes praise enemies and blame friends! "Directly a man assumes the moral attitude of a historian, he ought to forget all considerations" such as love of friends and hatred of enemies. Polybius was born about two hundred years after Xenophon wrote his memoirs of Socrates; his ideals are a fitting inspiration and guide for any writer of human history for all time.

Three great heroes are said to have saved Greece; but against Miltiades, Themistocles, and Pausanius we may set Thales, Xenophanes, and Heraclitus, and Pythagoras, Democritus, and Aristotle, as the saviours of civilization. And if to that sextet we add Herodotus, Thucydides, and Polybius, we have the fundamentals which distinguish the education open to Uncle Sam's children from that open to the children of Menes, Sargon, Moses, and the king of the Cannibal Islands. The Greeks thought things out as had never been done before, and thereby laid the foundation for a body of sound knowledge; modern science increased that knowledge a millionfold, and today it is built into machines that make nature drudge to do man's dirty work.

v

Xenophanes taught Parmenides, who taught Plato, who taught Aristotle, who taught little Alex who was to become the great Alexander, who was to teach more men, in less time, more things than did any other human being that ever lived. But this is too simple; besides, it does injustice to Alexander's father. Alexander sprang up like a mushroom in a lion's skin, but he sprang from rich soil. That spring illustrates what events can do when they conspire.

The rise of the Macedonian is not miraculous; it is wonderful, and it has been done thousands of times on American soil. It is the story of jumping from shirt sleeves to the top in three jumps. Many boys have had a tutor as good as Alexander's, but they have not had Alexander's father's and grandfather's tutors—no family tradition. The amount of energy that can accumulate in three generations of Will-to-Do-and-Be would be incredible if it were not so observable. Alexander, for example.

North of the Thessalian plains lay Macedonia, from which no "cry" had as yet come. To Athenians, cheering Pericles while he directed Ictinus and Callicrates in the erection of the Parthenon and his friend Phidias in its ornamentation, Macedonia probably seemed more remote than did Ohio to the "Boys of '76."

The Parthenon was opened to the public in 438 B.C., and with good reason could Aristophanes exclaim: "Oh, thou, our Athens, violet-wreathed, brilliant, most enviable city!" What a sight that Acropolis must have been on that opening day, with its dazzling snow-white Pentelic marble masterpieces! Which, of course, has nothing to do with far-off Macedonia. Well, that is the point. Macedonia was far off; nobody there but insignificant peasants, ruled over by no-account barbarian chiefs calling themselves kings.

But one Macedonian chief had an idea. If he could not reign regally, he would live artistically. He called in some talent: Zeuxis, the celebrated painter; Timotheus, the poet; Agathon, the tragic poet; that grandest tragic poet of them all, old Euripides; and Hippocrates, founder of the science of medicine, Father of the Art of Healing. That made a *court*; it would make one today. Into that court was born Philip, son of King Archelaos.

Philip had training other than that offered by barbaric Macedonia. It was the fate of war that he had to pass three years as a hostage at Thebes—the Seven-Gated Thebes of Bœotia, about fifty miles north of Athens. Thebes never did like Athens, had even favoured the Persians, and at this time was dominated by Epaminondas, a first-class fighting-man. The young Macedonian hostage learned about war from him. He also thought he saw signs of weakness all over Greece, which gave him a big idea; and the death of his brother gave him his chance. In 359 B.C., at the age of twenty-three, he became Philip II, king of Macedonia, and events soon proved that his idea was feasible.

How Philip rose to dominion over Greece by 336 B.C., when he was assassinated by Pausanius just after he had been chosen to lead the Greeks against the Persians, is not part of our story. But we may stop long enough to pay a tribute to our old friend Demosthenes, who thundered *philippics* at Philip with more patriotic zeal than statesman-like insight. Demosthenes, great Athenian as he was, was too patriotic to think things out. Athens could not unite the Greeks—no one could. They had to be clubbed together.

It was all right for Plato and other highbrows to dream Pan-Hellenism. But Athens had ceased to be a permanent power; most of her statesmen were ward politicians. Persia was still a menace. Somebody had to save Greece. Philip had proved that he was the man. His last act was to make himself virtual dictator of Grecian armies against Persia. Assassinated. But his son Alexander, now twenty years old, was to prove that Demosthenes had fought not only a losing fight but had put his money on the wrong stable. Had the great orator-patriot won we should all be here today, no doubt, but history would make different reading. Two years later this Aristotle-tutored boy-king continued the business of knocking jealous Greek heads together, and by 334 B.C. could start on a campaign which in just eleven years was to Hellenize the world.

We have already attended Alexander's funeral at Babylon in 323 B.C. Death, possibly, was never so calamitous to such colossal designs. The idea that he "sighed because he had no more worlds to conquer" does him grave injustice—or I misinterpret the fact of his sending, at the age of thirteen, hundreds of natural-history specimens to Aristotle in Athens. Or was it mere swelled-headed vainglory that prompted him to sacrifice to Artemis at Ephesus, to Melkarth at Tyre, to Mazda at Ecbatana, to Yahweh at Jerusalem, to Jupiter Amon at Siwa, to Ptah at Memphis? It was not superstition; it was a grand gesture on a grand tour—like a President kissing the handsomest baby at every capital city.

The East at any rate had its revenge. It was Hellenized, but, as Briffault says, it seized upon the jewels of Greece and wove them into mystic cabalistic webs, into gnosticisms and theologies. We shall see some of them crying from pediments in Roman forums to ensnare the passer-by. Had he lived twenty years longer, Alexander might have rid the East of some of its mental cobwebs, Hellenized it in spirit as well as in name. Certain it is that ideas of absolute monarchies and kings ruling by divine right bounced up out of the East like Jacks-in-the-box. To that extent Marathon and Salamis were hollow victories.

I think it time wasted to recount Alexander's victories; and in a sense there was none. On the plains of Troy he stopped and carefully trained a little army of 30,000 infantry and 5,000 cavalry. After a few pitched battles there was nothing more to do but let the fruit fall into his lap. Persia fell like a rotten tree. The Chinese in Bactria offered no resistance. The whole journey to Hyderabad in India was a huge royal picnic. He went out to conquer, but he also intended to investigate; in short, to make a gorgeous scientific expedition. He had designs on the East—to Hellenize it. He married Roxana, daughter of Darius III; eighty of his officers married Persian ladies; and ten thousand of his soldiers took Persian wives. His premature death put an end to his plans. Kandahar (Iskander, Alexander) in Afghanistan remains to perpetuate his name in Asia; Alexandria, in Egypt.

Some twenty years after Alexander's death, we find four kingdoms growing up out of the debris of his collapsed empire: Egypt, under Alexander's general, Ptolemæus, who founded the Dynasty of the Ptolemies; Syria, under the general, Seleucus, who founded the Seleucid Dynasty—out of which were to come the countries of the Galatians, Parthians, and the Jews under the Maccabees; Bithynia; and Macedonia.

In other words, Alexander's empire had died a-bornin'. But from his Hellenizing dreams were born many kingdoms which spoke Greek—at court, in law, and on decrees and coin of the realm; and such art, literature, and learning as they had were Grecian. Otherwise, apart from the kingdom of the Ptolemies, they did nothing to speak of in carrying on Greek science or sanity. But note that to conquer those kingdoms Rome herself had to learn Greek, to become Hellenized. And note, too, that it was Hellenized Byzantium that kept the Moslems off Europe's back until Europe could grow strong enough to stop them herself. Note also that Paul's Epistle to the Galatians was addressed to Aryan Celts or *Gauls*, who by 280 B.C. had invaded Greece and passed on into Asia Minor.

The chief thing to note is the kingdom Ptolemæus set up in Egypt with its capital at Alexandria. That city now became the Boston of the cultured world, the New York of the business world; and for three centuries was the centre of Greek civilization, the capital of the new Hellenistic Age. The Orient had to do business with Greek merchants; they had to learn Greek. So it was that Attic Greek, the tongue of Pericles, became the language of business, commerce, and education. Even the Hebrew Bible had to be put into Greek so that educated Jews could read it. Through and from Alexandria were disseminated science, art, literature, education, books, philosophy, religion, and architecture.

Alexandria is Alexander's own city. He chose the site wisely and then told his great architect, Deinocrates, to go ahead. He did not live to see it develop into what must have been for its time the best planned city in the world. Ptolemy I Soter (322-285 B.C.) and his immediate successors were wise and upright kings. The city, with its right-angled streets, regular blocks, underground sewage system, metal water-pipes (eleven were found under a pavement at one street crossing), its museums and libraries, steadily grew in size and power and was at its zenith in 48 B.C., when Cæsar stepped in to settle a quarrel between Ptolemy XIV and his sister. Even then Alexandria might have survived and gone on civilizing the world had that sister not been a girl named Cleopatra—she who upset the godlike Julius and drove Mark Antony mad.

Alexandria had a population of half a million and was a regular city in every sense of the word. Its great harbour was marked by a lighthouse 375 feet high—as high as a thirty-story skyscraper. It stood on Pharos Island; and gave its name "pharos" to "lighthouse" in Romance languages and its model to early church spires and minarets. It was one of the wonders of the world, and for sixteen hundred years remained the world's greatest lighthouse. Among Alexandria's other modern improvements Breasted mentions automatic door-openers; washing-machines—delivering water and mineral soap as needed; press for olive oil; automatic dispensers of holy water outside temples; fire sprinklers; levers, cranks, screws, cog-wheels, cables, water-wheels, endless-chain apparatus; missile-hurling war machines; running water in houses; shadow-clocks invented by Egyptians; and Greek water-clocks.

Ionian leavening was working—in Archimedes, for example. He lifted a three-masted ship by merely turning a crank. He in all the world first realized the enormous lifting power of a lever. His "give me a place to stand on and I will move the earth" sounds so modern that it is hard to realize it was said over two thousand years ago.

Now, the significant thing is not Archimedes and his ship-lifting endless screw and earth-lifting lever, but the fact that Alexandria was the kind of city which could use cranks. This Ptolemaic government was no French Republic so carried away by a Liberté-Egalité-Fraternité formula that it had no common sense left. It did not kill a man just because he was a scientist; it had use for scientists.

It founded a museum, not for fossils, dead or alive, but for the training of scientists. It was a national research academy—a combination Smithsonian Institution, Massachusetts Institute of Technology, and Royal Academy. It was government-founded and government-supported. It had refectory, gymnasium, reading-rooms; an observatory, a zoölogical garden, and an anatomical institute where vivisection was practised on condemned criminals. It furnished board and lodging for scholars in residence and for the scientific staff, which was appointed by the king and, everything considered, better paid and more highly honoured than are most modern staffs. They were not supposed to spend half their time worrying about mundane matters; they could devote their energies to scientific pursuits.

We shall look later at some of the results of this amazingly modern research institute, but here we may have a sample. Aristarchus demonstrated that earth and planets revolved around the sun, and computed the diameter of the earth correctly within fifty miles. Aristarchus—not Galileo; in 275 B.C., not 1625 A.D. Religion was not then enthroned.

The museum also had a library, which grew from 400,000 volumes under Ptolemy II to 900,000 volumes by the time Cæsar arrived. On its staff were excellent philologists, who edited standard texts of Homer and other Greek classics, and in 120 B.C. the first Greek grammar. The librarian said a big book was a big nuisance: to read one was like reading a roll of film; so he cut the long rolls into "books." Thus started the *books* of our Homer and other classics.

Cleopatra made a lot of trouble—but no Needles. As I said before, our Central Park "Cleopatra's Needle" is one of the obelisks King Thutmose III erected in front of his temple to the sun-god: they are sun symbols. It was taken to Alexandria in 23 B.C. and set up in front of the Cæsareum. Our interest here, however, is in the Cæsareum and not in the Needles. Why was it in Egypt? Because the Cæsars had grown bigger and the Ptolemies smaller.

Ptolemy XIII was succeeded by two of his children under the care of the Roman Senate, which appointed Pompey as their guardian. One of the children was Ptolemy XIV; he "banished" the other child, young Cleopatra, and had Pompey murdered. Enter Julius Cæsar as guardian. He took the girl's part, naturally, and defeated young Ptolemy XIV, who fell in the Nile and was drowned. Cæsar, despite his infatuation for Cleopatra, returned to Rome and became dictator. He appointed Ptolemy XV, a boy of eleven, co-regent with his sister Cleopatra. All this has carried us from 51 to 47 B.C. Two years later Cleopatra had young Ptolemy XV assassinated, whereupon Cæsar appointed their own son co-regent with Cleopatra. That co-regent was Ptolemy XVI Cæsar, also called Cæsarion. And the following year Julius Cæsar was murdered.

Enter Antony, 41 B.C. He did not go to Egypt to aid Cleopatra, as Cæsar had done, but to punish her for allowing her general to aid his enemies, Brutus and Cassius. He forgot his errand and lived riotously with Cleopatra so long that the Roman Senate outlawed him.

Enter young Octavius, grandnephew and adopted son of Cæsar. He defeated Antony at the battle of Actium (31 B.C.). Antony committed suicide when he heard that Cleopatra was dead. She wasn't, but rather than grace Octavius' triumphal chariot to make a Roman holiday, she, too, committed suicide—by poison, probably not snake. Thereupon Octavius made Egypt a Roman province and sailed away to Rome, where he celebrated three triumphs on the same day—closing the temple of Janus for the third time in Roman history. A few days later he changed his name to Cæsar Octavianus, to which title the Roman Senate four years later added the word Augustus.

*Exeunt omnes.*

Enter the Roman Empire.

Rome, the Eternal City. All roads lead to Rome. Even today it is one of the wonders of the world. What must it have been in the imperial heyday of the Antonines! Let us see. It is worth looking at. To understand Rome is a big step toward understanding modern civilization, for in a sense we are the successors of the Roman Empire. Their god was Power; ours is Success. Money was the emblem of Power; it is the sign of Success.

An Athenian would feel at home in the White House, the Century Club, or on Broadway; an Ionian or Alexandrian Greek would feel comfortable in a modern observatory, a research laboratory, or a graduate seminar; a Roman would feel equally at home in the United States Senate, Tammany Hall, or on the directorate of a Wall Street banking-house. Rome could and did rule. By sheer genius in military and civil engineering she rose to preëminence in power, dominion, and influence, but her actual contribution to the civilization we now enjoy was less than that of the aborigines of the American continent.

She gave Europe emperors and popes, one ruling in the name of God, the other speaking for God. *Pax Romana* sounds well, as does the Roman Catholic Church, but under Roman rule human rights disappeared, social values were rolled in the dust. There could be no honest privacy, no free speech, no free thought. The secret service and the confessional, gladiatorial shows and the Holy Inquisition, were the logical instruments for enforcing obedience to codified, canonized law. Tribute and obedience were the price of life. The nature of our inheritance from Rome may be fittingly symbolized by the extent to which that inheritance was nullified by the work of Lincoln and Darwin.

We have seen how Crete was wet-nurse to the civilization Greece fell heir to; we have seen Greece colonize Sicily, the shores of Lower Italy, and the Riviera; and we have seen the Cæsars in the Greek city of Alexandria. We have now to see how Rome rose up out of a Hellenized world and became the world's champion civilizer, and especially what civilization looked like when it had become Romanized.

Recall the 2000 B.C. Swiss Lake Dwellers. They were not all *Swiss*; some of them were Italian. On the debris of one lake village Venice was built and so stands today. When those Lake Dwellers reached the River Po, they got copper (or *cuprus*, as our chemists call it) from Cyprus; also a mixture of copper and tin from Brondesium, and so we call it bronze. Why they did not go farther south and get the three R's is unknown; possibly because the Etruscans blocked the way.

Who the Etruscans were or where they came from is unknown. They probably came from Asia Minor; they may have been Lydians or Anatolians (Hittites); possibly cousins of the Minoans of Crete. It is inferred that the Etruscans raided the Po delta as early as the thirteenth century B.C. By the tenth century B.C. they controlled the Italian coast from Naples to Genoa. By 750 B.C. they had crossed the Tiber, driven out the last Latin chief, and founded a city kingdom at Rome.

Note the strategic position of Rome: its hills commanding the last ford of the Tiber, and, in a way, Italy herself. Memphis, Babylon, Troy, Constantinople, London, Hamburg, all enjoyed strategic advantages. Rome was on a natural highway; it commanded the weakest spot in that highway.

Rome was Etruscan until about 500 B.C., when, judging from its walls, it was the greatest city in Italy, larger than the Athens of Pericles. With the destruction of their fleet in 474 B.C. by the Greeks of Syracuse, the Etruscans begin to pass from history; but they were civilized and left their mark on Italy, on the Latins.

Rome, therefore, is a mere upstart. Even in little Crete civilization had come and gone a thousand years before Rome began to be Rome. From the Etruscans the Romans got their start in tribal organization, religion, and architecture—and especially the arch, already hoary with age.

During those early centuries the Latins were also directly influenced by the Greek traders who were swarming all over the Mediterranean. From them they learned their letters, among other things; and had they not made certain changes in the alphabet, we should not now have to learn a new alphabet to read Greek. They also learned certain arts from the Phœnicians, and got from them a garment the Greeks called *kiton*, which they called *ktun*, and we call *tunic*.

Early Roman history begins in myth. The Romulus and Remus story, with their wolf foster-mother, is no more history than the Wichita story of Creation. There were Etruscan kings in Rome; there may have been Latin kings in Rome. There was a republic; there were consuls—as we know from a Greek historian—and they were attended by twelve lictors who bore bundles of rods called *fasces*. The rod-bearers are now called *Fascisti*.

Those primitive Romans, like the early Greeks, were small tribes, jealous of one another and always scrapping; but while the Greeks were sea-rovers, traders, pirates, the Romans (*Latins*) were stubborn, hard-headed, tight-fisted, abstemious peasant farmers. They traded and fought like South African Boers. Their later "patrician aristocracy" was based on nothing more than having been the first into town—like Chicago's aristocracy, who rode in on ox-drawn wagons in the pre-railroad days. They had no early idea of Progress or of Big Business, nor intention of world-conquest. Even in 390 B.C., when Juno's geese cackled on Capitol Hill, thereby saving the fortress from surprise, the Romans could not prevent the Gauls from sacking and burning their city. By 338 B.C., however, Rome was easily leader of the Latin tribes, and with her victory over the Samnites in the battle of Sentinum (295 B.C.) she was mistress of central Italy, had learned how to fight, and to love it. Rome was on her way. There was handwriting on the wall if anyone cared to read it.

Carthage—now a Greek city in culture—misread it and issued a challenge; and when the treaty of peace was finally signed (201 B.C.) after the Second Punic (Phœnician) War, Rome was the world's leading power—with Carthage in her debt for $11,000,000 a year for fifty years. That victory, you will recall, spelled defeat for the west wing of the Semite-Indo-European conflict. On which issue, says Breasted, "depended the character of civilization down to the present day."

Well, our side won; we beat the Semites. Then there was the war indemnity. Rome could win more victories now. The paradox is, as has been pointed out, that it was fate that called the turn. After the First Punic War, Rome decided on a "no more annexations" policy. After the Third Punic War came Scipio's Monroe Doctrine of "no expansion beyond the Italian Peninsula." Hadrian denounced Trajan's conquests—but when in all history did a nation turn a conquest loose? We too denounce, deplore—and find excuse enough to rule our empire-in-the-making.

The Carthaginians had already been driven from Spain, which now became, and remained for six centuries, a Roman colony. Rome also had become master of Sicily, capturing and plundering Syracuse in spite of its brave resistance and the engineering science of our old friend Archimedes. Rome then (200 B.C.) began to find excuses to reënter Macedonia; and its conqueror returned to Rome with such immense spoils (including 250 wagon-loads of Greek statues and paintings) that Roman citizens could stop paying taxes. Rome could now be said to be a *great* civilized power. Macedonia as a kingdom was no more. Seventy towns of Epirus were plundered and destroyed; 150,000 of their citizens sold as slaves.

Then came the Third Punic War (149-146 B.C.), with the elder Cato's *Delenda est Carthago*. Well, Carthage certainly was deleted, for after burning for seventeen days its remaining inhabitants were sold into slavery.

With the fourth Macedonian war (148-142 B.C.) Macedonia became a Roman province; Corinth fell without a blow—unless, indeed, Rome's sending Corinth's art treasures to Italy and selling her citizens into slavery could be called a blow.

The destruction of Carthage and Corinth was certainly a death blow to the Greek civilization of the world; and it was to deal the death blow to the Republic of Rome—and even to the gods in heaven. God was to become Cæsar. His court of saints and angels was to become the Imperial court, and the republican opposition was to be devils and imps.

Civil wars followed; reigns of terror; a slave insurrection in Sicily—Sicilian *Camorristi* and the *Mano Negra* are rooted in ancient times. The Gracchi appeared and disappeared. Jugurthine wars—Marius and Sulla.

In 100 B.C. Cæsar was a newborn babe. Within fifty years he had divided all Gaul into its three parts, and "came, saw, conquered" all of them; also Britain. We have seen Cæsar on the Nile; also Pompey. We have not seen Pompey extracting $12,000,000 worth of gold and silver treasure from the Jews' temple in Jerusalem. Sinews of war. Little wonder that *reason* was to drop from man's vocabulary; that faith was to reign in its stead; and that people everywhere in that Roman world were to hunger for prophets to do their thinking for them.

VII

With the death of Cleopatra, the three-centuries-old Alexandrian Greek dynasty of the Ptolemies ended.

Rome was really big now, big enough to wear a crown; but who was to wear it? Cæsar (48 B.C.) met Pompey at Pharsalia in Greece; Octavius (31 B.C.) met Antony at Actium off Egypt. Cæsar made a crown possible; Octavius proved he was august enough to wear it. We saw the Age of Pericles; we face the Age of Augustus: two centuries of peace—of a kind. Our old Mediterranean Hellenic world has become the Mediterranean nation, with Rome as its capital. *Pax Romana* not only ruled the waves, but the banks of the Thames, the Rhine, and the Danube. But those savages of the north were growing strong on raw meat; they could not for ever be denied their place in the sun.

Wars Europe had in plenty, but culture, civilization, fared badly. Not a single Cæsar was to measure up to Ptolemy Philadelphus the Greek; nor did one emperor of the Holy Roman Empire do anything for his subjects more worthy of respect than had been done by an Egyptian king three thousand years before. Wars do not beget, provoke, or produce civilization; they never did; they never will.

But let us get on. Let us look at this Age of Augustus, its big facts, its big ideas.

The first great fact was Rome itself. It was promptly reconstructed; police organized; fire and water departments established. The Cæsar built himself a royal house on Palatine Hill—and we have called kings' houses "palaces" ever since. Rome was very rich. Lucullus and Pompey had brought enormous riches from the East. In conquering, Rome had plundered the world, enslaved its people.

Never before and rarely since was there such a mania for wealth, such a fever to get rich quick. Machinery existed for getting rich; moral values to regulate the acquisition of power did not exist.

Between Rome and Nineveh climbing to power there was the difference between tweedledum and tweedledee; Rome was perhaps less murderous. But the difference between having one's throat slit on the spot and being fed to the lions after being dragged by a chariot in an emperor's triumphal procession, is nothing to cheer one up.

When Rome had conquered the world, she established peace. Of course; she wanted peace, and for the same reason that a farmer wants peace in his dairy barn. Rome milked the world, and not for the good of the cows but because she liked milk. She had to keep the cows at peace and build roads and viaducts to get to them and to bring the plunder home.

And all the time and everywhere she was fighting for "hearth and home." That is what every imperialist says. But old Tiberius Gracchus had called the turn on Roman generals fighting for any such reason: "They lie; not one of them possesses a hearth or a home, or even a family grave. That others may enjoy riches and pleasure, that is what they are fighting for, those Romans who are called 'masters of the world,' while they have not so much as a sod of earth that they can call their own." Tiberius Gracchus knew his generals; he had lived with them.

Rome became mighty—on ideas borrowed from Alexandria, architecture borrowed from Greece, statuary plundered from Greece. Not only in material things did Rome plunder Greece, but in politics, economics, philosophy, art, literature. Almost without exception, her great intellectuals were plagiarists. Of original work in philosophy, astronomy, mathematics, or medicine, there was none; nor one single inventor. She was a great builder—great amphitheatres, public baths, basilicas, bridges, aqueducts, triumphal arches; but she built with neither her own money, her own ideas, nor her own hands.

Italy soon became a series of vast estates worked by slave labor. Proconsuls drained the provinces without mercy; Verres, according to Cicero, in three years in Sicily reduced 773 landed proprietors to 318. Six landlords under the Cæsars owned half the province of

Africa. One estate alone could control literally hundreds of thousands of slaves. When slaves grew dear—as they must when the supply is not constantly renewed—a servile class was brought in to take their place: the agricultural serfs, or *coloni*. That an infamous caste system should develop in Rome was a foregone conclusion. Other conclusions were also inevitable.

Rome's fall, for example.

Rome was essentially false at heart. Military power means exploitation of every social service. Cæsar "wins" an election by purchasing 320,000 votes; gives a gladiatorial show at a cost of $40,000; pays $25,000 to one actor for one performance. Brutus lends the city of Salamis money at the rate of forty-eight per cent interest. A banking-house in Cæsar's time lends money to an exiled Ptolemy at the rate of one hundred per cent, and when the money cannot be collected, Cæsar so arranges African war contracts that the bankers recoup their losses. Slavery, usury, and shameless, brutal exploitation of the conquered provinces underlay Rome's dazzling splendour. If Cæsar as First Consul could steal three thousand pounds of gold from the Capitol, replacing it with gilded copper, we can easily guess what later Cæsars might do.

The probabilities are that the Roman emperors never were so black as the early ascetic fathers of the Church painted them. White thinks it likely that not more than one out of every twenty martyrdoms ever took place; the other nineteen were due to the morbid imaginations of mediæval monks in monasteries. To make a good martyr story, the torturer's callous brutality as well as the innocent victim's submissive meekness has to be exaggerated. Rome was black enough, but she was also great. With Nero as the focal spot, Rome looks very black.

Now note. Nero was driven from the throne by Galba, who became the victim of the revolt of Otho, who was overthrown by Vitellius, who was overthrown by Vespasian—in less than a year. Looks black; but it is exceptional. *Pax Romana* did rule for two hundred years—Tucker thinks as in no other period in the world's history.

Let us take a quick run through these two hundred years. Nero had a great fire. Vespasian crushed the rebel Jews in Palestine, and his son Titus destroyed Jerusalem. Trajan bridged the Danube, adding Dacia (Rumania) to the empire; he also added the 350-year-old Parthian kingdom of Armenia, Mesopotamia, and Assyria. With Hadrian (117-138) the Roman Empire became as great as Egypt's Ancient Empire had been thirty centuries before. With Marcus Aurelius, the finest of the line, a noble line ended. And *Pax Romana* ended as the Germans entered in 167 A.D.

That peace covered what is now Holland, Belgium, France, Spain, Portugal, Switzerland, Italy, Hungary, much of Austria, Rumania, Greece, Turkey, Asia Minor, Mesopotamia, Syria, Palestine, Egypt, Tripoli, Tunis, Algeria, Morocco, and the lower two-thirds of England. One could travel from Jerusalem to Rome, or from Rome to Cologne or Lisbon, without fear and with less danger than one can cross Halsted Street or Times Square. Roughly, 100,-000,000 population.

Travelling the queen of roads—the Appian Way—one would meet, says Tucker, merchants with slaves carrying bales; pedlars (probably Jews) with their packs; actors; tumblers; gladiators; a philosopher; a regiment of foot soldiers or cavalry; mounted dispatch-bearers; gigs; wagonettes; gorgeous coaches with outriders; litters; possibly Nero, with a thousand carriages; and possibly Poppæa herself, with her five hundred asses to provide the milk for her bath.

At Ostia, port of Rome at the mouth of the Tiber, one might see Claudius' three-masted 1,100-ton ship, and with far better passenger accommodation than that of the *Mayflower*. It is on record that one ship brought twelve hundred passengers from Alexandria. The boat Paul was wrecked on carried 276. From a Red Sea port 120 ships a year sailed for India to bring back the luxuries Rome easily absorbed.

A garrison or city guard of 6,000 men in barracks protected Rome within the walls; and in addition a gendarmerie of 7,000 men served as night watch and fire brigade. Outside the gates was the Imperial Guard of twelve regiments of 1,000 men each. There were smaller garrisons all over the empire, especially at Lyons, Antioch, and Alexandria.

That Spain, Portugal, France, and Rumania still speak Latin is a tribute to Rome's military and civil conquest. Augusta, Aosta, Augsburg, Autun, and Augst are reminders that Augustus was an

empire-builder. Amiens then was Ambiani; Rheims, Remi; and
Paris and Trèves were administrative centres of the Parisii and
Treveri tribes.

When Paul told the Ephesian Christians to put on the belt of
truth, the breastplate of righteousness, the shield of faith, the helmet
of salvation, and the sword of the spirit—"the whole armour of
God"—he named the equipment of a Roman legionnaire. A Roman
legion was our brigade: 6,000 infantry, 120 horse. The soldiers,
free-born and of good record, enlisted for twenty years, and were
then honourably discharged with a sum of money and a grant of
land. Legions were numbered and some had names, such as the
"Lark," the "Victorious," the "Indomitable." A company or regiment in disgrace, or insubordinate, was "*dec*imated," every tenth
man condemned to death being determined by lot. The Imperial
Guards were especially picked men. They wore gorgeous armour,
enjoyed special privileges, and served sixteen years with double the
regulars' pay. With Rome's vast frontiers she had to defend a longer
line than did the Allies in the Great War. To take care of her defence problem she maintained frontier posts not unlike ours when
we had frontiers. That frontier was garrisoned by 300,000 men.

The crossing of the Rhine in 406 by the northern barbarians
meant that the empire's defences had crumbled. Their frontier
legions had been annihilated in less than a generation; the nearly
thousand-year-old commonwealth was gone for ever.

Technically speaking, the emperor was not a sovereign nor Rome
an empire. It was a nominal commonwealth; the emperor its "first
man." The title of emperor had begun with Julius Cæsar, when in
48 B.C. he was given the new title of *Imperator*—which meant possession of the *imperium*, insignia of commander-in-chief or military
commander. So it was that on the anniversary of his accession on
January 1st, the army swore loyal obedience to him. His effigy was
on every regimental standard, in the centre of every camp. Roman
citizens, through the Senate, could depose him, but it could not get
rid of him without the army's consent.

The Patrician (or "ox-team") families controlled Rome up to
366 B.C.; the Plebeians, up to 69 A.D. Then Rome was controlled by
the Colonials until 381, when the Christian emperor, Constantine,
by edict divided the world into Christian and pagan. Otho, who

followed Galba the Patrician, was of a distinguished Etruscan family. Vespasian, first of the three Flavian emperors, was not born in Rome, nor was he of "royal" descent; he was of Sabine origin, and the first Colonial ruler. He was proclaimed emperor by the army in Alexandria. He and his son Titus were capable rulers, but were without the qualities which made the first two emperors, Augustus and Tiberius, so notably successful. Caligula, the third Cæsar and last of the Julian *gens*, was a cruel, crazy paranoiac. Claudius, of the Claudian *gens* and next in line, while not a complete failure, was weak-minded, and so henpecked by that notorious hussy Messalina that he very properly had her murdered. Nero—of whom more anon—was next. Then came the Black Year (69)—three Flavians.

Trajan, admirable ruler and excellent general, was not even an Italian, but was born in the Roman colony of Italica, near Seville, Spain. He was followed by another Spaniard and an even greater ruler and builder, Hadrian, whose mole beneath the modern castle of St. Angelo in Rome, and villa at Tivoli near by, are favorite tourist haunts today. He was followed by the peaceable Antoninus. Then came the highbrow meditator and Stoic philosopher, Marcus Aurelius (161-180). His *Meditations* still appear among the Gift Books, and his equestrian statue still adorns Capitol Hill.

The army now rather definitely took charge and for nearly a century appointed the emperors. Caracalla built enormous baths— to be imitated architecturally about seventeen centuries later by Washington and New York railroad stations. He murdered his half-brother and other thousands, and of course was murdered. With Diocletian (284-305) and his huge baths and general persecution of Christians we may stop, and look Rome over against this brief historic background.

We must not forget that the Roman Empire covered vast territory, and that its people included almost all then known colours, tongues, cultures, and religions. It is not to be wondered at if some of its rulers were vain, some mad, and some cruel. Not all popes were saints, nor are all presidents statesmen; nor have all tsars and kaisers been conspicuously successful rulers or notably creditable specimens of humanity. Few emperors were so cruel and vindictive as Richard I; nor could Nero match Edward I, who disembowelled

Wallace and hung him up to die in agony, hanged 280 Jews in the
streets of London, plundered sixteen thousand more, and drove
them out penniless. All things considered, Rome averaged up
pretty well.

Even Nero meant well and began well. He did not plunder Rome
because he was a plunderer, but because he was in debt; plunder
was a recognized method of collecting funds—a legitimate "racket."
Nor did he light up his garden with burning Christians because no
Japanese lanterns were available, but because he thought that anybody who hated the whole human race as madly as the Christians
did should be burned. Besides, it was a way of showing his love for
his friends who had been offended by Christians.

We saw Nero win a prize in the Olympian games: it was the ten-
horse chariot race. That is the kind of fool he was. Above all, he
was "arty." He competed with the champion minstrels; he "suped"
in the chorus. He sang, and played the harp, the flute, and the bag-
pipes. He danced. He dabbled in oils and clay. He "rolled the
bones"—for twenty dollars a pip. He imported $150,000 worth of
roses from Alexandria for one bouquet. It was a cruel fate that
made him emperor. He would have made a perfect rich man's
son. Given a floor of a Park Avenue apartment house and a studio
penthouse in the Village, he would as easily "burn up" New York
as he did Rome.

Nero Claudius Cæsar Augustus Germanicus (or, as they would
have called him on the Hill, His Highness Claudius Nero, Premier,
Commander-in-chief of the Forces, empowered to act as Tribune
of the People, and head of the State Religion) was rich in titles, but
he was cradled in crime. Look. His predecessor, Claudius, married
Messalina and killed her but not their son. He then married the
ambitious widow Agrippina, who had a son of her own, our little
Nero. She persuaded Claudius to pass over his own son and legal
heir, and adopt her Nero as heir to the throne; then, lest Claudius
change his mind, she poisoned him. Nero got his throne because
his mother married and killed an emperor, his stepfather.

That was a good start and Nero travelled fast. At the age of
sixteen he married Octavia, daughter of Messalina and Claudius,
his murdered stepfather. He then fell in love with a freed woman,
and then with the well-known Poppæa Sabina. He quarrelled with

his mother, who in a rage threatened to make emperor his brother-in-law Britannicus, brother of Octavia and son of the poisoned Claudius. So Nero, who had profited by his schooling, poisoned Britannicus, the rightful ruler; had his mother done to death; drove his wife off and had her executed; and married Poppæa.

But I do injustice to Locusta, the most celebrated poisoner of her time, forerunner of the celebrated poisoners of Christian Rome. She was a professional and there was no secret about her profession; she was for hire—a recognized instrument of crime. Agrippina hired her to poison Claudius; Nero, to poison Britannicus—and paid her a big price. Tradition says he struck her a sharp blow for not using her grade "A" sudden-death poison; and granted her official immunity for her art and settled a domain on her. She had her disciples, pupils. With Galba's house-cleaning of Nero's evil-doers, she was executed.

Seneca eulogized poverty; and at death by Nero's order, left a fortune of fifteen million dollars. Seneca was a real Stoic, but he was also Nero's tutor and the ghost-writer of his speeches and the funeral eulogy of the poisoned murderer, Claudius. According to the Roman historian, Dio Cassius, the revolt of the Britons was due to the brutal means taken to collect two million dollars they had borrowed from Seneca at exorbitant interest. I do not mean to suggest that Seneca, the philosopher, could have made a decent man of Nero; only that he did not practise what he preached and was accessory before a rare collection of most infamous goings-on. And that was the man who had moral scruples against taking part in politics!

"Hast thou appealed unto Cæsar? unto Cæsar shalt thou go." Paul was right to appeal to Cæsar; there were broader-minded men in the capital than in Judea. Caligula going to Gaul with a huge army and coming home with a pocketful of clam-shells, or spending over a million dollars in ten months, was an exception. So was Nero. The Prætorian Guard murdered Caligula. Nero committed suicide.

Nero's persecutions were in no way typical of the government's attitude toward aliens. Probably not a religion within the borders of the Roman world was without its priests and adherents in the Rome of Nero and Paul. There were indescribable sensual vices in that

Rome—as there are today in Paris, London, Berlin, New York, and Chicago. Nero plundered the provinces; and when they could not be plundered fast enough to meet his mounting debts, he began to plunder Rome. There was a tremendous outcry against both Caligula and Nero—from Romans, from Senators. If Nero was cruel to Christians, he was cruel to Romans. Brought up in the moral atmosphere of a Hell's Kitchen gang warfare, he was quite normal —setting a pace for Pope Alexander VI and other Borgias who were to appear when civilization was old enough to rediscover America.

Vice wedded to vanity, enthroned, or endowed by a rich father, spells folly, oppression, tyranny, crime. Look at Nero. Look at Lollia Paulina, "covered with emeralds, and pearls gleaming all over her head, hair, ears, neck, and fingers, to the value of $1,500,-000." Civilization has managed to get rid of its Neros; it still loves its Lollias. Of such virtuous and noble matrons as Cornelia, Valeria, and Volumnia, Rome probably had as big a share as most modern capitals.

Lollia, by the way, inherited her vast fortune from her grandfather—an infamous money-grubber and plunderer of provinces, despite the coat of whitewash Horace gives him. She was forced to divorce her husband and marry Caligula, who soon tired of her. As she had been an unsuccessful candidate for the place Claudius had made vacant when he murdered his wife, and which had been filled by Agrippina, her end can be easily guessed—and easily verified by Roman history. Agrippina, taking time by the forelock as was her wont, had Claudius banish her from Rome and then send a tribune to murder her. After all, there was no more reason why she should not have inherited tainted money than Nero a tainted throne; it was the custom of the country.

Paul, accused and facing trial, could demand as a Roman citizen that he be sent to Rome—though how he or his Jew father or grandfather became a Roman citizen is unknown. Jews were "foreigners" in Rome, but in their own province they might acquire Roman citizenship.

Above the Romans—people, commons, or third estate—were some ten thousand Knights or upper middle class, notorious plunderers; their minimum property qualification was fifteen thousand dollars. The top crust of the imperial system was the Senators, with a minimum qualification of forty thousand dollars. Some were worth twenty million dollars. Incomes of nearly a million dollars a year were not unknown. However "noble" a Senator of the days of the Republic may have been, the Senate of the Empire was a servile rubber stamp for the army-made emperor. Success was reaping its reward.

Let us look at some of the material manifestations of success, at monumental Rome of the days of the great Empire.

## VIII

When Cæsar wanted to reform the calendar, he had to import Greek mathematicians and astronomers from Alexandria. When Caligula wanted to become a god and so escape the assassins, he turned to Egypt for his plan; and after the Senate had duly declared him god and he had appointed prominent Senators priests, he took his place on the porch of the temple of Castor and Pollux and between the two images was sacrificed to with peacocks, pheasants, and flamingoes. His image in gold was set up in the provinces—even in the Holy of Holies in Yahweh's temple in Jerusalem. He even borrowed the old Egyptian idea of marrying his sister to keep the stock "pure."

But when the Romans wanted to build a good road or a masterpiece aqueduct, or drain a swamp or dig a mine, they could go ahead with Roman hands and improve on anything theretofore accomplished. In fact, in material processes and material achievements they got so far ahead of the world that it is just catching up.

Some of those great material achievements—practically all in ruins—can still be seen. Ruins, not because badly built, but because of earthquakes, Vandals, and the far more destructive pagan-smashing Christians. Rome itself was sacked by Alaric the Goth, Genseric the Vandal, and by the Germans—all within sixty-two years. But the real vandals were the ignorant, savage Christians from the north. Christian vandals swept across Roman Africa as an appallingly destructive force. What they could not smash they whitewashed—for, as White says, they could not worship in the presence of beauty. For a thousand years it was a Christian virtue to quarry in pagan buildings and wipe them out of existence. Bigoted clergy preached that it was a Christian duty to "burn, pollute, gut, deface, dismantle, wreck, and annihilate all pagan temples and their contents."

We know Imperial Rome's greatness only from what we can learn from the relics that escaped the savage onslaughts of the bigoted Christian mobs. Pious Christians, for example, thought a bath an abomination. We know Roman bathtubs from the specimens Vesuvius covered with ashes. We do not know the bathtubs the Mohammedans in Spain used, because there was no Vesuvius to bury them and there were Christian Ferdinand and Isabella to have them all smashed by royal edict.

Imperial Rome had already fallen, but after 381 the Christians made it their special business to see that its customs, products, idols, temples, statues, buildings, and books were burnt, smashed, or buried. They saw their duty; they did it like the men they were. In trying to look at Roman civilization we see, I repeat, the remains. From these remains we must reconstruct all that may be seen of Roman material culture, Roman art and literature. We think we have some Roman classics; we have some scraps.

Rome herself was a robber; but she robbed to keep, not to smash. Napoleon had the same true Roman spirit. He did not smash: he had things boxed up and sent to Paris—the bronze quadriga, for example, which was returned when Napoleon was exiled and which today leaps at you from St. Mark's in Venice. That is the only bronze quadriga that has come down from Imperial Rome. There were thousands of triumphal arches, most of them crowned with quadrigas; only a few arches remain, just that one quadriga. In one Etruscan town captured by Rome in 265 B.C. there were two thousand life-sized bronze statues. There were hundreds of thousands of such statues in Rome. How many remain? Trajan's magnificent bronze column stands—but only because it served as pedestal for a Christian saint. Rome's archives, *annals*, were kept on bronze plates and stored in vaults; there were millions of them. According to White, tens of thousands of tons of plates were melted down, to be coined or used for other commercial purposes.

Nearly every city in the Hellenic world, in addition to its temples, had *palæstræ*, or wrestling schools, for boys; also gymnasiums for men—colonnaded courts for wrestling, boxing, discus-throwing, jumping, pitching quoits, running; and tennis, racquets, handball, and squash courts. There were dressing-rooms and cold and warm baths. Such structures, built to last, were to be found wherever Greek influence was felt. Rome came along and added bridges, baths, temples, and theatres—all built for all time. Some of those structures, including bridges, might have lasted ten thousand years. Had the empire been taken over by a line of Hammurabis or Sargons, we might still have its 350,000 miles of roads, its tens of thousands of beautiful stone bridges, its thousand amphitheatres with their mosaics, reliefs, and hundreds of thousands of marble statues.

It was not Rome alone that was a real city, nor Rome alone that made the Empire great. Great was Diana of the Ephesians, for example; possibly greatest in the ancient world. This temple of Artemis (*not* Diana) was 425 by 220 feet, and had 127 columns sixty feet high. The Colossus of Rhodes was great; Rhodes itself a fine, rich, handsome city, with three thousand statues.

Hadrian's Empire had twenty thousand walled towns with modern and ancient improvements—sewers, aqueducts, baths, paved streets, open squares, basilicas, porticoes, temples, a hippodrome for chariot races, a theatre for drama; in the western part of the Empire an amphitheatre for gladiatorial and wild-beast shows; and in the eastern part an odeon for recitations and musical performances. Also excellent harbours with breakwaters and man-made inner harbours with fine stone docks. Of cities of more than 100,000 there were more than twenty, of which Rome, Alexandria, Antioch, Carthage, Capua, Aquileia, and Trèves were chief. Every city had its baths and aqueducts. Rome's baths are still stupendous; they must have been dazzlingly gorgeous. Rome had ten fine open squares, twenty great basilicas, and over sixty great colonnaded porticoes.

Hadrian's Rome was said to have had 400,000 life-sized statues in bronze or marble; 40,000 groups of life-sized statuary; 4,000 statues of superhuman size; 400 equestrian statues; 40 quadrigas; and four *colossi*. The man who counted them seems to run to fours. But not one of these statues presumably could compare as a work of art with the colossal gold-and-ivory Athene of Phidias in the Parthenon—of which not even a splinter remains. Possibly less of the Parthenon itself would have been left to serve as a powder magazine for the Turks if the fifth-century Christians had not con-

verted it into a church dedicated to the Mother of God. But even
Phidias' Athene seems to have been less marvellous than his forty-
feet-high chryselephantine statue of Zeus at Olympia, with its hair
and garments in gold, for that was the crowning masterpiece of the
Græco-Roman world of art.

Hadrian's tomb, or mole, as also that of Augustus, was not only
of huge size but of great artistic beauty—though neither, presumably, was as fine as the mausoleum at Halicarnassus; and that as a
work of art probably surpassed the Taj Mahal of Agra (which, by
the way, Lord Lytton, Viceroy of India, recommended turning into
lime to build barracks). And, speaking of Huns and Vandals, you
may have noticed that most of the sculptured figures on tombs in
parts of Spain and Portugal have no heads. What parts? Parts visited by the French armies in the Peninsular War.

The Persians passed through Egypt like vandals; but before
Theodosius the Christian began his clean-up of pagan gods, there
were hundreds of temples in Egypt as perfect as when built. White
estimates that at that time there were also twenty thousand Greek
temples in good repair—as against not one today.

Of the paintings of the Græco-Roman world we have only late,
mediocre Pompeiian copies and imitations. Pompeii was but a
seaside resort, though not so terrible as Brighton, England, nor
nearly so terrible as Atlantic City. But there were great painters in
those days, probably the greatest fresco painters the world has seen
or had seen since Knossos. Marvellous panel pictures by Zeuxis and
Apelles are known to have been extant up to 400 A.D. and were
comparable to the best of Titian or Raphael. Burnt-out, ash-covered,
seaside-resort Pompeii gives us only an inkling of the taste in furniture and all that goes with a cultured home, that went with the
Empire. Towns had their museums of such curios as grace the
Musée Cluny in Paris—an ancient monastery, by the way, built
into and upon the ruins of a great Roman bath. Of museums of
jewellery alone, Rome had five.

From the material, let us turn to the intellectual side of Roman
civilization. What did they read?

"When you go hunting," wrote the elder Pliny to his nephew,
"take my advice and carry your writing-tablets as well as your
luncheon-basket and flask; you will find that Minerva roams the

hills no less than Diana." I do not know the date of that letter; it might have been written in Nero's reign, for Pliny died in 79, the year Vesuvius buried Herculaneum in lava and Pompeii in fire, ashes, and mud. But, except for the reference to the "flask," that letter might have been written yesterday by an old-fashioned natural-history professor to a young nephew just out of college and off on a hunting trip. "Minerva roams the hills." Minerva, the Roman Athene, was the symbol for brains, for all intellectual activities.

The intellectual activity of our age is probably not one whit greater than it was in the days of Imperial Rome. Interest in intellectual pursuits was possibly never more widespread than it was during the first and second centuries. In fact, there was almost no difference between what was called "education" in my college days and education as it was taught in the days of Pliny. True, Pliny did not have to learn Latin, for that was his mother-tongue; nor did he have to learn Greek, for that was the tongue of his nurse, and probably of the "pedagogue" who accompanied him to school. But he had to know his Homer, his Vergil, and his Terence. Education, in short, was the same old classical education which up to forty years ago was the only education fit to turn a farmer's boy into a gentleman. I suspect that as regards fitting one for living the life of one's time, Roman education laid a better foundation for Roman citizenship than my college did for American citizenship. The Roman was not getting much science, nor did I in that "classical" course, but he did not have to learn two dead languages as "mental discipline" before he could begin to read the Classics which were to make him intellectual.

It has been said that neither Attic Greece nor Imperial Rome produced a single practical invention or made an important industrial discovery. Well, they did not have to; they knew enough to carry on. They were practical and their slaves were industrious, and for their times the Ionian and Alexandrian Greeks were scientifically minded. But the world was not yet ready to discipline its thinking; centuries had to elapse before China's paper, printing-press, gunpowder, and compass were so to recreate the world that man was forced to think about new things. The great world-shaking fundamentals of civilization had been discovered a thousand or more years before there was a Cæsar or a Cicero, and were at work throughout the Græco-Roman world. The Romans did not have to create art, literature, or the drama; the Greeks had done it for them. They could be intellectual, just as any Yankee could a few years ago, by exhibiting familiarity with the classics. My "classics," of course, included certain English prose and poetical "masterpieces."

The Roman citizen had certain duties to perform—domestic, political, religious; he was taught to perform such functions as his duties as citizen would demand of him. In that sense his education was practical; in that sense mine, so far as the four years' classical curriculum went, was not.

We were told much of what was sacred, what was sin—but not a word about the possibility of an observed fact being sacred, or that it was a sin to believe everything we were told. We heard much of virtues—but of the virtue of being curious, not an inkling; much of merit—but of the merit of critical scrutiny, not a word. We had a course in Greek Philosophy, but it was taught chiefly as a lesson: how much wiser the Greeks might have been had they had the Bible to curb their speculations. The Ionian Greeks, who alone in the ancient world developed a nose for facts and a lodestar for speculations, were swept away with a gesture because they dared to seem to question such "known facts" as Genesis sets forth; the Attic Greeks were praised because they knew so much about the soul.

In other words, critical thought, scientific procedure, were no easier in Pliny's day than they are today in thousands of counties in the United States. On the other hand, what passed then (and passes now) for Intellectual was much more widespread then than it is here now.

We laugh scornfully at Pliny's mistakes in natural history, but it was good enough for Christian Europe for over sixteen centuries, and nowhere is it on record that anyone ever worked harder to find out the facts of nature. He was not content, as was the intellectual habit then, to know himself by wearing *Gnothi* on a signet ring. He had the idea that he could know himself better if he knew more about the world he lived in, and he worked prodigiously to understand it. That nephew to whom he had recommended Minerva spoke in a letter to a friend of his uncle's keen intellect, his incredible zeal, his great capacity for wakefulness, his reading dur-· ing meals, and never reading anything without taking excerpts; much like Darwin. His primary trouble, also like Darwin, was that there was almost no natural history worth reading. That there was a world under the sea, under our feet, and under our skin, and that that was the only world we could ever know, and the world we had to know before we could know ourselves, was as yet unknown and undreamed of, except remotely by Lucretius and a few Ionians and Alexandrians.

Then, as now, it was so much easier to read than to observe, to accept what was said or written than to go out and prove it—to follow Diana than Minerva. Aristotle at times proved himself a sound thinker, but his credulity in accepting as facts assertions he could have proved false is almost beyond belief. Here are a few samples of his "facts": Men have eight ribs; men's hearts alone of animals *beat*; men have more teeth than women; women's skulls have only one suture; eggs float on sea water; sea water is drinkable in a wax vessel. Had the great logician never laid his head· on a woman's breast, or counted her ribs, or looked into her mouth or at her skull? When Nicias the Aristocrat, after Pericles' death, led the Athenians to their doom against Syracuse, he went wild over an eclipse of the moon, although Anaxagoras could predict it.

Against our background of science today, the best Greek and Latin thinkers seem incredibly credulous, uncritical, childish. Pliny as a natural scientist is, of course, quite absurd. But natural science is a *modern* science. Science is modern. The one outstanding differ- ence between 19 or 193 or 1730 and 1930 is science. A few names tower up out of the mediocre level of the ancient world; and a few tower up out of ours. But my guess is that the workers on the Parthenon or Hadrian's mole thought as straight and had minds as well disciplined as those who built the Empire State Building. They could sort out fiction from fact as well, and came just as close to regulating their thoughts by the very modern historic sciences of anthropology, sociology, philology, and comparative religion. Into the beliefs of that age we shall look presently; let us get on with our Roman school.

"Two feet make one step," said the Roman schoolboy; "two steps make one pace; one thousand paces make one mile"—*mille*. Ours has 1760 "yards," but is just as primitive. The French finally got to the point where they could throw a Roman school-book away; we still think it unpatriotic not to cling to our old feet. Cæsar's comment on hearing the boys sing-songing their lesson was: "If you are singing, you are singing badly; if you are reading, you are singing." We gave up singing our lessons only two generations ago; the Far East still sings on—in India, out under the trees, like bees hiving.

They also had their "problem" questions—or possibly it was an antique intelligence test: "Hannibal has beaten the Romans at Cannæ; shall he or shall he not proceed directly to attack? Answer the question as if you were Hannibal." Turned into a "Resolved," it reminds me of the debates in our old Ciceronian Society. Seneca's comment was: "We are learning not for life but for the school"— and that, I submit, is as sound a comment as was ever made on any school system.

Rome had no organized system of general education as we have, nor cheap newspaper print to supply the deficiency. Literacy, however, seems to have been the rule, and for four hundred years books were cheap and plentiful and the booksellers prosperous. With the disorders in Rome parchment became expensive and papyrus from across the sea almost unobtainable.

For centuries Rome was a great intellectual centre, a real book town—as some of our towns were in pre-flivver days. Of the thousands of towns in the Empire, thousands had public libraries. Rome alone had twenty-nine, containing hundreds of thousands of books and papyrus rolls. They had over ten thousand Greek comedies and thirty thousand tragedies. Where are they now? Of three hundred Greek writers of tragedy, we have parts of three only. Vandals. Adult ignorance hates a highbrow; add bigotry, and off goes his hat!

Early Christian brotherly love meant bitter hatred for pagans. Rome was Pagan, Scarlet, Sin; its books were so many passports to hell—as French books are today to Watch and Ward Societies— obscene, indecent, immoral, ungodly, poisonous. The early Christian mind was above such things. When Alaric sacks, loots, and ravishes Rome, Augustine the Saint writes a dissertation on: Would the outraged virgins be entitled to the crown of maidenhood in the next world? But in general the Church welcomed the German savages; it thought it could do better with "roughnecks" than with an Empire which had an official state religion. Down with Rome! Burn the books! A mere list of the Greek and Latin literary treasures known to be lost would fill a volume.

Livy wrote a monumental history of Rome; he was to the Romans what Herodotus was to the Greeks—the national historian. Of his 142 books, each a small work in itself, only thirty-five are extant: enough to stamp an impress on the history of the republican Rome that lasted to modern times. Trajan wrote up his conquest of Dacia, and for three centuries it was as popular in Rome as Cæsar's Gallic War: not one word extant. Of Rome's greatest poet, Ennius, only tantalizing fragments are left, though we may infer much about his *Divine Antiquities*, for Augustine drew heavily from it in his *City of God*. Varro—"most learned of the Romans" and close friend of Cicero—wrote between six and seven hundred volumes: less than one remains. No Latin history has come down to us complete. Of Cæsar's many writings, his *Commentarii* alone was preserved, because the army used it to study his methods of warfare. But why our girls are still asked to read it in a Quaker school, I do not know.

Latin and Greek poets fared badly. Homer was a text-book and so escaped, but no other Greek epic survived. Of the three great Greek tragedies, we have only such selections of Æschylus, Sophocles, and Euripides as were used in schools. A one-volume edition of Euripides was preserved by accident. For such Greek lyric poetry as we have we are indebted to school anthologies. Of Greek comedies we have Aristophanes only because he was used in Greek schools. Attic orators and Herodotus, Thucydides, and Xenophon survived in Byzantine schools only. Such parts of Aristotle as survived were deemed useful for educational purposes. Plato survived because he was congenial to the Christians for the support he gave to the idea of an immortal soul. Of the greater Greek philosophers we have practically nothing. Latin poets mostly perished. Vergil, Horace, and Ovid were too beloved to be allowed to disappear. Of the Latin tragic poets, Seneca alone survived. Cicero served practical needs and so was preserved.

The moral sentiments the Christians brought to Rome were in

no respect essentially new or different from those which were already familiar to the Roman populace. Cicero, Seneca, Epictetus, Marcus Aurelius, Plutarch, were in a way preachers of morals, and Romans crowded under the pulpits to hear such sermons. The novel in Christianity was its dogmatic character and its extraordinary mysticism.

The Stoic "philosophies" were really manuals of pagan righteousness. Sustain and abstain, as Epictetus said; the laws of nature are the mind of God; no one can disobey these laws with impunity. Live as nature directs. The divine mind is not, like man's, swayed by hopes, fears, griefs, exaltation, but by reason. Be reasonable; obey reason. There were pretenders and hypocrites, of course, among the Stoics, but theirs was a school of righteousness just the same and its messages were expounded by lecturers. In other words, there was nothing essentially new in the Christian idea of belonging to a church and sitting under a preacher. Stoicism was the most characteristic of Roman creeds, as Phariseeism was of the Hebrew.

To Epicurus, founder of the second great school of moral philosophy, happiness was the end of life. His chief maxim was that man should not be troubled about death. Death did not concern man at all—for he only is when death is not; when death is, he is no longer there. Desire health; eat simple, wholesome food.

To the professional Stoic and Epicurean philosophers of Athens, Paul was just a new kind of itinerant philosopher—an amateur charlatan. They called him a Picker-up-of-Seeds—a "quack-quack," so to say. Paul himself saw his dilemma. "The Greeks demand philosophy, but we proclaim a Messiah crucified"—which was, as he admits, "to the Jews a stumbling-block, and to the Greeks a folly."

Rome was quite familiar with itinerant preachers vowed to poverty and celibacy, calling upon the people to renounce the world and repent in God's name. There were then, as now, plenty of morons floundering about in a flood of superstition, wall-eyed with mysticism. The new "Science in Names and Numbers, the vibrations of which unconsciously affect one's thought and action" (as recently announced in San Diego, according to the *American Mercury*) would have had its devotees in Rome as it has in San Diego;

but it does seem that there is less excuse for such idiocy in our West than there was in Rome.

Rome, of course, as she grew rich, had many self-made men and the inevitable crop of vulgar *nouveaux riches* such as Petronius mocked because they imagined Corinthian bronzes made by an artist named Corinthus. The vulgarity due to the influx of great wealth can easily be seen making its way into every phase of Roman life—in buildings, in art, in drama, in religion, in philosophy. Big "butter-and-egg" men more and more demanded *realism*—and palmistry. Idealistic sculpture gave way to portrait busts; Greek drama, to custard pies. By Constantine's time taste and craftsmanship had almost disappeared; not one artist could do what thousands had done in the Augustan Age. Even Greek artists who used to turn out copies of copies of copies of Marble Fauns, Discus-Throwers, and Venuses for two hundred dollars each, had become extinct.

The old Empire was changing, reeking with superstition, floundering in doubt. In the early great days of the Empire, no one seriously doubted the reality of this world or asked if life was worth living. All that was taken for granted, as was also the belief that the Romans were Jupiter's chosen people and that he, greatest of all gods, had willed that Rome should rule the world.

And Rome had prospered. Now the old aristocratic families, guardians of the traditional beliefs, had virtually ceased to exist. They had been the pillars of the state religion, the keepers of Rome's dignity. With their passing went also the household chaplains who had helped to preserve the rites and ceremonies of the old religion, and the household philosophers who fought the East's idea that the world was a snare and a delusion and that inner spiritual life alone was real.

Stoicism itself had become an intellectual pastime for highbrows—a lay religion of the lawyers. Vergil's well known lines: "To these men I have set bounds neither of possessions nor time; I have given them sway without limit"—once known to every schoolboy and believed in implicitly by every Roman, no longer were the certainty they had been during the first two centuries.

Rome had put too much faith in her gods, had counted too heavily on their holding her up, pulling her through; had listened to Vergil rather than to Lucretius. Vergil was to the Romans what Homer was to the Greeks. Homer was his inspiration; his genius was his own. The *Æneid* is a great epic poem, but its influence was vicious. It became a Bible, confirming the Roman's unfounded beliefs, supplying them with sanctions for supernatural beliefs. Vergil flattered their vanity and gave them a false world to live in, a supernatural world to die for. He was a great poet, but he was orthodox and a fundamentalist. Hades became very real in his hands, fear of it a big factor in men's beliefs.

In early days the Romans buried food, playthings, utensils, money —for the soul's feeble replica of earthly life; also a coin in the mouth for the boatman. If unburied, the soul could not enter Hades but had to hang around shivering, watching Charon ferry the more fortunate across the river Styx. Hence it was a disgrace and a dishonour not to be buried. If the body could not be found, obsequies were performed, a cenotaph built. Even when the soul reached Hades it needed aid from friends on earth—periodic honours, etc. As it does today, and as the Church thoughtfully makes provision for.

Even Pliny believed in ghosts. One had prophesied a fortune for a friend; Pliny himself had heard the rattling of the chains and had seen the ghost.

During the seven days of games provided by Augustus, a comet appeared; it was declared to be Cæsar's ghost mounting heavenward. From that time on it was believed that emperors' souls mounted to heaven as divinities. In the Eastern Empire the Greek epithet *Soter* (Saviour), formerly applied to such high gods as Zeus, came to be given to kings.

It was an age when miracles grew like mushrooms, when emperors healed by laying on of hands, cured lame feet by stepping on them, blind eyes by the use of spittle. Vespasian was a famous miracle-worker. Apollonius of Tyana in Cappadocia, born 4 B.C., was even more famous. He had travelled far and wide—to Nineveh, to Babylon; had met Brahmans and was versed in Pythagorean lore; he also knew Spain, Africa, Athens. In Nero's time he met the funeral procession of an aristocratic virgin, dead on her wedding day. He touched her. She rose and returned home. He was a seer as well; and from Ephesus beheld Domitian being murdered in his palace in Rome.

The point is not that miracles were performed then, nor that people believed in ghosts or eagerly sought saviours or redeemers—for miracles are still performed and saviours are still sought daily; but that such an age could produce a Lucretius, a man who did not believe in ghosts.

In his sombre fanatical faith, in his scheme of the universe, and in his mission to rid the world of superstition, Lucretius reminds Shotwell of Dante and Milton. But his amazing evolutionary views of the origin of life remind biologists of Lamarck and Darwin. If there was a more marvellous anticipation of modern biologic science in all ancient literature, I do not know what it was or where to look for it.

Not inappropriately, Lucretius opens his great didactic poem of seven hundred thousand lines, *De Rerum Natura*, with a magnificent apostrophe to Venus, symbol of the powers of reproduction. But he knows nothing of any Golden Age, or Dawn of Innocence in an Eden of the Gods when there was no sin, no evil, no sorrow, when everything was lovely and harmonious and everybody innocent of error and desire; nor any fires of Vulcan. He was a thorough-going evolutionist; life had slowly evolved from lower to higher forms. "Ah! unhappy race of men," he cried, "when it has assigned such acts to the gods and joined therewith bitter anger! What groaning did they then beget for themselves, what sores for us, what tears for our children to come!" Nor is it piety at all "to bow down to stone, sprinkle altars with blood," etc., "but rather to contemplate all things with a mind at rest." Lucretius was born eighteen centuries too soon. His world was no more ready for naturalism than Egypt was ready for Ikhnaton's hymn to the sun.

The Greeks had their Golden Age, their attitude toward those of that age. Greece also had her Agnostics: men who said, "We don't know"; or, "Well, what of it?" But the Greeks also came more and more under the spell of the underworld ghosts, with the result that great cults grew up, became endowed, and exerted enormous influence in diverting attention from living here and now and directing it toward preparation for living in the gloomy by and by. Worldly-mindedness was being undermined by other-worldly mindedness; the will to live wisely, fully, virilely, was giving way to the will to renounce all human wants and desires in order to exist forever as pure phantom. The flesh was being mortified that the spirit might be freed to endure forever. Platonism was getting ready for Neo-Platonism. In short, Rome was in need of new gods; the Græco-Roman world was getting ready to turn Christian.

That "turn" was a logical step; it had momentous consequences. We can only understand it against a background of the beliefs it supplanted and the sequence of events which brought it about.

Rome became the centre of Christianity, but all the world of the Jewish composers and compilers of the canon of the Old Testament, of the saintly composers of the New Testament, and of the early preachers of the religion of the Bible, was a Greek world—Greek in language, literature, religion, science, and philosophy. From approximately 600 B.C. to 400 A.D. Greek things were the smart, the cultured, the intellectual things of such parts of the Mediterranean world as wanted to be smart, cultured, intellectual. Greek thinking was not universal thinking in that world—far from it; but it set a pattern for thinkers, furnished food for thought—whether digested or, for one reason or another, rejected.

We saw how rational Greek thinking could be at times; we saw something of the sanity and humanness of the Homeric gods. Why, then, should Athens, intellectual and artistic capital of the world, keep on building temples and continue to persecute such harmless old cranks as Socrates, such really wise men as Aristotle, such really great poets as Euripides? Was Plato a great philosopher or just a great mystic with extraordinary skill in mystifying credulous people who felt the urge to think and had nothing but words to think with?

Let us make certain of the facts, and of their significance. I know no better way to emphasize both than to say that what we call modern civilization was rooted in Greek culture. I am not talking of progress or of civilization in general. I speak of *modern* civilization, that advance in knowledge which makes for power. Our advance began where the Greeks left off.

One incident will suffice to show how deeply Greek influence had penetrated the ancient world. Alexandria during the third century B.C. was the science centre of the Græco-Roman world. It had also become an important Jewish centre. Those Alexandrian Jews, as we shall see, put parts of the Old Testament into Greek, in which form it came down to us. *Greek thought influenced those translators.* The Wisdom literature, so-called, deals with sensible, physical matters rather than with a supernatural world. It makes the heart the seat of understanding—not the liver, as do the Psalms and Proverbs; and in other ways it could be shown that those translators were familiar with Aristotle.

In short, the Greeks had begun to ask the only kind of questions that could get the approximate truth about things and about the really good in human relationships. Thales, Pythagoras, Democritus, and Aristotle are the real protagonists of modern science. Archimedes was a modern engineer and an inventor of the first rank. Zeno and Epicurus show far greater ethical sanity than Plato—or even Aristotle.

600 B.C.-400 A.D.

400 A.D.-1600 A.D.

With 1600, roughly speaking, modern science, modern civilization, begins where the Greeks left off. Something had happened—many things, in fact. Hypatia had been torn to pieces; Bruno had been burnt at the stake; the Inquisition had persecuted free thinkers as though they were infected rats bearing plague germs.

We speak of culminating epochs in history; 400 A.D. was such an epoch. The history of the rise and fall of the Roman Empire gives us only a part clue to the essential factors of that epoch—and not the most significant part. Christianity rose out of the ruins of the Roman Empire, true; but when Rome fell, Greek rational thought fell also. Christianity became more imperial than Rome had been, more superstitious than Athens had been.

Modern science began where Greek science left off; Christian religion began where Greek religion left off. Our legacy from Greece was not an unmixed blessing.

All credit to precocious Greek genius; but what we need now is more light, not on Greek art, or literature, or poetry, or the Parthenon, or the three thousand marble statues on an Olympian hillside, but on the religious beliefs and practices of the Greeks. The Parthenon is a ruin, but the Virgin is a living wonder-worker.

## IX

Greek religion is immortalized in Homer and Hesiod, engraved on the monuments to the dead, and depicted on the walls of Pompeii and the vases of graves and other soul-cult objects throughout the Hellenic world. That religion can now be read, thanks to modern scholarship; and upon Harrison and Rohde I have leaned unblushingly in the story which follows.

That story, may I point out, is worth knowing for its own sake and for the light it throws on Christianity-in-the-making and religion-in-the-making. The uniqueness of Greek religion, as I see it, is that it passed from primitive beginnings to high civilization as a folk religion and not as the word of a god speaking to mere human beings. It made no claim that the Word was the Truth, or that the Word had been handed down from on High. Greek beliefs, in short, were neither codified nor divinely revealed, and formal worship had become little more than a God-save-the-King gesture at the close of public functions.

But formal worship is often deceptive and may afford little insight into the fundamental beliefs which regulate social conduct. And when a genius for words like Plato so manipulates those beliefs that they can be made to fit into any religion, give verisimilitude to any faith, we have something a revealed religion can use as evidence. Did Plato believe in a hell or in immortality? He certainly believed in the code which forced the hemlock to the lips of Socrates and gave moral support to every gesture of mediæval intolerance. He was essentially a religious fanatic.

Homer knew nothing of hell, nor believed in immortality—except for Immortals. He knew that at death man's *psyche* hastened away to the "house of Hades"—darkness below the earth; or, more vaguely, sank into the earth. But his "psyche" was not our "soul" as opposed to "body." The body at death fell to pieces, became "senseless earth"; the psyche, freed only in death, was an invisible image, man's second existence, his soul. It escaped out of the mouth at death, or from a gaping wound.

Odysseus saw on the borders of Hades "images (like smoke) of those that have toiled." He recognized the images of his mother and of his companions of the Trojan War. Thus, too, the soul of

Patroklos appeared to Achilles one night—just like him in figure and stature. But only a *fabled* hero like Odysseus could reach the entrance to Hades; once across the river, souls can never return; they float unconscious in the murky underworld.

Patroklos' soul prayed Achilles for immediate burial that it might pass through the gates of Hades at once and not wander restlessly about below. Then, too, Elpenor's soul meets his friend Odysseus at the entrance to the shadow-land; hence his soul retains sense, even has a heightened consciousness. It cannot enter because its physical counterpart, the body, has not yet been destroyed. Fire alone destroys the body—and appeases the soul. The only funeral rite Homer knows is cremation. Why, then, mounds over graves, and headstones? That his fame might remain imperishable, said Homer; that future generations might not be ignorant of his history.

*Psyche* to Homer is also "conscience," "will," "double," "second self"; a shadow, a dream picture, impalpable to human touch. In Odysseus' journey to Hades there is no suggestion of sin or punishment. The life souls live is one of resignation, not of hope. The shade of Achilles laments that a live day laborer is better off than a dead prince—and points the moral better than Solomon's live dog being better than a dead lion. In Homer's dead land there are neither rewards nor punishments.

The gods only were immortal; gods and immortals are interchangeable terms. To be granted immortality is to become a god. Thus, Calypso wanted to make Odysseus "immortal and ageless for all time"; she wanted to keep him with her forever, and she could only do it by making him a god like herself. Thus, too, the gods carry Ganymede, most beautiful of mortals, to Olympus, where he dwells forever as the cup-bearer of Zeus.

But gods could remain gods only so long as they had magic food—ambrosia and nectar; by eating the gods' food, anyone could become an immortal.

Such, briefly, was the Homeric belief. Sacrifices were offered to the gods for favors expected; the worshipper shared the banquet with the god—the *dios*. Back of *dios*, in time and etymology, is that dire word *dirus*, which smacks more of black magic than it does of divinity. *Dirus*, in fact, had a double meaning: the "cursing and blessing that haunts all inchoate religious terms."

Within three centuries after Homer, Greek religion shows signs of fearing the gods' curses more than expecting their blessings. They began to see ghosts, bogies. Their religion was no longer, "I give that you may give," but, "I give that you may go away and stay away." They were no longer worshipping the Immortals on High Olympus, but vague, irrational, malevolent spirits. In other words, their worship had descended to the level of the Eskimo: their *beliefs* had become *fears*.

Athens had a great festival; the sacrifice was a holocaust—ostensibly to Zeus, but in reality to an underworld serpent whose worship had been superimposed upon that of Zeus. Xenophon, returning from Asia, ran short of funds, consulted a specialist, and was told that Zeus opposed him and must be appeased. Xenophon sacrificed a holocaust of pigs. But the Zeus he sacrificed to was Zeus in his underworld aspect, figured by his worshippers as a snake. In Greece he was figured as an earth-god in human form; he bore a cornucopia and his food was roast pork. Hence Xenophon's sacrifice of pigs. That was the Zeus-Hades of Euripides.

Greek religion in pre-Homeric days was essentially ancestor worship. It was based on the belief that souls freed by death lived on as powerful, consciously active spirits. Elysium, the Isles of the Blest, by Homer's time was already on the dim horizon, the circle of the Fortunate closed; the day of miracles was past. But the idyllic longings which gave rise to a picture of Elysium where souls lived untroubled lives of perfect bliss under benign skies, thought of these souls as without desire or activity; Elysium was unexplorable, far beyond the reach of discovery even in the distant future. Only in the Golden and Silver Ages did miracles happen.

With Homer, dead souls went to Hades, a vague, shadowy world. The soul, in other words, had no power; it could neither act on nor influence the living. There were burial rites, but their object was merely to bring about the more complete and perfect freedom of the soul that it might sink underground in peace.

Religion in the Golden Age of Pericles was something different. The Attic calendar was not unlike that of our Hopi Indians, each month of the year named after its principal ceremony. The ceremony made the month; the month belonged to the ceremony. Thus, the official Attic calendar began at the height of summer, and was celebrated by a great festival sacred to the city.

By mid-February the gods had done their worst. But the dead earth's awakening meant springtime also for the ghosts; they must be propitiated or there would be no crops. Hence the mid-February-mid-March month was called *Anthesterion*; its great ceremony, *Anthesteria*.

This ceremony, ostensibly sacred to Dionysus, was really a ritual to placate the ghosts so that they would keep away. The rites, therefore, were conceived of as a practical measure to promote good crops. It was, in short, primarily a Feast of All Souls; it became a revel to Dionysus—a Good Friday, for man is always ready to shift from a fast to a feast. Even in Hesiod's day the *Anthesteria* was an ancestral festival. Neither slaves nor servants were to be hindered from drinking wine. After stated days for opening the wine casks, for the cups, for the pots, there followed three days of revel—a holiday for the children, feasts among friends, a revelry for the servants. Everybody drunk, as pictured by Aristophanes. On one day the wife of the chief *archon* went to the temple of Dionysus and "wed" the god.

Who is this Dionysus? We know him as the god of wine, also as Bacchus, Bromio, etc., and with him associate satyrs and mænads. To the Greeks, Dionysus was not an Immortal on Mount Olympus, but the god of all growing things, of every tree and plant. Only later did he become the god of wine exclusively. His worship is the result of a mixture of two elements—a vine-god cult superimposed upon, affiliated with, or developed out of, a vegetation-god cult: the addition of a cup of wine to the primitive Greek's loaf of bread. With the breaking of bread they could renew the life of the body; with the drinking of wine they could renew spiritual life as well. Thought was thereby reborn, equanimity and magnanimity restored.

We peeping moralists think of wine in terms of slums, crimes, and Volsteads, but serious excess in drink has always been rare in Mediterranean lands. The Greeks were not a nation of drunkards; they realized that wine could lend lovely forms to art, stimulate to new thought. While Dionysian worship was essentially intoxication, it soon was transformed into something higher and deeper. Intoxication to the Greeks was "possession": one was literally possessed by the god, by something divine. It was also madness—but a divine madness. Sorrow and joy are obsessions, possessions.

Mysticism, a new religion, had appeared—as it so often does when the gods lose touch with life and reality and die of their own perfection. That is what had happened to the Olympian gods. Dionysian worship brought a new impulse of enthusiasm into Greece—a belief that man, through physical intoxication first and then through spiritual ecstasy, could pass from human to divine.

Dionysus was originally a Thracian god. The Thracians to the Greeks were powerful "medicine"-men; Herodotus thought them the greatest, except possibly the Indians. Dionysus was probably a tree-god before he was a vine-god. He was mothered by Semele (Mother-Earth) and conceived by a thunderbolt. That made easy his adoption by Zeus, who himself was god of the thunderbolt. As lions attend the Mountain-Mother in Asia, draw her chariot, guard her throne, so Dionysus, son of Semele, has a chariot drawn by lions, or is himself attended by a lion. On a vase painting he stands between two great prophylactic eyes, while a little doglike lion looks up at him adoringly: lions are no longer the dominant terror in Greece. He is also figured as a bull and as a tree. As Athene "takes" the olive, so Dionysus takes the ivy, pine, and honeycomb; ivy especially is sacred to him. For "inspiration" his mænads chew ivy leaves: as the Delphic prophetess chewed bay leaves.

Mænads are merely cult epithets, meaning mad women. Any woman, anywhere, who worships or is possessed, maddened, or inspired by the spirit of Dionysus, is a mænad. Grecian mænads also tended the god—frenzied, sanctified devotees of the worship of Dionysus.

Satyrs and centaurs, and our own devil with horns, hoofs, and tail, are born of the victor's infantile desire to relieve his hate of his fallen foe by making him as hideous as he can. Devils are always as ugly as angels are sweet.

As Ridgeway pointed out, conquerors look upon the conquered with hate and aversion—and with some reluctant awe. They also have a certain respect for the conquered as wizards—who alone are on speaking terms with the local ghosts, and hence are employed as sorcerers, as we employ "native" guides in a strange land.

The conqueror also imputes all known evil and bestial character-istics to the conquered. The conquered hide out in mountain haunts and make reprisals on the conquerors, who see them as satyrs and centaurs who carry off women and snatch babies from their cradles; hence horns, manes, tusks, tails, etc. Centaurs originally were wild men on horses—a terrifying sight at a distance if one had never seen a horse, or a man astride a four-footed animal. Satyrs never turned into horses, but remained wild men with horse adjuncts of ears, tail, and sometimes hoofs.

Dionysus brought his revel rout of satyrs and mænads with him from Thrace; peace is just what he did not come to bring. We now return to *Anthesterion*, the month which begins with mid-February.

February itself is *the* month of purification; *februum, februa*—"purifications." Strips of skin were fertility charms. They formerly sacrificed goats to placate ghosts: hence goat-skins have magic power, are "sacred." And so they used strips of skin in their puri-fication rites—just as we "beat the mischief out of him" or apply "good medicine" or make the sign of the cross.

With the month of May-June (*Thargelion*) came an early sum-mer festival ostensibly dedicated to Apollo. But *thargelos* means the first loaf made from the new harvest; also, a "pot full of seeds." *Thargelia* was a festival offering of the first-fruits of the harvest. The rites were directed primarily to expel, to get rid of, ghosts; the ceremony itself aimed at physical and moral purgation as a means of promoting and preserving fertility. "Bread and wine are sacri-ficial elements, but are far removed from being elemental."

But let us go up on the Acropolis at Athens to see a festival to Zeus himself—to Zeus Polieus. It is the *Diploia* ceremony in the merry month of *Thargelion*. Pericles himself will be present and other notables of this Golden Age. On the bronze altar of Zeus cakes of barley mixed with wheat are laid. Oxen are driven around the altar, and the ox which goes up and eats the offering is sacrificed.

This is how it is done. The ax and knife for slaying have been dipped in water by "water-carrier" maidens; the weapons are then sharpened and handed to the butchers. One fells the ox, another cuts its throat, while the man who has just felled it throws the ax from him and flees. The ox is then skinned, and all present eat; after which the hide is stuffed with straw, sewed up, set on its feet and yoked to a plough. The next step is a trial in the ancient law court, presided over by the "king," to determine who murdered the ox. The "water-carriers" accuse the sharpeners of the weapons, who blame those who handed the weapons to the butchers, who in turn blame the ax and the knife. Ax and knife are found guilty, condemned, and cast into the sea.

Now, this house-that-Jack-built hocus-pocus in the centre of civilized Athens was a rite of solemn import. It was a dreadful abomination to kill the ox; its ghost and the spirits of vengeance generally must be tricked or appeased: hence the pretence that the ox is not dead or has come to life. He ate the cakes of his free wicked will; we didn't kill him, but something did; we must get rid of it. The "pollution" is thrown into the sea.

Plutarch tells us that a hut resembling a king's palace was set up on a threshing-floor at Delphi every eighth year; it presumably held a snake. A boy was led up to the "palace" carrying torches which had been lighted according to ritual requirements. The hut was fired, and everybody fled without looking back. The boy too went off, fasted, then was dined and brought back crowned with laurel. Harrison infers this to be a mimetic representation of the slaying of the python and the banishment of Apollo.

*Python? Apollo banished!* We speak of religion as enacted, not as literature. The Olympian gods were high gods—far too high to soil their hands with such mysteries as snakes, children, and ghosts. True, the Greeks had their Trinity—their three chief divinities. True also, that we usually rate their religion high because they put Zeus, an old rain- or thunderbolt- or "sky"-god, at the head of their trinity; that Apollo, an old sun-god, was the best beloved because he could foretell the future; and that Athene, once an old Amazon in shining armour protecting cities, had become wisest of counsellors and first in peace, bearing an olive branch. True, too, that to these gods splendid temples were erected; but the point is that when we rend the veil of the temple we see the same old bag of tricks that we find Pawnee and Hopi making medicine with. Popes and priests make the same kind of medicine.

Superstition is superstition and Bibles are Bibles, no matter what language they are written in. And snakes are snakes—in Sumer and Akkad, in Palestine, in Greece, among the Hopi and Mayas, and in the Garden of Eden. And so are children. In superstitions they are rarely very far apart. A Greek peasant woman today hurries her child to baptism lest at any moment it disappear in the form of a snake.

The Greek festival of *Thesmophoria* is as far from Olympus as Thales of Miletus is from St. Paul, but it was Greek religion as practised and the gist of the Eleusinian Mysteries, Greece's most influential religious ceremony. It was so highly charged with potential dangers that even Herodotus had to preserve an "auspicious silence" about it. It was a three-day ceremony: the first day, *Kathodos* and *Anodos*, or the Down-going and Uprising; the second was fast day; the third was Fair-born or Fair-birth. It was exclusively in charge of the women and was an autumn sowing ceremony. Its business was to promote fertility in women and crops. That business was accomplished by magic rites. These rites were not addressed to God but to bogies, evil spirits. The business of the ritual, therefore, was to avert evil.

The women carried the *sacra*—the loaded things, the "medicine," supernatural stuffs, superhuman powers. Such *sacra* are taboo to the impure. The gist of a mystery is often the removal of the taboo. And so women, specially purified for the purpose, let pigs down into clefts in the rocks or into underground chambers. Then they themselves descended and brought up rotten flesh (presumably of last year's pigs). This flesh was placed on altars, and, mixed with seeds, served as a fertility charm. The pigs were sacrifices to the powers of the earth: snakes represented those powers, were their guardians.

A mystery to the Greeks meant a rite in which certain *sacra* were exhibited, but not until after the worshipper had been purified; purification was an essential of the mystery. When I *muo* in Greek, I shut my eyes or mouth. I am a *mystes* when I have vowed secrecy—sworn that I will not speak of the things that are about to be revealed. But in ancient Greece, as in the modern Greek fraternity, there was nothing to reveal because there was nothing to see; that is, nothing more significant than you will find in an Osage medicine-man's bundle.

In other words, secrecy was not the gist of the mystery; purification (initiation) was. After the purification one could handle, eat, partake of, the *sacra*. In the *Thesmophoria*, the women had to fast one day before they could handle the *sacra*. In the Eleusinian Mysteries, one had to sacrifice a pig before one could offer and eat first fruits. A mystery, therefore, is the doing of that which relates to a *musos*, a pollution: it is a purification ceremony—primitive magic, a practical end to promote fertility. The *Thesmophoria* women, by carrying the *sacra*, compelled nature. But they could not touch the *sacra* without removing the taboo inherent in them till purified. The gist of the mystery is to remove the taboo.

Our friend Cicero was initiated into the mysteries at Eleusis, and declared that he was taught not only to live happily but to "die with a fairer hope." He speaks as one who has just been baptized and hopes to go to heaven. The intimate splendour and social prestige of the mysteries of this little town of Eleusis, less than twenty miles from Athens, were due to Athenian boosters; they saw that Better Mysteries meant Bigger Business.

There were two festivals a year at Eleusis, synchronous with the death and rebirth of nature. Both were dedicated to Demeter, the Great Mother, worshipped under divers names all over Greece, and everywhere with mysteries; and in Asia Minor as Cybele with timbrel and cymbal.

Demeter's daughter, Persephone or Kore, was carried off by Hades (Pluto). Wearied by her long search for her daughter, Demeter, in the guise of an old hag, finally reached the little town of Eleusis, where she was hospitably received. That so pleased her that she gave the Eleusinian king seed corn and taught the four princes the art of husbandry. Hence the particular Demeter cult at Eleusis, with which the cult of Dionysus was affiliated later.

The most striking part of the festival was a torchlight procession along the Sacred Way from Athens to Eleusis on the night of the fifth day of the mysteries. Her great splendid temple was destroyed by Alaric the Goth in 395; but in a near-by church dating from about 1100, mosaics of the *Christos Pantakrator* and scenes from the life of the Virgin may still be seen.

Because Demeter herself had taught the Eleusinian princes her cult and the sacred *Orgia*, respect for the goddess prevented their being communicated to others. Hence her cult became a religious service in charge of a close corporation. The priesthood was hereditary and at first only citizens of Eleusis were admitted; but when Athens took charge, admission was thrown open to all Greeks of all countries and colours, male, female, or *hetairai*.

No details of the long-drawn-out festival have survived; but its secret *sacra* were presumably no more significant than the ball, mirror, and pine cone of the Dionysus mysteries or the "medicine" of the Navaho night chant. There may have been a symbolic celebration of the religion of nature, a dramatization with Demeter as Earth; Persephone, her daughter, seed corn; rape and return of Persephone, sowing of the seed, and the rise of young grain—in short, the yearly decay and renewal of vegetation. That presumably, or something similar, was taken over by the worshippers to signify their own rebirth, to image the fate of the human soul. And that was its real mystery; in substance not unlike the mysteries of the initiation ceremonies of Australian and Melanesian primitives.

All Greece grew interested in these mysteries, and in course of time they became a Pan-Hellenic festival, at which time a solemn truce of God was proclaimed as for the games at Olympia. In 440 B.C., at the height of her power, Athens decreed that yearly offerings of first fruits should be made to the temple at Eleusis, and invited all Greeks to make such offerings.

Egypt, presumably, was the first country to associate the idea of securing immortality for the soul by taking over the primitive rites of fertilization, but at Eleusis we find the first distinct promise of a blessed immortality. That promise drew worshippers from far and wide, for the door was thrown wide open; anyone could be saved, by initiation.

These mysteries were continued into Roman times, were infused into Christianity, are echoed by St. Paul, in the Fourth Gospel, and appear in the ceremony and ritual of the Christian Church. Joining church—confession—was to the Greeks an expression of faith or a confession of dogma: an avowal of rites performed. Therein lies the gulf between the ancient and modern religious attitude. The Greeks saw that uniformity in ritual can be preserved. Fasting, handling the *sacra*, can be done in the same old way whatever one's opinion or sentiment. There can be no such uniformity in thought. They left men free where freedom was important. In other words, a Greek could confess—and believe what he pleased.

But Greek civilization did more than open an Osiris career to confessors. It gave us angels and a host of other supernatural beings worth looking at. Also, and especially, Orpheus, the Good Shepherd. But before we look at this Sweet Singer, let us have a final look at some Greek souls, and other supernatural phenomena with which our own religion is not entirely unacquainted.

In its beliefs and practices the Greek cult of souls differed in no essential particular from that of the Trobriand Islanders of today. Corpses must be properly disposed of or the soul can find no peace; until buried, the ghost haunts the neighbourhood and may get angry and do a lot of damage. Burial, therefore, was less a mark of respect for the dead than a protective measure for the living.

The eyes and mouth of the corpse were closed by the next of kin. The body was then washed and anointed by the women of the family and clothed in clean garments. It then lay in state on a bier inside the house. Marjoram was strewn under the body, which rested on four vine branches; the grave also was lined with vine branches. Cypress branches outside the house door warned of death within, as do our mourning wreaths today. The head of the corpse was decked with garlands and fillets. The funeral dirge was sung by women of the immediate family. A law of Solon forbade women to tear their cheeks, beat their breasts, or otherwise inflict punishment upon themselves. It also forbade the sacrifice of animals before the procession to the grave, and excessive ostentation. Which means that mutilation, sacrifice, and ostentation were practised up to 594 B.C.

On the third day the corpse was placed on a funeral pyre and cremated. The ashes and bones were carefully gathered by a son, and enclosed in a box or urn. Although the soul was freed by cremation, it still had some connection with the body; hence household utensils, etc., were laid beside the urn.

One had best visit a graveyard in silence, Plato said, because the dead "hover" suspended over their graves; hence the law of Solon forbidding abusive language about the dead. The old warning *De mortuis nil nisi bonum* was prompted, not by respect, but by fear. If one spoke evil of the dead, its ghost might haunt one.

Plato never raises the question of the validity of the belief in souls; he discusses souls as though they were self-evident facts, like the Acropolis or the sun. He was a spiritualist and a theosophist, and the *psyche* of his psychology was soul-stuff pure and simple. In the *Apology* he asks whether death means complete unconsciousness like dreamless sleep, or the soul's passing to the Realm of Souls. To him souls are souls, and he discusses their nature, origin, and destiny.

Meanwhile the ritual of burial and the cult of souls ran its usual course. More and more the dead became objects of pious zeal; their resting-place grew in sanctity. State, city, and religion joined in taking steps to protect family tombs from profanation. Innumerable signs gave notice that violators of the peace of the grave must pay monetary fines into the public treasury. Inscriptions abounded placing the grave and its sanctity under the protection of the gods of the underworld; shocking curses, calamities, and torments now and for evermore, were invoked against profaners of tombs. Prayers that the departed might rest in peace became more and more common.

"Curse" tablets by the thousand have been found in Greek graves and sanctuaries. The curse is the essence of early law; no Commandment without a curse. Break the Commandment and something dire will happen. "Honour thy father and thy mother"—or the devil will get you. The old Greek curse was magic of another kind. When you "put a curse" on a man, you bound him down to do his duty by spells and magic. Written on those curse tablets was, "I bind you down."

In an Attic grave a little headless lead figure was found; its arms were tied behind its back, and through the centre of the body was a nail. *Attica*, not Uganda. Some centuries after that lead spell was made, the hands and feet of Theophilus, a Christian saint, were bound by magic; he could get no relief. Finally he was told in a dream to go fishing and whatever the fisherman drew up would cure him. The net brought up a bronze figure, bound hand and foot, with a nail through one hand. The nail was drawn out; the saint recovered . . . just like that!

This cult of souls it was which inspired the belief in a continued life after death; also the belief in a small army of supernatural beings. *Daimones*, for example—Meddlesome Matty souls wandering over the earth prying into human affairs, observing justice and injustice, and dispensing favours and riches, like the saints in heaven. Every Greek family was supposed to have its good *daimon*, some ancestral soul which had taken the family under its wing and become the guardian spirit of the house.

A murder trial to the Greeks was not primarily an affair of justice between state and living citizens. It was essentially a religious act; its business was to satisfy the damaged souls of the dead and the *daimones* which represented them. It was a rite of propitiation to the hosts of the lower world. Part of the "trial" was the purification of the murderer—the *katharsis* rite. With *katharsis*, the blood of the murdered man is everted; his soul will be appeased and will not wreak vengeance. And so the murderer *spits three times*. "No savage tribe," says Rohde, "ever had more primitive ideas or realistic symbolism than the classical Greek populace."

A modern Greek writes cholera with a capital "CH," just as his Attic ancestor would have done if "caps" and "lower case" had been in use. To both, cholera is a sprite—as are also hunger, pestilence, madness, nightmare, mumps, chicken-pox, any disease: spirits all, bad spirits, sprites. So are *Keres*.

*Keres* are not fates. Fates are fairly modern abstractions. Religion does not begin, or end, with abstractions. It begins with scary things, ghosts, evil spirits. The business of religious ritual is to propitiate them or shoo them away. The Greek *Keres* began as ghosts, and by Plato's time had become little winged sprites. They were like personified bacteria, to which all mortals are exposed. In the lives of most mortals, said Plato, *Keres* adhere "which pollute and disfigure them." One had to look out or a *Ker* would get one. And so they smeared pitch on the doors to catch them; and spat them out with the spittle of chewed buckthorn.

*Keres* are really death demons, messengers, souls that carry off souls, angels of death. Death as figured in early Greek art was a snatching away of the soul by storm ghosts, evil death-demons:

*Keres, Harpies*—in later times, *Nereids*. Harpies not only snatched souls away, but could bring things to life. Thus, a harpy mothered the horses of Achilles; *Zephros* was their sire.

Zephyrs snatched souls away and also begot life. Life only can give life; soul only can beget a soul. Hence winds are souls and also breaths. And so an Athenian about to go away prayed and sacrificed to his *Tretopatores* (Fathers to the third degree); to his forefathers, to his ancestors, and to the ghosts and the winds.

The *Keres* on the shield of Odysseus were pictured as vultures. That armed him, as the cobra armed the Pharaoh's crown; or as the Gorgon's head arms a Greek bake-oven: it makes an ugly face *at* you if you are trying to steal the bread, *for* you if you are baking the bread.

Of the three Gorgon sisters, Medusa is the most evil. Slain by Perseus, her terribly lovely face can turn men into stone. That face, essence of the Gorgon head, is potent only when severed. It was first figured as a grinning mask, with glaring eyes, tusks, and pendent tongue; the body was added later. As Harrison says, the ritual artifact comes first, then a monster is begotten to account for it, and finally a hero is invented to account for the slaying of it. "The highest divinities of the religion of fear and riddance became the harmful bogies of the cult of service; *the Olympians became Christian devils.*"

The Gorgon was an Evil Eye incarnate. It slew by the eye, by fascination: hence was the prophylactic eye; it could out-stare, out-evil, the Evil Eye. And so it is found on vases, shields, and prows of ships.

Fish-tail mermaids are modern creations, unknown to ancient art and literature. But "these feathers and these feet of birds" and "faces of fair maids" that whetted Ovid's curiosity came from old Greece. The Greek Siren is always a bird-woman, a *Ker*. In their religious zoo, she belongs to the same order as the Sphinx and the Harpy: monstrous forms expressing monstrous ideas; birds of prey with power to lure by their song. The Harpy is a ravening snatcher; the Sphinx has uncanny prophetic power; the Siren seduces by her voice, but is a Harpy at heart, a bird of prey. Sirens are cousins to *Keres*, demons of the underworld. Human-faced birds as souls are common in Egyptian, more common in Greek, art.

When Hades finally became a hell for the wicked, it was guarded by the dog-faced Cerebus; but the sentinel idea is thousands of years older, the Sphinx at Gizeh being the oldest form, though just what idea prompted its creation is not known. In Greece, the Sphinx is the incarnation of the plague. Like the Harpy, she carries men to destruction; she especially snatches off the young men of Thebes; she is, in short, a *Ker* specializing in young males. But she is also a fortune-teller and has the bad habit of asking riddles herself. Man the myth-maker put these two underworld bogies together and made her what she is, the Sphinx.

Cross a Sphinx idea with a Siren idea, and we have *Keres* as *Erinyes*—which in popular bogy form people the Christian hell. *Erinyes* are the angry ones; as the *Eumenides* are the kindly ones; the *Poinæ*, the awful ones; the *Maniæ*, the mad ones. Not proper names, just adjectival epithets. *Erinyes* began as *Keres* of human beings unrighteously slain; they are outraged souls of the dead crying for vengeance. They are articulate *Keres* administering vindictive torment. They are irreconcilable demons without a drop of the milk of human kindness. They are our own imps of Satan.

Man made gods in his own image, but it took him a long time to realize that he was a man and not a cross between a bull and something he thought he saw in the bottom of a cave. Ages had to pass before he even dared think of himself as strong as a bull or as clever as a snake. His early gods were animals or monsters. He was haunted by bird-women-souls, Gorgon bogies, Sphinxes, Harpies, and such. Only later came the kindly grape-gathering, flute-playing, snake-nymphs, the Charites who gave grace and increase. Their snake bodies do not mark them as malevolent, but as earthy; they are genii of fertility.

The Olympian gods are a patriarchal family: Zeus, supreme, father of gods and men; Hera, the wife, always in revolt; and sons and daughters quarrelling among themselves and revolting against Pa and Ma, but subject to Pa's final authority. But older, more fundamental, more potent, is the matriarchal family religion of the local cults. The Christian Church began with the anthropomorphic Father-Son relationship, but that was soon enlarged to include the Mother-Maid Mary. Hera reigned alone at Argos; Athene at Athens—and she was no god's wife; Demeter and Kore, mother

and maid, were supreme at Eleusis. Even Apollo, the oracle at
Delphi, was preceded by a succession of goddesses. Kore as *daughter*
is a child of mythology; mother-maid, mature-woman-virgin, were
the pre-mythmaking relationships.

Pandora, once goddess of the Earth and sacrificed to as such, by
the time of Aristophanes had become misty, her ritual archaic.
Patriarchal Hesiod made her the handiwork of Olympian Zeus.
Woman, as we have seen, in the early stages of the growth of agriculture, because of her magic power gained a false prestige. When
man—Hesiod, for example—outgrew his belief in her magic potency, he made her the handiwork of Zeus, or created her from
somebody's rib. Thus, from being a great Earth-goddess, Pandora
sank to a mere curiosity box in beautiful female form. She opens
the great grave-jar, *pithos;* and *Keres* flutter forth, bringing death
and disease; hope only remains. Pandora reëmerged later as
Aphrodite.

There are no male trinities in Greece, many female trinities:
three Charites; three Horæ, etc.; and three times three, or nine,
Muses. A murderer also spits three times to appease his victim's
ghost; invokes the dead three times; sacrifices on the third day;
mourns three days. And when eminent Athenians sat in court on
life-and-death cases, they sat on the hill where Ares (Mars) was
once tried for murder—Areopagus or Mars Hill, where Paul told
the Athenians what this "new doctrine is." Below that hill was the
shrine of Erinyes, the avenging furies of blood, euphemistically
called the Eumenides. That court sat three days—as the three ways
the threefold Hecate of the underworld was worshipped.

Paul did not tell the Athenians that he perceived they were in
all things "too superstitious," as the Authorized Version has it, but
that in all things they were "somewhat religious." Paul was a
Greek: he knew religion when he saw it; he knew better than to
call Greek religion "superstition."

Greek trinities began as dualities: Demeter-Kore, Damia-Auxesia.
The demands of art probably added the third figure; a central
figure of a mother with one daughter does not make good composition. Demeter and Kore had become too crystallized as two
persons to be trinitized. Divine pairs not beyond the adjectival
stage could easily be made three. But once the triple form is estab-

lished, the three forms are always maidens in Greece, mothers in Rome.

We pass by Helen of Troy and the judgment of Paris—that was merely a beauty contest—and look at a real goddess, Athene. She began—not from Zeus, not at all—as an adjective, the Athenian One, Maid, Pallas, our Lady of Athens. She became *the* maiden, *the* Parthenos; her temple is the maiden chamber, the Parthenon. She refuses natural motherhood—to become the foster-mother of all heroes, as conceived in matriarchal days. Athenian politics turned the local Kore into a non-human abstraction.

Aphrodite is Kore as eternal radiant youth, but not as virgin. She wants love, not marriage. She is *Nymphe*, the Bride, but bride of the old order. All fertile animals belonged to her, especially the dove and the goat. Being an island queen, she was sea-born. She becomes *Ourania*, the Heavenly One, sailing through heaven on a great swan. But the Greeks could not make her fit into the Olympus family. As life itself is a mystery, and as they had no explanation for the love that begets life, Aphrodite kept her godhead to the end. Eros, her son, eclipsed her for a while, but she reëmerged with new dignity as mother. The Venus Genetrix of Rome is but a radiant Aphrodite sobered by motherhood.

Hera, queen of Olympus, wife of Zeus, seems all wife, till you look at her closely. Then you discover that she is always pecking at Herakles, whom Zeus loves but cannot protect. Why doesn't she submit, like a good wife? Because she was forcibly married, was never really a wife; she leaves submission to Zeus' shadowy double, Dione.

In canonical Homer's theology, the Olympian gods are not creators. They are simply Immortals: death would mar their splendour. There is no question in Homer of whence man, or why good and evil. The Olympians lay no claim to being all in all. Where, then, did man come from, and why is there good, evil? But first, how did the gods come to be? How did the Olympians become gods?

Why do snakes infest tombs? A bearded snake is a human snake, a vehicle, incarnation of a dead man's ghost. Snakes are feared, but not worshipped. But a bearded snake is a transition stage between animal and man. The beard marks the snake's divinity in human form. When the marrow decays, a man's backbone, said

Ælianus in his *Nature of Animals*, turns into a snake. And as we have seen, a dead spirit could also take the shape of a human-headed bird. That bird was a creature of mythology; the bearded snake became the object of a religious cult.

Zeus on Olympus was not worshipped; Zeus *Meilichios*, the Kindly, Gracious, was—as a snake, the Great Snake, an underworld deity. Only after the gods had been sung on high was Olympus peopled with its patriarchal family. The real home of those gods was the grave, the caverns where they lived. They could be reached by prayers, by rites. When these ancient gods were turned into heroes, the Olympian gods appeared.

The difference between a Greek hero and a Greek ghost, then, is merely time. Hero worship began as ancestral ghost worship, and so in essence it remained. The word *hero* is adjectival—mighty, strong, noble, venerable. Homer's heroes are strong in battle; cult heroes are strong in death: the dead are the Better and Stronger Ones. Thus, Homer speaks of a certain traitor, seducer, murderer, and craven as the Blameless One. The title was appropriate, for he was speaking of a dead hero.

Many of the Greek army at Marathon saw the ghost of Theseus in full armour fighting in the ranks against the Persians. Athens a few years later brought his bones and buried them in the Thesion, where they could be more easily worshipped. Those who fell at Marathon were worshipped as heroes. A solemn procession was made each year to worship the heroes left on the field of Platæa. As early as 620 B.C. a Draconian law ordered that gods and national heroes be honoured according to ancestral usage; that is, with sacrifices, animals, blood, etc. Gods were heroes; national heroes were national gods. Where the hero was buried, there the god dwelt. The great games—Olympian, Pythian, Nemean, etc.—were celebrated in honour of the gods, but they were originally funeral games and it was understood that the games really repeated the funeral ceremonies of a dead man—a mode of appropriate worship.

They worshipped phantoms, symbols of ancestors; but they clung to the forms of ancient ancestor worship. Athens had her hero-general, her hero garland-bearer, and her very famous hero-physician, Æsculapius, who clung to his snake in token of his humble birth as the ghost of a mortal. But between his birth on Greek soil from a class of Well-Disposed Ones, and the birth of an African rain-doctor's fetish, there is no essential difference. A tribe in Africa or on a South Sea Island cannot afford to departmentalize its gods; it must be content with Jacks-of-all-trades gods. Æsculapius typifies the healing god of all higher religions that have not yet given up words for things.

Æsculapius came to Athens about 420 B.C. from Thessaly, where his cult rivalled Apollo. The chief part of his ritual was the "sleeping in." The patient came and slept in his sanctuary and in a dream was healed, or the means of healing was revealed. When the patient got it he was a Receiver, a *Dexion*.

Sophocles after death was styled *Dexion*. He had "received" Æsculapius in his own house and had set up an altar to him; hence his canonization. But the old poet was too alive and human even after death to be a success as a hero.

Plato, in his *Laws*, gives this sequence of objects in divine worship: Olympian and city gods; underworld gods; *daimones*, orgiastic worship; heroes; ancestral gods; and, finally, honour to living parents.

The *Keres* are the Downward, the Deathward; the *Erotes*, the Upward, the Lifeward. Eros was the god of life, the popular reflection of Protogonos, the All-god. His feet were on the flowers, he couched in their folds; he was of all life; he was Dionysus; he was Pan. He gave a soul to life, and reality to a monotheistic dogma. And then from "over the midnight sea a voice was heard crying, 'Great Pan is dead.' " Let us look at Orpheus.

Orpheus came from Thrace, not as a god but as a man, a magical musician. His work was to modify the rites of the god he worshipped. He is the Good Shepherd in Christian art—forerunner of the Ravenna Saint Apollinare, who one by one weeded out the bad wild beasts from his congregation of mild, patient sheep.

Orpheus was also a teacher and a prophet; he brought a new religion and sought to restore an old one. He was martyred; his tomb became a mantic shrine. His followers tried to raise him to Olympian rank, but—like Herakles and Æsculapius—he was too human to be quite divine. In his saintly and ascetic figure early Christianity saw the prototype of Christ.

Dionysiac worshippers, as we saw, were "possessed" by Dionysus, in their orgiastic rites became him—as, after death, the worshippers of Osiris became Osiris. Orpheus retained the old Dionysian faith that man might become a god, but he changed the concept of god and sought godhead not by physical intoxication but by spiritual ecstasy, by abstinence and purification. Orphism, then, was a worship of the mysteries of life, of powers and potencies, rather than of personal gods. It was a religious sect.

Orphic mysteries are first mentioned by Herodotus; it is presumed that there was no Orphic sect in Greece before the second half of the sixth century B.C. As the sect had a definite set of doctrines, it was thereby distinguished from Greek state worship and all other cult associations; it was a society of believers, practising a cult unknown or disdained by official worship.

As Orphism was a curious blend of spiritual asceticism and Dionysiac ecstasy, we may get closer to its mysteries by recalling the Dionysiac mysteries and looking at the great mysteries in Crete. Mysteries, as we saw, are chiefly concerned with elaborate purification preparatory to handling magical things, the *sacra*. But Orphism sought to make man magical, divine; to bring about his complete union with the divine. In Crete, that was done by eating the god, a union symbolically effected by the rite of Sacred Marriage, and union by adoption of the rite of Sacred Birth. Such rites of Sacred Marriage and Sacred Birth became ultimately the central Eleusinian mystery.

Titans, the primeval powers of evil, in the Orphic legend murder the god; they dismember the One into the Many. Their impiety thus disperses the divine One into the multiplicity of things. These many are reborn as one in a new Dionysus sprung from Zeus, who now destroys with lightning the Titans who had eaten the limbs of the god. This *One* torn to pieces by the Titans was Zagreus, almost unknown to Greek literature and the centre of a primitive cult, a ritual figure. In Crete, the bull, Minotaur, took its yearly toll of human beings; in their ritual it was the tearing and eating of the bull—"possibly a human child." A Greek vase extant pictures a

Thracian tearing with his teeth a slain child, while Zagreus looks on approvingly.

As Orpheus' forefathers, the Titans, had dismembered and eaten the god, they had to be punished with thunderbolts, even though good came of their evil deed; so Orpheus himself, their descendant, can become Bacchus.

In short, the Titans were once divine; they fell; their descendant can make you divine if you are initiated into the mysteries. There are Titanic elements and Dionysiac elements, body and soul, in man. The Orphic doctrine says that man's duty is to free himself from the claims of the body in which the soul lies fast bound like a prisoner. But the soul has a long road to travel before it is free. Death frees it for a time, but it must again suffer imprisonment in a body; again it flutters in the wind, to be borne by a breath of wind into a new body—and so on through the "cycle of necessity." Thus the "wheel of birth" ever returns upon itself in hopeless repetition.

That cycle could be ended, the wheel stopped, by joining Orphism and its Bacchic mysteries; there alone lay salvation. Orphics alone were saved; the only people who could greet each other as *pure*. The first reward of the Orphic initiate was to have his deathless soul led by Hermes into the intermediate region where souls must go. Special poems announced his terrors and delights. In Hades, judgment waited. The impious suffered punishment and purgation in deep Tartaros; those not purified by Orphic mysteries lay in the Pool of Mire. Orphic initiates could get from the gods below pardon and purification for dead ancestral souls by paying a penalty in the next world for their misdeeds. But a true *Bacchos* could dwell for ever in the fair meadows of deep-running Acheron.

Plato, in his *Republic*, speaks of seers and mendicant quacks who pester rich men's doors, trying to sell books by Orpheus, showing them how by performing certain sacrifices they could be released from suffering after death—or go to hell if they didn't. Orphic priests even sold indulgences.

And so the old fear of ghosts turned into ancestor worship, which in turn developed into hero worship. Cults grew up—cults of human souls who raised themselves above their fellow-men by special powers. Thus the idea was born that death does not end all existence, nor Hades' gloom swallow up all life. Orphism was the last word in Greek religion; its ritual revived ancient practices and gave them new significance.

With Harrison, we may see in Orpheus a revived, intensified spirituality, ardent, ecstatic enthusiasm, a high self-conscious standard of moral conduct, deliberate simplicity of life, abstinence from many things, temperance in all, great quiet of demeanour, marvellous gentleness; or the reverse: formalism, faddism, priggishness, lapse into arid symbolism, pseudo-science, pseudo-philosophy, ignorant revival of obsolete rites, an exhibition of ignoble thaumaturgy and squalid credulity.

But to me it looks as though "the voice from across the midnight sea" had diagnosed the case only too correctly. Eros to the Orphics was not a *theos* but a *daimon*; the great god Pan had been murdered. Rationalism is dead; philosophy loves wisdom less and sorcery more, and turns its energy to raising spirits; the High Gods are replaced by mobs of idols and swarms of devils; miracle. mongering becomes a learned profession; surmise and revelation are Big Business; life itself becomes faded and grey; and the old Greek civilization, about to breathe its last, begins to pray that its soul may rest in peace.

That civilization, as we have seen, was reborn in Alexandria; its basis was science, which knows no race, language, or political or natural frontiers. That rosy dawn of science was soon darkened by ominous clouds. We have yet to see what they were, where they came from, what their portent was. But we know that civilization's dying gasp on Greek soil was the speculative philosophy of Neo-Platonism. Its mission was not to take this world as a home to work and play and live in, and work to make it a better home, but to leave it, fly from it. In short, it helped so far as it could to prepare the way for the next step in speculation. The world was ready for the Christian faith.

Paul was a Greek. Whether he was an initiate of the Orphic cult, as Macchioro claims, is far from certain. It is certain that the philosophy of Plato and the religion of Orpheus prepared the way for ready credence in the new sacrificed and resurrected God Paul preached to the Greek world. It is also certain that Orphic symbols have been found in Christian catacombs. In Plato's philosophy of the supernatural, in his Logos as Divine Reason, his postulate of

Divine Artificer, and in his astounding genius for manipulating
prose, the church found just the support it needed to make its
doctrines attractive to the Intelligentsia. The Church Fathers out-
Platoed Plato; they were the real Neo-Platonists.

x

Before me is a nickel magazine with a large rural circulation.
One of its page advertisements is devoted to phonograph records.
In the section headed "Sacred" are these titles: "Are You Washed
in the Blood?"; "How Wonderful Heaven Must Be"; "Life's Rail-
way to Heaven"; "There's No Disappointment in Heaven"; "Jesus
Getting Us Ready"; "Where We'll Never Grow Old."

There is nothing in these or in any other titles of sacred music
I know of, to suggest that this earth is any good or that life on it
is worth while. Christianity to millions today is a religion of the
defeated. They accept defeat when they accept religion. Nothing
here is satisfactory. To desire satisfaction is vanity; to gratify desire
is sinful. That attitude makes sound, healthy living well nigh impossible. It is a selfish idea; it makes for inhumanity; it fosters
aloofness from this world; it sets a premium on misunderstanding
this world.

Man adopts a new god just as he adopts a new car—when the
new one seems safer, sounder, surer. The Romans adopted the
Etruscan gods and then identified them with the Greek gods.

Rome borrowed the Greek gods in the sense that Mexico borrowed the Hebrew gods. There is only the sky to roof mankind;
there is only one moon, one sun, one thunderer, one rain-maker;
all seas are salt, all rains fresh; every river has a source; every crop
must have its moisture; every village its hero; every hero his shrine.
Every human being, in short, is born of woman, lives on earth, in
air, under the sky, and must die—and "go somewhere." All mankind has names for attitudes toward "nature," toward such natural
phenomena as must be encountered during life. Whenever and
wherever this "attitude" takes the form of a belief in supersensible,
superhuman, supernatural things or forces or powers, and leads to
acts which make that attitude effective, we have religion. That is
what religion is. If it is not that, it is something other than religion.

It would be amazing if there were not great resemblances between Roman and Greek religion and religious practices. There were. It is somewhat amazing that Rome was so tolerant of outside religions. She was. She even sought divine guidance from the East, from any direction. Romans wanted what we all want—health, wealth, and immortality; and they prayed for them, prayed to any god that dispensed such necessities. Also for salvation from every conceivable thing—especially from shivering for ever outside Hades, and from *lemures* or vagabond ghosts with mean, vindictive dispositions haunting crossroads and highways. It is the business of priests to get all these things—or something just as good.

Since the fabled days of Numa, Rome had had her college of priests or pontiffs. Emperor Augustus, as head of everything, assumed the rôle of Chief Priest or Pontifex Maximus, as the popes or papas are still styled. Early in her career, Rome began formally to adopt certain Greek gods—but only after they had been approved by the College of Pontiffs and authorized by the Senate. But because Greek was the language of culture and of the Muses, practically all Romans knew Greek mythology, and soon fell into the habit of accepting Greek personifications and giving them their own interpretation. Other Greek gods and mythical anthropomorphic beings were taken over—even after the Greeks had relegated some of them to the nursery—and fitted to their beliefs or into their mythology.

The net result was that Rome had a state religion of a kind. The essence of that religion was to take the world in which man has to live—the world he naturally loves to wander through, explore, and manipulate, and in which he loves to hunt and kill and fish and catch and eat—out of his hands and put it in charge of hands he could not train, control, or slap. And that was a disadvantage.

What could they do? Well, they prayed to those invisible, intangible "hands." Erected magnificent temples to some of them, put priests in charge of some, Vestal Virgins in charge of others. Priests and Virgins had to be fed and lodged, and some of the "hands" liked the odour of roast pork or beef. To some, more costly sacrifices were deemed necessary; even human blood was not inappropriate or offensive. Toward all unseen hands there was *some* kind of attitude, some degree of fear, respect, veneration, or gratitude. And their response was regulated by the thermometer of their emotions.

Rome's College of Pontiffs was a state institution; the function of its officers was as definite as that of our Department of State. They attended to certain business. They were neither preachers nor moralists. They belonged to no church, had no Bible, no credo. They were not trying to make people moral or sober or righteous, nor were they trying to save souls, cure disease, or wash away sins. Rome had certain gods, protectors. These gods had been treated thus and so, and Rome had prospered. Keep on treating them thus and so. Belief in them and in their protecting care was no more questioned than we question our belief that ours is the Land of the Free and the Home of the Brave, or that God's in His Heaven and will keep on looking after fools and Americans.

There were certain rites to be performed on certain dates and in certain prescribed ways. It was the Pontiffs' business to see that all was properly done. If the Senate ordered something new or something extra, they were there to make the new or extra effective. They had also kept the annals of the state on bronze tablets, which, as we have seen, the Vandals used as a mine for cheap raw material.

Some Romans were monotheists, finding Jupiter sufficiently all-embracing, all-powerful; the majority were polytheists; some did not know and were agnostics; some were atheistic, and instead of calling on Flora when they wanted flowers or on Pomona when they wanted fruit, called on their own particular rabbit's foot. Practically everybody then had his or her pet superstition or collection of pets —just as today. But though their list of superstitions was probably never so long as is California's or a college athlete's, their infantile beliefs included omens, signs, portents, and the efficacy of expiation and purification. They feared bad dreams, and black birds on the wrong side of the road. Thunder, lightning, and earthquake scared them. They believed that it had rained blood, that an ox had spoken, and that a statue can bleed or turn around.

Whether health was Health, and if so, just who Hygeia was, few knew or cared much. They did know certain ways of preserving health. They may not have been the best ways, but they got along with them. In general it may be said that all the gods in the Roman pantheon, from the tiniest nymph to mighty Jupiter enthroned on Capitol Hill, were kindly, well-disposed gods. They had brought Rome through. Keep on doing the right thing by them and they will do the right thing by Rome. Respect for these gods—especially the great gods—was as much a part of a Roman's habitual behaviour as it is for a Southerner to applaud when "Way Down in Dixie" strikes up, or for men in uniform to salute the flag, or for us all to rise when the band starts up, "Oh, say . . ."

Our forefathers deliberately divorced religion from government, but we are still forbidden certain blasphemous acts and are asked to swear on the Bible. We are finally divorcing an anthropomorphic superhuman being, Israel's Yahweh, from our coinage; and whether the Bible is, can, or must be read in the schools seems still hanging in the balance. Rome had not moved even so far in separating religion from state. As we can show our loyalty by an oath and our patriotism by a gesture, so anyone in Rome could show loyalty and patriotism by doing as the Romans did: respecting the national gods and shrines; being loyal to the nation's religion.

Otherwise, one could believe in as many or as few gods as one chose, or in none at all. Rome for her age was in religious matters the most tolerant and broad-minded nation the world had ever seen. Rome no more questioned one's religious views or beliefs than our own government is supposed to. She asked what every Empire has asked, namely, that no view dangerous to the empire, its emperor, or to existing social order, be held.

A Jew could have his synagogue in Rome and practise Judaism —and did; a Roman might become a Jew—some did; or worship Isis or Mithra, Orpheus or Christ. It was all right, provided they did not flaunt their religion in ways detrimental to state and society. Rome was as tolerant toward a new god as most of us are toward a new cough cure: we will try it, and if it works magic we will adopt it, even though we have to throw away an old bottle to make room for the new. Before the end of the second century of the Empire, Rome was a regular county fair for venders of new cough cures. Never, except possibly today, were new saviours so much in demand as in the days when the Empire was definitely headed for the Fall.

The nice old long-whiskered, white-gowned Druids that Claudius mopped up in Gaul were roasting human beings in wicker cages. Human sacrifice was against the laws of nature and especially against the laws of Rome. New York or Chicago does not ask the religion of its car-barn murderers, or hang them (when it gets them) for their religion. Claudius "persecuted" the Druids because they were fiends, and drove the remnant into Britain because they were stirring up sedition—trying to prevent the legitimate business of the Roman governors.

Christianity was getting its foothold in Rome about the time Claudius was getting rid of the Druids in Gaul and his fourth wife, Agrippina, was grooming her own son Nero for the august throne. Nero persecuted the Christians. They were not Druids; they had been supposed to be merely a variant of Judaism and had not only been tolerated but protected by Rome. Now they were being persecuted. Had they, or had Rome, changed? They were not Druids. What were they?

Paul always got a square deal from the Roman Governor; it was the Jews who were after him because he was a renegade. Even in Rome he was acquitted on his first trial. So, too, the Roman governors in Egypt made no objection to the Egyptians worshipping birds, cats, and crocodiles. Rome even sought Egyptian and Asiatic gods to open offices on the banks of the Tiber. Why, then, did they persecute Christians?

Absolutism in any form of human relationship is unnatural and makes for madness. The Cæsars had gone mad. Nero not only persecuted Christians; he slew and banished philosophers, made it a crime to philosophize. Domitian crucified the scribes who copied any work criticizing him. Tiberius "put down foreign religions," pulled down the temple of Isis, crucified her priests, expelled the Jews and proselytes, and drafted young Jews into the army and sent them to unhealthy garrisons. Anything or anybody that threatened or seemed to threaten the state's solidarity was treason, that cast aspersion on the emperor was *lèse majesté*.

It takes a really virtuous emperor—or man in any rank of life— to make his virtue his armour and not depend on brutal oppression of the under dog to prove his virtuousness. Rome might be eternal. The Empire was changing. Change was inevitable.

Three centuries after Alexander's death the Mediterranean world had become a Mediterranean lake. Every town on every island and on every bay and inlet was doing business with and taking orders from Rome, and was under her influence. For two hundred years, roughly, the dominating voice around that lake was saying: This is a good world: *Dum vivimus, vivamus*. But between the Golden Age of Antoninus, "Father of the World," and the end of the reign of Marcus Aurelius, the Roman world had ceased to be a secure stage for life's drama and had become a world of pestilence, famine, earthquake, bedevilled by the hordes of savages pouring in on all sides. The two hundred years' peace was gone. And with it went rationalism. Philosophy turned to revelation. There was no certain light anywhere; life was drab and dreary. And as the old civilization was preparing to give up the ghost, men everywhere began to believe in immortality, and to seek the means of insuring it with an ardour hitherto unknown in the history of the world.

Such a populace—in Rome, Jerusalem, Los Angeles—is easy prey for venders of patent medicines, distributors of divine healings, preachers of new magic. Chaldean astrologers, Egyptian wonder-workers, Hebrew kabalists, Persian magicians, Syrian sorcerers, Indian fakirs, tonsured, mitred priests, took possession of Rome, mistress of the world. Mithraic clergy in solemn intonation (says Briffault) called upon the Lamb of God that taketh away the sins of the world; tinkling bells of acolytes announced the culmination of the mystery service, and in clouds of incense the priest turned to the kneeling crowd and raised aloft the sacred chalice filled with life-wine. Women found ineffable comfort in unburdening their sorrows before the Queen of Heaven bearing the Divine Son in her arms, and in mingling their sorrow in mourning the death of the god.

It was even worse in the eastern provinces. "In Antioch and Alexandria all the mysticism, occultism, and abracadabras of Jewry, magical Egypt, and Orphic Greece held their Sabbath of Unreason. Religions changed their symbols and rituals; worshippers passed from shrine to shrine. Mithraism, once a simple and pure popular cult, got the poor, lowly, and disinherited: master knelt by slave in the mysteries."

Mithraism had become thoroughly established in Rome, as had the worship of Isis and Osiris. By 217 Rome had fallen so low that she had to purchase peace from the Parthians and the army proclaimed a fourteen-year-old Syrian sun-priest emperor. That emperor in his four years' reign as Elagabalus (Heliogabalus) raised Debauchery Preferred to a new high; but in his successor, Severus Alexander, Rome could still give her people an excellent ruler, and a great jurist (Ulpianus) who, fifteen hundred years before Rousseau, declared that all men are created free and equal. Yet within thirty-five years Rome had again dropped so low that under Aurelian (270-275) imperial patronage became the official religion. There was some excuse for this, for Aurelian was a fighter and rightly styled Restorer of the World.

With Caracalla the storm broke. For a century ignorance and superstition reigned; also eighty emperors in ninety years. There were no small farmers left, no responsible statesmanship. Rude soldiers steered the ship of state. The Sassanian Persians had risen to power in the East to rival Rome. Zenobia from Palmyra ruled over Asia Minor, Syria, and Egypt.

Diocletian restored peace and reëstablished the Empire, ruling from Asia Minor like an Oriental despot; and having done his work, divided his empire among the best men available and abdicated—to return (305) to his farm in Dalmatia to plant cabbages with his own hands. He had found the Empire shaken by internal discord and rocked by external violence; he left it tight and snug, at peace within, and united from the shores of Holland to the Black Sea, from the Tigris to the Nile. But he deprived the Roman Senate of its last shred of power, and he persecuted the Christians.

The Christians, we may recall, were the sect Nero had used as torches to light his garden, the sect that had suffered general persecution in 250. That sect was now, within fifty years, to become the state religion under Constantine (323-337); and within sixty more years to wring from the dying Emperor Julian the admission, *Vicisti Galilæe!* Yes, the Galilean had won.

Julian (the "Apostate") was a Christian up to the age of twenty, but seems to have been turned from it by the bigotry, hypocrisy, and uncharitableness of the Christians. Especially was he displeased by the vileness and cold-blooded hypocrisy of Constantine the Great, who had embraced Christianity for political reasons only. Julian was not only a great emperor but a very remarkable man. He was also a great scholar and writer. He preferred his pagan philosophy. He hoped to see Rome's old state religion restored in a purified form, and did what he could to withdraw the privileges which Constantine had accorded the Christians.

But the tide had gone too far. On his death from wounds received in defeating the Persians at Ctesiphon, the army reëstablished a Christian on the throne with the appropriate name of Jovianus. Christianity was now the religion of the Roman Senate. The Romans had a new sign to conquer with; Yahweh had supplanted Zeus and Jupiter; Christ was Saviour, not Mithra nor Osiris; Heaven had replaced Hades. Humanity again—and more definitely than ever before—turned its back on the certain material good things of this world for the possible spiritual blessings of an unseen world.

What that religion might have become had it been born elsewhere and at another time is as futile a speculation as it would be to discuss the possible history of Greece had there been no Orient, or Rome's fate had there been no Greece or Christianity. There was an Orient, there was a Greece, there was a Rome. The Roman Church is inconceivable without Rome and Greece and the Orient. It was organized on a Roman politico-legal foundation; its theology and philosophy are rooted in Grecian philosophy and mysticism. The Neo-Platonists especially had turned more and more toward monotheism. The Christian God that grew up was a product of that philosophy and of Roman imperial despotism.

Christianity is as surely a historical product as is the Constitution of the United States or the latest model airplane.

History? We saw Cæsar in Alexandria; we spoke of the Cæsareum. We saw the Jews at work in Alexandria on the Old Testament. We saw the great school of learning that had been set up in Alexandria. Let us take one more look at it.

The Cæsareum is nothing now but a rubbish heap. The imposing thing in its vicinity is Pompey's Pillar, the largest ancient relic in Alexandria worth looking at. That great column of red Assuan granite was once part of a temple of Serapis; it was set up on its present site by Emperor Theodosius in 391, to celebrate a Christian victory over pagans and the destruction of heathen temples and monuments.

Pompey's Pillar does not mark his tomb; nor did Cæsar build the Cæsareum. Cleopatra began it as a great temple in honour of Antony. Augustus completed it as a temple where divine Cæsars might be worshipped. Even its site is not certainly known today.

It is known that Alexandria was soon in the throes of Christianity. It is a tradition that St. Mark preached the gospel there. It is known that some bones were removed to Venice, where, presumably, they are still venerated as the saint's relics in San Marco Cathedral. It is known that by 190 Alexandria possessed a theological school, and that Clement, an early Church father, at the beginning of the third century was trying to make a religion out of Christianity and Neo-Platonism; that despite persecution, especially by Decius, Valerian, and Julian the Apostate, it was headquarters for Christian erudition and the orthodox faith of the Athanasian Creed; and that in 230 it yielded spiritual hegemony to Constantinople, which now became the guardian of Greek thought and science. It is known that Theodosius ended pagan Alexandria; that its Christian patriarch showed unholy zeal in smashing pagan works; and that in 415 Hypatia, learned, modest, and beautiful daughter of the pagan mathematician Theon, was dragged from her chariot, stripped, torn to pieces, and burned by a Christian mob, because she was a pagan, and learned, and beautiful.

*Exeunt* paganism, learning, and beauty.

Enter Christianity and the Bible.

What is Christianity? What is the Bible? How did the Christians get to Rome, suffer persecution, and *win*?

# CHAPTER NINE

## The Myths and Mysteries of the East Become the Holy Bible of the West

1. "It Ought to Be an Unpleasant Thing for a Man to Be an Infidel." 2. The Promised Land; Its Chosen People and Their Literature. 3. The Canonization of the Bible, or "Inspiration." 4. Israel's Primitive Religion and God of War. 5. Israel's Messianic Hope and Last Prophecy. 6. The Witnesses; or, Evidences of Christianity. 7. "Search the Scriptures"; or, Make a Myth to Prove a Myth. 8. Saul of Tarsus Goes Roman.

### I

LANGUAGE, monogamous marriage, fire; discovery and invention of tools; domestication of plants and animals. Then man bent metals to suit his needs and had more time to think and to mould nature to suit his fancy. The cultivating, moulding, and disseminating processes were facilitated by the invention of phonetic writing. But man still lacked two great aids to security: he had no reliable guide for his movement over unknown lands and across unseen seas, nor a cheap and effective mechanism to put his written word into circulation. The compass and print paper, with movable type, supplied these deficiencies. They were in use by the time Columbus discovered America and are deeply embedded in our civilization. That civilization reached its culmination with pagan Imperial Rome; with Christian Rome it went into a thousand years' sleep. No other event in human history worked such havoc with man's handiwork, such momentous change in his outlook.

All that man had built through thousands of years of toil and effort, even the world itself and the joy of living, all—wife, home, friends, health, and happiness—were to be renounced in the name of a Saviour sent to bring, not peace, but a sword, into the world.

And the sword began to do the Lord's work with a ruthlessness that would have made Assyria's war lord green with envy.

Yet "it ought to be an unpleasant thing for a man to have to say plainly that he does not believe in Jesus Christ," said the Dean of Canterbury recently. Ought it? Not very long ago it was not only unpleasant, it was downright dangerous. Does the Dean's "ought" imply a longing for the good old pre-anæsthetic days, when the Church could practise vivisection on non-believers' bodies in the interests of the True Faith?

Those good old days are gone, for a while at any rate. Have we yet reached the day when it ought to be an unpleasant thing for a man to be a hypocrite? We *have* reached the day when the dogmas the Church asks us to accept may be examined in the light of reason and known facts. If these dogmas are founded in fact, no examination can overthrow them. If they are not founded in fact, we have a right to say so; and especially, it seems to me, we have a right to set forth the grounds of our infidelity if, having examined the evidence, we find it unconvincing, even though we once accepted the dogmas and professed faith in them.

This difficulty arises: does agreement with certain principles of Christianity make one a Christian, or can one be a Christian only by believing in Jesus Christ?

I need not point out that there are churches and churches, each claiming exclusive powers and privileges and some claiming to be the *only true* church. If one were to be dropped on this earth from another planet, let us say, with the intent to become a "Christian," how would one go about it, whose word would one accept as authoritative? Every church, I presume, would say, "Ours; our Bible is our authority."

Bibles differ, but agree in certain great fundamental dogmas, all of which have to do with the words or teachings not primarily of a man called Jesus, but of a supernatural being called the Christ.

This Christ was supernatural because he lived in the flesh—like a human; suffered for the sins of mankind; and after having performed many miracles or supernatural events, died and came to life again and ascended to heaven. Incarnation, Atonement, and Resurrection are the three basic Christian dogmas. Greatest of these is Resurrection. Christianity as revealed religion hangs, or falls, on the alleged fact of Resurrection.

The evidence for the alleged facts of Christian dogma is the Gospel narratives. The important question, then, is: are the Gospel narratives credible? Do they furnish such evidence as would normally pass as authentic or reliable history or would be admitted in a court of justice? Would any of the testimony offered by the Christian Bible in proof of the resurrection of Jesus be admitted as legal evidence in the humblest justice court in Christendom?

Evidence, to be legal, must be credible. Hearsay evidence is not credible; seeing and hearing evidence is. This does not mean that every witness is to be believed or that every bit of contemporary testimony is credible. But to be a witness one must have witnessed something, must have lived at the time of the event, must have been a contemporary.

A Jesuit father of the Catholic Church recently declared that "the Resurrection of Jesus cannot be attacked by history, because there is no historical evidence against it." Quite so; nor is there any historical evidence that Apollonius of Tyana did not raise the dead to life, or that at least a hundred American cult heroes did not ascend to heaven—to say nothing of the well-known resurrected gods of Greek, Roman, Hindu, and Chinese mythology.

"No historical evidence against it?" Did Paul's disciples in Corinth believe in the Resurrection? They did not. How else explain Paul's, "How say some among you that there is no resurrection of the dead. . . . If the dead rise not, then is Christ not raised?" When Paul wrote that, the Gospels were not yet written; the Resurrection was as yet a tradition only and not at all universally accepted by the early Christian churches. As we shall see, the idea of resurrection, not only of the Saviour, but of saviours, was and had been in the air for centuries.

Why does no single Gospel writer say, "I saw"? Why are there four, and only four, Gospels? When were the Gospels written? What, in short, is the credibility of the testimony in the Christian Bible as to the dogmas of the Christian religion?

But Christianity is a *revealed* religion. Well, who revealed it; and when and where; and what is it that was revealed? It seems certain that the revelation is seriously questioned, or there could not be so many kinds of Christian churches. To my youthful inquiry it was made certain that the Bible is the Book of books, that it all hangs together, is all divinely inspired. I could not "accept" this or that part, but must accept it all or none—like a nerve, according to Fechner's law. But whether I accepted it or not, I must treat it respectfully or I would be doubly punished. Our family Bible was as certainly a fetish as was ever wonder-working idol to African cannibal.

I respected and accepted it, but I could not follow it because my Christian community did not expect me to follow it; it had no more use for humility, poverty, and understanding than it had for tramps, waifs, and Catholics. It was enough that one go through the motions on Sunday and keep sober and out of jail the other six days. It was all right for a deacon to rob his widowed daughter-in-law—as long as he did it "legally"; and it was all right for another deacon to acquire a quarter of the town's property, so long as he only loaned widows money at five per cent a month and collected it in advance. It was all very mysterious, but so long as I was saved nothing else seemed to matter much.

Is Christianity wedded to civilization in an indissoluble mono-gamic marriage? If so, and we have less peace on earth and less security in our homes than in the year 30 throughout the Roman Empire, what is wrong with the wedded twain, and is it Christianity or civilization that is wrong? If these twain are to save the world, they should be up and doing. If the marriage is a failure, why not a divorce? If we are a secular nation, why pretend otherwise? If we cannot be good, perhaps we can be happy. If we cannot cope with evil, perhaps we can alleviate suffering. If we cannot love our fellow-men, perhaps we can hate the idols and superstitions which stand in humanity's way.

Our business now is to examine the Bible as we might examine Homer, or the Egyptian Book of the Dead, or the Persian Avesta. Who wrote it; when was it written and why; and what does it say? In short, what was the nature of the victory alleged to have been admitted in the dying Julian's *Thou hast conquered, O Galilean!*

And, first, who are the Jews?

## II

The Jews were not primarily makers of history, but rather were made by history. When they moved from the desert into the Land of the Book, great chapters of history had already been made by the great nations on either side of them. In the ensuing history of those nations, that of the Jews was but an incident.

The land that had been promised them is hardly what we should call a Promised Land. It was, rather, a poor, unhappy hunting-ground, across which great armies moved to conquest or at Megiddo met to fight it out. Behind them were other Semitic plundering nomads; in front, the Philistines and Phœnicians, with their own cults and gods. It was not a rich country. It was hardly to be expected that the Jews would develop a rich culture or make material contributions to civilization; and they did not. As soon as their walled hill towns got enough wealth to tempt a burglar, a burglar was upon them. Assyria ended the two-hundred-years-old kingdom of Israel and carried many Israelites into captivity, and had not Cyrus the Persian restored them to Palestine the Bible we are asked to swear upon and by would in all probability never have been written.

Note again, please, that the Jews who returned to Jerusalem were not *the* Jews, but only those who *wanted* to return, those who had necessarily been influenced by their sixty years' exile but had never become reconciled to Babylonian culture; in short, the fanatics in the tribal cult. Those who remained called them "the bran, the dregs of the people."

Those who returned—the Judaism of the Exile—were the makers of such contributions to civilization as especially interest us here. The career of the Jews as a nation, as a self-governing people, was, as we saw, brief and inglorious. To say that they had a genius for religion is to say what may be equally well said of the Egyptians, Chaldeans, Persians, Hindus, Aztecs, or Australians. Historically speaking, their temple at Jerusalem, like a Hindu or Aztec temple, was a shambles—just one sacrifice after another. It was a system of sacrificing flesh and blood to an anthropomorphic power for special favors.

After the Exile the Jews may be said to have specialized in one particular, and that is the phase of their activity which forms part of our Biblical inheritance. They began to compose systematic write-ups of their god Yahweh, to turn their own local deities into servants of Yahweh: and all written up with more regard for biographic detail than for historic truth. Moses and Joshua became the miraculous leaders of divine deliverance in prehistoric times.

Jew (or Hebrew) is not a term of race or blood, or even of language, but of politics—a name for a group of tribes, the confederation of the Bedawi. Each tribe had its own god, as did the tribes or city states in Sumer-Akkad. The Yahweh cult through historic circumstance prevailed, and in course of time was imposed upon the other tribes. But not all Hebrew kings were Yahwist; some of them were anti-Yahweh or polytheistic. Thus, one prophet saw Jerusalem with as many Baal altars as streets, and Judah with as many gods as cities.

Even the post-exilic monotheism, so-called, never put an end to the old ceremonial tribal god, who lived in the temple while the temple stood, and when the temple fell became Chief Rabbi on high. But whereas formerly he had spent three hours a day playing with Leviathan, he now spent his leisure instructing those who had died in infancy.

The synagogue became an institution only after the Babylonian captivity. Where the prophets formerly exhorted, they now predicted, à la Chaldean. Persian influence—Evil Power, etc.—more and more moulded ideas taken from the Chaldean star-gazers, seen, for example, in Jacob's zodiacal children and Joseph's dream.

Note, too, that in Isaiah (xlv: 1) Yahweh takes Cyrus under his wing, or rather takes him by the right hand, and calls him his anointed—Messiah, Christ. Without Cyrus, I repeat, we should in all probability have no Old Testament. Shall we thank Cyrus or the Assyrians?

Those Israelites of North Palestine had originally come in contact with the Canaanites, from whom they learned such civilization as they had, including the worship of the Canaanite god, Lord or Baal. Saul's son, Ishbaal, and Jonathan's son, Meribaal, were men of Baal.

The Jews in the south had clung to their old tribal god, Yahweh. They were pastoral people. Yahweh was the god of poor shepherds;

Baal, of rich town folk. The Tyrian Baal was Melkarth, "King of the city." But Elijah, enraged because Ahab (married to Jezebel, a Tyrian princess) had slain Naboth, went north and denounced Ahab; and finally his followers killed the whole northern royal family and the Canaanite priests of Baal. That made the shepherd a warrior, and Yahweh was now thought of as a war-god.

This was early in the ninth century B.C., the time of the prophets' struggle with the idolatrous northern Israelite kingdom. Jehu especially was a smiter of temples and a murderer of Baal's priests. There was nothing holy or sacred about Israel's wars; they sought revenge, booty. *Israel* was a war-cry; Israel's oldest monument is a war song. Deborah's ode is fine poetry, but its business is with war and not with religion. Jehu "restored" Yahwism as the state religion of Israel—but it was the old bull cult with a new name.

Yahweh long remained, and still is, a war-god: a hand on the banner of Yahweh! Yahweh has war with Amalek for ever. So let all thine enemies perish, O Yahweh. And when he had brought victory, he rested in his tent. When Joshua prayed for more time that he might finish off his enemies, "the sun stood still and the moon stayed, till the people were avenged on their foes." Such a war-god was worth more than an armoured tank.

With Amos, shepherd from the Judah hills of the south, came a new note. The south poor envied the north rich; so his god was a kindly father who was not pleased with rich living. Amos became a reformer. He denounced fine clothes, corrupt living, and everything beyond his reach. He was the first Hebrew reformer, but before Amos preached justice toward the poor, social justice and a humane code of ethics had been incorporated into religious practices on the Nile.

Amos lived about 750 B.C. The Jews had already borrowed an alphabet from Phœnician and Aramean merchants, had given up their clay tablets borrowed from the Babylonians, and were writing on papyrus with Egyptian pen and ink. Amos may have borrowed his idea of social justice also from Egypt. At any rate, he put his sermons into writing. They are not the earliest writings in the Bible, but they are among the oldest. Presumably, excerpts from the ninth-eighth century documents written in Judah were incorporated into the present Pentateuch and into Joshua, Judges, Samuel, and Kings.

In the Book of Kings are certain stories of the early prophets with a viewpoint earlier than that of Amos. As Deuteronomy was not written before 650, its theology post-dates the prophets of the Babylonian captivity, although it contains many ancient laws. Leviticus, the Holiness Code, was written about 600 B.C.; and the Priestly Code, as found in Exodus, about 500 B.C.

Let us now turn to their literature.

That Yahweh began as a primitive local god of the Hebrews there is no doubt. To us he seems unlovely. He was unlovable to the Hebrews. Gods are rarely born of love; worship of them is rarely inspired by love—whether in Palestine, Egypt, Greece, Yucatan, or the Fiji Islands. And as a matter of fact the Hebrews themselves in their despair thought Assyria's god stronger—better war-medicine—than theirs.

Of that despair the Prophets were born. Their business was to turn defeat into victory. They were moralists; their task, the moral regeneration of the despondent. Our Yahweh, they said in substance, is better than Asshur; he rules a wider territory. He only used the Assyrians to teach you a lesson for your wrong-doing. Be penitent, have courage, and you will see. He will punish those wicked Assyrians!

And when Sennacherib's army was destroyed by pestilence in the Nile Valley, the priests could shout: See! Didn't the Prophet tell you that Yahweh would send his destroying angel? And with Nineveh's fall a century later, still more prophecies were "fulfilled" —by editors, writing long after the events. Then came the Babylonians, and Judah followed Israel into exile. Some fled to Egypt, where Jeremiah tried to preach a spiritual God, but they had to have a temple to be spiritual in. Then arose an unknown prophet who, as we read in Isaiah (Chapters XL-LV) seemed to preach monotheism, and, according to the editorial headlines of my Bible, foretold Babylon's destruction, sent Christ, exhorted trust in Christ, spoke of Christ's "free redemption" and foretold his "sufferings." In fact, the amount of foretelling read into these chapters, and the deductions drawn therefrom as expressed in page and chapter headings in my Bible, are strictly in keeping with the psychology of makers of "inspired" texts.

The Book of Isaiah, as we saw, was possibly begun by 700 B.C. It was certainly added to, amended, and revised, in the sixth, fifth, fourth, third, and second centuries. The eighth-century Prophets were trying to turn a primitive religion of taboos and sacrifice into one of morals and upright living. They worked the old legends over to point morals—as the moralist compilers of the Pentateuch had plundered the past to point their moral. Shotwell calls them "high-minded" moralists—just why I do not know. To my way of thinking, it is no more "high" minded in a moralist to plunder and pervert than it is in a mother to lie to a son to improve his morals. This is certain: straight-mindedness seems incompatible with every kind of propaganda, moralist or otherwise. I venture the guess that it is especially difficult for any moralist to think straight.

When Cyrus loosed the exiles and allowed them to restore the temple in Jerusalem on a modest scale, the time seemed ripe to the Jewish priests to do what had been done before, and what was to be done so often thereafter—combine religion and politics in one man. The high priest of the temple became the ruler of the new state. The old religion now became the state religion, the official religion—"inspired," as is every state religion. The occasion necessitated a codification of the old religious laws, taboos, sanctions, etc. —the Pentateuch, the *Law*. There also finally emerged, says Breasted, a hymn-book of this second temple.

The Book of Psalms is that hymn book—a collection of one hundred and fifty religious songs. And a wonderful collection it is of the joys and longings, hopes and fears, penitence and grief over sin, sorrow and anguish over calamity, and gratitude for forgiveness and restoration. Also wild cries for revenge and the deep grief of despair. Also the hope of the coming Kingdom. Every human emotion and sentiment finds expression in the Psalter; "the whole range of human life," says Bewer; its joy and woe, light and shadow, its daily routine. Some of the songs are possibly as old as David, but the exact date of not one song can now be known. The Psalter as we know it was certainly not completed before the canon of Writings was completed.

The last song of all (Psalm CL) is especially interesting because it lists the musical instruments that accompanied the temple choir —trumpet, harp, timbrel, and cymbals. But all tradition of the temple music, says Bewer, has been lost. We know nothing of the melodies or tunes, only that they sang and danced before the Lord!

Yahweh dwelt, as does the god in a Hindu temple, in the inner-most shrine, the Holy of Holies. Within the temple they were liter-ally in his presence. To the temple all were expected to go three times a year for the great festivals: "Arise ye, and let us go up to Zion unto Yahweh our God"; and up they went, to the sound of songs and pipes. And when near the holy city possibly sang, "I will lift up mine eyes unto the hills, from whence cometh my help." Psalm LXXXIV shows how keenly the pilgrims longed for the tem-ple; Psalm CXXII, how joyfully they received the summons. "If I forget thee, O Jerusalem, let my right hand forget her cunning" (Psalm CXXXVII). And many have not forgotten it yet.

In Psalm XXIV, taken in conjunction with Psalm XV, Jewish religion reaches its crest; XXIV elevates moral purity, social moral-ity; XV says that only the righteous citizen is fit to dwell in the holy hill.

> And in thy high and holy hill
>     who shall a dweller be?
> The man that walketh uprightly,
>     and worketh righteousness,
> And as he thinketh in his heart,
>     so doth he truth express.
> Who doth not slander with his tongue,
>     nor to his friend doth hurt;
> Nor yet against his neighbour doth
>     take up an ill report. . . .
> His coin puts not to usury,
>     nor take reward will he
> Against the guiltless.
>
>             .    .    .    .    .
>
> Ye gates, lift up your heads; ye doors,
>     doors that do last for aye,
> Be lifted up, that so the King
>     of glory enter may.
> But who is he that is the King
>     of glory? who is this?
> The Lord of hosts, and none but he,
>     the King of glory is.

If Israel had only accepted that conception, Bewer quotes an eminent Jewish commentator as saying, "the religion of Yahweh would have become the religion of the world." Israel was too human. There was no human god yet, only a superhuman power to be feared and bargained with.

No, that crest is not the average of the songs. The high note sounded in Psalms xv and xxiv is more often a low note—a promissory note: Grant me so-and-so and I will do so-and-so; "burnt offerings of fatlings"; "with the sweet smoke of rams"; "bullocks with he-goats." "I will pay Thee my vows." "Blessed be Yahweh, who has not turned away my prayer."

The Psalms are religious hymns, collected from many that must have been sung by the Israelites through the ages. Yet many of them seem remote from spirituality of any kind. Printed today, they would be denied the mails because of their immorality. But when we turn to Chapter iv of the Song of Songs and remember that sister really means sweetheart, we have sexual pleasure so explicitly stated that we wonder how this, and Chapters ii and vii, ever got between the covers of a divinely inspired book. They are, as Bewer says, exquisite in form and in sentiment, but they are frankly erotic. And they were meant to be, warm-blooded love songs in the best Oriental imagery and as plain to an Oriental as a barn door.

Well, I Kings iv: 32 said that Solomon was a great song-writer as well as a maker of proverbs: "his songs were a thousand and five." The Song of Solomon was *The* Song of Songs, Solomon's best! They *could* not be mere warm love songs—as they appear to be and are—because Solomon was a paragon, not only of wisdom, but of piety. *Ergo*, The Song does not sing of earthly love, but of the love of Yahweh, the bridegroom, for Israel, the bride. The Christian Church did even better by itself: it accepted the Canticles as canonical and turned the Yahweh-Israel allegory into a Christ-church allegory. Thus, my Bible writes above Chapter ii, "The mutual love of Christ and his church."

Some of the songs seem older than the exile; most of them belong to the third century b.c. They are secular folksongs, and as such were sung, says Bewer, in wine-houses long after their canonization. The pity is that there are not more of them. Deep, passionate, human love, strong as death, marriage without the sanctification of religious rites, are a wholesome note in any Bible.

And enormously to its credit be it said, neither heaven nor hell is often brought out and placed on exhibition in the Hebrew Bible, nor is any devil painted as horribly as Plato depicted one. In fact, the Hebrew Bible was far from a cult book for the cure of sick souls or a guide for eternal bliss. Such ideas were in the air during the late centuries, but were not uppermost in the minds of the Jews. What they wanted primarily was not salvation, but revenge. The world had gone wrong. They had fine faith, as seen in the Psalms; narrow-minded fanaticism, as seen in Esther; the patience of Job and the pessimistic scepticism of Ecclesiastes; they had sorrows and disappointments, and successes which proved mirages. And if the Seleucid king Antiochus Epiphanes had left them alone instead of persecuting them unmercifully, they might have become Greeks in religion as well as in language and culture. He did persecute them. And after fourteen years' struggle and under the leadership of Judas Maccabæus, they were free again. And again they were persecuted—by Herod, king of Judea.

Then they became part of the Roman province of Syria. Still they did not turn to devil-dancing or ghost-hunting. They wanted revenge, divine justice, a new Messiah to reëstablish a kingdom of the Jews, where the lowly should be exalted and the high and mighty humbled. They did not want to reach heaven or escape hell; they wanted an earthly kingdom here and now. During the last two centuries many of them had seen the wish come true. They accomplished that, we may suspect, because they agreed with the Mishnah that "a man who philosophizes on what there is above the heavens or below the earth, what existed before creation or might have come since its cessation, would be happier never to have been born."

The Mishnah consists of texts begun under the Maccabees and compiled about 100 B.C. The Gemara was comments on the Mishnah. Together they form the Talmud. There is also a Palestinian Talmud codified in Jerusalem in the fourth century A.D.; and the much larger Talmud or codification of Babylonian rabbinic discussions of the fifth and sixth centuries. The Talmud is to the Jews what the New Testament is to Christians—an authoritative Word.

That, roughly, is the literature of the Jews—the "Christian Epic," as Santayana calls it. While there is much that may be termed good literature in it, the epic of a universe created in less than a week, with man's temptation, transgression, and expulsion from the lovely garden, etc., is neither great nor original—nor even consistent. It is far inferior to the great epics of India and Greece—or to its own Babylonian original. In fact, it seems likely that had there been no Babylonian captivity, there would have been no Christian epic. Certain it is that the laws of Moses, which underlie many of our customs and ideals, originated in Sumer, and are found in the Code of Hammurabi.

While the Christian epic differs from most epics in emphasizing the Fall and its evil consequences on the fruit of the womb, most epics and mythologic literature in general show keen observation and even what we may call intelligence. But makers of systems of philosophy and of religion felt no such need to observe or to use their intelligence. Hence the emphasis on sin in the Christian epic, on "mind" in the Greek philosophies.

Our interest, however, is not in Hebrew literature as such, but in our Holy Bible and its religion. We have now to see how our Bible was formed—the nature of its inspiration, so to say. How was it canonized?

### III

Writings in ancient times were committed to stone or bronze, or to clay tablets or papyrus—a kind of paper made from thin slices of papyrus reed pasted together crosswise. As Phœnician Byblos was a centre of export for papyrus rolls, it became the Greek word for book—*biblos*.

*Ta Biblia* to the Greek fathers meant The Books; but the Latin fathers used the word *biblia*, not as a neuter plural, but as a feminine singular. The Saxons did not use the word Bible for the Scriptures, but *Ge-Writ*. Coverdale, first to publish a complete Bible in English, called it *Biblia*. John Rogers first used the word Bible for the Scriptures in 1537.

A *testament* is the thing made when one makes a will or a disposition of one's worldly goods. Its use for the two parts of the Bible is inappropriate, and is due to a misunderstanding of the

Greek (*diathake*) for the Hebrew word for covenant. Thus, Paul in Corinthians speaks of "the old covenant" and of "Christ's ministers of the new covenant." Origen, in the third century, spoke of "the divine Scriptures, the so-called Old and New Covenants"; and so they should be called today.

Whatever it be called, the Bible is a book only because it is printed as a book. It is a unit in the same sense that all the things in an Indian medicine-man's bundle constitute a unit. The early Christian fathers did not regard it as a unit or as a book. Jerome in the fourth century called it the *Bibliotheca Divina*, the Divine Library. And so it is, a library of books.

Hebrew writings of any description appear late in history as compared with their neighbours. The oldest known Hebrew document is the Moabite Stone, now in the Louvre. It was erected about 850 B.C. by King Mesha of Moab as a tribute to his god Chemosh, to celebrate his victory over the revolting Israelites—although that is not quite how II Kings III:5 puts it. Next in time (about 700 B.C.) is the six-line Siloam inscription found in a pool in Jerusalem. It is of local interest only, but, like the Moabite inscription, is in Hebrew. From these only can any idea be had of Hebrew writing during the time of the Kings.

In 1616 an Italian traveller discovered in Damascus the enormously interesting and important Samaritan Pentateuch.

When Sargon II in 722 B.C. carried off 27,290 Israelites from around Samaria, he replaced them with at least nine other nationalities for safety's sake. These immigrants intermarried with the Hebrews and adopted their religion. The returning Exiles resented this, and expelled an Israelite high priest for having a foreign wife. This Israelite, says Josephus, was Manasseh; and he took with him a copy of the Pentateuch—all the Scripture the Jews then had.

This Pentateuch and the Siloam and Moabite inscriptions are the oldest known Hebrew texts; they are all in old Hebrew characters, not square, no vowels, consonants only, and the words separated by dots. The oldest existing Hebrew manuscripts date from the ninth century A.D. The characters are square, as they are today, and the words are not separated but are indicated by marks beneath the characters, as are the vowels.

Alexandria, as we saw, three centuries before the Christian Era had become the Highbrow and Big Business centre of the world. It had enough Jews to have a Jewish quarter, and they worshipped in an old Egyptian temple remodelled after the temple at Jerusalem. They spoke Greek, had their priests, and kept up their Jewish rites, but they could not read their Bible, so it was translated into Greek and called the Septuagint Version, or simply LXX, because, tradition says, seventy men did the translating.

Were they inspired? Certainly. That is what religion is—*inspiration*. No inspiration, no religion. But there are sceptics. Very well; inspire another story, reduce tradition to writing. So they inspired an epistle to the effect that an officer in Ptolemy II's army had told how seventy-two specially imported elders from Jerusalem began their translation on an island far from the madding crowd, each translator working quite by himself. That is, there were seventy-two translators. When all had finished they compared notes—and lo and behold, the seventy-two translations were identical! That "fact" guaranteed infallibility and divine inspiration. That officer story was a myth; the epistle, a forgery.

The known facts are that the "LXX" Bible was translated from Hebrew into Greek in Alexandria during the course of a century and a half, beginning about 280 B.C., and was finished by 130 B.C.; by whom is quite unknown. When the mythical LXX did their translating, not all the Old Testament was yet in existence. Ecclesiastes, for example, was written about 200 B.C.; Daniel and parts of Isaiah and Zechariah, still later.

That Greek translation or LXX Bible differs materially from the oldest Hebrew Bible extant. Matter was either omitted by the translators or added by unknown hands later. Which means that no one knows just what the Hebrew Bible of 300 B.C. was or said. Into the differences between what was supposed to be the Hebrew Bible and what is known as the Hebrew Bible we cannot go further than to note that the years from Adam to the Flood in the Greek translation are 2,262; in the Hebrew 1,656; and in the Samaritan Pentateuch 1,307. Abraham was born 1,170 or 940 or 290 years after the Flood, according to the Divine Word as found in the LXX, Samaritan Pentateuch, or the Hebrew version. That may be good guessing, but it sounds very human. The Hebrew differs from the Samaritan Pentateuch in some six thousand spots. Take your choice.

More important to note is the choice made in 100 B.C. It was really not a choice, for the Samaritan Pentateuch was buried sixteen centuries deep and the Hebrew Bible as now known was at least ten centuries unborn. In 100 B.C. the LXX was the only Bible available. It became, says Simms, the Bible of the Greek-speaking Jews not only of Alexandria but of the entire Mediterranean world. It was the Bible of Jesus, of the Apostles, and of the early Christian church. It is still the official Old Testament of the Greek Catholic, the Abyssinian, Egyptian, and Armenian churches.

By the beginning of the third century A.D. three other Greek translations of the Hebrew Bible had appeared. Meanwhile the LXX Bible had been copied and recopied—by more or less fallible human hands, each having no higher guide than his own conscience.

Of the *books* of our Bible, not one exists as it was written; there are no original manuscripts of any Old or New Testament book. They have been repeatedly edited and copied; and as the early Hebrew scribes wrote without vowels, there have been many long arguments as to just what certain words and phrases meant. If, for example, you take any sentence on this page and copy it without vowels, and then run the consonants together without spaces between the words, it becomes a puzzle of a sort and might easily be read in more than one way.

That is one reason why we do not know just what the Hebrews called their principal God, the Divine Name. They were afraid not only to take it in vain, but to take it at all. J H V H might be Jehovah or Jahveh; it was probably Jahveh and pronounced Yahweh. The Authorized Version (King James) uses Jehovah only four times, and it is never put on Jesus' lips. The word Lord (Adonai) was used instead.

To illustrate the difficulty in having to supply vowels to find out what a text is trying to say, Simms uses the three consonants B R N: they may be read barn, born, burn, barony, briny. The King James version is bad not only because it is in old-fashioned, antiquated English, but because it was based on faulty texts. But it got such a foothold as a fetish that many still think it represents the Original Revelation, so sacred that not one critical finger may be laid on one ambiguous or senseless word, not one comma displaced. As long as there are scholars with new points of view, as long as new texts are discovered, and as long as the English language changes, there will be revised versions. But so long as the Bible is a fetish, the King James version will be THE WORD.

The principal difficulty the modern translator encounters is to pick out the mistakes or corruptions which crept into and are found in all Biblical manuscripts. Many of them were mere "slips of the pen"; this was long centuries before printed books or "proof-readers." Can you make a perfect and exact copy of one page of the Bible? Probably, with great effort. But how many copies of your copy, copied by different persons unfamiliar with your chirography, will be perfect? For sixteen hundred years the Old Testament existed only in hand-copied manuscripts; the New Testament, for fourteen hundred years.

According to Simms, there are more than 150,000 variations in the extant manuscripts of the New Testament alone. Not only were there mistakes due to accidents and to normally fallible human hands, but some copyists did not hesitate to correct supposed errors, soften harsh sayings, or strengthen indecisive sayings, incorporate matter that was found in a margin, and add explanatory matter. Then, too, copyists were not always mere copyists; they were also human, partisan theologians. "Doctrinal tinkering," Simms calls it.

There are versions and versions, but of what? the Bible? There is no Bible. There are many Bibles. Our fundamentalist friends overlook this fact. Having their own Authorized Version of an original Revealed Bible, they laugh scornfully at palæontologists arguing the pros and cons of *Pithecanthropus*. But palæontologists trying to find true religion find more canonical Bibles than they can digest.

A canon is good only if it is straight; that is what canon originally meant, a *straight* rod, hence a measurer, a determiner, a ruler. A Bible is a library of *sacred* books; if a book is "sacred," it is *canonical*. Every church has had to decide for itself, or accept some one else's dictum, just what books are sacred, inspired—"*intended* by the Almighty," as Simms says, "for a place in the Sacred Library." But, as "God certainly gave no revelation conveying such information, and as no body of men has been divinely inspired and authorized to determine such matters," each church has used its own ruler in deciding which writings are canonical.

And so, as a matter of fact, there are today eleven canonical Bibles: Roman Catholic; Orthodox Greek Catholic; Syrian; Abyssinian; Egyptian or Coptic; Armenian or Gregorian; Latter Day Saints; Episcopal and Lutheran; Protestant; Jewish; and Samaritan.

The official Bible of the Roman Catholic Church is the old Latin Vulgate of Jerome revised by Pope Clement VIII in 1592 and known as the Clementine edition. It contains forty-six books in the Old Testament and thirty in the New—three of which are apocryphal. The Old Testament of the Greek Catholic Bible contains fifty books; of the two Protestant Bibles, thirty-nine. The chief difference between the Episcopal and Protestant Bibles is in the New Testament; that in the Episcopal contains the usual twenty-seven books, and in addition seven apocryphal books. The Bible of the English Church is not complete without the apocrypha.

Early Israel's literature—songs, myths, legends, rituals, etc.—was its religion. Hence a "book" was a myth, a legend, a poem, a history, a sermon, a ritual—or a hodge-podge.

Not all of Israel's early "books" were canonized. Thus, our Old Testament speaks of "the Book of the Wars of Jehovah," "the Book of Jashar," "the Book of Nathan," "the Book of Iddo the Seer," "the Acts of Solomon," etc., up to at least twenty-five. The Pentateuch as we have it in the first five Books of the Bible was compiled from at least four principal sources. These sources, as also the above-mentioned "Books," are quite lost.

In fact, the early Christian church thought that all the Old Testament had been lost during the Babylonian captivity; and that Ezra, "divinely inspired," dictated ninety-four Books to five scribes in forty days. That was a good miracle and firmly believed by many great Church fathers—Clement, Tertullian, Jerome, etc. It was founded on a legend in a 100 A.D. book called Second Esdras—still canonical in the Roman and Greek Catholic Bibles. That same question came up again in Luther's day—how had the canon of the Old Testament been fixed? "By a Great Synagogue (said a Hebrew scholar) presided over by Ezra." Luther accepted it, and with no more authority for it than that the sun had obligingly stayed aloft while Joshua finished a battle. There never was a

Great Synagogue; and very little is known as to just how or when the canon of the Old Testament was settled.

It is known that the Old Testament is far from unique in its claim to be a special revelation; also, that there was no creation; that the patriarchal histories are legend; that Moses did not write the Pentateuch; that David did not write the Psalms; that the Joseph story is a romance, the decalogue an expression of late ideals; and that the older Books were written at different times by different hands. A miscellany, Shotwell calls it—"legends from nomad camps, borrowings from Babylon, Egypt and Persia; annals of royal courts, laws, poems, prophecies; always being edited and reëdited, like the heritage of Greece preserved in a Bible." But it remains a great product. It is the record of national traditions, the outlook and aspirations of a "poor, harassed, semi-barbarous people, torn by feud and swept by conquest"; the expression of a people moving up from barbarism—sometimes savage Bedouins, often touched with exaggerations of hero-myths.

In that process of redaction the Bible as a library of ancient, semi-barbaric literature lost much of its effectiveness, charm, and simplicity. That inevitably happens in every attempt to make a book out of many books, especially when the book is edited with an eye to a propagandist end.

Later Jewish editors felt the need of "In the beginnings," and so it is that Genesis and the other Books of the Pentateuch—or Hexateuch, if we include Joshua—were among the last written. The Genesis story is badly done because it was compiled from two Creation and two Flood stories. There is not only duplication, but several sets of mythic figures: Cain and Abel, Tubal-Cain and Jabal. The curse of Ham is grafted upon the curse of Cain, making that the curse of Canaan. It tells the same offensive story twice, once of one patriarch and again of another. It gives a plagiarized, metaphysical version of the origin of death, life, and evil. It borrows the Egyptian Two-Brothers story or Adonis myth, as Joseph's history. It uses the names of several gods, always pretending that they stand for the same god. Stories about the mythic founders of the race are intermingled and repeated. And worst of all is the systematic effort to gloss polytheism into monotheism. The man Jacob wrestled with is the same man who talked familiarly with Cain,

Abraham, and Sarah—Yahweh. Even the finding of Moses and the Red Sea passage are variants of the myth of the man born to be king—Cyrus, Romulus, Oedipus, and many others.

Only as all this is kept in mind are the endless confusion and conflict of the Old Testament understandable.

To save Yahweh the indignity of running parochial errands, the Samaritan Pentateuch supplies him with angels. Zeus was given the same divine dignity in Greek mythology. Even Homer did not tell the worst he knew about the gods of Greece. Ham in rabbinical literature was the "black" son who dishonoured his father Noah. The Hebrew editors, for purposes of their own, edited, falsified, the text. They saw no reason why they should take a critical point of view.

A critical viewpoint, naturally, is not easy for believers to take; the essence of belief is the blocking of clear thought so that medi-tation may have a clear track. Thus, we can understand the incor-poration into the Hebrew canon of some of the later "books" which would be of interest and value to the Greek Jews, but whose slight prophetic element hardly fitted the hand of the Christian fathers hunting evidence that Jesus had been prophesied.

In fact, the Jews themselves resented the way the Christian fathers used their Bible as a source book for evidence of the coming of Christ. They denied the accuracy of the Alexandrian or LXX canon, and, as we have seen, made new translations of their Bible. Aquila's translation, made about 128, became thereafter the Bible of non-Christian Jews; but the one that became popular with the Christians was a later translation from Hebrew into Greek, done in that same century.

The chief difficulty in deciding what was or was not the exact text—and hence should or should not be included in the Old Testament—is that the oldest known manuscript dates from the ninth century. The crux of the controversy was over the so-called apocryphal books. Were they or were they not "inspired"? Judging from the number of *Susannahs at the Bath* in European art gal-leries, the Book of the History of Susannah, in the Latin Vulgate, had at least an inspiring influence on Christian art.

Apocryphal are "hidden" books, but whether hidden because secret—like an Eleusinian mystery—or because too deep for the masses, is unknown. The Latin Vulgate Old Testament contains no less than fourteen books (apocryphal) not found in the Hebrew Bible. Catholics consider all books held apocryphal by Protestants (except I and II Esdras and the Prayer of Manasses) as canonical (equally inspired) as all other books of the Bible.

Before looking at the apocrypha, let us see how the Jews divided their Bible. First is the *Torah*, or Law, as we call it, from the name the Alexandrian Greeks gave to the Pentateuch or five Books of Moses. Next, the *Prophets*, the "Former Prophets"—or four histories, Joshua, Judges, Samuel, Kings; the Latter Prophets—Isaiah, Jeremiah, Ezekiel; the Minor Prophets; and, finally, the *Writings* or Scriptures—Ruth, Psalms, Job, Proverbs, etc. This division in itself is evidence that the Jewish canon was not formed at one time and forever, but on the other hand was a growth, a matter of accepting, rejecting, compiling, editing, etc. It was a gradual process, the evolution of centuries.

The Law was the first canon formed, and presumably the only Sacred Book the Jews had when Manasseh went off to found his Samaritan church. That was not earlier than 432 B.C. "And Ezra the scribe . . . opened the book (unrolled the scroll, it should be). . . . Also caused the people to understand the law." That was after Nehemiah had returned from exile and had begun to rebuild the city walls. Ezra read the Law—something "sacred" and authoritative. That was about 444 B.C. and the book was doubtless the Pentateuch.

The canon of the Prophets was completed by 200 B.C. and was probably not more than a century in forming. The Book of Daniel is a prophetic book, but it could not be included because the Prophet canon was already closed when Daniel appeared (165 B.C.); so it was placed with the Writings, or third canon, begun about 160 B.C. and completed before the end of that century.

During the canonization of the Writings the editors did not hesitate to substitute historic hindsight for prophetic foresight. Thus, to Isaiah were added four whole chapters; to Jeremiah, one chapter. Not one of the Books, says Bewer, "escaped editorial revision." Judean editors "brought Amos and Hosea up to date in order that they might serve as guides and warnings to Judah, lest it also be engulfed in ruin. . . . Not only sentences and clauses but

whole new oracles were added." Many were the additions to bolster
the belief that Israel would be restored. And all this more than two
hundred years after Herodotus had placed history on a sane, sound
foundation.

But those editors were not historians, they were priests; and
ready, as priests always are, with their rationalizations and justifications. Yahweh had inspired prophetic words; he could inspire the
editors of prophets! But, said the Palestinian Jews, with Ezra and
Nehemiah Yahweh ceased to inspire! The test of a book's divinity,
therefore, was a question of date: if written before Ezra-Nehemiah,
it might be inspired; if later, it could not be. Psalms, Proverbs, Job,
Canticles or Song of Songs, Ruth, Lamentations, Ecclesiastes, Esther,
Daniel, Ezra, Nehemiah and Chronicles, passed the test and were
canonized: the Canticles and Ecclesiastes because "written" by Solomon, as the Writings.

The Alexandrian Jews, on the other hand, held that the Divine
Spirit was still inspiring writers; hence the dozen or more books
now called apocryphal which the Westminster Assembly (1643),
in agreement with the official Hebrew position, found "human
writings," without "divine inspiration" and "hence no part of the
canon of Scripture." But *they are*! said the Roman Catholic Church
at the Council of Trent; and if any man does not accept them entire
as sacred and canonical, "let him be anathema."

You must always take your choice. Do you want history, *facts*;
or religion, *proofs*? Is David the sweet singer of Israel, founder of
a temple, the author of a liturgy—as in Samuel and Kings; or a
king, warrior, statesman, founder of a kingdom—as in Chronicles?
We must always choose. As Shotwell says, the church for centuries
debated which should be regarded as the inspired Books, but the
eighteenth century sceptics reversed that doubt and asked why any
Book should be regarded as inspired. The asking of that question
was the beginning of higher criticism.

Let us now look at the canonization of the books of the New
Testament.

According to Simms, Jesus' followers were so confident of his
early return to inaugurate a new age that they felt no need to write
up his life; nor was anything at all written for more than forty
years after his death. Having once started, however, to reduce myth

and tradition to writing, a whole literature came into existence. About 150, the idea of a canon of New Testaments got started, but the idea was not put into effect until after the Council of Nicæa in 325.

For centuries the church believed that it was the Lord himself who decided which of the many little Greek books then claiming divine sanction had been truly inspired. Everything (so ran the legend) which had been referred to the Council was piled under the communion table; then "they besought the Lord that the inspired writings might get up on the table, while the spurious ones remained beneath—and it happened accordingly"!

As a matter of fact, the New Testament canon as we have it was first settled by Athanasius, Bishop of Alexandria, in 367; but for centuries the number of Books and the order of their arrangement varied. There is no intrinsic reason, for example, why Revelation should not be put first instead of last in the Bible—except possibly because it is an obvious forgery and based on an old Jewish diatribe against Nero.

Among the more important apocryphal books finally rejected as not "authentic" were the Gospels of Peter, of the Birth of Mary, of the Infancy of Jesus, and of Nicodemus. Also the Epistles of Clement, Barnabas, Ignatius, Polycarp, Jesus Christ, and of Paul to the Laodiceans; also the Acts of Paul and Thecla, and a Book called Paul and Seneca. But all these and more were read in the early churches, and some are still read in some churches. The Quakers, for example, use the Epistle of Paul to the Laodiceans.

Of the excluded apocrypha, one is worth special mention: the Protevangelion. This was ascribed to James, brother of Jesus. It exalted Mary, and furnished the basis for the dogma that Mary was never contaminated by sin. That dogma was proclaimed authoritative by Pope Pius IX in 1854. Christian dogmas are artifacts of history; the dogma of incarnation is equally a product of aboriginal America, all the way from the Algonquins to the Peruvians.

Besides the apocrypha above mentioned, twenty-six Gospels were also declared spurious; as were, according to Simms, no less than forty other books referred to by the early fathers. "In Catholic countries, in fact, these apocryphal writings have had vastly more influence than the Biblical narratives themselves. Especially from the twelfth century on did they furnish a mine for the poets and minstrels of Germany, France, and England. Numerous miracle plays represented incidents related in them." Their influence on Christian art was also profound.

The oldest known manuscript of the New Testament dates from the fourth century and belongs to the Vatican, where it was guarded from critical eyes until the last century. Of the six oldest and best manuscripts of the New Testament—all in Greek and all dating from the fourth or fifth century—not one was used in translating the King James version. The oldest known fragment of the New Testament (portions of the Matthew Gospel on papyrus) was found in Egypt in 1896, and dates from the third century.

Such, in brief, is the Christian church canon, official authority for Christian dogmas. It did not settle on this canon for hundreds of years; presumably it could not settle on just what Christianity was and what parts of the ever-growing literature would seem most convincing. That point settled, the literature becomes "inspired"—as is presumably every sermon today. If the pope's words are infallible, they *must* be inspired. The real question, then, is, what is behind inspiration?

The Father, God, Lord, Adonai, the Almighty, J H V H. He revealed himself to his Chosen People. His son is the central figure of Christianity. Let us look at the Father, at the Supernatural Being who walked and talked with Jacob just after he had deceived his blind father and shamelessly swindled his brother, who put Moses up to "borrowing" the Egyptian's jewellery as a ready way of looting it, who permitted Sarah to lie to him. In short, let us glance at the *religion* of the Jews.

IV

Our Bible, as we saw, is Authoritative. In that one word we have in a nutshell the difference between so-called primitive and civilized religions, between oral and written religion. To unlettered folk the essence of magic power lies in the *ritual*: if the right *things* are not done, the magic will not work. They may be hazy about the origin of magic, they may know that authorities disagree as to just which is the "true" version, but they know that there is only one key to force the lock of magic. But once the true version is decided upon and reduced to writing, we have a Scripture which in almost no time at all becomes the Word, the Logos, the Divinely Inspired Word, the Authorized Version. The world may change, the outlook on life may change, but the Word is changeless and the new outlook on life must be squared to fit the Word.

And so throughout history every "progressive" nation found ready-made excuses for a career of conquest, Divine sanctions for its war chief. He, the war chief, *must* have unlimited power; people *must* be disciplined! And in victory or defeat the cause lies in fortune or fate—some mystery, God's will.

We call it Progress, Advance of Civilization, Manifest Destiny, the White Man's Duty, etc. "It?" Anything we are ashamed to call by its right name—occupation of alien territory, for example, or removing the Indians from the path of progress, exploitation of the Negroes of Liberia, etc. The ancients at least were more frank. Sargon the Assyrian lists so many flayed, so many impaled, so many burnt: all because God was good to him—his list proves it! The Jews were equally frank—and quite as savage as the Assyrians. They left no such evidence of their savagery as the Assyrians because they had none to leave. They were between too powerful nations to go far out; they did the best they could.

They had their war-god behind them, and Israel swore to him: "If Thou wilt deliver this people into my hand, then I will utterly destroy their cities." "Of the cities of these peoples . . . thou shalt save nothing alive that breatheth." Jericho is "devoted," and a curse is laid on its site to prevent its being rebuilt. David, his "favorite," smote every male in Edom; and from Rabbah "brought forth the people that were therein and put them under saws, and under harrows of iron, and under axes of iron, and made them pass through the brick kiln, and thus did he unto all the cities of the children of Ammon."

Titus destroyed Jerusalem and took thousands of Jews slaves to Rome. But there is no record of any Roman displaying such fiendish cruelty as David or "devoting" a captured city to his war-god.

Asshur "gives" victory to the Assyrians; Marduk to the Babylonians; Chemosh to the Moabs; Yahweh to the Jews; God to the Christians; and so on down the line to Great Quahootze, who "gave" the victory to the Nootka Indians in answer to the oft-quoted prayer from Tylor: "Great Quahootze, let me live, not be sick, find the enemy, not fear him: find him asleep, and kill a great many of him."

Yahweh is a God of righteousness—of savages. A savage God, a superman, a superhuman being, but always in human form. Agag is done to death in his "presence." He accepts such blood feuds as make gang wars sacred. He demands vengeance for unintentional homicide. He is vengeful. He resorts to deceit. He swaggers, he struts, he menaces, he threatens. He is utterly unlovely. He is the God of plunderers, of torturers, of warriors, of conquest, of every savage passion.

This anthropomorphic monstrosity, born of cowardly fear and ignorant superstition, steals through the Garden in the cool of the evening, smells the sweet savour of Noah's sacrifice, and says he will never curse the ground again. Then, seeing that "Adam is become one of us," and being afraid that men will obtain too much power and build a tower to heaven—that "nothing will be restrained from them which they have imagined to do"—he "confounds" their language and scatters them abroad, with all the dignity of a jealous, angry child knocking down a pile of blocks. All this childishness was borrowed from Babylon; but it is still Bible, the Word of God, to millions. That anthropomorphic creation of superstition is still Omnipotence, Omniscience, Fate, Fortune, Creator, Judge, Father, to millions of Christians.

Before the Jews borrowed Eden and a Flood from Babylon and made over their own mythology to fit into the new, Yahweh was a real and undisguised primitive magician. So potent was his magic power that it was dangerous to go near him, whether in his thick darkness, in his burning bush, or among the cherubim of the Ark. Even the Philistines were afraid of him. "Gods," they cried, when the Israelites brought the Ark into camp, "are come into the camp; who can deliver us from the hand of these mighty gods?" That "Ark" was Israel's war "medicine"; it was Yahweh, a fetish. When the Philistines captured the Ark, it plagued them like smallpox; it was not their medicine, they did not know how to handle it. It was sacred!—in the sense that Jericho was "devoted."

Sacred is *sacer*, Greek for taboo, something magic, potentially dangerous. Know its secret and you can handle it—as an electrician does a high-voltage wire; but if you do not know how to work it, it may strike you dead. We have read so much soap and water into "purity" and so much childish awe and sentiment for family heirlooms into "sacred," that it is not easy for us to realize the significance of any ancient rite, much less the rites we believe in or are familiar with. The time is long overdue for a revaluation of the things that are pure, holy, sacred. Without such a revaluation there can be no sound thought on human worth, human rights, or humane ideals.

Sacred things to all ancients were tabooed things; they belonged to mysterious powers. "Devoted" Jericho is not holy or sacred as we use such terms; it is unclean, accursed, *taboo* to human touch. Yahweh alone could handle such an idolatrous city; his magic alone could destroy it.

The Ark was holy, sacred—taboo. It was essentially a "medicine" bundle; it contained the medicine, Yahweh. And mighty dangerous medicine, too. Uzzah touched it; men of Bethshemesh looked into it: fatal, all smitten dead. It had its counterpart in the chest in the mysteries of Bacchus, in Pandora's box, in Noah's ark, in the argo of the Argonauts, in the moon-shaped boat Isis used to gather the dismembered Osiris. It was the mystic womb of nature and of woman—symbol of rebirth, salvation, and redemption.

Our Indians used to keep their medicine bundles on tripods outside the *tipis*—too dangerous to keep in the house. No one dared open them but their keepers. Solomon's temple was a glorified "tripod" for housing the Ark.

And when Jeroboam bade Israel, "Behold thy God that brought thee up out of the land of Egypt," what did they see but the teraphim and golden bullocks such as were set up at Dan and Bethel? And what was Bethel itself—the one set up by Jacob—but an idol, the house of a god? El-beth-el meant "God of the house of a god." An apparition appears to Jacob in a dream and he concludes that Bethel is not only the house of God but the gate of heaven. In Joshua a stone is mentioned of which it was said, "It hath heard all the words of Yahweh which he hath spoken unto us." It was a pillar, a standing stone, an idol, where Yahweh lived; as were the sacred posts or asherim. Fetishes of fertility. Churches are full of them today. They have office hours, holy times when the god is in attendance.

Recall the pillars Solomon set up in front of his temple: *Jachin*—"he shall establish"; and *Boaz*—"in it is strength." They were crowned with pomegranates—female symbols crowning phallic emblems. What else are these but countersigns of rites performed in the temple of the Babylonian Venus Mylitta, where every woman repaired to have intercourse with a stranger? The Bible refers to the phallic emblems or images and the "groves" or female emblems of the Syrians. From Rehoboam's time it was the custom for men and girls to be attached to Jewish temples for such fertility ceremonies. It was an honour for a woman to be fertilized by a holy man—"children of God."

That the Israelites were familiar with the fertility cults of the East may also be seen in the parable of the vineyard in Isaiah v: 1-14. But what the prophet is parodying, according to Creighton, is not a vineyard, but a fertility cult song. Verse thirteen refers to the sensual practices of the cult which will be displaced by the naked frenzy of captivity. What is meant is that the people will go down to Sheol, where the fertility-goddess now goes alone in the spring-time to restore life in the world. *Sheol*, in preparation for their arrival, has enlarged its capacity.

Yahweh was the rain-maker of the fertility cult—and in fact was a better rain-maker than the Phœnician Baal. But he became so assimilated to Baal, Tammuz, and Adonai, Lord, that Jewish women celebrated the lamentations to Tammuz in the temple and often spoke of Yahweh as the Lord.

In Judges xxi:20 we have other references to Bacchanalian festive dances: "When the daughters of Shiloh come out to dance in the dances, then come ye out of the vineyards and catch you every man a wife." "Wife?"

Many of Israel's fetishes were holy trees; they had been planted by the patriarchs. As Robertson Smith says, all that was needed to constitute a sanctuary was precedent. All Canaan was a sanctuary, Yahweh's land, as Israel was his people. Canaan was so holy that killing game there was taboo unless the hunter "returned the life" to the god by pouring the blood on the ground.

"In every place (in Canaan) where I cause my name to be remembered, I will come and bless thee." "Ye shall reverence my sanctuary." And from the burning bush came Yahweh's voice: "Draw not nigh hither; put thy sandals from off thy feet, for the place whereon thou standest is holy ground." The place is not holy because Yahweh spoke to Moses, but because he lives there.

Holy places, hilltops, thickets with their shadows and presences. Most of us are afraid of thickets at first, but finally friendly spirits replace the demons we first peopled them with. Mount Carmel, sacred above all mountains and forbidden of access to the vulgar, says Robertson Smith, is still covered with thickets. Mount Horeb was so holy that it was taboo to man and beast: "Whosoever toucheth the mount shall surely be put to death." Holy? Yahweh dwelt there. Yahweh is "a jealous God, a consuming fire." To be in a "holy" state of mind was to be afraid. Religion begins in fear and awe, and later calls it respect and reverence.

Yahweh also lived on Mount Seir, whence he issued forth to battle; and "the earth trembled, the heavens also swayed; yea, the clouds poured water, the mountains quaked in the presence of Yahweh." He chose Mount Zion for a home; and Amos declared he would roar from Zion and utter his voice from Jerusalem.

Wherever Yahweh "dwells" is the appropriate place to receive altars, sanctuaries, sacrifices. Find a cathedral in Europe without its divine relics. On the site of the victory over the Philistines, Saul built an altar. Gideon and Manoah sacrificed in the places where they received divine messages. The patriarchs founded sanctuaries wherever Yahweh appeared to them.

An Islamic student has recently surveyed Palestine's holy spots— holy since Canaan and Hebrew days, down through Moslem to modern days. The same shrine may be "sacred" to modern Christian, Moslem, and Jew. Of shrines about Jerusalem only five per cent are in valleys or plains; all the others are on "high places," mountain-tops or hillsides. Pictographs often adorn the walls around the shrines—snakes, palm branches, human hands. To the Moslem peasant the hand is Fatimah's; to the Christian, the Virgin Mary's.

A sacrificial altar in every village, hilltop sanctuaries, sacred groves, haunted rocks, boundary stones that could curse. Horeb and Sinai compete for the honour of having entertained the lawgiver. But suppose that event never happened? Well, it is a good story. As

Shotwell says, it *may* have happened; it *must* have happened; it *did* happen. The story pleases so many that the sceptics cannot raise their voices. And so Abraham builds an altar, Isaac digs a well, and Jacob piles boundary stones at Gilead. And Naaman, told to bathe in the Jordan, gets angry: only the rivers of Damascus can purify *him*—the Jordan is healing only to Israel! In the grotto at the Jordan's source the ancient Israelites had a sanctuary to Dan; the Greeks and Romans, to Pan.

While they removed their sandals in holy places, during burial, and in the presence of a ghost of any kind, Moses hid his face when approaching holy ground on Mount Sinai, and Elijah wrapped his face up at the cave on Mount Horeb: "insulation" rites, lest they be electrocuted by the divine potency. But Saul stripped off his clothes and lay naked all night prophesying. Presumably that was the ancient Hebrew custom of ceremonial purification. The removal of the sandals was a compromise; as later the sackcloth or loin-cloth was a substitute for nakedness. Once "purified" and inside the sanctuary, they danced around the altar or standing stone. So they danced around the golden bullock—image of Yahweh; so danced the daughters of Shiloh at the annual feast. So David, in his loin-cloth, danced with all his might before the Ark. Hebrew "feasts" originally meant circular dances; they developed into processionals with music and song. Then the worshipper drew near and stroked or kissed the sacred object. To "entreat" the favor of Yahweh meant to stroke Yahweh's face. In Hosea we read of the people kissing the golden bullocks at Dan and Bethel.

"Thou shalt not take the name of the Lord thy God in vain," says my Bible; but what the Hebrew wrote was: "None shall appear before me empty" (handed). You pay for favors expected, bring a victim for the sacrifice.

The Hebrew name for sacrifice is *lehem elohim*. And that is what any sacrifice to any power higher than human means—food of deity. Call it a bribe, or call it hush money; some *human* hand gets it. Supernatural beings have neither teeth nor stomach. Is the patent never to expire on this invention? Must man for ever sit at the feet of a Voice from a mouldy tomb and feed and clothe its spokesmen? It does seem monstrous that the most useless and senseless of all ancient inventions should be the only one that man still worships, still talks about with bated breath, still builds altars to, and the one to which he still sacrifices his health, happiness, and virility, and the welfare of mankind.

Purification, dancing, etc., were mere preliminaries to the real act of worship: today, "thank offerings" or contributions; in early Hebrew days, an animal; in later Hebrew days, bread. Animal sacrifice—such as the first-born Passover festival ascribed to Moses—is an echo of the old nomadic days of sheep, shepherds, pastures, and spring lambs; but in absorbing Canaan they seem to have absorbed the Baal cult of an agricultural people, including the feast of unleavened bread. As we have seen, the Bible is not guiltless of references to human sacrifice.

That first-born children were sacrificed in early times there is no doubt. Not till after the Exile did the custom entirely disappear. In II Kings the sacrifice of children to "Melek" (Moloch, another name for Yahweh) is expressly forbidden. It seems evident from the passage that such sacrifices were considered oblations to Yahweh as king, and were consumed outside the town at the "tophet" below the temple. Tophet means funeral pyre; but as the Hebrews rarely burnt their dead, the passage must refer to human sacrifice.

Later, cattle were substituted for humans, but were not considered so potent; hence in time of need or on grave occasions, adult humans were offered. Thus, Jephthah sacrifices his daughter in fulfilment of a vow; Hiel, his eldest son, to lay the foundations of Jericho; and his youngest son when he set up the gates. The vow to destroy the people of a city if Yahweh gave them victory was simply a promise of abundant human sacrifice.

Animal sacrifices must be clean and without blemish. They might be burnt—wholly "consumed"—on the altar, or they might be partially burnt and eaten by the worshippers. But the blood was poured into the earth as a libation to Yahweh; hence animals accidentally dead might not be eaten, as their blood had not been ritually offered. Fat must be burnt on the altar. And as all first-born animals had to be offered to Yahweh on the eighth day after birth, there must have been many altars.

Covenant sacrifice, as mentioned in Exodus xxiv:8, where Moses took the blood and sprinkled it on the people, is symbolic of their eating it. The sprinkling of the blood of the Paschal on the door-posts extended the efficacy of the sacrifice to the entire household.

Jonathan "covenants" love and brotherhood with David—investing him with his garments, girdle, sword, and bow; as Glaucus and Diomede in the *Iliad* exchange armour in token of their old friendship.

Sacrifice in its original totemic days is, fundamentally, not payment or tribute, but a service of communion between man and his animal god; they jointly participate in the flesh and blood of their victim. Thus, Robertson Smith sees evidence of the reëmergence of a primitive totemic cult in the fact that the Hebrews after the Exile, thinking Yahweh had forsaken them, began to sacrifice "unclean" ("abominable") creatures, such as pig, dog, mouse, and "other vermin."

Many other references could be cited showing a tendency to hark back to primitive totemic days before the Hebrews had a god higher than a Digger Indian's. Yahweh was not their ancestral god, but the god of the Kenites of Sinai. He had taken pity on Israel, delivered it from bondage, and brought it into this milk-and-honey land. That proved he was a good god to tie to; and on this, says Paton, rested the ethical requirements of the old Hebrew religion. Leave out the exodus from Egypt and the conquest of Canaan, and the religion of the early Israelites has nothing to rest on but primitive animal totemism. Yahweh had shown that he was the best god and therefore alone worth worshipping. But as he had proved himself Israel's god, he demanded that the Israelites prove themselves his people.

Hence the reiteration *ad nauseam* of the jealousy idea and all that goes with it. Submission: "It is Yahweh; let him do what seemeth him good." To revolt against his authority, to revile him or curse his name, is a deadly sin, and death is the penalty. Obedience: "Keep my commandments always"; "Hearken unto the words of the voice of Yahweh"; "All that Yahweh hath spoken we will do." Trust: "Abraham believed Yahweh, and Yahweh counted it to him for righteousness." David "strengthened himself in Yahweh," and was rescued from his peril.

Yahweh was always a jealous god. There were plenty of other gods, but Yahweh alone must have the allegiance of the Israelites;

they could show allegiance by turning their backs on the other gods. Joshua, Judges, and the early Prophets again and again warn the Israelites not to serve the other gods. Elijah spends a lifetime warring with the Tyrian Baal. Hostility to the Canaanite gods demanded that their altars, shrines, sanctuaries, and images be destroyed, their customs avoided. There was to be no treaty with them, nor marrying them. Canaanites must even be annihilated lest they seduce Israel into worshipping their gods.

Whatever Yahweh was to become later to the Israelites of the kingdom, he was no more the one and only god than a kangaroo was the one and only totem to an Australian. He was the only god the Israelites were supposed to worship. Says Naomi to Ruth: "Thy sister-in-law is gone back unto her people and unto her gods." And Ruth says: "Thy people shall be my people, and thy God my God." Gods were cultural elements; when one changed one's culture or nationality, one changed one's gods.

Note the change in the tone of the post-Exile Israelites. They are now more timid, more pious; they act like clients of Yahweh, says Robertson Smith, who find themselves in a land where they have no rights but are dependent on Yahweh's bounty. Yahweh seems to have turned his back on his Chosen People. Rites become more conciliatory, holocausts more common.

After the Flood, animals could be killed and eaten if the blood were poured on the ground. Sacrifice began with the Mosaic dispensation. All slaughter became sacrifice; no beef or mutton could be eaten except religiously. By a Deuteronomic law, one could slay and eat domestic animals anywhere if one poured the blood on the ground. Yahweh could walk in the Garden in the cool of the evening, but he was never more than an enormously potent disembodied ghost. The most appropriate "food" for such spirits was blood. Yahweh has a fondness for blood which suggests the blood libations to Greek heroes, especially the ghosts in the *Odyssey* which greedily drink the sacrificial blood. Blood disappears into the ground more easily than flesh and so is more easily consumed by the god.

In II Kings xxiii:11 we find Josiah putting a stop to a practice of the kings of Judah—sacrificing horses to the Sun-god.

Wine was the "blood" of the grape: hence Jotham's "wine which cheereth gods and men." Robertson Smith thinks libations of wine an imitation of and surrogate for the blood of earlier sacrifice. But blood itself, because it contained the "life of the flesh," was too sacred for mortal consumption; it was devoted to the god at the altar. As the Greek pantheon had Goat-eaters, Ram-eaters, Bull-eaters, and even the Cannibal, so the idea that Yahweh ate bull's meat and drank goat's blood was never quite eliminated from the priestly ritual.

We have already seen the element of sacrifice in the Semite rite of circumcision. The Bible tells us that mourning rites included lacerating the flesh and shaving the head. Hair offerings to tombs or on pyres were common. A vow to cut one's hair at a sanctuary at a certain time or after a certain period, consecrated the hair and rendered it inviolable meanwhile. Thus, the long hair of a Hebrew Nazarite or a Greek Achilles marked its consecration. Achilles had vowed to dedicate his hair to the river-god on his return from Troy. As that return could never be, he laid his yellow locks in the hand of the dead Patroklos. Women worshippers at the feast of Adonis of Byblos had to sacrifice their hair or their hymen.

Why harp so much on sacrifice? Because sacrifice is so much harped upon today; because Christianity itself eternally harps upon sacrifice—yea, is founded on sacrifice. All right. But what is sacrifice? Who pays; who gets paid; and who gets cured, and of what? These are legitimate questions. We have as much right to look into them as we have to look into hell, or to look at a battle-field, or into an insane asylum or a slum.

Who is this God of Isaac we are asked to worship, who so bungled creation that he had to employ a snake and a fig leaf to find an excuse for a Flood, and then had to send his son to redeem mankind? As a child I was ordered to fear God and keep his commandments. Now I want to know why I should fear him or anybody, and whether or not his commandments are worth keeping. If I carry a load of guilt and am full of sin, I want to know just what guilt and sin are before I try to unload my guilt and wash away my sins. I see that unloading and washing process going on around me, but I have not been able to see that anybody is lighter or cleaner. The real question, as I see it, is whether the Bible itself is not the burden that weighs on humanity, the sin that makes for hypocrisy and social injustice and puts an insuperable barrier between human lives and sound, sane, healthy human living.

If the Bible is inspired, sacred, inviolable, nothing I can say can possibly injure it; if, on the other hand, it is a human document made by fallible human hands, it is altogether proper and appropriate that it should be so regarded. We seek the truth about it. What is its origin? What shred of evidence have we that a supernatural spirit in human form might not equally have inspired Billy Sunday, Mary Baker Eddy, Brigham Young, Spinoza, Plato, and Sappho, as well as Moses—or any poor simple-minded lunatic who behind the walls of an asylum claims to prophesy in His Name?

In Egypt, in Babylon, in Rome, throughout the Christian world, anything done in his name makes it holy, makes it right—whether it be slavery, prostitution, human sacrifice, class war, social injustice, any form of human oppression. We do not rely quite so much as the Babylonians and Egyptians did on saying the right words, speaking the right name, making the right kind of sacrifice conditional for success, health, and happiness; not quite—but we do tolerate an enormous body of superstition which sets more store on cleansing sins than it does on keeping clean and living like a sensible human being.

Superstition did not start, or end, on the Euphrates. Nor is the Babylonian brand essentially more inhuman than many other brands, but it is at the bottom of our Bible and at work in America today. Christian fervour began with the Chaldean priests of Babylon. When Cyrus repatriated the Jewish captives, he exported a load of Chaldean nonsense which is still exploited in pulpits as golden wisdom. Sacrifices once demanded by fertility cults are now demanded in the name of Civilization and Progress. We are still asked to make atonement for imaginary sins committed in a mythical Eden.

Ezekiel's laws of atonement are later than the Passover institution of Leviticus where blood was sprinkled as a magic rite of protection from evil spirits; but they aim at the same end—to put the worshippers under superhuman protection from supernatural dangers. Ezekiel provided for two days of atonement a year, in the first and seventh months. In their fasts and humiliation they recall the very widespread dramatization of the fertility god. In Canaan the Jews had met such a god and such a religious rite—Adonis or Tammuz, a local Canaanite Baal.

In Judges xix:29 we read: ". . . he took a knife, and laid hold on his concubine and divided her, together with her bones, into twelve pieces, and sent her into all the coasts of Israel." If we read this in a Babylon or Aztec Bible, we should want to know what such a murderous savage was up to; but in *our* Bible he is not a savage, nor is it murder: it was an approved way of doing just what Saul did (I Samuel xi:7) when he "took a yoke of oxen and hewed them in pieces and sent them throughout all the coasts of Israel." He was calling Israel to arms; it was a sacrament, a covenant.

Or, two parties could make a covenant with each other by cutting a victim in two and getting between the two pieces. Ezekiel's "This is the blood of the covenant which Yahweh hath cut with you" implies the same kind of covenant, but dividing there means eating the sacrifice and applying the blood. Later, "dividing" by eating was replaced by cutting the sacrifice in two. Standing between the pieces symbolized their union by the victim's mystical life.

From beginning to end, from cover to cover, religion is saturated with mysticism, haunted by ghosts. Ghosts of animals were more powerful, more potent, more fearsome, than human souls, just as the animals themselves were rated more this or more that. The church still exorcises devils from the catechumen before baptism, and still shouts hallelujahs of praise. But the hallelujahs the Hebrews shouted were wailings for the death of their sacrificed victims. Practically around the world, the skin of the sacrificed animal clothes its wearer in some of the sanctity of the victim. And so "unto Adam and his wife did the Lord God make coats of skins and clothed them"—and "the man is become as one of us."

Possibly none of the so-called Mosaic commandments has worked greater injustice or made the understanding of human nature more difficult, than that of a god so inhuman as to visit the iniquity of the fathers upon their children to the fourth generation. Eli's sons' sins were so inexpiable that they were visited on the whole clan—from "generation to generation." But there was at least one redeeming feature to this monstrously inhuman attitude—children of fathers who had eaten sour grapes were not to have their teeth set on edge.

We saw the Athenian house-that-Jack-built farce of discovering the guilty party and finally hanging it on a butcher knife. The Mosaic law was not only as senseless, but more cruel and more far-reaching in its consequences. The Mosaic law demanded that offending animals be slain. That law, of course, survived in Christian Europe; and not till 1846 was the law of Deodand (*Deodandum*, God-given) abolished in England. If a cart ran over a man and killed him, or a tree fell on him, the cart or tree was "tried," confiscated, sold for charity, and thereby "purified."

Religious purification has nothing to do with sanitation or hygiene; it has much to do with mental aberration. Without the shedding of blood there is no remission of sins! Blood washes away sins. One becomes purified when one removes a taboo, and is thereby immune from the danger of handling something sacred. Herodotus records that sexual intercourse among the Babylonians, etc., was followed by ablution and fumigation. Several passages in the Pentateuch imply that sexual intercourse was taboo to Israel's warriors —a very widespread taboo. Yet the taboo among the Hebrews, as Robertson Smith points out, cannot be directed against the act itself, for it applies to wives; nor can it spring from asceticism, because Hebrew temples were thronged with "sacred" prostitutes.

Biblical purifications are from "uncleanness," sin, anything sacred, taboo. Thus, the "consecration" of a red heifer on a sacrificial altar makes the heifer holy, sacred. The priest who performs the sacrifice must thereby purify himself after as well as before performing the holy function. So the priest "defiles" his hands handling Holy Writ, and must purify them. Living water is a good purifier, but blood is far better; and the ashes of the burnt victim are good. Also incense, unguents, fumigation. Especially good is frankincense, for the gum tree itself is holy.

Holiness (ye-shall-be-holy) meant freedom from the taint of the taboo of something holy, especially some other god than Yahweh. A temple prostitute was a "holy one"; a high-tension wire of any kind, dead or alive, animate or inanimate, anything free from defilement—all holy. Holiness had nothing to do with moral values, ethical attitudes, physical well-being; it had everything to do with magic power.

The Levitical law tells us that the mere touch of the carcass of "vermin" defiles; one must purify, wash. But that makes the water "unclean"; it can spread contagion. An earthen pot, for example: smash the pot. As they do today in India, by the million. But we also learn in Leviticus that a leper's impurity can be transferred to a fly-away bird, or a scapegoat; or, as we learn in Matthew, devils can be cast out—into a herd of swine. What are devils? Impurities, spirits, ghosts, unclean things? Anything, according to our Bible, connected with the worship of an alien god—and hence alien; all physical defects caused by evil spirits; all diseases, because due to evil spirits; sex activities, because they belong to Astarte, old Mother Earth goddess; everything connected with a corpse. To go into a temple or a sanctuary tainted was to invite Yahweh's death penalty. "Unclean" food could be got rid of by fasting. The taint of the sex act could be removed by abstention for a stated period before going on the warpath or entering Yahweh's presence.

Yahweh, in Amos, Hosea, Isaiah and Micah, begins to have some of the attributes of an honest, humane, human being worthy of the respect of mankind. But before and after, he is neither the God of useful love nor of human righteousness. Our Lenten song:

> Christian, dost thou see them
> On the holy ground,
> How the hosts of Midian
> Prowl and prowl around?
> Christian, up and smite them!

as Harrison says, could have been sung with equal propriety by Greek or Roman—or Chaldean or Israelite. It has the right spirit! The coincidence between the spirit of a pagan and a Christian warrior, or between Babylon and modern inhumanity, is not accidental; it is inherent in the frame of mind which elevates spirituality at the expense of humanity.

Beliefs in demons, hairy beings, and nocturnal monsters which haunt waste places and commune with jackals, roam all the way through the Bible from Isaiah to Luke. After all, the difference between a good spirit and a demon lies in the fact that no one likes a demon; it has no worshippers. Good spirits conquer bad just as men conquer wild animals. References to prohibitions against divination, enchantment, sorcery, charms, all spring from Yahweh's jealousy. Yahweh had his own magic paraphernalia: ark, ephod, urim, thurim; and his own inspired prophets. He would not tolerate Israel's using the charms, divinations, etc., belonging to rival gods or cults. It is always *our* magic, in religion or business, which is legitimate.

Nor did Yahweh tolerate worship of shades. He himself was a shade, a spirit: "Thou shalt have no other gods before me." That the Hebrews, as the Greeks and Romans, had an old primitive cult of the dead, there is no doubt; all their mourning rites point that way. They were tolerated, but they were too closely related to other gods not to contaminate the mourners, who were thereby tabooed from taking part in worshipping Yahweh until after proper purification rites. Samuel's ghost is called Elohim (God).

In connexion with this cult of the dead, recall the part played by snakes in Greek cults of the dead. The serpent in Eden is no Satan in disguise; it is an underworld demon. There is no mistaking its demoniacal character. There are also several references in the Old Testament to snake-charming, and expressions of the idea that by spells and incantations animals may be prevented from injuring flocks and fields.

Much is made of Israel's God's righteousness, and of the ethical monotheism of the prophets, Amos in particular. The prophets, we are told, were the "Protestant reformers" of ancient Israel. But in all seriousness, what did either reformation amount to, what was its outcome, what can we make out of the reformed Jewism that could not be made out of the ancient? Just what was it the prophets were trying to reform? Was it a ritual or a moral reformation?

Let us see if we can get a close-up view of the ethics of the old Hebrew Yahweh. He was primarily omnipotent. "Is there anything too hard for Yahweh?" they asked, as a trusting yet thoroughly disciplined child might ask of a father; and having answered in the negative, they ask of him anything they want and do not know how to get for themselves. It is always easier for the child in stress to ask for relief than to squirm around until it finds relief through its own efforts. The Christian God triumphed over other gods because he alone seemed to offer success through failure.

When the Jews wanted anything they prayed for it, and the closer they got to Yahweh the more certain it was that he would hear their prayer and the more likely that he would oblige. Hence the sanctuary (or church) was the best place to make divine appeal, and at specially set hours. In prayer they "spread out the hands," palms upward, as they are portrayed on Babylon monuments. They prayed in a loud voice—as they pray today on Sunday mornings over the radio. Eli saw Hannah's lips move, but as he did not hear her voice he thought she was drunk!

There were, says Paton, several classes of prayer: *invocation*, or calling upon Yahweh on entering the sanctuary; *declarations*—of righteousness, sinfulness, etc.; *petitions*—for personal or tribal deliverance from distress, for guidance, prosperity, children, etc., or for the distress of one's enemies, that they might be cursed, etc.; *promises* or vows—to murder everybody in a city if Yahweh would grant the victory, etc.; and *arguments* with Yahweh in prayer— "entreating the Lord" meant hammering away at Yahweh till they got it.

Not the faintest suggestion that "a man's a man for a' that." Our doctrine that all men are created equal and are endowed with inalienable right to life, liberty, and happiness, would be a congenital impossibility to any theology. Did, does, the Christian share his God with the heathen? Not unless the heathen puts on trousers and mumbles the right words. The Jews would not even share their Yahweh with their neighbours.

Even the Ark with its image of Yahweh—the *abbir yisrael* or "bull of Israel"—had become the throne, the dwelling-place, of Yahweh. In other words, from the time Sheshonk put an end to image worship by capturing both Ark and golden bull, to the time when Ark was a covenant, Yahweh was bound to the Ark, the exclusive property or "medicine" of the Jews. He was no god of their neighbours. With Yahweh shut up in a box, the neighbours had no god at all—only a guardian angel whom Yahweh punished with his nation when the angel went wrong.

The Jews had no neighbours; they did have fellow-Israelites. To the non-Israelite they assumed no moral obligations. Moral obligations toward neighbours and strangers have appeared on earth despite and not because of an ethical god or an ethical pantheon. Only in sophisticated modern times did man create a benign, beneficent, sympathetic, humane God—largely for window-dressing purposes.

Yahweh commanded Israel to exterminate the Canaanites, and they did it with as fine religious frenzy as one half of Christian Europe displayed recently in trying to exterminate the other half. Moses was commanded to blot out even the remembrance of Amalek. "Go and smite Amalek," says Samuel, "and utterly destroy all that they have, and spare them not, but slay both man and woman and suckling." And if David left a male Edomite alive, it was because of no tenderness of heart.

> By the waters of Babylon,
> There we sat down, yea, we wept,
> When we remembered Zion.
> Upon the poplars in its midst
> We hanged up our harps.

A great poem, let us say, and full of pathos and beauty; also of savagery which any Iroquois or Apache might with equal justification have uttered, but never did.

> Remember, O Yahweh, against the Edomites
> The day of Jerusalem;
> Who said, Raze it, raze it,
> Even to its foundation!
>
> O daughter of Babylon, thou destroyer,
> Happy shall he be, that rewards thee
> As thou hast served us.
> Happy shall he be, that takes and dashes
> Thy little ones against the rock.

Psalm cxxxvi catalogues Yahweh's miracles—creation, etc.— and his smitings and his slayings, for all of which "mercies" Israel is to give thanks! Similar tender mercies were cause for thanksgiving among Christian nations for nineteen hundred years. Israel was a tight corporation. It granted no legal rights to alien residents; even the 620 B.C. Deuteronomy code made it legal to sell carrion to aliens.

Not only is there no moral objection to slavery as an institution, but the Jews enslaved one another for debt. Truth as truth was no virtue, nor to be expected except under oath. Deceit as deceit is nowhere condemned; the successful liar is praised for his cleverness.

Their idea of peace, friendship, kindness, etc., never rose higher than and often fell below that of clansmen among our American Indians. True, Lot did give up his two daughters to save his guests from danger.

Their family relationships were no higher, no lower, than we should expect them to be. David, leader of a robber band, commits adultery with Uriah's wife Bathsheba, and then has Uriah murdered in most shameful fashion. Ammon rapes Tamar, his half-sister, and goes unpunished by David—and the one sin leads to Absalom's fearful revenge. It was a man-made code of sexual ethics. Polygamy was practised; also habitual concubinage. Abraham and Jacob take their wives' slave maids as concubines. Chastity was a virtue only among women; but it was no disgrace to be a prostitute, holy or unholy, nor to associate with one. The wife is a thing—stuff, along with a man's other personal property. A betrothed girl who yielded to seduction was stoned to death—as was a seducer or raper, for having violated property rights. Death was the penalty for an adulterous wife; adultery on the husband's part was no offence.

A father apparently had about the same right over his children as he had over any other property. Female infants could be exposed up to Ezekiel's time; children could be sacrificed to Yahweh or sold into slavery; daughters could be dedicated to temple or plain prostitution.

Building temples with slaves seems to have been the privilege of all Oriental despots. Solomon was such a despot, a brutal murderer, and an apostate besides. Yet he was called a prince of peace who was supposed to have shed no blood. He enslaved the Canaanites; but there were not enough of them left to build his Jerusalem into a royal city, so he levied thirty thousand Israelites in the good old-fashioned Egyptian way.

Egyptians, Babylonians, Assyrians, Persians, Greeks, and Romans made contributions to civilization; the Israelites were never even civilized. Of culture such as the Greeks practised they knew almost nothing. Drunkenness was no disgrace, nor was excessive gratification of food or sex appetite. They had no arts of their own, nor industries. But they feared God and kept his commandments! Yes, and the Yahweh they feared was a peculiar blend of super-savage chief and Oriental despot, with the same blend of moral attributes, and restrained only with difficulty by Moses, his Grand Vizier, from acts so rash that other nations would doubt his omnipotence. Human rights and reasonable conduct and common sense are no more advanced by the Old Testament than they are by the Bible of the Aztecs.

v

Malachi is the last book of our Old Testament and was written about 460 B.C. Nearly three centuries later Israel was to produce her final prophet. That prophet believed in a coming Messiah; he plundered the Hebrew Bible for evidence—as the Book of Daniel was later to be plundered to document the kingdom of Christ and to prove that Christ was the Messiah of the Hebrew Bible.

Daniel was written about 165 B.C. and was the last of the Hebrew Bible to be written, except the thirty-third chapter of Isaiah and the last seven chapters of Zechariah. These last prophecies are unintelligible without a brief reference to history.

In 198 B.C. Palestine became part of the Seleucid kingdom of Syria. That brought the Jews face to face with Hellenistic culture. Rich Jews especially succumbed to its influence. The very existence of Jewism seemed to hang in the balance. Then came one of those fateful moments in history, with far-reaching results.

Jewism was persecuted. Not Jews, *Jewism*. King Antiochus IV Epiphanes (175-164 B.C.) tried to hustle the Jews out of Jewism into Hellenism. Jason, a Jew with a Greek name, was given the high-priesthood and at once began to turn Jerusalem into a Greek city. Antiochus, to punish Jerusalem, looted the temple treasury, and two years later resorted to more drastic measures to Hellenize the city. Its walls were razed, services stopped in the temple, its books burnt, Sabbath and circumcision proscribed; and, crowning insult, an altar to Zeus was erected on the burnt-offering alter and *swine were sacrificed!* Even at country shrines Jews were ordered to worship and sacrifice to Zeus.

Yahweh himself would not tolerate that, and the Jews burst into flame. Judas Maccabæus, one of five sons of a small town priest, led the revolt. Within three years all Jerusalem but the citadel was in their hands, the temple purified of its defilement and rededicated to Yahweh.

Enter the Book of Daniel, purporting to contain Yahweh's revelations to his servant Daniel in dreams and visions during and just after the Babylonian exile, nearly four hundred years before! Why had no one heard of these revelations? "Shut thou up the vision, for it belongs to many days to come"; "go thy way, Daniel, for the words are shut up and sealed till the time of the end." As Bewer says, the author of Daniel did not mean to deceive, but to put his book over. It was not thought of as a fraud, for most apocalyptic writers used the same device. There is no fraud in magic if one plays fair with magic power.

At any rate, the Book of Daniel was not what it purported to be, and apart from the justification which God is supposed to extend to his prophets fighting with words or swords, would merit the stigma of plain fraud. Daniel, like the other apocalyptic writers of those centuries, was a new note; they represented a new school in Judaism. They held out the hope of personal resurrection. And the source of all that apocalyptic wisdom was Iranian Babylonia. That the Book of Daniel was later canonized was of enormous import.

And at that time (says Daniel xii: 1-3) shall Michael stand up, the great prince which standeth for the children of thy people; and there shall be a time of trouble, such as never was since there was a nation even to that same time: and at that time thy people shall be delivered, every one that shall be found written in the book.

And many of them that sleep in the dust of the earth shall awake, some to everlasting life, and some to shame and everlasting contempt.

And they that be wise shall shine as the brightness of the firmament; and they that turn many to righteousness as the stars for ever and ever.

That is *resurrection* as a Hebrew prophet saw it in December, 165, or in January, 164 B.C. But not *all* will rise—only "many." And the "end of times (when) the anointed one (shall) be cut off, without judicial trial," was due in June, 164 B.C. June came and went, but the hopes of the Jews were now too high to be snuffed out by a mere miscarried prophecy.

So a second Zechariah arose and added Chapters ix, x, xi, and part of xiii. He had real visions; he saw Syria, Phœnicia and

Philistia added to the Jewish kingdom. And he meant physical kingdom; the Jews were about to see their dream come true. Over that physical kingdom they will rule. . . . And again he predicts:

> Rejoice greatly, O daughter of Zion,
>   shout, O daughter of Jerusalem;
> Behold, thy king comes to thee,
>   he is vindicated and victorious;
> Lowly and riding upon an ass,
>   even upon a colt, the foal of an ass.

This was the Jews' Messianic hope. "And he shall dictate peace to the nations; and his dominion shall be from sea to sea, and from the River to the ends of the earth. . . . And Yahweh shall be seen over them, and his arrow shall go forth as the lightning; and the Lord Yahweh will blow the trumpet and will go with the whirlwind of the south."

Still the earth did not fall, nor the world become a Jewish empire. So about 135 B.C. a third Zechariah added three more chapters to the Book of Zechariah. The siege of Jerusalem impended, but Yahweh would save the day. More, "Yahweh shall be king over all the earth: in that day shall Yahweh be one, and his name one." Even the climate was to change: "Neither heat nor cold nor frost"; and even "at evening time there will be light." Jerusalem itself would be physically elevated and the surrounding country leveled to a plain, etc. And as for those who fight against Yahweh, "Their flesh shall consume away while they stand upon their feet, and their eyes shall. . . . " A gruesome prophecy.

But Jerusalem will be rich in plunder—"gold, and silver, and apparel, in great abundance." If any enemies are left alive, they will go to Jerusalem once a year to worship the King and to keep the feast of tabernacles—the harvest thanksgiving festival. If the "heathen" do not go up, Yahweh will smite them with the plague.

Even the bells on the horses, in that day, will bear HOLY UNTO YAHWEH. And "every pot in Jerusalem and in Judah shall be holiness unto Yahweh of hosts; and all they that sacrifice shall come and take of them, and seethe therein; and in that day there shall be no more the Canaanite in the house of Yahweh of hosts."

Jewish prophecy died hard, but whether any particular prophet of any particular faith should be called a religious leader or just a Brigham Young or an Alexander Dowie is a question for experts. One thing is certain: there is nothing in that New Jerusalem Empire that would appeal to an Athenian, a Roman, or to any human being on earth except a circumcised Jew who knew the ritual.

If one prefers the last word of the Hebrew Bible as it is printed in the Revised Version, we still have Yahweh the war-god smiting "the earth with a curse."

And it shall come to pass that, when any shall yet prophesy, then his father and his mother that begat him shall say to him, "Thou shalt not live; for thou speakest lies in the name of Yahweh"; and his father and mother that begat him shall thrust him through when he prophesies. And it shall come to pass in that day, that the prophets shall be ashamed every one of his vision, when he prophesies; neither shall they wear a hairy mantle to deceive; but he shall say, "I am no prophet, I am a tiller of the ground; for I have been made a bondman from my youth." And one shall say to him, "What are these wounds between thine arms?" Then he shall answer, "Those with which I was wounded in the house of my friends."

Between the howling dervishes of Elijah's time and the professionals in haircloth and with self-mutilated bodies in the third Zechariah's time, there was nothing to choose. But if the Prophet of Nazareth revived prophetic religion in its "original" purity, as Bewer says, and gave it its truest and highest expression, why did the Jews reject that prophecy and demand the death of the Nazarene? Accepting the record as facts, there are serious discrepancies. The one supreme fact is that the religion of the Prophet of Nazareth became the faith of Europe and of the Christian world. This, as has been said thousands of times, was a critical turn in the history of civilization; but to say, as has also been said thousands of times, that Christianity "saved" Europe or saved civilization, is, to put it bluntly, arrant nonsense. What did it save Europe or civilization from or for? And what is meant by "save"? Since man became man he has had only two saviours—his brains and his hands—and only one of his hands is *right*. Nor has he ever had anything to save but himself and his fellow-men—and they are not always worth saving.

Enormous significance has been read into the fact that Christianity *triumphed*. Over what? And whose was the victory? That "victory" was won fifteen centuries ago. Where are its fruits?

Christ, it is asserted, is the Prince of Peace; Christianity, the Light of the World. Do the facts of history bear out these assertions?

But, first, what is Christianity? What is the evidence? What do the witnesses say?

## VI

The New Testament canon has four Gospels, chosen from dozens. Four—because (said Irenæus) there are four cardinal points. There were also four influential churches: Jerusalem (Matthew); Rome or Alexandria (Mark); Antioch (Luke); Ephesus (John).

From the canonical four Gospels, the Acts of the Apostles, the twenty-one Apostolic Letters and the Apocalypse, let us turn to the "witnesses" themselves.

No Gospel was written by an eye-witness of the scenes and events narrated. The two statements in John (xix: 35 and xxi: 24) are later additions to the text.

With but one exception, no Christian writer quotes any of the Gospels before 150. That exception was Papias, who about 120 spoke of the story of Mark and the sayings of Jesus.

Mark was written sometime between 60 and 70; Matthew, not before 70 and probably between 80 and 90; Luke, between 80 and 100; John, about 130; the Apocalypse, in 93.

The three so-called synoptic Gospels (Matthew, Mark, Luke) do not agree except where they might naturally be expected to differ— in a series of long phrases. From which it is inferred that they must have had the same common source. Luke certainly compiled from other sources and cannot have known Matthew and Mark as we have them. Although Mark seems to have been the chief source of Matthew and Luke, it seems to have been based on a source earlier than Matthew. At any rate, the oldest known manuscript of Mark ends abruptly at what is the eighth verse in our Bible; the last twelve verses were added later. Burkitt characterizes Matthew as a "second edition of Mark, revised and enlarged."

The Gospel according to John was written neither by John nor by a contemporary of the other three Gospel writers. It was written by a theologian saturated with the theosophy of Philo the Jew. He seems to have known the three synoptic Gospels, but does not hesitate to contradict them. St. John's Christ, as Reinach says, was God himself; the object of the book was the spiritual teaching of Christianity. If John is history, Mark is fiction.

As "evidence," John is worthless; Luke at best a third-hand witness; Matthew and Mark, second-hand—and we know nothing of their authority. Mark does not even know about Peter. The three synoptic Gospels simply echo words and traditions repeated long after the death of Jesus and compiled by men influenced by Paul's preaching—and created to supply a demand. The alleged historic happenings are at best hearsay evidence which would not be allowed in any court of justice in America. Even St. Augustine declared he would "not believe in the Gospel if I had not the authority of the church for so doing." In other words, *the* authority for "authority" is the church.

Note in passing that the Gospels neither founded a papacy nor instituted Peter head of the church. Neither Mark nor Luke knew anything of Peter's primacy, and the "Thou art Peter" in Matthew was an interpolation—and bootless at that, as the church had already cut loose from the synagogue.

Jesus himself taught no dogma, said nothing about Christian sacraments, baptized no one, taught no doctrine of sin and justification. In asking us to love our enemies he asked the impossible— though if we could and did, this would be, as James said, another and a transformed world. That was a high note, and foreign to the times. It was not a unique note in human history, but almost unique, and good enough to found a religion.

Other sayings—such as, "I shall rise from the dead," etc.—are far from unique; in fact, they belonged to that age. There is no reference to human immortality in the first seven books of the Bible; nor do the Psalmists believe in it. As some one has said, Moses, judging from his alleged writings, had no more use for a future life than he had for the worship of crocodiles. To the Jewish world, what mattered was the Law of Moses and what counted was circumcision. Paul came along and said it was baptism only that mattered, belief only that counted.

Before the end of the century no one knew where Jesus was born or when, what he taught, or where or when he died. Paul knew much of a Christ, practically nothing of a historic Jesus; and even boasted, as Shotwell says, of his indifference to the details of the life of Jesus. Paul's Christian doctrine came from the desert and not from Jerusalem. His doctrine calls for the intelligence of blind, ignorant credulity, and for nothing more.

Paul himself was converted by evidence which, offered in a law court today, would call for a commission in lunacy. But there is no doubt of his conversion or of the enormous strength of his call to faith; there is nothing like it in history. It won because it asked nothing more than the credulity of a child told to shut its eyes and believe in miracles.

To make any miracle true, nothing more is needed than credulity —sometimes called "inner experience." The glittering premium put on faith made credulity an enormous virtue, incredulity a hideous sin. Even such scepticism as a man might be expected to display in a horse trade was sin. The reward for faith was immortality; the punishment for scepticism, eternal damnation. Paul's basic idea— redemption from guilt of original sin through expiation by the voluntary sacrifice of a superman—was as "original" as a Dionysiac mystery; the idea was already centuries old and had been condemned again and again by tough-minded people and even by Athens of the fourth century B.C.

Miracles are recorded by the Gospel writers; some fairly innocent ones in Mark, oldest of the four Gospels. Luke records a youth on the way to burial rising from his bier. But in John, last of the four Gospels, Lazarus, dead four days ("by this time he stinketh") "came forth." Any comment one might make seems flat and stale. When it is remembered that this magician, Jesus, is supposed to be the son of Israel's chief magician, Yahweh, who helped Jacob in shady transactions and was even defeated by Jacob in a wrestling match and had to bless Jacob before he would let him go, we begin to come to grips with the kind of mind which accepts the whole Bible as gospel truth.

The big problem of Christianity is not why it was so effective once it had got seated in the saddle, but how it got seated. Let a belief, no matter how irrational, which seems to solve every critical problem in life, once get the sanction of the Powers-that-Be, and it rolls on irresistibly—as did Christianity for centuries. The kind of honesty that Bishop Colenso in modern times was brave enough to exhibit is generally smothered before it is allowed to take its first breath. That story, as Carpenter records it, is so illuminating that it may be told again.

Bishop Colenso, missionary to the Zulus, told his flock how the Israelites had crossed the Red Sea in one night; whereupon the Zulus proved to him that if the Israelites had marched in close file *five abreast*, they would have formed a column a hundred miles long, excluding baggage, sheep, and cattle; one night would not be enough. Now, how would most bishops answer a puzzler like that? I know the reply I should have received: "The Bible says so; there is a special spot in hell for a doubter like you!" Colenso was not that kind of bishop. He agreed that the Zulus' point was well taken, and wrote *Pentateuch Examined*—thinking in his innocence that his church would be glad to correct such an obvious error. Glad? He was temporarily deposed from his bishopric, and 140 believers wrote 140 books to refute *Pentateuch Examined*!

Christianity, once enthroned, ruled men's minds with a red-hot rod. The fact that it did become enthroned seems miraculous enough in itself to supply grounds for belief in the supreme miracles of Christian dogmas. This point was earnestly insisted upon in my course on Evidences of Christianity: if Christianity had not been the only one and uniquely true religion, it *could* not have triumphed! With our scant knowledge of history and the critical edge of our curiosity already dulled, that seemed a valid argument.

Christianity, of course, is "true" religion. It succeeded, as we shall see, largely because its appeal was to mankind rather than to any one nation or people; and because at that particular time, and in fact ever since the break-up of the ancient world of Darius, there had been but two classes of society around the Mediterranean Sea—the ruler and the ruled.

Even the rulers were far from content. Seneca, Nero's tutor, made much of the spirit, little of the body: "The body is the burden and punishment of the spirit; it oppresses it and holds it captive." Put ye on the spirit of a great man, he says in another place; much like Paul's "Put ye on the Lord Jesus Christ." Similar passages are found in Mithraism. The ruled feared death as something terrible, whereas before it had been a brother of sleep.

Christianity is no more unique in its dogmas, mysteries, and miracles than the religion of the Aztecs or any one of the dozen religions clamouring for believers in the Mediterranean world between 200 B.C. and 300 A.D.

The central dogma of Christianity—resurrection—is without foundation in historic fact. Even the synoptic Gospels are irreconcilably discrepant on this point. But resurrection as the central theme of Christianity, as well as of other Oriental religions, is not only credible, but a logical deduction from any attempt to read human destiny in terms of mythical interpretations of changing seasons with recurring life and death. Every such attempt leads to a world religion, and in the attempt astrology, solarism, phallicism, symbolism, art, and the pseudo-historic principles of false etymology and euhemerism play their rôles, contribute their mite.

We are prone to think of Christian churches as unique, or at least as significantly different from Jewish synagogues or Chinese joss-houses or Egyptian temples.

Are they?

At the dawn of Christianity, and within the Roman Empire, there were temples to Yahweh, Zeus, Jove, Apollo, Dionysus, Hercules, Mithra, Adonis, Astarte, Baal, Osiris, Isis, and Horus. These temples were to gods, to superhumans. The gods had much in common —necessarily, because they were all born of the same human brain trying to answer the same question, What shall I do to be saved?

Apollo, Dionysus, Mithra, Adonis, Osiris, Isis—the Isis that was worshipped in a temple said to have stood on the spot where Notre-Dame de Paris now stands—were all, says Carpenter, born on or about December 25; of a virgin mother; in a cave or underground chamber; toiled for mankind; were called "Light Bringer," "Healer," "Mediator," "Saviour," "Deliverer," "Messiah," or "Christ"; were vanquished by the powers of darkness; descended into hell; rose from the dead; ascended to heaven; founded communions of saints and churches; baptized disciples; and were commemorated by eucharists. To those deities Christianity added one more—Jesus.

Osiris, for example, was born December 27th; travelled about; was supreme king; taught civil arts, music, gentleness, etc.; created corn and wine; was betrayed by Typhon, prince of darkness; was slain and dismembered; was placed in a coffin and came to life. His

Passion or mystery play—suffering death and resurrection—was enacted at Abydos.

The Hindu Krishna's birth was announced by a star; he performed miracles, raised the dead, healed lepers, deaf, and blind;
championed the poor and oppressed; had a beloved disciple, Arjuna
(John); was crucified on a tree or shot by an arrow; went to hell;
rose from the dead and went to heaven in sight of a multitude; and
will return to judge the quick and the dead.

Mithra was born December 21st, in a cave, of a virgin; travelled
as teacher and illuminator; had twelve companions or disciples; was
buried and rose from a tomb; his resurrection was yearly celebrated;
was called Saviour and Mediator; was figured as a lamb; was remembered by his followers in sacramental feasts.

And so on and so on.

We heard nothing of these "heathenish beliefs" in our Evidences,
but the makers of Christianity knew about them—even got excited
about them and thought they had to explain them away. The devil,
they said, had caused pagans to adopt facsimiles of Christian practices and dogmas to confound Christians. Justin Martyr spoke of
the Lord's Supper "which the wicked devils have imitated in the
mysteries of Mithra"; Tertullian, "The devil by the mysteries of his
idols imitates even the main part of the divine mysteries. . . . He
baptizes the worshippers in water and makes them believe that this
purifies them from their crimes."

Cortez complained that the devil had taught the Mexicans the
same things which God had taught the Christians. But if those same
Mexicans had not thought Cortez their saviour Quetzalcoatl, who
was born of a virgin, fasted forty days, was done to death, and expected to return any minute, Cortez would hardly have won so
pitiably easy a victory.

One wonders how Christianity could have survived without the
aid of the devil. Whoever the devil is, he certainly has not been given
his due by Biblical writers. To the early prophets Yahweh was not
only vengeful, but full of deceit. When Yahweh had to appear as a
good God, he was whitewashed by making Satan responsible for
man's fall from grace.

Satan, serpent, snake, fish. Fish story. But everywhere and over
all is the moon—the ever-living, ever-dying moon. Moon with horns;

snakes with horns. The snake is the moon's representative; the hope of resurrection. Re-read your Genesis; re-read your Old Testament. Recall the brazen serpent Moses sets up to save the Israelites from death. And as Moses lifted up the serpent in the wilderness, even so must the Son of man be lifted up; that whosoever believeth in him should not perish, but have eternal life, says John.

"But we little fishes," said Tertullian, "followers of our True Fish, Jesus Christ, are born of water; not otherwise can we obtain eternal salvation." The first saviour of Israel, Joshua, was also a fish—or rather a son of Nun, who was the son of a fish. And Nun was the true name of the Messiah before the sun was created: identical with Leviathan, who rose three days after his death. Adonis (Tammuz) was also a fish-god, as was Oannes of Babylon. Fables at best are reckless with their zoölogy. Fishes are cousins of snakes, lizards, crocodiles, etc.—and all had legs and tails once, are all equally guardians of the waters of life. "Not otherwise can we obtain eternal salvation!"

And where did Glaucus—he of the fishtail—get his secret of resurrection but from the serpent? What is a serpent? What is a fish? What is a human being? What is life? Where does the moon go when it goes out of sight? Science has one answer; children have another. The answers ignorance once made to such questions became embalmed in sacred myths, in revealed religions, in the Christian Bible. Snake stories. Fish stories. Five billion dollars in church property in the United States today because of a snake story.

Greek funerary art is rooted in a den of snakes. But the image of a fish, said Clement of Alexandria, was the badge of a good Christian and once was as common an emblem of true faith as the cross, which was originally a phallic emblem and widespread centuries before Christianity.

### VII

About the time Jeremiah was being persuaded by Yahweh to consecrate his life to prophethood, Nebuchadrezzar was making his accession prayer to Marduk, the one true and merciful God. Nabo, son of Marduk, was God's envoy to mankind. Jeremiah began his prophecy in 626 B.C. A year later the Chaldeans were to become the dominant power in the world, and so to remain for a century. What of it? This. We are asked to "search the Scriptures." The Jews who wrote the Scriptures were searching the new religions—on the Euphrates, and later that of Zoroaster with its Son of man, Satan, Archangels, and Last Judgment.

Everything kept going wrong for nearly everybody in the Near East. The times were ripe for saviours. The Jews especially were on the lookout for Messiahs. As the Hebrew Bible is brought within comprehension only by an understanding of Jewish history, so the Christian doctrines are intelligible only against the background of their genesis. They were not created in a day or in a year, but slowly, became fixed after centuries.

Judaism had failed; the Israelites had failed. Christianity, to succeed at all, must be a defeatist religion. Having none of this world's goods, it sprang up out of disaster—to blossom into hopes for a hereafter. Man cannot live by bread alone; but he can put up with poor bread if he believes he will feast for all eternity. Its triumph was a calamity—"a wellnigh insurmountable obstacle," as Shotwell calls it, to scientific inquiry, which has taken almost nineteen centuries to surmount.

"Search the Scriptures."

Origen, scholarly Alexandrian Greek father of the third century, searched them, and declared himself against accepting Genesis literally; such stories as the devil taking Jesus on a high mountain, he said, were fables or parables. Origen, says Shotwell, furnishes the ammunition for most of the sermons of modern theologians, who, in trying to reconcile religion with science, feel they must explain away the inherently impossible from the Bible to win the respect of men who are not entirely bereft of reason. They resort to allegories—as Origen had learned from the Greeks to do.

Salvation was the Christians' war-cry; salvation of souls. The old pagan world, especially the Græco-Roman, thought they had something more worth saving; besides, their souls would take care of themselves anyhow. Their primary interest was in living and making history here and now. They could make their mythology fit their facts. The Christians had to make their facts fit their beliefs in their mythology. They searched the Scriptures for "facts" to bolster up their beliefs; "history yielded to the demands of eternity."

And one of the first problems the church had to face was to find a setting for the new religion. "Who is this new Saviour? What are his credentials? Who vouches for him? What is his authority?" Well, he was not a Chaldean or a Persian who believed in a Messiah, nor yet one of the recent Mandean sect on the lookout for a Son of man Redeemer. He was a Jew—he whom the prophets foretold. He *fulfilled* the prophets! The Hebrew Bible was his "authority." His coming had been predicted for ages. The Hebrew Bible was forced to yield a theory of history and a scheme of chronology which would fit the then known Greek and Egyptian chronologies.

The church met that problem in two ways: it twisted obscure or interpolated references to a Messiah to fit a certain Jesus; it prepared a chronology to fit prophecy fulfilled. Its chronology succeeded because, as Shotwell says, the Old Testament offered no continuous chronology and because theology demanded that Christ be the centre of world history.

The first formal Christian chronology was prepared in the middle of the third century by Julius Africanus, who, drawing on Josephus, Manebo, and other pagan sources, arranged the Eras of the "old dispensation" in a series symbolical of the seven-day creation. The world was to last six thousand years, followed by a Sabbatical millennium. Christ was to be born fifty-five hundred years from Adam. And so it was arranged.

More important than the work of Julius Africanus was that of Eusebius of Cæsarea, Father of Church History, who in the third century worked out a world history which exercised an incomparable influence on the Western world. It carried, says Shotwell, not only Biblical, but Chaldean, Greek, and Roman history back to creation; and therein lay the "evidence" for the Christian world view—"a vast world scheme, the 'economy of God,' no longer a speculation but a commonplace." And when Eusebius' scheme was recognized by the Christianized Roman Empire, it became a "fact." As a fact it still does service in printed Bibles to refute the facts of nature recorded in the rocks as the scientist reads them, and the facts of history recorded on stone monuments as the historian reads them.

In the huge mass of conflicting opinion it seems impossible to separate fact from fiction, evidence from hearsay, as to the personality of the central figure of Christianity. Some take the position that no such person lived; that the entire story is a myth comparable to other myths which grew up around anthropomorphic solar personalities, vegetation deities, or culture heroes. Collateral evidence is certainly scanty and sometimes open to suspicion.

Robertson, for example, takes the extreme view that the Christ of Christianity is a synthesis of two of the most popular pagan myths, with some Judaic elements as a nucleus; "a compound of an already composite Gospel Jesus, an interposed Jesus the Nazarite, and a superimposed Jesus born at Nazareth"—and none of them Paul's Jesus, but each, in Paul's words, "another Jesus whom we have not preached." While Frazer seems to find the crucified Jesus the annually slain vegetation-god or sacred tree, Robertson finds his burial in a rock tomb suggestive of Mithra; and Jesus no more, no less, of a man-god than Attis, Adonis, Hercules, and Dionysus— and as was Samson originally.

The first mention of Christ by a non-Christian author is found in the fifteenth Book of the *Annals* of Tacitus, written about 100. The name "Jesus" is not mentioned; only "Christ executed in the reign of Tiberius." Christ, as we have seen, is Greek for anointed; Messiah, in Hebrew. Two references in Josephus to Jesus are, says Kautsky, third-century additions by Christian copyists offended because Josephus fails to mention Jesus, and are certainly a forgery.

Josephus was born 37 A.D. and was a Jewish warrior statesman and diplomat, born of priestly stock. He went to Rome in 63 to plead for the Jews, and became a Roman. His *Wars of the Jews* and *Antiquities of the Jews* are among the most ambitious works of ancient literature. Shotwell calls him the last and greatest Jewish historian.

The lengthy reference to Christ in the eighteenth Book of Josephus' *Antiquities* is obviously spurious or an afterthought. His reference in the twentieth Book to a high priest who had "James, the brother of Jesus, the so-called Christ, haled to court, together with a number of others, indicted as transgressors of the law, and stoned," is not obviously a forgery. It may be genuine, and if so, only proves that there was a Jesus, called the Christ. But Jesus was a not uncommon Jewish name, and for 150 years there had been many so-called Messiahs or Christs.

As to the statement in Luke that Joseph travelled to Bethlehem from Nazareth because of an imperial census and that Jesus was therefore born in Bethlehem, history shows that Judea was not then a Roman province, no census was taken until 7 A.D., and it was not necessary to go to Bethlehem for census purposes. Jesus was "born in Bethlehem" to "fulfil" Micah's "Out of thee (Bethlehem) shall he come forth unto me that is to be ruler of Israel." Joseph went from Nazareth to "fulfil" another prophecy: that the Messiah be a Nazarene; but Isaiah never said anything of the sort. Then, further, to fulfil Hosea's "Out of Egypt have I called my Son," the infant Jesus is taken on a mythical journey to Egypt. Jesus was also born of a virgin because Isaiah said a *virgin* would conceive—in the Greek Bible only; the Hebrew Bible says *woman*. In other words, some Gospel writer, knowing nothing of Jesus' birth but knowing of a Messiah, manipulated old prophetic writings to bolster up a fictitious biography.

The Jews were always looking for a Redeemer, a Messiah—just as a loser looks for a turn of luck; but the Jews of Palestine at this time were looking for a Messianic leader of Jews; that was the kind of saviour they wanted, not a world-saviour. Beyond Judea, even into Persia, a world-saviour was expected. Though Judea had repudiated Jesus as its Messiah, the Gospel writers did not hesitate to rifle the Hebrew Bible to authenticate their world-saving Messiah.

Note that Paul knows nothing of Jesus' virginal birth, nor is it mentioned in the original version of Matthew or Mark. Note, also, that at least a hundred culture heroes are immaculately or supernaturally conceived. *All Saviours in all mythologies have virgin mothers.* Only in modern times has anything been discovered about the physiology of reproduction. Belief in immaculate conception was universal. Pliny, Vergil, and St. Augustine believed that mares could be fertilized by the wind. For "Holy Ghost" read bathing in the sea, rain, sun, moon, eating cherries, a lotus flower, a swallow's egg, almonds, pomegranates, billberry, a worm; and in the case of Rebecca, Jacob's mother, fruit of the mandrake. Plato's father and mother were warned by Apollo in a dream that their child was to be virgin-born—as were Joseph and Mary warned in the Bible myth.

Nor is the myth of the divine child "taken on a journey" peculiar to Jesus. Isis brings Horus out of Phœnicia, as Mary brings Jesus out of Egypt. Hagar and Ishmael, Mandane and Cyrus, Latona and Apollo, Maya and Buddha, Æsculapius and Apollonius, are all brought forth "on a journey."

Mary and Joseph themselves are pure mythic creations with counterparts in dozens of mythologies. The whole story of conception, annunciation, birth, etc., is "a patchwork of a hundred suggestions drawn from pagan art and ritual usage." The New Testament canon says Jesus was born in a manger, an inn stable; the apocryphal books say in a cave: "ill-disguised adaptations of a wide myth." The cave shown as Christ's birthplace at Bethlehem was, according to Robertson, from ancient times a place of worship in the cult of Tammuz.

Note how the myth of Jesus' birth grows in the Gospels. Luke adds the shepherds; the apocryphal Gospels add still more. Shepherds belong to Cyrus and Krishna myths. The massacre of the innocents appears in a late preface in Matthew and is not found in Luke. It is "simply a detail of a universal myth of the attempted slaying of the child of the sun-god"; the disappearing stars at dawn suggest a massacre from which the child escapes. The same idea is found in the Moses myth, and in Egyptian and Indian mythology. Only Luke relates the absurd story of the twelve-year-old boy Jesus confounding the doctors in the temple with his wisdom—as Moses had left home at twelve to inspire, and as Samuel had prophesied at the age of twelve. It is a common myth motive. Twelve disciples, twelve signs of the zodiac, twelve months in the year.

How Jesus' birthday was settled we have seen in another chapter. Also how the times of the seasons and the solar year in general have been incorporated in our "Christian" calendar. Even into the Middle Ages, Christmas was celebrated in Provence with a Yule-log—often called the *Christ-log*—anointed with oil (as the image of Tammuz used to be) and burned to the accompaniment of this suggestive song:

> Rejoice, O Noël Log,
> For tomorrow is the Day of Bread.
> Let all good things enter hither,
> Let women bear children,
> Let goats kid,

> Let the ewes lamb,
> Let there be much corn and much bread,
> And of wine a vat full.

Such winter-solstice celebrations, with the burning of the Yule-log in a huge bonfire, were part of the worship of the god Thor in pagan Scandinavia.

To get at the facts behind the Temptation myth would take us farther afield than we can afford to travel. It would require looking at old Akkad-Sumer pictures of the Goat-god and the Sun-god on a mountain-top; at Osiris and his enemy, the Typhon; at Dionysus and Silenus fighting the Titans; at Zarathustra's temptation and at Buddha's; and especially at the climbing sun in Capricorn, the High One who rules the world. Mark barely mentions the forty-day temptation, says nothing of fasting; but Matthew and Luke elaborate the myth, while John is quite silent. Robertson thinks the coincidence between the Christian and Buddha temptation myths so close that one must have copied the other or both copied a third. In Zarathustra's temptation Ahriman (Satan) promises him a thousand years' dominion if he will renounce Mazda. Zarathustra refuses and predicts the coming of an unborn Son-Saviour who will destroy Ahriman and raise the dead.

January 6th, as we have seen, to the Eastern church stood for four kinds of epiphanies or magic performances; all four were pagan ideas. But turning water into wine is the special prerogative of Dionysus. Besides, at the feast in Cana the men had already drunk "well." Why produce six jarfuls more?

Dionysus also walked on the water, as did Poseidon, Hercules, and Jesus. Assyrian and Babylonian monument pictures show a scourge-bearing god. The same idea is embodied in Osiris—Saviour, Judge, Avenger—armed with a shepherd's crook. Apollo shot pestilence arrows of punishment among the Greeks.

The miracle of raising from the dead was a familiar one to the Greeks. Even in the time of Antoninus Pius, Æsculapius is said to have restored vision to two blind men. Matthew thought the idea so good he used it twice: in the ninth chapter the two healed men are charged to "see that no man know it"; in the twentieth, the miracle is performed before a multitude and there is no charge to secrecy.

The ghastly Lazarus miracle in John could not have been known to Luke, else he could not have told the parable of Lazarus and the rich man. The story of the raising of the daughter of Jairus parallels the Roman story of the miracle-performing Apollonius of Tyana. In that story the girl is the daughter of a consul; in Mark, of "a ruler in the synagogue"; in Matthew, of a "certain ruler."

The dramatic anointing story seems to be pure fiction, told by Matthew and Mark almost word for word. In Luke, the woman (and a sinner at that) anoints the feet and not the head. John has Mary anoint the feet and wipe them with her hair. There are other discrepancies, understandable when it is remembered that in the Hebrew Bible the Messiah is the Anointed One and that the battle priest was anointed with oil. Hence the necessity for the New Testament writers to anoint Jesus, but a Christ for Gentile consumption would naturally not be anointed by priestly hands; they would expect it to be done by women.

Matthew's "ass and a colt, the foal of an ass" should read, "an ass, the foal of a colt." The story is a myth anyhow, and goes back to a zodiac emblem of the Chaldees.

Peter seems to be a composite of two mythical figures, both military deities: the two-sexed Mithra; the two-faced Janus. Janus, originally a Sun-god, came to hold the subordinate position of Opener and Closer (of the day): hence he was the key-bearer, the gate-keeper, of the palace on high; he made peace and war; and was also the god of harbours. His symbol on coins was a ship. Roman Janus coins bore a ship on one side, a double head on the other. Where we say, "Heads or tails," the Romans said, "Heads or ships." The mythical Peter walked the waves, carried the keys, and was fickle. Note, too, that Peter is made to smite off Malchus' ear, walk after the policeman, take a seat in the high priest's yard, etc. —all that the Scriptures might be fulfilled!

The idea behind the eucharist or the Lord's Supper was not only widespread in the pagan world, but is behind all primitive medicine taken by the mouth. In the Dionysiac mysteries one became identified with or united to the god through the partaking of the "divine elements." The rite was part of Hindu, Egyptian, and especially of Mithra, cults. That Paul knew of the existence of such a cult is the obvious inference from: "Ye cannot be partakers of the Lord's table and of the table of devils." His devils, presumably, were the Mithraic. Mithraism was Christianity's chief rival in Rome. Tarsus, Paul's home town, was a Mithraic centre, from which the religion had already crossed over to Rome and into the Roman army. Its doctrine of communion with divinity through body and blood was precisely the doctrine of Paul.

Nor is there any uniqueness in baptism and confirmation; in fact, most of the savage world is acquainted with that doctrine of second birth. All primitive initiation rites are an "entering in" of one kind or another into one state or another: adulthood, the tribe itself, or some secret society. It was just as necessary to be born again to join the Mithraic or Dionysiac "church" as for the Christian. The Mithraic initiate was half drowned in the blood of the bull. Christians are "washed in the Blood of the Lamb," immersed or just sprinkled.

"Then shall the Priest say," says the christening service, " 'O merciful God, grant that the old Adam in this child may be so buried that the new man may be raised up in him; grant that all carnal affections may die in him and that all things belonging to the spirit may live and grow in him.' " And so the Christian child "puts on" Christ—a Christian totem; in the eucharist, he eats the totem.

Let all the sins of the world fall on me, said Buddha, that the world may be delivered. Tien, the Chinese Holy One, died to save the world. But it is inherent in all saviours who die or are done to death to save the world, that they do not remain dead; they rise again to immortality: Krishna, Indra, Osiris, Horus, Mithra, Hercules, Attis, Adonis, Jesus.

If, says Carpenter, in the Credo one read Dionysus, Krishna, Hercules, Osiris, or Attis for Jesus; Semele, Devaki, Alcmene, or Neith for Mary; and any corresponding terrestrial tyrant for Pontius Pilate: the Apostles' Creed fits the rites and worship of any pagan god.

In no other one respect did the Gospel writers have so much difficulty as in making a plausible myth of the death and resurrection of their Messiah. They had to fulfil the Scriptures, yet produce a Messiah who was not a Saviour of Judea only, but of the world. In their effort to be convincing, they resorted to such theatrical effects as, seen on a stage or read in sober-mindedness, must seem like amateurish melodrama.

A by-product of the Passion myth as formulated in the Gospels was the rousing of such hatred and contempt for the Jews throughout Christendom as nineteen centuries have scarcely sufficed to efface. Otherwise I think it highly probable there would be no Jews today.

The possible materials available to the Gospel writers were of three kinds: myths of deities dying and being restored to life again —such as the myths of the solar and vegetation gods; dramatic performances which annually reënacted these death-resurrection myths; and historic or pseudo-historic crucifixions.

Moses was transfigured on a mountain; Elijah was carried up to heaven: both were ancient Sun-deities. Sun-deities wore a crown or nimbus: Prometheus and Hercules wore mock crowns, in memory of their sacrifice for mankind. The sacrificial victim in Mithraic rites was crowned; in Egyptian ceremonies crowns of thorns were used.

Ancient Babylon in her festival of the dying-resurrecting god used a condemned prisoner as victim. He was allowed to "play" king for five days: robes, throne, etc. He was then stripped, scourged, and crucified for the good of the people. He was a scapegoat, in short. In Persian feasts of the Sacæa, the same crucifixion was enacted. Possibly the drama of Esther (Ishtar) and Mordecai (Marduk) was an ancient Babylonian mystery play.

Such a divine drama was enacted by a Roman garrison at Durostolum as late as 300 A.D. Thirty days before the feast of Saturn a mock king was elected by lot, and, as Saturn, was allowed thirty days' royal honours and free sexual licence. He was then supposed to kill himself on his own altar. But as the lot had fallen on Dasius, a Christian soldier, he refused to kill himself, and was killed by the soldiers. Antigonus, the last Ashmonean king of the Jews, was scourged and slain by Mark Antony. In Caligula's reign, according to Philo, the practical jokers of Alexandria dressed up a well-known lunatic named Karabas in royal purple, and, dragging him to the theatre, hailed him KING OF THE JEWS—all by way of mocking King Agrippa, then strutting around Alexandria in vast pomp on his way to his new kingdom of Jerusalem. This was in A.D. 38, and this king was the father of the Agrippa who was to hear Paul's defence in A.D. 60.

Finally, there is the Talmudic evidence of a Jesus Ben Pandira having been put to death on the eve of the Passover about a century before the death of the Biblical Jesus. Robertson thinks this the Jesus Paul spoke of as stoned and hanged on a tree. As the Greeks often used "hanging" for crucifixion, the "hanged on a tree" was left in Acts v: 30.

Of the crown of thorns, scourging, and kingly title, Paul seemingly knew nothing. Matthew's loud-voiced cry rending the veil of the temple, the earthquake, the rent rocks, the opened graves, and the saints rising from the grave, are palpably theatrical. What did the saints do after they had gone into the holy city and appeared unto Mary? And who was convinced by all this proof? Certainly not the high priests, nor the Pharisees; only the Roman soldiers— to fulfil the eighteenth verse of the twenty-second Psalm. They do not rend Jesus' mystical seamless inner garment; they divide his other garments into four lots. But this pious accommodation on the part of the soldiers to fulfil the Scriptures is the exclusive idea of John, who seems to have searched the Scriptures thoroughly. Note, also, that the "My God, my God, why hast Thou forsaken me?" Matthew and Mark (but not Luke or John) put into Jesus' mouth, is from that same twenty-second Psalm.

Burial, lamentation, resurrection, etc., show equally convincing evidence of the Gospel writers' knowledge of Oriental mythology. The synoptic contradictions in details represent variants of myths and mystical dramas.

This myth-making tendency is well illustrated in the last chapter of John, last of the Gospels to be written. A comparison of the end of that chapter (the twenty-first) with the last verse of the preceding chapter, seems conclusive evidence that the twenty-first chapter was an afterthought or an appendix added later.

Jesus appears to seven disciples by the sea of Tiberias. There is a big catch of fish. They eat; Jesus does not. In Mark, there was no sea; Jesus simply appeared to the eleven as they sat at meat. They are to cast out devils, heal by laying on of hands, and can take up serpents and drink poison with impunity. The object of the visit in John was to command Peter to feed his lambs and sheep. But in

Luke Jesus gives bread to only "two of them" on the way to a village, and later in the same chapter Jesus appears to the eleven. They
thought him a spirit, but he asked them to handle him—in flesh
and bone—to prove that he was no spirit. And still they did not
believe. So he asked for meat; and they gave him a piece of broiled
fish and honeycomb, and he did eat.

It all seems so childish, so primitive, so universal—and so confusing. Why invent a banquet at all? Was it because a Mithraic tomb
pictured seven rulers of sacrificial feasts, and was the Mark and
Luke banquet of eleven a still later invention to get away from the
pagan seven—one myth, as Robertson thinks, becoming the occasion for another?

Now that the earth is round and not flat as it used to be, and
heaven no longer a solid firmament, magic flights by superma-
gicians to heaven seem rather more fabulous than they seemed to
simple-minded myth-makers in the days when myth-making was
the highest form religious intelligence could take. The Enochs,
Elijahs, Krishnas, Adonises, Herakleses, Dionysuses, and Christs of
the old world that go to heaven can find an equal host of good
Indian cult-heroes that have already gone on high. No wonder the
exasperated early Christian shrieked, "The devil has his Christs!"

Myth-making did not stop with the Gospels. The church kept on
multiplying its myths, as Robertson says, on pagan lines, step by
step. Thus, the descent into hell, the seven martyrs, the Trinity, the
giant Christopher bearing the Christ-child, the Assumption of Mary,
the Immaculate Conception of Mary's mother Anna, Jesus' birth
in a cave, the worship of an ox and an ass, are all drawn from pagan
practices, as were the myths of the Gospels themselves and the machinery of priesthood. Lactantius makes Jesus twice-born, like
Dionysus. The pope wears a mitre, like Mithra and Dionysus, in
whose chair he sits. Peter, as we saw, was assimilated to Mithra and
Janus. By the Middle Ages the church had circumstantial descriptions of the "face"—as "authentic" as portraits of Apollo, Peter, and
Paul; all pretensions "to impose fantasy on mankind as a fact."

Jesus was tried by the Sanhedrin at a full meeting. The trial was
a travesty on justice, the proceedings radically illegal. Nevertheless,
the Sanhedrin found cause to deliver Jesus to the Roman authority

for execution. Pontius Pilate was the representative of Emperor Tiberius, but at the time of the trial he was procurator of Judea and subordinate to the governor of Syria. He had a bad record and was as much of a coward as were Peter and the other disciples. It was his business to preserve peace in a city of fanatics. The mob was in command; he had no time to send for troops from Syria. It was not Roman jurisprudence which executed Jesus, but a cowardly procurator doing what seemed to him his duty.

But if Jesus was a rebel and had called upon the Jews to refuse to pay taxes, Pilate had to condemn him, and the Jews should not have turned him over to Pilate. I read Matthew, then Luke, then John. Pilate says he is innocent—"I find no fault in this man." And Pilate's soldiers not only crucify Jesus, but scourge and deride him as King of the Jews. Now, I repeat, if he had acted like a King of the Jews, like a Messiah, why should the Jews, who were looking for some one to lead them out of Roman bondage, hand him over to their enemies? Did the Jews bribe the Roman soldiers to become the tools of their own base treachery? The whole trial, as related by discrepant second-, third- or fourth-hand witnesses, so violates both Jewish and Roman procedure as to seem like a badly done piece of fiction, an incident, like the Passion itself, in a composite myth.

But, myth or history, there is no doubt of one staggeringly big fact, namely, that during some three centuries a religion called Christianity was born and grew rapidly into a world-religion. It was born of the belief that a Saviour's appearance was imminent, and that that Second Coming was to be the final catastrophe. According as they could answer the summons, "Are you ready?" men lived their lives from day to day between ecstatic hope and abject fear. That belief paralyzed thinking, dammed all the joys of life, put a premium on ascetic impotency and gullible ignorance, outlawed intelligence, and raised bigotry to the highest price in the history of the known universe. What did? Christianity.

What is Christianity? Rome. Without a Rome to appeal to, Paul's blasphemous doctrine against humanity might today lie buried among the dozens of forgotten Oriental sects. Rome made Christianity what it is. Christianity is Rome, or nothing but an empty vessel into which one puts one's pet superstitions and one's own philosophy of life—in which case the label is as meaningless as the Iroquois *orenda*.

Let us make no mistake, and let us be honest with ourselves. The Bible no more solves any riddle of life than a shaman's kit-bag. There is no more originality or virtue in our Bible than in scores of other Bibles. All Bibles are man-made and when committed to writing are soon out of date. The Christianity which grew up in Rome and which is embalmed in our Bible had no light to shed on any social or political problem of the time, nothing that would free one slave for one single day or hasten peace on earth, goodwill to men, by one single hour.

Jesus, in Matthew, curses the Jews; and in Luke "foretells" the destruction of Jerusalem, including pregnant and nursing mothers, with a ferocity that would shame a savage. True, such ethics is sprinkled through the Hebrew Bible, but New Testament ethics at best is but Jewish ethics in a different setting. Jesus no more condemns war or slavery than did the ancient Assyrians. By implication, possibly. As Newman said, "There is little in the ethics of Christianity which the human mind may not reach by its natural powers; and which here or there . . . has not in fact been anticipated." And anticipated by Romans, Greeks, Persians, Egyptians, Hindus, Chinese.

Some of Jesus' moral precepts seem so unnatural as to appear grotesque; they simply cannot be taken literally. His reply to a disgruntled disciple, "Ah! how beautifully white are the dog's teeth!" reminds one of some of the cryptic platitudes of a recent Christian president of a certain nation. And what can we make of the Saviour of mankind cursing a fig tree? Grant that Jesus was supposed to be talking to Syrian peasants; that fact does not sanctify these sayings or put intelligence in them when the author of the sayings had more intelligence than Syrian peasants.

Celsus, writing of Christians early in the third century, hit the nail on the head: "It is only the simpleton, the ignoble, the senseless—slaves, womenfolk, and children—whom they wish to persuade or can persuade." But Celsus was a poor prophet; he prophesied the extinction of the churches.

A Jewish book of about 120 B.C., called the *Testament of the Twelve Patriarchs*, is loaded with moral precepts dealing with love and kindness. On such literature the Gospel writers drew. The Sermon on the Mount was no sermon and there was no mount—outside the mythical mount of the mystery play. Taken as it stands, it practically annuls the whole principle for which Jesus is supposed to stand—which was ideals, not precepts, ethical mysticism, love of God, goodness, truth, and so on. In the Sermon he is made to appear as a giver of laws, set rules for conduct.

The Sermon at best is purely gratuitous—a compilation of sayings from Isaiah, Psalms, etc. It was never preached; it may have been spoken in a mystery play. Such stringing together of ethical maxims for teaching purposes was a Jewish practice. The setting alone of the Sermon shows its handiwork. In Luke's version of the Sermon the poor are glorified, the rich condemned; but in Matthew the rich are let off; it is enough to be poor in spirit to be blessed. Luke is no Gospel for a rich congregation.

Note how savage Luke is against the rich. Class hatred is apparent in all the Gospels, but by Matthew's time the rich are no longer put on a level with thieves and bandits. Hence the title given Matthew of "favourite Gospel of the Church." Luke sends the rich man to hell, not because he is a sinner, but because he is rich; the poor man goes to Abraham's bosom; nor can a rich man enter heaven as a camel cannot pass through the needle's eye. And in the Luke Sermon, to be rich and enjoy life is a crime deserving cruel punishment. James also hates the rich and tells them to go to now and weep for the miseries that are to come upon them.

The Sermon teaching, "Swear not at all . . ." is taken literally by certain Christian sects; Quakers, for example, are supposed to refuse to take oaths. Suppose other Christian sects took the entire Sermon literally, what a picked brotherhood of superhumans would result! Would they be anarchists or just communists, and how long would they last in this Christian world?

The Lord's Prayer, says Robertson, was a formula officially promulgated by the Jews and originated in Babylon. An ancient Aramaic Kaddish prayer ends thus: "Magnified and sanctified by His great name in the world which He has created after His will. May He erect His kingdom in your lifetime and within the lifetime of the whole house of Israel."

The chapter just after the Sermon in Matthew has the oft-quoted passage of "Foxes have holes . . ."; but T. Gracchus in 130 B.C., in speaking of the Roman proletariat, put it this way: "The wild animals of Italy have their caves and their lairs in which they may rest, but the men who struggle and die for Italy's greatness possess nothing but light and air, because they cannot be robbed of these. Homeless and shelterless, they wander about with their wives and children."

Jesus threatened those who would not follow him with weeping and gnashing of teeth, but which Jesus are we to follow? The anti-Gentile, anti-Samaritan Jesus; the Jesus who came eating and drinking; the Nazarite Jesus; the Messiah Jesus who was to restore the fortunes of the Jews; the spiritual Messianic Jesus who preached universalism; Paul's Jesus who died Messianically but had no Messianic teaching; or the Jesus of the Fourth Gospel?

Is Mark *the* Gospel; Matthew and Luke mere partisan Gospels; and the John Gospel Christianity's first sacred book, its writer the Mohammed of the new religion? John was primarily a mystic; he preached neither Gospel nor Redeemer, but a principle—the *Logos*, the Word, God. This principle is triune—God, Spirit, Word: an adaptation of the Messianic myth of the Jews plus Greek and Persian ideas of the Logos, to Hellenic minds. His God is a blending of Mithra, Light of the World, and Dionysus, who offers his body and blood as a mystic sacrifice of salvation—a sacrifice, by the way, common in cults of the time, all the way from Greece to the Indus. To make his immortality doctrine more convincing, he has a decaying corpse restored to life.

### VIII

Paul preaching the Risen Christ managed to make it sound more reasonable and more certain than the Orphism with which his Greek auditors were familiar. That cult, the resurrection of the slain son of Zeus as Dionysus, was known not only throughout Greece, but up to the very walls of Palestine. The idea of Orphism is the idea of Paul's Risen Christ; both are mystery religions. Paul shows no more interest in the practical problems of his age, nor points any more toward any future solution of any of the real problems of life, than a Nautical Almanac. He saw serfs as beasts of burden on two legs and was of a mind with the Jews who thanked

God they were not born women. As Shotwell says, he preached everything from matrimony to pedagogy, but was careful not to interfere with any male prerogative.

For at least seven centuries before the Christian Era, the Orient had been busying itself with prophetic religions—Chaldeans, Jews, Persians; for three centuries they had worked on the doctrine of the End of the World, a Last Judgment, a Resurrection, a Paradise, and a Hell. From that doctrine arose not only the Christian but several other Salvation religions. With these Christianity had to compete—even with a Jewish Salvation Army.

Paul took a preëxistent yearning for salvation and built it into a certainty. There can be no reasonable doubt that Paul felt that certainty, or that it came to him on the road to Damascus in a "revelation." Jesus is the Redeemer, Paul is his prophet. Because of Paul, Greek became the language of the new religion, the city its home rather than the country; the country people, *pagani*, became pagans.

Paul (Saul of Tarsus) was a fire-eating Pharisee on the way to Damascus when he had his "vision." He preached at Damascus, and three years later returned to Jerusalem, where he met the apostles. He then went to Antioch, where he converted the Jews to Christianity. From Antioch he went to Cyprus, where he was so well received by the Roman proconsul that out of gratitude he Romanized his name, changed it from Saul to Paul. He returned to Jerusalem in 57. After a riot, Paul was sent to Cæsarea; but he demanded trial in Rome, where he was sent in 59. He presumably was put to death in Rome five years later. Mark went with Paul to Rome, and, says legend, became Peter's secretary. But Peter's visit to Rome is probably legendary, as are the movements of the other apostles.

Christianity's first battle was between Paul's idea of a church universal at Antioch and Peter's idea of a church for the Jews at Jerusalem. For communion in Paul's church one need not be circumcised or pass through the synagogue—as in Peter's. Paul preached salvation for Jews and Greeks—hence "Apostle of the Gentiles." Christianity owes more to Paul than to Peter, to Antioch than to Jerusalem.

But for a long time it was not at all certain whether Paul's Order of the Saviour or the Judean cult of Jesus would win out. Philo, an Alexandrian Jew, thought Judaism would become the religion of the world; he saw men everywhere being converted to Judaism. In the time of Tiberius, a petty king of an Assyrian district was circumcised and became a Jew. Nero's wife, Poppæa Sabina, became a Jewess. But renegades to Hellenism made artificial foreskins and changed their names. A high priest named Jesus changed his name to Jason; Menahem, to Menelaus.

Evidence of the competitive zeal for converts is shown in Matthew XXIII:15. "Woe unto you, scribes and Pharisees, hypocrites! for ye compass sea and land to make one proselyte, and when he is made, ye make him twofold more the child of hell than yourselves." The hostility of the pagan to the Jewish Christian developed into intense hostility to Judaism and to the Jews.

The destruction of Jerusalem by Titus in 70 ended two centuries of political unrest in the Eastern world. It also profoundly affected the fate of religion. The Messiah who had been expected to lead a rebellious people to victory was replaced by a Messiah who was crucified, not for rebellion, but as proof of God's infinite mercy to mankind. Congregations that had been organized to hold believers together to await a physical kingdom, now of their own accord grew in strength and conviction of the second coming of the Messiah: the Kingdom of God is at hand, this very generation! "The Lord himself," said Paul to the Thessalonians, "shall descend from heaven with a shout, with the voice of the Archangel and the trump of God: and the dead in Christ shall rise first: then we which are alive and remain shall be caught up together with them in the clouds, to meet the Lord in the air. . . ." The wish was father to the thought; the cumulative beliefs of the congregation made certain their belief in a Messiah coming in all splendour and glory. Ecstatic faith. But note that Enoch, most important of the Jewish apocalyptic writers, who wrote not later than 170 B.C., speaks of a Christ in heaven about to come to judge men, and called Son of Man.

Myths multiplied, the congregations grew, but still the Kingdom of God did not come. Then, out of such abundant materials as were available, faith created a Kingdom Come on high. Heaven is our home. But so far as the Gospels are concerned, no joy is to be found even there, but a common repast; no duty here higher than to God; no inspiration to help one's neighbours, only to save one's soul.

That is all: save one's soul. Nothing else matters; poverty is glorious; disease a sacred thing. Life is not worth living; deny yourself, scourge and mortify the flesh. Be proud of poverty and misery. Go into the desert and die of thirst. Live like a sour-grapes fox. Above all, get off in a corner and polish up your soul. Faith justifies all, anything. But make certain your own soul is saved. Nothing else matters. In following Him Who came to bring not peace but a sword, anything—however foolish, vile, cruel, savage, stupid, insane, unjust—may be for the glory of God and the good of one's soul, so long as an odour of sanctity may be thrown over it.

Christianity poses as an angel of light, but, as Carpenter says, it is discreet about its own dark deeds. It began by destroying, distorting, and denying its pagan sources. Bishops assassinated one another. It encouraged the Children's Crusade; the shameful murder of Manicheans, Albigenses and Huguenots; burned thousands of witches and heretics at the stake; and Greek, Catholic, Lutheran, and Protestant priests urged nations to slaughter one another with diabolic devices of science, glorifying the war-cry of patriotism in defiance of their principles.

There are still unwritten pages between man and the universe; but, as Shotwell says, it was a "paper bulwark which for centuries kept people from inquiring into the secrets of nature." That bulwark is the Bible; more specifically, the Gospels, whose contradictory teachings, says Robertson, are as oppugnant as Hegel, Kant, Comte, Arnold, and Ruskin. They belong to clashing sects, changing generations, to a hundred hands. They occur in documents visibly made up of shreds and patches, bound up with myths "gross as a mountain, open, palpable"; and always faced by the eternal veto of Paul's silence, who knows no word of Jesus' teaching.

In all that teaching I find nothing so far removed from Christian egotism as the words of the last of the Pandara brothers in the Indian epic, who, held up at the gate of Paradise by Indra himself, exclaimed: "O mighty Indra! I will not forsake this dog of mine, even for my own salvation."

Against that superb devotion to man's oldest and closest dumb friend set the price of salvation demanded by the Roman Catholic Church: "For any man who does not hold the unity of the Catholic Church, neither baptism, nor alms however profuse, nor death met for the name of Christ, can be of benefit for his salvation."

How did it come about that a universal, world-salvation religion became the exclusive possession of a church which could send souls to hell without waiting for a Judgment Day? How did it come about that a religion for the meek and lowly, which up to 100 A.D. numbered less than fifty communities, all of simple-minded people, and up to 180 A.D. less than seventy-five, by 325 A.D. numbered more than five hundred and fifty communities and included a Roman Emperor?

Again we move to Rome.

# CHAPTER TEN

## Christianity Enthroned

1. Wonders of the Invisible World; or, Modern Miracle-mongering.
2. What the Cult of Jesus Had to Dethrone. 3. Paul *Might* Be Right!
4. The Christians *Were* Right! 5. I Believe in . . . the Virgin
Mary; and the Double Standard. 6. Savage Europe Goes in for
Christianity and the Popes Go in for Power and Splendour. 7. The
Cross Fights the Crescent for Christ's Sake. 8. Heresies and the
Inquisition; and the *Witch's Hammer*. 9. The Jesuit Enigma. 10.
Luther's Little Popelet and Henry VIII's Love-affair Reformation.
11. "Has God Forgotten All That I Have Done for Him?" 12. Peace
on Earth, Goodwill to Men.

I

WHETHER or not we are a Christian nation, our civilization
is a child of Christian Europe; our early book of knowledge
was the Bible, our ethical platform was the ethics of Christian
Europe. And if knowledge of the Bible is the first step in wisdom,
and becoming a Christian the first move in becoming Christ-like,
a glance at the history of Christian Europe should be profitable.
For it was in Europe that Christianity became enthroned; it is from
Europe that a large section of the Christian world today takes its
cues, if not its orders.

Having already looked at the Bible as a one-volume library of
knowledge, we have now to inquire how Christianity became enthroned, what was the ethics of throne and pulpit, and how Europe
fared under Christian dispensation; in other words, what happened
to civilization while it was ruled by bishops and elders, and whether
from Rome by a pope or from a village by a Protestant reformer.

Not that the past determines the future, but that the past is a
story which can be read and that such a story can be evaluated.
*Something* happened to the civilization which the Græco-Roman

527

world had borrowed, begged, or stolen from the civilized Near East and then made its own. What was it?

What is happening—here, now? The present can help us to interpret the past; in fact, in many human affairs it is our best interpreter. And so let us make a pilgrimage to the shrine of a saint. We shall see some modern miracles; we shall meet some first-class wonders of the invisible world face to face. And our guide shall be the official guide-book of St. Anne de Beaupré.

All saints of all religions, the guide-book tells us, have miraculous power. St. Anne has more than any other saint because she is the grandmother of the Saviour. That makes her more dignified; endows her with special privileges; gives her power with God. She shares in the highest privileges of her beloved daughter, the Queen of Heaven. The greater our confidence in a saint, the more numerous are the favours and the miracles wrought by the intercession of that saint. No other saint can inspire more confidence than the mother of the Immaculate Virgin, grandmother of the man-God, our Lord and Saviour Jesus Christ.

Where did I learn all this? In Canada. What is Canada? St. Anne's inheritance, given her by Christ. She is Queen of our dear country; this basilica (of St. Anne de Beaupré) is her palace, scene of her royal bounty.

The crypt of that "palace" has twenty-six altars, twenty-five confessionals, and accommodates two thousand worshippers. The reliquary is a mass of gold, with nine turquoises, eight garnets, four amethysts, eight diamonds, and one "fire opal"; at the bottom is a gold plate studded with twenty-eight diamonds. It contains holy relics: a "pretty big fragment of a finger bone"; a second, third, and fourth bone from the hand; and a "Great relic"—a *bone from her wrist*—obtained from Pope Leo XIII in 1892.

Relics of what—sabre-toothed tiger, Cave-man, the Great Pyramid, the Parthenon? No; of *St. Anne*. But the *Bible* says nothing of St. Anne. There is "nothing curious about that; it is enough glory for her to have had the Immaculate Virgin Mary as her daughter." Still, "tradition" supplies her with a father named Stollen, "of the royal family of David."

Anne, we are told, "shared her time between prayer and the care of the children of the poor"; and died at the age of fifty-six in the arms of Mary, her beloved daughter. She was buried in Bethlehem in the ancestral tomb and then transferred to Jerusalem and placed in another tomb beside her husband, St. Joachim. And it is a *"historical fact"* (italics mine) that in early A.D. her body was brought to France by Lazarus, who, though once dead and decomposing, "became first bishop of Marseilles."

We began with tradition, "rather vague but accepted"; then we got a "historical fact." We come now to, "In any case it is certain" that Anne's remains, "to prevent profanation by barbarians," were placed in a grotto in the church's foundation and the entrance sealed and forgotten—until "divine providence was pleased to reveal it." The church—"it is certain"—was being reconsecrated by an archbishop. Among those present was a vast audience of clergy, army, and people; and Charlemagne.

Watch closely. A young boy, "blind, deaf, and dumb from birth, began gesticulating with hands and feet." They smell a prodigy and begin to dig. The boy keeps on gesturing. They dig deeper, and find "a lighted lamp" before a recess in the inner wall of the crypt. Such "unaccustomed splendour" attracted the emperor.

Now listen. "In this crypt is the body of St. Anne, mother of the blessed Virgin Mary, Mother of God." That is what the deaf-dumb-and-blind-from-birth youth said. He could talk now, and see and hear. A triple miracle.

They open the recess, find the relics in a wooden case wrapped in a veil, with this inscription "in Latin": *Here is the body of St. Anne, mother of the Virgin Mary*. They open the reliquary, and "a fragrance came forth similar to that of balsam."

But, author of the guide to the basilica of St. Anne de Beaupré, how do you know that *your* "relics" are genuine? Because St. Bridget of Sweden in her book of Revelations tells how St. Anne came to her in an apparition and testified in person to the authenticity of her relic preserved in said basilica.

From that guide I also learn about indulgences—ranging from two hundred days to plenary. Also how "God always favoured" pilgrimages, and "sovereign pontiffs and bishops never cease to encourage them." Also that holy mass "is the surest way to gain the favours of God, is the golden key to open the treasury of heavenly blessings": the gift of a precious article, the promise never to take part in certain amusements, etc. Candles and lights. Especially is perpetual mass of "infinite value." Price fifty cents. Guide? No; *perpetual* mass. "A share in a mass said every day for all time"!

Crutches, etc.—glorious trophies of Anne's many victories over spiritual and corporal infirmities, "unquestionable witnesses of the power of her intercession with the eternal Father and his divine Son. Hasten, then, devout pilgrims, cast yourselves at the feet of St. Anne," who "wears a diadem of gold and precious stones with which she was crowned . . . in the name of Pope Leo XIII."

St. Anne de Beaupré is presumably doing business today as she was when I visited her two years ago. She is *the* Church, the one true and logical Church!

If, as I was led to infer from a voice on the radio yesterday, I can receive balm for my broken heart, compensation for my faithless mate, and a solution of my financial difficulties, by writing a certain Baptist preacher in Michigan, why not get plenary indulgence after breaking hearts and robbing a bank? Why bother with a mere Baptist preacher when a vast mechanism exists which can bring pressure to bear on the grandmother of God, and will do it eternally for less than it costs to see a prize fight from the ringside? This is a machine age; if I want magic power or supernatural results, I shall go to the most perfect machine of its kind ever built by man.

The church is always a machine; a human machine which preys on gullibility, which is oiled, clothed, and fed by fearful ignorance.

St. Anne de Beaupré as a cult would have been at home in Antioch, Alexandria, Athens, Rome, or York, in 193 B.C. or A.D. She could have done business, got a hearing, had followers, performed her miracles. There is nothing new about miracles. Every rain in Africa—or in Kansas—is in answer to prayer, or the beating of a tom-tom, or the sacrifice of a tomcat. Aurelian performed miracles in Alexandria. Our cities today are full of divine healers.

A remark of St. Chrysostom sheds a flood of light on miracle-mongering: "Formerly the extraordinary endowments of the mind (magic power) were even bestowed upon the worthless, because the church then had need of miracles, but today (fourth century) they are not even given to the deserving, *because the church no longer is in need of them*." The church had won; why resort to more trickery? Judging from the steady supply of miracles reported these days, the church is in need of them.

Miracles pay—pay the church, pay the town. They make for bigger and better business. Lasserre, after long study, has estimated that nearly a million people visit Lourdes every year—more than any other tourist centre in France. The whole neighbouring country lives off them; agriculture, quarrying, and other activities normal to the region, have ceased. In 1928 there were forty garages and 203 hotels, and for every tourist there are four pilgrims.

Æsculapius at Epidaurus in pagan Greece was a divine healer, but he had no such following; nor were his disciples so rich as the "fathers of the Grotto"; nor did he have the official sanction of a pope, or the official approval of a great church for the miraculous cures by the intercession of the Virgin.

Three years, it seems, after the Virgin had been declared free (by a papal bull, 1854) from the taint of original sin, she appeared to a child and made the startling announcement, *I am the Immaculate Conception*. Did she, or did she not, appear? Well, if she did, it was a good business proposition. The pilgrimages to the Grotto of Lourdes began; its waters cure all diseases.

Grenoble began with the same kind of fraud. In 1846 a fanatic female, clad in a yellow robe and wearing a sugar-loaf hat, appeared as the Blessed Virgin to two little shepherds. A local legal inquiry pronounced her a fraud, yet the next year the bishop "confirmed the miracle"—and a congregation was formed to exploit it. Pilgrimages began; its waters still perform miraculous cures.

But the crowning insult to human intelligence is to be found in the sanctuary of Loretto, where one may find the "Holy House itself in which was born the Blessed Virgin Mary and in which the Word was made Flesh"—transported by angels from Palestine *via* Dalmatia in 1291. How may one know it is not a mere fairy tale? By a pronouncement of Pope Benedict XV in 1916, ordering that the Feast of the Translation of the Holy House be observed every December 10th. The voice of the pope is the voice of God, and since 1870 infallible. Loretto is visited by 100,000 pilgrims a year; provision is made for tattooing the goddess on their arms.

One church alone in the Eternal City of Ghosts and Holy Relics (St. Prassede) contains: the bodies of six saints; relics of Matthew,

Luke, Bartholomew, Philip, Andrew, Peter, Paul, and John the Baptist; some of the garments of Our Lady and a piece of the Lord's seamless robe; three thorns from the crown; and four pieces of the True Cross. In the chapel of St. Zeno (also in Rome) one may find the Holy Pillar of the Scourging brought from Jerusalem in 1223.

Just one more example to illustrate the alertness of the church in making the most of tradition to capitalize a superstition for business purposes. During an automobile show in Boston a few years ago, as related by Tozzer, hundreds of taxi-drivers attended a church service. The Italian priest invoked on them the protection of St. Christopher, and gave each chauffeur a pair of medals which had been "blessed," one for personal wear, the other to be attached to the car. On one side the medal bore a picture of Titian's famous St. Christopher bearing the Christ-child over a river; on the other, the words, "St. Christopher protect us."

Well, it was a good idea—if it is true that

> In whatever day thou seest the likeness of St. Christopher,
> In that same day thou wilt from death no evil blow incur.

But the difference between that kind of protecting magic and the magic the Trobriander puts into his canoe to make it go fast and keep him from a watery grave, is the difference between superstition in the illiterate South Seas and in Boston; or, shall we say, between savagery and civilization? But let us get on with the idea: see how a Boston idea works out in New York.

We now have on the East Side of New York what is known as the *Church of the Motorists*—formerly the Roman Catholic Church of the Holy Family. There is not only a special mass for motorists, but, according to the press, the priests in their vestments go out into the street and pronounce a blessing upon all cars parked nearby. "There will be no charge for the blessing, but if owners of cars wish to make a donation to the church, they may do so."

Does the Church officially approve? A cardinal has "given permission"; and a relic of St. Christopher recently received from Rome has been "authenticated" by the Chancery of the New York Archdiocese. The relic is "applied to worshippers" and is the excuse for a shrine which it is hoped "motorists from all parts of the country will come to visit." A statue of the saint stands beside the altar of the shrine.

There was a Christopher, and he was put to death in Asia Minor about 250 in the general persecution of Christians by Emperor Decius. Where he was buried is unknown. Not until the Middle Ages did he begin his career as a popular miracle-working saint. Shall we live to see his image hung up over street crossings, blinking red and green, and protecting all who look upon his face from sudden death? It is possible.

It was not the *cult of Jesus* that Rome persecuted or that triumphed over the cult of Isis, or the Great Mother, or Mithra; it was the *Christian Church* which was persecuted, the Christian Church which triumphed. It grew, not in humanity nor in meekness, gentleness or any so-called Christian virtue, but in power, organization, wealth. From lowly and humble origins it grew big enough for an emperor to experiment with. There were Christians beyond the Euphrates by 100 A.D., but so far as the Church was concerned they might as well have been in Hades. The Church was infinitely less interested in saving human beings from pain, poverty, and misfortune, than it was in saving its own skin. And that has been its big fight ever since.

Cult of St. Anne, cult of Mary, cult of St. Joseph, cult of the Bleeding Heart, cult of St. Christopher, of more saints than there are days in the year or were gods in the entire Græco-Roman world in the year 1. By gathering them all up, all the mysteries of life and death, of birth and pain, of seasonal changes; by adopting existing machinery; by appropriating the spiritual, magical, supernatural, and superhuman powers of all the other gods and goddesses; and by utilizing all the devices yet invented to secure a hold on undisciplined thought: the Christian Church at last won out. It needed no divine guidance, no sacred Scripture, no religion of a life of love and duty, no Golden Rule, none of the nobility of character, friendliness or democratic simplicity of Jesus. It furnished its own inspiration, guided itself by the exigencies of the times, put whatever interpretation it pleased on its Bible, and found in its Bible whatever justification it needed for war-cry and propaganda.

In fact, our Christianity has borrowed so extensively and has been reformed so many times that no two seem able to agree in defining it. As a result, more energy seems to go into wrangling over what it is all about, into explaining, propounding, defining, and defending it, than into Christian works. As death is just a job to the grave-digger, Christianity is largely a matter of jobs—and for a large number of people.

Before we look at the Church itself, let us look at the cults Christianity found to hand, ready to be built into a church.

## II

Samuel Butler said that we had never read the devil's side of the case because God had written all the books. It may have been true once. It certainly is true that thousands of books said to have been inspired by the devil were destroyed by the early Christians; hence information about the rival cults and creeds Christianity had to conquer before it was enthroned is scantier than it should be. Something is known, however, and it is necessary to have a brief look at it if we are to understand the growth of Christianity and the significance of its victory, civilization's set-back, and the decline of science.

We think of Paul speaking to Greek cities as something new on earth, of those early Christian communities as unique phenomena —and of both as divinely inspired. As a matter of fact, Paul was preceded by generations of Stoic missionaries who preached virtue in threadbare coats. There was no essential difference between their preaching that men should spend themselves in the service of their fellow-men, and the preaching of Jesus; nor anything new in Jesus' teaching that good should be returned for evil. Even in the field of sexual ethics Paul's austerity was not more than that of his contemporary pagan saint, Musonius Rufus.

Greek philosophy, once busied with metaphysics, had turned to ethics, and preached it with the fanatical zeal of an Amos or an Isaiah. Self-salvation was its creed; self-mortification, its ritual. The dead bones of an almost bankrupt world had been stirred. Among the Stoics were high-minded men of noble character. They had left their imprint on the Græco-Roman world; their ideals and terminology were appropriated by Christianity and were now shot at the masses with a dynamite charge of, *Do it now, and do it this way;*

*or* . . . The Stoics had no machinery for throwing the fear of God into men's hearts.

Again, Antioch—not Jerusalem—was the first home of Christianity. Antioch is symbolic of the fact that Christianity was nurtured in a Hellenized world. Jerusalem, Judea, as we have seen, would in all probability have succumbed to this Hellenizing process had not the blind and stupid zeal of Antiochus Epiphanes halted the process and aroused anew the Jewish nationalistic spirit. The net result of the Maccabean revolt was to proclaim Simon hereditary high priest, civil and military governor of the Jews, *"for ever*, till a trustworthy prophet should arise." Under his son John Hyrcanus, Judaism was a fighting religion once more. And such it was at the time Christianity appeared. It was a proselyting religion. It was against the Greeks; it was against the Christians. John was a forerunner of Mohammed.

The crisis which precipitated the Maccabean revolt was turning the temple at Jerusalem into a gymnasium. Sports meant everything to the Greeks, nothing to the Jews. The gymnasium was an intrinsic part of Greek education. It went wherever philosophers, teachers, poets, and rhetoricians went in the Hellenizing process of the Mediterranean world. The gymnasium meant not only sports, but baths and feasts in public eating-halls to the sound of music. "The cities are filled from end to end with the noise of harp-playing," says a historian of the century before Christ.

But not all people like music, gaiety, life, joy, happiness; some prefer to make a virtue of their aches and pains, and they easily turn reformer. The Græco-Roman world before and after the beginning of the Christian Era was fertile soil for the moral reformer. But it is never enough to reform morals for morality's sake; reformers must have a platform, slogans, something to shoot at. What is the best way to beat the grave, attain heaven? Magic; mystery. Some cult.

And so it was that the world then, as now, was busy joining something which had the magic passwords for solving the supreme mystery. Cult brotherhoods under the banner of this or that god or combination of gods were not so common then as they are in parts of our country today, but they were common enough to make the idea immediately available for communistic brotherhoods of the new Jesus cult.

That age also, as Box points out, was strong in forming new cults by combining certain features of two or more cults into one. Typical of this syncretic tendency was the Isis-Serapis cult, compound of Greek Eleusinian mysteries and old Egyptian religious elements. This cult had reached Rome by 80 B.C., and by Roman soldiers (soldiers are notoriously superstitious) was carried all over the Western world. This and similar cults played up the idea of salvation and worshipped what has been called a monotheistic pantheon.

We speak, in our ignorance, of the Unchanging East. The East is thousands of years older than the West. We cannot compare Babylon with New York or Damascus with Chicago and get anywhere; but Damascus today is one thing, in the days of Haroun al-Raschid was another, and in the days of Saul of Tarsus was a Greek city. It talked Greek, had Greek temples, Greek civilization. It set store by education; there were college professors and college students. And the students, then as now, were thinking not about what the lecturers said, but, says the historian Philo, about "ten thousand things about ten thousand different subjects . . . and the professor talks to an audience, as it were, not of men, but of statues."

The significant thing is not that the teachers seem to have been as dull and uninspiring then as now, but that there were so many things to think then on so many subjects. Life may have been bad, immoral; but there was life and plenty of it. Whatever it was, our picture of it has been distorted by Stoic, Jewish, and Christian moralists, and caricatured by contemporary satirists. The moralists did not like it. One need not be a Jew or a Christian to abhor luxury; only poor and out of luck, as were the Jews and Christians. And both Jews and Christians were ready to suffer martyrdom for the faith that was in them.

We generally think of the Romans as persecuting *Christians*. They played no favourites; Jews, Christians, what not, were fit subjects for persecution, if in the eyes of Roman law they were dangerous to the state. Even when Rome laid her hand most heavily on the Christians, there was no evidence of such a diabolical, sadistic spirit as we find in the Catholics of Prague of the Middle

Ages, who thanked God that they had Jews to persecute and could thereby show their love for Jesus. Still less do we find any of the spirit of that Christian saint, Augustine, who considered it unspeakably impious of the elect to pity the damned. The beatitude of the saints would be incomplete if deprived of the bliss of watching the sufferings of sinners.

The simple truth is that in the Græco-Roman world a Puritanical Fundamentalist was tolerated as long as he kept quiet and minded his own business; otherwise he was as welcome in Rome then as he is in New York City now. But in Rome, as in London (and not in New York) today, he could mount a soap-box, talk his head off, and get police protection as long as he kept his tongue off the good name of state and emperor.

Even in Hadrian's time Jewish rabbis preached that a Jew should suffer martyrdom rather than be guilty of idolatry, fornication, or murder. Appropriate respect for the flag—statue of the emperor—was, however, to the Jews equivalent to idolatry. Israel's jealous Yahweh was no less jealous when he became the God of the Christians.

Recall the sanctity which enveloped the Olympian Games. Greek drama also developed from tragedy which had a religious or supernatural background. The moralists, especially the followers of the one supremely jealous God, could not afford to be caught flirting with anything that smacked of foreign gods. They not only did not go to the shows because of their implied heathenism, but because they hated the idea of theatre, circus, games—useless, wasteful luxuries; better spend the money on alms!

The Greek was perfectly familiar with the idea of apotheosis. State worship of the emperor, to the Græco-Roman world, was merely the logical outcome of an attitude which had paid divine honours to living rulers since the days of Alexander. The Christian church itself was in time to adopt this idea and fill heaven with venerated saints; and to worship its Pontifex Maximus as the Infallible Word of God. But Jews and Christians could not afford to risk offending their own one and unique Holy Being, Supreme and Transcendent. Their God again and again had warned them what would happen if they went after other gods. The worship of a Roman Emperor was the one supreme blasphemy.

But Porphyry, a heathen philosopher, wanted to know how the Christians got around angels: "Are they not *just the beings we call gods*?" Then what is the dispute all about? And he was mean enough to ask the Christians to re-read Matthew xxii:30.

Augustine, in his *City of God*, described a religious rite he himself saw in Carthage—the worship of the mother of the gods, the *Magna Mater*. What he thought of the scenes at the time we cannot know, but by the time he had come to describe them their "obscene speeches and actions" were the quintessence of sacrilege and pollution—at any rate to one who feared the "wrath of the true and ever living God" more than the "displeasure of those accursed powers." Yet we infer from Augustine that the early Christians themselves were occasionally a bad lot. They certainly showed more zeal in wrecking pagan temples and blacking their wives' eyes for tempting them, than in putting into practice the moral precepts of the Sermon on the Mount.

As a matter of fact, the cult of this Phrygian goddess, Cybele, *Magna Mater*, had been brought to Rome and enthroned on Palatine Hill two centuries before the birth of Christ, and we can read about it in Vergil and Ovid. The rite was celebrated in Rome as late as 394. Its most significant feature was baptism in the blood of a bull, whereby the individual was purified and regenerated: *renatus in æternum*, "reborn into eternity." The cult had its priests, both men and women, choir, vergers, etc.; even a sacred college of those who bore the sacred tree in the processions.

The Isis-Serapis cult entered Rome in the first century B.C. Serapis was the "Protector and Saviour of all men," ever ready to assist when invoked in time of need. Christianity may be the only true religion, but how often has it produced a prayer of thanksgiving finer than that of Lucius Appuleius to the Queen of Heaven (Isis) after he had joined the Isis-Serapis "church," and recorded in his *Golden Ass*:

"Thou who art the holy and eternal Saviour of mankind, ever bountiful to the mortals who cherish thee, thou bestowest thy gracious mother-love upon the wretched in their misfortunes. No day . . . no brief moment ever passes without thy benefits. On land and sea thou watchest over men, and holdest out to them thy saving right hand, dispelling the storms of life. Thou dost undo the hopelessly ravelled threads of Fate, and dost alleviate the tempests of Fortune and restrainest the hurtful courses of the stars. . . . As for me my spirit is too feeble to render thee worthy praise, and my possessions too small to bring thee fitting sacrifice. I have no fluency of speech to put into words that which I feel of thy majesty. Therefore will I essay to do that which alone a poor but pious worshipper can: Thy divine countenance, and thy most holy presence will I hide within the shrine of my heart: there will I guard thee, and continually keep thee before my spirit."

Recall the "Apostate" Julian's dying words (which quite likely he never said, for most dying words are apocryphal): "Thou hast conquered. . . ." What had Christianity conquered? Cult of the Invincible Sun. No wonder the world grew dark! The invisible had conquered the visible; the insensible was elevated above the sensible. That cult, founded by Aurelianus ("Restorer of the Universal Empire") in 273, was imitated by the Christians and then destroyed by force. Based as it was on the cult of Mithra, Mithra literature was also destroyed. Of all the cults Christianity had most to fear, that of Mithra was supreme. Mithraism was so close to Christianity that the Christian fathers could smell its breath; to Justin Martyr and Tertullian it smelt like the devil's.

The cult of Mithra reached Rome about 70 B.C. and was carried by the army, to which it particularly appealed, right across the Empire. Ruins of its monuments have been found from the shores of the Black Sea to the hills of Scotland and all over northern Africa. At the time of its entrance into Rome it was already as old as the cult of Yahweh.

And to me—as it was to J. S. Mill and William James—it is one of the curiosities of fate that the Aryan world should reject the most reasonable, the most sensible, of all the gods man ever created, one created by Aryan-speaking peoples, and accept instead and bow down to a Semitic God of War who did not hesitate to stop the clock of our cosmic universe to let an Israelite polish off his enemies.

Mithra, as we have seen, was the Indian and Persian God of Light, co-ruler and joint creator with Varuna or Ahura, God of the Sky, of the universe. By 1400 B.C. Mithra was the national god of the Mitanni in eastern Asia Minor. To the Persians he became the god of truth, defender of the righteous. And such he was to the Achmænid kings of the Anatolian highlands who followed the break-up of Alexander's empire. Some of them even took his name —Mithridates. Greece favored Cybele, Serapis, and Syrian Baals, but frowned on Mithra, god of their greatest enemies.

What a race it was between the cult of Mithra and the cult of Jesus! And such a prize—the dominion of the world! No two cults ever ran such an even race or for such stakes. It was appropriate that on a battlefield the Semite War-God should triumph over the Aryan God of Truth, né God of Light.

Yet Mithra had carried the Roman legions to victory after victory. His followers were pledged to "fight the good fight." They were morally obligated to perform good deeds, and not lose themselves in good thoughts like mystics. Even in warring against sin and evil they could invoke Mithra's help. "His mighty aid could assure his soldiers of victory both against earthly and unearthly foes; salvation, deliverance, redemption, both in this world and in the world to come."

In fact—and here is another irony of fate—Mithraism was the ideal religion of a Roman Emperor, the beau ideal of one ruling by divine right. That idea was originally Persia's; their kings ruled by grace of the Supreme Being, Mithra. Grace was a halo, a nimbus, a corona of Helion fire. And so, beginning with Commodus (180), Roman Emperors styled themselves *Pius, Felix, Invictus. Felix* meant that he was illumined by divine grace; *Invictus*, that he was allied with the sun.

Mithraic priests preaching the doctrine of the divine right of kings made it possible for the Cæsars to erect their thrones upon altars. Christian priests smashed the heathen altars and put their church upon the throne. The Mithraism of Aurelian was as much a monotheism as the Christianity of Constantine. Which is beside the point. The point is that men in the times we speak of needed symbols. The Roman Empire needed a symbol to make it a coherent society; without an appropriate symbol it would fall apart. Worship of the emperor furnished the symbol. The ancient world was a world of believers. Patriotism alone could not hold a state together, nor could belief in gods or a god. Patriotism and belief combined could: witness the vast and enduring Roman Empire. It fell. The Roman Catholic Church was erected on its ruins.

## III

Any attempt to explain the rise of Christianity which leaves human nature out of the count must fail; and human nature in I A.D. or 325 A.D. was just what it is today. The world today is not what it was then; but the world today is not so different from that of Augustus or Constantine that every man can call his soul his own, or, to paraphrase Luther's words, is free from that quality of faith which wrings the neck of reason. Society now reveals the same startling contrasts of great wealth, luxury, and idleness, and abject poverty and back-breaking toil. It is as easy to feel lonely, wretched, and insecure in New York today as it was in Rome nineteen hundred years ago; just as easy to feel utterly insignificant, that there is no justice in the world, and that something ought to be done about it.

Pride, when not mated with pure selfishness or overweening ambition, has enormous value in human lives; but what pride can be left to the down-and-out, what shred of a feeling of security? Fate is no respecter of persons, but she does seem at times to deal her favours with outrageous partiality, with a malevolence which can appal, terrify, benumb.

Again, there is that about the city which to a stranger, to an empty stomach, to an aching heart, seems the very apotheosis of selfishness. To such, nothing seems more real than man's inhumanity to man—as real as poverty, as disease, as death itself.

But man is rarely so poor that he cannot afford a bit of canvas on which to paint his thoughts, or so lacking in words that he cannot build a word-world which rights all wrongs, a story-world where everything comes out right in the end. It was not Christianity that won; it was that Christianity as then presented filled a want which had grown insistent, and filled it more certainly and more completely than any other existing religion.

For every millionaire there were thousands who had between them and hunger and cold nothing but a copper and a rag. That *is* a terrifying state. And misery does find comfort in company. Such a company grabs at a hope as a drowning man snatches at a straw. The hope may not feed, clothe, or bathe them, but it can accomplish wonders in banding them together. They make it work further wonders.

The Christian God was no more real than Jupiter, but Christ was made to seem more real than the other saviours. If the poor man could not be one with a millionaire Senator, he could be one with Christ; and that, to his starved, terrified soul, was bliss enough, comfort for his poverty, a pacifier for his fear, a prop to his pride, a guarantee of life eternal. That was a great deal for a poor man to get for nothing. It cost nothing, neither a coin nor a day's work. Ask and ye shall receive; nothing more—except belief; just believe in Him. Think what *Christ's friendship* must mean to a man without a friend on earth, of the compensation he can get for an empty life by identifying himself with God, of the self-importance a social outcast can gain by going to church, or even by rehearsing his sins before his fellow-creatures.

Christianity was not only the most powerful magic then offered, it was the cheapest—unbelievably cheap; it offered so much for so little. It cost money for sacrifices to attain the bliss of Elysian Fields or Fortunate Isles, or even to join the mystery cults in vogue. The Christ mystery cult cost but a word, a nod of the head. And as heaven and hell were objectified as never before, made more real— heaven more blissful, hell more terrifying—the appeal of free salvation to a vain but credulous street-sweeper, pauper, slave, widow, was tremendous. Endless bliss on high while watching the hated rich sizzle below! Could an emperor aspire higher? One cannot get a favour from a Chinese joss without burning a stick of incense. But no incense, no flower, not even a stick of candy; not even one humane deed, much less the kind of effort one must put forth to win the respect of one's friends—Romans or countrymen. One did not even have to cherish one's wife, be dutiful to parents, loyal to the state or respectful to its emblems and insignia.

This does not mean, nor am I implying, that those early Christians had no virtues; but I *am* saying that it was and is easier to talk of a contrite heart and assume humility than to live humbly with a contrite heart. In Rome—as in New York until recently— one won respect by toil, zeal, industry, prudence, thrift, directed effort, playing the game like a man; such virtues now won less than repentance. If Calvary's penitent thief could attain Paradise in a day by a few words, why not any penitent sinner? If I were a professional criminal with any doubt about my soul, I should certainly want nothing less than a bishop to see me off. Fear of capital punishment might conceivably deter certain criminals from committing capital crimes were there not always available a mechanism for washing their slate clean at the last moment.

The pagan world swarmed with nymphs, sprites, elves, and ghosts of every kind; they became so many imps of Satan to lead men astray. Tartarus, which the pagans reserved for the incredibly wicked, now became a hell for unbelievers and backsliders; its old pagan jailers, performing their unpleasant duty without malice or vindictiveness, now became an organized band of fiends incarnate who loved to torture. Later, saintly Christians could anticipate hell's terrors and make them as real as the racks of the Inquisition.

Mithra was real, as was Isis-Serapis, as were all the gods of all the mystery cults, all the gods on High Olympus and in the Roman pantheon; but the Christian heaven and hell were *imminent*. Judgment Day might be any day. So strong is the hold of that belief today that well-meaning ignoramuses still pop up like Jacks-in-the-box to name the Fateful Day.

There never had been such a heaven, such a hell; souls had never seemed such hazards, nor the line between life and death so vague. Magic they had long been familiar with. The Nile, and especially the Land of the Two Rivers, had been exporting it for three thousand years. But no such marvellous, miraculous magic had ever come out of the East as was now coming out of the Land of the Book—for, had not some wicked people crucified the only Son of the only God, sent to save sinners' souls? Eternal life and bliss everlasting were to be had for the mere asking. The very idea of heaven was so alluring, of hell so frightfully appalling, that doubt in other and older ideas increased. *Paul might be right!*

The earliest converts to Christianity were the kind of people who on their first day in New York buy the Brooklyn Bridge, the Woolworth Building, or the Hudson Tunnel, while their wives at home are buying sets of subscription books on the instalment plan, chests of patent medicines, or having their fortunes read: the kind of people who want to get rich quick, get cured quick, and make up for an impoverished, misspent life in an opiate dream; the kind of people who have leaned on superstition so long that they have lost the use of their spine, who have depended on beliefs so long that they cannot think straight.

Slaves, serfs, paupers, pedlars, street-sweepers, beggars, tinhorn gamblers, cripples, chronic invalids, morons, widows, Reds, and unadjusted women. Not all of them, of course; but that is what they looked like to the Romans—a rabble of slaves, paupers, and criminals. Nor, as we may infer from Paul's Epistles to the Corinthians, were those early Christian assemblages always pure, meek, and model. We seem to detect signs of drunkenness and other carnal vices; they also quarrelled.

But I cannot agree with Kautsky that Apostles and Prophets were swindlers and impostors. Billy Sunday may be a crank and Elmer Gantry a crook, but there are no impostors or swindlers in religion. There is something of the hypocrite in us all, something of the swindler and impostor, too; and when I say that, I merely touch a weak spot in all human nature that remains sane enough to keep out of an asylum.

After all, the difference between Paul pushing his brand of magic and a great corporation broadcasting a cure-all, is a difference in degree, to be sure, but that it is a difference in kind I am not quite so sure. Paul believed in his wares and that the labourer was worthy of his hire. And didn't a Mosaic law say, "Thou shalt not muzzle the mouth of the ox that treadeth out the corn"? "Am I not an apostle? am I not free? have I not seen Jesus Christ our Lord?" Well, he had not seen Jesus Christ—except in a vision at the gate of Damascus; but he was an "ox," and he as much as told the Corinthians that they should free him and other apostles from manual labor and support them. As Cardinal Allen said, apostolic men should not only despise money, they should also have it!

An apostle was an *apostolus*, a traveller, a homeless circuit rider; especially concerned with organizing new church congregations. The prophets were the local medicine-men, and not always enthusiastic over visiting apostles who expected board and keep and travelling money from the congregation. The more money and glory the visiting pastor carried away, the less there were for the local prophet.

By 150 A.D. it came to be a rule that apostles were not to burden a community for more than a day or two. "If he remains three days or demands money, he is a false prophet." But how could these poor congregations support churches? How could poor congregations later build cathedrals?

The serf, the peasant, the washerwoman, are poor in earthly, but rich in spiritual, goods: "first-fruits"—of oil, wine, bread, cloth, etc. *If we have sown unto you spiritual things, is it a great thing if we shall reap your carnal things?* That looks fair. It was a great idea, though far from original with Paul. Magicians have always been ready to sow spiritual tricks and reap carnal harvests. But not all can be apostles or miracle-workers, for "*God hath set* some in the church, first apostles, secondarily prophets, thirdly teachers, after that miracles, then gifts of healings, helps, governments, diversities of tongues."

Though we "covet earnestly the best way," Paul will show us "a more excellent way"; and "the greatest of these is charity." No wonder the Rotarians claim Paul as their very own; he was an organizer, a clever salesman, "full of pep." He was of the stuff the church is made of, the forerunner of the Christian Fathers. Even such reason, sanity, tolerance, magnanimity, and sweetness of spirit as there are in the Gospels had little room to expand in Pauline theology. The advice to resist not evil and to love one's enemies— given also in India and China—was no part of Paul's more excellent way.

And so it was that small cult churches of the meek, lowly, and ignorant, meeting at common meals and aiding those even meeker and poorer, came in course of time to include also those who gave their all to the church, renounced the world, the flesh, and the devil, and became "holy," "perfect." Even today it is not unknown for a rich person who has tried everything and failed to find satisfaction, to try poverty as a last resort, to give all to the church, and live the life of a hermit or a beggar.

In this connection we may ask in all seriousness, is there anything in the Gospels which warrants or justifies the church, with its organization, its graduated hierarchy, its social distinctions? Jesus never spoke of a church; he did speak of an assembly, an *ecclesia*— just once! But man is so easily socialized that he may be called a "joiner" by nature. Let the idea spread that a rich man can enter heaven only as a camel can go through the eye of a needle, hence presumably *must* go to hell—and the church never deprecated either idea: the soil is seeded for a rich carnal crop for the church to harvest. Rich old widows, and especially rich old reprobates, are shining marks for contribution-plate passers.

The church communities seem originally to have been communistic organizations, sharing their goods and participating equally in their consumption. At first the apostles waited on the tables. As the flocks of the faithful grew in numbers, additional waiters were appointed—"deacons"; later, head-waiters or over-deacons—*episkopos*. *"Episcopi"* (bishops), said a Roman jurist, "supervise the food serving for the daily sustenance of the city population." There were originally deacons and deaconesses. The latter were usually widows, also useful not only for charity but for propaganda purposes.

The presiding elder of the assemblies was the *presbyter* (old man) or shepherd who leads his flock like sheep—not to the slaughter, but to the shearing. But, as Milton said, new *presbyter* is but old *priest* writ large. As the church perfected its organization the individual congregations gradually lost all control over their priests and bishops and became a claque, as Kautsky calls it, greeting their bishop with jubilant applause. And a claque they have remained. How many rulers on earth today are so firmly entrenched in their powers, privileges, and prerogatives, so free from having their words questioned or examined critically, as the priests both in and out of the Catholic Church?

Outlawed at first, as in a sense they were in Rome, the Christians met in private houses on Saturdays; later, on Sundays. They read from the Bible, baptized converts, and gave thanks through the *eucharistia*, the holy communion of bread and wine. Baptism for adults meant total immersion—"drowning" the evil spirits. The sick and dying were "anointed" with holy oil: bad medicine for any evil spirit prowling around.

The Church wisely gave up total immersion, for it is often inconvenient; sprinkling is much more thoughtful and considerate. But Paul's "blotting out the *handwriting* that was against us" (Colossians II) and *"putting off"* the body of the sins of the flesh" presumably can only refer to the traditional seal the devil fixed on Adam's forehead in sign of their compact. Early baptism was not a mere rite or an idle gesture or a mere washing away of sins; it was the business of washing out the "handwriting," drowning the devil, "*buried* with him in baptism." "Lie not one to another, seeing that ye have put off the *old man* with his deeds."

There was nothing new, of course, either to Jews or Romans, in the idea of cleansing from evil (*miasma*) or of exorcising devils; but no such definite promise or tangible results had been held out as did the Christians with their rite of baptism, or such dire consequences if baptism were resisted.

With the final dispersal of the Jews (*Diaspora*) after the destruction of Jerusalem (70 A.D.) synagogues or prayer-houses became more numerous in Rome; they were recruiting-grounds for the Christians. The Talmudic teaching that it is better to be persecuted than to be a persecutor, that God is always on the side of the persecuted, even though the persecutor be a just man, was made to order for purposes of church proselyting.

To Trajan, Aurelius, Decius, and Diocletian the Christians were Bolsheviks; and they were treated as such. From every point of view, three of the four were great emperors. Domitian, Commodus, and Caracalla, cruel, brutal emperors, tolerated—even favoured—the Christians.

Rome herself did not like Christians, did not like the company they kept, did not like their secrecy, did not like them at all. Rome did not understand them. And the more they were persecuted, the more the Christians were convinced they were right and the more earnestly did they spread their nihilistic doctrines—until they could afford to become conservative.

Paul was a good organizer, but note, too, that Roman society was fertile soil for men of the shrewd walking-delegate type, men who would rather talk than work and knew how to join up men who would rather destroy than create, or, if they could not destroy, would gladly accept something for nothing.

Heaven never is pictured as a land of the shovel and the hoe. The Bible speaks of the dead rising from the grave and of Christ risen in the flesh and eating broiled fish; but how about the fish and wine of the Hereafter? And who is going to wait on the table, do the dishes, catch the fish? Silence on all this; a dead silence about the sweat of the brow in that future state of bliss. No wonder the proletariat was ready to humour the walking delegates by joining that kind of union.

It is not surprising that Imperial Rome, which by long and arduous conquest had worked its way to the top of the world, should frown on a sect which proposed to attain a higher plane without an hour's work or the exhibition of a virtue a sensible man could live with. The Roman was no saint, no paragon of virtue, but he knew a social nuisance when he saw one, he knew an enemy when he saw one. To his way of thinking, the Christian was both. The Christians were against Rome's gods, Rome's business, Rome's ideals, Rome's joys and pleasures. They were disloyal kill-joys, meeting in secret and making friends with the dead. They were pacifists; their views were corrupting the army. Disloyal, dangerous, disingenuous, deceitful, liars, hypocrites, unprincipled scum: that is what they seemed to Imperial Rome. Nor is there any doubt that up to the end of the second century Christianity was numerically small and recruited almost entirely from the dregs of Roman society, or from simple-minded women, children, and slaves. Even the Christian Father Jerome spoke of them as "lowest rabble." Not till the reign of Severus Alexander have we Jerome's evidence that rich people and nobly born ladies had "received the message." The only known convert of rank before the reign of Commodus (180-192) was the consul, Flavius Clemens, executed in 95 for "atheism" —denying the gods of Rome! Not till 321 could the church, like a legal personage, hold and inherit property.

Nero especially was no plaster saint, but there is no evidence that he fired Rome, nor evidence that he burst a blood-vessel trying to stop it. There is evidence that Rome burned for nine days, and that he accused the Jews *and* the Christians of having fired it. They might have done it; they must have done it; of course—are not the Christians always talking about the last judgment and the world on fire?—they did it! They certainly were persecuted. Their religion was "a pestilent superstition," "a malevolent superstition"; it meant "hatred of the human race." They practised magic; they would not take the usual law-court oath; they had no interest in the Emperor or Empire, but instead talked of another king, of a coming kingdom; they met in secret. In short, they were to pagan Rome what Reds are to Christian Rome.

We are sojourners upon earth, said Tertullian; our home is in heaven. "We fear our God, not your governor. If your law errs, I conceive it was devised by man, not handed down from heaven." There is the answer in the words of a Christian Father. The Christians would neither defend the empire nor respect its laws or guardian gods. Impious nihilists: to the lions with them!

The marvel is that there was one Christian left to recount the tale of marytrdom. Rome of the first two centuries was surely more tolerant of foreign gods and beliefs than most Christian nations have been; much more so than Spain or Tennessee is today. In fact, pagan Rome never persecuted Christians as utterly as Christian Rome persecuted pagans.

Then, too, there was an extenuating factor in favor of pagan Rome: she persecuted Christians not because their beliefs were alien, Oriental, or Christian, but because the Christian God was inhuman; nothing pleased him which any ordinary, virile, healthy mortal could find pleasure in. People who worshipped that kind of anthropomorphic monstrosity must be insane; banded together in church communities, positively dangerous. Their presence threatened the sanity of society; their insults to the gods of the state could only end in disaster to the state.

All this seems reasonable only if we remember that those early church communities were quite as fanatical on many points as a few sects are today on a few points. The church had not reached its present advanced position. The early Christians saw a brigand in every soldier, a devil in every god, a sinful human being in every pagan priest and king, and all war as unspeakably wicked. Such views were corrosive sublimate in the Empire.

It is often argued that the mere fact that Christianity survived the lions and the torture proves that it is the one true faith. As well argue that because Christian Jews survived Spanish persecution and Christian Inquisition, Judaism is the one true faith. Most of our delusions, in fact, are founded on just such reasoning. Truths are not established on battlefields, nor errors stifled in torture-chambers. Mohammedanism, as we shall see, spread far faster than Christianity.

Torture-chamber procedure is an ancient practice and still the favourite weapon of brutal ignorance working in secret. Up to 150 years ago it was quite legal in England to cowhide Bedlamites to cure them. There are still Christians who think self-mortification of the flesh an evil-exorcising process, pleasing in the sight of the Lord.

Rome tortured maniacs to cure them. Most Christians were maniacs. Rome handed over her prisoners guilty of capital crimes to the lions for execution. Many Christians had committed capital crimes. Between a lion and an electric chair there may be a choice; personally, I think the lion preferable. We still have witnesses to our state executions, and I suspect public executions would draw well. They have only recently become private; generally, I suspect also, to the disgust of most victims, who have taken the only way they know to fame or notoriety.

Greek for "witness" is *martyr*. The early martyrs who suffered for their faith were "witnesses" of the faith that was in them. "To bear witness" and "to suffer" are synonymous. Those who survived torture were "confessors." Torture to the Græco-Roman world was the normal procedure in securing evidence from slaves; in fact, a slave's evidence was inadmissible except when obtained under torture. But torture was not a Roman pastime, nor was a Christian martyred every day. There were several organized persecutions, but never such a man-hunt as that organized by Christians last century to exterminate the natives of Tasmania. That was a *successful* organization!

Rome's never was; she waited too long, and knew no more psychology than a modern war lord. I suspect that the first Christian fed to the lions because of religion was the biggest advertisement Christianity could possibly have had. The spectators may have been thoroughly indignant, or may have shouted their satisfaction at seeing the end of an enemy of the state; but news is news, and when one Christian turned and bit the lion (as in *Ben Hur*) it was big news and everybody in Rome must have heard of it by supper-time.

Nor should we underestimate the power of slave Christians to carry the news of their new faith to their mistresses. The fact that a woman is rich or blue-blooded is no proof that she is tough-minded or above listening to back-stairs gossip. And as for one reason or another (and there were many) Rome had become mongrelized, Roman ideals confused, and Roman idols discredited, there was always the still, small voice whispering, "The Christians may be right!" Christianity, in fact, had travelled so far that by the third century it had less to fear from Roman persecution than Rome had to fear from internal dissensions and heresies.

The Roman Empire did not fall; it went bankrupt and fell into the hands of receivers. The receivers were primarily interested in their own affairs, on behalf of which they picked Rome to pieces. Rome became Christian. And within two hundred years Romans were so outnumbered by aliens from the north that they were the under dogs. It was not even the fashion to be a Roman.

We look at two dates: 100-200 or 300-400, for example. The time interval does not seem long, but a year then had as many days as it has now, and a great deal can happen in a hundred years. A century may prove enormously fateful for any country. One year, recently, was enough to out-date every code of ethics; four years, every map of Europe. What will four centuries do?

Rome was not built in a day, nor did it go bankrupt in a year. The same for Christianity. For both, the fourth century was full of dynamite. Many lives were lost, many ideas born, many idols smashed, many new idols set up.

## IV

Rome had applied the science of the Greeks, and applied it gloriously. But she had exhausted it; science had dried up at the source. She fell back on superstition. The Christians had the kind Rome needed. The Christians *were* right.

Before we look at a bare outline of the sequence of events which led to the enthronement of a pope in the chair of a Cæsar, let us note that without Alexander no Eastern Roman Empire would have been possible; without Paul there would have been no Christianity outside Palestine; and without Cæsar there would have been no Roman Empire to set the stage for the papacy—or for Charlemagne's Holy Roman Empire. Christianity, then, rests primarily on the foundation laid by Alexander the Great and Julius Cæsar; and it was Constantine who shaped the structure begun on that foundation.

Without Constantine the Great, Christianity could not have become identified with the imperial purple, which not only insured its triumph but gave divine sanction to the morals, laws, and ideas which dominated Europe in peace and war for fifteen hundred years. Whatever else Constantine was, he won his throne and ruled like an Oriental despot. Whatever Jesus was or the cult of Jesus stood for, Christianity became imperial, despotic, absolute. And for fourteen centuries Europe saw a succession of sovereigns and pontiffs committing murder in the name of Christ, who, judged by the standard of common delinquents, would have been hanged by the neck till dead. Christian throne and altar on St. Bartholomew's Day alone killed more men than did the French Revolution, September massacres, Reign of Terror, and all.

64. Nero persecutes the Christians and philosophers.

93. Domitian persecutes the Christians. Christian converts include a few Roman nobles and a few Senators.

230. Alexander Severus proposes eclectic hero-worship: Christ, Orpheus, Abraham, Cicero.

250. Decius. Organized general persecution of Christians; bishops of Rome and Antioch put to death: a fatal tactical error.

273. Aurelian performs miraculous healings in Alexandria by "laying on of hands," and calls himself God and Lord on his coins. Introduces Mithraism, a noble experiment; it had high standards of purity and a doctrine of immortality.

303. Diocletian, on behalf of Mithraism, which he favors, begins the last, greatest, most frenzied and most ineffective general persecution of Christians: so ineffective, so futile, that he abdicates (305) in disgust. Rome goes into the hands of six receivers—three Augusti, three Cæsars—all fighting for the crown.

307. Six Augusti: one killed; one resigned; one drowned while trying to get away from the Augustus who had killed one of the Augusti and whose name was:

312. Constantine, who had travelled so far from the old Roman gods that he was willing to try a new one. He did; his army was full of Christians. They bore the banner, so it is said: *Hoc signo vinces*. Israel's War-god, Yahweh, smiled on Constantine. His army won. He became patron of the Christians, who had been legalized by decree of Galerius the preceding year. Imperial patronage. Usual rush of the mob to climb aboard the band-wagon. Constantine now

allied himself with his brother-in-law (one of the three remaining Augusti), who defeated another Augustus, who then committed suicide. Then there were two—Constantine and his brother-in-law ally. They fought two battles; then there was one.

323-337. Constantine the Great. Christianity was Big Business now. Jesus had lived and died in vain. Constantine favored Christianity at the expense of paganism, made it the state religion, and allotted pagan endowments to metropolitan churches, making it profitable for thousands of money-grubbers to enter the priesthood and elevating greed above tolerance as the proper standpoint for viewing all things pagan. But Constantine himself was never more than a catechumen or neophyte; he was never baptized, or if so, it was on his deathbed.

325. First General or Œcumenic Council of the Church at Nicæa in Bithynia—of which more anon.

330. Constantine makes Byzantium his capital: *Nova Roma, Constantinopolis*, city of Constantine.

356. Statue of Victory removed from the Senate Hall in Rome.

361. Julian "the Apostate," anathema to the Church. The fact is that Julian was a fighter, an able man, wed to Greek philosophy. He thought the old religion good enough if purified of its abuses, and that was what he tried to do. It was really a reaction, a back-to-the-good-old-days movement. He not only did not persecute Christians but exhorted his followers to imitate their charitable institutions. Had he lived longer, history might have a different story to tell. He died of a wound received in battle against the Persians at Ctesiphon.

363. Jovianus the Christian, raised to the throne by the soldiers! Exit paganism, polytheism; enter Christianity.

379. Theodosius, co-regent. Very sick; recovers; joins church.

382. Gratianus. Altar of Victoria removed from Senate Hall in Rome; paganism definitely disestablished.

390. Theodosius, Emperor. Executes seven thousand revolting Thessalonicans and cruelly punishes remainder. Prohibits heathen sacrifices and orders all temples closed. Christian monks begin to tear them down.

408. Honorius. Closes all public offices to pagans by edict and appropriates the revenues of all pagan religions.

415. Hypatia, pagan daughter of a pagan scientist, persecuted by Cyril the Christian. Hypatia stripped, cut to pieces, and burnt. Cyril canonized and now a saint in heaven. I should prefer to meet Hypatia.

After the removal of Hypatia, symbol of science, Christianity had time to breathe and find out what it was all about. In that process *Christ*ianity became *Church*ianity. But first it had to find out what it believed in, what it could sell to the people.

With the Church wrangling about doctrines and dogmas, what may we expect to find in the way of advance in knowledge or science? Nothing. We find nothing. On the contrary, we find Justin Martyr of the second century proclaiming that the Prophets of Israel were a better source of truth than the Greek philosophers. We find Bishop Clement of Alexandria calling Greek philosophers robbers and thieves—of the Prophets! We find Tertullian, Church Father, declaring scientific research superfluous since Christ. We find the biographer of a saint speaking of the "rubbish and nonsense of such shameless poets" as Homer and Vergil, and asking how the writings of Sallust, Livy, or Cicero, and of Herodotus or Demosthenes, could serve the servants of God. We find the sainted John Chrysostom rejoicing in the reëstablishment of universal idolatry and practical polytheism in the name of the Christian creed; we find him also testifying to the normality of the vices the Church was supposed to have banished, and the use of churches, like ancient temples, as places of assignation. We find Origen, Church Father, declaring that certain God-names have magic power to cast out evil spirits, that the mere name of Jesus is potent to cast out demons. We find sainted Gregory asking, Will Latin grammar save an immortal soul?

What was the answer? The Great Hollow, the Middle or the Mediæval Age! A Church which canonized the persecutor of Hypatia; which set up emperors and then, to weaken them, allied itself with kings whom it crowned and made God's Anointed, thereby making submission to their sacred pretences a duty enjoined from On High; which persecuted Galileo; and which today rules, punishes, rewards, meddles, forbids and denounces this and that like a common scold—all in the name of the Sovereign of the State of Vatican City, Vicar of Christ, Successor of St. Peter, Bishop of

Rome, Archbishop and Metropolitan of the Roman Province, Primate of Italy, Patriarch of the West, Supreme Pontiff of the Universal Church.

"State of Vatican City": all that remains of the "eternal dominion over Rome, Italy, and all provinces of the West" which was handed to the papacy in the "Constantine Donation"—proved in 1440 to be a forgery. Even the title "Supreme Pontiff" was valid by the exigencies of history rather than by the forged "Decretals" of the ninth century attributed to the Spanish bishop, Isodorus: that "boldest and most magnificent forgery" which (says Voltaire) has "deceived the world for centuries."

Science, not at all; history, only if it justified faith—hence to be found only in Hebrew Holy Writ; art, only if it served the needs of the new religion; joy, gaiety, happiness, good fellowship. . . . But let Keble of the "Oxford movement" of early Victorian days answer: "It would be a gain to this country were it vastly more superstitious, more bigoted, more gloomy, more fierce in its religion." Back to normalcy, to the good old days when Rome did not have to content herself with scolding and denouncing, but ruled Europe as Squeers ruled Dotheboys Hall.

Note that while the enthronement of the church was definite by 408, the Roman Empire definitely and finally fell in 395. On its ruins were erected the Eastern (Byzantine or Grecian) Empire, with its capital at Constantinople, 395-1453; and the Western (Latin) Empire, 395-476. Of the Western Empire, Rome was the capital for only seven years; after 402 Ravenna was the capital. But this split, as Robinson says, did not end the fiction that the two emperors were supposed to govern one empire co-jointly and in unanimity; nor did the idea of one government for all civilization disappear until late in the Middle Ages.

Astounding and extraordinary as that Eastern or Byzantine Empire was—and it was both—it is too far outside our current of history for extended comment. As a record of Christian rulers mounting thrones with hands dripping with the blood of murdered wives, fathers, sons, and brothers, it is possibly unparalleled in all human history—although the record in Italy, with twenty-three popes and five anti-popes in one century, was not at all bad.

But that is only part of the strange story of uncanny, unique

Byzantium. On the unparalleled Bosporus there rose one of the richest, most prosperous, and dazzlingly beautiful cities the world has ever seen. Sacred palaces with ivory doors, jewelled basilicas, churches in polychrome mosaics. Rome herself was never so splendid nor had a hippodrome so bedecked with obelisks from Thebes, tripods from Delphi, statues by Praxiteles, art treasures from wherever there were treasures to be plundered.

Her very richness, splendour and luxury excited not only the emulation but the cupidity of Rome during later centuries, and the Roman Church and its crusading brigands were always torn between the desire to redeem the Holy Land and to loot Byzantium—to surrender in the end to the passion to loot in the Fourth Crusade.

While Byzantium was sole heir and repository of Hellenic civilization, and for ten centuries remained the European guardian of culture and the ark of civilization, she made no contribution to civilization, added no spark to rekindle free thought, furnished no impetus to progress. She had few scholars, and they were pedants and compilers; her literature was rubbish and largely of miraculous events. She taught nothing, learned nothing. The Arabs swept her fleets from the seas; Genoa and Venice captured her commerce. And Empress Irene, who won her throne by gouging out her son's eyes after having betrayed him, worshipped images, proposed marriage to Charlemagne, and was canonized by the Greek Church, gave history one of its most curious figures and Byzantium a figure typical of her savage Christianity. Just why the Empress was sainted my *Book of Saints* does not say, for Saint Irene was a Greek Catholic.

v

325. First General (Œcumenic) Council of the Church.

Now the chief difference, as I see it, between a church and a scientific council is this. Churchmen meet to reach an agreement on a creed; that creed becomes the law, believe it or *anathema sit!* Scientists foregather to exhibit their wares: these are my facts, this is my conclusion—I may be mistaken in some of my facts, in which case my conclusion is from nine to ninety-nine per cent off; the important thing is my finding of facts: are they *facts*, can you find them also, can anybody find them? Every time science follows religious procedure it commits suicide.

That "chief" difference is fundamental, and fundamentally important. It furnishes, I believe, the principal key to the Middle Ages, from which we are just emerging and from which a few European nations have hardly begun to emerge.

Christian converts are generally children. They are told what they shall believe before they are old enough to have learned the habit of forming beliefs from evidence. As a consequence, whole realms of facts go a-begging because they do not fit established beliefs. Not all Christian beliefs are tied in to the nervous system by fear of hell fire, and fewer now than a generation ago; but I have heard a college president threaten a senior with hell fire for questioning a belief. And it was no idle threat: it was made in deadly earnest, in "righteous" anger, and reinforced by a gesticulating clenched fist. Such threats, I suspect, are not entirely unknown even today.

The church not only threatened but murdered fellow-Christians, and not only for unbelief, but for differences of opinion. What becomes of the one true and only divinely revealed religion if it was so bunglingly revealed that after nineteen centuries its professed followers cannot agree upon a common creed? The fact that there are church histories in a dozen volumes and 212 separate and distinct denominations in the United States alone, is a fair commentary on the oneness and the truthfulness of the only revealed religion.

Into the history of conflicting creeds and discrepant confessions we cannot go, but it will be not without profit to follow the history of certain phases of the creed of the Universal Church.

As Rome was mistress of the world in the early centuries of the church's history, it was fairly inevitable that the head in Rome should become master of the churches of the Empire. But, as I have pointed out, there is not only no Biblical authority for a Petrine papacy, but the actual primacy of the Roman Church was not won without a struggle. Historically speaking, the primacy was Antioch's.

It need hardly be pointed out that every magician believes in his magic, and that if his magic is an anthropomorphic being he will talk to it and confess his faith openly; or, in the words of the Psalmist, "And I spake of thy testimonies in the sight of kings, and was not ashamed." The Egyptians, Babylonians, Persians, etc., were no more ashamed to declare their testimonies, nor less clever in reducing them to formal creeds.

To the Jews whose God was Yahweh and who became followers of Christ, it was enough to believe, with John, that "God so loved the world that he gave his only begotten Son, that whosoever believeth in him should not perish." But there was a long, rough journey between that short creed and the lengthy confessions of different sects, some with fifty or more chapters or articles.

Before the end of the first century there was what is known as the Apostles' Creed. Out of that grew what is called the old Roman or Baptismal Creed of about 150. There were also the Creeds of Antioch, Jerusalem, etc.

As the church became more and more distinct from Judaism, it faced the issue—one of the first it had to decide—whether Israel's God was a demon and Jesus Christ alone the Saviour of mankind, or Christ the Messiah who had been prophesied by the Israelites. We have seen how that issue was decided, and why, and how it was that out of that decision four Gospels were canonized.

The big question—battle, rather—at Nicæa was how the Father is related to the Son, how Father and Son are related to the Holy Ghost, and how all three are related to the Virgin Mary. It was a battle; at any rate blood was shed, for, as Julian said, "there is no wild beast like an angry theologian."

That battle began between Arius, a priest, and Athanasius, a bishop, both of Alexandria. God is superior to Jesus, said Arius. That is *heresy*, said Athanasius. The Nicene Council condemned the "Arian heresy," exiled Arius, burned his books, and declared: Jesus is the "Son of God, of the substance of the Father, consubstantial with him, begotten, not born, eternal like the Father, and immutable by nature." But the Arian heresy spread, of course; so the Council of Constantinople in 381 decided, after divine inspiration no doubt, that the Holy Ghost should be the third person of the Trinity, equal to the Father and the Son.

In case that was not clear to everybody, Bishop Vigilius in 490 declared: "We worship one God in Trinity, and Trinity in Unity, neither confounding the Persons nor dividing the substance."

I am not yet certain what the Holy Ghost of that Trinity is supposed to be. Religion might possibly have stuck to me if, mingled with the threats, fears, duties, and loves, there had been a mother in it.

It was good psychology that prompted the church to adopt the best-known, and so best-beloved, divinity of the Græco-Roman world. Adding Plato's *Logos* to the Fourth Gospel version of the same paraclete added nothing to Christianity a child could love or a man adore; adding Mary to the Holy Family gave heaven that "homey" feeling and Christian art a real inspiration.

But what to call her, where to place her—that was the question which split the church and still agitates the Christian world. Is Mary a female of flesh and blood and of use to humanity here and now, or is she a spirit divine to be worshipped from afar?—with one's back meanwhile turned upon sex as the one primal, blown-in-the-bottle, inherent sin. That was, is, the question.

Juvenal had marvelled at Cybeline priests making eunuchs of themselves for the Kingdom of Heaven's sake, and at the rich Roman lady who plunged into the wintry Tiber to propitiate Isis. These were pagan answers. As a matter of fact, many followers of Christ followed the practice of the Cybeline priests. Even the practice of making eunuchs of the Vatican choir boys was not given up until condemned by the amiable and learned Pope Benedict XIV in the eighteenth century—although the practice was prolonged another century to supply the Italian operatic stage with male sopranos.

Rome persecuted Christians because their religion seemed incompatible with good citizenship; they might equally well have persecuted them because their religion was incompatible with *mens sana in corpore sano*. They exalted faith in God above such human qualities as health, lovableness, fair play, open-mindedness, and integrity of character—qualities which have always had worth in human society but are made to seem minor virtues in the eyes of the Christian God. It is the business of the priest, if true to his religion, to oppose the principle on which all private life, in so far as related to sex, family, and the home, is founded. His very calling exempts him from the moral and social obligations of the ordinary citizen. But even to refer to the fact was to court the threat of hell fire. It is all right for the Catholic priests to claim spiritual descent from the Jewish priesthood, but we may recall that its best known members were the high priests Annas and Caiaphas.

A flock whose chief concern is to get God on its side may be a flock that merits the good graces of its neighbours, but it is not necessarily that kind of flock and often is not. Why worry about being likable, respectable, or honourable: have they not God with them? Expand "flock" into a snugly entrenched state church, and we have a potential despot that can turn the world into a hell's cauldron, into or out of which it plunges or lifts human beings as one drops onions into or forks them out of a pot of Irish stew.

Was Mary a woman or a goddess? Is Christianity's central figure the only god without sexual hunger? Jesus in his earliest portrayals is obviously fashioned on the lines of a youthful Greek god. In fact, the catacomb pictures of a beardless youth tending a flock of sheep and bearing a lamb on his shoulder might pass for Hermes; or, thrumming a lute among wild animals, for Orpheus. Jesus as portrayed in the Gospels says little about sex taboos; nor was the church itself at first particularly agitated about sex. Whether the cross is, as claimed, or is not a phallic emblem, there is after all nothing monstrous or insane in such an emblem. It was wellnigh universal in one form or another. And certainly the Syrian cults which elevated sexual orgiastic rites to a religion were more spontaneous, more rational, sensible, reasonable, than the opposite extreme of asceticism which drove Christian monks by the thousand into the Thebaid desert. There was, we may not doubt, great laxity of morals in decadent Rome: but no more, probably, than in Rome, Paris, London, or New York, today. Asceticism is no answer to such a condition, nor the foul insults the church hurled at women.

There is nothing new in the idea of a chaste god. Apollo was such a god; such were all the old gods, contended Julian; and such is the dominant principle in Buddhism.

Mary, Virgin Mother, Queen of Heaven, was no new figure to the Classical world. Demeter especially was widely known: her images would fill museums; her myths, libraries. But all the cults of the Bearing Mother and all the rites which promoted fertility and rebirth were founded on a flesh-and-blood personality. Nor is it certain that early Christian rites were free from such conceptions and practices.

It is certain that up to the fourth century Mary was a woman, and was by Chrysostom reproached for her vanity! Then began the acrid dispute which was not to be decided until Nestorius, Patriarch of Constantinople, said that Mary was the mother of *Christ* and not of God: that is, that she was just a mother and a human being and had borne Jesus without virginity. The *conception* may have been miraculous, but Mary herself was no miracle, no divinity; nor a virgin. Ambrose, founder of Western music—when Latin superseded Greek in the service of the Roman churches, the *Kyrie eleison* (*Lord, have mercy*) being a notable survival—lauded her perfection. And when Augustine, after sowing his wild oats as a young "Greek" philosopher in Carthage, became the church's great organizer and thinker and declared that Mary alone of mortals was without original sin, she was on the way to canonization. But was or was she not a goddess? A goddess was needed. The pagan world had goddesses. If Christianity was to capture the pagans, it must have a goddess.

And what more appropriate than that Mary should be turned into a goddess in Ephesus, home of the great hundred-breasted "Diana" of the Ephesians? There the Church met (431) in its third General Council and formally declared Mary the Mother of God—to the intense delight and patriotic shouts of the citizens of Diana's old town, who burst into a regular orgy of celebration.

"Divine Motherhood of the Virgin Mary" is how the Church now alludes to that momentous event. If you were in Rome this year—possibly in connection with the fifteen hundredth anniversary of the proclamation of the Divine Maternity of the Mother of our Lord—you saw of course what is perhaps the most remarkable monument of Italian art, the basilica of Santa Maria Maggiore, with its marvellous mosiacs just under the "triumphal arch" recalling the Council of Ephesus.

The pope's representative at that Council was that famous respecter of the rights of womanhood, St. Cyril, Patriarch of Alexandria. Cyril had already anathematized Nestorius for calling the

Mother of God (*Theotokos*) just a mother. There was nothing for the Council to do but depose him from his See of Constantinople, for "blasphemy."

Nestorius was deposed but was not without followers, who now founded the Nestorian Church in Persia, whence by 600 it had spread to the east from Tibet and China to Sumatra. Not until the thirteenth century, however, did Rome pay any attention to that far-away sect; had it done so sooner, all China might have been converted. A Nestorian church was established in Peking, but when the Mongols became Mohammedans there was a reaction against the Christians and the Nestorian churches perished. Not so in India, however, where a remnant survives on the Malabar coast, and where a few years ago I watched them celebrate Palm Sunday with curious archaic rites.

But that is not all. That Council of Ephesus would have been well advised if it had paid more attention to Nestorius and less to Mary; she could have waited a while longer. In driving Nestorius out, they let loose an instrument which was to return a thousand years later and rock the church to its very foundations. In that fateful split over the effort to monopolize Truth, Diocletian was proved right: Christianity had not saved the world; it had wrecked a world civilization.

According to Wigram, twenty-five metropolitan archbishops owed allegiance to the Patriarch of this Nestorian branch, or "Church of the Assyrians," as he calls it, in the days of Haroun al-Raschid. That church, entrenched in the land of Sargon and Sennacherib, suffered little from its Moslem neighbours, much from orthodox Christians. As a result, it helped the Persian Moslems to defeat the orthodox Christian armies of Heraclius; and Egypt opened her gates to the followers of the Prophet, preferring them to the Christians. Egypt and all northern Africa fell to the Moslems.

But more than all that, the Nestorians had carried the spirit, and more especially the written, record of Greek science to Syria and the Land of the Two Rivers. We shall see what the Arabs made of it; and how, through them, that spirit was rekindled in Bagdad, Damascus, Moorish Spain, and Saracenic Sicily, and finally crept up into Europe, restarting civilization on the course it is now running and we are trying to understand, even if we cannot catch up with it.

Mariolatry went merrily rolling along. By the eighth century she was, said John of Damascus, Saviour of the World. "We were sinners and afraid of the wrath of the Father," said Peter of Blois, "for he is terrible; but we have the Virgin, in whom there is nothing terrible, for in her is the fullness of mercy and purity."

To Albertus Magnus of the twelfth century, the Holy Virgin was the Great Goddess. *Ave Maria* was introduced into all the churches in that century. She soon had more worshippers than the male Trinity, especially in South Europe. God was thought too terrible to be approached; Christ was just a judge; Mary alone, Queen of Heaven, could be merciful to sinners. And what is Mary today to the masses of Spain, Italy, and the rest of the Catholic world, but an image to which one prays as images used to be prayed to in the world of B.C.

She became the miracle-worker *par excellence*. Her exploits fill volumes. The list of miracles attributed to her is longer than that of all the saints put together. Never, anywhere, had primitive man conceived such magic power possible in a single person. No wonder she was worshipped. Three samples must suffice.

A monk, in squalor and with an ulcerous nose, prayed to the Holy Virgin, reminding her of the services he had rendered her. She came right down in person and with milk from her own breasts instantly healed his sores. Again, the reverend abbess of a certain convent was in "trouble." What to do! The Virgin appeared in person, and, acting as midwife, delivered the abbess painlessly of a lusty boy, who was handed over to a holy hermit. Again, a nun, weary of convent life, put her keys on the altar and went to town to live a life of shame. But she tired of that, and again sought the quietude of the convent. She knocked, and the Blessed Virgin herself let her in! She had taken the sister's place while she was in town, and no one in the convent knew of her escapade. All this in the name of Christian religion. She is still the wonder-working Mother for millions. And we have seen her mother, Anne, in business at Beaupré.

To the sentimental poets of Provence Mary was "sweeter than the sweetest wine"; "a potion sweet of love"; "rosy dawn, morning red"; "bridal crown, all maids' delight"; "with heaven's golden splendour."

Such sacred sex aberration was matched by feminine worship of Christ. One example must suffice. "I desire, then," said Catherine of Siena, "that you withdraw into the open side of the Son of God, who is a bottle so full of perfume that even the things which are sinful become fragrant. There the bride reclines on a bed of fire and blood. There the secret of the heart of the Son of God is revealed and made manifest." Otherwise Catherine seems to have been quite sane and an excellent politician.

The Council of Ephesus may seem to have settled Mary's status in the Holy Family, but down through the centuries she was a bone of contention for the cult-makers. Much scenery had to be built around her before she could usurp Christ's original rôle of intercessor for our sins. How did she get to heaven? The Bible is silent; not so the myth-makers. She was carried to heaven by angels—as you can see for yourself in any of the glorious Assumptions.

The Feast of the Assumption, first instituted in 582, was adopted by the church in 750. But during the twelfth century the question of Mary's guilt (original sin) came up afresh. Her body was flesh and blood; it *must* be infected! Why, then, did she not transmit her infection to Jesus? Because an act of divine grace preserved her body from original sin when it received its soul. And that, the doctrine of the Immaculate Conception, became a dogma of the Catholic Church by Pius IX's papal bull of 1854.

Meanwhile, a sixteenth-century apprentice to the tailor of a Berne Dominican monk claimed that he had seen Mary "eye to eye." She did not like the Immaculate Conception doctrine and said so to the apprentice. For believing the apprentice, four Dominicans were burnt at the stake. The Dominicans, it seems, were sceptical about the doctrine anyway, for had not the Virgin revealed to St. Catherine that she was born in sin? But had not the Franciscans inside information that Mary had told St. Bridget she was born free from sin?

What Mary herself never divulged was what she thought of sex or sex morality. The church, however, still claims authority—Infallible at that—in such matters, so we may stop here and look at this important matter historically. All the more so since its victory over women is among the most notable of all Christian victories.

Sexual desire as the one great original sin, as represented in the Hebrew Bible, is comprehensible as one understands the history of that particular fable and the historic development of Yahweh alongside the naturalistic fertility cults of Israel's Syrian neighbours. Israel had become sophisticated; those Syrian rites were not so innocent as the Syrians thought. Why, sexual desire brought sin into the world—and like the old serpent it is, is always lying in wait to betray men! And so Israel, having been defeated on the battlefield, felt enormous pride in having won a victory over his better half.

The mediæval church picked the victory up where the Prophets had left off and turned it into a Christian victory. From its condemnation of the flesh and degradation of sexual intercourse sprang the most highly organized system of hypocrisy ever invented. That system could only spring from an unparalleled sense of shame and consciousness of guilt. When a Christian Father, a Catholic priest, or a Methodist bishop begins to hurl invective against "vice," it is time to inquire into his personal experience with women.

Sex morality or woman's status bears no necessary relation to the height or state of civilization. The famous Code of Hammurabi showed not only a high order of society but a high status of woman, and such recognition of her rights as a human being as are hardly equalled on earth today.

English law at the time of Blackstone practically denied woman's existence as a personality after marriage. She had almost no rights at all. From the time of the Norman Conquest until fairly recently, the English wife was her husband's *liege* subject. If she killed him she was punished, not for murder, but for petty treason—revolt against her sovereign. Her only redress for his maltreatment was a church court.

To the Hebrews, Eve was merely Adam's first *faithful* wife. Before her was that ravishingly beautiful she-devil, Lilith. She did not care much for Adam and one day left him. Three angels gave her a choice of going back to him or having a hundred of her children die every day. She did not go back—and revenged herself by strangling Eve's children. Hence this prayer to the three angels hung up in Jewish women's rooms: "God, let this woman give birth to a son; and let him get a wife like Eve and not like Lilith!"

Polygamy was practised up to Deuteronomy's time. Concubines also were permitted. Thus, Abraham takes Sarah's slave-maid; Jacob takes the slave-maids of Leah and Rachel—and Yahweh himself rewarded Leah because she gave so cheerfully! Chastity then was no more required of men before marriage, nor fidelity after, than they are today. Prostitution was a recognized profession in good standing, and it was no disgrace to patronize it; nor, in the eyes of the writer of Matthew, was it a disgrace to be the descendant of a prostitute. At any rate, Rahab (or Rachab) was a harlot and is named in the genealogy of Jesus in the first chapter of Matthew. The Hebrew word for "husband" means *owner*; the wife was a *thing*, a chattel.

The Hebrew bride was blessed with, "Be thou the mother of thousands of ten thousands!" The adulterous wife was killed. Wives could be divorced for any cause. Her "rights" as set forth in Exodus were life, food, clothing, and coitus three times a month. The father could kill his children. A daughter who was found to have lost her virginity before marriage was stoned to death as damaged goods; she had cheated her father out of the price of her sale.

In short, there is not one moral precept or one kind word for honest love in the entire Pentateuch. Nor is one ancient Athenian known to have married a free-born woman for love; in fact, the whole complex of marriage based on the love of two free individuals was alien to Greek thought. What the Greeks thought, the church preached—after adding another and possibly more fatal obstacle to the smooth course of true love. This idea came from the Levant, though it was not confined to the Near East.

The idea began in the belief that "woman is a well, a grave, a ditch; a sharp iron dagger which cuts man's neck," as an old Babylonian ritual put it. We shall never know where the double standard began, but it was well started when written history began. A lawyer's manual from Ashurbanipal's library, says Barton, quotes an ancient Sumerian law to the effect that a divorced wife could practise prostitution on the street and bring up girls in the profession—called, not without reason, the *ancient*. But man has managed to keep his blinders on and ignore the fact that in that particular profession he has played the rôle of Patron-Founder. The Babylonian might well have thought of that when he prayed to his gods to change his enemy into a woman—as the worst curse he could put on him.

Prostitution, it seems likely, could not have become so easily and early institutionalized had not women been made the chief vessel in the fertility rites that grew up with the growth of agriculture. The nature of these rites we have seen. We need only note the far-reaching consequences of that idea once it had started on its mad career.

One consequence was to give man an excuse for unbridled licence —all because the earth must be fruitful. Sumer-Akkad enthroned the idea in Ishtar, the eternal feminine, female principle of the cosmic universe. Babylon built a temple to her daughter, Astarte, the Goddess of Love. To her were sacrificed virtue, virginity, the mother and the child. Women decked in garlands sat in line, waiting their turn to be chosen by men who would "sacrifice" them. In her Syrian temple the drums and pipes played for a thousand years —for the orgies of men dressed as women, women as men, in all known forms of sex perversion. And all this insanity in the name of Religion.

Honest normal love was driven out lest it *pollute* an "innocent world"; was banned as "indecent." Unclean, unclean. Diogenes, the ascetic, practised onanism in the market place to show his contempt for everything connected with love—thereby climbing down the ladder of evolution to the level of a fish, as Bölsche says. More "noble-minded" Athenians practised pederasty. The besieged Greek colony of Lokria vowed to offer its women in Aphrodite's temple for sacred prostitution if the gods would give it victory. Then there is Lot's generous proffer of his two virginal daughters to a strange mob, to save his skin, as told in Genesis xix: 8.

Such, roughly, was man's opinion of woman in the early centuries when Christianity was fighting for its life against the mysticism of other Eastern religions. It was not a high opinion, nor a credit to human reason, nor a psychologically sound foundation on which to build a sane social order.

Many centuries had to pass before the church got complete control over the whole institution of marriage, but from the outset it tried to go two ways at the same time, both inimical to a sane, sound social life. The idea behind both was enough to drive society insane—and it did. That idea was that love—good honest sexual love—was sin, inherently wicked, Satan's way of thwarting God, and that it would drag men down to hell.

The church, therefore, simply had to take to celibacy. The difference between Diogenes and the celibate priest was primarily one of words: both were ascetics mortifying the flesh—a morality, as Bölsche says, which became the vulture that fed on Prometheus' liver. The Church Father, Tertullian, opened the kingdom of heaven to eunuchs; Origen castrated himself.

"How often did I fancy myself amid the pleasures of Rome!" exclaimed the ascetic St. Jerome, seeking peace from the flesh in the solitude of the desert under the burning sun. "I sought solitude because I was filled with bitterness. Sackcloth disfigured my misshapen limbs and my skin had become by neglect as black as an Ethiopian's. Tears and groans were every day my portion. I, who from fear of hell had consigned myself to that prison where I had no other companions but scorpions and wild beasts, fancied myself among bevies of young girls. . . ."

It did not seem to occur to anyone that there might be a reasonable compromise between sensual orgy and ritual purity. How could there be, with the Wisdom literature shouting: Give me any wickedness save the wickedness of a woman; with the whole Bible damning woman as temptress and destroyer, the source and fount of all sin on earth?

One could not serve flesh and the devil and then handle sacraments or perform spiritual duties. Asceticism, celibacy of priests, became inevitable. But somebody had to sin or there would be no sinners to save!—no excuse for religion. The church had to concede the weakness of flesh; it reduced marriage to the simplest possible terms—a mutual pledge without witnesses. Later it became illegal to marry outside the church. Thereafter adultery became the deadly sin; divorce, the cardinal immorality. There could be no divorce for those whom God had joined; but if it could be shown that God had not really joined them, the marriage could be annulled!

Meanwhile, and inevitably, virginity began to be glorified and was finally deified. John Chrysostom rated virginity as high above marriage as the heavens above the earth. Thomas Aquinas thought virginity alone made men as good as angels. The Council of Trent anathematized anyone who said that it was more blessed to marry than to remain virgin or celibate. With love cursed as the foulest sin, with families founded on concessions to sin, the wonder is that the Dark Ages were not darker. And they would have been had there not been so much saving grace in human nature itself.

According to the morals of our Teuton ancestors, a father could "expose" his children if he did it before they had had their first meal. He could kill them, and sell his wife into slavery. Up to the nineteenth century he could kill his wife for any reason which to him "seemed good." But King Knut of England forbade the sale of a woman to a man she disliked.

In an old Irish saga a rich man pays the chief two hundred head of cattle and a hundred ounces of gold for the use of his daughter "for one year." The chief is delighted, of course, and consents. The Queen of Connaught boasted to her husband that before marriage she always had a secret, as well as an official, lover.

These are samples of the morality which formed the background of Romantic love. The Age of Chivalry makes good reading—if one be not a stickler for chivalry. Arab morality, contrasted with that of the Crusaders, was refined and ladylike. Richard the Lion Hearted was a Red Indian avenging his wrongs, an out-and-out savage. The world has probably never seen a sweeter collection of privileged knaves than the Knights of Chivalry. Scarcely one of them would have escaped hanging by a western Vigilante. They stole cattle, robbed wayfarers, and were pirates at sea.

Having received their swords from the church and vowed to defend the faithful, they behaved like Chinese bandits. They robbed and ransomed Christians, treated the poor like dirt under their feet, and surrendered themselves to lust and licentiousness. The Age of Chivalry was an age of treachery, perfidy, lying, deceit, and cruelty, below the standard of a western cattle-thief.

How did love fare? Well, woman then as now loved a winner. "My lord," said a Provençal wife, reproached for infidelity, "you have no dishonour on that account, for the man I love is a noble baron, expert in arms—Roland, nephew of King Charles." That closed the debate; Roland held the honours. As Briffault says,

Henry VIII in the eleventh or twelfth century would have been quite normal. Anyway, he had no more wives than many New York business men—only he *married* them.

Romantic love as we think of it simply did not then exist. If a knight found a lady unprotected it was his business to "protect" her—even if he had to resort to violence; to do otherwise was dishonourable, an "unchivalrous" act. The order of chivalry was disorderly living.

Nor was it any disgrace to be a bastard. The mythical heroes King Arthur, Gawain, Roland, were all bastards, as were Charles Martel, Charlemagne, William the Conqueror, and Theodoric. Only when the church got control of marriage did bastardy become disgraceful.

Men's clubs, then as now, must also be counted among the forces against sound morality. There they lived, sang, drank, and danced, and recounted tales of war and of the valour of their ancestors. No woman's honour was safe among them. It was a man's world, "for men only"; only prostitutes, "club girls," need apply. Such were the women who bore the wounded warriors aloft to Valhalla, the eternal mead-hall where free love reigned, as it did in Moslem's flowery houri meadows. Clubs became barracks, or saloons with girls behind the bar, or remained clubs: enemies all of a sound family life, all accepting naïvely the principle of a double standard in morality.

Two other Middle Age phenomena bearing on the general question of morality can only be mentioned here. One was the continuance of the old pagan rites of fertility, in one form or another—festival times of sex licence. Such was the spirit of carnival and of the May Day festivities so hated by our Puritans as being the work of Satan. The other was more serious, more devilish, more destructive of human morality, more provocative of incredible credulity. But witches and vampires will be brought into court later. It may be noted here, however, that the church seemingly had to go stark mad before morality could begin its long uphill climb into the light of the sun.

For some thousands of years now our civilization has been plagued with a fatal disease. It has tried every cure but common sense, fought every conceivable evil phantom but the evils of darkness, ignorance, and bigotry; and in its wild pursuit of wealth and power today still rides roughshod over the one trait in man worth saving, the one trait that made him possible, the one trait that can possibly cure the fatal disease.

That disease is founded on the double standard in sex morality. The one human trait worth saving is marriage founded on sexual love. Brute strength cannot wage war successfully against honest love; it does triumph because true love has been forced to make way for sensuality, for cold asceticism, or for deaf, dumb, and blind resignation. Individuals can prolong existence in any of these three forms of sex aberration, and even achieve distinction in socially useful work, but they are *necessarily intolerant* of every ideal that makes for greater sanity in human society.

The historian of the future will, I suspect, discover no great difference between the celibacy the church forced on its priests and the celibacy Success and Progress force on unnumbered thousands. The modern employer of labour making his might "right" is degrees below the mediæval baron exercising his right to the first night of the bride. The baron was simply performing a social service; the employer of labour turns a fellow-worker into a slave to one element of society. "Labour?" clerks and stenographers, in banks, department stores, etc.; especially applicants for the stage, silent, loud speaker, or spoken. If sex love must lead a dog's life, it must become a pariah. In every age social disorders have borne a direct ratio to disorderly homes.

The girl whose first sex experience brings her face to face with bestiality is possibly even worse off than the boy whose first experience is with a prostitute. Neither has yet taken the first step in the only kind of love experience which leads to a happy married life; both have had the first lesson in morality which makes for immorality. Society does not seem to care, nor sees very much because it keeps its eyes closed.

After a few minutes, the naked South Sea Islanders seem no more immoral or immodest than a naked babe in its mother's arms. Celtic and Teuton warriors fought their battles quite nude. Yet we keep hanging tin fig leaves on works of art to cover their nakedness—thereby evoking the erotic element the fig leaves are supposed to disarm. What morality needs is facts, and it is as silly to cover them with fig leaves as with rose garlands. We cannot see with clean eyes when the ideas behind the eyes are obscene.

Even obscenity, used properly, can be put to social service if society is organized for social purposes. Evans-Pritchard has recently shown how certain African tribes during times of emotional crises —religious ceremonies and important joint economic activities— permit or even favour the suspension of taboos against free speech in all sexual matters. That makes for obscenity, but its free flow serves both as stimulus to effort and reward for greater effort.

Shocking—yes. But moralities are only prevailing customs in morals; and, as Briffault says, Socrates, Cæsar, Raphael, Titian, Shakespeare, Napoleon, the Duke of Wellington, and George Eliot were all morally unfit for the best Igorrote society. And as for ethics, where in all the "savage" world can we find a standard low enough to tolerate husbands who automatically became possessed of their wife's property on marriage and who could carry off her belongings, leaving her to fend for herself and her children and possibly amass more property—and then return and seize that and waste it in riotous living?

Such inhuman, brutal behaviour seems incredible, but it was legal behaviour in England not so very long ago. What our own recent attitude toward women was we may remind ourselves, if we have forgotten, by thumbing the pages of the life of Lucy Stone.

China, I suspect, has a longer record of emancipated woman than any other nation. Her categorical disabilities were fewer; her politico-economic rights were almost, and her social rights quite, as good as man's. Even her part in religion was not purely passive. But in our Middle Ages even woman's passive part in religion was far below man's, and with his stranglehold on all war activities she ceased to function in the social order. In Spain, for example, she was primarily a breeder of dupes. Working through her, the politico-religious machine had a regular supply of nourishment and waxed fat; but the nation sank to the status of a family trying to live by doing one another's wash.

Americans still believe that the male of the genus *Homo* is the only naturally endowed state animal; and so practically all state activities—politics, legislation, finance, business, justice, war, administration—are still closely grasped by the male hand. And hardly less than the Greeks, he still turns to the *hetairai* for his playmates; but, less courageous than the Greeks, he will not allow his Aspasias to educate his daughters or compose his funeral oration.

He will try everything once except the woman he proposes to marry. If his wife can run the flat and bear him an heir to whom he can leave his name and fortune, he is content, and will talk you deaf, dumb, and blind about the Sanctity of the Home.

Times are changing, and the foes of change are arming and uniting. It is not yet certain that we have permanently passed the stage in morals where woman must choose between being an heir-breeder, a form for the display of wealth, a doll for immoral purposes—or, as Madame de Staël put it, bear children or write books. Terence, in a Greek derived play, makes lovers lament because they have to get married. And Medea, in Euripides' play, complains about the high cost of husbands. We have not travelled very far from the immoralities of the Periclean Greeks.

We have not travelled far enough in understanding that love is the one fundamentally important source of power in human lives, just as the sun is the earth's power plant, primordial source of all earthly virtues. And the forces of nature focussed their attention on making the mother of the race the more efficient sex. Taking the animal kingdom by and large, the female is the better man by about fifty per cent. The burden nature lays on her she bears efficiently, healthily, vigorously.

Then man comes along and in the name of God so fills her up with sin and loads her down with rubbish, spiritual and material, that she cannot walk, let alone seek a mate or bear children. She drops out of sight for from two to five days of each lunar month, spends a thousand dollars to have her child delivered, and is too frail to feed or raise it. That is what civilization has done for the human race—reduced by fifty per cent the efficiency of one half of its number. Civilization is just as rotten as its women are. Half the gadgets our civilization turns out in carload lots are devices for driving women crazy. Anything pays—if it pays. And the sky is the limit. We speak of tyrants and the tyranny of nature: their power is as nothing compared with that of a smug, self-complacent civilization that is more concerned with Law than with human liberties; with High Finance than with sound health.

Even in the days of Ramses II the husband acknowledged "thy rights of wife; from this day forward I shall never by any word oppose thy claims. I have no power to say to thee, 'Thou art my wife.' It is I who am the man who is thy husband." As far back as we can go in Egyptian history, no career was closed in woman's face. It is recorded of one woman of the Old Empire that she was a clerk in her father's office, was promoted to administrative posts, was governor of a province, and commander-in-chief of a military district. She was one of the most important and wealthy citizens of her day.

"If thou art wise," says a maxim in the oldest book in the world, "keep thy home. Love thy wife and do not quarrel with her. Feed her, clothe her, anoint her. Caress her, and fulfil all her desires as long as thou livest, for she is an estate which brings much profit. If thou oppose her, it will mean thy ruin." Search the scriptures for a maxim as sound.

## VI

The early followers of Jesus were simple enough folk, but the shepherds of the flocks by the fourth century were neither children nor fools, and they knew how to handle both and make them pay. It was all right for Paul to talk about the ox being worth its fodder, but the leading lights of the fourth-century church were not oxen and they did not like fodder. They had been going to classical schools and learning the ways of Imperial Rome; and with a big Bible behind them and many apocryphal books, they could find authority for anything.

With Holy Writ as warrant, with Græco-Roman world splendours as model, and with the rites and cults of a dozen pagan religions to prompt them, they could build a church that *was* a church. And they did. All they had to do was to look around. The models were there by the thousand. Also ideas for rebuilding heaven, remodelling hell; for turning martyrs into saints with as many and as assorted attributes as all the gods of the pagan world; even halos for their saints—the aureoles of Syrian gods.

Even their churches were ready-made for them when they were ready to move out of cellars and catacombs into daylight. Roman churches are still called by the name Romans gave the *basilicas* in which they transacted their business. St. Peter's itself is but one end of an architectural story that began at Gizeh with a clerestory hall, went to a Nineveh palace for its façade, in Rome's triumphal arch found additional features, and in Rome's Pantheon its dome. That story covers thirty-five hundred years, to be sure, but then it was all above ground and easy to read. Justinian (527) in roofing a Roman basilica in Constantinople to make it into a St. Sofia, used ten thousand men and eighteen tons of gold. But to offset this gift to the world he had the laws codified and closed the schools of Athens, thus ending, as Breasted says, "all intellectual liberty in the ancient world."

Just the same, many churchmen of the fifth century were very clever, if distorted, thinkers; and the greatest of these was Augustine. He had not scattered wild oats and imbibed Greek philosophy for nothing. I cannot see that civilization owes him a nickel, but the church certainly would have been poorer without him. His implied recognition of Rome's leadership helped to make effective the myth that Peter had been the first Christian bishop and by transferring his authority to a successor had "founded" the holy office of Pontifex Maximus, or pope. Rome had become uniquely respected and its monuments had been too great to be wiped out by the Goths and Vandals; as the capital city of the church it was a first-class asset in its growth.

What would have happened when the savage Teutons invaded Rome had they not found the church in power, it is not possible to say. We can say, however, that whatever influence the church exerted in civilizing savage Teutons was not because the church was Christian, but because it was Roman. Rome had gone Christian and the church was all that was left of the power that once was Rome's. During the Middle Ages, Roman and Christian were synonymous terms.

Two factors contributed to convert the savages—monks preaching hell fire, and the glamour of a civilization that included a Pericles, a Plato, a Cæsar, and a Trajan. To be sure, these notables were not Christians, but the savages did not know that; they were "Roman," and what was Roman was Christian. The language of the church was Latin—no longer Greek; Latin was the bond which held Christianity together.

The western half of the Roman Empire ended in 476 with the deposition of that ironically named puppet, Romulus Augustulus, by the leader of the Teutonic hordes. With the Gothic kingdom that now rose out of Rome's ashes, or the other kingdoms that rose out of the ruins of the Empire, we are not concerned. Our concern is civilization—and that is something not easily found in the next five centuries of the rather Dark Ages but great days for the church.

Take it or leave it, the fact remains that the five centuries which saw Europe converted to Christianity also saw such a string of murders, parricides, fratricides, and poisonings, and such bestial, brutal, drunken licentiousness, as cannot be found in five thousand years of Egyptian history; nor anywhere, says Gibbon, more vice and less virtue in the same space of time. Let us look at a few of these Christian kings.

They are interesting as murderers; they are illuminating as pupils, not of Christianity, but of the church. It is Christianity that keeps going bankrupt, not the church. The church never did go bankrupt. Gregory the Great not only could "give banquets whose luxury surpasses that of the Emperor's table," but was the richest man in the Empire. It was the church's business to adapt itself to the age. The church changes doctrines from time to time, incorporates new ideas more fitting to the times, soft pedals on other doctrines that will not fill the coffers or confessionals. The church persecuted heresies; but Reinach defies anyone to name one heresy persecuted by the church the adoption of which would not have brought about a diminution in her revenues.

It was a warlike age; a rich and cultured world lay helpless at the feet of warlike savages. If the Gospels denounce anything, it is bloodshed; if Christ stands for anything, it is peace. But certain conditions, said Augustine, justify war. What conditions? Those the church decides on. He also and necessarily finds merit in the profession of the soldier. How otherwise organize a Christian army and equip it with adequate slogans? When Justinian closed the pagan schools he probably did not close much; sixth-century schools in Athens were not the Greek schools of Alexandria—now nine centuries remote. By closing pagan schools the church closed pagan argument, pagan speculation, moulder of pagan beliefs. That is one reason why those centuries were so dark: no new light to think by; the church told people what to think, and manufactured the machinery to make them like it. Other beliefs were heresy, capital crimes. Justinian not only closed pagan schools, but Christian as well—especially at Antioch and Alexandria. Rome could handle Christian theology without the aid of outside schools.

Voltaire thought that the church's conquest of half Europe was due to important female converts. Through Clotilde, queen of Clovis, western Europe was Christianized in less than a generation. Religion went with the flag; the flag was the ruler, king, duke, what not. The conversion of eastern Europe began with that of the Duchess Olga at Constantinople. Eastern Europe is largely of the faith of the Eastern Church with headquarters at Constantinople —Orthodox Greek. The split between the Eastern or Greek and the Western or Latin churches became definite in 1054, at which time they formally excommunicated each other, the Christian way of telling each other to go to Hades. That split, by the way, accounts for the survival of a modified Greek alphabet in Russia and Bulgaria today; for, as we have seen, the Roman Catholic Church formally adopted Latin in 400.

Conversion to Christianity never proceeded so rapidly or so spectacularly as did conversion to Mohammedanism, but in general it may be said that all Europe had become converted by the year 1000. Ireland, "Isle of Saints," says Reinach, got the best missionaries and was evangelized by Patrick in 450. The monk Augustine converted the Anglo-Saxons in 596; and Boniface the Germans between 689 and 755.

Thus far it had not been necessary to use violence, but in Charlemagne's time the Saxon chiefs were not so docile. He offered them a choice—be baptized or be killed; 4,500 Saxons paid for their stiff necks. Thereafter, with Europe converted as a block, the church's main business was with individuals—backsliders, idolaters, etc. Special bishops—forerunners of the Inquisition—were charged with dealing with such criminals.

Clovis was the first royal convert outside the Empire proper. He became king of the Franks by persuading a king's son to murder his father and then proceeding to crack the son's skull. He was baptized by Remigius in 496. The Merovingian Frankish kingdom was succeeded by the Pepins, or Carolingians, its last king having been deposed with the consent of the pope and retired to a monastery. The lowly Peter fishermen were now papal realtors of kingdoms.

Pepin the Short and his sons were "anointed" by the pope in 754 as kings of the Franks. Pepin styled himself "King by the grace of God" and gave the pope large slices of Italy, which grew, presumably also by the grace of God, into the Papal States. One of Pepin's sons, thanks largely to the pope, was to become our old friend Charles the Great (Charlemagne, 768-814). One of his sons tore out his brother's son's eyes; and a son of that son abducted his half-brother's daughter from a convent, put her in a cask, and set it afloat on the river. Meanwhile, Alboin of the Langobord kingdom had been murdered by his wife, Rosamund, merely because he had forced her to drink from her murdered father's skull! But there were extenuating circumstances. Rosamund had married her father's murderer and then had murdered him. A Burgundian king gained temporal power and security by killing three of his brothers.

Merovingian and Carolingian morals reeked with licentiousness, vice, and debauchery. Raoul de Cambrai, hero of a *chanson*, is said to have roasted a hundred nuns alive. One of Charlemagne's paladins cut off the nose, ears, hands, and feet of some ambassadors sent to treat with him; if he had then roasted and eaten them, he could have qualified as a Uganda king.

Following Odoacer the German, who in 476 had deposed the last king of the Western Roman Empire, came Theodoric, styled the Great. He founded the kingdom of the East (Ostro) Goths in Italy. He was a prime butcher, and was succeeded by a line each of whom mounted the throne by murdering his predecessor.

Savage Christians; but *savages*. Rome had conquered savages and civilized them; but these Teutons (Nordics) Christianized, in some ways suggest swine let loose in front parlours. Europe from the fifth to the tenth century was a pig-sty. All Gaul and Italy, says Briffault, were in ruin, squalor, and desolation. Cities practically disappeared; in Nîmes, the people dwelt in huts in the ruins of the amphitheatre; Mantua was submerged in stagnant waters. By the ninth century not one of the prosperous Roman cities of the Rhine was left; wolves, boars, bears, roamed among the ruins; the Roman villa atria were cloisters or dunghills; the reduced population lived in huts around the barons' lairs or monasteries, clothed in skins or sack-shaped wool, and could not go abroad for fear of beasts and robbers. Famine and plague were chronic; there were ten devastating famines and thirteen plagues in the tenth century alone. There were man-hunts for food; at Tournus on Saône human flesh was publicly sold. Anarchy reigned, absolute and unchecked: no law but the barons' will; no business but brigandage, private war, and riot; in their rush-strewn towers they lived, often using the halls for stables.

St. Boniface complained that under the pretext of pilgrimage a trail of Teutonic prostitutes was left over every part of Europe. Drunkenness was equally common among both sexes. The church could convert faster than it could tame. It became touched with savagery itself. The condition of the church and monasteries was appalling. "On no account," said a Carolingian regulation, "shall an abbot gouge out the eyes of his monks or mutilate them, whatever fault they may have committed." Incest was regulated down to details. A priest was allowed only one wife.

John XII, a vicious and unprincipled pope, was accused by the Roman clergy of turning his palace into a brothel; he was murdered by a wronged husband. Of the seven popes who reigned between 955 and 985, one died in exile, one was assassinated, one died in prison, and one was poisoned. Benedict IX resigned office and put the Chair of Peter up for sale.

Contrary to general opinion, celibacy is not a Roman Catholic dogma, but a doctrine, an affair of discipline. Egyptian Christians as early as 250 had copied a custom of the Essenes of Jesus' time and of the Pythagoreans of 600 B.C. who lived in communities— cenobites. As the Egyptian cenobites went into the desert (eremos), they were called hermits. Benedict was the organizer of the first cenobites in Italy into monasteries. They were vowed to poverty and manual labor—"He who works, prays." Many a monk found congenial work in copying and illuminating ancient manuscripts. They were not all fanatics, nor was every pope a Gregory, to burn all the Cicero and Livy manuscripts he could get his hands on. Celibacy to the monks was a virtue. A Church Council in Spain in 305 enjoined celibacy on the priesthood, but celibacy did not become a church doctrine till the twelfth century.

I once had a notion that Charlemagne was a great civilizing force in the Middle Ages, creator of a Renaissance, as it were. He did found schools—as the Puritans founded Harvard College— but they were abbey schools where priests could learn to read and write that they might fight paganism. Charlemagne's schools hardly survived his last breath, and had a primary-grade curriculum.

Here, for example, is an arithmetic lesson as taught by Alcuin of York, "most learned" man of his day and Charlemagne's intellectual prime minister:

An accurate acquaintance with numbers teaches us that some are even, others uneven; that of the even numbers, some are perfect, others imperfect; and further, that of the imperfect numbers, some are greater, others less. . . . Take, for example, the number VI; the half of VI is III, the third is II, and the sixth part I. The perfect Creator, therefore, who made all things very good, created the world in six days in order to show that everything that he had formed was perfect of its kind. . . . When the human race after the Flood replenished the earth, they originated from the number VIII; . . . thus indicating that the second race is less perfect than the first, which had been created in the number VI. . . . The sixty queens and eighty concubines (mentioned in the Song of Solomon) are the members of the Holy Church. . . .

That is a sample of learning in the Middle Ages. But, after all, what business has a consistent Christian priest with learning, anyhow? None, except to read and expound Holy Writ to converts. Theodoric, greatest of Teutonic kings, could neither read nor write, although he spent fourteen years at the Byzantine court. Merely to be able to read made a German noble distinguished for his learning.

The clergy, priests, alone could read; and some of them could even write. There were bishops who could not sign their own names to their canons. King Alfred lamented that from the Humber to the sea there was no priest who could translate simple Latin or understand the liturgy in its mother tongue. No, it was not the church that civilized Europe, nor the church that saved civilization.

It was out of such schools as Charlemagne founded that there grew up that subtle, hair-splitting, over-refined, infinitely minute learning known as Scholasticism. Its god was authority, archenemy of science.

"In all thy splendour," said Bernard of Clairvaux, "thou art the successor of Constantine rather than the successor of Peter. . . . Was Peter clothed in robes of silk, covered with gold and precious stones? Was he carried in a litter surrounded by soldiers and vassals?"

It may or may not be for the glory of God, but the pope carried through the enormous crowds that throng St. Peter's on festal occasions is a stunning spectacle. I cannot conceive of a Roman Emperor making a more spectacular entry. Bernard criticized the abuses of the church in vain. A divine ruler of a celestial city with streets of gold is not to be worshipped in a cow stable; he must be worshipped in munificence, magnificently. Tauler of the fourteenth century even dressed Christ up in the robes fitting his station as a Christian knight: "Christ's scarlet knightly robes for his knightly devotion; by his chivalric exploits he won these knightly weapons, which he wears before the Father and the angelic knighthood." To the Middle Ages, a knight; to this age, a Rotarian.

The pope even claimed suzerainty over the earth—as successor not of Peter, but of Julius Cæsar himself! And Hildebrand, Gregory VII (1073-85), showed the world. Before he became pope, he had handled the mundane affairs of five popes. He especially claimed overlordship of the territory ruled by Henry IV—since 962 known as the Holy Roman Empire. Its emperor had deposed a pope and forced Rome to promise to elect no more popes without the emperor's consent. For a century a merry war waged over this issue. Hildebrand thought the time ripe to settle it. He excommunicated Henry. Henry crossed the Alps in winter and in the garb of a penitent stood barefooted for three days before a castle in Canossa. Then Hildebrand let him in and gave him absolution. That was January 28, 1077. Three years later Henry was again excommunicated—but he was three years older. He went to Rome and created a pope of his own, and allowed Hildebrand to die miserably in exile. But Hildebrand was a great pope all the same, and presumably put the idea of conquering England into William the Norman's head.

At any rate, William did conquer England, like a true Christian savage; and a century later, in the reign of Henry II, Thomas à Becket was made Archbishop of Canterbury. Henry tried to make criminal justice an affair of state and not of church. Becket, a conspirator against the king, was murdered by four of Henry's knights. Henry of course was excommunicated, and forced by the pope to pay in money and in barefooted penance at Becket's tomb for his absolution. The uxorious Henry VIII was excommunicated, as was his daughter Elizabeth. But by that time the English Church could thumb its nose at Rome.

Excommunication was the strongest card in the church's hand, its most lethal weapon in political warfare, and few men dared brave it. An alley cat might have a moment's peace, but not an excommunicated man; he was a lost soul in hell and on earth bedevilled by all its imps. His only chance of salvation was, not Christ, but the church. All religious rites in the kingdom of an excommunicated king stopped—as though God had declared a strike against the kingdom, says Reinach; all oaths of allegiance to his person were automatically released. The ruler had to submit, if for no other reason, because driven to it by his terror-stricken subjects.

Pope Boniface VIII excommunicated Philip the Fair, king of France, and to Albert of Austria he gave a bull: "We give you, in the plenitude of our power, the kingdom of France, which belongs of right to the Emperors of the West." Note the "We give . . . which belongs of right." No prophet in Israel had ever dreamed that Yahweh would put so much power in any mortal's hands. Popes handed out large tracts of Europe to their favourites as one hands out slices of cake. In such manner were the crowns of Portugal, Spain, Hungary, Denmark, England, Aragon, Sicily, and France handed out.

No wonder treasure rolled into Rome. No wonder paganism was eclipsed in the splendour and gorgeous trappings of Christianity. Festivals were multiplied; basilicas became more and more magnificent; and countless candles borrowed from paganism sputtered away to the glory of God and in rivalry with the smoke of incense. Pay, pay; do as I say; submit—or I'll send your soul to hell and make you an outlaw among your fellow-men. Excommunication was a priceless weapon.

So great was their power that priests not only stripped citizens of all their possessions, but tortured, mutilated, and burned them alive—nor even spared the dead in their graves. A young English squire stole a priest's riding-crop; it cost him three years' exile, public penance in seven churches, and a fine of six hundred pounds! The ringleader of a mob which attacked a bishop did penance and paid a fine of six thousand pounds; fifty others of the mob, including a woman, were publicly scourged. Penance usually meant holding lighted candles, standing barefoot, while the crowd jeered.

No priesthood on earth was ever more shameless than that of ninth- and tenth-century Christianity. The church sold its favours more openly than a prostitute sells hers. Did a priest wish to keep a mistress: pay a tax to the bishop. As Reinach says, divine forgiveness was cheaper than a new coat. Bones of saints had their market price and made for better and bigger business. At least a ton of nails, and enough wood of the True Cross to build Atlantic City's boardwalk, were sold and worshipped.

The story that Philip the Fair had fourteen witnesses who "heard" a pope say: "How profitable this fable of Christ has been to us," may be calumny; but the fable certainly was profitable—especially for what was read into it. Purgatory, for example. There is not a word nor an idea of purgatory in the Gospels. There is the idea in Vergil and in the Orphic mysteries—a sort of probationary halfway house between pagan felicity and gloom. Souls appear before Minos for judgment; and can be purified by fire, as could a corpse to the ancient Greeks. The idea in St. Augustine's eyes seemed to have merit, especially as the Gospels made no provision for souls between death and the Last Judgment. Hence the Christian purgatory, long a doctrine, and a dogma of the Church since the Council of Florence in 1439.

Here is the idea. If you are really bad, sinful, wicked, you go straight to hell; but if you have a chance, you go to purgatory—on probation. You can buy perpetual mass and endow perpetual candles because the fate of your soul is not irrevocably sealed at death. The church can use its good offices on behalf of souls thought doubtful: intercede with the saints! And will—for a price and the profession of penitence.

Beginning with the eleventh century, the business of buying

dubious souls from purgatory became Big Business. What a weapon this was for brigandage in the hands of a church whose priests could be visited by the ghosts of souls writhing in torture in purgatory and facing the eternal fires of brimstone. *Why not buy them out?* There is no limit to pious credulity: the priests might be right. Why, said a Franciscan monk, the pope could empty purgatory at a single stroke!

The Dark Ages had to become stark mad before the worm turned. And possibly the turn would have been deferred more centuries had not the church organized, systematized, and perfected the institution of "squeeze" as no other institution was ever perfected.

Confess your faults one to another, said James. And so early church communities did. But it is not easy to confess one's faults to one's neighbours—not so easy as it is to one's parents, especially if they are sympathetic listeners. If they are, honest confession is good for one's peace of mind, and possibly for one's soul. At any rate, the church, always a master technician in dealing with children, women, and simple-minded people generally, saw possibilities in private confessions to priests.

What a hold it gave the church over guilty and tender-minded people! What a club in unscrupulous hands to hold over sinners! And what a money-maker! It took religion thousands of years to invent an idea so formidably tyrannical and so profitable.

Confession of a fault or misdeed to one's father meant a promise not to do it any more. Confession to a spiritual father meant penance. How does one show a penitent spirit? By deeds pleasing in the sight of God, such as building a chapel, or doing any deed that the church deems good. Out of that inspired idea grew up one of the most iniquitous practices ever devised by organized superstition: the compounding of felonies at so much per.

Gregory VII was a great pope, but Innocent III was the master builder of the temporal power for which his predecessors had been collecting the materials for four hundred years. Not the least potent of these materials was the weapon of excommunication.

Every human institution, it seems, must inevitably pay for its superman. Innocent III overdid it. He was not merely pontiff, king, or emperor; he was at one time the undisputed lord of the entire

Christian world. He excommunicated Philip Augustus, king of France; Otho IV, emperor of Germany; and John Lackland, king of England. He preached the Fourth Crusade, scourged the Albigenses, and made a hell on earth for heretics and Jews.

It was Innocent III who brought the idea of the confessional to its logical perfection. Perhaps some guilty parties were not taking advantage of this wonderful opportunity to confess and obtain absolution—at a price. That could be fixed. So, in 1215 the church made yearly confession obligatory—and it must be made into the ear of a priest! Not even an abbess was worthy to hear and absolve. It was this shameless traffic in indulgences, among other things, that set the Augustinian monk Luther to nailing up defiances on the church door.

With Innocent III the church reached the height of its temporal power, but not of its folly. Rulers could get up enough spunk to resist the church's greed for territory, but the people were still held, too spineless to resist the church's passion to control men's thoughts. Innocent's death in 1216 is a date in human history. The Fourth Crusade he preached is one of several dates in the history of organized brigandage and highway robbery in the name of Christianity. The Crusades failed, deserved to fail, and in failing certainly stirred up a mess which has not yet ceased to emit fumes.

VII

We soon shall see how a rival religion arose in the seventh century in Arabia and spread temporally and spiritually with incredible speed, turned Christianity out of Asia and Africa, and was stopped in Europe only after centuries of struggle and effort. Palestine, the Christian Holy Land, was in the hands of the followers of Mohammed within ten years after his death. For the first few centuries Christians were not denied the privilege of pilgrimage to the Holy Land, which had been going on ever since the famous pilgrimage of St. Helena, mother of Constantine the Great, when she "discovered" the True Cross and built a vault and a church for the Holy Sepulchre.

But Mohammedans are Mohammedans and Christians are Christians. The Mohammedans were also cousins to the Jews, and Yahweh was also their God and Christ one of their saints; otherwise

John Bull's mandate in Palestine might not be such a prickly pear. Mohammedans are said by Christians to be fanatics; but becoming converted to or being born into Christianity does not necessarily confer immunity from fanaticism.

When, in 1071, the Mohammedan Saljuk Turks gained control of the Holy Land, going on a pilgrimage to Jerusalem passed from one hundred per cent safe to one hundred per cent hazardous. The church would stop all that and make Palestine safe for a Cook's tourist. That was the burning passion behind the Crusades. It was a poor idea, but it did give such crusaders as escaped the infidels' and one another's swords a set of new ideas. And Europe was sadly in need of something new to think about.

The capture of Saracenic or Mohammedan Sicily by the Normans in 1071 was an additional factor in preparing the Crusaders' way: it opened up the Mediterranean again to the fleets of the Cross.

The idea of the First Crusade (1096-99) seems to have emanated from Pope Urban II: he had had a dream visit from our Lord; but it was Peter the Hermit of Amiens who preached the Crusade and the freeing of the Holy Sepulchre to France and Italy. An army of from 200,000 to 600,000 answered the call. After three years less than 22,000 of that army reached the holy city. There was a general massacre of Jerusalem's whole population, after which they made a pilgrimage to the Church of the Resurrection. They then erected Jerusalem into a feudal kingdom.

The Second Crusade was a total failure; it got no plunder at all. The Third (1189-92) gave us Richard of the Lion Heart and of a disposition even more cruel; also Saladin, who had conquered Jerusalem in 1182, and who now showed Christians that a Mohammedan could be a gentleman. In fact, he treated them with more magnanimity than they deserved. He allowed Richard to get away without rendering homage or paying a ransom—which was more than his fellow-Christian, Henry IV, Emperor of Austria, did, and he kept Richard prisoner for thirteen months besides.

The Fourth Crusade (1202-04), pet child of Innocent III, supposedly against Egypt, was prostituted by Venice into a raid on Christian Constantinople. That city was sacked and burnt, while the Christian army, vowed to fight infidels only, held bloody orgies in St. Sofia. Western Europe carried away immense booty in gold and silver, and enormous plunder in antiquities. It was then that Venice got her quadriga of bronze horses for St. Mark's Cathedral, and Paris the Crown of Thorns which Sainte-Chappelle was built to enshrine. That was not all: "Whatever was learned or holy, whatever was noble or valiant, rolled away into the independent states of Trebizond, Epirus, and Nice." It was a hideous orgy of massacre, arson, and loot. To Innocent III's credit be it said, he excommunicated the whole crusading, looting army; but that did not prevent the Greeks of two centuries later from declaring that they preferred the sultan's turban to the pope's tiara.

The Children's Crusade followed, unique in history and one of the foulest blots on Christendom. Led by Stephen, a miracle-working peasant, it gathered up an army of some thirty thousand boys and girls, mostly under twelve. They had been promised a dry path across the Mediterranean. One shipload foundered with all on board; but several thousands were carried across "for the sake of God and without charge" by slave-dealers, and sold into slavery.

The Fifth Crusade (1228-29) did recover Jerusalem but soon lost it, and so furnished excuse for the Sixth and the Seventh (and last) Crusade in 1270. The last two Crusades did one thing: they made a Saint of Louis IX of France, although he lost his entire army to the Sultan and only gained his own liberty after paying a heavy ransom in the Sixth Crusade. In the Seventh he lost most of his army by sickness, and the Christian world the last of its possessions on the coast of Palestine. But he had good, sound, Christian principles. One of them was: Don't argue with a blasphemer; run him through with a sword!

And so it is that the Crusades, which come to us invested with romance, are, as Jenkins points out, really the subject of tragedy. If there were great names among the Crusaders, there were even greater failures. If the banner of the Cross was carried high, it was more often dragged in the mire, and too often stained with the blood of innocent victims. In short, the Crusades were an exhibition of unbridled, unprincipled, unrestrained savagery in the name of Christ.

The logical conclusion to those two centuries of senseless, futile, plundering expeditions came in 1453, when the Moslem infidels entered Constantinople and took over the Greek or Eastern Empire. That was a real blow to European civilization.

Among other immediate results of the Crusades were: the increased hold of the papacy on all power and authority, and of princes over their subjects; great riches and power to the Italian republics; and certain orders of knighthood—samples of whose chivalry we have already seen.

Merchants of Amalfi in 1070 had founded the Hospital of St. John in Jerusalem, in charge of a brotherhood which was to serve those wounded in war. That brotherhood after the First Crusade became the Knights of St. John or the Hospitalers. They wore a black mantle bearing a white cross. When Emperor Charles V gave them the Island of Malta, they became the Knights of Malta.

The Templars, or Knights of the Temple (Solomon's), sprang from a handful of French knights in 1118. They wore a white mantle bearing a red cross. The Teutonic Knights began as a general hospital brotherhood, which was raised to the order of knighthood during the Third Crusade. They wore a white mantle bearing a black cross. They were dissolved in 1809.

All these orders numbered *knights, priests,* and *brothers* vowed to war against infidels. The greatest warring they did, however, was against one another. In one fight between Templars and Hospitalers, not one Templar lived to tell the tale.

Philip the Fair in 1307 arrested all the Templars in France and tried them on charges of idolatry and immorality. What he really wanted was their property. After torturing them for "evidence," he burnt fifty-four of them—an act of incredible and, from evidence now available, unjustifiable, inhuman savagery. Five years later Pope Clement V abolished the Templars, executed the Grand Master, and confiscated their property—which was not inconsiderable, for they were also bankers, though never so rich as the Hospitalers. Clement is even less justified by the facts than Philip.

We may note in passing that that same Philip the Fair also tortured Jews and lepers in his Christian zeal, but was man enough to quarrel with a pope for taking too much money out of France. The pope said he would take anything he wanted. Had not God set him over kings and kingdoms? His bull, *Ausculti fili,* said so. Philip burned the bull. That was 1301. The pope replied with another bull the next year, *Unam sanctum* (Spiritual is supreme over temporal power); and threatened Philip with excommunication. Philip's answer was such an indignity that the pope sickened and died.

Philip brought about the election of a Frenchman, Clement V. France and the church kissed and made up, and the pope moved to Avignon, which from 1309 to 1376 was the papal residence.

Times were beginning to change. Let us look at some heresies.

VIII

What rebellions are to kings, heresies are to popes. We look first at the heresy Innocent III tried to stamp out: the one in the South of France headed by the bishops of Toulouse and Albi, known as the Albigenses.

This sect, like the Waldenses and the *Cathari*, or "Pure," represented a revolt against certain church dogmas. It was a curious rationalistic blending of Buddhistic and Mazdean elements. Jesus was the good divinity; sensuality the evil, and represented by the devil. The leaders of the sect were the "Perfect." They were vowed to celibacy; ate fish, but no other flesh; substituted laying on of hands for baptism; and practised open confession. They probably were not perfect, but they were sincere and had high moral aims: and they were "heretics." Hence Innocent's crusade against them.

Southern France was invaded by an army of 300,000 men. It was really a crusade. The recruits were freed from paying interest on their debts, exempt from all law courts, and absolved from all past and future sins. No Assyrian army ever rode to war on so glorious a band-wagon or in such goodly company of priests, bishops, and nobles. For twenty years they murdered, plundered, burnt; men, women, and children. The motto (proposed by the papal legate) in storming Béziers (1207) was: *Slay all; God will know his own!* Twenty thousand were slaughtered. There were seven thousand bodies in one church; thousands rotted to death in obscure dungeons.

Why such inhuman ferocity against that particular part of France? Well, it was infested with heretics. Moreover, Provence, apart from Moorish Spain, was the most civilized part of Europe. For two hundred years it had been peaceful and prosperous. The university of Montpellier offered instruction in medicine, botany, and mathematics, to be found nowhere else outside Spain. There were also flourishing schools at Nîmes, Narbonne, and Carcassonne. It was civilized! But so thoroughly was its civilization blotted out that it did not recover for three centuries. Any heretics overlooked by the crusading army were exterminated by the Inquisition.

In 1124 the church had burnt one Pierre de Brueys for presuming to insist that the Bible was the only rule of faith. In 1170 Pierre Waldo, a rich man of Lyons, read his Bible, and liked it so well he had it translated into the vernacular. He took its teachings seriously and divided his property among the poor, for whom he founded a church. Its members were driven out and forced to take refuge in the Alpine valleys, where they founded the Church of the Waldenses and tried to spread the Gospel tidings. But Innocent III had declared that the faithful should not read the Bible. An office of the Inquisition was set up at Grenoble, and hundreds of Waldenses were burnt. Still the sect grew. A crusade was indicated! Whole bands were smoked to death in caves. Whole valleys were depopulated—largely by Irish mercenaries.

Even today Catholic lands are not noted for their literacy; in fact, the church never did deplore civil illiteracy. Pope Hildebrand in 1080 had declared that it was the will of God that His Word should be hidden. A Church Council in 1229 forbade the translation of the Bible into the vernacular and decreed that only the clergy should possess it—in Latin. And in 1536 William Tyndale was burnt alive in the public square, with his English translation of the Latin Bible.

While *inquisitors* had been called into existence by Innocent III in 1203, the Roman Inquisition as a regular tribunal for trying heresy cases was not established until 1229, by Pope Gregory IX. It retained that title until 1558, when it became one of twelve Congregations of the Pontifical Family—the Congregation of the Holy Office. That office, charged with safeguarding the Faith, presumes to pass upon what Catholics may read—a duty formerly belonging to the Congregation of the *Index Expurgatorius* and which it carried out in Italy by destroying whole libraries.

We think of the Spanish brand as the deadliest of the species, but the fact is, as Reinach says, that the Inquisition covered the entire Christian world with desolation and horror. It killed 100,000 in

Spain, but it burnt an equal number in Germany, and Albigenses, Waldenses, and Hussites, by the thousand. Hundreds were burnt in Lombard and Venetian valleys by Raphael's friend, Leo X. It lent its good offices to the English for the burning of Joan of Arc; to the Knight Templars for their war against the Teutons; and to any local politician who lusted for revenge. Reformers in France especially were persecuted with incredible cruelty. For speaking his mind about the worship of images and relics, Jean le Clerc was torn to pieces. Twenty reformers had their tongues cut out so that they could not speak to the mob, and were then burnt at the stake.

The Inquisition turned Spain into a "hell lighted only by the flames of the stake." And Spain has had little light since, for while Napoleon suppressed the Inquisition when he entered Madrid in 1808, it rose again as soon as he was out and was not finally abolished till 1834.

What a sight that old Plaza Mayor in Madrid must have been in the grand old days of Torquemada, confessor of Isabella, first Grand Inquisitor, when six thousand human beings were burnt, while King Ferdinand, bareheaded, sat on a seat lower than Torquemada and looked on. For such *autos-da-fé* (acts of faith) Torquemada was eulogized by Pope Sixtus IV; and from plundered infidel Moors and Jews the Spanish crown derived enormous revenue—for Isabella lied when she swore she had never appropriated the plunder.

Why was Torquemada never canonized? Loyola was—and in the very Plaza where Torquemada had played a rôle that might have fitted Nero. The church had canonized just as bloodthirsty Inquisitors. It inherited saints and even honours many who never lived, but since the twelfth century the pope alone could turn men into gods. Torquemada was zealous enough. He was a "good" man. He died in the conviction that he had "given his best to the service of God." Had the papacy been forced to have a conscience? In the usual pre-canonization trial had the *devil's advocate* been heard too insistently? I do not know; it might have been a factor.

It was not the heretics and infidels roasted to death that robbed Spain of her brains for centuries, or the books destroyed by the Grand Inquisitor, but the final forcible expulsion of a million and a half Jews and Moors. Their brains were not committed to beliefs which automatically closed eyes to a universe begging to be investigated.

"Fanatic" Moslems had tolerated Jews, yet Catholic Christians, before they were firmly seated on the throne, began to persecute and torture them, forcing them into baptism, taking away their books, treating them like dogs. Fanatical Philip II even laid the defeat of the Spanish Armada at their door, and set the machinery in motion which freed Spain not only of the remaining Jews, but also of the Moors. Lope de Vega joined in the national exultation, having already found solace for a personal bereavement in performing the duties of an Inquisitor.

The trouble with twentieth-century Spain is the same as that of sixteenth-century Spain: priest-ridden, no brains needed; paralysis from church and crown tyranny. But Spain again, and in the not distant future, will rejoin the stream of civilization. And we need not be too uncharitable. We have our own Judge Lynch, our Kluxers, our own Daytons—and a witch now and then, to remind us that we too are human. It is not at all certain that we shall never have a Torquemada; it is certain that we have the makings, the raw materials. We certainly have thousands who believe in witches and that the stake is only too good for infidels.

Torquemada was a Dominican—a clerical order of mendicant friars founded by St. Dominic in 1215. Their specialty was scholarship to confute heresy, which began a special career after the year 1000 had come and gone and still no sign of Judgment Day. The disorders in the papacy itself were a heresy-provoking factor. In one period of forty-five years (1003-48) six popes were deposed, two were murdered, and one was mutilated. With the inevitable rise of heresy due to the renaissance of science, the Dominicans reached the height of their power in the fourteenth century—when the devil himself openly stalked abroad, bidding against God for worshippers.

It is probably impossible for us today to visualize a society so utterly morbid, credulous, irrational, and insane as that of the fifteenth century, which made hell so real, the dread of heresy so appalling, the hope of salvation so remote, that thousands in utter despair offered their souls to the devil—redeemer of persecuted humanity; and for promise of pleasure here and now worshipped him in obscene parodies of the mass.

The great church itself had travelled far from its humble beginnings as small, obscure communistic communities practising the cult of Jesus. It had become the most efficiently organized mechanism the world has ever seen. That it assumes today to dictate the length of the dress of a not small fraction of the human race is, after all, but an echo from the age when it assumed nothing, but, on the contrary, ordered the very lives of the people of a continent as nature herself had never ordered them.

Into the making of that machinery went many devices, some extraordinarily clever and ingenious, some diabolical. At these we have already looked. What needs emphasis here, if we are to come within miles of understanding devil-worship and witchcraft, is the atmosphere the church felt it necessary to create to propagate the church. That, of course, is the primary business of every church once it has great vested interests in worldly goods. Propagating the Gospel way of salvation is one thing; propagating the machinery for Gospel salvation is another. That machinery requires an atmosphere of its own.

The forgery of "lives" of miracle-working martyrs was a prime fifth-century industry. But with the decree of the Council of Nice in 787 (reaffirmed by the Council of Trent, 1546) that no church be consecrated without a relic, a new and more profitable industry sprang up. Not only was the very air of the Middle Ages laden with invisible germs; the churches were filled with miracle-working relics and wax-doll saints that could wink and nod their heads. And for every angel hovering about there were legions of *incubi, succubi,* ghosts, vampires, goblins, devils, imps, and grinning gnomes. Swarms of ignorant, fanatical monks stalked across the land; other swarms hived in monasteries capping every habitable hill in Europe. It was not the king's palace or the robber baron's castle that dominated the landscape of superstition's darkest days, but vast monasteries of monks whose ignorance was matched only by their fanaticism.

They so filled the air with goblins and devils, and so earnestly and convincingly told their tales of magic and miracle, that they believed in it all themselves. They were not scoundrels by nature or profession; they were products of their time, and as honest as bootleggers, politicians, and moral censors.

Being products of their time, it was inevitable that they should love God less and fear the devil more—inevitable because they were human beings, animals with strong passions. They did not stop to inquire *how* that fact came about; they only knew that it was all because of Eve and the serpent. Eve was a woman; the serpent was the devil. Women were everywhere; the devil was equally ubiquitous—and more dangerous, because he could assume any shape and be in a thousand places at the same time.

We euphemize God as Nature, Goodness, Law, Spirit, etc., and the devil as guilty conscience, evil desire, flesh, etc., but not so the Middle Ages. God was as real as a pope; the devil, as an inquisitor; and hell, as a red-hot iron on a tender human body.

It was out of that morbid, diseased state of mind that Mariolatry grew up: the cult of the Virgin, Mary-worship. As the devil was the enemy of Mary, when that cult reached its logical climax was the time for the devil to reap his richest harvest. As the Dominicans were specially charged with the propagation of Mariolatry, they became the logical persecutors of witches, the enemies of Mary, especially of women "possessed" by the devil. They had to be hunted out and destroyed before the world could be safe for Mary.

Witchcraft is fundamentally bound up with all religions professing to save souls, dealing with souls, or believing in souls. This or that particular religion may object to my associating souls with witches or vampires or ghosts or evil spirits, but—and this is the point—the "evidence" for witches, vampires, imps, evil spirits, and ectoplasm is just as *conclusive* as is the evidence for souls.

I have at hand an *authority* on witches, vampires, and such figments of credulity. This authority is no other than the Roman Catholic Church itself, in the person of the Reverend Montague Summers—and not of the Middle Ages, but of A.D. 1928. In that year he published a translation of *Malleus Maleficarum* (*Witch's Hammer*), a fifteenth-century manuscript, which he calls one of the most pregnant and interesting books of the kind that deal with eternal things—the eternal conflict of good and evil. I should go further. With the addition of Mr. Summers' preface, it is not "one of" but *the* most pregnant and interesting book I know of for studying the limits of human credulity. An insane asylum is good, but this handsome volume is more easily handled. Besides, it is the very core of a great religion speaking. On its cover *Malleus Maleficarum* bears the magic crossed keys of Peter and the mitre of the Pope. It is the Infallible voice of the Church, the voice of God. What Innocent VIII believed in 1484, Pius XI believed in 1928.

Innocent VIII has heard, says his bull setting witch-trial courts in motion, that:

Many persons of both sexes, unmindful of their own salvation and straying from the Catholic Faith, have abandoned themselves to devils . . . and by their incantations, spells, conjurations, and other accursed charms and crafts . . . have slain infants yet in the mother's womb, as also the offspring of cattle, have blasted the produce of the earth, the grapes of the vine, the fruits of trees, nay, men and women, beasts of burthen, herd-beasts . . . vineyards, orchards, meadows, pasture-land, corn, wheat, and all other cereals. . . . They hinder men from performing the sexual act and women from conceiving, whence husbands cannot know their wives nor wives receive their husbands; over and above this, they blasphemously renounce that Faith which is theirs by the Sacrament of Baptism, and at the instigation of the Enemy of Mankind they do not shrink from committing and perpetrating the foulest abominations and filthiest excesses to the deadly peril of their own souls, whereby they outrage the Divine Majesty and are a cause of scandal and danger to very many.

And let no man harass the Inquisitors, warns the bull, for "upon him will fall the wrath of Almighty God, and of the Blessed Apostles Peter and Paul"—and presumably of the Inquisition itself, which knew well how to make Divine wrath effective here and now.

Innocent's bull was only one of a long record of such papal ordinances. Gregory IX, for example, in 1233, ordered Conrad of Marburg to "proceed against the Luciferians, who were overtly given to Satan." More interesting is a bull of Julius II (1503) with its solemn description of that "abomination" the Black Mass, central feature of worship of Totemists, "unhappily yet celebrated today in London, in Paris, in Berlin, and in many another great city."

Into the Black Mass history we cannot go; but before going on to Kramer we may profitably look at a wafer or two. Peter Browe, for example, has recently shown that the Eucharist was a well-known twelfth-century charm for love and riches, and an antidote against sterility, infection, and sickness, in man and beast; it was also a rain-maker and a wine-improver. In unscrupulous hands—

that is, those leagued with the devil—it was used for poisoning, inducing abortion, etc.; hence it was carefully guarded against sale and theft. Women especially were closely scrutinized when partaking of the Eucharist. During the thirteenth and fourteenth centuries priests and laity were imprisoned or burnt for using the sacrament as a charm. And such "abuse" today—unless a Spanish law of January 1, 1929, has been repealed—exposes one to the danger of from three to six years' imprisonment.

Returning now to Innocent's bull: any denial of its teaching, says Mr. Summers, "must traverse the Gospel accounts of demoniacs, the casting out of devils by our Saviour, and His divine words upon the activities of evil spirits." Of course it must. Innocent had plenty of Gospel grounds for belief in devils—though fewer grounds for roasting devils out of women by fire. Still, there is Exodus xxii, 18, "Thou shalt not suffer a witch to live."

A "divine command," says Mr. Summers. And the Benedictine monks were the proper persons to make the command effective, because St. Benedict's influence over "dark powers" was "remarkable." Even his medal is "extremely potent against all evil spells." Kramer, the Benedictine, charged by Innocent with the special witch inquisition, was a Master of Sacred Theology and distinguished by his zeal. This brings us back to the wafer.

In 1495 Kramer was lecturing in Venice on public worship and the adoration of the Most Holy Sacrament. *Should* this worship be with or without condition? Unconditional, said Kramer; and this is the reason why. A yokel collecting firewood in a copse near Padua found two pyxes ("Host" boxes) which had been stolen three years before from the village church. One pyx had been used to carry the "Lord's body" to the sick; the other, for its exposition on the Feast of Corpus Christi. The yokel reported his find to the priest, who found some Hosts in one of the pyxes.

Well, what does one do when one finds the Lord's body in a copse? Something must be done, that is certain. The priest brought a consecrated altar stone from the church, covered it with linen cloth, and placed the pyx underneath. Then he built a shrine around it. The place was watched, but the news got out, and people brought candles and placed them all around, crying, "Christ's body is here." And the news reached the Bishop of Padua.

Some priests, it seems, protested against the mummery and spoke of idolatry; some even said it was devil-worship. But why *argue* about the "Real Presence?" asks Mr. Summers. To save ambiguity, say "The Blessed Sacrament is God." And that is what Kramer said. The Most Holy Sacrament *is* God and should be worshipped without condition.

We learn further from Mr. Summers that a few saints have actually "seen our God in the Blessed Sacrament"; St. Veronica, for example, "with her bodily eyes." Then there was the Cistercian monk Vaulem, who saw the infant Jesus in the Host, holding a "crown of gold adorned with precious stones." St. Catherine of Siena saw Him under different forms; and even "at the fraction of the Host she saw how He remained entire in each part." And if there is still any doubt, Mr. Summers says that in the Cathedral of Orvieto he himself has "venerated the *Corporale* which is stained with blood that fell from the Host when a young doubting priest was saying Mass."

The somewhat Dark Ages were dark because everybody was in the dark; they were prolonged because even in this day of electric switches it is easier to shut one's eyes than to switch on a light.

Let us now look at Kramer himself, an honest woman-hater if one ever lived. If we are amazed at his misogynous trend, Mr. Summers suggests that he may prove "a wholesome and needful antidote in this feministic age, when the sexes seem confounded." And he quotes approvingly Peter's "Let wives be subject to their husbands . . . as Sarah obeyed Abraham, calling him lord."

Can witches dull generative power or obstruct the venereal act? Can they so contrive sleight-of-hand illusion that the male organ will appear to be entirely removed and separate from the body? Can witches disguised as midwives kill the fœtus and induce abortion; and if not, can they offer newborn babes to devils? What is the remedy for those whose virile member has been conjured away or who seemingly have been transformed into bestial shapes? How pass sentence upon a witch who has been accused by another who has been or is about to be burnt at the stake? How do women copulate with devils? Why are women chiefly addicted to evil superstitions? How can a bewitchment be distinguished from a natural defect? How do witches impede and prevent the power of procreation? How do witches enter the human body without doing any harm? How do they raise hailstorms and stir up tempests? How shall those parts of witches where they conceal devils' masks and tokens be shaved?

Dozens of such questions are solemnly raised and learnedly answered by the author of the *Witch's Hammer*. A world of fact? A bewitched, bedevilled world. And this poor deluded friar solemnly asks how the judges can protect themselves from the spell of a witch! One wonders if they always succeeded. But here is the recipe. Have some salt consecrated on Palm Sunday and some Blessed Herbs about your person, or, better still, "enclose them in Blessed Wax"—an *Agnus Dei*, a wax disc stamped with the figure of a lamb and worn around the neck as a charm.

An Inquisitor from Como "told us last year (1485) he ordered forty-one witches to be burnt after they had been shaved all over." If a witch does not confess the first day or cannot be terrified into telling the truth, she can be tortured the second and third day, or "another day." A preliminary trial by red-hot iron is useful. "We Inquisitors cut off the hair of the head, put a bit of Blessed Wax in a cup of Holy Water, and invoking the Most Holy Trinity, make them drink it three times on a fasting stomach."

Further details of the Third Degree as it was administered by Kramer may give our own civil inquisitors a new idea. "While the officers are preparing to question her, let her be stripped. If she will tell on other witches, she can be sentenced to imprisonment for life on bread and water"—provided the "other witches" are convicted. But she is not to be told that she is to be imprisoned for life— merely that she is to "do some penance." While she is being questioned, let her be frequently exposed to torture; then, if she will not tell, show her other engines of torture.

One is tempted to say: Father, forgive them; for they know not what they do.

It really is a great book. I know no other that takes us so close to the heart of the man of religion who has turned his back on all that is decent and lovable in human nature in order that he may do God's holy will.

Anyone haunted by the fear of being obsessed with a devil may be interested to learn that St. Peter's in Rome has a column from

Solomon's Temple which frees one of devils "because Christ stood near it when he preached." One may even insure oneself, family, and cattle against witches by sprinkling holy water on houses, barns, etc., meanwhile invoking the Most Holy Trinity and saying a Paternoster. Also use a Blessed Candle; and if you cannot light one, sprinkle its wax around the house. Sacred words bound to the body are also marvellously protective—if seven conditions for their use are observed. But the surest insurance for places, men, and animals against witches is to write in four places, in the form of a cross, the words *Jesus, Nazarenus, Rex, Judæorum*. To these add the name of the Virgin Mary and of the Evangelists, or the words of St. John: "The Word was made flesh."

Did the ape that became man possibly pay too dearly for the gift of words?

Kramer does not quote Plato on Logos; he does quote Aristotle on "Alterations"—in the human body. Greatest of these is the influence of the stars: devils cannot interfere with their movements. "This was also the opinion of Dionysus in his Epistle to St. Polycarp!"

Kramer also quotes Ecclesiasticus approvingly: "There is no head above the head of a serpent; and no wrath above the wrath of a woman. I had rather dwell with a lion and a dragon than keep house with a wicked woman." The word "wicked," of course, merely salts the wound. To those sex perverts "wicked" and "woman" were synonymous terms.

Women, says Kramer, are more impressionable than men and hence readier to be influenced by a "disembodied spirit." Women also have "slippery" tongues and are naturally weak; hence they find easy and secret ways of "vindicating" themselves by witchcraft. And, finally, woman is the "more carnal" sex; but she really cannot help that, for she is born crooked. Formed originally from a "bent rib, that is, a rib of the breast, which is bent as it were in a contrary direction to a man"—why, she has been just naturally contrary since the days of Adam.

And so, Kramer concludes, all witchcraft comes from carnal lust —in woman "insatiable." For further proof the reader of the *Hammer* is referred to Proverbs xxx.

St. Dominic is represented as a barking dog with a lighted torch in his mouth; his mother (also a saint) dreamt she had given birth to a dog bearing a lighted torch which was setting the world on fire. "Even to this day," says Kramer, Dominic's barking keeps the heretic wolves from the Christian sheep. But those Dominican witch-inquisitorial dogs did not stop with barking; they bit with red-hot jaws of iron.

One final word about the Reverend Montague Summers, for he is modern, learned, and speaks with the approval of a world power. He is a perfect example of what great "learning" (even in a Sir Oliver Lodge) amounts to when backed by infantile credulity. He typifies the entire crew of modern spiritualists, who can materialize anything from ghosts to ectoplasm. Mr. Summers recently wrote a book on vampires. He believes in vampires; in fact, he has no patience with such former church writers as presumed to be sceptical about them.

How do you know a "vampire" when you see it?

Open the coffin. If the corpse is fat and sleek and the face ruddy as in life, it is a vampire! The eyes will be lit up with a baneful glare; the snarling lips will reveal ivory-white, razor-sharp teeth; and from the mouth clots of blood may be seen to drip. Other evidence of the vampire's horrid feast may even be visible!

In all reality there is nothing so foul as the pictures man paints with words, in all nature nothing so monstrous as what he reads into them.

Our own witch episode has probably received more attention than it deserves. It happened in an age of witches; it was a mere flash in the pan compared with Europe's debauch (in the principality of Trèves alone 6,500 witches were executed); it is one of the few episodes in our history to which no one that I know of has ever pointed with pride.

The simple facts are these. Two West Indian slaves, full of spiritualist tricks and practising fortune-telling and palmistry, met some moron girls at a house near Salem in 1692. The girls were deeply impressed and soon began to act queerly. Encouraged by an equally gullible and superstitious audience, they progressed to spasms, contortions, and the making of funny sounds. They might have gone on in their mad career without attracting great notice had they not begun to shout in church—as though they were possessed! They *must* be possessed! But by whom? They named names, and nineteen human beings were executed for witchcraft; fifty-five more were tortured, and 150 were imprisoned.

Was there no one to protest against this crime? There was; but, said church, law, and education, to question witchcraft is to question the existence of the devil. Such doubters are *atheists*—people who want to lead godless lives and suffer no just retribution.

Belief in supernatural power cannot tolerate, and when in the saddle does not tolerate, honest doubt. The theocratic state pillories honest doubters or burns them at the stake, and sends their souls to hell as atheists or infidels. What should the secular state do with its honest doubters?

Whether a vision will land one in an asylum or among the saints on high depends primarily on time and place. One would like to think this age less gullible and more charitable to its visionaries. We are no doubt more charitable; we no longer torture, hang, or burn witches, nor officially flog those "possessed." Generally speaking, we are humane with idiots, imbeciles, and cranks. But gullibility still stalks about, and occultism, spiritualism, and such mysterious mummeries still thrive. The Society of Jesus still finds lodgment in our midst. In other words, the soil which favoured the growth of supernaturalism in mediæval times is not altogether sterile today; nor will it ever be sterile to such growths until man gets house-broken to the idea that earth is his home and on the whole a most desirable dwelling-place.

## IX

On Friday night, in the dimly lighted refectory of a certain Order, men may be seen on their knees saying grace with outstretched arms. Some are kissing the floor; some are crawling under the table to kiss the bare feet of those seated. Some are confessing the breach of some order and are being punished for their guilt with knotted whipcords.

*Men* I said, not dogs; and of the Society of Jesus—hence known as Jesuits; founded in 1534 by a saint—Ignatius Loyola.

Whenever you meet a man, said Carlyle, "believing in the salutary nature of falsehoods, or the divine authority of things doubtful, and fancying that to serve the good cause he must call the devil to his aid, there is a follower of Un-saint Ignatius." That sentence is quoted from ex-Jesuit Barrett's *The Jesuit Enigma.*

Ignatius—"degraded, ferocious, Human Pig and perfect scoundrel"—should have been decent enough, thinks Carlyle, to consent to be damned, "to cower, silent and ashamed, in some dim corner, and resolve to make henceforth as little noise as possible"; that would have been "modest, salutary." Possibly; but it would not have been saintly or have made Ignatius a god in the Roman Catholic pantheon. And the church was sorely in need of a new kind of soldier; the Reformers were at hand!

So Ignatius left his sword in the monastery of Montserrat (where it may still be seen in the Shrine of Our Lady) and after a night of vigil set out, garbed like a pilgrim, on foot, for Manresa. There in a cave he gave himself up, not to be damned as Carlyle said he should, but to penance and prayer; to the joys and terrors of unrestrained mysticism; to dejections, *élans* of love, visions of peace and horror. He was visited by angels and devils; he contemplated suicide; was distrait, almost crazy with fear of hell, and appalled at the idea of a long life of penance in purgatory. And could see no way out save by perseverance.

He must indeed have been a wicked rake. He had fought the French at Pampeluna, where he was wounded, walking thereafter with a limp. And he had perforce read the life of Christ and *Flowers of the Saints.*

He worked for a while on what was to become his famous *Spiritual Exercises*, and set off for the Holy Land with only his manuscript and a pilgrim's staff. He proved to be a marvellous archæologist, "discovering" Eve's birthplace. On his return he was hailed as a saint; and in Paris, where he received a Master of Arts degree, he secretly organized a little band of followers and at a shrine on Montmartre swore them in (1534). Six years later the Society of Jesus (S.J.) or Order of Jesuits was formally approved by Pope Paul III. One hundred years later, in an official publication, the church claimed that the Virgin in person had dictated *Spiritual Exercises* to Ignatius. If true, she has much to answer for.

In their fundamental doctrine, and as their chief weapon, the Jesuits turned a very old and very human dogma to religious ends. All's fair in love and war, said the world; all's fair in religion, said the Jesuit. Use strategy; lie, cheat, deceive, split hairs, be subtle. Victory is not to be won by love, but by craft and guile.

The church knew all that; the Dominicans used it in their witch trials; but this was the first time in the history of religion, so far as I am aware, that falsehood, craft, and guile were officially recognized (by Paul III's bull, *Regimini Militantis*, 1540), the first time the followers of falsehood were officially organized as a society—of Jesus! The church must have been in desperate straits. It was. The Great Heresy was on. And the soldiers of Ignatius, bound together by oath and under the slogan, *All for the Honour and Glory of God* (A.M.D.G.), marched forth to conquer the world. And without doubt some of them were very fine and noble characters and an honour to the human race.

How does one take *spiritual* exercise? There are many ways: the Christian Scientist's is one; the Indian Yogi's is another. Here is the Jesuit way. The exercitant is to imagine:

the length, breadth, and depth of hell; to see its vast fires and souls enclosed in fiery bodies; to hear the lamentations, howlings, exclamations, and blasphemies against Christ and his saints; to smell the smoke, brimstone, and stench of a kind of sink of filth and putrefaction. Also to taste those most bitter things, tears, rottenness, the worm of conscience. To touch those fires which burn the souls. And in meditating on the Passion, to ask for grief, anxiety, and other inward pains that he may suffer together with Christ suffering; by inward touch to handle and kiss the garments, places, footsteps, etc.

One may win spiritual exaltation, says Barrett, by mere contemplation: not by sitting cross-legged contemplating one's navel like a Hindu Brahman, but by kneeling on the ground, lying on the face or back, or by sitting or standing and composing oneself in the way in which one may hope most easily to attain one's desires. Keep that up long enough, and one can get, day by day, crazier and crazier in every way.

A Jesuit also eats by rule; he is to be so abstracted that he neither sees, smells, nor tastes his food. Upon woman, that "limb of Satan," he must look with profound distrust mingled with fear and contempt. "Our enemy the Devil," says the Constitution of Ignatius, "resembles the nature and habit of woman in puniness of force and obstinacy of spirit." Ignatius must have had a mother; one wonders what he will have to say to her in heaven—or are there no women in his heaven?

David was Yahweh's prophet. The Jesuit wears David's cloak, and thereby becomes the Almighty's prophet, the Messiah's selected companion, the predestined one—self-righteous, unbending, stiff-necked, arrogant. That is what Barrett says, and he has lived with them. A Jesuit abroad is so modest in the eyes of heaven that he is supposed to put on calico knickers when he takes a shower bath. Why not a step-in of lead—or are Heaven's eyes less sharp than X-rays?

Spiritual Exercises *may* be a contribution to religious life, but "they cause in the hearts of hundreds of thousands an immense wilderness of misery, depression, and weariness of soul." Barrett also speaks of "the tragic holocaust of fine young men, the continual sacrifice of generations on the altar of Jesuitism."

How remote—in gentleness, in decency, in everything that makes the human race admirable and worthy of respect—seems St. Ignatius. And what more damning commentary could be made on the Order of Jesuits than the mere citing of the facts that four popes tried to get rid of it, that it was banished *from Spain* in 1767, dissolved in Portugal in 1773, and even dissolved by the White Pope himself in 1773.

Even as early as 1741, Benedict XIV, for the better control of those "disobedient, contumacious, captious, and reprobate persons," had enacted stringent laws. But an Order founded on guile is not so frail; it has more lives than a cat. It was restored in 1814, to be again expelled from Russia, Switzerland, Portugal, and France, repressed in England, and banned in Germany. It still lives, even in England and Germany, and in this country numbers over four thousand. Its Black Pope (as the head of the Order is called) still rules an *imperium in imperio*; and, clever psychologists that they are, no other Order of the church has known so well how to lighten human chains that human beings might the more effectively be subdued.

No Order today does more to bring religion down to the worship of what Reinach calls white idols with gold, pink, and blue. The Jesuit trinity of Jesus, Mary, and Joseph is far fitter for morons than that of the old immaterial Father, Son, and Holy Ghost.

Under Jesuit influence Pius IX raised Joseph above Peter and

Paul as patron saint; he likewise instituted the Feast of the Sacred Heart of Jesus, worship of which had been sanctioned by Pius VI. The Jesuits proposed the adoration of the actual heart of Jesus; Pius IX again approved. Painted hearts appeared, and in 1875 a basilica was begun at Montmartre, Paris, dedicated to the Sacred Heart.

And all because a simple-minded girl in 1675 "confessed" to a Jesuit that she not only *saw* the bleeding heart of Jesus, but *exchanged hearts with Him*. From such puerilities grow great cults— and great basilicas, in Paris, in New York—in this age of science, some four hundred years after the Reformation.

## x

In my strongly anti-Catholic community I imbibed the belief that Catholics worship idols and Protestants God—all because Luther and the other Reformers had screened idolatry and other useless and ungodly dross out of Christianity, leaving only the pure gold of salvation. I also got the impression that the worth-while in our civilization was in some way hitched up with the Reformation. Luther was second only to Christ as a world-saviour.

The argument ran something like this. To a world sunk in solid sin and dense ignorance Christ came, and sacrificed himself for our sins. But the wicked Catholics had taken salvation out of Christ's hands, and the world again was no fit place for a decent Christian. The Reformation reformed the world, made it safe for Christians, and in the long run everybody would become Christian, including, possibly, the Catholics.

It was all rather hazy, but on two points I had strong convictions: that Protestants alone were "true" Christians, alone would be saved; that the Reformation had saved the world, our part of it alone being worth saving. Still, one ought to try to save the heathen. It was then that I decided on China.

Of the early long sermons I had to listen to, sitting on a hard bench, I recall next to nothing but "justification," "grace," "sin," and "baptism." Baptism washed sins away; one was justified by faith, hence was in good "grace." But suppose one fell from grace! Well, that was, and is, a big question in many churches, but as Christianity started as communities of saints, the question did not at once arise. Through baptism they had had their sins washed away; that saved them: they were saints. But flesh sometimes prevails. Now and then a saint would fall by the wayside, or rather fall from grace; more specifically, commit murder, adultery, fornication, or bow down to some particularly attractive idol. Those were grave sins and meant expulsion from the community of saints. But could one not be saved a *second* time? Was there no way by which one could climb back to grace? Yes, said the church; by a contrite heart and proving contriteness by doing an act of penance.

That "yes" was one of the most momentous decisions the church ever made. It started two things: it turned the community of saints into a community of human beings; it opened the way to penances. From these two things there grew up during the Middle Ages the loveliest system imaginable. There was ancient and widespread precedent for this system—in effect this: if I kill your wife or child, I may compound the murder or recompense you for the damage done to your property by paying you so many hogs, sheep, cattle, horses, or other commodities. The church took over that principle and fitted it to the times and circulating media.

This is how it worked. I am "saved," let us say. I commit a sin, which damns me forever. But I do not want to be eternally damned, so I repent, am contrite. How can I prove it? By confessing my sin and doing penance—giving alms to the poor, for example. But will God forgive me? "Yes," says the church; "if *I* ask him—and I will if you pay me."

It was a great system and I have already acknowledged its merit as a go-getter. The system reached perfection when it had developed a technique for committing sinless murder, or for "indulging" sins father had committed but which he hadn't time to do penance for before his throat was cut. It got to the point where one could buy absolution for blasphemy, treachery, murder, any form of crime or moral unscrupulousness.

There were causes for the *protest* against the church other than the mere sale of indulgences; otherwise the Reformation could not have succeeded, for the church was enormously powerful and had the machinery to crush the life out of any mere reformer.

That machinery, however, was odious to rulers, and especially were the Germans tired of Rome's eternal meddling in their temporal affairs. *Money flies over the Alps!* What was the good of kings ruling by divine right if Rome claimed exclusive power to interpret divinity? Then, too, the church was a gross caricature of Christianity; it was thoroughly selfish, despotic, opulent, corrupt to the core. The masses groaned under the priests' squeeze; the secular clergy resented Rome's exactions and the dominance of the various monkish Orders; the knights were jealous of the worldly rich abbots; and the princes feared and hated Rome's interference. The Germans especially wanted a place in the sun. The Reformation was a German reaction against Romanism.

It was also an age of devil-phobia and religious pessimism; an age of intolerance; an age which could produce a *Witch's Hammer*, a Luther, a Calvin, and an Ignatius Loyola. Then, too, Luther was an Augustinian, not a Dominican, friar; otherwise the church might be selling indulgences today in Dayton, Tennessee.

Funds, large funds, were needed to build the largest church in Christendom—St. Peter's, Rome. The job of raising funds in Germany was entrusted to German Dominican monks—under the pretext that the funds were to be used in a holy war against Turkey, astride the Bosporus since 1453. Possibly the Augustinians were jealous of the Dominicans.

Martin Luther was the son of a miner of Eisleben. He became school-teacher, monk, priest; had visited Rome and had been made a Doctor of Theology; and was professor of theology in Wittenberg University. For him, learning was the handmaid of theology.

In 1517 Tetzel, a Dominican monk, arrived in Luther's town and began peddling indulgences. "How soon will the donations take the soul of the damned out of hell?"

> *"Sobald das Geld im Kasten klingt,*
> *Die Seele aus dem Fegfeuer springt"*

is said to have been the reply Tetzel preached from the pulpit— just as soon as the coin jingles in the box! And that was the little spark that was to touch off the great Protestant Reformation.

At any rate, Luther (October 31) nailed upon the door of the Wittenberg court church a fulmination (answer) in ninety-five arguments, not against indulgences, but against the *abuse* of indulgences.

War followed: a word-war between Augustinian and Dominican monks. Leo X anathematized both houses. Luther answered with his *Captivity of Babylon*, which had nothing to do with Babylon, but much with the business of mass and *transubstantiation*—"a word not to be found in the Scriptures"!

Leo answered with a bull, which Luther burned in public in Wittenberg (December, 1520), writing a good-bye note: "Little Pope, little Popelet, you are an ass, a little ass."

That note, had Luther not had powerful backing, would have been his last. But he had—Frederic the Wise, Elector of Saxony. Frederic carried Luther off to a Saxon fortress in Wartburg, where he lived as Junker Georg and began his translation of the Bible. But even with Frederic's support Luther could hardly have survived had not the German Emperor, Charles V, had to leave Germany on business of war against Francis I of France. Denmark, Sweden, and other German states embraced Luther's doctrine, which he had introduced into public worship in Wittenberg and which the Diet of Worms (1521) had forbidden. At a diet at Spier in 1529 the Catholics tried to make the Worms Diet decree effective, but fourteen cities and several priests *protested* against this resolution—and that made the Reformation Protestant.

Luther died in 1546, and the Emperor again tried to crush the Protestants. But in 1552, by the Convention of Passau, they were formally conceded religious liberty. And Charles in disgust tore a page from Diocletian's life and resigned his German Empire to his brother Ferdinand, and his Spanish Empire to his son Philip— the same Philip II who watched infidels roast at Madrid's *autos-da-fé*, the same Philip who lost Spain's hold on the Netherlands in their war of liberation.

It must have been a blow to the pride of Charles V, for while he was a "good" man, even "clement beyond example," he was passionately devoted to the maintenance of the True Religion, and had decreed that every heretic should be beheaded, burnt, or buried alive. And that was the fate of over fifty thousand of his subjects in Holland.

While God reveals himself less spectacularly to Protestants than to Catholics, as Robinson says, he reveals himself no less convincingly. No pope had assumed a more authoritative tone in matters of dogma and practice than did Luther. He even presumed to do what no pope since Gregory had done: authorize the Landgrave of Hesse to marry a second wife while his first was still living. That second marriage might have been justifiable on many grounds; Luther did not authorize it on ethical or any other grounds which come within the realm of human mundane relations, but on supernatural grounds.

There was just as much religion in Europe with Luther as without, and as much superstition; but there was no more freedom of thought, and certainly no more disposition to read the Bible with a calm and critical eye. There were two voices of authority now where there was one before, and Luther was as certain his was *the* voice as the church was certain of its authority. *In fact, the old church had itself produced more efficient critics of its dogmas and doctrines than Luther ever was.*

The most Luther did was to eliminate certain mechanisms the church had found useful and profitable in capturing the simple-minded and in consoling widows and failures. And he did start an argument, which the church itself calmly ignores: that of masses, indulgences, pilgrimages, purgatory, wonder-working relics, and the papa-ship of the Bishop of Rome, the Apostles knew nothing, the Gospels say nothing.

Having eliminated these frills from his worship, there were to be fewer side-shows, more solemnity, in the big tent. No more mass, no pilgrimages, no more worship of relics, veneration of saints, no Mariolatry. But heaven was brought no nearer, nor hell pushed farther off; nor was the devil whitewashed, abolished, or his potency in any way impaired. Nor has the devil yet entirely parted company with Protestant literature; in fact, many Protestant sects quarrel with other sects for not getting more hell into their sermons. The number of saved and damned in the Presbyterian Confession of Faith is so certain and definite that it cannot be either "increased or diminished."

Faith, faith; justification by faith alone. Decency, playing the game, behaving like a thoroughbred, minding one's own business, keeping one's hand out of others' pockets: nothing saves one from sin but faith. What is sin? The devil. How does one get rid of the devil? By baptism. Baptism today, whether total immersion or a drop, is either a sacrament for purification from sin, an exorcism for casting out devils, as it was for Luther—or it is hocus-pocus.

Protestants in general nowadays soft pedal the devil and are inclined to euphemize sin, but the God they worship is a Trinity, and if they have no saints to worship they still have angels to believe in; in fact, their religion is no more monotheistic than was Ikhnaton's or the Stoics'. The difference between an ordinary Christian praying to one heavenly power, and a Stoic praying to the gods, is primarily linguistic and secondarily ethic: the Christian wants to be saved; the Stoic wanted to be worth saving.

In other words, the Reformation was in no sense an ethical reform, and it could not have succeeded had there not been church lands, enormous estates, to seize. Why hadn't the German princes seized the church lands before? Hadn't thought of it. The church could still excommunicate; the fires of hell were as hot as ever—possibly never so hot. But Luther and the other Reformers—as did Huss in Bohemia—so clearly formulated the outrageous pretensions of the church that they found the courage they needed to gratify their pent-up covetousness and avarice. It was greed that won in England, not an ethical reform. Scotland imitated Henry VIII's policy, and at the end of her Reformation the church estates had simply passed out of Roman dominion into the hands of a needy nobility.

Just when are plunder and murder and roasting human beings alive justifiable in the sight of the Lord? *Reformation* sounds well; but just what or who was reformed?

Luther set up a paper pope; hated tolerance as the devil hates holy water; was as devout in his belief in witches as Kramer; had as much regard for sweet reason as Dowie; and less use for Copernican astronomy than the pope himself. His Christianity asked the poor man to submit to despotism and tyranny. For the tolerance of Erasmus he had only harsh epithets: Godless, slanderer of Christ, an Epicurean, greatest knave alive. His Reformation succeeded because it was backed by promoters: princes, rulers who were promoting their own interests. Between his Bibliolatry and Rome's Mariolatry, speaking personally, Mary wins.

Justification by faith alone, said Luther. "We see, then, how rich a Christian or baptized man is, since even if he would, he cannot lose his salvation by any sins, however great, unless he refuses to believe; for no sins whatever can condemn him but unbelief alone." Of course Luther could dispense with most of the sacraments of the Catholic faith and all the gaudy trimmings of the Catholic Church. Salvation needed no more of that, nor even works fit for repentance. Have faith; belief alone saves. It was so simple, so easy. "Little popelet, you are an ass, a little ass!"

Five years after the Evangelical Estates had protested against the execution of the decree of the Worms Diet that Luther be driven from the German Empire, two Saxon priests had a burst of inspiration. Jesus, they said, was not baptized when a child, but only after he had grown up. Should not children be rebaptized? Their point was well taken; so well, that they thought they were warranted in preaching a holy war against those who did not rebaptize—Lutherans and Roman Catholics. That preachment was especially acceptable to the peasants all the way from Saxony to Lorraine, and led to what is known as the Peasants' War. Did Luther show any sympathy for the peasants? Not a drop. And they were destroyed—150,000 of them. And, said Luther, they *deserved* death of body and soul *many times over*! "Let there be no pity; it is the time of wrath, not of mercy. Princes can better merit heaven by bloodshed than by prayers."

Luther fulminated against transubstantiation. Well, what did he do with the communion mystery? He retained half of it. The Catholics ate God without bread; Luther ate God and bread. But Zwingli went still further. He declared that God was in neither bread nor wine; that is, that the Eucharist is a brotherly meal and not a magic performance.

Calvinists got their name as Americans get theirs, by a fluke. It was Zwingli who instigated the Reformation in Switzerland, not Calvin, and in 1518, the year after Luther nailed up his thesis. Zwingli was a parish priest in Zurich, a follower of Erasmus and the most open-minded of all the Reformationists. His followers soon included not only Zurich, but Berne as well. Lucerne and four other cantons waged war against Zurich and Berne. Zwingli fell in battle, whereupon the Catholics quartered and burnt his body.

Calvin, a young Catholic pastor in Picardy, had resigned and settled in Paris to preach reform under the protection of Margaret of Navarre, sister of Francis I. But in 1535 he was exiled from France, went to Basle, Switzerland, and thence to Geneva, where in 1553 he treacherously and malignantly murdered Servetus—largely because the latter in editing Ptolemy's *Geography* had said that Judea was not "flowing with milk and honey" but was a barren and meagre land. That, said Calvin, "inculpated Moses and outraged the Holy Spirit." Even ten years after Servetus had been burnt to death Calvin called him a "dog and a wicked scoundrel." Had Calvin been pope, Galileo would not have escaped with a mere recantation.

From Geneva the Reformation spread to France and to Scotland —*via* John Knox, who had been a refugee with Calvin. Knox was a real honest Calvinist; he was among the first to clamor for the head of Mary, Queen of Scots. His one paramount ethical ideal was the murder of every Catholic in Scotland.

The Reformation did not begin in England; it just was—by the Act of Supremacy, 1534. All because Henry VIII fell in love with sweet-sixteen, black-eyed Anne Boleyn, maid of honour to his wife, Catherine of Aragon, aunt of Charles V. A passing love-affair, as Voltaire said, had done what neither Peter's Pence, sale of indulgences, nor five hundred years of extortions could effect.

In marrying Catherine, Henry had already violated a church rule—for she was the widow of his older brother—but had been granted a papal dispensation. Now that he wanted to divorce her—because the marriage had been a "sin" and never had been "legal" —it was asking too much to expect the church to annul the marriage. Besides, the pope did not dare risk angering Charles V. He did suggest, however, that Henry follow Abraham's example and have two wives. Henry rejected that in favour of Cromwell's idea and became head of his own church. He married Anne, got his divorce, and as the representative of God plundered the church shamelessly.

In 1521 Leo X had given Henry the title of "Defender of the Faith" for his absurd and ridiculous thesis *Assertion of the Seven Sacraments* (in reply to Luther). Excommunicated by Pope Clement VII in 1531, he assumed the title "Protector and Only Supreme Head of the Church and Clergy of England."

Henry's Reformation was no more "Protestant" than Ignatius'

*Spiritual Exercises.* It was Henry's own Reformation, by Henry, for Henry. It reformed nothing, nor pretended to. It did confiscate the vast wealth of the abbeys, and made it a capital offence to be a Protestant or to believe in the pope. He had three persons burnt at the stake for denying transubstantiation and refusing sacrament at Easter, and on the same day executed three papists for loyalty to the pope. His treatment of Cardinal Wolsey and Sir Thomas More was typical of this heartless, brutal despot.

Henry's daughter, Mary Tudor, wife of Philip II of Spain, was a rabid Catholic and cruelly persecuted Protestants, burning three hundred of them, including Bonner, Ridley, Latimer, and Cranmer. I infer that Froude thought Cranmer merited his fate, for he said he knew nothing good of him except that he burnt well.

Meanwhile, during the reign of Henry's son, Edward VI, parliament had established uniformity in religious service, introduced a prayer-book, and published a Confession of Faith in forty-two articles. That prayer-book (1553) is the foundation of Anglican worship; and that its recent revision did not lead to bloodshed, if not to revolution, is evidence that the world has moved.

Elizabeth, daughter of Anne Boleyn (executed for adultery), had to be a Protestant or a bastard, for the church had not recognized Henry's marriage to Anne. She completed (1563) the establishment of the Anglican Church—Church of England or Episcopal Church, as it is called—and adopted thirty-nine of the forty-two articles of Edward's (Cranmer's) Confession of Faith.

As the Irish stuck to the old faith, Elizabeth forced Anglican priests into Irish parishes; and with that the trouble began. Protestants, to the Irish, have been synonymous with oppressors ever since.

While Elizabeth's Episcopal Church was essentially Protestant in dogma, it was really Catholic in hierarchy and cult—so Catholic, in fact, that it met much opposition; hence the "Non-Conformists" or "Dissenters." Among these was a little band of Puritans.

James I, first of the four Stuarts, had been brought up as a Protestant in Scotland, but was strong on the divine right of kings and of bishops—"No bishop, no king!" His politics and religion were all mixed up. Dissenters were no longer allowed to dissent in peace; in fact, so great was the pressure on them that three hundred

Puritan clergymen gave up their jobs, and in 1607-08 about a thousand extremists, led by their minister John Robinson, left England and settled in Leyden, Holland, becoming known as "Pilgrims." Twelve years later, nineteen families of that congregation (102 individuals), under a patent of the London Company of South Virginia, sailed from Plymouth, England, for Hudson's River. Winter overtook them on the Massachusetts coast, and there they settled (1620) with all their austerity and an incredibly large amount of furniture and crockery for a ship so small as the *Mayflower*. And that place is called Plymouth, the Holy Land of the New World.

Shortly after James I came to the throne, forty-seven ministers of the Established Church began a work which was completed in 1611 and which is now known as the King James Version of the Bible.

John Milton possibly, John Bunyan certainly, were Baptists—an early sect of dissenters. They were against infant baptism, for total immersion, and had no use for bishops, military service, or oaths. It was possibly the only sect in Christendom in which an early Christian would have felt at home.

Wesley, an eloquent Puritan preacher, about 1740 began a series of revival meetings in England with his friend Whitefield. It was essentially a revolt against materialistic eighteenth-century ungodliness and freethinking; but inasmuch as dissenting preachers had for eighty years been arguing that the only *method* of reaching happiness was by being virtuous, Wesley was called a "Methodist."

An offshoot of Methodism in origin is the Salvation Army, founded in London in 1872 but so called only since 1878. It is, as its name implies, military in organization, and as it is without sectarian bias, can devote itself exclusively to the Lord's business.

Of the many deranged mystics of the seventeenth century, Swedenborg probably has had the greatest influence. He talked with Jesus, Paul, and Luther; had even been "instructed concerning the state of souls after death." He was the official herald of the second coming of Christ.

The story of our own Smith, the pedlar, to whom an angel made revelations and presented gold-inscribed plates, is too well known to be retold here. We may observe, however, two things. Smith's martyrdom (1844) was an important factor in the survival of the grandiose delusions of a paranoiac. "Mormons" are *Mormons* because Mormon, a descendant of Joseph the Patriarch, settled on these shores in 600 B.C.; Joseph was a polygamist, hence polygamy.

Smith was a clumsy plagiarist, his Messianic revelation a palpable fraud; and where on earth but in America, Land of the Free and Home of the Brave, could a disciple of such a faked religion in thirty years build a cult that could defy a nation, and amass seventeen wives, fifty-six children, and two million dollars? Brigham Young picked the right place and the right time for his mundane existence. He rates high in America's galaxy of go-getters in the Lord's name

## XI

Protestant Puritan England reached American shores in 1620— to find Catholics on the north and Catholics on the south. In fact, it was Roman Catholics rather than Protestants who discovered and conquered America. And look at America today—or at Boston. But also look at Dayton—or at our *ante bellum* South, with its Protestant Christian clergy justifying Negro slavery because Noah had cursed Ham's line for having made light of an old man's drunken spree. That meant slavery by act of God and not as the result of savage warfare, and that the one supreme moral duty of the slave was blind and abject obedience. It was not a crime to fight for freedom; it was a sin—a sin against God.

The Reformation did do one thing—it reformed the popes. The papacy after the Reformation may not have been so strong-minded or so strong-armed as before, but the popes themselves were more respectable.

The Catholic Church itself even made a show of cleaning house. A great Council was convened at Trent in 1545, which lasted nearly twenty years. It did not put an end to the sale of indulgences; it did make the confessional-box obligatory. It also defined original sin and made marriage inviolable—which helped suffering humanity not at all. Nor did it do anything to end invoking saints or venerating relics; in fact, it anathematized anyone who rejected such props to salvation or doubted or denied purgatory or the validity of indulgences.

The church did have the new Order of Jesuits to make religion more palatable to the masses, and once they had accepted, to get a firmer hold over them. Sinners frightened away from sin by Luther's narrow road could be human now and then and still count on salvation. It was the business of the Jesuits to get around frail yet hopeful humanity. The church regained some of its lost ground—South Germany, Poland, parts of Switzerland and France. It had nothing to regain in Spain because the Inquisition had performed nobly, as it had in Italy.

The Sorbonne in 1521 had condemned Luther and his writings, and two years later the works of Erasmus; and had proclaimed that the "impious and shameless arrogance of heretics must be restrained by chains, by censures, nay, by fire and flame, rather than confuted by argument." Despite the fact, however, that the university and the clergy were against the Reformation, the time came when it began to look as though the crown of France might fall into the hands of a prince of the Reformation. So Pope Pius V wrote the young French king, Charles IX, son of Catherine de' Medici, to exterminate the Protestants, as the Albigenses had been exterminated three centuries before.

The result was the Huguenot Wars, which, beginning 1562, lasted thirty-six years. In the St. Bartholomew massacre in 1572 over three thousand were murdered in Paris alone, and in France over thirty thousand in one night. With the Edict of Nantes, 1598, the Huguenots, who had become a political party as well as a Protestant religion, were given full political, and certain religious, rights. The Edict was at best a pious fraud and had been forced on the Bourbon king, Henry IV, who had been a Protestant but had done penance and been freed from the papal ban. He had to end the war to save his crown and his country. Civil war was ruining France.

Just the same, the Edict marked a new deal in European politics, a deal that was not made really effective until our own nation started without a state religion. Thus far, the Reformation had nowhere overthrown the insidious alliance between religion and government. It had simply replaced a religion centred in Rome by national churches: Luther in Germany, Zwingli in Switzerland, Arminius in Holland, Calvin in Geneva and France, and Knox in Scotland. The English Church also had supported the monarchy, cultivated reverence for authority, and persecuted Puritans, Anabaptists, Quakers, and independents in general. Nowhere yet had the Reformation made for religious tolerance or for freedom of thought; it had made for nationalism.

Returning to France, we have to note that the Jesuits were insidiously working away at their business and had been steadily gaining ground in numbers and influence. With the third Bourbon king, Louis XIV, their ascendancy over the crown was complete. On their advice and under their pressure, the Edict of Nantes was revoked, in 1685: no more *reformed* religion in France; children *must* be educated in the Catholic faith; and no emigration from France.

In 1767 France was to drive the Jesuits from the country and be revenged for this monstrous advice, but the results of that Revocation were staggering—as fateful for France in one way as had been the expulsion of the Jews from Spain. Protestant pastors were banished, their churches demolished, their worship outlawed. Within three years more than fifty thousand families had fled. France had lost her most liberal brains; military leaders, including Schomberg; men of letters; and especially her artificers, who enriched Holland, Prussia, England, and Switzerland. For seventeen years this cruel persecution was kept up. And had Catholic Europe not provoked Bohemia to revolt on behalf of Protestant Europe, no Thirty Years' War would have been begun in 1618, Germany would not have been ruined for two hundred years, nor France elevated to the highest rank as a European power.

Louis XIV was a great king, no doubt, but he was to live to see Marlborough victorious over his army at Ramillies—and after the disaster to ask: "Has God forgotten all that I have done for Him?" Eighty-seven years after that, another Bourbon Louis (XVI) was to be executed by his people. Had there been no Revocation of the Edict of Nantes, there possibly would have been no French Revolution.

## XII

One of the stupidest experiments of the French Republic was to abolish God. Napoleon, however, found God useful in his business; indeed, one might say, parodying James I, it was with him, No God, no Emperor. We certainly can say, No Divinity, no King by Divine Right. But there is no justification for saying, No God, no civilization; or, No Christianity, no civilization.

Civilization is inherent in man himself. The form it takes is dependent on historic factors, on psychological elements. Some of the clearest thinkers known to history were born ages before Christ; just as there were civilizations in Rome, Greece, Crete, Egypt, and across Asia from Palestine to Japan, before Christianity. Civilization is no more inherent in Christianity than it is in Shintoism or Buddhism or Judaism or socialism.

"We have practised the Christian religion," said a French cynic a hundred years ago, "for nearly two thousand years; suppose we now try the religion of Christ." Well, suppose we do? Suppose you or I tried literally to follow the teachings of Christ as set forth in the Gospels? Such an effort might land us in heaven; it certainly would not land us in any church or office or college that I know of; it probably would land us in the poorhouse, if not in jail or in an asylum. For if the Gospel of Christ means anything, it is that we shall keep out of church, give our earthly goods to the poor, refuse to fight, and suffer adulterers to live. It is not necessary to suppose, like Stead, that Christ come to Chicago. Suppose he came to any city in the Christian world: would that prince of outcasts feel more at home among Rotarians or with the Salvation Army? I think it highly conceivable that he would find Trinity Church as worthy of rebuke as the banks of the money-lenders which line the street that Christian church overlooks.

There may be a difference of opinion whether Wall Street or the White House more appropriately symbolizes our Christian civilization, but it seems fairly certain that Christ would find himself as dead set against both as he was against the established order of his own day. It is not certain that Christ's fate today would be what the Gospels claim it was nineteen hundred years ago, but if he were to appear in person on the floor of the Stock Exchange or in the White House grounds and begin to preach, he certainly would be arrested, tried, and convicted of disorderly conduct, disturbing the peace, and being a public nuisance. A fourth conviction—in New York at least—would carry a life penalty; for, like the ancients, we Christians still try crimes, instead of living human beings who may or may not be criminals.

But all this is bootless. Christ himself, if he was anything, was what we should today call a "poor nut." The Christ the Gospels give us and whom we are asked to believe in was an artifact, a human product, and quite as bizarre as the men who created him. The divinity that inheres in him is the divinity that inheres in every supernatural wonder-worker—no more, no less.

To call ourselves "Christians" and to style our brand of civilization "Christian" is to say nothing more than that we have joined a church and that we are members of a civilization which finds Christianity useful in the same sense that Napoleon found God useful. So useful is it that we unblushingly pass it on from one generation to another, playing upon mother-love to make it efficacious. That was the hypocrisy Tolstoy denounced: "the infamous lie of a religion in which we do not believe ourselves, but which we forcibly impose on others."

Therein is the curse of every religion which gets its hands on power. Christianity, before it was three centuries old, became the most powerful single social engine on earth. Some of that power has been torn from its hands, but that it will ever voluntarily relinquish any of its power is more than we may expect of any mortal man who, like the Hebrew prophet or Fundamentalist preacher, can give vent to his sadism by calling cruelty "justice," and crush intelligent scepticism•by calling it infidelity or treason.

One has to hear with one's own ears or read with one's own eyes in a reputable paper that a certain amendment to our Constitution was "born of God," before one could believe anybody actually said it.

Religion is a disease. It is born of fear; it compensates through hate in the guise of authority, revelation. Religion, enthroned in a powerful social organization, can become incredibly sadistic. No religion has been more cruel than the Christian. Again and again it has raised its hands in protest against atrocities—but has it ever turned a hand to put an end to any one atrocity or social injustice? Has it diminished crime, stayed war; does it rate sincerity above hypocrisy, respect the conscientious objector, insist that treaties be kept in spirit and in truth, or hesitate to be the servile slave of any avaricious ruler or despotic power? To what church could a single oppressed minority today appeal for sympathy and understanding?

The Hebrew prophet knew right from wrong and had no trouble in getting Yahweh's approval of his brand of righteousness. Our Christian reformers show no less conceit in their pronouncements. Why should they, when they can quote Acts xv: 28: "For it seemed good to the Holy Ghost and to us"? What is the test today in ethics, morality, and all matters involving social behaviour— human happiness, justice, and fair play, or the approval of the church? It is not enough for one to be curious about this earth and to try to know oneself and one's fellow-beings so as to get along with them and live sanely and happily; instead, one must learn the will of God. And how does one learn that will? Not by reason, at any rate; for reason, said Luther, is a pretty harlot, and would blind us to the great truths of God as revealed in the Bible. But *whose* Bible—Luther's, the Protestant's, or the Catholic's?

May I again point out, as did Gibbon, that in substituting the Pauline doctrine of original sin, redemption, faith, grace, and predestination, for transubstantiation, Protestantism did nothing to lessen the socially destructive evils of authoritative religion. Was theocracy ever more brazen than under Laud and his Star Chamber? No pope could have made the Scottish princes tremble as did John Knox. Calvin out-poped the pope. And at the cry of "No popery" in England, every Catholic in the land trembled for his home, every priest for his life.

Religion is mysticism, supernaturalism, or it is nothing that need be called religion. There is no fundamental difference between Christian religion and any other anthropomorphic religion whose God is the image of the superman man would like to be. Belief in an ancient myth is no longer a valid substitute for such an understanding as we must have of this world if we are to enjoy and master it; nor will it fit us to mind our own business and keep our hand busy in socially useful activities to be always lifting it in supplication to some mystery we are afraid of.

Just think over calmly the demands Christianity makes on human reason and understanding: we children of wrath and sin are born under God's curse; God sacrificed his Son, Christ, as an atonement for our sins—but not unless we believe and are baptized. Having professed our belief and been baptized, we can sing, with Thomas of Celano:

> With thy favored sheep, O place me;
>   Nor among the goats abase me;
> But to thy right hand up-raise me.
>
> While the wicked are confounded,
>   Doomed to flames of woe unbounded,
> Call me, with thy saints surrounded.

Otherwise we burn forever in a brimstone lake.

Kimball Young, after examining nearly three thousand hymns used in Christian churches, found, as might be expected, that the majority deal with regression to infancy and with future reward. About sixteen per cent deal with sin, redemption, and purification; eight per cent exult over the blessings of redemption in the sweet by and by. Some fifteen per cent are definitely founded on struggling inferiority complexes—sadistic and masochistic projections being about equal. But deepest of all motives is that of coördinating unrequited infantile wishes with adult reality.

In other words, Christian hymns, like all religious rituals and rites, perform the definite function of *pacifiers*. They say in effect: Never mind if you are poor and lowly now; you will be rich and exalted hereafter. This life is but an empty dream anyhow—all vanity and delusion; it is the life eternal that counts, that is real. We may not be happy, but we can be good; we may suffer, but we need not be evil. We may be as spineless as jellyfish, but we can feel very brave as we unite in singing "Onward, Christian Soldiers," or as we "praise the Lord" in that less familiar hymn:

> The Son of God goes forth to war,
>   A kingly crown to gain:
> His blood-red banner streams afar:
>   Who follows in his train?
>
> Who best can drink his cup of woe,
>   Triumphant over pain,
> Who patient bears his cross below,
>   He follows in his train.

That Christianity has cheered countless weak and faltering human beings there is, of course, no doubt. Nor, I think, is there any doubt that religion, especially Christianity, makes for weakness and then plays the added rôle of supplying artificial crutches for weakness. The net result is that the Fundamentalist, the "true" Christian, hell-bent on possessing the Kingdom of God, has neither time nor inclination to try to understand this world or make it safe to live and love in. Believing as he does that we are here today and gone tomorrow, why should he bother about it? Why should he worry about the pain, suffering, and poverty, the monstrous social injustice, and the palpable breakdown of law and order, which surround him on every side, when nothing matters but the salvation of his own soul—and he can win that by mere faith? As a matter of fact, few Fundamentalists do worry much about such things, but they are human and some of them swell up like frogs over the power they find they can exert over their fellow-men.

We may not know what Goodness is; we do know when we are happy. We may not know what Evil is; we do know when we are in pain. We also think we know what makes for happiness in general among human beings, and what makes for suffering and distress. Further, it does seem to me that the most fundamental problems of this and every other nation today are how to increase happinesss and health, how to lessen suffering and distress. But I do not find that any church is tackling these two vital problems. I do find the Catholic Church agitating itself over and dictating fashions in clothes and taste in art, and taking a dictatorial tone in the most intimate relations between men and women. I do find the Protestant Church meddling in politics and resorting to the ethics of hijackers.

That one church does not burn women for showing their calves, and the other does not burn men for believing in Darwin, is no proof that either church has reformed or lost any of its hatred or conceit, for the pope is still God's mouthpiece and speaks with an Infallible voice, and the "anti" leagues are all "born of God" and hence can do no wrong. No, it is not the church that stands between female calves or male evolutionists and the fire.

We did not need James to tell us that it is not easy for us to love our neighbour as ourself, nor to point out that if we could this would be a new world; but if we cannot love our neighbour, we can try to understand why he is so unlovable. We can go further, it seems to me. We can hate the idol that tricks him, expose the superstition that deludes him, and fight the spokesmen of that superstition for whose upkeep and in whose behalf he surrenders his birthright.

That birthright, as I see it, is to live and learn, to love and enjoy, to create and beget, to be healthy and happy. To call me a sinner or expect me to be a saint is to interpret that birthright in terms of an Inquisition or a Ku Klux Klan. That would make it impossible for me to be a Freud, a Darwin, a Galileo, or a Bruno; or even be happily married, if marriages are made in heaven and indissoluble as the church says they are; or if I must marry to keep out of hell, "better," as St. Paul says, "to marry than to burn."

We call a sexual pervert who prefaces his pleasure by inflicting pain on his mate, a sadist. When the church says that suffering purifies sin and so is "good," it is simply rationalizing sadism—the tendency of our animal nature to get pleasure out of others' pain, if we have not learned the humane habits of compassion and mercy. To recount in detail the sadistic practices of the church through nineteen centuries would require volumes; but possibly the most brilliant item in that long catalogue of horrors is that of Spaniards baptizing Indian babies in Peru and then dashing out their brains.

Just recently the Catholic Church was at its old business of raising more Christian martyrs to sainthood. But what of the thousands and hundreds of thousands of Christians put to death by the Christian church? Such wholesale sadism of hurrying sinners to hell as soon as possible is unknown to any but the Christian God. Israel's God was jealous and even cruel, as is any war-god, but not so subtle in his cruelty as the God the Christian sadists created out of their perverted minds.

Again, my birthright, as I see it, includes a mother, father, brothers, and sisters. Even a pup has such a birthright and generally loves its mother. But, "Woman," asked Christ, "what have I to do with thee?" What indeed! Is it any wonder that society went loco when it began to found its ethics on one who came to set sons against fathers, daughters against mothers, and daughters-in-law against mothers-in-law?

Not only does Christianity make no demand on my inherent right to learn; it bids me retain the mentality of a moron, or rather of an imbecile:

And (Jesus) said, Verily I say unto you, Except ye be converted, and become as little children, ye shall not enter into the kingdom of heaven.

Whosoever therefore shall humble himself as this little child, the same is greatest in the kingdom of heaven.

A scientist may call himself a Christian, but nobody with the intelligence required these days to be a qualified druggist's clerk can call himself a "good" Christian. True, knowledge is no longer the sin it used to be when the church ruled men's minds; nor does every Fundamentalist believe the earth flat and that it was created 4004 B.C. But Catholic and Protestant Churches alike still rate infantile beliefs higher than scientific scepticism, and for every excuse they find for an intelligent understanding of sex they can offer a dozen rationalizations for morbid and perverse attitudes toward sex. For every gesture the church makes for a more enlightened attitude toward birth control and the stamping out of venereal disease, it finds a dozen rationalizations for war, famine, and disease—all preventable, as are most of the miseries, injustices, and cruelties which now plague the human race but which could be made as obsolete as the sabre-toothed tiger or King Dinosaur.

Religion cannot end war, famine, and disease, or increase earthly happiness, or wipe out human suffering. Man can. He can do it only over the dead body of religion. The start has been made, but remember, please, that the start toward all that has made this unique industrial age possible was made outside the church, in spite of the church, and by men pilloried by the church. The church has had its fangs pulled and its hands stripped of the red-hot branding irons it once loved to press against human flesh, but its curse is still so potent that some of our greatest scientists shy at being called Freethinkers, though they must admit that freethinking alone has begun at last to free mankind from the closed mind inherent in all religions. If our Osborns and Millikans are allowed to live, it is not because they are orthodox Christians, but because orthodox Christians no longer rule the world.

Given a fair field and an honest fight, man can beat superman every time. The natural is mightier than the supernatural; reality is more potent than unreality; fact is stranger than fiction. No church, however strongly entrenched behind the Word of God or strong in Vested Interests, can forever escape human scrutiny or withstand human hands. No religion can be better than human nature at its best.

# CHAPTER ELEVEN

## The Renaissance of Science and the Foundations of Modern Secular Civilization

1. The World Is Mine Oyster. 2. Roger Bacon Decides to Burn Aristotle. 3. The Turn in the Tide of Human Affairs. 4. The Flight from Mecca to Cordova. 5. Six Centuries of Preparatory Ferment. 6. What Everᵛ Mathematician Should Know. 7. Science: Pure and Impure.

### I

WE MAY preach isolation as fervidly as we please, or think ourselves as unique as we please; the fact remains that we are rooted in the historic past and will be related to the future. Let us make no mistake about this, nor be too certain of our superiority. Let us not, from the height of our wealth and material comforts, and to the music of the radio and the hum of machinery, rest content with "looking down" upon the ages that have gone before. A tenth-century Moslem could do that quite as well as we can or as an Alexandrian Greek could.

Those roots are deep; some of them are tap roots, reaching down to the very soil of human nature and feeding on the waters of life itself. These tap roots cannot be cut, nor possibly ever wholly known; but they can be, and are being, better understood. That better understanding is the achievement of modern times, made possible because hands were freed to dig for facts, because eyes were freed to look for fact-bearing soil. That soil is not found in books or by thinking; nor can the search for such soil be guided by any general principle which leaves human lives or the bare facts of human existence out of the count.

Rationalistic, æsthetic, spiritualistic principles have all been tried and found wanting. Water rises in a pump, said the rationalist, because nature *abhors* a vacuum. Hold firm to that idea and see how soon you can discover anything about atmospheric pressure.

Planets move in circles because a circle is the only *perfect* figure, said the æsthete—and so thinks the theosophist. Hold to that idea and see what you can make of the movements of the moon or the planets. Nothing is real but spirit, said the spiritualist, and sat down to contemplate ideality while some mere human being fed him the factual foods his factual flesh required to exist in a factual world.

Note, please, that neither the spiritualist's contemplation nor the ideality he discovered has done any more to make this world better known or more fit to live in than did, for example, Hegel, who ponderously evolved the cosmos in his mind and concluded—on the very day that a new planet was discovered—that there were no more planets to be discovered. Even Newton, who saw so far into matter, invented two absolute and independent entities to take care of matter. But, thanks to Einstein, Newton's postulated Time and Space have gone the way of all Absolutes—back to relatively limited brains for further investigation.

Many Greeks and a few Romans did what they could with their limited equipment to investigate this factual world, and to build such facts as they found into a theory of the cosmos. Their theories make better reading as mythology than they do as science; as philosophies they do not make good reading at all. It was nothing less than a misfortune that if any of Aristotle had to perish it did not all perish. In saddling civilization with the idea that intellectuality alone is the good life, he put an incubus on men's backs almost as deadly as Paul's spiritualism. Possibly the curse Paul laid on the flesh would have been sooner shaken off had not Aristotle been "moderate to excess." When critically minded men of the Middle Ages turned from Paul they embraced Aristotle, Apostle of the Intellectual Life, High Priest to the world of the Schoolmen.

And mere man was between the devil of Christianity and the deep sea of Intellectual foam. Man, said the church, is a miserable sinner, his every impulse is vile; it is against his very nature to act, feel, or think right; humanity is loathsome, personality a crime. But, said Aristotle, some are destined to rule, others to slave; for to some nature gives higher intelligence, to others brute strength. The master's right over his slave is like that of man over the beasts.

It was as easy for Aristotle to answer the argument of those who protested against such ethics as it is for us to rationalize our rule over our Little Brown Brothers. Here is the argument. The mere fact that a man is a slave, or that a people has been conquered, is in itself proof that they cannot reason and that the conqueror can. The conqueror is innately the superior man; the conquered, the inferior. Conquerors always rule subject peoples in their interest. Whose interest? The subject people's, say the conquerors. Barbarians, said Aristotle, are born to be slaves. Masses, says the Master Mind, are born to be exploited.

But, said the knights of the Middle Ages, the peasants are descended from Ham, whom Noah condemned to slavery; we ourselves are descended from those heroes of Troy who settled in western Europe. Frenchmen are descended from Francion, son of Hector! An early eighteenth-century Frenchman expressed his doubt of that Trojan origin—and was barred by the Bastile from further expression of such unpatriotic thoughts.

What our friends the Eugenists, if given a few years' absolute power, would make of the so-called science of heredity is frightful to contemplate. That they would be greater respecters of human liberties than an Innocent III is doubtful; that they would abolish all hereditary rights in property and all compulsory education—as they should to be consistent—is even more doubtful.

For thousands of years the world has been full of presuppositions and assumptions; they generally sufficed to furnish a religious or a moral sanction to any situation, however absurd, diabolic, monstrous, unjust, unethical, or inhuman. Certain assumptions and presuppositions were the weapon the church used to keep the masses in their places; they served equally well to keep rulers on their thrones, professors in their chairs. The priests were in charge of men's souls; rulers, of their bodies; professors, of their thoughts.

If souls are immortal, they may be trusted to look after themselves; but until it is recognized that life on earth can get along without souls, and that human beings are sane and sound and humane in direct ratio to their freedom from hope of future reward or fear of everlasting torment, self-confidence is likely to remain no higher than it was at the beginning of the Ice Age. With thousands of us it is not as high today as it was then, or as it is among so-called savages.

Whatever in our civilization makes for sane, rational behaviour in human lives, is largely due to the fact that human hands have been freed from the control of brains which claimed divine wisdom or gave up with, "I don't know, I'm sure." The professional gnostic is as useless to turn a wheel as the professional agnostic. With the attitude of neither can it be discovered that there is a wheel to turn or a human interest to be served.

To a bishop's rejoinder on being told that Christianity had failed, "It has never been tried," we may add, neither has common sense nor science. Science may fail; but science alone is one, hates no one, fears nothing, is the friend of all mankind, alone can serve mankind impartially, alone thrives on truth, alone is satisfied with nothing but the best truths, alone is the measure of progress, alone seeks the light and eternally wars on darkness and the supernatural. Only from a scientific point of view is man's Golden Age still in the future, the Garden of Eden a creation of human hands.

I did not say scientist; I said *science*, the scientific attitude. For it is true, as Lowie has observed, that there has been no fundamental change in the psychology of the scientist since the Reindeer Age; there has been retrogression in his ethics during the last hundred years. Nor is it without significance that our scientists have been compared, not to a host of guiding angels, but to a swarm of stinging bees, which must be housed, cherished, and multiplied at public expense for the honey they may possibly yield.

Religion seeks the divine vision through reflection, intuition, fasting, prayer; philosophy seeks reality through logic, pure reason, or pure mathematics. But some Greeks got the notion that the world of reality was an oyster man could open with his hands if only he would use patience, courage, honesty, and brains, and that they should do their thinking in the world they lived in.

That was an enormous advance; but their science failed in one fundamental respect: with the Holy Trinity of throne, altar, and sword they formed a holy alliance centred around the pen. As a result, they had too little regard for experimental evidence, too little use for their hands; and they never fully realized that they might put their hearts into the service of their fellow-men as well as into personal advancement.

However, as Burke said, you cannot indict a nation; nor, I may add, an age—not even the Darkest Age of Christian Europe. Human nature will not remain indicted; otherwise the human race would have become as sessile as a forest, as organized as a colony of termites, and ninth-century Christian Europe might have crystallized into a Christian Abyssinia.

The earth does move, and man is not a tree or an insect. The church—of Rome, Luther, and Calvin—again and again roasted the truth out of a man; but neither the gods on Olympus and Sinai nor all the devils in hell could keep man forever out of Eden or from tasting the fruit of every tree in the garden. What man lacks at birth, and what he desires before he is ready to cry quits, is knowledge. And had the church, by a real miracle, brought it to pass that human beings as punishment for their sins should be born blind, they would have found some guide to the tree of knowledge—even as deep-sea sharks developed electric torches to guide them to such crab-apples of wisdom as they needed in their dark and sharky business.

Centuries before Christian popes tried to crush wisdom by closing schools and burning books, an equally stupid Chinese emperor made the same foolish gesture, and with the same result. Confucius, burnt, arose as Immortal Wisdom; in attempting to crucify learning, the church deified it. No religion based on belief in the unseen, intangible, and insensible, and demanding nothing higher than childish credulity, can survive indefinitely in a world of human beings, for that world has an indefinite, indeterminate future—which no cult of the supernatural has.

We call ourselves a Christian nation, but all that makes modern secular civilization stand out in sharp relief from the civilization of Thutmose III or Augustus I, is not because but in spite of Christianity. I do not mean to imply that *bona fide* Christians have not made great contributions to knowledge and to the cause of civilization, nor that every pope was the enemy of science. Pope Sylvester II, for example, who sat at the feet of learning in Moorish Spain and returned its devotee, was a great forerunner of the scientific renaissance of the eleventh century.

Christians and popes are human beings—even while acting like devils and pretending to be saints; but the church, as keeper of a mystery, interpreter of magic power, and propagandist for a supernatural world, is and must be the enemy of free thought, free speech, and free press. Some churches claim to have severed all ties with the supernatural and to lend all their support to freedom in thought, speech, and press. And they go under many names. Whether they are *churches* or not, I do not know. I do know that to the orthodox Darwins the Unitarianism of the Wedgwoods was just a "feather bed to catch a falling Christian." I do know also that some very eminent scientists cannot close an address without an invocation.

That is the world we are gradually getting away from—a world of mysticism and supernaturalism, intolerant and indifferent to facts except as they seemed to fit into the philosopher's imagined world or served to edify an allegorical *Pilgrim's Progress.* The philosopher *thought* it all out; the Pilgrim *knew* it all: it had all been revealed in his Book. For the Christians, as Robinson says, built their theories on information received direct from God. To be arbitrary was to be Godlike!

Yet in that prison house was born an infant who within three centuries was to bestride the earth as no giant of men's imagination ever did. We call that infant the Man of Science. But, said Nietzsche, he is not a man, not even a human being—merely an instrument, the most costly, exquisite, easily tarnished. Incapable of love or hate, Nietzsche's philosophy was only an expression of his limitations. He said what Aristotle would have said, what early Tolstoy said, and what Wordsworth implied. It took Carlyle, however, really to hate science. The classical scholar, the intellectual highbrow, the æsthete, the moralist, the spiritualist, the humanist, all hate science, however fast they may drive their auto to the nearest painless dentist or antiseptic surgeon. Abuse is the refined substitute for fists when confronted by an argument which cannot be refuted. But read White's *History of the Warfare of Science with Theology.*

## II

The opinion is widely accepted that modern science is the child of the sixteenth-century Renaissance. That Renaissance had its own children; science was not one of them, though one Renaissance figure was both a superlative genius in art and one of the most versatile and scientifically minded men the world has ever known—Leonardo da Vinci.

While da Vinci was one of the greatest scientific investigators of all time, especially in biology, it is only fair to say that his employment of the scalpel as an aid to realism in art was but the culmination of a naturalistic movement which began in the thirteenth century with Verrocchio and Mantegna. Dürer, Michelangelo and Raphael all left anatomical drawings and made the scalpel first aid to the brush. But the time had finally come when the scalpel was to be used for anatomy's rather than for art's sake.

The forces which made science possible favoured the rebirth of art and literature. The Roman Church promptly adopted art and to the great artists paid honours once reserved for royalty. Certainly few kings have ever been honoured as Italy honoured such masters as Michelangelo, Raphael, Titian, Mantegna, and Brunelleschi; nor were Petrarch, Boccaccio, and Ariosto rated much lower. They were truly geniuses. They worked like Trojans and created such beauty as Europe had not seen for ages. They are to be reckoned among the forces which were changing men's outlook on the world as well as the world itself.

We shall look at these forces presently, but first let us look at a Renaissance foster-child—one which grew into the kind of intellectual monster that glowered down at me as a freshman from the president's chair in a Baptist college with the traditional classical course. That venerable grey-haired monster is not so spry as he was, though he is far from extinct, and still occupies many chairs in our colleges. His name is Classics; he presumes to educate youth by drilling it in the grammar of two dead languages. Such drill "disciplines the mind," "humanizes the intellect." One thereby becomes genteel and automatically develops into a Christian gentleman.

Not only was the Renaissance not genteel or refining; its very culture, as Briffault points out, was founded in corruption, unscrupulousness, and brutal selfishness. What could be expected of a civilization whose four great patrons were Leo X, Alexander VI, Cæsar Borgia, and Lorenzo the Magnificent—a despoiler of orphans, a murderer, a traitor, and a tyrant?

Roger Bacon could see which way the cat was going to jump,

and before the Renaissance was well into its stride he sounded the alarm in these pregnant words: "If I had my way I should burn all the books of Aristotle, for the study of them can only lead to loss of time, produce ignorance, and encourage error."

That was said six and a half centuries ago. And I look up at my eleven-volume edition and ask myself if I *could* burn it. Burn all the books of Aristotle? Perish the thought! "Produce ignorance, encourage error?" More so than the books of Moses or Mary Baker Eddy or Bernarr McFadden?

Aristotle was one of the world's greatest thinkers; a prodigy of learning, an untiring worker, an intellectual giant if ever there was one. Eleven great volumes, a library in itself—yet only a fragment of what he wrote. And what did he not write about! Logic, rhetoric, ethics, politics, physics, metaphysics, meteorology, astronomy, geology, morphology, psychology, biology. He was an evolutionist; some of his studies in embryology were astoundingly accurate. He was rich; his wife brought him added riches; his royal patron Alexander gave lavishly to his researches. Few scientists today have such resources at their command as had the Father of all the Sciences. And when Alexander died he was given the choice of hemlock or exile—because he hurt the trade in prayer and sacrifice! Athens did not like him because it hated Alexander; the priests did not like him because he put enlightenment above ignorance.

Bacon was a priest, a Franciscan friar, a doctor of theology of the University of Paris. Was that the reason he did not like Aristotle? Not at all. Bacon himself was a scientist and dabbled in alchemy at Oxford. He had travelled, and somehow had discovered that observation must precede knowledge. He had a high sense of the value of mathematics, and an even higher sense of the fact that mathematics could not take the place of experiment. Bacon was a modern in his point of view—too modern by four hundred years.

Bacon was tired of Aristotle as *authority*. He thought it time to dethrone him. Aristotle had reigned long enough as the intellectual sanction for scholastic debates—such as, how many angels could stand on the point of a needle. And five hundred years hence historians will note that in the year 1931 American universities were granting higher degrees for theses in certain sciences (so called) not one whit less scholastic nor one particle more scientific than the theses of the Schoolmen of the Middle Ages.

Bacon did not have his way; on the contrary, the rediscovered world of Greek literature was ransacked by Catholic and Protestant alike for anything that could serve the ends of theology. Even as late as 1883, says Barrett, the General Congregation of the Catholic Church declared: "Since the Society of Jesus has decreed *the utility of the philosophy of Aristotle for the ends of theology*, we are to adhere to it. . . ." To Protestants especially Greek philosophy was a godsend, because, as Hogbun says, it equipped their theology with a metaphysic, their democracy with a Utopia, and gave the modern world "an intellectual armoury in its revolt against ecclesiastical authority."

I said Greek philosophy. With the Fathers Clement and Origen, both Platonists—or rather Neo-Platonists—Scholasticism was on its way. Jesus' sufferings thereafter became the sole topic of epic import; Mary and the Apostles, the principal sources of romance. There could be no heroism, no poetry, no wisdom, no social justice. Even the two highbrow Classic religions, Stoicism and Epicureanism, fitted the Christian world like a pair of mittens; they cared nothing for human rights and had no more concern in making this world a better place to live in than had St. Francis of Assisi—or than that grand almoner to His Most Christian Majesty, St. Vincent de Paul, who visited the infamous hells of the French galleys as a messenger of love, calling sinners to repentance!

It is never the business of church or school—of philosophy or science—to fight for social justice, inveigh against social inequity, propagate ethical ideals, or evaluate moral conduct in terms of significance to human society. It is the business of science, however, to be honest and impartial.

The revived Greek learning above all gave the Scholastic mind a new intellectual toy—a cross-word-puzzle pastime which became the habit of the kept men of church and school. That habit is not entirely foreign to these shores, nor quite outmoded in our halls of learning. It is useless, meaningless baggage. It carries us nowhere in our search into human nature, nor furthers by one hair's-breadth our inquiry into man's place in or relation to nature. We cannot humanize this Machine Age with any or all of the dead languages, or play the part this age demands of us with any intellectual concept thought out in Athens and formalized by Humanistic pedants.

Bad as it was, and enduring as have been its vicious consequences, classical culture did give rise to Scholasticism, which in turn gave courage to Protestantism. And Protestantism did succeed in doing one thing that had to be done before man could stretch himself and begin to look around: it wrested the Book of books from the hands of the pope and brought it into the light of day. That was a big step, though taken in a roundabout way. While Protestants and Catholics quarrelled over "gestures and vestures" and wrangled over worn-out dogmas, new and more vital heresies had a chance to grow. But man might conceivably have escaped from the authority of the Book earlier had he had only the Roman bishops to fight and not the Book reinforced by that intellectual monstrosity, classical Humanism.

In other words, no Renaissance, no Sistine Chapel or Madonna della Sedia. Or, in the words of John Addington Symonds, no Renaissance, no dissolution of the Middle Ages; and no dissolution, no soil broken for the growth of modern science.

### III

Three centuries and a half after Roger Bacon had written his *opus magnum* and paid his respects to Aristotle, another Bacon, who was neither priest nor school-teacher, but Francis, Lord Verulam, Viscount of St. Albans, Lord Chancellor of England under James I, was to sum up the enormous change that had come over man's attitude toward his world, in these words: "I have not sought, nor do I seek, either to enforce or ensnare men's judgments, but I lead them to things themselves and the concordance of things, that they may see for themselves what they have, what they can dispute, what they can add and contribute to the common stock."

That marked a new turn of the tide in the affairs of men. It made the world an oyster again in man's hands. It was the beginning of wisdom, emblem of the spirit of modern science—not the words themselves, but the attitude behind them.

I do not mean to imply that Francis Bacon was a great scientist, for he was not; but with Bacon, with his attitude, science—all that is to be discovered, all that can be added to the common stock—became possible. Philosophers, logicians, rhetoricians, mystics, word-jugglers of every description, may hold their heads in their hands and look wise till all the souls in Sheol are as cold as absolute zero trying to find what is behind *die Dinge an sich* (things themselves), and not get as close to them as the naked children on the beach of a coral isle, for they can see for themselves what they have, what they can dispute, what they can add and contribute to the common stock.

It was all right for Augustine to live in a world complete enough to end any minute the inscrutable Will of a Divine Providence decreed; and it was all right for the Middle Ages to accept such a doctrine of Providence. Augustine could cite miracles in proof of his claim to be the spokesman of God, author of his *City*. The world of monks, miracles, martyrs, popes, emperors, knights, and Gregory the Great, of the Middle Ages, could accept that kind of Providence; but *we* are well along in the twentieth century, and it is well to keep reminding ourselves of certain great truths.

One is that every scheme of philosophy or of pseudo-science which assumes to replace Augustine's Providence must resort to mysticism or supernaturalism. Another is that any such scheme of Finality and Certitude can be as iniquitous and tyrannical in unrestrained human hands as ever was Christian scheme of salvation. Still another is that the hell of every social injustice and political oppression is paved with good intentions.

Another great truth that no scientist should ever forget is that science at best can only furnish better truths, closer approximations; and in the final analysis recognizes neither authority nor precedent. Yet how many halls of learning dare hang Bacon's words above their doors? And if they did, and if every teacher took them to heart and tried in all serious intellectual humility to lead his pupils to things themselves and not to enforce or ensnare their judgments . . .

But it is so much easier to feed youthful credulity than to encourage observation and cultivate scepticism in boys and girls. Possibly that is the answer to the dull moron mass of humanity that once every four years lays aside its gum long enough to cast a ballot, and between times lies an inert prey to the venders of every nostrum known to all the ages. It does seem certain that never before in human history was mere life so fool-proof, never before was it so easy for the Simple Simons to keep on living.

Contemporary with Bacon were Harvey and Galileo. Before Harvey was Vesalius; before Galileo was Bruno; before Bruno, Copernicus. All within a hundred years. Great names these in the history of intellectual freedom; great pioneers who boldly resolved, bravely dared look for themselves at things themselves. It is not what they saw that makes them great; it is that they dared look, that they dared question Destiny, Fate, God's handiwork, Holy Writ. They did not see far; they saw enough to shake the foundations of the world, shatter the old crystalline sphere to pieces, and restore the human body to human hands. They mark the transition from the age of Scholasticism to the age of modern science. They were the founders of modern science.

But who seeded the soil which yielded a Bacon, a Galileo, a Harvey? There must be seed or the richest soil is barren. An idiot can be brave and a moron can dare, but ideas which can be cashed at the counter of rational experience must not be counterfeit, nor can they be produced from nothing. Our business now is to trace these ideas back to their antecedents. We shall not find them in the Renaissance; we do find them in the eleventh, twelfth, and thirteenth centuries—far richer in sterling ideas than the Renaissance, whose art has blinded us to its poverty in scientific thinking. The hair-splitting of the Schoolmen who grew up out of the Dark Ages obscures the lights that were beginning to twinkle in a few universities.

Those early lights were Greek lamps which had been rediscovered, rewicked, rekindled, and kept burning by the "fanatical" followers of Mohammed. We must make a pilgrimage, not only for its intrinsic value, but because we are rulers of thousands of Moslems—such as the Moros of the Philippine Islands. After all, Mohammed has as many followers as Christ, and for ages they were more civilized than Christian Europe.

But before looking at the phenomenon of Moslem civilization, it will help us to understand what we shall see if we glance critically at our old text-book epochs of Fall of Rome, Middle Ages, Dark Ages, Renaissance, Protestant Reformation, French Revolution, etc.

Divisions—epochs, eras, dynasties, reigns, etc.—which serve book purposes are not necessarily rational or sharp divisions; they are conveniences, like punctuation marks on the printed page or milestones on a pike. As every naturalist presumably rebels against the necessity of dividing plants and animals into orders, species, genera, etc., so the historian of human behaviour must regret the implications that seem justified from cutting history into slices which can be consumed at one sitting. This observation seems especially applicable to the history of civilization.

Edison, for example, was born on a certain day of a certain year; the very hour may even be known. The date of birth is sharp and clear-cut. But Edison at five, at fifteen, at twenty-five, kept meeting ideas—new to him, but some of them thousands of years old, some born of the generation that produced Edison. After playing with some of these ideas he got one of his own, and put it to work in electric light. If *he* hadn't, it is certain that some one else would, for electric light was in the very air, a cultural ponderable was at work upon thousands here and abroad. The idea Copernicus used to smash the Christian world was older than Christianity.

Scientific, like aerial, *aces* are aces through accident, limelight, press, citation. They are unique or "irreplaceable" only to the extent that their contemporaries are unknown or unsung.

It is also unfortunate, as Robinson points out, that "Middle Ages" means everything from Rome's Fall to Columbus. The fact is that church, monasticism, religion, intolerance, mysticism, etc., started before and grew out of the Roman Empire. While they were growing, Rome was falling. What Christianity saved was what brought Rome down: infinite pains about things that were not so, and even if so, could not be remedied. The Roman world, as Harnack says, was intellectually bankrupt before the German savages plunged it into deeper ignorance and obscurity.

70 A.D. to 430, date of the death of Augustine, is, roughly, the period of the Christian fathers. Greek thought, such as had flourished in Athens and especially in Alexandria, disappeared. Knowledge fell far below par; nobody wanted any information about anything except religion, magic, and mystery.

430 to 1142, date of the death of Abelard, master intellect of the Middle Ages; seven centuries of from bad to worse—the Dark or

Middle Ages. Towns vanished, libraries rotted or were burnt, schools were closed—to be reopened after Charlemagne as monasteries or by some pacifist bishop.

Roughly, then, the Middle Ages cover a thousand years, from Theodoric the Great to Henry VIII, from Boëthius to Rabelais. Boëthius has been called the bridge between ancient and modern times. The passage from Middle to modern was not sudden; there was overlapping, much fusion.

With 1100, lights began to twinkle: the Renaissance of Science. An age of travel had begun. Italian priests became archbishops of Canterbury, chancellors of England. An Englishman became Chancellor of Sicily. Merchants trudged from Italy to Flanders. Priests, poets, students, Jews, went everywhere. Winchester, England, was in closer touch with Palermo, Sicily, than it is today. Europe had seen, and was to see, darker days than the eleventh, twelfth, and thirteenth centuries averaged.

Now let us follow the followers of Mohammed, see what we owe them, and discharge the debt—a debt, by the way, which only recently has been discovered: not because they kept us out of Mecca but because Christians are congenitally loath to give the devil his due. It is easier for us to say, "No Copernicus, no Newton," than to say, "No Arab astronomy, no Copernicus"; or to say, "No Judaism, no Christianity," than to say, "No Semites, no modern civilization."

But do not take that too literally; science was bound to come into its own sooner or later. Some group of men, somewhere, somehow, was bound to learn how to make thunderbolts, synthetic drugs, contraceptives, anæsthetics and airplanes, and to discover microbes, atomic weights, additional planets and conditioned reflexes. But the difference, so far as practical purposes go, between a Greek thinking atoms and Dalton weighing them, suggests the noble Russian lady weeping buckets of tears in her carriage over the hero's death in the play she had just seen, while her coachman froze to death on his box. Between thinking and weighing is where the Mohammedan Arabs came in, to save the world, for a while at least, from becoming a mad-house. Arabs and Jews were Semites, as were the Babylonians and Chaldeans.

Christian whites in their zeal to "civilize" the savage world might learn a lesson by pondering over what might have happened to civilization had there been no savages to save it after the Christian fathers and their savage German converts had done their best to destroy it.

IV

The Arabian desert of the seventh century was in the hands of tribes not one whit more civilized, and indeed more savage, than were our Plains Indians of the seventeenth century. Their favourite method of keeping the population down was to bury surplus girl babies alive. They were strong on blood feuds and great believers in the magic power of trophies. The grandmother of a caliph and a social light of Mecca, for example, had Mohammed's uncle's heart torn out and sent her as a trophy—for purposes of divination.

Mecca was an oasis of savage Arab tribes surrounded by a world of Jews and Christians, especially Nestorian Christians. One of these tribes, the Koreish, controlled Mecca's market place and shrine or idol—the Kaaba, or Black Stone, a meteorite. Chief of this tribe was Hashem. Being a good Semite savage, he emulated Abraham by trying to sacrifice his son Abdullah to the idol. Had he succeeded, that child would not have lived—to become Mohammed, the Prophet.

Mohammed was born in 571 and grew up in the midst of such monstrous idolatry, cruelty, bloodshed, and infanticide as would have shamed an Apache Indian. But the Hashems were rich merchants, and young Mohammed travelled far and wide and saw something of civilization. He rebelled against the gross superstitions and inhuman savagery of his people, and preached reform. "Science," he said, "is the remedy for the infirmities of ignorance, a comforting beacon in the night of injustice."

He also said that Moses was the first prophet to reveal God's will and purpose, Christ the second, and himself the third, final, and greatest. The Jews and Christians could not believe him, of course, for they were already sold on their own Prophets. But many Arabs did believe and accepted his *Koran* (Reading) as their Bible—the authoritative word of God and primary source of all Islamic law; himself, as the fount of manna.

The Koran, like the Old Testament in a way, is a collection of

Arabic legends and moral maxims. It rejects idolatry and polytheism and accepts one God—the God of Jews and Christians. It prohibits blood feuds, infanticide, cruelty, pork, and wine; stresses almsgiving, patience, and integrity. Like the Old Testament, it allows slavery and a limited polygamy. It reduced the number of superstitions, but stressed predestination, the fires of hell, and the joys of heaven.

Mohammed was as truly a prophet of reform as Semitism had ever produced. And the reform he preached meant here and now and by grown men in all their powers—not by ascetics or celibates.

To *submit* or be reconciled to the will of God was to become an *Islamite*; to *believe* that there was but one God (Allah) and that Mohammed was his Prophet, was to become a *Moslem*. That is to say, the religion Mohammed founded is Islamism; the followers of that religion are Moslems. On Moslems four duties were enjoined: prayer, charity, fasting on Ramadan (as discipline), and a pilgrimage to Mecca.

Mohammed was a reformer, not a fanatic. Early Moslems were not fanatics; they were too busy to go crazy. The Moslems who most nearly approached fanaticism were the Jewish and Christian converts to Islamism. It is the business of a new germ to *take*.

Mohammed did not enjoin celibacy or preach asceticism or the adoration of saints, but that did not prevent Moslems from assuming to lead saintly lives or worshipping at the tombs of their saints; nor would there have been any worship of saints' bones or hairs of the Prophet's beard had such relics not been regarded as miracle-workers. And there was no machinery for roasting a Moslem chief for declaring—as one did—that "if there were a God, I would swear by his name that I did not believe in him."

Islamism spread with dazzling speed because the Christians of Syria and Egypt had had a surfeit of theology and oppression. They *embraced* the new religion! They could live with and under their new masters and enjoy life as they could not under their Christian masters. Free thought, Moslem's crowning glory for eight centuries, and to which our civilization is so greatly indebted, was destroyed by its own orthodox clergy—as scholastic and as formalized as the Christian clergy in the days of Scholasticism. From the blight of five centuries of intellectual sterility the world of Islam is just now beginning to try to emerge.

Mohammed, owing to internal dissensions, fled from Mecca to Medina in 622; and died in 632 with all Arabia at his feet. The *Hegira* (flight) marks the year one in the Islamic calendar. It was under his first successor, or *caliph*, that the Koran was canonized. This caliph lasted two years, and was succeeded by huge, brave, honest, loyal Omar, one of Mohammed's greatest caliphs, one of the world's greatest unifiers. Omar rode into Jerusalem on a red camel, with a basket of dates and a skin of water.

No Christian army ever won such amazing victories as did the Islamic armies under Khalid, "Sword of God," and Amroo. In twenty years the Moslems had conquered 36,000 strongholds, destroyed four thousand churches and temples, and erected fourteen hundred mosques. The Sassanian king of the revamped Persian Empire of Darius was driven from his throne—thus ending a four-hundred-year dynasty; Babylon was captured, and Ctesiphon with its incredible wealth. Egypt and all North Africa fell before a handful of men. From the Nile to the Indus, from Antioch to Samarkand, there was no God but Allah, and Mohammed was his Prophet.

The Moors were in Spain by 711, where they destroyed the kingdom of the Visigoths on the plains of Guadalquivir. Nor was their march into Europe checked till they met Charles Martel at the battle of Tours—an even century after the Prophet's death.

What a march! And, as Breasted says, in following Islam's conquest of civilization we follow a rising trail. Pastoral Arabs were studying science while Germanic Christians were priding themselves on their brutish ignorance. To put it another way, while the ruins of civilization in Europe were being steadily shrouded in denser darkness, civilization was rising anew in the Moslem world. To that side we now turn, especially to the two new capital cities of civilization.

First, Bagdad. In 661 the caliphate was moved from Medina to Damascus, under the Sunnite Ommiads. In 750 it passed to the Abassids, and Bagdad, erected alongside Ctesiphon, became the capital. Within two hundred years Bagdad had become the world's most civilized city. It fostered science and rational thought, and tolerated atheism. All religions, said one of its blind poets, are equally absurd; the world holds two classes of men: intelligent men without religion; religious men without intelligence.

Brother of, and even abler than, Haroun al-Raschid of *Arabian Nights* fame, was al-Mamoun, Islam's Charlemagne, Bagdad's greatest caliph in promoting culture and science and encouraging the study of Greek literature.

Not since the palmy days of science in Alexandria had the world seen such an academy as Bagdad's ninth-century "House of Science." Aristotle, Euclid, Ptolemy, etc., were translated; Greek manuscripts, scattered since 529, were collected like precious stones; Brahmagupta and other Hindu mathematicians were studied and advanced. Christianity was tolerated as the Christians themselves had not tolerated divergent Christian sects. Mamoun even put a Christian at the head of the college in Damascus—for his science, not for his religion.

Imagine a Christian college making Omar Khayyám president— or even professor of mathematics! Yet Omar was one of the greatest mathematicians of his age. Much credit is due to the *Rubaiyat's* translator, FitzGerald, but, as Robertson says, the *thoughts* are Omar's. His epigrams have never been surpassed for echoing depth. Nor did he offer shibboleths for godlikeness, but sang of wine and roses and the joys of life—"putting into music the undertone of all morality," more to be preferred by refined intelligence than zeal for the hereafter. And what Christian father or Greek philosopher could with Omar say, *One for two I never did misread?*

While Omar could paint love with fine passion, woman in Arabian poetry generally came off badly—in fact, not so well as a female camel. The only love the poets sang was the love of sweethearts. But Europe had not yet reached even that height; in fact, when the bards of Provence were finally inspired by Arab poetry to sing of love, it was Mary who received their homage.

Where did these Moslems get their Greek literature, their passion for culture, their zeal for science, their predilection for free thought?

They were young yet; they were not already committed to this school or steeped in that tradition. The Nestorians, driven from

Byzantium, had carried Greek literature to Syria. Through Syrian Christians it passed to the Arabs.

Even before the Prophet's death, one of his relatives had carried presents to the Emperor of China and had obtained leave to found a Moslem mission. There were soon seven hundred mosques in Shantung alone. Ibn Batuta, a celebrated Arab traveller of the fourteenth century, pictures China permeated with Arab traders and merchants. At Hangchow he met a man from near his home town in Morocco whom he had met before in Delhi, India. The Eastern world was travelling; the world was growing smaller.

Before Christianity had got into North Europe, Islam had found its way to Java and the Sulu Seas. The Moslems conquered, proselyted; but they also observed, learnt. Excepting portraiture, banned by their religion—especially by the *Traditions of the Prophet*—they took over bodily the remains of Græco-Roman art, literature, science, and handicraft. In Egypt and along northern Africa, especially at Carthage, there remained scraps of science—agricultural knowledge, chemistry, astronomy, mathematics, medicine, botany. All this they gathered in and made their own.

The Moslems not only came, saw, and conquered; they remained to intermarry with the "natives" and be conquered. They planted Islam's seed deep in the soil. From that soil mosques sprang up. Every mosque had its school. Scholars were rated higher than priests or politicians. A caravan was as likely to be laden with manuscripts from India and Byzantium, and with botanical and mineralogical specimens from everywhere, as with silks and cottons. One Moslem travelled forty years collecting mineralogical specimens; another botanized over the entire Moslem world, comparing the flora of Greece and Spain with that of Persia and India.

It was a *thirst* for knowledge, a passion for the delights of intellectual culture; and shared by prince and courtier alike. Libraries, observatories, were part of life as it was lived in the courts of the caliphs and emirs; their delight was in listening to lectures on science.

It was a new game in human interests and never played more zealously. Had they cultivated the arts of dominion and government as assiduously as they cultivated the arts of peace, civilization today might be Moslem and not Christian. Even the Greeks—

Ionian or Alexandrian—had never played this game so hard or brought to it such a wide-open spirit of inquiry, or such methods of observation and investigation, weighing, measuring, counting, as did Arab scientists for five centuries. From their hands Europe got its start, its first lessons in astronomy, botany, chemistry, jurisprudence, mathematics, medicine, and philosophy. Yes, philosophy; for the greatest of all Middle Age expounders of Aristotle was Ibn Roshd, known to us as Averroës, least mystical, most rational of all Arab thinkers. Even to read Averroës was a sin in the Inquisitorial eyes of the church.

To the charge that Arab alchemy or chemistry was all magic, Thorpe, historian of chemistry, replies that it was Christians and not Arabs who imported theosophy and mysticism into alchemy. In fact, Europe clung to its infantile pastime of "reading" stars and searching for an elixir of life for centuries after it had discovered Arab chemistry.

By the sixteenth century there were over two hundred manuscript versions in Latin alone of a work from Damascus called the *Secret of Secrets* and supposed to have been written by Aristotle to guide Alexander—the essence of practical wisdom and occultism.

Superstitious Europe was as hungry for such secrets as is ignorant superstition today. Tycho and Copernicus were primarily astrologers, only secondarily astronomers. Copernicus moved planets with angels. Kepler was an astronomer; but he drew horoscopes. Newton squandered his genius working out astrological prophecies in the Book of Daniel. All the great European pioneer chemists dabbled in alchemic transmutations. Priestley was smart enough to discover oxygen, but quite failed to realize its astounding significance in every vital process—that being reserved for the great Lavoisier, the man slain by the new French Republic because it had no use for science!

The Renaissance of Art in Italy, I repeat, has blinded us to the Renaissance of Science in Spain. For it was to Spain, to Seville, Toledo, and especially to great Cordova, capital of the Cordova caliphate since 755, to Cordova, cradle of science, that students went to sit at the feet of the only masters of science then in Europe.

To Cordova went Michael the Scot again and again, to make translations, to search for manuscripts. To Cordova went Gerbert for the terrestrial and celestial globes with which he astonished his pupils—that Gerbert so avaricious for knowledge that he was to become the hero of fantastic Middle Age Faust legends as Pope Sylvester II.

Cordova was a centre of learning four centuries before Paris or Oxford; a civilized city, with water and lights and general culture, six centuries before Paris or London. Moorish Spain at one time had seventy public libraries; Cordova's library, 600,000 volumes. And in el-Hakim II, says Viardot, "the most zealous and enthusiastic protector that letters, science, and the arts had ever known."

Spanish Moslems, called *Moors* or Moriscoes, are a mixture of Arabs and Moroccan Berbers, and descendants of Phœnician, Greek, and Roman colonists. All North Africa up to 700 had been part of the Eastern Roman or Byzantine Empire. It was the Moorish general, Tarik, who landed at Gibel in Spain in 711 and gave his name to the hill of Tarik or rock of Gibraltar—in ancient days one of the two Pillars of Hercules. He soon made all Spain—except the little mountainous Christian kingdom of Asturias—a province of the Ommiad caliphate.

Moorish civilization reached the height of its brilliance in the ninth and tenth centuries—a height in many respects not yet attained by Christian Spain. Toledo and Cordova, once a city of a million people, today are but ghosts of Moorish glories; and, while Seville is an imposing city, its glorious cathedral is overshadowed by its more glorious Giralda, once minaret of a Moorish mosque and an astronomical observatory—the first ever erected on European soil. When Alphonso XIII visited Seville, he lodged in the remains of the old Moorish palace. When the sightseer visits Spain, he makes for Granada and its Alhambra. In Cordova he will find no seat of learning, nor even tradition of the site of its once famous university.

By the eleventh century the Christian end of Spain had grown from one to four kingdoms: Asturias—now become Léon; Castile; Navarre; and Aragon. Then Léon and Castile were united into Castile-Léon. The northern Christians began to covet the smiling gardens of the Moorish southlands. Cordova sent out an S O S call to the Faithful.

The call was answered by the Almoravides of Mauretania, a North African province since the days of Emperor Claudius. The

Almoravides stopped the Christians, and liked Spain so well they stayed. The caliphate of Cordova broke up (1031) into a number of small states, and the Almoravides became masters of Moslem Spain. They in turn were succeeded in the twelfth century by the Almohades. The Christians, however, kept pushing south, and by 1238 all that was left of Moorish Spain was the kingdom of Granada, still preëminent in science, industry, agriculture, and commerce among European lands.

The little kingdom of Granada carried on the grand tradition. Its wool, the finest in the world, was eagerly sought by the Flemish and French weavers; it was still the leader in horticulture and arboriculture.

That was the kingdom Ferdinand the Catholic and Isabella conquered in 1492. And when a few years later Ferdinand went to Cordova to behold the church his Christian fanatics had built in the very centre of one of the world's greatest mosques, he beheld, sighed, and exclaimed: "You have built here that which could have been built anywhere, but you have destroyed that which can never be built again."

1492. Columbus discovered some islands off a continent which Norsemen had discovered five centuries before and probably tried to colonize, but which had been discovered and colonized at least five thousand years before by Asiatics.

Why did Columbus sail west? Because da Gama had sailed east. The Portuguese had already found a sailing-route to India; it was a good route and they controlled it. Why discover another which possibly they could not control? And so when the Italian, Cristoforo Colombo, applied to the Portuguese for the job of finding a new route to India, they kept putting him off in the hope that he would die of old age. Instead, the Italian sailor, after hanging around for several years, entered the service of Isabella (1486)—and as a Spaniard, Cristobal Colon. But he had to wait till the Christians were through with the Moors before he was allowed to try out his idea.

Why this idea of sailing west to get east; and why take the idea to Portugal? To Portugal, because Prince Henry the Navigator was not a navigator nor even an able-bodied seaman; he was an epoch-maker, a maker of men who make history. He had founded a nautical academy at St. Vincent in southern Portugal. Navigation had become a science. The teachers in that academy were Arabs and Jews from Moorish Spain, land of science. Regiomontanus (Müller of Königsberg) had translated the astronomical tables of al-Batani, the Arab. From them he computed his *Ephemerides*. Navigation had passed from the sailor's hands into the scientist's. Columbus knew where to go to sell his idea. But da Gama had spoiled his market.

Moorish, Arabic, science slowly trickled, or rather was smuggled, into Christian Europe, and after studying, translating, and assimilating it for five centuries, Europe began to build her own structure on those Arabic foundations. But there is not a single great name in science in all Christian Europe before 1600 that cannot be matched by an Arabic precursor.

A Christian translates an Arabic work and astounds the Christian world—and must pay for it with his pride, liberty, or life! Regiomontanus went to al-Batani; Kepler, to Ibn Yunis; Vesalius, to al-Razi (Rhazes). Then there was al-Hazen, greatest of them all. How many sciences are not indebted to his work on optics and his discovery that the retina is the seat of vision—that we see because rays of light from external objects strike the retina. Felix Valyi says that even the author of Christianity's greatest poem, the *Divine Comedy*, according to recent discoveries by a Catholic priest in Madrid, got his inspiration from thirteenth-century Mohammedan Spain. Wiedemann compares the "extraordinarily great service" of these early Arab scientists to that of such pioneers as Newton, Faraday, and Röntgen.

Unchanging East! The East does not change fast enough to suit us, and when it does change we sneer at it. Unchanging Europe.

The printing-press and paper, centuries after their invention and use in the Far East, finally reached Europe; also gunpowder and the compass. Europe in time discovered that the earth was not flat like a pancake and was well worth looking at. And about five centuries after the Arabs had converted Malaysia and parts of China, a European discovered China. Marco Polo's account of what he saw on his trek from Venice to Peking still makes good reading, but to thirteenth-century Europe it was a Paul du Chaillu revelation—so much so that he was called a liar. At the court of Kublai Khan, the Mongol, he saw the ruler of nearly all Asia, outside India and Arabia. He crossed China when it was never more powerful or illustrious.

1492. But before Columbus or da Gama were Gutenberg, Marco Polo, Cordova; and that rare Christian Frederick II (1212-50), Emperor of Germany (Holy Roman Empire), King of the two Sicilies, cold to the obligations of his own religion, warm to free-thinking Moslemism, preferring the company of his Arabian ministers to any that Christianity then afforded. In short, Frederick did not like his church; he did like his Saracen (Moslem) subjects in Sicily—under Mohammedan rule from 902 to 1091.

The early flare-up of learning in South Italy is unthinkable without Frederick's fondness for the Moslem way of thinking. The Norman kingdom of Saracenized Sicily was the bridge for direct contact between early Greek writers and the twelfth-century Renaissance in law, natural science, philosophy, theology, and the classics in general. That was an epoch in the history of European intelligence. Only in Frederick's Norman kingdom did Greek, Latin, and Arabic culture meet in peace and tolerance. Saracens of Sicily, Greeks of Calabria, and Lombards, were allowed to retain their own language, religion, and customs.

Frederick II, grandson of the illustrious Emperor Barbarossa, has been called the Infidel Emperor, the Royal Heretic—and by Pope Gregory IX, "a forerunner of Anti-christ." He was in reality a forerunner of the scientific attitude, the first scientifically minded prince of Christian Europe—a link between Christian mediævalism and secular renaissance.

But it was the "man of Bath," Adelard, of the preceding century, who first assimilated Greek science—after long travel and exploration, and study in Spain, Syria, and Sicily. One of the most interesting and significant figures of the twelfth century, his is the greatest name in English science before Roger Bacon. "It is hard to discuss with you," he wrote his nephew, "for I have learned one thing from the Arabs under the guidance of reason; you follow another halter, caught by the appearance of authority, for what is authority but a halter?" He introduced the new Euclid and the new astronomy into the West, and was a real pioneer.

V

Copernicus is a great name in the astro-physical world and Vesalius in the bio-physical, but the sixteenth-century world in which they were born was preceded by no less than six centuries of preparatory ferment. The yeast of that ferment was Alexandrian Greek learning, carried to the Near East by Jews and banished Nestorian heretics and cultivated anew in the University of Bagdad. Not for eight centuries was Christian Europe to possess such a centre of learning. Bagdad was the successor of Alexandria, the precursor of Cordova and Seville, the inspiration of Amalfi, Salerno, and other early South European centres of science. Science was not to find itself at home in Paris and Oxford for still other long centuries.

Bagdad alone did more to keep the torch of learning alight than all the churches of Christendom. Ptolemy, Archimedes, Euclid, Hippocrates, Galen, and the Hindu mathematician Brahmagupta, all could have found chairs awaiting them in Bagdad's eighth-century university. And while Christian Oxford was trying to digest the first five propositions of the first book of Euclid, Moslem Cordova and Toledo were working out spherical trigonometry and the theory of numbers. Nor would Oxford have had any Euclid at all had not the Rabbi ben Ezra carried Greek algebra and Hindu decimal notation from Spain to London in 1158.

The great adventure of the European scholar, says Haskins, lay in the Peninsula, in Moorish Spain, where the twelfth-century Latin world went to seek the key to knowledge. But still other and more general cultural traits also crossed the Pyrenees and the Mediterranean, and helped to prepare the foundations of modern Europe.

Paper, compass, gunpowder—world-conquering devices, a powerful trinity. Paper, however, is merely paper until it is loaded with a human message. The best of compasses is but a toy without the navigator's science. Nor could gunpowder have spilled the armoured knight and ended Feudalism had there been no desire for political freedom. Paper, compass, and gunpowder came from the Far *via* the Near East, but commerce and industry also came to Moorish Spain and Sicily from the Near East.

Also from the Near East came goods—things to eat, to wear, to fight with, to ride on, to make music with. Muslins from Mosul, gauzes from Gaza, grenadines from Granada, damasks from Damascus, and moirés, crêpes, chiffons, satins, taffetas, and fine silks, linens, and cottons; marvellously fine, gorgeously coloured fabrics, in exchange for the coarse clothing of barbarous Europe. Our chemise and jupe are the old Arabic *kamis* and *jubba*. Christian knights rode on leather saddles made in Cordova and carried damascene blades made in Toledo or Damascus, and Europe in general learned to like Arab sweetmeats, confections, and water ices. At one time there were 16,000 looms in Seville alone; 130,000 silk workers in Cordova. Eastern dyes gave English wool a world market. And the old word *mauresques* tells the story of the Arabic origin of our stringed instruments; lute (*al-ud*); violin or rubeb (*rabab*); zither, tabour, guitar (*kuitra*); psaltery, early form of piano (*sautyr*).

We learned something of Norman England in our school days, but little of Norman Sicily or of the Saracenized court of Frederick II. Norman England was never out of touch with Norman Sicily. And all Christian rulers in Europe could employ Arab tutors for their sons and send to Cordova for the best doctors the world afforded. But for Frederick's enthusiasm for Moorish science and the refinements of civilization Christian Europe had no sympathy. For taking a bath seven days in the week he was denounced with horror and by Gregory called Anti-christ—"a pestilent king who affirms that the world has been deceived by three impostors, Moses, Jesus, and Mahomet." Nor did the church count it to his credit that he founded universities at Messina and Naples. Even the scholars he encouraged and his followers were anathematized as infidel unbelievers. Little wonder that he exclaimed to his friend Malik-al-Kamil, while they walked arm in arm in Jerusalem discussing science, "Happy Sultan who knows no Pope." The Sultan presented him with a big domed clock which showed the hours and the rising and setting of the sun and moon.

What was Frederick doing in Jerusalem? He went to Palestine as a crusader to escape Gregory's threat of excommunication. In the Moslem he found a good friend, and got a fine clock—symbols of the difference between Christian and Moslem world of the thirteenth century.

And the influence the Moslem exerted on the Christian world was primarily the influence which was to make our world possible. The first and most lasting result of this influence was the recreation of commerce and manufacture in Europe and the concentration of wealth and power in the hands of merchants and cities. Marseilles, Arles, and Nice became rich, cultured, and *free*: free republics as the Greek city states had been ages before.

Amalfi, Salerno, and Naples followed, and in 875 formed an alliance with Saracen Sicily and defied the excommunication of the pope. Later, Pisa, Genoa, and Venice became rich, powerful, free. Genoa and Pisa, coveting the fine wool of Saracen Sardinia, joined forces and conquered it. Lucca, having learned the art of weaving in Saracen Palermo, now became the leading centre of the woollen trade. But at the sack of Pisa the Lucca master weavers fled to Florence—to make that city great and rich and her merchants the bankers of Europe.

Those Italian cities rose to wealth through trade with the Moslem world. In fast, light sailing-ships caulked with tar, the Arabs had a monopoly of the sea-borne trade with India and with Africa as far south as Mombasa. They also kept open caravan routes to India, China, and the Malaccas. They introduced bills of exchange and other devices necessary to big business, all of which were adopted by the Italian merchants. The first well-known double-entry bookkeeping is that of Pisano, whose *Liber Abaci* (1202) remained the authority in accountancy for centuries. He introduced Arabic numerals, negative numbers indicating debit.

In other words—and to repeat—Europe's fifteenth-century Renaissance, apart from its paintings, is a joke. The difference between the Scholastics deifying Aristotle while trying to think clearly on such problems as whether the divine essence engendered the Father or was engendered by him, and whether the Holy Ghost did or did not appear as a real dove, and the Humanists who lighted their lamps before Plato's bust and begged for an arm bone of Livy, is the difference between a professional logomachist and a professor of classical languages: one loves to play with catchwords, the other to idolize his antiques; one talks himself to death, the other buries himself in words. Both are pedants, and in a society which has neither the Greek's concern for ideas nor the

Arab's for facts, easily become brilliant pedants. Their contribution to the sum-total of civilization is no more, no less, than that of a Methodist bishop and a bookworm. Such parasites are not all dead yet.

There was a university at Salerno by the ninth century and a law school in Bologna by about 1000. But during the eleventh and twelfth centuries, with the spread across Europe of a passion for learning inspired by Moorish Cordova, Toledo, and Seville, the beginnings of universities were made in Paris, Oxford, and Cambridge. At first they were mere guilds of masters and pupils. While they developed from the monastic schools, they derived their authority from neither church nor state.

The thirteenth century was marked by a passion for learning and a shifting from one university to another—to sit at the feet of learning wherever it could be found. Standards, from our point of view, were low, and the students themselves drunken and disorderly, turbulent and profligate. The medical schools of Salerno, Bologna, and Montpellier began as offshoots of Moorish Spain; their teachers were Jews from Spain.

Friar Bacon at Pope Clement IV's invitation wrote a treatise on science. His *Opus Majus* summarized Greek, Roman, and Arabic science. In 1268 he returned from Paris to Oxford, but the next pope condemned his books and he was imprisoned.

Whereas Thomas Aquinas and Duns Scotus, contemporaries of Bacon, had tried to reconcile Aristotle and the Bible, Bacon, as we saw, wanted to burn Aristotle and begin all over again. He was the father of the modern scientific attitude—observe, experiment, and verify every statement. In "cobwebs of learning," however "admirable for fineness of thread and work," he could see no "substance or profit."

One of Bacon's conclusions was that "the ocean between the east coast of Asia and Europe is not very broad." Columbus quoted that line two hundred years later—and died thinking he knew just how "broad" it was. But meanwhile Aristotle, once banned by the church from the schools, had been restored with almost divine honours, and the renaissance of science had to give way until a new star appeared in the heavens to prove that Aristotle's heaven was not so immutable as it seemed to be.

It was one thing for Bacon to cry, "Burn Aristotle!"; another, to expose Aristotle as an old fogy. Modern science dawned with Copernicus and blazed forth with Galileo. Galileo especially practised what Bacon preached: experiment, verify. Intellectual giant that he was, it was Aristotle's misfortune that he trained with Plato rather than with Pythagoras. It took twenty centuries to prove that this earth is neither fixed nor the centre of the universe. It need not have taken so long if Christian Europe had not canonized Plato and Aristotle.

Christian Europe believed; the Bible was authority for its beliefs; Plato and Aristotle were so much manna to the centuries which hungered for cross-word-puzzle toys. By solving such puzzles they could become intellectual and remain believers. Plato, who would have been as little at home in a chemical laboratory as in a coal mine, and Aristotle, who could talk about brains, hearts, teeth, and ribs, more easily than he could look at them, were the intellectual inspiration of the ages of superstition and faith. Bacon is typical of the revolt against Aristotelian logic and Platonic philosophy. There were others.

When Ptolemy's *Almagest* was translated from Arabic into Latin, Greek astronomy was again available to Christian Europe—to inspire Copernicus to take his immortal flight. When Hippocrates was restored to Europe—from a Jewish Arabic version—Vesalius was inspired to found anatomy anew. When it was discovered that Archimedes said he could move the world if he had a place to stand on, Tycho furnished the place; and Kepler, standing on it, moved the world.

Archimedes, ancient Greek science; Kepler, modern science. It took Europe four centuries to begin where the Greeks had left off two thousand years before. By the end of the thirteenth century Christian Europe knew as much science as Moorish Spain and Saracenic Sicily. Roger Bacon was not the greatest scientist in that renaissance of science, but no one that I know of in that age saw more clearly than he the inevitable and eternal enmity between abstract norms of creeds, cults, faiths, beliefs, systems, and philosophies, and the facts the eye discovers in the vast laboratory of nature in which men live and have their being.

Jews have often been called misers, but the Jews of the Middle

Ages collected facts quite as assiduously as they collected gold. They looked upon facts as interesting in themselves and as above the spoken or printed word. Even a president of the United States broadcasting over the radio dresses his speech in the cast-off intellectual garments of a social order once at home on the Nile, Euphrates, and Tiber. Such intellectual hand-me-downs should have no home on the Potomac.

We expect a bishop to look to God for his authority and can forgive him for slitting our throats in God's name, but we expect our rulers to look to the electorate for their authority and can hardly forgive them for forgetting that experience is the supreme guide in dealing with social problems.

Experience follows experiment. Man is by nature an experimenting animal. With words he can project an experiment or formulate a hypothesis. Will the project work, is the hypothesis sound? Try it, make the experiment, put it to the test. Thus, and only thus, does man become experienced, expert, skilful, a master, an authority. We speak of the experimental sciences—and no harm is done if only we keep in mind that we all, all human beings, are natural-born experimental scientists. Few get far because they are denied the opportunity to experiment, or because they learn to rely on second-hand experience; their authority for their life is the printed page. Sometimes they talk like God and act like imbeciles. And sometimes they live in the Ghetto and talk like wise men.

## VI

Seven persons have each seven cats, each cat catches seven mice, each mouse eats seven stalks of barley, each stalk yields seven measures of grain: what are the numbers and what is their sum?

I can't do that problem in my head; I probably could with paper and pencil. The Egyptians started such silly problems in geometric progression and reckoned with stones, a primitive comptometer, rather more primitive than the Chinese abacus, not so primitive as counting by fingers and toes. Toes are rarely used in higher civilization except for toe dancing and corn plasters, and fingers, I believe, are regularly used for mathematical purposes only upon the Stock Exchange. But to say that because fingers serve High Finance they are therefore to be spoken of in the first chapter of every book on the history of finance, is to be absurd. It is even more absurd to speak of finance as a science or of a great financier as a great scientist. Yet we speak of mathematics as a science and speak of finger and toe counting in the first chapter.

It is not true, as Hankel says, that "in most sciences one generation tears down what another has built," and that "in mathematics alone each generation builds a new story to the old structure."

Is mathematics the "science of treating exact relations between quantities or magnitudes and operations," as Webster says; or the "abstract science which investigates deductively the conclusion implicit in the elementary conceptions of spatial and numerical relations," as Murray says; or "the science of quantity," as the Century says? At any rate, there are mathematics and mathematics: "applied," for example, as when dealing with a series of problems the connection of which is *objective*; and "higher," or all "scientifically treated branches," which excludes such branches as "practical arithmetic, elementary geometry, trigonometry, and a part of algebra" —presumably Impure or Lower.

What, then, is Boole's *Mathematical Analysis of Logic*, forerunner, as Moritz calls it, of Boole's other mathematical work, the "immortal *Laws of Thought*," and also dealing with neither quantity nor form? Mathematicians presumably would call these two books Pure and Higher, and they must be mathematical because a mathematician wrote them, but I balk at calling them science; nor can I see how a *Laws of Thought* which deals with neither quantity nor form comes within the realm of science at all. The spiritual realm, yes; higher metaphysics, yes; intellectual pastime, yes. I can even see how mathematicians built themselves up in the social scale by drawing a distinction between themselves and those who merely measured the earth, the corn, or the cloth. A land-surveyor is a mere geometer, the corn measurer is a farmer or grocer, and the cloth measurer is a weaver or tailor; all employ mathematics, they measure magnitudes, quantities, forms. They use arithmetic—add, subtract, divide; geometry—in measuring the earth; trigonometry —in solving triangles; and algebra—in solving equations. But, bless you, that is not science, for these practical people are too direct; they are not even mathematicians, for mathematics deals only with indirect quantities—far off, inaccessible, even non-existent. The more inaccessible, the *higher*; the more inconceivably non-existent, the *purer*. Pure abstraction. A geometry of *Lage*, a *Mathematical Analysis of Logic*, a *Laws of Thought*. An Eddington, a Millikan, an Einstein.

The history of civilization, we are told, is the history of science. History has thrown up some great rulers of men, but it has remained for our generation to produce a colossus of mathematics so transcending that among the nearly two thousand million human beings on earth only six—or is it five?—can measure up to his Olympian heights! Ordinary mathematicians hardly dare gaze up at these icy-cold regions, so blinding is the light. They talk about Einstein as the Israelites talked about Yahweh; and when they try to lead us mere mortals to a point of vantage where the heights may be viewed, they give us a pair of smoked glasses in the preface and warn us in the first chapter that they themselves do not understand it. How, then, may *we* expect to?

I admit that I have to take my courage in my hands to write so seemingly irreverently about the reigning colossus of science—even as a Malabar pariah looks with fear and trembling upon a Konkany Brahman and leaves the highway for the field when he approaches. I too shall have to pay for my temerity, because science has quite as many castes as Hinduism, and its Brahmans, the mathematicians, look down upon the pariahs who try to describe in words such entities as their eyes see and their hands touch, much as Big Bankers look down on small "butter and egg men."

I am not presuming to say that differential equations are not *higher* than test tubes, nor to deny that the man who first describes God or the cosmic universe in mathematical formulas will not be entitled to the crown as having achieved the most amazing intellectual adventure possible to man. But, we may be permitted to ask, will that God or cosmic universe satisfy any human want or contribute one iota to human welfare? The Babylonian year of 365 days is not exact science, but it will be more useful in helping Mr. Einstein to handle his problems of taxation and death than all the mathematical formulas the Big Six—or is it Five?—could think up in a million years.

Plato's Republic is an intellectual achievement of the first order, but no Democratic ass or Republican elephant could live in it, much less a Jefferson or a Lincoln. So with the universe our mathematical physicists dazzle us with today: the disembodied shades of Vergil's Inferno are more real—for they are as true entities with sensible properties as the entities the pure scientist imagines, endows with properties, and then describes in mathematical terms. In short, the difference between the Greek philosopher's solution of the universe and the modern mathematical physicist's is merely in the symbols employed: neither solution solves anything except man's insane desire to grasp the Infinite. Insane? Well, it is quite as sane as man's attempt to be a god.

In other words, science no less than religion can "lure the weary inquirer, the footsore seeker, on through the wilderness of disappointment in the present by endless promises of the future: take him up to the top of an exceeding high mountain and show him, beyond the dark clouds and rolling mists at his feet, a vision of the celestial city, far off."

But, you may say, Einstein is not, Newton and Descartes were not, particularly weary or footsore; and if they saw the celestial city they have not described it, as did St. Augustine. True. Equally true is it that their mathematical "city" has no more sensible existence than that of the Christian saint; it will not support life, it will not prolong life, it will not help us understand ourselves or our fellow-men or our position in or relation to the universe in which we live. And that, I take it, is the real business of science. Arrogant snobbery in science can be as destructive of progress in human welfare as dogmatic authority in religion. The things that count in human welfare cannot be forced into mathematical symbols or described in philosophic terminology.

It might seem that such academic discussions of such purely academic matters have no bearing, or bear so remotely, upon our own social and cultural problems that nothing more—and rather something less—need be said. But that is the very point I am driving at. A cage of rats, or a crib of babies, in charge of an attendant sporting a doctor's degree and an up-to-date mathematical methodology, is academic, but it is also symbolic of the serried ranks of "batteries" now turned on four- and two-legged rats in the expectation that human society can be reduced to *laws*. Nowhere is it explicitly stated, but the inference is allowed to prevail, that as a result of all this, society somehow or other will become law-abiding.

In other words, there is a growing tendency just now to assume that the social sciences can take over the unfinished business of the church; that by experiment and mathematics they can accomplish what used to be accomplished by faith and prayer. It may be so. At any rate, there is a feeling that faith and prayer having failed, why not try the *experimental* method? Endowments for social research now fall as easily by a shake of the tree of golden apples as chapels used to fall. Even Big Business has been persuaded, and if the craze keeps up we shall soon find no bank without its Pure Mathematician, no emporium without its Chief Statistician, no beauty parlour without its Logical Analyser, no tobacco shop without its Rational Deducer.

An expert Wall Street statistician told me recently that his technique is now so perfect that he can predict everything about what stocks *ought* to do—but practically nothing about what they or any one of them *will* do an hour hence. The list of gamblers who have beaten Monte Carlo by statistics is notoriously short; yet their mathematics was perfect, their statistics actuarily fool-proof.

Experiment with rats and young criminals, of course; it can be done! But how direct can the experiment be, how clear-cut? And the results of the experiment can be measured, but can it be certain that other results are not also measured? Laws? Certain inferences, possibly; and never beyond the range of probability. A really good experiment has little need of statistical manipulation or statistical treatment. The worse the experiment, the more dependent it is on statistical manipulation—and the less certain the resulting inferences. Yet the social scientists (or some of them) are clamouring for more statistics, better methodology. What they need to improve is not their technique but their experiment. And from the nature of human beings—and rats and even plants—that is not easy. It is their major problem just the same.

As Wilson points out, we are all necessarily statisticians. Most of our practical thinking and doing is essentially statistical in nature. But we must also remember that:

The major premises in our syllogisms when we deal with reality are in the nature of statistically established inferences from our observations. It is true that in those general propositions like law or gravitation, or the simple laws of mechanics, and of electricity, and of chemistry, the statistical element is very largely eliminated because the law is without exception. . . . In those sciences—in which the natural complications are so great that no adequate formation can be made, at any rate in the present state of our knowledge, by the process of disregarding minor disturbances—in those fields of science, in short, where the distinction between major and minor disturbances cannot be drawn because there are so many factors of about the same intensity, it is necessary to resort frankly to the statistical method. The method itself is something that anybody can learn, but the application of any statistical method to material which in itself is not reliable is probably even more dangerous than to apply a well-balanced judgment to the material without statistical analysis.

In another place Wilson gets even closer to the weak spot in most of the investigations today on foot to determine "specific," and even general, *abilities*.

A method is a dangerous thing [he says] unless its underlying philosophy is understood, and none is more dangerous than the statistical. Our aim should be with care to avoid in the main erroneous conclusions. In a mathematical or strictly logical discipline the care is one of technique; but in a natural science and in statistics the care must extend not only over the technique but in the matter of judgment, as is necessarily the case in coming to conclusions upon any problem of real life where the complications are great. Over-attention to technique may actually blind one to the dangers that lurk about on every side, like the gambler who ruins himself with his system carefully elaborated to beat the game.

Yet our Freudians go right on deriving theories of human behaviour, as though the *laws* of human behaviour could be postulated. It follows necessarily that the data they collect are largely predetermined. That, I repeat, may be art, or skill, or what you will; it is *not* scientific procedure.

Logical thinking is, of course, important in the sizing up of the values of materials, the drawing of inferences as to the meaning of the data, and the determination of future procedure. Having said that, we have only said what is pretty generally known, and even preached, but not so generally practised. We are not born with a rational "mind," nor are children notoriously logical thinkers. That many never learn the art is because it is easier to give free rein to thought than to restrain thought by keeping it checked up with the material world of reality.

There is little enough excuse for the physicist to wander off into the shadowy world of mathematical analysis far beyond his power to check experimentally. What excuse can there be for the social scientists who take refuge in pure research? What validity can be assigned to their graphs? Aristotle's physics was bad enough; his metaphysics is still good for Jesuits.

Civilization, such as it is, we may remind ourselves, exists because man just naturally loves to monkey with things, to fool around, to try out his capacities, to make experiments. If he did not have that proneness to monkey and experiment, he would be lower than the monkey he apes. He has that proneness above all animals. As a result, he has made wonderful discoveries and inventions, some of which are so extraordinarily useful that they have lifted him immeasurably high above the animal world.

Religion, philosophy, and science are, I repeat, simply attitudes toward nature. Religion postulates the supernatural; philosophy is concerned with the nature of reality; science is a way of dealing with such realities as men can discover with human sense organs and with such extensions and refinements of these sense organs as can be made by human hands. The scientific attitude, therefore, differs fundamentally from the philosophic and religious attitudes. It alone permits man to accept his world as he finds it and to use his brain and hands to get as much out of it as he can. It alone brings him face to face with nature, allows him to explore nature, putter around with tangible things, wheedle secrets from nature that can be turned to human welfare.

Man's supremacy over nature today is the result of the exercise of the scientific attitude. Our own civilization, in so far as it is superior to other civilizations, is the measure of the extent to which this attitude has been employed in solving such vital human problems as the health and happiness of all its members. That it is vastly inferior to what it might be is because too many socially destructive interests are so heavily entrenched that they can defy all attempts at scientific revision.

Conceivably the time will come when "human wickedness," as Seneca called it, will have "fully developed." It is hardly likely that "human knowledge" will ever complete its whole task. But note Seneca's frame of mind; it was not the scientist's, but rather that of a philosopher with a moralistic bent. He thought, as did Socrates, that wisdom was *virtue*, something to be garnered and hoarded for its own sweet sake, as some librarians regard books, and misers gold. Many in this age take the same attitude toward time. Time is money, we say; and we speak of the "precious" minutes, the "golden" hours. Socrates had no illusions on this score. "Time is made for slaves," he said. But what slaves were made for, or why there should be slaves, was not within the province of ancient wisdom; nor was the question raised as to the virtuousness of a slave-owner.

The point is simply this. Man evolved from an ape and created civilization because he could talk. Language was his most valuable single weapon, the most important civilizing agency. Let there be no doubt about this; but let us also be clear that talk can no more clothe a naked body or fill an empty stomach than can the bull-frog's croak or the bird's song. The croak may be sweet music in a fellow-frog's ear and the song may sound a note of warning—but only if they are not uttered in a vacuum but within hearing of fellow-creatures. Even then the biologic chain is incomplete until the fellow-creatures have made appropriate responses.

Down through the ages man has been building systems in words, in symbols, in mathematical formulas. Grant that many of these look beautiful to the eye, sound beautiful to the ear; call them philosophy, literature, art, æsthetics, religion; speak of them as signs of fine culture, marks of rare intelligence, as evidence of divine inspiration or the spontaneous outpourings of intuition. To the extent that they transcend the facts of experience, and in so far as they do not accord with observable evidence, they are beyond the pale of science.

One step further. I may or may not enjoy a differential equation, Newton's *Principia*, Seneca's Morals, or Socrates' Wisdom— and whether I do or not is nobody's business but my own; but as an individual specimen of the genus *Homo*, holding as I do that human beings are the most important things to know, worshipping no other god but man, and conceiving no values higher than those which make for human happiness, I am entitled to ask whether such works can be made to serve human needs. In other words, will they work for me and mine, or did they ever work for the good of mankind? If the answer is yes, they have real value and meaning. If Seneca's philosophy and Socrates' ethics stand this test, they are worth-while contributions to civilization. If Newton's laws and Einstein's equations are tools whereby man can grasp his universe and so more easily mould it to human ends, they too must be rated not only as achievements, but as contributions to human liberty, mileposts in the advance of civilization.

We do not ask of a poem that it tell us anything, nor do we go to a prize fight for information; but when I open my Moulton's *Astronomy* I expect to find the facts I am seeking: knowledge about the stars, how big they are, how hot, how dense, how far away, what they are made of, why they differ in colour, why the moon waxes and wanes, why some stars seem to maintain the same relative position, what that comet is off there, and so on. I may even hope for an answer to a very old question: just how and in what way can the stars influence my "fate"—or is the "reading of horoscopes" as childish as "reading" tea-grounds or crystal spheres?

I do not expect my astronomy to be pure or high. All I ask of it is that it be honest, unbiassed, truthful, sincere, scientific; that it give me the latest and best body of factual knowledge there is about this universe—which may be chaotic and running down or up, but which does tolerate plant and animal life, including curious human beings. My curiosity may even extend far beyond my possible personal needs, and while no astronomer can conceivably foretell how many millions of years this earth will last, I do go to him—and not to a physician, banker, photographer, politician, or philosopher—for his best guess as to when some big star might possibly bump another piece off the sun and so upset the solar system again.

And may we note in passing that countless numbers of human beings have given more time to guessing the end of creation than to creating a critical attitude toward guessing. If we insist, however, on resolving the fate of this earth, the astronomer is our man, a man who studies, observes, draws deductions from hypotheses, tries them out, reformulates them, makes more observations, makes a discovery, draws another deduction, tries it out, improves his technique, invents new additions to human sense organs, applies his mathematics, measures forms, magnitudes, quantities, relationships, etc. But he knows that no mere mathematical formula will get him any deeper into any star than a mere digging-stick got his great-grandfather .into the soil. I infer that mathematical formulas, like digging-sticks, may be put to useful ends. Certainly no one gets far in a modern machine shop or drug store who cannot measure form and quantity.

The Great Pyramids are oriented with respect to the stars and prove knowledge of geometrical form; they are the best evidence we have of early Egyptian applied mathematics. A 1500 B.C. papyrus shows symbols for addition, subtraction, and equality; and evidence that the Egyptians could solve equations with one unknown quantity. They also had a clever way of finding the circumference of a circle of a given radius; and of finding the areas of isosceles triangles and trapezoids.

Upon Babylonian theorems, or skill in computing, and Egyptian geometry, or skill in drawing, the Greeks, beginning in the seventh century B.C., built a mathematics which came down to us as "Euclid." Euclid's *Elements*, or geometry of line and circle, served to introduce mathematics to youngsters for over two thousand years, and, though replaced in the last few decades, the name is still synonymous with elementary geometry. Adelard presumably translated it from Arabic into Latin in 1120. It was put into English in 1570, and not till after Newton's time was it demoted from the university to the lower schools. But that Euclid was a Greek and could not resist being a philosopher may be inferred from his work on *Phenomena*, or a *Geometrical Theory of the Universe*. In other words, Euclid seems to have inspired not only mathematics, but Boole, discoverer of Pure Mathematics—the "subject in which we never know what we are talking about, nor whether what we are saying is true," to use Russell's oft-quoted line.

In other words, if I understand the matter at all, mathematics—arithmetic, algebra, geometry, and so on—is a useful adjunct in building pyramids, bridges, skyscrapers, radios, and the cosmic universe; but such mysterious insolubles as time, space, motion, continuity, infinity, can be "solved" only by Pure Mathematics. To put it another way, Aristotle's Formal Logic, the favourite intellectual pastime of the Middle Ages and the life work of Leibnitz, has during the last seventy-five years been made the Science of sciences.

In fact, I infer that Formal Logic is now so perfect (Pure) or so nearly perfected, that not only are all philosophic noses out of joint, but all scientific noses as well.

For example, a scientific "nose" may conceivably be useful in discovering the truth about a certain cancer "cure" or about the contents of a bottle labelled Pure Gin, or Pure Ergot, or Pure Olive Oil; but how trivial seems the virtue of such a nose compared with that of Pure Mathematics, which alone can discover pure truth.

No longer can we say with Democritus that "we know nothing, not even if there is anything to know." The philosopher's stone has been discovered. Words are no longer needed to describe the universe, nor senses to learn the truth about anything in the universe or on earth: symbols only, and Formal Logic, Laws of Thought, Pure Mathematics. Aristotle would be pleased, the Schoolmen are justified, and Leibnitz' dream of a Universal Characteristic has come true. Pure Mathematics cannot discover how many angels can stand on the point of a needle—because to "stand on" implies space and space finds no place in pure geometry; but it can throw light on such "entities" as points—and, I infer, even on angels.

That is art; that it is science I cannot see. That anyone is entitled to pursue art for art's sake is, of course, to be frankly admitted; but that the study of pure mathematics is a valuable "mental discipline," or that it "purifies" thought or ennobles moral fibre, is in my opinion an intellectual hangover from the Pythagorean distinction between abstract mathematics and concrete mechanics, astronomy, optics, surveying, music, and computation.

In fact, Pythagoras himself classified mathematics into: arithmetic or absolute numbers; music or applied numbers; geometry or magnitudes at rest; and astronomy or magnitudes in motion. That was the basis of Boëthius' famous *quadrivium* of Middle Age learning; grammar, rhetoric, and logic forming the *trivium*, the other three of the seven "liberal arts" of Capella's early fifth-century compendium of Grammar, Dialectics, Rhetoric, Geometry, Arithmetic, Astronomy, and Music, which is not yet quite extinct.

Pythagoras himself was something of a naturalist, and in one important respect was some twenty-five hundred years ahead of his time: he held that fossils were just what they appeared to be, *fossils,* petrified plants or animals, and not freaks of nature as they had to be when viewed from the background of the Book. Conceivably, natural history might have had a chance to claim men's attention earlier had not Plato's School of Heavy Thinkers succeeded the Pythagorean school of keen observers; indeed, that school by the time of Plato had become speculative rather than scientific. With its incorporation into Plato's Academy it lost all touch with reality and was less scientific than a modern divinity school.

Now, it is one thing to see a fossil as a fossil, and quite another thing to see the *significance* of fossils. In fact, the entire history of certain modern sciences lies between looking at fossils as fossils, and at fossils as related facts which could fit into a theory or which could be resumed by a law or hypothesis. Darwin was by no manner of means the first man to see fossils as fossils, but he was one of the first to get so excited about them that he thought he had to do something about it. His very ignorance about fossils, plus his desire to dispel that ignorance, was vastly more helpful to him than two thousand years' false assumption of a knowledge of fossils.

Excepting phenomena sensible to man only because of artificial aids to human senses, we of this age see little that was not visible or had not been observed by the ancients. But we see it in a different way: the thing seen fits like a key to make clear the relationships in a whole sequence of things or a whole group of phenomena. Hundreds of generations had seen what could be done with digging-sticks and with wedges; but Archimedes saw that with the lever principle behind the digging-stick he could move the world, and with the principle behind the wedge he could split it. He was more than a mere digger and splitter; he was a pioneer in the engineering sciences. He formulated the general principles on which such sciences rest.

Again, Archimedes was not the first to notice that as he immersed his body in a tub of water the water ran over the sides, but he was the first to see the *significance* of that fact—and it so excited him that he jumped up and ran off naked, shouting *Eureka*! And why shouldn't he be excited? He had discovered the famous principle of hydrostatics—thereby giving birth to mathematical physics, which, as Whitehead says, came of age when Newton sat in his orchard and saw what millions had seen before, an apple fall. Archimedes begat Newton.

Back to the bathtub, for it illustrates a broad principle.

When Archimedes got in his tub he had something "on his mind." A gold crown had been decreed for one of the temple gods, and certain weights of gold had been turned over to the goldsmith for the purpose. The crown looked all right, but it was rumoured that the smith had substituted some silver. How to find out whether the crown was *all* gold was the problem that had been passed on to Archimedes. As he realized that the weight of his body forced out an equal weight of water, he shouted his "I have found it!"

*Eureka,* as a motto for California, means Gold discovered, but in Archimedes' mouth it meant the discovery of a far more precious element—the principle of specific gravity. He was a great engineer and a great geometer; he founded theoretical and practical mechanics and hydrostatics. And paid with his life because he flared up in anger when a Roman soldier spoiled one of his geometrical diagrams. But the Roman general built a monument to him and adorned it with a mathematical figure. Cicero, 137 years later, discovered that monument and restored it. Its site is still pointed out in Syracusa, Sicily.

Archimedes himself, apart from his share in Euclid, was almost unknown to Europe till Galileo's time—chiefly because he left no record of his mechanical ingenuity, for that would have been unworthy the noble profession of a philosopher! In fact, only when he forgot he was a philosopher did he act like a genius. Even at that, he was the most inventive of all the Greeks. Professional verbalism was the bane of Greek science.

VII

There are endless things yet unknown about life, but a vast deal is now known which was not known fifty, two hundred, or two thousand years ago. The more that is known we owe primarily, not to astrology becoming astronomy or to alchemy becoming chemistry, but to man's beginning to look at life, to explore it, to question it. As long as man was absorbed in trying to read his fate in the stars or in the palms of his hands, as long as he looked upon the universe as a vast allegory, and to numerals ascribed moral virtues and magic values, he learned precious little that he could smoke in his pipe or use in the business of life.

The Arabian alchemist hunted for a philosopher's stone, the Christian alchemist for an elixir of life; they found neither. Presumably, there is no stone which will transmute base metal to gold, nor any elixir of immortality. But they *hunted*; and they hunted for the two things dear to human hearts—ready money and long life. Their hunt was no armchair affair but "pure" *research*—as pure as that of the Cave-man hunting a herd of wild horses, and presumably equally good sport. They searched and searched again, diligently, indefatigably, and found neither gold nor immortality; but they did find out some striking facts about the nature of chemicals and medicines. Possibly the Cave-man did not always find his horses; possibly he found something tastier and handier than wild-horse flesh. Discoveries are made by explorers, investigators. And every human being is by nature an investigator—and easily learns to abide by and live with the results of his investigations.

"Pure science" begat modern industry, says Millikan in his *Science and the New Civilization*. Well, pure science also begat ham and eggs, and a digging-stick, sailboat, and a solar year. Millikan, I suspect, is trying to sell "pure" science to our Captains of Industry —as the church used to sell pure religion to the Captains of Men. Buy our pure science, you will get rich; buy our pure religion, you will get salvation. You profit by the deal, and I get a living out of it.

My quarrel is with Millikan's use of the word *pure*—that, for example, "pure" learning pays; and with his argument that science has no quarrel with the religious spirit, but that, on the contrary, science has promoted religion by destroying *materialistic* theories of the universe. True, the physicist has let the atom get out of his hands: one second it is mass and the next energy. Well, one second the physicist's face is wreathed in smiles and he seems sane enough, and a moment later he looks and acts like a raving lunatic. That does not signify that he is a spirit or that there is nothing the matter with his teeth, or that he needs spiritual consolation and not the services of a very materialistic dentist who thinks of teeth in terms of what has been discovered by exploring teeth and investigating nerves, and by experimenting with analgesics.

If science means *scientia* and *scientia* means knowledge, a scientist presumably *knows*. And as every physicist knows that he cannot lift himself by his bootstraps, whether this universe is matter or spirit, so he should know that knowledge is only gained through the exercise of human senses, and that in and by itself science has no more merit, virtue, or worth than unborn cosmic rays. The discovery of these cosmic rays (by Millikan) represents an intellectual achievement of the very highest order, but I can see no more merit or virtue in their discovery than in the discovery of an amœba, nor any difference in the purity of the science behind the discovery. Millikan was not hunting cosmic rays, he was fooling around—as was that giant discoverer Leeuwenhoek when he was hunting through a drop of his saliva to satisfy his curiosity. We may turn the knowledge of cosmic rays to power—as the knowledge of amœba has been turned.

Now Millikan could never have discovered cosmic rays, nor Leeuwenhoek amœbas and bacteria, with mere human sense organs; they had to have more penetrating eyes and better tools than nature gives us. And so, as our early ancestors supplemented their natural tools and weapons with such artificial devices as digging-sticks, hoes, arrows, cows, irrigation, etc., modern man has extended all his natural facilities for acquiring information.

The difference between what Copernicus could know in 1543 and what Newton did know in 1687 is chiefly the difference between the artificial extensions (often called scientific instruments) to human sense organs available to Newton and not available to Copernicus. Among them are the telescope, microscope, micrometer (making delicate adjustments of the telescope possible), thermometer, barometer, slide rule, and pendulum clock. Galileo had a telescope—in fact, he reinvented it—but he had no artificial clock, and so to test a hypothesis he counted his pulse to measure time.

The history of the advance in nearly all fields of knowledge in modern times is an incredible fairy tale without taking into account the enormous strides made in the advance of these aids to the tools by which alone man extends his knowledge. Harvey, for example, made one of the most revolutionary discoveries ever made—that the blood circulates; but he could not possibly discover capillary circulation without a microscope. Hence we may forgive him for believing, with Aristotle, in "spontaneous" generation.

No one knows what life is, but the microscope let man see so far into life that he has had to revise his old beliefs. With the aid of the microscope and the test tube, and modern physical and chemical technique, life is as mysterious as ever, but living things are known as never before. A body of knowledge has been built up from this modern scientific attitude and this modern capacity for getting at facts, which has brought life within the range of scientific understanding; many of its manifestations have been brought within a control that would have astounded the leeches who bled Washington to death to save his life! Biology may not be as "exact" a science as physics—or as spiritual—but it is as *pure*.

We are now ready to see what Europe made of science once it had really decided to become scientifically minded. But may we observe again that it took four hundred years to make the step; and, especially, that by the time modern science really began, the European world at large had been jarred to its foundations by the application of the mariner's compass, the use of gunpowder, and the printing-press. I say "especially" because it is the fashion in some quarters to attribute modern scientific progress to the universities. The truth, rather, seems to be that science all along the line progressed in spite of the universities. Civilization certainly did.

The point I would make, and I think it worth emphasizing, is illustrated by a story told of Herbert Spencer. After he had delivered a lecture by request to the inmates of an insane-asylum, the great philosopher was shocked to discover one lunatic convulsed with laughter. Pressed to explain his mirth, he exclaimed between gasps, "To think that *I'm* in and *you're* out!"

Well, Europe was *out* at last—out to discover a world forced on its attention by the great voyages and made available by the printing-press. The Crusaders had discovered the East; Columbus and Magellan, the West; Diaz and da Gama, the South. The world was larger than it used to be and people were rushing to and fro as fast as slow sailing-ships and horses could carry them. And there were new teachers, new sources of inspiration which had slowly made their way west and had finally got into the schools; especially the *Almagest* and Euclid, incorporating the mathematics of Pythagoras, Hippocrates, Eudoxus, and the later Greeks—Archimedes and Ptolemy. It was a Ptolemaic world that Copernicus smashed, a New world that Columbus discovered; and Magellan sailed around them both. Now they are all connected by telephone and wireless, by steamship and airplane, and lit up by electricity. And look at them!

Or, rather, let us first trace the growth of that body of knowledge which has transformed the world and which cries aloud to be applied to the transformation of human society.

# CHAPTER TWELVE

*Modern Knowledge of Inorganic Nature, or The Growth of the Physical Sciences*

1. The Macrocosm and the Microcosm. 2. Copernicus out-Joshuas Joshua. 3. What the Inquisition Did Not Do to Galileo. 4. Newton's Falling Apples and Rising Tides. 5. Faraday's Successful Days. 6. Madame Curie and Radium. 7. "Physicists Have Become Demons." 8. Alchemy Becomes Chemistry. 9. The Earth Gets a Historian.

I

A COMET was recently visible in the sky. That "sky" is part of man's "nature"; the comet itself was presumably visible to man alone. Conceivably, there are such complex aggregations of as yet indescribable, complex cells of such stuff as man and dreams are made of, on other planets or stars; and if so, conceivably they have invented telescopes. But because an idea is conceivable, it does not necessarily follow that it will prove fruitful; it may be idiotic or merely foolish. Our knowledge of what is "off there" is still rather scant, but what we do know has been learnt by observation —with modern observatories and other technical appliances for sharpening our senses, extending our reach.

Why bother about the comet, anyway, or whether life exists beyond our atmosphere? Because we like to explore our universe. Exploring comets may not be so immediately useful to man as exploring measles or the graves of ancient kings; but as prostitution is said to be the oldest profession, astronomy is the oldest science. At any rate, comets come and go, and without a by-your-leave; but stars behave better. An observing farmer can plant his corn by a bright star. He probably puts his crop in by an almanac, but his ancestors read time by the stars; the sky was their calendar—"the sun by day, the stars by night."

An astronomer today will predict an eclipse within two or three seconds; astronomers four thousand years ago, within one day—an exceedingly proficient performance. But it was Thales of Miletus who saw the moon, not as a rabbit or some other childish fancy, but as a dark object visible because the sun shines on it, and causing an eclipse of the sun at regular intervals but always ten or eleven days later. The phases of the moon, fruitful source of ancient mythology, were to Thales mere waxing and waning phases due to natural causes.

A pupil of Thales said that the sun was not the burnished shield of an anthropomorphic god, but a body very far off and much larger than the earth. A century later Pythagoras and his school drew still closer to the truth as it seems to us today. Not only was the earth not the centre of the universe, nor even its most important member, but a sphere enclosed by an atmosphere and without tangible support. A little later another Greek saw on the moon, not a face, but mountains and shadows.

Then Democritus (430 B.C.) said the Milky Way was not milk but a vast number of stars too feeble to be seen individually. Twenty centuries later the world discovered that the old Greek was a scientific observer and not an ape telling a bedtime story to amuse his children.

Twenty thousand years after man had travelled the world around, two thousand years after the Greeks had observed that it was round, and two hundred years after Bacon had estimated that it could be sailed around, the earth had so shrivelled up and flattened out that it was hardly fit to live on; and Ptolemy with his list of eclipses of the moon, Pythagoras with his earthly sphere whirling through space, and Aristarchus with his earth revolving about the sun, might as well, for all the church knew or cared, never have been born. In other words, the solar system as we know it today is essentially the one the Greeks knew twenty-five hundred years ago.

That the earth rotated on its axis was proposed by the Asiatic astronomer Seleucus seventeen centuries before anyone again dared venture such a theory. Two Alexandrian Greeks (Eratosthenes and Apollonius), by close approximations of the earth's diameter and circumference, laid a firm foundation of mathematical geography, but nothing was built on it till modern times—with Kepler, Newton, and Leibnitz. Even the astronomical instruments of that superb astronomer, Hipparchus, were not improved upon until the time of Tycho, seventeen centuries later.

Hipparchus not only worked out the precession of the equinoxes (that circular swaying of the earth's axis in 25,868 years whereby the celestial pole describes a circle among the stars, giving us Vega as pole star twelve thousand years hence), but discovered that the Chaldean astronomers' year of 365¼ days was eleven minutes too long!

Hipparchus (160-125 B.C.) was also the first known astronomer to observe a new star. That so stimulated him that he measured the positions of more than a thousand stars and assigned to them the six degrees of brightness we still use.

Three centuries later came Ptolemy, last of the great Alexandrian Greeks. His *Syntaxis*, or *Almagest* as the Arabs called it, records the deeds of his scientific forbears and his own contributions to knowledge: atmospheric refraction, whereby objects seem to be higher in the sky than they are, and the moon's deviation from a uniform speed in its revolution about the earth.

With Ptolemy the light went out in Europe. When, a millennium later, his *Almagest* got back into Europe, Europe again passed out of the twinkle-twinkle-little-star stage; or, rather, out of thinking like a microcosm morally and physically dependent upon a macrocosm or cosmic universe of which man himself is the epitome. We probably even owe that philosophic generalization to that rare fifth-century B.C. Greek genius Democritus, so rich he could entertain King Xerxes, so disdainful of riches that he spent his fortune in travel and study, and so foolish—from a modern point of view —that he said he would rather discover a few true causes than own the Persian Empire.

For a Democritus bent on discovering the causes of things and devoting his fortune and his eyesight to their discovery, a Christian Europe hell-bent for heaven had no use; but for his microcosm-macrocosm idea intellectual Europe developed a passion, and the idea itself into a system so fantastic that the old Greek would have wept could he have seen it.

## II

In 1473, in a house still standing in Thorn, Poland, there was born a male child who, like Darwin, was to study medicine and later be destined for the church, but who, unlike Darwin, was to become a canon in a cathedral, and at death leave a book which was to prepare the world for Darwin. Which is another way of saying that Ptolemy's world had to be destroyed before Darwin could discover a place fit to evolve a monkey into a man. And it is noteworthy that as Darwin foresaw the far-reaching consequences of his conclusions, Copernicus saw his work as a challenge, not only to the world of the Bible, but to the world of common sense. What he did not see, but Darwin saw clearly, was that if the Bible is not authority for the earth, it is not authority for man.

"The scorn which I had to fear," said Copernicus, "in consequence of the novelty and seeming unreasonableness of my ideas, almost moved me to lay the completed work aside." And so he dedicated it to and also wrote the pope to use his influence to defend him from those who might attack his theory "because of some passage of Scripture which they had falsely distorted for their own purposes."

Copernicus was no great astronomer; his actual observations were not as accurate as those of Hipparchus nearly seventeen centuries earlier; his greatness lies rather in his daring. He not only had the Bible—and Aristotle and Ptolemy—against him, but everybody who could "see as plain as day" that the sun revolved around the earth and not the earth around the sun as Copernicus declared. More, he had Thomas Aquinas, great thirteenth-century reconciler of science and religion, of Moses and Ptolemy, against him. As man was the *object* of creation, the argument ran, so the earth was the *centre* of the universe; and around it revolved the concentric spheres of air, ether, and fire. These "flaming walls," or crystalline spheres, carried the sun, stars, and planets. It was a beautiful theory, that geocentric theory of the universe. The church liked it—and, as I have said, anyone could see that it was so; one had only to watch a sunrise.

We do not yet know just what a sunrise is, but this old monk Copernicus was the first Christian to see it as it is and not as it seems to be. It was a staggering blow to intellectual pride. His *De Revolutionibus* was the best astronomical work since the *Almagest*, and even more revolutionary—so revolutionary, in fact, that a century had to pass before his vision was confirmed by Kepler and Galileo.

With Galileo modern physical science was on its way; with Copernicus it started. Copernicus picked up the earth where the Greeks had left it and started it turning on its axis around the sun; but he could not prove it—in fact, he had little scientific evidence for his theory. Galileo made the theory a scientific hypothesis which would stand the test of experiment and verification.

Now, does it really matter very much to you and me, or to Christians and pagans, or to Moby Dick and Alexander Dowie, whether the earth revolves around the sun or the sun around the earth? We *see* the run rise in the east, we *see* it set in the west. Is it really important that we learn the facts behind that seemingly perfectly obvious phenomenon?

I have raised that question, not to try to answer it, but rather to emphasize a fact often referred to in these pages. The fact is this. Not much is yet known about man, life, earth, sun, and stars; no one has yet really solved any riddle of the universe; nothing is yet known of Beginning or End, of First or Final Cause; no one knows precisely what man's relationship to this earth is, or just what man's place in nature is; nothing at all is known about human destiny. But we can say with the Soothsayer in *Antony and Cleopatra*, "In nature's book of secrecy, a little I can read."

Millions today proceed on the theory that to a certain limited extent the destiny of human lives lies in human hands—and is not to be read in palms or stars. What else is the story of man's rise to his present supreme position but the story of his progress in freeing himself from such accidents as tend to make his life insecure?

That story of progress is marked by long chapters written in the blood of failure and under the pangs of pain and starvation; but on the whole there has been progress. At any rate, we are not apes or troglodytes, nor are we fugitives from a world of sin seeking escape in monasteries or mortifying our flesh in the hope of heaven. We do not know what a *best* world would be, or what constitutes the *best* life, but most people today think this is a better world to live in than it was five centuries ago. There seems to be evidence that more people live better lives and get more out of life than their ancestors did when Copernicus propounded a theory which, if true, meant that this earth was not the centre of the universe nor created especially for man's benefit, nor so created that man could do nothing about it but hope and pray.

If the earth is not, as was supposed, a mere springboard for getting to heaven, and man himself a poor worm of a sinner, an insignificant speck tossed about by blind, inexorable, mysterious, titanic forces, what, pray, *is* earth and what is man? Need it be said again that the answers to these questions will not be all in as long as earth lasts and man's tongue wags; but the 1931 answers are not those made by 1531 tongues. Even Established Belief no longer tries to force earth and man to fit the Bible; it does seek to twist the Bible to fit the new earth and living man.

The church itself hardly realized how momentous was the challenge Copernicus made to the very foundations of its authority. That does not lessen its significance or the magnitude of that "triumph of reason over instilled and spontaneous prejudice"—a triumph won not by Copernicus, but by an army of revolutionary thinkers which began with less than a corporal's guard and now numbers tens of thousands.

What touched Copernicus off? What suggested to him that possibly the earth was not in the centre of a heavenly dome carrying fixed stars, and other crystalline domes carrying planets and sun and rotating at different speeds? Why wasn't he satisfied to accept established cosmogony?

He had gone to Italy, where he had heard that the Greeks themselves had not all agreed with the views set down in Aristotle and Ptolemy. He had heard that Pythagoras had the notion that the sun was a great central heating plant or fire, and that the earth moved around the sun. That is all. An ancient Greek had differed from a less ancient Greek. But Ptolemy was *the* authority; Copernicus, with his borrowed notion, questioned that authority for more than thirty years.

Three years after Copernicus died, Tycho Brahé was born—of a Danish noble who dedicated him to the state. But the stars willed otherwise. In fact, a brilliant new star appearing in 1572 in Cassiopeia, if it did nothing else, said Kepler, at least announced and produced a great astronomer. Now, Copernicus was no authority yet, but Aristotle was, and Aristotle had talked about the "immutable heavens." But what business had a new star to show up in an *immutable* heaven? Tycho, from his magnificent, royally built observatory, began to quiz that new star and to put the Copernican system to the test.

Then fortune smiled again and a brilliant new comet hove in sight. What is a comet? Nobody knows all about comets, but in Tycho's day a comet was more than a freak of nature, it was a freak of an inspired mind. Not a mind that *thinks* things out like a philosopher, but *reasons* them out like a child after consulting father. In fact, the doctrine of original sin is less puerile than the old Christian belief about comets. One idiocy can lead to another just as surely as one good turn can deserve another—and more inevitably.

Sinful, wicked human beings give off gas; that gas, like the hot air it is, goes up; God's anger ignites the poisonous stuff; it then falls down on people's heads and causes bad weather, pestilence, sudden death, and Frenchmen! Yes, *Frenchmen*. I do not know if the author of that definition of a comet was ever canonized by the church, but he certainly deserves a degree *summa cum laude*.

I go further and admit that the church's definition makes a far more interesting affair of a comet than the mere atmospheric phenomenon modern science makes it. It is true, as so often pointed out, that science has destroyed countless interesting and even beautiful beliefs. But, to go no farther afield, note how, attention having been withdrawn from looking upon comets as causing such varied mischief as bad weather, Frenchmen, and pestilence, it can be directed to inquiring into such an evil as pestilence and such phenomena as weather and Frenchmen.

Tycho, among other things, restored weather, sudden death, pestilence, and Frenchmen to the laboratory, where they could be observed. He himself was a thoroughly brilliant and practical astronomer—even though he rejected part of the Copernican theory. Had he not lost his nose in a student duel and married "beneath him," he might have been more of a noble and less of an astronomer royal. He did lose his nose; and in 1600 befriended a young man named John Kepler—"one of those rare spirits that nature gives to science from time to time for the purpose of causing the work of many centuries to blossom."

Hipparchus was present at the birth of a new star—and was inspired to be an astronomer. To measure angles and lines he greatly improved the trigonometry the Egyptians had used. Considering his times and facilities, he is close to the top of the world's astronomers. A new star seventeen hundred and six years later inspired Copernicus, an extraordinarily keen observer. Kepler succeeded him as royal astronomer to the Emperor of Bohemia, and for twenty-two years studied, fighting poverty and disease and fleeing religious persecution. But before he died, from the place Tycho had given him to stand on he had moved the world with the idea let loose by Archimedes.

Kepler was the successor of Hipparchus, predecessor of Galileo, Newton, Einstein—all *great* scientists. Kepler illustrates what I mean by great. He began his career by checking Tycho's observations on the orbit of Mars against his theory of planetary motions— held to be circular by everybody from the Greeks to Copernicus. He discovered a discrepancy of eight minutes. A *fact*—for there was no doubt about Tycho's observations. The theory would not stand the test of that fact. But how many men feel that they must abandon a theory just because it will not stand the test of a new fact— especially when the theory has the support of a Plato? And so, on the basis of that error of eight minutes, Kepler undertook, in his own words, to "reconstruct the universe."

Mars, planets in general, move around the sun, not by epicycles and eccentrics, but by ellipses. But *circularity* then, as Schlesinger says, was as much a matter of scientific creed as conservation of energy is today. Kepler's "laws," while less popularly known than Newton's, took the stars out of the hands of empiricism and placed them in the realm of scientific astronomy. It is significant that Kepler announced his third law in a book entitled the *Harmony of the World*—which, he said, "will be read in the present age or by posterity, it matters not which; it may well await a reader, since God has waited six thousand years for an interpreter of his words."

III

Before Kepler died Napier had invented logarithms, but Kepler had little benefit from this device, which, as he himself had said, triples the life of an astronomer. Nor did Kepler have that other and vastly more important device, the telescope.

Invented logarithms; and the telescope! A time-saving device; a device for seeing farther into space. But why should man want to save time, to see farther into space? It is his nature. Man is naturally curious about the things that stimulate his eye; he itches to get his hands on them so that he may manipulate them—analyse them, tear them apart, study their relationships, their "go," as David Faraday used to say. What makes them go? And having satisfied that first and entirely natural curiosity, man tries to see the connection between their "go" and himself. What is there in their "go" that can be made to serve human ends beyond the mere gratification of idle curiosity? Modern civilization is the answer. It is based on the application of the science of the last five hundred years.

Behind the brick and steel walls of our smoke-ridden cities it is not easy for us to realize the appeal the starry heavens made to our ancestors, especially to those in Eastern climes with clean air and clear skies. Not until man had been domesticated out of almost all semblance of a natural animal, not until he had begun to live like an animal in a cage, was he forced to take heed of his wretched condition and turn his energies toward pondering the problems under his feet. And so it was that ages before he had worked out a technique for studying the infinitely small near-by things that make or mar life, he had become skilful in reading the infinitely large remote things. Hence astronomy was the first, as it is also the most useless, exact science; and biology the last and least exact science, as it is also the most useful. So it is that the astronomer analyses and weighs remote stars far more easily and exactly than the biologist analyses and weighs molecules of protoplasm. That the astronomer can predict the behaviour of the stars far more certainly than the biologist can predict the behaviour of living beings is a now trite truism.

To return to the telescope: may we point out that the eye of the greatest astronomer is but a human eye, that it is not eyes that see, but human beings, and that human beings get curious slants. It is true in a sense that we see, not what we are looking at, but what we are looking for; it is even more true that no eye is so blind as the eye that refuses to look. We do not ask our pet chimpanzee to look through a telescope, or expect a moron to see farther or more clearly with one.

This brings us to that grand old soldier of science, Galileo Galilei, who almost alone and unaided fought a fifty years' fight against entrenched bigotry and enthroned ignorance. And because, when old, infirm, and nearly blind, the terrors of the Inquisition forced him into a momentary recantation, we must not be deceived as to either his greatness or his extraordinary courage. Peter himself denied his Master—and under far less trying circumstances.

Galileo—to call him by his "Christian" name—was born 1564, the year of Shakespeare's birth. America had been discovered, Mexico and Peru conquered, and the earth's rotundity proved by Magellan. Copernicus had been dead nearly twenty years; young Tycho was just entering on his career; and Giordano Bruno was a lad of sixteen in a Neapolitan Dominican convent, among the "hounds of the Lord."

Let us first follow Bruno to the stake, for the light of its fire will illumine the days of Galileo. It is easier for us to look upon the Inquisition as a curious extinct monster of antediluvian days than as a terrible engine of destruction of a scientific attitude which under another name still functions to control the beliefs of millions of people and burnt its last victim less than a century ago. Galileo is a colossus of modern science, but the scientific attitude could not have gained so secure a foothold in the modern world had not Bruno, valiant knight militant of freedom of thought, prepared the way. Intellectual freedom does not necessarily lead to good works any more than a scientific attitude. Before either could prevail in modern Europe, war had to be waged against orthodox unreason, whether Catholic or Protestant.

Bruno as a student had failed to be impressed by the doctrine of the Holy Virgin and had fled to Rome from Naples, where he had been ordained priest at twenty-four. When it was learnt that he was the possessor of such forbidden literature as the writings of Erasmus, he had to flee from Rome. In Geneva he laid aside his

Dominican habit and flirted with the "deformed religion," as he called Calvinism later. In Toulouse he took an M.A. degree and taught astronomy, but again had to flee religious persecution. To Paris next; then to Oxford, where he lectured on the Copernican theory; then a dozen years of wandering, debating, and lecturing, through Europe—Paris, Mayence, Marburg, Wittenberg, Prague.

Finally he reëntered Italy by invitation and in Venice was treacherously betrayed to the Inquisition, which in 1600 burnt him at the stake. His martyrdom to science naturally did not make Europe any safer from attack on orthodox superstition. If the Copernican theory was scientifically sound, Biblical cosmogony had to go by the board, and with it the orthodox attitude toward man's place in nature.

Nine years after Bruno's martyrdom Galileo, then thirty-five, heard that a Dutchman had been playing with magnifying lenses. The news fell on open ears, and he promptly proceeded to make a telescope which magnified thirty diameters. Why did he want a telescope? Because while a student at Pisa he had heard a lecture on the new Copernican theory. It had seemed quite mad to him, but an "intelligent and wary" friend told him it was not to be laughed at. So Galileo decided to look into it; a telescope might be useful. Within seven years he had seen so much with his telescope that his fame had travelled across Europe.

It is not certain that Galileo was the first to point a telescope at a star; he *was* the first to understand the stars.

Obviously, what he saw cannot be described here, but we may note that he saw what Anaxagoras thought he saw twenty centuries earlier—rugged mountains on the moon. Galileo measured some of them. He also saw what Democritus thought he saw: a Milky Way without milk but quite full of faint stars—though he possibly would not have agreed with Shapley that there are forty billions of them. He also saw what many others had thought they had seen, spots on the sun, but which they thought they should not see because the sun must be kept *immaculate*: hence sun-spots had been considered planets revolving around the sun near its surface. Then Galileo saw what no naked eye could see, the satellites of Jupiter.

Would the head of the Department of Philosophy like to look through the telescope and see Galileo's sights? He would not. He even tried to persuade the Grand Duke that Jupiter could not possibly have any satellites: they *are invisible to the naked eye, and therefore can exercise no influence on the earth, and therefore would be useless, and therefore do not exist. Besides,* (added this professional lover of wisdom) *the Jews and other ancients, as well as modern Europeans, have adopted the division of the week into seven days and have named them after the seven planets. Now if we increase the number of the planets, this whole and beautiful system falls to the ground.*

So it does; but it fell hard and was a long time falling. Galileo gave his system to the world in 1638, but not for more than a century did the church permit it to be *taught*, nor for more than a century and a half permit it to be taught as *true*. And not until 1835 was his book withdrawn from the *Index Expurgatorius.*

Galileo did more than establish the Copernican as the true system—which alone would have made him immortal. By extraordinarily keen observation and ingenious experiment he carried mechanics immeasurably beyond the point where it had been left by the great Archimedes and only less great Alexandrian barber, Ctesibus, nineteen centuries before. True, Archimedes' works had only recently been translated into Latin, and their study no doubt was a huge factor in spurring Galileo to study mechanics. But study he did; and to such good purpose that he was able to write the laws of motion and thus pave the way for Newton—born the year Galileo died (1642).

Of the two, Galileo was the greater scientist; and one of the hardest headed men of all time. Newton was not content to be a scientist; he dabbled in religion. Even Thomas Aquinas, thirteenth-century saint, was less religiously minded than Isaac Newton. Galileo is the real founder of modern science. The very fact that the church tried to silence him is evidence that it saw in him a dangerous enemy to written authority. The church saw then what many Christians and scientists fail to see now, that there can be no peace between dead authority and living observation, analysis, and reflection.

In thus paying tribute to genius, however, we may recall that genius cannot rise alone and unaided; it takes more than one man to make a genius. The day Galileo was born Michelangelo died:

significant, as has been said, of nature's passing the sceptre from art to science, and certainly ending the dominance of Aristotelian tradition. When Galileo at the age of thirty-six was sweeping the heavens with his telescope, fifty-four-year-old Tycho was scanning the heavens at Prague, and thirty-year-old Kepler was working out the orbit of Mars. The cultural soil was ready for new growths. But that does not by any means signify that society at large was ready to accept the new growths, or even to look at them with an open eye, much less to nourish them with the milk of human kindness.

Not by any means. "Society" to Galileo was Aristotelian philosophy and the Catholic and Apostolic Church of Rome. The philosophers were all against him; the church admonished him and then commanded him to relinquish the "false opinion" that the earth moves, that there are spots on the sun, etc. Not only false opinion, but *pernicious doctrine* and *altogether contrary to Holy and Divine Scripture*. But the old man kept on observing and studying, and finally, in 1632, published his *Dialogue* on the Ptolemaic and Copernican Systems. Whereupon the *Cardinals of the Holy Roman Church, Inquisitors-General, and Special Deputies of the Holy Apostolic Chair against Heretical Depravity,* invoked the Most Holy Name of our Lord Jesus Christ and of His Most Glorious Virgin Mother Mary, and found, pronounced, judged, and declared Galileo guilty of the heresy of believing what every schoolboy on earth today is taught to believe, namely, that the earth does move and is not the centre of the universe.

Let him that is without guilt cast the first stone! And let us remember that Galileo at seventy was old and bent, and that excommunication in 1633 in Rome was not ex-communication in 1931, anywhere. The earth has moved, and the church can be defied more easily today than it could be then. Galileo had to recant, to swear with his hand on the Holy Gospels that he abandoned his false opinions, and abjured, cursed, and denied his errors and heresies. To recant, or be ex-communicated and possibly roasted alive, was the price he paid for having appeared "openly upon the Theatre of the World as a Witness of the naked Truth." But, said the Inquisitorial Court, the naked truth is "absurd, philosophically false, and formally heretical because expressly contrary to the Holy Scriptures."

Now, with the passing of Galileo and the beginning of Newton, modern science had two centuries behind it; but the papacy was hardly aware of the fact, nor that since 1450 every attempt to enslave the physical world by Mosaic cosmogony and to bind human under-standing by Holy Writ had failed. It had taken Christian Europe four centuries to learn that there was such a thing as Greek science, and two centuries more to lay the solid foundations of our modern sciences.

While so far I have stressed the advances in the astronomical sci-ences during these two centuries, advances were made in other sci-ences as well. But these advances could hardly have been made had not the astronomers broken down the ancient walls which for more than a thousand years had kept men shut up in schoolrooms or monasteries, trying to find out just what some inspired idiot had meant when he poured out his soul on parchment. The *word* was law; there was no need for eyes to discover anything. Everything had been discovered—by Aristotle; or revealed—by the Holy Ghost. To be scholarly, one went to school; to be wise, one learned ancient wisdom; to be learned, one developed the gift of gabbling learn-edly. System. We go in for standardization; they went in for sys-tematization. Knowing next to nothing of the physical world, they became ingenious in manipulating metaphysical worlds which they felt impelled to reduce to a system—and then tested it by a back-ground of logic, as though that gave it reality or was a test of its truthfulness.

Galileo dealt that world of sanctified hot air and Holy Writ the hardest blow it ever received. His trial before the Inquisition adver-tised the fact. For, be it observed, Galileo saw more than the rings of Saturn and the moons of Jupiter and the earth revolving around the sun; he saw through the tricks of the planets—their motions proper to themselves and in relation to each other. His discovery of the fourth moon of Jupiter is one of the finest bits of all scien-tific reasoning, and would qualify him for ever for a place among the *Stelligeri*. More. Not only should those ignorant of astronomical observations not clip the wings of speculative wits with rash pro-hibitions, to use his own quaint words, but ignorance should justify no belief in anything that can be put to the test of observation and experiment.

And what old Galileo said, young Galileo had practised. He watched the slow swing of the lamp in the cathedral of Pisa—and discovered the regularity of pendulum vibrations. The cathedral was his laboratory; the swinging lamp, his tool to unlock a great mystery. He climbed to the top of Pisa's famous leaning tower and made it an experimental laboratory to discover the law of falling bodies: velocity of descent was *not* proportional to weight, no matter if Aristotle had said so. Will men for ever prefer the decision of a Master to the evidence of their eyes? His deducing by experiment and describing with mathematical precision the acceleration of falling bodies, it has been said, probably contributed more to the physical sciences than all the philosophers of twenty-five centuries. Galileo did not *see* the earth rotating about the sun; he proved it by the laws of mechanics he himself had discovered, and with the help of iron balls, inclined tracks, boards, rails, bits of string, and brains and ingenuity. He founded dynamics and made physical science possible.

IV

As it is infinitely improbable that any event will repeat itself, and as the precise value of any event is infinitely difficult to ascertain, we may agree with Lagrange that Newton was the greatest genius that ever lived, or with Newton himself, who likened himself to a boy on the seashore looking for smooth pebbles and pretty stones, "whilst the great ocean of truth lay all undiscovered" before him. "If I have seen farther than Descartes, it is by standing on the shoulders of giants." Certain it is that Newton then, as Einstein now, was the complete and overshadowing genius of his time. One then, as now, acquired merit by touching the hem of his garment.

I make no claim to merit for confessing ignorance as to what it is all about, but as nearly as I can make out Newton (in his *Principia*, 1687) reduced the universe to three laws of motion which, according to Pearson, form the starting-point of most treatises on dynamics. "Physical science, thus started, resembles the mighty genius of an Arabian tale emerging amid metaphysical exhalations from the bottle in which for long centuries it has been corked down."

Pearson forgets that the bottle had already yielded up Copernicus, who put the earth in its proper and relatively insignificant place; that Kepler had written the laws of planetary motions; that Galileo had founded mechanics anew and set the earth revolving around the sun; that Roman had been succeeded by Arabic numerals; that algebraic symbolism was almost completely modernized; that Napier had written tables of logarithms, and Descartes analytic geometry: in general, that there was enough mathematics in the air to lead Leibnitz to invent the differential calculus simultaneously with Newton and in better notation and form. Presumably, these were among the "giants" on whose shoulders Newton said he stood. We may also speak of them as the soldiers of science in the fight against ignorance.

Newton was a farmer's posthumous child, born Christmas day, 1642, in a village near Cambridge. Like many other boys destined to be gentlemen farmers, he was sent to the university to be polished. But at a county fair he picked up a book on astrology—presumably to read his fortune. It settled his destiny instead, for he was excited by its geometry and trigonometry. That led him to Euclid and to everything mathematical he could get his hands on. Within eight years after entering the university he had been made professor of mathematics. But before that, he had been driven from Cambridge by the plague, and had spent many months at his mother's home—just when, as he said, he was in the prime for invention and more mathematically minded than he ever was again. It was while on the farm that he invented the infinitesimal calculus and formulated the binomial theorem, and there it was that the alleged falling apple started him hunting for the laws of gravity.

In finding them he brought the apple within the law that moves heaven and earth and causes earth's tides to ebb and flow. That law says in effect that every particle of matter in the universe attracts every other particle with a force varying inversely as the square of their distance apart, and directly as the masses of the two particles. Hence tides. The moon attracts particles at the centre of the earth less than at the surface on the side nearest the moon and more than the ocean on the farther side. The sun also causes two similar daily tides, but they are less than the moon-caused tides because the sun is so far from the earth. Two centuries and a half later, Darwin's son George, after long study of relative equilibrium in rotating liquids, made a great advance in the science of predicting tides.

Falling apples, rising tides. But how can we raise better apples; how, especially, can we make an apple tree go in for more apples and less wood; and how can we harness the tides and thereby make the earth safer for harness-makers? Both problems, as I see it, are mechanical in nature: one biophysical, the other physical. The mechanics of apple trees now begins to be understood, but not so well as the mechanics of tides; and that is because the biophysicists have not yet found an adequate description for any biological phenomenon. The physicists can describe their phenomena. They know—or did till recently—what they mean when they use such words as energy, mass, force, velocity, weight, etc. Mechanics is an art, an applied science. This is a machine age—begun by Archimedes, advanced by Galileo, and reduced to a science by Newton. And to a metaphysic, by some of our modern physicists.

I have raised this point before; it seems worth raising again. Let us return to Newton. His title to immortal fame, we are told, lay in his discovery of the one law or mechanical principle governing the whole universe. And what is this universe to which he acts as lawgiver? Matter: in quantity, density, and bulk; in motion, quantity, and velocity; and having an innate force or an impressed or centripetal force. Now, that *may be* the universe, or it may not; it *is* the universe which moves according to Newton's laws or single mechanical principle. What is real about that universe is Newton's conception of it; it differs from the Greek concept of the world in that it embraces the idea of continuous space. Space to Newton was a physical entity, a reality like matter or time. Nothing else mattered; nothing was real in Newtonian philosophy but matter, space, and time.

What, no ether waves?

Man, too prone to jump on a fallen foe, is busy clearing the air of ether waves so that there may be no interference with the electric waves that now go on the air. But it seems worth while to point out that the man who invented ether waves was clear-sighted enough to realize that while the Alexandrian Greeks could see far, their theory of optics was all wrong. Light rays, said Euclid, are straight lines emitted from the eyes. Well, then, why don't we see in the dark? And what is "darkness"?

A tenth-century Arab revised the absurd idea of eyes "emitting" light rays, propounded the law of refraction, and probably was the first to note the magnifying power of a spherical piece of glass. Above all, he really studied the human eye. But, as usual, Europe trailed along some five centuries behind. Kepler was the first to formulate a sound theory of vision in terms of light rays or stimuli, retina and brain. Galileo had tried to estimate the velocity of light by means of signal lanterns, but failed, of course, because of lack of sufficiently delicate apparatus.

His immediate successor in physics was not Newton, but Huygens, a Dutchman. He too tackled the problem of the velocity of light, and, on the basis of Römer's observations of a satellite of Jupiter, estimated that it travelled 600,000 times faster than sound. But *in* what? Sound or mechanical waves travel in air, and slowly; light travels fast—in fact, three times faster than Huygens thought it did. He invented *ether* as its medium, and, despite Newton's authoritative opinion, held that light travels like a wave rather than like a ray.

Now note, this Dutchman did not know what light is, but he did have a theory about the way it travelled—a theory, by the way, about a century ahead of his time. For that theory he needed something else—something finer, harder, and more elastic than air. He hypothecated ether; and then went ahead and worked out a consistent theory to account for reflection and refraction.

Huygens also worked out an achromatic eyepiece for telescopes, studied polarization of light, and put spiral springs in watches and pendulums in clocks—and put them in on mechanically sound principles. He applied mathematics—not like a Galileo or a Yankee, but, considering his time, with great practical ingenuity. He invented "ether"; he had a sound theory about light. He died 1695. He ranks among the chief lights of the renaissance of the science of mechanics which began with Archimedes.

What is light?

## V

"I have at last," wrote Faraday in his diary, "succeeded in magnetizing and electrifying a ray of light, and in illuminating a magnetic line of force."

In the strictest sense of the word, that was *some* success; more, it was real progress, one of the most astounding steps man ever took, one of the last steps he had to take before he was finally freed of the ages-old accumulation of superstitious fears and fearful beliefs in supernatural powers and mysterious influences.

No man knows just what electricity is, but enough is known about it to force it to work for man. He no longer fears it—though he does handle it with gloves. He generates it and he controls it. And all because he found out that the mystery of the spark in the stroked cat's back is no more, no less, than the mystery in the thunderbolt of Jove. As Darwin restored man to nature as a natural phenomenon to be studied like any other phenomenon, so Faraday delivered the last stronghold of nature into human hands for human observation and manipulation.

Faraday announced his success in 1845—almost a generation after the end of a war whose soldiers' widows are still a charge on this nation. There is no innate connection between widows and Faraday, or between pensions and electricity; I am merely trying to emphasize the fact that some of us were born and married long before the dawn of the electric age.

The nineteenth was an amazingly fertile century—but whether more so than this one will prove to be, no one can yet say. If in three decades only we have invented a Space that will swallow up everything, conceivably we can invent a Frankenstein who will destroy everybody. Before we turn the corner into the twentieth century, let us note that certain agencies had been accumulating during the preceding two centuries which tended to make it not only possible but easier than ever before for man to throw off the academic hood and gown and the ecclesiastic cross and robe, and have a "look-see" on his own authority and without the traditional smoked glasses.

One greatly favouring condition was, of course, the complete smash-up of the world itself. It was really more than smashed; it was knocked out. Materially, by Columbus *et al.*; spiritually, by Copernicus. With the world-that-was gone, another had to be discovered. That necessity alone mothered new tools and appliances, new ways and means. Some of these we have already seen. Let us be more specific about a few of them.

The seventeenth century, as we saw, yielded many new devices for reckoning, measuring, analysing, comparing, etc. Also mathematical devices, or conceptual tools as they have been called: Napier's logarithms, Descartes' analytical geometry, Pascal's calculus of probability, Leibnitz'-Newton's differential calculus. There were also many equally important scientific instruments developed. As some one has said, a screw-cutting lathe can be as important an instrument of knowledge as the differential calculus. Telescope, microscope, barometer, thermometer, air pump, manometer, etc.

Take the thermometer from the scientist's hands—physicist or physician. Even Galileo anthropomorphized a natural phenomenon he but dimly comprehended, and repeated the old line that nature "abhors" a vacuum. Still, he did make some beginnings in thermometry, but it was his assistant, Torricelli, who carried on his master's experiments on heat expansion. He used mercury instead of water in his experimental tubes—long called "T. Tubes," just as the empty space above the mercury is still called the "Torricellian vacuum." The mercury did not rise thirty-three feet "as it should," but only a few inches. Why? Difference in specific gravity between water and mercury. The water or mercury does not rise in the tube because nature abhors anything, but because air is heavy and the atmosphere *forces* the liquid up the tube. That is why water rises in a pump thirty-three, and only thirty-three, feet.

*Nonsense*, said everybody. Well, if Torricelli is right, said Pascal, liquids will not rise as high on a mountain top as in a valley. The experiment was made. The atmosphere itself now became a new object of curiosity, and in the barometer (*baros*, weight) and thermometer man had invaluable instruments of precision. But not for another hundred years did he have the sense to learn that freezing and boiling points are invariable. And not until 1774 was it discovered that air is not a simple, indestructible, unalterable, elementary substance. Modern chemistry was born that year. And, still more curious, Watt's steam engine was not a *steam* engine: he merely used steam to produce a vacuum; he proposed to run his engine—an improvement on one invented by Newcomen—by atmospheric pressure!

Again, with the passing of one classical authority after another in the seventeenth and eighteenth centuries, Latin passed out in one country after another as the language of the highbrows. The vernacular became the medium of thought. Scientific thought thus also became nationalized—unfortunate but inevitable. Scientists themselves began to foregather to discuss their problems and perplexities in societies modelled after Plato's Academy and Aristotle's Lyceum, and the Museum at Alexandria.

The first scientific academy was founded in Naples, 1560; Rome, 1603, having Galileo as a member; London, the Royal Academy, 1662—among its early members, Huygens, Malpighi, Leeuwenhoek, and Newton; Paris, 1666. Leibnitz founded the Academy of Science in Berlin in 1700, and helped to organize those of St. Petersburg, Dresden, and Vienna—and, incidentally, was two and a half centuries ahead of our own doctors of education in realizing that it is next to impossible for us to learn to think straight in one language, much less in two.

We force our youth, said Leibnitz, to undertake the Herculean labour of mastering different languages, whereby the keenness of the intellect is often dulled, and condemn to ignorance all who lack knowledge of Latin.

As early as 1743 Ben Franklin proposed the founding of a Philosophical Society in Philadelphia, but it was not organized until 1769—with Franklin as its presiding officer until his death in 1790.

Franklin's kite was no toy, but a serious and even daring experiment. He was not the first to study electric or magnetic phenomena. Magnetic phenomena especially had excited the Greeks, who played with "lodestones," rubbed amber, etc. But apparently it was Gilbert, physician to Queen Elizabeth and twenty-four years older than Galileo, who began to make open-eyed experiments in magnetism and electricity. He proved that the earth itself is a lodestone, a great magnet, which accounts for the behaviour of the compass or magnetic needle. Also that glass, sulphur, resin, etc., could be so excited as to attract other bodies—like amber. What is it that does the attracting? *Vis electrica*, he said; and we still call it electricity.

He even formulated a hypothesis of electric *effluvia*; and we still speak of electric "juice." He also coined the phrase, "north and south poles." Galileo respected him and Priestley referred to him as the Father of Modern Electricity.

Early in the eighteenth century an electric spark had been compared to lightning. Franklin said it was lightning, and proved it by his kite experiment in 1752. He also showed that atmospheric and machine-made or frictional electricity are the same thing. But not till 1820 did the attempt to discover the relation between electricity and magnetism succeed. That discovery led Ampère to begin his epoch-making investigations in electro-dynamics; it also led Faraday to turn from chemistry to electricity.

Faraday fortunately had no university education to overcome. He came of age as a journeyman bookbinder and with an open mind. In binding a volume of the *Encyclopædia Britannica* he became excited over an article on science, so interested that he applied to the Royal Institution of London for a job. There he worked for some years as assistant to Davy, the great chemist. Then, alone and in penury, he turned to electricity—to make capital discoveries of far-reaching consequence both in the theoretical field and in practical application. The whole development of electrical engineering, says Bragg, hangs on a single day's work of Faraday in 1831.

What Faraday conceived—magnetic fields, electro-magnetic theory of light, atomic theory of electricity, and quantitative law of electrolysis—Maxwell and others established in the following generation. "Practically every experiment in physics is a modification of an experiment which has gone before." Carnot in 1824 had laid the foundation of all later work on heat. Gibbs a half century later showed that Carnot's principle or "cycle" (the Second Law of Thermodynamics) holds true throughout the entire physico-chemical world. Maxwell carried on, and identified heat with light, and both with electricity. He predicted electro-magnetic waves.

What Maxwell proved by mathematics, Hertz demonstrated by experiment. It is interesting to note just how this demonstration came about, for it is typical of most advances in human knowledge. Maxwell's *Treatise on Electricity and Magnetism* (1873) was an important book, but no one knew just how important. His foundation, as he himself tells us, was a thorough mastery of Faraday's

*Experimental Researches.* Being a master mathematician, he sought a way to express his master's hypotheses mathematically: What formula would supply the needs of electromagnetic forces, or, in other words, take the place of the hypothetical ether? He concluded, and mathematically proved, that the *medium* "good enough" for light phenomena was good enough for electromagnetic. From which he concluded that light is electromagnetic; which he expressed in the mathematical form of differential equations—often spoken of as a "world formula." For the time being it was science's highest attempt to say God in mathematical terms. It admittedly was an idealization. But it seemed to be ultimate and final.

Europe did not take too kindly to Maxwell's theory, but the great Helmholtz asked Hertz, one of his pupils, to look into it. Quite accidentally, a few years later, Hertz thought of a way of testing Maxwell's "inference that light consists in the transverse undulations of some medium which is the cause of electric and magnetic phenomena." He then began a series of brilliant experiments which completely verified Maxwell's inference. To do that he had to determine, not only the actual existence of electromagnetic waves, but their properties and speed as well. Then came Marconi, with marconigrams or wireless messages carried by electromagnetic or Hertzian waves; and a few years later, Radio Corp. and Radio Corp. pf., A and B—and all three moving up and down the Big Board according to no known human law.

Hertzian waves, 1888; Marconi's wireless telegraph, 1896; de Forest's wireless telephone or *radio*, 1909; etc. But in 1895 Röntgen discovered X-rays, in 1896 Becquerel discovered radioactivity, and in 1898 Madame Curie discovered radium—and in 1929 we presented her with a gram of it. To extract that one gram we had to treat five hundred tons of Colorado carnotite ore with five hundred tons of chemicals, to say nothing of the coal and water used in the process, or the thousand men and hundred thousand dollars.

That gram of radium, a nation's gift to a woman, and that woman, twice honoured with the Nobel Prize, discoverer of something more sensational, more epochal, than a continent or a planet, represent . . . Well, just what do they represent? A chapter in the history of civilization—a big chapter, an important chapter? Does it mean that Madame Curie herself is as big a figure in history as Cæsar, or as important to civilization as Napoleon? Dozens of equally foolish questions rise before me. I make room for only one more, one which requires no answer, for it answers itself: Is such a combination of events conceivable at any previous time in human history? And if there are such entities as human souls, I should like to think that among those present at that presentation ceremony were the ghosts of Franklin, Volta, Oersted, Faraday, Maxwell, Hertz, Röntgen, Becquerel—yes, and of Hypatia, Galileo, Bruno, and Pope Sylvester II.

## VI

What is *radium*—matter, a body, an element?

While we have been watching astronomers setting the world in order and physicists dragging the lightning down, and both calculating the distances of stars in light years (instead of in inches, feet, and miles), an allied group of scientists has been resolving matter into its primordial elements. But before we turn to that story, we need a fact to set the stage for what to me is the greatest of all melodramas in man's attempt to solve the universe between breakfast and supper.

We return to the good old days of 1895, when the purest scientists were sighing like prematurely senile Alexanders because there were no more worlds to conquer. Matter had been resolved into seventy-odd unchangeable and indestructible "elements." They not only had the elements' number, but their atomic weight, their laws. Not only had the laws been written for celestial mechanics, but for atomic mechanics as well; ether-physics and matter-physics were finished chapters. The whole universe, in short, was witness to man's ability to discover its fundamental principles of Mass and Energy, and the policemen Momentum to keep it moving. And chemist and physicist saw that it was good; in fact, they were just as pleased with their creation as Yahweh was with his Six-day Genesis.

I said "seventy-odd" elements. Yet when Columbus discovered America less than a dozen elements were known, and of these the ancients knew nine—though not as "elements" in the modern sense. Gold, silver, copper, iron, lead, tin, mercury, and sulphur were easily discovered and identified because they occur "native." Charcoal (carbon) was, of course, also early known. During the Middle Ages arsenic, antimony, bismuth, and zinc were added to the list; and cobalt, platinum, and nickel in the eighteenth century. But not till 1772 was it discovered that air was a mixture of gaseous *elements*. Nitrogen was the first discovered, and two years later oxygen. With the turn of the century twenty-eight elements were known. By 1839 the number was increased to fifty-five, and by 1886 to seventy-two. That was supposed to be final.

In the spectroscope modern chemists have had an enormously valuable assistant in analysing matter. That device takes advantage of the fact that light rays—from any substance heated to the stage of incandescent vapour—passing through a prism are broken up into lines and appear on a screen as a *spectrum* or band of colours—red, orange, yellow, etc. As each group of lines of colours in the spectrum is characteristic of one, and only one, element, the spectroscope is an invaluable instrument of precision in the analysis of compounds.

By 1860 the spectroscope had been used for analysing the composition of the sun and stars and for solving other astronomical problems. As each chemical element has only its own coloured lines with their own wave lengths, enormous advance was made in identifying the matter of the earth with the matter of the universe. And that had been done to everyone's satisfaction by 1893.

About that time Lord Rayleigh, in trying to find the density of the common gas nitrogen, discovered a new gas, *argon*, a new element. Within a few months a whole family of chemical elements had been discovered, including helium and neon.

For over a century, chemists had been suspicious of air. After removing all the oxygen and nitrogen they could from any given volume of air, there was always some gas left. That fact was known as early as 1785. Rayleigh, confining his attention to nitrogen, discovered his "air" nitrogen was heavier than *pure* nitrogen should be; so, with his assistant, he "burnt" the nitrogen—passed it over hot magnesium, with which it unites. Still there was some gas left. Because it is so lazy, "inert," they called it *argon*, Greek for lazy.

That is why argon is now used as filler for incandescent lamps using tungsten filaments—tungsten having been discovered about the time Cavendish discovered that there was something to be discovered in pure air besides oxygen and nitrogen. Just as we had been breathing argon without knowing it, so it is believed that the famous Damascus steel was famous because its steel contained tungsten, though its makers knew nothing of tungsten itself. As no other metal has such a high, and carbon alone of all elements a higher, melting point; as carbon filaments require nearly three times as many watts per candle power as tungsten for the same light; as argon makes a perfect medium for artificial illumination; and as its presence raises the boiling-point of tungsten: we use hundreds of millions of tungsten-argon bulbs a year, and at a saving of hundreds of millions of dollars.

Note also, as we pass by, that one man at a lathe with tungsten-steel tools can now do what formerly required the work of five men at five lathes. Figure that out in reducing the cost of all machine-shop work—in millions of automobiles, for example.

Helium, second of the argon family, was discovered by the spectroscope in the sun; hence its name (*helios*, Greek for sun). That discovery was made by Jannsen, French astronomer, in 1868. Helium was isolated by Rayleigh's pupil, Ramsay, in 1894. It also is inert, and very light, insoluble, conducts heat well, and liquefies only at an extremely low temperature. Its full possibilities are only just beginning to be recognized. Its adoption for dirigible balloons is comparable in a way to the adoption of argon in incandescent lights; and, in a smaller way, to the use of neon (the "new one") in neon lights. In 1914 helium cost two thousand dollars a cubic foot; now, less than ten cents. Almost any child can remember when there were no neon lights; now there are thousands of miles of them. A neon light is pure neon gas in a high vacuum tube—unknown before radio tubes, not yet ten years old—ionized by an electric current. The electric current is generated by a dynamo.

On August 29, 1831, Faraday noted in his diary the result of a certain experiment. That experiment was one of innumerable experiments to discover what, if any, were the connexions between electricity and matter (or the elements) and between electricity and light. Speaking of that August 29th experiment a few days later, he noted in his diary, "Probably build a machine up this way." He had discovered the principle of the dynamo; he had made a dynamo in principle. Some years later he wrote another of his prophecies—at which he was far superior to any Israelite: "Perhaps heat is the related condition of the forces when change of gravity occurs. . . . Hence chemical action is merely electrical action, and *vice versa.*"

By 1833 Faraday, after long experimentation with electrolysis, had anticipated the atomic theory of electricity. Passing over the work of Maxwell, Helmholtz, and others, we come to Crookes' experiments with vacuum tubes. He discovered that they conduct electricity; he called it "radiant matter," and spoke prophetically of the "borderland, where energy and matter seem to merge." That was in 1874. Hertz, Lenard, and others also experimented with vacuum tubes. But Röntgen in 1895 quite by chance discovered that radiations from Crookes' tubes mysteriously penetrated substances such as wood, fabrics, flesh, etc., supposedly impenetrable by any light rays. He called them X-rays; we call them X-rays, or Röntgen rays, and with them X-ray teeth and bones and make movies of the movements or action in our heart and alimentary canal.

The following year Becquerel experimented with X-rays and all the fluorescent material he could get his hands on: such material *might* also be a source of deeply penetrating rays! He discovered that any uranium compound gave off such rays—"Becquerel."

Uranium does not come from Uranus, but from pitchblende, in which it was discovered about a century and a half ago, and from other uranium ores, such as carnotite in Colorado. Also from cleveite, where Ramsay first discovered helium. The Curies took up Becquerel's clue and discovered something in pitchblende which was far more radioactive than pitchblende itself; this was barium-chloride, also a compound. From that they finally got radium chloride—millions of times more radiant than pitchblende. Professor Curie died, his wife carried on; and in 1910 isolated radium (*radius*, "ray"), a new element. Madame Curie's was more than a brilliant discovery; it was a world sensation.

VII

What is radium? What is matter? What is an element? No one knows. Nor am I trying to be facetious over what some consider the most serious problem in the universe, if not on earth. I am trying to emphasize what seems to me an important point, namely, that science or philosophy can get no closer to God or Absolute or Finality than religion. A scientific attitude, on the other hand, can get us closer to the things a human being should know in order to live more freely, more humanely, than any other point of view. And may I insist again that near the close of the last century two sciences thought they knew the physical world and had it amicably divided between them. Thus, chemists dealt with the matter of the universe; physicists dealt with its energy—light, heat, electrical, sound, mechanical, etc.

By further mutual agreement, matter was defined as anything that occupies space or has mass; energy, anything that can do work. As you and I obviously occupy space, which we can prove in various ways—as, for example, by stepping in a tub of water or on the scales—and as we can and do work, asleep or awake, we came within the ken of chemist and physicist. But as we are more or less alive as distinguished, for example, from a lump of coal which has long been dead, or from a lump of salt which never was alive, and as the Greeks called life *bios*, we have biochemists and biophysicists —although, when something goes wrong with our liver, which certainly has mass and is a regular chemical laboratory for work, we call in a physician and hope he has had a sound training in physiology. And the *physic* in both words is the same old Greek word we find in physicist and physics meaning *nature*, though physic also may signify a purge.

Well, mass to many suggests the liturgy of the Eucharist; to others, blue mass; to still others it suggests bulk—such as an elephant or a mob. To the scientist it means matter and can be measured and weighed, and once upon a time was thought indestructible. In other words, matter is what man thinks it is, and most of us think of matter as something we can see or feel or taste or smell, or sense by some refinement or extension of human sense organ.

But what was sensed by sense organs good enough for life in the jungle was one thing, and what must be sensed in this modern chemical age is another thing and not very old, either. In fact, modern chemistry may be said to have been born in 1661 with the publication of a book called *The Sceptical Chymist*. Boyle, the sceptic, allowed that chemists write "darkly, not because they think their notions are too precious to be explained, but because they fear that if they were explained, men would discern that they are far from being precious. . . . Not having clear and distinct notions themselves, they cannot write otherwise than confusedly of what they but confusedly apprehend." If those who "trouble the world with riddles and impertinences" would only keep still, we should "escape an inconvenience."

Our pharmacopœias are still burdened with Middle Age alchemies, but chemistry passed from "natural philosophy" to science when chemists began to distinguish quality from substance. As late as 1848, however, a text-book on chemistry spoke of heat and light as "subtile species of matter," although it had been shown a half century before that heat could be generated by friction alone, and though by 1839 Joule had begun an epoch-making series of experiments which showed that heat and work—electrical and chemical energy—were mutually equivalent; or, to put it another way, that heat and work are equivalent and interchangeable. "Energy is unperishable and immortal," said a hopeful chemist in 1843.

At a temperature of minus 273° Centigrade (minus 459° Fahrenheit) all internal activity constituting heat ceases; but even in the most charitably disposed person all internal activity ceases long before his temperature falls to mere zero. And it is only an hypothesis that the atoms of a hydrogen molecule cease all internal activity at minus 273° C. Absolute zero is but a closer approximation to the truth than zero old style. Conceivably, it is not the best approximation that can be made; it was the best the nineteenth century made, and was so good that it has not yet been bettered. At any rate, when one speaks of heat, one speaks of Rumford, Carnot, and Joule—and of J. R. Mayer, a German physician whom Joule plundered.

Joule was a pupil of the English school-teacher Dalton, who in 1808, in his *New System of Chemical Philosophy* (note the word "philosophy"), propounded the atomic theory of matter. That theory neither told all the truth about matter nor gave us very much information about atoms, but it was an honest theory and more truthful than any proposed before. Best of all, it was a useful theory —workable; so workable and so useful, in fact, that a vast edifice has been built upon it. What that structure is may too easily be seen for me to point it out. Dalton's hypothesis emphasized the atomicity of matter. Well and good. But emphasis also had to be laid on the fact that even matter in gaseous form exists, not as single, but as two or more, atoms. Only the rare inert gases already referred to are "monoatomic." The matter the chemist deals with is molecular—although under great temperature and at very low pressure most molecules can be atomized, or perhaps I should say monoatomized.

It was Avogadro who emphasized the molecular nature of matter, in 1811, by the famous law which bears his name. Mendeleeff's discovery (1869-71) of the "periodic law" of chemical elements, the generalization by which elements are now arranged in "natural" groups or families—halogens, alkali metals, inert gases, etc.—was so good that chemists, after calling the roll of the elements, predicted that certain "numbers" were missing. It was a prediction comparable to that by which Neptune's discovery was made possible and "missing links" probable. Several "missing" elements have already been found, one in the very year that Mendeleeff formulated his law.

Note the essential difference between moral and scientific law: one deals with *oughts*, the other with *musts*; one "views" with hope, the other with confidence—and when confidence has been lost in a law of science it is abandoned forthwith. One other point about Mendeleeff's law. The discovery of X-rays and radioactivity not only did not dethrone it, but on the other hand strengthened confidence in its soundness and usefulness. Even the physicists respect it, but, as we have seen, are undecided whether this universe is stuff or energy, coming or going, a creation or creating. Whatever it is that is primordial, there seems to be reason for hypothecating primordial electrons. At any rate, under Arrhenius' *Theory of Electrolytic Dissociation*, chemistry joined hands with physics in becoming a quantitative science, both equally blessed by the calculus. It was Mendeleeff who established modern inorganic chemistry; Arrhenius who founded physical chemistry, and largely on the basis of work done by Clausius, Faraday, and Davy.

"Unperishable" and "immortal" are human concepts; to project such concepts into energy (another human concept) is, among other things, an interesting intellectual pastime, and may conceivably be as reasonable a view of the universe as the suggestion put forth last year that the universe is committing "suicide." Why this pessimistic view? The Second Law of Thermodynamics says so. It is really distressing and somewhat confusing; but very important for man's peace of mind.

Now, man has not yet succeeded in making a perpetual-motion machine, but the idea has beset him for centuries. Nature is such a machine; so says the First Law of Thermodynamics. But that law presupposes not only a universe, but a wound-up universe. Stuff and energy exist. The stuff, like immortal souls, is eternal and indestructible; there it is, in the sun, moon, stars, earth, air, water, everywhere, all held together by gravity in one sweet, orderly system, moving along according to Newton's laws of motion, and kept for ever moving according to the First Law of Thermodynamics. Beautiful, orderly nature. Man may come and go, but nature goes on for ever. So sang the poets, and the scientists agreed; and the chemists had discovered the indestructible elements, themselves the home of immortal energy.

Dalton's atomic theory says in effect that every element—gold, mercury, oxygen, etc.—consists of minute particles or *atoms* specific for that particular element and differing in weight and other properties from the atoms of all other elements. That means, further, that in any compound we have a definite number of atoms of each element present in the compound. If, therefore, two atoms of hydrogen united with one of oxygen form the compound called water ($H_2O$), then two atoms of hydrogen united with two of oxygen form not water but an entirely different compound. And as a matter of fact hydrogen-peroxide ($H_2O_2$) is quite different from water—just as carbon-monoxide (CO) differs from carbon-dioxide ($CO_2$). The H, O, and C of these formulas represent single atoms of hydrogen, oxygen and carbon—the smallest conceivable amount of the element. The $H_2O$, $H_2O_2$, CO, and $CO_2$ represent molecules —the smallest conceivable amounts of the compounds. As all hydrogen is always hydrogen atoms, so all water (if pure) is always water molecules. In other words, H is always H and $H_2O$ is always $H_2O$ —even though, as we know now, lead molecules are not all the same.

It was a theory—a thoroughly workable theory, an extraordinarily useful theory. The theory alone enabled no one to see an atom;

it did enable chemists to manipulate elements, analyse compounds, synthesize compounds. To put the matter another way, there may in fact be no such thing as an atom, it may have no more existence than a ghost, but chemists handling elements as though atoms existed get precise results from their handling. Call the atomic theory a working hypothesis, say nothing about its correctness; it is a fact that with it chemists have worked wonders.

Now, consistent with the atomic theory was the theory that the hydrogen atoms in the molecules of water in my arm would remain hydrogen atoms to the end of time. That means that they could be recovered—by dehydrating my arm and electrolyzing the water. Thus treated, the water returned to its "elements"—two volumes of hydrogen to one of oxygen; and all the atoms of each element as good as new.

Electrolysis is a curious phenomenon. I can recover the water in my arm by decomposing it. There are several ways of decomposing animal flesh: heat is one; bacteria of decay, another. The simplest way to decompose water is to add sulphuric acid and pass a current of electricity through it—as Faraday demonstrated in 1834. During electrolysis the atoms act as though they were charges of electricity. The process itself may be called ionization—from the Greek *ion*, "going"; molecules are decomposed into atoms which go some place. An ion, then, is an atom or group of atoms carrying an electric charge, which may be positive or negative. Negative charges are called *electrons*—suggested by Stoney in 1891.

Is an electron mass or energy? Are atoms indestructible? These, roughly, are the background of the scientific world-wide war that has raged since the discovery of radioactivity at the close of the last century. Not only radium itself, but a half dozen additional "elements," including one called *ionium* or "wanderer," and one called *niton* or "the shining one," were discovered between 1903 and 1910, all radioactive. The war over radioactivity is not to be confused with radio activities.

Radium and other radioactive elements do not behave according to the laws of nature. So much the worse for the laws of nature; they must be rewritten—and that is what scientists are now trying to do: so to rewrite the laws of nature that radioactive elements can feel at home. The difficulty (and that is what the war is about) is that scientists cannot agree on the facts; but they are mostly open-minded and are watchfully waiting.

*The* fact on which there is agreement is that, whereas atoms of elements were supposed to be fixed, stable, and immutable, atoms of radioactive elements are not stable; they disintegrate under the scientist's eyes, and he can't stop the disintegration. They obey no known law. In their world the man-made laws of electro-magnetics do not hold. Again, every physical change known to physicist or chemist involves a definite amount of work or energy; but helium, for example, in disintegrating liberates a million times more energy than in any chemical change hitherto known.

Before radioactive days, the chemist dealt with atoms of elements not as atoms but as aggregates of atoms, and so infinitely small are they that before he could detect change—by spectroscope or chemical analysis—he had to have at least more of them than there are human beings on earth multiplied by hundreds—say, $10^{12}$.

How, then, can he know radioactive atoms or electrons? By their works. They shoot out particles which register as a flash on a screen. They shoot fast and with enormous energy. X-rays shoot through human bodies, wood, wool, etc. It takes a plate of iron a foot thick to stop the "gamma" rays. It is estimated that there is as much energy in a shovelful of radioactive elements as in a thousand tons of coal.

While radium is considered helpful in destroying cancerous growths, it is known to be dangerous to life unless proper precautions are taken. Many workers in radioactive substances died before it was learned how to handle them safely. It is known, for example, that even a few moments' exposure to X-rays suffices to kill spermatozoa. Hence the lead aprons worn by patients during X-ray photography.

The discovery during the past forty years of the sub-atomic structure of matter is conceivably the greatest man ever made; its future consequences are certainly far beyond living man's capacity to foretell. The discovery in itself forms a great chapter in science—just how great only the future can disclose.

Science has already been forced to revise its theories, not only of the cosmic universe, but of energy and matter as well. Only a few of the great names in this profoundly sensational series of discoveries have been mentioned, and it has not been possible to bring out the distinctions made by scientists in the various kinds of subatomic phenomena—such as X-, alpha-, beta-, gamma-rays, etc.; or to set forth certain amazing facts—such as the different rates of disintegration in the various newly discovered radioactive elements.

But we may note one more fact, for it bears on the revised age of the earth.

Rutherford in 1903, after intensive study of radioactive matter, formulated the following law or theory: "A definite small proportion of the atoms of each radioactive substance becomes unstable at a given time . . . the atoms break up . . . the disintegration is explosive in violence, and is accompanied by the ejection of an alpha particle with great velocity. . . ."

The theory worked, and it was found, as I have said, that some elements are more active than others. A bit of uranium, for example, is a slow worker; it will lose half of itself in $6 \times 10^9$ (6,000,000,000) years. Actinium will do the same trick in 0.002 of a second.

Now such radioactive elements, so far as known, decompose— very slowly or incredibly fast—and finally settle down as lead. Study of lead-bearing rocks necessitated revision of the age of the earth. The result of that revision we shall look at in the next chapter. But think of the energy given up or lost during the disintegration of radioactive elements. Some of them shoot their rays almost with the velocity of light. That means enormous energy. The unit of measure of energy expenditure is a calorie, a heat unit, the amount of heat required to raise the temperature of one gram of water from zero to 1° Centigrade. I have already spoken of the incredible energy in a shovelful of radioactive substance. The gram of radium the United States gave Madame Curie gives off 134 calories per hour—or more than enough to melt its own weight of ice.

During its decomposition to lead, one cubic centimetre of niton gives off seven million calories. It is not impossible that the earth's heat can be accounted for by radium alone. But there is no radium on earth today that has been here as long as the human race; and half of all the radium on earth today will have decomposed before 3600 A.D.

I spoke of these elements as shooting particles during disinte-

gration. Are the particles comparable to bullets fired from a gun?
Are they mass, *matter*, or just a *charge* of energy? I should like to
know. But there can be, it seems, no quarrel with Einstein's contention that mass and energy are interchangeable terms; nor can
there be any doubt of Einstein's experiment to test his hypothesis.
Light, all are agreed, is a form of energy; hence, said Einstein, it
must have mass. And if it has mass, it must be subject to gravity;
light rays from a distant star passing near the sun should be bent,
deflected. Observation of the solar eclipse of May 29, 1919, seemed
to confirm Einstein's hypothesis.

And so the old sharp boundary lines between material, electrical,
and ethereal phenomena have had to go. Also, the sharply defined
atom has disappeared; it is no longer the "uncuttable" unit of an
element, for it cuts itself, and in some elements with devastating
results. So far man has not been able to hasten or hinder this disintegrating process. And so we are reduced to a universe of mass as
energy and of energy as mass; and of mass we recognize, name, and
describe ninety out of a possible ninety-two elements, each a specific
substance beyond man's present power to decompose.

Talk about reconciling science and religion! It keeps one busy
these days reconciling physicists. Millikan catches the "birth cry"
of new elements in the "depths of space" and measures the cosmic
rays liberated when two hydrogen atoms unite to form a helium
atom by the rate at which they discharge an electroscope. And
Eddington in radioactivity hears the "moans of the suicide"—of
disintegrating atoms.

Is the universe decomposing, committing suicide, running down,
headed toward a state of uniform changelessness? It should be by
the Second Law of Thermodynamics, which says in effect that
while it is easy enough to transform the energy of coal into heat
and to convert forty per cent of that heat into work or mechanical
energy, it is impossible to keep steam up unless more coal is fed
to the furnace.

In fact, this Second Law of Thermodynamics seems to apply to
so many phases of life as man knows it that it is hardly to be wondered at that he applies it to the universe and proves it by catching
rays on sensitized plates. Water runs downhill; many are called,
few are chosen; *facilis descensus Averno*; all the king's horses can't

put Humpty Dumpty up again, nor can the king himself un-scramble an egg; and even astronomers run down without fresh supplies of fuel-food. Why shouldn't the universe run down? On the other hand, why should it? Certainly any universe made by *pure* science would run down: it would talk itself to death.

Eddington's cosmic suicide theory is new in name only. Clausius, seventy-five years ago, called it *entropy*. An "entropian" eye has an inverted or turned-in eyelid. When Clausius said that the entropy of the solar system tends toward a maximum, he was judging that system by the fact that man so far has been unable to see how heat of itself can pass from a hot-water bottle of eighty degrees to a stomach of ninety-nine degrees. At any rate, it doesn't; nor has man been able to make an ideal heat engine, although Carnot imagined one. Every heat engine ever made is only partially effi-cient; a certain large number of heat units disappear in the opera-tion. Heat does not pass naturally from a cold to a hot body. Eighty degrees is warm, but not warm enough to warm a stomach—unless, of course, it is an excised stomach on ice.

Clausius and others then, as Eddington and others now, saw the sun warming the earth. There is evidence that it has been warming it for two or three billion years. But sun and other million-odd suns we call stars should by all man-known laws be dead and stone-cold. Yet they blaze away, shooting their energy into space! Well, if space is eating matter, and if matter is energy, why can't space go on giving birth to little stars and nourishing them till they get big enough to blaze into suns?

Yet the astronomer suggests that we try to find a way to circum-vent the Second Law of Thermodynamics, unless we propose to sit idly watching the entropy run its course. We are trying, it seems to me, to circumvent too many laws now. If the universe wants to run down, let it run. Meanwhile, and for a billion or more years we are told, the sun will be our good friend and we shall have a lot of laws and ideas nearer home that need revision. But if, as Eddington has lately suggested, we can get the 200 horsepower a year with which Einstein endows every drop of water by merely raising its temperature 39,999,900 degrees above boiling point, let us by all means think less in terms of releasing souls from hell and more in terms of releasing subatomic energy from our vapoury exhalations. Meanwhile my curiosity goes so far as to wonder just how many horsepower would be required to heat matter up to a point where it begins to behave like a disembodied electron. And I am curious, furthermore, as to whether, once having freed these electrons, we should fare better at their hands than did our ancestors with their swarms of disembodied ghosts.

If we were not so mortal, so certain of nothing as of death and taxes, and yet so fond of life, is it conceivable that man, even an astronomer, would give the universe a life of billions of years, and in the same breath doom it to an ultimate and inexorable death—unless, indeed, something could be done about it? I should like to suggest that when better adventure stories are written, the astrophysicists will write them. Whereas astronomers used to cast horoscopes, thereby making astrology wet nurse to astronomy, they now forecast destiny for sheer glory, thereby making associations for the advancement of science occasions for enhancing personal prestige. What Faraday a hundred years ago considered worth no more than two lines in his diary, suffices today for a presidential address—to be expanded into a volume if time permits. But while *pure* scientists have withdrawn matter from the universe in order to discover its *ultimate* composition and constitution, and debate whether the electron is light, heat, or electricity, a corpuscle of matter or a wave, engineers have built radio sets and better battleships, chemists have made drugs and better ethers.

It is possible, as Lewis says, that physicists have become demons. It is certainly true that mathematical physicists today are the intellectual aristocrats of the earth, fawned on by High Society, the diversion of Big Capital. If Professor A. H. Compton were a Catholic, he certainly would be entitled to a papal dukedom as well as a Nobel Prize; and a century hence might be canonized—not for having studied atomic structure by X-ray diffraction, but because he, or "Science, particularly the new physics," according to an interview in the *New York Times*, has some "astonishing things" to say on the problems of free-will, immortality, and God.

What he is reported to have said would qualify him for a chair in the Athens Academy, but not in the Alexandria Museum. We have all wondered how a good, gentle, Christian deacon could turn into an inhuman tightwad between Sunday evening and Monday morning, but the deacon is slow beside the fast-working physicist who has only to bombard atoms to conclude that "possibly mind acts on matter."

"A survey of the physical universe indicates that mankind is very possibly nature's best achievement in this direction (intelligent minds). If in the world scheme *conscious* life is the thing of primary importance, what is happening on our earth is thus of great cosmic significance. . . . We find *strong reasons for believing* that in spite of his physical insignificance, man may be of extraordinary importance in the cosmic scheme" (italics mine). He also supports the "evidence against the view" that the "mind cannot survive the brain," and hence finds that "no cogent reason remains for supposing that the soul dies with the body." He speaks of the fire man must pass through to bring out the "pure gold of his soul."

If that is science, there is no difference between it and mysticism or religion, nor anything to "reconcile." I should also like to observe that if freshman Compton had used as many terms with nothing more behind them than the breath any talking ape uses when he expounds the secrets of the universe, or for his belief in the atomic theory could give reasons no more "cogent" than he can for his belief in minds, souls, etc., he would never have passed his midyear examination in physics.

Then here is Sir James Jeans giving Plato's Eternal Ghost a boost by discovering that the universe we live in consists of "pure thought —a Mathematical Thinker." All of which, I submit, throws a flood of light on an old and puzzling problem.

I cannot decide whether the new physicists are setting their souls in order to meet their Maker or are just playing politics in behalf of more heavily Endowed Chairs and larger Research Funds. There seem to be "cogent" reasons why a great physicist who can take a scientific attitude toward atoms, once he begins to think of molecules becomes maudlin. With such enormous aggregates of huge molecules as are found in human beings, he seems to become congenitally feeble-minded. Solving the riddle of the universe is simple compared with solving the secrets of a fertilized egg no bigger than the dot over an "i."

In all serious soberness, have we yet in our review of history found man denying that his thoughts are the most important thing on earth? Well, they *must* be of *cosmic* significance. Did anyone ever have to *prove* to us that our thoughts are so important that we are cosmically significant, even though we may be a runt physically? Why should Nobel Prize winners have to tell us all this when it is plainly stated in the Bible that even the hairs of our head are numbered; and what else can that mean but "pure" thought? Not even a doubting Thomas would have to wait for a Neophysicist to tell him what he felt in his bones.

It is not easy for anybody—Attic philosopher, Roman Epicurean, Old Stone Age hatchet-maker, or New Scientific Age physicist—to welcome the truth about himself or look at biologic facts with a calm, objective, unbiassed, impartial eye. Yet modern physicists feel at liberty to accept evolution—including that of physicists. "Biologically speaking," says Compton, "life is essentially continuous and eternal." Why "essentially"? Is it continuous or not? And what evidence is there that it is "eternal"? Eternity is a long time— as Einstein himself would presumably admit.

One word more before we leave Compton, for he also dabbles in psychology. "In some reflex actions and habitual acts we *may* behave as automata, but where *deliberation* occurs we feel that we choose our own course" (italics mine). "Thus, if there is freedom (of thought) there must be at least some thinking possible quite independently of any corresponding cerebral process." That "possible" argues mind over matter. And Einstein says there is nothing but space—which is busy consuming matter. And Millikan says there is no matter.

True, Millikan also says that neither he nor Jeans "*knows* anything about it." That fact, however, does not prevent him from suggesting that modern physics has "thrown the purely mechanistic view of the universe root and branch out of its house." Which, I suppose, leaves us room for pure thought: the triumph of mind over matter. But, "the one thing of which you all may be quite sure is that neither of us knows anything about it."

Enough is enough. We have passed the joking stage. When a physicist smashes his thumb he does not say *Damn!* with his cortex or by a reflex arc or with his sympathetic nervous system or with his vocal cords, but with his whole body. If he hits his thumb in a co-ed class-room, he may just think and feel *Damn!*—like the well-trained automaton he is; the naughty word itself may be spoken hours or days later, or never. There are endless ways a man may react to a smashed thumb, or to his animal instinct to live till he wears out; and as man till now has had next to no understanding of just what has taken place in a worn-out animal mechanism, although he has depicted senile decay vividly enough, he has thought hard how he could live continuously and eternally.

Compton's mind or consciousness is no more scientific than Plato's or Aristotle's; nor is his eternal life any more grounded in observable fact than Plato's or Paul's immortal soul. If one *must* live eternally, why isn't existence as a disembodied spirit as satisfactory individually, and as cosmically significant, as an electron? The physicist, of course, does not know what an electron is; nor does the spiritualist know what a disembodied spirit is.

But every anthropologist knows that all peoples satisfy their longing for life eternal by talking immortality—just as all peoples imagine themselves *the people*, and so far as they think in cosmic terms hold themselves cosmically important. Physicists are also people, but whether cosmically more important than frogs, who shall say?

We may perhaps remind our physicists, and ourselves, that we are close kin to amphibia and to them owe the voices with which we cry to high heaven and with which we claim in one breath to be children of God and in the next to be as eternal as electrons or cosmic rays. But have we any evidence beyond an amphibian thirst for eternal life, and our human voice to utter the Unutterable and the Infinite and Absolute and to cry Eureka! that *cosmically* speaking we are more important or significant than a frog?

The physicist's mathematical abstractions do represent a high type of art, an intellectual expression of emotion, and a refined extension of man's capacity to imagine life; but that such abstractions in and of themselves have more meaning in human lives than a love lyric, I cannot see. The lyric, if good, is scientifically sound; the abstraction may be—it may even be useful. In that case it will pay for its board and keep, but will thereby lose its purity and its philosophical dignity.

It certainly is true, as Bridgman says, that the rapid change in physical "progress" these days makes for breathlessness. It is also true that, whereas we used to have nearly a hundred elements or entities for our universe, we now seem to require only one. What an electron is I do not know. But if space, as Einstein predicts, is finally to survive as the "sole carrier of reality," and has, as he claims, already "annihilated" ether and time, and is about to swallow up the field and corpuscular theory, I do not see what I should or can do about it, especially when Eddington comes along and says, "We need ether"! Something can be done about that. $(C_2H_5)_2O$ is still an entity in tins in chain drug stores.

Radioactivity.

What, then, is this earth? What is its secret? Simply the electron: key not only to earth, but to the secret of the universe. The electron, the one basic component of all matter—here on earth, off there in the stars, throughout the entire cosmos. No wonder astronomers, physicists, and philosophers dog its footsteps. But what do they dog —a foot or a step, a noun or a verb, an entity or a concept, a bullet or an explosion, mass or energy?

If only Faraday and Maxwell had not discovered electromagnetic "fields"! Newton's world of geometry and space was so simple; he was its perfect Lawgiver. And now Einstein seeks to be Lawgiver to both. At any rate, he is reported to have said recently that he is looking for a system of equations which will take in all physical phenomena, including gravitation. "This would be an enormous gain in the picture of the uniformity of physical nature." It would indeed. But, he admits, the problem of getting that picture is not yet solved and will be difficult of solution. It will indeed.

And here is the strangest thing. It "appears that space will have to be regarded as a primary thing"; and matter, a "secondary result." "Space is now having its revenge, so to speak, and is eating up matter." It has already gobbled up time, for Einstein's theory of relativity "establishes the fact" that space and time must be united in a single four-dimensional continuum.

Space is not alone in having its "revenge"; philosophy is revenged for its slights and slurs. Einstein's insistence that "space is the sole reality" is still front-page news and carries as big a headline as the latest reality about German reparations.

The poor old ether we used to worry about is now merely something in a can to put us to sleep; time does not count any more;

and nothing matters. Space alone is real; and space, "analogous structurally to the electromagnetic field," even space has lost its absolute character and, like Vergil's woman, is a changeable and influenceable thing.

Merely for its historic interest we may note before returning to earth that the Greeks did not operate with space—that is, "scientifically;" in fact, the idea of space might possibly never have entered the realm of science at all had not Descartes invented analytic geometry. That was in 1637, a few years after he had written a treatise on the universe.

Descartes comes under our lead pencil because he, more than any other modern, carried on and by his great name propagated the classic superstition that there is inherent virtue in a mathematical demonstration; that wisdom can be found alone by following the path marked by mathematical symbols; that truth can be discovered only by the mathematician and described by mathematical formulas. It is not surprising to learn that Descartes dreamed some of his most "fruitful dreams" and did his "best thinking" in bed. In fact, Whitehead thinks Descartes in bed inventing the method of co-ordinate geometry an historic moment, comparable to Columbus sighting America, Galileo turning his telescope to the heavens, and Franklin catching a spark on the string of his kite.

Now, I can see the advantage of having the machinery of algebra available for the solution of geometrical problems, of a geometrical figure which makes algebra concrete and visible to the naked eye— just as two arms are better than one. And Descartes made that possible. But he did too many other things to cripple men's arms and bind men's eyes. For example, years ago I had an old clerk who had failed to solve the simplest problems in living; he was always on his uppers and at best shabby genteel. He really had no time for simple problems; he was solving the problem of the universe—by drawing vortices! Thousands of vortices. Descartes had argued that the universe could thus be solved: one vortex for the sun, one for each of the planets, etc.; the phenomena of the universe to be solved or described by one mechanical principle—the *vortex*. Not bedtime stories, but early morning inspirations in the "abstract regions of thought."

Of the six parts of Descartes' *Discourse*, one is devoted to the "reasons" by which he proves the "existence of God and of the human soul"; another, to the "difference which exists between our soul and that of the beasts."

Descartes was primarily a metaphysicist; he did not have to examine his premises—God, soul, beast; it was enough to keep his logic straight. And in this one line he succeeded pretty well: "Good sense is the most widely distributed commodity in the world, for everyone thinks himself so well supplied with it that even those who are hardest to satisfy in every other respect are not accustomed to desire more of it than they have." He also observed that the greatest souls are capable of the greatest vices as well as of the greatest virtues. But he knew no more about souls than a Hottentot, nor are his reasons for their existence more convincing. For, as his contemporary, Pascal, remarked in connexion with the paucity of students of the abstract sciences, "There are yet *fewer students of Man than of Geometry*"—and still are. Euclidean geometry—solid bodies, with points, lines, planes, and distance—plus Cartesian space, Gaussian coördinates, Hertzian waves, and Einsteinian matter-swallowing space, all combined, are far simpler problems, more easily studied and more readily described, than man.

To think of space swallowing matter is no great intellectual feat. Think of men swallowing swords and Einsteins! All honour to science, but every scientist had a mother and was born on earth. And this earth—or parts of it at least—is finally safe for childbirth. There has been some advance in the knowledge of organic nature. But before we turn to that story, let us see how the earth itself was restored to human hands—to find a human historian.

### VIII

It was formerly believed that somewhere, somehow, if man could only find it, there was a tree or an elixir of life; that stars, planets, and constellations, somehow or other, exerted an "influence" on human lives; and that there was a way, if it could only be found, whereby base common metals could be transmuted into precious uncommon metals. The casting of horoscopes, as we have seen, was pin-money for fairly modern astronomers, and today is a job for astrologers. With Copernicus the stars began to be stars again, not beneficent or malignant influences on poor mortals here below.

Astrology as a profession and as a pastime of priests, poets, philosophers, and physicians, gave way to alchemy.

Alchemy, as a science, was enormously handicapped by two basic
theories: that disease was an entity, youth could be renewed, and
life prolonged indefinitely; and that lead could be transmuted to
gold. Most Middle Age alchemists combined the two theories and
held that the elixir of life was liquid gold; that the discovery of one
"secret" would lead to the other. Hence the long search for *potable*
gold.

In other words, mediæval alchemy was an art and still in its
infancy; yet an eleventh-century Arabic treatise on alchemy was
obviously an attempt to advance a science rather than a guide to an
impossible art. Impossible, because mediæval theories of matter were
wrong. It was not only an anthropomorphic view of matter, but
the theory of life itself was wrong.

That theory was Indian in origin, and said in substance that
organic and inorganic are identical and essentially manifestations
of God; that just as the organic (man) attains perfection, becomes
one with God, by successive migrations of the spirit through rebirth
from one body to another, so *base* metals could be purified or transmuted into "pure" metals by successive stages. It was only necessary
to find the proper "spirits" or "souls" by which the transmutation
could be brought about. And as the love of gold replaced the love
of life, alchemy thrived—though it was generally practised in secret,
for only in recent times has love of gold become the major virtue,
and its possession, howsoever transmuted, ennobling.

Feverish search for an Elixir of Life or a Fountain of Youth
never quite ceased, and led to many interesting and some valuable
discoveries—the Mississippi River by de Soto, for example; but medicine could not get far from its ancient empirical stage until certain
facts were discovered to upset all ancient theories of life and vital
processes. There could be no science of biology, nor sound basis
for medicine, until there was a *science* of chemistry.

The furtive search for the philosopher's stone or for a process
of making a high-caste God from pariah materials, did lead to certain discoveries, but alchemy could not get far because the alchemist
was working on theories which were not only false but childish.
It was Boyle, the sceptic, who not only dared to question those

theories, but dealt them such a blow that new theories of matter had a chance to be born. Purified of its anthropomorphic childishness, alchemy gave way to chemistry.

Boyle, we note in passing, was but one of the group of men in the time of Charles II who inaugurated England's Classical Age in science and brought her to the front in Europe. Only in our own generation, however, were the sciences which form the backbone of our scientific education christened.

My father's Natural Philosophy, or Natural History as it was sometimes called, was a lineal descendant of the Ionian Greek natural philosophy. By the time I was entering college, chemistry and physics had started academic careers of their own; and of Aristotle's Natural History, geology, botany, zoology and physiology had taken form as separate sciences. I do not mean to say that there was no geology, for example, before 1880, for geology was placed on a scientific footing by Lyell in 1830; but that geology, botany, etc., and other *natural* sciences, began to exist as sciences, apart from or independent of "natural history," in 1880—even as chemistry and physics a few years before had cut loose from "natural philosophy." The distinction is still made, however, between the natural and physical sciences, though even these abstractions, as we shall see, are far from being air-tight or fool-proof.

While Treviranus of Bremen published a *Biologie, oder Philosophie der lebenden Natur* in 1802-05, and was the first known to use the word biology—or a science of life as against lifelessness—biology had to wait for the great naturalists of the Victorian Age to be securely founded as a science, as had the more specialized sciences of morphology, physiology, cytology, anthropology, bacteriology, pathology, etc. The old geology of Lyell's day also gave birth to many children: mineralogy, petrology, palæontology, etc.—all impossible without a sound chemism.

The recent historic development and the accomplishments of these special sciences are not my task, but that of a university staff with laboratories, libraries, and museums. The additions, or at any rate the output, of alleged contributions to science, for this year alone, will run into tens of thousands of printed pages and millions of words—all consuming, among other things, vast quantities of paper pulp and printer's ink, to say nothing of the amount of sugar burnt in the bodies of the scientists while they manipulated numberless frogs, mice, rats, cats, guinea-pigs, and dogs, peered through thousands of microscopes, incubated billions of microörganisms, embalmed miles of plants, tissues, etc.; and no count yet made of the raw materials the chemists use in their investigations or the power the physicists transform in their experiments. We seem to be dealing with supplies in army quantities, with costs in terms of battleships. Yet we cannot build jails fast enough to hold our criminals, or asylums big enough to house our lunatics—but our Morgans have the largest private yachts and our Fords the hugest fortunes in the world. We do lynch a Negro now and then, but we are civilized. Our civilization is based on science; and this is not only an age of science, but *the* Scientific Age.

About the time Boyle was putting Aristotle and the alchemists on the witness stand and asking them what they meant by their *Elements* and *Principles*—to "discuss them with you as working instruments for advancing knowledge"—a theory was advanced which, beginning with the Greeks, had guided all manipulation of material substances up to Boyle's day, and for a hundred years after. It had to be exploded before man could come closer to the truth about the nature of things.

Every material substance, said that theory, was a fragment of primordial matter plus more or less fire, air, water, and earth. That is to say, of *elements* as a chemist speaks of them today, ancient philosophers and mediæval alchemists knew nothing at all. On their theory that fire, air, water, and earth were elemental, and salt, sulphur, mercury, etc., fundamental principles, it was little wonder that their endless experiments could yield little more than silver threads among the gold. As a guide for manipulating the material world, it had as little practical value as the theory that God is good has for regulating human conduct.

We must distinguish, said Boyle, such *qualities* as hot, cold, wet, and dry from the *stuff* of matter. That was in 1661, but it was not until my grandfather's time that Mayer discovered the law of the conservation of energy. Nor in Boyle's day was there any idea that matter was indestructible; nothing was yet known of the composition of air; gases were not yet differentiated, nor was combustion understood.

Fire, one of man's very earliest friends; combustion, a chemical process that keeps the hearth fire burning and the living heart beating. We still speak, and not inappropriately, of the "spark" of life, of life "blazing up," "dying down," "going out." But where does it go when it goes out? Some said to Sheol, and some to heaven. After long experiment, two German contemporaries of Boyle announced a new theory of combustion—an amendment, as it were, to the theory of matter which had held men's thoughts and stayed their hands for two thousand years. It was really more than a theory; it is, said Stahl, one of the experimenters, a *substance*, "the combustible substance, a principle of fire, but not the fire itself." He called that "substance" *phlogiston*.

In other words, fire was more than a "principle"; it was an *element*; an element that "escapes" when a substance is burnt, like a "flame" from a blown-out candle, a "spirit" from a burnt-out human being.

That blow-out we now call "oxygen shortage"; combustion, "oxidation."

Mayow, the second experimenter, after watching burning camphor and living mice "go out" under a bell-glass, called it fire-air, but spoke of "spirit" as the *substance* common to air and nitre which brings about combustion.

Despite the falsity of that phlogiston theory, it required a century to dethrone it. The story of its dethronement is the story of the discovery of the nature of air, the differentiation of its various gases, etc. It cannot be told here in any detail, and only a few of the discoverers can be even named, though it is one of the most important discoveries ever made by man. In fact, the net results of eighteenth-century advances in chemistry and other sciences were quite as revolutionary as the political upheavals known as the American and French Revolutions: foundations were laid for the new structures of modern civilization. That century also marked the beginning of the most astounding industrial revolution in all history.

Nearly thirty years before Boyle studied gases and described his experiments, van Helmont, a Dutch alchemist, had experimented with charcoal. After burning sixty-two pounds of oak charcoal, he found he had one pound left—"therefore the remaining sixty-one pounds are *spiritum sylvester*. This spirit, hitherto unknown, I call by the new name of *gas*."

A few sticks of oak: it was not a big fire; it does not look like a big experiment. But it was a *scientific* experiment, and a most important one. The "woodland spirit" he weighed was carbon dioxide or carbonic-acid gas. That was its first mention as an end product of combustion, and the first time a gas was ever weighed or the word *gas* used.

Van Helmont also observed that the same gas is "expelled" in fermenting wine, bread, etc. That we also expel the same kind of gas because our energies come from internal combustion engines, he had not even the remotest idea. In fact, as a biologist he was worse than a Digger Indian, if, as is said, he wrote a recipe for "making" mice from corn and sweet basil.

Van Helmont discovered his gas about the time Galileo discovered Jupiter's satellites and the Pilgrims discovered Massachusetts. That seventeenth century was a great age of discovery. Europe, in fact, had gone in for discovery. Discoveries were piling up. Life was not so rich or complex then as now, but it must have been fun for the curious in that youthful period of the growth of modern civilization. Scientific societies were the meeting-places for young greybeards who displayed their discoveries to one another with the boyish enthusiasm normal to all healthy activity.

Descartes and Newton had rejected the Mosaic cosmogony, but it still had to be reckoned with. It was one thing for a Laplace to say he did not need an anthropomorphic divinity to create the universe as he conceived it; it was quite a different thing for ordinary mortals to think of sun, moon, stars, earth, living beings, man, as anything but gifts from the Creator. Discoveries could not outrun Authority; or, more precisely, Authority had to be opened up to question before certain discoveries could be made and before the significance or implication of discoveries could be faced with equanimity.

Thus, the expression *breath of life* seemed plain enough. Why question it, why try to resolve "breath" into its elements or "life" into its substances? But too many curious people were pottering with things at hand and underfoot and in the air and water, not to have discovered some fundamental truths of great import.

The air we breathe, the breath of life. How insignificant such things must seem to the Newtons and Einsteins; how trifling any discoveries that might be made about the nature of air or breath, compared with the Immutable Laws a Newton might discover or the Space-devouring-Matter concept of an Einstein! Yet, without the eighteenth century discoveries of the nature of air, little progress could have been made in chemistry and less in biochemistry—that science which delves deepest into the nature of life.

Stahl's bogy, *phlogiston,* had finally to be abandoned on the discovery that certain substances when burnt or calcined *gained* rather than lost weight. That was asking the bogy to explain too much— to work both sides of the street at the same time. That discovery, however, could not have been made except after long experiments on composition, decomposition, and chemical change. Such experiments were made in the seventeenth and eighteenth centuries because chemistry had ceased to be a hunt for a secret magic which would at once rejuvenate life and fill pockets with gold. The search for potable gold was among those "noble experiments" which man keeps making in the hope that God will reward the noble.

The Aristotelian "fact" of the duality of everything in nature— body or substance, spirit or soul—was gradually replaced in the seventeenth and eighteenth centuries by a theory of organic and inorganic, or animate and inanimate, nature. Whatever *anima* was —breath, wind, spirit, soul—all living beings had it and were therefore animate, or organic. Organic is still applied to the world of living beings; inorganic, to the world of lifeless things.

The distinction is now known to be less sharp than it seemed, for just a little over a century ago Wöhler made urea in his laboratory—by simply heating ammonium cyanate; and it was just as good urea as was ever secreted by man or beast. Urea is not life, of course, but it belongs, or did, to the animate or organic world. With Wöhler it became an artifact, a substance made by human hands. In the year 1828 the boundary line between organic and inorganic was crossed for the first, but by no means the last, time. And the chemist today knows nothing of organic chemistry, a great deal of the chemistry of carbon compounds.

Wöhler was begotten by the Leyden physician Boerhaave, whose

*Elements of Chemistry* (1732) was the first organic chemistry and marked an epoch in the history of that science.

While Boerhaave was preparing the way for a chemical study of living bodies, Hales, an English clergyman, rode a hobby to good purpose and prepared the way for a physical study of living beings. He was especially interested in atmosphere. With his manometer he measured arterial blood pressure. His best work was the invention of the *pneumatic trough*, a device by which gases could be collected in closed vessels over water.

A pneumatic trough does not seem much of an invention, but as we have seen before, some enormous advances in science and civilization have hung on devices simple in themselves but making it possible to manipulate enormously vast or complex phenomena. The equipment the freshman today finds awaiting him in a chemical or physical laboratory was not plucked from trees nor dug from the ground. Remove the microscope alone from the hands of the first-year medical student and he is back in the sixteenth century—and without foundation for a sound theory of pathology.

How was man ever to learn anything about breath if he could not catch it, control it, weigh it, and put it on the witness stand—give it the third degree, so to speak?

Breath is air. Hales found he could drive "air" off certain substances—limestone, for example—by heating them. Black, in 1750, found he could drive "air" from limestone by pouring acid on it; he collected it in Hales's pneumatic trough. He weighed it; then reversed the process, and got chalk. He was a pioneer *analytic* and *synthetic* chemist. And he got along without any phlogiston theory. The *air* he got from his experiment he called "fixed"—fixed in the limestone or chalk precipitate, and "air" because all atmosphere is air!

Next, Bergmann, a Swede, discovered, by the use of litmus, that Black's "fixed air" was an acid; so he dubbed it "aerial acid." He also found that it was heavier than air and soluble in water. Here, then, was aerial air, soluble in water, heavier than air, odourless, invisible, and an acid; present in human breath and in some mineral waters; would not support life; yet would attach itself to lime to form chalk; and was given off during fermentation. What was "fermentation"? What was this air that was "fixed," that was present in the human breath, and yet would not support life? Well, don't hold your breath till it can be analysed.

While Black in Scotland was finding "fixed" air, Cavendish in England was finding "inflammable" air. Unlike fixed air, it was *lighter* than ordinary air and burnt readily; yet, like fixed air, it was death to a candle flame or a mouse: it would not support life. Eight years later, in the very year Thomas Jefferson announced that it was time to reverse the rule that the sovereign had rights and the people only privileges, in the year 1774 to be exact, Joseph Priestley, a Unitarian preacher, made an equally revolutionary announcement. Conceivably, civilization of a kind could have gone on for centuries under the theory that sovereigns had rights and the people privileges only, but it is inconceivable that a science of life could have become possible under the reign of the ancient theory that air is an indestructible, unalterable, simple, elementary substance. That was the theory Priestley exploded. And with its explosion went the theory of phlogiston.

In fact, Priestley called his air *dephlogisticated* because he derived it from *burnt* metal—calcined mercury. By heating that reddish powder he drove off an "air" in which candles blazed higher and mice stepped livelier. Even charcoal "sparkled in it, exactly like paper dipped in a solution of nitre." Exactly. He had discovered *oxygen* and did not know it. He had made a discovery more vital to life than that made by any astronomer since the world began, and did not realize it.

In the following year Scheele, a poor Swede apothecary, yet a great chemist, independently discovered oxygen—and called it "empyreal" air, a far closer approximation to its real nature than Priestley's "dephlogisticated." But it required the genius of a Frenchman to build the first solid and enduring structure on the foundation stones laid by Black and Cavendish, Priestley and Scheele. His name, to be found among the immortals of all ages, is Lavoisier.

Feed a month-old baby one spoonful of milk a day for thirty days, and what happens? Well, there are several ways of observing. One is to *weigh* it. We can get good information about the weight of things by lifting them, matching their "pull" against the "feel" in our muscles; but when your prescription for a "tonic" calls for a specific small amount of some deadly poison, you hope your druggist will not weigh it with his finger but in a deadly accurate *balance*. Lavoisier was a crank on using the balance; he thereby founded qualitative chemistry on a scientific—honest, unbiassed, impersonal—basis.

Only a good theory can be weighed in the balance and not found wanting. Priestley, as we have seen, found dephlogisticated air: there must, then, be some phlogiston somewhere. Lavoisier "burnt" metals in air, and the "cinders" weighed more than the metals; but metals burnt in a vacuum did not gain in weight. The difference equalled the weight of the air. He heated the red powder of burnt mercury—and found that it lost the weight of Priestley's dephlogisticated air.

Further, he found that air in many acid compounds. He called it *oxygen* (acid-producer). He then burnt charcoal in pure oxygen—and obtained Black's "fixed air," Bergmann's "aerial acid." He analysed it and found it seventy-two parts oxygen, twenty-eight parts carbon; and called it carbonic acid. We call it carbonic-acid gas, or carbon dioxide. He burnt a diamond in pure oxygen—and got carbon dioxide. What is a diamond? Carbon, charcoal in another form. And finally he checked up on Cavendish's "inflammable air." As it unites with ordinary air or oxygen, Lavoisier named it *hydrogen* (water-producer).

By 1794 the French Revolution was on, and Lavoisier, with fifty-one years behind him, had possibly still greater triumphs before him, for he was an extraordinarily brilliant experimenter. But it was not to be, for radical politicians can be as stupidly savage as conservative theologians. He was guillotined in the name of Liberty, Equality, and Fraternity.

It looks as though we had taken a long time to discover oxygen and hydrogen, and that diamonds are but charcoal or carbon in another form. But note that meanwhile (1772) Rutherford had discovered nitrogen; and then note that with these four elements and a few pinches of mineral salts, it is possible to build a body good enough for man and beast. More important still, note that with the complete rout of the old Fire, Air, Water, and Earth theory, man could begin to get a new understanding of the earth itself and of everything below, on, or above it, including himself. That "new understanding" presumably never will be complete, but its visible consequences after less than two hundred years are so great that no one living, I suspect, can realize the possibilities of even the immediate future.

## IX

Given the four elements, air, fire, water, earth, plus some primordial stuff, said the Greeks, anything was possible. But the modern scientist needs about forty elements to build an earth, although he could build a man with half that number. In fact, he estimates he could make up about ninety-five per cent of the earth with eight elements, or three-fourths of it with only two; and of the twenty-odd elements needed for man, he would require large amounts of only four—and very common ones at that. Oxygen alone of the ninety known elements accounts for nearly half the known earth.

I said "could make"; he could if he had the recipe. I might know the chemical constituents of a cake down to the atomic weight of each component element; that fact alone would not help me to make a biscuit fit for a dog. Things—dogs, cakes, man, earth—are not so simple as that. Into their making many factors enter: time, heat, pressure, etc. Some of these forces are pretty well understood; for the understanding of others, possibly, thousands of years will be required. Man is only at the threshold of realizing the significance of the greatest of all his discoveries, the most important of all his known facts: the fact that this earth and all that is therein and thereon are his for unnumbered millions of years to do with as he wills.

I said "known" earth. Only ten miles of the crust are known by direct observation; the remainder, or core, is known by inference only. For example, as the density (specific gravity) of the crust is a little more than two, and of the entire earth a little more than five, the interior, presumably, is largely of the heavier elements or metals —lead, gold, tin, silver, etc.

Again, this "crust" is far from being the *original* earth's crust; it represents a growth, a development, an evolution, endless change, reforming, remoulding, weathering, eroding. More than that, it is largely the "skeleton" of incalculable numbers of plants and animals which made brief use of a few simpler, commoner elements for purposes of living and dying, and then bequeathed them to Mother Earth again—just as we borrow minute portions of these same elements for building our physical structure and for living purposes. A Heavenly Father may be preparing a home for us on high, but human life is inconceivable had not countless plants and animals, most of them so small they cannot be seen with the naked eye, prepared this earth for higher life.

While scientists have discovered new planets and new suns, and have gathered an astounding amount of information about other worlds, they have not yet discovered another as fit for life as ours; in fact, they have discovered but one earth fit for man and dog. And that this earth is fit for anything as high as an alga is because of the sun, supreme power-plant and original source of all living energy on this earth.

Of all the symbolic language man indulges in, none comes closer to strict scientific literalness than *Mother Earth* and *Father Sun*. Curiously enough, that view still prevails among many untutored peoples, and might have prevailed the world around had not certain men found that speculation, however absurd, could be sold to the man at the plough if dressed in fancy garb. In selling-talk there is little new under the sun, and none that I think of at the moment has cost mankind more than philosophic and theosophic cosmogonies.

The one we inherited, I need not repeat, was a curious mixture of Oriental and Classical speculation. While both Mosaic and Classical cosmogonies contain some shrewd guesses and are not entirely unworthy of respect, they came to be barriers to further speculation or even to frank, open-eyed curiosity. After all, why should anyone be curious about this earth if it was made in a week and is not our home anyway? With that idea prevailing, it is hardly to be wondered at that not until the nineteenth century did the earth have a historian worthy the name geologist.

I do not mean to imply that Greek pseudo-science and Christian orthodoxy regulated all Europe's beliefs about the earth up to the nineteenth century: only that such beliefs prevailed. Facts, fossilized or otherwise, had to be squared with such beliefs. That neither Descartes nor Newton accepted the Mosaic cosmogony had little influence in opening the way to such intelligent observation of fossils, rocks, and land formation, that a rational history of the earth could be undertaken.

That history is still being written—or, rather, rewritten; for, I emphasize again, knowledge of the interior of the earth can only be had by inference and deduction, from indirect observation. Presumably, not one square foot of the earth's surface today is just what it was a thousand years ago. Presumably, the oldest known rocks are derived from still older rocks—just as it is believed that the oldest known fossil forms of life are derived from still older forms.

Only in recent decades have competent observers fairly covered the earth's surface. New observations have necessitated revisions of many conclusions that seemed justifiable a few decades ago. Nearly half the earth's surface, and all its interior, yet remain to be explored; much is yet to be learned about the mechanics of the earth's movements; the origin of life is still beyond man's ken. The science of climates is less rudimentary than when Eratosthenes, librarian at Alexandria, invented seven climates, but no great advance has been made since von Humboldt, in 1817, defined isothermic lines and placed clime on a scientific zone foundation. The causes of variation are still far from known.

We may note that the speculations of Aristotle, Herodotus and Strabo, and of Ovid, Lucretius and Pliny, were closer approximations to the truth about the earth than anything produced by the Intellectuals of the Middle Ages.

Both Greeks and Romans saw through fossils—as did Leonardo da Vinci. To the Middle Ages they were "fermentations" or "exhalations" of the soil, or merely "freaks" of nature. An assistant to Pope Sixtus V called them "star seeds." An English antiquary said they sprang from seed-bearing vapours in the sea. And even when, by the middle of the eighteenth century, they were finally recognized as petrified plants or animals, they were regarded as proofs of and as caused by Noah's Flood. That made fossils acceptable to the church. Even as late as 1823 Buckland wrote a treatise on fossils, "attesting the action of a Universal Flood." And even Cuvier, a really great naturalist for his day, attributed them to the Flood.

In fact, not only fossils as organic facts, but facts of observation such as flat, tilted, folded, and buckled rock masses, were "explained" by the Flood or by earthquakes which had turned plains into mountains, seas into lands, etc. Woodward in 1695 went so far as to describe how the whole earth had been torn up by the Flood and then settled down as we now find it. But as time went on and observations increased, it seemed that one flood wasn't enough to account for everything "as we now find it." What then? Postulate more floods: as many floods as are needed to account for what is seen.

*Diluvialists,* they were called; nor was a breath of suspicion cast on their orthodoxy. When they could not make a flood account for some particular geologic phenomenon, they conjured up an earthquake; they delighted in "convulsions of nature," "emanations," "cataclysms," "débâcles." As Freud can find anything he needs for his theory in the Unconscious, the Diluvialists and Cataclysmists could postulate any natural "force" they needed for every phenomenon they found. And while the Neptunists said that the earth's crust was laid down in water, the Vulcanists revelled in hanging everything on fires and volcanoes.

"Phantoms," said Hutton, a hard-headed Scottish farmer, physician and chemist, in 1795, and in these words formulated the theory which underlies modern dynamic geology: "Amid all the revolutions of the globe, the economy of nature has been uniform."

In other words, the best interpreter of the past is the present; if we would know how rocks *were* formed, let us inquire how they *are* formed. Did the school-teachers jump at this safe, sane, sound, and logical theory? No; they jumped on Hutton. An Edinburgh professor called his researches "monstrosities." Inclined strata, said Authority from the Chair, were so formed "originally."

Again and again and again, it is the same old sad story. No advance without piercing the enemy's line. The man who gets through is generally killed, and is honoured for ever after as the Unknown Soldier. Hutton was a true pioneer, a revolutionist. Nobody calls him a great scientist; in fact, he is an almost unknown soldier. He broke through; his ammunition was the one weapon authority fears most—honest, sincere doubt. Once authority—on belief, on dogma—is questioned, some one is soon inspired to make war in earnest.

Hutton inspired Lyell, who blazed the way for Darwin, supreme general of all the forces against the supernatural. It was Darwin's opinion that the science of geology is more indebted to Lyell than to any other man. That opinion, so far as I know, has never been questioned. But Lyell himself would have given Hutton the glory.

Lyell's *Principles of Geology*, first published just a century ago, rescued the earth itself from the first, and its countenance from the seventh, chapter of Genesis. But it was de Laplace's *Exposition du Système du Monde* which accounted for the beginning of the earth without the need, as he told Napoleon, of God. He did it with a Nebular Hypothesis, inspired by Leibnitz, who a century before had traced the earth's hypothetical development from a glowing nebulous mass to a smooth solid globe. My old school-books talk of Laplace, but my new ones find Chamberlin's Planetesimal Hypothesis most in accord with present knowledge of planets, satellites, and nebulæ. Chamberlin's idea is that this earth is to the sun, its parent, as a drop is to a bucket of water—the "drop" having been spilled from the sun with other planetesimal drops, by a passing star.

That passing star—if one really did pass—in one sense was a First Cause so far as this earth and all thereon are concerned; and in another sense it was a catastrophe to the sun: it tore some of its stuff off. Conceivably, another passing star might bump into this earth. That would be a catastrophe, and might be called—if anyone were left to call it—a Final Cause. It may be, as Pearson points out, that such First and Final Causes are fairly common cosmic occurrences, but whether anyone but man ever speculates on such matters is very problematical. So far as is known, man is the only being that has developed a speculating medium.

How old is the earth? After long speculation on this matter, the Hindu philosophers decided it was "eternal"—thousands of millions of years. Less liberal with time were the Chaldean philosophers; their guess was 2,150,000. Zoroaster allowed the earth but 12,000 years; while the Hebrews, with what might be called a time-inferiority complex, did not allow the earth time to comb its hair. Bishop Ussher, after long study of Hebrew chronology, fixed the date of the earth's creation at 4004 B.C.; at 9 A.M., October 23rd, added Dr. Lightfoot, Vice-Chancellor of Cambridge University. And that "date," strangely enough, as Professor Gregory points out, although founded on not one fact, nor even buttressed by argu-

ment, rose to the dignity of a doctrine, and is still a test of orthodoxy for half the Christian world.

But when the earth was rescued from the church, and when its
study was taken from the armchair heavy thinkers and put on a
scientific basis, especially as more and more time had to be postulated to account for observed facts and logical inferences, it was
soon seen that, while the earth might not be as old as the Hindus
thought, it must be far older than the Chaldeans allowed. When
the geologist, for example, found layers of limestone thousands of
feet thick deposited by calcareous microscopic organisms; when he
found that if he added up all the series of stratified or "organized"
rock he had a deposit over ninety miles thick: he realized that he
was dealing with a problem which could not be solved with a few
thousands but only with many millions of years' time.

William Thomson (Lord Kelvin) tackled the problem from the
standpoint of sunshine and the principle of the dissipation of energy.
The sun, presumably, is no perpetual-motion machine which can
generate energy through all eternity. Thomson put its age at not
more than 100,000,000 and possibly not more than 40,000,000 years,
and of that allowed the earth only two-fifths—or, at the most, only
20,000,000 years for geologic time.

Why, exclaimed the geologists, that isn't enough time to lay down
the chalk and coal deposits! Still, Thomson was a great physicist
and set great store by mathematics. Figures cannot lie; that which
is Q.E.D.'d is mathematically demonstrated. His views held until
Perry in 1895 showed up their weakness. And then radioactivity
jumped up, as we have seen, and handed the geologists all the time
they needed to account for this earth—a billion years for the *old*
rocks alone.

# CHAPTER THIRTEEN

*Knowledge of Organic Nature,*
*or The Growth of the Biologic Sciences*

1. The Microcosm; or, Thinking Biologically. 2. How the Mysteries
of Life Became the Facts of Biology. 3. Taking the "Super" out of
Supernatural and Finding a Place for Man in Nature. 4. How the
Anatomists Rescued Man's Body from the Book and the Physiolo-
gists Restored It to Life. 5. Take Medicine: as Science or as Art.
6. Pestilence and Plague; and the Devils of Disease. 7. Antiseptics;
or, the Discovery that Godliness is Cleanliness. 8. Anæsthetics Rob
God of the Sweet Music of the Voice of a Woman in Travail.
9. From the Drug Store on Sacred Street of the Eternal City to
Chemotherapy. 10. Health is Wealth.

I

WHAT we call modern biologic science would not greatly interest Confucius or Buddha, St. Paul or Nero; for them it
would have no meaning or importance. They would marvel at
our motor-cars and possibly like to try a ride or even to go on the
"mike"; but our generalizations, universals, hypotheses, and other
language conveniences would not fit theirs nor serve their intellectual interests. They did not think our thoughts because such
thinking was not adequate to their times nor at all expressive of
their civilization. Our philosophy of life offers no substitute for
theirs: their orbits do not coincide anywhere; there is no point
where our experience could be substituted for theirs. In short, they
could learn from us only by becoming as a little child.

While biology is the most modern of all sciences, we may recall
that into the welter of priestly incantations, prayers, magic, and
drugs of a credulous world of twenty-four hundred years ago, came
Hippocrates—to inspire Aristotle and give the world its first great
naturalist and the science of the human body its most important
discovery. All things considered, Hippocrates was possibly as keen

and honest an observer as the world has ever known; all things considered, Aristotle was possibly the greatest naturalist the world has ever seen.

No real progress could be made in any biologic science until modern man had seen enough with his own eyes to discount what some ancient authority had thought out and written down. Rapid progress was made when so much had been seen that seeing, looking, observing, and experimenting became a more fascinating game than speculating about what had been seen. Modern science, as I see it, is an Aristotelian victory and a Platonic defeat. Modern biologic science, so far as it does not end in nature worship, is a triumph for the school of Hippocrates and a defeat for the school of Neo-Platonism, Gnosticism, and Theosophy.

And the triumph of science is the triumph of empiricism. But while I, an individual, may learn much by experience, I may add enormously to my knowledge by making use of the recorded experiences of others.

The modern biologic sciences offer a rational theory of life, supply a rational theory of disease. These theories are founded on facts, grounded in truths. They cannot disprove many commonly accepted beliefs in spirits, fates, prayers, or in any superhuman, supernatural or occult power, possession, or will; nor is it their business.

In the days of alchemy, at the time of Paracelsus, contemporary of da Vinci and Copernicus, it was generally believed that the signs of the zodiac, or the "luminaries of the firmament," had some mysterious connexion with the parts of our body and influenced the course of our lives; and that there was a spiritual significance and a moral relationship between human beings and the zodiac. Hence astrology, as a system whereby *horoscopes* ("hour-watchers") could be "cast." Some of the loveliest and gruesomest pictures from mediæval times represent semi-disembowelled human bodies surrounded by signs of the zodiac. Such pictures were used as we use crosses or angels today, or as our grandfathers used the skull and crossbones on their tombstones.

Now, if one *believes* that a skull, angel, cross, or zodiacal man is a fit mark for a tomb, or that one born on January 1, 1900, as against August 1, 1600, is predestined to success in love and failure in business, science neither cares nor objects; but the engraving of signs on tombstones and the casting of horoscopes are jobs—or professions, shall we say?—and the professors of carving and casting will certainly not object. Their care will be to sell bigger carvings, better castings.

Astrology—or, rather, beliefs which keep astrologers in food and raiment—was good business for the church. In fact, the rude but often sane and sound beginnings of anatomy and physiology among the Greeks, which culminated in Galen, were washed out when early Christianity in its struggle for existence took over the old Babylonian astrological system. The Stoics had made a philosophy of it; the Neo-Platonists, Gnostics, and Mithraists, a mystery. The system fitted beautifully into early Christianity; it can be made to fit any ten-year-old belief if told by one having authority.

The system gave birth to astronomy, but the mother of lies survived the operation and delivers more astrologers today than astronomers. The facts of astronomy are many and not easily seen through; they must be handled with patience, acquired with patience, with spectroscopic exactness, with mathematical precision, and with cold calculation. Astrology needs only such facts as any star-gazer can acquire, a lot of faith, and a childlike imagination.

Yet the master minds of the Humanistic period of the Renaissance played with this old vapid nonsense. They had more words at their disposal than the Chaldeans, but the net result of their theosophical and Neo-Platonic philosophy was to give a new lease of life to the old idea that Nature gives up her secrets to the man who talks about her rather than to the man who plays with her and lets her do the talking.

Out there is the universe; it is very beautiful; *ergo,* beauty is a manifestation of the divine Idea. What is the universe? The divine unity of the living All. But that is a clumsy phrase. Call it, then, the *Macrocosm*. What is one to do with the Macrocosm? Admire it! But it is easier to get lost in admiration of the universe than of the twaddle spilled in trying to discover the analogy between the Macrocosm and the man who called himself the microcosm.

The outcome of that intellectual search, begun when man decided that thinking it out was easier and more intellectual than digging it out, and raised to classical heights by the Aristotelian

Stoics, was that whatever the Macrocosm might be, man was its *quintessence*, the microcosm.

Now, that was all very well as a philosophy, but what is the good of my being the quintessence of all the cosmic powers if I have to work like a slave for a living and die like a horse before I have got all out of life I want? What indeed? asked the Humanists. Not satisfied with the scriptural answer to that genuine antique, they searched the Classics. They found that Pythagorean and Platonic elements sprinkled with Lucretian atoms (sired by Democritus) made a better Neo-Platonism than that of the Christian Fathers. They called it the Corpuscular theory—in the interests of science, I suppose. How is one to handle such a theory? With mathematics, of course. Especially with Neo-Pythagorean mathematics—charming, fantastic, childish number systems, number mysticisms, number symbolisms. Nor did they overlook the rabbinical Kabala.

No one knows what is in a cocktail any more. But if it is moonshine man wants, he is not likely to be particular about the purity of its source. It is the essence of magic that it be ever more magical; of fantasy, that it be ever more fantastic. A trusting and gullible age must ever have new signs, fresh wonders. The particular age we are now speaking of—and are not yet weaned from—was the age of theology. As God was the cause of all phenomena, there could be no physics as we use the term today, there could be only a theosophy; nor could there be chemistry as science, but there could be a theological chemistry.

It must be so. The supernatural world can only be caught with supernatural gloves. Theology, the "science" of God, demands theosophy—knowledge of Godlike things. And Europe, having compiled a theology from an Oriental Bible and Greek philosophy, sought what further the Orient had to offer that might fit into its theosophy—on the ground that if one is brewing wonder-working herbs to cure a wonder-worked disease, the more herbs the better; and that if one got enough herbs one could cure anything, everything, including senile decay.

As theology demands theosophy, as the macrocosm demands a microcosm, so astrology demanded alchemy. The Kabala was the theosophy of the Jewish rabbis—mystical interpretation of the mystery of mysteries, secret esoteric doctrine, drawn largely from Indian occultism or theosophy. Magic, pure and simple. Christian alchemy fertilized by Jewish Kabala could make gold! At least, that was the claim. Gone now are the alchemy and the Kabala of the good old days; our theosophists do not claim to make gold, but table-rappings and ectoplasm are still good for the "long green."

Think of three worlds: *Intellectual*—ideas, spirits, demons; *Celestial*—sun, moon, planets, and stars; *Elementary*—earthy bodies. These three worlds mutually "correspond"; whatever happens in one influences the other two. The go-betweens are not angels, as you might suspect, nor even ideas, but *emanations*—particles from earthly bodies.

That was the fifteenth-century world into which Paracelsus was born; a world whose best-sellers dealt with demonology, necromancy, astrology, chiromancy, alchemy; when the champion liar claimed to divine by means of a golden tooth he had miraculously grown in the mouth of a ten-year-old child. That was the world of Innocent VIII, father of sixteen children, and author of the famous bull to the authors of the *Malleus Maleficarum*; the world of astrology and alchemy, handmaids of ignorance, superstition, and evil.

It was an age that wallowed in witchcraft, revelled in demonology; an age that was ready for a master quack, Paracelsus; an age that produced those master forerunners of modern science, Copernicus and Vesalius. That man's place in nature is now reasonably secure and reasonably well understood is because science tore nature and man loose from the hands of the quacks; that quacks abound is because the hands of the quacks have not yet been torn loose from women and children.

Paracelsus (Theophrastus Bombastus von Hohenheim) was the son of a Swiss alchemist and physician. The son decided to go in for both. He saw no discrepancy between magic and science, but thought he saw good in both, and turned his master mind to synthesizing one supreme medicine from Galen and alchemy, from the Kabala and theosophy.

Same old story; he could not go both ways at the same time. He chose the easier. At his first lecture, as Professor of Medicine at Basel, he publicly burnt Galen's writings and boasted of his contempt for science—even as Christian Scientists do today. Why trouble to study smelly cadavers or pore over dry books when one can know God and everything by *intuition*! He did not seek facts—only a mystic insight by which one knows all things, communicates with God, and drives away demons. To renounce sensuality and obey the will of God is to become one with celestial reason and thereby possess the philosopher's stone.

Paracelsus was not the first fanatic, nor the last. A theosophist is a theosophist, whether of the school of Alexandrian Gnostics, Kabalists of the tenth century, Alchemists of the fifteenth, or Healers of the twentieth. They unite in their contempt for truths won at the cost of labour, in their belief in *minds* which alone impart wisdom and light to men, emanations of the Divinity.

Why study the human body or the processes of living if man himself is a theophany, a microcosm of the macrocosm? Why indeed! No theosophist does. Paracelsus did not. He sought the spiritual or astral essences; and having found them, sought their "signs" or "figures" in material or corporeal essences.

Into the system of "medicine" this divine healer worked out, we need not here enter. It is enough to say that it can still be found in drug stores, its principles heard in pulpits.

Now Paracelsus may have been right, the Christian Scientists may be right, the Theosophists may be right. Man may be a microcosm of the macrocosm, an emanation of Divinity itself—in short, a theophany. It may be that we can know things only through intuition, that only through mystical ecstasy can we enter into relations with all things and all beings and become one with Celestial Intelligence. It may be that Rabelaisian satire toward the "abstractors of quintessence" was misdirected energy.

Maybe the pope is infallible; maybe we are compounded of spiritual mind and material body, and only the mind is worth a cent. But it does seem to me that so much nonsense could not possibly have survived for so many centuries had not the interests vested in the business of magic, mysticism, and superstition been able to draw upon the two master minds of antiquity, Plato and Aristotle—especially Aristotle's pseudo-scientific speculation about mind, which until recently haunted psychology like a lost soul and still muddies thought about human nature and man's place in nature.

And as for *thought* or *thinking*, I think it no exaggeration to say that Aristotle's, Plato's, Descartes' and Kant's discussions of such forms of behaviour are as unscientific as a Trobriand Islander's discussion of the physiology of reproduction or Euclid's discussion of the phenomena of light-rays.

Biology is either the science of life or it is nothing. To set up a science of mind, as psychologists do, and a science of body, as some biologists do, is to split the most important of all sciences wide open. That house divided against itself cannot stand.

It may also be true, as Ecclesiasticus said, and as a Broadway hospital inscription says, that *Healing cometh of the Most High*, but my guess is that the nurses in that hospital proceed on the assumption that it is just as well to read the pulse and temperature now and then, and even consult the physician—though the inscription does make a good alibi if anything goes wrong!

In other words, there may be a factual foundation for any belief, no matter how absurd it may seem to be; on the other hand, there may be no such foundation for certain beliefs even though they seem as "plain as day." That science to a great extent is "remaking the world" is because innumerable beliefs have been stripped of their venerable rags and looked at with a pawnbroker's eye. Are they genuine, will they wash? that is the question; not, as the Inquisition told Galileo, are they contrary to Holy Writ—or any writ not on the Index.

Had the church but realized it, Holy Writ had already met a tougher foe of embalmed ignorance than Galileo or Copernicus. While Paracelsus was synthesizing a philosopher's stone, Vesalius was analysing a human being. If Galileo started up a cosmic universe out of the macrocosm Copernicus had shattered, Vesalius let daylight into the microcosm and gave man a chance to look at himself as he is in the flesh and not as he was in a book. The world has nearly caught up with what Copernicus started; it may never catch up with what Vesalius started. Every child has heard of Copernicus or Galileo or Newton, and knows something of the movements of the stars; how many know anything about the movements of their bowels or ever heard of Vesalius?

Millions of people have the idea that life is so mysterious it just *must* be some mysterious principle, some *vital* force. The Greeks had a word for it: they called it *psyche*. Driesch calls it *Vitalism*; spiritualists call it *ectoplasm*. Add these names together, and what have you? Enough material for a flea or enough energy to keep a bacterium moving? More specifically, do these names give us a better idea of life than a South Sea Islander has? They certainly give us no foundation for the study of embryology or of the physiology of reproduction or respiration.

True, some scientists say spirits have no factual basis; that souls are born of hope and fear and exist only as words or misinterpretations of various natural phenomena, including dreams. But, fortunately or unfortunately, as Pearl says, no one can *prove* that an impalpable soul does not live on after the body has turned to dust, ashes, or coal, nor can any scientist absolutely demonstrate that such persistence does not occur.

What, then, are the *facts*? On the one hand, ancient and widespread beliefs that souls exist; on the other, unbiassed examination of beliefs in souls—with the verdict that the evidence, while it might deceive the over-hopeful and hyper-credulous, would not hang a cat. Further, that just as the astronomer's theory of the cosmic universe requires no anthropomorphic Creator, so the biologist's theory of life requires no soul. Science cannot "examine" spiritualism because it cannot come to grips with any factual evidence which supports a belief in spirits; nor is anything known about living beings which supports a belief that life can exist apart from a mechanism, an organism, a material body.

As the "wind" does not blow where it listeth but where it finds itself pushed and pulled by natural forces acting on natural atmosphere, so no "ghost" could flit about or hold hands or make noises without oxidizing some carbon compound in a chemical engine. But a ghost with an internal-combustion engine is no longer a ghost; it is an object of scientific investigation.

Souls are figures of speech, and, as such, subjects of study by the linguist, the historian, and the anthropologist; objectively, they do not exist, and consequently are outside the realm of the biologist, who studies action in living objects. As no ghost can talk to a biologist, so no biologist can talk to a spiritualist. Biology, spirituality; materialism, mysticism; natural, supernatural; faith in the present, faith in and hope for the future; science, religion.

Inclusion of unreal "facts" prevents an approach to the reality of life. Such "facts" cannot serve as pegs on which to hang new facts, or as a background for a closer approximation to the truth of the facts one might discover. Beliefs in supernatural or supersensible beings or powers prevent man from taking, or trying to take, an honest and dispassionate view of life. No man with an immortal soul in dire peril can take a scientific attitude toward himself, his wife, his children, his neighbours, his enemies, his country, or the foundations of his beliefs. "Saved," such a man is one kind of social liability; "lost," another kind. Lost or saved, he cannot feel free to seek facts, welcome criticism, await proof, examine other points of view; he accepts his beliefs, seeks vindication, and thrives on inertia of thought. He is not in tune with this age, for he cannot think biologically.

No Huxley could write a *Man's Place in Nature* until man had been restored to nature. Or, consider the parable of the Sower. The farmers knew they could not keep on drawing from their banks without making a deposit now and then, but they thought they could do that with the soil. They found they could not—and began to ask questions. What is *soil*, anyway? "And some fell by the wayside . . . some upon a rock . . . some among thorns . . . and others fell on good ground and bore fruit an hundredfold."

But what makes ground *good*? Just dirt? Or bacteria, protozoa, microscopic algæ, moulds, fungi, and those incredibly valuable earthworms which also do their part in the breaking down and building up processes necessary to make soil? A pail of rich soil is a vast universe of life and teeming activity.

When all this was known—and *intuition* played no part in its discovery—agriculture, after ten thousand years, began to be a science. The old empiricisms would work no longer. Behind too many of the old symbols was an empty word, a silly superstition, a meaningless formula. In the laboratories and experiment stations are sought new truths, tangible facts, sensible entities. Chemistry and physics are the handmaids of this new science. Agriculture will be new again and the world incalculably enriched, when a cheap and easy way is found to crack the cellulose molecule into its sugars, for then man's optimum fuel will be as cheap as straw, cornstalk, and sawdust.

## II

It would be interesting to know if any of our Puritan ancestors had heard of that prematurely wise genius, Roger Bacon, who wiped Aristotle off the slate with one hand and with the other wrote hopefully of the time when people would realize that they had a culture and that it was in their own hands to develop it along rational lines. Not many, probably, for such ideas were not taught in those days. It took five hundred years to prove that Bacon was right; that the road to human happiness lay through the study of plain everyday things that could be seen and handled, that man gets control over nature by experimenting with the things of nature, that man could rationalize his own inventiveness, that through experimental science he would be able to travel in ships without oars or sails, ride fast on land in carriages propelled without animals, fly like birds through the air in machines, and cross rivers on bridges without supports! What a prophecy of the Brooklyn Bridge, the steamship, the motor-car, and the airplane!

Why no prophecy of the telegraph, telephone, and radio? Electric control was then as far beyond man's wildest dreams as were fertilized eggs, electrons, and atoms. True, Democritus had *thought* atoms—and it was an extraordinarily bold and shrewd theory; but, with the exception of Epicurus, Democritus little influenced the Græco-Roman world. And that world was certainly as far from ready to accept Epicurus as is our Fundamentalist world to accept Darwin. In fact, no man or age bowing in fear to invisible powers can stand the light of reason—even though he illuminate his Bible by incandescent light.

And may I again emphasize the fact that mere brilliancy, or meteor however big, cannot glow till it encounters oxygen, or kindle a fire unless it comes within the range of inflammable materials. Movements require leaders; but little, if anything, moves unless there are followers. It is easier to start a mob in motion than a community.

Initiative—the proponent of a political revolt, an original inventive genius—is one thing; setting and leadership are other things. The idea, for example, of planetary motions, basis of modern astronomy, began with Eudoxus and Calippus. Before Eudoxus and

Calippus, Pythagoras and Aristarchus had anticipated the Copernican theory. Aristotle certainly anticipated Darwin in the theory of evolution. But, as we have seen, the cosmology of the ancients was knocked sky-high by the Book of Genesis, and that Book still stands between Darwin and many devout people.

Such triumph as Darwin had—and it was great—was due primarily, not to his original genius or his compelling honesty and sincerity, but to the fire of a tiny band of followers, led by Thomas Huxley in England, by Asa Gray in America. Darwin himself, one of the gentlest souls that ever lived, saw the devastation in religious beliefs acceptance of his theory would entail, and declared he felt like a "murderer." But Huxley gloried in murdering the powers of darkness, as they seemed to him. No crusader for light and intellectual freedom ever won such a victory.

Aristotle, like Lucretius and to a lesser extent other ancients, anticipated the modern theory of evolution—the gradual processional change from the inorganic to the organic, from simpler forms of life to higher. That story is so plainly written in the plant and animal world, and even more plainly embalmed in the earth's crust, that the idea of evolution seems inescapable; but the idea never gets a chance with one who will not look or with one who says: "I care not what the rocks say; I have my own story of Genesis; it alone is authority, it transcends reason itself."

That curious crab, Carlyle, is not famed as Bible student or as moron; "intellectually" he was the peer of Darwin; yet he rejected Darwin's laws of natural selection with contempt. John Hampden persecuted Wallace (Darwin's ally in the theory of evolution) for twenty years for trying to convince him that the earth is round. Round? The earth is flat, said Hampden, and offered to bet five hundred pounds that it was. Alexander Dowie doubtless would bet as many dollars.

Aristotle's theory was an intellectual feat of high order, and not without some justice has he been called the founder of experimental science. But, unlike Roger Bacon, he never reached a point in his thinking where he could see human affairs as possibly open to investigation and hence possibly modifiable in ways suggested by such investigation.

Possibly that very failure of Aristotle to take a scientific instead of a philosophic attitude toward the realities of life fired Bacon to launch his rocket. Why *think* experimentally if you are not to *make* experiments and then proceed on the information your experiments give you?

Aristotle, thanks to the Arabs, was rediscovered by the Western world rather late in that tenth-thirteenth century period of astoundingly rapid development of the scientific attitude. After it had been "interpreted" by those wise churchmen Albertus Magnus and Thomas Aquinas, it was rendered innocuous, its "mistakes sanctified." Anything—book, belief, opinion—the church "reconciles" with the Bible thereby becomes just one more barrier to free thought, one more obstacle to scientific exploration, investigation, and experimentation, and the practical application of the obvious or reasonable deductions from such study of nature.

Not only was there nothing serious in Plato for the church to swallow, but very much, as we have seen, which it found useful; his doctrine of souls especially, and his emphasis on morals and metaphysical subtleties.

The Renaissance, I repeat, was not a scientific movement, nor did it mark progress in freedom of thought; it did mark a change in favourite Greek authorities. Plato was elected. The Reformation involved even less emancipation; for the Protestants there was just one Book. The Greeks were dangerous freethinkers! They were thrown over bodily.

To burn a witch is one thing; to inquire too closely into the morals or beliefs of a princely patron of the church is quite another. Being priest or preacher was a job in itself; for the higher clergy, a very fat job. As long as their living was secure and luxurious, why concern themselves with *material* things?

Again, how can church or censor know what is godly or good for men, women, and children, if they (church and censor) do not read all the possibly ungodly or bad books? How indeed! Some of the freest thinking that has ever been done has gone on under a tonsure.

Now, one of the by-products of the change engendered by the literary Renaissance and the spiritual Reformation was an added stimulus to inquire what it was all about. What people talk about they think about—and often discover that they have no great body of facts to think upon, and so read up. The discovery of the fact that the classics clashed was in itself stimulus to read the classics and then decide which was right. And centuries after the Arabs had discovered the lore of the classical world and made it its own, and had built upon it rather solid structures, Christian Europe rediscovered it. The immediate result was intellectual anarchy—which always ensues when men revolt against systematized intellectual despotism.

That "despotism," strange hybrid of Bible and Greek philosophy, was essentially Organized Belief. It was not only authority for life and existence, it was a wall beyond which men were forbidden to think, a norm or canon with which men were supposed to reconcile their thoughts. In other words, it was essentially the same old theocratic power thought which had been born on the Nile and again on the Euphrates. It was absolutism, as though no free-thinking, scientifically-minded Greek had ever lived in Ionia or Alexandria, Athens or Syracuse. Don't think; believe! But Bacon had said, Experiment!

Galileo experimented. He was a scientist; with him intellectual anarchy begins to become scientific discipline. The year Galileo died Newton was born. The facts his experiments revealed, and which he incorporated in his mechanics, are as true as the stars—and are all incorporated in Einstein. There are no revolutions in science; evolutions only, and due to new methods—the substitution of the physical for the metaphysical, the natural for the supernatural, the material for the spiritual.

A Martian visiting these shores in the days of Galileo in quest of information about living beings would have been referred to the Bible and the latest edition of some ancient Natural History. Possibly to a *Physiologus* or a *Bestiaries*—tales of centaurs and phœnixes, frogs and crows, allegories to point morals. Today, he would be invited to use his eyes and such adjuncts to understanding as are available; or he would be given a text-book on life, a Biology, or a Biochemistry, or a book on the Mechanism of Life or the Living Machinery or the Engines of the Human Body; or an organic chemistry.

Would he find anything about "organisms" in an organic chemistry? Nothing; but a great deal about alcohols, ethers, aldehydes, fats, oils, waxes, lipoids, amino-acids, proteins, uric acids, and various organo-metallic compounds of the aliphatic series or "open chain" compounds; and various hydrocarbons, amines, alcohols, phenols, ketones, quinones, dyes, stains, terpenes, vegetable alkaloids, and arsenic and mercury compounds of the aromatic series or "closed chain" compounds; and pigments, chlorophyll, enzymes, vitamins, and hormones.

What have these odds and ends to do with life? In bottles in a chemist's shop, nothing. Combined in proper amounts and under proper physical conditions, these odds and ends will make an elephant or beeswax, a whale or maple sugar, a human being or a silk dress. The chemist has not synthesized an elephant, a bee, a tree, or a man, but he has analysed them: he knows what they are made of and what makes them go; and he can make most of the substances they make or require for life. He can make wax, sugar, silk, and over two hundred thousand other organic compounds.

Nature makes a bee, the bee makes wax; man can make wax just as good. Nature makes a camphor tree, rattlesnake, cow; man can make camphor, snake poison, beefsteak. It is still cheaper to grow beefsteaks on the hoof and rubber on the trees than to make them in the laboratory. It took man less than a century to learn how to make beeswax; nature must have spent over a hundred million years throwing up a bee. Give man a thousandth part of that time.

The first steps are the hardest to make. It was a great step when a little over a century ago the old Logos ceased to be the kite of life and became the tail of biology.

What has been accomplished in the better understanding of ourselves and of all living beings since life became the object of scientific observation cannot be told here, nor short of a fifty-foot shelf of books. I have not tried to tell it, nor even to summarize it. I am trying to get so much of it before us as may be useful as a background against which to view the nature of our civilization, of ourselves, and of our relation to the day and age we face. Believing as I do that the enduring and the significant achievements of modern science are in the realm of organic rather than inorganic chemistry, and that an honest and unbiassed attitude toward ourselves and life in general is quite as important as a sensible attitude toward the sun, moon, and Orion, I think our progress in the biologic sciences quite as well worth emphasizing as in motor transportation and wireless communication. Why all the hurry if there is nothing but the grave at the end of the journey, why speed up communication if we cannot talk back from the grave?

If it be urged that life is still a mystery, I reply, so is an electron, a drop of water, a grain of salt. If evolution is a mystery, so are the materials out of which life was evolved, and the sun's rays which beat upon this earth and drive it to drink.

The sun is a power plant; it drives green plants to eat atmosphere; but the world of human beings had to wait long to find that out, or what plants do with atmosphere when they "eat" it. That genius, Malpighi, not only saw "a certain great thing" with his own eyes, but many great things. True, he had a microscope, but it was so poor it would be scorned today; but he saw into capillary circulation in animals, and far enough into the function of green leaves to begin a scientific approach to the world of "trees, shrubs, and herbs," as Theophrastus had called the vegetal kingdom. A Digger Indian would have made a better classification, but that was good enough for a Europe yearning for Kingdom Come.

The real Harvey of the plant world was Hales, whose *Vegetable Staticks* (1727) laid the foundations on which the present superb structure of plant physiology has been built. And may I point out the significance of the discoveries made by the botanists in the understanding of animal physiology? Animals cannot *eat* carbon, but carbon they must have. They get it from the plant world, which splits the carbon dioxide of the atmosphere, builds the carbon into compounds useful for animals, and sets the oxygen free in the atmosphere, where animals may find it and use it for oxidizing the carbon compounds they get from plants.

Life is one thing in plants, another in animals, but essentially the same thing—chemical reactions. The plant seeks a place in the sun; the animal seeks the plant. No plant life, no animal life. Living processes in animals involve chemical combustion, oxidation; the end product is water and carbon dioxide. Plants need both. There is water enough for all, but only through plants is carbon kept in circulation in such form that animal engines can keep up steam.

Plants liberate oxygen; it was Priestley, the chemist, who discovered that fact. Last year a hundred-mile belt of oxygenless water was discovered in the Pacific Ocean: that belt is lifeless!

Before we go further, let us go back a little—possibly to Roger Bacon, who found a pair of convergent crystal lenses "useful to old men and to those whose sight is weakened, for by this means they will be able to see the letters sufficiently enlarged, however small they may be." He was talking about a microscope; but no one could possibly have suspected in the thirteenth century just how useful a microscope could be, not only to old, but to young men, or how far they could see into the foundations of life. "Burning glasses," spectacles, etc., were known to the ancients, but for centuries were looked upon, like the compass, as curious toys. Nothing serious came of Bacon's lenses: to see letters, however small, was to see only what had been seen or was visible to any ordinary pair of eyes.

With the middle of the seventeenth century men began seeing things that human eyes were not naturally fitted to see. Through the telescope Galileo was seeing far out beyond human vision—into the realm of the infinitely large. With the microscope man began to see into the realm of the infinitely small, though it was not then realized just how much this earth was to shrink because of the new vision, or how far into the inscrutable mysteries of life man was to travel in less than three centuries: more with the microscope than in three million years without it.

Two centuries had to pass before man began to wake up to just what it was he was seeing. The microscope had opened a new world, but many facts had to be discovered before they could be viewed in relationships, or before the factual microscopic world could be related to the factual world revealed by human vision and by new techniques and new ways of comprehending that world.

What the seventeenth century saw through the microscope was duly reported to the then existing Royal Societies—to be talked over enthusiastically as curiosities of nature. With the eighteenth century these curiosities grew into large collections of curios. The nineteenth century brought arrangement, classification, order. The curios were no longer curios, but became parts, members, of the one vast articulate, living, breathing, organized body of knowledge we call biology.

A puzzle of infinite parts, many of which are well understood, some hardly at all; but the parts fit, and they can be fitted. The name of the puzzle is *Life*—neither more nor less puzzling than that other puzzle, the materials that build the bodies life resides in, the energies life employs in living.

Curiously enough, the first book written on what the microscope revealed (Hooke's *Micrographia*—little pictures—published by the Royal Society in 1665) was written to "sell" the idea of using a microscope; it was an intellectual toy, a new plaything for tired Highbrows. *Micrographia* described and figured the "little boxes" of organic structure—the unit or cell of organic protoplasm. Of such "little boxes" each of us is allotted some nine billion for brain use alone; and for carrying oxygen to and carbon dioxide from the ten million million cells of our body, some 30,000,000,000 per spoonful of blood. And every cell of our body, as is now known, is an extraordinarily complex and busy little world. To cite a single example, there are some 3,300,000,000 molecules in every single liver cell, and each bafflingly complex.

Hooke was a physician, a microscopist in his spare time, an ingenious observer. With him, and the discoveries revealed by the compound microscope in the hands of his contemporaries, the biologic sciences began to revive—two thousand years after they had first been called to life by Aristotle and his pupil, Theophrastus. In fact, it was some years before the microscope gave as much insight into plant anatomy as had been visioned by Theophrastus, the first real botanist, as Aristotle was the first real zoologist.

We smile at the master's classification of animals, at the pupil's classification of plants; but, I repeat, two thousand years had to elapse before Christian Europe caught up with pagan Greece. "I found no basis prepared; no models to copy," said Aristotle; "mine is the first step, and therefore a small one, though worked out with much thought and hard labour. It must be looked at as a first step and judged with indulgence."

There was a botanic garden connected with Aristotle's Lyceum. Theophrastus studied it, and with his pupils discussed such significant horticultural problems as grafting and budding. Pliny himself was no mean botanist, nor was Pedianus Dioscorides, author of a celebrated treatise on *Materia Medica* and master herbalist to the

Middle Ages. But, according to Coulter, Hippocrates himself, master of Aristotle, was the first real student of scientific botany.

Contemporaries of Hooke were: Malpighi, really great anatomist (parts of our kidneys and spleen bear his name) and founder of microscopic or cellular anatomy of animals; Grew, who did a similar service for plants; and Kircher and Leeuwenhoek.

Of these early microscopists, Leeuwenhoek was the real genius, and one of the rarest birds in human history. He had no business looking through a microscope; it was his business to grind lenses. But his hobby became his grand passion. The trouble was that he saw more than his age could digest. For what the Delft Dutchman curiously saw, accurately described and honestly figured in his reports to the Royal Society in 1683, was nothing less than bacteria, protozoa, and spermatozoa. He was the first bacteriologist, the first protozoologist, the first to see the tiny plant louse give birth to a live aphid, the first to see the male element of reproduction.

More remarkable still, he had the conviction that the whole world, including Aristotle, was wrong in believing in "spontaneous generation," that life grew out of putrefaction or corruption. He was looking for evidence to back up his conviction. And he found it! But the unlearned were not yet ready to give up their immortal souls, nor the learned their belief that *corruption* generates *life*. Two centuries had to pass before the fact was established beyond doubt that life springs from life and not from a decaying refuse heap of lifeless remains; before Huxley, sharpshooter at ignorance, could deliver his presidential address to the British A. A. S. on *Biogenesis and Abiogenesis*. That was only sixty years ago, yet:

> Thoughts that great hearts once broke for, we
> Breathe cheaply in the common air,

and sometimes get as chesty as though we had stood with Pasteur, Koch, and Darwin on the firing-line! With that address, spontaneous generation (abiogenesis) went by the board—for ever. Life is not generated in a scrap heap, but from life or the makings of life. *Omne vivum, ex vivo*.

Or, *Omne vivum, ex ovo*, as we sometimes say, and as Leeuwenhoek rightly concluded. But in higher animals, such as humans, who lays the egg? Man, said the Dutchman; and so says the Bible.

Did not Adam germinate Eve? There was some excuse for both opinions. De Graaf in the seventeenth century had discovered the follicles which contain ova and which now bear his name. He also gave the name "ovary" to what in woman was then called testicle. But the true human egg was not discovered until 1827. No one has yet seen a fertilized human ovum, nor even a human embryo less than ten days old. Leeuwenhoek was the first to see and figure a spermatozoon; he did not know what it was, so he called it the germ—an egg, as it were, to be "hatched" by the female. And having seen it wrong, it was easy for him to see something in it that wasn't there. He *thought* he saw a *homunculus!* Therewith began the school of Spermists as against the Ovists; "preformationists" both, and today as obsolete in biology as the theological school which saw all creation beginning in the Word.

Even a school of Spermists or Ovists marked a great advance over the Greek and South Sea speculations on the physiology of reproduction. How *could* they know anything of the physiology of reproduction when they would not even take the trouble to get at the facts of their gross anatomy?

The human uterus is not *bifid*, as in cows, but *simplex*, as in apes. Even a fifteenth-century professor of anatomy in Pavia wrote of it as "divided into two concave parts." He never looked: just handed on the original inference—that a uterus is a uterus and all look alike; that is, that the human uterus was like one seen two thousand years ago in some domestic animal. And stated this, not as inference, but as fact.

Having settled the "fact" that the human uterus was *bifid*, the Greeks proceeded to settle certain other facts, such as that the female develops in the left part, the male in the right. Why? Because left is west, darkness; right, east, light. Well, that is good philosophy: it begins with an inference, verifiable but unverified, and by a childish analogy draws another inference, not verifiable but utterly unjustified. At any rate, when man tells the story he is born right, and by nature comes from the east, where it is light.

Those Greek philosophers loved also to discuss the nature of the "generative fluid." Man has it. Do or do not women have it? Well, what is it, then? "Foam" from the *rich* part of the blood that flows drop by drop from the brain, said the Pythagoreans. Not at all, said the Apollonian Diogenes; it is a "subtle air" which escapes from the spermatic veins during coitus.

They discussed other phases of human reproduction and embryonic development just as learnedly and philosophically. One more sample. Woman, being of a warmer nature than man, has more heat, said Empedocles; hence menstruates—at the waning of the moon. Empedocles also made eyes of fire and water. In vision, fire goes out from the eyes to meet objects. That is why we shoot people with fiery glances!

Despite the advance in science, a Christian intellectual of a century ago could no more keep from anthropomorphizing creation than Aristotle could. Religion declares the will of God, says my Bridgewater treatise, and philosophy manifests his power. And who was *the* philosopher of 1830 England? Aristotle, "the great zoological and physiological luminary of Greece." For writers of Bridgewater treatises there was no science of life, no biology; there was Aristotle, and his *Natural History* could be drawn upon for any "fact" which might be twisted into evidence of God's Goodness— or, when "Goodness" was not so evident, his Power or Wisdom.

Even a "Pliny says" is enough to make a mollusc a good illustration of the Supreme Being's goodness and attention to the wants of his creatures—its byssus "has been long celebrated, for it is *mentioned* by Aristotle." God, as Supreme Intelligence, creates shellfish; but Aristotle only has to mention one to make it famous. In the Christian world not a hair falls unnoticed by the All-seeing Eye. In the Aristotelian world nature makes nothing in vain, nothing that does not justify the ways of God to man. In the Ptolemaic world of the Stoics, things move and have their being by superhuman forces of heavenly origin. The key to the human life cycle was to be read in the stars. They reveal, foreshadow, and control human destiny.

Great is our debt to the Greeks, but Bacon may have been right at that. Still, I should not like to burn Aristotle. Somebody had to start naming things and, having named them, with the names build schemes and theories and draw inferences and conclusions. And get enthusiastic about them and hand them on to the next generation to play with. Christian Europe did not like Greek intellectual toys, and spent a thousand years trying to smash them. And then, wearied of their own toys, in sheer ennui they sought something new, something to talk about, because, being intellectuals, they could do nothing else. They discovered that the Arabs had some curious toys, and began to like them. After about five hundred years, they found they could make things with them—new toys, new theories, new notions. And the more they manipulated them, the more they could manipulate them. Their technique improved, their tools improved, and their wits perforce were sharpened. They became more critical.

Now, note again that Galileo with his telescope could see new stars, more stars than anyone had ever seen before; could see more deeply into the cosmic universe than anyone had ever penetrated before. But a century and more had to pass before an engineer could take the stars, and such energies and forces as were known, and build the stars into an orderly machine. Then and there celestial mechanics became a science.

Hooke and his contemporaries saw further into life than had been seen before. Hooke even guessed that the existence of certain fossils in England suggested a phase of life on earth and that England once enjoyed a tropical climate. But no one was prepared to pick that guess up and try to see what could be made of it. No one was yet big enough to make anything of the tiny things seen under the microscope; there was no theory of life, no classification of living things, they would fit into, nor enough facts yet known to suggest a theory of living things. Genesis was the authority on all such recondite matters. More, the ardour which kept the early Leeuwenhoeks peering down brass tubes to see what they could see, slowed down—as though they had enough curiosities, why seek more.

I was speaking of the seventeenth- and eighteenth-century microscopists. The microscope before me is binocular, has two sets of paired Huygens eyepieces, and three achromatic objectives—one of which is for *oil* immersion. What that microscope cannot see of life (such as ultra-microscopic bacteria) can be picked up in a filtre; and what cannot be seen *into* may be seen *through* with X-rays. I resist the temptation to name other modern appliances which can be brought to bear upon life; they are numerous enough to stock an emperor's palace, ingenious enough to excite the envy of the creator of human sense organs. The point is, that a modern research microscope bears about the same relation to the one Leeuwenhoek used as Galileo's old spyglass bears to the instruments in the Lick Observatory.

Leeuwenhoek probably had no Huygens achromatic eyepieces, certainly no achromatic objectives—with the result that what he saw was spherical and surrounded by a coloured halo. Do we not often see things in the round when they should be seen in the flat, and endow things with a halo when they are as plain as mud? The far-seeing or the highly magnifying eye of science must be free from aberration, spherical or chromatic. And think of a *binocular* microscope!

Certainly modern instrument-makers have given man marvellous tools for prying into nature's secrets: more, and more precise, than nature allowed him. True, binocular vision came to us through our monkey ancestors, but the eyes nature gave us are so faulty an optician would be ashamed to let them out of his shop.

There are embryos, as Aristotle well knew. Where do they come from? How do they start? What is the female's share, the male's share? Aristotle discussed such questions, and in an answer of four words could have built himself a monument better than the Pyramid: "Damned if I know!" Nor did Harvey or any of his day know, yet he accepted Aristotle's ideas of parthenogenetic birth and spontaneous generation as though they were facts. In fact, his *On the Generation of Animals* with a preface by Aristotle would pass as a text-book in such parts of literate Melanesia as have been seduced to Christianity.

Harvey and the Middle Ages thought that by doing certain things they could produce or "generate" such things as honey bees, eels, etc. The boy of today who thinks, for example, that pianos and airplanes generate spontaneously in scrap heaps, has about as clear an insight into manufacturing processes as university-bred Europe of last century had into the biologic process of generating eels or honey bees.

I hold no brief for eels, nor charge against Harvey. He was a great man; at any rate, his demonstration that blood circulates in the animal body marked an epoch in understanding life. But look at eels now—with a genetic history of millions of years and a cyclic history of thousands of miles behind every eel. And look at bees now—and do not underestimate the rôles their honey and wax have played in human welfare. Wax is wax and honey is an extraordinarily valuable food for man. We do not know all about bees today, but enough to fill a fat volume, and when we want bigger and better bees our Department of Agriculture will breed them. Right now they are bent on breeding a bee with a bigger stomach, a larger thorax, wider wings, and a longer tongue, which will swarm less and breed more. It should also be more immune from contagious diseases, have a kind heart, a gentle disposition, and share its honey more generously with its keeper.

Will the scientists breed such a bee? Why not! Think of the old-fashioned milk cow, all horns and bones, and barely enough milk to support a wabbly calf. Think of the razor-back hogs and the hens that would rather gad than lay eggs. And think of cod-liver oil, and liverwurst; and the calves' liver the butcher used to give away because nobody would buy it, that we should have blushed to eat a few years ago, but eat now to bring a blush to pale cheeks. Thanks to Minot, liver now rates as a priceless boon in pernicious anæmia.

Anæmia—deficiency of blood or of red blood cells, or hemoglobin; a deadly disease. Why, the story of hemoglobin alone—and it was utterly unknown a few decades ago—gets closer to life than the combined knowledge of the entire world up to one hundred years ago.

This is not the place to "sell" liver or to indulge hepatic vein; there is too much in the liver, it does too many things, is too complicated in its genesis, embryological changes, anatomical parts, and especially and above all in the chemical processes it performs and on whose proper functionings our life depends. But compare our own attitude toward this huge vital organ with that of our grandmothers, when calves' liver was fit only for cats and their own had to fit stays ("tight-lace" or "corset" liver), or with that of the Roman *Haruspex* ("entrail observer"), who offered models of the liver to the gods to cure internal diseases.

What the ancients did, and some moderns do not, understand is that life is pretty tough and often "gets well" without benefit of clergy or medicine-man; and that what passed for spontaneous generation was sheer ignorance of how nature generates. Marshall's *Physiology of Reproduction* requires more words than there are in this book; and it is primarily for animal-breeders.

Just what does an animal-breeder do? Takes the raw materials nature offers him, looks them over, decides what he wants more of—butter, fat, bacon, eggs, juicy steak, honey—and breeds to that end. Animals inevitably vary in this or that respect, and such variations as are in man's favour man favours. He selects. The process is not unlike, but only roughly like, that followed by engineers who in the inanimate world make bridges out of iron mines or chemists who make drugs out of coal mines. The chemist could make coal, but it is still cheaper to dig it. The biologist cannot make cows or pigs; the chemist can make most of the things cows and pigs make, but as his time is worth more than that of cows or pigs, he lets nature grow the animals.

The great advance in both processes always involves the discovery of how nature did it. That discovery made, man can do it. It seems that nature spent long periods of time in producing such complex natural products as bees, eels, cows, and pigs—and human beings. Nature could throw up a diamond more easily than a diatom, but having once produced a diatom she easily grew more. The elemental forces as well as the raw elements needed for making diamonds are relatively fewer in number than those required for the simplest form of life.

Most boys today, I suppose, know more or less about galvanic batteries, coulombs, volts, watts, amperes, ohms, and farads; but how many know that Galvani, Coulomb, Volta, and Watt were all born in the same decade, and that they lived to see the birth of Ampère, Ohm, and Faraday? And how many know that Galvani was not a physicist at all, but a professor of anatomy at Bologna? Well, he was; and when, in 1791, he described how frogs acted as though they were shocked with electricity when touched with two different metals, he certainly started something. He thought the contraction electricity, and argued that it must be in the muscle itself. It isn't, of course. Muscle nerve is a good conductor of electricity—a fact made use of by the state in murdering its criminals. Action in nerves and nerve cells is bioelectric action. But biologists have not yet finished investigating the clues opened up by Galvani's frog-leg battery.

Galvani's seemingly insignificant discovery proved to be the factual wedge which opened up this astounding era of electricity. He was not trying to galvanize a frog: he had never heard of galvanism; he was an anatomist. His meat should have been a man's leg, not a frog's. But frog corpses are cheaper than human; and besides, it has required great courage to break through the accumulated taboos about human corpses. We are still so far from the end of these taboos that few boys or girls leave school with a practical view of their internal mechanisms. The final authority on human anatomy is the human body. Sound knowledge began to replace the authorized surmises, guesses, and observations of the ancients when corpses of criminals were sent, not to dunghills, but to dissecting-rooms. Our youth still studies biology in terms of fish-worms and frogs. And we call ourselves a practical people; ours, a practical education. Practical for what?

Galvani hung his preparations on copper hooks attached to an iron bar. When the loose end of the frog swung up against the iron, it twitched. He probably jumped at the unexpected phenomenon; but he was far enough along in a scientific age not to attribute a twitch in a dead muscle to the devil or to any other figment of frightened imagination. The twitch *looked* to him as though produced by an electrical discharge. And so it was, but that the discharge was generated in the muscle itself was all wrong. He should not have jumped to that conclusion. Volta of Padua, after monkeying further with the idea, discovered the rashness of Galvani's conclusion, and showed that it was not the muscle that generated the electricity, but the two *dissimilar* metals—copper and iron; or, better still, copper and zinc. Brought into *direct* contact, or *through* a proper medium such as a nerve or a dilute acid, the metals generated electricity. Thereupon Volta built his "pile"—of pairs of different metals separated by cloth wet with dilute acid.

The voltaic followed the galvanic battery in ten years. That same year (1800) Nicholson utilized the decomposing effects of chemical or "voltaic" electricity—as distinguished from common, physical, or frictional—to electrocute (decompose) water; and thereby disclosed the elemental hydrogen-oxygen skeleton of one of life's oldest and best friends and one of the four "primordial principles."

Seven years later Davy electrocuted two well-known substances till then rated as "elements": potash gave up its secret and decomposed into potassium, carbon, and oxygen; soda, into sodium, carbon, and oxygen. And the next year Davy produced an electric arc between carbon poles. Galvani's frog, 1790; Davy's arc-light, 1808. Progress. Also chemical electricity on a scientific basis, and electric batteries and electrolytic processes on a taxable basis.

What Galvani called "animal electricity" and is now known as bioelectricity, is still a deep and difficult problem, though much advance has been made since the Italian anatomist galvanized a dead frog's leg to life.

The mystery of life can only be solved by handling the things of life. As they become known a factual basis is built up. Out of that body of knowledge a science of life emerges—and in the hands of Wells and Huxley becomes a fascinating story in two ponderous volumes.

### III

The chemist compared his elements, discovered certain relationships, and from his comparative studies arranged his elements in series, groups, etc.; in short, prepared a Table of Elements. He rates this table highly and finds it useful in every chemical operation.

Similar tables, based on supposed genetic relationships, exist for living beings: one for plants, another for animals. If I wish to find my degree of kinship with a jellyfish, for example, all I have to do is to look in the table and find *Homo* and then *Cœlenterata*. I find nothing between me and a jellyfish—besides the fact that I draw a Latin, the jellyfish a Greek, name—but a few lines, a few figures, a few dates, all representing change in structure and method of living, growing, and reproducing: which took time.

In the books before me there are a score or more such tables. They do not agree in detail, and some are longer, more detailed, than others; but they do agree in their main conclusions. Are the conclusions true? They seem to be. One does not have to take them on faith; they may be verified against a factual background. That background is the earth itself, the fossil forms embedded in it, the observable facts of comparative anatomy and embryology, the facts revealed to the naked eye and to the microscopic eye—yes, and to the eye of chemist and physicist.

It was one thing for astronomers to upset Mosaic cosmogony and for the French and American Revolutions to upset social equilibrium and established authority; it was another and a bigger thing to bring order out of the plant and animal world and find man's place in that picture. Was or was he not created 4004 B.C.? Is or is not life spontaneously generated? Is man an animal or is he an exception, a *special* creation? Have plants and animals stood still since creation, or did they also fall? These seem strange questions now, but the answers—as epitomized in any of the above-mentioned tables—have been formulated only within the last hundred years; in fact, most of them are as Mid-Victorian as our Civil War.

With sound text-books on biology in the hands of high-school pupils and fine libraries of botanies and zoologies available on every side, it is not easy for us to realize that the entire world of plants and animals was practically unknown, unexplored, and unclassified when Washington was a schoolboy. Pliny would have satisfied his curiosity about the nature of things; Aristotle on Zoology and Theophrastus on Botany would have been "advanced" reading—Aristotle perhaps too advanced, for he found an animal in man and placed him with the animals. That might do for pagan Greece; it would not do for Christian Rome. No revealed religion has ever had any doubt as to man's place in nature, namely, out, above, *hors concours*, a *chef-d'œuvre*, only a little lower than the angels.

It was Linnæus, a Swede, who in 1735, in his *Systema Naturæ*, put man in his proper place in the order of *Primates* with the monkeys and the apes—but not with the bats, as he thought, though with more reason than appears on the surface. Linnæus, as Haddon says, was a genius in classification; order and method were his passions. He was a firm believer in Special Creation, but he had a high regard for facts and was little given to theorizing. Father of taxonomy, he has been called. He did put systematic zoology on a sound basis. He did put man in his proper place, and was the inventor of the binominal system of nomenclature now in use. He did place man in one genus (*Homo*)—though whether he should have added *sapiens* is open to question. *Stultus* has been suggested as more fitting. Maybe. Man is often foolish, but he is neither wise nor foolish by nature.

Vastly more is now known about varieties, species, genera, orders, etc., and especially about extinct species, but Linnæus' scheme worked; somewhat modified and revised, it still works, and is the backbone of the tables in use today. In 1758 Linnæus published the first volume of the tenth edition of his great work. He named and described 4,370 species of animals. The number of species of insects alone today is variously reckoned at from one to ten millions— with about half the earth still to be searched.

*Systema naturæ:* a *system* of nature. Nature so systematized that newly discovered plants and animals could be put in their places; just as the cosmic universe had been so reduced to order that new stars and new planets appeared not as new but as just having announced themselves; just as the elements had been so set in order that new elements could be assigned their position at once.

Let us be certain that we are clear as to what we are talking about. Those systems—of extinct and living organisms, of elements, of celestial bodies—are purely artificial; they are artifacts, man-made, and therefore frail; they can be no more perfect than man's capacity to make them so. They have no objective existence; they are abstractions and exist only as thought, spoken or in printed symbols.

The question is, rather, are they useful; do they work; are they conveniences; are they founded on realities or entities; have they a factual basis? And are they superior to national boundaries, religious creeds, æsthetic feelings? Do they serve no purpose but that which they claim to serve—to resume the observable facts of nature, of celestial bodies, of elemental matter? Science can do no more than that for or with any group of phenomena. It can never transcend honest, impartial observation or the reasonable inferences which may be drawn therefrom. It is not the business of science to explain man's position in the universe, but to discover it honestly and describe it faithfully. Man may want to govern himself accordingly, or he may want to govern others as though he himself were creator.

In 1788 the Linnæan Society was founded in London, with the great Swede's books and specimens as the nucleus of its library.

Nature study had now become a favorite outdoor sport in England. Even theologians had taken it up—to find "design" everywhere, proof that Moses was right. Butler's great work on the *Analogy of Religion, Natural and Revealed, to the Course and Constitution of Nature*, had appeared in 1736 as an answer to the scepticism which had been growing since Descartes had opened the floodgates of doubt. Paley's famous *Natural Theology* appeared in 1802. Nature was available for observation, for study; but it was all God's handi-work—*special* creation. There was no big problem about nature, only lesser problems of analogy and reconciliation. The Bible said so and so; nature was searched for the proofs. And who could inter-pret nature so well as the theologians, the Paleys?

For over a half century yet there was no natural science: natural history only. And most of its professors were clergymen. Buckland, professor of geology at Oxford; Sedgwick, professor of geology at Cambridge; and Henslow, professor of botany at Cambridge in Darwin's school days—all were clergymen of the Church of Eng-land. They were honest, earnest teachers; but the earth and the natural history they taught were an eternal, unchanging, immuta-ble world. True, there had been doubters, sceptics, and even hints that natural forces might account for the living world, but even up to the 'fifties of last century there was no hint that a theory of evolution had ever been propounded: it seemed, said Weismann, as though all the teachers in our universities had drunk of the waters of Lethe.

In other words, Linnæus' systematized world of plants and ani-mals was nothing more nor less than a classified Noah's ark. As God had created them, so they were—yesterday, today, and for ever, unchanged, immutable.

Lamarck, a French zoologist, in his great work on the *Organiza-tion of Living Bodies* (1801), and in his *Philosophie zoologique* (1809), had offered a revised version of the Greek idea of the gradual development of living beings as a substitute for special creation, which we now regard as a landmark in the history of evolution, if not one of the keys to evolution. But the fact that he died (1829) blind, in poverty, and a social outcast, shows what his contemporaries thought of the Lamarckian theory.

Cuvier, a contemporary of Lamarck, added enormously to the

foundation laid by Linnæus in systematic zoology and by the Hunters in comparative anatomy; but in his Mosaic cosmogony he was strictly orthodox.

St. Hilaire, another contemporary, in his *Philosophie anatomique* (1818-22), was the first to realize something of the significance of the great fact of similarity of structure or form which runs through all animals, as though they were formed on one plan, after one principle. He had hit on a profound truth, and his principle of *homology* is the basis of all subsequent studies on morphology. But Cuvier could not see it at all, and the two friends started a discussion which so excited Europe that Goethe, no mean naturalist, spoke of it as "this great event."

Goethe had reason to be interested. He had used the word *morphology* in 1817 and had clearly seen that form is never permanent. He had a prophetic vision but an idealistic philosophy. He had discovered the homologies of the parts of flowers, while Linnæus had discovered their sex organs. But it was a pupil of Linnæus who proposed a much better classification of plants than Linnæus. Candolle (1778-1841) so further improved that system that it remains the basis of botanical classification today. Curiously enough, the church allowed plants to be classified in a natural order—based on genetic relationship and implying evolution—without protest.

With the new microscope (without spherical or colour aberration) new crops of facts began to be harvested. Had the church but known what was good for it, it would have kept a closer eye on the revolution of 1828 than on the French Revolution of 1830. The French can have a revolution any time, but only once for all time can two "impassable" barriers in nature be passed in one year. Wöhler's discovery—purely accidental—that when he heated ammonium cyanate he had urea, has already been referred to; he had passed the supposedly divinely appointed barrier between inorganic and organic, a barrier passed every day now in thousands of laboratories around the world.

Equally, possibly more, important was von Baer's discovery that man reproduces, like chickens, by eggs. He was the first to see a human ovum; the first to put comparative embryology on a scientific basis; the first to prove Linnæus right in making an animal of man. Man was still high, but he was not out of sight of the other Primates, nor was there any longer a sharp line between reproduction in higher and lower animals.

Then came that astounding discovery of Schleiden and Schwann in 1839, of the cellular structure of both plants and animals. Yeast had been rediscovered two years before; as had been the vegetable parasite that causes Favus or "honeycomb" scalp, and the animal parasite that causes itch. In fact, from about 1875 on, the "world of the infinitely small" was no longer safe from the eye trained to peer through a microscope. A flock of new sciences came into being; old ones were put on a new footing; life itself began to have standing in the courts of science; and, best of all, death germs were brought within range of the guns of science. It is hardly likely that ever again in the history of the human race will so brief a span of time witness so many epoch-making discoveries so vital to human health and happiness, as were made between 1835 and 1885.

If crime today costs us seven and a half billion dollars a year, and ill health and preventable human wastage in accidents another five billions, it is only because science has made us rich enough to afford appalling dishonesty and hideous waste. Without our science, we should be little better off than China and no more civilized than were the Romans two thousand years ago.

Turn back to the last year of the eighteenth century. Was the world all explored by 1799? Well, Captain Cook's third voyage of discovery had come to an end with his death at the hands of the natives in Hawaii twenty years before, and he was the last of the *grands voyageurs*. The world was discovered—but it was not yet explored. In fact, the first great explorer in the modern sense of the word was Alexander von Humboldt; his first voyage, in 1799. His *Kosmos* is a monument of keen observation and profound reflection. It was to inspire the next generation, at home and abroad, to observe nature and think naturally; and in Germany, to place him beside Goethe.

Closely following Humboldt came Robert Brown's voyage to Australia. He brought back over four thousand species of plants till then unknown to botany. Von Baer, discoverer of the human ovum, explored nature in Nova Zembla (1838). Our own Dana explored the Pacific between 1838 and 1842; Huxley (in H.M.S. *Rattlesnake*), the South Pacific, 1846-51; Wallace, the Malay Archipelago,

1854-62. And the most famous of all explorers, Darwin, in H.M.S. *Beagle* (1831-36), remains to be mentioned.

The immediate result of these expeditions was, to use Sedgwick's words, to throw a flood of light upon the infinite wealth, variety, creative resources, and capacity of this earth and its plant and animal inhabitants, and to reveal countless and marvellous adaptations of organisms to climate, soil, and other environmental conditions. In other words, Buffon's *Natural History*, finished in 1804, in forty-four quarto volumes, neither contained all of nature nor covered all its history.

What was the meaning of this infinite wealth and variety of plants and animals which could adapt themselves to countless conditions of physical environment? No ark could possibly hold them all; no Mosaic genesis could create them all; nor could prevailing theory of fixed, unchanging, immutable species furnish any clue to what the eye could see. And the eye had ranged through Brazilian forests, Patagonian pampas, up and over the Andes, and all around the world.

The Lamarckian and Greek theories about the ways of nature might never have been uttered; Genesis was still the authority on all creation. But here were these facts, and here was Lyell taking the earth out of Genesis. And Cuvier in 1800 had published his work on living and fossil elephants. Other huge fossil remains began to be discovered: enormous reptiles and crocodiles in France; lions, tigers, and bears, in Belgium; and so on. A world of life was revealed beneath Europe's feet: old life, extinct life—like, yet unlike, living life.

Then came that "fanatic madman" as he was called, Boucher de Perthes, who in 1841 found near Abbeville-on-the-Somme a rude cutting implement of flint. It was not the first palæolith ever found, but it was the first one ever to be seen in its true bearing. Again and again old stone tools and weapons had been found, but, like fossils, they were regarded as freaks of nature, Jove's thunderbolts, or some other equally childish conceit. But, as we have seen, Hooke in the seventeenth century saw through fossils, and with the discovery in England, Belgium, and France of the fossilized remains of extinct animals or of those found only in tropical climes today, 4004 B.C. began to look like yesterday.

In 1846 de Perthes announced the finding of human implements in gravel beds that belonged to the Glacial Drift Age; in 1854 he found more human remains unmistakably associated with the fossil cave-bear and cave-lion. But no Academy called a special session to congratulate M. Boucher de Perthes on his find; in fact, it was almost twenty years before the world accepted his conclusions, and only after he had heaped up evidence. The "world"? Well, two English geologists: Sir J. Prestwich and Sir J. Evans; and then only after they had thoroughly examined the site of the discoveries. Their acceptance of the facts was announced to the Royal Society in 1860.

Curiously enough, a palæolith similar to the Abbeville specimens had for years been lying in the British Museum, labelled *Found with elephant's tooth*. But that Museum was then, as are many museums today, a curiosity shop; and it takes a curious turn for anybody to be curious about a rude flint implement even if found with an elephant's tooth. If the label had read "Found with angel's tooth," it would still have been a curio—but more likely to be in a church than in a museum.

The difference between a curio and a fact is not in its honesty— for not all curios are "mermaids" or "Cardiff giants"—but in the beholder's eye. That the facts and artifacts which began to burst upon Christian civilization at the beginning of the nineteenth century could be made to tell a story, that they were not curios but, when properly arranged, pages of history, was not yet recognized. Even so learned a man as Palgrave could say: "We must give it up, that speechless past; whether fact or chronology, doctrine or mythology; whether in Europe, Asia, Africa, or America: lost is lost; gone is gone for ever." Even then Paradise had been Regained. Why not the past ages of earth, and of man, and of civilization? Well, much of it has; Sir John would be surprised if he could come back.

Herodotus was good at recovering the past for such regions as he could cover in one short life. And what is geology—or zoology or anthropology—but a historic science? The dates came too fast; too many facts rose up from the dead past to shout their living story. They were hard facts and they would be heard.

For example, Darwin visited the Galapagos Islands off the coast of Ecuador. He was then a fairly ignorant youngster with little to his credit but huge curiosity and fearless honesty. He knew something of geology. The islands were evidently *new*—not geologically old like the mainland. Fine, he said to himself; here is where I see some of God's *new* creatures. But the birds and other animals he saw were just like those on the mainland. Yet not quite like: they varied this way or that. The variations all seemed to point in one direction—adaptations to the peculiarities of the harsh island environment.

Again, on that same immortal voyage in that impossible tub the *Beagle*, he discovered the fossil remains of enormous sloths and armadillos in Patagonia. Big, hard facts. The earth *was* old, as Lyell had said; and young Darwin had Lyell's book with him. Also an essay on *The Principle of Population* by one Reverend T. R. Malthus, F.R.S., Professor of History and Political Economy. That ponderous book was then in its sixth edition and can still be read with disapproval by all "anti's," and especially by the anti-contraceptionists and those who believe that a large proportion of the human race is doomed to premature death "by the inscrutable ordinations of Providence." Poverty, in Malthus' opinion, was not a Providential Ordination, but a check to population and a curable social disease. Without the roar of abuse which greeted his essay, it could not have gone through so many editions—nor, possibly, have aroused Darwin's curiosity sufficiently to make him take it to sea.

The gist of Malthus' argument was, that, as people naturally multiply faster than food, somebody must suffer. Darwin could have written his *Origin of Species* without Malthus' suggestion as to who would suffer first; but, being forced to the conclusion on the *Beagle* that species were *not* immutable, having already collected an enormous number of facts bearing on variations and adaptations, and realizing, as he was also forced to, that life was a struggle, it was the reading of Malthus which at once brought home to him that "under these circumstances, favourable species would tend to be preserved, and unfavourable ones destroyed. The result would be the formation of a new species. . . . I had at last got a theory by which to work." And he worked on it for twenty-two years.

Darwin wrote down the substance of his theory in his notebook in 1837, five years after the Patagonian fossils had convinced him that species were not immutable, and fifteen months before he read Malthus. Five years later, in 1842, he wrote out a sketch or abstract of his theory, and two years later rewrote the sketch in expanded form.

Looking back now, it seems so simple, so self-evident, such an inevitable conclusion. Yet, as Darwin wrote to a friend in 1844, to say that species were not immutable was like "confessing a murder." In other words, Darwin's unpublished 231-page sketch did what no ancient or modern had ever done—presented a scientifically sound hypothesis of evolution.

If species evolved, through natural selection, man himself evolved. Good-bye, Garden of Eden, supernatural origin, divinity, taint of original sin; welcome, jungle, cousin apes and monkeys. Darwin knew that his theory would, as Gladstone put it later, relieve God of the labour of creation and discharge him from governing the world. "Confessing a murder?" Of man's cherished, naïve, childlike faith that he was the son of God.

1735, Linnæus: *Systema Naturæ*.

1858, July 1: Special meeting of the Linnæan Society of London; joint paper by Darwin and Wallace, "On the Tendency of Species to Form Varieties; and on the Perpetuation of Varieties and Species by Natural Means of Selection." (Bentham, the great botanist, was to have read a paper at the next regular meeting *proving* the *immutability* of species. It was never read. Nor was there any discussion of Darwin's paper—its subject was "too novel, too ominous.")

1859, *Origin of Species by Means of Natural Selection*, or the Preservation of Favoured Races in the Struggle for Life.

1871, *The Descent of Man*, and Selection in Relation to Sex.

1882, *The Action of Carbonate of Ammonia on Chlorophyll-Bodies*.

1882, April 26: Darwin buried in Westminster Abbey, near Newton. Pall-bearers: Lord Avebury, Huxley, James Russell Lowell, Wallace, Duke of Devonshire, Canon Farrar, Hooker, Earl of Derby. "He thought," said the *Times*, "and his thoughts passed into the substance of the facts of the universe. And grass-plots, flowers, human gestures, and all the doings and tendencies of nature, build his monument and record his exploits. The Abbey's orators and ministers have swayed nations, but not one of them ever wielded over man and intelligence so complete a power as did Darwin."

Born 1809, February 12: Charles Darwin; Abraham Lincoln. Emancipator of human minds from the slavery to tradition; emancipator of human bodies from a no more real physical bondage— says Lull in his splendid *Organic Evolution* (1921).

Lull does not try to prove evolution any more than a modern text-book of chemistry tries to prove chemistry. He accepts evolution as a fact as the chemist accepts elements as facts. But the *mechanism* of organic evolution is still problematical; the number of facts, the proofs of evolution, have increased enormously since Darwin's day, and no animal, no plant, no bacterium, nor living organism of any kind, has yet been discovered which is meaningless or incomprehensible within the Darwinian hypothesis of evolution as against the then prevailing belief in a Mosaic cosmogony.

Darwin called it Natural Selection; Spencer called it evolution. The world at large calls it evolution. But, as Wheeler points out, as words in religions should be used in such a way as to connote the greatest possible number of meanings to give employment to theologians, so we have the following vocabulary for the single, simple, expressive word *evolution*: Heteropathic causation (Mill); Creative synthesis (Ward); Evolutionary naturalism (Sellars); Emergent evolution (Morgan); Emergent vitalism (Broad); Holism (Smuts); Organicism (Henderson). Darwin would be pleased— and, quite likely, amused.

IV

"In the voluminous literature on 'rejuvenation,'" says Carlson, "as related to the sex glands, are some records of serious and competent investigations, much frank fiction, some humour, more tragedy, but scarcely even the umbra of scientific support for the sundry 'rejuvenation' measures so carefully attuned to credulous minds."

Carlson does not say that rejuvenation has arrived, merely that the literature has. *Credulity*—enough of it to provoke voluminous literature, and backed by a wish intense enough to provoke the manufacture of rejuvenating remedies. Hundreds of them—as voluminous as the literature.

Business of mementoes; business of sex pills. *Memento mori*; rejuvenation. Remember you must die. Why die?

Biology today is a science. It could become a science because it formulates a hypothesis which works, which keeps the door open to analysis, to experimentation, to boundless discovery, and to a possible synthesis which is only now beginning to come into its own. It knows its materials, its energies; its hypothesis is mechanistic —as is that of physicist and chemist. It looks to the future, knowing what it can do today. What the bioengineer can do, no one yet knows. The advance that has been made is astounding, and it is real—as real as in the realm of copper and iron, steam and electricity. Biology today is the sum-total of the knowledge, actions, opinions, and beliefs of biologists, of men who study life.

And as no life is so precious—in our eyes at least—as human life, I want in the remaining sections of this chapter to look at knowledge primarily as a story of the growth of facts which forced the change in opinion whereby this age puts health as a preparation for life above faith as a preparation for death.

The first step in that momentous change was the rescue of the physical body from the insults heaped upon it by both Christian supernaturalism and pagan mysticism. And need I add that Aristotle, thanks to the weight of his mighty name, was almost as great a barrier to advance in anatomical knowledge as the Bible itself? His mistakes were handed on from generation to generation.

There was a medical school in Alexandria. Human bodies as well as animals had been dissected: first, possibly, by Herophilus about 300 B.C., called by Singer the Father of Anatomy. His distinctions between veins and arteries and between motor and sensory nerves were penetrating and sound. He also named the first twelve fingerbreadths of our small intestine so accurately that it is still the *duodenum*. The prostate gland also has kept its appropriate Herophilus name.

Then came Erasistratus, a few decades later. In realizing that arteries and veins communicate, he anticipated Harvey's discovery of the circulation of the blood, and postulated the existence of what could be detected by a microscope—the capillary circulation viewed by Malpighi in 1661, four years after Harvey's death. Conceivably, Harvey would never have had his attention turned toward circulation had he not, when a student of Fabricius in Italy, been shown *valves* in the veins. *Why* should there be valves in veins? In answering that question he let part of Aristotle's anatomy join the "duds" of science. But ears, in Harvey's time, were even less open to that kind of evidence than they were in Aristotle's.

Aristotle would have lent ear to such evidence. He was a fine observer, but after he had located intelligence in the heart and put his brain to cool it, it would have taken Archimedes and his lever to start the blood circulating in Aristotle's system—instead of moving back and forth like a pendulum, as he thought it did.

Even Hippocrates, greatest name in the history of medicine, did not see with his own eyes as much of the inside of a human body as a cook to a cannibal king. Aristotle never opened a *human* body. The Alexandrian Greeks did; but they were not Authorities. Da Vinci did; in fact, he dissected over thirty human bodies, male and female. He poked his nose in a thousand other things, and many of them he saw clearly. Only recently have his papers and sketches revealed his greatness as anatomist and engineer, even as he was known to be great as architect, sculptor, and painter. Even a fossil did not fool his eyes. But he was an artist; his time went in for art, not for science; and he gave them great art because it was founded on knowledge. They did not know that this "miracle of versatility" knew more about the human form he so divinely portrayed than Æsculapius himself, son of Apollo though he were and god of medicine; more even than Galen, greatest of ancient anatomists and crowning glory of the Empire of the Antonines.

Galen, son of a rich and celebrated architect and mathematician of Pergamum, was a great student, particularly of Aristotle. When he was sixteen, because of a dream his father had had, he was "dedicated" to medicine, and studied at Pergamum, Smyrna, and especially at Alexandria. In 157 he returned home, and for four years acted as surgeon to the gladiators. He went to Rome at the age of thirty, and became so successful as a practitioner that he was persecuted by jealous rivals and began a five years' wandering, but was persuaded by the Emperor Marcus Aurelius to return. He was not only physician and surgeon, but had his own drug store on the Via Sacra—the druggists would cheat! His shop was burnt during the reign of Commodus, in the great fire which destroyed the Temple of Peace where Galen gave public demonstrations and where his works were stored. Many of these were lost, for they had not all been copied.

Galen could not be called a physiologist in the modern sense of the term. He wrote—sixteen books on the pulse alone. His mistakes necessarily were numerous and often grotesque. His anatomy was the most complete picture of the human body produced by the ancient world. He described three hundred muscles, and his knowledge of the functions of the spinal cord as described in his work on *Anatomical Operations* was not extended until Bell's investigations in 1811. In fact, Galen's collective writings—on drugs, health, disease, etc.—formed a complete system of medicine: the *Galenic*. It ruled Europe, Asia, and Africa for thirteen centuries.

Galen's anatomy was based on studies of a human skeleton, an ape's muscles, an ox's brain, and a pig's viscera! Human anatomy must be based on studies of the human body—of both sexes, and from its beginnings as a fertilized ovum to death through natural senile decay.

Let us be clear about Galen. He was a great man and a genius in anatomy. He belongs to the immortals of all time and was as noble a figure in Imperial Rome as any in the Athens of Pericles. He was not only physician to the gladiators, but to two emperors, and probably the wisest in the world at the time. He was nearly the last of the great Greeks.

That was the trouble. Like Aristotle, he was too good, too great, too far ahead of his fellow-men to make a contest. His opinion, like Aristotle's, like Ptolemy's, ruled that part of intellectual Europe which found the Power, Wisdom, and Goodness of God manifest, not in the Book of Genesis, nor in the book of nature, but in the works of Aristotle, Ptolemy, and Galen.

Even up to the seventeenth century physicians were Galen's slaves. They saw, not what existed, but only what he had written. There could be no real physiology until there was sound anatomy. For 1,343 years he was the Word in human anatomy. He taught, for example, that there was an orifice in the septum which separates the ventricles of the heart; also that the heart contains an "incorruptible" bone—he had found a small bone in the heart of an elephant. It remained for Vesalius to show that, however hard the human heart may be, it is boneless; and for Servetus to question the porosity of the septum between the ventricles. No orifice, no mixture of food and air could take place in the heart as Galen had said.

Six hundred years before Galen became the Father of Anatomy, Hippocrates, Father of Modern Medicine, greatest of ancient physicians, genius in the natural sciences, Aristotle's guide in looking to nature for his philosophy and Galen's in his search for truth, founded the first school of naturalism. If the modern physician resorts less to Galenic medicines and more to Hippocratic doctrines, it is largely because Vesalius rediscovered the human body and modern biochemistry discovered how nature builds human bodies. The success of the modern healer in restoring the diseased body to health is a measure of the road biology has travelled since Hippocrates proclaimed nature the real philosopher.

It seems rather startling that man had to speculate about nature for twenty-five hundred years before he took Hippocrates seriously and decided to look at nature more and talk about nature less. Galen capitalized nature; biology capitalizes the facts of nature.

Galen, indeed, had he been alive a hundred years ago and a believer in the Christian God, could have qualified to write a treatise on the Power, Wisdom, and Goodness of God as manifest in creation, under the terms of the last will and testament of the Earl of Bridgewater.

Nature reveals God to man, and the stars control his destiny; but man himself, in his body, in his bones and muscles, and in his processes of living, justifies the ways of God to man. Man is perfect because God is wise; man's body reveals that perfection. Why go to the stars or the annals of the mysteries to find God, when he has revealed himself in us mortals? Let us study man. The knowledge thereby gained will better reveal God than any Christian or pagan mystery. That was the step Galen took.

And it was an enormous step in advance; no greater one was taken for two thousand years. Let us see. Galen accepted natural law, but sought the secret of its working in man's body rather than in the stars; he accepted a Divine architect, but sought the secrets of his building operations in human physiological processes rather than in magic or miracle.

Galen knew about Judaism and Christianity and in fact speaks of both, and with no great respect. In putting natural law above the Christian God as revealing divinity, he remarked that "in this matter our view differs from that of Moses."

But it did not differ so much that his *Anatomical Procedure* was anathema to the rising tide of Christianity. Christianity could use Galen—as it could use Aristotle and Plato and Ptolemy. No other pagan writer survived the Christian hatred of pagan science so completely as did Galen. Of the sixteen books of *Anatomical Procedure* no less than nine were handed down in Greek; the other seven reëntered Europe through Arabic translations.

With Galen's death in 199 a haze began to close down over human structure and function. Man's body began to sink in estimation. Under the contemptuous curse of the church it became unclean, contemptible, unworthy of its spiritual burden. Galen had left it something of a curiosity shop; the church let it rot, or tortured it with hot irons, or filled it with imps from hell. Vesalius rescued it; saw it, not as modern biology sees it, but as something worth seeing—as a *fabric*, a masterpiece of workmanship by the Master Craftsman, something high and noble, and worthy of God, the great Artist.

Not all the intervening centuries were a blank in the progress of anatomical knowledge. Many of them—too many for the good of civilization—were a blank; they did not even have Galen, or any use for him. Galen's death in 199 had rung down the curtain on scientific inquiry into human structure and function. Rome was falling; civilization itself was falling—falling before the savage hordes of the north. Even when Gerard of Cremona and others of the twelfth century, through their translations of Greek science from Arabic to Latin, had given Europe something to read and think about, nothing much came of it except the idiotic speculations of the Schoolmen. And so the thirteenth and fourteenth centuries passed without scientific observation or experimentation, or any study of nature worth a line in the history of biology.

Human bodies had been dissected at the University of Bologna, but rather as aids in memorizing the anatomical terms of Arabic authorities. There is no known record of a *post mortem* examination before 1286. Mondino's *Anothomia* of 1316 is the first modern work on the human body and the first book to picture the *human* uterus; but the fact that this "Restorer of Anatomy" hated to clean bones "owing to the sin involved therein" shows how hard it was for him to grasp facts by the hand. Sound advance in accurate knowledge of human anatomy hung on the material available for observation and study. Pope Sixtus IV had seen, from his medical studies at Bologna and Padua, the necessity for dissection. With him the church lifted its ban on dissection, and bodies could be opened with its permission. Dissection was officially recognized by statute at Bologna in 1405; at Padua, in 1429. Thereafter plenty of material was available.

As a developing science anatomy also suffered, even in the sixteenth century, from the warfare of terminology. Should Arabic anatomical terms or Latin and Greek—symbolic of the Humanist intellectuals—be used? The classic nomenclature won, and as a result practically all the thousand-odd parts of our body still bear their original Greek or Latin, especially Latin, names. Of the few Arabic names which won out and still survive, the most interesting are *retina* and *sesamoid*—the open "sesame" of Aladdin.

Meanwhile additional writings of the ancients had become available, and by the time Vesalius was ready to begin his revolutionary work of rescuing man's body from Galen's teleology, Europe commanded nearly all the medical classics and as much Galen, Hippocrates, and Aristotle as we do today. Practical anatomy was being taught at the University of Paris, where Sylvius, its first eminent anatomist, was discovering and describing the sphenoid bone of our skull and the aqueduct of Sylvius of our brain.

Vesalius, in short, was not a spontaneous generation. No genius ever is. The old Galenic science was his sire, the new realistic art his dam; he was, as Singer says, a true product of his time, even as Paracelsus was. But, unlike the quack, Vesalius really studied his Galen.

Born of a medical family in Brussels, Vesalius spent his boyhood dissecting everything he could get his hands on. After studying at Louvain he went to Paris, where practical anatomy was supposed to be taught and where Sylvius was lecturing to crowded houses. He promptly quarrelled with Sylvius, who was teaching what he had read in a book; Vesalius was arguing from what he had seen in a corpse.

At the age of twenty-three he was called to Padua as professor of surgery in the university and court physician to Emperor Charles V.

He *taught* anatomy—but not with books, nor even with models or through demonstrators; he was his own demonstrator and his demonstrations were on *human* bodies, dead and alive. At the age of twenty-eight his *De Humani Corporis Fabrica* appeared—and Galen disappeared as the authority on anatomy; man's body was allowed to speak for itself. The ancient microcosm became as truly Vesalian anatomy as the ancient macrocosm became Copernican astronomy.

Between 1543 and 1782 Vesalius' *Fabric of the Human Body* went through twenty-five editions and was plagiarized time and again—once by one Helkiah Crooke, who, says Singer, added insult to injury by accusing Vesalius of having *slighted* Galen!

Curiously enough, the first book printed in England using copper plates was a pirated edition of Vesalius, in 1545. It was later translated by the infamous Nicholas Udall, author of the drama *Ralph Roister Doister*.

May I emphasize the fact that the system Vesalius brought under observation was infinitely more complex than that brought by Copernicus; that the human and similar animal structures are so intricate in their mechanism, so varied in their parts, that only years spent on their study can give one a faint idea of their complexity, vastness, and intricacy. The most complicated man-made mechanism ever sent to a repair shop is a toothpick compared with the mechanism the stork delivers after one fertilized ovum has grown for nine months. The ovum itself is microcosm of more varied parts with more varied behaviour than the cosmic universe. That is the *nature* of life; that is the kind of stuff and force the biologist deals with. There could be no advance in understanding life, and no scientific attitude toward health, growth, normality, sanity, disease, old age, or the changes in recurring cycles of living beings, until man could be viewed from every aspect and in every process in every stage of growth, development, and decay, and in health and disease.

The real triumphs of science are drowned out by the loud speaker, the airplane propeller's roar, the auto engine's hum, and the rat-tat of the riveting machine, or are obscured by such death-dealing contraptions as submarines, Big Berthas, and aerial bombs; but my guess is that when man has stopped his inhuman war against man and takes time to look back at these last five centuries, he will rate the biologic sciences as the greatest of all human triumphs.

What is man? What are human beings? What is life? Why do we grow old and die? What is death? Is it inevitable, and is it the end of life? Are these *real* questions? And if so, whither shall we turn for the answers? Let us make no mistake about one thing: if man is a product of sleight of hand and life the gift of a master magician, the answers need not be sought in observation—no scalpel, no microscope, can reveal anything. And if all those who hold that man is supernatural, that life is vitalism, entelechy, or any other supernatural mystery, should vote to close up all biologic laboratories and all medical schools, they would only be consistent.

If, on the other hand, man in life and death is a natural phenomenon, the answers to all riddles ever propounded by man, woman, child, or sphinx are to be discovered by observation, and by observation alone. And it is up to man himself so to describe the results of his observations that they can be understood by all who think they live in a factual world and must depend largely on the honesty of the accumulated observations of their fellow-men.

The factual basis of living structure and vital processes was laid by the Greeks. But that basis was so faulty in so many respects that no man or animal could live a second with such a body by means of such processes. It was a fantastic body kept going by utterly impossible processes. Vesalius wrecked that preposterous body with its mouth of dog bones, for ever.

His genius was not in wrecking it, nor in destroying an authority idol; it was in observing so much and in such a short time that anatomy became *Vesalian*. His masterful drawings of the generative organs, for example, were based on six bodies only; of these, one was a murdered pregnant woman examined for legal purposes, one a woman who had been hanged, and one a six-year-old girl stolen by a student from a grave. He was charged with having opened the body of a dying nobleman while the heart was still beating, and was ordered by the Inquisition to go on a penitential journey to Jerusalem. He did go to Jerusalem, and lost his life in a shipwreck on the way home. He had dissected human bodies, thereby laying the scientific foundation of modern art in medicine and a cornerstone of all modern biologic sciences.

One of his pupils, Fallopius, in his *Anatomical Observations* (1561), was the first to describe the ovaries and the tubes (Fallopian) which conduct ova to the uterus. He also named the vagina and placenta. Coiter, also at Padua, and a student of Fallopius', took up embryology where Aristotle had left it, and after incubating eggs day after day left a remarkable account of the developing chick embryo. He was also the first to figure the skeleton of the human fœtus.

But greatest of all Paduans was Fabricius, also a pupil of Fallopius. The anatomical theatre he built at his own expense still stands. After 1604 he gave up teaching to devote all his time to study. He carried embryology far beyond Coiter; was the first to explore thoroughly and figure accurately the valves in the veins. *He taught Harvey!* And with Harvey, blood began to circulate in human beings for the first time in human history.

Vesalius sired Fallopius, who sired Fabricius, who sired Harvey. With Fabricius, gross anatomy becomes modern anatomy and embryology is off to a good start, awaiting the compound microscope to restart it on a career that is not yet finished. With Harvey (1578-1657) the interest shifts from the dead body to the processes of living. But it was not until 1802 that a chair of physiology was founded in England—and by a Paduan student, Sharpey. His copies of Vesalius, Fallopius, and other Paduan anatomists are still preserved in the University College of London.

What Vesalius had done to Galen's freak body, Harvey did to Galen's freakish ideas about how that body functioned. He could not have made that advance had he not had a real human body to look at. Such a body he saw at Padua. It is not too much to say that every medical school in the world today is founded on the traditions of Padua—not forgetting the enormous debt of medical science to Malpighi of Bologna (1628-94).

Malpighi it was who *proved* Harvey's theory and stamped his own name indelibly on many hitherto unknown parts of the spleen and kidneys. He started microscopic anatomy, thereby paving the way for morbid anatomy or pathology; and where he left embryology it remained, says Foster, till the beginning of the nineteenth century. In every sense of the word Malpighi was a scientist —objective, honest, experimental, critical, modern. "His was a magic hand which illuminated all it touched." "Do not stop to ask," he wrote, "whether these ideas are new or old, but more properly whether they harmonize with nature."

The sixteenth century had bridged the gap of fifteen centuries and given modern medical science something substantial to build on, a complete human body: not as complete as it is today, but complete enough to breathe and digest food. But it was all in the air about the nature of breath and food. It knew that as a last resort extreme unction could be administered, but no one yet knew that an administration of oxygen and an injection of adrenalin might postpone the last resort. In short, the chemists and physicists had to analyse the world life lives in before the biologist could discover what life is and what keeps its home fires burning.

Harvey died 1657; but Boyle, Hooke, Boerhaave, Hales, von Haller, Cavendish, Priestley, Lavoisier, Galvani, Rumford, and others had to clear the way before a Sharpey could find a place for a chair. Besides, as Voltaire had said, the business of the eighteenth century was to recover humanity's lost title deeds. He could not foresee it, but the achievement of the eighteenth century was to recover the breath of life. The new chemistry—Priestley and Lavoisier—performed that task.

To put the matter another way, the seventeenth century had exhausted the possibilities of the old-fashioned compound microscope, and the eighteenth century physical sciences had not yet given life the gas. One name stands out for notice, not so much for what he proved as for what he disproved: von Haller of Berne, at Göttingen in 1752. He cut muscles clear from nerves and bodies and made them contract. His work on sensibility and irritability, fœtal circulation, and the mechanics of respiration, laid the foundations of anatomical physiology, and through anatomical studies in general helped to clear the way for those two famous Hunters, John and William, to found comparative anatomy.

Think of trying to cure hysteria on the supposition that it is a disease which results from the retention of the menses in the uterus, which thereby goes "crazy"! But when a physician to Henry II of France showed that hysteria occurs in little girls, during menses and after the menopause, and in males as well as in females, hysteria could be pried loose from the uterus and looked at. Lepois looked at it, and his writings on hysteria, among other things, made modern neurology possible. That was 1618; but more than a hundred years had to elapse before a doctrine of nervous irritability could be established as a substitute for an imaginary "animal spirit" in a contracting brain ventricle which was thereby forced into hollow nerves!

How did they know the nerves were hollow? Somebody had said so. And who was "somebody"? Authority—Galen probably. And what was animal spirit? Well, it was something every authority had talked about: Aristotle, Plato, van Helmont, Descartes, Leibnitz —all the intellectual giants. Descartes especially had "investigated" nervous "fluid." Von Haller, the Swiss, spent a lifetime investigating sensitivity in nerves. He even experimented on nerves. He also wrote some two hundred works, practised medicine, and dabbled in poetry and novel-writing.

Sixty years later, Sir Charles Bell for the first time distinguished between motor and sensory nerves. With him physiology was securely founded on an experimental basis, and in such hands as Magendie, Hall, Müller, and Bernard soon became something like the structure it is today—a structure which gives support to health, which understands normal healthy activities: a court, as it were, which examines man at ease and thereby learns to rob disease of its mystery, to take it out of God's hands, away from the clutches of fate, black magic, and even to free it from the curse of original sin.

Human anatomy and human physiology—as fact, history, or the medical school's backbone—are neither short nor simple. They are today—and this is the point I would emphasize—on a firm and secure foundation. They are as scientifically founded as astronomy or chemics, and founded not on childish fancy or senile guesses, but on observation and experiment. It is now possible to think of life scientifically—as well as wistfully, hopefully, or scornfully. Even medicine may be looked at as science—or as art; and a drug store as a store or as a drug. Meanwhile we shall want to try to think about health scientifically—for if biology is a science it should furnish the background for a sane, healthy view of health.

v

Take medicine, said Harvey: as *art*, it is a habit with reference to things to be done; as *science*, a habit in respect of things to be known. Now, a Greek who could distinguish only fifteen kinds of pulses might conceivably be a better physician than a Chinese who could distinguish twenty-seven kinds; the greatest sphygmologist on earth might also conceivably be the world's worst mender of broken hearts, or could learn as much about his patient from fifty-seven kinds of pulses as might be learnt from one drop of urine or blood.

This pulse or that tells a story and may be valuable in diagnosis. A physician may become a great artist in diagnosing pulses, a great specialist even, in the highest-priced sense of the word; yet his prescription for my particular kind of pulse may be the very thing to drive me to a premature grave. For this reason: he is trying to fight my particular pulse, whereas what I need is health. For that I go to Hippocrates, who takes me, not as a pulse or a tongue or a drop of urine or blood, but as an individual who should be at ease and is now diseased. What has happened? What kind of accident has upset me? What can be done to restore my functional integrity?

Nature fitted man to fight for life; religion fits him to fight life, science to fight death. A war is always on somewhere.

Man for thousands of years has been familiar with life—in himself, in his fellow-men, and in domesticated and wild animals. But that he could *control* life as he had learnt thousands of years ago to control fire—that was a staggering idea, subversive of the Immutable Laws of Nature or the Eternal Will of God.

Yet that idea had to prevail before the abnormalities, aberrations, and diseases of the living could be placed on a scientific foundation. It *is* a staggering idea, the most forward step man ever took; and although it was taken since this country celebrated the centennial of its independence, there are millions of Americans who still think of life's control as in the lap of the gods or in the hands of God as interpreted by the Pope, Mary Baker Eddy, a book on astrology, or some other equally infantile superhuman, supernatural monstrosity.

How low pagan Greek science had sunk among the Christian Greeks may be inferred from the fact that after Galen there is not a Greek physician worthy of mention in the historic record, and that the Greek sovereigns of Constantinople sought the services of Arabic physicians.

But, as we have had occasion to remark so many times, before Greece was Egypt—long, long before. Pythagoras writing on the properties of plants and the use of squills in the sixth century B.C. seems modern compared to Imhotep writing a treatise on anatomy and the practice of medicine and surgery twenty-three centuries before Hippocrates was born.

It is well that we remind ourselves now and then of our debt to the Greeks; also, that from Egypt the Greeks got their drugs and their surgical instruments—but not the Egyptians' practical knowledge of anatomy or their often sound and penetrating physiological inferences.

How could the Greeks draw inferences about what goes on under the skin without knowing what is under the skin? They never opened a human body; the Egyptians did—even in the time of Imhotep, Breasted thinks. They had worked out a technique of surgery, took stitches, used adhesive tape, liniments, plasters, and tonics. They also used laxatives and enemas. Imhotep's observations on the heart as the central part of a distribution system had to wait forty-four hundred years for a Harvey to shed further light on the nature of the heart as a pump. His connecting paralysis of the limbs of one side of the body with injuries to the other side of the brain had to wait till our own generation for conclusive proof.

At death this great physician, scribe, and architect to great King Zoser was deified, and twenty-five hundred years later was identified by the Greeks, under the name Imouthes, as their own deified Æsculapius, the Homeric physician. A temple to Imhotep, says Breasted, was built at Memphis, and today "every museum possesses a bronze statuette of this apotheosized wise man, proverb-maker, physician, and architect of Zoser" of the Old Kingdom. An inscription now in the Vatican is the earliest-known mention of a king founding a medical school; but a preface to an Egyptian treatise on medicine in the reign of Ramses I, thirty-two centuries ago, says:

I have come out from the Gynæcological School of Sais, where the divine Mothers have given me their prescriptions. . . . I am in possession of the incantations composed by Osiris personally. My guide has always been the god Thoth, the inventor of speech and writing, the writer of infallible prescriptions, he who alone knows how to give reputation to magicians and physicians who follow his precepts.

That was a different tune from Dr. Imhotep's. Medicine had become a priestly affair—Couéism, laying on of hands, magic, incantations; and too much faith in the virtue of drugs and the influence of the stars.

By the time Herodotus visited Egypt there were "specialists" for diseases of the head, for abdominal affections, and for internal diseases; also dentists, oculists, and ophthalmologists. Cyrus and Darius both drew upon Egypt for their physicians. Breasted says that many Old Kingdom recipes handed down through the ages were carried by the Greeks into Europe, where they are still in use among the peasantry of the present day.

Known Egyptian remedies included squills, gentian, aloes, cedar, mint, myrrh, caraway, elderberries, and castor oil. And what is castor oil good for? To expel demons, calm vital spirits, assuage the Archæus, evacuate morbidic humours; and in more recent times, eliminate toxins, reduce blood pressure, and restore endocrine balance.

Early medicine in Greece was not a science but a cult: dreams, visions, magic, and certain Egyptian lore in the private and secret possession of the Æsclepiads or medicine-men attached to temples to Æsculapius, the most famous being Cos, Cnidus, Rhodes, and Pergamus, in Ionian Greece. Their medicine may be inferred from their anatomy and by two examples: the male generative fluid originates in the spinal marrow; the uterus is an animal that can be flattered by pleasant odours and will try to escape unpleasant— a belief, by the way, that persisted up to the middle of the sixteenth century. To draw up a fallen uterus the patient sniffed musk and sweet-scented herbs, and was exposed externally to the foul smell of galbanum and the smoke of burning feathers.

From the ninth to the fifteenth century, medicine was taught in well-organized medical schools in Bagdad, Damascus, Cairo and Cordova.

Of all those instrumental in helping Europe to recover the science the Nestorians had saved and the Arabs had resaved and made their own, Gerbert of Aurillac, head of Christendom in 999 as Pope Sylvester II, was second to none. Through him, as the first great translator, the Arabs were to repay to the "Christians of the Western world the services that had been formerly rendered to them by the Christians (Nestorians) of the East."

Gerbert had gone to Toledo to learn what was then unknown in Europe; he brought back knowledge and enthusiasm, and taught Islamic science to the Germanic world from Rheims and in Italy later as pope. The Crusades opened Europe's eyes to a new civilization; but science dribbled into Europe *via* Spain, Sicily, and Italy. Gerard of Cremona alone, in the twelfth century, translated over seventy Arabic works, including twenty-one medical works; he also turned Galen and Hippocrates, as well as Plato and Aristotle, into Latin.

Sylvester II was the exception that proves the rule. Not that the popes were uniform in their attitude toward science, nor all the monks averse to meddling with alchemy. But even such early schools of medicine as Salerno and Montpellier, and later ones at Padua, Bologna, Paris, etc., were in no sense part of the Christian state education. Christianity was against all science in general and medical science in particular.

With God as the immediate effectual cause of all phenomena, there was no need, no room, for science; there was room for theosophy. And so we find a motley crew of Oriental sorcerers, philosophers, and interpreters of all brands of Eastern occultism following Arab science into Europe and competing with it at every turn. Galenic medicine, such as it was, and Arabic pharmacopœia, such as it was, had to fight for their lives. What progress could medicine, as art or science, make with a theological chemistry and a belief that epidemics were caused by storms, comets, eclipses, earthquakes, volcanic eruptions, migrations of birds, swarms of insects, vermin, etc., and that disease was due to an abnormal mixture of "humours" or to a demon or the devil himself?

Anatomical facts and physiological principles came hard, for the truth about enormously intricate structures and mechanisms, and about vastly complex chemical and physical processes, could no more come to a Greek or a Schoolman by intuition than to a Hottentot. Greek physicians did make some discoveries; but such anatomical and physiological facts as they got from observation and the clinic had to square with a metaphysical theory of life. Such theories were easily spun, because they had few, and almost none of the really important, facts. They were seeking the essence of disease and not the causative factors of disease.

When Europe, after more than a thousand years, did recover Greek medicine, she spent the better part of five centuries arguing about it or interpreting it against the Christian or theological background—which at best was no improvement on pagan metaphysical theories of life. The Middle Ages did not study anatomy or physiology, nor life in health or disease; they studied the Old Masters. Not a treatise on circulation or what not, but a treatise on Hippocrates or Galen or Celsus or the Æsclepiads, or on some new metaphysical doctrine—Iatrochemical, Iatromathematical, Iatromechanical; and by the seventeenth century, on the less fantastic but not less metaphysical doctrines of Animism or Vitalism. While this or that pope might prefer this or that "school," no physician of the church could quarrel with any of the metaphysical schools, for they all postulated a soul—though hidden under such names as "Innate Heat," "Force," "Archæus," "Pneuma," "Vital Principle," etc. For nearly two thousand years the curse laid on life by the Christian emphasis on death was the great hindrance to rational observation of life.

The ancients made mistakes, but the great mistake Europe made was in thinking it a sacrilege to question ancient authority. There could be no advance along many lines because ancient opinions were accepted as truths and embellished with the academic freedom of highly trained parrots.

Loaded down as they were with "Aristotle said this" and "Galen said that," how could any advance be made in understanding life, health, disease, and death? When men paid less attention to Aristotle's facts and more to his methods, they began to discover some facts for themselves. Vesalius taking off his coat and deciding to discover some anatomy for himself, in 1543, was a turning-point.

Thereafter the physician of a Roman Emperor was less an authority on the human body than the cadaver of a pauper.

The ancients, of course, knew that the heart beats, but they had no more idea of its biologic significance than a Trobriand Islander has of sexual intercourse. No sound physiology—of respiration or reproduction—could be built on such childish speculations. Respiration, said Galen, is a *refrigeration* process; by breathing we get rid of the heart's "innate heat and fuliginous vapours"!

Galen was the greatest physician of his time, but he had the one great fault of nearly all physicians of all time—he could not admit there was anything he did not know. That may be meritorious in an artist and unavoidable in an emperor's physician, but why mask ignorance in a "fuliginous vapour"?

Respiration, a fundamentally vital process for plants and animals, was not to be guessed at, nor surmised, nor thought out intuitively, by all the Platos that ever lived. It is too complicated a process. Its understanding involves a knowledge of too many different kinds of structures, too many kinds of processes, before it becomes half-way intelligible.

Blood has always been a first-rate curiosity to man as well as a food and a fetish. It will be profitably studied for centuries to come. Life is in the blood, as the Hebrew said, but every Masai child knows that. The real question is, what is life? A knowledge of blood is an aid to the answer.

I am not trying to make fun of the Greeks. They were great scientists, honest men, and they went as far as their eyes and their tyrants would let them. Even Homer's heroes have clinically correct death agonies. Hippocrates left clinical pictures of childbirth, and of certain fevers and other diseases, which are scientifically sound; also such useful terms as *acute, chronic, endemic,* and *epidemic.* Aristotle dissected nearly fifty animals, ranging from a lobster to an elephant. But an artery in a dead animal is empty and looks like a blowpipe. How was anybody to jump at the conclusion that arteries are part of an extraordinarily vast and complex circulating system of a body of some twenty-six thousand billion individual cells?

Laugh at the four humours of Hippocrates? They were the Word for two thousand years of medical practice. This Greek, born 460

B.C. in Cos on the Ægean Sea, founded the noblest of all arts on a scientific basis. He was the Father of Medicine. We shall see him again. The Middle Ages could not see him for St. Paul and similar medicine-men. There was no time to fight ignorance; everybody was busy fighting demons.

In other words, there could be no rational theory of disease before there was a rational theory of health, of life itself. There is such a theory of life. It is not the Truth, but it is truthful and it is honest, and it works and is a guiding principle for the countless observations and experiments today being made in the biological laboratories of the five continents.

To get the contrast between modern and ancient attitudes toward disease, let us take a further glance at Greek physiology. It began with the usual four humours: *blood,* hot and moist; *lymph,* cold and moist; *yellow bile,* hot and dry; *black bile,* cold and dry. Change in those humours made for disease. Then they postulated three kinds of spirits: *natural,* a vapour arising from the blood which was formed in the liver, which passed to the heart, where it united with air and became *vital,* which then went to the brain and became *animal.*

These three spirits produced faculties: natural, vital, animal. The three faculties produced actions: natural, vital, animal—and each kind, internal or external. The natural faculty resided in the liver; the vital, in the heart—which through the arteries heated and lighted the body; and the animal, in the brain. And so on. But over and above these primordial faculties was a "primal force" which was the source and soul of all the faculties.

That *primal force* to Galen and Hippocrates was Nature; to the modern physiologist it is natural forces, chemical actions and reactions, etc.; to Barthez, writing in 1798 on the mechanism of movement, it was *vital principle,* the thinking soul—"the cause which produces all the phenomena in the human body." Between Galen's primal force, Barthez' vital principle, Bergson's Vitalism, and the psychologist's mind or consciousness, there is not much choice. Each generalization "explains" facts by a hypothesis, the hypothesis itself having no factual basis.

Physicians of the last century even invoked Molière's mythical peccant, crass, fuliginous and feculent humours as forces or entities to explain other hypothetical or misunderstood phenomena.

These metaphysical theories delayed sound biologic advance because they laid undue emphasis on certain phenomena and thereby prevented other and more important phenomena from falling within range of observation.

Take Paracelsus again: genius, quack, an extraordinary figure and well worth understanding, for he is not dead yet. He believed that stars "influence" human lives and that God's imprint may be found on plants, metals, etc. Further, that the body is composed of sulphur, mercury, and salt. And that disease follows when the mercury becomes precipitated, distilled, or sublimated; the sulphur, coagulated or dissolved; or the salt, calcined or coagulated; such changes being brought about through the action of heat or cold, dryness or moisture; and the elements themselves being under the direction of an astral body—vital force or Archæus—residing in the belly.

Very well. Disease is an *ens* (from *esse*, to be), an entity or inherent essence. Of which there are five kinds, because derived from five causes: *ens asterum,* stars; *veneni,* poisons in food; *naturale,* natural, entities controlled astrally; *spirituale,* spirits and demons; and *deale,* acts of God.

Now for the treatment. Find the remedy which corresponds to each disease; seek the spiritual or astral essence which resides in the material essence, the counterpart in the spiritual macrocosm for the spiritual microcosm. That is easy, because the form of a plant reveals the astral idea corresponding to the disease. After the plant is found, extract its essence. In short, for the old therapeutic doctrine of *Contraria contrariis curantur* he proposed *Similia similibus curantur*. And Hahnemann erected the doctrine into a medical school which is not quite dead yet.

There is nothing wrong with Paracelsus' system if one believes in primitive magic, spiritualism, or occultism—and millions of Americans do.

Yet Paracelsus burnt the great Galen; he did say, keep your hands off wounds and they will cure themselves; and he did use antimony, iron, lead, arsenic, and mercury, thereby starting medicinal chemistry on a new road, the end of which is yet far off.

Even a seventeenth-century chemist could make mice out of "corn and sweet basil," and talk about a soul containing a sentient soul, which contains an Archæus, which contains the *aura vitalis*. And then conclude that disease is a form of life, an "idea" of the Archæus.

*Archæus* looks imposing enough, but it has no more substance to it than archaic. It was simply van Helmont's name for vitalism; the invisible counterpart of the visible body, in the Paracelsian or Spagirist school of medicine. It is also called mind, consciousness, soul, ghost, ectoplasm.

Yet van Helmont's Archæus was an improvement on Aristotle's mind; it did have some physics and chemistry behind it. He did analyse blood and urine, and was the first to discover an acid and a ferment in gastric digestion; and, as we have seen, he did discover carbonic-acid gas. He too, however, suffered from too much Aristotle, and spent much time contemplating his soul—though, unlike Aristotle, he thought intelligence a human trait and not an emanation from the divinity within us. In another important respect he broke with the ancients; he found air no element, nor fire. He found that water can contain elements, that the earth is a compound of elements. He accepted the three elements of the alchemists—sulphur, salt, and mercury—and added gases, including the "sylvester" gas that comes from burning wood and fermenting wine. To the "material elements" he added the *blases*: such impetuous movements as earthquakes, thunder, emanations from stars or bodies, and movements within living bodies.

It was the *Blas humanum* that became the vital principle of Descartes, who was less chemically inclined than van Helmont but material enough to see man and animals as machines of materials in motion. Hence Vitalism to him was vital mechanics. Animals are machines; the soul is the motor. He located the soul in the pineal gland, from which point it stirs up the brain, thus generating vital spirits in the ventricles, which then spread throughout the body, causing the blood to boil up and develop heat. Vital spirits, then, were a kind of ether—and that, he thought, was the common substratum of everything in nature.

Then Leibnitz stirred the mud and discovered monads or human beings. Soul and body, spirit and matter, are related because of a pre-established harmony.

Well, philosophy is philosophy and generally only remotely related to human physiology. But on Galen's speculations about speculations was founded Galenic medicine. And on van Helmont's, Descartes', and Leibnitz' speculations were founded the three great schools of medicine of the seventeenth century—the Iatrochemical, the Iatromechanical, and the Vitalistic or Animistic. These schools lasted into the nineteenth century and their remedies are still to be found in drug stores.

Sylvius (1614-72) founded the Iatrochemical school. It could not go far because chemistry was still alchemy and the human body was chemically what it has always been—not the simple affair of Paracelsian mercury, sulphur, and salt, and van Helmont "ferments." Today one does not speak of a chemical-healing school; one does speak of biochemistry—and must know much of it to go far in medicine as a science.

It was inevitable that the philosophy of Descartes should provoke medicine to find a system to fit his living machine with the soul as motor. So Borelli (1608-79) applied mathematics and mechanics to medicine. *Iatromechanics* was born. That marked progress; but when seventeenth-century medicine went so far with mathematics and the physical and chemical sciences as to seem to minimize the importance of the soul as motor, the eighteenth swung back again and gave the soul a boost. Stahl's (1660-1734) man of materials activated by an immaterial and immortal soul, was the answer to Iatro-mechanico-mathematico-chemistry.

Animism as doctrine gave way before the view which began to become possible with Morgagni's discoveries of the nature of certain organs of the body and which was formulated by Borden in 1752 as the doctrine of Organicism. Life, as he saw it, is the sum-total of the lives of each particular organ. That doctrine at least ended the ancient humouralism; but it did not relieve the living body of its soul or vital principle. It was Barthez who in his *New Mechanics of Movement in Man and Animals* (1798) propounded the doctrine of "Duo-dynamism," because, as he said, he had to distinguish between man's "vital principle" and his "thinking soul."

"Thinking soul" thereafter passed from medicine to psychology, but vital principle hung on a while longer. John Hunter (1728-93), while not rejecting the principle of vitalism, was great enough physiologist to realize that what is called life or living principle is the most complex concept in all nature because no other principle is so complex in its effects. With the dictum of that great physician, surgeon, anatomist, and physiologist, we come close to the end of the eighteenth century and may close our review of metaphysical medicine.

Before passing on to the agnostic nineteenth century, may I emphasize the important fact that there could be no biology, no science of life, no solid foundation on which medicine could build securely and rationally, until all theories of life, living processes, disease, and death were stripped of their sanctity and shorn of their authority. That, please note, came about only as men turned from theories and sought facts; closed their books and went to Nature herself; gave over pure reasoning as to the *why* of things to discover perchance the *how*. The whys might be the more interesting story, but the hows had real value—values that were to transform every phase of life in human beings, values that could be built into added years of health and happiness and freedom from pain and disease.

Hunter could not know just how complex living beings are— nor does anyone yet; but he saw a great truth. That truth is not to be explained away by a mathematical formula, or by any simple formula, whether it be Emergent Evolution, God, Vitalism, Organicism, Pneuma, Archæus, Anima, or Psyche. And what is biology itself but a half-hundred or more "disciplines" or sciences which tackle this or that phase of everything we call life, which includes Nature herself?

What Lister saw in compound fractures of bones was nothing more than Hippocrates saw and described twenty-four centuries ago: that the patients generally died, and that "it is a spasm that kills them."

Hippocrates well knew both septicæmia and pyæmia. He did not know tuberculosis as it is known today; he did know what a tubercular sufferer looked like, and that if he hung around the city he would die, but if he got out in the hills in the sunshine he would probably get well. His reputation lasted twenty-five centuries; his *vis medicatrix naturæ* will last as long as Nature remains the great healer. What is aseptic surgery today but a successful effort to keep out bacterial invasions and give Nature a chance to heal the wound, repair the broken tissue?

Therein lay the greatness of the Father of Medicine. Health is natural; disease has a natural cause. "It is thus," he said, "with regard to the disease called Sacred; it appears to me to be nowise more divine nor more sacred than other diseases, but has a natural cause from which it originates like other affections." Even Sydenham, the "English Hippocrates" and a great figure in the history of medicine, could only see the Great Plague as a "scourge for the enormity of our sins"—a vision not one whit sounder than that of the Puritans, who laid the plague to the evils of monarchy. Some of the evils tied to democracy's tail are as solidly grounded in unreason.

Hippocrates was not only the first clinician, he was a master in diagnosis and ætiology. He correctly associated diarrhœa and dysentery with contaminated water, and childbirth fever and suppurating wounds with tainted hands.

As Haggard says, he saw so keenly and described so accurately that not for eighteen hundred years were his observations of disease equalled in accuracy. For certain pathologic conditions they still stand as models, and will for no one knows how long. For, as Hippocrates said, *Life is short and art is long, the occasion fleeting, experience fallacious and judgment difficult*. In other words, the best of men is only a man for a' that and has human limitations.

Think of the spade-work which had to be done before anything vitally important could be discovered about blood-poisoning, or before pus-forming bacteria could be discovered. Only the compound microscope and a Pasteur could prove Hippocrates' marvellous genius in seeing into the causes of disease. His oath—still administered to graduates—does credit to the human race and alone redeems Greek civilization; his medicative power of nature is a monument to civilization and the greatest single discovery in the science of health.

And no sooner was he dead than he was deified, his origin traced back to Æsculapius and Herakles.

Vesalius, van Helmont, Harvey, Malpighi, Boyle, Stahl, Boerhaave, Linnæus, von Haller, Hunter, Spallanzani, Cavendish, Priestley, Galvani, Lavoisier—sixteenth-, seventeenth-, eighteenth-century sight-seers: three centuries of manipulating things with human hands, seeing with living eyes. And such facts as they did bring home, such fundamental facts as they did discover! Not enough to make a baby, nor to prevent a baby catching smallpox, but, heaped together, enough to look at babies rationally, enough to make the plateau out of which lofty peaks were to rise in the nineteenth century.

Lister, Pasteur, and Koch were the mountain peaks; but they stood on the high plateau of facts built up by men who saw, as Hippocrates saw, that facts themselves are the final authority; that they can be found only by keen-eyed observation; and that any deduction not factually founded, while it may serve for conversation or as a basis for a book for an intellectual education or a text for an encyclical, can never make the grade in science.

Man and living processes then and forever were transferred from the realm of religion into the light of science. Priests did not close the church doors, nor relinquish their hold on humanity—and never will till humanity learns to depend on itself. Man and living processes are not completely solved riddles yet, nor conceivably ever will be, but such solving as has been done—and it is considerable—has been done by men who were interested in saving lives, and not by those who made a livelihood by saving souls.

When man began to realize that he was neither dust nor the son of God, he began to create more marvellous things out of dust than his primitive Heavenly Father dreamed of. When Pasteur created pathogenesis and Darwin delivered all life into human hands, man for the first time in human history became the arbiter of human destiny. Medicine thereupon ceased to be a Rabelaisian farce played by three actors—physician, patient, and disease; and life itself ceased to be a mystery play of magician, soul, and body. It does seem, however, that some centuries must still pass before a generation can be born which will face life's drama with its hands free, and not tied by the generations which have gone before.

A civilization with the tools of the gods of creation and the *mores* of the imps of hell, is a menace to humanity.

Rome fell; Christianity rose; and upon Europe hell loosed its swarms of demons, devils, and imps, its plagues, pestilences, and epidemics. In that atmosphere medical science could not thrive, and promptly fled to the more genial climes of the Euphrates and the Indus. There were times during the seventeen centuries between Galen and Pasteur when parts of Europe were not only a pest-house but a mad-house.

Man's upward climb has depended primarily on health and happiness. Without one he could not live long; without the other there was nothing to live for. But millions have put up with wretchedness in the belief that there is virtue in misery and in the hope that they would get their reward later on. That belief and that hope took the ache out of hunger and pain and the sting out of death. But while asceticism may be a virtue, biologically speaking it is race suicide, psychologically speaking a disease, and socially speaking a vice. The race is not to the poor in spirit or to the weak in flesh, nor ever was.

Health—enough of it to live out the normal life cycle as a member of society and not as a parasite; happiness—enough of it to keep buoyant: vitality, at ease, freedom from disease. Pain is disease; fear is disease. Pain and fear are often indistinguishable, often fanciful, often unjustified by the facts; but in the presence of pain or fear there is no factual world—escape only, flight from reality.

Disease, then, in its broadest sense, is what man has been fleeing from for a million years—trying to escape death. Has he made progress? Is death itself a disease, a preventable disease?

Thomas Parr probably lived a hundred but is said to have lived a hundred and fifty-two years, on a diet of coarse hard bread, subrancid cheese, milk in every form, and "small" drink, generally "sour whey." With less *rich* fare and purer air than was to be found in London, he could have lived longer, Harvey concluded after examining the body at the command of Charles I. How much food do we require? What is the best food for building a human body and keeping it in repair and good working order? What kind of food is necessary to sustain life, to prolong life, to prolong life indefinitely? Do we ever die a "natural" death, or does something kill us?

Progress? Think of going back to the good old pre-aseptic, -antiseptic, -anæsthetic days! If progress in health and longevity is of paramount importance to man, then the tool which has enabled man to see farthest into the causes of disease and premature death is man's paramount tool. That tool is the microscope.

Religion is either supernaturalism or it is nothing. Human destiny is either in human hands or in superhuman clutches. Disease is either a natural phenomenon and caused by violation of the rules of health, or it is a supernatural phenomenon and caused by God knows what. Do our ailing popes, bishops, and clergy—did those of a thousand years ago—rely on their magic power to heal themselves, or do they call in the best doctor in town?

The difference between a Martin Luther declaring that pestilences and fevers were nothing but the devil's work, an Emperor Maximilian issuing an edict that syphilis was an affliction from God for the sins of men, a Cotton Mather calling it the just judgment of God, or the Scottish clergy calling smallpox an affliction from God —the difference between these and the fact that syphilis and smallpox can still take toll of human lives is not the difference between the twentieth and the eighteenth or the sixteenth century; it is the difference between what can be done in the name of science and humanity but is not allowed to be done in the name of God.

Are these harsh words? Are they *true*; are they founded in *fact*? That is the real question.

Which have stopped more deaths from typhoid—wire screens or prayers? In the Boer War typhoid killed more men than did bullets. During our Civil War one soldier out of every hundred died of typhoid; in the World War, one out of every 20,000. Of the 1,300,-000 British soldiers on the western front in that war, just 266 died from typhoid. The French, who did not use preventive measures at first, had over 12,000 typhoid fatalities in the first sixteen months. Of 12,800 soldiers in our army in 1912 who received preventive treatment, only two developed typhoid. Of 108,000 in camp during the Spanish-American War, 20,000 developed typhoid. Of the millions of our troops in the World War, only 227 died of typhoid.

Lepers facing the most ghastly form of lingering death known to man presumably got some comfort from being called "Christ's poor"; presumably, also, a papal absolution to a victim dying of

bubonic plague was a great comfort. And comfort is fine; but life
is finer. Surely, if there be healing power in any name, it should
be in that of a saint who was called back to life from the grave—
to become Bishop of Marseilles and patron saint of all lazarettos.
I wonder how many of "Christ's poor" St. Lazarus has healed? Of
these "tombs of the living dead" there were, says Haggard, nineteen
thousand in western Europe alone during the days when the church
ruled men's thoughts. That was one way to get rid of "Christ's
poor"; another was to pile them up and burn them, as did Philip
the Fair.

Leprosy is hard to catch or cure; it can be stamped out by fire
or by being buried alive. But it is not on record, outside fairy books,
that any leper was ever cured in any lazaretto or by any prayer to
St. Lazarus. It is a fact that leprosy today is a curable disease. There
is no known reason why it should not become as extinct as the
dinosaur.

During the sixteenth century no one year was free of bubonic
plague, with its terrible mortality, often as high as ninety-nine per
cent. In fact, from the outbreak of the famous Black Death pestilence in 1348 till the beginning of the eighteenth century Europe
was a plague-ridden land. Little wonder its civilization was hard,
narrow, artificial, and unwholesome.

The thirteenth century Children's Crusade was a mad disease, and
cured at an awful price. In 1374 an epidemic of St. Vitus' dance
(*chorea*, "dancing") was spread from town to town by thousands
of convulsionaries as though it were a contagion.

Cerebrospinal fever (*encephalitis lethargica*), or sleepy-sickness,
broke out in Emperor Maximilian II's army in 1566, and spread
through the Rhineland. Scurvy again and again carried off thousands of soldiers, sailors, prisoners, and paupers, like a scourge;
not until the nineteenth century was it known to be a food-de-
ficiency disease.

All malignant fevers were formerly called *pestilential*. Not until
modern times was true pest or bubonic plague definitely distinguished from what is now known as typhus. Typhoid is typhus-
like. A visitation of Black Plague would be met by bands of simple-
minded idiots going about the country singing hymns while they

scourged themselves with whips to appease the divine wrath or whatever they thought it was that took delight in public masochism.

The sixth-century plague at the height of its three months' visitation cost Constantinople alone, according to Gibbon, ten thousand lives a day. What it cost other parts of Justinian's empire is not known, but so much "in some of the fairest countries of the globe" that they have not yet recovered.

Fourteenth-century plagues cost Europe some twenty-five million lives—and incidentally gave Christian borrowers excuse for burning thousands of Jew lenders for taking interest, then forbidden by the Christian Bible. *The Jews had spread the plague!* Some Christians today have equally pious views as to how some things spread, and would like to murder the spreaders.

Boccaccio, who fled Florence to escape the plague and meanwhile wrote the *Decameron*, estimated his city's loss at a hundred thousand. "Shrift there was none; churches and chapels were open, but neither priest nor penitent entered—all went to the charnel house. Sexton and physician were cast into the same deep and wide grave; the testator and his heirs and executors were hurled from the same cart into the same hole."

That was 1348, the year the Black Death reached Rome. It was also Holy Year. So Pope Clement VI offered not only absolution to all Christians who might die on the way to Rome or back, but the assurance that their souls would skip purgatory and go straight to heaven. What a bait! Nearly a million and a quarter swallowed it, and a tenth of the pilgrims got home alive, "home" being all Europe. But think of the enormous offering to the church!

The Pope did not contract the plague; he was at Avignon. When the plague reached that town he shut himself up in one room. Petrarch's Laura died at Avignon of that "divine manifestation" —as, finally, did the Pope's physician, Guy de Chauliac, a famous surgeon from the school of Montpellier. He left descriptions of both the 1348 and 1360 epidemics at Avignon.

The year following Clement's Holy Year saw the plague in London—to end 317 years later with the Great Fire. Pepys, as Haggard points out, was more interested in the loss of property by fire than in the loss of life by plague. Defoe's *Journal of the Plague Year* is largely based on the plague in Marseilles, for Defoe presumably was born in 1661, while the London plague reached its height in 1665.

Napoleon, it is said, to stop the plague in Jaffa, ordered the victims poisoned—which was a surer way to stop its spread than by touching their sores (*bubos*) as he is pictured in the Louvre painting.

The first known official *quarantine* against suspects was made by Venice in 1348. The period was forty days: had not Moses and Christ been quarantined *quaranta giorni* in the desert? Because Napoleon in returning from Egypt to France in 1798 violated the quarantine law, it was moved in the National Assembly that he be shot. Think what the loss of that motion cost the world! And give a priest credit for having made it, for it was the Abbé Sieyès— of the church which six years later consecrated Bonaparte Napoleon I, Hereditary Emperor of the French.

Civilization has wiped out plague! Well, if it has, there can be no harm in looking a fact or two in the face. One is that we of today are no more *immune* from plague than was mediæval Europe. A few years ago, three months of plague cost Manchuria sixty thousand lives. In 1900 plague cost San Francisco not quite two hundred human lives and California the lives of twenty million squirrels. That it did not cost this nation twenty or sixty million human lives we owe, not to civilization, but to science. In fact, civilization, guised as the Good Name of San Francisco, said, "There is no plague!" But there is, said science, in the name of physicians charged with protecting the nation's health. Did San Francisco welcome an investigation? Did it want to find out the facts? It did not. As health had little chance to be heard when everybody was busy fighting Satan and getting ready for the Judgment Day, so truth—about disease, about social evils and social injustice—has to yell to be heard above the clamour for Progress.

Fifty years ago the rest of the nation could have quarantined San Francisco and let it pay for its Local Pride with the lives of its citizens. And possibly the disease could have been confined to the city or the state, just as the lower Mississippi region used to be quarantined for yellow fever.

We forget that no part of the nineteenth-century world, or of the American colonies, or of the United States, was free from epidemics.

Epidemics of yellow fever, smallpox, diphtheria, childbed fever, visited our eastern seaboard cities again and again. The toll of children in New York City alone in 1840 was forty-five hundred; in Philadelphia in 1793, ten per cent of the population. In eighteenth-century Europe smallpox took toll of sixty million lives. It and similar diseases early reached these shores and played havoc with our aboriginal population; but it's an ill wind that blows nobody good, for, as that devout Christian Cotton Mather observed, it almost cleared the woods of those "pernicious creatures to make room for a better growth."

Napoleon broke quarantine to return to France, but he had his troops promptly vaccinated after Jenner, in 1798, had proved that cowpox protects from smallpox. And fourteen years later some American "savages" sent a wampum belt to Jenner—"In token of our acceptance of your precious gift, and we beseech the Great Spirit to take care of you in this world, and in the land of spirits." Quite different from the answer Christian fanaticism made to one of the greatest triumphs in human history. It said that smallpox was a "visitation from God"; cowpox, the product of "presumptuous, impious men."

And that is the spirit of the "anti's" today: anti-vaccinationists, anti-vivisectionists, and every sect, cult, church, school, or society which does not, cannot, or will not think rationally about disease, disease in every form, venereal, social, physical, or "mental." Put any one of the anti-scientific minorities in supreme power, and within twenty years what was left of our population would be quarantined by the world.

"To know is one thing," said Hippocrates; "merely to believe one knows, is another. To know is science, but merely to believe one knows is ignorance." But, as Haggard says, the danger to the scientific spirit, to the advance of medicine, and to the integrity of modern civilization, does not come from ignorant masses, but from the so-called intelligent shapers of civilization who cannot think rationally; from "sentimental and idle people in whom the primitive instinct escapes from repression and rises to prevent thought. They revive in modernized form and terminology the religious healing cults of primitive peoples, or join forces with the anti-vivisectionists and revel in the contemplation of cruelties which exist only in their imagination."

The actual beginnings of infectious diseases can in all probability never be known. Williams believes that smallpox, cholera, leprosy, bubonic plague, mumps, glanders, measles, anthrax, and rabies are of high antiquity in Europe, and thinks the high antiquity of malaria, tuberculosis, yellow fever, and syphilis less certain.

It is believed, but not *proved*, that syphilis originated in the New World. Before 1495 there is no clinical account of the characteristic symptoms of the disease caused by the micro-organism of syphilis. The evidence *seems* conclusive that the germs were carried to Europe by the sailors of Columbus from the island of Hispaniola (Haiti), where it was indigenous and among the natives a curable disease.

There is evidence that the disease appeared first in Barcelona, where Ferdinand and Isabella received Columbus on his return. A book dated 1521 and written by a physician who practised in Barcelona in 1493, speaks of the "Reptilian Disease, commonly called in Spain the Buboes." Oviedo, who spent forty years in America, argued in favour of its American origin.

It is known that many Spaniards joined the army of Charles VIII of France on his military expedition into Italy in 1494-95. After pausing at Genoa and Florence, they spent four weeks in Rome and three months in Naples. Charles reached Lyons in November of 1495. His army of dissolute ruffians and adventurers scattered in every direction.

The consequences were momentous. Italy lost the intellectual leadership of Europe to England, France, and Germany. She acquired syphilis—first at Genoa, and throughout Lombardy in less than two years. In Naples it became a virulent and devastating epidemic.

By 1497 syphilis was so prevalent in southern France that the Paris Parliament tried to control it by regulations. By edict, Emperor Maximilian I recognized the danger of this new and unheard-of scourge. It was carried by Swiss mercenaries to Switzerland, and reached England from French and possibly Spanish ports by 1497. It reached Russia the same year, and had reached the Netherlands the previous year.

"This virus of prostitutes will soon infect the entire universe," was the prophetic remark of a physician who had closely observed the spread and ravages of the disease after the battle of Formio. It was soon in China, the Indies, and Africa, and all too soon had overspread the earth.

The French called it the "Neapolitan" disease; the Italians, the "French"; the English, Scots, Dutch, and Germans, the "Spanish pox"; the Persians, the "Turkish" disease; and the Portuguese, the "Castilian" disease. The Spaniards called it the "Italian measles," and also the "disease of Hispaniola." Its name first appeared in print in Frascatoro's poem, *Syphilis sive Morbo Gallico,* in 1530, though a work devoted to the *morbum Gallicum* or *morbum Neapolitanum* had been published in Venice in 1497.

In a treatise dedicated to Cæsar Borgia and published in Rome in 1497, Torella gave the first clinical picture of the "horrible and contagious" disease, and begged pope, emperor, king and lords to take prophylactic measures to prevent its spread. He proposed the examination of all public women by specially appointed matrons, who were to send the affected to a special hospital to be treated by special physicians.

Mercury then, as now, was the treatment, and monkeys then, as recently, were the experimental laboratory for disease. It was Metchnikoff and Roux who inoculated monkeys with the virus in 1903, clearing the way for Schaudinn's discovery in 1905 of the protozoon *treponema pallidum,* the cause of syphilis. Five years later, Ehrlich and his Japanese assistant, Hata, announced their syphilic specific "606."

The use of mercury, like all treatments for all diseases until recently, was purely empirical. Mercurial ointments had long been used for any disease of the skin, and syphilis was supposed to be a skin disease—as it is at first. Rhazes, the Arab physician, had learned from experimenting on monkeys that mercury administered internally in pure form was not very pernicious; but that calomel, and especially sublimate, were very dangerous; and that the "emanations of mercury" led to paralysis.

What Rhazes and other ninth-century Islamic physicians knew was known in the medical schools of Salerno and Montpellier of the tenth and eleventh centuries. But there was a profound difference between our savage Nordic ancestors embracing Christianity

and priding themselves on their ignorance, and the pastoral Arab
followers of the Prophet translating and absorbing Greek science.
For science, as the Prophet had said, "is the remedy for the infirmities of ignorance, a comforting beacon in the night of injustice. The
study of the sciences has the value of a fast; their teaching, the value
of a prayer; in a noble heart they inspire the highest feelings, and
they correct and humanize the perverted."

"God has not inflicted diseases upon us," said the Prophet, "without at the same time giving us the remedies." As Cumston says,
the Arabs started out to search for the remedies, and accomplished
in one century what Europe required several to absorb.

Ehrlich's salvarsan, or "606" (1911), was a mercurial derivative
which was fatal to the organism of syphilis and not to its host. But
the difference between Rhazes and Ehrlich was far less than that
between empirical medicine and chemotherapy. Rhazes was on the
way. The Arabs were the first to use chemical preparations in treatment of disease—the first chemotherapists. And a thousand years
before we had a pure-drug law (violated daily) the Arabs had made
pharmacy a government institution and druggists responsible for
the purity and prices of their drugs.

Progress? Progress could now be made. We are ready for a
Lister: a man who could stand on the giant Pasteur's shoulders and
make the world safe for lacerated flesh and woman in labour.

VII

"Science" discovers, we say, thereby possibly concealing the profound truth that it is man who makes discoveries. His motive may
be as divergent as an empty stomach, an empty pocket-book, or the
desire to add another hundred millions to his account. Whatever
the motives which prompt men to hunt, few have led to greater
discoveries than sheer curiosity, the love of discovering something.
That is why many men have ridden to fame on a hobby-horse.

Columbus was not looking for America, nor Wöhler for urea.
Leeuwenhoek was not looking for anything; he was just looking
through something. What he saw through his microscope, had he
but known, might have scared the wits out of him, but he was not
at all scared, only more curious, and he went on looking—probably

at a financial loss to his business of grinding lenses. But think of the joy he had in the discoveries he made!

The story of the discovery of microbe organisms begins with that Dutchman and what he saw. That story is an open book today and one of the most fascinating in all history—and an infinitely more important chapter in civilization than the Hundred Years' War, or the Napoleonic Wars, or even the World War. That is, of course, if the saving of a human life is more important than the destruction of millions of human beings. That the story of the germ-killers is not as interesting to as many people who can read as the story of the man-killers, is because our education fits us for Big Game Hunting rather than for civilized living. Human warfare is the biggest of Big Game Hunts, and it is a poor specimen of humanity who cannot be thrilled by poring over the records of famous man-hunters and human-power wielders.

Does anyone know where Pasteur is buried? Is there anyone who has not visited Napoleon's tomb? Is there an American schoolboy who has not heard of listerine, or many who have heard of Lister? Are as many familiar with Jenner as with Mesmer, with Koch as with Coué?

"One ought to be ashamed to make use of the wonders of science embodied in a radio set, the while appreciating them as little as a cow appreciates the botanic marvels in the plants she munches," said Einstein to a radio audience last year. "Appreciation?" Why, they receive *adulation* compared with the appreciation given those who have made the world fit to live in! Or is death from lockjaw or bubonic plague preferable to being run over by an automobile or electrocuted by a live wire?

How many yeast-eaters have the faintest notion what it is they eat or what happens to yeast when it lands in their stomach? Or the significance of its rediscovery in 1837, more than a century and a half after the Dutch lens-grinder had discovered that yeast is a living, growing organism? But not till 1859, and after epoch-making studies, did Pasteur discover that yeast, a microbe, causes alcoholic fermentation. That discovery threw other thousands of speculations upon the scrap heap of worn-out thinking. And while the South was fighting for Slavery and the North for Union, still other great victories over nature were won by science. "Spontaneous generation" was laid to rest for ever. Instead came knowledge of the bacteria of putrefaction and decay. The light of science, as Tyndall said, was being let in upon the murderous dominion of our foes. It was indeed.

By 1865 Pasteur had discovered the bacterial agents of other fermentations: butyric, in sour milk; acetic, in cider vinegar. It is now known that bacteria produce acids, alkalis, fermentation, light, pigments, poisons, proteins, putrefaction, ptomaines, sulphur, iron, enzymes, excretions. And perform many other wonderful things such as are duly set forth in Jordan's eight-hundred-page text-book of a science founded by Pasteur and made an independent biologic science by Koch. Destroy that text-book and the knowledge therein, and man again is at the mercy of all the quacks in Christendom.

We celebrate the '76s, and properly, for it was in 1876 that man won his greatest victory in the fight for freedom. In that year Koch *proved* the connexion between a disease and a bacterium! A millennium hence, which will be the bigger date—1776 or 1876? For, please note, no one before 1876 had ever proved a causal connexion between any specific disease and any specific bacterium. Man could think straight between death and a head split by a battle-ax; he could also think straight—Hippocrates did—between health and fresh air, sunshine, and nourishing food. But civilization does not produce a Hippocrates every millennium; and by 1876 she had produced an Industrial Age, with its crowded cities, tenements, slums, factories, mining towns, squalour. That age could not live without bacteria; it could not survive without knowing how to fight them. But first it had to discover them.

By 1879 the bacillus of typhoid was discovered; tuberculosis, in 1882; Asiatic cholera, 1883; tetanus (lockjaw), diphtheria, and syphilis, 1884; gonorrhœa, 1885; bubonic plague, 1895. What voyages into the world of the infinitely small things which work infinitely profound changes in big things! The prodigious capacity of the tiny things to multiply, to cause changes in the earth itself, in the soil, in the thousand and one things on which our lives, health, and prosperity hang! They are into everything, up to everything. They made the earth fit for higher forms of life. They transform the very dead into materials fit for use by the living.

Again, the discovery of how microbes get at us, into our blood, into our heart, into our alimentary canal, into our spinal cord, into our brain; and once in, how they multiply, and what their multiplication subtracts from our health and adds to our fevers—that discovery is another story and one that has cost many valuable human lives. Monuments to known and unknown soldiers, but how many monuments can you see to those who knowingly risked their lives that the transmission of death-dealing germs might be definitely discovered? In that search, which led around the world—into cholera-infested camps, yellow-fever swamps, sleeping-sickness jungles—strange facts were uncovered; the rôle rats, fleas, flies, mosquitoes, etc., play in carrying disease; the rôle water, air, food, dirty hands, etc., play in spreading disease. Nor is the story yet all told or the need for brave soldiers yet past. As I write these words one of my friends is investigating an unknown, yet known deadly, disease. In his laboratory he faces possible death as certainly as though he were afoot in a tiger-infested jungle.

We forget that life on earth is a struggle, that for a million years man has had to keep improving his technique to survive the struggle. He has cut himself loose from natural selection. We no longer kill off the aged and infirm or expose surplus babies to the elements; we have assumed responsibility for living above and beyond the natural life with a devil-take-the-hindmost and might-makes-right, but there is need to remind ourselves that this world is not yet foolproof, nor by any manner of means safe for monkey curiosity, infantile tricks, youthful daydreams, or old-age sighs for the good old times.

The 1918-19 influenza epidemic cost us nearly a half million precious lives; India, six million. Most of us have already forgotten its rapid spread, its great morbidity, its predilection for radiant youth. But we should not forget that its bacillus is not yet positively known, its mode of transmission not at all known; and no one knows where it has gone or when it will return.

There is so much that is yet to be discovered about infectious diseases and immunity therefrom! So much that yet needs doing before this age becomes as expert in its fight against germs as the old age was in fighting devils. Man's million-year fight for freedom has just begun anew, with new weapons, new tools, new outlook, and new ideals. And if progress in that fight seems slow, encouragement may be had by contrasting the last five hundred with the last five thousand years or the last hundred with the last hundred thousand; or this generation with all the generations which have gone before.

Think of the mortality of the World War; then think of what that mortality would have been without antiseptic surgery. Think of the young men foredoomed to death during the Civil War if they so much as got a scratch on their skin; with more serious wounds they could die with the stench of their own putrefying flesh in their nostrils—and too often in sight of maggots crawling in that dead flesh. Think of the frightful mortality from childbed fever in the good old days; for every laceration of maternal flesh a host of death-dealing germs ready to hurry the mother to the grave before she had time even to name her child.

Medical science has done its part—and we assume we have done ours. But a fact we can find no joy in is that between 1912 and 1925 the rate of maternal mortality in the United States practically stood still. Which means that about twenty years ago we were so busy viewing progress with pride we forgot how changing this world is and that every view-with-pride should face forward and not backward. We certainly cannot view with pride the fact that for the last six years our maternal mortality rate is the *highest* of all nations of the so-called civilized world.

We have Ministers of War, and of Commerce, and of Agriculture; but of Education or of Health, none. Britain has both. Its Health Ministry, says the *New York Times*, is concerned *because British mothers die in childbed only two-thirds as regularly as mothers in this country*. Progress in wealth is fine—but what is wealth? What is septicæmia?

Too many British mothers die in childbed because they do not take care of themselves during the prenatal period; doctors or midwives make mistakes; facilities for medical care are insufficient; mothers do not follow doctors' advice. And at that they are only two-thirds as bad as American mothers! Horse sense is fine for horses, but what humans need is health sense. With plenty of that, our Sairy Gamps would lose their jobs, every physician would be a competent obstetrician, and every expectant mother would know what to expect if she neglected the P's and Q's of healthy maternity.

Pneumonia and influenza alone of all known acute communicable infections are still beyond effective control. That is because of the newness of the science of bacteriology. Possible control is one thing; "effective" control is another, and depends on public health-mindedness. We became motor-minded in twenty years, radio-minded in less than ten, and in possibly another century we may be health-minded.

The movement in that direction began in 1842 with a report on sanitary conditions among the labourers of England. The report that that condition was appalling was one thing; what to do about it was another. Equally appalling reports had come regularly from hospitals, especially surgical hospitals. Every case of abortion is a surgical operation, and not so long ago every case of difficult labour was a surgical operation.

A great surgeon of the nineteenth century was great because of his skill in amputating a leg or an arm or performing a Cæsarean section in a jiffy. He really was skilful, really quick. But what happened to the patient after being unstrapped and loosed from the operating-table was of less import to the greatness of his reputation. A mortality of twenty per cent was normal; of Cæsarean operations, eighty; of maternity in general in some hospitals, ninety per cent.

Stromeyer, great military surgeon of the Franco-Prussian War, amputated thirty-six legs through the knee-joint—with thirty-six deaths. Nussbaum amputated thirty-four legs—thirty-four deaths. Other surgeons operated with one hundred per cent failures. Hospitals were cesspools of pyæmia. French hospitals housed more horror than the Crimea; of 13,173 amputations, including fingers and toes, 10,006 were fatal.

Hospitals endowed with the accumulated wealth of centuries were public curses. In Munich's big—and because of the city's rapid industrial growth, overcrowded—hospital, deaths from hospital gangrene mounted from twenty-six to eighty per cent in two years. It was like an epidemic. Nussbaum, its director, was in despair.

Surgery of any sort was quite possibly fatal and most probably painful. Painless surgery—from circumcision and pulling teeth to Cæsarean sectioning and tonsillectomy—is only a few years older than the writer of these pages; antiseptic surgery, not a year older.

When Vesalius was a medical student a hemorrhage was stopped with boiling oil, molten pitch, or a red-hot iron. In Galen's time ligatures were used to stop hemorrhages; but the Arabs wisely preferred cauterization: it sterilized the wound. Paré, great Middle Age surgeon, revived the use of ligatures and was enormously successful—not in tying cords but in saving the lives of his patients. After Paré, the mortality in surgery depending on ligatures steadily increased.

Why? Infection. "I dressed the wound, and God healed him," Paré said of an officer who departed gaily on a wooden leg. He had *dressed* the wound; infection was kept out. Infection then, as now, was not necessarily fatal; it depended on the part infected. Paré, for example, dared not open the abdomen, nor amputate an arm at the shoulder or a leg at the hip; infection would be fatal!

"I dressed the wound"—and the wound healed itself! The trick was in the dressing. Called to take charge of wounded soldiers in besieged Metz, he never could "forget the ragged bandages . . . rewashed only once a day and dried at the fire, and hard as parchment"; and the washing done by "four big fat prostitutes." Paré *nursed* his patients. He spent two months nursing a French marquis, nearly dead with an abscessed thigh, back to life.

Even up to 1857 London hospital nurses were frowzy frumps who drank—and had worse habits. In fact, Oliver Wendell Holmes declared he would prefer Hahnemann to Hippocrates as a physician if he could have Florence Nightingale to nurse him, as against Sairy Gamp with Hippocrates. Which means that Holmes saw what Paré saw: that in surgery, dressing takes precedence over God; that Godliness is next to cleanliness.

Possibly the oldest mention of nurses is in the *Rig-Veda*—the four pillars of medicine: the physician, the drug, the nurse, and the patient. Asoka in the third century B.C. is known to have founded many hospitals. An 1185 Angkor-wat inscription in Cambodia speaks of two hundred and two hospitals and even describes the nurses' uniforms.

Moslems built the first hospitals worthy of the name; the one at Bagdad had a staff of twenty-four physicians, and kept records of case histories. Egypt had sanitary police and a well-endowed, celebrated hospital in Cairo, and a special hospital for women. "Cleanliness is piety," said the Prophet. Hygiene was a corner stone of Islamic morality, an impetus to medical progress.

Early Christian monasteries encouraged nursing; but in spite of St. Francis' attempt in the thirteenth century to revive the profession, it soon sank to its former low level. The first secular nursing society was the seventeenth-century Sisters of Charity of the Order of St. Vincent de Paul, and it is today the largest in the world. But the idea of *training* women to take the place of inefficient and drunken females in caring for the sick was born in the brain of a German pastor in 1836. To his Kaiserwerth Deaconesses' Institution at Düsseldorf went rich and proud Florence Nightingale. She knew nothing about streptococci or staphylococci or any kind of bacteria, but she was a lady and knew dirt and filth when she saw them.

When Florence Nightingale went to the Crimea with forty nurses in 1854, and began trying to scrub up the grimy wounded and to let sunlight and fresh air into foul hospitals not fit for cattle, she was roundly blessed by the general staff there and at home as a meddlesome busybody. But she never gave up; she cleaned up the foul hospitals, got her men clean, gave them clean food, fresh air, sunlight, and pure water. She acted, in short, as though she were a true daughter of the Father of Medicine.

In 1860 a school for training "new-style nurses" was established at St. Thomas's Hospital with the "Nightingale Fund" of fifty thousand pounds. An orphaned Negro baby in Kenya Colony today can get better treatment than could be had by the King of France in the sixteenth century. Vesalius and Paré together could not save Henry II, wounded during a jousting tournament.

Seven thousand hospitals, nine hundred thousand beds, care for our ten million patients a year—at a cost of about a billion dollars a year. Yet our investment in hospitals is two billion dollars less than our investment in churches, and no provision is made for the adequate and systematic training of competent executives, without whom hospitals deteriorate as rapidly and easily as boardinghouses. What may be seen in some of our hospitals—if one can really get behind the scenes—is unpleasant, unsanitary, unethical.

What Hippocrates, Paré, and Holmes saw, Semmelweis saw more clearly and penetratingly in the big maternity hospital in Vienna.

This almost unknown man was quite as keen an observer as Lister.

That hospital had two sections, "A" and "B." In "A," mothers died at the rate of 100 per thousand; in some years at the rate of 158. In "B" they died at the rate of thirty-three per thousand. Why? Semmelweis tried out one reason after another: climate, crowding, fear, tolling bell announcing priest's arrival to administer comfort to the dying, poverty; or was it "wounded modesty"—for labour in "A" was in charge of medical students; in "B," of midwives. He could hang the discrepancy on none of these. The great fact kept haunting him: *heavy* mortality from childbed fever in "B"; *frightful* mortality in "A." He saw no light.

Then Kolletschka, a colleague, cut a finger while performing an autopsy. A few days later he sickened and died. And Semmelweis saw "with irresistible clearness that the disease from which Kolletschka had died was identical with that from which I had seen so many hundreds of lying-in women die." "Day and night" the vision haunted him with ever-increasing conviction. "Did the individuals whom I had seen die from an identical disease have *cadaveric* material carried into the vascular system? To this question I must answer, Yes!"

And well might he have exclaimed, Eureka! "Childbed fever" was *wound infection* from blood fever, blood-poisoning. The women got it from the cadaver-stained hands of the medical students, their childbirth attendants; or a clean hand could carry the infection from one infected woman to an as yet uninfected woman; as Holmes put it, "from bed to bed, as rat-killers carry their poison from one household to another."

Thereafter Semmelweis made every student wash his hands in a chlorate-of-lime solution before making an examination. In seven months, maternity mortality in "A" fell from 120 to twelve per thousand!

Everybody rejoiced, of course? Nobody that could be heard above a baby's cry. Semmelweis' enthusiasm was met with apathy; his success, with petty official injustice. And after a lifetime devoted to eradicating puerperal fever from maternity hospitals he died of the same disease, but under the name of blood-poisoning—probably from a scratch on his finger during an operation. Thus ended on

August 13, 1865, as Haggard says, a chapter in the conquest of death at birth.

For sixty-five years puerperal fever has been known to be a preventable infection; yet the death rate from childbirth in the United States is as high today as it was thirty-one years ago, septicæmia causing forty per cent of the deaths, toxæmia twenty-five per cent. In this, the richest country in the world, over seven thousand mothers die every year from this preventable disease—a higher rate than in any other civilized country on earth. Compared with Sweden, in this delicate test, we are a disgrace to civilization. And the public at large does not seem to care. Child-bearing is not Big Business, nor reduction in maternity mortality Progress.

For his discovery of vaccination the state awarded Jenner thirty thousand pounds. Lister, by invitation, made a triumphal march through the universities of Munich, Leipzig, Berlin, Halle, and Bonn; London withheld recognition. But in 1883 he was given a title—not a very big one, a mere baronetcy, when he should have been created a duke or an earl at least. In 1897 he was elevated to the peerage, the first time in history an honest medicine-man was made a lord. He died in 1912 and was buried in Westminster Abbey.

Every surgical operation today, says Haggard, is a monument to Lister. But behind every antiseptic surgical operation is the immortal Pasteur's discovery of the connexion between bacterial invasion and infection. It was because of Pasteur's discoveries that therapeutics was transformed, surgery reborn. It was Lord Lister himself who in 1892 addressed these words to Pasteur at his jubilee celebration:

Truly, there does not exist in the entire world any individual to whom the medical sciences owe more than they do to you. Your researches have . . . lightened the baleful darkness of surgery, and transformed the treatment of wounds from a matter of uncertainty and a too often disastrous empiricism into a scientific art of sure beneficence. Thanks to you, surgery has undergone a complete revolution, which has deprived it of its terrors and has extended almost without limit its efficacious power.

"Almost" without limit. Will the limit have come when a surgeon takes our works out and cleans them—as a jeweller a watch? Possibly; and by that time, conceivably, the physiologist will have learned how to grow new parts. Think of going to a hospital for a new mainspring! New glands are already on the market, though not yet home grown.

"Cadaveric material," Semmelweis called it; heaven alone knows what a spiritualist or a mathematical physicist would call it. But if there is anything real behind any generalization in this vale of tears, it is the cold corpse of a loved one. No less real are the bacteria of decay—of which there are several varieties, all as real as elephants, some as murderous as machine-guns. It is easy enough to kill a bacterium; the trouble is in getting it out in the open where it can be safely fired at. Most of the cells of our living body are as alive as a bacterium—and are as easily killed. And as our blood is the living environment of our living cells, it is not easy to insert a bacterium-killer in our blood which is not also a cell-killer. Our blood carries its own crew of bacteria-killers—or *eaters* rather (*phagocytes*)—and they can generally take care of bacteria so long as they can be confined to the surface of a wound. In fact, an old medical saying was, *Bonum et laudabile pus* (good and laudable pus). The idea was that if a wound was suppurating it was doing finely. But once bacteria are in the blood-stream itself—that makes for blood-poisoning, septicæmia, pyæmia, death.

Pus is a mud puddle; blood-water full of the living, dying, and dead soldiers of a battle. Inflammation is generally a sign of pus. Suppuration is pus; and an abscess or "gathering" is a pocket of pus, a veritable sink of iniquity whether in a jaw or joint, mastoid process or mammary gland, spinal column or spermatic cord. How do these internal abscesses originate? From external. Bacteria from an infected gum, perhaps, may be carried by the blood to the heart, where they settle down in a valve, begin to multiply, and fight phagocytes and form pus, abscess. Our tonsils, teeth, and sinuses are fine breeding-grounds for pus-forming bacteria. From such foci of infection they may be carried to joints, to the appendix, heart, middle ear, etc.

In short, it is a long and murderous story for this busy age, with its bad teeth and go-getter's record of thirty-five thousand deaths and about one million injured a year in automobile accidents, and the numbers steadily rising. That is what makes antiseptic surgery such a boon and Lister such a saviour of human lives.

When Joseph Lister began to operate in the Glasgow Royal Infirmary in 1860, a compound fracture was so dangerous that the arm or leg was amputated with about a fifty-fifty chance of recovery. But fractured bones not protruding through the skin healed when set, and without pus. An amputated arm or leg healed, if at all, with pus. Why? That was Lister's problem: why *no* pus when the skin is not broken; why *always* pus with an open wound or when the skin is broken?

He got his clue from Pasteur: no bacteria, no fermentation; putrefaction is kin to fermentation; *ergo,* no infection, no pus.

Problem: what to do? Pasteur had found he could kill bacteria by boiling ("pasteurizing," sterilizing). But that would not do for living flesh, so he sought a chemical sterilizer or antiseptic. And as carbolic acid had already been used as a deodorant, he decided to make an experiment. That was in March, 1865. The patient died. He tried again and again, on a compound fracture. He then used pure carbolic acid and tried a different technique; the wound healed, there was no infection. That was the beginning of antiseptic surgery.

Even in 1860 he had written a paper *On the Antiseptic Principle in the Practice of Surgery.* Did surgeons like his principle? Not at all; in fact, they failed to see the point; they thought he was using carbolic acid as a medicine! But bacteriology was not yet a science, and the air was still thick with fantastic theories about disease in general; there was as yet no clear line between infectious and other diseases, nor were infections themselves at all clearly differentiated. Those epoch-making discoveries were to start their as yet unfinished career in 1876.

The antiseptic surgery of Lister has become the aseptic surgery of the modern hospital operating-room. A pathogenic organism has a slim chance of getting near an open wound. As we saw, Paré himself never dared open an abdomen. Appendicitis, extrauterine pregnancy, etc., were no less common last century than now— though appendicitis is now on the increase for some unknown reason; but the best "cure" then was the curate.

What a surgeon cannot and does not cut out today is hardly worth mentioning. The patient does not always recover, but death is not from septicæmia. No surgical operation today has any terror for the operator. But no patient can be expected to live, however "successful" the nephrectomy, if he has, to begin with, only one kidney, as was discovered recently in a post-mortem examination.

Just why Nature keeps on experimenting with the masterpiece of creation is not known, but she does: a heart on the wrong side, only one kidney, a tubal gestation, dermal cysts, tumours, etc. Such experiments and faulty growths may happen in the best regulated families. Many of them can now be corrected, eliminated— even cancerous growths, if caught in time. But formerly such growths among the vital organs were almost always deadly growths.

A tubal pregnancy, for example. The first operation for such misplaced confidence was performed in 1883 by the famous gynæcologist, Dr. Tait, who has left his name on a knot, a law, a method, and an operation—all parts of the modern technique of safely delivering human infants. His tubal operation was a success; he thereafter performed forty such cases—and lost just one! So far had Lister's antiseptic surgery travelled in fifteen years. That is progress!

### VIII

*For I have heard a voice as of a woman in travail,* says Jeremiah, *and the anguish as of her that bringeth forth her first child, the voice of the daughter of Zion, that gaspeth for breath, that spreadeth her hands, saying, Woe is me now! for my soul fainteth before the murderers.*

The introduction of anæsthesia in childbirth prompted a clergyman to speak of chloroform as "a decoy of Satan, apparently offering itself to bless women." But, he prophesied, "in the end it will harden society and rob God of the deep, earnest cries which arise in time of trouble for help." Well, if woman by nature is the scum of the earth and childbirth "the primal curse," the anguished voice of a woman in travail must be sweet music in God's ear. "In sorrow shalt thou bring forth children," God had said. Painless childbirth was contrary to religion and the express command of Scripture!

A sixteenth-century priest used the same argument when it was suggested that a canal be cut through the Panama Isthmus to join the Atlantic and Pacific Oceans. What God had put asunder let no man join together! But Simpson, as Haggard points out, in his answer to the fanatic sadists who fought anæsthetics in childbirth, called attention to the fact that God in his surgical operation for a rib from which to make an Eve, used an anæsthetic. What else was the "deep sleep" he caused to fall upon Adam?

What would the Pope do if he were so unfortunate as to contract tetanus or dislocate his hip? Suffer such torture as to suggest the execution of a would-be assassin of a king of France; submit to the "engines," as they were called, which might have served the torture chamber of the Inquisition—the engines used as late as 1820 to reduce dislocation? Those engines were efficient; they did not always reduce a dislocated joint, but they could tear a limb off.

"The patient was *untied* and returned to bed." Young Darwin, son of a famous physician, went to Edinburgh to study medicine, and the first time he entered a clinic was met by the agonized scream of a girl on the operating-table. Such screams may be sweet music in some monster's ear, but one was enough to shock that humane young man out of the clinic forever.

Yet for three hundred years physicians had known ether!

Why had it never been used? Why, when a patient entered a hospital for the reduction of a dislocation or a surgical operation, was he first submitted to the "unholy trinity of bleeding, purging, and puking" and then tied or held down by Sandows, or hitched to the "engine"—to suffer the tortures of the damned? No wonder surgeons became so renowned for their dexterity that one could boast of doing two hundred amputations in a single day.

Why this three hundred years' delay? Because, says Hunt, "the physicians were convinced that they knew enough to state positively that such results as were caused by ether would never be obtained by any drug, and because they had not yet learned to appreciate the value of experiments on animals."

*A voice, as of a woman in travail!* The cold sweat of perfect agony; the convulsions of strychnine; the excruciatingly painful cramps of lockjaw. And earache, toothache, stomachache, headache. And gout, rheumatism, stricture, lumbago, *angina pectoris.* And dislocation, fractures, cuts, burns, bruises. What chambers of horrors we poor mortals can be when wracked by pain! But scream on, woman-in-travail; shriek and sweat, man, woman, and child in the agony of pain; let no one rob God of the deep, earnest cries which arise in time of trouble for help!

It is a rather terrifying thought that progress in alleviating pain and suffering had to fight not only religion, which is naturally morbid on disease, but also human nature, which is prone to accept the habitual as the limit of possible achievement. Anæsthesia—and asepsis—came, says Hunt, when the medical profession had demonstrated to its own satisfaction that they were *impossible*.

But come they did. And the hour Weir Mitchell spoke of—*none so sweet, as when hope, doubt, and fear watched 'mid deepening stillness, one eager brain with God-like will, decree the Death of Pain*—came on October 16, 1846. ETHER DAY! Haldane anticipates an even greater day—a day when most of the pain in human life can be wiped out at a stroke—to come when a drug can be found as good as morphine, one-tenth as poisonous, and not a habit-former.

The year following Morton's successful demonstration in the Massachusetts General Hospital of ether as a pain-killer in a surgical operation, Simpson of Edinburgh discovered the anæsthetic effects of chloroform on human beings. Not only religion, but medicine as well, fought against its use in maternity cases. The pain of childbirth, said a Dr. Meigs of Philadelphia, is "a desirable, salutary, and conservative manifestation of life force." Even Queen Victoria's acceptance in 1853 of chloroform for the delivery of her seventh child (Prince Leopold) was frowned upon by the medical profession; but when in 1857 she again accepted it, chloroform became anæsthesia *à la reine*. It was like putting a new cosmetic on the market—with royal approval. There could be no opposition thereafter.

Two years after Simpson first used chloroform in childbirth, he reported that he had used it successfully in over forty thousand cases of childbirth and surgical operations. Sir Walter Scott, on learning that Simpson was to be knighted, suggested a "wee naked bairn" for his coat-of-arms, with the motto, "Does your mother know you're out?"

Ether, chloroform, morphine, cocaine, novocaine, acetanilid, opium, atropine, nitrous oxide, etc., are drugs, and merely to mention drugs is to open up what may prove to be *the* decisive battle in human history. At any rate, the discovery of ether as an anæsthetic has been called the most important event in surgery and one of the most important events in human history. Certain it is that the torture the human body has been subjected to, and the concoctions that have been put in human stomachs in the name of Cure, are unbelievable.

Therapeutics is far from an exact science, but probably the prize drug of all time was *theriaca*—compounded by Nero's physician of seventy-eight different ingredients, and, according to Cumston, prescribed in the middle of last century for smallpox, measles, and other malignant fevers.

Before we enter the drug store, however, let us look at a barber shop.

Do you know the derivation of the words *chirurgeon* and *cancer*; can you give the Latin and Greek equivalent of each?

Cancer to the fifteenth century was something that required handwork—a chirurgeon. As England in that age specialized in handwork, the cutting of cancers, beards, etc., was under the protecting ægis of a chartered company—the Barber Surgeons. Their sign was a dish with a piece bitten out so as to fit snug around the neck under the chin when the patient was to be bled. And bleeding the patient was no figure of speech. To be a master Barber Surgeon one underwent a long apprenticeship and passed an oral examination—of which the above is a sample question. In 1540 the Barber Surgeons Company became the College of Surgeons, leaving the barbers holding the dish. But the term "surgeon and barber" appears as late as 1618; the word physician began to appear in the sixteenth century.

The main difference between cancer now and in 1531 is, as I see it, that biologic science today is keenly alive to one great fact: it knows where its knowledge ends and its ignorance begins. It knows nothing of cancer's cause or causes, and practically nothing of its control or cure. It knows that it is not contagious, that it can be treated successfully in its early stages when it is still purely local, that delay is dangerous, that it is ravaging humanity, and that it is a national threat of increasingly formidable proportions. Because of that fact, cancer may be forced to surrender its secret before these words see printer's ink; on the other hand, its secret may be buried so deeply in the nature of life itself that a century must pass before it need fear anything but the surgeon's knife or a speck of radium. That it must eventually yield its secret, let no one doubt.

Galen would hardly feel at home in the corner drug store; he would be enormously interested in a chemotherapy laboratory. There could be no true drugs until there was real chemistry. And it is quite as important that our drugs be honest as that our currency be sound. Aseptic surgery may save the infant, an anæsthetic deaden the mother's pain—and all that progress go for naught in her death from an *impure* drug.

## IX

What, besides wall-paper, books, sandwiches, candy, tobacco, poker chips, lipsticks, telephone booths, and postage stamps, does one find in a drug store? Any drugs? Are drugs medicine, and is a pharmacist a medicine-man? Do medicines cure disease? Is anything that cures disease a medicine, and is every medicine a drug? Is an anæsthetic a drug, or a contraceptive, or a germ-killer? And where does science come in—as propaganda for quack cures, as Haldane said, manufactured by the rich for diseases of the poor, who need better food and houses, and for the rich who only need work? Or just where does science enter a drug store?

That drugs, cures in general, began in and with magical practices I need not again emphasize. But it does seem astounding that as late as 1779 an amnion should be advertised in the *London Times* —price twenty guineas; and that as late as 1848 an amnion had a market value of six guineas. Why a hundred dollars for a fœtal membrane? Because amnions then were not merely fœtal membranes but "lucky hoods"—or, as they were called in Italy, "Virgin Mary's little shirt." They were *sacred*; the child *must* wear one. Midwives bought them. A lawyer wore one concealed as a lucky charm. It was *good* medicine! Drug stores have carried tons of medicine not so good.

I have no statistics, but I infer that this country consumes tons and tons of drugs a year. I infer that no matter what your ailment, you can get from one to one hundred different prescriptions, each in some one's opinion a *cure*. I also infer that the more obscure the nature of your disease, the larger the variety of prescriptions available and the wider the divergence of the ingredients. I also infer that most people judge their family physician by his promptness in prescribing something that can be had only from a drug store or from his own now almost obsolete medicine-chest. I know, for I can see with my own eyes, that the drug store is not what it used to be; but is it better, and if so, how much better, than Galen's drug store on Sacred Street in the Eternal City?

The drug store of my boyish days had, among other things, magic extracts of syrups, and gilded, silvered, and sugar-coated pills. The syrups were organic; the pills were strange compounds of both organic and inorganic substances. That drug store was not a lineal descendant of Galen's, but it was not unlike Avicenna's pharmacy, which went up in smoke with Galen when Paracelsus made a public exhibition of his swelled head. Avicenna was a pharmacologist; Paracelsus, an alchemist.

Avicenna was one of the three greatest of all Islamic physicians; Cumston thinks there possibly never was a more facile or wider intelligence—or more precocious and indefatigable. Christian Europe was centuries catching up with his *Canon*—and with Rhazes' *Continens* and Avenzoar's *Assistance*.

Had not religious scruples prevented Islamic physicians from performing autopsies, medicine might have passed more quickly from mediæval Salerno and Montpellier to modern medical science. They were not ignorant of anatomy, but they did not know enough anatomy to support sound reasoning in physiology. That they reasoned as clearly as they did on such knowledge as they had, is a tribute to their level-headedness. Some of them certainly knew more anatomy than Galen—and as one of them said, "If anatomical knowledge be ignored, mistakes will be made and the patient will be killed." The fact that they distinguished between a patient dying and being killed may account for their high repute in and out of Spain.

It also accounts partly for their pharmacology. When they did not know what a drug would do, they tried it out on the dog— or, still better, on a monkey. "I noted that he twisted and clenched his teeth and grasped his belly with his hands," etc.—and that the monkey did not die. It was hard on the monkey, but it was the beginning of experimental medicine, which today tries it not only on monkeys, but on dogs, cats, rabbits, and guinea-pigs. For finding the action of a drug on the abdomen, a monkey is far handier than a dog.

To the Greeks, opium was a very dangerous drug. The Arabs experimented with it, and in their hands it became one grand cure for pain. They even used it as it was used when *Castoria* was a coughing child. Opium will stop a cough and put a child to sleep—and children certainly used to cry for it!

Opium stops coughing, but is it a cure for a cough; does it treat a symptom or a disease? It will put me to sleep, but will it cure my insomnia? But what is insomnia, or cough, or disease? I raise these questions merely to point out again the difference between medicine as art and as science—and between a body that functions normally under normal conditions and abnormally when conditions make for disease. The Arab physicians could see far enough, at any rate, to know that drugs do not *preserve* health; also that drugs could be abused, that their continued use would lessen or break down natural resistance.

When Dr. Sanman gives me a drug I presume he knows just what the drug is and just what it will do to me. But does he, or rather, *can* he, know? There must be a lot of faith on both sides: on my part, in him (which is easy, for I have had good luck with him); on his part, in the soundness of his medical education in general, in the honesty of the drug itself, and in me. Patients are notorious liars about themselves and careless about taking their medicine. When he prescribes a certain drug, it may be on the supposition that certain specific foods or liquids or drugs are already in my stomach, intestines, or blood.

Again, there is no use in my using ultra-violet rays to supply Vitamin D if I freeze to death for lack of infra-red rays; nor of giving me insulin for my diabetes if I become so absorbed in writing a book that I forget to replace my broken syringe.

A patient or a community can get the full benefit of a physician's intelligence only if it is accepted and applied intelligently. We suffer from this or that, catch this or that, die from this or that, because *we* are at fault, and not the art of the physician or the science of medicine.

Picking a physician or a drug, like choosing a wife or a president, is less an exact science than picking a motor-car or a radio set. Clarity on this point, it seems to me, is an asset to intelligent thinking—not only about individual health, but about social diseases as well.

Further, sound thinking about drugs for any ailment and cures for any disease just now is not easy, because we live in a mixed haze of primitive superstition and childish faith, unscrupulous charlatanism and sincere scientific efforts to discover the materials medical science needs for a sound *materia medica*.

There can be no sound therapeutics until pharmacy is a fine art and pharmacology an exact science. And that time is yet far off—how far may best be seen by reviewing such progress as has been made and understanding how it has been made.

Note, please, that *therapeutics* (the art of medicine) does not necessarily imply a drug store. Many a prayer, many a faith healer, has done what no pharmacist could do. Mondeville's fourteenth-century counsel was for its time good medicine: "Keep up your patient's spirits by music of viols and ten-stringed psaltery, or by forged letters describing the death of his enemies, or by telling him that he has been elected to a bishopric, if a churchman."

Witches are as real to people who believe in witches as is a pathogenic bacterium, and they can kill. If I, a denizen of a Congo forest, am bewitched, I am as good as dead: no Hippocrates need apply; I want a witch-doctor—and the best the Congo affords. The medicine most of us want is the medicine that will put us at our ease, and most of us learnt the magic touch of a gentle hand, the soothing sound of a reassuring voice—and we learnt it early. And if we learnt to depend on laying on of gentle hands and soothing voices, a competent Reader can perform wonders.

Power of mind over matter, it is often called; also Christian Science. But let us be reasonable and keep our feet on the ground. Miracles can be performed, and are daily and by thousands—and in Christian Science churches as well as at Lourdes, St. Anne de Beaupré, and in the Congo. Any good witch-doctor can cure a witch. Witches and similar "diseases" have been cured by the million for thousands of years.

Nature—time, food, etc.—has power to restore not only broken hearts but broken bones. Of course the heart may never again be as good as new—no heart is; and the bone might heal straighter with a splint. And so the ages-old search for restorers, prolongers, rejuvenators. In that search, which circled the globe and tried everything, discoveries were made. Thus there grew up what is called *empirical* medicine.

In empirical medicine there need be, and generally is, no *known* connexion between disease and drug. I suffer, for example, from gout. What is gout—a disease, or a symptom of high living? One thing is certain—with gout I am far from easy. I want ease. What does the physician prescribe? It depends on the physician and on my age, pocket-book, etc.; but in general he prescribes some *physical* medicine—massage, heat, etc.—and some *material* medicine—a drug, such as lithium salts or arsenic or colchicum.

Colchicum, let us say—meadow saffron. The "active principle" of its seed and stalk is a bitter alkali. Fed to dogs or apes, it produces symptoms not unlike those of pure mercury; but, unlike mercury, the distressing abdominal symptoms mean death. A half grain of colchicum, the active principle, is fatal to man and beast. Why have it in the drug store?—there are plenty of other poisons. Because in small doses, say one one-hundredth of a grain, it has been found useful in gout. Why in gout? Just because; experience; empiricism. It is empirical therapeutics. It does not always work; it does not necessarily work. It is also a good example of the pains man has taken to ransack field, forest, and all outdoors, for cures.

Take meadow saffron again. What else is it but a drug? Well, it is a plant, and every plant has carbohydrates—cellulose, sugar, starch, or gum, etc. These may be excellent foods, but they have no pharmacologic action. Besides these common chemicals in common combinations, thousands of plants contain oils, resins, balsams, ferments, alkaloids, acids, and toxins. From these, organic drugs are extracted and compounded, and dispensed as vinegars, waters, solutions, decoctions, infusions, syrups, elixirs, spirits, wines, honeys, lotions, extracts, masses, pills, powders, lozenges, ointments, and plasters.

They are administered by the mouth or by inhalation, or by the hypodermic needle and syringe into tissue; or, if still quicker action is desired, directly into a vein, which puts the drug into circulation throughout the body in half a minute. Through mouth and alimentary canal, drugs may not take effect for hours. Alcohol, among certain other drugs, does not take so long; most of it never passes beyond the stomach. Drugs are also administered per rectum and by inunction—but it takes a thin skin to get fat from "skin foods."

What do these drugs cure? Most of them, nothing. They do not pretend to cure; they *act* on something—and the something is generally a system and not a disease. Roughly, they are stimulants or depressants or excitants—on heart-beat, pulse rate, on various parts of the nervous system, brain, spinal cord, motor nerves, sensory nerves, sympathetic nerves, etc.; or vaso-constrictors and -dilators; or digestives, cathartics, or diuretics, tonics, etc.

Because they act thus and so on this or that system or part of a system, they are applied in treating diseases of this or that system: circulation, digestion, respiration, nervous system, genito-urinary, skin, etc.

So far, not much of this would have been Greek to an Arab physician of Bagdad, Cairo, or Cordova. They created pharmacy; they created the pharmacist—and, as I said before, put him under government control as to the prices and quality of his wares. The Krabadin, or Islamic Codex, was a mediæval forerunner of the big *Text-Book of Therapeutics* before me.

Avicenna had no stethoscope with which to explore the chest, for that did not come into use until Lænnec in 1818 reported his results; nor did he have absorbent-cotton dressings for wounds, for they were invented by Guérin in 1866; nor did he have a hypodermic syringe, although both principle and syringe have long been well known to every cobra and copperhead. Man did not inject drugs under the skin until Rynd started it in 1845, and Pravaz so popularized the syringe that it still bears his name and is the most popular instrument in the dentist's office.

There are, of course, many more non-drug remedial measures available to physicians than were known to mediæval medicine; electricity, for example, and radium and X-rays, and a large assortment of gadgets by which the physician looks into our eyes, ears, nose, sinuses, stomach, and other dark and gloomy recesses of our anatomy. Also new and costly ways of letting blood, puncturing the spine, and flooding us with sunlight at midnight.

Actinotherapy, radiotherapy, röntgenothedapy, were then, of course, in the lap of the gods. But Avicenna and his times were up on opotherapy and organotherapy; in fact, they were more justified in prescribing dried fox's lung for asthma than most of the drugs prescribed for that affliction at the beginning of the twentieth century. A fox is a long-distance runner; he must have long-winded lungs. Dry the lungs and feed them to a breathless patient. When they prescribed fresh bone marrow and fresh blood for anæmia they anticipated Minot, and that was a real triumph for empirical therapeutics. But to infer that a diet of dried kidney will cure kidney trouble, or that eating dried gonads will cure old age, is like attempting to cure idiocy with a diet of brains.

The difference between organotherapy and chemotherapy is the difference between mediæval and modern medicine. Chemistry then was alchemy; it is a science today. Chemotherapy is just beginning to struggle up on to a scientific foundation. Must it advance little by little, even as Hippocrates said, and not reach its highest point "until a great number of generations have come and gone," or can advance be speeded up, as the attainment of other human goals has been hastened, by the application of more scientific methods?

That is a real question, and possibly the most serious of those on which hangs the future of the human race. Before looking at it, however, let us be more explicit about Avicenna's drug store.

Was there in it any specific drug for any specific disease? It did have drugs, honest drugs, known tried-and-true drugs, drugs which were used by the Egyptians and by the Greeks, and drugs which the Arabs themselves added to the pharmacopœia, drugs which are drugs today, drugs in daily use and found in official pharmacopœias; laxatives such as rhubarb, senna, and cassia; stimulants such as *nux vomica* and camphor, and aconite, and Indian hemp, colocynth, santal, ergot, and sulphates of copper and iron, many metallic oxides, silver nitrate, sulphuric and nitric acid, and alcohol. I emphasize this point because it helps to emphasize another: the Islamic pharmacy was mostly pharmacologically sound.

The toe bone of a saint may "cure"; ground and put up as pills, it may still pass as "medicine"; but as a matter of fact it is as inert in a human alimentary canal as powdered coal or horse hair.

Potatoes used to bring fancy prices in Europe—not for their starch or food value, but as *medicine*. A sick ambassador of Queen Elizabeth to France was given a mixture of musk, amber, gold, pearl, and unicorn—and if some brick dust, sawdust, mummy dust, and

Pittsburgh soot had been added, he would have died just the same. Such stuff is not a drug—though it may be a drug on the market. We eat our peck of dirt and live. It passes through us no more changed, nor more changing us, than the pennies and grape seeds we swallowed in childhood. Arsenic, ergot, and alcohol are drugs; they act on us; they are pharmacological stuffs.

The Arab physician did not prescribe mummy dust. Christian Europe did—even into the seventeenth century; and when the genuine article was scarce, they went to the gallows for their raw material. Unicorn's horn was the prize remedy of the Middle Ages. It was good for all sorts of ailments, and was an antidote for poison. Pope Clement VII's present to his niece Catherine de' Medici on her marriage to the Dauphin of France was a scrap of unicorn horn—to destroy poisons in food!

There is no unicorn; there are narwhals. Narwhal's "horn," elephant's ivory, and our own ivories are all the same material; but in the *materia medica* of superstition they may range in value from a nickel to a thousand dollars a pound. If Henry II's constable, Montmorency, had but known it, he might just as well have sent the king's daughter a chip off his ivory-headed cane as a piece of unicorn horn to cure her smallpox. Even that good sceptic, Robert Boyle, kept the sole of an old shoe in his pharmacopœia; ground fine and taken internally, it was good for dysentery!

A favourite Middle Age "remedy" was crocodile dung. The drug stores complained that the importers were adulterating it! Cardinal Richelieu on his deathbed drank a mixture of horse dung and white wine prescribed by a charlatan. Urine as a mouth-wash for toothache was a good eighteenth-century remedy—and quite likely will be prescribed in the twenty-eighth century if man does not get over his something-must-be-done-about-it, try-this habit.

Even spices, according to Haggard, were put into circulation as drugs and not as condiments. They came to be rated so highly that their control was the chief factor in the long struggle for the Eastern trade—not in *spices*, but in *drugs* worth more than gold. Aloes, opium, pepper, sandalwood, rhubarb, cloves, and nutmegs were the prizes Genoa, Venice and Portugal fought for. For a century Lisbon was the drug capital of the world; then the Dutch; and, after "torrents of blood shed for the inoffensive clove," the English.

If Europe of the seventeenth century A.D. had embalmed her dead as carefully as Egypt of the seventeenth B.C., what a sweet mess of drug-store goods could be had from rich, noble, and royal viscera! Charles II after a convulsion was separated from a pint of blood, then gave up eight ounces more by the "cupping" process. He was then given an emetic and a purgative, and another purgative. He then had room for an enema—of antimony, sacred bitters, rock salt, mallow leaves, violets, beet root, camomile flowers, fennel seed, linseed, cinnamon, cardamom seed, saffron, cochineal, and aloes.

But that is less than half the torture forced upon that dying man by physicians set on "leaving no stone unturned." They certainly overlooked no bet, for before they finally killed him there had been added to his internal collection melon seeds, manioc, slippery elm, black-cherry water, extract of flowers of lime, lily-of-the-valley, peony, lavender, gentian root, extract of thistle leaves, mint, rue, angelica, nutmeg, quinine, cloves, dissolved pearls, and extract of a human skull! Also doses of "Raleigh's antidote"—compounded of dozens of herbs and animal extracts. His head was shaved and blistered; he was given sneezing powder and "brain-strengthening" powder; and a plaster of pitch and pigeon's dung was put on his foot.

That was the best medicine could do for royalty in 1685; no wonder Charles turned Catholic as a last resort! In 1860 Oliver Wendell Holmes, in a passage quoted by Haggard, said that— opium, wine, anæsthetics, and "a few specifics which our art did not discover," excepted—he firmly believed that if the whole *materia medica* then in use "could be sunk to the bottom of the sea, it would be all the better for mankind and all the worse for the fishes."

The great merit of Holmes was that he did not, like Paracelsus or Hahnemann, propose a new and equally fantastic set of drugs or system of therapy. His remedy was sweeping: sack the lot, except opium, wine (a food, he called it), anæsthetics, and a few specifics. And the opinion he voiced signalized the enormous seventeenth to nineteenth century change in attitude toward drugs.

That that 1860 attitude has not been put into general circulation is, of course, not because of any compassion for the fishes, but because a *drug* store is a drug *store*, and its business is not the betterment of mankind, but to carry and dispense the drugs the public wants. It is conceivable that if all Sunday schools substituted Haggard's *Devils, Drugs, and Doctors* or Clendening's *Human Body* for the Holy Bible as a text-book, it would be all the better for mankind; but who is brave enough to suggest the move, and how is such a suggestion going to be received by Sunday-school teachers and Bible publishers? Think of Congress making such a proposal, or even one congressman! And then think of what the drug interests did and do to a law, not to throw drugs out, but merely to make them honest; and of what the Bible interests have done and are doing to Congress, and to anyone who proposes sweet reason as a humane substitute for sour religion.

What are the "few specifics" Holmes mentioned? Mercury for syphilis, and quinine for malaria, seem to be specifics—chemically known drugs for physically known diseases. Digitalis is good for heart disease; but what is heart disease? Also, what is digitalis? "Galenic" digitalis is one thing, or rather several things, such as digitoxin, digitalin, digitonin, and other "principles" the modern chemist wrings from "galenic" extracts, fluid extracts, tinctures, etc. To discover all the active principles in all galenic preparations has been a huge task and impossible without modern chemistry.

Holmes would also have included colchicum for gout, iodine for goitre, and ipecac for dysentery. But, as is now known, there is dysentery and dysentery, goitre and goitre, gout and gout. For example, certain kinds of dysentery are now presumed to be due to certain specific microörganisms not unlike those which seem to thrive in our mouth without endangering our health. But the *dysenteric amœba* is a tropical beast. The best cure for that germ is to kill it in boiling water. Once lodged in the human intestine, ipecac is the only known specific. And that it is specific is only empirically known.

Goitre is not a specific disease; it is a symptom of abnormal thyroid. The thyroid is a gland, and its business is to find iodine in our food and secrete it as the body needs it. Iodine is no longer the drug it used to be, for the chemist now makes the drug the thyroid should make.

Before we look at these marvels of modern biochemistry, or chemotherapeutics, let us look at the drug store's bible—the U. S. P., as it is called, or the U. S. Pharmacopœia. It is standard and official;

it does for drugs what a cook-book does for foods. Started in 1820, it is the oldest of all modern national pharmacopœias. It is revised every ten years by a national committee and presumably ranks high among the best sellers, for there are nearly sixty thousand drug stores in the United States—or one to less than three physicians, or six times as many in proportion to our population as in Germany.

Any possible connexion between our wealth of drug stores and our poverty of contribution to the list of important drugs made available during the last fifty years, or between our college population, ten times larger than Germany's, and the fact that we read fewer books than Germany—or than Scandinavia, or France, or Holland? Probably.

The U. S. P. of 1820 is not the U. S. P. of 1930. In one period of thirty years alone, 573 drugs were dropped. But the *Useful Drugs* of the American Medical Association, the largest of its kind in the world, lists 365 drugs—not because there are 365 days in the year, or so many bones in the human body, or so many diseases known to the profession, but because they are considered useful. The World War was waged with fewer munitions. Yet "physicians are criticized for not prescribing more and still more drugs," as Professor Reid Hunt said last year in his presidential address before the U. S. Pharmacopœial convention.

But who does the criticizing—pharmacists, dealers in drugs, or patients greedy for drugs? The most significant fact about the whole drug business, as I see it, is its present chaotic condition; and that, presumably, is inevitable. And will remain so as long as pharmacy is pulled one way by the wants of the medical profession and another way by the panderers to human frailty.

More exact knowledge of disease will be useful in prevention or cure; but, as Hunt says, progress in this topsy-turvy world has not proceeded logically. Smallpox and yellow fever are now effectively controlled—and their causes are yet unknown. Malaria and syphilis were more curable before their cause was known than are pneumonia and tuberculosis, about which much is known. On only a most imperfect knowledge of pathogenic bacteria, Lister revolutionized surgery and medicine.

Nature heals; but with cancer, syphilis, tetanus, amœbic dysentery, yaws, diabetes, hookworm, etc., we may heed Rush's remark—

that nature should be turned out of doors and efficient art substituted.

"Efficient art" formerly came from empiricism, but the drugs which have proved useful in ancient or modern times have been discovered by experiment. Galenic digitalis was good, but digitalis therapy is now a science. Medicine could not cross the line from empiricism to science until organic chemistry made chemotherapy possible.

Some twenty organic compounds are added daily to the 258,000 already described—and every one a *possible* drug; but the physiological effect of not more than three or four thousand is yet known. What a vista is opened up! No one can foretell the effect of this or that organic compound upon this or that group of cells of the human body. Take, for example, methyl alcohol: it will destroy the cells of the retina, causing total blindness, but without injuring any other organ or tissue of the body. Atropine paralyzes the endings of certain nerves of the sympathetic system. Quinine finds and destroys the organisms of malaria. Emetine, the alkaloid of ipecac, goes after the amœba of dysentery. A chemotherapy may even be discovered for cancer before its cause is known.

*Selective* action. Finding drugs which, put into the human body, perform like animals trained to ferret out and slay other animals. Our body is an affair of biochemicals, regulated in growth, in rate of growth, in sex, colour of skin, rate of metabolism, in immunity to toxins and proteins, etc., by drugs. Our body secretes these drugs. One gland secretes one drug, another another. We have many drug-secreting glands, and are, as Barker said, the beneficiaries and the victims of the chemical correlation of their secretions.

Many of these glands, and among them the most important, are not only physiologically but even anatomically new. To lay them bare in all their import has required the combined efforts of thousands of investigators, and the story is yet far from complete. Some of the drugs they secrete are of astounding potency, but equally astounding is the fact that they can be and are made or synthesized by the organic chemist.

Ehrlich's discovery of "606" has been called a happy accident, and so in a way was Wöhler's discovery of urea; but Ehrlich was no accident, nor was Wöhler: they were *chemists*. The great merit of

Ehrlich was his aiming high and from a broad and firm foundation. Nearly thirty years ago he declared that the future of medicine lay in pharmacology—chemotherapy. He could not have gone so far ("606" is only incidental in his great work) in laying the foundations of a new science had he not had a chemically-minded nation behind him. The great modern contributions to scientific therapy—the arsphenamines, cocaines, and other local anæsthetics, the effective hypnotics, all the pain-killers, the salicylates, the nitrites, bromides, antitoxins, most of the antiseptics—came mostly from Germany. Even today, says Hunt, there is "scarcely a university pharmacological laboratory in the United States the equal of a number in Germany forty or even fifty years ago," nor an institute "comparable to the one founded for Ehrlich at Frankfort."

We had talked of preparedness, but when we entered the World War we had no local anæsthetics, no modern arsenicals, and few hypnotics. We have now, and make our own dyes besides; but the control of the manufacture and sale of drugs by chain stores is not likely to hurry the progress of chemotherapeutics.

Last year, in a Congo village of 126 people, 83 went down with sleeping sickness—a terrible, lingering death. Tryparsamide was injected. Within one year the 83 were fully convalescent. And that is just one little story, one tiny drop in the ocean of joy the human race owes to the modern organic chemist, to chemotherapy.

Homicide, insecticide, germicide, bactericide; Trypanosoma, trypanocidal. It is the *cide* (cædere) that kills; the *ide* is the chemist's way of conveying definite information about compounds: tryparsamide is trypanocidal for trypanosomes. Now, just as there are many ways of killing a *Homo*, so there are many ways of killing Trypanosoma. One way, of course, would be to kill man, its host, but that would be almost like destroying the earth to get rid of a man. That is just what was done for years to prevent the spread of sleeping sickness over large areas of Central Africa: destroy all the animals not already destroyed, remove all the people not yet dead, and clear the area of all vegetation. But think of having to resort to such drastic measures to stop the spread of plague, smallpox, etc. It is still a moot question, I believe, whether or not certain areas of Africa should be stripped of game, fauna, and flora, and the human population removed elsewhere, to check the spread of one of the most terrible diseases known to man.

One step further. Trypanosomes—like the *treponema pallidum* of syphilis—are not bacteria; they are minute single-celled protozoa. Protozoology is one of the new biologic sciences, and like bacteriology dependent on the sharp-eyed microscope to bring the facts to light.

How many kinds of protozoa there are is not yet known; hundreds of genera are known, and of these many are known to lead a parasitic life and to be more or less fatal to their host. Presumably, not all species of the more or less deadly amœbas or trypanosomes are yet known to science; certainly not all species of bacteria are yet known. Search for such enemies of the human race is quite as important as search for poles or polo ponies, and any nation whose Safety First campaign omits provision for extending knowledge in such fields must depend on nations which do make provision, when the cry goes forth, "Save me, or I perish!"

We think ourselves tremendously smart in being able to lend a hand to remaining pestilential areas of the earth; and so we are, but we should remind ourselves that we too used to be plagued by malignant contagious diseases, that we went through one only recently, and that we have no guarantee about anything save death and taxes. As it is, our domesticated plants and animals are far from free of destructive parasites—nor conceivably ever will be. The fight has only begun. Munitions are fine, but what use are munitions if we do not know who our enemies are and what their habits? The more exact that knowledge, the easier it will be to discover ways of destroying them.

Munitions. We of this country need no barricade against Trypanosoma, nor have we personal use for munitions against it. We are *immune*; but our immunity proceeds from the fact that the carrier of trypanosomes, the *tsetse* fly, which carries the germs from the dying to the living or from the infected to the non-infected, is not native to this continent. We have no guarantee, however, that this continent will never be invaded by a tsetse fly or something just as good. I presume we always shall maintain a quarantine against certain specific foreign parasites harmful to our fauna or flora.

Man seems to be naturally immune from certain organisms fatal to certain plants and animals. From certain other pathogenic organisms we *acquire* immunity, either by surviving an attack or by a specific anti-bacterial treatment. Thus, having had smallpox, we acquire immunity. We also acquire immunity by exposing ourselves ("vaccination") to cowpox—the same disease once removed. The cow seems to slow down the virulence of the disease—as a cotton vest may slow down a bullet. Smallpox is *variola*; cowpox is *varioloid*. For many diseases, *passive* immunity may be acquired by vaccines or by serums—*antitoxins*, or specific *antibodies*.

A few years ago it seemed that the business of bringing bodily resistance to infection had been established on a sound basis; and so it may be. At any rate, Immunology was born, as little sister to Bacteriology. And look at those children now! Merely to relate the *Newer Knowledge of Bacteriology and Immunology*, editor Jordan called upon eighty-two authorities from all parts of the world; and they took twelve hundred large pages to tell their story of progress. Since Pasteur, Koch, and Ehrlich? During the past *ten* years! What a book!

Well, one thing seems certain: vaccine-therapy and serum-therapy are not so simple as they seemed. And why? Because, as Manwaring says, no man is a hundred per cent biochemically pure. In other words, I am as "specific" as the specific *antibody* which may be injected into my arm to immunize me from a specific foreign *body*, an "organized colony of dominant human colloids, biochemical echoes of ancient and mediæval infections, ceremoniously adopted personal diseases, and incompletely homologized undigested dinners." Before an antibody can become specifically fitted to me, my specificity must be determined.

Four specific diphtheria antibodies have been discovered in the last three years. No one yet knows that any one of them is identically the same as the antibody my body would form were I down with diphtheria.

Looks discouraging, doesn't it? It must be for the young, conscientious medical student. But this Newer Knowledge, as I, a layman, see it, is as epochal a step in man's scientific progress as any ever made.

That medicine, biology, all the sciences dealing with the phenomena of life and death, are still cursed with pagan, mediæval,

Christian and Mid-Victorian physiology, is inevitable. That they will remain under that curse indefinitely is not so inevitable.

Neither philosophy, metaphysics, nor religion has yet satisfied man's quest for an answer to the Whither, Whence, and Why; biology may not, nor is it its business, but it can today tell us enough of the Whithers and Hows to make the Whences seem senile and the Whys childish. And once really divorced from pagan and Christian magic and mysticism, and from Mid-Victorian idealism and pietism, what a future opens up for biophysics and biochemistry, and for the security of the human race as long as the sun shines in the heavens and the earth keeps rolling along!

### X

1492. Columbus: *America.*

1543. Copernicus: *De Revolutionibus.*

1543. Vesalius: *De Humani Corporis Fabrica.*

1930. Ransdell Bill; National Institute of Health established in Washington as successor to the Hygienic Laboratory of the Public Health Service; $750,000 appropriated for new building; and a gift (No. 1) by the Chemical Foundation of $100,000 to endow "basic chemical research."

Loud cheers; great progress; "the most forward step ever taken by the American Government;" civilization at last on a scientific foundation; war declared on disease; Washington, the clearing-house of health for all the world.

War claims its millions, disease its tens of millions. Having won the war to make the world safe for morons, we shall now wage war to keep the morons healthy. A Napoleon of science is to lead an army of scientist experts in medicine, pharmacy, physics, biology, bacteriology, pharmacology, dentistry, and allied professions, against invading microbes and disorganized body functions.

With that war won, no more common colds, which now cause more deaths and economic waste than any other disease; no more influenza, measles, pneumonia, tuberculosis, cancer, childbed sickness, infantile paralysis, Bright's disease, anæmia, heart lesions, venereal diseases, leprosy, or malaria. Preventable diseases alone cost us over two billions a year; the economic value of the lives sacrificed to ignorance and neglect is six billion dollars more; the human repair bill runs to a billion more. 2+6+1=9. Nine billion dollars. Enough money to dignify a war debt.

I learn further from Senator Copeland's pamphlet that the "intent of the Act is to promote the health of human beings, improve their earning capacity, reduce their living expenses, increase their happiness and prolong their lives." And that, while our federal government in five years spent *four* million dollars in the study of human beings' diseases, it spent *fifty-four* studying hog and hominy diseases. The inference is that it is now sold on the idea of fighting human as well as animal and plant diseases, has arranged for a building, and has already collected $100,000 in the contribution plate.

I do not mean to be flippant about a vitally serious subject, and I feel almost like joining Mr. Garvan of the Chemical Foundation in gratitude to Senator Ransdell for the long forward stride taken for the good health of the country—"in so far as it lies within the will of God." Why the string to the gratitude? Without the string, yes—and without qualification; with it . . . Well, money for a research which is to underwrite the nation's health, but only in so far as God wills, is, it seems to me, tainted money.

For this reason. But let me say first that neither Mr. Garvan nor the Chemical Foundation enters this discussion in a personal manner at all. I know next to nothing about the Chemical Foundation, nothing at all about its president. They are as impersonal as the Holy Catholic Church or Paracelsus. Mr. Garvan is, or was, according to *Who's Who*, a Catholic, a trustee of the Catholic University, a member of the Catholic Club, and presumably orthodox. And if the Reverend John A. Ryan of the Catholic University may speak for Catholics (and if I correctly interpret his article on Catholicism and Liberalism in the *Nation* of August 6, 1930), Mr. Garvan's only way of finding out how far my future good health hangs on the National Health Institute or the will of God, is the Holy See. "It is wrong for a Catholic to disregard the authority which Christ has conferred upon the Church. The thinking and the reading which the Church forbids is, generally speaking, harmful to true faith and to sound morality."

But what is true faith and sound morality—or good health? How may one find out? How can one ascertain the truth or falsity of the *fact* implied in the "which Christ has conferred upon the Church"? Was such authority actually conferred? Is there a historic fact behind that calm implication? May one go to the authorities for evidence? Yes, if one goes to such books as the Church accepts as authoritative. But one may not read such authorities as the Church puts on its Index of Prohibited Books, as, for example, Gibbon's *Rome*, Darwin's *Species*, the *Book of Common Prayer*, or Bertrand Russell's *Marriage and Morality*. One may not even send one's children to schools where the truth or falsity of such books may be investigated. In short, within a year Catholics have been *forbidden* to read certain books, *commanded* to send their children to certain schools.

What has all this to do with health or the National Institute of Health? Directly, nothing; indirectly, everything. Absolutism in religion makes for good religion; acceptance of the Church's "unconditional authority"—imperative for all good Catholics—to lay down the principles of faith and morals, and the rules for testing the validity of faith and what the morals fit one for, makes for superstition.

I can see how a good Catholic might make a good president of a Chemical Foundation; but blind acceptance of any authority never made a good chemist. A chemist today may not know what to think about a chemical experiment which has gone wrong, but if he attributes failure to God's interference, he is not likely to find out how to make an experiment go straight.

There is no absolutism in science, and progress has been made despite authority. That we make rapid progress today is because the pace is so fast that no one authority occupies the throne long enough to become sacrosanct. Absolute—as Truth or as Authority—ends, like perfectly logical conclusions, in nihilism, just where it began. Absolutism in religion is and must be as dangerous to sound ideas in health and disease as absolutism in government is and must be inimical to sound ideas in economic and social values. But no Mussolini can be so deadly to the scientific attitude on which future advance in civilization depends as a Pontifex Maximus.

But let us look further at this Health Institute. Let us grant that a nation going in for health, a national research for knowledge of the nature of the enemies of health, is a unique move. Let us grant, further, that the Institute sooner or later removes cancer, pernicious anæmia, Bright's disease, and kindred ailments from the dread category of incurable to curable diseases; that infantile paralysis, influenza, and pneumonia are no longer as fatal as they were a century ago—are, in fact, not fatal at all. Grant all this, and where are we?

Well, the economic welfare of the country will be promoted, says Senator Copeland; there will be fewer broken hearts and fewer broken lives. Necessarily? Science conceivably may stock every corner drug store with the necessary chemical bullets to slay every known angel of death, whether in the guise of a specific microör-ganism or the failure of a specific vital organ or gland to function: will that scientific victory necessarily promote economic welfare or reduce the number of broken hearts or broken lives? In my humble opinion, it will not. The victories of science cannot become the victories of society—though they may be of a special section or class of society—until society is educated up to the point of being able to profit by the victories.

Are we as a community, a society, a commonwealth, a nation, organized to educate toward that point? Let there be no mistake: just as long as our educators must put patriotism, creed, or any special interest or spiritual authority above honesty and strict and impartial respect for ascertained or ascertainable truth, we must expect to go on as we have been for millenniums, handing down infantile beliefs and senile attitudes toward life, health, happiness, and social justice.

"An epoch in the history of welfare legislation." So was the Eighteenth Amendment to the Constitution. Welfare legislation which is not an expression of public opinion grounded in welfare habits of thought, speech, bodily action, and cultural attitudes, is simply more jobs for lawyers, doctors, nostrum-venders, and undertakers. I may be wrong, but I cannot see how a National Institute of Health could possibly serve ignorance, Christian Scientists, Catholics, Theosophists, Spiritualists, or Fundamentalists, of whom we have millions. Why not? They do not want to be served. Painless dentistry probably, and possibly antiseptic surgery in removing facial blemishes, tonsils, adenoids, and vermiform and caudal appendices; but the truth about healthy ways of living, about the fundamental facts of life, about the findings of the biologic, psychologic, social, or historic sciences—no.

Are venereal diseases social diseases, and is society prepared to take a scientific attitude toward them? Are ignorance and poverty social diseases, or are they merely limitations to social health and inherent in human nature, so ordered by the inscrutable will of God? Are the crimes and lunacies of ignorance, poverty, and greed, social diseases, and if so, how can they be cured? Are they preventable, and whose business is it to cure or prevent them?

We should remind ourselves that lunacy and crime have been torn from Satanic hands within the last hundred years. That both are products of psychological causes and social environment, is a modern idea, and not yet in general circulation. In this connexion we may recall the words of the Massachusetts preacher who was trying to account for the "present [1799] licentiousness of youth." It was not, he said, *wholly* to be attributed to reigning infidelity, nor to the pernicious example of unprincipled men; *"much is owing to parental negligence."*

Agencies now at work will discover the *nature* of cancer, let us say, on July 4, 1935; are there any agencies at work which will make it unlikely, or even more unlikely, that on that day there will be any less demand for the services of faith healers, or for new kinds of faith healers, or for new books on astrology, mysticism, and spiritualism, or for the latest wares of the most up-to-date alchemist? None that I can discover. But I can discover more books on astrology, mysticism, theosophism, spiritualism, and more of the wares of the alchemist in my home town than I could have discovered in Nero's Rome. And it is not because more New Yorkers are interested in the history of the "occult" sciences, but because there is today more demand for occultism than for history, more demand for magic than for science.

I hope I have not exaggerated; I have not meant to. I simply make the inference that seems warranted from what I see advertised as cures for the failures inevitable to occult striving. The Bible is the perennial best-seller; fake psychology grinds out its large crop of fake successes and pays almost as well as sound fiction. As I view our times, there is nothing that would seriously embarrass Paracelsus if perchance his elixir should restore him to life or prevent him from founding a school or a church and amassing a very tidy fortune. Our laws would protect him, the radio would carry his voice and the mails his doctrine and his nostrums. I doubt if all these blessings of our civilization would be equally open to Margaret Sanger, J. B. S. Haldane, or Bertrand Russell. We are *organized* for Success and for the salvation of souls, but not for the salvation of human lives.

Barnum was no fool; he gave the people what they wanted. That is business; he made it Big Business. But a physician who gives the people what they want is called a quack. Paracelsus is called a quack; he was really an alchemist, a prophet, and a genius.

Born the year after Columbus discovered America, he died two years before Copernicus smashed the macrocosm and Vesalius opened up the microcosm. So we are told; and allowed to infer that alchemy was buried with Paracelsus. Alchemy became chemistry; astrology became astronomy; and *melothesia* (zodiacal man) became anatomy and physiology. True enough, but no human being ever knows as much as that at birth; and while such information is easily acquired today—outside parochial schools—it is not so easy to acquire the habit of living up to the light of the information.

In other words, millions of people live as though chemistry had not superseded alchemy nor astronomy astrology. The chemical age? Yes; but age of astrology, too. Natural man? Yes; but zodiacal man also.

Now, zodiacal man should have given up the ghost with Galen. Did he? Look at any monkish parchment of the Middle Ages. He should have gone out with Vesalius. Did he? Look into any old barber-surgeon handbook, or your grandfather's almanac, or at the latest astrological text-book. It is one thing to discover, after diligent search and research, that there is no possible or plausible causal relationship between the signs of the zodiac and the lines of man's palms, or between the movements of the heavenly bodies and those of human viscera, or between the macrocosm and a microcosm, or between a system of astrology and the findings of biology; it is quite another thing to get these discoveries written into the drama of civilization or to get people to view themselves in the new rôles.

If the history of science, of free thought, of rationalism, or of common sense, teaches anything, it is that anything that makes for freedom—a new discovery, new vista, new inference, new hypothesis or new weapon with which to fight ignorance; or a new light to human understanding and to closer approximation to the truth— no matter how valuable it may be, does not and can not get a hearing, much less a foothold, unless it can be adjusted to the old or substituted for the old. A supergenius may arise to see things with rare insight, but how often does civilization accept the new view and govern itself accordingly? Individual habits are hard enough to change; the inertia of a hundred million people is comparable to that of continental land masses.

Old beliefs are to be laughed at or cherished as priceless heirlooms, but the beliefs that last longest and die hardest are the beliefs which simplify life by postponing, evading, or cheating the realities of life. We laugh at the childish beliefs of the Chaldean astrologers —and order our lives on a set of beliefs as infantile, and cherish them as priceless heirlooms while deluding ourselves that they are scientific because we live in an age of science.

It is the business of a scientist to get on with his discoveries; it is the business of the historian of science to record in chronological order the findings of scientists. I am making it my business here to try to discover why it is that our own civilization is still an asset to quacks and charlatans, knaves and robbers—and thereby a liability to every honest citizen. And among the reasons must be numbered the fact that there are too many predatory agencies and interests—some heavily entrenched, some heavily capitalized— which exist on ignorance and thrive on gullibility. If there is a will of God, there is a limit to learning the ways of nature and a limit to man's responsibility to man. Human society, presumably, must always be a Limited Society, but man himself should respect no limits but those of his own inherent limitations—and just what they are is not yet known.

I do know that I have often marvelled at the progress man has made in substituting simple, honest conclusions for the fanciful beliefs of a too credulous past—and have come to with a start to realize that among us today beliefs no less fanciful nor more grounded in fact form the mainsprings of action of this or that class, this or that church, this or that caste or party. Ignorance prevails because ignorance is valuable to everyone who has a fake to sell. Our selling organization controls the ignorance-dispelling machinery.

If this age is, as we are often told, spiritually bankrupt, it is rich in Spiritualists, Fundamentalists, Christian Scientists, faith healers, vegetarians, and anti-vivisectionists, who with one accord fight medical science and hate biologic science in general. They do not understand science; they think they do understand disease—which is either punishment for sin in general or failure to live according to their "light." Whenever you hear the "spiritually bankrupt" wail, look for the disappointed vender of a nostrum or a spurious brand of ethics.

Among the forces which make for disease must be reckoned those who make a living from ignorance, ranging from the itinerant medicine-man to the chain drug store, from individual food cranks to organized faith healers. It was bad enough in the old pre-science days to suffer epidemics of cholera, etc., for the good of our souls and as punishment for our sins, but why should deaths from tuberculosis cost this nation a billion and a half dollars a year and the care of tubercular victims another eight hundred millions?

It is all to the good that the death rate from tuberculosis within thirty years has decreased from 194 to 79 per hundred thousand; that the death rate from typhoid and paratyphoid has decreased from 34 to 5 per hundred thousand; that deaths from diphtheria have decreased 95 per cent; that cholera, typhus, and yellow fever have almost disappeared; that our death rate has been halved; and that health education alone, according to the report of the American Medical Association, saves the nation three and a half billion dollars a year. But the nation still pays billions of dollars for preventable disease—an appalling toll to negligence, pig-headedness, ignorance.

We still harbor a million sufferers of malaria a year; of tuberculosis, seven hundred thousand; of hookworm, over a million. We still have up to a hundred thousand cases of smallpox in a single year; six thousand deaths from typhoid; nine thousand from diphtheria. And, says Dr. Lyman Wilbur, "thousands of women are sterile or semi-invalids because of gonorrhœa. There is much paralysis, locomotor ataxia, and mental disease, and there are many handicapped children because of syphilis. All of this is correctable, and should be corrected. It is a scientific error, if not a crime, for a child to be born with congenital syphilis." *Crime?* Can a rich nation commit a crime? Then ours must be reckoned among the great criminals of history. A sick list of two millions a day, 365 days of the year—and mostly *preventable*. Too many deaths, too much suffering, from known preventable diseases.

Today we die of heart disease, apoplexy, nephritis, cancer, and pneumonia—all controllable with the application of preventives or with early diagnosis and prompt treatment. Fifty years ago tuberculosis, diphtheria, typhoid, diarrhœa and scarlet fever were the chief causes of death. While these, except tuberculosis, have almost disappeared from among the primary causes of death, they are still too common secondary causes; they leave their unhealed wounds to weaken heart, kidneys, lungs, etc., and lower resistance to new attacks on health.

Why die of any preventable disease? Why subject any child to any contagious disease which, though not fatal, may wound for life? Because medical education must make terms with vested interests which have cures to sell. Because knowledge of method in therapeutics is still at the mercy of theotherapy. Because disease is still related to magic, or to impiety or unbelief, or to God; hence to be treated by rites, incantations, pence, prayer or sacrifice, charity or philanthropy. Because it is easier to take pills than precautions. Because we learn to recognize symptoms and get in the habit of calling on outside help for the remedy—and the average patient's only criterion of a "good" doctor is his ability to apply the remedy neatly and skilfully and without ruffling the patient's feelings.

In short, because we today, like our ignorant ancestors, confound "cures" with medicine, and seek them without the instinct which guides a cat to catnip. Unless medical knowledge becomes more general, unless the young generation can be more thoroughly grounded in the basic principles of health and disease, we shall be between the devil of unscrupulous drug trusts and the deep sea of occultism, either of which would make Middle Age alchemy and Kabala green with envy.

The Lord may give as of old, but he does not take away as regularly as he used to. Godliness may be fine in its place, but in a maternity hospital it must be second to cleanliness. The grimmest page in history was the regularity of childbirth mortality in hospitals in pre-aseptic surgery days; the next grimmest page was the appalling infant mortality. Of all the triumphs of man over nature, that of the discovery of the nature of disease is the greatest. That discovery could not have been made as long as health was in the hands of fake healers, divine or otherwise. That discovery cannot be made really effective until we are so organized socially that it will be as easy and as "good business" for the facts of the biologic sciences to get into circulation as it is for those of the physical sciences.

The family physician can do much and must be the first recourse in disease, and the public health officer can do much to enforce sanitary surroundings. But, as Dr. Emerson has recently pointed out, public health is but the sum of individual health. The family physician is the original health officer; the home, the first and best unit of every health centre.

There has been enormous improvement; but the improvement, while impressive in ratios and percentages, is, after all, only what should have been expected once the nature of such formerly deadly diseases as scarlet fever, diphtheria, diarrhœa, etc., had been discovered. The point is that they are not yet extinct, as they should be. Our cities do not expect to lose lives because of rattlesnakes or wolves: why, then, because of diphtheria or tuberculosis? One should no more expect to be bitten by smallpox these days than by a snake; yet there are fifty thousand cases of smallpox a year in the United States—some years as high as a hundred thousand cases. Influenza, "colds," and pneumonia still plague us, and infantile paralysis and sleeping sickness are as deadly threats as ever; their nature is as yet unknown, but they can be controlled, confined.

Then think of the amount of tuberculosis, syphilis, gonorrhœa, malaria, and hookworm yet roaming about freely. They can be controlled; they should be extinct. They can be extinguished. According to a recent estimate in the *American Journal of Syphilis*, there are over 1,100,000 venereal cases *constantly* under medical care in the United States, costing twenty-one million non-effective days a year. This is a national disgrace.

It is fine, I repeat, to note the progress made in fifty years in checking and controlling disease; nor do I know of anything which better symbolizes this progress than the change which has taken place in women's dress and the changed attitude toward what is or is not ladylike for little girls. But heaven alone knows how soon women will begin to sweep the streets with petticoats and lace their viscera above or below their belts. That a change of attitude has taken place toward food, exercise, rest, play, sex, etc., there can be no doubt. But here again there is no foretelling how soon the pendulum will swing too far in any one direction, or swing back again.

Death from diseases of the nervous system have declined in New York City 85 per cent in fifty years; but deaths from heart disease have increased 187 per cent, from diseases of the arteries 663 per cent, and from diabetes 1,150 per cent! Is this merely a replacement of old enemies by new, asked Dr. Emerson in the *Times*, "strange brutalities crowding out familiar ones?" They are, at any rate, twentieth-century diseases, and we now face a "rapidly increasing array of occupational or industrial diseases, and the accumulating disorders of nutrition—over-indulgence in certain foods, under-indulgence or deficit in certain others."

The average person knows that his motor will not run without certain fuel and some particular care; true, he depends on the filling station and the garage, or on his chauffeur. About his own body or the simple essentials of health he is densely and profoundly ignorant; and after he has violated every rule of right living for fifty years, wonders why his physician cannot perform a miracle and make a new man of him. And when now and then some genius of a physician or dentist does perform the miracle for him, he yells "Robber!" if he is asked to pay for it.

The Black Death lasted ten years less than, and ended three years before the end of, the Hundred Years' War between France and England. One born that year (1453) might *expect* to live eighteen years; born in 1815, thirty-three years; today, sixty years: but only if he survived the first year. It is the first year that is hardest for babies. Fifty years ago it was a four-to-one shot that any baby born in New York would outlast the first year; today it is seventeen to one.

According to the American Child Health Association, the average infant mortality for 1929 in 729 American cities was 66 per thousand births. But in several cities the rate was as low as 42; and even as

low as 15 in one of the smaller cities. In other cities it was as high
as 112, 119, 125; in a Pennsylvania mining town, 157! To the question asked by the New York *World*, "Need so many babies die?"
the answer obviously is, *No*.

Some cities still make cleanliness next to nothing; they harbour
plague spots, disease-breeding centres: ignorance, poverty, over-
crowding, impure water, unwholesome milk, faulty sewage, filth.
A city is as clean as its filthiest alley, as wholesome as its most overcrowded tenement. Man may have a spiritual nature, but he must
be born in physical surroundings; and if those surroundings are
not conducive to sound health and socially useful habits, we may
expect disease and crime, or such a miracle as an intelligent mother
can perform now and then.

How to attain an intelligent attitude toward health and disease
is society's problem, not science's. If every disease-bearing germ were
known by its first name, and if a magic bullet in the form of a
specific drug were known for every such germ, and if the ætiology,
symptomatology, and diagnosis of every such disease were perfected, we might in course of time exterminate the germs—even of
tuberculosis, syphilis, and gonorrhœa; but disease would just as
inevitably follow excess as it does now. Sunstroke, frost-bite, gluttony in food or drink, and malnutrition—from insufficient diet or
ceaseless worries, rages, etc.—are excesses that make for disease
and death.

There is such a science as hygiene; its laws are not to be violated
with impunity. Hygiene and war are incompatible, and always have
been; hygiene and poverty can form no enduring alliance; but
with dark, damp squalour there can be no hygiene at all. For
Hygieia, as the Greeks knew well, is the daughter of Æsculapius,
son of Apollo, god of light, healer and saviour of men, and protector of crops from blight, mildew, and vermin.

What percentage of Americans have the slightest notion that
there is anything *new* in the belief that such a disease as diphtheria
is due to a specific living organism? Most people, I suspect, accept
the existence of diphtheria and germs as naïvely as they do thun-
derstorms and fevers. The proportion of people who think of
cyclones in terms of God's wrath, and who call in a priest instead
of the family doctor, is less than it was a few years ago. It is one

thing to live in an age of motor-cars, radios, and antitoxin serums, but why call this a scientific age if it lacks the two essentials of scientific advance—proper respect for facts, and willingness to abide by them? It is astounding that between such respect and willingness there has been a three-thousand-year-old barrier: a God built in the image of man who talked like a paranoiac with delusions of grandeur and demanded that men act like obedient morons. That barrier is down; God has become nature; man has become considerably less than the angels, but has already outsoared and may even outlive them.

We speak of "safeguarding society" and impress upon our children the necessity of shunning bad company and avoiding debt, while school and church add their injunctions; yet how many parents or wage-earners are alive to the seriousness of bad health or know anything of the risk to health inherent in certain occupations?

Is it not, asks Dr. Emerson, as important that our suicide rate for each hundred thousand has increased from five to nineteen, as that the death rate from diabetes has increased at about the same rate?

Can the probabilities of stealing and truancy be estimated on the basis of today's records of boys who have motherless homes or breakfastless mornings? Why is it less the province of a doctor of public health to concern himself with the incidence of temper tantrums than with the prevalence of rickets in a community? If half of the boys who get into trouble with the police have suffered from bad companionship, is that not as important a social fact demanding preventive community expenditures as that half the babies who die of diarrhœa and enteritis had unpasteurized milk?

"Safeguarding society." By frowning on females in white robes who tell fortunes by cards; or by fawning on males in black robes in tax-exempt churches who dispense absolution from guilt of crime, hold the keys to heaven and hell, promise rewards in heaven for slights on earth, and in God's name declare what is and is not sin?

We need a complete and thorough overhauling of our notions about health and disease. And in that process every notion which today rates economic above biologic, spiritual above vital, supernatural above natural, superhuman above human, values, must be swept away. Every business, I care not how big or how high-powered its advertising salesmanship, which takes a predatory attitude toward public welfare and thrives on ignorance and gullibility, is a public enemy.

Health is wealth; to put wealth before health is to put the cart before the horse. There can be no sound foundation for enduring national health until sex love, family affection, and conception have been freed from any taint of sin and every dictum of an Infallible Voice. Human life at best is heir to enough natural evils; they are not to be met by the palliatives of magic and mysticism, but by wisdom, courage, fortitude, serenity, and a certain resignation. Not more superhuman, but more human, is the answer to greater progress toward freedom from the ills the flesh is heir to.

## PART THREE

## WHAT SHALL WE DO TO BE SAVED?

## CHAPTER FOURTEEN

### Progress and Democracy in the Machine Age

1. This Is *the* Machine Age. 2. There Has Been Progress, but . . .
3. Business Is Business, and 4. War Is Hell. 5. Democracy Demands
a Democratic Education.

I

THIS is *the* Machine Age; civilization now runs by machinery.
Willy-nilly, we who are here are part of it, and it is well that
we should understand it. This chapter is an attempt to look at it
sympathetically and understandingly.

We did not have to wait for radios and drugs until science had
resolved the ultimate constitution of matter; nor for improved methods of communication and more effective drugs shall we have to
wait for science to discover how it can beat its own man-made laws
of thermodynamics. The universe may run down eventually; but
if it were known that Gabriel would sound his trumpet next Fourth
of July, the firecracker factories would not shut down.

Probably we all realize that we are going to snuff out some day—
and as geologists reckon time the day is near at hand. That fact
does not reconcile us to senile decay, nor can I discover that senility
has ever been elevated to a cult, though it is easy to discover cults
which have hastened the onset of senility. It is even easier to discover throughout history a tendency of man to try to be superman:
to stay young, to discount creaking joints and wrinkled skin. How
else can we interpret religious phenomena but as an attempt to beat
Nature at her own game? What else is the history of civilization
but an expression of the progress made toward that end?

Achievement. Man's place in nature today, whether we call it
good or bad, high or low, is characterized not so much by what
he gets out of life as by the way he lives. He has always been an
energetic animal; he supplements his energy. He easily acquires
skill; today he becomes skilful along a certain line or in a certain

field. He has always been a social animal; he finds himself today a member of a vast society which has become so dependent upon coöperation that a shut-down or a prolonged strike in any one basic industry would disrupt society.

It required no more intelligence to build the Panama than the Corinth Canal, or the Empire State Building than the Parthenon. The important difference between building then and now is in the amount of coöperation required, the highly specialized technique or skill demanded, and in the use of superhuman power.

A machine does not necessarily make for health, happiness, or longevity, but there is as much sense in railing at this Machine Age as at the age of ox-carts and hand-mills. Machines make for advance in human freedom and in human progress just as surely as did digging-sticks and flint knives. To charge such palpable stupidities of this age as disease, poverty, crime, and war to machinery is to close our eyes to human nature, to fail to distinguish between what is and what might be, between what has been done and what might be done.

Engineering is a science, politics is a job, and we suffer ourselves to be governed by job-hunters. We can think of iron ore in terms of steel rails and battleships, and of crude oil in terms of dyes and drugs, but we still think poverty, crime, and disease are laws of nature because it suited certain vested interests to rationalize fortuitous and historic social conditions. That acceptance of the *status quo* in human social conditions is no more a mark of sound thinking or of a scientific attitude than it would be to accept the earth with its natural resources as a law of nature and hence beyond man's capacity to change.

Man has dug out the ores and pumped up the oil, and in fifteen years has learned to get more power out of combustion engines than there is in all the muscles of all the horses, elephants, oxen, and men combined. Even human muscle has increased its efficiency by fifty per cent in fifteen years. The story behind these two achievements is one of the most astounding in all history. And it is an amazing fact that there is available today in the United States a billion horse-power electrical energy, enough to give six horse-power to each person—the estimated equivalent per man, woman, and child in the United States, of the labour of 142 slaves.

Few of us realize that we each have 142 slaves working for us—I know some people who work themselves like slaves; and each of us, I suppose, has a theory to account for the fact. But of all the rationalizations about labour that I have come across, the neatest, I think, is the Reverend J. Townsend's, whose words presumably will be a gospel message for at least another century as they have been during the last.

It seems to be a law of nature [said the divine] that the poor should be to a certain degree improvident, that there may always be some to fulfill the most servile, the most sordid and the most ignoble offices in the community. The stock of human happiness is thereby much increased whilst the more delicate are not only relieved from drudgery, and freed from those occasional employments which would make them miserable, but are left at liberty without interruption, to pursue those callings which are suited to their various dispositions, and most useful to the State. . . . When hunger is either felt or feared, the desire of obtaining bread will quietly dispose the mind to undergo the greatest hardships, and will sweeten the severest labour.

A "law of nature," the Reverend Mr. Townsend called it; and that to many people today means God's law, for, they argue, laws of nature are inexorable and immutable, hence eternal, and therefore divine. I think it well that we keep reminding ourselves that no law of nature, nor any word of God, is above suspicion or exempt from a court of reason.

Nothing that I have said, however, is an argument for throwing the past out of the window or for poking a finger of scorn in the eye of every authority. Nor, on the other hand, am I in favour of shouting *Eureka!* every time somebody takes out a patent or a copyright. Most of our machines and machine-made products are as essential to us as horse flesh was to our ancestors a half million years ago. We are as truly dependent on our culture as Cave-man was on his.

This is an industrial age, as that was; but industry today. . . . Well, I know a Baker, a Brewster, a Potter, a Fletcher, a Hooper, a Cooper, a Weaver, a Taylor, a Painter, a Carpenter, a Goldsmith, and dozens of Smiths—all more or less industrious and all presumably descendants of followers of once homely occupations, but that any one of them today follows the industry implied in the name is unlikely. Brewster may do a bit of home-brewing, but it is a thousand to one that Baker does not bake. In fact, if we traced a slice of bread back to the soil, we probably never would be out of sight of a machine of some sort driven by superhuman power. Today, about the only "human" touch in bread is in the eating—after it has been toasted by electricity.

Industry—but through machines in charge of engineers. Dozens of kinds of engineers, from those who engineer legislation through Congress to those who engineer tunnels through mountains. There are engines and engines. Man could not have become man without becoming more and more *enginous*. His long climb up out of animality is marked by an ever-increasing dependence upon engines, instruments; by increasingly better engines; by more highly developed technique in getting engines to do his work. I like to think that my days have coincided with those which provided engines to do woman's work as well. Sweeping a carpet or scrubbing a floor is an engineering job; there is as much sense in having it done by machinery as there is in having wheat threshed or cigarettes rolled by machinery.

To charge our social and economic evils to modern industry, as do many, and to sneer at this Machine Age, is, it seems to me, as unreasonable as it was for our ancestors to blame the devil for anything they did not understand and hence disliked.

It has recently been said that when science gives man a machine which will do the work of a hundred men, he begets ninety-nine children to consume the surplus, and the social condition remains unchanged. That may be true; it is true that millions live today where there were only thousands or hundreds a century ago. It is also true that the vast wealth which has been made possible through machines and labor-saving devices in general has often gone into projects devoted to the accumulation of more wealth or into peaceful luxury and war-time extravagance.

But the uses wealth is put to and its distribution, equitable or otherwise, among those who created it, are quite a different thing from the fact that this technically engineered Machine Age has made it possible for more human beings to work less and play more than ever before in human history. To argue that there are too many people on earth, or in China, or on Manhattan Island, is merely to suggest that they should go in for fewer babies and more golf, or for less buncombe and more information in advertising, politics, and contraceptives.

Sixty-odd per cent of the jobs in a Ford plant, they say, can be filled by men after only one day's training; and only six per cent of the jobs require more than a week's training. And a moron can learn to drive a Fordson. Marvellous. Really.

But note, please, that these labourers are not treated, housed, fed, and bossed like serfs. No doubt the arm that feeds a mere machine, that participates no more than one turn of one screw in the finished product, does not feel the warm glow of an arm that chips a perfect flint knife.

Grant that no labourer in a Ford plant takes the same pride in a Ford car that the ancient flint-worker took in his knives, or that the tinned salmon I ate tonight would have tasted better if I had caught it and my wife had broiled it over a smoky fire: and what have we granted? Labour is not what it used to be! Nor is life, for that matter. When a shelter was built over that fire and the fire itself brought under control in a fireplace with a chimney, labour of cooking was made easier.

What else were fire, bow, spear, ax, hoe, plough, wheel, and shelter but labour-saving devices; or spring, loom, pot, pan, poker, soap, needle? Labour-saving devices. Lighter labours. Make work as easy as possible. Conceivably, it is good for man's soul that he earn his bread by the sweat of his brow; conceivably, sweat is the price we pay for original sin. It is also conceivable that the man who invented that notion expected to get his bread without sweat.

In short, the story of civilization is shot through and through with recurring inventions designed to lighten labour, to get bread without sweat: and not all of them by any means have been machines of parts whose motions were so constrained as to transform natural energy into work. Many of these labour-savers consisted of nothing more ingenious than Tom Sawyer's idea of getting paid for letting his neighbours whitewash his fence.

Tom's was an ancient idea. Thousands of years ago man discovered that besides the natural energy in sunshine, wind, and rain, and in beasts of burden, there were additional reservoirs in his fellow-men which, properly handled, could be transformed into work. In fact, all so-called highly organized societies for five thousand years have assumed, more or less naïvely and always rationalistically, that certain classes were natural labourers, other classes natural parasites on labour. Practically all of our laws of inheritance are based on that assumption. And Holy Writ can be cited as additional evidence that the distinctions between those who have and those who are meek in spirit are part of a divine plan which needs a Hereafter for its justification.

Many Americans still labour under the delusion that it is quite in accordance with the divine plan and natural law that the "Superior" should exploit the "Inferior" races. It was pure historical circumstance rather than enlightened opinion that stayed the hand of the white despoiler and exploiter in Africa, Asia, and the islands of the Pacific. Even as it is, it will require decades and possibly centuries to repair the damage already done.

By historical circumstance I mean, of course, the change that has been brought about by the substitution of mechanical for human energy. Now, whether we *like* this Machine Age or not is beside the point. The point is that it is here and that its very presence has changed the world we live in. This changed world has changed us. When our ancestor changed his stone for a steel ax and his slingshot and crossbow for a shotgun, his world was thereby changed and he himself a different man. His behaviour was changed to meet environmental changes. New outlooks, new horizons; new techniques, new avenues of freedom, new manners of living.

Think of the thousand and one changes in business brought about by the typewriter alone; or in architectural art and housing conditions in general, by the elevator. The typewriter did not make business, nor the elevator houses or architecture; they do form part of the machine-power complex which makes this age unique.

More. This ever-increasing development of and dependence upon machine power has changed national quite as much as individual outlooks. The mediæval guild crafts, with their rigid rules of apprenticeship and monopolistic control of certain industries, had to give way before the factory system, as ruthlessly tyrannical as the world has seen. There was a limit, not to the cruelty an outraged master might display, but to the amount of labour which could profitably be expected. A Hindu or a Sicilian will beat and ill-treat his beast of burden, but he stops short at permitting it to die of starvation or beating it to death with a club. The early nineteenth-century factory magnate needed no such compunctions—and often had none at all.

It was *natural* that women and children should work fourteen hours a day on starvation wages. The Lord gave; and the factory took away—and about as fast as the Lord gave. It was natural; it was the divine plan; it was Economic law! Nature, Bible, and text-book all agreed; and the factory magnate ruled Britannia's wave and her Parliament. And England—and America—still thought in terms of man- and horse-power. Horses were bred, for speed on turf and strength in commerce; and men were exploited heedlessly, ruthlessly. Our immigration policy was dictated solely by the needs of factory and plant, railroad and mine, for new labour. And the Great Powers carved up the "empty" spaces with an eye to future needs for man-power and raw materials.

But why grow man-power when it is so much easier to develop coal, gas, oil, water, and other natural sources of energy? Today, these are the objectives of national power-thinking. Science today can make as good sugar as Cuba, or as good rubber as Para, can grow; but it is still cheaper to grow them than to make them. That condition, presumably, will not continue indefinitely, for the chemist already has the exact formula of many of man's necessary ingredients for life, and new sources of energy are being discovered. That does not mean merely that man can imitate them, but that he can make them—and make them just as pure. Many of the drugs necessary for life and growth and sexual desire can now be made in chemical laboratories—and every whit as good as man naturally develops or secretes in his own body. One would be rash indeed to set a limit to the chemist's power to make or synthesize enormously complex compounds out of very simple, common elements. But our political engineers still work on the theory that a public trust is a private trough—and if we include their friends, each has more feet to get in the trough than a millipede.

In other words, this age, which makes it possible for man to fly like an angel and talk like a streak of lightning, makes it profitable for him to think like a hog and act like a racketeer. Doesn't it seem strange that civilization should have had to wait for this nation to develop the most deadly, insidious, and costly form of social parasitism known to the human race? Or do I err in thinking three billion dollars a big price to pay annually for our national racket industry? The principle behind the industry, of course, is as ancient and honourable as that of any theocracy, and the idea of levying tribute is no more modern; but the technique of collecting money at the point of a sawed-off shotgun, with the aid and connivance of an arm of the law, is unique. It is also, be it noted, not out of keeping with a national spirit which ranks get-rich-quick as a major virtue and finds no merit in honest failure.

It seems inherent in human nature that whenever the god is gold the devil is the metallurgist. The symbol of our god is the dollar sign, and a bank account is the proof that our prayers have been answered. Wealth can commit no wrong and a rich life is measured by riches. The real sin is poverty; the height of folly is work. The one word Success sums up the rite, ritual, and creed of the national religion; and our "most important work is to care for boys and girls, give them a happy childhood, and equip them for a successful life"—as President Hoover told the National Education Convention last year.

Hence our task, said the President, is to give every child the opportunity to grow up with a healthy body, a trained mind, a disciplined character, a cheerful faith in himself, and a devotion to our form of government. But as to whether public-school teachers might "allow" schoolroom discussion of such controversial subjects as *tariff* and *prohibition*, the Council of that Education Convention was afraid to express an opinion.

Certainly such subjects should not be discussed. How could such discussion simplify our "task" or make our public-school system a more "distinctive and magnificent ally of the home in the most precious trust"?

Most *precious* trust? Power and Light, or just what "trust" did the President have in mind? Certainly our public press cannot be depended upon to dispel ignorance, break down prejudice, or promote sanity, for we, the public, still prefer scandal, sensation, and crime to an honest recital of illuminating facts or enlightened opinion on public policies and trends. And we, the public, prefer gossip because our public schools institutionalize faith and devotion and crown the cheer-leader with success. Why not turn our public-school system over to the Catholic or Christian Science hierarchy? They are organized to turn out cheerful Faithful and Devoted, and they certainly understand the art of discipline.

The devil is the metallurgist, and Tubal Cain was "an instructor of every artificer in brass and iron." The devil, whether in brass or iron, or as electric furnace or coal-miner, is man-made or a living human being. And as I am trying to encompass human behaviour in the large, the devil—as coal-miner, blacksmith, steel bridge, Leviathan, Machine Age, or material civilization—is caught up in my net and hence worthy of notice, if not respect.

This Machine Age we are living in has been indicted as a monster, sordid, horrible, and by many is hated as the devil in person used to be hated. We have lost, we are gravely told, all the sweetness of life, and most of the finer, higher, more intellectual, and more spiritual realities of life—and all because our civilization has become *materialistic*. The machine has done it. Damn the Machine Age!—especially the automobile and wireless, though I notice that the Pope has installed a broadcasting station in the Vatican, that he may fight the devil with his own weapons.

Obviously, a Buddhist monk in a Tibetan monastery or a Christian monk on Mouth Athos, or even a *Pithecanthropus erectus* of Java, could see no good in a motor-car or a radio set. Possibly there is no *good* in such gimcracks. But among the things our ancestors went in for were better means of transporting themselves and their goods across land and sea, and more effective means of getting their thoughts across. Their efforts in such directions led them up out of monkey-land. Civilization from the beginning was *material*: better control over the materials of life, over the things that mattered in life.

Now, the improvements man has made in the three decades of this century in transportation of materials and communication of thoughts, are nothing less than astounding. There are still wide seas, high mountains, and Chinese walls of international prejudice against free trade, and probably will be for centuries; but this material age has made this world a potential unit. I expect to live to see popular-priced excursions to the South Pole, and while on one of them to talk back to the girl I left behind me.

In other words, man is finally beginning to cash in on the fact that he is born human; to realize that there are still many worlds to conquer and that he is the man to conquer them. By and by he will learn that if he does not like this world he can leave it, but that the only way to make it more likable is by doing his share of the work.

The ancients had their wonders of the world—*seven* in number, of course: Pyramids of Gizeh; mausoleum at Halicarnassus; temple of Artemis at Ephesus; hanging gardens of Babylon; Colossus at Rhodes; Phidian Zeus at Olympia; and the lighthouse at Alexandria. Against these put our seven wonders, as determined by a *Popular Mechanics* referendum a few years ago: wireless telegraphy; telephone; airplane; radium; anæsthetics and antitoxins; spectrum analysis; X-rays. No mention at all of the automobile or tractor, and television then unknown!

*Material* Age? Why, this is the least material of all ages! It is almost human. Suppose we could recall, spotless and unblemished, the seven wonders of the ancient world, and that we owned them. And suppose our only child was down with diphtheria, that a Cæsarean section impended for friend wife, and that our leg had to be amputated, would we not trade all seven wonders and all the faith behind them for just two of our modern wonders? Is any miracle imputed to antiquity as wonderful as those performed hourly by anæsthetics and antitoxins, or by radium, or the radio, or the airplane, or X-ray photography?

To be historically minded, it seems to me, is to be fortified against the claims of authorized bigotry and arrogant intelligence; also, to have confidence restored in one's fellow-men.

Civilization was possible because man discovered by handling things how he could make them himself. Civilization advanced, progress was made, commensurately with restricting the handling of things to the common weal. Often it is not possible to discover a common weal. Commonwealths in name are common enough; in reality, all too uncommon. Nor, when we speak of the general public, is it always easy to think in terms comprehensive enough to include everybody or all classes. Certainly, few in our own country would agree as to just what is meant by the term "public welfare."

Now, I am not here concerned with politics or with government, but with this Machine Age of ours. I am not arguing that a motor-car, for example, or cocaine, is an advance; nor, on the other hand, that either is a curse because, improperly used, each is an instrument of death. Either motor-cars and cocaine are advances or there is no such thing as civilization: one beats time, the other pain. Both are easily made today—an impossible feat a few years ago; both are enormously valuable, yet the motor has enormously complicated life, and cocaine presumably will complicate it still further.

With the exception of a few accessories, the motor-car is synthesized from a carload of iron ore; cocaine, from a bucket of coal tar. We are just beginning to realize the possibilities of iron ore; hardly at all of coal tar. Ford supplanted Rockefeller in wealth and millions of horses in jobs, but think, if you can, of the possible fortune awaiting the man who can control the output of the potential sugar and starch in sawdust and the potential edible fats and oils in the coals and oils down in the earth. Russia alone, as Haldane suggests, if she became chemically minded, could not only revolutionize the world's food supply but bankrupt the farmers of the world.

We already have laws for motor-cars in relation to crime, insurance, public utilities, taxation, licence, chattel mortgage, torts, etc. We have laws regulating the sale of cocaine, even of alcohol, but nature herself makes alcohol under our eyes and cocaine can be made by a sixteen-year-old chemist, and pretty soon he will be able to synthesize morphine, which is even more valuable than cocaine.

What is to be the solution of the problems which will inevitably arise with new synthetic drugs and foods? More laws merely, or a sharp shift in ideals and a thorough revision of our conceptions of social organization? I raise the question only to drop it after pointing out that every society which went in for any ideal incompatible with the common weal sooner or later went through a revolution.

No matter what it is—a new law to redress a social wrong, a new theory to square with a new fact, or a new tool to save a man's arm or a woman's back—there is always somebody to sneer or throw a brick. One of the bizarre chapters of history would recount the reactions of authority—church, state, mob, profession, finance, business—to every advance in civilization and science. Man's inhumanity to man has wrought more woe, but man's hostility to anything new forms a longer and, viewed in retrospect, a really comic, chapter.

But while laughing at human nature for declaring that an iron ploughshare "poisoned" the earth and "insulted God," let us not forget that it is the same human nature which today in another form prophesies disaster to every measure which violates "Nature's Fixed Economic Laws." Whenever the cry of nature's "fixed" laws, economic or otherwise, is raised, it is fairly certain that the cry is voiced by ignorance or entrenched privilege. Marx, who lifted the lid from the horrible abyss of sweated labour and questioned the respectability of those who grew rich on that labour, is today as much anathema to certain classes as Darwin is to certain communities.

We have already had some examples of man's hostility to anything new. Here are a few more.

The man who first opened an umbrella in Philadelphia was arrested; who first drove a sawmill by water power in England was mobbed; and the inventors of stoves, railroads, and telegraph were "crazy." George III said the lightning-rod was impious. Jenner, who invented vaccination, was scorned by the medical profession; and Harvey, for discovering and demonstrating the circulation of the blood, was called "crack-brained" and his doctrine branded as "new-fangled" and "dangerous." Lister, who founded antiseptic surgery, was blackballed by the London Surgical Society. Napier fought the introduction of steam power in the British navy. Walter Scott called gaslight a pestilential innovation. Up to 1845 a Boston municipal ordinance made bathtubs unlawful except on medical advice; the doctors themselves said bathing was dangerous to health. Even a book on comparative anatomy and physiology, in 1816, was denounced by the famous Dr. Abernethy in a lecture before the College of Surgeons, as aiming to "loosen those restraints on which the welfare of mankind depends." If we could go back in history we should find the bow and arrow denounced as fit only for treacherous cowards. Firearms were declared to be the invention of the devil and destructive of all nobility and chivalry. The first railway was fought in the British Parliament.

Sugar, before the cultivation of cane in the West Indies began to make it readily available in Europe, was, as J. W. Emerson points out, a medicine, or at best a luxury of the rich and beyond reach of the poor. As its price fell its use increased, and as almost nothing was then known of the chemistry of nutrition it soon became a "harmful" substance and its use a *sin*. Antisaccharites got busy, and the war against sugar was on. It is clearer than light (said a London physician in 1647) that sugar is not a nourishment, but an evil; not a preservative, but a destroyer. Too much licentiousness? Sugar! Did tuberculosis and scurvy rage? Sugar!

Sugar, in fact, to the seventeenth century was on a par with wine, nutmegs, and tobacco as purveyors to man's carnal appetites, as leaders-down-to-hell. Science had not investigated sugar, but an "eminent physician" had. His "clearer than light" dictum was quoted from the pulpit. Nay, more, the scientists of the day united in condemning sugar as evil. With Liebig's discovery in the middle of the last century that sugar is not only a food but the optimum source of human energy, it ceased to be a villain in the human drama.

Tea, "a Chinese drug" to an essayist in 1766, was pernicious to health, obstructed industry, and impoverished nations—was a "many-headed monster" in fact.

Coffee, said a physician in 1523, intoxicates the head and is prejudicial to health. Some ten years later a Cairo mob, roused by a fanatic's tirade against its use, "Carrie-Nationed" the coffee-houses and abused the people present. In Constantinople also the coffee-houses proved more attractive than the mosques; so coffee was declared to be a sin and prohibited by the Law of the Prophet. Coffee-houses were also outlawed by Charles II of England.

Sugar is a food. Tea and coffee are stimulants; so is tobacco. Anti-tobacco laws still come and go. By a Colonial law of 1646, one could not smoke except on a "journey of five miles or more from any town." And in 1629 the settlers in Massachusetts were prohibited from planting tobacco "unless in small quantities, for physic, to preserve health."

It is not that somebody is always taking the joy out of life, but that man is naturally timid and eternally hates to admit that he does not know; that he is prone to look askance at the man who dares, and to hate him if he seems to be enjoying himself. A hundred years from now we may have a really scientific verdict on the rôle of certain specific "stimulants"—such as tea, coffee, tobacco, alcohol, etc.—in human behaviour. With that verdict it will be possible to take an intelligent attitude toward their use. Present-day "scientific" conclusions about alcohol seem to be just a shade higher than six-teenth-century conclusions about sugar, tea, coffee, and tobacco: full of propaganda based on emotional slants, empty of scientific investigation of the physiologic function of stimulants.

What is the melting-point of ice? But here is a lump of *hot* ice— even at a temperature of 180° it will not melt. Then it can't be ice, you say. But it *is* ice, says the physicist, and it can't melt because I've got it under 300,000 pounds pressure. Liquid air and hot ice are not freaks of nature; they are natural products of (to us) "un-natural" conditions. We are accustomed to air in the form of a gas, to 31° as the melting-point of ice; but we are also accustomed to air and ice under an atmospheric pressure of fifteen pounds to the square inch.

Bridgman in his laboratory plays with materials under conditions of his own choosing. As against the usual atmospheric pressure of fifteen pounds, he can impose a pressure of over a half million pounds per square inch. Under such unusual conditions, old familiar friends take on unusual behaviour. Some of them are so impressed that they remain impressed even when he lets them out from under the thumbscrew.

Human beings are like that: they can be so impressed that they are crippled for life, deformed out of all semblance of humanity. There is a limit to our capacity to breathe rarefied or vitiated air, a limit to our capacity to thaw out. It is conceivable that our civiliza-tion, with its supernatural pressures, lays a burden on us that only superhumans could bear. Our universe may be infinitely larger than our forefathers thought it, but our greatest men continue to be born of woman as of old and require no larger amount of sod to cover their mortal remains than did their forbears in the days gone by.

Great are the achievements of science, and vast are the fortunes amassed in business, but scientist and business man alike may recall the *Memento te hominem esse* of the slave who followed the tri-umphal car, reminding Cæsar that he was but a man, after all. We who live in this business age of applied science may also remind ourselves that even as a digging-stick was good for digging graves as well as roots, and could be used in an emergency for cracking skulls as well as cocoanuts, a motor-car can outrun human needs as well as human legs and is as easily turned into a weapon of destruction as into an aid to the journey through life.

In other words, just as no modern scientist can be more than human, so no product of modern science can be put to higher use than humane ends. If there is anything to be read in the mirror of history, it is that civilization falls hardest when it rides highest over the elementary principles of justice, honesty, and humanity.

Modern science provides power, in staggering amounts, and great stores of knowledge of things innumerable; and directions and suggestions for turning this knowledge into more power pour forth in endless streams of printed pages. There are more things in the catalogue of one mail-order house than were dreamed of by ancient philosophy or were known to the world of George Washington. Yet we live in a social order which primarily views us as purchasers and taxpayers in time of peace, and in war as machines on two legs which can carry arms and are run by internal-combustion engines requiring nothing but food and water.

Scientific differs from social progress because it is easier to discover a fact than to change a habit. Ptolemy was a great authority, but he had been dead a long time when Copernicus brought forward facts to undermine his opinion. True, the church had adjusted itself to Ptolemy, but the existence of the church was not dependent on a Ptolemaic universe—as it is on a sinful universe. Social inequalities persist because the heritors of power—the social authorities—are very much alive and in control.

Enormous advance has been made in society—but from the necessities of a political situation faced with a practical, industrial Machine Age, and not because entrenched power has changed its mind about the inevitableness of class distinctions. Our notions of the rights of private property are hardly more modern, or scientific, than those of ancient Egypt and Babylon. The Old Testament is still authority for social injustice.

Only today I heard a coloured woman "explain" to her mistress that it was the "lot" of the dark-skinned peoples to work for the whites; and she cited drunken Noah's curse upon Canaan as though it were testimony comparable to such facts of nature as motherhood and sunshine.

Science makes a vacuum cleaner available for human hands, and the white housewife turns it over to hands born to clean. Genesis IX: 25 may have seemed a reasonable rationalization to its author; it may have been a valuable guide to conduct and a warrant for the existing social organization; but that did not make it true then, and it seems shocking to hear it quoted today as authority for social organization.

Now I can state more explicitly the point I wish to emphasize, namely, that science—as method, as achievement, as power, as possession—does not make civilization, nor emancipate humanity, nor insure health, happiness, or longevity, nor release peoples from servitude and sweat. But, as method, achievement, power, and possession, science can serve civilization, can help humanity in its ages-old struggle for greater freedom from the asperities of life, toward more liberty to enjoy life.

This point of view, it seems to me, is worth emphasizing, because man is more prone to accept existing conditions as natural and hence unalterable, than to make the effort to find out how the conditions came into existence and then take pains to change them. Creature of habit as he is, man finds it easier to fight change than to change his mind, easier to make a goat of innovation than to realize that he himself is the butt, not of innovation, but of his false rationalizations about innovations.

The prevailing fashions in rationalization just now are motor-cars, Eighteenth Amendment, Soviet Russia, materialism, and the Machine Age.

Satisfied, blissful ignorance. We smile at London and Paris satisfied to wade ankle-deep in mud, through narrow, crooked, dark streets, seven centuries after Cordova had miles of paved and lighted straight streets. Are we not satisfied with incredible waste in sickness and inefficiency and social parasitism, years and years after such physical and social diseases have been scientifically diagnosed and remedies discovered? We are satisfied with decrepit grandmothers on their hands and knees scrubbing marble floors of banks bulging with wealth, while their owners sleep in silk or seek the joys of the tired, lonely business man.

We profit enormously by the application of scientific methods to modern industrial problems and to agriculture and medicine—and to war; but we have not even got to the point where we can think scientifically about our social, political, economic, or juridical problems, much less bring scientific procedure to bear on their solution. We accept a Machine Age and easily become air- and radio-minded, for neither machine nor wireless defies spiritual or intellectual authority; but we are still prevented by our spiritual and intellectual authority inheritance, from recognizing the false prophets who deluge us with their own theories for the salvation of home, family, and nation.

If there is an art of war, there must be an art of peace; if efficiency of human work, then efficiency of human play. If nature can be moulded, controlled, why not human nature? If man is a brotherhood, why not let him live? If knowledge is power, why lose so much time on such mental toys as cross-word puzzles? If disease is preventable, why not prevent it? If the classics are dead, why not bury them? If there is a scientific attitude toward wealth, why not put it to work? If patriotism can become a vice as easily as a virtue, let us look at the nation truthfully. If our social parasites are too expensive, let them be put to work. If our intellectual garments are antiquated, let us make some that are better adapted to the needs of this age. If a scientific attitude can create a Machine Age, why can't it create a humane age? If smart business can capture politics, why can't fair play? If there is no inherent virtue in a white skin nor demerit in kinky hair, why not end this stupid feud between White and Black?

If we must worship an idol, reverence an idea, salute a flag, cherish a shibboleth, cheer a slogan, or follow a leader, let us do it with enthusiasm and the courage of our convictions—after due investigation has shown that idol, idea, flag, shibboleth, slogan, or leader is alive, human, worthy, honest, sound, wholesome, unselfish, tolerant, and humane.

## II

That there has been progress we are all, I presume, agreed. But does it mean anything? And if so, just what? Of what does it consist, what direction is it taking? Merely to ask these questions is to assume disagreement. Disagreement is a fact.

It is also a fact that most disputations about progress are futile; the disputants rarely agree because each has a different concept of progress and a more or less particularized cultural background from which to examine it. I do not propose to join that verbal contest. I do propose to look at progress from the standpoint of such knowledge of nature and her forces as is now available, and then to review as critically as I can the factors of our civilization which seem to make for or retard progress.

Progress—in plant or animal world—is security; and judging from the record embalmed in earth, security had meaning in one of two respects: the organism was simple enough or sufficiently generalized to be adapted to almost endless change in environment; or it was facile enough to meet change with change. One made for lower life, the other for higher. *Fixity,* on certain low levels of organization; *plasticity,* on ever higher levels. Such conditions and processes—incalculable in number and complexity—are conveniently resumed by the one word evolution.

Security in very low forms is generally won at the price of short life and rapid reproduction; the individual enjoys the flame of life, so to speak, for a fleeting moment and passes it on to the next generation. Growth is primarily reproduction. Recall Woodruff's pair of paramœciums occupying the known cosmic universe in a few thousand years if unmolested and endowed with longevity. But what would the paramœcium do then?

Security in very high forms is generally won by prolonged individual effort. Growth is not primarily a process of endless reproduction, but of slow growth, from one stage to another, each stage involving progressive change in structure and mode of behaviour. What is involved is primarily a learning or acquiring process. Life is not merely life; it is accomplishment, achievement, learning and living, living and learning. Security does not pass from one generation to the next through the germ-plasm or in the process of reproduction, but from hand to hand. Life is learnt, in its infancy is led by the hand. Even the reproductive cycle is strictly limited in time; twins are abnormalities.

In these very high forms (man ranking highest) security is not inborn, but acquired. Ample time and fitting mechanisms are available for such acquisition. Individual longevity results; and also the continued existence of the species, for enough time is allowed to insure reproduction.

Man especially depends upon the use of his brain to help him find security. That larger brain is his natural equipment for discovering means and methods of security. Success depends upon his use of it; he fails when he does not use it. He cannot get the most out of it when he is moved by fear. Whatever banishes fear makes for security; adds to his capacity to use his time and energies for the purpose of discovering what has to be done to promote security, and then to live out his life in peace, health, and happiness.

Has there been progress in this regard? The first fire kindled, the first word spoken, the first tool fashioned, the first animal tamed, the first plant cultivated, were steps in progress. That progress, enormous progress, has been made in man's conquest of the forces and materials of nature he must conquer or perish, there cannot be the slightest doubt.

And may I again emphasize the fact that the turning-point in man's progress from an ape was speech. The key to the importance of speech is to be found in abstractions: abstract words, simple symbols which express categories of qualities, attributes, states, activities, etc., and generalizations. Speech itself is not progress from a simian past, nor freedom from perils which beset human lives; it is an instrument which makes progress possible. I may be drowning in a gallon of carbon dioxide within sight of a tank of oxygen, but to be saved I must get some of that oxygen into my lungs. That is why we now equip our firemen with pulmotors as well as with fire extinguishers. Speech does make progress possible; abstractions and generalizations make for speed in progress.

Note also, please, that the first move in the step from Galvani to galvanized life and iron was no accident. Galvani was no accident, only the incident. He saw. He did not draw a sound inference, but he described what he had seen, and did it honestly, impartially. No *law* of science can do more. The wider the application of the "law," the greater the number of phenomena its description resumes, the greater the law. No law is greater, or rises higher, than the collective wisdom of its creators. The thunder speaks, but in so far as it speaks to man it is man who interprets its message; and that can only be done by symbols which have meaning only in terms of other symbols which by custom have become media of exchange between human beings.

To deny progress or to doubt the reality of progress these days is to quibble or to pass into the realm of metaphysics—a realm in which, I confess, I cannot breathe.

Accepting progress, then, as a reality or as a valid concept, and my rough sketch of its biology as factually founded, we must infer, it seems to me, that man, in the future as in the past, must expect to find security in his hands guided by his brain rather than in breeding better hands or more brains. Man is amply endowed, bountifully provided for, by nature. In strict literalness, his fate is in his hands. But burnt hands, or hands trembling with fear, are poor hands for doing the work which man must do to find the joy in life his nature has so lavishly allotted him.

How about eugenics, then? Let a geneticist speak—and do not quarrel with me for taking the liberty of employing italics to emphasize these few lines from Jennings' *Biological Basis of Human Nature*:

It appears indeed *probable,* from the present state of knowledge and the trend of discovery, that the following sweeping statements will *ultimately* turn out to be justified: (1) All characteristics of organisms may be altered by changing the genes; *provided* we can learn how to change the proper genes. (2) All characteristics may be altered by changing the environmental conditions under which the organism develops; *provided* that we learn what conditions to change and how to change them. (3) Any kind of change of characteristics that can be induced by altering genes, can likewise be induced (*if* we know how) by altering conditions.

Now, breeding a red-eyed *Drosophila melanogaster* is one thing; breeding a kind-hearted, tough-minded *Homo sapiens* is another and—I believe Jennings would agree—a yet far-off thing. But that is what is needed now. When an expert, for example, after profound investigation, can discover that "sex is the cause of prostitution," we need enough clear thinking to find the man behind prostitution—or rather that unholy trinity of pimp, policeman, and politician.

Progress is not made by discovering causes which excuse or rationalize facts, but by finding the facts and then doing something about them. Some of the facts in our midst might, with propriety and all due regard for progress, be strung up on a lamp-post.

If we are looking for *progress* while thumbing the pages of our universal history, we do not find it, as a rule, under *strong* rulers, theocratic or political; rather we find that the healthy disgust with the *status quo* which does useful things, is born among the people and comes to the front when they are not forced to follow a leader. They, the workers, the practical people, the people whose experience gives them common sense, are the makers of progress—and of rational reform and serviceable science. That is all science is: refined, sublimated common sense. And if any one point has become clear by now, it is that to expect the "study" of the Bible or any other Writ to *build* character, is groundless and harmful. Man ever changes his ethical ideals, and these historic changes can be read in books, but the habitual practice of social, ethical, and moral conduct is not fostered by books; it can be learnt only in the school of practical experience.

Most of us, I presume, are proud—I certainly am—that we are Americans; but there can be no harm in examining America or ourselves, or in trying to discover just what it is we have to be proud of. Are *we* making progress?

Material progress, yes; amazing progress. The first day I put foot in a school there was not a telephone, electric light, gasoline engine, automobile, airplane, moving picture, or radio on earth. My grandchildren are growing up in a world of telephones, radios, movies, and the endless machines now driven by electricity. They will accept them as naïvely as I accepted coal-oil lamps and the one-horse shay. But will they grow up in the same old world of human beings? Will their world overcome hindrances to general pleasure and happiness as ruthlessly as it sweeps away every obstruction to progress? Will it fear ignorance only, will it be beset by fears which paralyze action and restrict freedom? Will it fear death and personal annihilation, and mask that fear under the "death of civilization"? Will it justify war, murder, theft, crime, wrong-doing, injustice, in the name of state, church, custom, or class? Will it look upon well-trained children as we look upon well-trained animals? Will it give its approbation to a grafting politician if he is a good fellow, to a thief if he belongs to the right church, to a bootlegger if he is successful, to an exploiter of thousands if he is a philanthropist? Will it fear the implied threats of glamorous advertising?

In short, will it be prepared to scrutinize the moral code it inherits as freely, frankly, and honestly as it scrutinizes its means of transportation? Are we?

It has always been wrong to murder, to steal, to lie, to cheat. From the beginning there has been no people without its moral *Oughts*, its *Be goods*. The thirteenth century was just as unctuously moral as we are today.

Walter Lippmann in his *Preface to Morals* held that scepticism was never so rampant as today. The idea seems to prevail also that we are more radical than ever before, but that our sceptics lack David's confidence in challenging the giants of social reality, though they can grapple with the cosmos with the arrogance of a pope. If I read my history aright, we are daily becoming more conservative, more afraid of breaking with the grand tradition.

Name one doctrine or propose one measure of general social morality which seems to threaten the prestige or reduce the income of our rulers, priests, landlords, lawyers, doctors, or teachers, and it will be met with scorn and derision. Even the labourer puts loyalty to his union higher than loyalty to the public at large. Yet in our democracy today most of us are citizens, customers, clients, employés, patients.

Ours is a republic, our form of government a democracy. Is that progress? Is it an advance in civilization?

Merely to ask these questions is to raise the lid of a Pandora's box. To answer them is to invite approval or the charge of traitor or the cry of Red, so emotionally loaded are our attitudes toward our government and toward politics. I am neither socialist nor politician. I have voted and I have served on juries and I have studied human society. Certain facts seem plain; certain conclusions seem warranted. There is, there must be, a scientific approach to anything and everything relating to man—as individual, as society, as American nation. What I set forth seems—to me at least—to be reasonable, factually founded, and worth setting down.

The beginning and end of morality, or ethics, or peace in family, tribe, or nation, is social justice. Social justice is the final test of civilization, the enduring foundation of all progressive civilization. It means nothing less than altruistic behaviour of the type which had biologic value when the human race was a family, which has value today, and will as long as man is human and not a mere animal who would tyrannize over his fellow-men for sheer love of power or of self.

We are constantly having the law of the jungle thrown in our faces; but where is the jungle that would tolerate, must less sanction, a state where one, in Dr. Johnson's words, could starve to death surrounded by "the potentiality of growing rich beyond the dreams of avarice"? If there is such a jungle, I do not know it. I do know of such a state. We think of the inequalities of past ages, and shudder at the thought that they were glossed over by appeal to Fate or the inscrutable will of God; but, as some one has suggested, King Alfred could never have believed that God would allow one small family to have six big houses, six automobiles, and a steam yacht, while six hard-working people half starved in one room.

Would the six richest men in America today deny that the distribution of wealth is anomalous, ridiculous, monstrous? Would they admit that such distribution is potentially dangerous and necessarily anti-social? Let us admit, as we must, that our really rich men spend more in advancing science and in encouraging its application to human ends, and less on ostentatious display, wanton luxury, and sheer gluttony or animal pleasures, than any other six enormously rich men in human history: we are still confronted by the obvious fact that they are the possessors of power over the destinies of millions of lives such as was once wielded by despots in God's name and today has no higher sanction than such economic myths as *laissez faire*, the Economic Man, and the Iron Law of Wages.

May I again point out that it is next to impossible for a man set above his fellow-men to think clearly about social justice or to feel humanely about his fellow-men. If history shows anything, it is that power over men, like a habit-forming drug, leads to lust for more power. That is especially true of the man whose passion and hobby are the making of money. Success in that respect is his sole criterion of values, the only way he has to enhance his importance in his own eyes.

So great has been the progress made in applying the discoveries of science to the art of life, that our wealth could be produced by half the population if its production were intelligently organized. Just how that can be brought about I do not know. I do know that such organization is compatible with a democratic form of govern-ment, and only with such a form. It is not possible in a democracy which has as many false idols as we worship today. I do know that such organization is not possible with a competitive system which makes machines and factories faster than they are needed. Class war, war between capital and labour, are not signs of progress, nor marks of a healthy civilization.

This is an industrial age. Are we making progress toward an industrial democracy? Is our civilization a healthy going concern, a real enterprise founded on faith in humanity and the righteous-ness of reason and truth?

May we remind our business men and our captains of industry, as well as our war colleges and rulers in society and politics, that they hold no commission from on high, nor need they expect to enjoy the benefits of a democracy if they do not play the game. Nor need they think they can insure their power and possessions by wav-ing a flag, brandishing a shibboleth, calling names, or solemnly uttering *Hands off!* In a democracy nothing should be served but social justice, there should be nothing holier than humanity.

Democracy means living and working together. Homes once were the training schools for such socially necessary education as under-lies a sound democracy. If we beat the world in the number of murders for money—and we do; and if three-fourths of our mur-derers employ firearms—and they do: there must be a reason. Be-hind that reason is the great fact that our democracy has not yet learnt to be honest with itself.

History teaches that the way to safeguard society is not by owner-ship, persecution, torture, excommunication, Inquisition, *Index Ex-purgatorius,* or the guillotine. Such expedients will be employed as long as any values are rated higher than human. To look upon a man, woman, or child, or any class, or any colour, or any section of the human race, as raw material or property to be controlled, ex-ploited, or governed, is to make a society which needs safeguarding.

We are a republic, but where is our *res publica?* What is our commonwealth or our common weal? We have a democracy, the only form of government or social contract consistent with social justice ethically permissible, socially justified. It is a meritorious form of government, but merit is inherent in it only as it is meritoriously conducted.

Let us be clear about this, for it is vital and concerns us all. We revolted from the rule of a ruler. Our fathers broke with the rule of caste—military as well as religious. How far have we progressed from caste rule if we hand our government over, as we do, to Big Business?

Is Big Business a figure of speech? Possibly; but who dominates our national policy at home and abroad, controls our manufactures, trade, and finance, subsidizes our education, and builds our cathedrals? Does church or school dare question the philosophy or ethics of Big Business—Off with its roof! The church accepts its morality and the educator writes its text-books. Is Big Business moral? It is immoral to question its morality. Is it patriotic? It is unpatriotic to question its patriotism.

When man discovered a worthy theory of the universe, he began to have worthy ideas about the world he lived in. We must have worthy ideas about human beings before we can have worthy ideas of human relationships. Our anthropologists have buried themselves in ruins and our sociologists have buried themselves in words. There is danger of our settling down again in false security—to come to when Business decides to precipitate another earthquake. The ancients sacrificed to Moloch and to Yahweh; we sacrifice to Big Business—the motor-car factory and the prison. Should the punishment fit the crime or the criminal, or the society which does a good business out of criminality?

Our democracy is necessarily an enormously complicated piece of machinery. It is run by Vested Interests in behalf of Vested Interests—through claptrap, ignorance, folly, and demagogy. It fears great moral principles and has no machinery to make them effective, no means of making them practical, nor courage to employ wisdom and honesty in being effective.

We accept democracy as we accept the motor and the telephone, expecting some one to furnish us with as much of them as we need or can afford, and to keep them in repair and good running order.

That is not progress, for against that background of expectation progress and decay are interchangeable terms. Heraclitus (500 B.C.) said that belief in progress stops progress.

Evolution follows a path, though no one knows where the path may lead; it is known that it follows no straight line. Progress is lawless and at best a man-made term, an anthropomorphic concept, born of desire. Desire is good and ideals are often useful substitutes for reality, but they neither create reality nor prepare the way.

We assume that democracy also is evolving—through amendments to the Constitution—and suppose that that inevitably makes for progress. We also seem to think that riding on the clouds lifts mankind on to a higher moral plane, and that because the physicist has weighed the earth and finds nothing wanting, we too, our civilization, our democracy, our social order, leave nothing to be desired. But a critical survey of history lends grounds for the belief that our social order is no less founded on rationalized, legalized theft than that of ancient courts was founded on legalized theft and murder. Democracy, with all its stupidities—and they are not inherent—is, I repeat, the only form of government consistent with progress in morals and in ethics. And morals and ethics mean social justice or nothing. A civilization stressing lapses or irregularities in sex morals while condoning dishonesty in high places and setting metallic or paper values above human values, strains at a gnat and swallows a bolus, which invariably results in acute indigestion and ultimate death.

It is not criminals that bedevil us or poverty which shames us, but a social order which is founded on hypocrisy and deceit and the infamous rule that possession is nine points of the law, that property is sacred and transmissible, and that mere possession is the mark of divine approval.

This is not an argument for something, nor is the question one of like or dislike. It is stated as a fact, and the real question is, is it a fact? There is no moral law in nature, nor will any appeal to any "immutable law" of nature suffice to block inquiry into the facts of nature. All that makes for human values, yesterday, today, and forever, is honesty, fair play, decency, justice—socially useful behaviour, not hoggish behaviour nor dog-eat-dog behaviour.

Oh, that's sentiment, a hopeless ideal, a Platonic dream! Sentiment, yes; an ideal, yes; a dream, yes—but not Platonic, for his dream included slavery. The real point is, is the sentiment healthy, the ideal in the line of human progress, the dream a plan which can be made practicable if we will only leave our canopied bed of mediæval morality long enough to find out why so many are forced to fit the bed Procrustes allows them, and then apply our knowledge to make the dream come true?

Progress in civilization has always meant accomplishment—and generally of what seemed preposterous, hopeless, or incomprehensible. We send a letter across the continent in a few days for two cents, our voice across the earth in a few seconds for a few dollars. Would there have been anything Utopian or preposterous in this to Ben Franklin? And would not our ideals, if not most of our practices, of criminal procedure without torture, have seemed soft sentiment to the civilized world of a few generations ago? To Richelieu, a foreign service without bribery was a dream. Government service today—local, state, and national—without bribery is still a hope. Innocent III thought a church without graft a hopeless ideal. With that thought I shall not quarrel; I shall merely point out that every militant church in America today does not hesitate to blink at facts or to resort to any unethical procedure to gain the victory.

Progress has been made in our own day and in so many respects that we are bewildered, but behind that bewilderment is the feeling that we have progressed *all along the line*. And so, in one sense, we have; but history proves that *excessive* advance in some one direction or in some particular respect generally turns out to be a weakness. Millions of people in motor-cars: but where are they going, what do they do when they get there, what price speed, what penalty luxury?

Murderers stole Job's herds, lightning killed his cattle, a storm killed his children, and poor Job himself was afflicted with boils. But he could still eat! We have an adequate answer for his sufferings, his abuses, and his boils. Yes; but only yesterday—and it was Sunday, in the richest city in the world—a girl fainted from hunger in a bread line and was dead before she could be rushed to a hospital. But no one starves to death in America; that is no longer possible! Parodying Louis XIV, God would not let an American starve—and a girl at that—after all America has done for him!

We are cruel in many respects, we do tolerate a great deal of injustice; but we have made progress. Let there be no mistake about this, and above all let us understand the significance of the progress made and being made in ethics and politics, in moral as well as in material progress. The municipal government of New York today seems to reek with graft, bribery, corruption; it seems to be a mere sordid machine for caring for its own selfish and greedy ends. Utterly cynical and indifferent to the rights of its citizens and taxpayers, as a municipal government it is not unique, nor possibly the worst in the world. Note, however, that the people of New York do not accept that condition as the will of God or condone it on any ground. If Einstein is front-page news, so are crime, evil, injustice; and not primarily as crime, evil, or injustice, but as a paid official of the government who has shamelessly violated the moral code as well as broken his oath of office.

That is moral progress. That kind of progress is being made right around the world. A young brute of a Belgian may kick a helpless Negro in the face (as I have seen with my own eyes), but the world at large, the bar of public opinion, does not approve such outrages. Before that bar, the Belgian atrocities had to stop. We think of the Civil War, and especially of Lincoln, as having freed the slaves. They were already freed before the bar of civilized public opinion.

That is progress in world morality, in universal social justice. That kind of progress is real. Never before in the history of the human race has there been so powerful, so general, or so insistent an appeal to the sentiments of decency, fair play, justice, and humanity. Never before was a great metropolis like New York so sensitive to and so arrayed against suffering, abuse, oppression, crime, vice, and injustice in every form.

Think of Liverpool a few generations ago, its docks lined with slave ships, other ships loaded with minors and petty thieves sold to the colonies for a dollar a head. Think of the public executions at Tyburn and elsewhere—a mere poacher, a young shoplifter; an heretical publisher in the pillory at Charing Cross or Temple Bar. Think of the old pressgangs that shanghaied men for the navy or the East India trade. Think of the utter callousness of the coal- and salt-mine owners, and of the squalour of the potteries, factories, and mills—predial slaves, half starved, living in rags and squalour, and dying under such a welter of cruelty and injustice as most of the world today would not tolerate for dogs. Even Constantinople was shamed into ridding its streets of half-starved curs.

Turn back still another century—to Paris, Rome, London, Madrid —to the days of *autos-da-fé* and the *Witch's Hammer*. Thousands flayed, impaled, torn in two, quartered, roasted, boiled; when only the prince and the priest had human rights; when unspeakable infamy of such forms of injustice as are beyond our ken was not only prevalent but sanctioned by religion, sanctified by law, and acquiesced in by gentlemen who found their pleasures in brothels and their delight in cock fights and the prize ring. To lift a voice against that social order was not to be called a Red, but to win a crown of martyrdom. So low was that age that it even taxed the peasant's plough.

We forget that our civil rights are less than 150 years old, that we had millions of slaves within the memory of the generation only now passing off the stage; that England less than a thousand years ago had seven times as many slaves and half-free men as free men, and that if one were thrown into prison he was more likely to rot there than to get out. There has been progress.

Human rights, humanity, humaneness, the kind of get-along-together behaviour that had survival value in an ape colony a million years ago: there has been progress along that line; and never at a pace so fast as now or in so many directions. Nor was clear thinking ever so valuable or more needed.

### III

Business is business, and largely a gamble unless it is Big; and the Stock Exchange is the gambler's paradise. One need not roll a bone, deal a card, buy a chip or a ticket, nor even look the horses over. No form of gambling has ever been made so easy or so simple or has put so small a premium on brains. A lucky fool—bootblack or weeping widow—can't lose; an unlucky Solomon can't win. But win or lose, like every game run by a "house," it is the *house* that eventually gets the money. True, the house, like the Canfields of old, furnishes easy chairs, free cigars, ticker tape, and endless tips and *dope* sheets; but it is the house, the kitty, the rake-off, the overhead, the Street, that keeps the gamblers hustling for margins.

Let us be honest with ourselves and deal frankly with the facts. I am no more "against" the Stock Exchange than I am against tea, coffee, or soap. Man by nature is a gambler. Youth especially is prone to take a chance on Fate—or, more specifically, to make a bet on any proposition, however hazardous. Gambling is a kind of war, a contest, a struggle, a fight; one pits oneself, or pieces of one's projected self, against an adversary. If the war is serious or the contest important or the bet big, it is a fight.

The biology of fight is the physiology of adrenalin, and the business of adrenalin is to help kill somebody. When man is angry enough to kill, he is for the moment a madman—a threat to his adversary, a danger to himself. It is the business of the professional gambler—that is, one who has learnt by experience that headwork can outrun footwork and that intelligence can beat brute strength—to keep a cool head.

Why is it not possible today to walk into a gambling-house in every city in America? Why do the more enlightened nations of the world today frown upon or control or outlaw gambling? Why have we no more public lotteries like those of Spain, Italy, and Latin America? Because gambling is a sin or wicked? No; because it easily becomes a vice, an evil. Because it is not a business, a trade, an industry, or an art; because it is a gamble, and, like morphine, easily becomes a vicious habit which travels on its own and too often disregards prudence, the rights of family, and the property of employer or associate.

Human struggles, human contests, yes; games, sports; competition, even keen competition. But the gambling proclivity of youth is wasted biologic endowment if it leads to no experience which can be cashed in at the bar of public opinion or over the counter of human social values, and which has value at the family altar.

So much for honesty's sake. What are the facts?

The first and most fundamental is that the underlying principle of gambling is economically false and morally vicious. Why? Because the man, woman, or child who speculates in stocks expects—or shall we say hopes?—to make money without making goods, or without rendering services which might favour or help in the making of goods. Yet, as Carver says, "the whole organization of the Stock Exchange is so designed as to make it possible for men to gamble." What Wall Street wants and must have is *commissions.* It is as indifferent to the source of these commissions as a gum-vending slot machine. When I sell a bushel of wheat or a share of copper "short," I have made a bet—no more, no less, than when I bet on a horse-race or a roulette wheel. Now, betting on a horse or a colour or a number may not be gambling, it may be sheer idiocy; the world at large calls it "gambling," and the man who tries to make a living out of Wall Street a *sucker.*

I am not proposing, nor even suggesting, a remedy; I am suggesting that a sound industrial system, a sound banking system, sound business, and a healthy, sane society, are not compatible with a Stock Exchange so designed as to make it not only possible but all too easy for men to gamble. We seem competent to think straight about morphine and even about gambling; but we are so beguiled with white marble and other evidences of success that we cannot think straight about the most vicious gambling-house the world has ever seen.

Business was never so old nor so big as it is now. It is big enough to be capitalized and powerful enough to be a god. That makes it worth looking at, for anything so big and so powerful is a possible menace to civilization and a probable threat to progress.

The primary business of business, as I see it, is trade; and a fair trade is a square deal. If I trade a penny fish-hook for a carved human skull (as I have repeatedly) it is a fair trade—if my fish-hook is good steel and the skull is bone and not papier-mâché. It is a square deal, even though the skull in London or New York is worth twenty-five hundred fish-hooks; there are more skulls in New Guinea than fish-hooks, and *vice versa.* True, we do not carve skulls, nor can the Papuan make fish-hooks; but he can live on fish and the best of skulls can catch none. Our natives of Central America made fish-hooks of gold. Gold is poor hook metal; presumably they would have traded a hundred gold hooks for one of steel. A fair trade again and good business for both parties.

The first business man was probably the fortunate possessor of a lot of gold (or copper) nuggets. In almost any Ohio mound evidences of widespread trade may be found: mica from the Carolinas, obsidian from the Yellowstone, shells from the Mexican Gulf, etc. The possessor of gold (or copper) nuggets was a capitalist; he could do business with them, live off them. His capital was "saved" wealth. His gold was wealth because people wanted it; they would trade goods for it. That, and that alone, made it wealth. If nobody had cared for his nuggets nor would trade anything for them, his wealth so far as his nuggets went was precisely *nil*.

The second stage in business grew out of fertile fields—surplus grain for trade purposes. Ancient nations stored wealth—metals, grains—as trade goods for war; thus they could buy men and equip armies and fleets. King, priest, and landlord acquired wealth through taxes, tolls, fines, rents, and gifts—all representing surplus from soil or mines. Exploitation in a sense. It became a habit, a custom, and acquired sanctity—like a "law of nature" or the "will of God."

With the Middle Ages, saved wealth began to accumulate in certain "logical" centres: the treasuries of the papacy, of the knightly orders, the higher feudal nobility, royalty. Also in certain cities where the modern business man began his growth. Venice, Milan, Naples, Bologna, Florence, Paris, London, Barcelona, Seville, Lisbon, Bruges, Ghent, Antwerp, Nürnberg, Cologne—all took their turn as financial centres.

Great estates necessitated business brains for their successful management: rent collectors, stewards, bailiffs, reeves. Part of the collected wealth stuck to their fingers and they began to share in the wealth and to see justice in terms of natural or God-given distinctions. But up to the time of Elizabeth there was no sharp line between landed and moneyed interests.

The Crusades, as remarkable in their failure as in provoking change in European society, were mighty forces in breeding money-lenders. As every Crusade was in the nature of a glorious gamble for superb stakes, the Crusaders spent recklessly and borrowed usuriously. And all Europe found itself in debt to Italy, Flanders, and the German banking-houses or loan sharks. The Renaissance inaugurated an era of luxury and bred social centres.

Italian luxury and magnificence rested on the exploitation of the Mediterranean world. Portugal, Spain, Holland, France, and England, in turn grew rich from destroying Arab civilization and from plundering Africa, South Asia, the West Indies, Mexico, and Peru.

Genoa, Pisa, Venice, enriched themselves by plundering Cæsarea, Acre, Sidon, and Tyre. The break-up of the Eastern Empire especially threw a colonial empire into the lap of Venice. With Moslem slaves alone, the Italians swelled Crete's population from fifty thousand to two hundred thousand. All rights and possessions in men, women, and children, says Hobson, passed to the new feudal superiors. Under Henry the Navigator, fifty thousand slaves were added to the population of Portugal.

But, as we have seen, Europe profited little from these predatory measures and the ruthless exploitation of goods and peoples. There was neither rhyme nor reason in getting or spending. King, noble, knight, church, sought wealth for war, ostentation, or alms-giving. It was an age of get-rich-quick—by rapine, plunder, extortion, confiscation. The great powers were frankly pirate states, and while we speak of the voyages of Columbus, Magellan, Drake, etc., as voyages of discovery, they were essentially quests for plunder, gold, ivory, spices, slaves—anything they could get their hands on that could be used at home. The natives they encountered had no more rights than the wild animals. We are prone to forget that if sixteenth-century civilization went far, it went armed and was no respecter of persons.

Easy come, easy go. Riches were squandered on luxury, vice, and ostentation. Of social amelioration or justice, of advance in hygiene or in knowledge leading to sound progress in material and moral welfare, there was none. Famine, plague, and war kept Europe's population down. Infant mortality was enormous.

Up to the eighteenth century the rate of increase of population in Europe was very slow—in that one century, in fact, none at all. France under Louis XIV had less than eighteen millions; Italy remained at eleven millions up to the eighteenth century; Spain declined enormously during the sixteenth and seventeenth centuries; Elizabeth's England did not exceed five millions; in 1800 it had less than nine millions. In Defoe's time there were fewer miles of good roads in England than in the time of Roman sway. One had to go two hundred miles from London to find a turnpike. Cattle could not enter London after October, for there was no bottom to the roads.

Out of those Middle Age days of mud, disease, witches, knights, popes, plagues, wars, cruelties, piracy, savagery, squalour, unspeakable poverty, incredible social injustice, came machines: levers, pulleys, wedges, screws, mechanical contrivances for doing work, methods of harnessing wind, water, steam, and electricity. Labour-saving devices, power-creating devices, undreamed of by all the ages that had gone before. Methods of economy nature herself had never discovered. Even dirt, garbage, and refuse proved to have unsuspected value. It was a new world. The discoveries of science were being applied to human ends.

A few paragraphs, or at most a chapter, would suffice to enumerate the advances made in this or that respect for one, two, five thousand years; a volume is required to set forth adequately the advances made in a generation or a century.

Business became big because the world of goods, of marketable goods, had become big, and because the world had speeded up its rate of increase in population.

Peru, India, China, grew cotton two thousand years ago. Kay's flying shuttle in 1738 led to better spinning thread. In 1769 came Arkwright's water-frame; in 1770, Hargreaves' spinning-jenny and Crompton's mule; in 1785, Cartwright's power loom. Then the world had better facilities for weaving than it had for getting raw cotton.

With Whitney's cotton-gin in 1793 cotton cloth became so cheap one could sew the world up in a cotton tick—and soon afterwards with a sewing-machine. The man who invented that marvellously efficient labour-saving device was mobbed and nearly murdered—less than a hundred years ago. It was a poor, clumsy machine, anyhow, but it was an idea. The idea was improved by Hunt and Howe, and with Singer grew to be the tallest building of its time in the world— for the natives, from Greenland's icy mountains to India's coral strand, had gone in for sewing-machines. I have encountered hand sewing-machines and kerosene lamps in incredibly out-of-the-way places.

Europe got gunpowder in the fourteenth century, and within two hundred years civilization had been profoundly affected: gunpowder represents accumulated power, condensed and easily loosed energy. In 1845 Schönbein invented guncotton. Two years later Sobrero invented nitroglycerin—which Nobel, a Swedish engineer, mixed with gunpowder, making it practical for blasting rocks. In

1867 he diluted nitroglycerin with inert siliceous earth, and the result was dynamite—and a fortune of nine million dollars for Nobel Prizes "for the good of humanity."

For the good of humanity. Is power good for us? Digging-stick, hoe, shovel; slow, back-breaking. With Nobel's explosives, one hundred men in ten months can do as much work as could thirty thousand men in eleven years in the days of Claudius. A steam shovel picks up fifteen tons as easily as I can pick up my hat. A throwing-stick is good: with one I can outthrow Babe Ruth; with gunpowder I can throw a half-ton of metal thirty miles; a smaller shell, seventy miles. People now talk of throwing themselves up to the moon. Why not? It is not very far. Science has not begun to exhaust the power of explosives. Think of a stone hammer—and of a steam hammer that can strike a hundred-ton blow or a tap so light it would not crush a hair; of spindles moving at ten thousand revolutions a minute.

Power. Horse, ass, aurochs, ox, buffalo, yak, reindeer, dog, camel, elephant, llama. They gave power; as did the wind. As a matter of fact, the ancient world had practically all the power devices and machinery known to man until he decided to generate power. This industrial power-driven Machine Age is less than two hundred years old. The problem Fulton solved with his *Clermont* on the Hudson in 1807 was solved two thousand years ago by a paddle-wheel moved by oxen on a boat carrying a Roman emperor to Sicily. But up to 1834 an English king could make no better time from London to Rome than Cæsar could make from Rome to London.

Yet men had been tinkering with steam since before Cæsar's day. But, if there are 150 parts in a watch no larger than a dime, think of the parts in a big steam-engine—or rather of the things that had to be discovered, invented, improved, and put together, before the world had a steam-engine which could pull the burden of a million human carriers.

Nearly a century before Cæsar went to Egypt, Hero of Alexandria had worked out a toy steam-engine on a principle which Branca, an Italian, was to rediscover in 1629, and Parsons in 1884 was to turn to reality in a steam turbine engine. Into the details of the history of the steam-engine we cannot go, but a large part of that story centres around such prosaic affairs as cranks, pistons, and cylinders which would hold steam. Watt thought himself lucky if his cylinders came within three-eighths of an inch of being true, and he could not have got results so good had there not been invented a machine for boring cylinders. That machine today works to one one-thousandth of an inch.

Symington in 1802 put a steam-engine in a tug to pull a canal boat. Think of the canals and business that tug started. In 1769 Cugnot's steam-engine ran through the streets of Paris at the incredible speed of three miles an hour. Brunton's monstrosity of 1813 kicked itself along on poles like a grasshopper. But with Stevenson's "Rocket" in 1829 the world had its first successful locomotive. Compound engines came later, and in 1867 the first successful gas-engine.

Not till 1819 was steam used to drive a ship across the sea, nor till 1870 had steam power come to exceed water power. But as early as 1764 steam-driven machinery began to be used in industry. Machine Age: work done by a machine (tool) set in a mechanism driven by power. A flint knife is good; shearing-machines will cut steel half a foot thick.

Three weeks was the time between Boston and New York by the first post-riders in 1673; six days by the first coach service in 1783. Our first transcontinental railroad was completed by 1869.

Iron Age. Iron is about as old as writing in human history; but, as the world could not be sewn up in cotton till an abundance of cheap cotton was available for the swiftly moving power looms, so there could be no real Iron Age until an abundance of cheap iron was available. There was a blast furnace in Belgium by 1350, but not till 1750 did the blast furnace really begin to work like a modern plant. Coal and coke made that possible. A modern blast furnace will do the work of a quarter of a million men in the early days of iron. The first railroads used wooden rails; then came iron rails—with a life of three months. With Bessemer's process, rails would last six years. That was the beginning of modern railroading and modern building.

Our roads were then, and up to 1890, the worst in the civilized world. True, we had had no Romans to lay the foundations, but we had had slaves. I have no figures of the amount of money we have spent on roads since 1890; it must be a staggering sum. They are today the best in the world and carry over twenty-five million automobiles. Thirty-five years ago there were just four autos in the United States—and one was in a museum and one would not run. Up to that time automobile speed in England was limited by law to four miles; in the cities, to two; and each gas buggy had to be preceded by a person carrying a red flag. 1896.

Lenoir's internal-combustion engine dates from 1860; Daimler's benzine engine for gas carriages, from the late '80s. And today half the horse-power generated in the United States is found in automobiles.

The horse-power unit idea began with Watt trying to estimate the amount of work his engine did. The work of a dray-horse, he thought, was equal to lifting thirty-three thousand pounds one foot in one minute—one "horse power."

On the second voyage of Columbus the native lads of Haiti were seen playing with balls—of "the gum of a tree." But rubber remained soft—a plaything, or at best a "rubber," till Goodyear in 1839 treated it with sulphuric compounds—"vulcanized" it. That plaything of rubber has grown into a mighty business of politics, finance, colonial policy, international competition, golf balls, rubber heels, balloon tires, and zeppelins.

There was a successful balloon ascension in 1783, but no zeppelin till 1900. In 1903 the Wrights flew over the sand dunes of North Carolina for twelve whole seconds—a world's record! The next year they had made such vast progress that they could turn around in the air, and in the following year they beat their own world record with a flight of thirty-three minutes and seventeen seconds. They invented the airplane. With Curtis' flight from Albany to New York in 1910, the conquest of the air had really begun. Aircraft today fly over the earth at the rate of 100,000,000 miles a year, and one has attained a speed of 367 miles an hour. I doubt if Roger Bacon would admit that possible.

Let us look for a moment at a real miracle, at real progress. It is not easy for us to realize that only one generation on earth has had really good light, one century only fair light, and all the thousands of ages before wretched or no light at all; or that real comfort in heating and cooling houses has run a parallel course.

There wasn't a match on earth until 1827. In that year an English chemist made the first friction match. Phosphorus put sandpaper out of fashion in 1833; but as late as 1904 it was advisable to be provided with sandpaper when using California matches, for they were sulphurous and frictional. Safety matches were invented in Sweden.

Nearly two hundred years ago Clayton produced gas from coal heated in a closed vessel or retort. In 1792 Murdock lighted his house with it; also the House of Commons—but the members touched the pipes gingerly and with gloved hands, "feeling it out"; they thought the light came through the pipes. Gas supplanted the old whale oil for street lights in 1830. Kerosene became available—and a better light—about 1850. But with the Welsbach mantle in 1886 gas became really effective for lighting purposes. The first lamp chimney was a happy discovery which we owe to a young brother of Argand, the Swiss chemist, who broke the bottom out of a bottle to see how it would work. It worked beautifully.

At our Philadelphia Centennial in 1876 there were just two electric-light exhibits, and not until 1882 was there a central power station for generating electricity. While the beginnings of that story go back to the Greeks playing with amber and calling its capacity to attract a straw when rubbed "amber-soul," it really begins with Volta's pile generating a continuous current and Faraday's 1831 machine moving wires past a magnet in an orderly manner. That was the first time electricity had been "harnessed"—the first dynamo. But not till 1873 was this current made to run a motor. High-pressure transmission became practical in 1893.

While de Moleyn had devised an incandescent light by 1841, it was Edison who in 1878 created the first incandescent bulb; and today our output of electric-light bulbs is more than 300,000,000 a day, and of electric light the equal in illuminating power of more than two billion candles. That may or may not be progress, but it is Big Business, and electric light is amazing progress. Candles still gutter on the altars, but the Basilica of St. Peter's is really lighted.

When Dom Pedro, Emperor of Brazil, heard Bell's voice at the Centennial, he exclaimed: "My God! it talks!" But Congress shook its head for three years before it would grant thirty thousand dollars to build a telegraph line from Washington to Baltimore, although Morse had already sent messages through three miles of copper wire. Fourteen years after that line was completed, Field had laid the first transatlantic cable, 1858. New York first talked with Chicago in 1892; with San Francisco, 1915. And after eight years' experimenting with Hertzian waves, Marconi in 1896 began wireless communication.

Electricity: amber, cat's fur, furry things, curios, curiosities of nature; a central *power*-house—one, at 257 Pearl Street, Manhattan, 1882; today, four thousand central stations, costing eleven billion dollars and serving twenty-five million customers. Progress? A revolution—in life and industry! Dynamic Age. Founded on science. There are millions in it today.

Does Big Business wait for another Faraday, Volta, Galvani, Hertz, Crookes, Maxwell, Steinmetz, Thomson, or Langmuir? It does not. It has no need for the amateur of the last generation. On their discoveries it has built a mighty structure of its own; and in the astounding laboratories of the American Telephone and Telegraph, the Western Electric, the Westinghouse, and the General Electric, it develops its own experts. It does not even need the university or the technical school. It nurses its children; it controls the light that shines and the voice of the Loud Dynamic Speaker; and, I infer, seeks to control the "white coal" of all falling waters. Science enlightens the world and Big Business controls the light.

A little over a century ago a Frenchman heated food in a closed vessel and sealed it while hot. Canned food was important business by the time of our Civil War, but not the Big Business it is now. With McCormick, in 1834, ploughs and harrows were raised from their five-thousand-year sleep. Threshing and spraying machines came with the centennial of our Independence. Since then there has been enormous progress in machinery for butter, cheese, and milking; and improved processes for preserving milk, eggs, and meat. Refrigeration was not common before 1880. The first cargo of fresh meat was sent from this country to Europe in 1879. With the electric refrigerator and a properly insulated wire, fresh meat and vegetables could be sent to Sheol. No one there or here need ever die of scurvy.

Take the business of the cinema and recall that poor Swede druggist, Scheele, who discovered oxygen and first mentioned the word *gas*. The movies owe him nothing for that, but they are indebted to him for playing with the effect of sunlight on silver chloride. It was

Wedgwood, however, who in 1802 made the first photograph. But he could not *fix* his pictures. Daguerre did that after thirteen years' experiment, in 1839. The collodion film got its start in 1850.

Big Business, yes; but try to conjure up a world without one single photograph—not even an old daguerreotype on copper! What a mighty force for the making of honesty the camera has been, for bringing home a factual world to replace the world of fabled monsters of a few centuries ago.

Do not think of the movies as they are under the incredible stupidity of the censors and Hays, but of what they might be in making the facts of life so plain that they could not possibly be misunderstood or mistaken. In their hands even the camera is forced to lie; truth, honesty, sincerity, vitality, art, great art, true art, fine art—all are sacrificed to a narrow morality and a paralyzing fear of hurting somebody's religious feelings or class prejudices.

The industrial revolution is but 150 years old, if we date it from Watt's use of a steam-engine in the coal-mines of Cornwall; the physical sciences are but 300 years old, if we date them from Galileo. The first miracle of biochemistry is just over 100 years old, if we date it from Wöhler.

Synthetic urea, 1828; synthetic silk, now an industry of over a hundred million dollars. Over one hundred million pounds of synthetic dyes; over two million pounds of synthetic flavours; a million and a half pounds of synthetic perfumes; thirty-one million pounds of synthetic resins; of synthetic drugs, over five million pounds; and of synthetic gin, I do not know how many barrels. Tons, millions of dollars' worth, of dyes, drugs, antiseptics, anæsthetics, perfumes, flavours, etc.—all synthesized, made to order because the chemists patiently analysed coal tar. Synthetic chewing-gum, wool, wax, leather, hair, ivory, fire-proofing. Analysis, synthesis. Modern miracles.

"Dry ice," solid carbon dioxide; forty carloads a day of this new method of preservation from the bacteria of decay now go out to all parts of the United States. Fresh, *strictly* fresh eggs, butter, and poultry can now go direct from His Tarrytown Estate to His Winter Home in Florida. And in a former age He would have been put out of the way as a useless encumbrance! Progress, in preserving eggs, in preserving human life.

Just one more illustration of what happens when an old idea meets a new method of "getting results." Is the idea worth the paper it is printed on? Print paper: enough made in the United States each year to build a plank road sixteen feet wide around the world. I spoke of a world sewed up in cotton cloth; we could more easily wrap it up in paper.

Enough paper pulp each year to make a plank road sixteen feet wide, twenty-five thousand miles long; 150 pounds of paper pulp per capita! How many trees cut, how many acres of forest cleared, how many hands employed in cutting, clearing, and moving the timber to the mills; how many tons of chemicals, etc.? What a story, what a business!

Moabite Stone, Rosetta Stone, Behistun inscription. Inscriptions on stone, on copper; writings on papyrus, on tablets, on soft clay. A Homer on snakeskins in letters of gold. Writings on parchment; writings washed out to make room for more writings: illuminated vellum. Writing with chisel, brush, hollow reed, quill, pen, fountain pen, typewriter, movable type. Three centuries from Gutenberg's clumsy wooden press to Stanhope's iron press. A half century between the first machine for beating pulp and a machine which would turn out an endless roll of pulp paper, and by 1840 the conviction that wood pulp could supply paper for the world. Age of wood-pulp paper. A revolving cylinder press in 1812; two years later, a power press—eight hundred papers per hour! Hoe press, 1845; linotype, 1884; monotype, 1888. And stop, look, listen to the presses now!

Machine age, power age, iron age, steel age, electric age. Power: steam, electricity. Machines, mechanisms: mechanical age. Yet there are those who decry it, deplore it, hate it. Why?

But first, just who is it that deplores machinery? The same people, it seems to me, who find the term mechanism odious when applied to man or other living beings. To do that is to rob man of his mystery. One cannot get along with a machine by filling it full of mystery or by talking about it mystically. Prejudice, sophistry, deception, misrepresentation, casuistry, have no value at all in helping us understand a machine or in getting results out of it. Calling it names helps not at all, nor does endowing it with virtue. The test of a machine is not its vulgarity or its respectability, its morality or immorality, its orthodoxy or its heterodoxy, its spirituality or materiality.

There, it seems to me, is the real reason for the astounding progress now being made in supplementing our indifferent innate equipment for satisfying routine human wants. We may monkey with a machine and thereby learn to use it, or think up a more useful one, but we cannot trifle with it if we are to understand it and make it do our bidding.

The first element behind every human enterprise which can stand the test of universality is sincerity, honesty. It is the application of that principle to industry which has transformed the world. One may lie, dissemble, cheat, deceive one's fellow-men, and seem to have a measure of success; one cannot successfully take that attitude with one's machine, whether it be radio, tractor, or sewing-machine.

That our marvellous mechanical equipment is still the slave of those who would pervert it to mere personal aggrandizement or unconscionable greed, or employ it as a weapon in fratricidal wars, is to be expected. Social control has always lagged, for it is easier to scrap a machine than the voice of divine sanction. It was all right to speak of "divine sanction" in the Middle Ages, but it does seem puerile in an industrial age.

Astronomy became a science and gave us the art of navigation; biology became a science and gave us the arts of medicine and agriculture in all their manifold phases; anatomy became a science and gave us the art of surgery; chemistry became a science and gave us the arts of the synthetic magician; and the historian, anthropologist, and psychologist have given us a scientific background against which all problems of human social behaviour can be viewed honestly, impartially and rationally.

But we still await the engineers who can cut through antique theories, sacrosanct conventions and consecrated sentiment, and direct the mighty forces now available toward real social progress. Not only should no human being on earth today have to starve to death, no human being should have to starve æsthetically or intellectually. There should be not only no lack of food, there should be no lack of opportunity, and there should be such organization that sheer luck or accident of place or incidence of birth would have less value for getting on in the world than moral integrity and earnest effort. For it is true, as Hobson says, that "life without industry is guilt, industry without art is brutality."

But while most of us can see and even deplore the iniquity of the caste system in India, with its "unspeakable untouchables," how many of us hold, with du Bois, that it is a self-evident truth *that a disfranchised working-class in modern industrial civilization is worse than helpless. It is a menace, not simply to itself, but to every other group in the community. It will be diseased, it will be criminal, it will be ignorant, it will be the plaything of mobs, and it will be insulted by caste restrictions.* Or, and this is more to the point, if we do hold it to be a self-evident truth, would we turn our hand over to do anything about it if we thereby imperilled one red cent in our pocket or our social prestige by one jot or tittle?

In one hundred years the earth's population has tripled; its shipping tonnage has increased tenfold; its iron output, sixtyfold; its coal production sixty-fivefold; its railroad mileage fifteenfold; its international commerce fiftyfold. To that brief evidence of progress add the incredible advances in output of *new* things undreamt of a hundred years ago—all making for power, speed, and incredible security, including that most marvellous security device since our primitive forbears tried to hold population down to a reasonable level by performing abortion with a club, and not yet put into circulation because useful knowledge of humane contraceptives is against the law. Whose law? To whose interest is it that there should be free and unrestricted flow of human infants? Unnatural? So is poverty. Unethical? So is supernatural power. Immoral? So is inherited power. Not good for business? Whose business?

Forward America.

Business is Good; Keep it Good.

Nothing can stop U.S.

A hundred years ago an English lord who habitually drank himself under a table groaning under a load of meat, fish, and game, approved the hanging of a child for the theft of a fish. It was *justice*; good for king and church; necessary for Established Law and Order.

Just now we are told: Buy till it Hurts; a few years ago it was: Save till it Hurts. One is a business slogan; the other was a war slogan. Times change. Business right now is Bad. Let us see what War is Good for.

## IV

It is a great tribute to our efficiency, Professor Wheeler thinks, that we make everything so fool-proof a baby termite might envy us our individual security. "Security?" Secure against what—famine, plague, war?

Automobile accidents in the last year and a half cost the United States more lives than the World War. Industry has cost her fifteen times more lives than have been lost on all her battlefields. Fatal accidents in industry alone cost this nation nearly 400,000 man-years of labour per annum; permanent disability, another 350,000 man-years; and less serious injury 3,000,000 weeks.

Security? Somebody pays. Industry may be efficient; automobiles certainly are, but they are not fool-proof. Even in normal years our average daily unemployed is two and a half millions, with another two and a half millions daily average illness. Our tuberculosis bill is estimated at $500,000,000 a year; malaria costs another $100,000,000; typhoid, $135,000,000; hookworm, $250,000,000; accidents, well over $2,000,000,000. The cost of life shortened by tuberculosis is reckoned at $5,000,000,000.

We have 25,000,000 people with defective vision; 53,000 totally blind; 400,000 deaf; and nearly 100,000 insane. And in fairly prosperous years, no less than 10,000,000 people in poverty.

How much of that staggering toll in lives, health, and wealth is preventable? How much of our brain do we use? We can say that we put less than five per cent of our natural and acquired resources to wise and humane uses. We can say that our press will give a front-page write-up to one avoidable accidental death, and be oblivious to a thousand deaths that same day due to preventable and avoidable disease. Death from any preventable disease should be news—sad, shamefaced news—to any community in the civilized world. We accept it with no more concern than our ancestors accepted plague; just as we accept the fact that one-fiftieth of our people own more than fifty per cent, and two-thirds only one-twentieth, of our wealth.

Efficient, yes. Security . . . ? It is not only that there are twenty-three thousand fatal accidents a year in American fool-proof industry, but that in proportion to population we have nearly twice as many such preventable deaths as any other country in the world. That at least should hurt our pride enough to make us curious. We can't expect a baby termite to envy our security if, despite all our fool-proofness, industry is so fatal to a mere labourer. Termites are workers; they have to earn their living. That is why we tell the sluggard to go to the ant. (Yes, I know a termite is not an ant.)

A can of fruit is a miracle of science, but we have over one thousand thirteen-year-old children working in the canneries; some even under eight. That is a vastly better showing than could have been made a hundred years ago. Then they would have had to work fourteen hours a day; we think twelve hours long enough for child labour. Canned fruit is sanitary fruit, but canning fruit, even in a New York flat, is hot, steamy work. The U. S. Children's Bureau finds that sanitary conditions where the children work are pretty primitive. Not *too* primitive of course, for that would create disfavour; but far more primitive than they should be in a rich country which can afford canned fruits.

Now, a thousand children canning fruit twelve—and some sixteen—hours a day (or night) in hot, steamy, badly ventilated canneries is not a very big potato, but it is one of the straws eventually making for the big stock of man-power loss this nation puts up with because it still thinks of human lives as crude oil from which something can be extracted by the cracking process.

Efficient? Not with fifteen per cent of our population at poverty level; or with four million people sixty-five years old without even a black-bread income; or with a five-billion-dollars a year loss from our physically non-effective, mentally, morally, and socially deficient, and the mentally and nervously ill. That is the *direct* cost, Bossard reckons, of our social ill-being; the indirect cost he places between twenty and twenty-five billion dollars a year.

While we are writing a check for that bill, let us look at another. It also is a big bill and one to which no American can point with pride, even although it comes under the heading Big Business. For crime is Big these days—bigger than it has ever been in the history of the world. It is a great and a paying business.

Sixteen thousand million dollars a year. Financial losses from fraudulent bankruptcy, etc., three-quarters of a billion dollars a year. Forgery, two hundred million dollars. Worthless stocks and bonds, five hundred millions. One billion dollars a year in forbidden drugs: morphine, cocaine, heroin, etc.—one-fifth as much as we spend on our fifty million school children, including their schools, playgrounds, and welfare work.

One-sixth of the nation's income. Tribute money: tribute to our inefficiency; tribute to criminals and racketeers. Five million people arrested a year; an army passing in and out of our bulging prisons.

Tom Sayers fights forty-four rounds for five pounds sterling. Dempsey fights Tunney thirty minutes before 145,000 spectators and a $2,658,660 "house"; Dempsey takes $750,000, Tunney $450,000. Big Business, licensed by the state, financed by bankers, and attended by Society. Six million "Red Grange" chocolate bars sold in one month. Gertrude Ederle received a million dollars' worth of offers—but what for she probably does not remember now.

Who pays these bills? Imperial Rome would have gagged at such an overhead.

Nothing can stop us. The non-stop piano endurance champion played sixty hours, five thousand selections, hit the keys over four million times, smoked two hundred cigarettes and fifty cigars. Tree-sitting contests, Spitting contests, Pick-bathing-beauty contests, Hog-calling contests.

Insect pests cost the farmers a tidy sum, estimated at from one and a half to two billion dollars a year. That brings our fool-proof bill to . . . call it forty billions. And the real war not yet begun.

Sherman called it Hell; Napoleon, a Grand Game: and *What Price Glory* proved that both were right. And the last war—the war to end war—proved that history can repeat itself if given enough time. True, no particular credit was claimed by the Brass Hats for killing babies, women, and old men; nor were such deaths listed with the blood-lusty savagery of an Assyrian warlord. But babies, women, and old men were killed—from afar, by long-range guns, aerial bombs, and poison gas.

Sherman quit fighting when the war was won; Napoleon, when he became Emperor—to lose his crown and his freedom finally on the battlefield. But it was a Grand Game while it lasted—for him; it was Hell for the rank and file.

We cannot end wars on a printed page, but we can talk about war in a page or so. We can even try to think about war rationally and honestly. I do not know that we can succeed, for the business of war is murder and no one in a murderous mood can think rationally or honestly about anything. In war one does not have to think, only to kill.

And so it is, it seems to me, that we need never expect to find a professional soldier taking a sane or rational attitude toward war. Psychologically speaking, the warrior is congenitally blind to the blessings of peace. Loyalty, for him, means hatred of foreigners. To be a good killer, one must be a good hater. Hence the floods of propaganda loosed in every war; more in the World War than ever before because machinery is now available as never before for letting propaganda loose. The real "atrocities" of the late war were committed so far behind the firing-line that no blood or mud could bespatter their authors to shame them.

War is necessarily shameless, dishonest, ruthless, cruel. It deliberately flouts every generous quality, every decent aspiration, every humane motive, every critical attitude. It denies the usefulness of, and scornfully rejects, every sentiment and virtue man has found useful in his long climb up from the jungle. It scornfully and cynically rejects every altruistic motive that lifts man above the savage beast.

And note this, please. No savage beast has ever risen one tiny fraction of an inch in the scale of animal life by warring on its own kind. Man alone of all the animals the sun shines on seeks to advance by warring against his fellows. Being a Napoleon conceivably is a Grand Game; but Napoleon himself was game—and of a deadly parasitic species. With our increased capacity and incredible facilities for hate-provoking propaganda, for organizing violent behaviour in new and unheard-of ways, war has passed beyond the stage where a nation or a continent or a hemisphere can afford that kind of parasite. The world cannot support it. The world of man still has its enemies—presumably always will have, certainly will have for centuries to come. To survive, man must wage relentless war against the forces of nature and the inertia of ignorance and stupidity. He cannot win that war by cutting men's throats or by bombing children.

Is any human being on earth today hungry or in pain, or in want of any of the comforts of life? Is there a slave, an aching tooth, a broken back, or a rational, reasonable, unfulfilled want anywhere in the civilized world? Is there anyone anywhere this minute dying of a preventable disease? Or a boy or girl in America who lacks the opportunity of play or is in need of sound wholesome food, shoes, school books, teachers, or medical care?

Our crime-disease bill is not far from forty billions of dollars. What our vain, senseless, stupid, monstrous luxury bill is, I do not know. I only know that in two years of the World War this country spent more than in the previous century. Pershing recently casually mentioned a three-day bombardment he witnessed in 1917. Three days of fireworks for the benefit of the god of war—$75,000,-000. And that represented just what one man could see, in one sector, from one side, in a four years' war. Is it any wonder France's national wealth decreased by one-third; England's, by one-fourth; and that the combined cost of the war is estimated at two hundred and fifty million billions of dollars?

Thirteen million people were killed; not babies, not senile men and women, not statesmen, diplomats, politicians, or professors in war colleges or Tom Browns at Headquarters, but soldiers, young men, boys out of school, off the farm, taken away from their jobs. Boys who were not really old enough to hate; they had to be lashed to frenzy to join in the Grand Game. Hell? Hell was turned loose before the boys left their home towns. Church joined school to swell the rulers' brag and bluster; flags waved, national anthems blared, uniforms paraded, and patriotism—God, King, Country— was exalted as the one sole virtue to lift man above the beasts of the field.

It was a Grand Game; hearts beat faster; big-game hunting; human beings could be shot with impunity—nay, could be blown to bits, ground up in the mud of their blood and bowels; charge bayonets, throw the bombs, loose the gas.

Man's inhumanity to man makes countless thousands mourn. Thirteen millions dead—every one leaving one or more mourners. We are more efficient than in Burns' day. It would probably be impossible to compute the exact number of mourners: not countless thousands, but—shall we say?—thirty-nine millions, for a war to end war.

The insidiousness of that cry—the war to end war! Just one more drink and I'll stop. Never again. We are going to clean this up so thoroughly it will stay clean forever. And Wilson was honest; we were all honest—at any rate, as honest as we could be with a war on. Truth and honest thought go one way—but that is not the way of successful propaganda for an offensive drive against civilization. Nor, I repeat, can militant diplomacy afford the luxury of cold honesty.

That is the really destructive, devastating, uncivilizing aspect of war. It is not its original cost. The world could have lost a hundred million young men and every ounce of gold on earth—and got off cheaply, if it could have gained courage to face the truth, to be honest about the facts of life.

In 1920 the Royal Belgian Academy awarded a prize for a school book for children from ten to twelve which "proved" the Germans racially perverse, innately malicious and cruel, robbers, plunderers, and murderers by nature, without a single human instinct or idea of any kind of right and justice, understanding of honour, or sense of humour.

What makes for patriotism makes for a fool's paradise whose last resort is war. Let us be clear about this. Untold millions of men have been slaughtered because Egyptian, Babylonian, Hittite, Persian, Roman, Hapsburg, Bourbon crowns claimed something that did not belong to them. War was a business. The prize was arable land, taxable subjects, and any accumulated wealth that might be carried off or destroyed. The soldier's pay was insignificant compared with his chance for adventure, plunder, loot, rape. It was a Grand Game; legalized gain, plunder, loot; and much was forgiven the soldier: he could defy every code of humanity, morality, or decency. Debauchery and unbridled licence were compatible with the banner of Crown and Cross.

We have moved up a stage—not too far; but why deceive ourselves that war to end war, or war for country or for civilization, is more virtuous than war for land or slaves? The New York politician or the Chicago hijacker is actuated by no "higher" purpose; he is out for gain, for graft, for loot. Apart from two or three important purchases, we have moved across this continent, not for a higher purpose, but because we wanted the land. And for every day's occupation of the Philippines or of Haiti we can easily find a thousand sham moralities and plausible rationalizations.

To talk of the nobility of nationalism is to talk like an imbecile. To think of civilization as hanging on to the coat-tails of the politics of this or that nation, and to ask us to respect the opinion of the politicians and follow their banner to battle—else civilization is lost! —is to bring civilization down to the level of a huckster.

"My country, right or wrong," is the motto of every bully, every cheat, every crook, every despot; the most ignoble of all forms of patriotism.

Rome rose and fell, Spain rose and fell, and so on and so on. But just what was it that rose, how old was it when it fell, what did it look like? The Grand Game, an ancient cultural complex, militarism, as a system for getting something by inhuman means. Did it pay? Did it settle anything? Oceans of blood have been shed for things, ideas, principles, that no self-respecting ape would take seriously. And the attendant agony and the hangover wrecks were all that Sherman said war is.

Meanwhile everybody gets ready for the next war. It is taken for granted that it will come; and we argue about the size of the guns instead of looking at a few simple truths which go a-begging.

Civilization moves on, now slowly, right now swiftly; it cannot stop; it is too heavily entrenched to be turned out; it moves on. But the old army game moves round and round in the same old vicious circle. The Old World has not yet unscrambled the omelette Cæsar made of it; for how many generations shall we be unscrambling the Versailles omelette? One thing is certain: those eggs cannot be restored by war.

I am not underestimating the hold on our thinking of the symbols we inherited from the Old Testament or from the law codes of the Roman Empire. Property is still more sacrosanct than human lives; we still talk of virtue in terms of armour, shields, swords, and gauntlets. Recall Paul's armour-clad Christian. Recall also Rome's fight against the Infidel. But how much civilization or faith was spread by the Inquisition? Just as much as the *Kultur* that was spread by the Kaiser's war-machine. Was the church really interested in faith, or in its own coffers? Was the Kaiser interested in *Kultur*, or in his own aggrandizement and vainglory? Most of us could glorify God if we could wear the crown and let the soldier bear the cross.

Germany had *Kultur* and a marvellous system of education. Her scientists were leading the world; her application of science was making her great, rich, prosperous. Her chemists alone had laid the foundations for world conquest in the arts of peace. But that was not enough. Her war lords were not enough to the fore. They preached ideals which were incompatible with liberty, for they demanded obedience to irrational whims. Education was not enough; there must be military discipline, blind submission to the voice of God's anointed. Germany, in short, put her trust, not in education, but in her war-machine.

Are we not possibly putting our trust in our money-machine? We fear loss—of money; we swell with pride—over heaped-up capital. The very thoroughness of Germany's war-machine was her undoing. Surrender on our part to a money-complex, with its pretence of disciplining our thoughts and actions, could be our undoing. It is a menace. Let it rule as a divine institution endowed with holiness, and our boasted bill of rights is a dead letter, our liberties lost.

The world today groans from hard times—and spends $4,300,-000,000 a year on arms—twelve years after the war to end war, and after several disarmament conferences and a few armament-reduction treaties. Sindbad's Old Man of the Sea never bore so heavily on human backs. Most of our own budget goes to the Old Man. In fact, of the $1,800,000,000 we spent from July to December of last year, over one billion dollars went to war costs.

It is now sixty-six years since Lee surrendered at Appomattox Court-House and ended the Civil War; and for that war we are still paying in pensions alone $140,000,000 a year. Nine widows of soldiers of the war of 1812 are still drawing dole. On that basis we shall be paying for the World War in the year 2048. I am not blaming the widows or the veterans; merely pointing out that veterans and widows of veterans are long-lived and Congress has never been able to resist them. But just when is a dole a pension and when is a war ended?

War, crime, corruption, debauchery, and cruelty are spawn of the same false and vicious psychology. Thus, it should cause us no surprise to learn that since the late war the menace to childhood from abuse, neglect, and depravity has doubled, and that all records for cruel and inhuman treatment in the last half year have been broken. "Surprise?" Who cares—even to the point of being surprised? There was a flutter of indignation at the exposure of venality in the framing of young women in the vice—or so-called justice —courts; but no Justice has been mobbed yet or put behind the bars, nor, so far as I know, barred from polite society. Some of them must be church members; I have heard of no expulsions, no excommunications.

It is just news, that is all; a passing shower in a great city parched for scandal. The news "made" the papers; but the facts made scarcely a ripple on the surface of life. The country is sound. Business is Good. But we can, I hope, and without charge of *lèse majesté*, agree with President Angell that "a nation which has become cynical or tolerant and complaisant in its attitude toward injustice or corruption in public or private life, which has become morally torpid, is in grave danger."

While injustice and corruption in public and private life are the legitimate offspring of war, we could not have become so complaisant toward them had we not forgotten our liberties.

Liberty? Freedom from the three evil fates: war, pestilence, and famine. The millions of human beings who have starved to death the last few years may have died happy, but it was a short-lived happiness and any philanthropist is entitled to try that brand of happiness on himself if he chooses. Pestilence weeds out the unfit, we are told; but "unfit" for what? Since when have our professional moralists submitted to the ordeal of plague to prove their fitness?

War is a biologic necessity, we are also told. Pure rot. War is no more necessary than cannibalism or rape; and, biologically speaking, it is more indefensible. Well, it makes for civilization; and if we do not agree, we are sneered at as *pacifists*: "Pacifism is an amiable philosophy!" Well, anti-pacifism is a despicable and an inhuman philosophy, and war is the most appalling of all destroyers of human values. Pending the end of that evil fate by human intelligence, I will agree to commit hara-kiri on behalf of civilization—if the next champion of the Anti-Pacifist League for Better Civilization will start another war and go over the top first.

What a democracy needs is a democratic education. What this

democracy demands is an Industrial Age democratic education. Is it getting it?

V

In thirty years (said August Heckscher, the philanthropist, on his eighty-second birthday) the United States will see the end of dire poverty, disease, and unnecessary suffering.

It *could*. Will it? I am just as hopeful as Mr. Heckscher, but my guess is that 1961 will see some dire poverty and disease, and altogether too much unnecessary suffering. Poverty is a disease, of course, as is crime; as are scurvy, beri-beri, and rickets. *Deficiency* diseases; deficiency of vitamins, deficiency of socially useful habits, deficiency of the wherewithal to pay for food, clothing, and shelter.

Progress in understanding these individual and social diseases has been made; great progress; and that understanding is the beginning of wisdom, the great tool for making living an art. But only if we use the tool. And who knows if we will use it? I do not know; I cannot predict three days ahead, much less thirty years.

The chief difference, as I have tried to point out before, between the ancient Greek and our modern attitude toward knowledge is in its application. To Socrates, knowledge was virtue: something esoteric, good in itself, an end in itself, its own reward. But reward for what? What virtue is there in the knowledge that Big Business is predatory, that overcrowded slums breed crime, that poverty is a social disease, famine a breakdown of distribution, war a madman's paradise, injustice the weapon of the bully and the snob and of a social philosophy which accepts inheritance as the Fundamental Law of Nature, if that knowledge be not applied to cleaning up the conditions which make for crime, famine, disease, war, and injustice?

Whose business is it to clean up iniquitous, unsanitary, unwholesome conditions? The custodians of wisdom, the virtuously wise? Or the professionals—the teachers, preachers, doctors, lawyers, journalists, social workers? Or the politicians? Certainly not; or, at any rate, no more than it is your business and mine. And *we* do not move out of our tracks because . . . Because we assume that it will be done by the machinery we help to support which is supposed to do it. What? Keep this Land of the Free and Home of the Brave eternally fit for freedom, hospitable to bravery.

More specifically, we accept the theory of democracy's inherent virtue and the further theory that we elect men to keep it running in good order and to make such repairs as are needed from time to time. Are the men we elect the best men? Well, they are representative: they represent us; and *we* are all right because we have been educated in the rights, duties, privileges, and responsibilities of citizenship.

That is why we have *free* and *compulsory* education. With that system we cannot go astray; our democracy can do no wrong. Education thereby becomes the palladium of security, its system the chief object of our solicitude. We point with pride to the fact that we spend on *public* education from kindergarten to college two and a half billion dollars a year—even though we spend three times that amount on candy, soft drinks, tobacco, and amusements, or five times that amount on passenger automobiles; in fact, our Lady Nicotine bill alone is just about equal to the cost of our devotion to the goddess Minerva.

Was Diogenes right in the line Voltaire (in *A Dialogue*) put into his mouth? "So long as it endures, the world will continue to be ruled by cajolery, by injustice, and by imposition." That was the question our American Fathers thought they had answered, and answered in the negative so emphatically that it could never arise again in this country.

Yet, according to *Science*, a New Jersey minister of the Gospel declared that "we are going to drive every Modernist out of our pulpits, seminaries, and editorial chairs *if it takes our lives to do it.*" A Fundamentalist "geologist" has attacked—of all parties—the U. S. Coast and Geodetic Survey, as "a wholesale official propaganda in favour of the evolution theory." And the Reverend William Ashley Sunday in a Los Angeles sermon is reported to have said—and it sounds like him: "If a minister believes and teaches evolution he is a stinking skunk and a liar. . . . The consensus of scholarship can go to hell, for all I care. . . . Old Darwin is in hell."

Some one has suggested that the anti-evolutionists oppose evolution because it never did anything for them. It does seem like a waste of breath to take a Billy Sunday seriously; but this Doctor of Divinity was a delegate in 1918 of the Chicago Presbytery to the General Assembly of the Presbyterian Church, U.S.A., and I am not aware that that church has repudiated the Reverend Sunday—or his doctrine. I have a feeling that the Presbyterian Church is Fundamentalist and a conviction that it does not hesitate to join forces with other Fundamentalist churches in trying to impose their will upon legislation and education. Politicians are notorious cowards; educators are congenitally weak-kneed and conservative by conviction.

But what, you may ask, has evolution to do with education? Let us see.

Now, man's place in nature is approximately what modern science says it is, or it is what the Bible says it is, or what an Egyptian or Chaldean priest, or a Wichita or Fiji medicine-man, says it is. Is the Fijian say-so as good as Chaldean, Egyptian as Judean? Or is it what modern science says it is?

Modern scientist, Judean, Egyptian, Chaldean, are human; all speak with human voices and none is infallible or omniscient. But if we split man's-place-in-nature into man and nature; "man," into cells, organs, glands, bones, muscles, nerves, etc.; and "nature" into sunshine, air, earth, food, bacteria, etc.: it does seem as though a modern scientific viewpoint should give us a more reasonable definition of man's place in nature than the one that prevailed when Copernicus was a canon of the church or when the church's Bible was written.

What is a gland? No scientist knows; no scientist knows what a vacuum tube is. But science knows about two hundred ways of using vacuum tubes, and enough of several glands to manufacture the kinds of drugs they secrete. If my pancreas secretes no insulin, I can buy it in the drug store. If I prefer to hear a book read by the author and to watch him while he reads, instead of writing one myself, it will be possible within a few years—and I shall probably be able to buy the "set" from the same drug store.

Perhaps an insulin-fed patient would be better to take his natural medicine and die at once of diabetes; possibly the radio is a curse, and perfected television, when it comes, a calamity. Conceivably, possibly. How about steam-engines? Shall we go back to water-wheels, windmills, and oxen, or farther back, to human muscle?

We can go to Halifax and back, but back in time we cannot go—except to review it as it has been recorded in our own or others' experience. But it is possible that our civilization will go to seed again—as it always has when rulers rule it in the name of supernatural authority.

Modern science, I repeat, is enormously indebted to the Arabs, and hardly less so to the Jews, who were the primary disseminators of scientific facts in western Europe. Knowledge of astronomy, chemistry, medicine, or mathematics, spelt culture for the Jews. They cultivated wisdom to the point that they became wise. No Fundamentalist today feels comfortable in a Jew's presence. Few Puritan universities open their doors wide, lest the whole Ghetto move in. Respectable Christian gentlemen are not above a sneer at the science of a Jew; they will accept the authority of an old Jewish Book, but not the findings of modern Jewish anthropologists.

Man's place in nature is now presumably fairly secure and probably for millions of years to come. This does not signify that some "spiritually" minded person is not this minute exhorting some gullible human being to castrate himself and abandon all earthly joy because the spiritual kingdom will dawn next year. But by the great majority nature is now regarded as so grand and man's place so enviable that even a Methodist bishop is not above using the back door to Wall Street. The spiritual kingdom may come, but the secular opportunity is here.

Insulin, radio, and steam power are also here—potent and innumerable voices crying in what once was a wilderness and heard around the world. They will be heard for ages to come. It is hardly likely that they can be routed by Inquisitions or silenced by excommunications. Our immediate danger is not that the open-minded experimental attitude may become theosophical again, but that it may become philosophical or intellectual; neither attitude is so inhuman as the theosophical, but both are quite as barren in humane works.

Because thousands have taken an open-minded experimental attitude toward the problems which concern man, an enormous number of human problems have been made easier and simpler. To say, however, that this scientific attitude has yet been applied to the larger problems of humanity, or that we govern our lives or order our society from the standpoint of such an attitude, is to camouflage the fact that while we have become secular- rather than religious-minded, we have not yet reached a stage where we rate the authority of experience over the authority of the Schoolmen.

We expose children to a slightly modified course of Scholasticism and call it education; and because hundreds of thousands are exposed annually, popular education is supposed to follow. And because education is supposed to be a liberalizing influence, it is assumed that the colleges turn out a million liberally educated youngsters a year. If liberal education is a good thing, a liberal education for all is an ideal thing—a goal for the nation to shoot at.

And so we fit our children to live here and now by giving them a liberal education: that is, by making them "study" what the Greeks studied. But Greek education was the product of a certain social organization. That organization was as different from ours as the Acropolis is from Coney Island or a Marathon runner from a Lindbergh.

What fitted one for life then cannot fit one for life now any more than what fitted one to live in the Stone Age of Greece fitted one to live in the Golden Age of Pericles. This age, we should remind ourselves, has its own special problems, new problems, which the Greeks could not have dreamt of. We speak of the blessings of our civilization—and they are real; but among our "blessings" are some very hoary anti-social ideas: such, for instance, as that a liberal education emancipates the mind from narrow provincialisms, whether of egoism or tradition, as James Russell Lowell said it does. But what is a *liberal* education? Four years' exposure to the Classics! Such exposure Lowell thought the necessary "apprenticeship everyone must serve before becoming a free brother of the guild which passes the torch of life from age to age."

Exactly. College is an apprenticeship to the Fine Arts Guild. But Liberty's torch is now lighted by electricity, and the passing of the torch of life now requires fertilization and oxygen and an expensive obstetrician. Our liberal education makes no provision for expensive obstetricians, or even for safe and simple contraceptives; yet, because it is popular and has failed, *popular* education is called a "sinister menace."

Our primary concern is not whether it is a menace or not, but rather the reason for its failure; and that, I think, lies in our cultural inheritance. That "inheritance" says in substance that custom is God—or a Law of Nature. The Greeks were accustomed to slaves; we are accustomed to labourers. The Greeks were accustomed to call certain pursuits ennobling, intellectual, liberalizing, educative, and ends in themselves—as though one became moral by studying Morality; virtuous, by studying Virtue; wise, by studying Wisdom; learned, by studying Learning; humane, by studying the Humanities; liberal, by studying the Liberal Arts. We have advanced beyond that in this respect: we think we become scientific by taking a "course" in science.

More, we still think of education in terms of such intellectual snobbery as inspired Sir W. Hamilton to say that the perfection of man as an *end* and as a *means* or instrument is not only not the same but opposite—and hence, as these two "perfections" are different, training must be different. The perfection of man as an end requires a cultivation of the liberal branches of knowledge; as a means, of the professional or lucrative branches. He also distinguished between liberal and lucrative sciences.

We have progressed this far: that, whereas in Hamilton's time the same liberal education which could fit young Darwin to take Holy Orders could also fit him for the post of naturalist on the voyage of the *Beagle*, to enter Holy Orders today a liberal education is not enough—one must be trained also in the professional or lucrative branches.

I realize, of course, that practical needs seem to require that educational curricula be cut up into courses, departments, etc., and that degrees may be useful as tags to distinguish the sheep from the goats. But here are two sheepskins which inform us in the purest of Latin that the bearer of one is a *Master* of Science, another of Arts; or, one is a *Doctor* of Science, the other of Laws.

Grant that this tomfoolery has been handed down from a preprinting-press, pre-paper era: does that make it so sacred that we should accept it and be forced to reconcile our twentieth-century outlook to it? As a matter of fact, we do; and, what is more to the point, we pay a high price for the tomfoolery. In emphasizing certain false distinctions we obscure reality. The college degree itself is guilty enough in that direction, for it signifies that the holder is *educated*; but to call this young woman a *Master* of Arts and that young man a *Doctor* of Philosophy, is to prolong the myth that some supervirtue inheres in two or three additional years' exposure to the "batteries" of *disciplines*.

But what is more important is that this tomfoolery forces human nature into a false position. Human nature finds its keenest joys in living artistically; human beings find life freest who live sensibly, and such freedom is had only by living in accordance with the known facts of life.

It is unfortunately true, as Dr. Macfie Campbell says, that:

> The student may pass through his college course without its being necessary at any stage for him to review the principles underlying human behaviour; without his being required to take stock of the hidden source of his own interests and beliefs and habits and moods; without his becoming aware that these moods and beliefs and interests, which are going to give to his individual life its special value, have definite biological determinants which work according to certain definite laws, and some knowledge of the control of which may make all the difference between stability and instability of his life. A college education does little to prepare anyone to meet the fundamental issues of life any better than the ordinary individual.

That is a real arraignment; and, I repeat, unfortunately true. College degrees dominate the pages of *Who's Who*; but degrees do not keep college men from supplying their quota to the prisons and asylums. In fact, some parasitic classes are regularly recruited from the upper classes of the college mill. Nor need we forget that the Delphic Oracle, Athanasian Creed, Inquisition, Geocentric Theory, Divine Right of Kings, Doctrine of Papal Infallibility, Burning of Witches, Sanctity of Slavery, Holiness of War, Inherent Virtue of Capital, and Mount Sinai's Eternal Verities, were incorporated into civilization with the backing of the Highest Seats of Learning.

And nothing less than a D.D., LL.D., could find opprobrium befitting male vanity to mark man's assumed superiority to mere woman. The arguments used less than a century ago to prove that woman should not be admitted to full rights in Higher Learning would fill a joke-book. Education would sterilize her! She would collapse on the campus from sheer "mental" exhaustion! I still recall the shock I got, on telling my old professor of Latin that college girls really did not seem to have as big families as they might, when he exclaimed, "Then *I* say, DAMN Higher Education for Women!" It was possibly the only time in his saintly life he ever gave way to a curse word!

But even that outburst was rather less sweeping than Chesterton's wiping out the whole Royal Society just because one scientist claimed to find a phallic emblem in a church spire!

What is wrong with education? Nothing. Many of our prevailing *ideas* about education are wrong. I shall try to enumerate the most important.

Our educational ideals are high—never before or elsewhere were they so high; and our endowments, especially for investigation, are prodigious. And that is all to the good. But, as has been pointed out repeatedly, we face thereby two dangers. One is that we make an experiment sanctimonious in itself; the other, that anyone who has made an experiment is thereby qualified to teach.

We deride Sanctorious weighing himself three times a day for forty years, and Weismann cutting off the tails of mice for twenty-two generations; but for every Sanctorious we have a hundred and for every Weismann a thousand, and most of them have not even a hypothesis to test, nor breadth to recognize a hypothesis if their experiment suggested one. Fools can ask questions, but those who have contributed to human progress and knowledge asked worth-while questions.

Too many question-askers today are job-seekers; and too many guardians of research funds are too easily fooled by plausible graphs and the idea that mathematical procedure leads to worth-while results, or that mere methodology is a major virtue, which, if persisted in long and patiently, will bear fruit.

In general, we may say that science does not advance or civilization progress when affairs—of experimentation or of state—are in the hands of professionals. The professional of necessity must be guided by precedents and be governed by authorities. Science acknowledges no authority, is guided by no precedent. It is no longer a heinous sin to search for God's secrets, as it was a few hundred years ago; but each year it becomes increasingly difficult for an amateur like young Darwin or Faraday to get the chance to study, observe, and experiment, unless he can satisfy some authority with fixed notions of the truth.

For a great Foundation controlling annual disbursements of millions of dollars for research to become allied with the interests of this or that class of professionals, is as bad as that all scientific investigation should be controlled by the state—through grants to state institutions; both policies can easily lead to results as disastrous as those which befell Christianity when it became the state religion of the Roman Empire.

Chemistry, for example, advanced with the gathering of facts. Now, endless pages can easily be filled on the nature of a "fact," but we must take a short-cut. A chemical "fact" is something that passes as coin in a chemical laboratory, something that can be used by a chemist in his business. Such facts are discovered by what we call the scientific attitude. They are not easily discovered by fear, desire, ambition, or greed. Hence science in general tends to slow down during war; and in peace time may easily be perverted if its development is controlled by professional scientists.

From facts, every science proceeds to generalization, theory, hypothesis, law; its *logic*, as Barry says, is always retrospective. One new fact may dethrone a theory which has reigned for a decade, a century, a millennium.

There are those who would say there can be no true science till all the facts are known. That may be; hence we may drop the "true" and remain intellectually potent by taking any science for what it is worth. Has it enough facts on tap to enable man to quench his thirst for knowledge? Is there enough salt in the facts to provoke new thirst?

Newton saw himself a slave to philosophy. "I will resolutely bid adieu to it eternally, except what I do for my private satisfaction, or leave it to come after me; for I see a man must either resolve to put out nothing new, or become a slave to defend it."

Times have changed, but human nature remains the same. Science advances in the same old way, but few scientists have to be cajoled, as was Newton, into making their discoveries public. Indeed, one might infer from the yearly flood of "papers" that the rate of the advancement of science is measured by the advancement of scientists and in terms of the number of papers published—eighteen thousand titles in one branch of one science alone, in one year.

One need no longer be a slave to defend something new; one must be a slave to keep up with the output. Meanwhile we assume that increase in quantity goes hand in hand with progress in knowledge. A more serious assumption is that increased knowledge signifies increased application of knowledge to the general welfare.

The mere mention of general welfare need not, presumably, convict one of anarchistic tendencies, but it does seem worth noting that Newton's plaintive cry was forced by that trait in human nature which responded to "Blessed are the meek: for they shall inherit the earth" by despising the meek, crucifying him who said it, and then making all square by worshipping his Holy Name.

Meanwhile the alliance between business and science daily grows closer, and with success as its motto offers a new heaven in this new dispensation of the Machine Age. Business success is measured by intake of dollars; scientific, by output of *papers* based on "research." Are the dollars won on sound ethical principles? Are the "papers" significant, the "research" on which they are based trivial, the authors themselves incompetent? Or are such questions simply not asked?

We put too much stress on book-learning. It is true, as a sage said three thousand years ago, that a student who acquires his knowledge by much reading is like an ass with a load of sandalwood on his back: he feels the weight, but does not know its value.

In the last two chapters I named many men who went far in discovering the world as we know it today—and discovered it so well that much has been done about it. Practically all these men were *self*-educated. Not that many of them did not have college degrees—I do not mean that; I mean that what they did was *extra*-curricular, and that their initial impulse or spark of ambition came before entering college or outside the college walls. In short, the college did not *train* them, nor fire them with zeal.

Many of these observations and much of the experimentation these days represent nothing higher than white-collar jobs; but some of us—thanks to luck and the peculiarities of our system of taxation—are so rich we cannot spend our income, and the man who takes to counting spots on butterflies' wings, or to fertilizing sea urchins' eggs with every conceivable device but nature's, may stumble on a fact which will throw light on a hitherto dark spot of life which would repay investigation. It may require more than one century before the "fact" brings home enough bacon to feed a million people or slay a billion enemies of man.

Our *natural* enemies are not men, but the powers of darkness. They can be fought successfully only as the light of understanding is turned upon them. They are real, and as pitiless as a hurricane, a drought, a mosquito, a typhus bacillus. These are the principalities, the powers, the rulers of darkness of this world, with which we wrestle—no longer by prayer and incantation or with humility and resignation, but with all the weapons in the armoury of science, all the devices known to science. *There* is warfare for you, a war as old as man himself, a war that will never end, a war that will tax man's capacity to the utmost, that deserves the enlightened attention of every thoughtful citizen.

If life offers more today, it demands more—and from every member of the community. Sound views of life, sound beliefs about life, are as necessary for health as sound foods or sound sleep. A lump in the throat, a pain in the heart, can kill as surely as carcinoma. *Bacillus botulinus* is as real as a bullet; sixty pounds of them are enough to wipe the human race off the earth.

History tells of the wars we have had with our enemies and we are nationally conscious of the ships we build to carry death to any foreign foe, but how about the death-carrying germs? Science discovers these germs in its dispassionate quest of the foundations of life and the causes of death; but science cannot, nor is it its business to, prolong life, cure disease, or prevent death. Its discoveries are tools, weapons, instruments, useful for the good of humanity. They should be available for every member of the human race. That they are not in more general circulation is because our social and political machinery is geared to cure rather than to prevent.

Cures are marketable goods, intrinsic parts of the selling game; prevention is public service. The public is not educated to the idea of public service, nor will it have the intelligence to realize what it lacks or the will to participate in the fight to get it, until our educational system stops aiming to please anybody and begins teaching youth that there is another world to keep up with than that of the Joneses.

The world of the Joneses with which our children think they have to keep up is a primitive, parochial world of hyper-credulity, knavery, and sham mysticism. Its problems are insoluble because it is built of elements as unreal as those which engendered witches and kings ruling by divine right. The vain imaginings of their untrained minds seeking selfish satisfactions beyond man's earthly capacity to satisfy, are as fatal to progress in physical, intellectual, æsthetic, and moral well-being as were those of the monks and knights of the Middle Ages.

I venture the guess that the boy who enters college without some fire in him will go farther on the road to usefulness to himself and to his fellow-men if he is fired out than if he is coddled and allowed to dawdle through. It is significant, as Thomas points out, that so many creative men were "failures" in school: "Being poor in school was an unconscious protective device for escaping from a multiplicity of learning with no relevance to their aptitude; in view of what was going to happen, they had to be the worst pupils." My further guess is that many teachers realize this—but how many schools dare flout success? How many colleges in America are free from the *Bigger* bugbear?

Hence the four years, hence the long list of offences against a sound theory of education, put up with just to keep pace with rival institutions, all of which help to keep poor chalk-laden, platitudinous, anæmic social misfits warming faculty chairs which they use as pulpits to express something they have not got.

That kind of teacher and that kind of student are social parasites —even if the student "makes the team" and the teacher makes intelligence tests. "Testing intelligence" may be highly conducive to "culture"; it may even be the mark of high intelligence to conduct such tests intelligently; but to me it looks like a game, a form of amusement—or possibly an alibi for honest toil. That there may be a more efficient test than that in vogue when I was in school to determine whether I had "passed" in Cicero and hence was prepared to take up Vergil, I can well believe. But "passing" Cicero is one thing; being able to think for myself about life is quite another.

It is astounding how these testers hang on. They could not if the public were not utterly indifferent and parents densely ignorant or culpably complaisant. They have been exposed again and again; but they are as oblivious to criticism as the professional mind-readers. They have squandered huge sums in alleged research, and as H. M. Johnson says, have "pronounced judgment on the 'general intelligence,' 'moral discernment,' and the various 'special abilities' of thousands of children, on grounds that warranted no judgment whatever."

If these seem harsh words—and they do—let me add Professor Wheeler's remark, that intelligence testers and psycho-analysts have shown it to be increasingly difficult for most of us to advance beyond, or increasingly easy to lapse into, juvenile or infantile modes of thought, feeling and behaviour.

War in the name of Yahweh is as excusable as testing intelligence in the name of science. It is well that we heed Johnson's warning that whenever anyone not a physicist or an astronomer tells us he has measured something indirectly that has never been measured directly, we are justified in asking to be excused from further exposure to his nonsense. Most parents, of course, have no idea what it is all about, or are complaisant or helpless. Compulsory education means compulsory submission to the system. And we entrust our children to the care of teachers and truant officers not fit to break a colt to harness or to train a dog to stand on its hind legs.

Remedy? More education. And we ask boys to hang on in school to an age when Nelson was a naval officer, Napoleon an artillery lieutenant, Alexander Hamilton a political writer, and Mozart and Beethoven famous musicians. As Thomas points out, Newton had discovered the law of gravitation, integral calculus, made discoveries in light, developed the binomial theory, and Linnæus had discovered the sexual system of plants, at the age of twenty-four. Ludwig, Brücke, Helmholtz, du Bois-Reymond, were reforming physiology at the average age of twenty-five. Mayer, Joule, Colding, Helmholtz, were all under twenty-eight years of age when they did their work on the conservation of energy. Goethe, Schiller, Byron, Keats, Shelley, Liebig, Sadi-Carnot, are also striking examples of creative work at an early age.

We think of education as we used to think of religion: join the church and you are saved—hence virtuous, moral, kind, generous.

Go through college and you are educated—hence wise, intelligent, intellectual, learned. It is a fine idea, a noble experiment, if you please, but it is too simple. We know now that it is not the church that makes for Christian virtue, or the school that makes for wisdom. One learns virtue by being virtuous; wisdom is learnt by being wise. Fundamentally, these are character traits; they are rooted in emotional slants. *The* teachers of emotion are parents. Home is the natural school. In the home—and too often the alley is the boy's real home—the foundation is laid for the attitude which is to keep trying things out.

The school is, of course, enormously important in its rôle of weaning the individual from the nest, socializing the youngster, but the best school in the world—and it is rarely encouraged by the public—can hardly undo vicious habits, can do but little to socialize the youngster if there is nothing to build on. The school can encourage, can guide, can direct—if there is something to work on; it can also, and too often does, so immunize the child against so many useful "disciplines" that school is left behind as a hated burden is left or a loathsome disease dropped.

We go on the general theory that school prepares us for "making a living" and emphasize the idea of "making the school practical"—instead of starting with the idea that we expect the school to help youngsters make a life that is worth living. That cannot be done by messing around the ruins of structures destroyed by modern science and industry.

This is an age of industry. It is even more an age of biology. It should be so taught that it *lives*. But as Haldane says, we shy at human physiology because it upsets our prejudices; at the physiology of digestion, reproduction, and excretion, because it is indecent; and at the physiology of our brain because it is irreligious.

Our children must depend on the schools—and with the disintegration of the family, more and more on the schools—for such awakening of their interest as will make them worldly wise, politically minded, socially responsible, courageous, and humane. They cannot be expected to approach with confidence the ever-recurring and increasingly complex problems of twentieth-century democracy unless they have met them face to face, have become acquainted with them, and have some understanding of them; and that can only be brought about by their participating in them, by taking hold of them, manipulating them—in words, at least, until the hands are trained.

Sheltered, cloistered halls sound romantic, but there is nothing romantic about a jail, an asylum, or a county poorhouse. This is a practical age, and because of that fact life should be lived on a higher plane of artistry than ever before.

We have the schools—more and better than ever before. The progress in housing students and in caring for their physical requirements since my barefoot days at the little red brick schoolhouse has been as rapid and tangible as the motor-bus which now gathers the children up from the ends of the township. Let us not doubt this, nor fail to appreciate the enormous improvements made in our schools. But let us not overlook the great fact that the best educational intentions in the world must fail our democracy if we continue to tolerate devil's workshops where criminal ideas are hatched and youthful delinquents spawned. Twenty-seven per cent of crime careers, according to William Healy, begin at the age of fourteen or under; seventy-five per cent at sixteen or under.

Why should we have to keep a standing army of four hundred thousand men to guard our lives and property? Why should our robberies and homicides be so relatively more numerous than England's?

"Mental deficiency," they tell us: a psychologist's way of saying "God's will." Piffle! What are the facts of the juvenile courts? Seventy per cent of juvenile delinquents so normal mentally that there was no excuse at all to resort to that subterfuge. Removed from vicious surroundings and placed in a healthy environment, seventy per cent of children with both parents criminals were restored to society; eighty per cent restored where one or both parents were alcoholics; and eighty-one per cent where one or both parents were "mentally defective" or otherwise abnormal.

We used to hear about the rejoicing in heaven over the return of one lost sheep. We now know that at least seventy per cent of the lambs supposedly lost forever can be restored if placed in a good environment. How about the other thirty? They can be saved too, eventually. That more are not saved now is because their bad habits are tied in too tightly and that "good environment" does not get hold of them early enough.

Saved from what—from the penitentiary or the hangman's noose? Not at all; saved from becoming the unwitting means of making this country a jungle where one is never free from the threat of armed thugs and the brutalizing tyranny of an army of police.

Age of science. Let us apply it. Enough has already been applied to make slavery, serfdom, child labour, and subjugated women as obsolescent as ox-carts or triremes. We need only press forward in the further application of knowledge to bring about a more success-ful democracy, a true democracy, founded on sound universal edu-cation and equality of opportunity for all. We cannot advance in that direction so long as we remain complacent about our ignorance or certain that our prejudices are founded in fact and grounded in moral law.

Our attitude toward crime and the administration of criminal justice has begun to change, has made great progress, in fact. That must be kept up. It can only be placed on a sound and rational basis by a critical examination of all our inherited notions of property, morality, religion, and education. Are those notions sound, are they humane, are they in keeping with the known facts; or are they outmoded, childish, inhuman, and in need of revision?

A true democracy demands, I repeat, a democratic education. Our civilization rests on science. Every profession today is scien-tifically founded; and none, not even the physician's, rests on a more solid scientific basis than that of the farmer. One is appalled at what a physician is expected to know and at what the farmer could and does not know. But medicine is a white-collar art, as it was in the days of Hammurabi; farming is a horny-handed job, as it always was. And though the "dignity of labour" may soften the farmer's feelings, it will not soften his hands, nor pay interest on the farm mortgage when he guesses wrong.

Our civilization, like all "higher" civilizations, is rooted in agri-culture. Our agriculture is on a modern scientific basis, but the farmer may starve to death for all science cares. It is not science's business to feed farmers, or to teach them how to farm or how to vote or what to eat; its business is to mind its own business, without fear or favour. But whose business is it to have a care that this nation has the intelligence and education required to support the civilization science has made possible, or to prevent this or that minority from wrecking it for their own pleasure?

Our own adult idea of government is perhaps most at fault. For thousands of years we have been *governed*: bought, sold, traded, like the stones of the field which pass with the title-deed to the land. This thing we call civil liberty is more modern than a printing-press. It was won at great price. It can be retained only with great effort. That effort must be brain-work, clear-headed thinking. Sound thinking in education, legislation, health, currency, industry, transportation, social relationships—in everything that makes for a rational, civilized democracy.

Our domestic and social economy must be sound, so sound that no politician can fool us with the old rationalized smoke screens— disguising the lust for power and excusing the display of arms on the part of those who by training and profession know no other route to self-expression. The professional soldier is more excusable than the politician whose idea of statecraft is dissimulation, perfidy, and sanctimony.

But think of the progress in education and democracy we have made since the curate of Epigny, Jean Meslieu, to vent his pent-up rage, left a deathbed testament declaring he had never believed a word of his teachings and hoping that the *last king might be hanged with the entrails of the last priest!*

## CHAPTER FIFTEEN

### *We Have Developed a Great Civilization*

W E HAVE finished our long journey; or rather we have made the circuit, for we are back where we started: *We have developed a great civilization!*

We have indeed; and in our journey we have met the man *We.* In fact, we have tried never to lose sight of him, for to do that were to fail to understand the civilization he developed, to fail to realize just how great that civilization is, and signally to fail to realize the price he had to pay to bring it to us who are now here, alive and enjoying its blessings.

"*We*" is human nature. Not Wise Man, certainly not Idiot Man; just man, humanity, human nature.

*Civilization* is man's handiwork; human artifacts; things, ideas, notions, to live with, by, and for.

*Developed.* Created, step by step, slowly, laboriously, valiantly. And for his loved ones: wife, children, fellow-men, the family, the tribe, the state, the nation—and some day perhaps may be added, the whole brotherhood of man.

*Great.* Never before was civilization so incredibly great. We who are in the midst of it can hardly realize how great it is, so new is it, so rapidly does it change and advance before our eyes and under our very feet.

And, finally, *price.* That is the issue I wish to discuss a little further in this closing chapter. Not that it has not been the theme of all the pages that have gone before, but that in my opinion it is *the* main issue today.

I do not mean to say that the millennium is just around the corner, but I do think a crisis in human history is here now. How serious it is, and especially what its outcome is to be, I do not know, nor can anyone foretell. Prediction, however, based on the fundamentals of human nature and on the facts of history, is, it seems to me, possible to a certain limited extent, beyond which point no science can go.

By way of illustration, let us refer again to a crisis in the course of civilization successfully met at the very dawn of history. A few years ago my illustration might have seemed rather academic or possibly trite, but with millions of human beings depending on doles for the scant necessaries of life as I write these words, with other millions underfed or half-starved, and with as many beggars to the mile in New York City as we once thought normal to Naples, food, bread, the staff of life, ceases to be academic—even though the academies as yet seem to have suffered no hunger pangs—and agriculture ceases to be just a matter of interest for the readers of *Farm and Fireside*.

Agriculture resolved one—in some respects the greatest—crisis man ever faced. The domestication of plants—especially of such body-building, energy-producing foods as grains and cereals—at once lifted human society out of day-by-day drudgery; with a few months' toil there was enough food for a year. But the mere fact that there was an abundance of food was itself a culture-provoking factor leading to new and diversified activities—such as better ways of harvesting, adequate ways of transporting, storing, distributing, and so on. For such new or additional activities as were suggested or provoked by abundant harvests, time and energy were available. One thing led to another. Life became not only vastly more complex than before, but, I think it fair to say, richer and fuller, more abundant and abounding. We need not call it nobler, because nobility implies class distinctions which are founded on man's exploitation of his fellow-men.

If it be urged that class distinctions are no more artificial than certain other cultural traits, and that all culture traits are artificial, I shall have to agree; but I should like to urge that that fact alone does not make them biologically useful or psychologically healthful. Tuberculosis also is artificial, a cultural trait human beings acquire only when living under certain conditions. Conceivably, consumptives may make great contributions to civilization. Stevenson, I believe, is the shining example of what a consumptive may be inspired to produce. But I am not aware that anyone has proposed that we all go in for tuberculosis as a means of advancing the cause of civilization—although feeble-minded thinkers do suggest that the slaughter of many able-bodied youths from time to time is a factor making for progress in civilization.

The ancient astronomer served a useful purpose—the purpose of agriculture—and was promptly annexed by the state. His labours made for human freedom, but they also made imperial expansion possible: more power, wider sway for the rulers, agricultural serfs more valuable to the king. They did not necessarily contribute to the freedom of the man with a hoe or at all increase his power of initiative.

Because of agriculture, human society developed along two lines; and all because man learnt that by doing certain things in certain ways he could get certain results—increase his food supply fivefold, diminish his working hours per year fourfold.

Agriculture was born from man's taking a scientific attitude toward certain specific problems. Because of that attitude he made a great discovery, an enormously useful discovery. It tied him to the soil, to be sure, but it also set him free for other activities—some useful, some pleasurable but not thereby necessarily useless. We need not attempt to define pleasure, but we can assert that no man goes far unless he puts all of himself into his work, gives himself up to it whole-heartedly. He cannot do that if he is pushed or driven by fear; he can do it if he is pulled by the joy of it or impelled by the love of it. Such men have *initiative*; to such men comes easily that elusive and indefinable thing called insight or intuition.

Agriculture—as a scientific approach to nature—made such activities possible; made man's position in nature more secure, gave him more freedom to behave in such ways as human beings can behave and apes cannot.

And may we who love to salute achievement with enough gunpowder to blow up a fortress of political corruption, or with a line of marching men long enough to clean up miles of filthy streets, again remind ourselves that the name of the man or men, tribe or society, who placed man's food supply on a scientific foundation, is unknown. Nor, it may be repeated, do we know the name, or even the colour of skin, of the man or men who "invented" language, fire-making apparatus, the digging-stick or lever, the stone knife, the hoe, pottery, basketry, sandals, rafts, canoes and sails, bows and arrows, domesticated animals, writing, alphabet; or who was the first artist, the first weaver, or the first metallurgist.

We pay homage to the Unknown Soldier—and to none so appropriately if we must disguise the fact that we cannot get along with our neighbours without pitting our soundest blood against theirs; but I suspect that if we critically scrutinized the list of all the names to whom homage has been paid, we should find that a large majority of them were enemies of mankind rather than benefactors of the human race, and that others had served humanity no more than do the meteors which burn themselves out in their flight across our oxygen-laden atmosphere.

To continue the Unknown idea a moment longer: I like to find myself in agreement with Bacon, who held the unknown inventor of the mariner's compass a greater benefactor of mankind than a thousand Alexanders and Cæsars—or ten thousand Aristotles. Why rate the compass so high? What makes any invention or discovery "high"? Effectiveness in human hands to control nature for human ends. Man had paddled and even sailed the wide seas for ages before there was a compass, but with it he gained an immeasurably greater victory over the sea than ever before. It not only gave him a new and extraordinarily valuable sense organ, as it were; it made the world one place. It was the first and most gigantic stride in making far-flung peoples people, mankind, humanity.

Unknown soldiers in the fight for freedom. It is pretty well known that the light-skinned peoples of northern Europe were among the last to be converted to the type of civilization which began in Asia, and that their contribution to the fundamentals of the three R's was precisely *nil*. Is it possibly to be their destiny to invent a peace-complex which will satisfy the world at large and signalize the birth of a higher, more universal freedom?

Much depends on the solution of this twentieth-century crisis. But let us get on with our story.

Having severed political ties with the mother country, we were spurred to try out new forms of political administration. Our Constitution and present form of government were the result. The problem was solved; it worked. Was it the best solution? Does it work now? The mere asking of the questions is in some eyes sacrilegious—like questioning the mercy of Providence. But in cold, calm reason, does it seem likely that the framers of a Constitution for a handful of thinly populated states along the seaboard, in stage-coach and mud-road days, could have been so hypermetropic as to make the best possible solution of a scheme of government for these states as they are today, or for this Union of forty-eight states, Alaska, Hawaii, and the Philippine Islands?

The Constitution would have been a veritable miracle of a unique order if they had. Yet to many that Constitution is a document so sacred, magical, and mysterious, that even to look at it questioningly is to court death and destruction. People who are afraid of touching the government should stick to the one-horse shay on a plank road.

Some day, conceivably, our civilization will be higher; then we shall all be more humble, less self-centred, and nationally less vainglorious. That day is yet far off; it means as radical a change in our social and economic attitudes as we are now witnessing in our attitude toward health and hygiene. It will mean that duty does not end with merely keeping out of jail or being respectable; that our national resources are not prizes to be won in class wars, nor their present possessors a privileged class to rule through their dummies as though by divine right; and the dethronement of our national complex of concealing the truth and repressing the facts.

How, then, did we get *our* civilization? Most of it by borrowing; some of it by invention. We continue to borrow; we continue to invent. We borrow from our neighbours—in these days the entire world. Borrowing is easier than inventing, but perhaps dearer in the long run. Inventions arise through the workings of what Boas has called the "inner forces" of society. These forces may be and usually are complex and not easily or always distinguishable.

It would be comparatively easy to pick out a few striking American inventions and to isolate the inner forces of our civilization which called them out and then put them into general circulation. I have particularly in mind the sewing-machine, telegraph, telephone, and electric light. But these inventions belong to an inventive age *par excellence*. They were made possible because this age specialized in certain knowledge and because the times were ripe for putting its knowledge to work. Scientific investigation and human hands coöperated in a way, to a purpose, never even conceived of before. This age is still with us and moulding us as no people was ever moulded before.

We may here recall that a telegraph-complex, fairly crude but thoroughly serviceable, was submitted to the British Admiralty a little over a hundred years ago, before it was even contemplated as a possible enormously useful public utility. The Admiralty played with it for a year, then turned thumbs down: "We do not find it useful"! Trust any Admiralty to be afraid of anything new. No inventive genius can get results if he cannot get a hearing. Usually he requires from one to two generations to be taken seriously. Now and then his idea is allowed to sleep for centuries, in clay tablet, parchment scroll, or printed book—as idea and nothing more.

Note the far-reaching consequences of the cotton-gin, which confirmed slavery in the South and called into existence dozens of new inventions to put this cheap and serviceable fabric into circulation. And one would be bold indeed to attempt to predict the end of the consequences of the automobile or radio. As one good turn deserves another, so one good invention, by transforming the environment, provokes not another but dozens or hundreds of others.

Man being what he is, it is inconceivable that the individual has ever been completely dominated by his cultural environment. Even in the most primitive societies "a man's a man for a' that." His individuality may be, and generally is, submerged, but in every tribe or nation's history there comes a time when there is a crying need for a new idea, a new god, a new way of getting across the sea, a new weapon to protect the home; a new leader, in short. The crying need is not always heard; often there is no one with vision keen enough to see around a corner or through a wall.

Our inventive genius sprang from hundreds of needs suddenly created by millions of newcomers from Europe and the opening up of our vast continent with its extraordinarily rich supplies of natural wealth crying out for exploitation. And behind that genius was sweat working toward a set purpose.

Our sudden mushroom outburst of invention was mothered less by necessity than by opportunity. It was a concatenation of circumstances which conspired to make invention, as invention, a primary stimulus. As settlers, we were a forward-looking people in a backward country. We came to America with all the advantages of European civilization and freed of some of its disadvantages. We could climb high in a few decades because we started from a high level. We may with profit remind ourselves of this fact when we compare our achievements with those of "effete Europe" or of more backward peoples. Primarily, our achievements are due to opportunity rather than to innate ability. Because some of our cultural complexes are very complex, we need not conclude that they make for healthy living or sound society; nor is the number of patents granted each year or decade a measure of progress.

When we pin medals on ourselves for our inventiveness, we should not overlook the fact that our stage is set for that kind of activity as no stage was ever set before. It is not that our inventors are unique; it is that the opportunity to invent and the monetary and social rewards of successful inventive activity are unique.

In evaluating our civilization, we must take another factor into consideration: everything had to be done! It was not a question of turning on the water, gas, and electricity, laying the table, and turning down the bed; the *house* had to be made. But the water, wood, coal, gas, and oil were here. The Mississippi Valley is not the Amazon, or the Nile, or the Euphrates, or the Yangtze. The water, wood, coal, gas, oil, were here—yes; and the iron, copper, silver and gold, and a virgin soil. Our uniqueness was, and still is, in our opportunity.

That we are especially or uniquely receptive to new ideas, I doubt; to some ideas along certain lines, probably; to reforms in such conspicuous complexes as education, religion, politics, and war, probably not; they are too strongly entrenched, too heavily endowed.

We cannot easily dispossess ourselves of the idea that some cultures must be better or higher than others, or stop rating cultures by the amount of their divergence from ours. We call the Japanese imitators or borrowers because they have recently taken on certain culture-complexes from European culture—forgetting meanwhile that we European settlers in America have contributed fewer cultural complexes to mankind than did the aborigines we dispossessed. We brought most of the civilization we have with us—and still go back for more; and of the complexes we brought with us, the majority are older than the Pyramids.

Coal and iron did not create Pittsburgh or South Chicago; man did—in a coal-and-iron age. Our forefathers on this continent took over the Indians' corn and maple sugar, their buckskin garments and snow-shoes, and on the frontier became hunters and trappers and in general lived a life not unlike that of their ancestors two thousand years ago—neither better nor worse, higher nor lower. They did not borrow or imitate all of the aboriginal culture, for they had their own social, political, and religious complexes. They borrowed what they needed and what could be fitted into their culture. Certain results the Indians achieved by methods which were so different from those of the pioneers that they aroused antipathy; other methods were enough like their own to arouse their curiosity, and these they tried their hand at.

This nation did not invent or destroy slavery; it did accept it and make it its own. It is worth looking at. Since the World War that last century crisis seems remote, possibly remote enough to illustrate our thesis.

"I want Cuba; I want one or two Mexican states; and I want them all for the same reason, for the planting and spreading of slavery. I would spread the blessings of slavery, like the religion of our Divine Master, to the uttermost ends of the earth."

Some years ago, half in jest, I ventured the opinion to my father that the Civil War was a mistake: that the South should have been allowed to cut loose from the North, and then made to stay loose till she begged to get in again. I have not yet forgotten the look of horror on his face. The mere idea was sacrilege! The Union was the most sacred thing in the world; to disrupt it was to tear the world asunder. Far better to fight it out with the South, even though it took the last able-bodied man north of Dixie. The Union was deeply embedded in his philosophy of life. Anything that endangered it threatened his life.

Senator Brown of Mississippi some eighty years ago voiced, in the words quoted above, the philosophy of the South; and he was as honest in believing slavery a blessing as my father was in believing the Union sacred. The South was ready to fight Spain for Cuba—or anybody else—to spread the "blessings of slavery"; the

North was just as ready to wage its holy war for the Union. The South was "for" the Union, but it had a "higher cause" and was willing to fight for it. The Union was not next to Godliness; slavery was.

The point is outside the merits of the Civil War, the blessings of slavery, or the sacredness of the Union. It is that families, tribes, states, nations, get that way; and that *that* way is sacred, blessed, rational, the only way—to be fought and died for.

The North-eastern states did not originally hate slavery, nor did the South originally look upon slavery as a blessing comparable to Christianity. When, however, the invention of the cotton-gin made slavery profitable, the South soon made slavery the foundation of its social and domestic economy, and became accustomed to it. Slavery was its great cultural complex: rational, plausible, normal, a blessing, a divine institution. Psychologically speaking, there was no difference between the South seceding to retain its main cultural feature, and the North fighting the South to retain *its* main cultural feature. Each side was "right," of course—morally, ethically, politically; right in every respect. And each had been getting more right for decades, thereby making the impending conflict inevitable.

The impression I get from the South is that it is still convinced it was right, still believes that slavery was a blessing, and that it was entirely justified in seceding. It feels, I suspect, not unlike a raped virgin, who, having recovered from the physical shock, turns her shocked honour into a family cultural trait.

In so-called higher civilizations, one culture trait tends to follow another with astonishing rapidity. We elevate this tendency to a compulsion neurosis. We are supposed to scrap our decorations, jewellery, clothes, hats, shoes, furniture, motor-cars, shaving-soap, perfume, etc., from once to six times a year just to keep in *style*. We lose interest in the old, not primarily because it is old or worn out or no good, but because, like the pampered children we are, we think we must have a new set of toys every new moon. Keeping us spoiled has become a vital part of Big Business.

I can estimate how far our red blood corpuscles, placed end to end, would reach, but who could compute the mileage of our scrapped automobiles so placed? We have become so civilized that we seem to have elevated the mere accumulation of wealth and rapid change in style to major vital activities; and call it Progress. But how much progress, except in terms of moron wish-fulfilments, have we made in some of the hideous facts of life? As a nation, we are not comfortable or happy, sane or sound. Crime and vice are freely and openly arrived at; inequality before the law, injustice in our social, economic, and political institutions, and stupidity in our educational system, are, *all things considered,* the worst in the history of the world.

As a nation, we are united in nothing but name, held together by slogans and the opportunity to amass wealth. Our neighbours hate, fear, or distrust us, and we pity or despise our neighbours; and our national smugness is paralleled only by our ignorance of our neighbours. Despite automobile, telephone, and radio, certain communities in America are as inert and as isolated as Uganda, and their prejudices more exploited by their masters.

It was right and proper for our ancestors to offer human sacrifices to the god of germination; at least they were logical, and there was glory in being sacrificed for one's country. But where is the glory now? Before we try to sell ourselves abroad, let us at least try to see just what it is we are trying to sell.

Our national culture-complex is salesmanship; our biggest business, to sell the benefits of our civilization to the world—especially such as we produce in excess of our capacity to consume. Salesmanship is our national religion; the fact that so many people are indifferent to the blessings of our civilization is our national bedevilment. Now, that may be a good religion; but is it not, like all other religions, founded on a myth—the myth of Progress and the Blessings of Civilization?

Of all the baits to catch fools, this rationalization of Progress stands next to Divine Right. There is, I repeat, no *law* of progress. We have, I repeat, outdone our immediate ancestors in our capacity to manipulate our physical environment and to project our voice, bodies, and chattels across space; and we have made great advance in combating certain preventable ailments. We have, in short, made notable progress in catching up with the evils inherent in our extraordinarily unnatural and artificial mode of living. Progress may mean decadence as well as increased human happiness; civilization is often highest just before mankind sinks back to lice, squalour, black bread, and serfdom, or destroys itself in civil war, chaos, and anarchy.

And one of the stupidest blunders in all cultural history—next to making love a sin and hatred a virtue—has been called by our President a Noble Experiment!

But, again all things considered, where or when in all history has it been possible to discuss existing conditions as freely, or with as clear insight into their history, or with as sound understanding of man's biologic needs and the psychological consequences of social disorders and disease, as it is today? Therein, it seems to me, lies the hope of tomorrow—the promise of today.

Now, is it or is it not true that *there never has been a time in our history when crime has been so prevalent, so well organized, so profitable and so audacious?*

Are these words, recently uttered by the chief city magistrate of the richest city the world has ever known, true? And if they are, do they constitute a *crisis*? Of course, you cannot indict a nation; but a nation can be *characterized*, and the question is, is not New York City—all our cities—suffering from a calamitous breakdown of morale? And when we say "cities," have we not said every R.F.D. in the nation open to the automobile?

It is a commonplace that society—New York, the U. S. A.—gets the ills and crimes it deserves. It should be equally self-evident that a nation which disregards ethical principles must expect its citizens to flout them too. If, to take a single example, our recently enacted tariff law is founded on any tried and true principle of ethics, national or international, then I frankly confess I am in utter, outer darkness.

I realize that the tariff is a loaded and a complex subject, and I admit my inability to discuss it in the weasel words of a politician or the technical jargon of a political economist; but can or cannot it be viewed from a scientific standpoint? And does or does not enduring peace rest upon national justice, enduring prosperity upon economic justice, and enduring social order upon social justice?

More specifically, are we, as President Hoover recently said we are, "able in considerable degree to free ourselves of world influences and make a large measure of independent recovery (from world depression) because we are so remarkably self-contained"?

Are we? And if so, are we proud of it? Is it Assyrian or Christian ethics to proclaim a national holiday of thanksgiving because "we have been blessed with distinctive evidences of Divine favor," and because, "as a nation, we have suffered far less than other peoples from present world difficulties"?

Well, if we are blessed with Divine favour, it must be pleasing in God's sight that in the face of a world-wide economic débâcle we enact what Raymond Fosdick characterizes as a blow at the economic stability of sixty nations, "the blind, desperate effort of a great country to hang on to the top of the ladder by kicking at every other country."

More. That Tariff Act of 1930, as I understand it, was not even honest with us, you and me, citizens and taxpayers of the United States. Its ethics. . . . How expect social justice when Liberty herself in the guise of Congress turns her back on the world and cheats her own children?

In the beginning God created fear; and man finally discovered that fear does not pay, that he has a brain which can be used in the service of truth, and that thus used it pays enormously.

The world has indeed moved since the days of Galileo, but, as Carlson says, it has not moved very far in some places. "Why, the handful of liberal and informed people who have worked their way out of the cocoon of supernaturalism does not even make a respectable leaven in the college-graduate group."

What has supernaturalism to do with tariffs, politics, justice, world débâcle, crime, crisis? Too much. It has dogged man's footsteps for thousands of years; it curses every nation that depends on it; it wrecks every plan that is not founded on verifiable experience and an intelligent use of the good old procedure of trial and error; it stifles honest, unbiassed inquiry, and hence eternally wars with science.

The crisis our civilization faces will not be resolved in a day or a year: early conditioned emotional reflexes are not easily reconditioned in the light of experience and experiment. Nor can it be resolved with the ethics of supernaturalism; it can be resolved with the ethics of science—the only ethics that has yielded enduring results in man's becoming the highly civilized animal he is.

This world today is sick, discouraged, weary, disorganized. There are bread lines; millions (six millions, today's paper says) of men and women can find neither food for their bodies nor work for their hands. There is work to be done; there are surplus stores of food; there are violence, graft, corruption, injustice. Of course; if they cannot live socially, they will live unsocially. But where is the social engineer to start the intellectual machinery in motion which will make it possible to get the facts behind this crisis out into the open where they may be seen for what they are, in order that the fitting things may be done? What agency, what force, is at work to help this nation, this world, to think in terms of twentieth-century light as well as ride in twentieth-century conveyances?

Light? Science. Science alone is universal; its language alone is that of the human voice. That voice today travels across the earth in less time than it takes my pencil to move across this page, or my voice to cross the street by the air-wave route. And it has been heard around the world. The world at large has not yet plumped for science, but each year does see increasingly large numbers of its denizens learn to use, like, and depend upon an ever-increasing number of the appliances modern science has made available for freeing man from the natural fetters of a natural existence.

We list the great names in science, but how adequately can we characterize individuals, or organizations of individuals, who deliberately turn the achievements of science to purely selfish ends, and, having insured their own existence in luxury at the expense of thousands of their fellow-men, prate of the "blessings" of civilization? I do not know. I do consider such an attitude inhuman and reckon such individuals among the enemies of humanity; and I suspect that so far as their names are preserved in history, they will be so rated. It is not necessary to burn Christians at a garden party to be rated with the Neros; nor to hunt runaway slaves to be a Simon Legree.

Let us be clear about this. Science is not magic, nor a way of salvation, nor a superstition, nor an object of worship. It is a method of procedure whereby man can increase the material wealth necessary to maintain a material body in this material world under a material sun.

That our civilization is rich and powerful is because the physical part of the universe has been set free for wide-open manipulation;

that a world crisis impends is because in its legal, economic, political, and religious aspects it is in many respects no more enlightened or more socially efficient than it was in the year Christ was born. The science which has come into circulation is the science that lays the golden eggs in business and serves the interests of class greed. The science which makes for more efficient social organization, which would make poverty, disease, crime, insanity, and war as obsolete as a suit of chain armour, has not yet become business because Big Business can get along with poverty, disease, crime, and insanity; and because some businesses thrive best on war.

Whatever thrives is *right*. Nothing succeeds like success. In no other age has success paid so well or been so honoured as in ours. Looked at calmly and dispassionately, our proneness to worship success—as Success, regardless of what the achievement signifies, means or stands for in human welfare or human usefulness—is astounding and borders on insanity: it can only spring from a diseased society. A city of seven million people that thinks nothing of "honouring" some perfectly useless, foolhardy stunt with a hundred-thousand-dollar parade passing within a block of a bread line a mile long, and calmly accepts degeneracy, bribery, corruption, graft, poverty, insanity, dirt, confusion, murder, robbery, crime-breeding tenements, and more million-dollar-a-year incomes than all the rest of the world, is as far from being a healthy social organization as is a richly dressed, hump-backed leper with syphilis, trachoma, and the hookworm, in an advanced stage of *dementia præcox*. That humpback may be a success, but in the name of sound common sense let us not call him Progress; and if we speak of him as Civilization, let us make certain we are not deceiving ourselves.

But, you say, we no longer naïvely accept syphilis, leprosy, trachoma, and hookworm as the will of God. Well, why not? Our ancestors did, and even today the average man on the street speaks of syphilis as "Serves him jolly well right!"

We do not accept disease as Blind Fate or Divine Justice or Punishment, because, after a war lasting three centuries, the chains which bound men's minds have been broken, with the result that man today can look at anything with a freedom which was once restricted to cats. Do not be misled by my use of the word "chains."

Behind that figure of speech is a fact as plain as the Great Pyramid or the Washington Monument.

That freedom to think, won after a three hundred years' war, is often called "intellectual" freedom. There can be no objection to that if we understand what we mean by intellectual. But to make intelligence an entity and endow it with our own personal repertoire of reactions to certain verbal stimuli, is to pass into the realm of philosophic nonsense.

To think straight about life is conceivably the most important thing a human being can think about. The extent to which life—human beings, any or all kinds of life, life in health, at ease, and in disease—and nature, the physical environment which supports living organisms, can be thought about freely and frankly, is the measure of our intellectual freedom. That such freedom is vastly greater today than it was three hundred years ago is as true as that it is far from being as free as it might be—or in my opinion will be.

It may help us to understand why it is still far from free if we recall the opponents of that long and as yet unfinished fight. Yes, unfinished. Dayton, Tennessee, often looked upon as a major engagement, was just a skirmish, a tiny pimple on a huge surface beneath which the old fever of intolerance rages as fiercely as it did when witches were hanged in Salem and Bruno was burnt in Venice.

But—and this is the important point—human nature easily learns to take very selfish individualistic, anti-social bents. Otherwise, no man could find his "most" in life by robbing children of the chance to be healthy; otherwise, no nation which exploits ignorance and builds itself up in power and riches through sheer brute strength could call itself civilized and boast of its humaneness; otherwise, no church could count itself a moral agency which administers Extreme Unction when oxygen is indicated.

These selfish anti-social bents, when organized and in power, make it possible for groups of men to live upon the toil of other men as biologic parasites. Whether we call them hookworms or bookworms is of little consequence, nor need we stop to inquire whether they satisfy human ends or supply human needs.

No doubt most of us would be healthier, happier, and saner if some froth and frivolity could be mixed with the pessimism which came down to us from mediæval times—than which no pessimism was ever gloomier. That man by nature is a "joiner" means that he is readily organized and easily managed, provided he be caught young—and the easiest way to catch him is through his mother.

For every organization of human beings on truly mutually co-operative lines whereby the individual's well-being was the common weal, history shows hundreds of organizations with special privileged classes who neither toiled nor spun but expected to be kept in luxury or in harems because they were born that way: for such are the workings of an inscrutable Providence. Even laws of primogeniture and of inheritance in general are supposed to be natural laws, if not to have the sanction of the Divinity Himself.

Now, to a king desiring great luxury and large armies, a man who sleeps all day and lies on his back all night gazing at the stars is a non-productive worker, worth less than a boy with a hoe or even a good rat-catching dog. But once the idea got firmly entrenched that the gazer had discovered something which would be useful to everybody with a hoe, star-gazing became a useful profession. To the extent that the gazer was accurate, restrained his imagination, kept a tight rein on his observations and repeated them year after year, he was following a method suggested by common sense and called scientific. He was, in short, a scientist—an early astronomer. He could not do what Galileo did, for he had no artificial aid to human eyesight. Galileo had—and discovered Jupiter's moons. That discovery in itself was quite useless, but it started other men off, and man finally discovered mankind.

That whole nations still shy at the idea of the brotherhood of mankind because loath to accept its implications, is no more evidence of unreality behind the idea than refusal to accept the implications behind the idea that man is a talking, thinking ape is evidence that man can become a talking, thinking, disembodied ghost, or that he ever would have become man at all had it not been for the evolution of his larger brain and more perfect upright gait.

If I have said all this before, I say it again—lest we forget. It is so easy to turn our backs on reality when high-pressure salesmen are bent on dazzling us with their gilded idols. That gold-brick game is at least as ancient as the first man who ruled by divine right or was carried up in a cloud and entrusted with the confidence of the Almighty. The game is far from up, or we could laugh at the antics of the salesmen and tell them to save their breath to cool their porridge and take away their slogan billboards that turn landscapes into compulsory school-rooms for the standardization of morons.

The gold-brick game thrives because we are morons. And before the smash it was all too easy for a moron to make a living. The application of the scientific attitude to labour problems made that possible—and in a single century. A machine-tender today with the brain of a chimpanzee and the patience of a chipmunk can earn more in less time than an assistant professor of bacteriology. Seven hours' work a day will give him enough food, a decent house, comfortable clothes. If he works ten hours he can have money to burn. He does. The incentives for working ten hours—or for picking a pocket—are overwhelming.

What boots it if the chemist makes more drugs than the human body or a quarter of a million compounds unknown to all nature —and he does; or if the physiologist knows to a gram, as he does, just how many calories a six-weeks-old infant weighing twelve pounds requires, if that infant is brought up in a cellar on "soothing syrup"?

One man, almost alone and single-handed, fought for twenty-three years to get pure foods written into legislation. Dr. Wiley himself is authority for the statement that a president of the United States grew purple with rage when told a certain drug was injurious to health, and declared that anybody who said so was an "idiot."

Food free of poison: what a crusade for a man to have to lead in this age! And was Dr. Wiley joined by thousands of Christian soldiers in shining armour, ready to give up their lives if necessary for one of the holiest causes that ever confronted a bedevilled civilization? He was not. He did not even have the enthusiastic support of all the presidents he laboured under.

Vast quantities of food can get to the tables of millions of families in this country only *via* much handling and treatment—generally in tin or glass containers. The amount of science involved in one tin of beans and bacon is enormous and to a former age would have been incredible. Certain chemicals, however, are not only deadly to the bacteria of decay, but also to the living cells of the human alimentary canal.

Well, what of it? Who cares? Whose business is it to look out for the living cells of a human alimentary canal? Certainly not that of the makers and venders of opiates for children or poisoned foods for grown-ups; they do not have to take the stuff, they just make and sell it. And that making-and-selling has come to be the holiest of our idols. It rates higher than church, higher than nationality itself, for it is the prop of the church, the visible ear-mark of the progress of the nation.

One can easily understand the church doing its best to prevent people from taking a scientific attitude toward such matters as health and life. But why this nation should not encourage its citizens to think biologically, and in every possible way and with the utmost, widest freedom. . . . That is part of the problem I am now trying to solve.

What is behind the nation? One hundred million human beings who were born here or are descended from those who came here hungry or in debt, or because the old home was not good enough for them. Some of them may have died of starvation; some may be more heavily in debt than when they came; and some may have come to the conclusion that the old home was not so bad as they thought. The mere fact that they came implies a certain amount of thinking things over, of having come to a rather important conclusion, and of having taken a decisive step: all of which was sane behaviour along scientific and rational lines.

But they brought some notions with them which prevent their descendants from making further experiments. To a good Catholic, for example, there is no factual world of organic or inorganic nature that cannot be reversed at any moment. Whatever an alleged miracle may be to a court of science, to a Catholic it is a *fact*. It *happens*; it is an *event*, as it used to be in the days when God himself walked on earth in the cool of the evening. It is not ignorance that fails to see through a miracle: it is blind faith that refuses to look. It is not that it cannot see, but that it will not: "There is nothing to see!" The cornerstone of faith is belief. The foundation of belief is truth. But at least the Catholic does call his Christianity "religion" and not *Science*.

I can talk to a Catholic; we do not agree on many things, of course, but I understand his language. I know what he means to say when he speaks of man, sin, spirit, soul, life, etc. I cannot talk with a Christian Scientist; good old words with honourable antecedents seem to evaporate in thin air, and I am confronted with a vocabulary that seems deliberately to have been invented (borrowed, rather) for the sole purpose of drowning reality in dephlogisticated air. Presumably they, like the Catholics, accept the reality of motor-cars, but they transcend the Catholics in denying such realities as *Spirochæta pallida*, *Bacillus tuberculosis*, or biliary cirrhosis. Thousands of people have gone to the stake for denying less obvious realities.

That I do not press the point may be construed as evidence of my desire not to "attack." That is not the issue. Medical schools and medical education are enormously expensive; health is a vital problem, not only for individuals, but for communities and nations. If medicine is all humbug and health nothing but make-believe, now is an excellent time to know it, that we may govern ourselves accordingly. Why live in the twentieth if the tenth century was just as good?

Christianity is an old friend and I feel tender-hearted toward it, but Christian Science is a modern upstart and I can easily feel tough-minded toward it. If I were disposed to attack it I might point out that in misappropriating the word science it puts itself on the level of a charlatan who offers a cancer cure in bottles "with the approval of the entire medical profession." I shall do nothing of the sort, but, rather, emulate Cicero's restraint by passing over in silence the fact that this woman encouraged her husband to die of diabetes when insulin was at hand, that those parents aided and abetted Klebs-Loeffler bacilli to choke a sweet child to death with a diphtheritic membrane across its throat.

"Well, it's *their* affair." I suppose so. But not long ago it was "their affair" if parents strangled their children with their own hands or sold them into slavery or prostitution. We send medical missionaries to the heathen Chinese. Why not to the Christian Scientist? We scrap the Decalogue, but murder is still a crime, and so is criminal negligence. We pasteurize milk with one hand and cultivate the germs of ignorance with the other.

Ignorance, gullibility: two useful abstractions if not abused and if the facts behind them justify their use. But are we not, am I not, prone to overwork or overload these two words? Have we not possibly reached a stage where it is wellnigh impossible to talk about our own civilization or culture in terms of a factual background?

Such terms must be largely abstract: generalizations must abound to a large extent. But are we more intent on settling arguments and solving and resolving problems with the first ready-made abstractions that come to hand, or on getting at the facts? Without attempting to answer that question, I stop long enough to point out that our recent advance in capacity to mould the material world has been possible chiefly because we have assumed an honest attitude about it. The old emotional ideas about the world have been replaced by: Let us look at this world and find out for ourselves what it is—and above all let us use our eyes, and let us be honest about it. If our ancestors thought it impious to travel faster than four miles an hour, that was their lookout. Our outlook is different. This is 1931, not 1831. Some of our ancestors thought it impious to eat pork. It is to laugh; pass the pork and beans!

Nor can we cover as with a blanket of charity the aggregate mentality of miracle-mongers, faith healers, and original-sinners, with the one word *gullible* or *ignorant*. Many among them are A.B.s, Ph.D.s, LL.D.s and D.D.s, college professors and presidents, millionaires, editors of magazines and newspapers. And how many of us were not once almost persuaded? Or are still troubled by doubts or fears?

Have we or have we not reached the point where, as Coutts says in his *American Road to Culture*, a public school text-book dare offend the D. A. R., the G. A. R., the O. C. V., the K. of C., the American Legion, the K. K. K., the A. F. L., the English-Speaking Union, or the U. S. Chamber of Commerce? To that list must be added the special interests the newspapers dare not "offend."

What a picture! Or rather what an indictment of our capacity to stomach the truth with good grace. Just imagine trying to write a biology, a sociology, an anthropology, or a history, which would pass such a board of censors as the D. A. R.s and the Kluxers, the English-Speaking Union and the Knights of Columbus! What chance has an honest and unbiassed treatment of the hard facts of life before these Vested Interests of Politics, Economics, Society, and Religion? The issue forced thereby is not, "Is it true?" but, "Will it offend this interest or that?" In no event must it offend the Catholics, the Protestants, the Jews, or the Christian Scientists. Why I do not mention Business is evident: the ark of Yahweh himself was not more carefully guarded from hurt. It has become the nation's god, at whom no one may thumb his nose.

True, infidels are not roasted—but Negroes are; and thought is free—if not subversive of Established Order, of which we have more brands and varieties than pre-Christian Athens, Alexandria, or Rome.

Ignorance? It is not so much that millions of Americans are ignorant of the main facts of the modern biologic sciences—zoology, anatomy, physiology, embryology, pathology, anthropology, etc.— but that their notions of life, of living beings, of man, and of health and disease, are such that modern scientific points of view are not welcome. They will install a radio among their antiques, and insist upon an electric toaster, but an idea that does not match their antique mental furniture is an "affront to their intelligence," a "slur upon their morality," or a "reflection upon their religion." Under such circumstances what chance has an idea to get a hearing?

Scientists may, as Robinson pleads, humanize their knowledge till they are Methuselahs, and in words of the utmost clarity, but they will be crying in a wilderness so long as our educational system rates fear of offence higher than love of truth. Science by its very nature is as honest as sunshine, as impartial as a drought. Any Interest that stands in the way of a scientific approach to any human problem, stands between man and human freedom.

It is human nature to trim one's sails to the breeze, but man has never found a policy that pays better in the long run than honesty; nor is honesty born of fear, but of courage. No book that fears to offend anything but the truth is fit for any school.

It tickles our pride to think that such old masters as Thales, Eratosthenes, Aristotle, Archimedes, Pliny, Lucretius, and many others, including Hypatia, and even many Egyptians and Babylonians, would soon feel at home in some of our halls of learning; but is there a quack, fakir, healer, mystic, spiritualist, crystal-gazer, star-gazer, fortune-teller, mind-reader or ghost-raiser known to an-

tiquity or to the Middle Ages who could not do a profitable business on any street in New York, Chicago, or Los Angeles, or fill a
pulpit in many churches of the land?

Could Herodotus teach history, for example, in Oberlin College;
or would his calm, dispassionate, critical mind disqualify him for
the chair?

Why pick on Oberlin? I don't. It is a fine college. It just happens that my eye lit on a book by a professor of history in that
large educational plant. True, his chair is Church History, and his
book is now six years old; but 1925 is fairly modern, and Oberlin
is not in China, but in Ohio, maker of Presidents; and even a
church historian is, I assume, supposed to know as much zoology
as a high-school graduate. This particular historian, as a matter of
fact, is a B. A. of Cambridge University, a D. C. L. of King's College, and an Inner Templar of London to boot. He even claims to
have travelled extensively. And among his many writings is the
one before me, *Christian Monasticism.*

St. Paul, says Hannah, but without specifying which particular
one, was the first Christian monk. Which fact, if fact it be, leaves
me cold. What interests me is that after Paul had lived as a monk
for 113 (!) years, he was visited by St. Anthony, who was directed
to his cave by a friendly but fearsome beast, a hippo-centaur: half
man, half beast. "This monster, after gnashing out some kind of
outlandish *utterance*, in *words* broken rather than spoken through
his bristling lips, at length finds a friendly mode of communication,
and extending his right hand points out the way desired." True,
Hannah quotes St. Jerome as his "authority," but with no suggestion that he was amazed, as St. Anthony himself was, at a talking
centaur. But it was a she-wolf that pointed out the very cave where
saint met saint and "exchanged the kiss of peace." For supper that
night the raven which had been bringing Paul's food for sixty years
brought double rations!

If it happened once, it could happen again! No fake that Barnum
could think up failed to find admiring believers.

Now, the point is not that the "higher" criticism has passed over
Hannah's head, but that our "natural history" inheritance came
straight down to us from the fabulous age—and that that fabulous
nonsense is still cultural background enough to qualify one to hold

a chair of history in a well-known American college. There is nothing unique about Hannah or about Oberlin; there are plenty of them in America. Their existence is a barrier to a more enlightened civilization; more specifically, to a general acceptance of the notion that if we have lost our way there must be a reason, and that the reason may be discovered if we will take the pains to look for it. Facts may be painful, but they will cure more ills in the long run than faith. Too often we view "with danger" when the case calls for an open-eyed view. And no such view is possible if we wear blinders or have too many blind spots.

As Jelliffe recently pointed out, there are millions—and not all in Tennessee—"whose horizons are still filled with the thought fossil forms of mediævalism, and still more millions whose devil has shifted a few points higher in the cultural scale. Our Comstocks, Watch and Ward Societies, and Fundamentalists are but a few of the persisting tendencies of the Jehovah complex that played so large a rôle in the early mental life of the Colonists. The foundation of our amazingly rich crop of religious cults, richer than anywhere else, is to be traced to the admixture of many racial strains of closely related cultural horizons."

We are not born with blinders, nor naturally endowed with more than one blind spot. We in this country are born into a civilization unique, on the one hand, in its confusion and ugliness, its ignorance and doubt, and on the other in the number and character of the paths opened up to reality and in the technique of discovering and opening up more and better paths. Why, then, this gulf between the most brilliantly illuminated reality the world has ever seen and a social chaos that only poets love and parasites adore?

An education which must steer such a straight course that it offends no minority with ten votes, may lead to heaven; it never can lead to the shores of reality. Reality? Motor-cars and radio sets, or criminals and lunatics? We boast of one, and accept the other with a shrug or a frown, or say: "Forget it! Aren't we *the* people? Look at our science!"

Of the many millions of boys and girls in our schools today who expect to become business men, housewives, etc., at least one million, says Dr. Williams, will end up in the insane asylum, if present ratios continue. Of the other millions who will escape insanity by taking to crime, I have no figures on which to base a prediction. But, after all, the number of our youth destined to become burdens to this and the next generation is beside the point, which is, that they are "destined"—or at least the great majority—not by fate or by nature, but by a theory of social values which puts a premium on success, penalizes honesty, sneers at truth, and trusts no one but the Trust Company.

Many of us still think of civilization in terms of exports, and cannot conceive of the world as civilized until every family has at least one motor-car and two suits of clothes. Some even think civilization impossible without motor-cars and clothes.

Autos and clothes do not make civilization. They, with thousands of other things, do make for the kind of civilization we live in now. They are useful contrivances, part of the universe to which mankind around the world is adapting itself. There are no natives any more, nor native heroes. The native does not want to meet God or live like Arjuna; he wants to meet somebody who can pull a tooth or lend him a cigarette, and he wants to live like Doug Fairbanks or Tom Mix.

Man comes, man goes; nations wax fat and die of heart failure; but this earth changes, and all thereon. Change is brought about by varying circumstances, sometimes fast, sometimes slowly—just now very fast. We want to know the reasons for these changes. We are not yet all satisfied with the earth as it is, nor with our own lot or that of our fellow-men; we would bring about more changes. We would, especially, know how change has been brought about—in the belief that conceivably such knowledge would be useful, and if not useful, at least interesting and not harmful.

Have we a philosophy of life, or of civilization? We do have what we call laws, generalizations, hypotheses, about life and about our civilization. And we systematize our thinking along many lines and in many respects. But is our thinking adequate? Do we follow ideals? Or do we simply make Names idols and ourselves worshippers of systems? More specifically, does disease outstrip health; insanity, sanity; social anarchy, the common weal? And is progress in industry made only at the price of physical and social deterioration?

If our philosophy of life outstrips our capacity to live soundly, freely, and with due regard for our responsibilities as members of society, and if our criterion of success is keeping up with the procession, most of us, I suspect, are failures, and all of us are in for a hard time. And the best medicine I know of for muddy thinking along these lines is the lesson history furnishes us of man's proneness to think metaphysically while he is rotting physically. Too many of these ancient metaphysical systems still draw interest though they pay no taxes, still meddle in human affairs though their sole professed interest is in spiritual, or intellectual, or moral, systems.

To put it another way, while twentieth-century civilization enjoys the benefits of twentieth-century science, it carries a huge burden of ancient superstition. It thinks scientifically enough about flat feet and fallen wombs, but it thinks of flat purses and fallen women against a background compounded of Moses, Plato, and the Virgin Mary. We can even think of a billion dollars or a billion gonococci soberly enough, but with what coloured glasses do we view a Billionaire or a Gonococcal!

We have twelve million boys and girls in Sunday school; and each year expend what amounts to the interest at six per cent on more than thirteen billion dollars, on organized religion. What do the boys and girls learn in their Sunday school, or how much supervision is there of the parochial schools? And as for organized religion in general, as Professor Smith says, "The sight of several churches mutually anathematizing each other's dogmas, criminating and recriminating each other, and giving each other the lie, suggests to the puzzled seeker for truth that possibly all of them are right in their mutual accusations, though each fails in its own claims."

Let us now look at another fact of great importance, it seems to me, in the attempt to see ourselves as we are or as others see us; not the fact that motor-cars killed more people last year than diphtheria, nor that from the most marvellous application yet made of a scientific discovery to meet human needs we get such incredible piffle as the radio delivers hour by hour, but the fact that a man has only to win a Nobel Prize to be accepted by the public at large as Omnipotence. Nor is that all: the prize-winner himself accepts the additional honour without blinking an eye.

In fact, just now we seem to be dominated by a trinity of Authorities: movie stars and society dames, on what to smoke, eat, drink, wear, and sleep on; billionaire capitalists, on everything relating to government and business; and Nobel Prize winners in physics, on everything relating to life.

If life is continuous and eternal, and if this earth will support human life for untold millions of years more, why bother about Ultimates or boast of our cosmic importance, when we have not paid for our last war or found out what it was all about, when we have not enough jails to house our criminals or enough asylums to shelter our insane? Why be important in the universe if we cannot be useful to our fellow-men?

Useful is the word I used, knowing well that it is the custom of many to sneer at it. Useful to human beings, in human society. That may not be the absolute test of values; it is a test which most human beings can understand. It involves no cult, is not esoteric, strains no human sense organ. It also solves no problem as to *why* we are here or the *purpose* of life. It requires no *system* of religion or metaphysics to give it meaning. It has meaning against a factual background of millions of human beings on this earth who for one reason or another (mostly preventable) will be prevented from living out their days in health, vigour, and happiness.

If my use of the word useful is a valid test of worth, why should it be easier to get adequate endowments for "pure" research than for a scientific research laboratory to study impure teeth? Why is a great physicist "higher" than a good dentist or an honest judge?

The answer is as long as human history and as deep as human nature, but, briefly, is somewhat as follows.

Our cultural traditions go back to a time when, as an ancient sage said, an astrologer could command more respect by telling one truth to a hundred lies than an ordinary man could by telling a hundred truths to one lie; to the time when anyone who supplied an *authority* by which to live, or a *purpose* in life, or a satisfactory rationalization of existence, was looked upon either as inspired or as an intellectual colossus. What the Magi did for the Babylonians, the Prophets for the Hebrews, the Philosophers for the Greeks, the Bible for the Christians, and the Mathematicians for European Intellectuals, Pure Research does for twentieth-century U.S.A. In short, if there is no hard and fast line between what are today called "the sciences" and what was formerly called Philosophy or the Humanities, scientists have only themselves to blame.

Ours is frequently spoken of as a Christian civilization; we call ourselves a "Christian" nation. We divide the world into Christians and heathen. We are believers or unbelievers; we belong and are saved, or are damned because we are heretics or infidels. We speak of the power and freedom of the press, but where is the press powerful enough or free enough to proceed on the supposition that ours is a secular and not a Christian nation, a secular and not a Christian civilization? The press, it is said, is secular, no respecter of persons, an impartial purveyor of news, a merciless exposer of fraud and sham in high or low; yet this monstrous social fraud, this gigantic hoax, goes rolling along as though it were the one social institution above criticism, above reproach, so sacred in its origin, so potent in its good, that it cannot be questioned aloud. What is the press afraid of: the God who first made fear on earth, the susceptibilities of its readers, or the wrath of its advertisers?

So readily excused is flagrant hypocrisy, so perilous is honest silence, that our politicians and even our Presidents show the same awe toward God and the Bible; and the flag of the Cross—a thirteenth century B.C. symbol at Tel-el-Amarna, or, coupled with a crescent, a twenty-sixth century B.C. Pyramid symbol—goes up, above the emblem of the nation, on our battleships every Sunday morning. And taxpayers must support this arm of the service also, whether they be Christians, Moslems, Buddhists, or just taxpayers. A Secretary who advocated the abolition of Christian clergy from the navy might find himself in hotter water than one who advocated the abolition of modern surgery.

Are press, big business, and politics in the same boat as that notorious sceptic, Napoleon, who left religion alone because it paid? "What is it," he asked, "that makes the poor man think it quite natural that there are fires in my palace while he is dying of cold? That I have ten coats in my wardrobe while he goes naked? That at each of my meals enough is served to feed his family for a week? It is simply religion, which tells him that in another life I shall be only his equal, and that he actually has more chance of being happy there than I. Yes, we must see to it that the floors of the churches are open to all, and that it does not cost the poor man much to have prayers said on his tomb."

We must not open the church to all, but we must open soup kitchens for the down-and-outs—and send the murderer to the gallows with a priest by his side to make his peace with God. Christian civilization thereby saves its face. And if I am crippled and penniless, and my children half starved, I am told that poverty is a virtue and because of it I shall the more easily enter the kingdom of heaven. What I want is less virtue and more food and some human sympathy; and I should get both sooner from a Cave-man than from the average civilized Christian.

Christianity makes for peace, we are told. When, where, how? In 1914?

> To God the embattled nations sing and shout
>     "God strafe England" and "God save the King";
>     God this, God that, and God the other thing.
> "Good God!" said God, "I've got my work cut out."

Did it make for peace in Christian Europe during the centuries since Europe "embraced" Christianity, or in Christian Europe transplanted to American soil?

This much is certain: we need not expect much change for the better until it is recognized that, however small potatoes, bigotry and obscurantism are Big Business heavily entrenched, hold white-collar jobs, sit in endowed chairs, feel free to concern themselves with every taxpayer's business, and are feared by all politicians, most newspapers, and many schools of Higher Learning.

Hundreds of thousands of boys and girls go out from our schools each year more or less familiar with the stories of Moses and Joshua, Cæsar and Charlemagne, Napoleon and Josephine; they study the Bible and "history." But is there a school in these United States which requires its students to become even remotely familiar with the story of the discovery of the fundamental facts which have brought about the most astounding revolution in human history and which make this a new world, with new ideals and such possibilities as only inspired genius can realize?

The answer to Dayton, Tennessee, is the answer to multi-millionaire by inheritance, to organized censorship, to organized crime, to widespread graft, to the pace that kills, and to any voice that speaks the language of any vested interest incompatible with human and more humane interests: education in honest thinking, backed up by habits of honest living. As it is, we are hanging disease and punishing ignorance; we are not hanging the right people. Bigotry never got to the bottom of a disease, nor dared face an honest and impartial justice court.

During the course of a million years or so man has learned to travel in seven-leagued boots, on magic carpets, and on wings faster than the wind. With his new-fangled arms he tunnels mountains, reaches down into the bowels of the earth, and on his reinforced back carries loads which would have staggered Atlas. Hercules himself was never so omnipotent. No Apollo could have foreseen, nor Pluto discovered, what modern man foretold and then caught on a gelatin film—the light of the new trans-Neptune planet, Pluto. No Æsculapius could have discovered the causal connexion between one mosquito and a chill followed by five degrees of fever; nor could Hygieia have cured malaria.

Sheer magic; such magical power as our forefathers never dreamed of. They had not learned how to *make* dreams come true and then to dream still wilder dreams and make them come true: just as we grow by living and live by growing.

We do not grow faster than we used to, we do grow more surely; we may not live longer, we do live more securely and freely and with less fear and trembling. To the fullness and richness of the earth there have been added countless other blessings to enrich life, give it zest, increase its pleasures, and lessen its pains.

We not only make one acre yield what used to require two, but make it possible for one mother with two children to be as certain of having done her biologic duty to the race as was her grandmother who bore a dozen children. Better than that, women have been restored to almost complete membership in good standing in the human race. That, to my way of thinking, is a more notable achievement than airplane or radio, and is equally due to honest thinking. That her complete membership must be qualified by "almost" is due to the fact that it is not as easy for men to look upon women, or upon any human relationship, as truthfully and hence as impartially as upon means of transportation and communication. Behind that "fact" is a cultural inheritance of a misogynous Pauline doctrine.

But facts are facts—until they are shown to be frauds; nor does that necessarily end their existence. Certain sections of society do all their trading with counterfeit money. The hardest facts of an insane-asylum are its brick walls and iron bars. Facts, like truths, are illusive, relative, subject to change with change in point of view. There are individual points of view, and political, ecclesiastical, scholastic, national, etc. Also, scientific.

The difference, for example, between a scholastic and a scientific point of view in regard to woman is that one says, She can do so-and-so; the other asks, What can she not do! Take another example. The church says, Do so-and-so and you will be saved; the scientist asks, What do you mean by salvation, what is it you propose to save, and what price salvation?

Again, from the national point of view a man is a taxpayer and a soldier; from the scientific point of view the big question is, What is he? And the scientist discovers no more reason for accepting man's word for his supernatural origin than for accepting the thunder's roar as omnipotence.

"It has taken man ages to assert himself," says Prometheus in Garnett's *Twilight of the Gods*, "nor has he yet, it would seem, done more than enthrone a new idol in place of the old." Probably more ages must pass before man can unite on an idol which will satisfy his longings and yet prove acceptable to all mankind. Certain it is that any other idol will prove false.

No idol of marble or bronze will serve, nor shibboleth or formula, nor unattainable ideal, nor impossible Utopia. Nor science either. With hundreds of laboratories bursting with science and thousands of granaries bursting with grain, over six million human beings starved to death in China, after incredible suffering and appalling cannibalism. Boccaccio saw hogs rooting among the dead plague victims in Florence, and Defoe saw people, crazed by the terrible sight of rotting plague victims, rush from their houses and jump into the river. Is it possible, Petrarch asked, that posterity can believe these things, when we who have seen them can scarcely believe?

That was six centuries ago. Europe was just emerging from the Dark Ages. This is 1931, age of science, era of incredible wealth, of incredible speed in transporting thought, bodies, and goods: yet there have been hungry bread lines in our cities and millions of our fellow-men done to death for the lack of three grains of corn.

What is our idol? Whatever it is, it is false; it is not even wise enough to recognize a human being except when dressed up in its own clothes. While these lines of humans were waiting for bread, and those Chinese were waiting for death, the Christian civilized nations of the world were haggling as to whether their war-weapon bill for the next few years would be two or only one thousand million dollars. And Wall Street shut down one whole day because it was *Good* Friday.

Do we have to go on forever paying for the mistakes of the Chaldees, worshipping Israel's God of War? That a superstition has ruled for two or twenty thousand years, or has been believed in by a million or a million million people, does not make it a fact or lift it out of the realm of ghosts or the region of folly.

There are millions of Americans today, whole states full of them, with no more love of science than Augustine had. For them, as for the fifth-century saint, the world is complete just as it is, a poor place anyhow and not worth bothering about; they are bound for the Celestial City.

They tolerate science as it comes to them in an automobile, a radio, or even a new serum, but the intelligence which prompts them to accept the sign hung on their door by the health officer is on a par with that which prompted plague-stricken London to paint a red cross on its doors and a "Lord, have mercy upon us."

They tolerate science because they like to ride in an automobile, talk over the telephone, listen in on the radio, and save the life of their child. They may even tolerate a scientific laboratory in their midst as a kind of additional magic power-house. At the same time they cling to the miracles they assimilated in childhood and the Glorious Fourth brand of patriotism of their youth—as though God had performed before their very eyes and endowed their politicians with exclusive wisdom. Let a scientist or a historian display scepticism or review miracles or patriots critically, and they are ready to go as far toward hanging him as the law allows—or, as Judge Lynch or a K. K. K., to take the law in their own hands.

It should be the inalienable right of every American citizen these days to live an interesting life, eternally to renew his youth in a loved pursuit: to be an amateur in life and not a professional.

The professional, to use Conklin's phraseology, lives by his profession; the amateur lives for his hobby. And it does seem, as Conklin suggests, that in the field of living things the amateurs have contributed more to our knowledge of nature than the professionals. Hooke, Leeuwenhoek, Swammerdam, Ehrenberg, Trembley, Sprengel, Gilbert White, Hudson, Gosse, Avebury, Darwin, Fabre, Mendel, all were amateurs, observing life because they loved living things. They sought, and in pursuit of a course they loved they found, what may well be man's highest happiness—æsthetic and intellectual pleasure. They sought neither material nor professional gain, but on the other hand put their time, money, and even their reputations, into their pursuit. "It may be doubted whether any great work has ever been done in any other spirit."

What makes a "work" *great*? Every age has had its own answer. One could easily collect a hundred answers today, each meritorious and possibly all divergent. Let us see if we can frame, not a definition, not a formula, but a background, as it were, against which "works" may be evaluated.

Is it not obvious that, whether the reality of earth's rocks, snows, and rains, or even of life itself, be denied, there can be no denying the fact that living human beings who are neither obsessed with fear of death nor hypnotized by the hope of cheating death, are more at home on earth and to more people than those who are dejected by fear or held up by false hope? To put it another way, is there not in every man that which the entire human race recognizes as an essentially human quality?

That quality is more easily felt than described. Radiant health perhaps best expresses what I mean. With that gleaming from the eyes and lighting up the countenance, a man may travel far into the heart of the savage, into the heart of humanity of every age and clime.

Radiant health is incompatible with insincerity, mendacity, and dishonesty—qualities which again and again have been elevated to the rank of high gods and for a while have seemed to lead to victory. But in all that man has won since he parted from his speechless ancestors, all that makes for health, sanity, power, and energy in our civilization may be credited to the fact that among men on earth honesty is the best policy. Nothing else has paid so handsomely, nothing else has given our civilization so much that makes it worth while to be alive here and now.

Untold numbers of human beings have followed that policy earnestly and eagerly, and have found joy, happiness, sanity, peace, prosperity, and loving friends. But what nation, or which civilization, what era or epoch, may be said to have held that policy high above all others? Why has no Power ever elevated that policy to a primary virtue? Chiefly because, as I read my history, every Power has had its own shibboleth, emblem, idol, god, so firmly embedded in its mind that it could not think straight about the realities of life. It could think honestly, rationally, intellectually, sincerely, only up to a certain point, to a certain dead wall beyond which it not only could not think but could not tolerate thought at all. It killed its free or non-conforming thinkers, and turned its loudest or most bloodthirsty conformists into national heroes or heavenly saints.

The difference between worshipping a shibboleth (such as, My Country, Right or Wrong) and an idol (such as the Immaculate Virgin or the Bleeding Heart of Jesus) is not the difference between one religion and another, or between one form of superstition and another; it is the difference between worshipping an idea which leads to anarchy and war and an idea which leads to futility and imbecility. Both ideas are inhuman, unsound, unhealthy, destructive of a more reasonable, more sensible, more lovable and more humane earthly environment.

That that environment can be made more lovable and more humane is to me as obvious as that this house in which I write is more lovable, more humane, than a Congo jungle or a Dordogne cave.

Now, I have admitted, as we must, that there was merit in the jungle and in the cave, but there were many more things besides: an incredible number of enemies in the jungle, and in the cave such hardship and discomfort that life can have been no great joy. We have passed far beyond the jungle and the cave; but have we passed far enough, have we passed as far as we might reasonably be expected to have passed, taking into account the enormous number of years since we roosted in trees with the jungle fowl or shared our cave with the remains of our relatives and the bones, gnawed clean by our teeth, of the animals slain by our hand?

If not, why not? Why, in the richest city of the richest nation in the world, is human life not less precarious than in Cæsar's Rome, and human beings only not quite so poor in health, happiness, and prosperity, and quite as full of superstition? Why will the battered head of a Greek god by unknown hands bring a higher price than any work any living human hands can turn out? Why is it easier to sell fakes than facts? Why . . . ? But why go on. The Bible is still a best-seller, exceeded only by the combined sale of fictitious confessions and fraudulent psychologies. For every reader of a journal of opinion there are a thousand readers of the journals of belief.

Words, words, words, words: fictitious words, fraudulent words, Holy words. Are the readers of these words prosperous and happy, are they healthy, wealthy, and wise? What do they seek among these millions of words—the secrets of life, aids to a richer, saner, robuster life, or culture, or personal advancement?

From the Holy words they seek compensation for the emptiness of their world; from the confessions and psychologies they seek scandal—the second-hand experience they are too timid and too fearful to try first-hand. And what they do not find in the weeklies and monthlies they get from the tabloids, which purvey goods and scandal to the masses as they were once peddled at back doors by itinerant purveyors of tinware and gossip.

I am not quarrelling with those drudges trying to fill empty lives by reading themselves into soulful bliss or by vicariously enjoying fornication or the commission of a murder with the aid of printer's ink. I am trying not to quarrel with anybody or anything. I am trying to find out what has happened to this civilization of ours. It is not as lovely, it seems to me, as it might be, and we recently discovered that it is appallingly expensive—in human goods, in human lives, in human passions. Any civilization which in four years costs thirteen million human lives and divides the world into two hostile camps, hating one another, suspicious of one another, and lying about one another, is a very expensive luxury—more expensive, possibly, than the human race can afford. And anyone, it seems to me, has a right to question it.

That, as I see it, is the supreme advantage of being alive just now; that, and not the fact that we can *fly* to Paris or *talk* with New Zealand, is the glory of this age and the hope of the future. It is much more important for the world of human affairs that it be allowed to make some observations and to ask some questions than that it can fly faster than the wind or send its voice as fast as lightning. Straight thinking is quite as important as straight flying.

Long before man thought he had found a way to fly to heaven like an angel, birds had been soaring in the heavens without any thought at all. When man stopped wishing he could fly like an angel long enough to ask *how* a bird flies, he soon learned enough to beat the bird at its own game—and it took nature many millions of years to make a good bird.

As President Hoover is reported to have said some time ago, the crowd only feels: it has no mind of its own which can plan. It is "credulous. It destroys, consumes, hates, and dreams; but it never builds." But it does elect Presidents, it does pay taxes, it does slave; and just now some of it is hungry and down-and-out. One would like to ask the President what he proposes to do about it, if anything. For it is true, as he also said, that the "mob functions only in a world of emotion," that the "demagogue feeds on mob emotions," and that "if Democracy is to secure its authority in morals, religion, and statesmanship, it must stimulate leadership from its own mass."

But why in the name of Saints Augustine and Ignatius and all the saintly souls of the Quaker Church, should Democracy *secure its authority* in morals or religion? What triumphed in 1928: a leader stimulated "from its own mass" or a demagogue who fed on mob emotion and profited from party organization? I do not answer the question; I merely ask it. I also ask, why is it that the great majority of American citizens are collectively nothing more than a crowd, a mass, without mind of its own but with the emotions of a mob—food for demagogues? One need not expect straight thinking from City Hall, New York, but one does from the White House, D. C.—especially when its occupant is an engineer.

The occupant of the White House just preceding Mr. Hoover

reminded us that we cannot remind ourselves too often that our right to be free, our support of our principles of justice, our obligations to one another in our domestic affairs and our duty to humanity abroad, the confidence in one another necessary to support our social and economic relations, and the fabric of our government, "rest on religion." Piffle; and the four men who had most to do with laying the foundations of our government would agree. What we want in our government is more honesty, more sincerity, more humanity; less buncombe, less hypocrisy, less superstition.

Mr. Coolidge was frank enough to admit that "the most casual survey of our own country reveals the existence of conditions which require constantly increasing efforts for their redress." The "forces of evil are constantly manifest." "Organized government . . . can do much . . . but without the inspiration of faith, without devotion to religion, they are inadequate to serve the needs of mankind."

I weigh these words and again say, Piffle! *Faith* in what, *devotion* to what religion?

Between Maine and California are all the religions known to mankind, and between Minnesota and Louisiana is faith in everything from Holy Writ to a rabbit's foot. What serves the needs of mankind? What has served these needs in the past? What lifted man above the jungle and out of the cave? Faith in his good right arm and devotion to his wife and children. And the farther he got from faith in himself and devotion to his fellow-men, the farther he got from being the kind of human being Abraham Lincoln would have loved to touch or humanity to sleep with.

Man's business is to live on this earth and with his fellow-men. No other business can transcend that or yield richer returns. Anything that comes between man and earth or sets man against his fellow-men is an enemy of the human race, an impediment in man's speech, a hindrance to his footsteps. Faith in anything beyond the sensible, devotion to anything beyond the reasonable, is such an enemy. All that civilized man has done that would shame a polecat, degrade a hyena, and make a cur hang its head, has been done in some god's name and on behalf of some absurd, insane, or monstrous faith. It was not necessary to know the world; it was only necessary to be prepared to abandon it on a minute's notice. The world was not made tidier or sweeter, because . . . "What's the use, if it is so soon to be abandoned?" Nor did human conduct become more human, because . . . "Why be human, when one can be a saint or a devil?"

As Robinson suggests, the *test* of a sermon, editorial, or presidential address is whether it throws some light on actual problems or complications in human affairs, or evades and obscures such problems in current abstractions—such as, Americanism, Bolshevism, Liberty, National Honour, Morality, Progress, Rise of Man, Science, Error, etc. These abstractions alone and of themselves are good for anything in the sense that a new-born babe is good for anything. This nation has paid a staggering price for worshipping more idols than a Roman citizen of 1 A.D. was supposed to worship to retain his self-respect and the good opinion of his fellow-citizens.

Why should a President of the United States tell us what every man who has earned a living by politics for the last ten thousand years has known, and what had already been put so well by Sir Auckland Geddes? "In politics, in the affairs with which governments have to deal, it is not accurate knowledge that matters—it is emotion!" Of course it is.

And for every four who order their lives and their business by rationally thought-out convictions and would like to see their government so ordered, there are ninety-six who live without order and move only by emotion and sentimentality. These ninety-six have never learned to walk alone; they must be led—and are ready to tear the man apart who questions their idol in religion or politics. And how often in history has the idol—in church, politics, or education—so much as admitted by nod or wink that it was not above reproach or criticism? Such admissions from those in the seats of the mighty have been painfully rare in human history, including our own and up to now.

All of which, no doubt, is *lèse majesté*—infamous, unpatriotic. So mote it be. But history lists kings, popes and presidents by the hundred who have been held blameless and above criticism—but who have been execrated and reviled after death for the stuffed shirts they were while alive. Some of the energy that goes into post-mortem execration might better be spent in looking living majesty over with a critical eye and an open mind.

Granting that out of every hundred American citizens ninety-six of us cannot lead but must be led, let us realize that our leaders are no longer clothed in spiritual authority or endowed with divine wisdom. Let us admit that they are always entitled to respect when they stick to the job they schemed to get and make a good job of it —and otherwise are entitled to considerably less than respect. And that, whether they do their job well or not, they are entitled to no more reverence or subservience than a waitress or a bootblack.

And may we note here that the modern tendency to brand socialists as anarchists—as the Middle Ages branded heretics as atheists—and to treat them as the bearers of a contagious disease, is quite as destructive of human rights of speech as was the policy of the church in the days of Torquemada, and with less show of reason. The church then was *the* Vested Interest of society. It did not stop to inquire just what the heretic did believe in or what were the grounds of his heresy; it was enough that he did not swallow the church's dogmas, hook, line, and sinker. He was not a believer: he must be an atheist—traitor to church and God. To Sheol with him!

But the difference between one who believes in a whole lot more government than we have, and one who believes in no government at all, is the difference between a communist and an anarchist. We have vested interests, and from what we know of human nature those interests will be well looked after. Our system of government, as I understand it, is not, among other things, a vested interest— like oil, steel, railroads, or denominational colleges; it is an agreed-upon method of regulating certain affairs of certain states and peoples and of dealing in certain respects with other states and peoples. That agreement can be revised and amended—has been, will be again presumably, possibly scrapped entirely and written anew.

Whenever I hear a Vested Interest or a politician brand somebody as an anarchist, a Red, or a Bolshevist, I am curious to know where he got his authority—especially just what brand of emotional fire is warming him up. We have laws which are supposed to protect ballot boxes and the lives of human beings, but none that I know of which may constitutionally interfere with my preaching from a pulpit or a soap-box that our government give as much heed to tuberculosis in citizens as it does to that disease in cattle—or on any other noble experiment that may enter my head. Such, for example, as that the citizens of this country should own and control all public highways and all public carriers of goods, persons, and words. Of course the Vested Interests would call that Socialism, or, more likely, Bolshevism; and they would also point out (with pride?) that The People cannot run anything and hence are fit only to be driven. Public ownership takes away all initiative! It may all be true; if it is, there should be a remedy. But to what Vested Interest are we to look for the remedy?

An enlightened democracy will be very chary about branding any man, will make very certain that it knows just what it is branding and what interest is served by the branding. It is not money that curses us, but faith—faith in symbols, formulas, and remedies which have come down to us from the ages that were timid and dark, fearful and bloody. Our advances have been possible because we could and did take less for granted than they did.

Thanks to the radio and the movies, we now hear and can see all mankind for what it is and not as we thought it was. That gives us an enormous advantage over all preceding ages: we can love our neighbour as he is and not as he ought to be. Of all the blessings of our civilization none is so great as that, none can do so much to transform the world. That transformation requires neither metaphysics nor theology; merely good judgment, sound thinking, and faith in man. No nation that thinks of civilization as man's gift to humanity can ever be held up to reproach, nor will the concept of a civilization freed of political barriers need defence.

Our civilization will not be saved by our politicians or by any one class of society. It is the business of every class to save itself, and it naturally fights anything and anybody that seem to threaten its hold on its prerogatives. Every class, profession, religion, trade, business, has its ideals, customs, beliefs, and codes; these collectively govern its actions, shape its ends, mould its opinions, warp its judgments.

The greater the solidarity of these classes, the stronger their vested interests, the less may be expected of them in such honest thought as civilization requires if it is to be vital, healthy, sane, humane. The professional classes have notoriously closed minds. Their aloofness from the common herd, lest they be cheapened, is quite as reasonable as that of the a-b-c-darians who eschewed letters lest they be corrupted by learning.

Every reform in morals has been forced on the church; every reform in education, on the college; every reform in medicine, on the profession; every reform in government, on the politicians; every reform in law, on the lawyers. And most of these reforms have been forced by men who had learned to trust their senses and had some common sense.

Scepticism, yes; agnosticism, yes. History is what it is largely because there has been a dearth of hard-boiled thinkers, too few men who dared doubt or come out with a flat "I do not know." But there is a gulf between honest doubt or frank ignorance and the conventional class thinker who has his mind so made up for him that he cannot even look at a new idea. No group, class, or profession is quite free to entertain a new idea or form a rational opinion; but certain classes, by the nature of their calling, are more segregated from society in general than other classes. Thus medicine-men, from primitive shamans to modern priests and doctors, are essentially closed societies; their traditional ideals are especially sacred, to be kept from the profane at all costs. Their minds are automatically closed to new ideas.

New ideas, in other words, are not put into circulation like new currency. Civilization itself determines whether the idea shall be allowed a hearing, its author allowed to live. The political leader moves along well-worn paths; the artist is controlled by vogues and technique; the superstitious, by the prevailing superstitions. Even God must conform to the fashion in ideas. To the Feudal Ages he was Overlord; to the rationalizing eighteenth century he was First Cause; to this age, so conscious of time, he is Wilful Nature with a destiny to be worked out through time. Perhaps it is not too much to hope that a saner age will discover him in humanity trying to live humanely and finding no odour of sanctity in anything but honest, sweet, healthy, joyous human lives.

We do enjoy a certain kind of freedom hitherto denied most of the human race, but it is just as well to keep reminding ourselves that we are bedevilled as never before by cunning and insidious propaganda to be something, do something, buy something we do not need and cannot afford. This propaganda is fitted to us and knows us better than we know ourselves, knows how to get under our skin.

Our "skin" is a complex affair, not unlike a section of the earth's crust of strata jumbled by earthquakes. The result is that in some of us the monkey idea of trying-anything-once is more easily laid bare than in others. Over that deepest layer is our family heirloom coat of many colours. Over that is an academic gown varying from three small r's to Big Degrees of assorted sizes and colours. Then there is class-consciousness, varying from Some Class to an alley gang apprenticeship. Also the special garb of our profession: high, reversed, celluloid, or no collar at all; hair-cut, hat, gloves, boots, and jewellery, to match; the immaculate garb of bishop, bellhop, or movie-palace usher; the sailor's dungarees; the jailbird's stripes. And we all have our coat of national sentiment: skin-colour and nose-shape prejudice, political doctrine, religious dogma. Encased in that armour as we are, let some one try to get a new idea under our skin! It sheds new ideas as the proverbial duck's back sheds water.

Nor is that all. These crusts of superorganically imposed customs, traditions, and habits rule us, make up our minds for us, tell us what to think, what to do. Ask us any question you please—How's business? What do you think of the tariff? Should we scrap battleships? Is Henry Ford a better man than J. P. Morgan? Are bare legs immoral?—and we have a pat answer. And most of our answers are no more logical, founded in reason or factually based than were the answers our Cave ancestors made to quiet their curiosity.

That Cave ancestor was a pragmatist, like ourselves; but the basis of his pragmatism was tangible, sensible values; the basis of ours is gold—and mostly gold-brick at that. Fear of an empty stomach led our ancestors around the world. That fear still haunts us; gold only lays the ghost. Our economic, political, and even our social life are all on a gold basis. Gold-bricks are shinier and more plentiful than ever; even "tainted gold" now wears a halo once reserved for heroes and angels.

Our professional saviours will not save our civilization; to expect it of them is to believe in magic and trust in miracles. The cure must come from the man in the street, in the factory, behind the plough; from men and women who are sold on nothing but sane, sound, and healthy human beings; who put their trust neither in Aristotle's nor in Billy Sunday's God, but in their own and their neighbour's strong right arm; who can see through fine sophistries, sacred conventions, plausible formulæ, prejudiced propaganda, subtle misrepresentations, venerable opinions, specious platitudes, and absurd distinctions between good and bad, moral and immoral, respectability and vulgarity. Only as such false coins and spurious values are withdrawn from circulation can human beings again devote their energy to socially useful ends and thereby build a civilization fit to live in.

The next time you are asked to subscribe to an Immutable Principle, have a good look at it first. If it cannot be transmuted into something that will nourish a baby, deaden pain, or promote health and happiness in you and your neighbours, it is pretty certain to be a fake in high-sounding words, a disingenuous idea masked as disinterestedness.

Nor may we expect to find that very rare and very precious virtue, humility, at home with ignorance or vested interests. The cocksureness of adult ignorance is to be matched only by the brazen assumptions of those in authority. With both classes, a little learning is a dangerous thing; but the difference between the miracle-mongering of the ignorant and the windy patriotism of the vested interests is the difference between squinting through smoked and rose-coloured glasses. They seek no light; they are beyond the reach of facts; they are interested only in further proofs of the righteousness of their position. The ignorant find the proofs in their magic; the interests, in the fact that their movements are chronicled as news and their faces reproduced in rotogravure or in the paid advertisements.

We have our colossus of this and of that. All history proves that colossi do not pay; yet most of the history we read plays up the doings of these psychopaths mad for power, for glory, for triumph, for victory, for dominion over men. Their lives make thrilling reading: but so do the doings of earthquakes, cyclones, tidal waves, plagues, and famine. We do something about these cataclysms: seek better ways to avoid them, to outride them, to make them impossible. We are much less sensible about our biologic monstrosities, our social parasites, our money-mad monsters.

Are our criminals better organized, our bread lines longer? Well, our list of million-dollar incomes is longer too. Over five hundred incomes of a million or more dollars in one year are no laughing matter, especially as they register net profits of nearly $750,000,000 on the sale of assets held two or more years. If that is not evidence, *distinctive* evidence, of Divine favour, Yahweh is not in his heaven, nor any justice on earth.

Civilization is not an *end*; it is a *way* of living. There are civilizations and civilizations, but behind each is the same old Man renewing his youth through his children. That is the only way human nature keeps alive. We proceed on the misleading hypothesis that civilization is a unit, and that man is a sort of zoological garden of domestic, semi-domestic, and savage animals. That hypothesis is wrong; in practice it makes for biologic insecurity, psychologic insanity.

Our civilization differs from Minoan or Assyrian; but you and I could have learnt to live like a Minoan or an Assyrian just as easily as like a Samoan or an up-to-date hijacker. One civilization afforded an opportunity to live one way; another another. Did any afford more than that?

Into a civilization each one of us is born with what Ferenczi calls *unconditional omnipotence*. But has our civilization advanced beyond that of Imperial Rome, which allowed men to live as selfishly as though the physical and sensual universe had been called into existence merely to gratify their infantile longings for omnipotence?

Kill them off? Certainly not. That would no more resolve the crisis than electrocuting Tammany's Tiger Cat or closing the churches and putting the bishops to ladling soup for the bread lines. Violence is no cure. Enlightenment is—if applied.

Why shouldn't the churches begin the process? There are enlightened men in the churches, both in pulpit and in pew. The churches are here, they are roomy, most of them comfortable; they pay no taxes and some of them are amply endowed. Collectively, they wield enormous influence. Collectively, they could transform the world. Yahweh fostered a war-complex; let the churches invent a peace-complex which will satisfy the world at large and signalize the birth of civilization in fact as well as in name—a peace on earth in fact as well as in the realm of ideality.

It can be done. But only if the churches turn their vast energies, now dissipated in carrying out the orders of some supernatural power or anthropomorphic god, to exclusively humane ends; only if they seek the kingdom of justice here and now; only if they courageously grasp the nettles of ancient and primitive beliefs, theories, and "revelations," and realize that they are no more divine sanctions for our habits, customs, moralities, and ethics than is the Rig Veda, the Koran, the Book of Mormon, or the divine teaching of Mary Baker Eddy.

Such a step would require courage. Such a step would be in line with all the steps man has taken in his climb up out of the jungle. The church has thrown the fear of God into man; let it now resolve to throw its weight against every ugly, silly, unsocial, unlovely, inhuman, unjust, unethical habit, custom, theory and authority. Let it fear dishonesty and (to borrow Carlson's words) reinterpret Paul's aphorism to read: Faith is of the past; hope should be chastened by experience; and charity is misdirected benevolence. What remains? The endeavour toward understanding, the hunger for beauty, and the urge for justice: and the greatest of these is justice.

And the greatest of these is justice.

It could be done. It would require courage. There are courageous men in the pulpits. They have less to fear than Business, Press, or Profession. They need serve only humanity; they need worship only truth; they need employ only scientific honesty. They have shown courage. It took courage for the Federal Council of Churches of Christ to hold that birth control is morally justified and to give even a "guarded" approval through its committee on marriage and the home.

That took courage; it is a step forward. It means the substitution of the human voice for a supernatural sanction in intimate human affairs. Anything, any relationship, so released from Divinity's hands, becomes natural, human, again.

Suppose the churches kept up that attitude for a generation, a century; stopped their anathematizing; turned to investigating; ceased thundering, threatening, and damning, and became human, inquiring, and devoted to truth and justice? Boys and girls, having less to learn, would learn better; teachers, having less to teach, might find time to educate; society might become social again; families might learn to live in homes; and as a nation we might learn to

mind our own business. And the example might become contagiou:
and the sun might travel around the world and not find Mars
anywhere.

It could be done. The churches could do it.

Man has built a great civilization, and this nation is the greatest
force in the world today.

I am glad I am alive and I am proud to be an American. But I
am even prouder to be a human being; and our nationalism today,
it seems to me, is humanity's great enemy, civilization's greatest
threat. Nor is that fact to be brushed aside by branding me Traitor
or sneered out of court as Utopian or contrary to Economic or
Natural Law or Divine Providence.

# INDEX